The Routledge Handbook to Global Political Economy

The Routledge Handbook to Global Political Economy provides a comprehensive guide to how Global Political Economy (GPE) is conceptualized and researched around the world. Including contributions that range from traditional International Political Economy (IPE) to GPE approaches, the *Handbook* gathers the investigations, varying perspectives and innovative research of more than sixty scholars from all over the world.

Providing undergraduates, postgraduates, teachers and researchers with a complete set of traditional, contending and regional perspectives, the book explores current issues, conceptual tools, key research debates and different methodological approaches taken.

Structured in five parts methodologically correlated, the book presents GPE as a field of global, regional and national research:

- historical waves and diverse ontological axes;
- major theoretical perspectives;
- beyond traditional perspectives;
- regional inquiries;
- research arenas.

Carefully selected contributions from both established and upcoming scholars ensure that this is an eclectic, pluralist and multidisciplinary work and an essential resource for all those with an interest in this complex and rapidly evolving field of study.

Ernesto Vivares is a Professor at the Department of International Studies and Communication, FLACSO Ecuador. His publications include *The IPE Puzzle of Regional Inequality, Instability and the Global Insertion of South America*.

The Routledge Handbook to Global Political Economy

Conversations and Inquiries

Edited by Ernesto Vivares

LONDON AND NEW YORK

First published 2020
by Routledge
2 Park Square, Milton Park, Abingdon, Oxon OX14 4RN

and by Routledge
605 Third Avenue, New York, NY 10017

First issued in paperback 2022

Routledge is an imprint of the Taylor & Francis Group, an informa business

Publisher's Note
The publisher has gone to great lengths to ensure the quality of this reprint but points out that some imperfections in the original copies may be apparent.

British Library Cataloguing-in-Publication Data
A catalogue record for this book is available from the British Library

Library of Congress Cataloging-in-Publication Data
Names: Vivares, Ernesto, editor.
Title: The Routledge handbook to global political economy : conversations and inquiries / edited by Ernesto Vivares.
Description: 1 Edition. | New York : Routledge, 2020. | Includes bibliographical references and index.
Identifiers: LCCN 2019050888 (print) | LCCN 2019050889 (ebook) |
ISBN 9781138479883 (hardback) | ISBN 9781351064545 (ebook)
Subjects: LCSH: International economic relations. | International finance. | Free trade. | Economic development–Developing countries. | Environmental economics.
Classification: LCC HF1365 .R678 2020 (print) | LCC HF1365 (ebook) | DDC 337–dc23
LC record available at https://lccn.loc.gov/2019050888
LC ebook record available at https://lccn.loc.gov/2019050889

ISBN: 978-1-03-240012-9 (pbk)
ISBN: 978-1-138-47988-3 (hbk)
ISBN: 978-1-351-06454-5 (ebk)

DOI: 10.4324/9781351064545

Typeset in Bembo
by Wearset Ltd, Boldon, Tyne and Wear

An eResource is available for this title www.routledge.com/9781138479883

Contents

Contents

Figures

Tables

Boxes

Contributors

Alberto Acosta is a Professor at the Department of Development, FLACSO Ecuador. Some of his works are *From the Ghost of Development to Buen Vivir*; *Post-Economía*; *Salidas del laberinto capitalista – Decrecimiento y Postextractivismo*.

Leticia Araya is an Associate Professor at the Department of Public Administration and Policy at Universidad de Santiago de Chile, Chile.

Craig Berry is a Reader in Political Economy at Manchester Metropolitan University. His books include *Pensions Imperilled: The Political Economy of Private Pensions Provision in the UK* and *Austerity Politics and UK Economic Policy*.

Andrea Bianculli is an Assistant Professor at the Institut Barcelona d'Estudis Internacionals (IBEI). Her publications include *Negotiating Trade Liberalization in Argentina and Chile: When Policy Creates Politic*.

Matthew Louis Bishop is a Senior Lecturer in International Politics at the University of Sheffield, UK. His works include *Rethinking the Political Economy of Development beyond 'The Rise of the BRICS'*.

Mark Brawley is a Professor at the Department of Political Sciences, McGill University, Montreal, Canada. His works include *Political Economy and Grand Strategy*. His most recent article applies intra-industry firm heterogeneity to politics: 'And We Would Have the Field'.

Hubert Buch-Hansen is an Associate Professor at the Department of Organization, Copenhagen Business School, Denmark. His works include *The Prerequisites for a Degrowth Paradigm Shift: Insights from Critical Political Economy*.

Stephen Buzdugan is a Senior Lecturer at the Manchester Metropolitan University Business School, UK. Some of his works include *Impact of International Business: Challenges and Solutions for Policy and Practice* (with Tuselman, Cao, Freund, Golesorkhi).

Lester Cabrera is a Lecturer at the Department of International Studies and Communication, FLACSO Ecuador. His works include *Territorial Discourses Opposed in the 21st Century'*.

John Cajas-Guijarro is a Professor of Political Economy at the Central University of Ecuador. His works include *Los capos del comercio. Concentración, poder y acuerdos comerciales en el Ecuador*.

Francisco Castañeda is a Professor at the Faculty of Business and Economics at Universidad de Santiago de Chile, Chile. His publications include *State Owned Enterprises (SOEs) and the Industrial Development in Latin America.*

Philippe De Lombaerde is an Associate Professor of International Economics at Neoma Business School, Rouen, France and was Associate Director at UNU-CRIS. He edited the four volumes on *Regionalism* (with F. Söderbaum).

Melisa Deciancio is currently the Coordinator of the MA in International Relations of FLACSO, Argentina. Her publications include *La construcción del campo de las Relaciones Internacionales argentinas: contribuciones desde la Geopolítica.*

Gian Delgado Ramos is a Tenured Researcher and Professor at the Center for Interdisciplinary Research in Sciences and Humanities of the National Autonomous University of Mexico (UNAM). His publications include *Asentamientos Urbanos Sustentables y Resilientes.*

Gustavo Durán is a Professor at the Department of Public Affairs, FLACSO Ecuador. His publications include *Agua y pobreza en Santiago de Chile: Impacto de la privatización en la emergencia de nuevas formas de exclusión urbana (1977–2009).*

Emrah Karaoğuz is an Assistant Professor in the Department of International Relations at Kadir Has University, Istanbul, Turkey. His publications include *The Developmental State in the 21st Century: A Critical Analysis and a Suggested Way Forward'.*

Bent Greve is a Professor in Social Science at the University of Roskilde, Denmark. His publications include *Technology and the Future of Work. The Impact on Labour Markets and Welfare States.*

Martin Hearson is a Research Fellow at the Institute of Development Studies at the University of Sussex, UK. He is currently working on the book, *The North-South Politics of Global Tax Governance.*

Eric Helleiner is a Professor in the Department of Political Science and Balsillie School of International Affairs, University of Waterloo, Canada. His most recent books include *Governing the World's Biggest Market* (co-edited with Stefano Pagliari and Irene Spagna).

Johannes Jäger is a Professor and Head of Economics Department at the University of Applied Sciences BFI Vienna, Austria. His publications include *Asymmetric Crisis in Europe and Possible Futures.*

Bonn Juego is a Postdoctoral Researcher and University Teacher in International Development Studies at the University of Jyväskylä, Finland. His recent publications are on the theme of the Crises of Development, including the concepts of authoritarian neoliberalism and populism.

Abigail Kabandula is a Lecturer at the Josef Korbel School of International Relations, University of Denver, US. Her published work includes 'Rising Powers and the Horn of Africa: Conflicting Regionalisms' (with Timothy M. Shaw).

Johannes Karremans is Lise Meitner Fellow at the Department of Political Science at the University of Salzburg, Austria. His publications include *Responsive versus Responsible? Party Democracy in Times of Crisis* (with Zoe Lefkofridi).

Sung-Young Kim is a Senior Lecturer at the Department of Modern History, Politics and International Relations, Macquarie University, Australia. His publications include *Hybridized Industrial Ecosystems*.

Max Koch is a Professor in Social Policy at Lund University, Sweden. His publications include *Capitalism and Climate Change*.

Mustafa Kutlay is a Lecturer at the Department of International Politics at City University of London. His works include *Political Economies of Turkey and Greece: Crisis and Change*.

Zoe Lefkofridi is an Associate Professor of Comparative Politics at the Department of Political Science, University of Salzburg, Austria. Her publications include 'A Step Closer to a Transnational Party System' (with Alexia Katsanidou).

Liliana Lizarazo Rodríguez is a Researcher and Lecturer at the Faculty of Law of the University of Antwerp. She has published on constitutional and economic law and International Monetary Fund conditionality, among other topics.

Michael Lukas is an Assistant Professor at the Department of Geography, Faculty of Architecture and Urbanism at the University of Chile. His works include *Global Urban Governance between Neoliberalism (2015–2018)*.

Cheryl Martens is an Associate Professor in the Department of Sociology at the University of San Francisco Quito. Her publications include *Questioning Technology in South America*.

Syed Javed Maswood is an Associate Professor in the Department of Political Science at American University in Cairo, Egypt. His publications include *Trade, Development and Globalization*.

Gustavo Matiuzzi de Souza is a Researcher at PCURS (Brazil). Some of his publications are *Cross-border Paradiplomacy in Mercosur* (with N. Oddone) and *Notions of Border in Regionalism Theory and Praxis*.

Fabiola Mieres is a Technical Officer on Labour Migration at the International Labour Organization based in Geneva. Her most recent publication is *Migration, Recruitment and Forced Labour in a Globalising World*.

John Mikler is an Associate Professor at the Department of Government and International Relations, University of Sydney, Australia. His publications include *The Political Power of Global Corporations*.

Jens Mortensen is an Associate Professor at the Department of Political Sciences, University of Copenhagen. His publications include *Seeing Like the WTO: Numbers, Frames and Trade Law*.

Stephen Nelson is an Associate Professor at the Department of Political Science, Northwestern University. He has published *The Currency of Confidence: How Economic Beliefs Shape the IMF's Relationship with Its Borrowers*.

Shawn Nichols is a Lecturer in the Department of Politics at the University of California, Santa Cruz, USA. Her publications include *Transnational Capital and the Transformation of the State.*

Anthony Payne is a Professorial Fellow at SPERI at the University of Sheffield, UK. He was the founding managing editor of the journal *New Political Economy.* His publications include *Civic Capitalism* (with Colin Hay).

Daniel Pontón is a Professor and Dean of the Security and Defense Center at the Instituto de Altos Estudios Nacionales, Ecuador. His publications include *Organized Crime, Police and Regionalism.*

Germán C. Prieto is an Associate Professor at the Department of International Relations of the Faculty of Political Science and International Relations, in Pontificia Universidad Javeriana (Bogota, Colombia). His publications include *Identidad Colectiva e Instituciones Regionales.*

Michael Pugh is a Professor Emeritus at the University of Bradford. He has published extensively on peace and conflict from a critical perspective. His publications include *Precarity in Post-Conflict Yugoslavia: What About the Workers?*

Cintia Quiliconi is an Associate Professor at the International Studies and Communication Department of FLACSO, Ecuador. Her publications include *Competitive Diffusion of Trade Agreements in Latin America.*

Leonardo Ramos is an Associate Professor of International Relations at Pontifical Catholic University of Minas Gerais (PUC Minas), Brazil. His publications include *A Decade of Emergence: The BRICS Institutional Densification Process.*

Andrea Ribeiro Hoffmann is a Professor of International Relations at the Catholic University of Rio de Janeiro, Brazil. Her publications include *Democratic Theory Questions Informal Global Governance* (with Herz).

Fredy Rivera is a Professor and Researcher at the Department of International Studies and Communication, FLACSO Ecuador and Director of the *Latin American Journal of Security Studies – URVIO.* His publications include *Microtráfico y criminalidad en Quito.*

Ignacio Sabbatella is an Assistant Researcher and Professor at the University of Buenos Aires, Gino Germani Research Institute, and CONICET, Argentina. Published work includes *Neoliberalism and* De facto *Integration in the Southern Cone.*

Marcelo Saguier is the Director of the undergraduate program in International Relations at the School of Politics and Government of the National University of San Martín, Argentina. His publications include *Dams, Chinese Investments and EIAs.*

Thauan Santos is a Researcher and Professor at the Brazilian Naval War College (EGN). His publications include *Evaluating Energy Policies through the Use of a Hybrid Quantitative Indicator-Based Approach.*

Sören Scholvin is a Research Fellow at the Institute of Economic and Cultural Geography, University of Hanover. Hhis publications include *Value Chains in Sub-Saharan Africa: Challenges of Integration into the Global Economy*.

Timothy Shaw is a Research Professor and Graduate Program Director in Global Governance and Human Security at the University of Massachusetts, Boston, USA and Emeritus Professor at the University of London, UK. He has edited the International Political Economy series for Palgrave Macmillan for more than 30 years.

Zhang Shengjun is a Professor and Director of the Institute of International Relations, School of Government, Beijing Normal University, China. His research and teaching areas are global governance and China's role, and China's foreign policy.

Aseema Sinha is the Wagener Chair of South Asian Politics and George R. Roberts Fellow at Claremont McKenna College in California, USA. Publications include *The Regional Roots of Developmental Politics in India: A Divided Leviathan*.

Leonardo Stanley is an Associate Researcher at the Center for the Study of State and Society (CEDES), Buenos Aires, Argentina. His publications include *Emerging Market and Financial Liberalization; The Changing Problem of Regional Development Finance in Latin America*.

Merisa S. Thompson is a Lecturer in Gender and Development at the University of Birmingham, UK. Her publications include *Critical Perspectives on Gender, Food & Political Economy*.

Nicolas Thompson is an Assistant Professor of Politics at the University of South Florida, US. His publications include *Economics & Politics* and *New Political Economy*. He is currently finishing a book about the Federal Reserve System's development.

Elizabeth Thurbon is an Associate Professor in International Political Economy and Scientia Fellow at the School of Social Sciences, UNSW Sydney, Australia. Her publications include *Developmental Mindset: The Revival of Financial Activism in South Korea*.

Diana Tussie is a Professor and Director of the Department of International Relations, FLACSO, Argentina. Her publications include *La Genealogía de la Economía Política Internacional: Rutas, Debates*.

Javier A. Vadell is an Associate Professor at Department of International Relations and Program of Graduate Studies of Pontifical Catholic University of Minas Gerais, Brazil. His publications include *A expansão econômica e geopolítica da China no século XXI*.

Maximiliano Vila Seoane is a Postdoctoral Researcher at the School of Politics and Government of the National University of San Martín (UNSAM), Argentina. His publications include *Cultura Viva: A Challenge to the Creative Economy Policy Discourse in Brazil*.

Ernesto Vivares is a Professor at the Department of International Studies and Communication, FLACSO Ecuador. His publications include *The IPE Puzzle of Regional Inequality, Instability and the Global Insertion of South America*.

William Vlcek is Senior Lecturer in Global Political Economy at the School of International Relations, University of St Andrews, Scotland. His publications include *Offshore Finance and Global Governance: Disciplining the Tax Nomad*.

Linda Weiss is elected Fellow of the Academy of the Social Sciences in Australia and Professor Emeritus in Government and International Relations at the University of Sydney. Major works include *States in The Global Economy*.

Owen Worth is Professor at the Department of Politics & Public Administration. His publications include *Hegemony, International Political Economy and Post-Communist Russia*; *Resistance in the Age of Austerity*.

Li Xing is a Professor and Director at the Department of Politics and Society, Aalborg University and Distinguished Professor by Jiaxing University, China. His recent edited volume is *International Political Economy of the BRICS*.

Acknowledgements

With the passing of the time, in the academic world, one comes to learn that social knowledge is an endeavour, historical, contextual and collective creation, based on research, learning and teaching, never unquestionable. Global Political Economy (GPE) is an ideal case of that. Beyond some partisans claim, it is plural, eclectical and unbounded to a particular epistemic community, language or methodology. The reason behind that is not the absence of a superior research agenda, conceptual and methodological corpus, but its complex and varied ontologies that range from the whole dimension of development themes to the vast issues of conflict in global and regional perspectives. These diverse and related ontologies make GPE a research field where different disciplinary versions coexist more than a unique discipline. GPE is created through different scientific means, always seeking to comprehend how the reality comes about or how to improve that for fairness, asking who wins and who loses. Thus, time, space and people shape and reshape our comprehension of reality and how the final outcomes of that takes form. Even if I am the circumstantial editor, this handbook is global, collective product about GPE, which could not have been written without the support, absences, feedback, suggestions, critiques, sharp observations and inspirations shared by many colleagues both at the North and South, West and East. The vision of the original design and the final outcome varied, as some authors were unable to contribute, but this did not change the geographical and research extension and mission of the handbook. A map is never the reality but helps to find new ways and to discover an unexpected group of great scholars and contributions. This production of the handbook followed my different stances and academic exchanges starting in Ecuador, continuing in Argentina, Brazil, Denmark, Canada and the UK, concluding again in Ecuador. To start with these thanks, I am truly grateful to FLACSO Ecuador for funding and support, as I had the opportunity to work on it during my sabbatical. For institutional backing and inspiration to the Balsillie School of International Affairs, the Institute of Political Economy at Carleton University, FLACSO Argentina and the Department of Cultural and Global Studies, Aalborg University. Thanks to my young and loyal assistant Paula Cordoba for the hard work. Thanks to Robert Crosby and Claire Maloney from Routledge for invaluable advice, and professional and personal encouragement. For inspiration, my sincere recognition goes to to Timothy Shaw, Benjamin Cohen, Diana Tussie, Li Xing, Linda Weiss, Anthony Payne, Eric Helleiner, Mark Brawley, Alberto Acosta, Cintia Quiliconi, Fredy Rivera, Javier Vadell, Leonardo Ramos, Melisa Deciancio, Marcelo Saguier, Owen Worth, Michael Pugh, Aseema Sinha, Sung-Young Kim, Syed Maswood, Abigail Kabandula, Barbara Göbel, Robert Muggah, Andrea Bianculli, Andrea Hoffman, Johannes Jager, Ralph Leiteritz, John Ravenhill, Jane Parpart, Laura Macdonald, Derek Hall, Belen Albornoz, Juan Ponce, Fredrik Söderbaum and Cecile Mouly. Last but not least, thanks to Cheryl, Genaro, Ayel and Alexander for everything.

Abbreviations

A

AARP	American Association of Retired Persons
AC	Andean Community
ACBF	African Capacity Building Foundation
ACP	African, Caribbean and Pacific group of states
ACSC	ASEAN Civil Society Conference
AfDB	African Development Bank
AGRA	Alliance for Green Revolution in Africa
AI	Artificial Intelligence
AIIB	Asian Infrastructure Investment Bank
AKF	Aga Khan Foundation
AKP	Justice and Development Party
AL	League of Arab States
ALADI	Latin American Integration Association
ALALC	Latin American Free Trade Association
ALBA	Bolivarian Alliance of the People of our Americas
ALMP	Active Labour Market Policy
AMISOM	African Union Mission in Somalia
AML	Anti-Money Laundering
AMV	Africa Mining Vision
APEC	Asian Pacific Economic Community
APF	ASEAN Peoples' Forum
APP	Africa Progress Panel
ARPEL	Assistance of National Oil Companies of Latin America
ARWU	Academic Ranking of World Universities
AS	American School
ASEAN	Association of Southeast Asian Nations
ASEM	Asia–Europe Meeting
AU	African Union

B

BAT	Baidu, Alibaba and Tencent
BEPS	Base Erosion and Profit Shifting
BISA	British International Studies Association

BMPE	Black Market Peso Exchange
BRICS	Brazil, Russia, India, China and South Africa
BS	British School

C

CAF	Andean Development Corporation
CAFTA	Central America Free Trade Agreement
CAIS	Central American Integration System
CAN	Andean Community
CAREC	Central Asia Regional Economic Cooperation Program
CARICOM	Caribbean Community and Common Market
CASCF	China Arab-States Cooperation Forum
CASS	Chinese Academy of Social Sciences
CBD	Central Business Districts
CBDR	Common but Differentiated Responsibilities
CBL	Commodity Back Loan
CCETCF	China–Caribbean Economic and Trade Cooperation Forum
CCP	Chinese Communist Party
CDB	China Development Bank
CDD	Customer Due Diligence
CDMA	Code-Division Multiple Access
CDSB	Climate Disclosure Standard Board
CELAC	Community of Latin American and Caribbean States
CEPD	Council for Economic Planning and Development
CETA	Canada Comprehensive Economic and Trade Agreement
CFT	Combating Financial Terrorism
CFTA	Canadian Free Trade Agreement
CHEXIM	China Export–Import Bank
CID	Corridors of Integration and Development
CIER	Regional Energy Integration Commission
CIGS	Copper, Indium, Gallium and Selenium
CIPE	Critical International Political Economy
CIS	Commonwealth of Independent States
CMI	Chang-Mai Initiative
CMW	International Convention on the Protection of the Rights of All Migrant Workers and Members of Their Families
CoE	Council of Europe
COMECON	Council for Mutual Economic Assistance
COMESA	Common Market of Eastern and Southern Africa
COSIPLAN	South American Council of Infrastructure and Planning
CPERN	Critical Political Economy Research Network
CPICF	China–Pacific Island Countries Forum
CPTPP	Comprehensive and Progressive Agreement for Trans-Pacific Partnership
CRA	Credit Rating Agency
CSE	Civil Society Europe
CSO	Civil Society Organization
CSR	Corporate Social Responsibility

CU	Customs Unions
CWUR	Center for World University Rankings

D

DBS	Developmental Bureaucratic States
DCs	Developed Countries
DEİK	Foreign Economic Relations Board
DFLA	Development Finance in Latin America
DNFBP	Designated Non-Financial Business and Professions
DNS	Developmental Network State
DPJ	Democratic Party of Japan
DR–CAFTA	Dominican Republic–Central America Free Trade Agreement
DRC	Democratic Republic of Congo

E

EAC	East African Community
EC	European Commission
ECA	Economic Cooperation Administration
ECB	European Central Bank
ECLAC	Economic Commission for Latin America and the Caribbean
ECOWAS	Economic Community of West African States
ECSC	European Coal and Steel Community
EDB	Singapore's Economic Development Board
EEC	European Economic Community
EES	European Employment Strategy
EIA	Economic Integration Agreements
EITI	Extractive Industry Transparency Initiative
EKC	Environmental Kuznets Curve
EM	Emerging Market
EME	Emerging Market Economy
EMNCs	Emerging Multinational Companies
EMU	European Monetary Union
ENI	Ente Nazionale Idrocarburi
EOI	Export-Oriented Industrialization
EP	European Parliament
EPA	Economic Partnership Agreement
EPB	Economic Planning Board
EPSR	EC Communication on the European Pillar of Social Rights
ERDF	European Regional Development Fund
ESA	European Sociological Association
ESF	European Social Fund
ETA	País Vasco y Libertad (Euskadi Ta Askatasuna)
ETF	Exchange Traded Funds
EU	European Union
EURATOM	European Atomic Energy Community

F

FAANG	Functional Annotations of Animal Genomes
FAO	Food and Agriculture Organization
FAR	Federal Acquisition Regulation
FARC	Revolutionary Armed Forces of Colombia
FATA	Federally Administrated Tribal Areas
FATCA	Foreign Account Tax Compliance Act
FATF	Financial Action Task Force
FDI	Foreign Direct Investment
FEAD	Fund for European Aid to the Most Deprived
FEALAC	Forum for East Asia–Latin America Cooperation
FETCCPC	Forum for Economic and Trade Co-operation between China and Portuguese-Speaking Countries
FFP	Fund for Peace
FIFA	Federation Internationale de Football Association
FLACSO	Latin American School of Social Sciences
FOCAC	Forum on China–Africa Cooperation
FPI	Foreign Portfolio Investment
FPÖ	Austrian Freedom Party
FPSO	Floating units of Production, Storage and Offloading
FPTP	First Past The Post
FSRB	FATF-Style Regional Body
FSRU	Floating Storage and Regasification Unit
FTA	Free Trade Area
FTA	Free Trade Agreement
FTAA	Free Trade Area of the Americas

G

GATT	General Agreement on Trade and Tariffs
GAVI	Global Alliance for Vaccines and Immunizations
GaWC	Globalization and World Cities
GCC	Global Commodity Chain
GCM	Global Compact for Safe, Orderly and Regular Migration
GCR	Global Compact for Refugees
GDP	Gross Domestic Product
GFC	Global Financial Crisis
GHG	Greenhouse Gases
GIF	Global Innovation Fund
GM	General Motors
GNP	Gross National Product
GPA	Government Procurement Agreement
GPE	Global Political Economy
GPN	Global Production Network
GSP	Global Social Policy
GVC	Global Value Chain

H

HAS	Hemispheric Social Alliance
HPAES	High-Performing Asian Economies
HPP	Hydroelectric Power Plants
HST	Hegemonic Stability Theory

I

IACHR	Inter-American Commission Human Rights
IACtHR	Inter-American Court of Human Rights
IADB	InterAmerican Development Bank
IBRD	International Bank for Reconstruction and Development
IBSA	India, Brazil and South Africa
ICANN	Internet Corporation for Assigned Names and Numbers
ICC	International Chamber of Commerce
ICC	International Criminal Court
ICGLR	International Conference on the Great Lakes Region
ICISS	International Commission on Intervention and State Sovereignty
ICSID	International Centre for Settlement of Investment Disputes
ICT	Information Communication Technology
IDA	International Development Association
IDB	Inter-American Development Bank
IDPC	International Drug Policy Consortium
IEA	International Energy Agency
IFC	International Finance Corporation
IFIs	International Financial Institutions
IGAD	Intergovernmental Authority on Development
IGDS	Institute for Gender and Development Studies
IIRSA	Integration of Regional Infrastructure in South America
ILO	International Labour Organization
ILWU	International Longshore and Warehouse Union
IMF	International Monetary Fund
INCR	Investor Network on Climate Risk
INGO	Intergovernmental Organization
IOC	International Olympic Committee
IOs	International Organizations
IoT	Internet of Things
IP	Intellectual Property
IPBES	Intergovernmental Science-Policy Platform on Biodiversity and Ecosystem Services
IPCC	Intergovernmental Panel on Climate Change
IPE	International Political Economy
IPE&E	International Political Economy and the Environment
IPEG	International Political Economy Group
IPR	Intellectual Property Rights
IPSS	Institute for Peace and Security Studies
IR	International Relations

ISA	International Studies Association
ISDS	Investor–State Dispute Settlement
ISI	Import Substitution Industrialization
ISIS	Islamic State of Iraq and the Levant/Syria
ITRI	Industrial Technology Research Institute
ITU	International Telecommunications Union
IVTS	Informal Value Transfer Systems

J

JIT	Just in Time

K

K-MEG	Korea Micro Energy Grid
KCL	King's College London
KSGA	Korea Smart Grid Association
KYC	Know Your Costumer

L

LAFTA	Latin American Free Trade Association
LDC	Least Developed Countries
LDP	Liberal Democratic Party
LEI	Liberal Economic Integration
LIBOR	London Inter-Bank Offered Rate
LNG	Liquified Natural Gas
LRBIO	Liberal Ruled-Based International Order
LTE	Long-Term Evolution
LTTE	Liberation Tigers of Tamil Eelam

M

MDB	Multilateral Development Bank
MDGs	Millennium Development Goals
MENA	Middle East and North African Region
MERCOSUR	Southern Common Market
METI	Ministry of Economy, Trade and Industry
MFI	Multilateral Financial Institutions
MFN	Most-Favoured Nation
MITI	Ministry of International Trade and Industry
MNC	Multinational Corporations
MNEs	Multinational Enterprises
MOFCON	Ministry of Commerce
MOTIE	Ministry of Trade, Industry and Energy
MOU	Memorandum of Understanding on Cooperation
MSIP	Ministry of Science, ICT and Future Planning
MÜSİAD	Independent Industrialists and Businessmen's Association

N

NAFTA	North American Free Trade Agreement
NAIPE	North American IPE
NARP	North American Regional Perspectives
NATO	North Atlantic Treaty Organization
NAZCA	Non-state-Actor Zone for Climate Action
NBI	Nile Basin Initiative
NCCT	Non-Cooperative Countries and Territories
NDB	New Development Bank
NEP	New Economic Policy
NGFS	Network for Greening the Financial System
NGO	Non-Governmental Organization
NICs	Newly Industrialising Countries
NIEO	New International Economic Order
NOCs	National Oil Companies
NORAID	Irish Northern Aid Committee
NSA	National Security Agency
NTB	Non-Tariff Barriers to Trade
NTS	Non-Traditional Security

O

OAS	Organization of American States
OBOR	One Belt One Road
OCDE	Organisation for Economic Cooperation and Development
ODA	Official Development Assistance
OECD	Organization for Economic Cooperation and Development
OEP	Open Economy Politics
OFDI	Overseas Foreign Direct Investment
OFDMA	Orthogonal Frequency-Division Multiple Access
OLADE	Latin American Energy Organization
OMA	Orderly Marketing Agreement
OMC	Open Method of Coordination
OPEC	Organization of Petroleum Exporting Countries
OPIC	Overseas Private Investment Corporation

P

PAP	People's Action Party
PCGG	Presidential Committee on Green Growth
PEP	Politically Exposed Person
PIIGS	Portugal, Ireland, Italy, Greece and Spain
PIPE	Pluralist IPE
PMCs	Private Military Companies
PR	Proportional Representation
PSA	Partial Scope Agreements
PSCs	Private Security Companies

PT	Partido dos Trabalhadores
PV	Photovoltaic

R

R&D	Research and Development
R2P	Responsibility to Protect
RECs	Regional Economic Communities
ROSCs	Reports on the Observance of Standards and Codes
RTA	Regional Trade Agreement
RVC	Regional Value Chains

S

SAARC	South Asian Association for Regional Cooperation
SADC	Southern African Development Community
SAL	Structural Adjustment Loans
SALISES	Sir Arthur Lewis Institute of Social and Economic Studies
SAPS	Structural Adjustment Programs
SAPSN	Southern African People's Solidarity Network
SAS	Small Arms Survey
SCO	Shanghai Cooperation Organization
SDGs	Sustainable Development Goals
SEM	Monitoring Group on Somalia and Eritrea
SINEA	Andean Electrical Interconnection System
SiPErg	Sheffield Interdisciplinary Political Economy Research Group
SME	Small-Medium Enterprise
SOE	State-Owned Enterprise
SPERI	Sheffield Political Economy Research Institute
SPID	Sectoral Plans for Industrial Development
SPS	Sanitary and Phytosanitary Measures
SRF	Silk Road Fund
SSC	South-South Cooperation
SSE	Steady-State Economy
SSRC	Social Science Research Council
STR	Suspicious Transaction Report
STS	Science and Technology Studies
SWAC	Sahel and West Africa Club
SWF	Sovereign Wealth Funds

T

TBTs	Technical Barriers to Trade
TCC	Transnational Capitalist Class
TEEMA	Taiwan Electrical and Electronic Manufacturers Association
TEU	Treaty on the European Union
TFTA	Tripartite Free Trade Agreement

THM	Transnational Historical Materialism
TIM	Turkish Exporters Assembly
TJN	Tax Justice Network
TMD	Turkish Contractors Association
TNC	Transnational Corporation
TNS	Transnational State Apparatus
ToA	Treaty of Amsterdam
TOBB	Turkish Union of Chambers and Commodity Exchanges
TOC	Transnational Organized Crime
TPF	Total Productivity Factors
TPL	Tariff Preference Level
TPM	Trigger Price Mechanism
TPP	Trans-Pacific Partnership
TRIMS	Trade-Related Investment Measures
TRIPs	Trade-Related Aspects of Intellectual Property Rights
TSGIA	Taiwan Smart Grid Industry Association
TTIP	Transatlantic Trade and Investment Partnership
TÜBİTAK	Scientific and Technological Research Council of Turkey
TÜSİAD	Turkish Industry and Business Association

U

UEMOA	West African Economic and Monetary Union
UN	United Nations
UN–ICCP	United Nations–Intergo
UNASUR	Union of South American Nations
UNCTAD	United Nations Conference on Trade and Development
UND	International Transporters Association
UNDESA	United Nations Department of Economic and Social Affairs
UNDP	United Nations Development Programme
UNECA	United Nations Economic Commission for Africa
UNECLAC	United Nations Economic Commission for Latin America and the Caribbean
UNESCO	United Nations Educational, Scientific and Cultural Organization
UNFCCC	United Nations Framework Convention on Climate Change
UNHCR	United Nations High Commissioner for Refugees
UNICEF	United Nations International Children's Emergency Fund
UNIDO	United Nations Industrial Development Organization
UNODOC	United Nations Office on Drugs and Crimes
USMCA	US Mexico Canada Agreement
USTR	United States Trade Representative
UWI	University of the West Indies

V

| VER | Voluntary Export Restraint |

W

WACD	West African Commission on Drugs
WB	World Bank
WBG	World Bank Group
WDR	World Development Report
WEF	Water–Energy–Food
WHO	World Health Organization
WIOD	World Input–Output Database
WOA	World Order Approach
WTO	World Trade Organization

Y

YMCA	Young Men's Christian Association

Z

ZEDEC	Specific Zones for Controlled Development

Introduction

Ernesto Vivares

In 2009, Mark Blyth, the editor of the comprehensive and substantive first version of the *Routledge Handbook of International Political Economy*, defined it as not "a textbook" seeking to establish what International Political Economy (IPE) was, but a picture of a pluralist field that was flourishing internationally. Indeed, a long list of scholars has contributed to enhancing IPE, defining its multidisciplinary character with insights from history, sociology, gender studies, postcolonialism, postdevelopmentalism, geopolitics and security. Few field studies are so lively and challenging given its wider range of diverse traditional or heterodox perspectives, and methodologies to grasp issues of development and conflict.

Briefly, for some, IPE is still the subdiscipline of International Relations bond to North American traditions of Political Sciences (Maliniak and Tierney 2009). For others, it is a Global Political Economy (GPE), defined by multidisciplinarity and plurality (Ravenhill 2017); a field of inquiry that gathers multiple and varied conversations about development and conflict within a world order. In this *Handbook*, we assume that both perspectives are legitimate, as they mirror two academic identities of the vast and heterogeneous academic field that goes from IPE to GPE. Two sides that, whatever the focus and resources of these perspectives, share a common element, that is to comprehend how the struggle for power and wealth bring about development and conflict in the intersections between international–domestic, state–market, regional and global, formal and informal realities of development.

This *Handbook* is a contribution to the vast array of work on IPE and GPE and is designed as a tool for research-oriented teaching and learning at postgraduate level, with plural, multidisciplinary and global criteria. It does not seek to explain the traditional schools or present universal definitions, ontologies or methodologies of either IPE or GPE but to strengthen the academic development of IPE and GPE from multiple perspectives and interests. The *Handbook* surveys the large variety of orientations and paradigms followed, as well as theories, central concepts, methodologies and types of evidence used in the field at global level, with and beyond the Western academy. It breaks away from the typical edited format that gathers the *flor y nata* (crème de la crème of scholars) in the field, to incorporate new perspectives, topics and research issues, which are reorienting the field. One of these new features is to include and go beyond the geography of mainstream approaches, generally self-referenced and self-legitimated. Second, the *Handbook* covers a range of traditional and non-traditional theoretical and methodological

IPE and GPE perspectives, in order to revitalize global conversations, the exchange and plural openness of the field. Third, it provides access to a Companion Website where scholars will find the classical and most referenced works for teaching learning and research in IPE and GPE, such as the chapters of Robert Gilpin (1987) and Benjamin Cohen (2019a; 2019b), questions for essays and exams and further readings. This approach prioritizes the progress of global scholarly rather than to focus on universal and ahistorical views, theoretical or methodological antagonisms, or academic chauvinisms revolving around different schools. Fourth, nearly the majority of the works are contributions from scholars of varied regional origins and orientations. Last but not least, the *Handbook* has contributions from a significant number of female scholars and contains feminist perspectives, something frequently overlooked in edited collections in the field.

Handbooks in the field commonly summarize academic orientations, debates, limits and contributions of specific schools or orientations of either IPE or GPE. These diverse IPE perspectives are not random ideas but indeed different IPE orientations and academic comprehensions concerning the global order. This therefore makes them useful tools for teaching, learning and research. In the first edition of the *Handbook*, Blyth opted to present a picture that extended the geographical scope of IPE to other global conversations in Asia and Latin America, although it remained mostly focused on Western directions (2009). The concept of "conversations" was Blyth's bold contribution to divert the debate and go beyond the boundaries set by Cohen's dichotomy of North American IPE versus the British School (2007; 2008). A decade later, with a world in flux, reality rechallenges our field, this time for responses to unforeseen global and regional issues of development, conflict and transformation, within and beyond the West. The second edition of the *Routledge Handbook* is about GPE as a tool for teaching, learning and research at postgraduate level. Thus, the *Handbook* is designed to further and deepen both the scope of IPE and GPE, within and beyond the Western traditional approaches, by supporting the global academic development of postgraduate students and scholars at postgraduate level. The strength of the *Handbook* is the methodological complementarity of its diverse contributions, set in a sequence of sections that groups specific chapters defining their pluralist, historical, geographical and development contributions. The format of the book, therefore, supports, complements and extends concepts covered in a vast array of similar texts, in terms of approaches, debates, traditional and new research topics, and also presents diverse methodologies. Despite the poor academic idea that there is only one version of IPE or GPE, we present here the wider range of faces, approaches and research orientations that populate IPE and GPE.

As a postgraduate instrument, the *Handbook* contains several foundational texts and will be enhanced by some prior knowledge concerning the debates and theories of IPE and GPE, especially concerning the comprehension and identification of the significant Western approaches and global discussions, and methodologies.

A handbook for teaching, learning and research

In a time of shock and high levels of uncertainty in the international, regional and national scenarios (Hay and Payne 2017), the main aim of the *Handbook* is simple: to contribute to *the academic development of IPE and GPE as a research-oriented field widening their boundaries* (Ravenhill 2017; Seabrooke and Young 2017). The justification of that is simple. The unforeseen developments of the last 20 years demand a recalibration of the missions and bridges between IPE and GPE, assuming their different ontological and epistemological parameters that are not always combinable (Lake 2013). We assume that this work must take place in light of finding responses to the tidal wave of disillusionment concerning the liberal order, world power transitions, the rise of nationalism and xenophobia, inequality, humanitarian crises, environmental disasters and increased unemployment related to technological advancements that are more and more replacing human labour. In response, GPE is becoming more oriented by pluralism and multidisciplinarity in growing conversations among different disciplines, geographical networks, epistemic communities, factions and hubs fostering new research (Seabrooke and Young 2017). This provides evidence of the rapid transformation of a field of inquiry beyond divides and dualisms around the paradigms, theories and methods that used to characterize the field of IPE (Maliniak and Tierney 2009; Seabrooke and Young 2017).

IPE and GPE

IPE and GPE are complementary and overlapping in their foci, but not the same. While GPE is generally produced out of the local circumstances to cover themes such as development, growth, conflict and more (Grosfoguel 2006; Tussie 2018). IPE, in contrast, tends to start with general themes and definitions that are thus applied to the local, sometimes with the risk of transferring interpretations from one context onto different contextual realities (Hobson 2013; Helleiner and Rosales 2017). GPE and IPE both, however, need to recuperate the big questions of our time. Besides, there are methodological and epistemological differences within both IPE and GPE: For some the field is scientific, and for others, an interpretive endeavour, indeed, the division between IPE and GPE is part of a logical progression within the Social Sciences.

IPE and GPE are, therefore, somehow different, yet connected pools where research, teaching and learning interconnect local and global thematic concerns, using varied disciplines and area studies to comprehend the realities of development and conflict and why these are taking place in one way and not in another. Beyond that, indeed, there are essential distinctions in each field. Mainstream English-speaking IPE is classically liberal in its conceptual framework, and how to assume development, its central point of reference and gravity is North America and its history and is often considered a subfield of International Relations (Lake 2011). The hallmark of mainstream IPE is its actor-oriented, liberal institutionalist and neoclassical domestic economic perspectives tied to empiric–positivist methodologies that converge in the so-called Open Economy Politics (OEP) (King *et al.* 1994; Frieden and Martin 2002; Lake 2009; Oatley 2012).

The problem with mainstream IPE is that it leaves out significant North American contributions and absorbs Canadian (Germain 2009) and Australian (Seabrook and Ellias 2011) schools as well as the North American left (Murphy 2011; Cohen 2019a, 2019b). Also, GPE can be seen to include IPE perspectives, but not vice-versa, as they have different ontological and epistemological status and research orientations. Assuming the separation of this pragmatic definition, IPE and GPE's ontologies vary from the very different contextual and historical realities that they reflect. While mainstream IPE defines itself as an international American paradigm (Lake 2011), GPE covers a broader range of perspectives and research orientations, to comprehend development and conflict according to the history and latitude of the theme of study (Hobden and Hobson 2002; Helleiner 2015). That is central due to the existence of the African, the Latin American, Asian, East Asian and Middle Eastern political economy approaches, which cannot be overlooked any longer. Different ontologies and research agendas mark each one of these regional and thematical strands since they have different concerns about development and conflict, uneven international insertions, vast inequalities, and massive informal, conflict and security and undercover sectors. Therefore, it is logical that they share, to a great extent, the tools of IPE, but they tend to see the same global issues from different ontological and epistemological lens.

Undeniably, unforeseen global developments bring into question the traditional boundaries of teaching and research within IPE and GPE. Occurrences such as the rise of right-wing politics of Trump, Farage, Orban, Salvini, Conte and, in Latin America, Bolsonaro, all defined by their shift to mercantilism, nationalism and xenophobia, shows the fractures in the values, major institutions and goods that for decades have been guaranteed by the global liberal order. Mainstream IPE's concern in the 1980s and 1990s was the architecture of this order, the liberal democracy, free-market economy and multilateral systems, which are all questioned today, to a great extent because of inequality and elites impunities. For instance, the central tenet of democracy is that it stems from the free-will individuals, but where does that legitimacy remain when companies such as Cambridge Analytics can manipulate electoral results? If the market is a logical result of the sum of individual rationalities seeking to maximize benefits generating equilibrium in the distributions of wealth, why are markets also primary sources of inequality? If free markets are the centrepiece of wellbeing, how can we explain that work is no longer central for individuals, families and society? If the multilateral order was built to protect liberty and human rights, why are wars, environmental disasters, nationalisms, hidden worlds and migration not included in our research field?

Observed from the top, the picture of the Liberal Order's decline would seem to have limited or few explanations from formal IPE, except to blame populist politics and lack of values from societies (Edwards 2012; Mearsheimer 2019). However, approached from below, in terms of political–economic insertions, conflict and development, ultra-conservative politics look more like a Polanyian circle (which provides another option of interpretation). That is the result of a historical political–economic dynamic, where neoclassical economies and unleashed markets generate inequality and political conflict (Polanyi 2001). Some would argue that this cycle, in turn, calls for Cesarean leadership to avenge fragmented and denigrated societies to establish new orders that counter the liberal order and its elites. The Frankfurt School had similar concerns in the face of the rise of European Nazism and fascism, and the totalitarian Western rationalism (Jeffries 2016). In stable times, the knowledge that explains reality tends to crystallize and become like technologies (Cox 2000), but in times of change, the research speaks, and that is one of the main challenges for both IPE and GPE today.

The academic challenge of GPE is not something new, and in recent years several leading scholars have argued in favour of these new directions (Acharya 2011; Ravenhill 2017; Shaw *et al.* 2019; Tussie 2018), the contributions in this *Handbook* fall along those lines. The main argument here is the need to extend the geographical, topical and methodological boundaries to advance towards IPE and GPE, nurturing teaching, research and publishing to the comprehension of complex realities of development and conflict today. Some scholars will undoubtedly wonder how far these limits might be extended, but that answer is a collective endeavour that rests on what we will make of the field.

The essence of this *Routledge Handbook* is not to present contributions from certain factions or to develop a universal school (typical in our field). This *Handbook* seeks instead to reflect part of the vast and varied global array of theoretical and methodological contributions from a wide range of global origins, diverse perspectives and specific inquiries concerning developments and boundaries in IPE and GPE. The *Handbook* is organized in five parts and gathers fifty-one contributions of sixty-eight scholars. It contains different theoretical, methodological, thematical, geographical and research-oriented contributions, to facilitate the research-oriented teaching and learning of GPE and the plurality of approaches and multidisciplinary in its focus. The following section provides a short synopsis of the contents of each part of the *Handbook*.

Part I: Historical waves and diverse ontological axes

The first part includes some of the most established and dominant approaches in IPE and the significant contributions that expand on these approaches. These identify some of the significant shifts and convergences about how IPE was and is nowadays academically comprehended and educated. The six chapters in this section present multiple and conceptual contours in the development of the field. It starts in the Introduction with some reference to the conceptual cornerstones of Gilpin's holy trinity (Liberalism, Realism and Marxism) and the geographical epistemic divide of Cohen (American and British Schools). These two principal contrasting contributions are essential to the framing of mainstream IPE and are significant contributions to their field and the teaching, learning and research within the fields of IPE and GPE. The following chapter discusses and questions the state of British IPE, how it is limited to a small number of influential scholars and subordinated to the North American IPE, losing its identity and the real big question, development. The subsequent analysis discusses the necessary ontological shift from IPE to GPE by exploring its historical roots out of the Western world in order. History and geography, accordingly, is the first key to expanding the limits and conceptual cages in the field. The following chapter centres on the two chief propositions fuelling Western neoliberal IPE. The next analysis also inquiries these boundaries of mainstream based on two main arguments. The first is that poverty can be reduced by market means without industrialization and that under globalization; the role of the state in development is minimal. This is logically followed by an examination of the extent to which we are witnessing a hegemonic shift with the rise of China, or how to epistemologically approach that from a GPE. Thus, once the global discussion is open, the subsequent two works aim to give voice to regions. Tussie's chapter first explores the Latin American IPE, unfolding must-read insights for the field of GPE, then Shaw's chapter about Africa mainly explores the theory and practice of the field in the continent.

Part II: Theoretical methodological perspectives

In Part II, the *Handbook* presents some of the most used and varied IPE perspectives, where scholars will find a significant range of conceptual chapters, pedagogically designed, with a classroom orientation to contribute to syllabi, theoretical frameworks and literature reviews. The section starts with the deployment of the detailed conceptualization and methodologies of the Open Economy Monetary Politics; followed a substantive analytical work about theory, concepts and methodology of the Open Trade Policy. The contributions continue with a consistent and systematic picture of the themes of the global commodity chains, global value chains and global production networks. This links the readings with a pedagogical conceptualization and examines the underexplored topic of regional value chains and after a consistent and substantive work about Constructivist IPE. The next chapters focus on exploration and analysis of a set of central concepts in the field, such as the world order and perspectives, Marxist and Gramscian IPEs as well as the elusive category of the Hegemon, as well as the new approach of Post Development. All these chapters are outstanding analytical pieces for use in classrooms and research.

Part III: Beyond traditional perspectives

The chapters in this section are devoted to a broad set of topics that go beyond the traditional boundaries of the fields of Political Sciences and Economics and present different global research patterns. Postgraduates students and academics will find a wide range of substantive perspectives, ideas and approaches for inspiration. The first chapter provides an in-depth analysis of the complex issue of Brazil, Russia, India, China and South Africa (BRICS) within the changing dynamics of the world order. The next chapter analyses the reality and battles concerning Global Economic Governance and different and opposite post-war perspectives. Giving continuity to IPE conceptual contributions, the next chapter follows the extensively disputed topic of regionalism and considers the range of perspectives to study regionalism both theoretically and methodologically and considers the limitations and conceptual cages that become evident when trying to apply Eurocentric and North America mainstream approaches to other regions, such as South America. The following chapters provide an essential set of perspectives. These include the work on transnational class, a chapter on ecological economics, degrowth and welfare, as well as discussions on extractivism, the work on national borders and regionalisms, the IPE of war and liberal peace and the topic of transnational organized crime.

Part IV: Regional perspectives and inquiries

The scholarly essays in this fourth part address the essential topic of a GPE that is the conversations and inquiries from regions towards the global order and mainstream IPE on all sides and at all levels of development and conflict. The section includes a wide range of regional contributions from Africa, Europe, Latin America, the Middle East, and Southeast Asia. It opens with a comparative essay about the IPE of China, Africa and Latin America. It follows with a discussion about the political–economic tensions inherent within the configuration of the Europe Union, and next, a groundbreaking study on the IPE of development in Southeast Asia. This ties in with an in-depth and sharp analysis of East Asia's development estate. The Eastern side of the global order is further discussed in the chapter about the IPE of rising India. The following chapter voices issues from Africa concerning the IPE of human security. The next chapter develops a discussion of the Turkish perspective concerning Middle East regionalism. The following chapter provides one of the most complete studies about the IPE of development finance in Latin America, followed by a unique constructivist analysis about the IPE of Regionalism in South America. The section closes with the advanced study of the IPE of Caribbean Development.

Part V: New research arenas

This section mirrors a significant part of new research topics that are expanding the traditional limits of IPE. As a research-oriented field, what defines the scholars of GPE are both the traditional and new investigations characterized by their multidisciplinarity and pluralism. The essays here are central for scholars interested in new avenues of research. The section begins with a detailed and comprehensive examination of the global social governance, followed by the substantive work about global production networks, and the innovative research about global tax governance. As part of new research issues in GPE, the next chapter considers the impact of new technologies on labour markets, followed by a study of the research agendas of cyber politics in the Global South. The next chapter presents an investigation about regional energy integration, followed by a work that undertakes a critical exploration and analyses the polemical industrial policy in Latin America, all vital texts for research. That is followed by an investigation about global corporations, while the next piece explores the transdisciplinary research issue of cities, migrations and crises. All of that is complemented by an in-depth analysis of the different approaches in the IPE of the environment. Finally, the *Handbook* presents two innovative studies of IPE and economic intelligence, and the examination of money laundering and terrorism.

The chapters here cover a wide range of studies from empiricist to interpretivist approaches with their possible research links or connections, in a theoretical and methodological blend of different GPE orientations. The *Handbook* also includes traditional Anglo-Saxon approaches aiming to offer a complete picture of IPE and GPE, showing the ontological lines of debate and rupture, to finally deploy global orientations of research in theoretical, regional and developmental issues.

References

Acharya, A. 2011. "Dialogue and Discovery: In Search of International Relational relations Theories and Beyond the West". *Millennium: Journal of International Studies* 39(3): 619–637.

Blyth, M. ed. 2009. *Routledge Handbook of IPE: IPE as a Global Conversation*. New York: Routledge.

Cohen. B. 2007. "The Transatlantic Divide: Why are American and British IPE So Different?" *Review of International Political Economy* 14(2): 197–219.

Cohen. B. 2008. "The Transatlantic Divide: A Rejoinder". *Review of International Political Economy* 15(I): 30–34.

Cohen, B. 2019a. *Advanced Introduction to International Political Economy*. Cheltenham: Edward Elgar.

Cohen, B. 2019b. The Multiple Traditions of the American IPE. In Blyth, M. ed. *Routledge Handbook of International Political Economy*. London: Routledge. 23–35.

Cox R. 2000. Political Economy and World Order: Problems of Power, Knowledge. In Stubbs, R. and Underhill, G. eds. 2000. *Political Economy and the Changing World Order*. New York: Oxford University Press.

Edwards, S. 2012. *Left Behind: Latin America and the False Promise of Populism*. Chicago: University of Chicago Press.

Frieden, J. and Martin, L. 2002. International Political Economy: Global and Domestic Interactions. In Katznelson, I. and Milner, H. eds. *Political Science: The State of the Discipline*. New York: W.W. Norton. 118–146.

Gemain, R. 2009. Of Margins, Traditions, and Engagements: A Brief Disciplinary History of IPE in Canada. In Blyth, M. ed. *Routledge Handbook of International Political Economy*. London: Routledge. 77–91.

Gilpin, R. 1987. *The Political Economy of International Relations*. Princeton, NJ: Princeton University Press.

Grosfoguel, R. 2006. "From Postcolonial Studies to Decolonial Studies: Decolonizing Postcolonial Studies: A Preface". *Review* 24(2).

Hay, C. and Payne, A. 2017. The Great Uncertainty. SPERI paper No 5. http://speri.dept.shef.ac.uk/wp-content/uploads/2018/11/SPERI-Paper-No. 5-The-Great-Uncertainty-389KB.pdf.

Helleiner, E. 2015. "Globalising the Classical Foundations of IPE Thought." *Contexto Internacional* 37(3): 975–1010.

Helleiner, E. and Rosales, A. 2017. "Peripheral Thoughts for Global IPE." *International Studies Quarterly* 61: 924–934.

Hobden, S. and Hobson, J., eds. 2002. *Historical Sociology of International Relations*. New York: Cambridge University Press.

Hobson, J. 2013. "Part 1 – Revealing the Eurocentric Foundations of IPE". *Review of International Political Economy* 20(5): 1024–1054.

Jeffries, S. 2016. *Grand Hotel Abyss: The Lives of the Frankfurt School*. London: Verso.

King, G., Keohane, R. and Verba, S. 1994. *Designing Social Inquiry. Scientific Inference in Qualitative Research*. Princeton, NJ: Princeton University Press.

Lake, D. 2009. "Open Economy Politics: A Critical Review". *Review of International Organizations* 4(3): 219–244.

Lake, D. 2011. TRIPs across the Atlantic: Theory and Epistemology in IPE. In Nicola, P. and Weaver, C. eds. *International Political Economy. Debating Past, Present and Future*. London: Routledge.

Lake, D. 2013. "Theory is Dead, Long Live Theory: The End of the Great Debates and the Rise of Eclecticism in International Relations." *European Journal of International Relations* 19(3): 567–587.

Maliniak, D. and Tierney, M. 2009. "The American School of IPE". *Review of International Political Economy* 16(1): 6–33.

Mearsheimer, J. 2019. "Bound to Fail: The Rise and Fall of the Liberal International Order". *International Security* 43(4): 7–50.

Murphy, C. 2011. Do the Left-Out Matter?. In Phillips, N. and Weaver, C. eds. *International Political Economy: Debating the Past, Present and Future*. London: Routledge. 160–168.

Oatley, T. 2012. *International Political Economy*. New York: Routledge.

Polanyi, K. 2001. *The Great Transformation: The Political and Economic Origins of Our Time*. Boston: Beacon Press.

Ravenhill, J. 2017. *Global Political Economy*. Oxford: Oxford University Press.

Seabrook, L. and Ellias, J. 2010. "From Multilateralism and Microcosm in the World Economy: The Sociological Turn in Australian International Political Economy Scholarship". *Australian Journal of International Affairs* 64(1): 1–12.

Seabrooke, L. and Young, K. 2017. "The Networks and Niches of International Political Economy". *Review of International Political Economy* 24(2): 288–331.

Shaw, T., Mahrenbach, L., Modi, R. and Yi-chong, X., 2019. *The Palgrave Handbook of Contemporary International Political Economy*. New York: Palgrave Macmillan.

Tussie, D. 2018. La Genealogía de la Economía Política Internacional: Rutas, Debates, y Desafíos en América Latina, in Urrego Sandoval, C., Leiteritz, R., Jiménez Peña, G. and Fuentes Sosa, N., eds. *Economía Política Internacional en America Latina: Teoría y Práctica*. México: CIDE.

1

Global conversations and inquiries

Ernesto Vivares

GPE: a growing research field

Global Political Economy (GPE) as a research field is expanding, although it is still limited in its scholarly outputs both in the North and South, East and West. Different research contributions in Western countries, Africa, Asia, Latin America and the Middle East make this evident (Seabrooke and Young 2017; Shaw 2019; Tussie 2018). GPE and International Political Economy (IPE) have different ontological, epistemological and methodological status. By IPE, the primary referent is mainstream and English-speaking IPE that defines itself as an international American paradigm (Lake 2011), while GPE presents a broader range of pluralistic perspectives and research orientations, to examine development and conflict according to the history and latitude of the themes of study (Helleiner 2015; Hobden and Hobson 2002). Under this pluralist and eclectic categorization, Critical IPEs, Feminist, Critical Geopolitical Economy, Post Colonial and Post Development IPEs, among others, can be considered segments within GPE. Therefore, GPE includes IPE but no vice-versa, as they have different ontological and epistemological standing and research orientations defined by diverse historical, geographical and methodological elements that set in different ways very diverse approaches. That is from empirical positivist OPE to the most radical Post Developmental and Feminist GPEs.

Accordingly, we assume that GPE is not a counter-hegemonic approach in contrast to Western thinking or a means to throw away all done in IPE. Instead, GPE emerges as an ongoing set of conversations and inquiries to the world order from diverse perspectives focused to a significant extent upon the wide conceptual umbrellas of development and conflict. In that sense, GPE may includes all strands of thinking, under the common factor of addressing development and conflict, within the coordinates between politics and economics, domestic and international, in the formal and informal pursuit of wealth and power in the world order (Cohen 2019a; Frieden *et al.* 2017; Gilpin 1975; Oatley 2018; Shaw *et al.* 2019; Underhill and Stubbs 2000). There are boundaries that impede to set a unique and universal definition for the field and the essential limitation to consider it as a traditional discipline.

Beyond that, the central concern of IPE and GPE assumed in this *Handbook* are related to the development of structures and orientations of their scholarship, and the vital task to update and reassess their missions today, as, in particular, IPE still bears the orientations set out four decades ago to explore the liberal world order (Ashworth 2002; de Carvalho 2011; Hobson 2012). Indeed, the central approaches of the English-speaking IPE were developed between the 1970s and 1980s (Cohen 2019a). IPE thus emerged as a subfield of International Relations (IR), bringing into IR the debate about the power of markets and financial globalization. IPE was, however, not an alternative to IR, but a door that broadened the scope of power with wealth, state and markets. The end of the Bretton Woods system, the Cold War and the rise of globalization consolidated the dominant idea that nothing was going to take back the liberal order and its universal standards. In other words, the ensemble among liberal democracy, the market economy and international conduct as standards of civilization (Bull and Watson 1984; Hobson 2013). English-speaking IPE was born within the optimistic limits of the liberal order and was vulnerable to its decline. However, reality changes and, nearly four decades later, we realize that historical responses concerning development and conflict in the international order were already developed in the early eighteenth century in different parts of the world (Helleiner 2015; Hobson 2013). In the 2020s, the mission of IPE is outdated, limited and rather insufficient for GPE, the former showing severe constraints in its scholarship when it comes to comprehending unforeseen changes forty years ago (Lake 2013).

There is a long list of issues that IPE is not prepared to address, and that is due its ontological and epistemological orientations defined to produce knowledge between the formal economy and politics in their links with the international (e.g. trade, finance, institutions, regimes, economic integration and others). Issues such as power transitions and hard tensions between a declining neoliberal order and rising nationalisms remain outside the scope of mainstream IPE. Indeed, mainstream IPE has never claimed to be able to deal with themes such as media manipulating democracies, xenophobia, security conflicts, humanitarian crises, environmental disasters, informal worlds and regionalisms, let alone the uncontrollable technological revolution, and the increasing inequality between countries and within societies. IPE and GPE constitute two different perspectives whose tools and big questions have to converge open and plurally in teaching, learning and research.

At some point, IPE lost its focus on the questions concerning development and conflict in world affairs and became more technological sets that function to explain and justify the liberal political–economic order. Thus, its main strength turned into its major weaknesses today, that is its lack of adaptability and dialogue with other epistemic groups and factions out of the West. Instead of undertaking a search for universal answers, GPE develops scholarship by exploiting the possibilities of pluralistic debates, problematizing realities and widening global inquiries drawing on an eclectic range of tools.

Indeed, these dynamics are experienced by students and lecturers alike who have to deal with opposite and outdated interpretations about what IPE is, narrowing the development of the scholarly. While mainstream approaches can be self-referential and lack dialogue with other perspectives, we can also find a loose sense of how IPE approaches in the Global South are applied and reproduced (Deciancio 2018). Beyond Western approaches, IPE features by epistemic segmentation and, in many cases, parochial orientations in terms of conversations and exchange with the dominant academic communities (Tussie 2018).

The central problem behind dominant interpretations about IPE in the Global South is the tendency to have an insufficient dialogue with inadequate or lack of access to global, regional and developmental voices, for epistemic academic progress. Narrowing the scholarly research even more, in some cases mainstream IPE is still taught as a formal field of study laying in-between two fields of studies, political science and economics (Cohen 2019a). For graduates that is a necessary introduction but for postgraduates it is a poor teaching. Furthermore, it is taught as the study of power within the liberal order on the intersections between states and markets, and the domestic and international (Gilpin 1975: 43). All the abovementioned have been the great tools of IPE up to now but are not enough for teaching GPE and the new world dynamics of development and conflict, wherein we still do not unlock the new transformations and role of power and wealth.

The picture of mainstream IPE is useful, however, as considering the state of world affairs, plagued of unpredicted developments and crises, we need to offer more to students and scholars for teaching, learning and research in GPE. The idea that IPE owns a formal object of inquiry and shares standards to certify specialists and legitimize their research and academic publications is more a definition for specific epistemic communities than for the whole, and does not help (i.e. Cohen 2019a). Even in the Anglo-Saxon IPE that is not present. According to Seabrooke and Young (2017), between five and seven organizational logics at work in IPE can be identified that defines how it is reproduced and how scholars are educated (Seabrooke and Young 2017: 323). Traditional divides in IPE dominate in classrooms, while Western control over the generation of theories or their questioning prevails in the top publications (ibid.).

However, with the production of IPE in other latitudes other than that of the West, similar limitations appear. In the Global South, IPE generally resembles more a global imported and local-oriented, either orthodox or heterodox, field of research about development and conflict but with different tonalities of exchange (Leiteritz 2005; Madeiras *et al.* 2016;). There the dialogues with the Anglo-Saxon IPE derivate either in mechanic importations, dependence, hybridizations or even resistances to the epistemic relationship (Tickner 2003; Tickner and Weaver 2009). The barrier in the South is its centrifuge parochialism and segmentation in small factions, generally defined by gatekeepers, their lack of conversations with other epistemic communities and the strong tendency to hydride concepts to explain current political tendencies.

Box 1.1 Conceptual cages

In his *The Protestant Ethic and the Spirit of Capitalism*, Max Weber warned how the successful ideas and projects of one era had been turned into political *iron cages* of another (2017). According to Weber (2017), the use of certain concepts for current research, removed from their original meaning, and the political purposes given to them by their founders, usually justify the survival and expansion of existing powers rather than explaining social change. Weber calls such historical ideas, namely those with a strong political sense in their orientation of development, "long lasting iron cages" of ideas, derived from rationalized forms of how reality functions in one historical context (2017). The Weberian metaphor might be a useful concept as a basis to identify and analyse the theoretical and methodological elements that are necessary in order to avoid the biases in teaching, learning and research.

Despite limitations, GPE is growing in the Western world, into that beyond the old traditional and peripheral traditions of IPE. For instance, the research of Seabrooke and Young highlights how IPEs are moving towards the contributions of evermore junior scholars (2017:322). Hence, IPE is moving towards multiple IPEs and to the wide field research of GPE, and this *Handbook* is only part of that evidence. If we consider that the nature and orientation of social knowledge are tied to time, space and social structures, then, it follows that GPE is no different from other fields of social knowledge. It reflects regional and local historical orientations similar or different to dominant Western IPE and GPE perspectives, given their diverse international insertions, orientations and outcomes of developments. Today, we know that IPE and GPE did not start in the Anglo-Saxon world as different research shows, but still, we teach that around a core of academic myths (de Carvalho *et al.* 2011; Hobson 2013). Evidence demonstrates how international and global political–economic contributions have been raised as historical responses in different parts of the world throughout history (Helleiner and Rosales 2017a, 2017b).

The existence of the Western core mainstream does not necessarily invalidate the presence of other political economic perspectives, as conversations with the world order, based on knowledge process of either import, dependence, hybridization or resistance (i.e. Grosfoguel 2009; Tickner and Waever 2009). On the contrary, Western IPEs would benefit from the opening up of the horizon for a broader and inclusive range of different understandings of IPEs, and this is why the first section of the *Handbook* is devoted to different ontological and epistemic architectures, research scope and historical shifts of the multiple faces of IPE and GPE.

We need to bear in mind something about GPE. Whatever the orientation of IPE, one concept remains common to all its varied strands and orientations: that is the promise to bring new insights to the comprehension of development and conflict. That is the result of the formal or informal pursuit of wealth and power in the connections between state and market, politics and economics, and international and domestic. All IPEs fall somehow within some part of these ontological coordinates, creating a multiplicity of alternatives for teaching, learning and research that we define here as GPEs. In this *Handbook* we are rephrasing the study and research of how the political power and wealth production and distribution, formal and informal, have been intertwined throughout world history, in different latitudes shaping international, regional and local orders in terms of development and conflict (Braudel 1979; Payne and Phillips 2010). Exploring one way to globalize the field, Helleiner, for instance, as well other scholars (de Carvalho *et al.* 2011; Hobson 2013) have evidenced that, in order to engage in a real global conversation, the teaching, learning and research of IPE must review the limited history of North American and European thinking, developing a more global intellectual history (Hobson 2012). Moreover, positively, different contributions identify the significance of the IPE approaches in diverse parts of the world (all quoted by Chin *et al.* 2014; Helleiner 2015: Özveren 2015; Sartori 2008).

Variations about the teaching, learning and research in IPE and GPE populate the IPE, and usually, they are inundated with different divides such as Realism, Liberalism, Marxism, OPE, North American–British, positivist versus interpretivist methodologies and more. These divisions are reproduced in classrooms and are thus translated into research, which in many cases dominates epistemic communities, factions or clusters, claiming to educate the real discipline of IPE and GPE (Cohen 2019a; Mignolo 2016; Seabrooke and Young 2017: 324).

Two main issues arise as a result of this bias. The first is related to how in several international and regional academic programmes, scholars are taught and trained in the field. That, in turn, frames the orientations and chances for the academic growth of the field. Second, these limited parameters of study produce a methodological bias, due to omissions, within the research that deals with issues and different approaches to political economy – this is the importance of pluralistic teaching, learning and research within GPE.

The debate about what is GPE and what types of knowledge the field produces varies depending on the range of the diverse ontological and epistemological positions in the field (Ravenhill 2017). These include the contentions and controversies in the field, whether they are normative, scientific, interpretivist, or an alternative discipline or research enterprise. Seabrooke and Young (2017), present one of the last pictures of political economy today, mapping its varied communities and orientations concerning teaching, researching and publishing (291) but they remain focused on the English-speaking academy. Language is a serious barrier in the field. Paradoxically, most of the academic communities make an effort to produce or translate their scholarship to English, something that does not happen the other way. That raises the question as to where the rest of the world falls on the map when academic communities do not speak English. The problem related to this is an academic cage of self-reference and self-legitimacy, a common mistake of the diverse analyses in the field of IPE (see Figure 1.1).

Teaching GPE

The dominant formats of teaching political economy are generally tied to the ahistorical and essentialist ideological division among liberalism, economic nationalism and Marxism, the Transatlantic divide, or related to the (North) American Open Economic Politics style (OEP), actor-oriented and neoliberal institutionalist approaches (Cohen 2019a. 2019b; Frieden *et al.* 2017; Gilpin 1987; Oatley 2018). This *Handbook* begins with the part "Historical waves and diverse ontological axes" discussing the chapter of Professor Robert Gilpin "Three Ideologies of Political Economy (1987)". We consider that this historical academic piece continues to provide a central conceptualization to grasp the liberal retreat and the return of nationalism and mercantilism with all their perils. Gilpin points out:

> Economic liberalism, Marxism, and economic nationalism are all very much alive at the end of the twentieth century; they define the conflicting perspectives that individuals have concerning the implications of the market system for domestic and international society.
>
> *(1987: 23)*

While some scholars may have preferred to start by questioning the traditional or mainstream frameworks in IR (e.g. Strange 1986); we considered it necessary to begin with the dominant conceptual apparatus in the field in order to broaden the discussion of foundational academic tools. Each format taught, we need to bear in mind, brings particular approaches to address some of the concepts within the coordinates identified above, although a central lesson is that each of those are defined specific methodological architectures for research, in terms of the varied combinations between ontology, epistemology and methodologies. Furthermore, they

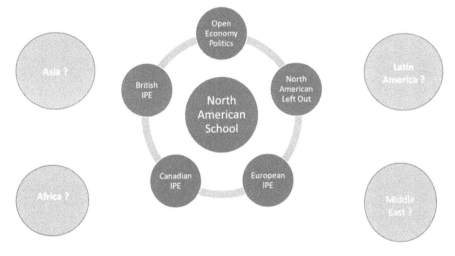

Figure 1.1 Global political economy

Source: Author Teaching Resources.

define how our research in GPE is analytically related to history, geography, development and conflict.

There is a consensus among the scholars that the North American school is the dominant format of teaching IPE and GPE. Increasingly the so-called (North) American Open Economic Politics style (OEP), actor-oriented and neoliberal institutionalist approaches converge due to their emphasis on formal political economy (Frieden and Martin 2002; Krugman and Obstfeld 2006; Lake 2009; Leiteritz 2005; Oatley 2018). For them, the North American and the trinity formats (Realism, Liberalism and Marxism) are the central academic assets, while contributions from other regions are usually peripheral, except the Latin American IPE, from several decades ago. Professor Cohen (2007, 2008), however, taking an internalist approach, managed to break the mould of the Holy Ideological Trinity and the North American School, by explaining the (North) American and British school divide. As in the case of Gilpin's work, Professor Cohen's contribution thus provides another critical tool for the academic formation in our field: "The American School" and "America's Left-Out" (2019a, 2019b) are included in the first part of the *Handbook*. This text remains, for many, a fundamental conceptualization and discussion in the Anglo-Saxon Political Economy that has highlighted several essential debates (Ravenhill 2017; Seabrooke and Young 2017: 324).[1] The controversy around the teaching of IPE, however, softened somewhat, due to the surge of another conceptual innovation within IPE. In 2005, John Ravenhill changed the ontological orientation of the debate by arguing that rather than a disciplinary discussion, IPE should be considered as a "field of inquiry" and therefore as a GPA, a field with many missing middles of research in-between different dual conceptions (2005). Thus, IPE can be distinguished by its ontological and epistemological varied formats to inquiry realities, focusing on the interrelations between public and private power, and in the allocation of scarce sources, to see who gets what, when and how. Briefly, Ravenhill opened the middle space in the divide, although still aligning the notion of IPE research to formal IPEs, that is, the relations between formal politics and economics, domestic and international (2005).

Moderating the debates, Blyth thus introduced the open and pluralist concept of "global conversations", opening up possibilities for teaching within an umbrella that included the holy troika: (North) American, British and the quantiative–qualitative divides in the first *Routledge Handbook* (2009). His contribution was defining IPE as multiple versions of teaching and research, but this work continued entrenched in the self-referenced side of the Anglo-Saxon Political Economy. That is because of the focus on the scholarly of the North American perspectives, and some past contributions from the South, such as Dependency Theory and Developmentalism.

Indeed, many scholars still find it unscientific and of little use to teach without universal definitions, issues, concepts and methodologies. The argument put forward here is that, within GPE, and we need to view this as a productive pedagogical challenge, the classroom is the best laboratory for testing and refining knowledge. The classroom is a unique collective of sharp young scholars with whom to explore, discuss and reflect on IPE and GPE from a plurality of perspectives in order to avoid reproducing bias or factions within the academy. Unfortunately, still, some scholars remain tied to the idea that scientific IPE and GPE often remain set on searching for unique and universal definitions, which can be misleading and lead to the reproduction of partisans and factions rather than scholars and academic communities.

The reality is that different strands of thought make up GPE, and those are based on different ontologies and epistemologies. For example, Diana Tussie from FLACSO Argentina argues that the structural difference between international and regional IPEs, despite their limitations, is that their contributions lay in the strength of their different ontologies (2018). Latin American IPE departs from the regional global insertion thesis to explain the international–domestic link rather than wars, institutions or casino capitalisms, as it is discussed within mainstream IPEs (Krasner 1994; Strange 1994; Tussie 2018:5). She contends that Developmentalism and Dependency Theory departed from how domestic–international interactions and dynamics framed regional development in the liberal world order of the Cold War. She shows that the central contributions of Latin American IPE, by then, were rooted in the political–economic history of global insertions concerning development models and type conflicts in the region, ontologies that even today mark regional IPEs (Tussie 2018).

Box 1.2 Ontology, epistemology and methodology

"Ontology," Norman Blaikie suggests, "refers to the claims or assumptions that a particular approach to social [or, by extension, political] inquiry makes about the nature of social [or political] reality—claims about what exists, what it looks like, what units make it up and how these units interact with one another" (1993:6). Ontology relates to *being*, to what *is*, to what *exists*, to the constituent units of reality; political ontology, by extension, relates to *political being*, to what *is* politically, to what *exists politically*, and to the units that comprise political reality". (Extracted from Political Ontology. Colin Hay. *The Oxford Handbook of Political Science*. Edited by Robert Goodin 2011. www.oxfordhandbooks.com/view/10.1093/oxfordhb/9780199604456.001.0001/oxfordhb-9780199604456-e-023).

Ontology in GPE always takes us to different assumptions that we keep clear concerning the theoretical perspective followed:

1   Nature of the dynamic of power in the historical and geographical context.
2   Nature of the dynamic of conflict and development.
3   Nature of the dynamic and relations between state and markets.
4   Nature of the dynamic and relations between the international and domestic.
5   Nature of the dynamic and relations between agency and structure.
6   Nature of the dynamic and relations between ideas and power.
7   Nature of the dynamic and relations between the world order and regions.
8   Nature of the dynamic and relations between international institutions and world economies.
9   Nature of the dynamic of conflict and development.

"Epistemology is the "science" or "philosophy" of knowledge. In Blaikie's terms, it refers "to the claims or assumptions made about how it is possible to gain knowledge of reality" (1993, 6–7). In short, if the ontologist asks, "what exists to be known?", then the epistemologist asks "what are the conditions of acquiring knowledge of that which exists?" Epistemology concerns … the extent to which specific knowledge claims might be generalized beyond the immediate context in which our observations were made, and, … how we might adjudicate and defend a preference between contending political explanations…. Epistemological assumptions are invariably ontologically loaded—whether knowledge is transferable between different settings for political analysis and hence whether we can legitimately generalize between "cases" (an epistemological consideration) depends on (prior) assumptions about the ontological specificity of such settings" (Hay 2002).

One way to be inclusive of the varied orientations within the field is to conceptualize GPE as heterogeneous, plural and eclectic, whereby each student, scholar or practitioner can choose their options concerning their academic aims and aspirations. We thus understand GPE as a heterogeneous field of inquiries, methodologically eclectic and oriented to the study of power, development and conflict in the dynamics and intersections between ideas and power, politics and economics, the international and the domestic, agencies and structures in a socio-historical and geographical context. GPE is unique today as a field of inquiry as teaching and learning within the field demands the sorting out of fundamental multidisciplinary tensions between the fields of philosophy, social history and geography, which are intertwined with each other in order to grasp how the realities of development and conflict come about (see Figure 1.2).

Furthermore, the full range of possibilities for the combination and connection of different ontologies, diverse epistemologies and methodologies are in themselves essential lessons for scholars, helping to bridge socio-historical and geographical contexts in order to guarantee the consistency and coherence of research. A survey about how IPE and GPE are taught and used in research paradoxically shows that the application of unique methodologies in the fields represents only a small fraction of the whole, even in the Anglo-Saxon world (Madeiras *et al.* 2016). Scholars, according to several studies, tend to apply mixed methodologies and complex combinations of the methodologies (Madeiras *et al.* 2016; Seabrooke and Young 2017). Moreover, the key to GPE's teaching and learning are the indissoluble links between ontology, epistemology and methodology but also have to consider the bridges between them and socio-historical and

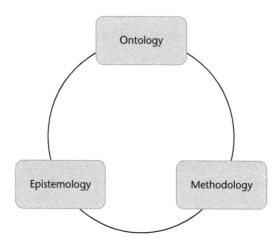

Examples of types of ontologies

1. Agency – Structure
2. Domestic – International
3. Historical Process – Ideas or Identities
4. Regional – Global
5. Value – Institutions
6. Politics – Economics
7. Formal – Informal
8. Security – Conflict
9. Formal and Informal Political Economies
10. Inequality – Development
11. Decolonialization
12. Post Development

Figure 1.2 Basic methodological architecture of research

geographical contexts. This will help to take us out from conceptual cages and universal affirmations based on assumptions that erase different knowledges of the specificities of context and time. These are the cases with Eurocentrism, hegemony, complex interdependence and other similar notions that impose their conceptual, political meanings into different scenarios.

Undeniably, GPE lacks the infrastructure and power of the organized mainstream IPE, especially its self-referencing and self-legitimization capabilities of their research institutions and leadership in research and publishing. Nevertheless, the North American and European academies are in a unique and unsurpassable position to unpack the crucial task of opening the doors to new conversations and inquiries. Unfortunately, the images and frameworks of the North in the political economy in the Global South are so entrenched, and, in some cases, although scholars may use its conceptual apparatus, they adopt of the term IPE because of its focus upon pro-Western formal political economy. Indeed, orientations from the North and South today take scholars to different academic paths in IPE and GPE, and that does not necessarily have to be like this. In the same regard, these opposite views can, however, become, complementary under specific methodological strategies based on more complex ontological and epistemological frameworks. Besides, as we can see in the *Handbook*, that kind of research can count for missing dimensions of the global political realities of development and conflict today in different contexts, concerning critical issues.

While there is no one, universal definition and methodology for IPE or GPE, it is possible to see the common ontological grounds and potential, connections and dialogues among their different practices, and the opportunities for teaching are vast. The intellectual history of IPE in the world is a substantive source to start and set different interpretations at the same level to teach and research the dialogue, something that shows how non-Western thinkers, well before 1945, developed similar ideas to those of liberalism, mercantilism, and Marxism (Helleiner and Rosales 2017a; Hobson 2012). These types of contributions are focused on how locating a broader global intellectual history of IPE allows us to avoid Eurocentric and Anglo-Saxon worldviews of IPE. In a significant contribution, Cox defines the purpose of IPE (2009: 324):

> Different approaches to IPE have to be understood historically. The English-Speaking world, long hegemonic in the dissemination of thought about Global affairs, will need to listen more carefully to the other voices in a global dialogue. It is when scholars are confronted with the full variety of perspectives that the work of intellectual bridge building can seriously begin.
>
> *(2009: 324)*

In summary, the institutionality, extension and power of the English-speaking IPE community are central to the development of the field, but the field needs to develop beyond this. GPE thus demands that we account for a broader range of perspectives to become global (i.e. Acharya 2011). The key to understanding requires seeing GPE as a research field to overcome the limitations in the teaching and research about world political economy orientations, affairs, agencies and structures (Ravenhill 2017).

Research in GPE

Research is not a linear process, but a series of different stages and processes, continuously overlapping and adjusting, which works on different levels, with diverse ends, means, analytical formats and protocols (Burgess 1982; Sautú *et al.* 2005). Popular textbooks have extended the distorted idea that research is a linear process, which may initially help students to identify stages throughout the process of a research project but ends as a conceptual limitation deforming the real tasks of knowledge production at postgraduate level (Jackson 2011; Sautú *et al.* 2005). It is central to bear in mind the abovementioned at the time of designing programmes for teaching and learning research in GPE, since research is a critical skill in the education of undergraduate and postgraduate students. Bearing this in mind, we selected the chapters for Part V of this *Handbook*, "New research arenas," independently to the different methodological formats and approaches of each scholar. What the chapters on research in the *Handbook* demonstrate is that only a few scholars, as Seabrooke and Young conclude (2017), pursue a pure lineal model of research. On the contrary, most of their approaches are marked by pluralism and eclecticism about some theoretical basis and ontological assumptions (Burgess 1982; Hay 2002).

According to the literature, we can identify three types of circular patterns or stages, which overlap with one another during the research, where the researcher continuously goes back and forth adjusting the objective, research strategies and outcomes (Jackson 2011; Sautú *et al.* 2005). Different specialists in methodology have stressed, in different ways, the importance of this methodological concept, but this is still weak in the scholarly field (Hay 2002; Jackson 2011). Methodology for research is still a poorly developed tool in the field, vastly dependent on traditional Political Sciences, being a pending subject that limits the growth of GPE (Madeiras *et al.* 2016; Seabrooke and Young 2017).

In 1982, Burgess argued that "research does not occur in separated "stages" and does not follow a linear path but instead is a social process, whereby overlap occurs between all areas of the investigation" (211). The central issues thus become focused on understanding the role of theory in research (Creswell 2014; Lake 2013; Sautú *et al.* 2005) (see Figure 1.3).

There are two main ways of teaching and learning how to explore in the field in order to produce research (White 2009). One is through studying the small group of great thinkers; the other by exploring what is taught, researched and published from the diverse IPEs. The first path is useful but limited, as great thinkers of our time are generally mainstream thinkers from the relatively homogeneous network of scholars, or what David Lake has defined as the "white man's IR" (2016). Their opinions crowd the media and journals, which are predominantly made by and for Western academia. They commonly act as owners of interpretations, gatekeepers that typically appear with a similar mantra or are quoted in different top-ranked textbooks and journals. Another line of exploration takes us to a more substantial learning process and represents an excellent academic habit of being nourished by new and old scholars. That is to explore, concerning our area of interest, what is presented, taught, researched and published in the field from international to local conferences and classrooms in different places (White 2009). The assumption here is that knowledge is always historical and situated. It is created for some reason and someone, and in that sense, different configurations and scholars produce distinctive orientations of not one, but several Global Political Economies.

The consensus is that there are different definitions about what IPEs and GPEs are an academic asset. That allows us to address the presence of different ontological, epistemological and methodological assumptions in the field, and second, to find the endless and possible alternatives of methodological combinations and research designs. These open different doors and raise new issues for research in IPE, representing the prime strength of the scholarship within the field.

The critical point in the teaching and research of IPE and GPE is not the definition of what it is or what it is not (something impossible to delineate in simple terms) but to identify their significant strands of thought (like Weberian ideal types). Thus, how they, in particular, methodologically based on specific rationalities, can play complementary roles in diverse research designs. Indeed, any academic attempt to tie postgraduate teaching to universal and unique definitions of GPE would become an inoperable effort and another academic conceptual cage.

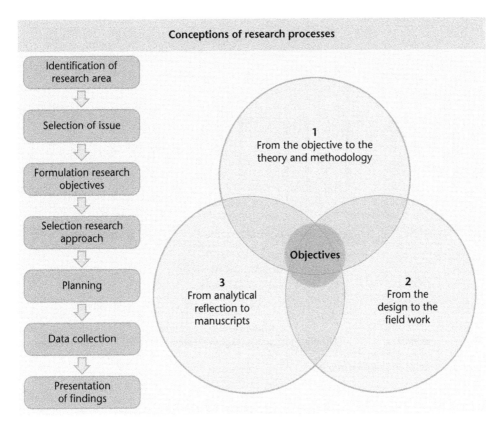

Figure 1.3 Conceptions of research processes

Teaching how to use concepts for research must be focused on helping students to open doors to varied and nuanced comprehensions of the political economy. IPE and GPE research outputs, in most cases, can be complementary to each other. Several scholars have already identified some of these common elements, doors or bridges, for instance, Cox (2000), Underhill and Stubbs (2000) and Lake (2003) have demonstrated cases for sharing common assumptions about IPE. Figure 1.4 provides a simple and easy way to grasp different methodological strategies and combinations. It illustrates the most commonly used approaches in GPE in their closer or distant relations with the most-known ideal-type research designs on the basis of contributions of different scholars (Creswell 2014; Hay 2002; Jackson 2011; Lake 2013). The vertical dimensions range from the role of theories in GPE at the top, location of research approaches, the methodological lines to types of evidence construction that define them. That combines the ontological, epistemological and methodological levels of any investigation (Hay 2002). Seen from the horizontal axis, the diagram ranges from the more empirical positivist designs to the further interpretative views (Creswell 2014; Jackson 2011). For instance, the methodological possibilities of design research combining the two extremes of the horizontal axis are fewer than seeking merging between closer strands of thoughts, while all research must logically gather all the levels. The picture is limited but convenient for introducing types of research in the classroom.

GPE brings about a meaningful set of research lines that cut across major concepts such as development and conflict, domestic and international, technology and welfare, globalization

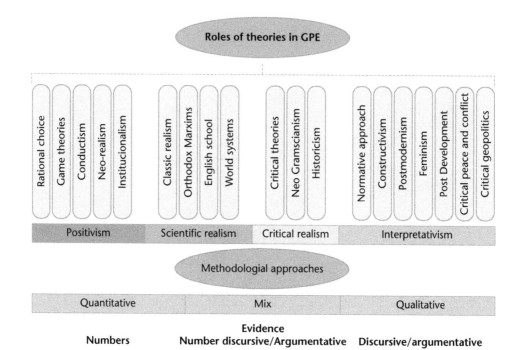

Figure 1.4 Roles of theories in GPE

and transition powers. Some of these lines are: Global Governances (Cooper 2019); Transition Powers (Paul 2018; Xing 2018); Development Finance (Ocampo and Johns 2019); Trade Wars (Lau 2019); technological change, labour and welfare (Greve 2018); Organized Crime (Ponton and Guayasamin 2018); Armed Conflict (Goodhand 2008); Media Power (Freedman *et al.* 2016); Bid Data (Balsillie 2018; Saetnan *et al.* 2018); Productive and Commodity Value Changes (Scholvin 2015); Inequality (Boushey *et al.* 2017; Milanovic 2016) and Migration (Lindley 2014). Moreover, we can also mention other lines such as the decline of the liberal order (Luce 2017); globalization (Maswood 2013); the return of nationalism and xenophobia (Ruzza 2018); informal economies (Medina and Schneider 2018); regionalisms (Söderbaum and Shaw 2003); warfare (Gow *et al.* 2019); cities (Sassen 2018) among others.

The demand for plurality and interdisciplinary conceptualizations is a condition *sine qua non* for the existence of GPE, what it means to understand GPE as a research-oriented and diverse field, whose common factor is a complex dynamic ontology that falls in the coordinates of state–market, international–domestic, formal–informal development and conflict. However, this focus demands a critical effort on the development of research methodologies as critical assets to bridge methodological, ontological and epistemological relations between the dimension of social life that are studied and the different disciplines and methodologies involved. Therefore, any attempt to expand the boundaries of mainstream IPE requires consideration that it is a research endeavour oriented to improve dialogues and epistemic exchange more than to replace formal IPE, and we can only consider this endeavour to be but a starting point.

However, the magnitude and importance of this change are not minor for both IPE and GPE in terms of research. For instance, today more than 50 per cent of real-life in the Global South develops in informal worlds, shadow economies, malign regionalism and the covert world (Medina and Schneider 2018). These are distinct and growing areas of research that have a central impact upon development and conflict at a global and regional level. Given the academic reference in the historical Western and Anglo-Saxon experiences, it is undeniable that the formal mainstream of IPEs insufficiently addresses these kinds of realities that distinguish the Global South. In terms of research, both North and South, depending on the type of research, tend to demand different ontologies. The regions of the Global South are not only the most unequal in the world but also those with the highest levels of informal and shadow economies, which has been made evident thanks to GPE research in this area (Abdih and Medina 2013; Feld and Larsen 2009; Medina and Schneider 2018).

The abovementioned research issues within GPE cannot be denied and deserve a more thorough research agenda within the field. These are just a few of the distinctive central issues that have not been on the radar or within the ontologies of formal IPEs. New research on organized crime, drugs trafficking, laundering money, solidarity urban and rural economies, guns trafficking, illegal mining and informal work as well as migration are all central issues that impact on the Global Political Economy, yet these have received very little attention in formal IPE and GPE research. One exception is the study of public policies or international regimes, although usually seen from the top of the agency without a clear comprehension of its formal and informal dynamics. Something that highlights the difference today between the concept of migration and current tendencies of exodus as the result of national disasters and conflicts.

The fast technological growth of biotechnology and infotech are other research lines emerging in GPE. Scholars and students should consider in global and regional power the increasing rise of issues of big data, cyber politics and security, global cities and their governance. They are becoming more and more important for investigation in GPE given their rise in parallel to the decline of liberal order and impact on the capacity to control corporate, social media, finance and above all democracy (Balsillie 2018). The revolutions in biotech and infotech are giving states and big corporations the control to engineer and manufacture life on an unprecedented scale. Technological change, inequality and the disruption of the ecological system by humans are the quintessence of the liberal order decline today and are necessary to address with new research. Thus, the old promises of the liberal order such as liberty, work and equality are quickly vanishing with the rise of an unpredictable world (Harari 2018).

It is also important to consider that today, geopolitics in a world order are in transition. The power of states to do damage is more significant than in the past centuries, and this is why the GPE must also take this into consideration as another research area in combination with geopolitics. IPE was born with a focus and ontology on interstate wars and international anarchy. Wars and state security remain relevant research issues since they can trigger other occurrences such as nuclear war. However, since the 1980s until nowadays, global realities have changed to the point that the only foreseen future seems one marked by inequality, environmental depredation and technological manipulation of democratic societies. Whatever the definitions of GPE, this must start with an updated mission and research focus in order to put the inquiry in perspective. If IPE rose as the study of interstate wars in an anarchical world, GPE needs to start with a focus on new, complex and dynamic ontologies and move beyond state-centric models to look at state–market and international–domestic research concerning development and conflict today. There is a famous quote from Lao Tzu (2019) that exemplified that: "Why is the sea king of a hundred streams? Because it lies below them."

Some additional research lines should be based on the new tendencies of development. For instance, according to Our World in Data, a non-profit organization integrated to SDG-Tracker. org, today the majority of people die from cardiovascular diseases, cancer, respiratory diseases, diabetes, blood pressure, neonatal diseases, road incidents, tuberculosis and HIV/AIDS. That means, in simple terms, that today we die mostly for our way of manufactured life and the inequality between and within societies, produced by a specific format of development, poor welfare and environmental issues, all themes generally absent in formal IPE, but on the radar of GPE.

Cities constitute another new research line in GPE since these are the locus of the outcomes of different kinds of development and conflict at the global, regional and national scale. The GPE of cities constitutes another growing line of research of significant importance in the field, being the central anchor where time and geography of development and conflict meet in intertwined dynamics (Weber 2017); although the concept has been central in social sciences it has not been relevant for IPE. Perhaps, with the primary focus of IPE on institutions, agencies and nation-state, mainstream perspectives have not seen one of the central geographical stacks in the dynamics of the GPE. Cities are urban geographical anchors and metropolitan centres where development and conflict become tangible in daily lives, from inequalities, shadow economies, violence, gender and migration, up to environmental issues. Contributions in these areas are growing in the region and are already considered as significant research focuses on GPE (Macdonald 2017; Muggah 2015).

This *Handbook* map out new lines of inquiry rather than promoting divides by bolstering universal definitions of IPE or GPE. However, this raises challenges such as: To what extent should the field be opened? So the answer is that this is something currently ongoing as the result of innovative research beyond the essentialists, ahistorical and divides of international and regional IPE. The *Routledge Handbook to Global Political Economy* aims to contribute to broadening and updating notions concerning political economy and the shift from IPE to GPE, making it important for scholars to decide how far and at what pace to go in this transition.

Note

1 Nonetheless, later Cohen would improve with the inclusion of other Anglo-Saxon contributions such as the (North) America "Left Out", the Canadian and Australian "Far Outs" (2014). Something again extended by Cohen lately in his book *Advanced Introduction to International Political Economy* (2019a).

Bibliography

Abdih, Y. and Medina, L. 2013. "Measuring the Informal Economy in the Caucasus and Central Asia". *International Monetary Fund*, WP/13/137.

Acharya, A. 2011. "Dialogue and Discovery: In Search of International Relational relations Theories and Beyond the West". *Millennium: Journal of International Studies* 39(3): 619–637.

Ashworth, L. 2002. "Did the Realist-Idealist Great Debate Really Happen? A Revisionist History of International Relations". *International Relations* 16(1): 33–51.

Balsillie, J. 2018. "Data is Not the New Oil – it's the New Plutonium". *Financial Post*. Available https://business.financialpost.com/technology/jim-balsillie-data-is-not-the-new-oil-its-the-new-plutonium?utm_source=cigi_newsletter&utm_medium=email&utm_campaign=what-you-need-know-about-grand-committee-big-data-privacy-and-democracy.

Blaikie, N. 1993. *Approaches to Social Enquiry*. Cambridge: Polity.

Blyth, M. ed. 2009. *Routledge Handbook of IPE: IPE as a Global Conversation*. New York: Routledge.

Boushey, H., De Long, B. and Steinbaum, M. 2017. *After Piketty: The Agenda for Economics and Inequality*. Cambridge: Harvard University Press.

Braudel, F. 1979. *Afterthoughts on Material Civilization and Capitalism*. Baltimore: Johns Hopkins University Press.

Bull, H. and Watson, A. 1984. Introduction. In Bull, H. and Watson A., eds. *The Expansion of International Society*. Oxford: Oxford University Press.

Burgess, R. 1982. The Role of Theory in Field Research. In Burgess, R., ed. *Field Research: A Sourcebook and Field Manual*. London: Routledge. 209–212.

Chin, G., Pearson, R. and Yong, W. eds., 2014. "IPE in China: The Global Conversation." *Review of International Political Economy* 20(6): 1145–1299.

Cohen. B. 2007. "The Transatlantic Divide: Why are American and British IPE So Different?" *Review of International Political Economy* 14(2): 197–219.

Cohen. B. 2008. "The Transatlantic Divide: A Rejoinder". *Review of International Political Economy* 15(I): 30–34.

Cohen, B. 2019a. *Advanced Introduction to International Political Economy*. Cheltenham: Edward Elgar.

Cohen, B. 2019b. The Multiple Traditions of the American IPE. In Blyth, M. ed. *Routledge Handbook of International Political Economy*. London: Routledge. 23–35.

Cooper, A and Alexandrof, A. (2019) "Assessing the Variation of 'Leader-focused Status' in contemporary global governance." *Contemporary Politics* 5(2): 532–548

Cox R. 2000. Political Economy and World Order: Problems of Power, Knowledge. In Stubbs, R. and Underhill, G. eds. 2000. *Political Economy and the Changing World Order*. New York: Oxford University Press.

Cox, R. 2009. "The 'British school' in the Global Context". *New Political Economy* 14(3): 315–328.

Creswell, J. 2014. *Research Design: Qualitative, Quantitative and Mix*. London: Sage.

de Carvalho, B., Halvard, L. and Hobson, J. 2011. "The Big Bangs of IR: The Myths That Your Teachers Still Tell You about 1648 and 1919". *Millennium. Journal of International Studies* 39(3): 735–758.

Deciancio, M. 2018. "La economía política internacional en el campo de las relaciones internacionales argentinas". *Desafíos*, 30(2): 15–42.

Edwards, S. 2012. *Left Behind: Latin America and the False Promise of Populism*. Chicago: University of Chicago Press.

Feld, L. and Larsen, C. 2009. *Undeclared Work in Germany 2001–2007 – Impact of Deterrence, Tax Policy, and Social Norms: An Analysis Based on Survey Data*. Berlin: Springer.

Freedman, D., Obar, J., Martens, Ch. and McChesney, R. eds. *Strategies for Media Reform: International Perspectives*. New York: Fordham University Press.

Frieden, J., Lake, D. and Broz, L. 2017. *International Political Economy: Perspectives on Global Power and Wealth*. Manhattan: W. W. Norton & Company.

Frieden, J. and Martin, L. 2002. International Political Economy: Global and Domestic Interactions. In Katznelson, I. and Milner, H. eds. *Political Science: The State of the Discipline*. New York: W.W. Norton. 118–146.

Gilpin, R. 1975. *U.S. Power and the Multinational Corporation*. New York: Basic Books.

Gilpin, R. 1987. *The Political Economy of International Relations*. Princeton, NJ: Princeton University Press.

Goodhand, J. 2008. War, Peace and the Place in Between. Why Borderlands are Central. In M. Pugh, N. Cooper and M. Turner, eds. *Whose Peace? Critical Perspectives on the Political Economy of Peacebuilding*. New York: Palgrave Macmillan.

Gow, J., Dijxhoorn, E., Kerr, R. and Verdirame, G. 2019. *Routledge Handbook of War Law and Technology*. London: Routledge.

Greve, 2018. *Routledge Handbook of the Welfare State*. London: Routledge.

Griffith-Jones, S. and Ocampo, J. 2019. *The Future of National Development Banks*. New York: Oxford.

Grosfoguel, R. 2009. "A Decolonial Approach to Political-Economy: Transmodernity, Border Thinking and Global Coloniality". In *Kult 6 – Special Issue* Epistemologies of Transformation: Roskilde.

Harari, Y. 2018. *21 Lessons for the 21st Century*. New York: Spiegel & Grau.

Hay, C. 2002. *Political Analysis: A Critical Introduction*. New York: Palgrave.

Helleiner, E. 2015. "Globalising the Classical Foundations of IPE Thought." *Contexto Internacional* 37(3): 975–1010.

Helleiner, E. and Rosales, A. 2017a. "Peripheral Thoughts for Global IPE". *International Studies Quarterly* 61: 924–934.

Helleiner, E. and Rosales, A. 2017b. "Towards Global IPE". *International Studies Review* 19(4): 667–691.

Helleiner, E. and Wang, H. 2018. "Beyond the Tributary Tradition of Chinese IPE". *Chinese Journal of International Politics* 11(4): 451–483.

Hobden, S. and Hobson, J., eds. 2002. *Historical Sociology of International Relations*. New York: Cambridge University Press.

Hobson, J. 2012. *The Eurocentric Conception of World Politics*. Cambridge: Cambridge University Press.

Hobson, J. 2013. "Part 1 – Revealing the Eurocentric Foundations of IPE". *Review of International Political Economy* 20(5): 1024–1054.

Jackson, T. 2011. *The Conduct of Inquiry in International Relations: Philosophy of Science and Its Implications for the Study of World Politics*. New York: Routledge.

Krasner, S. 1994. "International Political Economy: Abiding Discord". *Review of International Political Economy* 1(1): 13–19.

Krugman, P. and Obstfeld, M. 2005. *International Economics: Theory and Policy*. United States: Pearson International Edition.

Lake, D. 2009. "Open Economy Politics: A Critical Review". *Review of International Organizations* 4(3): 219–244.

Lake, D. 2011. TRIPs across the Atlantic: Theory and Epistemology in IPE. In Nicola, P. and Weaver, C. eds. *International Political Economy. Debating Past, Present and Future*. London: Routledge.

Lake, D. 2013. "Theory is Dead, Long Live Theory: The End of the Great Debates and the Rise of Eclecticism in International Relations." *European Journal of International Relations* 19(3): 567–587.

Lake, D. 2016. "White Man's IR: An Intellectual Confession". *Perspectives on Politics* 14(4): 1112–1122.

Lau, L. 2019. *The China-US Trade War and Future Economic Relations*. Hong Kong: The Chinese University Press.

Leiteritz, R. 2005. "International Political Economy: The State of the Art". *Colombia Internacional* 62: 50–63.

Lindley, A. ed. 2014. *Crisis and Migration*. London: Routledge.

Luce, E. 2017. *The Retreat of Western Liberalism*. London: Little and Brown.

Macdonald, L. 2017. *The Politics of Violence in Latin America and the Caribbean*. New York: Cambridge University Press.

Madeiras, M., Barnabe, I., Albuquerque, R. and Lima, R., 2016. "What Does the Field of International Relations Look Like in South America?". *Revista Brasileira de Political Internacional* 59(1).

Maswood, S. 2013. *Trade, Development and Globalization*. London: Routledge.

Medina, L. and Schneider, F. 2018. "Shadows Economies Around the World: What Did We Learn over the Last 20 Years?" *IMF: Working Paper* 18/17. Available at: www.imf.org/en/Publications/WP/Issues/2018/01/25/Shadow-Economies-Around-the-World-What-Did-We-Learn-Over-the-Last-20-Years-45583.

Mignolo, W. 2016. "Global Coloniality and the World Disorder. Decoloniality After Decolonization and Dewesternization After the Cold War". *World Public Forum "Dialogue of Civilizations"*. Available at http://wpfdc.org/images/2016_blog/W.Mignolo_Decoloniality_after_Decolonization_Dewesternization_after_the_Cold_War.pdf.

Milanovic. B. 2016. *Global Inequality. A New Approach for the Age of Globalization*. Cambridge: Harvard University Press.

Muggah, R. 2015. "A Manifesto for the Fragile City". *Journal of International Affairs* 68(2): 19–36.

Oatley, T. 2018. *International Political Economy*. New York: Routledge.

Özveren, E. 2015. Turkey and the Turkic Linguistic Xone. In Barnett, E. (ed.). *Routledge Handbook of the History of Global Economic Thought*. London: Routledge.

Paul, T. V. 2018, Restraining Great Powers: Soft Balancing from Empires to the Global Era. New Haven: Yale University Press.

Payne, A. and Phillips, N. 2010. *Development*. Cambridge: Polity.

Ponton, D. and Guayasamin, T. 2018. Organized Crime, Security and Regionalism: The Governance of TOC in LA. In Vivares, E., ed. *Regionalism, Development and the Post-Commodities Boom in South America*. New York: Palgrave Macmillan. 270–290.

Ravenhill, J. 2005. *Global Political Economy*. Oxford: Oxford University Press.

Ravenhill, J. 2017. *Global Political Economy*. Oxford: Oxford University Press.

Ruzza, C. 2018. *Populism, Migration and Xenophobia in Europe*. London: Routledge.

Saetnan, A., Schneider, I. and Green, N. 2018. *The Politics and Policies of Bid Data: Big Data, Big Brother?* London: Routledge.

Sartori, A. 2008. *Bengal in Global Concept History*. Chicago: University of Chicago Press.

Sassen. S. 2018. *Cities in the World Economy*. London: SAGE.

Sautú, R., Boniolo, P., Dalle, P. and Elbert, R., 2005. *Manual de metodología. Construcción del marco teórico, formulación de los objetivos y elección de la metodología*. Buenos Aires: CLACSO.

Scholvin, S. 2015. *A New Scramble for Africa: The Rush for Energy Resources in Sub-Saharan Africa*. London: Routledge.

Seabrooke, L. and Young, K. 2017. "The Networks and Niches of International Political Economy". *Review of International Political Economy* 24(2): 288–331.

Shaw, T., Mahrenbach, L., Modi, R. and Yi-chong, X., 2019. *The Palgrave Handbook of Contemporary International Political Economy*. New York: Palgrave Macmillan.

Söderbaum, F. and Shaw, T. 2003. *Theories of New Regionalism*. New York: Palgrave Macmillan.

Strange, S., 1976. "The Study of Transnational Relations". *International Affairs* 52(3): 333–334.

Strange, S. 1986. *Casino Capitalism*. Manchester: Manchester University Press.

Strange, S. 1994. "Wake up, Krasner! The World Has Changed". *Review of International Political Economy* 1(2): 209–219.

Stubbs, R. and Underhill, G. 2000. *Political Economy and the Changing World Order*. New York: Oxford University Press.

Tickner, A. 2003. "Hearing Latin American Voices in International Relations Studies". *International Studies Perspectives* 4(4): 325–350.

Tickner, A. and Waever, O. 2009. *International Relations Scholarship around the World*. New York: Routledge.

Tussie, D. 2018. La Genealogía de la Economía Política Internacional: Rutas, Debates, y Desafíos en América Latina, in Urrego Sandoval, C., Leiteritz, R., Jiménez Peña, G. and Fuentes Sosa, N., eds. *Economía Política Internacional en America Latina: Teoría y Práctica*. México: CIDE.

Tzu, L. 2019. *Tao Te Ching. The Book of the Way*. US: Ancient Renewal.

Underhill, G. and Stubbs, R. eds. 2000. *Political Economy and The Changing Global Order*. New York: Oxford University Press.

Weber, M. 2017. *The Protestant Ethic and the Spirit of Capitalism*. New York: Vigeo Press.

White, P. 2009. *Developing Research Questions. A Guide for Social Sciences*. London: Palgrave Macmillan.

Xing, L. 2018. *Mapping China's "One Belt One Road Initiative"*. London: Palgrave Macmillan.

Part I
Historical waves and diverse ontological axes

2

The sick man of IPE

The British School

Craig Berry

Introduction

The British School (BS) is a fictional character – one with a vital part to play in the story of International Political Economy (IPE). Of course, all communities are imagined, to some extent, and scholarly communities are no different. The question is whether the imaginary of the BS – and indeed IPE – serves a useful purpose for scholarship in political economy, and the social sciences more generally. Does the BS label or grouping provide a platform for enhancing our ability to critically assess the political and economic processes that constitute and shape key dimensions of the human experience? This chapter argues not. The notion that there exists a slightly more diverse and eccentric school of IPE scholarship which originates in Britain serves to reinforce the deeply damaging notion that mainstream IPE – centred imperialistically in the United States – is hospitable to subaltern accounts of the global economic order, and that the English-speaking world remains uniquely able to explain globally significant political and economic conditions. Furthermore, the continuing force of the fiction of the BS serves to inhibit the development of political economy scholarship in Britain itself, by strictly delineating what counts as IPE – despite its self-image as a heterodox community – and isolating itself from broader traditions of social science scholarship which may represent a more substantive intellectual challenge to the so-called American School (AS).

The chapter begins by outlining the emergence of the BS in interaction with American-centred IPE, outlining its key progenitors, and key omissions. It then discusses an alternative reading of the lineage of the BS, that is, classical political economy scholarship in Britain – but argues that the present-day BS cannot be situated in this territory in a meaningful sense. The third section discusses the conceptual and empirical issues that preoccupy BS scholars, and the final section concludes with a warning about the future of political economy in British universities, if the BS imaginary is not decentred. The tone of the discussion is avowedly polemical. It generalises for the sake of clarity and brevity, but this should not be mistaken for a failure to appreciate the reflexive and nuanced nature of political economy scholarship, or a failure to notice the existence of countervailing movements against the dominant story of the BS. No one scholar, or even body of scholars, represents straightforwardly the BS's worst tendencies; for this reason, the chapter elects not to cite, or implicate, many specific examples of BS scholarship (although it does cite contemporary contributions to disciplinary debates). But the BS's flaws are no less serious for this, and a radical rethink of how to support and promote political economy in Britain therefore no less necessary.

The special relationship between the British and American schools of IPE

Box 2.1 Key points

- The foundational myth of the British School is that Susan Strange and Robert Cox, critics of the American-centred IR and IPE disciplines, opened international studies up to post-positivist perspectives, enabling a more critical account of power and ideology in the global economic order.
- However, the British School remains narrowly fixated on its special relationship with the American School, and attempts to reorient IPE towards older traditions of classical political economy have been relatively unsuccessful.
- The British School also has a curiously strained relationship with development studies, mirroring the disjuncture between development studies in the English-speaking IPE community more generally.

The BS is not a creature of its own creation, but rather has been conceived in opposition to the AS. In this account, there is a distinct field of IPE scholarship, with scholars and research generally sorted into two main camps on either side of the Atlantic. The self-image of the BS as intellectually heterodox derives directly from the accepted story of the AS as a more positivist endeavour, emerging from the interaction of the disciplines of International Relations (IR) and international economics (a branch of neoclassical economics). The world is composed of nation-states seeking advantage, and hegemony, but they (increasingly) interact economically as well as diplomatically and militarily, and indeed the accumulation of wealth and the accumulation of power by nation-states is (increasingly) mutually reinforcing. International organisations institutionalise this interaction, to a greater or lesser degree, and indeed have served to enhance the cross-border nature of economic processes. As such, in this account, IPE grew out of the study of international 'regimes', in order to consider the ways in which political processes shaped international economics and, probably more importantly, to apply neoclassical assumptions about human behaviour to the activity of states in the international policy arena. The AS, the accepted core of IPE scholarship, was, and remains, a sub-section of IR, with the International Studies Association (ISA) forming its premier professional body.

The BS apparently constitutes, on the one hand, everything that did not fit neatly into positivist IPE. Epistemological openness is a prized characteristic of the BS, even if the reality rarely fits the ambition. Yet its genesis is often associated with just two scholars: Susan Strange and Robert Cox. Strange, British political economist and former financial journalist, was a central player in the emergence of IPE in general, on both sides of the Atlantic. She is rightly seen as a colossal figure in British political economy, but we should be wary of the way in which the self-image of the BS often identifies, implicitly or explicitly, Strange's critique of the IR-based study of international regimes as a – or *the* – key foundational moment in the emergence of a version of IPE more sceptical of positivism and neoclassicism. Strange was at least partly responsible for some of the most important elements of the BS. From the early 1970s onwards, she made the case for an integration of IR and international economics, while simultaneously calling for an interdisciplinary approach to the study of the world economy. In her landmark text *States and Markets* (Strange, 1988), she made the case for political economy scholarship that focused on how political authorities and private economic actors act upon each other, and identified these interactions as central to the influence of 'structural power' across four domains, including knowledge. Strange's focus on finance as a domain of structural power was a distinguishing feature of her work, and one quickly vindicated by real-world events. She helped to institutionalise her alternative approach to IPE in Britain through the British International Studies Association's International Political Economy Group (IPEG), before briefly leading the US-based ISA.

Cox, Canadian labour theorist and former International Labour Organisation official, was established as a major presence within the emerging field of IPE after the publication of 'Social forces, states and world order: beyond international relations theory' in the journal *Millennium* in 1981. In this paper, Cox outlined his 'historical structures' methodology for studying the global political economy. An historical structure, for Cox, is a fit between particular configurations of forces, namely ideas, institutions and material capabilities. Crucially, however, any historical structure identified should not be seen as a fixed entity, but rather a framework for political and economic interactions, as dominant and alternative ideas about world order both motivate and condition real-world agency. Cox's legacy was soon co-opted by neo-Gramscian scholarship, a variant of neo-Marxism, migrating from the margins of IR to IPE via the British School. Cox's emphasis on strategic agency and the role of ideas was seen to be aligned to the neo-Gramscians' account of the ideological hegemony of neoliberalism as a manifestation of the power of a transatlantic economic elite. Cox of course disavowed the label 'neo-Gramscianism', despite acknowledging the influence of Marxist intellectual and activist Antonio Gramsci on his approach (see Cox, 1983), but the neo-Gramscians soon became an important element of the British School, particularly well-represented in Canada (with some neo-Gramscians claiming that their approach itself constituted a 'school' of IPE, unencumbered by geography).

One of the organising myths of IPE is that the BS and AS represent the two wings of a coherent field of study (see Cohen, 2008). It is a notion powerfully critiqued by Ben Clift and Ben Rosamond (2009), whose alternative history of IPE in Britain is discussed further below. An important secondary myth involved in the construction of IPE is that, while the AS offers empirical rigour, the BS serves as a gateway to a more diverse set of social science traditions, and as such enables critical and post-positivist approaches to political economy find a perch in IPE. In this account, the BS is seen implicitly as the heir to centuries of critical theory, albeit internationalised in accordance with the emergence of global interconnectedness. Are we confident that the BS – or the version of IPE practised in Britain – can really sustain such claims? As much as the BS's advocates might protest against Cohen's rather AS-centred account of the AS/BS duopoly within IPE, it is for most a purely theatrical rebellion. The space for genuine heterodoxy is in practice rather limited. An AS-centred view of the BS might be intellectually uncomfortable for some, yet insofar as the BS identification represents a route to stateside recognition, it is also a propitious niche within which to plot a career as an academic political economist, with little engagement with, or scrutiny from, the wider social science community.

In *Foundations of International Political Economy*, Matthew Watson (2005) made a rather inspirational attempt to reboot the BS. He endorses Strange's critique of the AS, but argues we have learned the wrong lessons, mistaking the legacy of Strange as an imperative to study the relationship (or balance) between states and markets, demarcating the field of inquiry narrowly as the extent to which public institutions seek to regulate private economic activity. Strange, of course, actually sought to decentre IR's statist ontology from IPE, and generally examined the role of private power in conditioning state behaviour. IPE's mission, for Watson, is to interrogate states *and* markets as mutually constitutive structures. For this endeavour, Watson seeks to reintroduce

IPE to the classical tradition of political economy, represented in this account by three key thinkers. First, and perhaps least surprisingly, Karl Polanyi (with a generous sprinkling of Marx), albeit a Polanyian perspective resituated from the rather narrow account of Polanyi's work which often prevails within the BS. For Watson, Polanyi offers an account of the historical and politically contingent processes through which different forms of economic relations are institutionalised and normalised. Second, and perhaps most arrestingly, Watson re-evaluates Adam Smith's work, arguing for an IPE grounded in an interrogation of the moral basis of economic relations. Third, Watson utilises Thomas Veblen's work to offer an account of habituation which challenges the rationalist tendency of institutionalism within IPE. For Veblen, institutions were not simply frameworks for regularised interaction, but manifestations of habits of thought which serve to socialise economic relations, and as such institutional change both requires and reflects the reconstitution of human agency.

Sadly, a decade and a half on – and with no blame attached to its author – we must see *Foundations* as a failed reboot. Watson's perspective has undoubtedly influenced many, without necessarily disrupting the dominant framings of BS scholarship. We should note that, among post-positivist perspectives, post-structuralism has found a perch within the BS – or at least a form of post-structuralism which sits alongside the prevailing variants of neo-Gramscianism and neo-Marxism (see de Goede, 2006). For example, in recent years, the Political Economy Research Centre at City University of London has provide a fertile home for the interaction of post-structuralism and heterodox economics in assessing finance sector practices, as exemplified by the work of scholars such as Ronen Palan and Anastasia Nesvetailova. An opening to post-structuralism is perhaps a natural consequence of Strange's interest in power–knowledge dynamics and Cox's interest in the ideational. But what place is there for, for instance, feminism, ecological political economy or queer theory; that is, critical, post-positivist perspectives whose *raison d'etre* is, in part, to interrogate the disciplinary boundaries which discourage a holistic account of the power dynamics underpinning the interaction of social, political and economic relations? Or indeed for Watson's appeal to moral inquiry within political economy? To claim such perspectives have even a *marginal* role within BS scholarship would probably be an over-statement. We could all point to impressive examples of each – although not nearly enough – but the more important point is that they have not been integrated into the central concerns of 'mainstream' IPE via the BS to any meaningful extent. Paul Langley (2009; see also May, 1996) argues, moreover, that even post-structuralism's influence has been rather constrained – precisely because of the limitations of Strange's understanding of knowledge as a power resource, which is not quite the same as the post-structuralist insight that agents, and their power, are constituted by prevailing ideas about knowledge and truth. Strange opened a door, but not far enough – and a disconnection between British political economy and post-structuralist scholarship in other social science disciplines (in Britain and elsewhere) was one of the consequences.

A final curiosity worth mentioning is that development studies, while acknowledged by the BS as part of the accepted canon, is firmly a marginal field of inquiry. Leonard Seabrooke and Kevin L. Young's (2017) study of 'social clustering' in IPE globally finds that the small group of British (and Canadian) scholars interested in development issues who engage with IPE journals and conferences are an 'island unto themselves' (2017: 308). (Watson's *Foundations* book had sought to recentre development through an application to international institutions focused on development of Polanyi's and Smith's insights). Anthony Payne and Nicola Phillips (2010) condemn the separateness of development studies from mainstream IPE, and indeed call for the notion of development studies as a sub-field to be abandoned. Alas, despite the origins of classical political economy in the study of early capitalism, the development of capitalism outside the West is not considered central to global economic order, beyond the depiction of 'developing' country populations as the victims of Western-centred trends. This is especially odd given the allusions to Karl Marx's legacy often found in BS scholarship – yet it is mainly via the neo-Gramscian fixation on the global (neoliberal) elite rather than, say, Immanuel Wallerstein's account of capitalist development, international exploitation and core-periphery dynamics (see Wallerstein, 2004) that Marxism has found its way into the BS. Almost by definition, low-income or 'peripheral' countries are marginal to the governance of international regulatory regimes, which are an important focus of scholarship in IPE. With the study of development marginalised, the BS has been rather slow to recognise China's role in *re*-ordering the global economy. Development studies is an important component of IPE, but to some extent British-based development theorists who identify as political economists tend to bypass the BS to engage directly with American-centred IPE, and by extension neoclassical development economics.

An alternative history of British political economy?

> ### Box 2.2 Key points
>
> - Ben Clift and Ben Rosamond situate the British School, or British IPE, in the longstanding British tradition of classical political economy, and as such challenge the 'origin story' of British School which is focused on Susan Strange and Robert Cox.
> - There is a very rich history of empirically grounded political economy scholarship in Britain, organised around abiding interests in imperialism, economic decline and statecraft.
> - However, there are few signs that this tradition is in good health within British universities, and few signs of engagement between scholars who engage with IPE and scholars committed to the broader enterprise of British political economy.

In the 2009 version of this handbook, Ben Clift and Ben Rosamond offer a different account of the origins of the BS. Contesting Cohen's view of the BS's contribution IPE, they argue instead that IPE scholarship in Britain has long focused on 'the degree to which the historical resolution of social and economic struggles have become inscribed upon the state and predispose it to certain types of action' (Clift and Rosamond, 2009: 107). We need not accept this as a definition of classical political economy – arguably it focuses attention a little too much on the political sphere – to appreciate it differs somewhat from actually-existing IPE. However, the significance lies not in this definition, but rather, first, in the argument that such scholarship pre-dates Susan Strange and Robert Cox, and second, in that IPE in Britain was established on the back of a set of empirical agendas, not epistemological predispositions. It is these real-world concerns that help us understand not only *how* the BS differs from the AS, but *why*. Clift and Rosamond outline four main 'drivers' of IPE scholarship in Britain that explain the transatlantic divide.

The first driver is the longstanding tradition of scholarship on British imperialism, which has inflected the study of capitalist development in Britain with an important historicist perspective. This allows for the identification of overlapping political, economic and philosophical influences, and an emphasis on the mutual constitution of the domestic and international realms. Early twentieth century economist (and critic of neoclassicism) J.A. Hobson is identified as a key progenitor of this understanding of imperialism, foretelling the later emergence of neo-Marxism in Britain. (The anti-Semitic elements of Hobson's work are rarely, if ever, acknowledged.) The second driver is a body of more 'policy-oriented work' in the post-war period focused on the unravelling of the British Empire and Britain's hegemonic – but unsustainable – position in international finance. Clift and Rosamond actually locate Strange's early work in this field. We can clearly see the influence of Keynesianism in this work too – but as much Keynes' own praxis as a public intellectual and policy-makers, as his general theory. Political economy flourished as Britain was presented with 'wicked' (admittedly, this was not a term in vogue at the time!) real-world problems regarding its international role which mainstream economics seemed unable or unwilling to address.

The third driver is scholarship on Britain's political and economic decline, and indeed the influence of 'declinism' among political elites. We can perhaps date this scholarship to the early 1960s (although clearly it overlaps with the second driver, as well as building upon the historicism of the first), but it was given momentum by the 'stagflation' crisis of the 1970s, and indeed the emergence of Thatcherism in the 1980s as an apparent remedy for decline. Scholarship on decline emanated from economic sociologists and historians, while clearly borrowing from classical political economy. The international determinants of British decline are central to much declinist scholarship, but there are few discernible overlaps between this body of work and the field of IPE that was emerging around this time. Even those political economists we can broadly associate with declinist scholarship who have become major figures in British political science, such as Andrew Gamble, Michael Moran, Michael Kenny and David Coates, arguably remained rather aloof from IPE throughout their careers. The fourth driver is one that arises from both some of the key dimensions of declinist scholarship and the much older traditions of classical political economy. For Clift and Rosamond, disputing one of the main rallying cries for the BS of IPE – and indeed one which was taken seriously by many AS scholars – 'there never was a need to "bring the state back in"', because in British political economy, it had never really gone away. The recurrent suggestion by IPE scholars associated with the BS that the state is missing from, or marginal within, analysis of some or other aspect of the global economic order is a perfectly valid one, when pitched at an IPE audience. Yet for those familiar with or schooled in the political economy traditions identified by Clift and Rosamond, the centrality of the state is the kind of thing that does – or at least should – go without saying.

The problem, however, is that British political economy does not really look like this (anymore). Outside a handful of pockets of strength for classical political economy, and the British-focused ancestry outlined by Clift and Rosamond, it would be difficult to argue that these traditions are in good health – which helps to explain the limited impact of Watson's attempt to recast the BS and IPE in general. There are relatively few major figures in British political economy who can be said to embody the alternative history Clift and Rosamond espouse, in contrast to the rather sanitised political economy of the BS. We can probably include Watson, Clift and Rosamond themselves in the former category (although Rosamond is now based in Denmark), as well as influential political scientists such as Helen Thompson and Colin Hay (although noting that Hay is also now based overseas, in France) and state theorist Bob Jessop. Some neo-Gramscian and neo-Marxist scholars based in the politics departments of British universities, notably Manchester and Nottingham, might dispute this characterisation, arguing that the line drawn here between British political economy and the BS is too strict, not least because their own perspective(s) are present in both lineages. There would be some empirical merit in this argument, but probably not enough to undo my general account (and, as noted below, the space for neo-Gramscians and neo-Marxists in IPE does appear to be disappearing).

Interestingly, the BS has arguably outgrown IPEG, and found its own niche within British political science that enables scholars to engage directly with US-based IPE communities without the conduit of the British International Studies Association (BISA). IPEG has actually moved away from the BS and IPE, to some extent, under the recent leadership of (feminist) political economists Johnna Montgomerie and Daniela Tepe-Belfrage, and greater participation of scholars not strongly attached to political science. It is also worth noting my own relatively new role as co-founder and co-convenor of the Political Studies Association's British and Comparative Political Economy Specialist Group, alongside Jeremy Green. Such developments might represent an increased contestation of Strange's legacy, or indeed a rediscovery on insights from Strange's work that appear to have been lost (or a bit of both). More generally, the real-world political–economic environment since the 2008 financial crisis clearly has something to do with this infant resurgence. There are, as such, grounds for hope that the BS may yet reconcile with richer traditions of British political economy to offer a more genuinely valuable perspective on social, political and economic relations. Sadly, and in keeping with this chapter's polemical spirit, in my view the crisis of the BS has actually solidified in recent years, meaning that, despite some encouraging signs, British political economy remains in great peril.

The British School's preoccupations

Box 2.3 Key points

- Leonard Seabrooke and Kevin L. Young's study of 'niche proliferation' in IPE demonstrates the marginalisation of some key domains ostensibly associated with the British School, as well as the ongoing subservience of British School scholars within IPE networks dominated by US-based or US-trained scholars.
- The British School focuses on the study of institutions, often with little reference to the economic processes that are mutually constitutive of institutional practice.
- More critical examples of British School scholarship are often framed by the financialisation concept or a cultural political economy framework, but tend to focus on micro-level policies and discourses, deemed emblematic of a wider accumulation which is itself under-investigated.
- The British School is also unduly preoccupied with intractable ontological, epistemological and methodological debates, at the expense of empirical depth.

This chapter's first section noted Seabrooke and Young's (2017) analysis of IPE's social clustering, drawing upon data on IPE publications, conference participation, post-graduate study and teaching. Their analysis challenges the notion that there exists distinct British and American schools of IPE (although this remains a dominant trope of how the discipline is taught). The discipline is characterised instead by an organisational logic of 'niche proliferation' whereby groups of scholars have developed specialist communities within the broader field, both providing paths to recognition via self-sustaining scholarly networks, and, to some extent, insulating niche members from the critiques that might arise from substantive engagement with a more diverse IPE community. While Seabrooke and Young do not explicitly infer this point, their analysis serves the present argument rather well. They demonstrate that scholars who might be considered as members of either the BS or AS actually belong to the same intellectual and organisational niches, but that US-based or US-trained scholars dominate *every* niche. In studying niche proliferation over time, they show also importantly that the main niches have become less geographically concentrated. The implication is that BS scholars are quite content as the junior grouping in the AS/BS duopoly of IPE, making critical contributions to the field but primarily, now more than ever, within professional channels overseen by the AS. For the sake of political economy, we must resist this 'if you can't beat 'em, join 'em' logic, no matter how lucrative the path may be.

Crucially, Seabrooke and Young (2017: 310–311) demonstrate that whereas scholars interested in 'global value chains' (GVCs) were a core part of IPE network before 2009, this is no longer the case: their 'hunch' is that such scholarship has migrated primarily to business studies and economic geography. They also find that Marxist-inspired IPE has migrated to specialist journals, and is no longer a major presence in mainstream disciplinary outlets. Alongside the apparent isolation of development studies within IPE, this represents a quite astonishing turn away, in the wake of economic crisis, from some of the main approaches through which structural inequalities in the global capitalist order can be identified, explained and, perhaps, addressed. While not mentioned explicitly in Seabrooke and Young's paper, it appears also ecological research appeared only fleetingly in core IPE networks (while the study of climate *politics* abounds within networks focused on international institutions). For Seabrooke and Young (2017: 309–310), the 'meat and potatoes' of IPE are: a network of scholars primarily interested in issues such financial and intellectual property regulation steeped in organisational theories; a network interested in policy networks, primarily those inhabiting the transnational financial architecture; and a network interested in the structure and power of international institutions more generally. Even a cursory look at such scholarship would acknowledge that the BS plays an important role in (and across) these networks and literatures – but certainly not a dominant one.

Obviously, this is not the beginning and end of the present-day BS. It is important to understand not *where* BS scholars are present, in the disciplinary map of IPE, but also *what* they are contributing. What are the concepts and approaches that BS scholars are most often to be found championing within IPE? We can identify five main signifiers. First, an explication of the 'varieties of capitalism' (and relatedly, nationally constituted varieties of specific features of capitalist development). The influence of Peter Hall and David Soskice's 2001 book *Varieties of Capitalism: The Institutional Foundations of Comparative Advantage* has been profound, although neither Hall nor Soskice are political economists in the classical tradition (in contrast to David Coates, whose slightly earlier *Models of Capitalism: Growth and Stagnation in the Modern Era* (2000) failed to achieve the same paradigmatic impact). Without questioning the value of Hall and Soskice's original work, the 'varieties of capitalism' framing has inspired a generation of descriptive research, as simply outlining differences between a relatively small sample of developed countries became permissible as an original contribution to political economy scholarship. Despite its conceptual debt to the French regulation school's analysis of capitalist accumulation regimes, the main explanatory power of varieties of capitalism lies in its relationship with rational choice (neo)institutionalism, as state actors are shown to behave rationally insofar as they conform to existing institutional practices (see Bruff *et al.*, 2015). As noted above, it is a far cry from the Veblenian institutionalism advocated by Watson. As one instrument in the toolkit of social science, there is nothing wrong with rational choice theory – and rational choice theory's assumptions about elite behaviour make it rather amenable to Marxist analysis of public policy – but it is not classical political economy. Of course, BS scholars, in contrast to the AS, have resisted the path from varieties of capitalism to rational choice. The concept of capitalist variety has instead been used in a more basic sense to echo the BS's foundational claim that states matter, by way of countering the notion that the world economy had become 'globalised' and that globally constituted marketplaces had escaped national jurisdictions, a trope which became dominant in IPE scholarship in the 1990s.

As an aside, it is surely this obsession with restating the state's role, in the abstract, that accounts for the disappearance of scholarship on GVCs from IPE networks. A concept that clearly resonates with classical political economy more so than Americanised IPE, the concept also ostensibly acts to decentre the state from analysis, and therefore disrupts part of the rationale for the BS's role as junior partner in the IPE duopoly. Of course, even the most rudimentary understanding of GVCs would require recognition that states serve to constitute, rather than inhibit, transnational production processes. The problem is simply a presentational one: in the rigid and conservative publication formats that dominate academic research (and which advocates of the BS has done little to challenge), it is difficult to showcase analysis of GVCs without *appearing to* eschew the BS's enduring (and narrow) theoretical concerns. (We might point also to the difficulty political science-trained political economists tend to have in researching economic processes *alongside* state behaviour; in studying GVCs, the economics cannot simply be bracketed off as a product of political processes.)

Second, the study of international institutions, including their internal processes, and the wider political and economic communities they are constituted by. There is nothing wrong with such a focus at the level of the individual scholar or research project, but when, as in Seabrooke and Young's account, it becomes the 'meat and potatoes' of IPE scholarship, then something has probably gone wrong. Even within the more critical BS, with its Marxist allusions, formal institutional processes appear to be receiving rather more attention than the economic processes that they ostensibly act upon. We risk missing the forest of capitalist development, while we busy ourselves with only the trees; that is, the institutional mechanisms and functions within which accumulation regimes are represented and reproduced. Relatedly, it is rather odd, for a perspective that claims roots in Marx's work, for class-based analysis of political–economic processes to be such a rarity.

Third, the concept of 'financialisation' has become extremely important to the BS. A vast and growing literature on financialisation probably represents the best interface we have between IPE's BS and classical tradition of political economy, insofar as the concept denotes a transformation in capitalism encompassing overlapping (and mutually reinforcing) social, political and economic change. It clearly has intellectual roots in British political economy, among other places. Alas, financialisation is not really a concept that was developed or popularised within the BS itself, but rather the fringes of the economic discipline in the United States. American economist Gerald Epstein's (2001) definition of financialisation as 'the increasing importance of financial markets, financial motives, financial institutions, and financial elites in the operation of the economy and its governing institutions, both at the national and international levels' prefaces a remarkably high proportion of research outputs and commentary related to financialisation by BS scholars.

It is worth outlining the fourth main signifier of the present-day BS at this point: a growing body of work on 'everyday' political economy, which overlaps with a new zeal for 'cultural economy' among some British-based political economists, heterodox economists and economic geographers. At the risk of over-simplification, approaches associated with this literature seek to show how politically contingent outcomes are normalised, and effectively depoliticised, by their grounding in everyday behaviour and cultural norms (although some also identify new forms of resistance to capitalist accumulation at this level too). It is worth including this work in any outline of the BS, not least because of its association with Montgomerie and Tepe-Belfrage, and their leadership of IPEG. However, its impact on the global community of IPE has probably been rather limited, and there are few signs this is likely to change.

Crucially, and bringing together my third and fourth signifiers, it is largely through studying everyday and cultural practices that the BS has focused its contribution to the financialisation literature. Among British political economists trained in political science, the focus in accounting for financialisation certainly seems to have been on how the process is manifest at the micro-level, rather than the macro- or meso-level economic drivers of financialisation, or even (with some notable exceptions) the political and ideological projects that have sustained financialisation. Readers might be reminded here of Mark Blyth and Matthias Matthijs' (2017) critique of IPE's 'missing macro'. They were of course referring primarily to the AS of IPE, and the pervasive influence of the neoclassical-inspired 'open economy politics' (OEP) paradigm, which is strangely uninterested in the international sphere, and focuses on how domestic political institutions aggregate, through bargaining processes, the interests of individuals, firms, industries, etc. Kathleen McNamara had warned earlier (2009: 73) that the influence of OEP risked 'leaving unsolved the big, important real world puzzles'. Such critiques are imbibed ostensibly with a BS sensibility, but a similar critique of the BS itself would not be wide of the mark. (Blyth is one of the few British exponents of classical political economy who engages extensively with IPE, which is no doubt partially explained by the fact he is now based in the United States.)

Many British-based political economists are content to focus on micro matters, such as very minor policy measures or very minor examples of political discourse. Unlike in OEP research, the wider, global capitalist order is not ignored; instead, the micro is deemed to be *emblematic* of the macro. The problem is that the macro (neither the macro-economic nor the macro-political) of which the micro is emblematic is rarely investigated or articulated in any meaningful way. British scholars of development are perhaps the main exception to this (see Bishop *et al.*, 2018) – which might explain their apparent marginality in professional networks. It is interesting that, notwithstanding their focus on American IPE, and despite Blyth's championing of the BS in the 2009 edition of this handbook, Blyth and Matthijs do not point to British political economy as a path to overcoming IPE's flaws in their 2017 paper. Accounts of British political economy's resurrection have, it seems, been greatly exaggerated.

Finally, and briefly, the BS tends to be preoccupied with (largely irresolvable) ontological, epistemological and methodological debates. Angus Cameron and Ronen Palan (2009) rightly defend the empiricism of the BS, against the implicit (and sometimes explicit) accusation of AS IPE that the BS lacks empirical rigour. For Cameron and Palan, a post-positivist BS is, at its best, more genuinely empirical insofar as it includes in inquiry the nature of the research subject itself – states, firms, households, etc. – rather than assuming that its characteristics are 'logically prior to it' (2009: 119). Unfortunately, however – and despite the veneration of Susan Strange, who barely wasted a moment on such matters – too often BS scholarship devotes far too much space to debating (or restating) ontological, epistemological and methodological issues, rather than simply getting on with the job. Articulating the vantage point from which research is conducted is obviously essential. But the sheer extent of theoretical navel-gazing evident in many ostensibly empirical research outputs – partly driven, no doubt, by the demands of journals' peer-reviewers – is not only indulgent, it presents a barrier to genuine engagement with other disciplines whose members are invariably not as well-versed in the rather esoteric language in which IPE discusses itself. Structure matters, and agency matters. The ideational matters, and the material matters. Past practice shapes, but does not completely determine, the present. Individuals and institutions have some autonomy vis-à-vis their environment, but not complete autonomy. We can conduct research methodically, without being a slave to methodology. Got it.

Concluding thoughts: (un)doing political economy

Box 2.4 Key points

- Political economy in Britain has become entrenched in British political science, which is itself aligning with the positivist epistemologies which dominate American political science. This location is intellectually stifling, but nevertheless affords scholars opportunities for career progression via sub-disciplinary niches.

- The failure of the British School to defend a broader classical political economy tradition has left the mantle of British political economy vulnerable to acquisition by neoclassical political economists, who ironically fit comfortably within the American School of IPE's understanding of political economy.
- The British School label and grouping inhibits meaningful interaction with political economists working in other disciplines of social science in Britain, Europe and North America.

A theme that has run throughout this chapter is that British political economy is now far too entrenched professionally in political science. Other disciplines are kept at a convenient distance, if not ignored altogether. This actually helps to explain the BS's intellectual trajectory, since British political science increasingly apes the United States' rationalist, positivist and strangely apolitical political science tradition, which is now very much evident in stateside International Relations and IPE. The vast majority of British political economists are attached to political science departments – but many of Britain's *best* political economists are not (irrespective of whether they adopt the political economy labelling). Development studies is isolated in IPE, but flourishing elsewhere in British universities, notably in geography and urban studies departments (but also some business schools).

The intention here is not to offer a naïve or utopian account of inter-disciplinarity in the social sciences, an agenda that is actually often designed implicitly to empty critical perspectives of their critical content. Social science needs political economy, but political economy is not answering the call. Most self-styled political economy institutes in Britain, at least in Russell Group universities, are quite explicitly focused narrowly on contributing to IPE, whether alluding to the BS or not. This trend is not wholly unidirectional, and there have of course been attempts to situate such groupings in the broader traditions of British political economy, or to situate activity in disciplines other than political science. But they tend to be short-lived. Another *mea culpa* required here is that my own disciplinary background is in political science. It is probably correct, and perhaps inevitable, that most political economists will find themselves drawn towards political science departments, due to the synergistic focus on power dynamics within both intellectual enterprises. Just as social science needs political economy, political economy needs political science. But political science should not be the only 'way in' to IPE. That British political science is the BS's major shareholder is problematic, insofar as it renders British political economy dependent on the broader relationship between British and American political science.

One of the implications of this relationship is that what it means to be a political economist in Britain is increasingly up for grabs. There has been a resurgence in a version of political economy, associated with rational/public choice theory, which imports the assumptions of neoclassical economics into the study of policy-making processes. The classical/neoclassical divide obviously resonates rather less in the United States, and as such Britain's neoclassical political economists can happily interact with the AS of IPE while bypassing the BS altogether. We can detect the emerging conflict in the establishment of a Department of Political Economy at King's College London (KCL); it is staffed largely by neoclassical political economists, while KCL's Department of European and International Studies department remains a key site of classical political economy. Similarly, the University of Sheffield's Department of Economics has established the Sheffield Interdisciplinary Political Economy Research Group (SiPErg), hosting an annual political economy conference, quite separately from the Sheffield Political Economy Research Institute (SPERI; where I was previously based), which is now part of the Department of Politics. (While the intellectual distance between political science-based and economics-based political economists is perhaps understandable, the distance between SPERI and the outstanding *heterodox* economists at Sheffield's Management School is far more regrettable). There is nothing essentially problematic about political economy's neoclassical variant: the methods its adherents employ can lead to unique insights into political processes. Yet if British political economy comes to be defined primarily in neoclassical terms, then something will have been lost. The question we must ask is whether the BS is helping to make the case for classical political economy in Britain, or instead simply offering a comfortable niche in which such challenges can be shirked.

It is obviously important to dispel any sense that this chapter seeks to offer an anti-American account of political economy. Heterodox economics is stronger in the United States than in Britain, and an important contributor to political economy, broadly conceived. There is also a strong tradition of political economy among sociologists in the United States – a community that appears to engage with sociology-based political economists in continental Europe more so than British political economists do. It is simply the case that American-dominated IPE is rarely a conducive home for classical political economy. Canada, often depicted imperialistically as merely an offshoot of the British School, is arguably the most important site of classical political economy in the English-speaking world, exemplified most notably by scholars such as Jacqueline Best at the University of Ottawa, and the Coxian and neo-Gramscian influence at York University in Toronto. Figure 2.1 offers a stylised map of the geographical and intellectual relationships which help to define the identity of the BS.

It is also worth noting that, insofar as IPE is represented in the universities of Western Europe, scholarship generally conforms to the AS rather than BS variant, and is similarly concentrated in political science departments. There is of course much more to European political economy than the discipline of IPE, especially in other parts of social science, but cross-channel

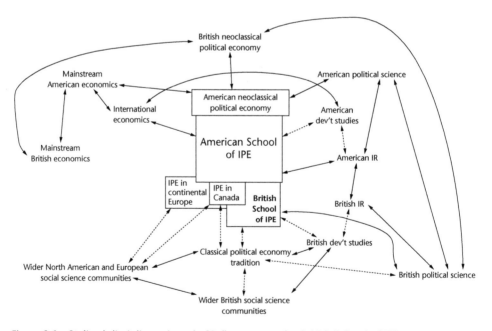

Figure 2.1 Stylised disciplinary 'map' of influences on the British School of IPE

Note
Dotted lines indicate weak or problematic relationship.

contact with British political economists in this regard is sparse, given the BS's reverence the for American-centred IPE community. For example, few British IPE scholars engage with the continental network around the International Initiative for the Promotion of Political Economy (IIPPE), despite it serving as a major platform for the European and American communities of political economists and heterodox economists, and indeed UK-based heterodox economists. It is generally supported in the UK only by the Greenwich Political Economy Research Centre at the University of Greenwich, by leading figures such as Özlem Onaran (the centre's members are generally *not* British-born). Similarly, there is seemingly little interaction between the BS and the European Sociological Association (ESA's) Critical Political Economy Research Network (CPERN). Of course, most British political economists are members of CPERN's formidable mailing list; yet engagement barely extends any further. For instance, only a handful of scholars who could plausibly be associated with the IPE sub-discipline in the UK presented at ESA's 2019 conference, despite CPERN being highly visible at the conference – and despite the fact it was held in Manchester, one of the key homes for BS scholarship. Engagement with the Society for the Advancement of Socio-Economics (SASE) is similarly limited, save for a handful of hardy enthusiasts on the fringes of British political economy. The ISA's annual conference in North America remains by far the most significant gathering for the BS, despite the marginality of political economy within the organisation.

It is also important to conclude by reiterating that it would be inappropriate, and indeed impossible, to implicate individual scholars in the crisis or failure of British political economy. It is a collective action failure, a very long time in the making, and in many ways reinforced by the incentive structures confronting academics in British universities. That said, we can, and must, do more. The omnipresent imperative to conduct inter-disciplinary research, while rather superficial, can be appropriated to rebuild a classical political economy that genuinely reaches out beyond political science to study the multiple dimensions of capitalist development. It should also be noted that British political economists, especially those who engage with IPE, are overwhelmingly male and white, and from privileged backgrounds – in my estimation, more so than other areas of social science, including political science more generally. (British political economy also has remarkably few adherents who, like Susan Strange and Robert Cox, have experience of professions other than academia.) Political economists should be at the forefront of efforts in higher education to create more inclusive workplaces, not dragging our heels at the back. Our failure in this regard surely contributes to the narrow intellectual agenda of British IPE. We need to cut the BS and bust open the closed shop of British political economy.

Bibliography

Bishop, M. Payne, A., Sen, K., Breslin, S., Öniş, Z., Muzaka, V., Booth D., Lindsay, C. and Yeung, H.W.-C. (2018) 'Revisiting the developmental state', SPERI Paper No. 43. Available at: http://speri. dept.shef.ac.uk/wp-content/uploads/2018/11/SPERI-Paper-No.-43-Revisiting-the-developmental-state.pdf.

Blyth, M. (2009) 'Introduction: IPE as a global conversation', in M. Blyth (ed.) *Routledge Handbook of International Political Economy: IPE as a Global Conversation* (London: Routledge), pp. 1–20.

Blyth, M. and Matthijs, M. (2017) 'Black swans, lame ducks, and the mystery of IPE's missing macro-economy', *Review of International Political Economy* 24(2): 203–231.

Bruff, I., Ebenau, M. and May, C. (2015) 'Fault and fracture? The impact of new directions in comparative capitalisms research on the wider field', in M. Ebenau, I. Bruff and C. May (eds) *New Directions in Comparative Capitalisms Research* (Basingstoke: Palgrave), pp. 28–44.

Cameron, A. and Palan, R. (2009) 'Empiricism and objectivity: reflexive theory construction in a complex world', in M. Blyth (ed.) *Routledge Handbook of International Political Economy: IPE as a Global Conversation* (London: Routledge), pp. 112–125.

Clift, B. and Rosamond, B. (2009) 'Lineages of a British international political economy', in M. Blyth (ed.) *Routledge Handbook of International Political Economy: IPE as a Global Conversation* (London: Routledge), pp. 95–111.

Coates, D. (2000) *Models of Capitalism: Growth and Stagnation in the Modern Era* (Cambridge: Polity).

Cohen, B. (2008) *International Political Economy: An International History* (Princeton, NJ: Princeton University Press).

Cox, R. (1981) 'Social forces, states and world orders: beyond International Relations theory,' *Millennium: Journal of International Studies* 10(2): 126–155.

Cox, R. (1983) 'Gramsci, hegemony and International Relations: an essay in method', *Millennium: Journal of International Studies* 12(2): 162–175.

De Goede, M. (2006) (ed.) *International Political Economy and Post-Structural Politics* (Basingstoke: Palgrave).

Epstein, G. (2001) 'Financialization, rentier interests and central bank policy', paper prepared for *Financialization of the World Economy*, University of Massachusetts, December 2001. Available at: www.peri.umass.edu/fileadmin/pdf/financial/fin_Epstein.pdf.

Hall, P. A. and Soskice, D. (2001) (eds) *Varieties of Capitalism: The Institutional Foundations of Comparative Advantage* (Oxford: Oxford University Press).

Langley, P. (2009) 'Power-knowledge estranged: from Susan Strange to post-structuralism in British IPE', in M. Blyth (ed.) *Routledge Handbook of International Political Economy: IPE as a Global Conversation* (London: Routledge), pp. 126–139.

May, C. (1996) 'Strange fruit: Susan Strange's theory of structural power in the international political economy', *Global Society: Journal of Interdisciplinary International Relations* 10(2): 167–190.

McNamara, K. R. (2009) 'Of intellectual monocultures and the study of IPE', *Review of International Political Economy* 16(1): 72–84.

Payne, A. and Phillips, N. (2010) *Development* (London: Polity).

Seabrooke, L. and Young, K. L. (2017) 'The networks and niches of international political economy', *Review of International Political Economy* 24(2): 288–331.

Strange, S. (1988) *States and Markets* (London: Pinter).

Wallerstein, I. (2004) *World-Systems Analysis: An Introduction* (Durham, NC: Duke University Press).

Watson, M. (2005) *Foundations of International Political Economy* (Basingstoke: Palgrave Macmillan).

3

Globalizing the historical roots of IPE

Eric Helleiner

Introduction

Susan Strange (1991: 33) famously argued that the field of International Political Economy (IPE) should be "an open range" that was "accessible – as the classical study of political economy was – to literate people of all walks of life, from all professions, and all political proclivities". In recent years, however, many IPE scholars have worried about a narrowing of perspectives arising from the fact that the field has become increasingly dominated by scholarship from the United States and Europe – or what I will call "Western" scholarship in this chapter. They have argued that the study of IPE requires a more "global conversation", particularly in an age when power in the global economy is rapidly diffusing away from the West to the non-West (e.g. Blyth 2010; Chin, Pearson and Yong 2013; Tussie and Riggirozzi 2015). As Robert Cox (2009: 327) put it, "Susan Strange's appeal for an open range now requires an openness to and understanding of the perspectives of all the civilizations that encounter each other in every world crisis."

Strengthening "global conversations" must involve more than just greater dialogue among contemporary scholars from diverse regions of the world. Also important is the geographical widening of the *historical* roots of the field. At the moment, IPE textbooks usually inform students that modern IPE builds on classical political economy debates from pre-1945 period involving Western thinkers. These debates are commonly depicted as involving the Western thinkers who developed the three ideologies of economic liberalism (e.g. Adam Smith; David Ricardo; Richard Cobden), neomercantilism (e.g. Alexander Hamilton, Friedrich List, Henry Carey), and Marxism (both Marx and later European Marxists theorists of imperialism).[1]

Drawing on a growing literature in IPE as well as the field of intellectual history, this chapter highlights some ways to widen the historical roots of the field beyond Western thought. It outlines a number of non-Western thinkers whose ideas before 1945 made important contributions to debates about IPE issues. Some of these thinkers put forward modifications of the three well-known ideologies identified above. Others developed similar ideologies but independent of Western influence. Still others advanced quite different ideologies that are not well captured by the three-way debate described in IPE textbooks. A final group contributed by influencing the development of Western thought. After providing examples of each of these kinds of contributions, I conclude this chapter by highlighting four reasons why the historical origins of IPE thought need to be widened to include these broader contributions from beyond the West.

Localizing Western ideology

The first set of contributions involved modifications made to the ideologies of economic liberalism, mercantilism, and Marxism that were prominent in the West in the pre-1945 years. Take, for example, the arguments of Western economic liberals such as Smith (1976 [1776]), Ricardo (1948 [1817]) and Cobden (Cain 1979), who advocated free trade to boost global peace and prosperity as well as to expand individual liberty. The economic liberal case for free trade represented the first ideology of IPE to achieve truly global reach, as it picked up supporters in the nineteenth century not just in other Western countries but also outside the West (e.g. Coller 2015; Helleiner and Rosales 2017a; Sartori 2008; Schwartz 1964). When free trade ideology diffused beyond the West, however, it was often adapted – or "localized", to use Amitav Acharya's (2009) terminology – in creative and important ways to fit with local conditions.

One such localization process involved the mixing of free trade commitments with strong nationalist goals. For example, many Latin American revolutionaries in the early nineteenth century linked free trade with their nationalist cause of throwing off Spanish colonial rule and its oppressive mercantilist trade regulations. In this context, free trade was associated with more revolutionary nationalist aspirations than it was in the writings of Smith, Ricardo and Cobden. After independence, some Latin American free traders also endorsed much more active state regulation of the domestic economy than did European economic liberals at the time. In order to maximize benefits arising from their countries' role as commodity exporters, they urged their national governments to take an active role in areas such as importing foreign technology, building infrastructure, investing in education and agricultural improvement, encouraging crop diversification, and even managing public monopolies in key export sectors (e.g. Helleiner and Rosales 2017a).

Another important localization of European free trade thought involved the rejection of the Eurocentric ideas that often accompanied it. In the nineteenth century, European economic liberals often argued that free trade would bring not just economic and political benefits but also cultural ones in the form of the spread of what they perceived to be superior European civilizational standards. This message was not opposed by all free traders beyond the West; indeed, some Europeanized Latin American elites embraced this rationale for free trade with enthusiasm in the mid-nineteenth century as part of their efforts to consolidate their domestic position and ensure continued imports of European luxury goods that distinguished their class (Gootenberg 1989; Rojas 2002). But in other contexts, it met opposition. For example, while advocating the opening of his country "everywhere to commercial intercourse", the prominent Liberian thinker Edward Blyden (1971 [1883]: 39) urged West Africans in the late nineteenth century to reject European civilizational standards in favour of what he called the less materialistic and individualistic "African personality" (Mudimbe 1988). To those Europeans who talked down African civilization, he reminded them of Africans' role in contributing to Europe's progress (Blyden 1969 [1880]: 243).

Western mercantilist and neomercantilist economic nationalist thought also diffused around the world in the nineteenth and early twentieth centuries, particularly Friedrich List's (1885 [1841]) ideas about the role that strategic tariffs could play in fostering industrialization. Like European free trade thought, however, List's ideas were also often modified in important ways when they imported into non-Western contexts. For example, the prominent follower of List in late nineteenth-century colonial India, Mahadev Govind Ranade, showed much more interest than List had in analysing the economic impact of colonization on the colonized. In his writings, Ranade (1906 [1893]: 106) developed innovative analyses of how British colonization had turned India into an economic "Dependency" that was "growing raw produce to be shipped by British Agents in British Ships, to be worked in Fabrics by British skill and capital, and to be re-exported to the Dependency by British merchants to their corresponding British Firms in India and elsewhere." He was also critical of the deindustrialization and "ruralization" of India under British colonial rule, as well as of Britain's extraction of wealth – or "tribute" – from its colony (Ranade 1990 [1881]: 151, 1906 [1892]: 29).

Ranade also called for different policies than List because British colonial authorities had no interest in raising India's tariffs to promote domestic industry in the late nineteenth century. As he put it in 1890 when comparing India's situation to that of the United States and European countries, "[w]e cannot, as with the Government of these Countries, rely upon Differential Tariffs to protect Home Industries during their experimental trial … it is useless to divert our energies in fruitless discussion, and seek to achieve victory over Free trade" (Ranade 1906 [1890]: 202). As an alternative, he advocated mechanisms to support Indian industrialization such as subsidized loans for local companies, targeted government purchase policies and voluntary initiatives to encourage Indians to consume local manufacturers.

Listian followers in other regions departed from the German thinker's advice in even more substantial ways. For example, as the new state of Turkey was coming into being after World War One, Listian ideas attracted much attention but they were combined with advocacy of a much more statist economic development strategy than List himself had endorsed. Particularly influential were the ideas of Ziya Gökalp (1959: 311–309) who called in 1923 for a kind of "state capitalism" for Turkey in which high tariffs would be combined with state-owned companies and "a national economic plan". Although inspired by List, Gökalp argued that this larger state role in the economy was needed to promote industrialization in a context of limited local skills and entrepreneurship. He also suggested that it was in keeping with local culture: "Turks are temperamentally étatists. They expect the state to take the initiative in everything new and progressive" (Gökalp 1959: 310–311).

Followers of List outside the West also rejected Eurocentric assumptions in his thought. List argued that only "temperate zone" countries were fit to industrialize, while those in the "torrid zone" – which included Asia, Africa and South America – were destined to be agricultural and raw material producers forever (List 1885 [1841]: 270). Many supporters of List in these latter regions simply ignored this dimension of his writings. Others challenged List's assumption explicitly. For example, while not mentioning List's work directly, Ranade in 1892 cited a number of arguments about why "torrid zone" countries such as India had the capacity to industrialize, including the impressive past economic achievements of Indian civilization. As he put it, Indian manufacturers used to find "a ready market in temperate kingdoms and excited such jealousy as a to dictate prohibitive sumptuary laws both in ancient Rome and in modern England" (Ranade 1906 [1892]: 27). In 1923, Gökalp (1959: 307–308) also highlighted how his country had housed a "rich industry" before the Ottoman Empire embraced free trade in the nineteenth century.

Marxism was the last of the three Western ideologies to spread globally, a process strongly encouraged by the 1917 Russian revolution. Once again, Marxist ideas about the global economy were modified as they diffused around the world. For example, in the 1920s, the Peruvian Marxist Jose Mariátegui went well beyond European Marxist theorists of imperialism in analysing various negative impacts of economic imperialism in his country, such as the role of foreign capital in exploiting local indigenous groups in alliance with local elites, exporting wealth from the country, inhibiting industrialization, and turning Peru into an "economic dependency" (quoted in Helleiner and Rosales 2017b: 679). In the same time period, Japanese Marxists also debated the unique dynamics of Japanese imperialism, with some arguing that it deserved their support (Hoston 1986). In a high-profile debate in Comintern in 1920, Indian Marxist M.N. Roy also questioned Vladimir Lenin's anti-imperialist strategy of working with national-bourgeois movements in colonized regions instead of more radical ones (d'Encausse and Schram 1969). In the 1930s, Caribbean Marxists such as George Padmore also critiqued European Marxist theories of imperialism for not devoting more attention to the role of race as a source of oppression. His Jamaican colleague Amy Ashwood Garvey also called for more attention to be devoted to gender issues (Malakani 2011).

Mixed in with these and other localizations were broader criticisms of the Eurocentrism of European Marxist theories of imperialism. For example, Mariátegui's one-time colleague Víctor Raúl Haya de la Torre became increasingly disillusioned with European Marxists in the 1920s who offered lessons to Latin America, a region that he argued they did not understand. As he put it in 1928, "we do not need to go to Europe to ask advice or to receive lessons in struggling" (quoted in Helleiner and Rosales 2017b: 670). Haya was also critical of Latin American Marxists who were "unthinking repeaters of an imported creed" and he called on anti-imperialist thinkers in his region to throw off the "mental colonialism" of European theory in order to develop analyses that better reflected the "historical time-space" of their region (quoted in Helleiner and Rosales 2017b: 670–671). Both Haya and Mariátegui also highlighted how socialist values emerged not just from Europe but also from the values, culture and history of the indigenous peoples in their own country. As Mariátegui put it, "We certainly do not wish socialism in America to be a copy and imitation.... We must give life to an Indo-American socialism reflecting our own reality and in our own language" (quoted in Helleiner and Rosales 2017b: 684).

Local origins of similar ideologies

In addition to localizing the three Western ideologies in these important ways, thinkers from other parts of the world also contributed to IPE thought in the pre-1945 era by developing similar ideologies independently. For example, arguments for free trade in non-Western contexts did not emerge only as a result of exposure to the ideas of Western thinkers such as Smith, Ricardo and Cobden. In China, the prominent eighteenth-century official Chen Hongmou – who had no knowledge of Western political economy – had already developed arguments for free trade before Smith's *The Wealth of Nations* was published in 1776. Rowe (2001: 421–422) describes Chen – who lived between 1696–1771 – as a "consistent champion" of trade liberalization, arguing that trade would provide mutual economic benefits for China and foreigners both in terms of the goods exchanged and the creation of "productive livelihoods (*guangsheng*) for the merchants and transport workers themselves". Rowe continues: "Chen also periodically advanced the Smithian notion that systematic commercial linkages between peoples help ensure peaceable intercultural relations more generally." Chen even shared the interest of European economic liberals in the link between free trade and the diffusion of civilizational norms, albeit from a distinctive Sino-centric perspective. As Rowe (2001: 422) puts it, Chen was interested in "the role of trade in bringing non-Chinese into closer touch with the Qing's civilized social model."

As Rowe (1997: 18) notes, Chen's ideas were part of his broader interest in markets and the idea that they "governed by rationally inferable laws of economic behavior". Like European economic liberals, Chen believed that self-interest, profit maximization and market dynamics could be socially beneficial and encouraged to work for the public good. Although Rowe

(2001: 204) cautions that Chen did not endorse "a blanket policy of laissez-faire", it is important to recall that Smith did not either. In comparing Chen's ideas to Western thought, Rowe (2001: 455) argues: "Chen's combination of taking agrarian proprietorship as the basis of the economy with an emphatic embrace of the 'the market principle' seems to place him closest to the eighteenth-century French physiocrats." He also references the work of Helen Dunstan (1996: 327) who has examined other Chinese proponents of markets at this time and reached the following conclusion: "The position of the present author is … that a rudimentary form of economic liberalism did exist in eighteenth-century China and that it was indigenous."

Neomercantilist thought also had important indigenous roots in the East Asian region. The case of Japan is particularly interesting and important. Analysts often attribute Japan's neomercantilist economic nationalist policies after the 1868 Meiji Restoration to the influence of imported Listian ideas from the West (e.g. Fallows 1993). But a growing body of historical scholarship shows convincingly that they had much more important local roots (Metzler 2006; Metzler and Smits 2010; Roberts 1998; Sagers 2006). Beginning in the early eighteenth century, Japanese scholars began to popularize a new kind of *kokueki* thought that urged local *daimyo* to enhance the wealth and power of their local domains by maximizing trade surpluses vis-à-vis other domains through activist government economic policies, such as export promotion, restrictions on imports, support for local artisans and merchants, and government-owned firms and monopolies. These mercantilist ideas had endogenous origins; as Mark Metzler and Gregory Smits (2010: 5) put it, "it is important to note the lack of any clear direct influence of European mercantilist thought on Japanese *kokueki* thinking". They emerged from Tokugawa Japan's distinctive political–economic environment characterized by inter-daimyo competition, high levels of commercialization and literacy, and financial pressures on daimyo to maintain costly residencies in the capital city of Edo. *Kokueki* thinkers also invoked Confucian ideas about rulers' duties to "order the realm and save the people" as well as the commitment of the ancient Chinese legalist thinker Shang Yang to a "rich country, strong army" at the time of China's Warring States (Sagers 2006: 24, 67).

Although *kokueki* thought initially was conceptualized for local daimyo, its advocates increasingly began to consider its relevance for Japan as whole as Western powers began to challenge the country's seclusion policy. After Japan's forced opening in the 1850s, this idea of scaling up *kokeuki* goals to the national level gained prominence and then served as a major influence on key officials in the post-1868 Meiji government. When reacting against Western free trade and economic liberal thought, Japanese officials drew upon the *kokueki* mercantilist tradition to develop innovative neomercantilist ideas and policies that were often quite different from advocated by List.

The success of Japan's post-1868 neomercantilist policies then had considerable influence on other East Asian countries (as well as beyond, particularly after Japan's military defeat of Russia in 1905). After Korea's forced opening in the 1870s, advocates of a new kind of neomercantilist thought invoked Japan's experience and were influenced by specific Japanese neomercantilist thinkers such as Fukuzawa Yukichi. Like their Japanese counterparts, the Korean neomercantilists also cited the ancient Chinese legalist tradition and experience of the Warring States period as well as the ideas of some advocates of economic opening in their own country from the late eighteenth century. List's ideas played little role in the development of Korean neomercantilism in the late nineteenth century; they were not introduced to Korea until after 1900 (Chey and Helleiner 2018).

List's ideas were also not introduced into China until the same time period. Well before this, however, thinkers such as Zheng Guanying and Wang Tao had already pioneered Chinese versions of neomercantilist thought in the wake of the Opium Wars (Helleiner and Wang 2018).

Like their Korean counterparts, both Zheng and Wang invoked Japan's post-1868 experience and advocated similar policies as those that Japan had pursued. They were also influenced by earlier Chinese thought, including not just that from the Warring states period, but also more recent "statecraft" thinkers such as Wei Yuan. In a famous 1844 book, Wei had urged reforms, including economic opening, to cultivate wealth and power in face of the new Western challenge in the wake of the first Opium War. Wei's book was also widely read in Japanese and Korean reformist circles, as were the ideas of Zheng and Wang (Helleiner and Wang 2018). These interconnections highlight how East Asian neomercantilist ideas emerged in the context of a region-wide intellectual environment that had strong indigenous historical roots.

Were there also examples of Marxist theories of imperialism emerging outside the West without reference to European ideas on this topic? One example can be found in the ideas of Kōtoku Shūsui who was the leading socialist in Japan in the early twentieth century. In 1901, he wrote an important work titled *Imperialism: Monster of the 20th Century* (that was also quickly translated into Chinese in 1902 and Korean in 1906). This publication appears to have been provoked by Kōtoku's concerns about Japan's involvement in repressing China's Boxer rebellion in 1900. What was distinctive about Kōtoku's work was the fact that he linked his analysis of imperialism to the cause of anti-capitalist revolutionary politics many years before Lenin (1970 [1916]) and other well-known Western Marxist theorists of imperialism did (Tierney 2015).[2]

Like Lenin, Kōtoku drew heavily on liberal anti-imperialist literature in the West at the turn of the century. While Lenin drew on Hobson's 1902 work, Kōtoku's key source was John MacKinnnon Robertson's 1899 *Patriotism and Empire*, which blamed imperialism on capitalist speculators and excessive patriotism in the imperial powers. Kōtoku made a similar argument about the causes of imperialism but drew a more radical political conclusion. While the liberal Robertson called for domestic reform such as the building of welfare states, Kōtoku argued that imperialism and its negative consequences – including exploitation and growing global military conflict – could only be ended by a socialist revolution that created an economy "in which the workers own all in common" (Kōtoku 2015 [1901]: 206). Unlike Lenin, he was also sceptical of anti-colonial nationalist movements, seeing them as holding a kind of false consciousness that interfered with his goal of worldwide socialism. As he put it, "There is only one solution. We must launch a great cleansing of the state and society or, in other words, start a revolutionary movement worldwide in scope" (Kōtoku 2015 [1901]: 206).

Local origins of different ideologies

A third kind of contribution of pre-1945 non-Western thinkers was that they developed ideologies about IPE issues that were distinct from the three Western ones usually presented to IPE students. Here, I provide just a few examples of some of the politically prominent ideologies of this kind. The first involved arguments defending economic autarchy; that is, the ability of a country to be economically self-sufficient (without necessarily refusing all trade). Advocates of autarchy were not absent from Western thought in the pre-1945 period; works such as Fichte's 1801 *The Closed Commercial State* (Nakhimovsky 2011) or Keynes's (1980 [1933]) case for "national self-sufficiency" at the height of the Great Depression are sometimes cited by contemporary IPE scholars. But the arguments in these works usually receive much less attention than those associated with the other three ideologies in standard IPE work (although they are sometimes folded into a category of "economic nationalism" that includes List's ideas). In non-Western thought in the pre-1945 period, the case for autarchy assumed a very prominent place. It also had quite different content from the ideas of Fichte and Keynes.

Given that Japan was one of the most famous cases of a country that pursued autarchic policies, it is not surprising that Japanese thinkers developed some of the more prominent arguments for autarchy. Although Japan had begun to tighten controls on its economic links to the world as far back as the 1630s, its turn towards greater autarchy became more pronounced in the late 1700s, prompting Japanese scholars to begin to talk of a policy of *sakoku* (national isolation). After a government order in 1825 went further to forcibly repel foreign ships that attempted to land in Japan, Aizawa Seishisai published a defence of the new policy in a work titled *Shinron* (New Theses). The work was only circulated privately initially, but it was later published in 1857 when became "a virtual bible to activists in the "revere the Emperor, expel the barbarian" movement" after the forced opening of Japan in the mid-1850s (Wakabayashi 1986: ix). While advocates of *kokueki*-style neomercantilist economic nationalism wanted Japan to compete in an open world economy for national power and wealth, Aizawa outlined a rationale for resisting engagement with the world economy instead.

At the core of his case was a socio-cultural argument associated with what Wakabayashi (1986: 9) calls a form of "proto-nationalism": autarchy was seen as a way to preserve and strengthen Japan's distinct identity and society. Aizawa critiqued international trade for providing foreigners with opportunities to promote alien religions that could undermine the loyalty of the Japanese to their country. He also saw autarchy as a way to boost this loyalty and the country's spiritual unity by challenging what he perceived as the growing decadence of Japanese society and restoring Japan's traditional culture and agrarian-focused economy. He believed that imports were largely "luxury items" and "useless commodities" paid for by mining the country's limited supply of precious metals, and that exports encouraged cash crop agriculture which undermined traditional Japanese agriculture and domestic food needs (quoted in Aizawa 1986 [1825]; 239). As he put it, he preferred to see agriculture returned "to its proper place of primacy in society", "decadent city dwellers" returned to their villages, "avaricious merchant princes" prevented "from garnering exorbitant profits and trampling underfoot small proprietors", and the Japanese people taught "to curb their acquisitiveness" (quoted in Aizawa 1986 [1825]: 240).

This socio-cultural case for autarchy contrasted with the arguments of Fichte and Keynes which were more centred on economic issues (particularly the need for policy space to pursue economic activist policies) and which explicitly endorsed enduring cross-border flows of ideas and culture. This socio-cultural line of argument continued to find supporters in Japan even after the country tuned towards neomercantilist economic nationalist policies after the 1868 Meiji Restoration. For example, in the 1870s and early 1880s, the leading Buddhist public intellectual Sada Kaiseki led boycotts of foreign products on the grounds that they undermined Japan's cultural autonomy. While the Meiji leaders imported modern Western technologies such as railways, steamships and mass production, he praised local artisan methods of production, arguing "inconvenience must be esteemed" and that Western-style development brought ecological costs such as deforestation, soil exhaustion and the depletion of finite resources such as fossil fuels (quoted in Sugiyama 1994: 1). In place of externally oriented production-driven industrial growth, he also argued that domestic prosperity could be better fostered by focusing inward on the greater consumption of local products and an agriculturally-focused economy (Rambelli 2011).

Similar arguments for autarchy can be found in other non-Western contexts. In colonized Ghana, for example, the prominent conservative anti-imperialist thinker Kobina Sekyi also argued in 1917 that autarchy would allow his people to insulate their culture and nationality from "evil" European civilization and enable an autonomous "unwesternized" development path (Sekyi 1979 [1917]: 244, 250). Just before Korea's opening in the 1870s, thinkers such as

Lee Hang-ro also defended autarchy as necessary to preserve Korea's traditional culture and agrarian-centred social structure which had been inspired by Chinese neo-Confucianism. From Lee's perspective, economic opening would cause an inflow not only of Western ideas but also of Western consumer goods and profit-seeking behavior that would undermine the neo-Confucian values of frugality and modesty (Chey and Helleiner 2018). His warning phrase "exchange of commodities, exchange of immorality" became a rallying call for opponents of the neomercantilist advocacy of economic opening (quoted in McNamara, 1996: 62).

Perhaps the most famous advocate of autarchy was the anti-imperialist Indian thinker and political leader Mohandas Karamchand Gandhi. Beginning in the early twentieth century, Gandhi urged his fellow Indians to focus on buying clothing and other goods that were produced in local village and cottage industries. He famously promoted the spinning wheel as a symbol of the kind of economic self-sufficiency – or *swadeshi* – that he sought for India: one focused on appropriate technology and decentralized village-based economic life. In contrast to neomercantilist economic nationalists such as Ranade (and later Jawaharlal Nehru), Gandhi questioned the value of large-scale industry and the modern centralized nation-state, arguing that these inventions of modern Western civilization generated concentrations of wealth and power that were exploitative, violence-prone, dehumanizing, and incompatible with individual freedom (e.g. Trivedi 2007).

In addition to ideas about autarchy, non-Western thinkers also developed distinctive transnational economic ideologies that did not fit clearly into the three classical ideologies outlined in IPE textbooks. One of these was developed by the Jamaican activist Marcus Garvey in the early twentieth century who applied what Ramla Bandele (2008) calls "diaspora politics" to IPE in creative ways. Garvey was a prominent supporter of the pan-African movement at the time he sought to promote the wealth and power of Africans and the African diaspora via a political entity – the United Negro Improvement Association (UNIA) – which he conceptualized as an embryo for a future independent African nation-state. Through UNIA, he sought to protect and boosted the economic self-reliance of Africans and the diaspora in ways that also fostered their common transnational identity and economic power (Bandele 2008; Ewing 2014; Shilliam 2006).

His most famous economic initiative in this area was the creation of the Black Star Line in 1919–1922, a shipping company in which Africans and members of the diaspora could purchase shares. In his view, the company was "the property of the Negro race" (quoted in Ewing 2014: 82) and it aimed to improve shipping connections between the US, the Caribbean and Africa with better routes, services and prices than those of the established lines. As Bandele (2008: x) puts it, Garvey hoped this company could "develop a black enclave economy and ultimately a black nation-state in West Africa" (see also Shilliam 2006). Garvey himself outlined his goals in 1919 as follows: "If we are to rise as a great [people] to become a great national force, we must start business enterprises of our own; we must build ships and start trading with ourselves between America, West Indies and Africa" (quoted in Bandele 2008: 94). Although Garvey's initiative floundered in the face of internal management problems and external opposition, it attracted much enthusiasm in these regions and beyond. Through his commitment to fostering a kind of protected "enclave economy" with the ultimate goal of the creating a wealthy and powerful independent African state, his ideology might be described as a creative type of "diasporic neomercantilism".

Another example of a distinctive transnational economic ideology was developed by supporters of the pan-Islamic movement that began to grow in political prominence in the late nineteenth century (e.g. Aydin 2017). Many of the initial supporters of this movement showed little interest in linking pan-Islamic thought to economic issues, but an early exception was the

Ottoman sultan Abdulhamid II, a figure who cultivated a kind of "imperial pan-Islamism" during his rule between 1876 and 1909. In 1900, he announced plans to build a new railway connecting Damascus to the holy cities of Mecca and Medina, describing it as a "sacred line" that would facilitate pilgrimages and strengthen Muslim solidarity worldwide (quoted in Özyük-sel 2014: 39). While most railway projects in the Ottoman Empire were financed and operated by foreigners from the West, he noted that this Hejaz railway was to be run by the Ottoman government, built with Muslim engineers, and financed with both official funds and voluntary donations from Muslims worldwide. Although the project served some specific Ottoman strategic interests, he depicted it as a joint Muslim economic project that would demonstrate the power and solidarity of the Islamic world (Özyüksel 2014: 69–70). This vision was initially very well received, with one journalist noting that the sultan "became at one shot the most popular man of the Islamic world, and hero of the day" (quoted in Özyüksel 2014: 60). Religious groups across the Islamic world promoted the project, with donations financing close to one-third of the project, an outcome that Özyüksel (2014: 217) suggests was "quite unprecedented in economic history".

A more significant and theoretical effort to link pan-Islamic thought to economic issues was made later in the early 1940s by the Indian scholar Savyid Abul-Ala Mawdudi. His writings at this time are usually seen as having pioneered an "Islamic economics" movement, a movement that became increasingly influential in the post-1945 years (e.g. Kuran 1997). Rather than fighting for an independent Muslim state, Mawdudi urged Muslims worldwide to defend themselves against foreign domination through a cultural revival that prioritized a comprehensive Islamic way of life. Because of the growing importance of economics to daily life, Mawdudi argued that this way of life needed to encompass economic activities through the promotion of initiatives such as bans on interest payments, wealth redistribution, and broader Islamic norms of economic behaviour.

In the early 1940s, Mawdudi also discussed the dynamics of the world economy, arguing that moral failures of excessive greed and selfishness, combined with the unwillingness of the wealthy to redistribute resources domestically, generated "antagonistic competition" between countries and the rise of imperialism. These trends caused wars, trade restrictions and exploitation wherein "a handful of bankers, brokers, and industrial and business magnates so completely gather in their clutches all the economic resources of the world that the whole of humanity is reduced to a state of dependence upon them" (Mawdudi 1966 [1941]: 24). In his view, this "satanic system" also adversely affected "world's moral outlook" with "the whole of humanity having been reduced to the lots of an economic animal" (Mawdudi 1966 [1941]: 14–25). Islamic economics, he implied, was the solution and one with universal aspirations. As he put it in 1939, "the truth is that Islam is not the name of a "Religion", nor is "Muslim" the title of a "Nation". In reality Islam is a revolutionary ideology and programme which seeks to alter the social order of the whole world and rebuild it in conformity with its own tenets and ideals" (Maududi 1976 [1939]: 5).

Influencing Western thought

A final kind of contribution of pre-1945 non-Western thinkers consisted of their influence on Western IPE thought. For example, some scholars have speculated about the influence of Chinese political economy on the thought of prominent eighteenth-century French physiocrat Francois Quesnay, whose economic ideas influenced Adam Smith (e.g. Clarke 1977). In 1767, Quesnay held up China as an economic model for a prosperous society because of its perceived focus on agriculture, markets and limited government. As noted earlier, there were indeed remarkable similarities between the ideas of Chinese thinkers such as Chen Hongmou and French physiocratic thought. It is important, however, not to overstate the influence. I have seen no evidence that French physiocrats were aware of the specific writings or ideas of Chen Hongmou. Instead, they were inspired more by the model of Chinese policy as described to them by Western observers of the country than the ideas of specific Chinese thinkers like Chen.[3] If Chen had an influence on Western thought, it appears to have been through the quite indirect channel of helping to shape Chinese economic policy in directions that then inspired Quesnay. For IPE scholars, it is also important to note that Quesnay praised China's limited trade and its prioritizing of domestic commerce, while Smith was critical of aspect of the Chinese model and of its trade restrictions (Millar 2011).

Another European thinker inspired by the example of non-Western economic practices was the German thinker Englebert Kaempfer. He was the author of *The History of Japan* published posthumously in English in 1727 (the original manuscript had been written in 1692) that provided a detailed description and analysis of Japanese society. Among other issues, Kaempfer (1906 [1692]: 301–536) prominently praised Japan's relative economic self-sufficiency (although the country had not yet shifted to the more autarchic policies of the late eighteenth and early nineteenth century). From Kaempfer's standpoint, Japan showed not just the viability of doing without most foreign goods, but also the desirability of this policy in discouraging foreign subversion, promoting international peace and ensuring policy autonomy to promote a consolidated virtuous domestic commonwealth. His case for autarchy rarely receives any attention in contemporary IPE writings, but his book was an "immediate best-seller" at the time and shaped European understandings of Japan until well into the nineteenth century (Matthew Perry had a copy with him when he opened up Japan) (Bodart-Bailey 1999: 7; see also Mervart 2009).

Unlike Quesnay, Kaempfer drew these conclusions from direct experience: he had lived in Japan between 1690–1692. What remains unclear, however, is the extent to which Kaempfer drew on the ideas of Japanese thinkers in developing his ideas. As we have seen, the most prominent defence of Japanese autarchy – that of Aizawa – did not appear until a century later and this defence was not entirely the same as that of Kaempfer. We do know, however, that Kaempfer became knowledgeable about Japanese thought during his time in the country and that his arguments for autarchy overlapped with some of the Japanese rationales for tightening economic restrictions. One further piece of evidence that Kaempfer's ideas overlapped with endogenous Japanese thought comes from the fact that his book was very well received in Japan when it first made its way to the country in the 1770s. As Japan moved towards greater closure after the 1790s, Japanese authorities ordered its translation into Japanese in 1801, giving it the esteemed position of being the only work of Western political economy invoked so prominently to support Japanese policy before the mid-nineteenth century. Indeed, the term *sakoku* came from the title given to his work by the Japanese translator (Mervart 2009; 2015). Kaempfer's work provides a particularly interesting example of how ideas about political economy flowed from East to West and back again.

The willingness of both Quesnay and Kaempfer to learn from the non-West may have been encouraged by the fact that they developed their analyses at a time before the West came to dominate the world. As Western power grew in nineteenth and twentieth centuries, many Western thinkers adopted more closed-minded, Eurocentric attitudes. But we can still find some interesting examples of the influence of non-West on Western political economy in this period.

One involves Dadabhai Naoroji, a very prominent Indian thinker in the late nineteenth and early twentieth centuries who – like Ranade – was very critical of a number of dimensions of British colonial rule. Through detailed statistical analyses, he focused particularly on how the

British drained economic resources from India in way that generated growing "extreme impoverishment" in the colony (quoted in Masani 1939: 428–429). Naoroji devoted much of his career to educating the British public and government about the issue, becoming very active in intellectual and political life in Britain where he chose to live for much of the time between 1855 and 1907. He even became the first Indian to be elected as a member of the British House of Commons in 1892.

Although Naoroji himself was a liberal, his greatest direct impact on British thought was in socialist circles. At a time when many European socialists were either uninterested in the impact of imperialism on the colonized or even supportive of imperialism, his analysis encouraged more attention to its economic costs for India and attracted some support. For example, his "drain theory" was embraced in the late 1870s by Henry Hyndman, a critic of British imperialism who created Britain's first socialist party in the early 1880s and went on to play a significant role in the Second International. Naoroji worked closely with Hyndman at various moments, including at the 1904 Second International's meeting in Amsterdam where he received a standing ovation and critiqued the drain as well as British treatment of India as a form of "barbarism" (quoted in Masani 1939: 432). According to Manu Goswami (2004: 338fn38), Naoroji also "carried on an extensive correspondence" with Karl Kautsky, another prominent European socialist analyst of imperialism. Goswami (2004, 227) also argues that Marx himself drew on Naoroji's drain theory in his writings about India.

Another non-Western thinker who influenced Western thought on IPE issues was the Chinese thinker and political leader Sun Yat-sen. From the mid-1890s onwards, Sun emerged as a prominent supporter of neomercantilist ideas and policies, inspired initially by pioneers of Chinese neomercantilism such as Zheng Guanying. In the immediate aftermath of World War One, however, he also advanced one of the first proposals ever for a multilateral lending institution could mobilize capital from wealthy countries to support the economic development goals of a poorer country such as China. Although Sun's (1922: 227) proposed "International Development Organization" was never created, the arguments he put forward in promoting the ideas were later invoked by American liberal internationalists who became interested in creating a multilateral development lending institution during the planning for the post-World War Two era (Helleiner 2014; 2018).

Sun's arguments focused on how borrowing and lending countries alike could benefit from this new kind of international institution. The former, he suggested, would acquire much-needed foreign capital to support their economic development more effectively than lending provided by foreign private financiers. The latter would gain economically as they found a productive international outlet for their surplus capital and goods. More broadly, for both sets of countries, he argued that the cause of international peace would be fostered by this new kind of international development cooperation. These arguments about the positive sum nature of international development cooperation helped to build support for the creation of the World Bank at the Bretton Woods conference of 1944 (Helleiner 2014, 2018).

Conclusion

This chapter has attempted to show some ways in which the historical roots of ideological debates about IPE issues can be broadened to include some contributions of non-Western thinkers from the pre-1945 period. There are many others that could also be cited. Let me conclude by suggesting four reasons why these and other historical contributions of non-Western thinkers deserve more attention from IPE scholars today. The first is simply that a more complete global intellectual history is provided when the historical origins of IPE thought are widened in this way. I have argued that Western-centric intellectual histories overlook at least four kinds of contributions made by non-Western thinkers before 1945: those that localized the well-studied Western ideologies of economic liberalism, neomercantilism, and Marxism; those that developed similar ideologies but independently; those that developed different kinds of ideologies from those three; and those who influenced Western thought (either directly or indirectly).

A second reason why the historical roots of IPE should be located in a broader global intellectual history is that much of the familiar cannon of classical Western political economy is infused with Eurocentric worldviews (Hobson 2013). As noted in this chapter, many pre-1945 non-Western thinkers highlighted this point, critiquing Western thinkers for assuming the superiority of European civilizational standards and for downplaying the agency of non-Western peoples. Contemporary IPE scholars risk reproducing these Eurocentric worldviews when telling the history of their field only through the lens of Western thinkers. They also miss opportunities to discuss how earlier non-Western thinkers suggested various ways of overcoming Eurocentrism and of addressing civilizational issues in IPE analyses.

Third, the study of pre-1945 non-Western IPE thought is important because of its contemporary legacies in non-Western regions of the world. Although many of the ideas of the thinkers discussed in this chapter find no place in IPE textbooks, they are often familiar to thinkers in their country/region of origin where they have helped to shape local intellectual trajectories over time. If IPE scholars today are seeking to foster more of a global conversation in their field today, they need to become more knowledgeable about such locally-rooted diachronic intellectual histories. Indeed, Robert Cox (2009: 324) suggests that this task is one of the most important facing IPE scholars today:

> Unlike economics, IPE cannot be an abstract science. Of its nature, IPE incorporates human concerns and intentions for social transformation and ethical values, and cultures and civilizations differ about these things. These aims and values are framed by people's innate sense of how the world works – a sense that has been shaped by a people's history. The impact of the *longue durée* in shaping mentalities provides the framework for thinking about policy. Different approaches to IPE have to be understood historically. The English-speaking world, long hegemonic in the dissemination of thought about global affairs, will need to listen more carefully to the other voices in a global dialogue. It is only when scholars are confronted with the full variety of perspectives that the work of intellectual bridge building can seriously begin.

Finally, the study of the historical contributions of non-Western thinkers is also important for reminding us that "global conversations" about IPE issues are not unique to the contemporary age. In the pre-1945 years, IPE debates were often informed not just by locally specific diachronic intellectual contexts but also by globally synchronic ones influenced by the circulation of ideas across the world in any given era. Contemporary scholars seeking to foster greater global mutual understanding in a more pluralistic world economy may be able to learn some lessons from the experience of earlier past global conversations. One such lesson is the importance of power relations in shaping global intellectual contexts. In the nineteenth and early twentieth century, the rise of Western power ensured that Western ideas became a key intellectual reference for thinkers across the world. Indeed, it is this very phenomenon that has led contemporary IPE scholars to focus so heavily on Western thought when analysing the historical origins of IPE thought in that era. But that narrow focus overlooks a second lesson: the non-West was not simply a passive recipient of ideas diffusing internationally from Western centres of power. Even in a context of highly unequal power relations, non-Western thinkers localized Western ideas in important ways, and also generated their own ideas that were influential locally and beyond. Contemporary efforts to strengthen global conversations in IPE today must be open to these complexities of power, localization, and multiple directionality associated with the global circulation of ideas both now and in the past.

Notes

1 "Neomercantilists" revised earlier mercantilist thought in the wake of Adam Smith's critique of mercantilism in the *The Wealth of Nations*. It can be defined as an ideology that prioritizes policies of strategic trade protectionism and other forms of government economic activism with the goal of maximizing the wealth and power of a state. This ideology is sometimes called simply "economic nationalism", but that label is a problematic one for reasons I have explained elsewhere (e.g. Helleiner 2002).
2 There were some less well-known Western Marxists who had already made this linkage in the late nineteenth century such as Henry Hyndman. Kōtoku also did not mention his work. Contemporary IPE scholars also rarely mention it. I discuss Hyndman briefly later in this chapter.
3 Clarke (1997: 50) suggests the Quesnay was influenced by Chinese idea of "wu-wei" which he argues was translated into French as "laissez-faire". Although this argument has been repeated by others, Jacobsen (2013: 28) notes that there is in fact "no direct textual evidence in the literature for this claim" and thus "one must regard the direct coupling of wu-wei and the economic concept of laissez-faire as a myth".

Bibliography

Acharya, A. 2009. *Whose ideas matter?* Ithaca: Cornell University Press.
Aizawa, S. 1986 [1825]. New theses. In: Bob Wakabayashi, *Anti-foreignism and Western learning in early-modern Japan.* Cambridge: Council on East Asian Studies, Harvard University Press.
Aydin, C. 2017. *The idea of the Muslim world.* Cambridge: Harvard University Press.
Bandele, R. 2008. *Black star.* Urbana: University of Illinois Press.
Blyden, E. 1969 [1880]. Africa's Service to the World. In Henry Wilson, *Origins of West African nationalism.* London: Macmillan.
Blyden, E. 1971 [1883]. The origin and purpose of African colonization. In Hollis Lynch, ed., *Black spokesman: Selected published writings of Edward Wilmot Blyden.* London: Frank Cass and Co.
Blyth, M. ed., 2010. *Routledge handbook of IPE: IPE as a global conversation.* New York: Routledge.
Bodart-Bailey, B. 1999. Translator's introduction. In: Engelbert Kaempfer, ed., *Kaempfer's Japan.* Honolulu: University of Hawaii Press.
Cain, P. 1979. Capitalism, war and internationalism in the thought of Richard Cobden. *British Journal of International Studies* 5(3): 229–247.
Chey, H. and Helleiner, E. 2018. Civilizational values and political economy beyond the West. *Contemporary Politics* 24(2): 191–209.
Chin, G., Pearson, M. and Yong, W. eds., 2013. IPE in China: the global conversation. *Review of International Political Economy* 20(6): 1145–1299.
Clarke, J. 1997. *Oriental enlightenment.* London: Routledge.
Coller, I. 2015. African liberalism in the age of Empire? *Modern Intellectual History* 12(3): 529–553.
Cox, R. 2009. The 'British school' in the global context. *New Political Economy* 14(3): 315–328.
D'Encausse, H. and Schram, S. 1969. *Marxism and Asia.* London: Penguin.
Dunstan, H. 1996. *Conflicting counsels to confuse the age.* Ann Arbor: Center for Chinese Studies, University of Michigan.
Ewing, A. 2014. *The age of Garvey.* Princeton: Princeton University Press.
Fallows, J. 1993. How the world works. *Atlantic Monthly* (December), 61–87.
Gökalp, Z. 1959. *Turkish nationalism and Western civilization.* Translated and edited by Niyazi Berkes. New York: Columbia University Press.
Gootenberg, P. 1989. *Between Silver and Guano.* Princeton: Princeton University Press.
Goswami, M. 2004. *Producing India.* Chicago: University of Chicago Press.

Helleiner, E. 2002. Economic nationalism as a challenge to economic liberalism? *International Studies Quarterly* 46(3): 307–329.

Helleiner, E. 2014. *Forgotten foundations of Bretton Woods*. Ithaca: Cornell University Press.

Helleiner, E. 2018. Sun Yat-sen as a pioneer of international development. *History of Political Economy* 50(5): 76–93.

Helleiner, E. and Rosales, A. 2017a. Peripheral thoughts for global IPE. *International Studies Quarterly* 61(4): 924–934.

Helleiner, E. and Rosales, A. 2017b. Towards global IPE. *International Studies Review* 19(4): 667–691.

Helleiner, E. and Wang, H. 2018. Beyond the tributary tradition of Chinese IPE. *Chinese Journal of International Politics* 11(4): 451–483.

Hobson, J. 1902. *Imperialism: A study*. London: George Allen and Unwin.

Hobson, J. 2013. Part 1 – revealing the Eurocentric foundations of IPE. *Review of International Political Economy* 20(5): 1024–1054.

Hoston, G. 1986. *Marxism and the crisis of development in prewar Japan*. Princeton: Princeton University Press.

Jacobsen, S. 2013. Physiocracy and the Chinese model. In Ying Ma and Hans-Michael Trautwein, eds., *Thoughts on economic development in China*. London, Routledge.

Kaempfer, E. 1906 [1692]. *The history of Japan*. Translated by J.G. Scheuchzer, volume 3. Glasgow: James MacLehose and Sons.

Keynes, J. 1980 [1933]. National self-sufficiency. In Donald Moggridge, ed., *Collected writings of John Maynard Keynes – activities 1931–39*. Cambridge: Cambridge University Press.

Kōtuku, S. 2015 [1901]. Imperialism. In Robert Thomas Tierney, *Monster of the twentieth century*. Berkeley: University of California Press.

Kuran, T. 1997. The genesis of Islamic economics. *Social Research* 64(2): 301–338.

Lenin, V. 1970 [1916]. *Imperialism*. Moscow: Progress.

List, F. 1885 [1841]. *The national system of political economy*. London: Longmans, Green and Co.

Makalani, M. 2011. *In the cause of freedom: Radical black internationalism from Harlem to London, 1917–1939*. Chapel Hill: University of North Carolina Press.

Masani, R. 1939. *Dadabhai Naoroji*. London: George Allen and Unwin.

Maududi. S. 1976 [1939]. *Jihad in Islam*. Lahore: Islamic Publications.

Mawdudi, S. 1966 [1941]. *The economic problem of man and its Islamic solution*. Lahore: Islamic Publications.

McNamara, D. 1996. *Trade and transformation in Korea, 1876–1945*. Boulder: Westview.

Mervart, David. 2009. A closed country in the open seas. *History of European Ideas* 35(3): 321–329.

Mervart, D. 2015. The republic of letters comes to Nagasaki. *Transcultural Studies* 2: 8–37.

Metzler, M. 2006. The cosmopolitanism of national economics. In Antony G. Hopkins ed., *Global history*. Basingstoke: Palgrave Macmillan.

Metzler, M. and Smits, G. 2010. Introduction: The autonomy of market activity and the emergence of Keizei thought. In Bettina Gramlich-Oka and Gregory Smits, eds., *Economic thought in early modern Japan*. Leiden: Brill.

Millar, A. 2011. Your beggarly commerce! Enlightenment European views of the China trade. In Guido Abbattista, ed., *Encountering otherness*. Trieste: Edizioni Universitá di Trieste.

Mudimbe, V. 1988. *The invention of Africa*. Bloomington: Indiana University Press.

Nakhimovsky, Isaac. 2011. *The closed commercial state*. Princeton: Princeton University Press.

Özyüksel, M. 2014. *The Hejaz railway and the Ottoman Empire*. London: I.B. Tauris.

Rambelli, F. 2011. Sada Kaiseki. In Roy Starrs, ed., *Politics and religion in Japan*. New York: Palgrave Macmillan.

Ranade, M. 1906 [1890]. Industrial conference. In Mahadev Goving Ranade, *Essays on Indian Economics*. Second edition. Madras: G.A. Natesan and Company.

Ranade, M. 1906 [1892]. Indian Political Economy. In Mahadev Goving Ranade, *Essays on Indian Economics*. Second edition. Madras: G.A. Natesan and Company.

Ranade, M. 1906 [1893]. Present state of Indian manufacturers and outlook of the same. In: *Essays on Indian Economics*. Second edition. Madras: G.A. Natesan and Company.

Ranade, M. 1990 [1881]. Review of "Free Trade and English Commerce" by Mongredien, A. In Bipan Chandra, *Ranade's Economic Writings*. New Delhi: Gian Publishing House.

Ricardo, D. 1948 [1817]. *On the principles of political economy and taxation*. London: Dent.

Roberts, L. 1998. *Mercantilism in a Japanese domain*. Cambridge: Cambridge University Press.

Roberston, J. 1899. *Patriotism and Empire*. London: Grant Richards.

Rojas, C. 2002. *Civilization and violence*. Minneapolis: University of Minnesota Press.

Rowe, W. 1997. Economics and culture in eighteenth-century China. In Kenneth Lieberthal, S. and Young, E. eds., *Constructing China*. Ann Arbor: Center for Chinese Studies, University of Michigan.

Rowe, W. 2001. *Saving the world*. Stanford: Stanford University Press.

Sagers, J. 2006. *Origins of Japanese wealth and power*. New York: Palgrave MacMillan.

Sartori, A. 2008. *Bengal in global concept history*. Chicago: University of Chicago Press.

Schwartz, B. 1964. *In search of wealth and power*. Cambridge: Belknap Press of the Harvard University Press.

Sekyi, K. 1979 [1917]. The future of subject peoples. In Jabez Ayo Langley, *Ideologies of liberation in black Africa, 1856–1970*. London: Rex Collings.

Shilliam, R. 2006. What about Marcus Garvey? *Review of International Studies* 32(3): 379–400.

Smith, A. 1976 [1776]. *An inquiry into the nature and causes of the wealth of nations*. New York: Oxford University Press.

Strange, S. 1991. An eclectic approach. In Craig Murphy and Roger Tooze, eds., *The new international political economy*. Basingstoke: Macmillan.

Sugiyama, C. 1994. *Origins of economic thought in modern Japan*. London: Routledge.

Sun Yat-sen. 1922. *The international development of China*. New York: G.P. Putnam's Sons.

Tierney, R. 2015. *Monster of the twentieth century*. Berkeley: University of California Press.

Trivedi, Lisa. 2007. *Clothing Gandhi's nation*. Bloomington: Indiana University Press.

Tussie, D. and Riggirozzi, P. 2015. A global conversation. *Contexto Internacional*. 37(3): 1041–1068.

Wakabayashi, B. 1986. *Anti-foreignism and Western learning in early-modern Japan*. Cambridge: Council on East Asian Studies, Harvard University Press.

4

The state of development in a globalized world

Perspectives on advanced and industrializing countries

Elizabeth Thurbon and Linda Weiss[1]

Introduction

How does globalization impact on the ambitions of state actors and the capacities of states to positively shape development outcomes? This is not just a question for developing countries seeking to catch up. It is also an issue for already industrialized countries that seek to upgrade technology, mitigate economic inequality and align economic with environmental goals. We thus approach the study of development in the classical sense to embrace not only the study of poorer countries, but also the study of large-scale socio-economic change that entails continuous technological transformation, regardless of the time or place in which it occurs.

Before globalization began to dominate debates in the 1990s, there was broad agreement that development involved structural transformation of the economy, notably the transition from agriculture to industry. Where scholars disagreed over obstacles and drivers, they were most deeply divided over the role of the state in the development process. The dominant view gave prominence to the role of property rights and related regulatory reforms that sustain a liberal market order (North 1990). This regulatory view downplayed the state and its economy-building centrality and continues to inform the understanding of 'why nations fail' and, conversely, why they succeed (Acemoglu and Robinson 2012).[2]

The limitations of this regulatory view became starkly apparent following the impressive rise of Japan and its former colonies, Taiwan and South Korea. To make sense of their rapid and unprecedented socio-economic transformation, revisionist scholarship soon put the state and its transformative capacity at the centre of the development story (Johnson 1982; Amsden 1989; Wade 1990; Weiss 1995). As Chalmers Johnson's seminal work on Japan sought to show, pace Cold War rhetoric, there was more than one kind of political economy in the world of capitalism – not just the free-market (regulatory) version promoted by the United States, but also the state-guided version practiced by the East Asian three.

As the last vestiges of the Cold War disappeared, however, two emerging trends combined to help shift the focus of debate: on one hand, growing global economic integration through ever increasing flows of goods, finance and capital, and on the other, the dominance of market fundamentalism. First, increasing economic openness appeared to many observers to shrink policy space, reduce political choice and ultimately sideline the national state's role in the development process. Second (and somewhat paradoxically), as companies in advanced countries began to globalize their manufacturing requirements, production itself all but disappeared from the development story. With this shift in focus, a new understanding took hold of the development agenda. This was the idea that a country could lift people out of poverty without promoting industrialization, and that whether in a developing or advanced setting, the state would have a very limited role to play in the endless challenge of economic transformation.

Our chapter challenges that understanding by addressing two connected issues that emerge from recent research. First, can there be development without production? Second, to what extent does globalization reduce or sideline the state's developmental role? To set the scene, we first examine how both the state and production became marginalized in understandings of what it takes to grow the economy, lift people out of poverty and pave the way for continuing prosperity. In the second part, we introduce an empirically and conceptually informed argument to explain why manufacturing production remains pivotal to economic prosperity, and why the state is still central to the development story, even gaining perhaps a renewed importance now that economies are deeply intertwined.

Removing the state from the development story

As is well known, an abundance of literature has told the story of the state's demise, decline and transformation as an economic actor. This story has been so well told that we touch on it only briefly below. Suffice to say here that despite conflicting evidence, by the closing decade of the twentieth century, the state's retreat had become one of the most widely accepted understandings in the scholarly community. What made it seem credible was that it resonated with real-world developments and political ambitions. First, the Americans, driven by rivalry with the Soviet Union, sought to promote a 'small-state' solution to the world's economic and social problems. As the Cold War thawed, political and economic leaders in the Anglo-American sphere reoriented their economies to prioritize markets and minimize the role of government. This shift towards what became known as market fundamentalism, enthusiastically promoted by the Reagan and Thatcher administrations, dovetailed with the rising policy influence of neoclassical economists whose theories promoted the state as problem and the market as solution to the pursuit of prosperity (for critiques see: Weiss 2010; Stedman Jones 2014).

Second, in the European arena, the push to broaden and deepen the European Union (EU), which first emerged as a response to Europe's violent past and gained momentum during the Cold War, received further impetus as the Berlin Wall came down. In distinction to the small-state ethos of the Americans, the Europeans envisaged a supra-national entity that would in many policy areas override the autonomy of its nation-state members. Concerned to bind Germany more closely to the European project, for example, the French, as a prelude to monetary union, led by example with the liberalization of capital movements (Abdelal 2006: 7). This move soon had a ripple effect across the entire global economy, as other advanced economies, not least the United States and Britain, sought to capitalize on the perceived advantages of financial openness. By the 1990s, 'globalization' had entered the lexicon, and in the EU it had become a different way of talking about 'Europeanization' (Weiss 2005).

Third, at the global level, we see the repurposing of the World Bank and the International Monetary Fund (IMF) as advocates for market opening, and the creation of the World Trade Organization (WTO) as an instrument of domestic institutional transformation. Under this new trade regime, the idea of trade openness shifted dramatically from one that prioritizes removal of tariffs and subsidies to one that reshapes national rules and regulations in line with a global

standard shaped by the wealthiest countries. From the 1990s onwards, these international organizations began to articulate a clear and consistent message for less developed economies (LDCs):
the golden keys to development are to be found in economic openness (*aka* globalization) and
institutional convergence. So, if as a country you wish to develop, you must limit the state's role
to providing 'good governance' by enforcing private property rights and establishing a framework of rules in which the free market can operate.[3]

These developments provided the context for a new era of state denial. By state denial we
refer to 'the proliferation of theses which portend the diminution or displacement of states as
primary power actors in the domestic and international arenas' (Weiss 1998: 3). These developments, often presented under the umbrella of 'state transformation', range from the 'death
of industrial policy' and the 'collapse of the welfare state' to the 'end of national diversity' and
the 'demise of the nation state'. In this era, the state came to be viewed in varying degrees as
weakened, hollowed out, or 'transformed' (see e.g. Hirst and Thompson 1996; Held and
McGrew 1999). Underpinning these views is the conception of a globalizing economy integrated chiefly by transnational capital and the market. By the turn of the century the idea of a
global economy dominated by stateless corporations and borderless finance had come to prevail.
As capital, finance and technology flow effortlessly across state borders, many concluded that
globalization is a zero-sum game – one that strengthens market players while disempowering
national governments. The end point is a state rendered largely irrelevant as an influential actor
in its own economy. Political choice and domestic institutions had little place in this
narrative.

A further deepening of these 'powerless state' views occurred as the Asian region was hit by
the full force of financial turbulence. The so-called 'Asian financial crisis', which saw a number
of its 'miracle' economies begin to unravel in the wake of capital liberalization, was broadly
interpreted as the failure of state intervention (for a critique, see Wade and Veneroso 1998). In
policy circles, the dominant understanding was that global integration brooks no alternative to
a market-led regime. Even a decade later, as the world was gripped by the Wall Street-induced
financial meltdown, the state's critical interventions were confined to short-term rescue efforts
rather than to more long-term remedial strategies. This response was (and remains) especially
true of the United States where financial institutions and their Congressional supporters have
vigorously resisted regulatory reform (Wilson 2012).

Downplaying the importance of industrial production in development

As mentioned earlier, many academic and policy actors, notably (though not exclusively) in the
Anglosphere, have not simply sidelined the state. They have also dramatically downplayed
manufacturing production as a building block of national prosperity. As the world's leading economic authority, the United States provided the crucible for the idea that production no longer
mattered in the 'post-industrial', knowledge-intensive economy. Beset by fierce competition
from East Asia, the dominant view that took shape in the US setting was that advanced countries
no longer needed to make things. Instead, they could – and should – focus on services and
knowledge-intensive activities. Again, these ideas seemed credible because they resonated with
broader changes in the global economy. Most significant was the migration of US manufacturing that began in response to Japan's rise as a serious competitor in America's high-technology
markets. In a number of sectors, US firms respond the Japanese challenge by fragmenting their
production processes and offshoring manufacturing to lower-cost destinations (Sturgeon 2002).
Beginning in the early 1980s, Japan also promoted offshore production to the region, giving rise
to the idea of a 'flying geese model' (Hatch and Yamamura 1996). How Japan dealt with this

and avoided extremes of de-industrialization discussed below, opens questions for further research.

America's offshoring trend was hastened by changes in the financial sphere, such as the rise of private equity firms and shareholder activism. Combined with the new ideology of 'maximizing shareholder value', first propagated by Harvard Business School, these developments had a profound impact on corporate decision-making. Short-term profit and share-price maximization became the ultimate managerial goals (Lazonik and O'Sullivan 2000). In this context, offshoring became the default response of American corporate executives under intense pressure from investors to rapidly reduce costs, boost profits and focus on 'core competencies' related to their company's intellectual property. In this offshoring story, the WTO also played its part by easing restrictions on foreign investment and globalizing US intellectual property laws.

By the 2000s, American firms, though by no means the only players, were leading the creation and coordination of global production networks. As companies in all advanced countries began to follow the American lead, the contribution of domestic manufacturing to both employment and GDP gradually declined. It was not long before scholars were pronouncing 'de-industrialization' as yet another inevitable outcome of globalization. Far from viewing the withering of production as a threat to national prosperity, US commentators gave it a positive spin. They claimed that advanced economies should focus on services, while leaving 'the rest' to specialize in the less intellectually demanding activities appropriate to their stage of development.

In the LDCs, a different set of considerations led to the downplaying of manufacturing production. In this context, 'poverty alleviation' and 'human development' replaced the earlier emphasis on industrial transformation. This substitution occurred at two different levels. At the macro level, international development bodies like the World Bank themselves retreated from the development project by embracing political objectives: good governance rather than economic development became the focal point. This new agenda reflected the growing influence of neoclassical economic thinking within international organizations like the World Bank; it involved a newfound faith in 'globalization' (understood as market opening, privatization, and deregulation) as the panacea for overcoming obstacles to development (Baghwati 2004).[4]

At the micro level, the good governance agenda complemented the embrace of a 'human-centred' approach[5] to development that focused on individual empowerment and culminated in the so-called Millennium Development Goals (MDGs). Rather than an effort to put countries on to the first rung of the development ladder or to keep them moving up the ladder, the MDGs proposed to reduce extreme poverty by combatting the three Ds – Disease, Debt and Disaster (like drought). Primary education, health and individual empowerment have occupied the centre stage in development discourse, while individualized poverty reduction schemes such as microfinance or conditional cash transfers, have been promoted as 'development' policies (for important critiques, see Amsden 2010, 2012; Andreoni and Chang 2017: 176). Although admirable and necessary, the MDGs (and their successor, the Sustainable Development Goals) do not put real tangible development on the agenda.[6] What's missing is the fourth D – Development – notably, an industrial development strategy to comprehensively lift poor countries out of poverty through structural transformation of their economies and mass employment creation. By excluding collective action for structural transformation, this individualized, bottom-up approach has marginalized production (Amsden 2012). The result has been a 'retreat from development'. The G7 states, which run the World Bank, have increasingly viewed that institution as an agency dispensing relief – a form of 'welfare colonialism'[7] – rather than as an agency to help developing countries improve mass living standards.[8]

Why production and the state matter

There is robust evidence that production is fundamental to long-term national prosperity. Manufacturing is not just an engine of job creation and productivity. It also drives technological upgrading and innovation (more on this below). So, if development is the goal, the question is what can be done to advance the productive capacity of the nation? We know from the past that the creation and expansion of productive capabilities generally demands some kind of central coordinating intelligence, and that with few exceptions, states have historically undertaken this role (see Weiss and Hobson 1995). What scope then remains for state activism in an integrated world? While global economic integration may impose new constraints, it can also enable state actors with developmental ambitions to seek ways around those constraints. In particular, the economic and social costs associated with integration can generate new demands that call for state intervention. How national governments respond to these demands, however, can vary considerably, depending on the domestic institutional setting and international environment (Weiss 2003).

In the following discussion we connect several strands of research that show why production remains essential to development, why this valorizes a role for the state, and why even in an epoch of economic openness states still have room to move. First, we consider why production is so important for development, remaining essential to national prosperity even in the twenty-first century. We then briefly examine the phenomenon of manufacturing decline and probe the extent to which globalization has been the driver. This brings us to consider the role of the state in fostering productive capacity and the conditions that enable or constrain policy responses to the pressures of globalization.

Why the decline of manufacturing is problematic for development?

It is now well established that almost every country that has succeeded in moving up the socio-economic ladder has done so by developing its productive capacities. Recognizing the strategic nature of manufacturing, even early industrializers like Britain and the United States set about deploying the tools to promote their infant industry (Chang 2002; Reinert 2008). A substantial literature explains the strategic value of manufacturing in the pursuit of national prosperity. Indeed, there is a robust body of research on the links between growth, development and manufacturing (see e.g. Mathews 2016). It is the sector most conducive to the uptake of productivity-enhancing equipment and processes, hence, the main source of productivity growth in the economy (Amsden 2012; Andreoni and Chang 2016). It is also responsible for most of the research and development that generates technological innovation. Moreover, the manufacturing industry is the sector that drives productivity growth in other sectors, which are often major end-users of manufactured inputs: think the use of chemical fertilizers in agriculture, and the use of electronic hardware like computers and telephones, routers and fibre-optic cables in almost all service industries.

In less developed settings, industrial transformation is especially important because, in comparison with agriculture, it creates physical, non-perishable goods that are more tradeable and less exposed to the dramatic price fluctuations of commodities. It thus generates more stable, higher-skilled and better-waged employment for large numbers of people. Seen in this light, the recent emphasis of the international development community on promoting 'human capabilities' (education, health) to the exclusion of 'productive capabilities' is deeply problematic. Both human and productive capabilities are central to development over the long term. However, as Rodrik observes, the cultivation of human capabilities is a slow and expensive process, and the growth payoffs tend to be limited until a sufficiently broad range of capabilities has been accumulated. Structural transformation on the other hand – at least in the early stages – does not rely on highly developed human capital. Poor economies can experience rapid industrialization – bringing job creation and growth – even in the presence of relatively weak skills (Rodrik 2013: 5). Of course, industrial upgrading eventually requires the upgrading of human capabilities. Over the longer term, the East Asian countries succeeded because they fostered *both* human and productive capabilities. The experience of Sub-Saharan Africa reveals the more likely scenario when the exclusive focus is on human capabilities at the expense of productive ones:

> Sub-Saharan Africa's failure to slay the dragon of poverty is due to a logical flaw in its policies: the remedies to reduce poverty don't address the causes. Poverty is caused by unemployment … but grass-roots poverty alleviation measures are exclusively designed to make job-seekers more capable although no jobs are available…. To create employment requires capital investments to expand entrepreneurial opportunities and increase productive jobs.
>
> *(Amsden 2012: 114)*

As a more general point, manufacturing production has a multiplier effect that makes it complementary, and increasingly integrated, with services.[9] Transport, finance, insurance, logistics, info tech, for example, are all producer related. Complementarity is evident in the well-established finding that manufacturing has a larger multiplier effect than any other sector, both in jobs and in GNP.[10] In advanced manufacturing, each job has been estimated to create up to 16 jobs in other sectors – electronic computing having the largest effect (Bonvillian and Weiss 2015: ch. 4). One reason why manufacturing typically generates many more jobs outside the sector is because firms that make goods often depend on extensive local supply chains that draw on primary, secondary and tertiary inputs. The flipside is the subtraction effect: when a manufacturing firm closes down, the impact reverberates along the supply chain, causing job losses throughout the wider economy. The growing seamlessness of advanced manufacturing and services is also evident in the extent to which producer companies increasingly straddle research, design and service provision.

The dramatic flow-on effects for jobs and income have been widely observed, but there are also serious ramifications for innovation that have been less well appreciated. A growing body of research finds that in many industries, production and innovation are inextricably linked, and that as production declines, so innovative capacity is weakened. This is important because technological upgrading and innovation are widely recognized as a foundation of economic prosperity. As the most extreme case of declining onshore production, the recent experience of the United States is instructive: decades of offshoring in both advanced and traditional manufacturing sectors have degraded the domestic supply chains to such a point that large gaps are now evident in the industrial ecosystem critical to generating breakthrough innovations (Berger with the MIT Task Force 2013). A growing body of research reports that as the production of sophisticated products migrates abroad, this diminishes the capacity to design and create next-generation products and reduces opportunities for identifying and developing new industry sectors (see Fuchs and Kirchain 2010; Pisano and Shih 2011).

For all the reasons outlined, manufacturing plays a substantial role in promoting national prosperity, regardless of the level of industrial advancement. In the section that follows, we examine the recent decline in manufacturing and probe the role of globalization in that process.

The decline of manufacturing

Over the past two decades, manufacturing activity as a share of GDP and employment has declined throughout the industrialized world, while most developing countries have failed to establish or upgrade local productive capabilities.[11] This trend may explain why manufacturing activity has come to be widely downplayed, if not overlooked altogether, in the development debate. Generally referred to as 'de-industrialization', the decline of manufacturing has been widely perceived as an inevitable result of global competition that pressures companies to pursue more cost-effective strategies or to increase market share.

As Rodrik (2016) observes, since the 1970s, all advanced countries have experienced industrial decline (measured in terms of manufacturing's share in employment). Importantly, however, so-called de-industrialization only set in once significant structural transformation had been achieved.[12] The developing countries of today are experiencing a very different pattern. In the emerging economies, for example, de-industrialization is setting in much earlier. In China, manufacturing employment peaked at around 15 per cent in the early 1990s. In Brazil, China and India, de-industrialization set in at the $5,000, $3,000 and $2,000 per capita mark respectively. The trend appears to be that emerging economies are now turning to services (chiefly hospitality, tourism, transport, real-estate) much sooner than their more advanced counterparts.

If we consider these trends in the aggregate, it might appear that globalization is responsible for most of the decline of manufacturing in advanced countries. In a more nuanced account however, we would observe that countries are located along a continuum that ranges from moderate to extreme de-industrialization.[13] This differential positioning suggests that contextual factors make a difference, among which we would include domestic institutions, political preferences and policy priorities as well as the technological specialization of a country's firms. Thus, for example, all advanced countries have experienced the migration abroad of labour-intensive manufacturing, and this can clearly be attributed to aspects of globalization such as trade and investment openness, technological advances (digitization and the internet), and declining transport costs. These globalizing opportunities have allowed firms in most advanced countries to relocate or outsource labour-intensive production to lower-cost jurisdictions. Where capital- or knowledge-intensive industry is involved however, different degrees of industrial decline suggest more complex factors at work that might include automation[14] and financialization,[15] as well as intellectual property rights (Weiss and Thurbon 2018).

Beyond the advanced economies, very few LDCs have managed to follow in the footsteps of East Asia's late industrializers and expand their manufacturing base (China being the outstanding example, discussed below). Globalization is implicated in this story in two main ways. One is that today's trade and investment rules have eliminated or outlawed most of the basic industrial policy tools that are needed to kickstart industrialization. Another is the creation of global value chains as a new way of organizing production. As we will see, both developments challenge the state's traditional role in the development process. It is to the state's changing role in development to which we now turn.

What room for the state?

If production is vital to development, what does it take to establish a viable manufacturing industry, and speed the transition to new growth sectors? Historically, this process has required some kind of central coordinating intelligence and, with some important exceptions,[16] national political institutions have assumed this role (Rodrik 2013). In almost every industrialized country, the state has sponsored the early development of the market economy and industrial enterprise. Once an industry is established, however, industrial policy has a lesser role to play in that sector. But this simply changes rather than obviates a role for the state, insofar as the development process is a continuing story of technological advancement. Even at or near the technological frontier, research finds that the state still retains a significant role in fostering emerging growth sectors (Breznitz 2007; Koh and Wong 2005). So, if techno-industrial transformation demands something more than market rules, if it involves some kind of coordinating intelligence, the relevant question is what scope remains for national states today to act in that capacity? Does globalization so restrict the state's policy space that pursuit of a techno-industrial strategy is no longer viable?

The policy constraining features of globalization – as distinct from Europeanization[17] – chiefly in the form of trade openness and financial flows have been well rehearsed. At the macro level, the liberalization of capital controls imposes new constraints on monetary policy, limiting the scope for interest and exchange rate interventions that might support domestic industrial expansion. At the micro level, trade rules now largely prohibit a variety of measures – tariff protection, local subsidies, the reverse engineering of intellectual property (IP)-protected goods – that the now advanced countries once deployed in their own climb up the development ladder (Chang 2002; Wade 2003; Dicaprio and Gallagher 2006). To these widely acknowledged constraints we should add the growing phenomenon of profit shifting, aided and abetted by intellectual property-intensive production, accounting schemes of multinational corporations and the proliferation of tax havens. Indeed, so massive are the profits being shifted to low- or no-tax jurisdictions (in 2017 estimated at $2.5 trillion in the US alone) that national tax revenues are diminishing across the globe, most notably in the advanced world (Seabrooke and Wigan 2017; Weiss and Thurbon 2018).

Beyond the constraints however, globalization also has an enabling dimension in so far as it generates new pressures and pathways for state activism. By removing barriers to trade, for example, global flows engender a political logic of competition that produces pressures on companies, creating incentives for governments to take initiatives that will in turn mitigate the effects of openness (Weiss 2003: 15). For example, as the Uruguay Round came to a conclusion and the WTO was established, the most advanced countries ensured that the new trade regime would endorse the promotion of science and technology (S&T). In this way, the new constraints of global competition helped to deepen state involvement in industrial governance by requiring states to 'elaborate a more complex range of supportive endeavors that mesh with an increasingly technology-intensive economy' (Weiss 2005: 725). For the already advanced countries, S&T policy has thereby become the new 'infant-industry policy' focused on spawning the high-tech industries of the future.

For the developing world, however, launching oneself onto the first rung of the techno-industrial ladder is now rendered much more challenging as the WTO's trade and investment rules have shrunk policy space. These rules now prohibit most of the instruments that enabled industrialized economies to achieve their goals. Aside from the externally imposed constraints, a number of LDC governments have also embraced the prescriptions of multilateral development institutions (the so-called Washington Consensus) and elected not to intervene to promote local industrial transformation (on Uganda, see Kiiza 2008). Here again there are important national variations. Rwanda, for example, appears to be bucking that trend in order to pursue a development strategy that has echoes of the East Asian strategy (Mann and Berry 2016). Although premature to draw big conclusions from a small sample, the existence of such cases would repay further research. At the very least they suggest that global constraints notwithstanding, political choice and domestic context remain significant. A similar story can be told for the impact of global value chains, as we see next.

> **Box 4.1 WTO agreements that can stymy or limit development policies**
>
> **TRIPs** (Trade-related Aspects of Intellectual Property Rights)
> **TRIMS** (Trade-related Investment Measures)
> **GPA** (Government Procurement Agreement)
> **GATT** (General Agreement on Tariffs and Trade)
>
> For a discussion, see Chang (2002)

GVCs as problem or solution?

The advent of global value chains (GVCs) has opened a fresh debate over the developmental benefits of globalization. So-called GVCs decompose production into smaller tasks that are then outsourced to multiple locations. This form of globalized production has been hailed by many economists as a boon for small and medium-sized enterprises (SMEs) in developing countries. Ostensibly it provides them with the opportunities to become integrated in the production networks of the world's leading firms, and to develop their local industrial base. From this perspective globalized production chains were deemed to open up a new development pathway. Yet as the WTO's 2017 report on GVCs makes clear, the potential benefits of GVCs for developing countries do not flow evenly or automatically. In many instances, the globalization of production has led to stasis, curtailing the constant upgrading that is needed to close the technology gap with the advanced economies. This is largely because GVCs embody power asymmetries that pervert development outcomes by constraining movement up the technology chain (Ravenhill 2014). As lead firms seek to monopolize technologies and higher value-added activities, they typically contract out only the least profitable activities to firms in LDCs. Moreover, foreign multinationals that lead the supply chains not only monopolize control of the technology; they also aggressively squeeze the profits of their suppliers. This leaves firms in LDCs with few resources to pursue upgrading and localize technology. Not surprisingly, then, industrialization in an era of decomposed production often fails to deliver economy-wide benefits (Baldwin 2011; see also Rodrik 2018). The prime case has been Taiwan which, for the past half century, has specialized in contract manufacturing and struggled to break out of its dependence on foreign companies which control the supply chains and apportion the value (Amsden and Chu 2003; Chu 2009).

Where GVCs have yielded more positive development outcomes, the research finds that governments have been actively involved in leveraging the strengths of local enterprise. As new research comes to light and greater attention is paid to states and public authority, the heavily firm-centric view of GVCs is thus being challenged. Building on these themes, recent research has identified up to four governance roles that states play within global production networks – as facilitator, regulator, buyer and producer (Alford and Phillips 2018; Horner 2017). In China, as one of many examples, local governments work closely with firms to identify and leverage their particular strengths with the aim of finding and accessing suitable niches in global production networks (Breznitz and Murphree 2011). As well as acting as gate-keepers to the local economy, identifying relevant partners, they also enter into negotiations with lead international companies and provide resources in exchange for specified development outcomes. However, effective bargaining depends on at least two conditions – market size and the capacity to monitor the bargains that have been agreed on (Ravenhill 2014). Understandably, China, with its sizable market and centralized control has been especially well positioned to capture the benefits of GVCs. As Rodrik (2013: 47) has argued: 'it is impossible to account for China's success in taking advantage of global supply chains without understanding the myriad state policies Chinese policy makers used to crowd in investments that would not otherwise have been made'. Market size is also a major factor in this story: as well as directing subsidies to its own firms, the leverage of market size enabled Chinese policymakers to insist on local content requirements (despite WTO rules) and, in some cases, the transfer of intellectual property through technology licensing (Lewis 2014).

China clearly has some exceptional advantages. Much work remains to be done on the bargaining efforts and effectiveness of other LDC governments as they seek points of entry to GVCs for their own firms. We also need more research on the willingness of multinational firms to negotiate investment agreements and the extent to which this propensity may vary by institutional capacity of the host country (Bakir 2015; Murtha and Lenway 1994). If there is a more general lesson that can be drawn from the Chinese case it is this: in the context of fragmented production, targeted industrial policy based on 'governed interdependence' (Weiss 1995) – a collaborative government-industry partnership – remains as central as ever to the development project (see, for example, Rodrik 2013).

Yet while globalization does not uniformly eliminate opportunities for developmental initiatives, there is no guarantee that state actors will seek to exploit that policy space, or that their efforts will be effective. Political choice matters. Much will depend on the ambitions of national policymakers and the crucible of domestic and international conditions that favour or frustrate their preferences. Does the political elite share a commitment to well-articulated national goals? Do they see the need for an industrial strategy as a nation-building project? Such a mindset was characteristic of East Asia's so-called 'developmental states' over the post-Second World War period (Thurbon 2016a). In Japan, South Korea and Taiwan, what we might call strategic activism was understood as the means to achieving the national goal of techno-industrial catch-up. Ambitions not related to development per se may also motivate states to take strategic initiatives that have long-term economic outcomes. In the United States, as a response to and legacy of the Cold War, national security ambitions have profoundly shaped the techno-industrial landscape. Military primacy was the driving ambition, and technological leadership the means. As the public–private partnership that underpinned the national security enterprise succeeded in pouring out numerous radical innovations, the commercial payoffs abounded (Weiss 2014).

Yet as we have indicated, national mindset and the political choices it informs mean little in the absence of a domestic and international setting that is conducive to strategic activism. It is the interplay of these factors that has done most to shape different national responses to pressures emanating from the global environment (Weiss 2003). To see how these conditions might play out in different settings, we briefly consider five cases.

Political choice matters: five cases

In Korea, the story of the past decade has been the resurgence of developmental ambition and the revival of strategic activism, largely in response to intensifying competitive pressures (Thurbon 2016a). Since the early 2000s, a combination of domestic and international pressures have fuelled perceptions of vulnerability among policymakers and the wider public. These include China's rapid rise, energy insecurity, rolling financial crises and stagnating private sector investment, not to mention growing income inequality. By fuelling deep anxieties about Korea's future, these concerns have served to galvanize the developmental ambitions of the policymaking elite, fostering public calls for state involvement in the economy. In response, successive Korean governments have significantly scaled up initiatives aimed at upgrading existing industries and kick-starting industries of the future. In pursuit of their goals, policymakers from both sides of politics have drawn heavily on pre-existing institutional strengths such as a strong, mission-oriented bureaucracy and a healthy suite of national development banks. Despite growing enmeshment in regional and bilateral trade deals, Korean policymakers have been careful to preserve (and make creative use of) their policy room to move (on government's ICT and smart-grid strategies see Campbell 2012; Kim 2012, 2019; and on the frontier technology of robotics, see Thurbon and Weiss 2019).

In China, the catch-up ambitions of the political elite have informed a similarly strategic approach to industrial governance, especially since joining the WTO in 2001. By signing up to the global rules of the game, the Chinese government narrowed its policy options *in principle*. In practice however, as noted above, the nation's size has afforded it greater leverage – and thus greater policy space – than many other developing nations. Using the lure of their local market, Chinese policymakers at national, local and provincial levels have been able to enlist foreign firms as 'voluntary' partners in development initiatives across a range of industries.[18] It must be said however that China's size has at times hindered central policymakers in their developmental objectives by demanding high levels of coordination between central and local government agencies that have often exceeded capabilities, even of the state's most ambitious planners (Chu 2017). Yet to this point, policy failures do not appear to have dampened those ambitions. Indeed, the Chinese state faces a host of domestic and international challenges that are likely to keep it focused on development as a political survival strategy as well as a way of reclaiming its status as a great power.

While the planets have aligned for South Korea and China, they have not been so propitious for Taiwan whose developmental consensus has been fractured by a divided political elite. Although Taiwan faces many similar challenges to those of Korea, not least the rise of a powerful China, its ability to respond strategically has been undermined by the emergence of a political opposition whose priorities are partisan rather than developmental. So while the organizations historically associated with strategic activism in Taiwan still exist (the Council for Economic Planning and Development and the Industrial Development Bureau in particular), their effectiveness has been compromised by contradictory, politically motivated policies aimed at eliminating the legacies of the KMT (Chu 2014; Thurbon 2019).[19]

Although from a completely different environment, the Australian experience shows how domestic politics can similarly override the policy space afforded national governments. In this case, the policy proposal in question was a 'super-profits' tax on the country's mining industry that drew the hostility of powerful multinational companies. Their threat to exit might seem to highlight the structural power of business because the government soon relinquished its ambition. In reality, researchers argue that it was not the threat of exit that motivated the policymakers' change of heart for they did not believe that a new tax would undermine investment. Rather, the federal government believed that as a result of a ferociously effective industry campaign, voters were convinced that the tax would harm the economy, and that as a result the governing party would lose electoral support. Thus, domestic politics triumphed over national economic interest (Bell and Hindmoor 2014). In Australia, this failure to take advantage of policy space is not an isolated instance. The broader picture is marked by a striking hands-off approach most evident in the mindset that substitutes trade policy (market openness) for strategic industry policy (see Thurbon 2016b).

Our final case reveals the paradoxes of globalization that create new avenues for state involvement. The United States has been not only the lead promoter of globalized production, but also the country most affected by de-industrialization. As explained below, in its efforts to counter some of these effects, the US has been bolstered as well as hindered by conflicting ideational forces.

US corporations have led the decomposition and migration of manufacturing offshore and spearheaded a new business model centred on the creation of global production chains (Sturgeon 2002). The massive offshoring of manufacturing and the decline of America's industrial base have for some time been implicated in job loss, wage stagnation and rising inequality. But it is the longer-term impact of that migration on techno-supremacy and national security that has done most to catalyse remedial initiatives at the federal level. In an environment marked by a powerful anti-state sentiment, the formation of a national security mindset has played an important anchoring role around which a semblance of elite cohesion has evolved. In particular, the strength of America's pro-security mindset has served to offset an 'anti-state' (small government) tradition which decries strategic industrial policy initiatives; importantly, the national security priority enables significant state activism in the techno-industrial arena, when it promotes innovations with dual-use applications (Weiss 2014).

Rather than being guided by an economic bureaucracy as in the case of South Korea, the US innovation engine has been catalysed by a cluster of federal agencies with security-related missions which act in partnership with the private sector (industry and university contractors).[20] As mentioned earlier, the innovations emerging from this cluster have strong commercial payoffs that are sometimes misleadingly attributed to an industrial policy. Most recently, the national security imperative has generated support for federal initiatives aimed at re-building America's degraded industrial ecosystem. In 2012, for example, the Obama administration introduced a $1.5 billion initiative to create advanced manufacturing institutes and partnerships across the country, most of them led by the Department of Defense. However, it remains to be seen whether domestic political opportunism under a leadership determined to eradicate Obama's legacy will scale back or jettison these initiatives.

Conclusion

Although widely eclipsed from the development story, two things are clear from recent research. First, industrial production – whether more labour-intensive in the developing world or more technology-intensive in advanced settings – remains foundational to national prosperity. Second, state actors often occupy a key position in the process of techno-industrial transformation. While globalization has removed some of the traditional policy tools available to state actors, it has by no means eliminated their policy space. Moreover, the perceptions of vulnerability stemming from economic openness have created new pressures for dedicated state action. A decade on from the world's most damaging financial crisis, marked by deepening economic inequality, slow–low growth and economic uncertainty, energy insecurity and climatic stress, these demands show no sign of abating. The disruptive consequences for domestic politics are all too evident in such phenomena as the populist shift of politics across the globe and the election of candidates promising to restore national autonomy and reinvent their economies. While the mandate for activist states exists, the determining factor is whether governing bodies, new or existing, are both enabled by their internal arrangements and motivated to move in developmental directions. Our key conclusion must be that development is as much a test of political choice, commitment and capacity as it is of the room to move afforded by globalization.

Notes

1 As frequent co-authors, we rotate first authorship.
2 By contrast, as some have wisely observed, property rights can just as easily hinder as help development. Historical examples include the Italian and Latin American latifundia landowning systems that empowered a large landowning class at the cost of agrarian reforms necessary for industrial development. Contemporary examples show how intellectual property rights can stymy innovation and industrial development in advanced settings (for references, see Weiss and Thurbon 2018). For a recent study of how high rates of productive investment in a developing context can occur under conditions of legal uncertainty and uneven protection of property rights, see Hamilton-Hart and Palmer (2017).
3 These policy prescriptions form part of the so-called 'Washington Consensus'. For the original articulation see Williamson (1993).
4 The literature on this topic is extensive. For a succinct critique see Stiglitz (2002).
5 The pioneer of this approach was Amartya Sen (1999).
6 Indeed while individual-focused interventions like microfinance can initially improve the lot of a small number of enterprising men and women, a substantial literature has shown that the long-term outcomes can be detrimental, failing to produce any meaningful economic transformation, while often locking individuals into repeated cycles of debt (Weber 2014).
7 To use the words of Reinert *et al.* (2016: xxvi).
8 On the 'unintended alliance' between neoclassical economics and the 'human-centred' approach since the 1990s, see Andreoni and Chang (2017).
9 For example, many advanced manufacturing firms are spinning out business services that form an integral part of their product. Even erstwhile software 'service' companies like Google are now venturing into the design and production of hardware – consumer devices – in order to gain hold of big data that will enable them to market new services (Bergen *et al.* 2017).
10 Estimates vary between 2.5 and 2.9 jobs in other sectors and higher still in high-tech production where the estimates range from 5.2 to 16 jobs for every one production job created (Bonvillian and Weiss 2015: 44).
11 For time series data on the contribution of manufacturing value added to GDP across the globe see the World Bank Data Set: https://data.worldbank.org/indicator/NV.IND.MANF.ZS.
12 That is to say that once manufacturing's share of employment had reached between 25 and 35 per cent, and per capita income around $9000–$11,000 (at 1990 prices, US, Britain, Germany and Sweden).
13 For example, according to World Bank data for 2016, manufacturing as a percentage of GDP ranged from as low as 7 per cent (Australia) to as high as 23 per cent (Germany) and 29 per cent (South Korea). See note 11 for source.
14 According to the International Federation of Robotics, the major driver of automation is the automotive industry, which buys some 40 per cent of all industrial robots worldwide (see Muro 2017). For a debunking of the link between automation and jobless growth, see Eichengreen (2017).
15 See the Berger 2014 and the Forum responses to same.
16 In his pioneering study of late industrializers, economic historian Alexander Gerschenkron (1962) argued that in late nineteenth-century Germany, it was the banks and large industrial firms that provided the coordination necessary to industrial transformation.
17 Rather than a 'mesocosm' of globalization, the European Community emerged initially as a collective security measure and has evolved as a response to pressures emanating from other regions (especially the United States and East Asia). Despite the impact of European integration, national pathways of adaptation to the larger forces of globalization have been well documented by analysts of Europeanization (see Kassim and Menon 2002; Schmidt 2002; Weiss 2005).
18 On development initiatives in renewable energies see Mathews 2017; in ITC see Breznitz and Murphree (2011).
19 The Kuomintang (Taiwan's Nationalist Party) has been the bastion of developmental leadership in that country.
20 Weiss (2014) refers to this cluster as the National Security State. See Chapter 2 for the range of defence and non-defence agencies that drive techno-innovation informed by a national security rationale.

Bibliography

Abdelal, R. 2006. Writing the rules of global finance": France, Europe and capital liberalization. *Review of International Political Economy*, 13(1): 1–27.

Acemoglu, D. and Robinson, J. A. 2012. *Why Nations Fail: The Origins of Power, Prosperity and Poverty*. New York: Crown.

Alford, M. and Phillips, N. 2018. The political economy of state governance in global production networks: change, crisis and contestation in the South African fruit sector. *Review of International Political Economy*, 25(1): 98–121.

Amsden, A. 1989. *Asia's Next Giant: South Korea and Late Industrialization*. New York: Oxford University Press.

Amsden, A. H. 2001. *The Rise of 'the Rest': Challenges to the West from Late Industrializing Countries*. Oxford: Oxford University Press.

Amsden, A. H. 2010. Say's Law, poverty persistence, and employment neglect. *Journal of Human Development and Capabilities* 11(1): 57–66.

Amsden, A. H. 2012. Grass roots war on poverty. *World Social and Economic Review* 1: 114–131.

Amsden, A. and Chu W. 2003. *Beyond Late Development: Taiwan's Upgrading Policies*. Cambridge, MA: MIT Press.

Andreoni, A. and Chang, H. J. 2016. Industrial policy and the future of manufacturing. *Economia e Politica Industriale* 43(4): 491–502.

Andreoni, A and Chang, H. J. 2017. Bringing production and employment back into development: Alice Amsden's legacy for a new developmentalist agenda. *Cambridge Journal of Regions, Economy and Society* 10(1): 173–187.

Baghwati, J. 2004. *In Defense of Globalization*. New York: Oxford University Press.

Bakir, C. 2015. Bargaining with multinationals: why state capacity matters. *New Political Economy* 20(1): 63–84.

Baldwin, R. 2011. Trade and industrialisaton after globalisation's 2nd unbundling: how building and joining a supply chain are different and why it matters. *NBER Working Paper* 17716.

Bell, S. and Hindmoor, A. 2014. The structural power of business and the power of ideas: the strange case of the Australian mining tax. *New Political Economy* 19(3): 470–486.

Bergen, M., Browning, J., Chen, L. Y. and Ellis, S. 2017. Google buys HTC talent for $1.1 billion to spur devices push. *Bloomberg*. Available at: www.bloomberg.com/news/articles/2017-09-21/google-buys-htc-engineers-for-1-1-billion-to-aid-hardware-push.

Berger, S with the MIT Task Force on Production in the Innovation Economy. 2013. *Making in America: From Innovation to Market*. Cambridge, MA: MIT Press.

Berger, S. 2014. How finance gutted manufacturing. *Boston Review*. Available at: http://bostonreview.net/forum/suzanne-berger-how-finance-gutted-manufacturing.

Bonvillian, W. B. and Weiss, C. 2015. *Technological Innovation in Legacy Sectors*. Oxford: Oxford University Press.

Breznitz, D. 2007. *Innovation and the State: Political Choice and Strategies for Growth in Israel, Taiwan, and Ireland*. New Haven, CT: Yale University Press.

Breznitz, D. and Murphree, M. 2011. *Run of The Red Queen: Government, Innovation, Globalization, and Economic Growth in China*. New Haven, CT: Yale University Press.

Campbell, J. R. 2012. Building an IT economy: South Korean science and technology policy. *Issues in Technology Innovation* 19: 1–9.

Chang, H. J. 2002. *Kicking Away the Ladder: Development Strategy in Historical Perspective*. London: Anthem Press.

Chu, W. 2009. Can Taiwan's second movers upgrade via branding? *Research Policy* 38(6): 1054–1065.

Chu, W. 2014. Challenges for the Maturing Taiwan Economy. Chapter 7 in Diamond, L. and Shin, G. (eds) *New Challenges for Maturing Democracies in Korea and Taiwan*, 216–252. Stanford, CA: Stanford University Press.

Chu, W. 2017. Industry policy with Chinese characteristics: a multi-layered model. *China Economic Journal* 10(3): 305–318.

Dicaprio, A. and Gallagher, K. P. 2006. The WTO and the shrinking of development space: how big is the bite? *Journal of World Investment and Trade* 7(5): 781–803.

Eichengreen, B. 2017. Two myths about automation. Project Syndicate. Available at: www.project-syndicate.org/commentary/two-myths-about-automation-by-barryeichengreen-2017-12.

Fuchs, E. R. H. and Kirchain, R. 2010. Design for location: the impact of manufacturing offshore on technology competitiveness in the optoelectronics industry. *Management Science* 56(12): 2323–2349.

Gerschenkron, A. 1962. *Economic Backwardness in Historical Perspective*. Cambridge: Belknap.

Hamilton-Hart, N. and Palmer, B. 2017. Co-investment and clientelism as informal institutions: beyond 'good enough' property rights protection. *Studies in Comparative International Development* 52(4): 416–435.

Hatch, W. and Yamamura, K. 1996. *Asia in Japan's Embrace: Building a Regional Production Alliance*. Cambridge: Cambridge University Press.

Held, D. and McGrew, A. 1999. *The Global Transformations Reader*. Cambridge: Polity Press.

Hirst, P. and Thompson, G. 1996. *Globalisation in Question*. Cambridge: Polity Press.

Horner, R. 2017. Beyond facilitator? State roles in global value chains and global production networks. *Geography Compass*. Available at: https://doi.org/10.1111/gec3.12307.

Johnson, C. 1982. *MITI and the Japanese Miracle*. Stanford, CA: Stanford University Press.

Kassim, H. and Menon, A. 2002. *The European Union and National Industrial Policy*. London: Taylor & Francis.

Kiiza, J. 2008. Mercantilism and the Struggle for Late Industrialization in an Age of Globalization. Chapter 9 in Mensah, J. (ed.) *Neoliberalism and Globalization in Africa: Contestations on the Embattled Continent*, 177–201. London: Palgrave.

Kim, S. Y. 2012. The politics of technological upgrading in South Korea: how government and business challenged the might of Qualcomm. *New Political Economy* 17(3): 293–312.

Kim, S. Y. 2019. Hybridized industrial ecosystems and the makings of a new developmental infrastructure in East Asia's green energy sector. *Review of International Political Economy* 26(1): 158–182.

Koh, W. T. H. and Wong, P. 2005. Competing at the frontier: The changing role of technology policy in Singapore's economic strategy. *Technological Forecasting & Social Change* 72(3): 255–285.

Lazonick, W. and O'Sullivan, M. 2000. Maximizing shareholder value: a new ideology for corporate governance. *Economy and Society* 29(1): 13–35.

Lewis, J. 2014. *Green Innovation in China: China's Wind Power Industry and the Global Transition to a Low-Carbon Economy*. New York: Columbia University Press.

Mann, L. and Berry, M. 2016. Understanding the political motivations that shape Rwanda's emergent developmental state. *New Political Economy* 21(1): 119–144.

Mathews, J. A. 2016. Latecomer industrialization. Chapter 32 in Reinert, E. S., Ghosh, J. and Kattel, R. (eds) *Handbook of Alternative Theories of Economic Development*, 613–636. Cheltenham, UK: Edward Elgar.

Mathews, J. A. 2017. *Global Green Shift: When Ceres Meets Gaia*. London: Anthem Press.

Murtha, T. P. and Lenway, S. 1994. Country capabilities and the strategic state: how national political institutions affect multinational corporations' strategies. *Strategic Management Journal* 15(2): 113–129.

Muro, M. 2017. Where the robots are. *Brookings Institute*. Available at: www.brookings.edu/blog/the-avenue/2017/08/14/where-the-robots-are/.

North, D. 1990. *Institutions, Institutional Change, and Economic Performance* Cambridge, UK: Cambridge University Press.

Pisano, G. P. and Shih, W. 2011. *Producing Prosperity: Why America Needs a Manufacturing Renaissance*. Portland, OR: Harvard Business Review Press.

Ravenhill, J. 2014. Global value chains and development. *Review of International Political Economy* 21(1): 264–274.

Reinert, E. S. 2008. *How Rich Countries Got Rich and Why Poor Countries Stay Poor*. New York: Public Affairs.

Reinert, E. S., Ghosh, J. and Kattel, R. (eds). 2016. *Handbook of Alternative Theories of Economic Development*. London: Edward Elgar.

Rodrik, D. 2013. The past, present, and future of economic growth. *Global Citizen Foundation Working Paper* 1.

Rodrik, D. 2016. Premature deindustrialization. *Journal of Economic Growth* 21(1): 1–33.

Rodrik, D. 2018. New technologies, global value chains, and developing economies. *NBER Working Paper No. 25164*.

Schmidt, V. 2002. *The Futures of European Capitalism*. Oxford: Oxford University Press.

Seabrooke, L. and Wigan, D., 2017. The governance of global wealth chains. *Review of International Political Economy* 24(1): 1–29.

Sen, A. 1999. *Development as Freedom*. New York: Alfred Knopf.

Stedman Jones, G. 2014. *Masters of the Universe: Hayek, Friedman, and the Birth of Neoliberal Politics*. Princeton, NJ: Princeton University Press.

Stiglitz, J. 2002. *Globalization and Its Discontents*. New York: Norton.

Sturgeon, T. J. 2002. Modular production networks: a new American model of industrial organization. *Industrial and Corporate Change* 11(3): 451–496.

Thurbon, E. 2016a. *Developmental Mindset: The Revival of Financial Activism in South Korea*. Ithaca and London: Cornell University Press.

Thurbon, E. 2016b. Trade agreements and the myth of policy constraint in Australia. *Australian Journal of Political Science* 51(4): 636–651.

Thurbon, E. 2019. The future of financial activism in Taiwan: the utility of a mindset-centred analysis of developmental states and their evolution. *New Political Economy*. https://doi.org/10.1080/13563467.2018.1562436.

Thurbon, E. and Weiss, L. 2019. Economic statecraft at the frontier: Korea's drive for intelligent robotics. https://doi.org/10.1080/09692290.2019.1655084.

Wade, R. 1990. *Governing the Market*. Princeton, NJ: Princeton University Press.

Wade, R. 2003. What strategies are viable for developing countries today? The World Trade Organization and the shrinking of 'development' space. *Review of International Political Economy* 10(4), 621–644.

Wade, R. and Veneroso, F. 1998. The Asian crisis: the high debt model versus the Wall Street-Treasury-IMF complex. *New Left Review* 1(228): 3–24.

Weber, H. 2014. Global politics of microfinancing poverty in Asia: the case of Bangladesh unpacked. *Asian Studies Review* 38(4): 544–563.

Weiss, L. 1995. Governed interdependence: rethinking the government-business relationship in East Asia. *Pacific Review* 8(4): 589–616.

Weiss, L. 1998. *The Myth of the Powerless State*. Ithaca, NY: Cornell University Press.

Weiss, L. 2003. *States in the Global Economy*. Cambridge, UK: Cambridge University Press.

Weiss, L. 2005. Global governance, national strategies: how industrialised states make room to move under the WTO. *Review of International Political Economy* 12(5): 723–749.

Weiss, L. 2010. The state in the economy: neoliberal or neoactivist? Chapter 7 in Morgan, J., Campbell, C. C., Pedersen, O. K. and Whitely, R. (eds) *The Oxford Handbook of Comparative Institutional Analysis*, 183–209. Oxford, UK: Oxford University Press.

Weiss, L. 2014. *America Inc. Innovation and Enterprise in the National Security State*. Ithaca, NY: Cornell University Press.

Weiss, L. and Hobson, J. M. 1995. *States and Economic Development: A Comparative Historical Analysis*. Cambridge, MA: Polity Press.

Weiss, L. and Thurbon, E. 2018. Power paradox: how the extension of US infrastructural power abroad diminishes state capacity at home. *Review of International Political Economy* 25(6): 779–810.

Williamson, J. 1993. Democracy and the 'Washington consensus'. *World Development* 21(8): 1329–1336.

Wilson, G. K. 2012. The United States: the strange survival of (neo) liberalism. Chapter 4 in Grant, W. and Wilson, G. K. (eds) *The Consequences of the Global Financial Crisis: The Rhetoric of Reform and Regulation*, 51–66. Oxford, UK: Oxford University Press.

WTO. 2017. *Global Value Chain Development Report 2017: Measuring and Analyzing the Impact of GVCs on Economic Development*. Co-published by the World Bank, the WTO, the Institute of Developing Economies (IDE-JETRO), the Organisation for Economic Co-operation and Development (OECD) and the Research Center of Global Value Chains at the University of International Business and Economics.

5

The international political economy of the rise of China and emerging powers

Traditional perspectives and beyond

Li Xing and Zhang Shengjun

Introduction: the placement of discussion

In studies of world politics and International Relations (IR) and International Political Economy (IPE), the concept of "hegemony" is often applied to describe different enduring aspects of an order in the international system. The concept is a useful analytical tool in conceptualizing and understanding the dynamic and dialectic interplays in the world order, IR and IPE. The chapter intends to further develop an alternative concept of hegemony – "interdependent hegemony" – as an alternative concept that can better catch the essence of today's situation, and through which the IPE of the rise of China and emerging powers can be better conceptualized and analyzed. Through studying the increasingly proactive roles in the IPE of an emerging world order by China and other emerging powers, the chapter claims that there is no existence of standalone or static hegemony, rather, hegemony in today's world order is becoming a dynamic and dialectic phenomenon in which shared or antagonistic, exclusive visions, projects and strategies co-exist. This chapter provides an analytical framework for conceptualizing the IPE of the rise of China and other emerging powers as a process embedded with dual aspects of both hegemony and counter-hegemony, i.e., two sides of the same coin – opportunities and challenges. The chapter concludes that China/emerging powers and the existing hegemons are intertwined in a constant process of shaping and reshaping the world order in the IPE nexus of national interest and economic, political and security agenda.

Conceptual/theoretical discussion

In the studies of IR, IPE and world politics/world order, "hegemony" is an indispensable concept that is often applied to describe different enduring aspects of an order in the international system. It is a useful conceptual instrument in understanding the dynamic and dialectic interplays in the world order and international relations/systems. Likewise, the concept is seen as a good lens to conceptualize the IPE hegemony of the rise of China and emerging powers.

Hegemony, connoted as either domination (coercive power) or leadership (soft power or influence), is a highly debatable concept throughout IR literature. The concept is applied to

---

Box 5.1 Hegemony

Hegemony is an indispensable concept often applied to describe different enduring aspects of an order in the International System. It is a useful conceptual instrument to understand the dynamic and dialectic interplays in the world order.

---

explain the relationships between the dominant and dominated. The dominant actors pursue hegemony by underlying conditions to establish and maintain hegemony. In mainstream IR theories, such as realism and liberalism, states are seen as the dominant actors, and hegemony refers to the ability and capability of the dominant actors to shape the international system through coercive or non-coercive means. In practical terms, hegemony implies aptitude in the influence or control of the structures of the international system.

In terms of conditions for hegemony, different variables are emphasized by different IR theories: hard power in neo-realism, soft power and institutionalism in neoliberalism, norm and value in constructivism, mode of production and division of labor in world system theory, and interactive mixture of all them in neo-Gramscian theory along with social forces.

The rise of China/emerging powers – realism's perception

Realism in general perceives hegemony as the dominance by one leading state in interstate relations, such as in the concept often used by realism "hegemonic stability." Such concept maintains that world order requires the existence of a hegemonic or dominant power.[1] Realists claim to describe the world as it is, but in fact they are reinforcing the ruling hegemony in the current world order. Classical realism uses the notion "hegemony" in a relative sense and understands it as substantial superiority of a dominant state over other states. Hegemony in realism's conceptualization refers to a condition of disequilibrium of power in the international system, in which one state (rising power) becomes so powerful that it can exercise leadership or play a dominant role in the international system. The realism's perception of hegemonic superiority can be summed up: "the constitutive elements of hegemonic power include military capabilities; control over raw materials, markets, and capital; and competitive advantages in highly valued good."[2]

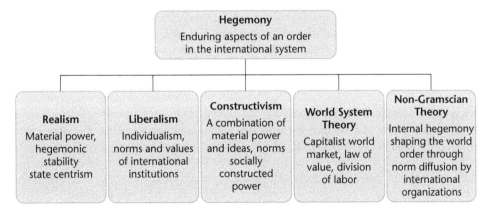

Figure 5.1 The understanding of "hegemony" from different theoretical perspectives

Source: Authors' own.

Box 5.2 Realism

Realism in general perceives hegemony as the dominance by one leading state in interstate relations, such as the theory of "hegemonic stability." Realism's awareness of the rise and fall of hegemony is expressed by the "power transition theory."

One of the most prominent advocates of the realism's hegemony conception is the "power transition theory."[3] The theory explores those dynamic factors that explain how and why transformation occurs in the global power structure. It examines power accumulation and the effect of dynamic power imbalance, which may lead to the emergence of new competitive/adversary relationships among nation states. One by-product of divergent power projection is the high potential for conflict when a rising hegemon (for example, China) and an existing hegemon (for example, the US) reach the stage of comparative equivalence of power. Gilpin also sees the "balance of power" between the existing dominant powers (the US) and the emerging powers (China) as one of the key causes leading to interstate warfare. This is because the former is exhausted by its global overstretch that "creates challenges for the dominant states and opportunities for the rising states of the system";[4] while the latter seeks to remake "the rules governing the international system, the spheres of influence, and most important of all, the international distribution of territory."[5] Reflecting a pessimistic view on power transition in the world order, Mearsheimer,[6] a proponent of realism, concludes that China's rise will not be peaceful due to the high degree of uncertainty and distrust between the rising revisionist hegemon (China) and the existing defensive hegemon (the US). In line with these perspectives of understanding, the BRICS (Brazil, Russia, India, China, South Africa), albeit it is not a sovereign state, is nevertheless seen as a counter-hegemonic power unit in terms of its purpose to break through the balance of power status.

The rise of China/emerging powers – liberalism's understanding

Hegemony, in line with liberalism's viewpoint, takes a non-statist approach and emphasizes the cooperative spirit of human being, the active role of civil society, the normative and cooperative mechanism of international institutions along with the IPE of complex interdependence, and transnational aspect of IR and the unclear line between domestic and foreign politics/policy.[7]

Liberalism tends to identify economics and other non-military factors as playing a more determining role in global governance. Liberal institutionalism, in particular, regards hegemony as being embedded in the interactions of each individual at the bottom, and in the norms and values of international institutions as rule-settlers at the top. Liberal institutionalism posits that despite the fact that international order may be a product of hegemonic power, it is not reducible to it, because international regimes have an independent causal affect in world politics. A strong representative of this argument is Robert Keohane, who argues that the international system could continue to function through its established international institutions even after the withdrawal, decline or collapse of the hegemony that had created it in the first place.[8] In line with this understanding, the international order governed by international institutions and regimes can continue its own life even though it is a product created by a hegemon.

Liberal-minded scholars are generally less pessimistic toward power transition in a world order that is structured by a rule-based system with well-developed international institutions. Neoliberalism regards the neoliberal world order led by US hegemony as benign and globally beneficial. The neoliberal order can be characterized as an open, rule- and institution-based global system emphasizing norms of non-discrimination and market openness.[9] According to this line of understanding, China's rise together with the BRICS phenomenon is an outcome that these later-comers' expanding and intensifying integration within the US-led capitalist world system. For example, the reason why China is currently a winner in the era of globalization is precisely because its economic growth and wealth accumulation has been generated from within, not from without, the US-led capitalist world order.[10] The same explanation goes also to other members of the BRICS.

Box 5.3 Neoliberalism

Neoliberalism sees the neoliberal world order led by US hegemony as benign and globally beneficial. China's economic success and its global rise is achieved from within, not from without, the US-led capitalist world order.

It is a dialectic nexus between the US-led/West-dominated existing world order (hegemony) and the emerging world order driven by the rise of China and other emerging powers (counter-hegemony). Seen from the liberal point of view, the rise of China and non-Western emerging powers symbolizes the resiliency the US-led world order that is able to accommodate the growing and catching up of other states. In other words, China's rise through the integration in the existing world order shows the *strength* of the liberal world order rather than its weakness.

The rise of China/emerging powers – the constructivism's interpretation

Constructivism in international relations sees hegemony (in terms of combination) as a dual construct of both material weight and symbolic value, i.e., a combination of material power and ideas. One of the attentions brought about by constructivism since the 1980s is on the dichotomy of structure vis-à-vis agency in IR. The point of departure of constructivism rejects the basic premise of conventional IR theories that assume an ontological predominance of the international system's structure/configuration over the system's agency/actor. This implies that constructive theory is critical to most IR theories' structural premise that the system's structural capacity, i.e., military, economy, resources, etc., fundamentally determines the actors that compose the international system (IS). Jackson and Sørensen[11] point out four common elements in all constructivist theories of IR: (1) international relations consist of ideas, values and norms and not only of material power and physical conditions; (2) common intersubjective beliefs and shared values between countries and people constitute the central ideological elements of the theory; (3) common creeds compose and express people's interests and identities; and (4) the theory must ascertain the means in which these relations are formed and expressed.

Box 5.4 Constructivism

Constructivism emphasizes the mutual generation between material capacity, and ideas, values. The rise of China and emerging powers will unavoidably bring about the spill-over effect of their economic power on norm diffusion.

It is important to draw attention to the fact that the constructive IR theory does not deny the decisive role of material capacity in IR; however, it emphasizes the mutual generation between material capacity and ideas, a mutually enforcing relationship. In other words, global "reality" is an outcome co-constructed by ideas and actions, and by agents and structure. It is the weight attached on the common ideas, norms and values among agents/actors of the international community that differentiate the constructive IR theory from other conventional IR theories. A hegemon is identified as a player that is both able to initiate, impose and enforce these ideas, norms and value, and able to inject them in IR/IPE relationships via international institutions.

One good example of putting China's rise in the context of constructivist perspective is Beijing's One Belt One Road Initiative (the OBOR Initiative). This gigantic project that attempts to link most countries across the Eurasian regions seeks to directly build itself on the narrative linkage for historical and cultural understanding and economic prosperity as well as on a medium of non-coercive diffusion of policy principles rooted in "state neoliberalism."[12] In line with the Chinese principle of "respecting national sovereignty" and "individual choice of development path," the OBOR Initiative will inevitably facilitate norms, ideas and principles of policy-making that have the potential to affect the behavior of others and alter their trajectory.[13]

Another example, in which constructive IR theory has a good point, is the China-led Asian Infrastructure Investment Bank (AIIB). The AIIB's role in China's normative power can be examined from three angles: normative principles, norm diffusion, and external perception. The AIIB embodies not only China's explicit economic power, but also its implicit ideas, values and norms that are in the process of being accepted by international institutions. The AIIB's policy framework has already inherited some Chinese norms on bank loan principles: (1) political non-conditionality; (2) the emphasis on investment in infrastructure; (3) the majority of voting power for Asian developing stakeholders.[14] The AIIB is a successful story of China's norm diffusion as a soft power mechanism.

The rise of China/emerging powers – world system theory's perspectives

The world system theory's conception of hegemony emphasizes state-based class and material forms of a hegemony that is shaped and maintained by a global division of labor. This division of labor constantly generates and regenerates unequal exchange, and that, in turn, differentiates the strong/rich versus the weak/poor, not only economically, but also politically and militarily. This theory is more historical and holistic, reaching beyond the perspectives of both realism and neoliberalism.

The explanations by world system theory[15] are based on the long-term history of the evolution of the world system, which reflects a series of "cyclical rhythms," i.e., the rise and fall of the system's contradictions and crises as well as the upsurge and decline of successive system-guarantors, with each one shaping a particular pattern of control and governance. These cyclical rhythms are still moving, expanding and are continuously bringing about minor but structural shifts in certain directions. The history of the world system shows that the division and re-division of labor within the capitalist world economy result in the movements of commodity, labor, and capital across different geographic areas through chains of production and exchange, as well as in comparative advantages. The capitalist world system is perceived to have constantly been integrative and expansive because it allows for the possibility of "upward mobility" and increasing "room for maneuver" for latecomers.

Box 5.5 World system theory

World system theory sees the rise of China and emerging powers as a contemporary evidence of the system's cycles in an upward mobility. Rising powers will have to follow the system's law of value, but their ways to adjust to the system's mode of production and to govern global affairs are shaped by individual history and culture.

The rise of China and other new emerging powers, seen from the perspectives of world system theory, serves as a contemporary evidence that the historical "cyclical rhythms" are still in operation, and are successively incorporating other parts of the world into its division of labor. Accordingly, the phenomenon of emerging powers demonstrates that the capitalist world system has been expanding beyond its core territories and incorporating new centers of capital accumulation and new spaces for capitalist relocation and investment. It also shows that enlargement of "room for maneuver" does exist within the system, and "upward mobility" is possible for certain countries, not for all, to upgrade their position in global division of labor.

The rise of China/emerging powers – the Gramscian and the Neo-Gramscian perspective

Derived from Antonio Gramsci's notion of hegemony,[16] Robert Cox further elaborated the concept of hegemony by extending the level of analysis from a national context to the international realm. Cox argued that hegemony is an important instrument and mechanism for understanding how a system or an order maintains stability through looking at the different interconnected components – ideas, material capacities, institutions, social forces, forms of state, world orders – and their interactions between national and international actors and institutions. Seen from Cox, hegemonic orders emerge from a national base: "a world hegemony is an outward expression of the internal (national) hegemony established by a dominant social class."[17] In other words, a world order emerges from changes in the mode of production (economic force), and the rise of new socio-political forces, which leads to constructing new forms of state.[18] The most powerful state, the United States, has been attempting to refashion the international system in its own image, a US-shaped "world order."[19] The hegemony of a world order is an outcome of power and norm diffusion through international organizations led by institutionalized coalition of the US and its powerful and wealthy allies.[20]

One central question on hegemony vs world order in the current context of the rise of China/emerging powers is to what extent an emerging hegemonic actor is well placed to shape the world order. Cox conceptualized "world hegemony" as the interplay between national and international pattern of relationships crossing social, economic and political configurations:

> Hegemony at the international level is thus not merely an order among states. It is an order within a world economy with a dominant mode of production which penetrates into all countries and links into other subordinated modes of production. It is also a complex of international social relationships which connect the social classes of the different countries. World hegemony can be described as a social structure, an economic structure, and a political structure; and it cannot be simply one of these things but must all three.[21]

Box 5.6 Neo-Gramscian IR theory

Neo-Gramscian IR theory looks at the different interconnected components – ideas, material capacities, institutions, social forces, forms of state, world orders, and explores how these interactions between national and international actors are projected outwards to shape the international order.

Understanding the neo-Gramscian comprehensive concept of hegemony of international relations as a combination of "structural power" and "superstructural forces," we can see some limitations of many existing literature that are exclusively centered on China's hard structural power in analyzing the rise of Chinese hegemony.

"War of position" is one of the important concepts of Gramsci's hegemony theory.[22] The notion implies a gradual and protracted political struggle in order to weaken the influence and foundation of the existing power structure. During the past four decades, China has been engaging in a foreign policy approach based on "Tao Guang Yang Hui" (韬光养晦).[23] The concept is derived from a Chinese idiomatic expression, which literally means "to hide brightness, and to nourish obscurity." It reflects a strategic way of thinking, namely "to be patient and to wait for a time when one is ready to assert a big role and to make a challenge." China's upgrading its position from a cheap commodity exporter to the largest exporter of hi-tech products, from a technology importer to a dominant player in AI technology, mobile, computer and satellite industries, is pushing the country toward a higher position in the stratification of the world economy. The awareness of "war of position" is reflected in Beijing's strategic plans, such as the 13th five-year national plan (domestic industrial and technological upgrading), "Made in China 2025" (dominant position in global high-tech manufacturing), and the One Belt One Road Initiative (shaping the regional economic order).

Today China is adopting a war of position strategy in occupying a pivotal position in global governance as a new and alternative provider of global financial public goods, which is making China an emerging rule-maker in setting norms and standards. Today China is the world's largest provider of finance, offering more loans than the World Bank, and it is the most proactive player of infrastructural investment for developing countries. The Beijing-led AIIB is seen as challenging the world economic order shaped and dominated by the United States, i.e., the so-called Bretton Woods institutions – the International Monetary Fund (IMF), the World Bank – which have been in place since the end of World War II. Both the IMF and the World Bank continue to be controlled by the United States and western European countries, Britain, Germany, and France. China's voting power in the IMF has increases substantially, but its voting share is still lower in proportions to its share of economic contribution. The IMF's approval of the Special Drawing Rights status for the Chinese Yuan's (SDR) in 2016 marked the entrance of the Chinese currency as a major world currency.

The implication of the IPE of China's global rise: redividing the divided world?

The IPE of the capitalist world system was historically shaped through a long historical process including slave trade, colonialization, "free trade" and world wars, and it has successfully brought multiple cultural systems into a single integrated market system and has incorporated various parts of the world into its division of labor.[24] The system has been maintained through fixed "social, political, and economic arrangements."[25] These arrangements are what we know as the IPE of "world order," and "they are the result of human decisions taken in the context of man-made institutions and sets of self-set rules and customs."[26]

The instrumental and analytical perspectives of IPE provide the framework for conceptualizing the global "structural power" that preserves those arrangements. By structural power it refers to "the power to decide how things shall be done, the power to shape frameworks within which states relate to each other, relate to people, or relate to corporate enterprises."[27] As Susan Strange clarifies, IPE enables us to conceptualize why "global arrangements are not divinely ordained, nor are they outcome of blind chance. Rather they are the result of human decisions taken in the context of man-made institutions and sets of self-set rules and customs." Historically and fundamentally, the hegemony of the successive global powers is based on the possession of structural power.

The IPE of the Chinese mode of capital accumulation and expansion

During the past four decades, great transformations have been taking place in the political economy of Chinese *state capitalism* in which the Chinese economy transformed from one that was owned and controlled by the state to one that is supervised and regulated by the state in combination with market mechanisms. One of the distinctive features of the Chinese political economy is the political, economic and socio-cultural *innovations* in developing state capitalism with "Chinese characteristics." The so-called "Chinese state-led capital accumulation model" actually bears two sides of the same coin: one aspect of the model entails free market capitalism, such as competition, liberation, privatization and entrepreneurship; while another aspect of the model emphasizes the decisive role of the state in economic macro planning, on financial and political control, and in promoting state-owned enterprises (SOEs).[28]

What has been drawing global attention nowadays in recent years is China's One Belt One Road Initiative. Seen from the internal perspectives, the OBOR Initiative implies that the Chinese economy is looking for a new growth model, a new mode of capital accumulation that is designed and structured beyond China's borders. Externalizing the Chinese system of accumulation would enable China to reorganize its economy especially those industrial sectors that are facing the problem of overcapacity. The OBOR Initiative is precisely advocating "production capacity cooperation" in cooperation with various international partners along the Belt and Road regions, particularly those Central Asian countries. By facilitating connectivity through massive infrastructural construction and the free flow of trade, labor, capital, people, and information, the OBOR is aiming to achieve deep market integration and expansion, and creating multiple cross-regional economic cooperation frameworks. Through enhancing Eurasian economic connectivity, the OBOR project has positioned Eurasia as one of the pivotal centers of China's foreign policy strategy. Beijing will be able to not only turn its historical vulnerability (a border with 14 nations) into a strategic asset, but also to consolidate its partnership with Russia and integrate Eurasia into a system of accumulation with Chinese characteristics, i.e., "authoritarian state-centric capitalism."[29]

While the IPE of the OBOR Initiative aims to provide platforms to facilitate a new round of Chinese production relocation and capital mobility, it is perceived by the existing world powers as one of Beijing's hegemonic political economy projects, i.e., occupying a hegemonic position in trade, production, and finance, and providing financial and infrastructural "public goods" to pave the way for an emerging world order with "Chinese characteristics." As one European Parliamentary report states, the OBOR will enhance China's "regional and international profile as a responsible global power by providing public goods, … and by assuming significant financial risks involved in individual projects from which other investors would have shied away."[30] OBOR has the potential to grow into a model or a vision for alternative rule-making within international politics and economics. This development will inevitably intensify global geopolitical and geoeconomic competition especially among the core economic powers.

However, some critics both inside and outside of China are questioning whether it is economically rational for Beijing to pour such huge investment into slow-return projects and high-risk countries/regions, especially with regard to the massive infrastructural projects which are conditional for the success of connectivity. Althoug the OBOR Initiative, as a grandiose foreign policy ambition, has a solid rationality in an attempt to reconfigurate and restructure China's economic landscape, it may overstretch China's strategic resources. In an era when China and the US are in a unprecedented trade war with the Trumpt Administration fiercely opposing "Made in China 2025" and demonizing the OBOR Initiative, the tough question is whether the OBOR Initiative will create an uncertain future for China's development trajectory. In addition, considering the fact that the Middle East, South Asia, Central Asia and the South China Sea are the areas and regions where the interests of major powers regularly clash, and political and security challenges are rampant, China has limited experience and involvement in dealing with geopolitical and geoeconomic problems in these regions.

Beyond the conventional IPE perspective: "interdependent hegemony"[31]

Since the global financial crisis in 2008 with the gradual weakening of the hegemonic dominance of the US-led world order, the rise of China and emerging powers has successfully penetrated into some power areas in terms of economic competition, capital accumulation, political and economic influence as well as technical and material capacities. China in particular is performing outstandingly in terms of its global share of GDP growth, global trade, high-tech manufacturing commodities, financial competitiveness as well as foreign aid and overseas investment. It is therefore argued by the authors that the world order is entering into an era of *interdependent hegemony*, implying that the sources and capacities to maintain the areas of structural power and monopoly are no longer dominated exclusively by the US/West, and to a large extent they are dependent on the contributions from China/emerging powers.

Box 5.7 "Interdependent hegemony"

"Interdependent hegemony" denotes a dialectic process of mutual challenge and accommodation engaged by both existing and emerging powers. It symbolizes a dynamic situation in which the existing system's defenders and challengers are intertwined in a constant interactive process of shaping and reshaping the world order.

Notwithstanding the concept of "hegemony" as an important tool for understanding and analyzing politics and international relations, "interdependent hegemony" is argued to be a better concept in both describing and analyzing the changing world order and imagining a conceivable emerging world order. The concept of "interdependent hegemony" implies a dialectic process of mutual challenge, mutual constraint, mutual need, and mutual accommodation engaged by both existing and emerging powers. It symbolizes a dynamic situation in which the existing system's defenders and the emerging system challengers are intertwined in a constant interactive process of shaping and reshaping the world order.

Figure 5.2 indicates that hegemony can be decomposed into many tangible aspects. China and some emerging powers have successfully occupied a position of power sharing (hard power, see Figure 5.2, left side) in a number of areas, such as economic competition, capital accumulation, political and economic influence, financial contribution as well as technical and material capacities. However, China/emerging powers are still in a relatively catching-up position in the areas of international norm- and value-setting, global governance, cultural and ideological leadership, and media control (soft power, see Figure 5.2, left side, the ??blue?? color).

The multifaceted aspects of "interdependent hegemony"

1   The notion of "interdependent hegemony" is conceptualized as a primarily interactive and dynamic relationship between China/emerging powers and the existing power constellation of the world order. It is a dual complexity of both "intended consequence" and "unintended consequence." On the one hand, the phenomenon of the rise of China/emerging power is an "intended consequence" brought about by the motivation of the established powers to purposefully invite and push China/emerging powers to be integrated in globalization and capitalist world economy so that these countries are able to develop themselves *within* the defined structural mechanism of global capitalism and world order. It is also an "unintended consequence" because the economic success of China/emerging powers is unprepared and their accumulated capacities are underestimated as a rising challenger to the existing order. The Chinese case as an unintended consequence, in particular, is well observed by Chris Patten, the last British Governor of Hong Kong, who described the rise of China both as "a threat to Western democracy" and as "the first example of a country which has done astonishingly well in this international system, but challenges its basic foundations."[32] It implies a dual complexity in which China's success is achieved from its integration in the capitalist world system, while at the same time the factors behind Beijing's success contradict or challenge some of the existing world order's basic norms – the two

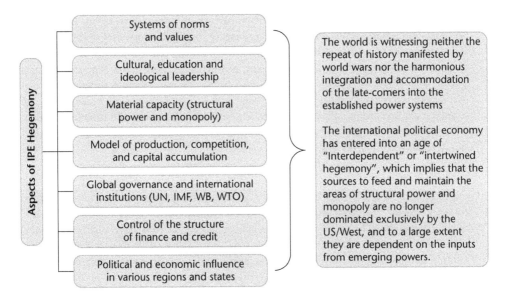

Figure 5.2   The interdependent hegemony of the world order in a new era
Source: Authors' own.

sides of the same coin. To put it in a nutshell, China's economic success is leading the country toward a more positive structural position in the distribution of global wealth while it is also a challenge to many "enduring aspects" and "global arrangement" defined by the core powers of the existing world order.

2   Interdependent hegemony indicates the fact that globalization and global capitalism is leading the world into a stage of "varieties of capitalism" in which capitalist agencies and classes are not only private economic actors but also states, and state-owned entities, such as Chinese SOEs. The effective integration of state interests and capital accumulation is helping some emerging power, particularly China, to win a "war of position"[33] by redefining the systems of alliance and reshaping the terrain and parameters of global social, economic, and political relations. The so-called "Beijing Consensus" as a "norm diffusion" of the Chinese development model reflects a unique IPE of "state capitalism."[34] China's increasing global financial role with its newly led AIIB Bank and BRICS Bank can also be transformed into Beijing's increasing norm-setting and rule-making leadership role in global governance.[35] The AIIB is identified by some as "China's normative power in international financial governance."[36] China is clearly in the process of changing its position from a rule-follower to a rule-maker in the international system.

3   Interdependent hegemony implies that the world is entering into a post-US hegemony era in which there is no dominant hegemony of norms and values defined by one single country (the US) or by a core cultural civilization (the West). China's economic success is opening for the accommodation and inclusion of alternative development strategies and policies. The so-called "Chinese model" is also opening for multiple factors and alternative explanations regarding mechanisms that make nations grow, i.e., a set of mutually interdependent relationships between ownership (property rights) and economic growth, between rule of law and market economy, between free currency flow and economic order, and, most importantly, between democracy and development. These norms and values are becoming "intertwined" – open, less rigid, and non-universal.

4   Interdependent hegemony depicts new counter-hegemonic alliances among various emerging powers, but these alliances are often issue-based rather than norm-based. Both China and other emerging powers are not aiming to create a new alternative hegemony, but they will continue to be a counter-hegemonic socio-political and socio-economic force in order to promote multilateralism. Most emerging powers in general and China in particular pursue very pragmatic foreign policy so as to find the balance between defending their "national interest" and resisting the hegemonic dominance of the existing order. China, for example, has no specific unified global strategy grounded on norms and principles; rather, it has different strategies, tactics and policy approaches to different global political, economic, and security problems on a case-by-case basis.

5   Interdependent hegemony offers China and emerging powers a good opportunity to develop a collective "positioning" strategy and "balancing" tactics. However, interdependent hegemony also illustrates the fact that China and emerging powers are not yet able to form an organic "historical bloc" and to create a substitution for an independent and universal hegemony. This is because China and emerging powers have different national agendas and priorities, different competitive or contradictory IPE relationships with the existing powers, and different regional and global influences. Some emerging powers, like China and India, still have unresolved bilateral political and historical problems. Even within the BRICS, as a non-western alliance, there are unbalanced power relationships among the five countries. It is more relevant to see the degree and consequence of their emergence and to explore how important BRICS cooperation is to individual BRICS

members' foreign policy strategies and potential relevance as leaders in regional and global governance.

6   Interdependent hegemony entails a new type of global IPE relationships brought about by the rise of China and emerging powers that is intensifying globalization and interdependence in the world order. The IPE relationships between the established and emerging powers exhibit intertwined complexities in which the conventional core-semiperipheral-peripheral stratifications and the traditional North-South axis show their limited applicability in analyzing the complexed relationships between them.[37]

Interdependent hegemony between the existing and emerging powers

As discussed above, "interdependent hegemony" views the relationship between the rise of China and emerging powers and the existing world order as being more interdependent than conflictual. The rise of China, for example, should not be one-sidedly dichotomized to the decline of the US-led existing world order. On the contrary, liberal-minded scholars actually interpret the success of China and other emerging powers as the result of their integration in the US-led world order and as a convincing evidence of the functioning and vitality of the existing liberal order.

Therefore, it is necessary to adopt a dialectic approach to understanding the current world order in which patterns of IPE relationship among nation states are shaped by the historical evolution of the hegemonic structure and with which emerging powers are politically and economically integrated and embedded. Both the challenge from China/Emerging powers and the structural barriers of such challenge has been conceptualized through the discussion of "interdependent hegemony" in the previous section. It is argued that seen from interdependent hegemony perspective, the emerging power phenomenon shows a clear limitation in terms of constructing alternative hegemony and an alternative world order. Interdependent hegemony entails a dialectic interplay between on the one hand, the dynamic and inclusive nature of the capitalist world system and, and on the other hand, the contradictions embedded in the system in the process of integrating non-western economies and non-western norms and values.

Hence, globalization/transnationalization process is a double-edged sword to both the existing hegemons and to China and emerging powers as well – both opportunities and challenges are two sides of the same coin. In line with this understanding, the discussion is to what extent the rise of China and emerging powers has indeed challenged the many aspects of the existing world order in terms of functionality, scope, legitimacy and authority. However, it has not yet fundamentally changed the IPE *structural power* of the existing world order. Structural power refers to "the power to choose and to shape the structures of the global political economy within which other states, their political institutions, their economic enterprises, and (not least) their professional people have to operate," and it contains four interconnected features: the security defense capacity, the control of system of production of goods and services, the control of the structure of finance and credit, and the dominance of knowledge and ideas.[38]

In the current era of transnational capitalism, it is less likely for China and emerging powers to establish a new world order with alternative hegemony. One unique feature of the IPE of the emerging world order can be characterized as a dual complexity: on the one hand, the world is witnessing the return of the historical "great power rivalry" characterized by security conflicts and zero-sum power competition, such as the China–US rivalry; while on the other hand, the capitalist world system is entering into an era of "interdependent hegemony" characterized by the system's continuous resilient capacity in accommodation and integration of new powers.

The new IPE relationships shaped by China's rise

The world system theory[39] provides a broad theoretical perspective to understand the historical development and transformative trajectory involved in the evolution of the modern capitalist world system. This capitalist world system evolved and expanded over a long historical spectrum and continuously brought different parts of the world into its law of value and division of labor. The hegemonic structure of the world system is a perpetual relationship of inequality in international division of labor, marking a permanent condition of economic stratification of inequalities among nation states. Under this global division of labor within one single global market, an IPE structure consisting of sovereign states and multiple cultural entities interacts within the framework of an interstate system. The world system is conceptualized as a dynamic one in which changing positions within the system's structural morphology is not easy, but possible by taking advantage of global capital mobility and relocation of production. Historically, the division of labor within the capitalist world economy brought about and resulted in flows of commodities, labors and capitals across different geographical areas through chains of production, trade and investment. China and India are seen as the last reserves (unexploited areas) that have been brought into the capitalist world system.[40] World system theory attempts to explain the system's dynamics as well as embedded inequalities in which nation states occupy different economic positions and are located in different development stages within a seemingly unified global economy. In line with the theory's conceptualization, different national positions located in different international division of labor, and the unceasing change of patterns of competition and competitiveness have planted the system from the very beginning with inherent inequalities and contradictions.

Seen from world system theory, the capitalist world system is understood to be embedded with fundamental features, characterized by a series of cyclical rhythms, i.e., economic prosperity or crisis, and upward or downward mobility. Likewise, the current phenomenon of the rise of China can be interpreted as a strategic policy success in which China took the advantage of the system's rhythmic cycles in upward mobility by its open-door policy to global division of labor, capital relocation, and production outsourcing since the end of 1970s. In other words, the Chinese success reflects the essential features of the world capitalist system. When China is becoming more successful as an emerging global economic power, the country is believed to be motivated or driven to act as a new political and economic system-guarantor due to its economic integration and market dependence on the functioning of the system's mode of production and capital accumulation. The historical evolution of the modern world system shows that the series of cyclical rhythms was followed by the rise and decline of new guarantors (new hegemons), such as the UK and the US, with each one having its own unique pattern of governance and control.[41] The rise of China is believed to be no different.

Nevertheless, new emerging powers, especially China, are also described as a challenger to the system's existing dominant guarantor and other core powers because they have different political and economic governing cultures. Realism believes that China has a strong interest in establishing a "sinicized" world order. However, seen from the world system's perspective, even if the future world order were to be injected with Chinese characteristic, it would simply be a reflection of China's internal economic, political and cultural extension without altering the fundamental architecture of the world capitalist system.

"Room for maneuver," "upward mobility," "promotion by invitation," "seeing the chance"

Hence, contrary to the pessimism of conventional IPE realism, world system theory does not view the rise of new successors (emerging powers) as a threat as long as the system's fundamental law of value – mode of production and capital accumulation – is maintained. This is because the advance of the latecomers is hugely dependent on and benefits from their integration in international division of labor and active participation in the process of capital and wealth accumulation. Accordingly, the rise of China and emerging powers is understood as part of the never-ending cyclical rhythms of the system, which symbolizes the strength and success of the world system in bringing more untapped parts of the world to the logic of capitalism without changing the fundamental relations of inequality within the system. World system theory's logical argument is clear: when China is successfully moving toward the core, it still needs semi-periphery and periphery, and perhaps even more so.

Figure 5.3 shows that China's rise is generating different implications and impacts on different parts of the world. On the one hand, it may be argued that China is becoming an emerging counter-hegemonic social force to the "core" of the existing world order; while at the same time, it can also be seen as a new rising hegemon to the semi-peripheral and peripheral parts of the world. This means, as an emerging power, China is standing in a transitional juncture from a world order that was dominated by conventional hegemony to a one that is increasingly shaped by interdependent hegemony. With its accumulated power and wealth brought about by its upgraded position in the world economy, China´s continuous rise is providing more "room for maneuver" and "upward mobility" to semi-peripheral and peripheral countries. As a rising "hegemon" China must not be identified as a new member of the conventional "core," rather, it should be understood as a nation whose power is characterized by global relationship and relevance.

Historically, it was in similar pivotal moments that opportunities for upward mobility within the system were generated and regenerated (promotion by invitation).[42] The post-war United States emerged as a dominant political, economic and military power in the international system, and it played a significant role in contributing to world economic development in the postwar era, particularly in the regions of western Europe and East Asia. For economic, security and political reasons the US committed itself to the revival of a liberal international economy, an international division of labor, and resource and market access that benefited itself and its allies.

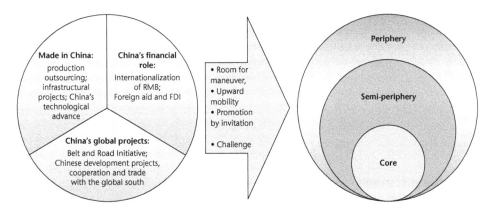

Figure 5.3 The multiple effect of the rise of China on the capitalist world system

Source: Authors' own.

The entire role played by the United States since the end of the Second World War is theorized by the realist IR school as "hegemonic stability" through providing the "public goods." As benign hegemon, the US leadership during this period was *structural leadership*, i.e., "the ability to direct the overall shape of world political order" based on resources, capital, technology, military forces and economic power.[43]

China's high economic growth in the past decades is another good story reflecting the positive spill-over effect of taking advantage of the system's upward mobility by seizing the chance of global outward foreign direct investment (FDI). "Room for maneuver" refers to the external conditions for "upward mobility" in the world capitalist economy that is conducive to internal development. Seen from a long historical perspective, the global core-semiperipheral-peripheral hierarchy has been a relatively stable structure over centuries. The system's rhythmic cycles and the rise or decline of hegemonic powers provide both upward and downward mobility. A positive effect of upward mobility can be generated by the combination of external forces in "promotion by invitation" (trade and investment), and internal forces in "seizing the chance" (policy and strategy). As mentioned above, the post-war role of the US in promoting global economic growth was a clear example of a force for promoting "upward mobility," and so was China since the 2010s. What is interesting regarding China is that the country was both an initial receiver and later on a contributor of room for maneuver and upward mobility.

"Promotion by invitation" refers to an "invited" upward mobility path enjoyed by a semi-peripheral or peripheral country, whose geopolitical or geoeconomic position is vital during the period of global power struggles, or whose internal resources and labor condition are favorable to global capital mobility and production relocation. The "promotion" is stimulated by the favorable external environment created by a hegemon, or by a group of nations, for the sake of their own IPE interests. In East Asia, Japan and the East Asian Newly Industrialized Economies (NICs), including post-Mao China, are historical good examples of this type of invited/promoted upward mobility driven by the US strategic interest.

"Seizing the chance" indicates a country's internal capability in taking advantage of a favorable development situation or condition that is taking place in the IPE of the world order as well as its mobilizing capacity in adjusting its internal comparative advantage and competitiveness to the new externalities accordingly.

The rise of China together with its capital outward expansion and global hegemonic strategy seemingly represents another rhythmic cycle of the rise of a new hegemon. It is both an opportunity in terms of room for maneuver and upward mobility for some countries, and a challenge and downward mobility for others, or a mixture of both. For example, the China–Brazil economic relations during the past two decades represent the coexistence of both opportunities and constraints. On the one side, China is now Brazil's largest trading partner, and Chinese investment in Brazil and Brazil–China trade relations are becoming more and more important to Brazil, bringing tangible benefits to the country in terms of enlarging its room for "political maneuver" and generating its "commodity boom." On the other side, the bilateral unequal exchange of trade, with China exporting manufactured products and Brazil exporting commodities and raw material, is making Brazil a primary commodity exporter to China and is therefore bringing about heated discussions on whether China is "deindustrializing Brazil."[44]

Concluding remarks

The global debates on the rise of China and emerging powers tend to locate themselves within the concepts and conceptualizations framed by the different conventional IPE schools of international relations in hypothesizing the binary choice faced by both the existing and emerging powers: the former is endeavoring to assimilate the latter into the defined structure and mechanism of the existing order, while the latter is struggling to benefit from challenging and adjusting the system.

This chapter takes its point of departure from the central analytical apparatus centered around the notion of "hegemony." It further develops this notion and provides an alternative framework of "interdependent hegemony" to understand the global impact of the rise of emerging powers brought about by globalization and the transformation of international relations and the international political economy. This alternative framework is considered to be a better conceptual tool in analyzing the nexus between the role of emerging powers as a counter-hegemonic socio-political force and the hegemonic resiliency of the existing world order. The chapter regards the capitalist world system as dynamic system that is under continuous changes over time, whereas certain basic features of the system remain in place. The geographic expansion of the capitalist world economy will never end. Despite the rise of China and emerging powers, the functioning of the world economy will always generate inequalities despite of some positional changes in the stratifications of the core-semiperiphery and periphery structure. The rise of China is fundamentally a positive driving force to the world system, perhaps not to the existing hegemon in some aspects, as a provider of upward mobility and room for maneuver for the majority of the Global South.

It is expected that the IPE of the world order will unceasingly be in a process of transition and transformation. The relationship between the rise of China and emerging powers and the existing order will continuously be based on a dialectic relationship of waxing and waning. The dynamic interaction between them will continue to be in a motion of flux and reflux, rather than in a purposeful forward (integration and accommodation) or a backward (conflict and war) movement as anticipated by realist ideologies. This is because a more horizontal world order brought about by China's global rise both creates more spaces for interaction and competition and generates both opportunities and challenges. For the time being there is a multifaceted interplay of realism, liberalism, altruism, hope and fear between China and the core western powers. In the years ahead the rise of China and the core powers of the existing world order will have to go through a considerable period of struggle, adjustment and tension.

Notes

1 Kindleberger 1973; Gilpin 2001.
2 Ikenberry and Kupchan 1990: 287–288.
3 Organski, Fimo, and Kugler 1980.
4 Gilpin 1981: 186.
5 Gilpin 1981: 187.
6 Mearsheimer 2010
7 Keohane and Nye 1989.
8 Keohane 1984.
9 Ikenberry 2008: 23–37; 2011: 56–68.
10 Ikenberry 2008.
11 Jackson and Sørensen 2003: 341.
12 Vangeli 2018.
13 Vangeli 2018.
14 Peng and Keat 2016: 736.
15 Wallerstein 1979; 2004.
16 Gramsci 1971.
17 Cox 1983: 171.
18 Cox 1981: 138.
19 Cox 1983: 171.

20 Cox 1981: 126–155.
21 Cox 1983: 171.
22 Gramsci 1971.
23 It is a Chinese idiomatic expression, which literally means "to hide brightness, and to nourish obscurity." The notion reflects an implicit strategic way of thinking, namely "to be patient and to wait for a time when one is ready to assert a big role and to make a challenge."
24 Wallerstein 1979; 2004.
25 Strange [1988] 1994: 18.
26 Strange [1988] 1994: 18.
27 Strange [1988] 1994: 25.
28 Huang 2010: 31–47.
29 Clarke 2015.
30 Grieger 2016.
31 "Interdependent hegemony" is the author's own concept. See Li 2016.
32 Quoted in *BBC News* 2008. Available at: http://news.bbc.co.uk/2/hi/asia-pacific/7719420.stm.
33 The notion is derived from Antonio Gramsci, who refers to a slow and protracted political strategy of ideological struggle that aims to occupy the critical terrain of popular "common sense." The concept intends to be distinguished from another notion termed by Gramsci as "war of maneuver," which refers to a direct, violent and immediate assault on the state for achieving political power (Gramsci 1971).
34 Li 2016: 18–31; Li and Shaw 2013: 88–113.
35 Feng and He 2015.
36 Peng and Keat 2016.
37 Li 2019.
38 Strange 1987: 551–574.
39 Wallerstein 1974: 387–415, 1979, 1997, 2004.
40 Li 2008.
41 Wallerstein 1997.
42 Wallerstein 1979.
43 Ikenberry 1996: 389.
44 Dantas and Jabbour 2016; Jenkins 2015.

Bibliography

Clarke, M. 2015. Understanding China's Eurasian Pivot. *The Diplomat*. Available at https://thediplomat.com/2015/09/understanding-chinas-eurasian-pivot/.

Cox, R. 1981. Social Forces, States and World Orders: Beyond International Relations Theory. *Millennium: Journal of International Studies*, 10(2): 126–55.

Cox, R. 1983. Gramsci, Hegemony and International Relations: An Essay in Method. *Millennium: Journal of International Studies*, 12(2): 162–75.

Dantas, A. and Jabbour, E. 2016. Brazil and China: An Assessment of Recent Trade Relations. *Economics of Agriculture*, 63(1): 313–322.

Gilpin, R. 1981. *War and Change in World Politics*. Cambridge: Cambridge University Press.

Gilpin, R. 2001. *Global Political Economy: Understanding the International Economic Order*. Princeton: Princeton University Press.

Gramsci, A. 1971. *Selections from the Prison Notebooks*. Quintin Hoare and Geoffrey Nowell Smith (eds.). London: Lawrence & Wishart.

Grieger, G. 2016. One Belt, One Road (OBOR): China's Regional Integration Initiative. *European Parliamentary Research Service*.

Feng, H. and He, K. 2015. *Running the AIIB*. China Policy Institute: Analysis. Available at: https://cpianalysis.org/2015/05/28/the-aiib-what-will-china-do-next/.

Huang, Y. 2010. Debating China's Economic Growth: The Beijing Consensus or The Washington Consensus. *Academy of Management Perspectives* 24(2): 31–47. Available at: http://neeley.tcu.edu/uploaded files/academic_departments/management/zol002102933p.pdf.

Ikenberry, J. 1996. The Future of International Leadership. *Political Science Quarterly*, 111(3): 385–403.

Ikenberry, J. 2008. The Rise of China and the Future of the West. *Foreign Affairs*, 87(1): 23–37.

Ikenberry, J. 2011. The Future of the Liberal World Order: Internationalism after America. *Foreign Affairs*, 90(3): 56–68.

Ikenberry, J. and Kupchan, C. 1990. Socialization and Hegemonic Power. *International Organization*, 44(3): 283–315.

Jackson, R. and Sørensen, G. 2003. *Introduction to International Relations: Theories and Approaches*. London: Oxford University Press.

Jenkins, R. 2015. Is Chinese Competition Causing Deindustrialization in Brazil? *Latin American Perspectives*. 42(6): 42–63.

Kindleberger, C. 1973. *The World in Depression, 1929–1939*. Los Angeles: University of California Press.

Keohane, R. 1984. *After Hegemony: Cooperation and Discord in the World Political Economy*. Princeton: Princeton University Press.

Keohane, R. and Nye, J. 1989. *Power and Interdependence: World Politics in Transition*. Boston: Little, Brown and Company.

Li, M. 2008 *The Rise of China and The Demise of The Capitalist World Economy*. New York: Pluto Press.

Li X. 2016. From "Hegemony and World Order" to "Interdependent Hegemony and World Reorder". In: Christensen, S. and Xing, L. (eds.) *Emerging Powers, Emerging Markets, Emerging Societies: Global Responses*. London: Palgrave Macmillan.

Li, X. 2016. Understanding China's Economic Success: 'Embeddedness' with Chinese Characteristics. *Asian Culture and History* 8(2): 18–31.

Li, X. 2019. China's Dual Position in the Capitalist World Order: A Dual Complexity of Hegemony and Counter-hegemony. In: Li, X. (ed.) *The International Political Economy of the BRICS*. London: Routledge.

Li, X. and Shaw, T. 2013. The Political Economy of Chinese State Capitalism. *China and International Relations*, 1(1): 88–113.

Mearsheimer, J. 2010. The Gathering Storm: China's Challenge to US Power in Asia. *The Chinese Journal of International Politics*, 3(4): 381–396 ·

Organski, A., Fimo, K. and Kugler, J. 1980. *The War Ledger*. Chicago: University of Chicago Press.

Peng, Z. and Keat, S. 2016. *The AIIB and China's Normative Power in International Financial Governance Structure. Chinese Political Science Review*, 1(4): 736–753.

Strange, S. 1987. The Persistent Myth of Lost Hegemony. *International Organization* 41(4): 551–574.

Strange, S. [1988] 1994. *States and Markets*, 2nd edition. London: Pinter.

Vangeli, A. 2018. A Framework for the Study of the One Belt One Road Initiative as a Medium of Principle-Diffusion. In Li Xing (ed.) *Mapping China's One Belt One Road Initiative*. London: Palgrave Macmillan.

Wallerstein, I. 1974. The Rise and Future Demise of the of the World-Capitalist System: Concepts for Comparative Analysis. *Comparative Studies in Society and History*. 16(4): 387–415.

Wallerstein, I. 1979. *The Capitalist World-Economy*. New York: Cambridge University Press.

Wallerstein, I. 1997. *The Rise of East Asia, or The World System in the Twenty-First Century*. Available at: www.binghamton.edu/fbc/archive/iwrise.htm.

Wallerstein, I. 2004. *World-Systems Analysis: An Introduction*. Durham: Duke University Press.

6

The tailoring of IPE in Latin America

Lost, misfit or merely misperceived?[1]

Diana Tussie[2]

Cutting out the cloth: it might have been IPE from birth

International Political Economy (IPE) focuses on the politics of international economic exchange. It is a substantive field of inquiry, rather than merely a methodology. IPE as a recognized field in Latin America is making its way as a loose field with heritages in International Relations (IR), in Economics,[3] Sociology, Economic History and development studies at large. Is it emerging as a subfield, a field in its own right, an inter-discipline? Does it focus on the special nature of the global system, along the lines of more traditional International Relations, or does it unearth its roots in the intellectual movements that emerged as development studies, in turn, branching across the broad range of social science traditions in Latin America? Can it bring these together? Despite some fuzziness, the field is the focus of much debate and grows in terms of recognition, output and importance, evident in the number of conferences such as the sequence of FLACSO conferences held by the Latin American School of Social Sciences better known from its Spanish acronym (FLACSO) and the publication of books and special issues.[4] Over time it has attracted a wide variety of backgrounds. Susan Strange had described the field she was promoting to as a minestrone that could incorporate many ingredients in incremental fashion. While many scholars in Latin America have emerged from development, others from Economic History, others merely feel alien (to a greater or lesser degree) to the clout of so-called "securocracy" of International Relations in Latin America. More recently, even in established Political Science, a narrow and excluding discipline, with strictly policed boundaries there is some acceptance that as Latin America is increasingly more integrated in the global system, national politics can no longer be treated simply as watertight compartments on their own. Political Science, as the respected discipline of the state, is also coming to terms with the notion that global material interests cannot be hived off as mere interferences in government.[5] In the same manner Economics has come to acknowledge that first best or one size fits all prescriptions can sink as a result of a political process. To take up trade as an example, there is a world of difference between trade policy and trade negotiations, whereby in the latter international and national interests struggle for distribution; hence the intrinsic centrality of politics emerges strongly. For IPE the "free" trade ideal and the "protectionist" backwater are constructions at best made in heaven (or hell). Real preferences are pragmatic choices situated along a continuum where neither one ever reigns supreme. Once we move away from first best we are called upon to navigate a sea of contending perspectives in which IPE has a lot to contribute on the "state market condominium".[6] This state–market condominium operates simultaneously through the competitive pressures of the market and the political processes that shape the boundaries and structures within which that competition (or lack thereof) takes place.

As academic turf protection has tempered, the time is ripe to re-visit how IPE is unfolding in Latin America. Moreover, global power shifts visibilize the action of the apparently powerless. In the case of Latin America, the prevalence of a theoretical model in which the United States was seen as enjoying "perennial predominance"[7] over a region seen as a dependent and defenceless object has lost sway. There are also powerful drivers coming from the global field of IPE at large which is in need of opening up to global conversations.[8] This has enabled spaces for situated knowledge and, even more important, methodologically, for considering wider conceptions of agency. For a field that has been framed in terms of stark, binary oppositions between rule-takers and rule-makers, disciplinary change augurs healthy results affecting what is IPE and how we study it. This chapter will argue that the diversity of origin and of analytical approaches in Latin American IPE militate strongly towards interpreting the field as much as an offshoot of traditional International Relations, as rooted in the broad tradition of political economy and sociology embedded in Latin America.

As soon as we enter the messy work of understanding what is around us we encounter multiple traditions and concepts. Left unexamined tradition is destined to cast a shadow over our minds. Whatever the importance of (usually dissidenting) IR scholars in fostering the phenomenal growth of IPE in the last decade, coming out of the closet, the field has reduced the erstwhile aura of securocratics. The chapter aims to provide the reader with an overview of field building in Latin America. It is meant to be a selective overview of conceptual devices, far from an exhaustive account of the "state of the art". There is no intention of looking at who is "there" and who is not. Instead, we develop a picture of the core questions and issues. The argument develops in three parts, beginning with a critical review of IPE field building in Latin America, its recurrent themes and questions, together with a description of its mixed nature at a crossroad between various scientific fields and without precise boundaries. In the second part, we investigate the regional fabric of Latin American IPE, signalling the inter-generational significance of "centre-periphery" as a conceptual device together with its evolution while providing the reader with a theoretical overview on what can be considered IPE in the Latin American context nowadays. Despite the academic consensus that dependencia was a foundational moment, it leads to a nostalgia for paradise lost that obliterates the quality and quantity of wider contributions with less fatalistic connotations.[9] The purpose of this chapter is to dispel the ostrich like view. The grounds for disagreement with this view are manifold as we hope to argue. Without turning to crude empiricism, as more nuanced work has seen the light Latin American IPE was able to move away from binary oppositions to construct relational approaches that stress process as much as structure. That is why in the third part we address the most recent developments with legacies of the past profoundly reconfigured and finely rebranded to account for the new place that Latin America holds in a deeply transformed world, its revised perspectives and goals, as well as various epistemic "turns". Finally, a conclusion draws together our reflections and allows us to highlight the main themes. The point of this chapter is to overcome the notion that Latin American contributions to IPE were significant but remain in the past. Yet to paraphrase Anna Leander, "reflexivity"[10] enables an inter-generational dialogue. It allows us to appreciate the "mental construct" that has taken form and better understand where a field's ideas come from – how they originated, and how they move over time.

Reflecting on roots

The main transformative event of the twentieth century may well have been decolonization, rather than World War I and II, in the sense that it systematized a set of relations and provided an anchor to continuous global restructuring of politics. Acharya and Buzan[11] confronting *faux* universalism explored "regional" sites of theory construction paving the way for the intersection between history and concepts. While IPE has long been appropriated as an undeniably Anglo-Saxon and Western field of narratives and assumptions,[12] the argument is that without comprehending agency in the Global South a good deal of the world is left untapped. Over the last decades the field has engaged in major self-reflection about Anglo-Saxon ontologies and epistemologies, debating its expanding frontiers. There has been a transversal effort to recover various homegrown conceptual contributions.[13] The result is the building of synergy between disciplinary and area studies approaches, unearthing an indigenous "school" that, without quite presenting itself as such, has analysed the region and its relationship with the world since the early entry into the system of states at the end of the nineteenth century to the present. This effort has shown how central were the conditions laid out by the IPE to state identities and thus on national interests and policies. There was no missionary zeal in Latin American international thinking but acute awareness of hostile hands that could affect states' prospects for survival. Long before International Relations was structured as a distinctive discipline, Latin American concern with "the international" was haunted by the international economy. The struggles for independence were a rallying cry against the monopolistic trade corset imposed by Spain. The colonial inception of Latin American states and the following status of commercial dependency contributed to blur the distinction between the economy and politics and between domestic matters and international ones, much in line with IPE's research programme. Settlers in Spanish America considered themselves part of a *Patria Grande* sharing cultural and historical ties, but more profoundly, as the struggles for independence proceeded, colonialism and foreign intervention constituted the idea of Latin America between West and non-West. If we accept this birthmark of a Latin America concerned with the two French invasions into Mexico, the territorial expansion of the US or the grabbing of Malvinas, it helps to understand how important was the double movement to tame the powers and enable business to proceed as normally as possible. In this sense, we argue that since its very beginning, Latin American International Relations have been largely a matter of political economy, with the region close to being an invisibilized pioneer on the edges of the mainstream.[14]

Economic relations have always *occupied* the spotlight and were the concern of a variegated range of schools and traditions. Well before "interdependence" was conceptualized by North American IPE, Latin American scholars and policy makers were aware of the utmost importance that economic links hold for those on the fringes of the system. Susan Strange had insisted on the puerility of the "mutual neglect of politics and economics".[15] She saw herself as representing a marginalized position and pulling ideas from many quarters (Latin American *dependencia* or French economists) into the mainstream.[16] *Par contra*, there was hardly a trace of mutual neglect in Latin America's vision of the world. While the experiences of state formation in Europe can be summed up in Charles Tilly's classic aphorism "war makes states, and states make war" for Latin America, we could tweak this dictum to a different codependency: "markets make states, and states make markets". Insertion and decolonization make up a distinctive ontology.[17]

Alternatively posed: was state formation critical for the formation of the market, or was it market formation that triggered state formation and associated modalities of governance? The struggles for independence and the coetaneous conformation of republics were ultimately about the making of capitalism, be it in the form of English trade covetousness or the desire of domestic elites to break free of the colonial monopoly and link up to the profitable English commercial networks. In many senses, Great Britain was Spain's inheritor, a monopoly supplier requiring reduced barriers to trade while offering sweet finance. Many authors have traced the roots of Latin American nation building to the organization of money, custom houses and external trade.[18] In this sense, widespread intellectual agitation accompanied the independence process since its early days, concentrating on issues such as commercial insertion; Bunge's proposal of a "custom union of the south";[19] the role of debt in reproducing colonial relations, as demonstrated by the elaboration of "defensive" jurisprudential Drago and Tobar doctrines. These contributions, as suggested by Helleiner and Rosales in relation to the Mariategui/Haya de la Torre debate,[20] must be recognized as forerunners of Latin American IPE, whose history is yet to be written in English and framed as IPE, but that socially concerned and politically motivated students in the 1960s and 1970s read intensely together with Marxist authors from all parts of the world. The extent of Latin America as a coherent composite category may be disputed, but there is no denying that problems were shared and that ideas flowed profusely.

This said, it is obvious that topics of relevance to Latin America have simply not been captured in mainstream IPE that grew entrenched in a highly specific and narrow set of conceptual and empirical foundations. Compounding this neglect, inputs from Sociology or theories of development, or theories of the peripheral state (such as Hamza Alavi or Alfred Hirschman) were hardly brought in. This resulted in two parallel tracks that barely touched each other – one that looked at the trees that that shaped the "whole system", and another that analysed chains of dependence, domination or simply abuse by more powerful actors. In the process, relations among some countries and regions that comprise the global political economy were ignored, and development in these regions were seen, if at all, as simple reflections of the "global" process.

To take up the influence of Sociology and marking a contrast with *how* the field has been shaped and not merely *what with*, it is difficult to overestimate its sway in Latin America. As a badge of professionalism, the Latin American Association of Sociology was established in 1950. Leading scholars at the time were trained in Sociology rather than Political Science which hardly existed and was just part of Law faculties. While the development of Political Science lagged and was not fully institutionalized until democratic transitions were more or less completed in the early 1990s (with the exception of Mexico and Colombia were stability had come earlier) Sociology was the mother discipline. After Seymour Lipset's and Gino Germani's seminal work, sociologists in the 1950s and 1960s researched the relation between levels of development and the prevalence of democracy.[21] There was a widespread acceptance that capitalist development in Latin America would eventually eradicate *caudillismo* and political instability, rooted in the weakness of capitalism, and would thus finally provide a solid basis for democracy. Such reformist hopes suffered a cruel blow with the rise of bloody dictatorships and neoliberalism in the Southern Cone of the 1970s. Debates about openness and political regimes became particularly urgent. While development economists were hard pressed to understand the "anomaly",[22] Marxists[23] as well as social democrats held that further capitalist development would require disciplining labour, violation of human rights and dismantlement of democratic institutions. By serving external interests, the local state was the predator against its own citizens, not the protector of internal violence but the purveyor. Put differently, if the European states aimed to ensure a social contract, many Latin America states made internal violence an everyday reality. In short, there is a vast literature examining Latin America's political economy in the twentieth century that focuses on the intersection of the international liberal order and domestic politics which then flowed into the legendary intellectual tradition associated with dependency as well as substantive critiques of governance as "dependent development".[24] The consensus on dependencia as a foundational moment cannot be understood without reference to the long standing sociological contributions that were neither part of International Relations narrowly defined as the discipline of war and peace nor of the bounded field of IPE in the Anglosphere that emerged beginning in the late-1960s and early-1970s. But the vagaries of the world economy were always closely inspected for understandable reasons. If creditors mattered to the Anglosphere, debtors were what mattered in Latin America. While Susan Strange's seminal work on international monetary relations of the Western world published in 1976[25] concentrated on creditors she delegated her last chapter on the Paris Club to Christopher Prout; that same year Rosario Green,[26] a prominent Mexican academic, later turned diplomat, published on the global crisis in a Sociology journal, showing dialogue *with* and uptake *from* sociologists. A coetaneous field of enquiry was then the so-called new international economic order. Even if today dependency theory is hardly taught, the real-world concerns that lent it credence endure. Latin American IPE has developed in an intellectual context that has borne this imprint. But the field does not admit of a dominant perspective or focus of enquiry.

Transdisciplinarity leads to the difficulty in stating where IPE starts and where it ends. Scholars have covered an extraordinary range of subjects in international economic relations. There are regional or country specialists who make contributions to IPE, for example in the field of regional integration or South–South cooperation, both vast and vibrant "IPE-like" fields. Others have focused on particular economic sectors or issues (trade, finance, energy or natural resources), or social groups (labour, landless peasants, global business community). Nevertheless, the central issues revolve on how politics conform markets, and markets conform states. International insertion, organizational or associational power, policy space, asymmetry, regional integration, are only some of the "core themes" of Latin American IPE, so embedded in the international thought of the region that have evolved over the years and through different historical phases. The role of politics in shaping IPE can be seen in the evolving issues taken up, from fixation with the US and the nefarious effects of its multinational corporations to more nuanced views in which the room for agency comes out. The relative resiliency of these conceptual devices owes quite a bit to Spanish's and Portugnol's forte as a *lingua franca* and the dearth of translations of English texts. The only textbooks translated were Joan Spero in 1977 and Gilpin, the latter both into Spanish and Portuguese.[27] Absence of translations precluded socializing via IPE scholarship from the Anglosphere, while Alfred Hirschman, Gunnar Myrdal, Frantz Fanon, Gramsci or the French regulationists were translated and widely read. For better or worse it left ample spaces for homegrown research enquiries albeit dispersed in a wide variety of journals.[28] The region itself became the epistemic foundation. While English was never able to topple the combined energy of Spanish and Portuguese, it also failed to bring the field together more tightly, which then grew in the interstices, in sharp contrast to the boost in China. As China repudiated the cultural revolutions, several foundational Western IPE books were translated into Chinese[29] and anchored the field via the Anglosphere. In the absence of this incursion, the Anglosphere was not as successful in its (re)production of academic hierarchies. And since the lead time of "hidden" publications in Spanish and Portuguese to be taken up in academic circuits in the Anglosphere is next to infinite, Latin Americans were able to speak to each other or to Latin Americanists. A stark indicator of this segregation is the number of attendees to the conventions of the to the International Studies Association in contrast to the Latin American Studies Associations in which conversations could be carried out in one's one language. Ties with French sociologists and Latin Americanists were never displaced. In parallel another feature of Latin American flourished: its policy orientation. Thinking and research are problem and change oriented, never sealed off from the real world, never quite in an ivory tower,[30] or as put by Arlene Tickner, "the primacy of lo práctico" was the mover.[31] We know from the William and Mary Teaching and Research in International Politics surveys that scholars are as interested in being involved in policy debates as in affecting the views of other scholars. The emphasis is on explanation and understanding rather than formulating laws or concern with building grand theories, as in all social sciences when first trying on clothes they are demanded by policy. The process demonstrates that IPE has lacked a sense of boundary maintenance though this diversity and ecumenism is not to be deplored.

The regional cloth as epistemic foundation

To take up inter-generational legacies, centre-periphery was a core concept in the understanding of the structure of the international political economy in Latin America. In his "manifest" – as Albert Hirshman called it[32] – "Latin-American development and its principal problems",[33] Prebisch contributed with an original analysis of the international system that would mark Latin American IPE and set the basis for the structuralist and developmentalist schools of thought that held enormous sway. The widely influential Economic Commission for Latin America and the Caribbean (ECLAC) articulated theories on centre-periphery showing how this structural dynamic was, to a great extent, detrimental. This was a pioneering vision proposed and projected by Latin America in the world, to the extent that it strongly influenced global policies such as special and differential treatment for developing countries in the General Agreement on Tariffs and Trade (GATT), the creation in the 1960s of the first regional development bank, the InterAmerican Development Bank (IADB) hand in hand with the Latin American Free Trade Association (LAFTA) and subsequently the United Nations Conference on Trade and Development (UNCTAD) in 1964.[34] As first Secretary General of UNCTAD, Prebisch was instrumental in uniting the developing countries and forming the Group of 77 (G77). He understood the need to boost exports and to remedy the unbalanced and iniquitous trade structure. In this way, Latin American structuralism, even though initially restricted to the region, was eventually extended to deal with the broad questions of insertion in the global economy. It is thus intimately related to the *problematique* of constrained autonomy or policy space. A major conceptual development concerning IPE as we understand it today was made by the dependency school. In their book *Dependencia y Desarrollo en América Latina*, Cardoso and Faletto[35] concentrated on the manner of integration of national economies in global markets, concluding how dependency is not simply external exploitation and coaction, but relies on intimate associations between the dominant local and external groups – which they called *elites*. In this sense, these authors highlighted the interconnection between internal and external factors and the nefarious role of international structural factors, first and foremost the US influence, the role of the international financial institutions, and the transnational presence of multinational corporations for development. Dependencia is "celebrated as the first genuine peripheral approach to development and international insertion".[36] This conceptual tool putting economic development at the forefront of international negotiations has been a fundamental pillar in Latin American IR and IPE as it considers development (or its lack) as the reflection of the international structure. North–South issues became a rallying point. There was a decided tension between the demands of development and democracy to the point of intellectual confrontation between "developmentists" drawing on insights from Prebisch and Furtado[37] and more "rupturist" *dependentistas* advocating for social revolution such as Ruy Mauro Marini,[38] Vania Bambirra,[39] Theotonio Dos Santos,[40] Andre Gunder Frank[41] and Samir Amin,[42] of the so-called "Marxist Dependency" school, rooted not only in socialist ideas but, also at times, in the Latin American heritage, ranging from Catholic intellectual traditions to the Mexican revolution. Marini, in particular, anticipated some of post-dependencia findings in proposing a more complex understanding of global structure that included intermediate powers such as Brazil and in capturing the beginning of the process of "internationalization" of domestic markets.[43] Notwithstanding the differences or precisely because of them, development became the object of a new problematization. Such issues were hardly matters of serious research in the IPE in the Anglosphere, which hived them off either to area or development studies.[44] Insertion and dependency extended to the realm of foreign policy and thus became related to the *problematique* of constrained autonomy[45] or in IPE parlance "policy space".[46] Talking to Economics naturally ready to abandon the idea of separate national economies and understand the world of negotiations was easier than to Political Science or International Relations, both infant disciplines at the time, both struggling to gain respect in the expanding university systems, the first one stressing methodological nationalism, the second one trying to extract the issue of defence and security from the realm of the military.

Today as university departments are more established and national science councils have stepped up funding IPE and International Relations are able to grant each other mutual acceptance and sit together more easily. Both share a growing recognition of agency and organizational power. The tendency to privilege structural factors over agency is not laid to rest but there is a fresh interest and growing research on agency, some of it propelled by the neo-Gramscian influence. This is demonstrated empirically through case material, whether it is on global financial markets or energy (see Sabbatella in this volume), international trade or the association of neoliberal polices and authoritarianism, all highlighting how politics lives in the economy and how the economy needs politics. The focus may be on the governed market to borrow from Robert Wade, the role of the state, or the contested interpretation of such structures.[47] Power and agency thus matter greatly. Some show the multiple layers of governance, global, inter-regional, regional, state and substate. There is more play given to regions, regional powers and regionalisms than the American-led order. The advent of the multiplex world order[48] is at least partly a result of the relative improvement in the economic conditions in the non-Western world. Some of these are directly associated with the so-called rising powers, a group spearheaded by the likes of China, India, Brazil, South Africa, etc. Some of these manifestations of agency – which have involved rejecting attempts by the major Western powers to create privileged space for their interests as well as collaborating with them to organize and manage global governance. In both directions they sketch patterns of agency such as cooperation, disputation, evasion and modification in the construction and the enactment of norms.

Taken together, IPE as an analytical field remains fundamentally based on a political reading of the international economy and the unearthing of its roots at the national level. It states that both levels are co-constitutive and that this process is not just "out there" as mere context. It has structural consequences, as it organizes internal relations in specific ways. Its proposed goal is to analyse the dual, opposing and simultaneous logic of economics and politics. Today IPE is a rapidly growing field, though far from representing a single intellectual tradition or a homogeneous school. The body of research is the result of a thematic convergence between several disciplines, Economics, Economic History, International Relations, Political Science and Sociology. What holds the field together are relatively simple conceptual devices, as outlined elsewhere:[49] (i) political and economic domains cannot be separated in any real sense, and even doing so for analytical purposes has its perils; ii) political interaction is one of the principal means through which markets are established and in turn transformed; and iii) there is an intimate connection between the domestic and international levels of analysis, and that the two cannot meaningfully be separated off from one another. These assumptions show a common denominator with the IPE in the Anglosphere, but also acknowledge its insufficiencies. The path to the common denominator may have started on theoretical grounds, or as a result of empirical enquiry or a combination of both. This has led to a considerable commitment to disciplinary ecumenism and an innovative willingness to draw insights from fields as diverse as the scholarly backgrounds of the IPE pioneers themselves. How much room exists in governance structures for policy space or political agency? Can cooperation happen? Are governments the helpless pawns of market forces? New "big" normative questions have arisen. The lines of analysis can be distinguished by the conception of the international order and the elements and main actors that the study assumes. They also focus on different levels of inquiry: the structure of the international system, the nature of government and competition within institutions, the role of interest groups and social forces. However, a key question unites them all: what is the actors' scope, and how can we explain their preferences, actions and consequences of these within the international political economy? By connecting these lines of research, we can see that the shared objective of the IPE is to understand both the construction of the international system and the foreign policy of each country, asking with each step "*Cui bono?*" Who benefits or could benefit from a certain situation? Who wins, who loses? How did we get to where we are? What policy space is there? Evident is the overarching concern for the impact of the global economy *on countries*.

And now what?

It is obviously the case that fields of social science including IPE, as well as their impact on reality, are bound to vary with the context.[50] Context sets the pace even if the academic incursion from the Anglosphere did not happen as intensely as in China. All the same the core matters of IPE have staged a break in. There has been a major boom in all things IPE ever since the end of the 1980s[51] with the scourge of the debt crisis, both in the public agenda and in academic studies. Immediately afterwards, structural adjustment, debt led trade liberalization,[52] the mushrooming of trade blocs showed how high the political stakes were. Latin American IPE then reacted focusing on "new" issues, while prompting renewed consideration of conceptual approaches as well. Promptly Latin American scholars tried to make sense of economic transformations under way and examined economic opening and burgeoning international alliances and commercial coalitions.[53]

It would be unfair to try and summarize these ideas too briefly. They can be expected and deserve to have a significant influence on the direction and course of much research and teaching over the next decade at least. An inherent uneasiness with the rules of the game as a given and a concern for reform is obvious. Studies of regionalism have thrived. Although the purpose of regionalism has shifted from period to period, the logic and methods of regional cooperation have demonstrated considerable continuity and it retains pride of place in the literature.[54] Region building is considered to have multiple payoffs insofar as it can deliver development space or accomplish full statehood. Regionalism has not only been important for accruing international legitimacy but also for bolstering the domestic agendas of governments. It is conceived as the bedrock of international insertion[55] either as an entry ticket into globalization or as the search for policy space.[56] While "insertion" is the path to overcome marginalization, regionalism has been the leading concept to deliver agency and enable recognition and participation. The concept of "international insertion" has become a focal point for the so-called "Brasilia school",[57] now distinguished from its early dependency robes.[58] For Alcides Vaz it accompanies the global projection undertaken by Lula's Brazil.[59] "Insertion" implies the enactment of domestic policies such as the adoption of neoliberalism *a outrance*, or opening policy spaces with Africa, Asia and very particularly China. As Latin America was swept off its feet into a world of criss-crossing permanent negotiations, scholars from all disciplines were shaken and opened their eyes to "the stuff of IPE". Economists, political scientists and sociologists had to subject their research agendas to the new world that was breaking into their protected nests and thus portion after portion of methodological nationalism were shed. For some this meant recovering and adapting old concepts out of a rich and long tradition of the radical Latin American critique of imperialism, neocolonialism; for others it meant building new, more pragmatic hybrids and taking charge of institutions long held to be foreign.[60] There are, indeed, people working both at the macro level where structure is of greater relevance, and there are others basing their work on the mezzo level research in which agency can be delivered. Instead of absolutist iron dilemmas framed as a choice between dependency and autonomy, a post-dependence mindset can be recognized. As we accept that agents can act and in fact do act agent-oriented narratives have emerged,[61] showing not only acceptance but construction, rejection, evasion, deflection, reconstitution and transformation of global and regional orders. IPE shows itself as an extremely diversified topic and as a topic that advances in the shape of a loose constellation. With legacies of the past reconfigured and rebranded, recent research has moved away from an essentializing view and focused on process as much as context. Different perspectives and scholars emphasize diverse aspects of the normative agenda, and much of the underlying debate is ultimately about priorities, not simply analysis and research tools. Advancing in minestrone fashion, the era of essentializing and of knowledge missionaries has long ended.

Sectors have begun to be unpacked, such as health,[62] infrastructure,[63] with an increasingly prominent role of civil society, social movements and networks of transnational cooperation.[64] The new Latin American IPE relies on hegemonic differentiation and competition among North America, Europe and Southeast Asia,[65] while at the same time witnessing the emergence of other powerful extraregional gravitational actors (China or Russia) as well as the leadership struggle between regional ones.[66] The Brazil, Russia, India, China and South Africa (BRICS) coalition and Chinese statecraft, with its accruing economic, commercial and investment penetration in the region in recent years,[67] are also accepted realities and central topics, along with the formation of megablocs[68] and the internationalization of "translatina" business-winning South American markets.[69] The effect of globalization on the reconfiguration of the state and on poverty, immigration and inequality are key issues in contemporary studies.[70] As with many questions in IPE, the normative content of these debates is important, indeed central.

Besides the unpacking of issues and experiences, Latin American IPE has continued to branch out and flourish loosely, unshackled from the cultural bedrock of the West, as a space to embrace insights, arguments and questions that are part of daily life and daily struggles such as the relation between society, ethnic communities, race, natural resources and nature as a whole. In this sense political economy and economic sociology are coming into closer interaction.[71] IPE – as all other Latin American social sciences – are witnessing the epistemological turn of the decolonial wave and have incorporated indigenous worldviews away from the white, European, dominant one inherited by colonialism.[72] The focal points of critique is the ideal of "modernity"[73] and the "coloniality of power" that together contributed to shape a Latin American society based on exploitation, racism and patriarchy.[74] Far from being only an academic debate, Native American cosmovisions were adopted by scholars, activists and politicians to the point that both Bolivia and Ecuador reformed their constitution following the precepts of Andean "Buen Vivir" (Sumak Kawsay) philosophy, a more balanced lifestyle with respect to "Mother Earth" (Pachamama).[75] Linked to the emergence of these alternative epistemologies is a reloaded awareness of "extractivism" such as mining, agribusiness and fracking. "Post-extractivist" or "post-developmental" perspectives argue that the world economy forces reprimarization, a return to complex rentier states and neglected asymmetries and inequalities.[76] These scholars have shown that export earnings have been able to finance poverty-reduction programmes, improve wages and expand social expenditures but inflicting serious damages to local communities, not least severe health problems. The control or lack thereof over natural resources requiring new thinking has grown very considerably in importance.

Beyond the search for conceptual devices that have contributed to field building, recent research is taking up theory testing in order to go global.[77] This entails attempting to falsify general claims against empirical evidence. The neopositivist approach rests on generating hypotheses and subsequently test if they can survive being applied to other contexts. The objective is then to discover systematic cross-case covariations. Much has been written about the neopositivist approach and the associated methods. We need not go further into this debate, but just to highlight neopositivist theory testing as the avenue in which younger scholars trained in the US are travelling. A neopositivist approach is most suitable for scholars with a commitment to the philosophical–ontological wagers of phenomenalism and mind–world dualism working with strict explanatory theories. Not everyone believes that theories are only strictly explanatory in the neopositivist sense. As Buzan notes

> Many Europeans use the term theory for anything that organizes a field systematically, structures questions and establishes a coherent and rigorous set of interrelated concepts and categories. Many Americans, however often demand that a theory strictly explains and that it contains – or is able to generate – testable hypotheses of a causal nature."[78]

The understanding of theory in the Latin America so far is closer to the European understanding than the American. Yet these more formal and quantitative rational choice contributions under the "open political economy" label represent a shift and overlap with the wider approach in the field. Together they show agency in a decentred world compounded by the absence of a singular and stable essential Latin Americanism and the presence of an inescapable plurality of values and multiplicity of alternative analytical perspectives. The value of this work is that it is starting new conversations, and building new authorities, concepts and theorizations that will become influential in their own right.

To close this section, one can see that IPE has somehow taken off. Scholars in fact define their own field through its openness to a variety of empirical problems, to a corresponding diversity of theoretical approaches, and finally to the discussions and debates coming from a variety of academic disciplines. Some prominent scholars aim to establish a Latin American school integrated into the global scholastic field and publishing networks in English. Others regard this as an unnecessary, even harmful exercise and insist on speaking and publishing in Spanish and Portuguese so that the field continues to be useful and to advance knowledge instead of getting lost in the fog of "normal science". Such divergences point to the existence of a vibrant community of scholars disagreeing on fundamental philosophical, theoretical and methodological issues.[79] As is true in many other communities of knowledge constituted by strong disagreements, their competing approaches play out in a finite space of attention and prominence where value is given to being part.

Prospects and options

The melancholy view of "a tale of lost vitality"[80] might have a kernel of truth so long as one does not worry about burying one's head in the sand and only looking inside. One can understand that it may be due to faculty factions or the political and economic structure of academic life in California and Cambridge. However, more humbly out, it is undignified to offend established sentiment or to argue *ad hominen* so will readily admit some of the points. One can fully agree with Palma's point that the founding fathers of dependencia abandoned academia when democratic transitions allowed taking up government posts. Their turn to politics emphasizes the social and political commitments that had driven them in the first place, the very real interest in reform. Yet life has gone on and the point today is to open the minds of those ploughing the field, studying, doing research and publishing in a variety of outlets – and not to pose hindrances to understanding or to close down minds. While the place of such distinguished "founding fathers" (very literally *fathers* rather than *parents*) of dependencia requires no further justification and is explainable with regard to disciplinary dynamics of repositioning of the older male generation, what matters much more for us is the cancelling out of the younger members of the scholarly community as active contributors.

Without throwing away the legacy, indeed even supporting its ongoing revaluation[81] and preserving the Olympus for them if need be, we need to move on and visibilize the various *milieux* in which scholars presently now work, without the funding or the infrastructure of the central committee that ECLAC had provided for such a long period of time. That the field is coalescing in a context of intense scholarly debate, some disputation as to what is the "right" mix between agency and structure, and with considerable input from other social science fields, particularly Sociology, is to be welcomed. Before outsiders jump in to reject this view and the prospects before it, we should remember the obvious: field building in across a wide continent with 20 countries can never be as compact or as homogenized as easily as the British school or the Canadian or French school.

Latin American IPE is introducing a variety of theoretical approaches, forms of argumentation, empirical data and consolidating today via debate and research on regionalism, global insertions, extractivism, international institutions, debt and new global–regional issues of development and action. The cognitive enterprise of the younger generations has moved away from the utopianism that reflected the ideal of a "national free will", an imagination of what the society could have been had it not been intercepted along the way. The community shares a sense of belonging, and organizes periodical regional conferences, many convened by FLACSO and intellectual and professional networks which is a key condition of field building and a precondition against parochialism. A lot of this owes its energy to the entrepreneurship of key individuals with haphazard access to funding. Institution-building lags behind. There is no single powerhouse playing the role of beacon and funder in the way that ECLAC did. Publishing outlets are few and far between. Some scholars go to International Relations journals, others to Political Science, Sociology or development journals such as *Problemas de Desarrollo*, *Desarrollo Economico* or *CEPAL Review*. With regards to the introduction of courses and programmes of study in IPE in the university system, there are scattered places where the field is taught now, moving from under the umbrella of the Economics faculty and becoming part of International Relations syllabuses.

Latin American IPE constitutes today a heterogeneous, pluralist and transdisciplinary field of research bound to different conversations and inquiries of development and conflict within the hemispheric and in the global order as a result of reciprocal interactions between economic and politics and the domestic and the international. In doing so, it represents the new and growing less-deterministic academic wave of the field. Nonetheless, a question remains: will it really coalesce into a field? This is difficult to foresee. Ironically, even as the "dialogue of the deaf" between disciplines seems to be overcome and a regional epistemic network takes shape led by a cluster of institutions, recognition is in its infancy. If IPE permeates approaches (to the extent of being almost a shared culture) institutionalization lags behind. Autonomization and legitimations happens differently in different academic *milieux*. The homegrown turn[82] in IPE adds an external driver paying attention to peripheral non-Western IR's position at a time of gradual post-Westernization, both in the world and within the discipline.[83] If there is an acceptance of the contingent and local value of knowledge it does not mean that we cannot do better.

How then does that leave our options? First of all, we posit that we need interconnected progress, simultaneously taking from each other and from the grand narrative of IPE that sits on a pedestal. That narrative was never complete so interconnections are needed both ways. Second, the global rise of China (as well as other "emerging" countries) and the steady coalescing of IPE inside Latin America, give cause to reevaluate the so-called "consensus" that since the era of dependencia the field has lost vitality. Consequently, recognizing the vastness of contemporary IPE studies in Latin America can help us understand the existence of *multiple versions* of IPE, and that there is something important to be gained from conscious bridge building across distinct national and cultural spheres of IPE. However, despite the difficulty in stating where IPE starts and where it ends, we would like to hold that IPE remains based on the premise that the dynamics of state and market are intertwined. Also, it bears the obligation of preserving the centrality of the research on power, development and conflict, and on the interactions and dynamics of the region–world order from different perspectives, at a time when formal IPE appears so limited in terms of framing research. In doing so, IPE in Latin America insofar as it can so easily tap into the very rich tradition of economic sociology might be able to liberate itself more easily from "the prison of political science"[84] and remain the space with open boundaries, where defying or refusing disciplinary boundaries is not only tolerated but encouraged.

Even if disciplinary change is under way, it seems highly unlikely that IPE will become more concentrated around a specific research programme placing a protective belt in Lakatos fashion within which progress (of the kind Cohen seems to think we need) can take place. The best way to proceed is with the politics of inclusion. As Leander has argued, Susan Strange's minestrone approach has become (one of the) central theoretical reference points in IPE. As we proceed to open our homes and invite our guests for dinner, incremental strategies aimed at adding new ingredients to Susan Strange's minestrone are rewarding and fruitful. The claim is not a drawback but an invitation. Please come in. The table is set. As cooks we take up the responsibility to make our meal fit for dinner.

Notes

1 This chapter owes a lot to discussions with colleagues at FLACSO and their gentle prodding but their hard questions that have pressed me to reflect on the journey and indeed the very existence of Latin American IPE. I am particularly grateful to the successive workshops and conferences at FLACSO, to Melisa Deciancio, Cintia Quiliconi, Pablo Nemiña, Juliana Peixoto, Pía Riggirozzi and Ernesto Vivares. We owe a very particular debt to Ralf Leiteritz and the generous colleagues he convened for kickstarting the process. Parts of this text reformulate the text to be published in Spanish in the handbook Leiteritz, Gabriel Jimenez Perez, Carolina Urrego Sandoval and Ninfa Fuentes Sosa are putting together. We thank Ernesto Vivares for the opportunity to continue reflecting and to come out in English. Neither our colleagues nor the readers may be fully satisfied with the text but it may help to sharpen further questions and continue the incremental process of field building.
2 With the assistance of Dario Clemente.
3 "International Relations" or "International Political Economy" (in capital letters) refer to the field not to the object of study such as "international political economy" (in lower case).
4 Jiménez-Peña, Leiteritz, Urrego, "Estado del arte de la Economía Política Internacional en Latinoamerica".
5 For a candid assessment from a leading political scientist of the want of analysis of the role of the market in the vast literature on transitions to democracy see Lechner, "El debate sobre Estado y Mercado".
6 Underhill, "State, market and global political economy: Geneology of an (inter-?) discipline".
7 Smith, *Talons of the eagle: Dynamics of US–Latin American relations*, 4.
8 Blyth, *Routledge handbook of international political economy (IPE): IPE as a global conversation.*
9 Palma, "Why did the Latin American critical tradition in the social sciences become practically extinct?"

10 Leander, "Do we really need reflexivity in IPE? Bourdieu's two reasons for answering affirmatively", 6.

11 Acharya and Buzan, "Conclusion: On the possibility of a non-Western IR theory in Asia".

12 Cohen, *International political economy: An intellectual history*.

13 Tickner, "Hearing Latin American voices in International Relations studies"; Tickner, "Seeing IR differently: notes from the Third World"; Tussie and Riggirozzi, "A global conversation: rethinking IPE in post-hegemonic scenarios"; Deciancio, "El regionalismo latinoamericano en la agenda de Relaciones Internacionales".

14 Deciancio, "La Economía Política Internacional en el campo de las Relaciones Internacionales argentinas".

15 Strange, "International economics and international relations".

16 Leander, "Theorising international monetary relations: Three questions about the significance of materiality".

17 Chagas-Bastos, "Recognition and status in World world Politicspolitics: A Southern southern Perspectiveperspective".

18 Centeno, *Blood and debt: War and the nation-state in Latin America*; Almeida, *Kemmerer en el Ecuador*.

19 Deciancio, "La Economía Política Internacional en el campo de las Relaciones Internacionales argentinas".

20 Helleiner and Rosales, "Toward global IPE: The overlooked significance of the Haya-Mariátegui debate".

21 Ianni, *Colapso do populismo no Brasil*; Di Tella, "Populism and reform in Latin America".

22 Diaz , "Open economy, closed polity?"

23 Borón, "Latin America between Hobbes and Friedman".

24 Dos Santos, "The structure of dependence"; Frank, "The development of underdevelopment"; Cardoso and Faletto, *Dependency and development in Latin America*.

25 Strange, *International monetary relations*.

26 Green, "Una respuesta tercermundista a la crisis de la economía mundial".

27 Edelman Spero, *Política económica internacional*; Gilpin, *La economía política de las relaciones internacionales*.

28 As late as 2007, scholars published in the long standing and respected *Revista Paraguaya de Sociología*.

29 Chin, Pearson and Yong, "Introduction: IPE with China's characteristics".

30 Deciancio, "La Economía Política Internacional en el campo de las Relaciones Internacionales argentinas".

31 Tickner, "Latin American IR and the primacy of lo práctico".

32 Hirschman, "The political economy of import-substituting industrialization in Latin America".

33 Prebisch, "The economic development of Latin America and its principal problems".

34 Margulis, *The global political economy of Raúl Prebisch*.

35 Cardoso and Faletto, *Dependency and development in Latin America*.

36 Tickner, "Hearing Latin American voices in International Relations studies", 327.

37 Furtado, *Desarrollo y subdesarrollo*.

38 Marini, *Subdesarrollo y revolución*.

39 Bambirra, *El capitalismo dependiente latinoamericano*.

40 Dos Santos, *El nuevo carácter de la dependencia: Gran empresa y capital extranjero*.

41 Frank, *Capitalism and underdevelopment in Latin America*.

42 Amin, *El desarrollo desigual*.

43 Clemente, "Los aportes de Ruy Mauro Marini a los estudios internacionales desde América Latina".

44 As an example of this other long standing mutual neglect, see Underhill's (2000) survey of IPE after Strange's manifesto. While development is hived off as a field in itself, IPE is about what the big powers do. Exceptions to this trend are included in this volume, Tim Shaw, Tony Anthony Payne, Eric Helleiner, most evidently.

45 Jaguaribe, "Autonomía periférica y hegemonía céntrica"; Puig, *Doctrinas Internacionales y Autonomía Latinoamericana*; Vigevani and Cepaluni, "Lula's foreign policy and the quest for autonomy through diversification".

46 Quiliconi and Tussie, "World Trade Organization and development".

47 Diniz, Boschi and Gaitán, "Elites estratégicas y cambio institucional: la construcción del proyecto post-neoliberal en Argentina y Brasil".

48 Acharya, "After liberal hegemony: The advent of a multiplex world order".

49 Tussie, *La genealogía de la economía política internacional: Rutas, debates, y desafíos en América Latina*.

50 For an approach that discusses thinkers' connection to concepts (in their local settings) see Cervo, "Conceitos em Relações Internacionais" and Cervo, "Conceptos en Relaciones Internacionales". His distinction between "thinkers of national expression", (national) "political and diplomatic thought" and the thought patterns of scholars working in academic and research centres is useful to the extent that it enables us to better comprehend intra-national differences among the local scholars in various national contexts.

51 Fajnzylber, *Industrialización en América Latina: de la caja negra" al" casillero vacío": comparación de patrones contemporáneos de industrialización.*

52 Tussie and Glover, *Developing countries in world trade: Policies and bargaining strategies.*

53 Lima, *The political economy of Brazilian foreign policy: Nuclear energy, trade and Itaipu.*

54 Petersen and Schulz, "Setting the regional agenda: A critique of posthegemonic regionalism".

55 Chagas-Bastos, "La invención de la inserción internacional: fundaciones intelectuales y evolución histórica del concepto".

56 Ferrer, *Hechos y ficciones de la globalización: Argentina Y El Mercosur en el sistema internacional*; Van Klaveren, "América Latina: hacia un regionalismo abierto".

57 Bernal Meza, *América Latina en el mundo: el pensamiento latinoamericano y la teoría de las Relaciones Internacionales.*

58 Cervo, "Eixos conceituais da política exterior do Brasil"; Lafer, *La Identidad internacional de Brasil.*

59 Vaz, "O Governo Lula: uma nova política exterior?"

60 Vivares, *El Banco Interamericano de Desarrollo en la década neoliberal*; Nemiña, "La relación entre el FMI y los gobiernos tomadores de crédito. El aporte de la EPI centrado en la incidencia de los intereses"; Riggirozzi, "The World Bank as conveyor and broker of knowledge and funds in Argentina's governance reforms".

61 Kingah and Quiliconi, *Global and regional leadership of BRICS countries*; Ramos and Scotelaro, "O estado da arte da Economia Política Internacional no Brasil: possibilidades para se pensar (e praticar) uma EPI a partir de baixo"; Fernández Alonso, "Diplomacia financiera en la periferia global: entre la cooperación y la coerción. Aproximaciones teórico-empíricas a partir de las relaciones crediticias de Argentina con Venezuela y China"; Pose , "Ideas y política exterior económica en el mundo en desarrollo. El caso de la salida de Uruguay de las negociaciones del TiSA".

62 Herrero, Loza and Belardo, "Collective health and regional integration in Latin America: An opportunity for building a new international health agenda".

63 Antúnes, *Infra-estrutura na América do Sul: Situaçao atual, necessidades e complementaridades possíveis com o Brasil.*

64 Riggirozzi and Tussie, *The rise of post-hegemonic regionalism.*

65 Estay and Sánchez, "Una revisión general del ALCA y sus implicaciones"; Riggirozzi, " 'Regionalism through social policy: collective action and health diplomacy in South America'; Sanahuja, "La construcción de una región: Suramérica y el regionalismo posliberal".

66 Clemente, *El regionalismo post-hegemónico en perspectiva crítica: una mirada neogramsciana. Brasil, Venezuela y la opción contra-hegemónica.*

67 Tussie, "Set to shake up global economic governance: Can the BRICS be dismissed?"; Vadell, "Las implicaciones políticas de la relación China-América Latina: el Consenso Asiático como red de poder global y el caso brasileño"; Ramos, "Potências médias emergentes e reforma da arquitetura financeira mundial?: Uma análise do BRICS no G20"; Slipak, "América Latina y China: ¿Cooperación Sur-Sur o 'Consenso de Beijing' "; Urdinez, Mouron, Schenoni and De Oliveira, "Chinese economic statecraft and U.S. hegemony in Latin America: An empirical analysis, 2003–2014"; Quiliconi and Peixoto, *Los desafíos del crecimiento sustentable con inclusión en América Latina.*

68 Katz, "El abismo entre las ilusiones y los efectos del ALCA".

69 Trucco, *Socios en la integración productiva. La estrategia asociativa de las empresas en el Mercosur;* Tussie, "Shaping the world beyond the 'core': States and markets in Brazil's global ascent"; Casanova, "La inversión extranjera directa en América Latina y las multinacionales emergentes latinoamericanas".

70 Trucco and Tussie, *Nación y región en América del Sur. Los actores nacionales y la economía política de la integración sudamericana.*

71 Nemiña, "Acción económica e incertidumbre: el aporte de Jens Beckert a la sociología económica".

72 Quijano, *La crisis del horizonte de sentido colonial/moderno/eurocentrado*; Mignolo, *La idea de América Latina*; Vivares, Lombardo, Torres and Cvetich, "Enfoques y cárceles conceptuales en el entendimiento de los nuevos regionalismos latinoamericanos".

73 Escobar, *Encountering development: The making and unmaking of the Third World*; Mignolo, *Histórias locais / Projetos globais: colonialidade, saberes subalternos e pensamento liminar*.
74 Garcia, Mendonça and Borba, "International political economy in Latin America: Redefining the periphery".
75 Vivares and Dolcetti-Marcolini, "Two regionalisms, two Latin Americas or beyond Latin America? Contributions from a critical and decolonial IPE".
76 Svampa, "Consenso de los commodities y lenguajes de valoración en América Latina"; Gudynas, "Diez tesis urgentes sobre el nuevo extractivismo"; Acosta, *El Buen Vivir Sumak Kawsay, una oportunidad para imaginar otros mundos*; Delgado, "Sociedades posneoliberales en América Latina y persistencia del extractivismo".
77 Urdinez, Mouron, Schenoni and De Oliveira, "Chinese economic statecraft and U.S. hegemony in Latin America: An empirical analysis, 2003–2014".
78 Buzan, *From international to world society?: English school theory and the social structure of globalisation*, 24.
79 See for example the discussion in the closing panel of the 2017 FLACSO conference on the governance of research and whether Spanish should be abandoned in favour of publishing in English.
80 Palma, "Why did the Latin American critical tradition in the social sciences become practically extinct?"; Cohen, *International political economy: An intellectual history*.
81 Loza, "Stavenhagen and the nation: Ethnicity, community, and political project"; Katz, *La teoría de la dependencia, cincuenta años después*.
82 Kuru, "Homegrown theorizing: Knowledge, scholars, theory".
83 Acharya, "Global International Relations (IR) and regional worlds: A new agenda for International Studies".
84 Rosenberg, "International Relations in the prison of political science".

Bibliography

Acharya, A. 2014. Global International Relations (IR) and regional worlds: A new agenda for International Studies. *International Studies Quarterly* 58, no 4: 647–659.
Acharya, A. 2017. After liberal hegemony: The advent of a multiplex world order. *Ethics & International Affairs* 31, no 3: 271–285.
Acharya, A. and Buzan, B. 2007. Conclusion: On the possibility of a non-Western IR theory in Asia. *International Relations of the Asia-Pacific* 7, no 3: 427–438.
Acosta, A. 2013. *El Buen Vivir Sumak Kawsay, una oportunidad para imaginar otros mundos*. Barcelona: ICARIA.
Almeida, R. 1994. *Kemmerer en el Ecuador*. Quito: FLACSO.
Amin, S. 1975. *El desarrollo desigual*. Barcelona: Fontanella.
Antúnes, A. 2007. *Infra-estrutura na América do Sul: Situaçao atual, necessidades e complementaridades possíveis com o Brasil*. Santiago de Chile: Naciones Unidas Comisión Económica para América Latina y el Caribe (CEPAL).
Bambirra, V. 1974. *El capitalismo dependiente latinoamericano*. México: Siglo XXI.
Bernal Meza, R. 2005. *América Latina en el mundo: el pensamiento latinoamericano y la teoría de las Relaciones Internacionales*. Buenos Aires: Grupo Editor Latinoamericano.
Blyth, M. 2009. *Routledge handbook of International Political Economy (IPE): IPE as a global conversation*. Oxford: Routledge.
Borón, A. 1981. Latin America: Between Hobbes and Friedman. *New Left Review* 130 (November/December).
Buzan, B. 2004. *From international to world society?: English school theory and the social structure of globalization*. Cambridge, UK: Cambridge University Press.
Cardoso, F. and Faletto, E. n/d. *Dependency and development in Latin America*, México: Siglo XXI.
Casanova, L. 2010. La inversión extranjera directa en América Latina y las multinacionales emergentes latinoamericanas. *Boletín Elcano* 128, no 7.
Centeno, M. 2002. *Blood and debt: War and the nation-state in Latin America*. Philadelphia, PA: Penn State Press.
Cervo, A. 1998. Eixos concetuais da política exterior do Brasil. *Revista Brasileña de Política Internacional* 41: 66–84.
Cervo, A. 2008. Conceitos em Relações Internacionais. *Revista Brasileira de Política Internacional*, no 51: 8–25.

Cervo, A. 2013. Conceptos en Relaciones Internacionales. *Relaciones Internacionales*, no 22: 149–66.

Chagas-Bastos, F. 2017. Recognition and status in world politics: A southern perspective. *SSRN Electronic Journal*.

Chagas, F. 2018. La invención de la inserción internacional: fundaciones intelectuales y evolución histórica del concepto. *Análisis Político* 31, no 94: 10–30.

Chin, G., Pearson, M. and Yong, W. 2013. Introduction: IPE with Chinese characteristics. *Review of International Political Economy* 20, no 6: 1145–1164.

Clemente, D. 2017. *El regionalismo post-hegemónico en perspectiva crítica: una mirada neogramsciana. Brasil, Venezuela y la opción contra-hegemónica*. Mexico: Observatorio Latinoamericano y Caribeño.

Clemente, D. 2018. Los aportes de Ruy Mauro Marini a los estudios internacionales desde América Latina. *Análisis Político* 31, no 94: 75–92.

Cohen, B. 2004. *International political economy: An intellectual history*. Princeton, NJ and Oxford: Princeton University Press.

Cohen, B. 2008. *International political economy: An intellectual history*. Princeton, NJ: Princeton University Press.

Deciancio, M. 2016. El regionalismo latinoamericano en la agenda de Relaciones Internacionales. *Revista Iberoamericana* 16, no 63: 93–110.

Deciancio, M. 2018. La Economía Política Internacional en el campo de las Relaciones Internacionales argentinas. *Desafíos* 30, no 2: 15–42.

Delgado, J. 2016. Sociedades posneoliberales en América Latina y persistencia del extractivismo. *Economía Informa*, no 396: 84–95.

Di Tella, T. n/d. Populism and reform in Latin America. In: Veliz, C. (ed.). *Obstacles to change in Latin America*. Oxford: Oxford University.

Diaz, C. 1981. Open economy, closed polity? In: Tussie, D. (ed.), *Latin America in the World Economy: New Perspectives*. Aldershot: Gower.

Diniz, E., Boschi, R. and Gaitán, F. 2012. Elites estratégicas y cambio institucional: la construcción del proyecto post-neoliberal en Argentina y Brasil. *Revista de Estudos e Pesquisas sobre as Américas* 6, no 2: 14–53.

Dos Santos, T. 1967. *El nuevo carácter de la dependencia: Gran empresa y capital extranjero*. Santiago de Chile: Cuadernos del Centro de Estudios Socio- económicos, Universidad de Chile.

Dos Santos, T. 1971. The structure of dependence. In: Frann, K. T. and Hodges, D. C. (eds), *Readings in U.S. Imperialism*. Boston: Porter Sargent: 226.

Edelman Spero, Joan. 1977. *Política económica internacional*. Buenos Aires: El Ateneo.

Escobar, A. 1995. *Encountering development: The making and unmaking of the Third World*. Princeton, NJ: Princeton University Press.

Estay, J. and Sánchez, G. 2005. Una revisión general del ALCA y sus implicaciones. In: *El ALCA y sus peligros para América Latina*, 17–106. Buenos Aires: CLACSO.

Fajnzylber, F. 1990. *Industrialización en América Latina: de la caja negra" al" casillero vacío": comparación de patrones contemporáneos de industrialización*. Santiago de Chile: CEPAL.

Fernández Alonso, J. 2018. Diplomacia financiera en la periferia global: entre la cooperación y la coerción. Aproximaciones teórico-empíricas a partir de las relaciones crediticias de Argentina con Venezuela y China. *Desafíos* 30, no 2: 43.

Ferrer, A. 1997. *Hechos y ficciones de la globalización: Argentina Y El Mercosur en el sistema internacional*. Buenos Aires: Fondo de Cultura Económica.

Frank, A. 1966. The development of underdevelopment. *Monthly Review* 18, no 4: 17–31

Frank, A. 1967. *Capitalism and underdevelopment in Latin America*. New York: NYU Press.

Furtado, C. 1964. *Desarrollo y subdesarrollo*. Buenos Aires: EUDEBA.

Garcia, A., Mendonça, M. and Borba, M. 2016. International political economy in Latin America: Redefining the periphery. In: *The Palgrave handbook of critical international political economy*: 431–452. London: Palgrave Macmillan.

Gilpin, R. 1990. *La economía política de las relaciones internacionales*. Buenos Aires: Grupo Editor Latinoamericano.

Green, R. 1976. Una respuesta tercermundista a la crisis de la economía mundial. *Revista Mexicana de Sociología* 38, no. 4: 767–781.

Gudynas, E. 2012. Diez tesis urgentes sobre el nuevo extractivismo. Contextos y demandas bajo el progresismo actual. Centro Andino de Educación Popular (ed.). Quito: CAAP y CLAES. In: *Extractivismo, política y sociedad*, 187–225. Quito: CAAP y CLAES.

Helleiner, E, and Rosales, A. 2017. Toward global IPE: The overlooked significance of the Haya-Mariátegui debate. *International Studies Review* 19, no 4: 667–691.

Herrero, M., Loza, J. and Belardo, M. 2019. Collective health and regional integration in Latin America: An opportunity for building a new international health agenda. *Global Public Health*, 14, no. 6–7: 1–12.

Hirschman, A. 1968. The political economy of import-substituting industrialization in Latin America. *The Quarterly Journal of Economics* 82, no 1: 1–32.

Ianni, O. 1968. *Colapso do populismo no Brasil. Civilizacao Brasileira.* Rio de Janeiro.

Jaguaribe, H. 1979. Autonomía periférica y hegemonía céntrica. *Estudios Internacionales* 12, no. 46: 91–130.

Jiménez, G., Leiteritz, R. and Urrego, C. 2018. Estado del arte de la Economia Politica Internacional en Latinoamerica. *Revista Desafíos* 30, no 2: 9–11.

Katz, C. 2001. El abismo entre las ilusiones y los efectos del ALCA. *Nueva Sociedad*, no 174.

Katz, C. 2018. *La teoría de la dependencia, cincuenta años después. Batalla de ideas.* Buenos Aires: Batella de Ideas.

Kingah, S. and Quiliconi, C. 2016. *Global and regional leadership of BRICS countries.* Cham, Switzerland: Springer.

Kuru, D. 2017. Homegrown theorizing: Knowledge, scholars, theory. *All Azimuth: A Journal of Foreign Policy and Peace* 7, no 1: 69–86.

Lafer, C. 2003. *La identidad internacional de Brasil.* Buenos Aires: Fondo de Cultura Económica.

Leander, A. 2002. Do we really need reflexivity in IPE? Bourdieu's two reasons for answering affirmatively. *Review of International Political Economy* 9, no 4: 601–609.

Leander, A. 2015. Theorizing international monetary relations: Three questions about the significance of materiality. *Contexto Internacional* 37, no 3: 945–973.

Lechner, N. 1992. *El debate sobre Estado y Mercado.* Santiago de Chile: FLACSO.

Lima, M. 2013. *The political economy of Brazilian Foreign policy: Nuclear energy, trade and Itaipu.* Brasília: FUNAG.

Loza, J. 2018. Stavenhagen and the nation: Ethnicity, community, and political project. *Latin American Perspectives* 45, no 2: 95–106.

Margulis, M. 2017. *The global political economy of Raúl Prebisch.* Oxford: Taylor & Francis.

Marini, R. 1969. *Subdesarrollo y revolución.* México: Siglo XXI Editores.

Mignolo, W. 2003. *Histórias locais/Projetos globais: Colonialidade, saberes subalternos e pensamento liminar.* Humanitas: Belo Horizonte.

Mignolo, W. 2007. *La idea de América Latina,* Barcelona: Gedisa.

Nemiña, P. 2015. Acción económica e incertidumbre: el aporte de Jens Beckert a la sociología económica. *Equidad & Desarrollo*, no 23: 9–33.

Nemiña, P. 2019. La relación entre el FMI y los gobiernos tomadores de crédito. El aporte de la EPI centrado en la incidencia de los intereses. *Desafíos*, 31, no 2: 341–373.

Palma, J. 2009. Why did the Latin American critical tradition in the social sciences become practically extinct? In: Blythe, M. (ed.). *The handbook of International Political Economy*: 243–265. London: Routledge.

Petersen, M. and Schulz, C. 2018. Setting the regional agenda: A critique of posthegemonic regionalism. *Latin American Politics and Society* 60, no 1: 102–127.

Pose, N. 2018. Ideas y política exterior económica en el mundo en desarrollo. El caso de la salida de Uruguay de las negociaciones del TiSA. *Desafíos* 30, no 2: 89.

Prebisch, R. 1950. The economic development of Latin America and its principal problems. Available at: https://repositorio.cepal.org/handle/11362/29973.

Puig, J. 1980. *Doctrinas internacionales y autonomía Latinoamericana.* Caracas: Instituto de Altos Estudios de América Latina Universidad Simón Bolívar.

Quijano, A. 2010. *La crisis del horizonte de sentido colonial/moderno/eurocentrado.* Havana: Casa de las Américas.

Quiliconi, C. and Peixoto, J., ed. 2014. *Los desafíos del crecimiento sustentable con inclusión en América Latina.* Buenos Aires: Teseo.

Quiliconi, C. and Tussie, D. 2013. World Trade Organization and development. In: Currie-Alder, B., Kanbur, R., Malone, D. M. and Medhora, R. (eds). *International Development Ideas, Experience, and Prospects.* Oxford: Oxford University Press.

Ramos, L. 2014. Potências médias emergentes e reforma da arquitetura financeira mundial?: Uma análise do BRICS no G20. *Revista de Sociologia e Política* 22, no 50: 49–65.

Ramos, L. and Scotelaro, M. 2018. O estado da arte da Economia Política Internacional no Brasil: possibilidades para se pensar (e praticar) uma EPI a partir de baixo. *Desafíos* 30, no 2: 127.

Riggirozzi, P. 2006. The World Bank as conveyor and broker of knowledge and funds in Argentina's governance reforms. In: Stone, D. and Wright, C. (eds). *The World Bank and governance: A decade of reform and reaction.* Abingdon: Routledge.

Riggirozzi, P. 2014. Regionalism through social policy: Collective action and health diplomacy in South America. *Economy and Society* 43, no 3: 432–454.

Riggirozzi, P. and Tussie, D. 2012. *The rise of post-hegemonic regionalism.* Dordrecht: Springer.

Rosenberg, J. n/d. International relations in the prison of political science. *International Relations*, 30, no. 2: 127–153.

Slipak, A. 2014. América Latina y China: ¿Cooperación Sur-Sur o 'Consenso de Beijing. *Nueva Sociedad*, 4, no 250: 103–13.

Smith, P. 2000. *Talons of the eagle: Dynamics of US-Latin American relations.* Oxford: Oxford University Press.

Strange, S. 1970. International economics and international relations: A case of mutual neglect. *International Affairs* 46, no 2: 304–315.

Strange, S. 1976. *International monetary relations of the Western world.* Oxford: Oxford University Press.

Svampa, M. 2013. Consenso de los commodities y lenguajes de valoración en América Latina. *Revista Nueva Sociedad*, 244, no. 4: 30–46.

Tickner, A. 2003. Hearing Latin American voices in International Relations studies. *International Studies Perspectives* 4, no 4: 325–350.

Tickner, A. 2008. Latin American IR and the primacy of lo práctico. *International Studies Review* 10, no 4: 735–748.

Trucco, P. 2016. *Socios en la integración productiva. La estrategia asociativa de las empresas en el Mercosur.* Buenos Aires, Argentina: FLACSO.

Trucco, P. and Tussie, D. (eds) 2010. *Nación y región en América del Sur. Los actores nacionales y la economía política de la integración sudamericana.* Buenos Aires: Teseo.

Tussie, D. 2016. Shaping the world beyond the "core": States and markets in Brazil's global ascent. In: Germain, D. (ed.). *Susan Strange and the Future of Global Political Economy*, 73–86. New York and Abingdon: Routledge.

Tussie, D. 2018. Set to shake up global economic governance: Can the BRICS be dismissed? *Global Governance: A Review of Multilateralism and International Organizations* 24, no 3: 321–330.

Tussie, D. 2020. La genealogía de la economía política internacional: Rutas, debates, y desafíos en América Latina. In: Urrego, C., Leiteritz, R., Jimenez, G. and Fuentes, N (ed.). *Economía Política Internacional en America Latina: Teoria y Practica.* Mexico: CIDE.

Tussie, D. and Glover, D. n/d. *Developing countries in world trade: Policies and bargaining strategies.* Ottawa, ON: IDRC.

Tussie, D. and Riggirozzi, P. 2015. A global conversation: Rethinking IPE in post-hegemonic scenarios. *Contexto Internacional* 37, no 3: 1041–1068.

Underhill, G. 2000. State, market and global political economy: Geneology of an (inter-?) discipline. *International Affairs* 76, no 4: 805–824.

Urdinez, F., Mouron, F., Schenoni, L. and De Oliveira, A. J. N. 2016. Chinese economic statecraft and U.S. hegemony in Latin America: An empirical analysis, 2003–2014. *Latin American Politics and Society* 58, no 4: 3–30.

Vadell, J. 2014. Las implicaciones políticas de la relación China-América Latina: el Consenso Asiático como red de poder global y el caso brasileño. *Comentario Internacional. Revista del Centro Andino de Estudios Internacionales*, no 1. 4, 135–161.

Van Klaveren, A. 1997. América Latina: hacia un regionalismo abierto. *Estudios Internacionales*, 30, no. 117: 62–78.

Vaz, A. 2006. O Governo Lula: uma nova política exterior? In: *O Brasil e a conjuntura Internacional–Paz e Segurança Internacional*, 85–96. Rio de Janeiro: Gramma: Fundação Konrad Adenauer.

Vigevani, T. and Cepaluni, G. 2017. Lula's foreign policy and the quest for autonomy through diversification. *Third World Quarterly* 28, no 7: 1309–1326.

Vivares, E. 2013. *El Banco Interamericano de Desarrollo en la década neoliberal.* Quito: FLACSO.

Vivares, E. and Dolcetti-Marcolini, M. 2016. Two regionalisms, two Latin Americas or beyond Latin America? Contributions from a critical and decolonial IPE. *Third World Quarterly* 37, no 5: 866–882.

Vivares, E., Lombardo, K., Torres, P. and Cvetich. 2014. Enfoques y cárceles conceptuales en el entendimiento de los nuevos regionalismos latinoamericanos. In: Alvarez, I. and Bonilla, A. (eds). *Desafíos estratégicos del regionalismo contemporáneo*, San José: FLACSO.

7

The international political economy of Africa in theory and practice

Timothy Shaw

Introduction

This contribution suggests that the quarter of the world's states that are African can yet contribute to international political economy (IPE) theory and practice (Shaw *et al.* 2019) as the North enters a period of ambivalence about, if not retreat from, positive global engagement. Each actor based in or concerned about the continent, state and non-state alike, advances a 'foreign policy' to reflect its interests, often in coalition with others. This entry builds on the contributions of Pieterse (2011) on East–South relations and Stuenkel (2015, 2016) on a non-Western world, also using current collections on South–South Cooperation (SSC) by Gu *et al.* (2016) on The BRICS in International Development and van der Merwe et al. (2016) on the Emerging Powers in Africa.

The diversion away from international order and peace of the US under Trump, the UK under May, and the European Union (EU) and Europe, the latter characterised by unanticipated immigration and endless eurozone crises, can be positive for 'African' agency and development; i.e. if the continent can seize the unprecedented space to advance its own 'developmental' states and regionalisms. Such possibilities of Africa's enhanced prospects are situated in terms of a changing global political economy in which 'new' economies (Noman and Stiglitz 2015), companies and technologies (Kabandula and Shaw 2016, 2019) are 'emerging' along with, contrary, non-traditional security threats. In response, novel forms of transnational 'network' governance are being conceived and charted (Roger and Dauvergne 2016) to advance sustainable developmental states and regionalisms through innovative 'foreign policy' stances outside established, but increasingly dysfunctional and ossified, interstate institutions.

The South has risen at an unprecedented speed and scale. By 2050, Brazil, China and India combined are projected to account for 40 per cent of world output in purchasing power parity terms. The changing global political economy is creating unprecedented challenges and opportunities for continued progress in human development. (UNDP 2013: 1–2).

Africa's economic growth remained resilient in 2015 amid a weak global economy, lower commodity prices and adverse weather conditions in some parts of the continent. Real GDP grew by an average of 3.6 per cent in 2015. Africa remained the second-fastest growing economy in the world (after emerging Asia) (OECD 2016).

Ironically, as many in International Relations (IR) and IPE seek to make their field more 'global' (Bergamaschi et al. 2017), two leading established and historically 'liberal' Western governments – US and UK – plus many 'alt' right parties and movements in the EU and the rest of Europe, seek to limit even reverse 'globalisation'; an unanticipated divergence as 'global IR' has become accepted and celebrated in Africa as elsewhere (Bichoff *et al.* 2016). And African contributions to the globalisation of IR and IPE come from its own cities, civil societies, companies, medias, middle classes, supply chains, technologies, think-tanks and universities, not just foreign ministries or president's offices, as corollaries of 'emerging' classes and markets powers and states, and even universities.

So African IR and IPE theory and policy go beyond traditional 'Northern' perspectives like realism and constructivism to issues, factors and frameworks that reflect the continent's own experiences of and responses to 'global' IR; for example, transnational conflict, culture, ecology, regulation, religion and technology (Cornelissen *et al.* 2015; Dunn and Shaw 2013; Warner and Shaw 2018). When African foreign policy was first defined and articulated between the recapture of autonomy by Ethiopia at the end of the Second World War and the formal declaration of independence for Ghana, it was preoccupied by the assertions and formalities of 'sovereignty'. By the middle of the second decade of the twenty-first century it had become all too conscious of the multiplicity of 'global' issues and the modesty of its ability to respond to, let alone impact or determine international affairs, despite enhanced prospects for 'African agency' (Shaw 2015). And clearly many African states have less foreign policy leverage than its 'non-states', like its ubiquitous diasporas both on (e.g. Zimbabweans) and off (e.g. Ethiopians and Somalis) the continent; e.g. digital communications like DStv and MTN, franchises like Nandos or Protea (now Marriott), Intergovernmental Organisations (INGOs) and think tanks like Institute for Peace and Security Studies (IPSS), multinationals like Dangote or De Beers, M-Pesa mobile finance, Nollywood, Pentecostal churches and preachers, Star Alliance airline hubs like Egyptair, Ethiopian and SAA.

The contrast between the external and other policies of developmental and fragile states is instructive: state policies of the former are more authoritative than the latter, in which non-state transnational relations thrive; cf. the foreign policy of Mauritius (Tang *et al.* 2019) versus Somalia or Democratic Republic of Congo (DRC). In the latter, the transnational, cross-border connections of non-state, even informal or illegal, actors may take precedence; e.g. the essential, continuous flow of remittances to Somalia and the myriad impacts of Somali pirates offshore and Al-Shabab in the Horn.

And, for an example of exponential divergence, contrast Europe and Africa at the end of the decade as the EU)and African, Caribbean and Pacific (ACP) group of states anticipate hard negotiations on a post-Cotonou world from 2020 onwards (Montoute 2019, Montoute and Virk 2017). Europe and the EU in 2018 to 2020 will confront an unexpected trio of challenges impacting any prospect of further 'developmental regionalism' (DR) – or collective external connections – in the Southern African Development Community (SADC) and elsewhere on the continent (Adejumobi and Kreiter 2016), both for the EU's continuing 27 members but also for its established networks in the Global South (Thiel et al. 2019):

a   the relentless crises of the Eurozone PIIGS (Portugal, Ireland, Italy, Greece and Spain) especially Greece and Italy (and briefly Iceland as another I);

b   the unanticipated waves of migrants – immediate aspects of 'new' 'non-traditional security issues' (NTS) exacerbated by transnational organised crime (TOC) and mafias – now combined with;

c   the British vote to leave the Union early in 2019, compounded by the continuing negative fall-out from the failed coup in Turkey: in NATO but not the EU. Onto a fraught if not failed Brexit in early 2019.

This contribution argues that the diversion of the US, UK and the EU away from 'global development' towards their own 'internal' difficulties may be positive for Africa, giving it unprecedented space to advance its own 'developmental regionalism' (DR) (Shaw 2016). 'African agency' (Shaw 2015) may yet be able to advance sustainable development and global goals in part through DR. Thus, in the middle of 2016, East Africa declined to sign an Economic Partnership Agreement (EPA) with the EU but the Tripartite Free Trade Agreement (TFTA) also remains unimplemented, with implications for the possibility of an effective Canadian Free Trade Agreement (CFTA) (Luke and Macloed 2019). And over the next five years, Eastern Africa will be pumping oil and gas from South Sudan, Northern Kenya and Uganda to northern Mozambique.

The articulation and advocacy of DR for SADC by Adejumobi and Krieter (2016) are timely as a form of regional external relations as EU formulations or 'models' are losing their salience compared to their leverage a decade or more ago, perhaps less in terms of security but more in terms of economics. Their formulation of a post-neoliberal 'new' regionalism is especially welcome as a) they encourage non-state actors like civil society, from local to global, and always transnational, as drivers (Montoute 2019; b) they recognise peace and security to be essential for sustainable regional development; and c) they advance 'common regional citizenship and identity' to sustain such DR (2016: 11, 16–17). Indeed, their rejection of xenophobia in Southern Africa resonates with fears of similar exclusive nationalisms in today's Europe, both inside and outside the EU, let alone Trump's America and his Islamophobic Executive Orders. However, the EU continues to advance an African Peace and Security Architecture (APSA) (Kabandula and Shaw 2016), increasingly as part of its fear of migrants and radical jihadist youth; i.e. NTS.

Africa and 'global IR' and global governance

As a contribution to comparative as well as African IR and IPE, this chapter seeks to juxtapose notions of interstate foreign relations with emerging debates around the 'sharing' or 'gig' economy: 'the internet of things' (IoT), especially the work of Manuel Castells on 'information'[1] and Clayton Christensen on 'disruption'.[2] The former has recently produced an edited collection on *Reconceptualizing Development in the Global Information Age* (Castells and Himanen 2014). And the latter has been chided by *The Economist* (2015b) for trying to monopolise the notion of 'disruption' by limiting it to low-end newcomers when it may have become more widespread than Christensen originally conceived two decades ago; hence the non-state, transnational Functional Annotations of Animal Genomes (FAANG) acronym superceding BRICS as the icon for growth, at least until 2019. Think of the threat that Google poses to carmakers, Facebook to newspapers and Apple to television stations. Back in 1995, Mr Christensen struck fear into executives by warning them that they could be put out of their jobs by companies they had never heard of. Today the biggest threats may come from people that talk about them every day.

Such disruption raises the question of whether 'African agency' (Brown and Harman 2013) may be a fleeting or sustainable phenomenon, compatible with a variety of active African schemes. So is the United Nations Economic Commission for Africa (UNECA) (2011/2012) advocacy of 'developmental state' aspirations a pipe dream? Can earlier preoccupations of the EU facilitate developmental inter-regionalism in Africa? Can the continent refocus on realising

Sustainable Development Goals (SDGs) after its disappointments with the Millennium Development Goals (MDGs)? (Kararach, Besada and Shaw 2015). And are 'fragile states'[3] or 'ungoverned spaces' readily separable from others as myriad, dynamic mobile communications enable the diaspora to connect and remit 24/7? (Laakso and Hautaniemi 2014).

In short, Africa presents some interesting cases of IT innovation,[4] particularly from the repair of second-hand Japanese cars and trucks, especially mini buses, to proliferating uses, legal and otherwise, of cellphones. Especially given distances on the continent, sensors on cars and trucks for tyre or oil pressures as well as for more secure logistics for supply chains are invaluable; similarly, biochip transponders on or blockchain monitoring of wild or domestic animals or monitors on pipelines and communication towers. If DR can advance such IoT, then it is likely to be adopted, despite the decline of the EU (see IDS 2016 on ten frontier technologies). Ubiquitous transnational African global networks would thereby be reinforced.

Today, a quarter-century after the end of the Cold War, transnational cross-border connections are increasingly non- or extra-state, from Africa Progress Panel[5] to West African Commission on Drugs[6] through Kofi Annan[7] and Mo Ibrahim Foundations[8], all contribute to African 'foreign policy'.

Similarly, peoples, goods and ideas, legal, legitimate or otherwise, flow across borders with minimal regulation as indicated by: the ebola virus 'crisis' 2014 to 2015; the regular delivery of 'ghat' to Somali communities (at least the men) around the Horn; the cross-border networking of Islamic fundamentalists connected to IS, Boko Haram and Al-Shabab, especially in West and East (e.g. US Embassy bombing and Westgate Mall attack etc. in Nairobi) Africa; inter- and intra-religious tensions between, say, Sunni and Shiite, orthodox Christians like Anglicans and Catholics, as well as heterogeneous Coptic and Orthodox churches and the 'born-again' as the latter, Pentecostals, proliferate throughout the Global South, especially Latin America and Africa; i.e. how compatible and cumulative are its foreign relations?

Meanwhile the notion of a 'global' IR and IPE (a more globalised, inclusive analysis and practice of 'International Relations' and IPE) is beginning to gain traction, with implications for the character of South–South relations (Bergamaschi et al. 2017 and van der Merwe et al. 2016). It was initially advocated by Tickner and Waever (2009) and was then espoused by the leading IR professional association, the International Studies Association (ISA)[9] as its theme for its February 2015 annual conference – 'Global IR and Regional Worlds: A New Agenda for International Studies'. I was pleased that my two coedited collections on African IR went into revised paperback editions mid-decade (Cornelissen et al. 2015; Dunn and Shaw 2013), reflective of the growing recognition of African and other contributions to 'global IR'.

Prospects for regional development: African human development and security post-2015

Advancing analysis of the prospects for a heterogeneous foreign policy – human development and rights and security on the continent – means to build on the increasingly familiar and compatible concepts (Roger and Dauvergne 2016) of 'the transnational' (Hale and Held 2012; Mukherjee-Reed et al. 2012) and 'global governance' (Harman and Williams 2013; Weiss and Wilkinson 2014a, 2014b) as together they advance analysis of transnational African relations and regulation symbolised by the Kimberley Process (KP) and Extractive Industries Transparency Initiative (EITI) (c.f. Bernstein 2011 on another KP – Kyoto Protocol – and Isealalliance), and now the Africa Progress Panel (APP).[10]

My own perspective on contemporary transnational relations on the continent was informed by being a graduate student at Makerere in the late 1960s with Ali Mazrui (Shaw 2017). His then-unfashionable concern with transnational culture, language, race and religion has since proven to be prophetic as evidenced by powerful legacies edited by Adem and Njogu (2019) and Njogu and Adem (2017); seminal contributions to a very authentic African voice in global IR and IPE.

Symbolic of a hopeful as well as innovative Africa was the advocacy by the UNECA of an African 'developmental state' at the start of the second decade of the century (2011, 2012), reminiscent of the activist role of the UNECA for dependent development in a previous era: an African variant of earlier Asian newly industrialising countries (NICs) with dirigiste regimes. These obviously need to be distinguished from the many classic 'fragile' states, which are concentrated on the continent.[11] In short, there are several 'Africas' just as the Global South is hardly homogeneous (Bergamaschi et al. 2017; Modi 2012; van der Merwe et al. 2016).

This stark contrast – say between Botswana and Mauritius on the one hand and DRC and Somalia on the other – poses difficulties for a singular approach to both analysis and practice of 'African' IR. What are the 30 so-called 'fragile situations'? So, what is and are development, development policy and development studies today with the rise of the BRICS, EMs and FMs, but also given the persistence of fragile states (Laakso and Hautaniemi 2014); and local to national inequalities with implications for sustainable human development and security given the rise of fundamentalisms and radicalisms?

Different reports on the continent asked whether Africa can 'bridge the development divide?' Similarly, *The Economist* (2015a) led its Middle East and Africa section from Lokichar in the distant North-west of Kenya on how 'Wild, ancient and oil-rich Turkana shows how fast the continent is changing' under the title of 'Oil in the Cradle of Mankind: A Glimpse of Africa's Future'.

Furthermore, given the ubiquity of 'private' regulation (c.f. Bernstein 2011 on Isealalliance), such as fair trade and organic certification (Hudson et al. 2013), even developmental states and regions do not really and authoritatively control burgeoning new sectors like mobile phones and finance, broadband internet, brands and franchises, logistics (particularly South African), and ATMs (SWIFT is a non-state, increasingly digital and virtual, network controlled by the world's banks[12]). A range of non-state rules on conflict-free minerals, diamonds, fish and forests symbolised by EITI, FSC, KP, Isealalliance and MSC,[13] set limits on statist or presidential ambitions, even corruption, capital flight and money-laundering.

Finally, can African global networks reflect a changing world in which the BRICS, especially China and India, are displacing the EU as the 'second world'; quite a cry from the non-alignment of the early 'Third World' of a bipolar moment: beyond Bandung?

Such a transformation has led Jan Nederveen Pieterse (2011: 22) to assert that the established North–South axis is being superseded by an East–South one in the second decade of the twenty-first century (Christensen and Xing 2016), that of 'emerging economies' or companies or classes or powers or technologies:

> the rise of emerging societies is a major turn in globalization … North–South relations have been dominant for 200 years and now an East–South turn is taking shape. The 2008 economic crisis is part of a global rebalancing process.

African IR in the post-2015 global political economy

As global investment in the BRICS and other Emerging Powers and Markets (EMs) peaked (Armijo and Katada 2014), Africa became the continent with the most promising 'frontier markets' (FMs). Africa is increasingly able to attract new sources of finance such as non-traditional donors (Sumner and Mallett 2012) like the Gulf states, Korea and Turkey, SWFs and global pension funds, remittances from myriad diasporas and new foundations like Annan, Clinton, Gates and Ibrahim.

Its growth trajectory may outlast that of many of the BRICS even if the risks are greater; so continent-wide and country-specific Exchange Traded Funds (ETFs) have proliferated (e.g. Van Eck Vector Africa Index ETF[14] and South Africa's first from the Johannesburg Stock Exchange (JSE)[15] at the start of the new century, now over 20 available). In 2013 to 2014, Africa's stock exchange performance was enhanced by financial and telecommunications sectors rather than energy or mining and by small–medium enterprises (SMEs) rather than large-caps. And at the start of 2017, Canada's Fairfax launched its own US$56m African investment fund with a focus on political economies like Botswana, Egypt, Ethiopia, Kenya, Mauritius, Nigeria and Rwanda. Its risk assessment reads like a comparative politics text, citing the Ibrahim Index, and it emphasises demand from the continent's emerging middle class;[16] again, criteria of successful schemes.

In turn, especially in Africa, 'contemporary' 'global' issues – wide varieties of ecology, gender, governance (de Waal 2015), health, norms, technology etc. – have increasingly confronted established analytic assumptions and traditions, actors and policies, leading to myriad 'transnational' coalitions and heterogeneous initiatives, processes and regulation schemes as previewed in Bernstein (2011), Dingwerth (2008), Hale and Held (2012) and others. These impact prospects for economic, environmental, health and natural resource governance in Africa as elsewhere, serving to define IR for and by Africa, not the EU: a unique mix of high and low tech, advancing human security as well as human development.

African IR has always been quite transnational or non- and semi-state: it is becoming more so as the continent's non-state sectors – centred in the worlds of civil societies (Africa Civil Society Secretariat)[17] and companies (e.g. Sub-Saharan Africa Chamber of Commerce[18] and Corporate Council on Africa)[19] – expand. African business schools have proliferated this century to augment the trend away from the state,[20] public administration and policy. They are increasingly ranked globally as by the Academic Ranking of World Universities (ARWU),[21] Center for World University Rankings (CWUR), the *Financial Times*, QS[22] and THES, such as those in Lagos, Pretoria and Stellenbosch.

Emerging economies, states, societies, think tanks and universities

Africa's economy is growing steadily. Last year average growth was 3.9 per cent and it is set to accelerate this year. Foreign Direct Investment (FDI) is helping to spur growth. It is expected to reach US$55 billion in 2015, 20 per cent higher than in 2010. Inflows of capital are increasingly focused on less resource-rich countries, as investors target the continent's booming middle classes. The amount of investment into technology, retail and business services increased by 17 percentage points between 2007 and 2013. FDI is also becoming a two-way affair. Last year Africa's outward investment hit US$11.4 billion, up nearly two-fifths since 2011–2012. (*The Economist* 2015a: 89).

The salience of 'emerging markets', largely outside both the EU and Africa, has led to debates about the similarities and differences among emerging economies, middle classes, multinational companies, states and societies (Christensen and Xing 2016), and now universities and business schools etc.; for example, the rising role of Chinese, Korean, Turkish and other analysts from TICK (e.g. the Turkish Open Access journal *Rising Powers and Global Governance*).[23]

These are informed by different disciplinary cannons: e.g. by contrast to Andrea Goldstein (2007) on emerging multinational companies (EMNCs), Pieterse (2011) privileges sociologically informed 'emerging societies'. In turn, there are burgeoning analyses of emerging powers, regional and otherwise (Flemes 2010; Jordaan 2003), in Africa as elsewhere. Despite the US subprime and EU euro crises early in the twenty-first century, FDI in Africa continues to grow, reaching $50 billion in 2013, more than double Official Development Assistance (ODA), primarily from outside the Organization for Economic Cooperation and Development (OECD): China, India and Turkey and myriad SWFs and State-Owned Enterprisesd (SOEs). The drivers are increasingly services for the burgeoning middle class (for example, banking, insurance, real estate, retail, telecoms and tourism) (see, for example, www.fairfaxafrica.com); plus food and energy (see: www.un.org/africa/osaa) that 'Africa's clicking'; and I would add that the clicking is by the poor in informal sectors as well as by middle classes in the formal. Hence the need to rethink 'development' beyond traditional industrialisation and towards the digital and IoT, including bottom-up.

With new energy discoveries and investments, a second tier of oil producers has emerged after Nigeria and Angola: Equatorial Guinea, Congo-Brazzaville, Gabon, South Sudan and now Ghana, with Kenya and Uganda (Mbabazi 2013) eager to join (Hicks 2015).[24] Liquified Natural Gas (LNG) is now exported from Nigeria, Equatorial Guinea and Mozambique, with the latter able to challenge the dominance of Qatar and Australia by 2020. Hence the interest of Exxon-Mobil (US$2.8 billion in March 2017) and Qatar buying into Ente Nazionale Idrocarburi (ENI) and Anadarko holdings in northern Mozambique from mid-2016 to early-2017.

Varieties of development

By the turn of the century, the newly industrialising countries (NICs) then BRICs/BRICS pointed to another way to development other than the EU's offer to the ACP of Economic Partnership Agreements (EPAs) or traditional inter-regionalism; such 'developmentalism' (Kyung-Sup et al. 2012) has now reached Africa (Hanson *et al.* 2014; UNECA 2011, 2012). But, while the 'global' middle class grows in the South (Dayton 2015) – increasingly major cruise companies like Carnival, Royal Caribbean and Norwegian sail out of Shanghai and Singapore as well as Miami – so do inequalities along with non-communicable diseases (NCDs) like cancers, heart and diabetes.

In turn, global health insurance agencies provide coverage and care globally; BUPA alone has 29 million subscribers in 190 countries serviced by 80,000 employees (www.bupa.co.uk).

Africa has advanced as well as benefitted from mobile technologies, extending its own IoT, from cell phones to mobile finance such as M-Pesa, developed in Nairobi at its iHub (see: www.ihub.co.ke), its mini-MIT or – Waterloo or – Cambridge (UK). After a decade, in 2016, it totalled six billion transactions. IBM opened a research lab in Kenya's capital mid-decade and now a trio of Kenya's major universities are building a basic laptop computer for over a million school children with an initial US$170 million from the government in 2015. Several Nairobi universities are offering an MSc in mobile finance supported by M-Pesa, Safaricom etc. and the latter has developed its own Kenyan version of Uber hailing app. iHub partners with several local and global IT companies such as Chase Bank, Google, Hivos, Intel, IBM, Microsoft, Omidyar, Oracle and Nation Media Group (connected to the Aga Khan Foundation (AKF), hence the AK University especially medicine, hospital and Serena Hotels), Safaricom, Samsung et al.[25] And during its late-October 2016 Huawei Southern Africa Partner Summit at the Huawei Innovation and Experience Centre in Johannesburg, Huawei signed music cooperation contracts with global and local music vendors,[26] an indicator of African 'sort power'.

Under the global digital wave, Africa shows great demand for digital services like music, game, video etc. According to Huawei's analysis, in five years, year-on-year growth will be around 40 per cent. However, there still remains a big gap between the growing demands and the digital productions.

New developmental regionalisms as foundations of IR

The proliferation of states along with capitalisms post-bipolarity has led to a parallel proliferation of regions (Haastrup and Eun 2014), especially if diversities of non-state, informal even illegal transnational 'regions' are so considered rather than just traditional interstate organisations (Fanta et al. 2013). And the eurozone crisis concentrated in the PIIGS, now reinforced by the unprecedented migration 'invasion' and the drama of Brexit, has eroded the salience of the EU as a model, leading to a growing recognition of a variety of 'new' regionalisms (Flemes 2010; Shaw et al. 2011).

In turn, inter-regionalisms have proliferated from those around the EU and the Association of Southeast Asian Nations (ASEAN) towards novel multilateralisms around emerging donors – e.g. Forum on China–Africa Cooperation (FOCAC)[27] meeting in South Africa at the end of 2015, Japan's parallel TICAD gathering in Nairobi mid-2016[28] and a proliferation of focused arrangements ex-China, such as its Asian Infrastructure Investment Bank (AIIB),[29] Chang-Mai Initiative (CMI) and CMI Multilateralization, SCO,[30] the BRICS' New Development Bank[31] and now the very macro-regional Belt and Road Initiative (BRI) (Xing 2019). Will the EU's difficulties mid-decade impact the hierarchy of inter-regionalisms, leading away from North-South and towards more East-South?

Mid-decade, emulating China and its AIIB, African Development Bank (AfDB), African Capacity Building Foundation (ACBF), donors and African companies have established Africa 50 for the continent to finance its own infrastructure through indigenous developers and investors[32] as reflected in Africa Investment Report 2016.[33]

Such regionalisms can now be claimed to include instances of DR or 'African agency' (Brown and Harman 2013; Lorenz-Carl and Rempe 2013), like South African franchises and supply chains such as MTN and DStv reaching to West Africa plus the recently formalised Trilateral Free Trade Agreement (FTA) among the Common Market of Eastern and Southern Africa (COMESA), East African Community (EAC) and the South African Development Community (SADC) (T-FTA) (Hartzenberg et al. 2012). Also there are new regional formulations around older and newer regional conflicts like the Nile Basin Initiative (NBI) and International Conference on the Great Lakes Region (ICGLR) plus the regional as well as global dimensions of, say, piracy off the coast of Somalia and the Intergovernmental Authority on Development's (IGAD) role in the endless conflicts in Somalia and South Sudan (ACBF 2014; Hanson 2015). Such piracy has proliferated and intensified off West Africa too as oil generates illegal as well as legal supply chains; so-called 'bunkering'.

Yet the development of formal inter-governmental SADC has been advanced by compatible forms of sub-regionalism, such as the Maputo Corridor and cross-border peace parks between South Africa and Botswana, Mozambique and Namibia. And elsewhere, Africa is installing pipelines as well as broadband cables in the Sahara, coast of West Africa and, shortly, Eastern African oil and gas fields (Hicks 2015);[34] symptomatically, in Mozambique national oil companies (NOCs) from China, India etc. partner with Anadarko and ENI, and now ExxonMobil: some US$25 billion will be required to construct the LNG trains.

As climate change increases, the continent is likely to need water pipelines too for irrigation. Global value chains (GVCs), hubs, logistics and brands, all part of 'development' and DR mid-decade, are largely defined by 'private' or transnational interests and rules rather than states, impacting the balance in African IR.

'New' non-traditional (in)securities (NTS)

Africa may have been growing at an unprecedented rate in the twenty-first century but it has also had to confront a growing range of unanticipated and unfamiliar security challenges (Hentz 2014), which complicates its IR (Kabandula and Shaw 2016, 2019). And, encouraged by the EU and the US, its interstate regional institutions – the regional economic communities (RECs) – have been further redefined in terms of African Union (AU) 'regional security' roles, especially conflict prevention and peacebuilding (Kobayashi 2016). Given the closeness of Euro-African ties, Non-Traditional Securities (NTS) cannot be isolated South of the Mediterranean, despite EU attempts in agreements and monies with Turkey, West Africa and the Horn such as the mid-decade Africa Trust Fund of €2 billion.

Such NTS threats and myriad novel and orthodox responses stretch from intra- and extra-continental migrations and flows of drugs and guns – citizen insecurity – to fundamentalist or radicalised jihadist networks, loosely connected to global al-Qaeda or 'Islamic State'; e.g. Al-Shabab in the Horn and Boko Haram in West Africa.

Varieties of private security – formal and informal, legal and illegal – have also developed on the continent particularly since 2000, from ubiquitous guardians of property, now especially land and food, to banking, cyber, migration and remittances security. Some private security professionals learned their trade with the US Army in Afghanistan or Iraq and demand shows no signs of abating given recent Al-Shabab attacks in Kenya and Al-Qaeda in Mali. Moreover, such jihadist groups may profit from informal trade, including oil, as well as attract radicalised youth, primarily male, from the Global North (Kobayashi 2016).

Thus the former drug supply chain has been recognised through the West African Commission on Drugs (WACD),[35] another form of IR; the latter – terrorist threats – through media and regional military responses (Kobayashi 2016). WACD (2014) published its report on 'Not Just in Transit' in mid-2014 and a variety of analyses, confidential and otherwise, have been produced about the dangers of 'radicalisation' in both East and West Africa (Harman 2014). Al-Shabab generates particularly difficult dilemmas for Kenya and neighbours like Djibouti and Ethiopia, given their established, sometimes affluent, Somali citizens, especially around 'little Mogadishu', the nearby Eastleigh suburb of Nairobi (Carrier 2015). The mix of immediate and distant diasporas as sources of remittances along with ideas and weapons presents challenges for states and Non-Government Organisations (NGOs) alike, let alone global franchises like Western Union and Money Gram and now Dahabshiil,[36] what *The Economist* referred to end-2015 (2015b: 78) as the 'Somali star' of banking in Africa.

And given seemingly exponential climate change, increasing recognition of the emerging nexus of 'water–energy–food' land (WEF) is likely to generate novel forms of tension, juxtaposing so-called 'global' issues and NTS.[37] Climate, energy, food, land and water security are likely to generate exponential demand post-COP21 (Paris Climate Conference) as Africa's population expands, particularly its middle class: African IR should anticipate such pressures in future.

In response, the Gates Foundation with others[38] has advanced the Global Alliance for Vaccines and Immunizations (GAVI)[39] and the Alliance for Green Revolution in Africa (AGRA).[40] The ubiquity of the Gates Foundation in African development this century, especially health and now agriculture (Moran 2013), is symptomatic of burgeoning transnational relations on the continent which trump established inter-governmental institutions like the World Health Organization (WHO) or Food and Agriculture Organization (FAO). Africa post-2015 will be different, but not necessarily as anticipated in UN debates around SDGs and global goals.[41] Similarly, the continent will benefit from the $200 million Global Innovation Fund (GIF) of four major OECD donors (Australia, Sweden, UK and US) plus the Omidyar Network, intended to improve the lives of the world's poorest people[42] as global commodities crash.

Conversely, TOC is increasingly transnational with the proliferation of (young and male) gangs from myriad states. In response, the fields of African, development and global studies as well as IPE need to develop analyses and prescriptions from the established informed annual Small Arms Survey (SAS) and Latin American then Global Commissions on Drugs and Drug Policy and Health.[43] As supply chains shifted away from Central America and the Caribbean to West Africa – 'shadow regionalisms' – in response to the 'war on drugs', the Kofi Annan Foundation created a pre-emptive West African Commission on Drugs;[44] another instance of African IR (Shaw 2015), in this instance encouraged by the International Drug Policy Consortium (IDPC).[45] Together, these led towards the UN global conference on drugs of April 2016[46] orchestrated by UNODC[47] and the Open Society.[48] As already suggested, African and Global IR include a percentage of informal and illegal relations. In the next section we look at how they also relate to the transnational.

Varieties of transnational governance and developmental regionalism

Just as 'governance' is being redefined and rearticulated, so the 'transnational' is being rediscovered and rehabilitated (Dingwerth 2008; Hale and Held 2012) following marginalisation after its initial articulation at the start of the 1970s by Keohane and Nye (1972): they first identified or labelled major varieties of transnational relations such as communications, conflict, education, environment, governance, labour, multinational companies (MNCs) and religions. After OP, KP and EITI[49] along with the Mo Ibrahim governance index[50] these reinforce any African claims to agency as illustrated in the comparative analysis of the Kyoto Protocol and ISealalliance in Bernstein (2011).

To fully capture the scope of African IR, we should add contemporary transnational issues such as brands and franchises; conspicuous consumption by emerging middle classes; world sports, such as the Federation Internationale de Football Association (FIFA) and the International Olympic Committee (IOC); global events from World Fairs to Olympics and world soccer; logistics and supply chains (legal and formal and otherwise); mobile digital technologies; new film centres such as Bollywood and Nollywood including diasporas, film festivals, tie-ins etc.; new medias such as Facebook and Twitter; i.e. the spill-over of FAANG into Africa around mobile communications. Such heterogeneous transnational relations and perspectives including KP, EITI and the Africa Mining Vision (AMV) deserve further attention in terms of their contribution to contemporary African IR.

The 'third sector' of civil society and think tanks has been developing on the continent along with its economies, companies, supply chains, etc., especially in the fleeting decade of commodities' boom. This is particularly the case for higher education, some of which, especially burgeoning business schools, is now for profit, and related networks of policy developers. In an era of mobile, hand-held IT devices, Africa's infrastructure deficit is no longer an obstacle to continental collaboration or developmental regionalism in the social sciences, from more traditional CODESRIA[51] and OSSREA[52] to more innovative AERC (see: www.aercafrica.org) and now PASGR.[53] Many national think tanks have been advanced by support and connections from ACBF (most members of the AU)[54] and IDRC's global Think Tank Initiative supported by Gates and Hewlett Foundations (Moran 2013) and Western ODA from the Dutch, Norwegians and Brits[55] (Smith and Reilly 2013). And the continent can boast its own regional top 50 along with others in the established Penn State think tank rankings; almost 10 per cent of the total 7,000 of such agencies are located in Africa.[56]

Some of the global INGOs are now based in Africa as well as elsewhere in the Global South (e.g. ActionAid to Jo'burg[57] where CIVICUS[58] was already established, now generating is own civil society index and producing is own annual report on the sector. And almost all of them work on the continent, now including some from elsewhere in the Global South, like BRAC (a non-profit foundation in the Netherlands) now in five states in Africa: Liberia, Sierra Leone, South Sudan, Uganda and Tanzania.[59] Yet CIVICUS still ponders whether such changes really advance global governance in a sustainable way.[60]

African capitalism and African IR and IPE

African capitalism 2019 may be different from others because it might yet find its own niche as some BRICS, EU and emerging market (EM) economies decline if not shrink. The mid-2016 combination of UK Brexit and failed coup in Turkey, following the eurozone crisis and migration 'invasion', has further increased the space for African definitions of IR and IPE as both those political economies have had leverage on the continent. The BRICS may linger as an interstate ginger group but are no longer global drivers (Cooper 2016). And ACP post-2020 will be less neo-colonial and more diverse and flexible than before to reflect exponential global divergencies (Montoute 2019; Montoute and Virk 2017).

Rather, African IR and IPE need to connect to FAANG and the 'sharing economy' as both have an interest in 'disruptive innovation', even if Silicon Valley is as yet unaware of such a possibility. Global Sovereign Wealth Funds (SWFs) and African ETFs have a mutual interest in connecting FAANG to Africa, and then extending it to China's Baidu, Alibaba and Tencent (BAT). 'Africa rising' is different from earlier forms of industrialisation such as the NICs: can its post-industrial developmental states connect directly to the IoT so leapfrogging earlier, traditional stages? The heady mix of EU internal preoccupations and African articulation of agency make a distinctive definition of African IR and IPE more possible.

In conclusion, let us consider five changes that may impact governance in Africa and African IR and IPE towards interstate and transnational organisations, reinforced by the disarray in and around the EU and US mid-decade:

a the world monetary system is now triangular – the euro and yuan as well as the US$ (Vermeiren 2014) – but global growth is largely a function of another trio of markets – China and India as well as the US, but not the EU, especially after Brexit;

b shift in the direction and concentration of global supply and value chains, including broadband internet, and airline and container hubs away from South–North towards South–East (Christensen and Xing 2016; Pieterse 2012);

c 'young shoots' of a digital revolution advancing a 'sharing economy' through the 'Internet of Things', but this may exacerbate inequalities between generations and the urban–rural divide unless managed judiciously: onto further dependency and/or agency;[61]

d continued evolution in heterogeneous, hybrid, multi-stakeholder communities to incorporate SOEs, SWFs, pension funds and ETFs, especially from the BRICS and other EMs and FMs (Besada and Kindornay 2013; Hale and Held 2012; Mukherjee-Reed et al. 2012; Sumner and Mallett 2012); and

e in response to inequality and alienation, further escalation of radicalisation and fundamentalisms leading to redefinitions of human and citizen security and regional and global citizenship (Adejumobi and Kreiter 2016): onto the redefinition and reordering of global goals.

In short, if Africa can continue to rise, then it may itself become a disruptor by 2025, advancing its own variety of IR and IPE in which its IoT innovations and related services – such as design, drones, fashion, film, foods, mobile finance and crowdsourcing (IDS 2016) and music – facilitate its global role beyond commodities; all reinforced by its global diaspora, continuously connected by IT. But if the continent slips back towards helplessness then its fragile states may come to disrupt us all given their global connections (Laakso and Hautaniemi 2014): the delicate balance between connectivity and radicalisation.

Notes

1 Available at: www.manuelcastells.info.
2 See: www.claytonchristensen.com; also see: www.christenseninstitute.org.
3 See: www.foreignpolicy.com.
4 See: www.itnewsafrica.com.
5 Available at: www.africaprogresspanel.org.
6 See: www.wacommissionondrugs.org.
7 See: www.kofiannanfoundation.org.
8 See: www.moibrahimfoundation.org.
9 See: www.isanet.org.
10 See: www.africaprogresspanel.org.
11 See: www.foreignpolicy.com.
12 See: www.swift.com.
13 See: www.isealalliance.org.
14 See: www.vaneck.com.
15 See: www.jse.co.za.
16 See: www.fairfaxafrica.com.
17 See: www.askafricanow.org.
18 See: www.ssachamber.org.
19 See: www.africacncl.org.
20 See: www.aabschools.com.
21 See: www.shanghairanking.com.
22 See: www.qs.com.
23 See: www.risingpowersproject.com.
24 See: www.africanoilcorp.com; www.tullowoil.com.
25 See: www.ihub.co.ke.
26 See: www.itnewsafrica.com.
27 See: www.focac.org.
28 See: www.mofa.go.jp.
29 See: www.aiibank.org.
30 See: www.sectsco.org.
31 See: www.brics6.itamaraty.gov.br; www.g8g20.utoronto.ca; www.thebricspost.com.
32 See: www.africa50.com.
33 See: www.analyseafrica.com.
34 See: www.tallowoil.com; www.africaoilcorp.com.
35 See: www.wacommissionondrugs.org.
36 See: www.dahabshiil.com.
37 See: www.water-energy-food.org; www.weforum.org.
38 See: www.gatesfoundation.org.
39 See: www.gavialliance.org.
40 See: www.agra-alliance.org.
41 See: www.post2015hlp.org; www.post2015.org; www.beyond2015.org.
42 See: www.globalinnovation.fund.
43 See: www.globalcommissionondrugs.org.
44 See: www.wacommissionondrugs.org.
45 See: www.idpc.net.
46 See: www.ungass2016.org.

47 See: www.unodc.org.
48 See: www.opensocietyfoundations.org.
49 See: www.eiti.org.
50 See: www.moibrahimfoundation.org.
51 See: www.codesria.org.
52 See: www.ossrea.net.
53 www.pasgr.org).
54 See: www.acbf-pact.org.
55 See: www.thinktankinitative.org.
56 See: www.gotothinktank.com.
57 See: www.actionaid.org.
58 See: www.civicus.org.
59 See: www.brac.net.
60 See: www.civicus.org.
61 See: www.ihub.co.ke; www.itnewsafrica.com.

Bibliography

ACBF. 2014. *Africa Capacity Report. 2014: Capacity Building for Regionalism in Africa*. Harare.

Adejumobi, S. and Kreiter, Z. 2016. *The Theory and Discourse of Developmental Regionalism*. Swaziland.

Adem, S. and Njogu, K. (eds). 2019. *Global African and Universal Muslim: Essays in Honour of Ali A Mazrui*. Banbury: Clarke, A.

Armijo, L. and Katada, S. (eds). 2014. *The Financial Statecraft of Emerging Powers: shield and sword in Asia and Latin America*. London: Palgrave Macmillan.

Balogun, E. 2019. *ECOWAS*. Abingdon: Routledge.

Bergamaschi, I., Moore, P. and Tickner, A. (eds). 2017. *South-South Cooperation Beyond the Myths: A Critical Analysis of Discourses, Practices and Effects*. London: Palgrave Macmillan.

Bernstein, S. 2011. Legitimacy in Intergovernmental and Non-state Global Governance. *Review of International Political Economy* 18(1), February: 17–51.

Besada, H. and Kindornay, S. (eds). 2013. *The Future of Multilateral Development Cooperation in a Changing Global Order*. London: Palgrave Macmillan for NSI.

Bichoff, P., Aning, K. and Acharya, A. (eds). 2016. *Africa in Global International Relations: Emerging Approaches to Theory and Practice*. Abingdon: Routledge.

Brown, W. and Harman, S. (eds). 2013. *African Agency and International Relations*. Abingdon: Routledge.

Carrier, N. 2015. *Little Mogadishu: Eastleigh, Nairobi's Global Somali Hub*. London: Hurst.

Castells, M. and Himanen, P. (eds). 2014. *Reconceptualizing Development in the Global Information Age*. Oxford: Oxford University Press.

Christensen, S. and Xing, L. (eds). 2016. *Emerging Powers, Emerging Markets, Emerging States: Global Responses*. London: Palgrave Macmillan.

Cooper, A. 2016. *The BRICS: A Very Short Introduction*. Oxford: Oxford University Press.

Cornelissen, S., Cheru, F. and Shaw, F. (eds). 2015. *Africa and International Relations in the 21st Century*. London: Palgrave Macmillan. Revised paperback edition.

Dayton, J. (ed.) 2015. *Latin America's Emerging Middle Class: Economic Perspectives*. London: Palgrave Macmillan.

De Waal, A. (ed.). 2015. *Advocacy in Conflict: Critical Perspectives on Transnational Activism*. London: Zed.

Dingwerth, K. 2008. Private Transnational Governance and the Developing World. *International Studies Quarterly* 52(3): 607–634.

Dunn, K. and Shaw, T. (eds). 2013. *Africa's Challenge to International Relations Theory*. London: Palgrave. Revised Classics pb edition.

Fanta, E., Shaw, T. and Tang, V. (eds). 2013. *Comparative Regionalism for Development in the Twenty-first Century: Insights from the Global South*. Farnham: Ashgate for NETRIS.

Flemes, D. (ed.). 2010. *Regional Leadership in the Global System*. Farnham: Ashgate.

Goldstein, A. 2017. *Multinational Companies from Emerging Economies*. London: Palgrave Macmillan.

Gu, J., Shankland, A. and Chenoy, A. (eds). 2016. *The BRICS in International Development*. London: Palgrave Macmillan.

Haastrup, T. and Eon, Y. (eds). 2014. *Regionalising Global Crises: The Financial Crisis and New Frontiers in Regional Governance*. London: Palgrave Macmillan.

Hale, T. and Held, D. (eds). 2012. *Handbook of Transnational Governance*. Cambridge: Polity.

Hanson, K. (ed.). 2015. *Contemporary Regionalism in Africa*. Farnham: Ashgate.

Hanson, K., D'Alessandro, C. and Owusu, F. (eds). 2014. *Managing Africa's Natural Resources: Capacities for Development*. London: Palgrave Macmillan.

Harman, S. 2014. *Terror and Insurgency in the Sahara-Sahel Region*. Farnham: Ashgate.

Harman, S. and Williams, D. (eds). 2013. *Governing the World? Cases in Global Governance*. Abingdon: Routledge.

Hartzenberg, T., Erasmus, G., McCarthy, C., Sandrey, R., Pearson, M., Jensen, H., Cronje, J., Fundira, T., Vojpen, W. and Woolfrey, S. 2012. *The Trilateral Free Trade Area: Towards a New African Integration Paradigm?* Stellenbosch: Tralac.

Hentz, J. 2014. *African Handbook of African Security*. Abingdon: Routledge.

Hicks, C. 2015. *Africa's New Oil: Power, Pipelines and Future Fortunes*. London: Zed.

Hudson, I., Hudson, M. and Fridell, M. 2013. *Fair Trade, Sustainability and Social Change*. London: Palgrave Macmillan.

IDS. 2016. *Ten Frontier Technologies for International Development* (University of Sussex, November. Available at: www.ids.ac.uk.

Jordaan, E. 2003. The Concept of Middle Power in IR: Distinguishing between Emerging and Traditional Middle Powers. *Politikon* 30(2): 165–181.

Kabandula, A. and Shaw, T. 2016. *African Multinational Forces in the Twenty-first Century: Challenges, Progress and the Future*. Paris.

Kabandula, A. and Shaw, T. 2019. Rising Powers and the Horn of Africa: Conflicting Regionalisms. *TWQ*, 39(12): 2315-2333.

Kararach, G., Besada, H. and Shaw, T. (eds). 2015. *Development in Africa: Refocusing the Lens after the MDGs*. Bristol: Policy Press (pb edition 2016).

Keohane, R. and Nye, J. (eds). 1972. *Transnational Relations and World Politics*. Cambridge: Harvard University Press.

Kobayashi, K. 2016. Pax Integrationem? Exploring Institutional Responses to Regional Security Challenges. Bruges: UNU-CRIS, October. Working Paper 2016/5.

Kyung-Sup, C., Fine, B. and Weiss, L. (eds). 2012. *Developmental Politics in Transition: The Neoliberal Era and Beyond*. London: Palgrave Macmillan.

Laakso, L. and Hautaniemi, P. (eds). 2014. *Diasporas, Development and Peacemaking in the Horn of Africa*. London: Zed for NAI.

Lorenz-Carl, U. and Rempe, M. (eds). 2013. *Mapping Agency: Comparing Regionalisms in Africa*. Farnham: Ashgate.

Luke, D. and Macleod, J. (eds). 2019. *Inclusive Trade in Africa: The CFTA in Comparative Perspective*. Abingdon: Routledge.

Mbabazi, P. 2013. The Oil Industry in Uganda: A Blessing in Disguise or an All Too Familiar Curse? 2012 Claude Ake Memorial Lecture (Uppsala: NAI). Available at: www.nai.diva-portal.org; www.isn.ethz.ch.

Modi, R. (ed.). 2012. *South-South Cooperation: Africa in the Centre Stage*. London: Palgrave Macmillan.

Montoute, A. 2019. *Civil Society and Global Trade: the ACP Group and the EU*. Abingdon: Routledge.

Montoute, A. and Virk, K. (eds). 2017. *The ACP Group and the EU Development Partnership: Beyond the North-South Debate*. London: Palgrave Macmillan.

Moran, M. 2013. *Private Foundations and Development Partnerships: American Philanthropy and Global Development Agencies*. Abingdon: Routledge.

Mukherjee-Reed, A., Reed, D. and Utting, P. (eds). 2012. *Regulation and Non-State Actors: Whose Standards, Whose Development?* Abingdon: Routledge for UNRISD.

Njogu, K. and Adem, S. (eds). 2017. *Critical Perspectives on Culture and Globalization: The Intellectual Legacy of Ali A Mazrui*. Nairobi: Twaweza Communications.

Noman, A. and Stiglitz, J. (eds). 2015. *Industrial Policy and Economic Transformation in Africa*. New York: Columbia University Press for IPD.

OECD. 2016. *African Economic Outlook 2016*. Paris. Available at: www.africaneconomicoutlook.org.

Pieterse, J. 2011. Global Rebalancing: Crisis and the East-South Turn. *Development and Change* 42(1): 22–48.

Roger, C. and Dauvergne, P. 2016. The Rise of Transnational Governance as a Field of Study. *International Studies Review* 18: 415–437.

Shaw, T. 2012. Africa's Quest for Developmental States: "renaissance" for whom? *Third World Quarterly* 33(5): 837–851

Shaw, T. 2015. African Agency: Africa, South Africa and the BRICS. *International Politics* 52(2): 255–268.

Shaw, T. 2016. African Agency Post-2015: The Roles of Regional Powers and Developmental States in Regional Integration. In Levine, D. and Naga, D. (eds). *Region-Building in Africa*. London: Palgrave Macmillan: 109–126.

Shaw, T. 2017. Transnational Africa(s): Ali Mazrui and Culture, Diaspora and Religion. In Njogu, K. and Adem, S. (eds) *Perspectives on Culture and Globalisation: The Intellectual lLegacy of Ali A Mazrui*. Nairobi: Twaweza: 37–63.

Shaw, T., Grant, A. and Cornelissen, S. (eds). 2011. *Ashgate Research Companion to Regionalisms*. Farnham: Ashgate.

Shaw, T., Mahrenbach, T., Mody, L. and Ying-Chong, R. (eds). 2019. *The Palgrave Handbook of Contemporary International Political Economy*. London: Palgrave Macmillan.

Smith, M. and Reilly, K. (eds). 2013. *Open Development: Networked Innovations in International Development*. Cambridge: MIT Press for IDRC.

Stuenkel, O. 2015. *IBSA: The Eise of the Global South*. Abingdon: Routledge.

Stuenkel, O. 2016. *Post-Western World*. Cambridge: Polity.

Sumner, A. and Mallett, R. 2012. *The Future of Foreign Aid*. London: Palgrave Macmillan.

Tang, V., Shaw, T. and Holden, M. (eds). 2019. *Development and Sustainable Growth of Mauritius*. New York: Palgrave Macmillan.

The Economist. 2015a. Oil in the Cradle of Mankind: A Glimpse of Africa's Future. (416) 8946, 11 July: 43–44.

The Economist. 2015b. Schumpeter: Disrupting Mr Disruptor. (417) 8966: 63.

Thiel, M., Maier, S. and Beringer, S. (eds). 2019. *EU Development Policies: Between Norms and Geopolitics*. London: Palgrave Macmillan.

Tickner, A. and Waever, O. (eds). 2009. *International Scholarship around the World: Worlding beyond the West*. Abingdon: Routledge.

UNDP. 2013. *Human Development Report 2013: The Rise of the South: Human Progress in a Diverse World*. New York.

UNECA. 2011. *Economic Report on Africa 2011: Governing Development in Africa: The Role of the State in Economic Transformation*. Addis Ababa.

UNECA. 2012. *Economic Report on Africa 2012: Unleashing Africa's Potential as a Pole of Global Growth*. Addis Ababa.

Van der Merwe, J., Taylor, I. and Arkhangelskaya, A. (eds). 2016. *Emerging Powers in Africa: A New Wave in the Relationship?* London: Palgrave Macmillan.

Vermeiren, M. 2014. *Power and Imbalances in the Global Monetary System*. London: Palgrave Macmillan.

WACD. 2014. *Not Just in Transit. Drugs, the State and Society in West Africa*. Geneva: West Africa Commission on Drugs.

Warner, J. and Shaw, T. (eds). 2018. *African Foreign Policies and International Institutions*. New York: Palgrave Macmillan.

Weiss, T. and Wilkinson, R. (eds). 2014a. *International Organization and Global Governance*. Abingdon: Routledge.

Weiss, T. and Wilkinson, R. 2014b. Global Governance to the Rescue: saving international relations? *Global Governance* 20(1): 19–36.

Xing, L. (ed.). 2019. *Mapping China's 'One Belt One Road' Initiative*. London: Palgrave Macmillan.

Part II
Theoretical and methodological perspectives

8

Open economy monetary politics

Nicolas Thompson

Introduction

A decade ago, David Lake (2009) christened open economy politics (OEP) an "emergent paradigm," setting it as the normative and methodological standard for International Political Economy (IPE) scholarship. OEP sees international cooperation as built from the ground up, rooted ultimately in the preferences of individuals. Neoclassical economic theory provides the deductive foundation for determining individual preferences, which are aggregated and transformed in domestic institutions into foreign economic policies or national ideal points for bargaining. OEP sees the global political economy as jointly produced by parallel national processes. International regimes rise and fall as states respond to the changing demands of their citizens.

OEP monetary research is structured around the macroeconomic trilemma, which holds that states cannot simultaneously achieve stable exchange rates, capital controls, and monetary policy independence. In a financially integrated world, this decision is narrowed to a choice between currency stability and monetary policy autonomy (Frieden 1996). OEP researchers study the determinants of currency preferences, the impact of domestic institutions, and global interactions among states and investors. Taken together, these processes explain the episodic nature of international monetary cooperation, as well as the evolution of the global monetary regime through time.

In the decade since Lake offered his paradigmatic appraisal, scholars from both sides of the Atlantic have questioned OEP's core assumptions, empirical strategies, and disciplinary dominance. Some criticize the practice of decomposing world politics into parallel domestic processes, which Thomas Oatley (2011) calls OEP's "reductionist gamble." Benjamin Cohen (2017) sees OEP's rigid epistemology as inviting an excessive focus on domestic politics. In his view, OEP's disciplinary ascent has stunted systemic-level theorizing on the IPE of money. Stephen Chaudoin and Helen Milner (2017) disagree. By surveying recent research, they show that OEP practitioners have productively altered their research strategies to account for the influence of macro-level processes and international power dynamics.

This chapter leverages this debate to assess scholarly progress across each of OEP's three research frontiers: individual preference formation, institutional aggregation, and global interactions. It begins by problematizing OEP's interdisciplinary ambition, observing that OEP's goal of building bridges with economics creates tensions with scholars representing other IPE traditions. The chapter then overviews OEP's explanation of the rise and fall of fixed exchange rate systems. The chapter's core surveys emerging OEP research. It finds that OEP practitioners have fruitfully engaged their critics, expanding our knowledge of contemporary monetary politics. Scholarly rapprochement has come at the cost of relaxing core OEP assumptions, however. The conclusion argues that this heterodox turn among positivist scholars invites a reappraisal of OEP's paradigmatic boundaries.

Interdisciplinarity and bridgebuilding

American scholars forged OEP with goal of establishing an "interdiscipline" with the field of economics (Lake 2006). Neoclassical economic theories are used to derive individual preferences and model domestic and interstate bargaining processes. Political scientists contribute rational choice comparative politics models to this interdisciplinary division of labor. Global outcomes are understood as growing from a bottom-up policy process. Firms, investors, and workers derive preferences over policy outcomes from their objective positions within the international economy. Institutions aggregate and transform preferences into foreign economic policies or ideal points for interstate bargaining.

The OEP explanatory framework sees both foreign economic policies and world outcomes as rooted in national-level struggles among winners and losers from globalization. The paradigm's core assumption is that individuals recognize their stakes in an opening world economy and demand policies which advance their interests. Deriving preferences from economic theory is OEP's "fundamental innovation," anchoring research in "prior, falsifiable, and empirically robust theory" (Lake 2009: 227). It also provides OEP with firm microfoundations, linking state behavior to the incentives of individuals. By highlighting globalization's distributional impacts, economic theory provides a roadmap for identifying relevant societal actors and theorizing which coalitions will form to undertake collective action.

The second frontier of OEP research gauges the impact of domestic institutions on policy outcomes. Institutions are understood as regulative mechanisms which aggregate societal preferences with varying degrees of bias. They determine which groups have access to national policy levers, and on what terms. Researchers study the impact of institutions ranging from micro-level differences in electoral rules and central bank structures among democracies to broad differences across political regime types. Within the realm of monetary affairs, scholars study the influence of institutions on national decisions of whether to fix or float the currency, raise or lower the exchange rate, or enact capital controls. Each of these choices impact national economic performance and have distributional consequences. Consequently, studying how institutions influence policy outcomes remains an important OEP research program.

The OEP policy process theoretically extends to a third level of interstate bargaining. International monetary cooperation is rare, however, because the costs of coordinating monetary policies often outweigh the benefits (Frieden and Broz 2013), and no global monetary institution exists to incentivize bargaining (Chaudoin and Milner 2017). Cohen (2017: 661) laments that the "OEP paradigm has come to rule the IPE of money," because "mainstream scholarship over the last 20 years has come to focus primarily on the domestic politics of monetary or exchange-rate choices." Chaudoin and Milner (2017: 684) see this critique as missing the mark, however, because "national governments are making these policy choices, not some global government."

The question of whether OEP adequately engages macro-level variables and processes is revisited later in the chapter. For now, it is worth noting that Lake sees room for intra-disciplinary conciliation on this front. He encourages researchers to relax peripheral assumptions in OEP models, such as the small state assumption, to account for the market power wielded by the United States and other large countries. Large states' policies influence global prices and, by extension, "politics and policies in other countries" (Lake 2009: 235). Lake argues that acknowledging realities of structural power will make OEP into a more dynamic theory, capable of tackling issues of historical contingency and systemic change, which critics consider an OEP blind spot (e.g., Cohen 2017; Keohane 2009). Emerging research, surveyed below, reveals that scholars are taking up Lake's advice with encouraging results.

Lake sees less room for compromise with critics of OEP's domestic politics model, particularly those who question OEP's practice of deriving individual preferences from global market structures. Constructivists claim agents' structural positions are rarely obvious, and shared ideas are often necessary to form preferences (Keohane 2009). Others argue that agents' interests are also shaped by institutions. Peter Katzenstein (2009: 126), for example, urges OEP researchers to take seriously the historical institutionalist insight that institutions have "constitutive powers … that shape actor preferences and interests through identities." Lake (2009: 231) dismisses these critiques as "inherent in the paradigm." On fundamental issues of where preferences come from and how institutions matter, OEP sides with economists and rational choice institutionalists over IPE scholars calling for a more eclectic approach.

The remainder of this chapter surveys the recent evolution of OEP monetary scholarship in the shadow of this debate. It first provides an analytic overview of OEP's approach to explaining patterns of international monetary cooperation, which is generalized to explain the evolution of the global monetary regime. It then assesses recent progress along each of OEP's three policy stages: individual preference formation, institutional aggregation, and global interactions and outcomes. The conclusion argues that OEP practitioners have successfully modified their research programs to address many of the concerns raised by their critics, but much of this progress has been achieved by swaying from OEP orthodoxy.

International monetary cooperation from the ground up

OEP explains patterns of international monetary cooperation through the evolving incentives and constraints faced by individuals. Fixed exchange rate systems emerge from national decisions to fix the value of their currency to a commodity, such as gold, or the currency of a trading partner. Fixed currency regimes act as focal points around which states can coordinate national policies (Frieden and Broz 2006: 589). Stable currencies promote international trade and investment by reducing exchange rate risk. Fixed exchange regimes can be self-reinforcing because their benefits increase with membership (Broz 1997). As more states stabilize their currencies, the opportunity costs of allowing the exchange rate to fluctuate increase. By contrast, falling regime membership reduces incentives for individuals in all countries to demand currency stability.

Sustaining fixed currency regimes is difficult because doing so requires ongoing national sacrifices to keep nominal and real exchange rates aligned. The *nominal exchange rate* is the number of domestic currency units required to purchase a unit of foreign currency. States which join a fixed currency regime declare a fixed ratio at which it will trade domestic currency units for foreign currency known as a parity. The *real exchange rate* modifies the nominal exchange rate to account for diverging inflation rates across countries. By joining a fixed exchange system, states promise to direct their monetary policies toward replicating monetary conditions prevailing abroad. Many individuals prefer steering monetary policy toward domestic goals, however, such as macroeconomic stabilization. Currencies grow overvalued as domestic inflation rates surpass those prevailing abroad. Overvaluation invites trade deficits by inflating the domestic currency's international purchasing power and reducing the competitiveness of the tradeable goods sector. External deficits can be financed temporarily by borrowing from foreigners, but investors eventually demand policy adjustments to remedy the underlying causes of overvaluation (e.g., relatively inflationary policies).

States can respond to adjustment demands by choosing among internal and external devaluation strategies (Walter 2013). Internal devaluation entails adopting contractionary policies, including fiscal surpluses, high interest rates, and structural reforms, to push down domestic prices. This path of austerity is necessary to sustain a fixed exchange rate (also known as a currency peg) but is painful for individuals whose fortunes are tied to the domestic macroeconomy. External devaluation, by contrast, entails lowering the nominal exchange rate to restore international balance. Holding other factors constant, a 10 percent devaluation equals a 10 percent subsidy for exporters and a 10 percent tax on imports (Broz and Frieden 2001: 333). Devaluation thus can improve the trade balance by stimulating exports and making imports costlier. While devaluation lowers national income in the short run, these costs are spread widely across society and are partially offset by rising competitiveness. Since exchange rate and trade areas overlap, currency misalignments often spill over into trade disputes (Broz and Werfel 2014; Jensen, Quinn and Weymouth 2015).

Fixed exchange regimes are fragile because many individuals oppose austerity. An "anti-integrationist" bloc of import-competing firms, non-tradeable goods producers, and their workers, prefers currency devaluation as the international adjustment strategy. These groups rely on expansionary monetary policies in hard times to stay afloat and bear a disproportionate share of austerity's associated losses of income, jobs, and business failures (Frieden 1991). An opposing "integrationist" bloc of export-oriented firms and international traders and investors, by contrast, prefers internal devaluation because its members can substitute foreign customers and assets for domestic when the local economy slumps. Further, these winners of globalization gain improved terms of trade with the domestic sector when austerity pushes down domestic wages and prices.

In most societies, the median citizen is employed in domestically oriented sectors and thus prefers flexible over fixed exchange rates (Bearce and Hallerberg 2011; Steinberg and Malhotra 2014). This stylized fact provides considerable leverage in explaining the OEP monetary literature's most robust finding, that democracies tend to adopt more flexible currencies, while dictatorships tend toward pegs. Since democratic leaders are accountable to a greater mass of citizens than authoritarian regimes, they are loath to accept the external discipline provided by a currency peg.

The simple insight, that democracy's advance upends stable currencies, goes a long way toward explaining the evolution of the global monetary regime over the last 150 years. The classical gold standard flourished from 1870 through 1914 within a context of rising globalization and limited democratization. Great Britain led the way by fixing the pound's value to gold (Eichengreen 1996). Other states followed suit to facilitate international trade and investment and attract British capital. The major beneficiaries of currency stability, internationally oriented merchants, investors, and exporters, wielded power in pre-democratic political systems. Labor was widely disenfranchised. Beyond these brute power arrangements, the classical gold standard was supported by a shared belief among investors and politicians that the existing parity structure was permanent, and a shared commitment to orthodox fiscal policies. It was further stabilized by apolitical administration by central banks which collaborated to avoid balance-of-payments crises and contagious financial panics.

World War One shattered the classical gold standard and its domestic institutional supports. Countries experienced varying inflation rates during and after the war, depreciating their currencies at uneven rates. Afterward, public debates broke out over whether currencies should be restored to the gold standard at their prewar parities, or if they should be devalued to account for wartime inflation. The internal devaluation path would require sustaining contractionary policies for extended periods to force domestic wages and prices to fall to their prewar levels. Re-pegging to gold at a lower rate, by contrast, would alleviate the need for austerity, but was untried. Currency debates unfolded in an evolving institutional context, as many European states democratized after the war. London financial interests carried the debate in Great Britain in 1925, which restored the pound to its prewar parity. France later devalued the Franc before returning to gold. Overvaluation hurt British industries, and austerity compounded domestic suffering. Meanwhile, French exporters boomed, and France stockpiled gold. As international trade and financial flows fell after 1929, Britain's commitment to gold grew less credible. In September 1931, after months of speculation, Britain made the fateful decision to float the pound. The gold standard again unraveled as other states followed suit by devaluing or floating their currencies.

The United States and Great Britain designed the Bretton Woods fixed exchange rate system during World War Two. Bretton Woods was designed to deliver the benefits of currency stability while enabling states to tailor their macroeconomic policies to domestic circumstances. This would be accomplished through two mechanisms: a fixed but adjustable parity system and capital controls. States would declare fixed parities with the International Monetary Fund (IMF), but could change them in instances of "fundamental disequilibrium." States could also restrict currency convertibility to regulate capital flows. This system became fully operational in 1959, when currency convertibility was fully restored in Europe. It was weakened throughout the 1960s, however, by speculation against the British pound and the U.S. dollar. These core countries ran persistent external deficits, depleting their gold reserves. In 1967, Britain bowed to speculative pressure by devaluing the pound. Waning U.S. support caused Bretton Woods to collapse, however. Surging inflation in the late 1960s caused the dollar to grow progressively overvalued. Richard Nixon closed the Treasury gold window in August 1971, refusing to continue exchanging dollars for gold at the $35 dollar per ounce parity.

In the ensuing decades, the global monetary regime evolved along differing tracks. Since 1973, the U.S. dollar has floated on foreign exchange markets. It remains the global reserve currency, used by states and firms around the world as a unit of account, store of value, and medium of exchange. Ninety governments peg their currencies to the dollar and eight others use the U.S. dollar as their domestic currency, a practice known as dollarization (Oatley 2014: 61). After Bretton Woods, Europeans worked to sustain currency stability, charting a different course. The German Deutschemark became Europe's anchor currency with the formation of the European currency "snake" in the 1970s. Monetary cooperation became more formalized in 1979, with the establishment of the European Monetary System. The introduction of the Euro in 1999, and subsequent denationalization of Eurozone currencies, began an unprecedented experiment in international monetary cooperation. The Eurozone crisis of the past decade has revealed the institutional fragilities of the currency union, as well as the domestic and international coalitions which work to sustain it (Frieden and Walter 2017).

OEP's bottom-up approach to explaining international monetary politics stands in stark contrast with a geopolitical approach which has been influential since IPE's inception (e.g. Cohen 2015). The state-centered approach sees currency relations as reflecting and reinforcing international economic power imbalances. Issuers of currencies used in international transactions receive substantial benefits, including seigniorage revenue, preferential access to foreign savings, and an ability to avoid international adjustment pressures. These advantages accrue most dramatically to issuers of global reserve currencies (Cohen 2006; Oatley 2014). Cohen (2017) argues

OEP's domestic orientation leads researchers to ignore this and other important systemic-level variables and processes. Chaudoin and Milner (2017) offer a sunnier assessment, however, casting systemic-level research as a bustling and productive OEP frontier. The next sections build on their approach by assessing progress along each of OEP's three research frontiers: individual preferences, domestic institutions, and global interactions.

Individual currency preferences

Governments face two fundamental currency decisions: choosing the exchange rate regime and level (Frieden and Broz 2006: 591). The exchange regime question is often presented as a simple choice between fixing or floating the currency. Exchange regimes vary along a continuum, however, from a free float, where market forces alone determine the currency's value, to a currency union, where states relinquish national currencies. Between these extremes lie at least seven intermediate regimes which variously trade off the costs and benefits of currency stability and monetary policy flexibility (Frankel 1999). Most states occasionally intervene in markets to influence their currency's value, so full floats are rare. States choosing intermediate regimes must also decide the currency's level. Overvalued currencies boost national income and purchasing power but hurt the competitiveness of the tradeable goods sector. Undervalued currencies, by contrast, boost competitiveness while lowering national income.

Jeffry Frieden (1991, 2015) separates currency regime and level choices for analytic purposes to build a typology of currency preferences. Applying insights from open economy macro-economics and the specific factors (Ricardo-Viner) model of international trade, Frieden predicts differing coalitions will form along each currency dimension. The regime decision pits internationally oriented sectors, including export-oriented firms and international traders and investors against domestic sectors, including import-competing firms and producers of non-tradeable goods and services. The international bloc prefers a stable currency to lower exchange rate risk, while domestic sectors prefer a flexible currency to enable an activist monetary policy. The currency level question divides society differently, aligning tradeable goods producers, which favor an undervalued currency, against international investors and the non-tradeables sector, which benefit from inflated purchasing power associated with an overvalued currency.

Frieden (1991) presented his seminal currency preference typology as a midrange theory suitable for testing and refinement. Scholars have since taken up this task with vigor. Much research investigates whether currency lobbying coalitions form along the sectoral lines that Frieden predicts. While measuring group preferences can be difficult (Broz and Frieden 2001: 327), survey instruments are increasingly used to ask firms and managers about their currency preferences directly. Survey data provides uneven support for Frieden's hypotheses. Analyzing World Bank Business Environment Survey data, Broz, Frieden, and Weymouth (2008) find evidence that manufacturing firm managers are sensitive to sudden exchange rate appreciations. Duckenfield and Aspinwall (2010) find mixed evidence among British firms, however, finding support for the link between trade exposure and a preference for currency stability, but also confounding evidence that exporters sometimes prefer a stronger pound. Albertos and Kuo (2018) also find greater support among Spanish exporters to the European Union (EU) for remaining in the Eurozone than among non-exporters, supporting the link between trade and currency stability. Bearce and Tuxhorn (2017) find that American businessmen's currency preferences are primitive, however, and when informed tend to break down along firm-based dimensions rather than sectoral lines.

Given this mixed body of evidence, scholars have looked to other structural factors to explain currency preferences. One important firm-level variable is the degree of product specialization.

Producers of standardized goods compete directly on price considerations and therefore benefit more from a depreciated currency than producers of specialized goods (Frieden 2002). A second significant firm-level variable is the extent to which imported inputs are used in production processes. Firms reliant upon imported inputs see those costs rise with depreciation, eroding competitiveness gains (Helleiner 2005). A third key variable is balance sheet considerations. Individuals sometimes respond to high local interest rates by borrowing from abroad in loans denominated in a foreign currency. This practice entails assuming currency risk. If the currency falls, the cost in local currency units of servicing foreign debts rise (Walter 2013). Frieden's (2015) updated currency preference model acknowledges these structural realities: that firm currency preferences are conditioned by their degrees of product differentiation; net foreign currency liabilities; and the ratio of foreign to domestic inputs used in production processes.

A different research program explores how firms have adapted to financial globalization by developing strategies to manage currency risk. Firms reduce their exposure to currency volatility through financial and operational hedging strategies. Financial hedging involves using forward currency markets and financial instruments to self-insure against currency risk (Knight 2010). Operational hedging entails internationalizing production processes (Kinderman 2008). Both forms of hedging lower firms' stakes in national currency decisions, reducing the likelihood that they will expend effort lobbying policymakers.

Frieden's currency preference model is pitched squarely at the first step of the OEP policy process. It abstracts away from institutional differences across societies, arguing that globalization flattens such differences and renders group politics ascendant everywhere (Frieden 2015: 15). The pluralist assumption boosts the portability of the model, making it adaptable to societies across space and time. Limited evidence of sectoral lobbying on currency issues has led some scholars to question the pluralist assumption, however (Frieden and Broz 2001: 328). Some argue financial sector preferences are most important (Shambaugh 2004). Others look to political parties to explain how sectoral preferences are aggregated and transformed into policies (Simmons 1994). Still others argue voters play an important role in shaping currency choices (Bearce and Hallerberg 2011; Walter 2013). These competing claims are arbitrated on OEP's second research frontier, institutional impacts on policy outputs.

Before turning to that next level of analysis, however, it is important to note that some OEP practitioners are challenging OEP's analytic division between preferences and institutions. David Steinberg's (2015) conditional preference theory, for example, holds that manufacturers' currency preferences are conditioned by their institutional settings. Endorsing Frieden's basic logic, Steinberg argues manufacturers only develop a clear preference for an undervalued currency in developing countries with state-controlled financial and labor markets. Manufacturers recognize that the costs of sustaining an undervalued currency, such as high local interest rates and rising wage demands, can be high. Manufacturers only demand an undervalued currency when they are confident that the state will suppress wage demands and steer them subsidized credit from state-dominated banks.

While positivist and anchored in materialist microfoundations, conditional preference theory borders on OEP apostasy. Lake (2009: 231) argues that OEP conceives of preferences as "thinly social," formed in relation to "a larger set of social interactions, the international economy." Domestic institutions are bypassed. By endogenizing institutions into the preference formation process, conditional preference theory embraces the historical institutionalist insight that institutions shape interests (Steinberg 2015: 42). Traditional OEP research, by contrast, sees institutions as mechanistic preference aggregators.

Domestic institutional impacts

Institutions play a "central explanatory role" in OEP by transforming preferences into policies (Lake 2009: 225). Institutions determine which actors can influence policies and their optimal strategies for doing so. Early OEP institutional research focused on how globalization presents states with a shared challenge of building credibility with investors. This literature focuses on how states use monetary commitment devices, including independent central banks and currency pegs, to reassure investors. More recent research explores how broader institutional differences across states influence currency decisions. This section first overviews the monetary commitment device literature before surveying research on democratic and autocratic institutions.

When capital moves freely across national borders, interest rates are set in global markets and investors exploit international arbitrage opportunities. Monetary policy becomes an ineffective demand management instrument in this environment because expansionary monetary policies place downward pressure on the exchange rate (Clark and Hallerberg 2000). To attract mobile capital and avoid interest premiums, states must convince investors that they will not devalue their investments through surprise inflations. The time–inconsistency problem makes this difficult, however, as changing circumstances lead governments to renege on monetary commitments. To demonstrate inflation-fighting resolve, states can delegate monetary policy authority to an independent central bank or relinquish it by adopting a currency peg. Under the former scenario, monetary policy is delegated to central bankers who are shielded from politicians by legal walls. Under the latter, the state promises to replicate foreign monetary conditions, disavowing discretionary interest rate policies.

Scholars debate whether these monetary commitment devices are complements or substitutes (Bernhard, Broz and Clark 2002). Some see them as complements, meaning the presence of one reinforces the other. Pegs and independent central banks are increasingly seen as substitutes, however, meaning the presence of one negates the need for the other. Some argue this is the case because independent central banks prioritize domestic price stability over external currency stability. In the interwar era, some of the world's most independent central banks destabilized the gold standard by enacting restrictive policies which exported deflationary shocks (Simmons 1996). In the post-Bretton Woods era, European states with pegged currencies which undertook fiscal expansions often sought accommodative monetary policies to prevent rising interest rates from attracting foreign capital and causing currency appreciation. More independent central banks were less likely to accommodate these demands (Bearce 2008). By keeping interest rates high to squash inflation, they signaled their prioritization of domestic price stability over external currency stability.

To the extent that currency pegs and independent central banks are indeed substitutes, exchange rate regime and monetary commitment technology choices are intertwined. Central bank independence pairs best with a flexible currency, while a currency peg renders central bank independence unnecessary. This finding supports observed outcomes in the modern world, as democratic states tend to adopt flexible currencies and establish independent central banks, while authoritarian states tend to peg their currencies.

Scholars offer varied explanations for why democracies choose more flexible currency regimes than autocracies. One view holds that democratically elected politicians face high political costs for enacting austerity to sustain a peg. Since autocrats do not rely on elections to stay in power, they can more easily adjust their economies to the peg (Leblang 1999). Others argue that features inherent in democracies, such as transparency and political competition (Bodea and Hicks 2015), are needed to unlock the credibility advantages of central bank independence. A third view holds that median voter preferences drive policy outcomes in democracies, and the average citizen is a domestically oriented producer with a preference for a flexible currency (Bearce and Hallerberg 2011).

Electoral processes further imperil fixed currencies in democracies. Despite monetary policy's limited effectiveness as a demand management instrument under conditions of financial globalization (Clark and Hallerberg 2000), elected officials often seek expansionary monetary policies before elections to engineer short-term booms which will pave the path to reelection (Frieden and Broz 2006: 593). Fears of punishment by voters also lead incumbents to delay choices between austerity and currency devaluation until after elections (Leblang 2003). When citizens have foreign currency denominated loans, adjustments are sometimes delayed indefinitely, creating conditions which invite speculative currency attacks (Walter 2013).

Central bank independence is often viewed as an institutional cure for inflationary-tendencies built into democracies. Many OEP theories assume that the only significant difference among central banks is their degree of legal independence from politicians. An emerging research program opens the central bank black box to explore their internal politics, however. Christopher Adolph's (2013) career theory of central bank behavior, for example, problematizes the common assumption that central bankers are apolitical technocrats. He argues central bankers' monetary policy preferences are tied to their career trajectories, which vary across central banks and cohorts. Central bankers drawn from government, for example, are often more inflation tolerant than those drawn from the financial sector. Consequently, the influence of an independent central bank on its environment is shaped by the preferences of its leaders. When central banks are unable to forecast and control inflation with precision, politicians can change their behavior by appointing inflation-tolerant doves, eroding their credibility advantages (Ainsley 2017).

A different research vein explores the mediating role of political parties in transforming societal preferences into policies. Right-leaning parties traditionally ally with internationally oriented interests which benefit from currency stability, while left-leaning parties represent broader sets of groups which gain from monetary policy activism. Right-leaning governments can therefore be expected to deliver higher degrees of currency stability than left-leaning governments. Empirical tests of the partisan hypothesis yield uneven results, however. Cross-national evidence supports the partisan hypothesis in the post-Bretton Woods era (Berdiev, Kim and Chang 2012), but left-leaning parties in the interwar era more frequently sustained the gold standard (Simmons 1994).

National currency policies often depart from their IMF declarations. Some states which declare currency pegs allow their real exchange rate to fluctuate, while others which declare a floating currency achieve real exchange rate stability. Such gaps between *de jure* and de facto exchange regimes occur more often in democracies than autocracies. David Bearce (2013) explains this divergent outcome through the regimes' differing constituencies. Democracies must respond to interest group pressures and voters, whereas autocrats answer to interest groups alone. Democratic politicians respond to this dilemma by treating *de jure* and de facto exchange regimes as short-run political substitutes. Flexible currencies are declared to please domestic sectors, while international sectors are appeased through policies which promote real exchange rate stability. Bearce's distinction among the channels by which societal influence is wielded across regimes reflects a broader shift in how the OEP literature conceives of authoritarian institutions.

Authoritarian regimes are often understood as anachronistic political systems which are the foil of democracies. Whereas democracies are open and free, autocracies are viewed as opaque and insulated from society. In the conventional literature, the arbitrary nature of autocratic rule makes it difficult for dictators to credibly delegate authority to an independent central bank

(Bodea and Hicks 2015; Broz 2002). Autocrats are thus attracted to pegs by necessity, because the fixed currency commitment provides transparency which their political system lacks. This same logic holds for transitioning economies. Young democracies do not have reputational resources to draw upon, so they struggle to build credibility with investors. This makes a currency peg an attractive commitment device in the short run, while the reputational advantages of democratic rule accrue (Frieden, Leblang, and Valev 2010). OEP practitioners are increasingly following developments in comparative politics, however, by more carefully scrutinizing institutional differences across the authoritarian world. Autocratic regimes can be usefully divided into three subtypes based on the rules by which their leaders gain and sustain power: civilian dictatorships, military dictatorships, and monarchies. Steinberg and Malholtra (2014), argue that civilian dictatorships, like democracies, are more likely to adopt flexible currencies than other authoritarian regimes because they answer to a broader swath of society.

By influencing national currency choices, institutional impacts extend outward to configure the global monetary regime. Indeed, critics allege that most OEP research stops at this second level of analysis (Cohen 2017; Oatley 2011). The next section shows that researchers have successfully evolved their strategies to incorporate macro-level variables and processes. The next section surveys this research.

Global interactions and outcomes

International monetary cooperation is rare in the modern world. Where it exists, primarily Europe, it is closely scrutinized. Outside of Europe, however, interstate bargaining over currency policies is exceedingly rare. Bowing to this reality, OEP researchers seek to explain relevant international monetary phenomena, including the determinants of currency crises, the resilience of capital controls, the Eurozone crisis, and U.S. monetary power in world finance.

Speculative currency attacks occur when investors decide a currency has grown overvalued and seek to liquidate their holdings of that currency before an inevitable devaluation. In the 1990s, speculative attacks hit the United Kingdom, Mexico, and several Asian countries. Such attacks present states with difficult choices between defending a peg or allowing the currency to fall (Walter 2013). Defenses entail spending down foreign reserves, and enacting austerity and structural reform programs. State promises to defend a peg ring hollow, however, if investors are unconvinced that the government will sustain a disinflationary program. Successful currency attacks result in large depreciations which reduce national income and purchasing power. OEP scholars explain how societal pressures and institutions interact to steer societies toward and away from currency crises.

Substantial research looks to elections and institutions to explain the timing of speculative attacks and policymakers' responses. Uncertainty engendered by elections, divided government, and changes in the composition of government is associated with the onset of speculative attacks (Leblang and Bernhard 2000; Leblang and Satyanath 2006). This literature models interactions between officials and market participants in periods around elections to explain their impacts on investor expectations and behavior. Broz, Duru, and Frieden (2016) extend this logic to explain the progression of state adjustment strategies before elections. Election-minded officials seek to avoid visible adjustment strategies which impose high costs on society, such as raising interest rates, depreciating the currency, or enacting trade restrictions. Consequently, democracies tend to respond to adjustment demands by first spending down foreign reserves or enacting capital controls before turning to more transparent and politically costly alternatives.

Another research program looks to broader institutional differences to explain divergent national proclivities toward currency crisis. More transparent states, those which regularly disseminate data to the World Bank and IMF, are less prone to currency crises than more opaque states (Kim 2018). Likewise, monarchies experience currency crises less frequently than democracies and other autocracies, because their leaders are relatively insulated from society and have long time horizons (Steinberg, Koesel and Thompson 2015). Scholars interested in learning more about currency crises should consult Amri and Willett's (2017) recent survey of the political science and economics literature.

Another empirical puzzle OEP scholars seek to explain is the uneven spread of capital account liberalization. A generation ago, scholars argued financial globalization had rendered capital controls obsolete (Frieden 1996). The global dismantlement of exchange restrictions was widely seen as imminent. Capital controls have not disappeared, however. Some scholars link capital account liberalization to democratization (Eichengreen and Leblang 2008; Milner and Mukherjee 2009). In this view, the global diffusion of democracy should lead to the universal removal of capital controls. Steinberg, Nelson and Nguyen (2018) refine this hypothesis, however, by arguing that democracy only spurs capital account liberalization when "proximate" countries, including neighbors, trade partners, and capital competitors, also open their capital accounts. This contingent understanding of democratization's impact helps explain the uneven pace of capital account liberalization as well as recent reversals.

Two other pillars of the contemporary global monetary regime, currency union in Europe and the international dollar standard, are the subject of ongoing OEP research programs. European Monetary Union (EMU) is a long-standing OEP research puzzle. Currency union is the firmest of fixed exchange rate systems, requiring states to relinquish national currencies, as well as control of monetary policy and the nominal exchange rate. The Eurozone was established in 1999 as the successor of the post-1979 European Monetary System and the 1970s "currency snake." Under these earlier fixed regimes, national currencies could fluctuate against the German Deutsche Mark within narrow bands. Occasional devaluations were permitted. Such flexibility was omitted from EMU, however, which delegated monetary policy control to a supranational European Central Bank.

Economists warned that the Eurozone did not match Optimal Currency Area criteria and proposed structural Eurozone-wide reforms to better meet those conditions. Despite some progress in this direction, such as the Stability and Growth Pact which committed states to keep deficits below 3 percent of gross domestic product, joining the Eurozone remained a risky endeavor. Southern Europeans traditionally relied on devaluation to shield their tradeable goods sectors from international competition. Germany and other northern European countries, by contrast, prioritized currency stability and low inflation to benefit export-oriented firms and creditors. The Euro's introduction did not eliminate such national differences, including varied growth models, labor regimes, and tendencies toward inflation (Iversen, Soskice and Hope 2016; Johnston and Regan 2018; Nolke 2016). In the Euro's first decade, interest rate convergence in the Eurozone and surging north-south capital flows concealed underlying problems.

The Eurozone crisis first manifested itself as a Greek sovereign debt crisis in 2009 (Frieden and Walter 2017). In the first decade of EMU, sluggish growth in Germany and other mature economies led northern creditors to invest in fast-growing peripheral economies, especially Portugal, Ireland, Greece, and Spain. Southern European governments, firms, and citizens took advantage of low interest rates to finance increased consumption, investment, and real estate development. Rapid growth caused income levels and housing values to rise, providing an asset base for further borrowing. The 2007–8 global financial crisis slowed north-south capital flows, however, as investors reassessed their risks. Housing bubbles in Ireland and Spain collapsed. Unemployment surged. Investors began demanding steep premiums to finance sovereign debts of Greece, Italy, and Spain. As Greece's debt servicing costs exceeded its capacity to pay, its leaders sought bail-outs to avoid default.

The Euro was founded on a promise to avoid sovereign bail-outs, but this commitment was never credible (Frieden and Walter 2017). Northern states demanded that southerners enact austerity and implement structural reforms for access to debt relief. Southerners demanded that northerners bear more of the adjustment burden by accepting haircuts, mutualizing sovereign debts, and stimulating their own economies. Since northerners brought more power resources to bear on negotiations, southern countries bore the brunt of the adjustment burden. While many societies resisted austerity, states have demonstrated varied capacities to sustain painful reforms (Walter 2016).

The Eurozone crisis has renewed questions of whether the Euro's costs exceed its benefits (Höpner and Spielau 2018; Matthjis 2016). If southern European states had national currencies, they could lower their exchange rates to spur exports and ease the adjustment burden. Because existing debts are denominated in Euros, however, devaluation would provide little debt relief. This balance sheet effect helps explain the lack of sustained mass uprisings against the Euro. Emergency lending facilities designed by the Troika, a commission of representatives from the European Commission, the European Central Bank, and the IMF, and expansionary policies enacted by the European Central Bank, also helped maintain support for the Euro (Howarth and Quaglia 2015).

Eurozone weakness stems from insufficient fiscal and regulatory integration (Baerg and Hallerberg 2016) as well as diverse labor regimes (Johnston and Regan 2018). An emerging literature analyzes Eurozone reform negotiations (e.g. Frieden and Walter 2019). One preliminary finding is that states with greater international financial exposure favor deeper political integration to rebalance the Eurozone, while states with weaker financial ties remain skeptical. This cleavage cuts across north-south divisions between debtor and creditor states (Târlea, Bailer, Degner, Dellmuth, Leuffen, Lundgren and Wasserfallen 2019).

The Eurozone crisis did not emerge in a global vacuum, however. It came on the heels of a global financial crisis with roots in the United States. OEP has been criticized for failing to anticipate the crisis and America's role in propagating it (Cohen 2017). In recent years, OEP practitioners have taken up the challenge of theorizing the sources and impacts of U.S. monetary power.

The United States has long been recognized as benefitting from the dollar's status as the global reserve currency. Governments and firms around the world hold dollars and dollar-denominated assets to process international payments and earn income. Currency held abroad is effectively interest-free loans, providing the U.S. government seigniorage revenue. Some see the U.S.'s "exorbitant privilege" of issuing the global reserve currency as a source of financial power which enables it to ignore international adjustment demands (Cohen 2006) and cheaply finance external deficits (Oatley 2014).

Scholars have adopted divergent strategies for analyzing the sources and impacts of dollar power. One approach follows the OEP template by dissembling the global dollar regime into its national units. Liao and McDowell (2016) argue some states' increased holdings of Chinese renminbi reflect a global preference shift away from an international order based on U.S. hegemony and toward a Chinese alternative. Others counter that the U.S.'s domestic institutional strengths, including its large and dynamic capital markets, transparency, and rule of law, reinforce the dollar's incumbency advantage (Prasad 2015). China's corresponding fragilities, including stunted financial markets, capital controls, and opaque governance, limit the renminbi's attractiveness as an alternative reserve (McDowell and Steinberg 2017).

Other research probes the mechanisms of U.S. monetary power. America's central position in global financial networks shields it from financial problems originating elsewhere in the world, while asymmetrically exposing others to its internal problems (Oatley, Winecoff, Pennock and Danzman 2013; Winecoff 2015). Rising and falling U.S. demands for foreign capital drive a global boom and bust capital flow cycle (Danzman, Winecoff and Oatley 2017). When U.S. borrowing surges, peripheral countries struggle to attract foreign capital and rarely develop financial problems. By contrast, when U.S. borrowing falls, surging capital inflows fuel developing world asset bubbles, paving the path to crisis.

Others investigate the impact of U.S. bilateral pressure for exchange rate adjustment. U.S. officials have historically responded to mounting trade deficits by pressuring trade partners to revalue their currencies. Weiss and Wichowsky (2018) find that the U.S. is most effective in extracting exchange rate concessions when officials across government branches are unified in their demands. They show that China responded to U.S. demands for renminbi appreciation before the 2010 elections, a period when U.S. policymakers were unusually unified in their demands. This shows that the U.S. still wields power through exchange rates, even though the dollar's own level is shaped by global market forces.

This section has shown that emerging OEP research has evolved to explain a broad range of systemic-level monetary phenomena. Like progress modeling domestic political processes, however, some systemic-level theoretical innovations push OEP's paradigmatic boundaries. The concluding section argues OEP monetary research programs have grown more diverse and eclectic in recent years, successfully answering many of OEP's external criticisms. Much progress has come at the cost of relaxing core OEP assumptions, however, suggesting the need for a new paradigmatic appraisal.

A maturing intra-discipline? Assessing progress in the IPE of money

This chapter surveyed recent works in the open economy politics monetary literature within the context of a dialogue between OEP critics and practitioners. Its main finding is that OEP researchers have answered David Lake's (2009) call to build bridges with other IPE scholars wherever possible. This concluding section reflects on how scholars working within positivist, materialist theoretical frameworks have advanced our understanding of world monetary affairs while deviating from OEP orthodoxy. Their successes demand a reassessment of OEP's paradigmatic borders.

Scholars are increasingly challenging OEP's domestic politics model, which links individual preferences to the world economy and relies on rational choice institutionalist models. Steinberg's (2015) conditional preference theory relaxes the first assumption, arguing that domestic institutions factor into manufacturing firms' cost-benefit calculus. This violates OEP's "hard core assumption … that interests are determined largely by a unit's production profile or position in the international division of labor" (Lake 2009: 231). Adolph's (2013) career theory of central banking similarly problematizes the common assumption that central bankers are apolitical technocrats. He shows that central bank behavior is shaped by the career trajectories of their leaders, challenging the rational choice view the only meaningful difference among central banks is their degrees of independence. Each of these theories violates core OEP assumptions about how individual preferences are formed. While each departs from OEP's standard template, they remain rooted in materialist microfoundations and are supported by robust statistical evidence. If OEP's paradigmatic boundaries are redrawn, there is a good chance that the familial resemblance of these types of positivist theories will be enough to warrant their inclusion.

It is less clear that network analytic theories of American monetary power would make the cut. Although Lake (2009: 235) encouraged researchers to recalibrate their models to account for structural power, this research program threatens OEP's core assumption of unit independence. Cast within the New Interdependence approach, which holds that international factors can be as influential as domestic (Farrell and Newman 2014), network analytic approaches reveal that the U.S. benefits from its position atop a steeply hierarchical global financial network (Winecoff 2015). If all crises are indeed now "global" and driven by changing U.S. demands for foreign capital (Bauerle, Winecoff and Oatley 2017), it is unclear what explanatory role remains for the domestic factors OEP privileges. Indeed, while methodologically sophisticated, it is hard to separate the implications of this body of work from critical approaches more popular across the Atlantic.

This chapter has argued that over the past decade, OEP practitioners in the field of monetary politics have effectively answered their critics. We now have a better understanding of a broad range of systemic-level monetary phenomena, including contagious currency crises, the diffusion of central bank independence, the Eurozone crisis, and America's monetary power. Researchers have adopted eclectic strategies to tackle these challenges, relaxing common OEP assumptions in search of richer, more accurate theories. This eclectic turn has yielded important insights and narrowed the transatlantic divide in the IPE of money. The diversity of positivist monetary research programs has eroded OEP's coherence, however, suggesting the need for reassessing its boundaries. Future scholars should take up this task.

Bibliography

Adolph, C. 2013. *Bankers, Bureaucrats, and Central Bank Politics: The Myth of Neutrality*. Cambridge: Cambridge University Press.

Ainsley, C. 2017. The Politics of Central Bank Appointments. *The Journal of Politics*, 79(4): 1205–1219.

Albertos, J. and Kuo, A. 2018. The Structure of Business Preferences and Eurozone Crisis Policies. *Business and Politics*, 20(2): 165–207.

Amri, P. and Willett, T. 2017. Policy Inconsistencies and the Political Economy of Currency Crises. *Journal of International Commerce, Economics and Policy*, 8(1): 175–199.

Baerg, N. and Hallerberg, M. 2016. Explaining Instability in the Stability and Growth Pact: The Contribution of Member State Power and Euroskepticism to the Euro Crisis. *Comparative Political Studies*, 49(7): 968–1009.

Bauerle, S., Winecoff, W. and Oatley, T. 2017. All Crises are Global: Capital Cycles in an Imbalanced International Political Economy. *International Studies Quarterly*, 61(4): 907–923.

Bearce, D. 2008. Not Complements, but Substitutes: Fixed Exchange Rate Commitments, Central Bank Independence, and External Currency Stability. *International Studies Quarterly*, 52(4): 807–824.

Bearce, D. 2013. A Political Explanation for Exchange-Rate Regime Gaps. *The Journal of Politics*, 76(1): 58–72.

Bearce, D. and Hallerberg, M. 2011. Democracy and de facto Exchange Rate Regimes. *Economics & Politics*, 23(2): 172–194.

Bearce, D. and Tuxhorn, K. 2017. When are Monetary Policy Preferences Egocentric? Evidence from American Surveys and an Experiment. *American Journal of Political Science*, 61(1): 178–193.

Berdiev, A., Kim, Y. and Chang, C. 2012. The Political Economy of Exchange Rate Regimes in Developed and Developing Countries. *European Journal of Political Economy*, 28(1): 38–53.

Bernhard, W., Broz, J. and Clark, W. 2002. The Political Economy of Monetary Institutions. *International Organization*, 56(4): 693–723.

Bodea, C. and Hicks, R. 2015. Price Stability and Central Bank Independence: Discipline, Credibility, and Democratic Institutions. *International Organization*, 69(1): 35–61.

Broz, J. 1997. The Domestic Politics of International Monetary Order: The Gold Standard. In: D. Skidmore, ed., *Contested Social Orders and International Politics*. Nashville: Vanderbilt University Press: 53–91.

Broz, J. 2002. Political System Transparency and Monetary Commitment Regimes. *International Organization*, 56(4): 861–877.

Broz, J., Duru, M. and Frieden, J. 2016. Policy Responses to Balance-of-payments Crises: The Role of Elections. *Open Economies Review* 27(2): 207–227.

Broz, J. and Frieden, J. 2001. The Political Economy of International Monetary Relations." *Annual Review of Political Science*, 4(1): 317–343.

Broz, J., Frieden, J. and Weymouth, S. 2008. Exchange Rate Policy Attitudes: Direct Evidence from Survey Data. *IMF Staff Papers*, 55(3): 417–444.

Broz, J. and Werfel, S. 2014. Exchange Rates and Industry Demands for Trade Protection. *International Organization*, 68(2): 393–416.

Chaudoin, S. and Milner, H. 2017. Science and the System: IPE and International Monetary Politics. *Review of International Political Economy*, 24(4): 681–698.

Clark, W. and Hallerberg, M. 2000. Mobile Capital, Domestic Institutions, and Electorally Induced Monetary and Fiscal Policy. *American Political Science Review*, 94(2): 323–346.

Cohen, B. 2006. The Macrofoundations of Monetary Power. In: D. Andrews, ed., *International Monetary Power*, 1st ed. Ithaca: Cornell University Press: 31–50.

Cohen, B. 2015. *Currency Power: Understanding Monetary Rivalry*. Princeton: Princeton University Press.

Cohen, B. 2017. The IPE of Money Revisited. *Review of International Political Economy*, 24(4): 657–680.

Danzman, S., Winecoff W. and Oatley T. 2017. All Crises are Global: Capital Cycles in an Imbalanced International Political Economy. *International Studies Quarterly*, 61(4): 907–923.

Duckenfield, M. and Aspinwall, M. 2010. Private Interests and Exchange Rate Politics: The Case of British Business. *European Union Politics* 11(3): 381–404.

Eichengreen, B. 1996. *Globalizing Capital*. Princeton: Princeton University Press.

Eichengreen, B. and Leblang, D. 2008. Democracy and Globalization. *Economics and Politics*, 20(3): 289–334.

Farrell, H. and Newman, A. 2014. Domestic Institutions Beyond the Nation State: Charting the New Interdependence Approach. *World Politics*, 66: 331–63.

Frankel, J. 1999. No Single Currency Regime is Right for All Countries or at All Times. *NBER Working Paper*, No. 7338.

Frieden, J. 1991. Invested Interests: The Politics of National Economic Policies in a World of Global Finance. *International Organization*, 45(4): 425–451.

Frieden, J. 1996. The Impact of Goods and Capital Market Integration on European Monetary Politics. *Comparative Political Studies*, 29(2): 193–222.

Frieden, J. 2002. Real Sources of European Currency Policy: Sectoral Interests and European Monetary Integration. *International Organization,* 56(4): 831–860.

Frieden, J. 2015. *Currency Politics: The Political Economy of Exchange Rate Policy*. Princeton: Princeton University Press.

Frieden, J. and Broz, J. 2006. The Political Economy of Exchange Rates. In: B. Weigast and D. Wittman, eds., *Oxford Handbook of Political Economy*, 1st ed., Oxford: Oxford University Press: 587–600.

Frieden, J. and Broz, J. 2013. The Political Economy of International Monetary Policy Coordination. In: G. Caprio, ed., *The Encyclopedia of Financial Globalization*, 1st ed. Boston, MA: Elsevier Publishing: 81–90.

Frieden, J., Leblang, D. and Valev, N. 2010. The Political Economy of Exchange Rate Regimes in Transition Economies. *The Review of International Organizations*, 5(1): 1–25.

Frieden, J. and Walter, S. 2017. Understanding the Political Economy of the Eurozone Crisis. *Annual Review of Political Science*, 20: 371–90.

Frieden, J. and Walter, S. 2019. Analyzing Inter-state Negotiations in the Eurozone Crisis and Beyond. *European Union Politics*.

Helleiner, E. 2005. A Fixation with Floating: The Politics of Canada's Exchange Rate Regime. *Canadian Journal of Political Science*, 38(1): 23–44.

Höpner, M. and Spielau, A. 2018. Better Than the Euro? The European Monetary System (1979–1998). *New Political Economy*, 23(2): 160–173.

Howarth, D. and Quaglia, L. 2015. The Political Economy of the Euro Area's Sovereign Debt Crisis: Introduction to the Special Issue of the Review of International Political Economy. *Review of International Political Economy*, 22(3): 457–484.

Iversen, T., Soskice, D. and Hope, D. 2016. The Eurozone and Political Economic Institutions. *Annual Review of Political Science*. 19(1): 163–185.

Jensen, J., Quinn, D. and Weymouth, S. 2015. The Influence of Firm Global Supply Chains and Foreign Currency Undervaluations on US Trade Disputes. *International Organization*, 69(4): 913–947.

Johnston, A. and Regan, A. 2018. Introduction: Is the European Union Capable of Integrating Diverse Models of Capitalism? *New Political Economy*, 23(2): 145–159.

Katzenstein, P. 2009. Mid-Atlantic: Sitting on the Knife's Sharp Edge. *Review of International Political Economy*, 16(1): 122–135.

Keohane, R. 2009. The Old IPE and the New. *Review of International Political Economy*, 16(1): 34–46.

Kim, N. 2018. Transparency and Currency Crises. *Economics & Politics*, 30(3): 394–422.

Kinderman, D. 2008. The Political Economy of Sectoral Exchange Rate Preferences and Lobbying: Germany from 1960–2008, and Beyond. *Review of International Political Economy*, 15(5): 851–880.

Knight, S. 2010. Divested Interests: Globalization and the New Politics of Exchange Rates. *Business and Politics*, 12(2): 1–28.

Lake, D. 2006. International Political Economy: A Maturing Interdiscipline. In: B. Weingast and D. Wittman, eds., *The Oxford Handbook of Political Economy*, 1st ed. New York: Oxford University Press: 757–777.

Lake, D. 2009. Open Economy Politics: A Critical Review. *Review of International Organization*, 4(3): 219–244.

Leblang, D. 1999. Domestic Political Institutions and Exchange Rate Commitments in the Developing World. *International Studies Quarterly*, 43(4): 599–620.

Leblang, D. 2003. To Devalue or to Defend? The Political Economy of Exchange Rate Policy. *International Studies Quarterly*, 47(4): 533–559.

Leblang, D. and Bernhard, W. 2000. The Politics of Speculative Attacks in Industrial Democracies. *International Organization*, 54(2): 291–324.

Leblang, D. and Satyanath, S. 2006. Institutions, Expectations, and Currency Crises. *International Organization*, 60(1): 245–262.

Liao, S. and McDowell, D. 2016. No Reservations: International Order and Demand for the Renminbi as a Reserve Currency. *International Studies Quarterly*, 60(2): 272–293.

Matthijs, M. 2016. The Euro's 'Winner-Take-All' Political Economy: Institutional Choices, Policy Drift, and Diverging Patterns of Inequality. *Politics & Society*, 44(3): 393–422.

McDowell, D. and Steinberg, D. 2017. Systemic Strengths, Domestic Deficiencies: The Renminbi's Future as a Reserve Currency. *Journal of Contemporary China*: 801–819.

Milner, H. and Mukherjee, B. 2009. Democratization and Economic Globalization. *Annual Review of Political Science*, 12(1): 163–181.

Nolke, A. 2016. Economic Causes of the Eurozone Crisis: the Analytical Contribution of Comparative Capitalism. *Socio-Economic Review*, 14(1): 141–161.

Oatley, T. 2011. The Reductionist Gamble: Open Economy Politics in the Global Economy. *International Organization*, 65(2): 311–341.

Oatley, T. 2014. The Political Economy of the Dollar Standard, In: T. Oatley and W. Winecoff, eds., *Handbook of the International Political Economy of Monetary Relations*. London: Edward Elgar Publishing: 54–68.

Oatley, T., Winecoff, W., Pennock, A. and Danzman, S. 2013. The Political Economy of Global Finance: A Network Model. *Perspectives on Politics*, 11(1): 133–153.

Prasad, E. 2015. *The Dollar Trap: How the US Dollar Tightened its Grip on Global Finance*. Princeton: Princeton University Press.

Shambaugh, G. 2004. The Power of Money: Global Capital and Policy Choices in Developing Countries. *American Journal of Political Science*, 48(2): 281–295.

Simmons, B. 1994. *Who Adjusts? Domestic Sources of Foreign Economic Policy during the Interwar Years*. Princeton: Princeton University Press.

Simmons, B. 1996. Rulers of the Game: Central Bank Independence During the Interwar Years. *International Organization*, 50(3): 407–443.

Steinberg, D. 2015. *Demanding Devaluation: Exchange Rate Politics in the Developing World*. Ithaca: Cornell University Press.

Steinberg, D., Koesel, K. and Thompson, N. 2015. Political Regimes and Currency Crises. *Economics & Politics*, 27(3): 337–361.

Steinberg, D. and Malhotra, K. 2014. The Effect of Authoritarian Regime Type on Exchange Rate Policy. *World Politics*, 66(3): 491–529.

Steinberg, D., Nelson, S. and Nguyen, C. 2018. Does Democracy Promote Capital Account Liberalization? *Review of International Political Economy*, 25(6): 1–30.

Târlea, S., Bailer, S., Degner, H., Dellmuth, L. M., Leuffen, D., Lundgren, M. and Wasserfallen, F. 2019. Explaining Governmental Preferences on Economic and Monetary Union Reform. *European Union Politics*, 20(1): 24–44.

Walter, S. 2013. *Financial Crises and the Politics of Macroeconomic Adjustments*. Cambridge: Cambridge University Press.

Walter, S. 2016. Crisis Politics in Europe: Why Austerity is Easier to Implement in Some Countries than in Others. *Comparative Political Studies*, 49(7): 841–873.

Weiss, J. and Wichowsky, A. 2018. External Influence on Exchange Rates: An Empirical Investigation of US pressure and the Chinese RMB. *Review of International Political Economy*, 25(5): 596–623.

Winecoff, W. 2015. Structural Power and the Global Financial Crisis: A Network Analytical Approach. *Business and Politics*, 17(3): 495–525.

9

The politics of trade in an open economy

Domestic competition over policy

Mark Brawley

Introduction

International trade generates contentious politics both between and inside states (Alt, Frieden, Gilligan, Rodrik and Rogowski 1996). Economists have shown that international trade can produce more wealth for participating states, but conflict arises from the distribution of those gains. These conflicts have made pure free trade relatively rare historically, though today most countries have opened their borders to inflows and outflows of goods and services. As more states have liberalized trade, our focus has shifted to the internal struggles over policy. The open economy approach uses the liberal perspective to analyze empirical evidence (Alt and Gilligan 1994; Moravcsik 1997; Lake 2009). Based in liberalism, it assumes individuals (including households and firms) are the key actors in political economy. Because trade redistributes wealth inside countries, individuals take up varied positions on trade policy. As trade becomes an issue, individuals who share particular preferences organize together to compete for control over policy. Understanding who controls policy in various countries then informs the negotiations between states as they make or break trade deals.

While this isn't the only way to model the formulation of trade policy, it has become the standard approach among political scientists. Debates continue, of course, because we face choices at each step-in modeling this "bottom-up" political process. How should we understand the basis for individuals' preferences? Do individuals find it easy to gather together to mobilize for political action, or do they find it difficult? How do political institutions shape the relative power (or voice) of the rival groups? Below, I sketch out the basic choices researchers can make, to reveal the advantages and disadvantages associated with particular options.

Identifying the array of domestic interests

Economic models of trade's redistributive impact

Adam Smith demonstrated the advantages of market-based exchange long ago; for more than a century afterwards, economists argued that free trade benefited each country in the aggregate. Trade made society as a whole richer. This proposition posed several puzzles regarding politics, however. If free trade was so clearly beneficial, why wasn't it more popular? Why weren't more states liberalizing trade? These questions prompted economists to examine how the benefits from trade are distributed inside countries. This question could only be answered once economists gained a better understanding of the sources of comparative advantage.

Stolper–Samuelson vs. sector-specificity

In the 1920s, Eli Hecksher (1919) and Bertil Ohlin (1933) tackled an essential question concerning international trade: if the gains from international trade come from specialization, how do states understand where their comparative advantage lies? Their answer focused on countries' endowments of the inputs used to make other goods. In their thinking, the cost of any good reflects the inputs needed to make it. Each good requires a rough mix of inputs (or factors of production); often the production of a good rests heavily on one specific input. If that input happens to be in abundant supply in one country, compared to others, that input is relatively cheap in cost (compared to other inputs). The good intensively using the locally abundant factor of production could therefore be made cheaper compared to a country where that same input was rarer (and thus more expensive). Heckscher and Ohlin thus concluded countries' endowments of the factors of production determined their comparative advantage. This insight has informed economists' efforts to understand the composition and direction of the flows of goods and services ever since.

Using the Heckscher–Ohlin set up, Wolfgang Stolper and Paul Samuelson (1941) addressed the question raised above: if free trade is beneficial to society as a whole, why isn't it more common? In particular, they asked why a democratic country would adopt protectionist legislation. They were intrigued by the experience of the United States they had recently observed. Their argument was simple. If the U.S. economy was characterized by abundant land and capital compared to elsewhere (implying labor was relatively scarce), then land and capital were cheap inputs, compared to much of the rest of the world. Labor costs were comparatively high. The Heckscher–Ohlin framework suggested the U.S. would export land- and capital-intensive goods successfully, while importing labor-intensive goods. Stolper and Samuelson then considered the impact of trade on the American economy; trade liberalization would increase the price of land and capital but reduce the earnings of labor. Since workers exercised votes in the political system, they protected their interests by limiting trade. This extension of the Heckscher–Ohlin model, known as the Stolper–Samuelson theorem, gave a plausible explanation for how the gains from trade were distributed inside countries.

Box 9.1 The Heckscher–Ohlin economic model

The Heckscher–Ohlin economic model provides our basic understanding for the basis of national comparative advantage. Most of the interpretations of the domestic distribution of the gains from trade build off this model.

For several decades, the Stolper–Samuelson theorem dominated economists' understanding of trade's impact. Political scientists only incorporated this information into the analysis of domestic politics in the 1980s. Ronald Rogowski (1989) employed the Stolper–Samuelson theorem to explain why some rather odd political groupings had emerged in the past. Rogowski demonstrated that trade could bring together domestic groups that otherwise shared very few interests.

In the basic three-factor version of the Stolper–Samuelson theorem, each country is evaluated in terms of its endowments of land, labor and capital. Relative abundance is determined by the ratio of each factor to another, with the resulting ratio compared to those from other states. Each state therefore has a comparative advantage in at least one area, and disadvantage in at least one other. Since the theorem describes economic interests in terms of land, labor and capital, this translates into expected alignments of the owners of these different inputs when trade becomes a significant issue. (The theorem generates factor-based, or as more commonly described, class-based politics.) For example, the owners of land and capital may have little in common, or in some settings even be likely enemies; yet if these two factors of production are relatively scarce, the owners of land and capital share a preference for protection. Rogowski demonstrated that trade could promote such political coalitions across a wide number of settings.

Box 9.2 The Stolper–Samuelson theorem

The Stolper–Samuelson theorem predicts that trade liberalization rewards the owners of the relatively abundant factors of production, while reducing the earnings of the owners of the relatively scarce factors of production. This produces factor-based (or class) cleavages.

Even as political scientists were finally integrating the Stolper–Samuelson approach into their own work, economists were questioning the utility of the theorem. To keep their analysis simple and clear, Stolper and Samuelson relied upon a couple of key assumptions. One concerned the speed of trade adjustment; they assumed it happened rapidly and completely. Another assumption addressed the substitutability of each unit of a single type of factor of production; they assumed one worker would be readily substituted for another, and so on. Assumptions are simplifying statements we treat as true, knowing they are false. We evaluate an assumption in terms of how well it helps the model provide useful answers to our questions. In truth, trade adjustment takes time to unfold – this process describes the reorganization of production, which may include the need for physical relocation of assets or people, new training for workers, and so forth. Also, this process would be altered by differences between individual units of each factor of production. Some units might be more easily redeployed into other uses, compared to others. This would determine which units of land, labor and capital might easily switch from one occupation to another, while others might find it extremely difficult to be used to produce an alternative good.

In some cases, the obstacles to adjustment are too great to overcome. Imagine a sophisticated piece of machinery designed to create a particular form of plastic. It might be quite challenging and costly to adapt this equipment to do any other task (let alone one in an area advantaged by trade). This piece of machinery could be described as "sector-specific," since it was particularly suited to employment in the manufacture of one good only. (A sector or industry is defined by the good it produces.) Economists began incorporating this assumption into their models of the distribution of the gains from trade in the 1970s (Mussa 1974).

To make a specific good, you combine a mix of inputs; we can describe any good by the mix of inputs required to produce it efficiently. As Robert Mundell (1957) observed, trade in the good mimics movement in inputs. Trade liberalization therefore expands exports of those goods that embody (intensively require) the locally abundant factor(s) of production; trade liberalization increases imports of goods intensively requiring the locally scarce factor(s). Trade adjustment involves the expansion and contraction of industries. This adjustment will not be complete, however, since some individual units of land, labor or capital cannot actually shift from their current use to another. In terms of understanding preferences on trade policy, this gives us a different sense of the likely cleavage evoked. Whereas the Stolper–Samuelson theorem anticipated the fissure to run between owners of assets (i.e., a factor- or class-based cleavage), the sector-specific approach predicts trade will pit the land, labor and capital in exporting industries versus the land, labor and capital employed in import-competing industries.

Box 9.3 Assuming individual units of factors of production

Assuming individual units of factors of production are usually specific to the sector they are employed in, changes how the gains from trade are distributed. Now, gains and losses follow industry lines, producing sector-based cleavages.

Sector-specificity vs. intra-industry firm heterogeneity

As with any model, the sector-specific approach also includes simplifying assumptions. While it allowed for variation in the qualities and utilities of individual units of land, labor or capital, it assumed that the firms participating in each sector operated alike. (Put differently, sectors are defined by the good produced; participants in each sector were assumed to incorporate the same mix of inputs, in the same fashion.) When economists surveyed firms in certain industries in the late 1990s, they discovered a puzzling pattern (Bernard and Jensen 1999). In some exporting sectors, the data indicated a surprisingly few firms executed the vast majority of the international trade. To explain this outcome, they examined how the firms operated. The research revealed that in some sectors, firms were relatively similar (in terms of size, technology, use of inputs, etc.), but in other industries firms varied considerably. In the heterogeneous sectors, the most efficient firms were the ones dominating the engagement in international trade (Bernard, Jensen, Redding and Schott 2011).

When researchers tinkered with the assumptions of the sector-specific model to take into account intra-industry heterogeneity of firms, their models produced some surprising results (Bernard, Eaton, Jensen and Kortum 2003; Melitz 2003). In a sector comprised of heterogeneous firms, trade liberalization would disproportionately reward the most efficient firms. As these firms expand output to meet foreign demand, some of their goods naturally find their way onto the domestic market; since they are the most efficient firms, their goods are cheapest, and will depress the domestic price. Meanwhile, the expanded production of these most efficient firms drives up the costs of inputs. In short, trade liberalization squeezes the margins of all firms in the sector. The most efficient firms can increase profits by selling a larger volume of goods, but the least efficient firms cannot — they might even be forced out of business.

Intra-industry firm heterogeneity therefore predicts that trade policy can produce cleavages inside a sector, if that sector is composed of heterogeneous firms. This new approach has now been brought to bear on evidence from politics. Early research applied this insight to lobbying – comparing sectors with heterogeneity to those more homogenous, to demonstrate the intra-industry cleavage could be observed in political behavior (Bombardini 2008; Osgood 2016, 2017). This remains some distance from showing such cleavages have an impact on political outcomes, though other studies have tied intra-industry divisions on trade to later stages in the political process described above (Kim 2017). To understand why, we need to look more closely at those later stages in the open economy approach, described below.

Intra-industry firm heterogeneity presents several opportunities for future research. On the one hand, it suggests a method for explaining some curious or challenging episodes from the past. For instance, in the 1890s and early 1900s, three of the largest wheat exporting countries – all democracies – adopted not just protectionist tariffs, but tariffs on wheat. In national elections dominated by trade policy, grain growers adopted diverse positions on the tariff. There are other historical cases where neither the Stolper–Samuelson nor the sector-specific approaches capture political dynamics accurately. Intra-industry firm heterogeneity may provide the key to understanding outcomes obviously inconsistent with either the Stolper–Samuelson or sector-specific approaches.

Box 9.4 Intra-industry firm heterogeneity

Intra-industry firm heterogeneity takes the sector-specific approach, and relaxes the assumption that all firms in an industry operate alike. This allows for the possibility that the gains and losses from trade vary across the participants in a sector, potentially creating a cleavage within an industry.

Trade-offs associated with each model

As just described, economists offer us several different ways to understand how the gains from trade are distributed inside countries. Researchers must choose between the three in the initial step of the open economy approach. Having just reviewed the three economic models of trade's domestic impact, we can now compare the features of each – they vary in how easily they can be applied, the detail of their predictions, and in other ways. By appreciating these differences, scholars learn when to rely on one rather than another.

Data availability

One very important way in which the economic models of the distribution of the gains from trade vary, concerns the ease with which they may be applied to empirical cases. (This holds whether we're talking about historical research or efforts to conduct contemporary analyses.) Applying the Stolper–Samuelson theorem requires some basic information: the economy's endowments of land, labor and capital. The ratios of these inputs can then be used to establish the country's comparative advantage vis-a-vis others, thereby identifying the expected dominant cleavage on trade policy. For applications in the political process, we would then need to know about the distribution of the owners of each of these factors. (More on that below.) This information is not particularly difficult to come by, even for historical episodes a couple of centuries in the past.

The sector-specific approach requires a bit more detailed data. Instead of the country's aggregate amount factors of production, we now need to understand the main products being made, and the inputs each of those major products required. This means getting a sense of the national economy's output, the composition of its trade, and the sectors employing the most people, land, and capital. We need this information in order to focus our attention on the sectors that are economically and/or politically important. Finding such data for current cases may not be difficult, because most countries monitor their trade and also survey economic activity. As we go further back in history, however, the number of countries with accurate data gets slimmer. Many European countries (as well as the United States and Canada) introduced the national census in the nineteenth century. Therefore, there are useful amounts of data from a fair number of countries reaching back a century or more, allowing us to describe the relevant sectors of economic activity in terms of sectors.

Of the three economic models described here, intra-industry firm heterogeneity requires the most detailed information, which is also the most difficult to obtain. We need the same information as with the sector-specific approach, and more. We also need to know the composition of each sector. If there is heterogeneity among the participants, we then need to isolate the most efficient firms. Economists often sort producers by size; in manufacturing larger size serves as a useful proxy for efficiency. This can be misleading at times, however, because in some sectors small-scale would be associated with efficiency. (This could be especially relevant for certain agricultural sectors, where smaller operations can produce an item more efficiently.) Understanding variation in firms' practices can be difficult to ascertain, because production processes tie to competitiveness. The most competitive firms may not want to reveal much about how they combine their inputs to make the good that defines their sector.

Luckily, modern data collection provides a good sense of the composition of sectors. Indeed, the theory itself arose from survey evidence gathered by economists. Information about individual firms can be found through two other routes. Sometimes it can be reconstructed from the census data mentioned above — that is, if we have a sense of the total output of a sector, and the number of participants, and then some way of observing different portions of those firms, then we can observe whether heterogeneity exists; from there we can then explore which differences in firms' efficiency. Alternatively, companies themselves might have kept records that indicate their inputs, outputs, and relative profitability. Among larger manufacturing firms, the practice of releasing annual reports began in the early twentieth century and has become more common. Here again, the necessary information may be more readily available for contemporary analyses, but difficult to find for historical cases.

Accuracy in interests vs. observations in political activity

The next characteristic of these economic models to consider is their relative accuracy. The Stolper–Samuelson approach is considered relatively accurate, though it does describe outcomes in vague terms. All domestic actors are lumped into one of three groups, and each member in each category is then considered to have the same sort of interests. In the sector-specific approach, actors are placed in the different categories based on their employment (or the employment of their means to an income). This integrates more detail into the classification, though the outcome is also quite simple: actors are placed in either exporting or import-competing sectors.

Intra-industry firm heterogeneity is much more detailed in its descriptions. On the one hand, it necessarily captures everything in the sector-specific perspective. It then builds on that by separating out those sectors composed of heterogeneous firms and allowing us insight into how those producers would have different preferences concerning trade policy. If the information can be tied to specific firms, then we can develop extremely detailed portraits of the political behavior of workers or executives linked to those companies. This can be quite valuable when concentrating on certain types of political behavior, such as lobbying.

Another dimension where these economic models vary significantly, is the time-period they describe. The assumptions embedded in each model make each one more relevant for certain sorts of questions. For example, the key assumption differentiating the Stolper–Samuelson theorem from the sector-specific approach concerns the costs of adjustment. If you are interested in the politics of trade observed over a generation, then you care about the long-run interests of domestic actors. Over the course of several decades, the costs of adjustment can be discounted. The Stolper–Samuelson perspective may be entirely appropriate then. If, however, you are interested in political activity over the course of a few months or a single year, then the costs associated with adjustment appear quite significant. Under those conditions, it would make much more sense to employ the sector-specific view (Magee, Brock and Young 1989). (If one could gather the relevant data on the composition of sectors, then applying intra-industry firm heterogeneity makes even better sense.)

In summary, the three main economic models of the domestic distribution of the gains and losses from trade are not equal. Some require much more detailed information than others; some provide clear but general pictures of expected preferences on trade, while others depict the distribution of preferences in much greater detail. Data availability may force a researcher to use one model rather than the others. Knowing the desired time-frame for the question at hand is also important for choosing the appropriate economic model to employ. These questions are quite important, since any errors or problems with the information developed in the initial stage will affect the overall results, regardless of decisions made in the following steps.

Box 9.5 The first stage of the open economy approach

In the first step of the open economy approach to the politics of trade, an economic model describes the array of interests in the domestic setting. This description informs each of the following steps, giving the overall argument key characteristics.

How individuals organize for political activity

The second step in the politics of trade in an open economy describes the way individuals come together to engage in domestic politics. If economics lays down the basic distribution of interests, then we need to understand how disagreement between rival viewpoints gets resolved. Political power matters; not all individuals wield the same power. Moreover, individuals rarely act alone in domestic politics. Instead, those who share interests come together to influence outcomes. Scholars have argued, however, that various latent groups do not share the same probability of uniting for effective political action.

Barriers to collective action

Some of the most important contributions to the study of collective action were made by Mancur Olson (1965). Olson's observations concentrated on the factors allowing some individuals to gather together easily, compared to those that could only form a group with great difficulty. These observations continue to inform our understanding of the first steps in the translation of preferences into political action.

Interest groups' inherent attributes

Olson noted that some latent economic interest groups found it easy to mobilize for political action because they already shared characteristics. Take for instance a set of farmers who grow the same sort of crops; they are participants in the same economic sector. Let's assume they therefore share a preference on trade policy, because the good they grow is exported. Can these producers unite to mobilize for political action on trade? Consider whether these individuals physically gather together for other reasons, such as social interaction. If the majority of these farmers belong to one religion, they may join together for regular services in the same place and the same time. This would facilitate discussions where they could formulate plans for taking action collectively.

Olson also considered the geographic distribution of the individuals in a latent interest group to be a factor in the difficulty of mobilizing for collective action. In our example above, we considered the circumstances confronting farmers. Typically, farmers have worked in isolation. (Occasionally, farmers gather together to harness their group strength, when they share in an activity such as a barn raising or to harvest crops.) If individuals are very widely dispersed, this distribution can be an obstacle to collective action. On the other hand, urban interests tend to be geographically concentrated. If we compare our farmers to workers in a large factory, the workers would surely find it much easier to gather together. One should note that the impact of geographic dispersion may be offset by technological improvements in the means of communication between individuals; advances in social media illustrate that thousands of individuals can now rapidly communicate with each other in ways that would astonish previous generations.

The number of individuals in the latent interest group also matter. In the case of industrial workers in one industry, or farmers in one sector, we could be describing tens of thousands of individuals, if not hundreds of thousands. If we were thinking about the owners of some businesses, on the other hand, there may simply be few in number. For much of the twentieth century, there were only a handful of major automobile manufacturers in the U.S.; they were known as the "Big Four." If you only need to coordinate actions between the corporate executives from a few companies, then the challenges to collective action are clearly lower than if you need to get agreement among tens of thousands of individuals.

When considering intra-industry firm heterogeneity, the nature of the products in the sector matter as well (Bombardini and Trebbi 2012). In some instances, output can be considered a commodity – where there is little differentiation between one firm's product and that of others. In other instances, products may be quite differentiated. This too can influence lobbying, by setting up both potentially diverse preferences on trade, but also creating the opportunity for trade policy to deliver different treatments within one category of goods.

In summary, scholars focused on understanding collective action have identified several key factors shaping the relative ease for individuals in latent interest groups to mobilize for collective action. The presence of existing shared characteristics can come in to play; the geographic dispersion is a second key factor; the number of individuals potentially involved in the latent interest group also matters. While these shape the odds individuals sharing an interest will actually form into a group, there are also ways politicians can help tilt the odds in the favor of successful unity.

Overcoming barriers to collective action

Scholars such as Olson have noted how groups can act to overcome these obstacles. Political actors can create formal groups, then formulate positive incentives to membership. By offering some form of inducement, the political leader can attract followers; individuals will then join the group. The organization can then be a vehicle for collective action.

If geographic distance is an issue, then the individuals seeking to organize the group can create incentives to draw the potential members physically together. For example, in the late nineteenth century, the politicians interested in organizing farmers in the United States needed to develop some means of attracting individuals from a widespread area to a single location at the same point in time. The National Grange came up with an effective solution: provide meetings where technical information was shared, and farmers could receive training about new equipment or methods. These educational sessions drew in farmers from broad areas, creating the opportunity for the Grange's leaders to speak to farmers about their political positions. The National Grange successfully mobilized many rural voters around several issues, including the American tariff.

In the section above, the number of individuals in a latent group was considered an obstacle to collective action; the greater the number, the harder it would prove to organize them into a single body. Being numerous can be turned into an advantage, however. If the potential group is quite large, it can wield economic power as consumers, for instance. An organization able to gather a significant number of individuals into one body for purchasing can often negotiate better deals; any discounts earned can then be offered to all potential members, so that the organization pulls in more representatives of the latent group. This tactic has been used by a variety of organizations, ranging from labor unions to activists behind the American Association of Retired Persons (AARP). (AARP now claims 38 million members.)

In short, leaders seeking to mobilize individuals in a latent group have methods for overcoming the barriers to organization. By crafting incentives, the leaders can get more of the potential members involved. This is true for any latent economic interest group, but it matters for our understanding of the politics of trade, because economic interests alone don't get us far in our understanding of policy outcomes. Understanding which groups are likely to organize and exert political pressure gets us into the domestic political process. Armed with better information about the potential groups holding rival views on trade policy, we can start to depict how they will compete in domestic politics.

Box 9.6 Although the economic models may identify individuals

Although the economic models may identify individuals who share preferences on trade policy, not all groups get heard. Theories of collective action help us understand how easily groups can form to articulate their preferences.

Incorporating other cleavages

When it comes to understanding contests between trade-based interest groups, we tend to describe them in terms of cleavages (i.e., who stands on each side of the issue) (Dalton 1996). It is important to note that trade policy does not always command political significance. There are certainly times when trade policy has dominated the political agenda in many countries, of course, but we shouldn't expect to observe it taking prominence consistently (either across time or across countries). Other issues will always be in play. Trade, as a matter affecting how groups compete, interacts with these other policy issues.

Preexisting cleavages

Other economic or social issues generate their own cleavages. In the past in western Europe, religious divisions were often prominent, with Catholics and Protestants adopting different visions about a number of policies, such as the role of civil authorities in managing education or handling social welfare. That preexisting cleavage could be critical for understanding politics, because this split determined the basic means for political expression (such as political parties). Linguistic divisions inside countries have historically played a similar role in shaping political alignments. These cleavages were often more significant politically than those based on any economic interests, let alone trade policy.

The presence of these other cleavages can make it easier or harder for interest groups centered on trade policy to form. In some historical situations, for instance, individuals who owned one factor, or belonged in one sector, found it difficult to come together around trade policy. In Imperial Germany, small farmers grew similar crops, meaning they shared a preference on trade policy, yet for many years they were unable to rally together. The small landowners in the southern regions belonged to the Catholic party, whereas the small farmers in the north backed Protestant parties; these different parties declined to work together. In comparison, the very large landowners in Imperial Germany concentrated production on a single crop (rye); more importantly, as Protestants of the same social standing, they naturally joined the same party. These large landowners easily rallied together to support a single political party that focused its effort on maintaining a protective tariff on grains. The large landowners enjoyed much greater success in the pursuit of the trade-based interests, compared to the small farmers.

The trade-based cleavages have to be integrated into the more complex image of domestic politics. Other issues often take precedence in domestic politics. The way in which these other cleavages operate can increase the importance of the trade-based cleavages or overwhelm them. Understanding the presence of other cleavages is rather important, because these may exert powerful influence on the divisions over trade policy identified in the initial step of the analysis.

Are cleavages reinforcing or crosscutting?

Sometimes these other cleavages fall along the same general lines as the trade-based split; we refer to these as reinforcing cleavages. In other instances, the more prominent cleavage runs in an entirely different direction; we refer to these as crosscutting. As an example of a reinforcing cleavage, imagine a country such as Canada or the United States, which expanded geographically as its frontier spread westward. The pace of that growth was bound up with immigration. If immigrants came in waves, with many leaving their place of origin simultaneously because of natural disasters or political upheaval, they often settled in the less populated frontier areas together. This produced frontier regions largely populated by farmers with a common immigrant background (which could entail shared linguistic, ethnic and/or religious traits). Meanwhile, their concentration in a specific geographic area often pushed them to produce the same agricultural product.

These conditions produce reinforcing cleavages, making it easier for the members of this latent interest group to overcome the barriers to collective action. In the example of the frontier farmers, they have opportunities to gather at religious meetings, or shared holidays. A classic example of this pattern occurred in the late nineteenth century, when Scandinavian immigrants populated the upper Midwest of the United States; these settlers in a state like Wisconsin concentrated on dairy production. The fact they shared a single religion, an old-world language, and common cultural traditions facilitated their collective action in politics.

Crosscutting cleavages have a different impact. These cleavages can undercut efforts to mobilize for collective action. If in our example, instead of all local farmers belonging to the same ethnic background or sharing the same religion, they were divided by those traits, yet they produced the same crop, they would face difficulties in recognizing their shared economic interests. Crosscutting cleavages open up opportunities for politicians to manipulate situations in different ways. If in our example, there are political leaders interested in getting the farmers who grow the most important crop in the region together (despite the farmers' differences) for the purpose of promoting trade liberalization, they may come up with incentives to draw the farmers together; opposing politicians, however, could play on those other cleavages, by raising the salience of an alternative issue. Speaking up about religion or linguistic differences or proposing an adjustment on an existing policy relevant in these areas, can reduce the likelihood the large trade-based group will form. Of course, in some situations the trade-based cleavage might be the one played up for political purposes, to divert from another.

These insights point to the need to map out the most significant cleavages in any given political context, in order to identify how the latent trade-based interests interact with other cleavages. This suggests that some portion of the time, the cleavages generated by trade get submerged or distorted in the jumble of competing policy areas that motivate political activity. The trade-based cleavage can be the dominant one in play, when the stakes involved in trade are high. Also, if cleavages reinforce one another, trade policy can take on more political significance, as a glue that holds otherwise disparate groups together. Rogowski's application of the Stolper–Samuelsson theorem demonstrated how often this could occur (1989).

Box 9.7 The second stage of the open economy approach

In the second stage of the open economy approach to the politics of trade, a political analysis captures the relative power of the various groups interested in shaping policy. This includes understanding their size, but also the intensity of their interests, as well as their ability to organize.

Expressing preferences in politics

Once groups form successfully, what sort of action do they take? The most obvious is lobbying – asking governments to alter trade policy to their advantage. Groups' efforts vary depending on the political arena they operate in. Such actions may be more easily observed in democratic settings, but it is entirely applicable to non-democratic situations as well. Efforts to influence policy necessarily concentrate on political competition. Groups might participate in competition directly. More commonly in democracies, political parties' aggregate interests into broader coalitions, giving voice to their supporters' policy preferences, and implementing those preferred policies once in office. Similar processes take place in non-democracies – they are simply harder to observe.

Lobbying

When we think of lobbying, most of us will picture a couple of more precise activities: representatives of narrow interest groups going to politicians to explain or elaborate their policy preferences, or those same representatives donating funds to the politicians they believe will implement their preferred policies if the politicians assume power. Lobbying involves both elements – the expression of preferences by groups, but also the provision of some sort of resource that enhances the ability of the political representative to compete for control over policy (Grossman and Helpmann 1994).

Resources interests' groups bring to bear

Which resources do political actors desire most? The answer depends on the nature of political competition. In modern western democracies, where politicians compete for votes, the ability to purchase advertising in mass media appears critical. Money can be the best resource in those settings, because it can be used to purchase all sorts of different services. Lobbying is often measured in monetary sums contributed to individual candidates or political parties. At the same time, new forms of social media have opened up different channels for reaching the masses, where money seems less important.

Other assets also matter. Volunteers willing to work on campaigns can be critical for electoral victory. Getting volunteers out to canvas tightly contested neighborhoods can be critical – that may be a more powerful way to connect to voters than simple radio or TV ads. The changes in mass media have also become so diverse, that people can easily avoid certain types of advertising. This may make the actions of volunteers more important than ever, since they can go door-to-door to speak with potential voters. Ride-sharing and other forms of volunteer activity on election day may also increase voter turnout.

The quality of individuals associated with a campaign effort also matter. All social or mass media does not carry the same impact. Having skilled operators providing support can be more critical than the total amount of funds spent. A poorly made ad, shown over and over, may actually damage a party's image. Celebrity endorsements have also proven powerful in a number of different electoral contests. Getting "star power" behind a candidate or a party can be very influential in democratic contests.

Since elections are popularity contests, the number of individuals in a particular group may matter as well. Reflect on the original observation Stolper and Samuelson made; they asked why a country such as the United States preferred protectionist tariffs. The argument is remembered for its economic logic – the owners of relatively scarce factors of production prefer protection, the owners of relatively abundant factors of production prefer freer trade. Yet the particular case they described also identified an important political component: in their case, the relatively scarce factor of production was labor. Labor could dominate the policy choice in the United States because the working class contained more voters than the capitalist and land-owning classes combined. Groups that can deliver ballots clearly have a resource politician in democracies seek.

In non-democratic settings, the key resources for effective lobbying presumably overlap with the ones mentioned so far. The ability to engage policymakers may be an essential resource. Anyone familiar with policy-making mechanisms in monarchies knows how important it is for lobbyists to gain access to the king or queen. Intrigue in the court has been the fuel for many historical episodes of trade policy change. Court favorites received privileges during the mercantilist era; often they promised to increase the kingdom's wealth, but just as often they shared profits with rulers.

In some non-democracies, the lack of transparency makes it difficult for us to formulate or apply our arguments. One may easily do the economic calculations regarding the distribution of interests on trade for a country such as the Peoples Republic of China, but without a better sense of who has the central government's ear, we may find it difficult to predict future Chinese trade policy decisions. At the same time, we know that in all these political settings, there are some sort of channels allowing constituents to communicate their preferences on policy to decision makers, and the people taking the decisions need to maintain some minimal amount of legitimacy to remain in power.

Institutional settings and the value of different resources

Understanding the way competition takes place suggests there may be some very subtle differences in the sort of resources that wield the most power in lobbying. Modern countries practice democracy in a wide variety of ways. Parliamentary systems focus all attention on the legislature, and voters typically have a simple choice (selecting a candidate based on party affiliation alone). Presidential systems usually separate the election of the head of the executive branch from the choice of representative in the legislature. This opens up several alternate possibilities for mixing up ones vote across races. The American system may be the best known of the presidential systems. In it, individual candidates can often operate quite independently from the national party leaders, whereas parliamentary systems tend to have quite strong party discipline (i.e., from the leader down to party members). In the American system, fund-raising takes place across all levels, and in many different directions; in parliamentary systems, parties typically control the most funds.

Box 9.8 Domestic institutions shape how groups compete

Domestic institutions shape how groups compete. These rules shape which resources matter in this competition.

This observation also holds when applying this approach across historical settings. Britain's initial turn towards free trade in the 1840s provides us several key examples. In the previous decades, Britain had maintained tariffs on foodstuffs (and grain in particular) as measures designed to ensure the country could feed itself during wartime. The growth of the population, coupled with urbanization and industrialization, left the price of bread and other basic items quite high; newly rich manufacturers understood they would benefit from freer trade because that would enable them to sell more abroad, but also provide more for urban residents to consume. There were also a couple of clear obstacles for reducing tariffs, however. Tariffs were legislated, and in those days the electorate for the House of Commons was tightly restricted. To vote, one had to have a particularly high income, or own land. The Anti-Corn Law League, a lobbying group, raised funds to challenge the tariffs. It spent its money on speakers and pamphlets, spreading its message – but also to aid its own followers in the purchasing of land. By purchasing land, these supporters earned the right to vote.

A concentration of resources can be important in the parliamentary settings, since the party leader tends to matter more than the individual candidates in the separate electoral districts. Since voters are bound to the local party candidate if they wish for that party's leader to serve as the prime minister, they may not care much about the quality of the local candidate. In a system such as the American, however, where voters can split their votes across parties (endorsing one party's candidate for president, but another's for Congress), the quality of the lower-level candidate matters very much. Lower-level candidates that can develop their own resources can operate more independently from their own party leadership.

Political parties

As mentioned above, we think of political parties as the conduits for political interests, and this is true whether we speak of democratic settings or not. In non-democratic settings, membership in a political party can be key to gaining access to policy making – just think about states ruled by one party, such as the old Soviet Union. In democracies, parties are the vehicle for competition. Parties serve in this capacity by gathering different groups of voters together into a larger organization.

Parties as aggregations of interests

The role parties play as the means for gathering interests together is especially apparent in American politics. Institutional arrangements press for the creation of broad coalitions; this setting pressures groups to coalesce into two large parties. These parties necessarily stretch to encompass diverse interests. Groups prioritizing different issues have to meld together to form an effective national political party. (As Roy Rogers once quipped, "I'm not a member of an organized political party, I'm a Democrat.")

While this process of joining together takes time to develop, there are moments where the joining together becomes concrete. Historically, these moments occurred at national conventions. American elections occur on a regular schedule; presidential elections take place very 4 years. Once the primaries are over, and different potential candidates have their supporters in line, they all gather to select the party's nominee; but this is also the opportunity to sort out the party's goals and establish which to emphasize in the coming campaign. After much debate, the results can be seen in the party's platform, its statement of positions on the most important issues of the day. A quick glance at many past party platforms will illustrate how important trade policy has been at times.

Convention debates shine a light on this process. These debates provide excellent examples of the process of interest aggregation. The platform is shaped in ways the party leaders expect will attract the most support among voters. These discussions can provide important evidence for establishing whether our picture of the underlying interests is accurate, as various delegations voice their preferred stance on trade. We then also see how trade policy fits with other issues, in terms of priorities.

Parties as channels of influence

Political parties transmit the messages and policy positions of the groups they rely on for support. In democracies, this is done via competition in the electoral cycle, where the party works hard to get its message out – it describes its agenda for future policy to voters. The party's campaign materials lay out how the party would govern, should it gain office.

In the original version of this analytical version of liberalism, Moravcsik (1997) assumed the state served the interests of the dominant groups in society. In other words, once the party competition ended, the basic version of this approach takes it as given that the government then follows the instructions it receives. This is in contrast to other approaches that assume the government has relative autonomy; the many variants of Realism adopt this alternative view. Neo-Classical Realism, for instance, would consider the interests of domestic actors, but place them in opposition to the state, with the state primarily focused on delivering security from international threats (Brawley 2017a).

Box 9.9 Political parties aggregate domestic interests

Political parties aggregate domestic interests into broader coalitions, capable of competing for control over state policy.

For members of the party in office, the platform determined before the election becomes a measuring stick for voters to use to evaluate the elected officials' performance. Whether voters truly do retrospective evaluations of governing officials is the subject of a good deal of debate (Guisinger 2009). Nonetheless, we generally expect the governing party's performance to be judged in the next round of competition by how well that party delivers the policies its supporters requested. This naturally includes how the governing party implements the preferred trade policy of its backers.

Competition within institutional settings

The rules of the political game shape the competition that parties engage in (Powell 2000; Rickard 2015). Readers in North America may be most familiar with elections based on "first past the post" (FPTP) competition within geographically circumscribed districts. In other words, the candidate with the most votes will win the right to sit in the legislature to represent the voters from a specific area. This is hardly the only form of democratic practices, of course. Some countries use "proportional representation" (PR), a system where large areas of the country (or perhaps even the entire country as a whole) chooses representatives from a number of party slates; each party then receives the number of seats proportional to the percentage of votes its candidates earned. Institutional practices vary in many other ways, and these differences exert a powerful influence on the nature and number of parties (Farrell 2011). That in turn can shape the relevance of trade-based interests in domestic political competition.

Lobbying and legislation

Institutional rules clearly shape the role of lobbying (Mahoney 2007). In many democracies, voters have come to question the significance of money in politics. Regulations have been introduced to cap the amount any one individual or group may donate to political parties or particular candidates, though these have proven hard to enforce. Institutional arrangements determine several key parts of the lobbying equation. Institutional arrangements dictate where decisions get made, who is involved, and thus where lobbying efforts get concentrated.

Where in the government does trade policy get made? Over the centuries, we have observed several different loci of activity on trade policy. In the mercantilist era (from the seventeenth to the early nineteenth century), most states weren't democratic. Instead they were ruled by monarchs. Policy originated in the royal court. Lobbying necessarily focused there. Those seeking to change trade policy typically exerted efforts to gain access to the advisors closest to the monarch, and then used their resources to tilt those advisors towards their own preferred policy.

In the nineteenth and twentieth centuries, tariffs comprised the main component of trade policy. As a form of tax, the tariff tended to be crafted as legislation. This meant trade policy emerged from legislatures, with hearings conducted, bills drafted and debated in committees, then final versions approved. On the one hand, this process identifies key legislators lobbyists would concentrate their attention on: the chairs of committees engaged in formulating the legislation. On the other hand, it also shows the need to create broad coalitions of support to get a majority behind one's preferred legislation.

In more recent times, the trade policy-making process has often returned to the hands of executives, and away from legislatures; this trend reflects the growing importance of existing international commitments governing trade policy. In the late nineteenth and early twentieth centuries, states often made their policy choices in rough isolation, whereas today they participate in international organizations overseeing trade (such as the WTO). Since the executive usually conducts these negotiations first, then reports them back to the legislature for approval, the executive can in effect set priorities, choose where to give concessions, and so on. The final product may not be easily altered by the legislature. This has naturally drawn lobbyists to focus more of their efforts on the executive element of government once again.

Elections

The rules governing competition in democracies clearly shape which voices get heard, and which do not (Rickard 2012; Ardelean and Evans 2013). As noted above, democracies come in several different forms. The most widespread may be the British-style Parliamentary style, where the executive commands a majority of seats in the legislature. The legislature is composed of seats representing geographically bounded electoral districts. Each seat is won by the candidate earning the greatest number of voters (i.e., a plurality) in that district. In such a set-up, groups that can mobilize for collective action that have some geographic concentration may be consistently rewarded with representation.

Where electoral districts are geographically defined, groups will need to be somewhat dispersed in order to be truly powerful. Let us consider an example, using the sector-specific approach. Most of the participants in the production of a certain export item may operate in a rather limited region; think of iron and steel production, which historically developed where sources of coal and iron ore were both readily available. If the elements of land, labor and capital tied up with iron and steel production share a preference for trade liberalization, then those interests will be heard in this specific region. How many seats in the legislature does that translate to? There will be a strong consistent representation for the iron and steel sector, to be sure, but one needs more than one loud voice to get policy shifted. Sometimes, it is better to have the sector's participants widely distributed across regions, so that the sector has political weight alongside voice.

Box 9.10 This approach can be used to explain why states

This approach can be used to explain why states prefer protection, even when this fails to maximize the gains for society as a whole. Trade policy merely serves the desires of the politically dominant domestic group, regardless of how narrow it may be. Power in the domestic setting determines who sets policy goals.

In other institutional settings, such issues may not matter. In a country relying on large districts with proportional representation, the sector's relative geographic concentration will simply be less important. Overall numbers of supporters will matter more. Understanding how domestic institutions shape the ability of domestic actors to express their preferences comes from comparative politics; it may be the most important area in the entire open economy framework where theories and models from political science contribute to our understanding of the politics of trade.

Box 9.11 The third stage of the open economy approach

The third step in the open economy approach to the politics of trade addresses the domestic political competition between the various groups, as they vie for control over policy-making. Analysts use models from comparative politics to understand which groups win.

Implementing the preferred policy

As just noted, the location of policy making has varied over time and across cases. Trade policy itself has come in many forms, as well. In the mercantilist era, regulations covering trade emanated from the monarch. As more democratic institutions and constitutional changes constrained monarchical power in the nineteenth century, tariff legislation more typically controlled trade. In the twentieth century, governments became more deeply involved with regulating the economy, opening the door to non-tariff barriers to trade (NTBs) (Mansfield and Busch 1995). These NTBs could emerge from legislation but might also arise from bureaucratic regulations. The emphasis on international commitments (via regional treaties and multilateral institutions) has perhaps brought decision-making on trade back into the hands of chief executives, as they typically dominate international negotiations.

Forms of trade policy

Trade policy decisions come in many different forms. We naturally address tariffs – the tax governments impose on goods when they cross an international border. (Export duties have become relatively rare, but they also mattered in some past cases.) While non-tariff barriers are more common now (such as the use of environmental regulations to block imports), there are examples from previous centuries where health and safety issues were implemented to block foreign goods from entry.

Legislation

As noted above, tariffs comprise an element of tax, created through domestic legislation. This provides us plenty of detailed evidence to test out our expectations. For example, in my own work on American trade policy in the early 1900s, I applied intra-industry firm heterogeneity (Brawley 2017b). This was relevant to several important manufacturing sectors, where large trusts had just been created. As the economic theory would predict, several very large efficient companies dominated American exports for their sectors. These exporting firms' efforts to shape trade policy could be seen via their endorsement of certain parties or candidates, especially during national elections. Once elections ended, the winning party members took their seats in Congress, and began formulating the new tariff. This process would often involve the gathering of testimonies from experts, which would include executives from different firms. The legislators themselves would then debate the various options, generating more evidence to consider, before writing the new legislation. The proposed tariff would then be voted on.

Because so many countries relied on tariff legislation in the nineteenth and early twentieth century, we have a large number of empirical cases to examine. These often provide excellent ground for testing (and contrasting) various applications of the different versions of the first stages of the open economy approach. Law-making bodies are composed of representatives, often with particular legislators tied to specific geographic locations. This allows us to use data regarding economic activity in local settings to develop expectations about trade policy preferences, which we can then look for in the collective action undertaken by voters, the lobbying any such groups will do, the campaigning politicians undertake, the party platforms as crafted in the electoral competition, and then the voting that took place.

Tariffs are notoriously complex. Typically tariffs rates are determined separately for each good involved in trade. This categorization can be developed into very specific niches. In the tariffs applied by the U.S. or Germany in the late nineteenth century, imports were separated into thousands of separate categories, with rates changing across them. Consider a broad category such as textiles; it would be subdivided into clothing, rugs, and so on. The clothing category would be divided further, depending on whether the item was produced for men or women, the sort of clothing it was, the fibre it was made from, and so on. For the example of the United States circa 1900, imported rugs were not only separated into categories depending on the fibre used, but also by thread count. Rates were then tailored to effectively block imports of the sort of rugs American textile firms manufactured. In these ways, legislation could be crafted to deal not only with sector-level competition, but even to the sort of good only a handful of American firms produced.

While tariff bills could be large and complex pieces of legislation, the process was fairly transparent, and we have the legislation itself to examine. When countries deploy NTBs, or when executive agencies implement trade policy, the impact can be more discreet and marginal – making it harder to observe in the first place. This is also true of the political process underlying such actions. The use of NTBs rests on the premise that the government has the duty to regulate the safety, health and environmental impact of goods, and thus should take action not only through legislation but through bureaucratic matters to serve its constituents' welfare. Yet this opens up the possibility the state will employ rules discriminating against imports. The combination of the opaque process plus the claim that other issues are paramount, make these more difficult to analyze (Mansfield and Busch 1995).

International agreements

Tariffs set by legislation were open to constant fluctuation, depending on the power of the competing domestic interests. If political institutions push for a two-party system, and the two parties adopt rival positions on trade policy, then every time the government changes hands, the dominant party has the opportunity to reverse the trade policy implemented by its predecessor. Tariffs were also adjusted in much of the period before World War II, as one of the primary tools governments hoped to use to manage the country's macroeconomic performance. Thus, it was not unusual to see tariffs constantly adjusted in some countries. (This was quite true of the U.S., though we can also identify others, such as Britain, which maintained fairly stable tariffs for many decades.) The advent of the Great Depression induced the U.S. and several other countries to employ tariffs in an effort to stimulate the economy. These efforts only reaped disastrous results. Not only did higher tariffs fail to stimulate domestic growth, they also triggered retaliations that destroyed exports (Eichengreen and Irwin 2011). The broader lesson learned by the western industrialized economies emerging from World War II was that trade should be liberalized, and tariffs used sparingly (Ruggie 1982).

One way to commit a country to a specific stance on trade is to implement that policy via a treaty with another country. That sort of promise often "ties the hands" of later governments. The Great Depression and World War II had decimated existing trade relations. This event wiped the slate clean in many respects, creating the opportunity for countries to rethink what sort of practices they would ideally adopt. The representatives of a wide range of countries gathered in Havana in 1948 to choose a new set of norms and rules to regulate their trading arrangements but failed to reach an agreement. A subset of countries — the western industrialized states — settled on a vague set of principles for guiding their international trade policies, based on the experience of the 1930s. Their agreement, GATT (General Agreement on Trade and Tariffs), promoted several key ideas. GATT stressed the need for liberalization of tariff levels, and for the avoidance of discriminatory tariff rates.

GATT grew in membership over the decades, and eventually evolved into the World Trade Organization (WTO). As of 2018, the WTO has 164 members; these states have signed on to rules that continue to reflect the original GATT principles. The number of members, and the inclusion of all the world's largest economies, speaks to the importance of international negotiations and commitments in the contemporary formulation of trade policy.

As the number of states involved in the GATT and then WTO negotiations increased, the talks grew in complexity. It became increasingly difficult to make further progress in trade liberalization. It had appeared in the 1990s that some sort of grand bargain was being struck, where western Europe and Japan would make concessions in agricultural protection, economically developing countries would open up their economies to liberalized trade in services, and the United States would accept improved dispute settlement mechanisms (Ostry 2002). These promises have been difficult to implement in the ensuing decades. Both the larger number of states, and the increased diversity of interests involved, has made current negotiations difficult to complete.

As a result, states wishing to continue to liberalize trade (by expanding liberalization to cover new areas of economic activity, or by cutting tariff rates even lower) have turned to bilateral or regional negotiations in recent decades. Here again we have the use of international commitments to bind the hands of successive governments. These are often quite effective as well, since they can be focused on a set of countries that trade intensively with each other.

The international structure of preferences

The open economy approach focuses first and foremost on explanations for the policy preferences of a single state. If one executes simultaneous analyses for a second country, the preferences of the two countries can be compared; this process can then be repeated for more states, creating a bigger picture. This larger portrait, what Moravcsik (1997) referred to as the structure of preferences, gives us insight on the possibilities for international cooperation or conflict (Betz 2017). If several states share a desire to liberalize trade at the same time, they clearly have the potential to strike a deal. If, on the other had, states bring conflicting preferences to the table, the likelihood of reaching an agreement is clearly diminished.

Bilateral relations

The simplest depiction of interaction at the system-level involves the interaction of two states. As described above, this can be done by applying the bottom-up process to two states, then reflecting on the interaction of their preferences. This can be fairly simple, when the two countries share economic and political characteristics. More often however, the two states have very different traits, meaning the analysis for one does not look like the analysis done for the other.

Note that this requires access to information about both countries' economic characteristics, the ability of their domestic groups to organize, the political competition inside each, and so forth. The analysis may look quite different in the two, since the political processes may vary in important ways. In his work on the impact of trade policy on the Anglo-German rivalry in the first decade of the twentieth century, Papayoanou (1996) executed such an analysis. He examined the domestic interests driving the trade ties between the two countries but noted the economic significance of the pro-free trade groups in Germany did not translate into control over foreign policy due to Imperial Germany's political institutions. It remains an interesting example of how to describe a bilateral trade relationship using the open economy framework.

Regional international trade agreements have also gained in popularity in recent decades. Consider the deals made to create the North American Free Trade Agreement (NAFTA). To understand how this agreement was reached, we would need to examine the domestic interests inside the three countries (Canada, the U.S. and Mexico). These economies are not necessarily alike, nor are their political systems. Yet if we execute such research, we would discover the grounds for the three coming together around a shared preference for trade liberalization at a particular point in time.

The open economy approach can be used to examine regional arrangements, though it should be apparent that the amount of work needed rises as the number of states involved increases. Some regional agreements include only a few states, such as NAFTA; the Trans Pacific Partnership (TPP), a proposed agreement that has not come to fruition, would have had a dozen members. Executing the open economy approach to these many states would require a researcher a good deal of time and effort. Reporting the results would also require more space than could be easily fit inside a 25-page journal article. In short, the open economy approach becomes somewhat unwieldy as we examine broader systemic outcomes.

International regimes

Scholars wishing to characterize practices at the level of the international economy developed the concept of international regimes (Krasner 1982). This concept refers to the rules, norms, practices and procedures around which actors' decision-making revolves. These rules or norms can be prohibitive or prescriptive; they can also be implicit or explicit. They have varied over the centuries. These international economic regimes are typically described in terms of their nature (do they promote opening up of economies, or their closure), their scope (what all do the rules or norms cover), and their strength (do they bind states' behavior, or are states relatively free to do what they want?).

Prior to the nineteenth century, the international trade regime was characterized by closure, as almost all powers employed mercantilist practices in efforts to control trade flows. Since most of the European powers were monarchies, it is easy to see how the open economy approach would focus on the internal dynamics of royal courts, as monarchs gave privileges to favorites. In return, anyone receiving privileges often shared benefits directly with the monarch. One of the most important exceptions to this pattern, the United Provinces of the Netherlands, tried to pursue freer trade. This can be explained, via the open economy approach, as the result not only of a powerful merchant class, but also because of the internal political institutions of the Dutch Republic. The United Provinces practiced a complex representative government, so that the merchants' broader voices controlled policy. Yet, with few other states receptive to Dutch offers, the systemic outcome has to be described as primarily one of closure.

The situation only changed in the mid-nineteenth century, when a number of the major economies removed their tariffs. This produced a rapid expansion in the volume of international trade in the 1860s and 1870s. Britain led the way in these reforms, through a series of changes to its trade policy legislation in the late 1840s. The approach described here again works well to capture the process in Britain; we can observe the shifting balance of domestic interests over time and trace its impact on politics. The final decisions remain misunderstood however, since the most dramatic step was taken by Sir Robert Peel's government; Peel had taken office as a protectionist. Further problems emerge when we apply this approach to the other major powers that followed Britain's lead. It is not entirely clear that free trade interests really held the upper hand politically in many of these subsequent liberalizers.

Those who study systemic outcomes often avoid examining the domestic political processes associated with all the participating states, because this is too difficult. (Data may be unavailable, the amount of cases becomes too great, and so forth.) Instead, they concentrate on the handful of most important players in the system at one point in time. This allows the researcher to concentrate on the states whose preferences are most likely to be felt anyway. Put differently, we look at Britain's trade policy preferences in the mid-nineteenth century, because we know that when other states' preferences clashed with Britain's desire for more openness, the British view would more often prevail. British power (in both its military and market forms) would tilt the balance in its favor.

Researchers don't have to concentrate on a single country, they can examine the top set of economic powers to get a picture of the likely systemic outcome. Someone using the open economy approach to predict what the international regime governing trade will look like 30 years from now would want to examine the roots of the policy preferences of the U.S., China, India and perhaps even the European Union. With those actors' preferences understood, the amount of future cooperation or conflict in the system could be estimated. However, note how difficult it might be to project the domestic economic interests and political processes at work in the EU or in China. Knowing how to do it, does not necessarily make it easy.

Box 9.12 The fourth stage of the open economy approach

The fourth stage in the open economy approach to the politics of trade moves from the analysis of a single country's policy, to the interaction of two or more countries. This jumps from comparative foreign economic policy to systemic outcomes. It uses states' preferences to describe whether states will find partners to cooperate with, or find clashing interests.

Recognizing trade policy's feedback

The best way to depict the open economy approach is as a circle. We start at the bottom with individual actors inside states, who then gather together based on shared trade preferences. Those groups then engage in the domestic political competition for control of the state, or at least of trade policy making. As the state then seeks to implement the policy preferred by the dominant domestic interests it engages other states. The results achieved at the level of the international system then determine the composition and volume of trade that takes place. As trade flows change, they have a direct impact back on domestic actors.

The economic impact of a change in policy

Once a country has adjusted its trade policy, our arguments expect that the change introduced affects economic activity, thereby redistributing wealth domestically. Political scientists often stop their analysis at the point where a new policy is selected and fail to consider whether the policy did in fact deliver the desired benefits to the groups that successfully demanded policy change. If trade is liberalized, the incentives to specialize kick in, and adjustment should occur. If trade is protected, then this process is halted, or perhaps reversed. In either case, there are some obvious implications.

Redistributing wealth

Trade liberalization should have two observable effects on the domestic economy. First it should increase the aggregate wealth in the country, all else being equal. We therefore think of trade liberalization as a motor for growth. Second, trade liberalization should prompt specialization towards the country's comparative advantage. This process may take time; expectations concerning the way it would unfold would depend upon the particular economic model one employed to begin with. But the entire framework is premised on the idea that individuals, acting rationally, engage in domestic politics to shift policy to their advantage. The whole process concerns earning benefits from trade policy.

If protectionism is adopted, then we can again formulate expectations on economic change. First, protectionism stifles trade, and denies one source of growth. This should hinder the economic potential of the country in the aggregate. More specifically in the open economy approach, we can predict the impact of protection on the distribution of wealth. According to the Stolper–Samuelson theorem, protection will increase the wealth of the relatively scarce factors of production; in the sector-specific approach, it increases the wealth of the import-competing sectors; and according to intra-intra-industry firm heterogeneity, protection rewards the less competitive firms across sectors affected by trade (in import-competing or exporting industries).

Importantly, protectionism often also rewards the state. If the form is a tariff, a tax on goods as they enter, then the imposition of a tariff generates additional income for the state. This incentive for protection introduces an additional actor into the equation – the state itself. In traditional applications of the approach described here, the state is merely a servant of the dominant domestic groups. (Other models, less popular in international political economy, focus on the state as a potentially important actor, separate from domestic groups, as mentioned above.)

This connection also identifies an interesting link between trade liberalization and changes in domestic tax regulations. In the nineteenth century, most national governments relied heavily on tariffs for their revenues. The adoption of free trade therefore raised a practical problem; the national government needed a new stream of revenue. This made some of the domestic fights over trade liberalization complicated, because that debate entailed the imposition of new financial burdens on constituents (Stein 1984).

Redistributing political power

In his groundbreaking application of the Stolper–Samuelson perspective on trade to politics, Rogowski (1989) emphasized how trade policy could create coalitions that otherwise were unlikely to form. Improvements in technology created opportunities to trade – raising the economic stakes. Class-based interests became salient, with certain class alignments forming around shared preferences on trade; those class coalitions then lived on, influencing other policy outcomes.

Part of Rogowski's argument hinges on the economic feedback just described. If the groups that dominate politics can set their desired trade policy, they should gain additional wealth compared to their opponents. Since we saw how wealth can be an important resource in lobbying and domestic political competition, control over trade policy has economic repercussions, and these in turn can redistribute political power. Often the groups able to determine trade policy invested a portion of their new-found wealth in ensuring they maintained political control for the future.

When the proponents of free trade gain control of the state, and implement their preferred trade policy, they not only gain additional wealth, but trade adjustment alters the composition of domestic economic activity. As Richard E. Baldwin and Frédéric Robert-Nicoud (2008) have argued, this political economic process can feed back, gaining momentum. This is clearest in the sector-specific approach, but also works in the intra-industry firm heterogeneity perspective. In the former, trade liberalization causes the economic activity of exporting sectors to increase, while the import-competing industries shrink. Adjustment involves the reallocation of factors of production from import-competing industries to the exporting sectors. The protectionist interests are not only poorer but decline in number as well. Intra-industry firm heterogeneity describes a similar process, since trade liberalization will eliminate the firms most desirous of protection.

Trade policy does not always get locked in, of course, because change can come from different sources. Consider how many steps the argument has worked through to get to this point. Disruptions can occur within any one step. Underlying economic interests can be changed by new forms of technology, shifts in population, or other forces. The ability to organize might change with new forms of communication. Domestic upheaval or a revolution might alter political institutions. While it remains true that trade policy will likely reinforce the political success of the dominant groups, we can identify many reasons to expect trade policy to be remade.

Why trade's impact matters

We focus on trade policy because it impacts both the total wealth of a society, but also the distribution of the wealth across domestic actors. To return to one of the initial points raised in this piece, economists identified these stakes long ago. Yet historically, we know that free trade has been relatively rare (Alt et al. 1996). In addition, we know that the wealth of a society is often associated with other outcomes, such the attainment of international power, prestige and a range of other societal goals.

Economic changes

Evidence from the last quarter century demonstrates just how important trade policy can be. In the 1980s, a number of economically developing states were experimenting with trade liberalization. These included two of the world's most populous states: India and China. Each had experienced frustration with their efforts to promote industrialization from behind tariff barriers. They both began opening up their economies to increasing amounts of trade in the 1970s and 1980s. Exports have fueled improvements in both countries' wealth and even of economic activity.

When the Cold War ended, and the Soviet Union collapsed, a wide number of states abandoned state-managed economic practices. The ideological shift prompted reconsideration of trade policies, with many states converting to more open trade practices (Milner and Mukherjee 2009). GATT began in 1948 with less than 20 members; today the WTO has 164 participating states, with another 24 states involved as observers. Participation in trade liberalization in this era has also proven to be economically advantageous. Trade liberalization generates wealth, but also improves productivity; the growth produced typically lifts more people out of poverty (Winters, McCullouch and McKay 2004).

Noneconomic outcomes

Increases in trade are associated with negative outcomes as well. As noted early on, the gains from trade come from specialization. Specialization entails adjusting what one makes, as well as how one makes those goods. This adjustment is disruptive – and while the discussion above centered on the economic processes, those economic processes often involve dislocations of where people live, levels of inequality in society, and so on. While specialization can increase aggregate wealth, the country itself may be hit with undesirable side-effects. (This also includes the possibility of environmental damage.) Economists might point out a simple notion: the wealthier the country, the better positioned it is to address these side-effects. On the other hand, some of these consequences to trade may be difficult to manage precisely because they impact society in unpredictable ways.

The growth in the volume of trade is also associated with imports of certain types of goods that may influence local culture. This has been tied to the political backlash against globalization. For all the economic benefits freer trade may deliver, the social disruptions can trigger great hostility. Tom Friedman's book *The Lexus and the Olive Tree* (1999) captures the ambivalence many feel towards trade liberalization. People desire the wealth trade creates, symbolized by the Lexus. Yet people want to retain their cultural roots, represented by the olive tree. Political leaders seek to strike the right balance between these goals, as they manage their trade policy.

Economic wealth is also considered the root of other desirable attributes. In international relations, we recognize states desire their own security and autonomy. Economic wealth is clearly one of the sources of international power. Governments recognize that wealth can infer them with legitimacy; trade has become an important tool for non-non-democratic regimes to maintain their popular support (Wu 2015). (We see this in how international sanctions have become a powerful tool to pressure all states, include the non-democratic ones.) Trade becomes the vehicle to wealth, which then contributes to the pursuit for many other goals.

Box 9.13 The last stage of the open economy approach

The last stage of the open economy approach to the politics of trade "closes the circle." It examines the impact of a change in trade policy itself, to understand where actual gains and losses are distributed in the domestic arena.

Choosing the right tools for understanding the politics of trade

Having reviewed the basic choices within the open economy approach, we can now review some of the consequences associated with the particular decisions researchers make. From the initial stage forward, each decision influences the work that follows. Certain options necessarily constrain later choices. These decisions shape the traits of the results produced.

Opportunities and constraints with economic models

The most important decision in the open economic approach arises in the very first step. Choosing one economic model to capture trade's impact will shape everything that follows. The three basic economic models can be compared in terms of parsimony, accuracy and generalizability. Each one embodies a particular balance of these characteristics.

The Stolper–Samuelson approach is the most parsimonious of the three. It has the simplest view of the distributional impact of trade. It also has a very vague picture of trade adjustment however. It appears to be accurate in the long term, though not in the short run. It is very generalizable, since it can be easily applied across both space and time. Utilizing this approach makes the later work easier, since we only need to identify the owners of assets to make predictions about the chief cleavage on trade. (This means we require comparatively less information about the domestic political economy.) This also sets us up to talk about broad political movements.

The sector-specific approach adds in more complexity, asking us to understand where particular units of each factor of production are employed. This will raise informational requirements (compared to the Stolper–Samuelson view), but the trade-off is in gaining a more detailed picture of the interests at stake, as well as of the trade adjustment process itself. This approach too appears to be generalizable across space and time. The data required to employ this perspective can then be used to make more informed and detailed predictions about diverse political opinions on trade; here we can shift from broad political categories to more particular coalitions constructed around trade.

Intra-industry firm heterogeneity is the least parsimonious; it requires information not only about the country's endowments of the factors of production relative to other states, and about the distribution of sectors, but also about the composition of those sectors. Although it requires more information, it also produces the most detailed picture of the competing interests. This also makes the political analysis a bit more difficult, however, since it requires a more detailed look at the political competition. This can be rewarding when the necessary information is required. It may not be very generalizable, however, for two reasons. First, not all sectors demonstrate heterogeneity (leaving one to utilize the sector-specific approach). Second, the information required (for either the initial step or the later ones) can be difficult to obtain, preventing researchers from using this approach.

Modeling the political processes

As a discipline, political science contributes to the open economy approach by incorporating theories of domestic political competition in to the framework. This works in several discrete stages – the organization of individuals and firms into groups mobilized for collective action, the channeling of interests into aggregations (typically political parties), and then the competition between those larger bodies for control of the state.

This sets us up to appreciate several different locations in the framework where change can originate. The economic models suggest change would come from the engagement of new states into international trade or some domestic shift in the factors of production (such as the expansion of land via frontier settlement, the union of two states, or the amassing of savings). The political models suggest we might see change in trade policy due to alterations in the methods (or circumstances) affecting groups ability to act collectively. This has been used to explain why policy changed at points in time (as when newsprint became cheaper, allowing flyers and newspapers to be more widely disseminated).

Alterations in political institutions – the "rules of the game" in domestic politics – clearly affect outcomes. We associate the advent of democratization as a empowering the voices of actors previously ignored. The trade liberalization that initially swept the global economy in the mid-nineteenth century was often determined by a select set of the richest members of society. These wealthy individuals often held particular assets, because republican systems only enfranchised property owners. As states adopted more democratic arrangements in the twentieth century, working class members participated in politics – power was redistributed. This has been especially true as democratization spread after the end of the Cold War.

The other way that the open economy approach recognizes a role for politics occurs in the interaction between states. In Moravcsiks' description (1997), we would build pictures of individual state's preferences, then consider the degree to which they match or collide. If one state desires to liberalize its trade, it may do so by itself. On the other hand, it can find willing partners with complementary attributes, the gains from trade will surely be higher. With greater stakes, the ability to deliver benefits increases. Changes in the international system can drive changes in options, leading to alterations in policy itself.

Limitations of the open economy approach

While pointing out the strength of the open economy approach to the politics of trade, it is worth noting a basic criticism. In this analytical version of liberalism, powerful domestic actors control the state. Governmental leaders serve the dominant interests. In reality, however, politicians – whether in office or leading opposition parties – are strategic actors. They seek power in the domestic setting. Since each policy issue evokes its own cleavage, political leaders can package policies together when they build powerful coalitions (Lake 2009). This means they may ignore trade as an issue at times; it also means they may want to combine trade with other policies. Political leaders in office may be able to introduce policies in the domestic arena that alter the interests of individual actors. We set up artificial boundaries around trade policy as a domain of study. The open economy approach utilizing the analytical liberal assumptions is powerful at answering the questions we pose, but we should also recognize it will not always capture the complexity of the political process accurately.

Bibliography

Alt, J. E., Frieden, J., Gilligan, M., Rodrik, D. and Rogowski, R. 1996. The Political Economy of International Trade. *Comparative Political Studies* 29 (6): 689–717.

Alt, J. E. and Gilligan, M. 1994. The Political Economy of Trading States. *Journal of Political Philosophy* 2 (2): 165–192.

Ardelean, A. and Evans, C. L. 2013. Electoral Systems and Protectionism: An Industry-level Analysis. *Canadian Journal of Economics* 46 (2): 725–764.

Baldwin, R. E. and Robert-Nicoud, F. 2008. A Simple Model of the Juggernaut Effect of Trade Liberalisation. *CEP Discussion Papers* No. 845.

Bernard, A. B., Eaton, J., Jensen, J. B and Kortum, S. 2003. Plants and Productivity in International Trade. *American Economic Review* 93 (4): 1268–1290.

Bernard, A. B. and Jensen, J. B. 1999. Exceptional Exporter Performance: Cause, Effect, or Both? *Journal of International Economics* 47: 1–25.

Bernard, A. B., Jensen, J. B., Redding, S. J. and Schott, P. K. 2011. The Empirics of Firm Heterogeneity and International Trade. *NBER Working Paper 17627*. Available at www.princeton.edu/~reddings/papers/NBERWP17627.pdf.

Betz, T. 2017. Trading Interests: Domestic Institutions, International Negotiations, and the Politics of Trade. *Journal of Politics* 79 (4): 1237–1252.

Bombardini, M. 2008. Firm Heterogeneity and Lobby Participation. *Journal of International Economics* 75 (2): 329–348.

Bombardini, M. and Trebbi, F. 2012. Competition and Political Organization: Together or Alone in Lobbying for Trade Policy? *Journal of International Economics* 87 (1): 18–26.

Brawley, M. 2017a. Analytical Liberalism, Neoclassical Realism, and the Need for Comparative Cases. In: Thompson. W. eds. *Oxford Encyclopedia of Empirical International Relations Theory*. Oxford: Oxford University Press.

Brawley, M. 2017b. And We Would Have the Field: U.S. Steel and American Trade Policy 1908–1912. *Business and Politics* 19 (3): 424–453.

Dalton, R. 1996. Political Cleavages, Issues, and Electoral Change. In: L. DeLuc, R. Niemi and P. Norris eds., *Comparing Democracies: Elections and Voting in Global Perspective*, Thousand Oaks: Sage: 319–342.

Eichengreen, B. and Irwin, D. A. 2011. The Slide to Protectionism in the Great Depression. *NBER Working Paper*.

Farrell, D. 2011. *Electoral Systems: A Comparative Introduction*, New York: Palgrave.

Friedman, T. 1999. *The Lexus and the Olive Tree*, New York: Farrar, Straus & Giroux.

Grossman, G. M. and Helpman, E. 1994. Protection for Sale. *American Economic Review* 84 (4): 833–850.

Guisinger, A. 2009. Determining Trade Policy: Do Voters Hold Politicians Accountable? *International Organization* 63 (3): 533–557.

Heckscher, E. 1919. The Effects of Foreign Trade on the Distribution of Income. *Ekonomisk Tidskrift* 21: 497–512.

Kim, I. S. 2017. Political Cleavages within Industries: Firm-Level Lobbying for Trade Liberalization. *American Political Science Review* 111 (1): 1–20.

Krasner, S. 1982. Structural Causes and Regime Consequences: Regimes as Intervening Variables. *International Organization* 36 (2): 185–205.

Lake, D. A. 2009. Open Economy Politics: A Critical Review. *Review of International Organizations* 4 (3): 219–244.

Magee, S., Brock, W. and Young, L. 1989. *Black Hole Tariffs and Endogenous Policy Theory*. New York: Cambridge University Press.

Mahoney, C. 2007. Lobbying Success in the United States and the European Union. *Journal of Public Policy* 27 (1): 35–56.

Mansfield, E. and Busch, M. 1995. The Political Economy of Nontariff Barriers: A Cross-national Analysis. *International Organization* 49 (4): 723–749.

Melitz, M. 2003. The Impact of Trade on Intra-Industry Reallocations and Aggregate Industry Productivity. *Econometrica* 71: 1695–1725.

Milner, H. V. and Mukherjee, B. 2009. Democratization and Economic Globalization. *Annual Review of Political Science* 12: 163–181.

Moravcsik, A. 1997. Taking Preferences Seriously: A Liberal Theory of International Politics. *International Organization* 51 (4): 513–553.

Mundell, R. 1957. International Trade and Factor Mobility. *American Economic Review* 47 (3): 321–335.

Mussa, M. 1974. Tariffs and the Distribution of Income: The Importance of Factor Specificity, Substitutability and Intensity in the Short and Long Run. *Journal of Political Economy* 82 (6): 1191–1203.

Ohlin, B. 1933. *Interregional and International Trade*, Cambridge MA: Harvard University Press, Cambridge.

Olson, M. 1965. *The Logic of Collective Action*, Cambridge MA: Harvard University Press.

Osgood, I. 2016. Differentiated Products, Divided Industries: Firm Preferences over Trade Liberalization. *Economics and Politics* 28 (2): 161–180.

Osgood, I. 2017. The Breakdown of Industrial Opposition to Trade: Firms, Product Variety and Reciprocal Liberalization. *World Politics* 69 (1): 1–48.

Ostry, S. 2002. The Uruguay Round North-South Grand Bargain: Implications for Future Negotiations. In: D. Kennedy and J. Southwick, eds., *The Political Economy of International Trade Law,* New York: Cambridge University Press: 285–300.

Papayoanou, P. 1996. Interdependence, Institutions and, the Balance of Power: Britain, Germany and World War I. *International Security* 20 (4): 42–76.

Powell, B. 2000. *Elections as Instruments of Democracy: Majoritarian and Proportional Visions*, New Haven: Yale University Press.

Rickard, S. J. 2012. Electoral Systems, Voters' Interests and Geographic Dispersion. *British Journal of Political Science* 42 (4): 855–877.

Rickard, S. J. 2015. Electoral systems and trade. In L. Martin, ed., *The Oxford Handbook of the Political Economy of Trade,* Oxford: Oxford University Press.

Rogowski, R. 1989. *Commerce and Coalitions*, Princeton: Princeton University Press.

Ruggie, J. G. 1982. International Regimes, Transactions and Change. Embedded Liberalism in the Postwar Economic Order. *International Organization* 36 (2): 379–416.

Stein, A. 1984. The Hegemon's Dilemma: Great Britain, the United States, and the International Economic Order. *International Organization* 38 (2): 355–386.

Stolper, W. and Samuelson, P. 1941. Protection and Real Wages. *Review of Economic Studies* 9 (1): 58–73.

Winters, A. M., McCulloch, N. and McKay, A. 2004. Trade Liberalization and Poverty: The Evidence so Far. *Journal of Economic Literature* 42 (1): 72–115.

Wu, W. 2015. When Do Dictators Decide to Liberalize Trade Regimes? Inequality and Trade Openness in Authoritarian Countries. *International Studies Quarterly* 59 (4): 790–801.

10

Global commodity chains, global value chains and global production networks

Sören Scholvin[1]

Introduction

Geography offers various tie-ins to International Political Economy (IPE). Geographical concepts and theories that deal with the interplay of economics and politics are abundant and diverse, and it is not possible to present all of them in a single book chapter. This chapter focuses on global commodity chains (GCCs), global value chains (GVCs) and global production networks (GPNs). While the latter is a genuinely geographical approach, GCCs and GVCs have been coined by sociologists. All three have found wide application in Economic Geography, shaping the way representatives of the discipline see the geographies of global production. Research on GCCs, GVCs and GPNs has been widely published in the *Review of International Political Economy*, demonstrating that there is a considerable interest in these approaches among scholars and students of IPE.

The empirical backdrop to GCCs, GVCs and GPNs is globalisation: processes of production and consumption are increasingly linked across national borders. By now, exports of intermediary goods exceed exports of final and capital goods. More and more components are traded internationally for subsequent use in production. As Gereffi (2014) remarks, there has been a strong shift from trade in goods to trade in capabilities, tasks and value added. Others speak of offshoring/spatial relocation in this regard, and Cattaneo, Gereffi and Staritz conclude that due to the increasing fragmentation of production across the globe, transnational value chains 'have become the world economy's backbone and central nervous system' (2010: 7).

This phenomenon is not as new as it seems. Prior to research on GCCs, GVCs and GPNs, scholars such as Dicken (1976) and Watts (1981) pointed out that countries from the periphery of the world economy became sites for the more routine, low-skilled segments of increasingly globalised production. Other activities – marketing as well as research and design – remained in economically more advanced parts of the world. 'Branch plant' investment offered little in terms of linkage opportunities, reinvestment of profits, skill formation and technology transfer. A different pattern emerged with the rise of 'performance plants'. These are marked by autonomy, complex functionality, specialised markets, heightened product and processes technologies as well as qualified workforces (Phelps *et al.* 2003; Pike 1998). New opportunities arose for the host regions of such plants because of their embeddedness – for instance through deeper localised backward and forward linkages (Turok 1993). The extreme cases of branch plants and performance plants point at the range of developmental outcomes in globally fragmented production. Explaining these outcomes is the purpose of research on GCCs, GVCs and GPNs.

This chapter begins with an overview of GCCs and GVCs, introducing the frameworks that have been developed in this context and showing how the two approaches have evolved since the mid-1990s. It then summarises extensions to GVC research. The third main sector deals with the analytical framework advanced for GPNs, including recent efforts to turn it into a theory. The last main section builds inroads into better incorporating the state into research on GVCs and GPNs by focusing on industrial policy. Throughout the text, I provide empirical examples from my own research on value chains and production networks in the oil and gas sector.

It should also be said what this chapter is not. It is not an in-depth survey of research on GCCs, GVCs and GPNs. Instead, key conceptual contributions are presented to provide readers with an overview that may serve as a starting point for further engagement with the corresponding literature. Some related concepts – in particular the filière approach by French scholars and Michael Porter's contributions on value chains – are not covered. While I mention varieties of capitalism and suggest how this branch of research may enrich the GPN approach, other potential tie-ins such as new regionalisms are not addressed. Further to that, I do not address the increasingly large policy-oriented literature that refers especially to the GVC approach, most importantly by the International Monetary Fund, World Bank and World Trade Organization.

Commodity and value chains

Research on GCCs goes back to an edited volume – *Commodity Chains and Global Capitalism* (Gereffi and Korzeniewicz 1994) – published in 1994. It brings together papers presented at a conference on 'the political economy of the world system' held two years earlier. In distinction from the often state-centric analyses of that time, the starting point of *Commodity Chains and Global Capitalism* is the conviction that industrial production has 'dispersed to an ever expanding network of peripheral and core nations alike [...]. In today's global factory, the production of a single commodity often spans many countries, with each nation performing tasks in which it has a cost advantage' (Gereffi, Korzeniewicz and Korzeniewicz 1994: 1).

These transnational networks – clustered around single products – constitute GCCs, which are represented as linear and sequential chains. As depicted by Figure 10.1, each node within a GCC comprises the interaction of all players involved in the acquisition and organisation of inputs, including labour, their transport, distribution and consumption. The dynamics of GCCs result from organisation strategies and competitive relations between firms. The main analytical purpose of the approach is 'to focus on the creation and distribution of global wealth as embodied in a multidimensional, multistage sequence of activities' (Gereffi, Korzeniewicz and Korzeniewicz 1994: 13). In other words, the competitive relations in and strategic organisation of globally fragmented production is meant to explain the global distribution of wealth – that is, uneven development in the capitalist world economy.

The idea of better understanding the capitalist world economy by analysing individual products along chains predates *Commodity Chains and Global Capitalism*. In a seminal article, Hopkins and Wallerstein define a commodity chain as 'a network of labor and production processes whose end result is a finished commodity' (1986: 159; see also: Arrighi and Drangel 1986; Hopkins and Wallerstein 1977). They suggest that after having identified the chain from resource extraction to manufacturing to consumption, researchers should focus on four aspects: (1) the

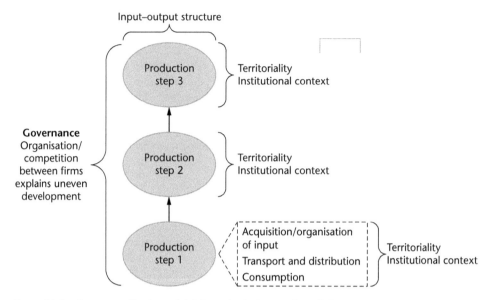

Figure 10.1 Conceptualisation of GCCs and relating analytical dimensions
Source: Author's own compilation.

flows to and from each node in the chain as well as the operations that occur around it, (2) the organisation of production within the node, (3) the dominant organisation of production throughout the chain and (4) the geographical location of each node. Gereffi (1994) converges these analytical steps into three dimensions of GCCs: input–output structure, territoriality and governance. In another publication, he (1995) adds the institutional context as a fourth dimension. It has received rather little attention ever since.

While input–output structure and territoriality constitute mostly descriptive dimensions, analyses of governance allow for explanations of geographically uneven development.[1] Gereffi (1994) distinguishes between buyer-driven and producer-driven chains. The latter are controlled by large conglomerates – for example in the automotive sector. Production is capital and technology-intensive, which creates entry barriers. Innovation occurs in production (through new production techniques, whose development is expensive). This means that lead firms can hardly pass full production on to suppliers because potential suppliers lack the necessary technologies or would share them with competitors. Import substitution strategies – in particular in Latin America prior to the 1980s – concentrate on producer-driven GCCs, with the state intervening in the economy through joint venture obligations, the creation and support of state-owned enterprises and similarly intrusive measures. Corporatism and the nationalisation of industries considered of strategic relevance also mark this approach.

Buyer-driven GCCs – most common in the apparel sector – are controlled by hollowed-out firms that do not engage in production. They control design and marketing, which constitute critical entry barriers. The reason for this is that in buyer-driven chains, innovation lies in design and marketing. Production does not require much capital or sophisticated technologies. It is intensive in labour. Hence, production can easily be outsourced via contract manufacturing. Buyer-driven GCCs stand at the core of export-oriented industrialisation, as exemplified by several countries in East and South-East Asia. The state – albeit often being labelled 'developmental' and in fact taking a decisive role for industrialisation – primarily assumes the role of a facilitator that creates conditions conducive to development through the provision of adequate infrastructure, easy access to credits and similar means. Foreign investment and a bias towards capital vis-à-vis labour, leading to low wages and weak trade unions (or their outright absence), play a major role for such development strategies.

The dichotomy of buyer and producer-driven chains must not be misunderstood as a simplification. There is considerable variety within the two categories. The distinction of buyer and producer-driven GCCs guides analyses by pointing out which firms decide how the respective chain is organised. It is not a final outcome of such investigation. For example, Taplin's (1994) paper on strategic organisation of GCCs in the apparel sector reveals that even within the boundaries of single sectors, generalisation is hardly feasible: outsourcing for fashion-oriented apparel is very different from outsourcing for mass product apparel, although both chains are buyer-driven. Thus, it is misleading (yet common) to speak in singular of *the* apparel GCC or *the* electronics GCC. Commodity chains are not sector-specific, but they vary at the level of individual firms and products.

At a workshop held in the year 2000, leading scholars agreed to adapt the rather incoherent terminology in their publications, from then on speaking of value chains instead of commodity chains. In addition to the new label, governance has been refined. A fivefold typology – drafted by Gereffi, Humphrey and Sturgeon (2005) – helps to describe and explain the main differences among various forms of chain governance.[2] The three authors argue that the form of governance that marks a particular GVC depends on the complexity of transactions, the feasibility of codifying transactions and the capabilities in the supplier base (see also Table 10.1):

- In market relations, the costs of switching to new partners are low for all parties. Such linkages depend on easily codified transactions, simple product specifications and the availability of suppliers that have the capability to make the products in question with little support from the buyers. Market linkages do not have to be completely transitory, as it is typical of spot markets. They can persist over time, with repeated transactions.
- Suppliers in modular value chains make turn-key products to a customer's specifications. Turn-key products are less generic and more complex than those interchanged in market relations. Supplying complete modules allows for the internalisation of tacit information and reduces transaction costs, including the buyer's need for direct monitoring. Technical standards simplify interaction by reducing component variation and by unifying process and product specifications.

Table 10.1 Governance of GVCs and its determinants

Type of governance	Complexity of transactions	Feasibility of codifying transactions	Capabilities in the supply-base
Market	Low	High	Medium
Modular	Medium	Medium	High
Relational	High	Medium	Very high
Captive	Low	High	Low
Hierarchy	Very high	Low	Very low

Source: Adapted and altered from Gereffi, Humphrey and Sturgeon (2005: 87).

Note
Gereffi, Humphrey and Sturgeon only distinguish between high and low. The finer differentiation in Table 10.1 reflects my own description of the types of governance from the previous lines.

- In relational value chains, interaction between buyers and sellers is very complex because of high levels of asset specificity. The availability of highly competent suppliers – a key condition for relational GVCs – provides a strong motivation for lead firms to outsource so as to gain access to complementary competences. Tacit knowledge must be exchanged. The mutual dependence that arises can be regulated through reputation, social and spatial proximity and the like.
- Captive relations involve small suppliers that are dependent on much larger buyers. Control and monitoring of production is high because of low supplier competence. Captive suppliers are confined to a narrow range of tasks – for example, they are mainly engaged in simple assembly. They depend on the buyers for complementary activities such as design, logistics, component purchasing and process technology upgrading. The suppliers hence face significant switching costs.
- Hierarchy or vertical integration is about managerial control, flowing from headquarters to subsidiaries. When product specifications cannot be codified, products are complex and/or competent suppliers cannot be found, the corresponding production must take place in-house. This form of governance may also result from a need to exchange tacit knowledge between value chain activities as well as a need to effectively manage complex webs of inputs and outputs, controlling key assets such as intellectual property.

This fivefold typology is more than a refinement of the distinction of buyer and producer-driven chains. GCC analysis is focussed on firms driving chains. Research on GVCs, meanwhile, has shifted to governance as coordination. It concentrates on inter-firm relations within specific chains, whereas the distinction of buyer and producer-driven chains implies a focus on lead firms. As Bair (2005) points out, research on GCCs stands in the tradition of world system analysis because it aims at showing how the periphery of the world economy is dominated by the core. It is meant to uncover how commodity chains structure and reproduce a stratified and hierarchical world-system. The more recent literature, conversely, is influenced by Business Studies. It aims at deriving policy implications.

Following this re-orientation, GVC research is driven by a strong interest in the prospects of development in value chains. A first proxy for such development is the distribution of profits and risks among all parties involved. It relates to the question of who is powerful and who is not, as powerful actors capture more profits and make others take risks to a disproportionate extent. The five types of governance illuminate power asymmetries. In captive relations, power is exerted directly by lead firms on suppliers, which is analogous to the direct administrative control that headquarters exert over subsidiaries of a vertically integrated firm. In relational value chains, the power balance is more symmetrical, given that all parties contribute key competences. Modular GVCs and markets are characterised by low asymmetries because suppliers and buyers work with multiple partners and switching partners is relatively easy (Gereffi5and Lee 2012). With regard to regional development, this implies that relational GVCs lead to better outcomes for the host region of the suppliers, whereas captive GVCs and vertical integration are disadvantageous. Modular and market relations stand somewhere in-between.

The last component of GCC/GVC studies that needs to be addressed in this overview is upgrading. In GCC research, upgrading is not an issue of major interest (because GCC research concentrates on uneven development in the capitalist world economy, not on the prospects of development therein). The term appears only in two chapters of *Commodity Chains and Global Capitalism*, being understood as a continuous process towards more sophisticated, more value-adding activities (Korzeniewicz 1994; Lee and Cason 1994). To research on GVCs, meanwhile, upgrading is central, as it is seen as the path towards development. Humphrey and Schmitz (2002; see also: Kaplinsky and Morris 2001) identify four types of upgrading:

- Process upgrading means that firms manage to transform inputs into outputs more efficiently by re-organising the production system or introducing new technologies. This matters particularly to firms new to global markets and GVCs, as their key challenge is to attain consistency in quality and to increase the speed of production.
- If firms upgrade their products, they will move into more sophisticated product lines. Suppliers usually start by catering for the low end of the market and then move on to upper market segments. They learn by exporting, but such sequences do not necessarily occur and face various obstacles.
- Functional upgrading entails acquiring new functions to increase the overall skill content of a firm's activities. Having started with mere assembly, suppliers may take control over the entire production process, including the acquisition of inputs. They later move on to design and marketing, and eventually sell their own brands.
- In chain upgrading, firms move into new but often related industries. For example, small enterprises that used to provide equipment and services to the fishing industry have benefited from Cape Town's efforts to position itself as an oil and gas hub, now servicing the offshore hydrocarbon sector.[3] Engineering companies that once produced tanks for sugar refineries in Mauritius sell tanks to petro-chemical complexes today because the technical details of production are similar.[4]

Suppliers – or, more generally, firms that seek to upgrade – enjoy considerable advantages in some of these forms of upgrading, but they suffer from major inconveniences in others.[5] These also relate to GVC governance. Generally speaking, if governance is asymmetric, suppliers will have easy and quick access to knowledge needed for process and product upgrading – most typically in captive relations. Opportunities for the other forms of upgrading, which are more promising regarding increasing value capture, are limited. Conversely, if chain governance is rather symmetric, suppliers are more likely to move to related industries and/or acquire new functions. The reason for this is that symmetric governance is associated with suppliers developing capacities on their own, especially in modular and relational GVCs. Yet, chain upgrading and functional upgrading depend on substantial investment and support from local institutions. Collective action through business associations, export consortia and local research facilities or the transformation of some local firms into large enterprises are necessary (Humphrey and Schmitz 2000).

Extensions of the GVC approach

In recent years, valuable extensions of the GVC approach have been made. This section cannot present all of them. It nevertheless builds inroads into important debates.

Considering that the GVC approach has its roots in Sociology, it tends to neglect the territoriality of value chains. Scholars with a background in Geography have further explored this dimension. Fold (2014) provides a framework for analysing the diversification of rural settlements, showing the impact of GVCs at this level. He suggests that the GVC approach has to better address how the creation, enhancement, capture and distribution of value affect places. In a similar vein, Neilson and Pritchard (2010) reveal the uneven insertion of ethical and fair sourcing schemes in India's coffee and tea plantation districts into GVCs. These mostly benefit large-scale plantations, which meet compliance criteria, while smallholders are unable to carry the cost of training and certification.

Bair (2005) goes beyond these approaches, ascribing explanatory value to territoriality instead of conceptualising it as an outcome of other features of GVCs. She argues that GVCs are influenced by their political and social embeddedness. Foodstuff GVCs, for instance, cannot be understood without taking into consideration regulatory mechanisms at various points of the chain (Ponte 2002; Stevens 2001). Salmon farming in Chile reflects historically developed social relations in the countryside (Phyne and Mansilla 2003). Arguably, these forms of embeddedness rather correspond to the neglected fourth dimension of GVCs: the institutional context. Nonetheless, the key message is that place-specific conditions shape GVCs, not just forms of governance.

Seeking to overcome a different weakness of the GVC approach, Bolwig et al. (2010) concentrate on horizontal dynamics. Horizontal dynamics are about the various relationships within a specific node of a value chain – for instance between migrant workers at a commercial farm and the owner of the farm. The typically vertical GVC perspective neglects these relationships. It fails to capture, for example, the numerous sources from which poor households generate income: food and cash-crop farming, harvesting of wild products, off-farm work and migrant remittances. These are individual chains, but what happens in one chain cannot be understood without taking the horizontal dynamics into consideration.

Dussel Peters (2008) criticises that the GVC approach conceptualises upgrading with regard to firms. For this reason, it leads to wrong conclusions on regional development. Dussel Peters highlights the contrast between the success of Mexico's apparel exports and the lack of broad-based benefits generated by the industry for its host regions. He concludes that in processes of upgrading, firms (or regions) must avoid the 'commodification trap'. They should concentrate on process innovation instead of product innovation so as to prevent simple assembly in captive relations. By taking the commodification trap into consideration, it can be explained whether the integration into a specific GVC contributes to socio-economic polarisation among and within regions or, alternatively, holds opportunities for broad-based development.

Taking these thoughts a step further, upgrading describes how a firm changes its position in and across GVCs. The developmental impact of such dynamics goes far beyond the individual firm and is not necessarily positive. For example, the upgrading by a specific firm may have negative effects on its suppliers if they fail to adapt to new requirements and hence drop out of the GVC. Bair and Werner (2011) accordingly criticise GVC literature for its inclusionary bias.[6] Indeed, GVC research deals almost only with cases of successful integration into value chains, but the changing geographies of global production reflect moments of inclusion and exclusion. Processes of disconnecting or expulsing from GVCs merit more attention, as they are a vital feature of uneven development.

There is also a certain lacuna in early GVC literature regarding upgrading as a socially beneficial process.[7] The concept of social upgrading closes this gap. Social upgrading refers to the improvement in the entitlements and rights of workers and the enhancement of the quality of their employment. It means analysing labour as socially embedded instead of seeing labour as a productive factor. The prospects of social upgrading depend on numerous characteristics of different types of work, ranging from small-scale, household-based activities to knowledge-intensive professions. Beyond that, social upgrading results from bargaining between capital and labour, which is strongly influenced by the enabling legal framework. In consequence, irregular and outsourced workers are less likely to benefit from social upgrading than regular workers (Barrientos, Gereffi and Rossi 2011).

Starosta (2010a; 2010b) criticises that the GVC approach – and research on GCCs alike – typologically describes outer manifestations of global capitalism (the form). It fails to uncover underlying forces (the content). This becomes apparent regarding power: powerful firms dictate, most importantly, who captures the profits generated in the chain. The fundamental question of why some firms are more powerful than others is left unanswered, at least in Starosta's reading of the aforementioned literature. What is more, the core interest of GVC research is the creation and capture of value. The approach operates without a theory of value, however.

Within the limits of this chapter, it is not possible to adequately summarise Starosta's complex application of Marxian theory to value chains. His articles and a contribution by Taylor (2007) may serve as a starting point for readers interested in GVCs from the perspective of Radical Economic Geography. As a side note, these lines also hint at the unfortunate fact that Marxist thinking is largely ignored in the mainstream research to which this chapter provides an introduction.[8]

Production networks

Geographers from Manchester and Singapore have advanced an alternative yet related analytical framework: GPNs. The key difference between GCCs and GVCs, on the one side, and GPNs, on the other, is that the GPN concept pays greater attention to the territorial dimension, meaning to how production networks interact with regions at a subnational scale.[9] Because the GCC and GVC approaches have been shaped by sociologists, social relationships – or, more precisely, lead firm dominance and inter-firm coordination – stand at their respective cores. The GPN approach, meanwhile, reflects the principal interest of economic geographers: the mutual influence of firms and regions.

By applying a network heuristic, the GPN approach emphasises the diversity of horizontal and vertical connections in production processes. They are multi-scalar and comprise non-firm actors. Coe, Dicken and Hess accordingly argue that the approach provides a framework that aims to 'incorporate all kinds of network relationships'. It 'encompass[es] all relevant sets of actors' involved in the production of a specific good or the provision of a particular service (2008: 272; on the network heuristic, see: Dicken et al. 2001). In other words, the GPN approach is highly inclusive with regard to actors and structures that shape the geographies of global production, and hence account for development trajectories that mark different regions. Arguably, research on GPNs therefore covers more actors than GCC and GVC studies do, in particular non-firm actors such as public authorities and trade unions.

Laying the groundwork for research on GPNs, Henderson et al. (2002) propose three analytical categories to systematically examine how a specific place plugs into a specific GPN (see Figure 10.2, further below). First, value refers to the conversion of labour power into actual labour and to economic return or rent that results from the production of goods and services. The latter understanding has become much more important to empirical assessments. It implies

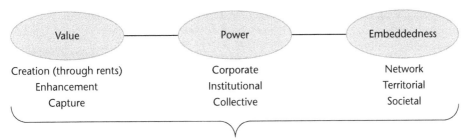

Figure 10.2 Value, power and embeddedness in GPNs

Source: Author's own draft, based on Henderson et al. (2002).

that value may be created through the control of human and natural resources (resource rent) and technologies (technological rent), uneven access to the financial system (financial rent) and infrastructure (infrastructure rent), the development of organisational capabilities (organisational rent), the harnessing of inter-firm relationships (relational rent) and the prominence of brand names (brand rent). If companies manage to influence policies in their favour, there will be a policy rent (Kaplinsky 2005). Different firms are able to create and generate different types of rents to different extents. Regions are marked by individual strengths and weaknesses regarding the creation of rents, which implies diverse ways of integration into GPNs.

Box 10.1 Value creation through rents in the Brazilian oil and gas sector

Brazil's oil and gas sector is dominated by the semi-statal giant Petrobras. Petrobras creates value from different rents. It benefits from a policy and resource rents because legislation on local content grants Petrobras privileged access to Brazil's vast hydrocarbon reserves, especially off-shore, pre-salt deposits found in 2007. Petrobras is also the core player at a science and technology parks in Rio de Janeiro. At that park, foreign service providers such as Halliburton and Schlumberger adapt their technologies to the geological specificities of the Brazilian reserves. Other oil majors do not have the same access to these networks. This leads to an organisational rent. Petrobras itself is the technology leader for ultra-deepsea exploration, meaning that it benefits from a technology rent too.

Source: Scholvin et al. 2020.

Once created through rents, value is enhanced. Existing goods and services are made better in intra and inter-firm processes. They become more valuable because of knowledge and technology being incorporated into them. Demand for skilled labour increases at locations where value enhancement takes place and local firms are able to move towards more sophisticated types of rents of their own.

Yet, it is one thing for value to be created and enhanced in a region that has plugged into a GPN but quite another for value to be captured locally. Inter-firm relations are always about power, and power constitutes a proxy for who benefits more. As Coe and Yeung argue, a GPN 'can be seen as a series of exchange relationships, and variations in the power balance along the network will affect the ability of its members to capture value' (2015: 17). Value capture is also about bargaining between lead firms and the regions that plug into GPNs. The pertinent issues related to value capture are therefore matters of public policies that affect laws on ownership structures and repatriation of profits (Henderson *et al.* 2002). 'For the purposes of economic development, value must be retained within firms, or the parts of firms, based in the territory under question' (Coe and Yeung 2015: 172).

The second analytical category that Henderson and his co-authors suggest is, hence, power. GPNs – and value capture in particular – are influenced by three forms of power: corporate power is about lead firms controlling their partners; subnational, national and international public authorities exercise institutional power, for example prescribing a certain local content or limiting the repatriation of profits; collective power is wielded by business associations, trade unions and similar organisations. Coe et al. (2004) add that cooperative relations between business associations, public authorities and trade unions – meaning organisations that often pursue opposed interests – are essential for plugging into and benefitting from GPNs.

Bringing power and value capture together, Coe and Yeung (2015) distinguish between the strategic partners of lead firms, specialised suppliers and generic suppliers. Strategic partners offer complete or at least partial solutions to lead firms by co-design or development in manufacturing and services. Specialised suppliers are not involved in these activities. They provide intermediate goods and services to lead firms, wielding less power and capturing less value. The input by specialised suppliers differs from that by generic suppliers regarding sophistication. The latter supply highly standardised and low-value products and services to lead firms, being even less powerful and capturing even less value.

Box 10.2 Strategic partners, specialised suppliers and generic suppliers in the oil and gas sector in Ghana

Oil and gas resources were found in Ghana in 2007. The town of Takoradi has become the hub for oil field operators such as Anadarko, Kosmos and Tullow. Because of the high risks that mark oil and gas exploration, such lead firms hardly ever take a specific block on their own. They cooperate with corporations of their like, which serve as strategic partners, bringing in capital and expertise. Firms such as Baker Hughes and Oceaneering are specialised suppliers. They possess outstanding skills in drilling and other technology-intensive activities outsourced by the oil field operators. Ghanaian enterprises are mostly generic suppliers. They handle in-country transport for the lead firms and specialised suppliers, for example.

Source: Information obtained by the author during field research in Ghana in October 2017.

The third category from the seminal article by Henderson and his co-authors is embeddedness. Network embeddedness captures the economic, institutional and social relationships in which firms participate in GPNs, for example the stability of their relations with other firms or the relevance of the network to their business. Territorial embeddedness is about the anchoring of GPNs at specific places – because of dependence on markets and resources or sophistication of local networks of small and medium-scale enterprises, for instance. Successfully plugging into a GPN means reinforcing the territorial embeddedness of lead firms, virtually tying them down. Hess (2004) adds societal embeddedness. It covers how firms are positioned within the wider cultural and historical context of a place or region. This form of embeddedness connects to the literature on 'varieties of capitalism'.

As noted, regional development depends on how local firms plug into GPNs. This means that endogenous factors are not sufficient for regional development. Coe *et al.* (2004) argue that regional assets – which range from labour and resources to technologies and organisational forms such as clusters – interact with regional institutions (see Figure 10.3). Business associations, labour organisations and public authorities transform such assets. In the ideal case, regional assets are moulded so that they meet the demands of GPNs in terms of value creation and enhancement. Using the words of Coe and his co-authors, regional assets must fit with 'the strategic needs of actors in the global production network' (2004: 471), providing relevant economies of scale or scope. Localisation economies occur as a consequence and GPNs are held down, thus unleashing the economic potential of the region in consideration.

This implies that there is bargaining and cooperation between lead firms and regional institutions. These relations do not only aim at transforming regional assets. They also affect industrial and social upgrading, growth trajectories and, most importantly, value capture (for example with regard to local reinvestment of profits). Merely plugging into GPNs does not necessarily

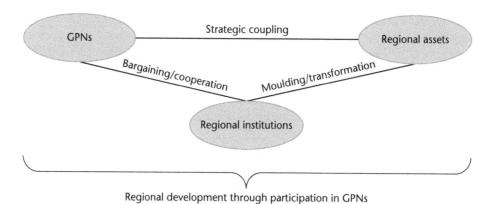

Figure 10.3 Regional development from the GPN perspective

Source: Author's own draft, based on Coe et al. (2004).

Note
Strategic coupling is explained further below.

lead to positive development outcomes. Regional institutions are the critical enablers not only of participation in GPNs but also of development through these networks.

In their recent book *Global Production Networks*, Coe and Yeung (2015) seek to turn the GPN approach into a theory. They suggest calling GPN research prior to this publication GPN 1.0 – that is, most of what I have summarised in the previous paragraphs. Their book, meanwhile, presents GPN 2.0. In order to advance a GPN theory, Coe and Yeung identify three drivers of market dynamics that have shaped the geographies of globalised production through increasing competition since the early 1990s: cost, flexibility and speed. Firms have to reduce costs, especially production costs, so as to remain competitive. This is achieved mainly by offshoring/spatial relocation – labelled a 'spatial fix' by Coe and Yeung. Flexibility results from firms specialising in the production of single components. Such a shift to core competences equals an 'organisational fix'. Speed is due to technological innovation that facilitates the exchange of data over long distances and alters production in numerous other ways. It constitutes a 'technological fix' to increasing competition.

Coe and Yeung propose to begin with firm strategies. These reflect the just mentioned dynamics, and also comprise imperatives of creating new markets, achieving financial discipline (so as to perform well at stock markets) and mitigating risks that range from market volatility to natural hazards. Generally speaking, strategies aim to position firms better with regard to their cost–capability ratios. For example, lead firms in the electronics sector outsource production in order to decrease their costs. They remain highly capable because research and design is done in-house. Producers of mass apparel, conversely, depend on corresponding inputs from their buyers. They have low capabilities but also low costs.

Similar to the aforementioned fivefold typology of GVC governance, Coe and Yeung distinguish between intra-firm coordination, inter-firm control and inter-firm partnerships. Intra-firm coordination means the internalisation and consolidation of value-adding activities. While inter-firm control combines externalisation to subordinate generic suppliers with strong control by the lead firm, inter-firm partnerships are about collaboration with strategic partners and specialised suppliers. The two authors derive the form that GPN governance takes from cost–capability ratios as well as the imperatives of market creation, financial discipline and risk mitigation. If all four determinants are high, inter-firm partnerships will dominate (as in electronics). A low market imperative and moderate risks lead to inter-firm control (for example in the automotive sector). Intra-firm coordination results from low pressure on cost–capability ratios and a low financial imperative (as in retail).

The outcome of firm strategies are trajectories of value capture.[10] These reflect continuous processes of coupling, de-coupling and re-coupling with GPNs. I elaborate on 'strategic coupling' in the next section. For now, it is sufficient to define it as 'the dynamic processes through which [...] strategic interests between local actors and their counterparts in the global economy' are coordinated (Yeung 2009: 213). Since the specificities of strategic coupling – it can be divided into different modes and types – are a proxy for value capture, they have far-reaching implications for regional development.[11] Figure 10.4 summarises the causalities that shape global production networks:

Without disregarding the insights gained through the GPN perspective and the progress that the concept has made since the beginning of this century, I close this section by elaborating on shortcomings of GPN 2.0.[12] Coe and Yeung's book is somewhat thin on political and socio-economic context factors. For example, the two authors name different forms of regional integration and paradigms for economic policy at the national level, but these would have to be better integrated into their analysis, especially to make GPN 2.0 more attractive to IPE scholars with a background in Political Science. Varieties of capitalism are mentioned. There is, however, no in-depth engagement with the corresponding literature, which would be particularly insightful because Coe and Yeung's thinking is guided by their own research experience on the Global North and the tiger economies in the Far East. I doubt that their approach can be transferred to other parts of the world without better recognising how these are different. To provide an example, it is fair to say that state-owned companies in many sub-Saharan African countries are not driven by considerations of cost, flexibility and speed.

Beyond that, further efforts are needed for the theory building that Coe and Yeung promise. Theories simplify reality through models in order to concentrate on a limited number of factors in causal relationships. If conditions A and B are met, outcome C will occur. Conditions D, E, F and G are put aside, being largely neglected as noise in the background. Of course, the causal chain from dynamics of contemporary capitalism to firm strategies to trajectories of value capture to regional development meets this definition of a theory. Throughout their book, Coe and Yeung tend to cover everything they find relevant, however. For instance, the conditions concerning value capture trajectories range from natural resources and labour markets to financial incentives for investors to the presence of other firms and the local knowledge base. Such a

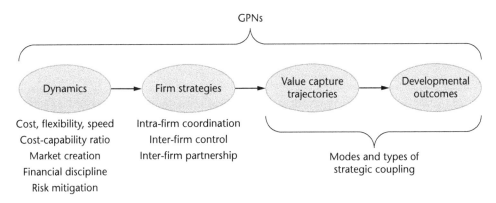

Figure 10.4 Causal chain according to GPN 2.0

Source: Author's own draft, based on Coe and Yeung (2015).

catch-all framework makes for a valuable starting point, but it complicates the reduction necessary for theory building.

It has also been criticised that GPN analysis recognises territoriality only as far as it influences the production network in consideration. Place per se has received less attention. Yet, there are place-specific dynamics beyond the creation, enhancement and capture of value. These ought to be better reflected. As Kleibert and Horner (2018) suggest, GPNs of corporate services, especially financial services, are most suitable to showing the impact of plugging into GPNs on uneven development, for example in terms of a rural–urban divide or within world cities – that is, regarding places and regions from a more inclusive perspective.

Strategic coupling, the state and industrial policy

The last main section of this chapter serves the purpose of better tying research on GCCs, GVCs and GPNs to core interest of political scientific IPE, namely the interaction of economics and politics. Politics is not absent from the approaches presented here, but as Neilson, Pritchard and Yeung (2014) admit, politics – in particular the state – has received little attention in corresponding studies.[13] This is not surprising because GCCs, GVCs and GPNs stand in a scientific tradition that seeks to overcome state-centrism. As Bair (2005) notes, research on GCCs and GVCs also emerged at a time when most countries abandoned state interference with the economy, favouring laissez-faire approaches and liberalisation instead.

Coming from the GVC perspective, Mayer and Phillips (2017) point out that states have facilitated the emergence of value chains by advancing policies of economic liberalisation, making GVCs a tool of development policy and accepting market concentration, meaning the increasing dominance of lead firms. States also regulate GVCs, now having largely privatised such regulation, for example via corporate social responsibility. They furthermore shape distributive outcomes, most importantly by pursuing policies that aim at competitiveness through less progressive taxation and the reduction of social welfare. Although Mayer and Phillips show that states outsource policies (and responsibly) across these three dimensions, states take the very decisions to do so.

Neilson, Pritchard and Yeung more narrowly argue that 'state action […] creates the enabling conditions that shape whether and how firms, regions and nations are able to engage with global markets, and their capacities to upgrade these engagements' (2014: 3). Tariff and tax policies, the provision of education facilities and transport infrastructure as well as the state's role in wage setting matter. These ideas are part of the aforementioned concept of strategic coupling. Strategic coupling is much more than state action though, as it captures the interaction of GPNs and regional institutions – the latter include countless private and public organisations. Coe and Yeung (2015) concentrate on forms of strategic coupling and their respective impacts on regional development, not on public policies. They distinguish three modes of coupling:

- Indigenous coupling is about inside-out processes. Local firms reach out of a region to participate in GPNs (or create new ones). These firms are autonomous and capture a considerable share of the value generated in the respective GPNs.
- Companies that meet the needs of a GPN perform functional coupling. The autonomy and value capture of companies involved in functional coupling are less than in indigenous coupling, although functional coupling is not necessarily an outside-in process that would merely aim at the host region of the firms in consideration.
- Structural coupling is limited to outside-in processes. Extra-regional lead firms connect a region to a GPN because of the region's assets. Structural coupling is marked by little autonomy and little value capture for the regional firms.[14]

To avoid misunderstandings, strategic coupling is not always successful and certainly not automatic. Once achieved, the specificities of strategic coupling change over time, reflecting a continuous process of bargaining among all actors involved (Coe and Yeung 2015). In other words, regional development is not simply an outcome of the functional integration of firms from that region into a GPN. Rather, it 'depend[s] on the ability of this coupling to stimulate processes of value creation, enhancement and [most importantly] capture' (Coe et al. 2004: 469). This leads back to the aforementioned interaction between lead firms and regional institutions or, in a different wording, the relationships between the state and transnational companies.

GPN 2.0 provides little information on state–firm relations. Coe and Yeung (2015) dedicate six pages of their book to how lead firms bargain with public authorities on market access, property rights and non-economic issues. They point out that institutional capacities – and thus the ability to bargain successfully – vary from one state to another and that states are in a disadvantageous position in a highly interconnected global economy. This framework leaves much room for expansion, but readers of *Global Production Networks* are likely left with the impression that in the end, lead firms matter, whereas states do not.

Thinking about GCCs, GVCs, GPNs and industrial policy offers a way to better integrate the state into the concepts presented in this chapter. After neoliberal convictions guided economic policies for almost three decades, many states are once again heavily involved with the economy, pursuing industrial policy so as to bring about development. Arguments for state involvement with the economy – especially in the Global South – are that corporate power remains concentrated in the core of the world economy, in spite of an increasing integration of developing countries and emerging economies into global economic processes. Powerful corporations appropriate an increasing share of profits, leaving little for their subsidiaries and suppliers in the Global South (Kaplinsky 2005; Milberg and Winkler 2013). Due to non-tariff barriers such as high-quality standards, firms from the Global South often fail to upgrade (Dolan and Humphrey 2004). Manufacturing in such chains and networks, both for exports and domestic markets, tends to come along with inputs being imported instead of local backward linkages being created (Barnes and Kaplinsky 2000).

Against this backdrop, the apparent question for governments in the Global South is: how to replace uneven development by processes of catching-up with the Global North? The answer appears to be a well-designed industrial policy – one that not only facilitates strategic coupling but also moulds it in a way that brings about advantageous outcomes so as to structurally transform the economies of the Global South.

In research on GPNs, the state tends to be conceptualised as a mere facilitator of strategic coupling. Studies that refer to the GCC and GVC concepts hardly ever overcome such a perspective on the state and upgrading. The state acts as an inter-scalar mediator, taking initiatives to bring local networks and global lead firms together. Observations on economic policies are usually limited to issues such as export and import quotas, tariffs and free trade agreements (exceptions are: Bhatia 2013; Bridge 2008; Horner 2014). Horner (2017) builds inroads into better analysing the role of the state in GCCs, GVCs and GPNs. He suggests that the state not only shapes them as a facilitator of strategic coupling (through incentives for local production and subcontracting, for example). The state is also a buyer and producer – in the case of electricity generation, this covers public procurement of electricity generated by private firms and electricity generation by state-owned enterprises. Being a regulator, the state moreover controls prices, enforces local content and regulates capital–labour relations.

Providing an alternative framework that is focused on types of industrial policies instead of roles taken by the state, Gereffi and Sturgeon (2013) distinguish between (1) horizontal policies that affect an entire national economy (through the provision of cross-cutting public goods such

---

Box 10.3 The state, industrial policy and Argentina's oil and gas sector

Argentina is home to considerably large unconventional oil and gas deposits. These are exploited in joint ventures that involve the semi-statal company YPF and various private corporations. The government encourages the development of the hydrocarbon sector by guaranteeing natural gas prices far above the market level. Corresponding agreements are signed before exploration in a specific area begins. Hence, the state acts as a critical buyer. Taking the role of a facilitator, the government has also advanced the construction of a railway line that will connect the largest unconventional plays to the port of Bahía Blanca so as to reduce transport costs. In Argentina, legislation on local content – an essential means of regulating value chains and production networks – refers to the provincial level. It ensures that lead firms and specialised suppliers engage in subcontracting close to the sites where they operate.

Source: Information obtained by the author during field research in Argentina in
May and November 2017.

---

as education or transport infrastructure), (2) vertical policies that target particular sectors in order to leverage dynamics along a complete value chain and (3) GVC-oriented industrial policy, which concentrates on specific segments of a few value chains. The latter is presented by the authors as the best option. It aims at capturing investment and improving a country's value-adding position by attracting global suppliers (instead of pressuring lead firms to invest locally), specialising in GVC niches (instead of intending to build vertically integrated domestic industries) and encouraging relationships among global suppliers and local firms.

Conclusion

Research on commodity chains, value chains and production networks has generated major insights regarding the geographies of global production and related uneven development. The three approaches provide corresponding analytical concepts and frameworks that have been presented in this chapter.

Research on GCCs began as an effort to advance world-systems analysis in a non-state centric manner. The main research interest was (and still is) how the core of the world economy dominates the periphery in transnational production processes, conceptualised as chains from resource extraction to final consumption. Focusing on lead firms, GCC analysis distinguishes between buyer and producer-driven chains. The input–output dimension and territoriality of GCCs have remained largely descriptive components. The institutional context has received little attention.

The GVC approach conceptualises governance as inter-firm coordination. Following Gereffi, Humphrey and Sturgeon (2005), five types of governance (market, modular, relational, captive and hierarchy) are distinguished. They derive from the complexity of transactions between firms, the feasibility of codifying these transactions and the capabilities among potential suppliers. Studies on GVCs aim at explaining the prospects of development instead of uncovering uneven development, which is the core interest in GCC research. For this purpose, four forms of upgrading (process, product, functional and chain) have been defined. They relate to GVC governance and the distribution of power among the chain participants.

Extensions of research on GVCs shed light on further critical aspects. These include development at particular places, place-specific conditions as determinants of GVCs, horizontal dynamics, the exclusion of actors and regions from value chains as well as social upgrading. It has been pointed out that upgrading by firms must not be confused with regional development, as the former only captures how individual firms change their position in and across GVCs. Such dynamics do not allow drawing conclusions on broad-based development. Marxist scholars have criticised GVC research for its lack of a theory of value.

The GPN approach is different from the GCC and GVC concepts insofar as it concentrates on the mutual relationship of firms and regions. The territorial dimension of production networks – in particular their institutional context – plays a critical role in addition to governance, which is the sole core of GCC and GVC research. What is more, the GPN approach is based on the conviction that one should focus on firms, especially lead firms and their strategies regarding cost–capability ratios, as decisive actors, not on products. One may add that GPN scholars appreciate complexity, where those who refer to GCCs and GVCs opt for simplification.

GPN 1.0 comprises three analytical categories: (1) value, which is created, enhanced and captured, (2) power wielded by corporations, institutions and collective actors, and (3) embeddedness within production networks, territories and societies. Politics is part of corresponding research since strategic coupling is conceptualised as continuous bargaining and cooperation between lead firms and regional institutions. The latter mould regional assets so that they fit the needs of GPNs. In GPN 2.0, efforts are made towards theory building. Coe and Yeung (2015) suggest that dynamics of contemporary capitalism explain strategies chosen by firms, for example vertical integration instead of outsourcing. These strategies stand at the core of GPN analysis because they account for trajectories of value capture, which explain regional development (or the lack thereof). Further to that, lead firms, specialised suppliers and generic suppliers are distinguished. They can be associated with various real-world types and three modes of strategic coupling (indigenous, functional and structural).

Still, GPN 2.0 remains thin regarding the impact of political and socio-economic contexts. The state tends to be conceptualised as a mere facilitator of strategic coupling, which is similar in GPN 1.0 as well as the GCC and GVC approaches. I have shown pathways to better reflect on politics and the state by relating the approaches presented in this chapter to industrial policy. Industrial policy can be seen a means to overcome uneven development through strategic coupling. It rests on the state not only being a facilitator of such processes, but also engaging with the economy as a buyer, producer and regulator. Coming from the GVC/GPN perspective moreover offers an alternative design of industrial policy, which does not have to be horizontal or vertical but may refer to specific segments within selected chains and networks.

Footnote

1 Acknowledgements: I am grateful to Jana Kleibert for comments and suggestions provided on the first draft of this chapter.

Notes

1 Since its very beginning, research on GCCs has been marked by a sharp contrast between, on the one side, scholars seeking to advance world-systems analysis and, on the other, researchers who hold a largely positive attitude towards the prospects of peripheral development in the capitalist world economy. Gary Gereffi, who has shaped the GCC and GVC approaches more than anyone else, belongs to the second camp.

2 In a similar but less cited approach to GVC governance, Sturgeon (2002) distinguishes between (1) commodity suppliers, which provide standard products through market relationships, (2) captive suppliers, which make non-standard products, for example by using machinery dedicated to the buyer's needs, and (3) turn-key suppliers, which produce customised products, for instance by relying on flexible machinery to pool capacity for several customers. The complexity of information exchanged between firms and the degree of asset specificity in production equipment determine which type of suppliers mark a specific GVC segment. Humphrey and Schmitz (2000, 2002) suggest that there are four types of firm interaction in GVCs, which reflect the need for inter-firm coordination. In addition to ordinary market relations and vertical integration/hierarchies, firms may interact in networks, which bring together partners with complementary capabilities, or quasi hierarchies, in which there are asymmetric capabilities.

3 Information obtained by the author during field research in South Africa in February 2014 and August 2016.

4 Information obtained by the author during field research in Mauritius in September 2017.

5 Further to that, the idea of upgrading as 'moving up the value chain' in order to obtain better results has been criticised as misleading by Ponte and Ewert (2009). Firms obtain better results through various strategies. Some of them equal upgrading, whereas other are actually about downgrading.

6 The same bias applies to research on GPNs, as Werner (2016) shows.

7 Admittedly, there is now an abundance of literature on labour in GVCs, with the edited volume *Putting Labour in Its Place* (Newsome et al. 2015) being a recent example of outstanding relevance.

8 There is, however, research on GVCs – and also on GPNs – that can be best labelled 'critical'. This includes the aforementioned studies on social upgrading and recent contributions on the exclusion of people and regions from production networks/value chains. For instance, Werner (2016) makes reference to Marxist terms, in particular to 'devaluation' as a driver of uneven development. Orthodox Marxist theorising – as pursued by Starosta – is absent from her article, however. McGarth (2017), meanwhile, applies Marxism in his critique of fundamental concepts from the GPN approach. He also shows pathways towards incorporating Marxist thinking – for example on 'primitive accumulation' – into analyses of what he calls articulations and disarticulations in GPNs. The empirical cases he presents are not related to Marxist concepts though.

9 As noted, territoriality is part of research on GCCs and GVCs, albeit a rather descriptive one. Further to that, territoriality in the GCC/GVC approach addresses a high level of spatial aggregation – core and periphery in the world economy, not the subnational region.

10 Value capture trajectories are meant as an alternative to the concept of upgrading, which is more common in GVC analyses. Coe and Yeung (2015) criticise that the upgrading account appears deterministic, mostly fits low-end suppliers and insufficiently reflects on institutional conditions. Most importantly, it tends to confuse means – that is, the enhancement of a firm's functional position in a GVC/GPN – with ends (a greater share in value capture), as indicated in endnote 5.

11 The modes of strategic coupling are presented in the next section. They constitute an abstract framework. The types, conversely, reflect real-world examples such as assembly platforms and innovation hubs. These types can be related to modes that mark them, relevant sectors, the likelihood of decoupling and, in consequence, trajectories of regional development.

12 More detailed reviews of this seminal book have been written by Dörry (*Economic Geography*, 93(2), pp. 209–211), Kleibert (*Journal of Economic Geography*, 16(2), pp. 539–540) as well as Scholvin, Revilla Diez and Breul (*Zeitschrift für Wirtschaftsgeographie*, 61(2), pp. 117–118).

13 A noteworthy exception is an article by Smith, who shows how the state, acting on different scales, is critical to the economic relations between the European Union and Tunisia. He concludes that 'the state continues to be centrally involved not only in setting the context within which [GPNs] operate, but also in the very constitution of forms of economic integration through GPNs[,] which articulate [...] interests across the EU and its southern neighbours' (2014: 22).

14 With regard to the aforementioned typology of firms and the example provided in Box 10.2, one may add that strategic partners of transnational companies and transnational companies themselves carry out indigenous coupling. Functional coupling applies to specialised suppliers and structural coupling to generic suppliers.

Bibliography

Arrighi, G. and Drangel, J. 1986. The Stratification of the World-Economy. *Review* 10(1): 9–74.

Bair, J. 2005. Global Capitalism and Commodity Chains: Looking Back, Going Forward. *Competition & Change* 9(2): 153–180.

Bair, J. and Werner, M. 2011. Commodity Chains and the Uneven Geographies of Global Capitalism: A Disarticulations Perspective. *Environment and Planning A* 43(5): 988–997.

Barnes, J. and Kaplinsky, R. 2000. Globalization and the Death of the Local Firm?: The Automobile Components Sector in South Africa. *Regional Studies* 34(9): 797–812.

Barrientos, S., Gereffi, G. and Rossi, A. 2011. Economic and Social Upgrading in Global Production Networks: A New Paradigm for a Changing World. *International Labour Review* 150(3–4): 319–440.

Bhatia, U. 2013. The Globalization of Supply Chains: Policy Challenges for Developing Countries. In: *Global Value Chains in a Changing World*. Elms, D. and Low, P. (eds): 313–328. Geneva: World Trade Organization.

Bolwig, S., Ponte, S., Du Toit, A., Riisgaard, L. and Halberg, N. 2010. Integrating Poverty and Environmental Concerns into Value-Chain Analysis: A Conceptual Framework. *Development Policy Review* 28(2): 173–194.

Bridge, G. 2008. Global Production Networks and the Extractive Sector: Governing Resource-based Development. *Journal of Economic Geography* 8(3): 389–419.

Cattaneo, O., Gereffi, G. and Staritz, C. 2010. Global Value Chains in a Postcrisis World: Resilience, Consolidation, and Shifting End Markets. In: *Global Value Chains in a Postcrisis World: A Development Perspective*. Cattaneo, O., Gereffi, G. and Staritz, C. (eds): 3–23. Washington: World Bank.

Coe, N., Dicken, P. and Hess, M. 2008. Global Production Networks: Realizing the Potential. *Journal of Economic Geography* 8(3): 271–295.

Coe, N., Hess, M., Yeung, H., Dicken, P. and Henderson, J. 2004. 'Globalizing' Regional Development: A Global Production Networks Perspective. *Transactions of the Institute of British Geographers* 29(4): 468–484.

Coe, N. and Yeung, H. 2015. *Global Production Networks: Theorizing Economic Development in an Interconnected World*. Oxford: Oxford University Press.

Dicken, P. 1976. The Multi-Plant Enterprise and Geographic Space. *Regional Studies* 10(4): 401–412.

Dicken, P., Kelly, P., Olds, K. and Yeung, H. 2001. Chains and Networks, Territories and Scales: Towards a Relational Framework for Analysing the Global Economy. *Global Networks* 1(2): 89–112.

Dolan, C. and Humphrey, J. 2004. Changing Governance Patterns in the Trade in Fresh Vegetables between Africa and the United Kingdom. *Environment and Planning A* 36(3): 491–509.

Dussel Peters, E. 2008. GCCs and Development: A Conceptual and Empirical Review. *Competition & Change* 12(1): 11–27.

Fold, N. 2014. Value Chain Dynamics, Settlement Trajectories and Regional Development. *Regional Studies* 48(5): 778–790.

Gereffi, G. 1994. The Organization of Buyer-driven Global Commodity Chains: How U.S. Retailers Shape Overseas Production Networks. In: *Commodity Chains and Global Capitalism*. Gereffi, G. and Korzeniewicz, M, (eds): 95–122. Westport: Praeger.

Gereffi, G. 1995. Global Production Systems and Third World Development. In: *Global Change, Regional Response: The New International Context of Development*. Stallings, B.:100–142. Cambridge: Cambridge University Press.

Gereffi, G. 2014. Global Value Chains in a post-Washington Consensus World. *Review of International Political Economy* 21(1): 9–37.

Gereffi, G., Humphrey, J. and Sturgeon, T. 2005. The Governance of Global Value Chains. *Review of International Political Economy* 12(1): 78–104.

Gereffi, G. and Korzeniewicz, M. (eds) 1994. *Commodity Chains and Global Capitalism*. Westport: Praeger.

Gereffi, G., Korzeniewicz, M. and Korzeniewicz, R. 1994. Introduction: Global Commodity Chains. In: *Commodity Chains and Global Capitalism*. Gereffi, G. and Korzeniewicz, M. (eds): 1–14. Westport: Praeger.

Gereffi, G. and Lee, J. 2014. Economic and Social Upgrading in Global Value Chains and Industrial Clusters: Why Governance Matters. *Journal of Business Ethics* 133(1): 25–38.

Gereffi, G. and Sturgeon, T. 2013. Global Value Chains and Industrial Policy: The Role of Emerging Economies. In: *Global Value Chains in a Changing World*. Elms, D. and Low, P. (eds): 329–60. Geneva: World Trade Organization.

Henderson, J., Dicken, P., Hess, M., Coe, N. and Yeung, H. 2002. Global Production Networks and the Analysis of Economic Development. *Review of International Political Economy* 9(3): 436–464.

Hess, M. 2004. 'Spatial' Relationships?: Towards a Reconceptualisation of Embeddedness. *Progress in Human Geography* 28(2): 165–186.

Hopkins, T. and Wallerstein, I. 1977. Patterns of Development of the Modern World-system. *Review* 1(2): 111–145.

Hopkins, T. and Wallerstein, I. 1986. Commodity Chains in the World-economy prior to 1800. *Review* 10(1): 157–170.

Horner, R. 2014. Strategic Decoupling, Recoupling and Global Production Networks: India's Pharmaceutical Industry. *Journal of Economic Geography* 14(6): 1117–1140.

Horner, R. 2017. Beyond Facilitator?: State Roles in Global Value Chains and Global Production Networks. *Geography Compass* 11(2).

Humphrey, J. and Schmitz, H. 2000. *Governance and Upgrading: Linking Industrial Cluster and Global Value Chain Research*. IDS Working Paper 120.

Humphrey, J. and Schmitz, H. 2002. How Does Insertion in Global Value Chains Affect Upgrading in Industrial Clusters? *Regional Studies* 36(9): 1017–1027.

Kaplinsky, R. 2005. *Globalization, Inequality and Poverty: Between a Rock and a Hard Place*. Cambridge: Polity Press.

Kaplinsky, R. and Morris, M. 2001. *A Handbook for Value Chain Research*. Available at: www.ids.ac.uk/ids/global/pdfs/VchNov01.pdf.

Kleibert, J. and Horner, R. 2018. Geographies of Global Production Networks. In: *Handbook of the Geographies of Globalization*. Kloosterman, R., Mamadouh, V. and Terhorst, P. (eds): 222–234. Cheltenham: Elgar.

Korzeniewicz, M. 1994. Commodity Chains and Marketing Strategies: Nike and the Global Athletic Footwear Industry. In: *Commodity Chains and Global Capitalism*. Gereffi, G. and Korzeniewicz, M. (eds): 247–265. Westport: Praeger.

Lee, N. and Cason, J. 1994. Automobile Commodity Chains in the NICs: A Comparison of South Korea, Mexico, and Brazil. In: *Commodity Chains and Global Capitalism*. Gereffi, G. and Korzeniewicz, M. (eds): 223–243. Westport: Praeger.

Mayer, F. and Phillips, N. 2017. Outsourcing Governance: States and the Politics of a 'Global Value Chain World'. *New Political Economy* 22(2): 134–152.

McGrath, S. 2017. Dis/articulations and the Interrogation of Development in GPN Research. *Progress in Human Geography* 42(4): 509–28.

Milberg, W. and Winkler, D. 2013. *Outsourcing Economics: Global Value Chains in Capitalist Development*. Cambridge: Cambridge University Press.

Neilson, J. and Pritchard, B. 2010. Fairness and Ethicality in their Place: The Regional Dynamics of Fair Trade and Ethical Sourcing Agendas in the Plantation Districts of South India. *Environment and Planning A* 42(8), 1833–1851.

Neilson, J., Pritchard, B. and Yeung, H. 2014. Global Value Chains and Global Production Networks in the Changing International Political Economy: An Introduction. *Review of International Political Economy* 21(1): 1–8.

Newsome, K., Taylor, P., Bair, J. and Rainnie, A. 2015. *Putting Labour in its Place: Labour Process Analysis and Global Value Chains*. London: Palgrave Macmillan.

Phelps, N., Mackinnon, D., Stone, I. and Braidford, P. 2003. Embedding the Multinationals?: Institutions and the Development of Overseas Manufacturing Affiliates in Wales and North East England. *Regional Studies* 37(1): 27–40.

Phyne, J. and Mansilla, J. 2003. Forging Linkages in the Commodity Chain: The Case of the Chilean Salmon Farming Industry. *Sociologia Ruralis* 43(2): 108–127.

Pike, A. 1998. Making Performance Plants from Branch Plants? In: Situ Restructuring in the Automobile Industry in the UK Region. *Environment and Planning A* 30(5): 881–900.

Ponte, S. 2002. The 'Latte Revolution?': Regulation, Markets and Consumption in the Global Coffee Chain. *World Development* 30(7): 1099–1122.

Ponte, S. and Ewert, J. 2009. Which Way is 'Up' in Upgrading?: Trajectories of Change in the Value Chain for South African Wine. *World Development* 37(10): 1637–1650.

Scholvin, S., Serra, M., Françoso, M., Bastos, P., Mello, P. and Borges, A. 2020. *Densidade, distância, divisão e as redes de produção globais: o caso do setor brasileiro de petróleo e gás*. Economia e Sociedade [forthcoming].

Smith, A. 2014. The State, Institutional Frameworks and the Dynamics of Capital in Global Production Networks. *Progress in Human Geography* 39(3): 290–315.

Starosta, G. 2010a. Global Commodity Chains and the Marxian Law of Value. *Antipode* 42(2): 433–465.

Starosta, G. 2010b. The Outsourcing of Manufacturing and the Rise of Giant Global Contractors: A Marxian Approach to Some Recent Transformations of Global Value Chains. *New Political Economy* 15(4): 543–563.

Stevens, C. 2001. Value Chains and Trade Policy: The Case of Agriculture. *IDS Bulletin* 32(3): 46–59.

Sturgeon, T. 2002. Modular Production Networks: A New American Model of Industrial Organization. *Industrial and Corporate Change* 11(3): 451–496.

Taplin, I. 1994. Strategic Reorientations of U.S. Apparel Firms. In: *Commodity Chains and Global Capitalism*. Gereffi, G. and Korzeniewicz, M. (eds): 203–222. Westport: Praeger.

Taylor, M. 2007. Rethinking the Global Production of Uneven Development. *Globalizations* 4(4): 529–542.

Turok, I. 1993. Inward Investment and Local Linkages: How Deeply Embedded Is Silicon Glen? *Regional Studies* 27(5): 401–417.

Watts, H. 1981. *The Branch Plant Economy*. London: Longman.

Werner, M. 2016. Global Production Networks and Uneven Development: Exploring Geographies of Devaluation, Disinvestment, and Exclusion. *Geography Compass* 10(11): 457–469.

Yeung, H. 2009. Transnational Corporations, Global Production Networks and Urban and Regional Development: A Geographer's Perspective on Multinational Enterprises and the Global Economy. *Growth and Change* 40(2): 197–226.

11

The IPE of regional value chains

Philippe De Lombaerde and Liliana Lizarazo Rodríguez

Introduction

One of the characteristic features of the current wave of economic globalization, and globalization *tout court*, is the fragmentation or 'second great unbundling' of production (Baldwin 2016; OECD 2013), made possible by technological innovations, including digitization and leading to decreasing communication and transportation costs, in combination with liberalizing (trade and investment) policies since the late 1980s. This led to a re-thinking of the structures of the (real) international economy in terms of (global) value chains (GVCs). A novel understanding thereby was that, in contrast with a market network of connected trading partners, GVCs imply some degree of vertical coordination (De Backer *et al.* 2018).[1] This means that value chains, in contrast with arms-length trade, may involve more long-term (structural) relationships and a stronger concentration of power in the hands of the 'coordinating' multinational companies. This in itself already justifies a political–economy reading of GVCs.

The concept of 'value chains' can be traced back to Porter (1985) and was then linked to the globalization phenomenon to become 'global value chains' (Gereffi *et al.* 2001, 2005), but alternative concepts like 'global commodity chains' (Gereffi 1994) or 'global production networks' (Coe *et al.* 2008; Henderson *et al.* 2002) also surfaced. Although GVCs have attracted increasing academic attention (mainly in the economic and management disciplines, less in the political and political economy disciplines), it has been argued that there is still a research gap with respect to the 'multiple causal mechanisms connecting (national, regional and international) institutions and GVCs' (Eckhardt and Poletti 2018: 6).

As will be shown below, from the early days of the study of GVCs it became clear that the scope of value chains is not always global, but often rather regional. This chapter looks precisely at those 'regional value chains' (RVCs) and does this through an IPE lens. It explores how they can be thought of and understood as trans-border spaces where economics, policy, politics and law intersect. The structure of the chapter is as follows: we first consider the scope of value chains and ask the question whether a distinction is relevant at all between GVCs and RVCs. We then show how regional economic spaces have been created in which RVCs are likely to emerge and develop. In the following section, it is shown how these spaces can be used for policy-making, geo-political strategy and political contestation. Finally, we show that RVCs can also be conceived as relevant spaces for re-regulating economic behaviour. We will thereby focus on the role of regional organizations.

The reach of value chains: global or regional?

The empirical literature on GVCs recognized early that the scope of value chains is sometimes, or often, regional rather than global. The distinction between GVCs and RVCs is usually not a neat one though: many value chains have regional *and* global features. Distinguishing between the two is a matter of relative regional density and/or autonomy of the networks. In addition, the architecture of the value chains matters. A typical RVC architecture is, for example, the 'spider' kind of value chain (Baldwin and Venables 2013) in which goods are assembled from various parts and components that are regionally sourced before being exported to the global customer. So, even if the final products are sold on the global markets, it has been observed in many cases that most of the core manufacturing activities are distributed among countries that belong to a particular region (Baldwin 2012; Baldwin and López González 2013; Guy 2009, 2015).

Complementary evidence has been presented by Rugman and colleagues (Oh and Rugman 2014; Rugman 2005, 2008; Rugman and Verbeke 2004). Using data on sales and assets of the Fortune top 500 firms, they showed that multinational activity of the world's largest firms is regionally concentrated rather than globally organized. In Oh and Rugman (2014), longitudinal data were used for the period 1999–2008. They found that around 80 per cent of the top 500 firms should be classified as 'home-region oriented' (i.e. they have more than 50 per cent of their sales or assets in the home-region). Overall, around 70 per cent of both sales and assets of the top 500 firms are 'regional' (i.e. belonging to the home-region in the triad). Over the ten-year period under study (1999–2008), the authors did not find any increase in the share of sales or assets defined as 'global'. There was a slight increase of the intra-regional shares though, at the cost of domestic sales or assets. These aggregate figures do not allow to distinguish between final and intermediate products as far as sales are concerned, nor do they allow to distinguish between vertically and horizontally organized firms as far as assets are concerned. So, they only give a partial view of the patterns of (intra-group) value chains, but they still give an indication of the importance of the regional dimension in the activities of lead firms in international value chains.

Value chain architectures have first been assessed via case studies of specific value chains, but more recently quantitative approaches have become more prominent. While initially, trade in intermediaries was distinguished from trade in final goods on the basis of the UN Broad Economic Categories to study the patterns of trade in parts and components, especially the work that involves linking input–output tables (and the analysis of the derived trade in value added[2]) has allowed to obtain a clearer (and quantified) view of the patterns and importance of value chains and the distribution of value added among participating countries (De Backer *et al.* 2018; Koopman *et al.* 2014).

In their review of the empirical evidence on GVCs based on data from the World Input–Output Database (WIOD),[3] Miroudot and Nordström (2015), for example, reached the conclusion that value chains are primarily still regionally organized. Trade in intermediates is regionally concentrated, while final products are transported over longer distances in the context of GVCs. At the same time, it is equally true that an economy-wide trend can be observed towards more international supply chains over time (De Backer *et al.* 2018; OECD 2013).

From Table 11.1 it can be seen that the extra-regional value-added shares in the value chains in EU-27 and the North-American Free Trade Agreement (NAFTA) have – on average – increased from around 10 per cent to around 16 per cent.[4] This means that, in spite of this

Table 11.1 Intra- and extra-regional value-added shares and production stages for EU, NAFTA and Asia-6, 1995–2011

		Value added shares (%)		Production stages (%)	
		1995	*2011*	*1995*	*2011*
EU-27	Domestic	71.6	65.3	73.1	66.5
	Intra-regional	17.7	17.4	17.3	17.4
	Extra-regional	10.7	17.4	9.6	16.0
NAFTA	Domestic	79.8	78.3	78.1	74.8
	Intra-regional	11.4	8.2	12.4	8.3
	Extra-regional	8.8	13.5	9.5	16.8
Asia-6	Domestic	82.5	72.9	83.5	75.3
	Intra-regional	6.1	8.7	6.2	10.0
	Extra-regional	11.5	18.4	10.3	14.6

Source: Miroudot and Nordström (2015: 21–22).

Notes
The percentages are simple averages of region members. Asia-6 is defined here as China, India, Indonesia, Japan, South Korea and Chinese Taipei.

increase, more than 80 per cent of export values is still sourced domestically or intra-regionally. A similar picture appears when looking at the production stages that are embedded in exports. Intra-regional value added shares and production stages in the EU-27 are higher than in NAFTA but these numbers are influenced by the size of the region and the countries, as well as the number of countries that the regions contain.

It has further been established that when input–output tables are split on the basis of firm size, relatively larger firms (including multinationals) are more involved in GVCs than relatively smaller firms (including small and medium-sized enterprises (SMEs)), which are part of smaller networks (including RVCs) (Cadestin *et al.* 2018). This points to a distinct political economy of GVCs and RVCs as they are populated by different sets of firms.

Social network analysis can also be used to study value chains by focusing on consecutive trade in intermediaries and final products (De Lombaerde et al. 2018). And studies along those lines also tend to confirm their strong regional dimension. In an analysis of the world textiles and apparel value chains and the electronics industry value chains, for example, regionalization patterns are still found to be important, especially in the topology of the electronics industry value chains. Endogenous geographical sub-networks are found that are based on geographical proximity as well as on preferential trade links, even if regionalization might recently be slightly receding (Cingolani *et al.* 2018). Regional clustering of production activities can take place around different economies that acquire centrality in different production stages (upstream, midstream or downstream) (Cingolani *et al.* 2017).

The creation of regional economic spaces

The development of RVCs is driven by companies but it strongly interacts with the policy and institutional context, and more specifically with the regional liberalization of trade and harmonization of rules. By lowering or eliminating barriers to trade regionally and facilitating cross-border trade, governments reduce cross-border transaction costs and 'supply' favourable conditions for the development of RVCs, while the latter create a 'demand' for (further) regional trade liberalizing policies. This nexus between trade policy and the development of value chains has been signalled at the regional level (for example, in the Central American context, Padilla Pérez and Quiroz Estrada 2017: 88–90) but mostly at the global level, where it has been shown through case studies as well as in large *n* studies (Begg *et al.* 2003; Curran 2015; Frederick *et al.* 2015; Kowalski *et al.* 2015; Miroudot, Rouzet and Spinelli 2013).

From a conceptual point of view, the World Trade Organization (WTO) distinguishes between various types of 'regional trade agreements' (RTAs): customs unions (CUs), free trade areas (FTAs), economic integration agreements (EIAs), and partial scope agreements (PSAs), depending on the level of commitment of the signatories (see Box 11.1). As of March 2019, 471 RTAs were in force in total (Table 11.2). Of these RTAs, 5 per cent corresponded to PSAs, 55 per cent to FTAs, 34 per cent to EIAs and 6 per cent to customs unions.

Box 11.1 Types of regional trade agreements, according to the WTO

Partial Scope Agreement (PSA)

PSAs are as such not defined in the WTO Agreement, but the WTO refers to them as agreements that cover only certain products and that are notified under paragraph 4(a) of the Enabling Clause.

This Clause refers to the Decision by GATT signatories on *Differential and more favourable treatment reciprocity and fuller participation of developing countries* of 1979 which allowed certain derogations to the most-favored nation (MFN) principle in favor of developing countries. More specifically, paragraph 2(c) of this Decision enables developing countries to enter into preferential arrangements on goods trade among themselves: Regional or global arrangements entered into among less-developed contracting parties for the mutual reduction or elimination of tariffs and, in accordance with criteria or conditions which may be prescribed by the CONTRACTING PARTIES, for the mutual reduction or elimination of non-tariff measures, on products imported from one another.

Free Trade Agreement (FTA)

FTAs refer to free trade areas and are defined in paragraph 8(b) of Article XXIV of GATT 1994 as […] a group of two or more customs territories in which the duties and other restrictive regulations of commerce (except, where necessary, those permitted under Articles XI, XII, XIII, XIV, XV and XX) are eliminated on substantially all the trade between the constituent territories in products originating in such territories. This article should be read in combination with the Understanding on the Interpretation of Article XXIV GATT 1994.

Economic Integration Agreement (EIA)

EIAs are defined in Article V of GATS. According to its paragraph 1 [t]his Agreement shall not prevent any of its Members from being a party to or entering into an agreement liberalizing trade in services between or among the parties to such an agreement, provided that such an agreement: (a) has substantial sectoral coverage, and (b) provides for the absence or elimination of substantially all discrimination, in the sense of Article XVII, between or among the parties, in the sectors covered under subparagraph (a), through: (i) elimination of existing discriminatory measures, and/or (ii) prohibition of new or more discriminatory measures, either at the entry into force of that agreement or on the basis of a reasonable time-frame, except for measures permitted under Articles XI, XII, XIV and XIV bis. Paragraph 3 of the same article provides for flexibility for developing countries.

Customs Union (CU)

CUs are defined in paragraph 8(a) of Article XXIV of GATT 1994 as […] the substitution of a single customs territory for two or more customs territories, so that (i) duties and other restrictive regulations of commerce (except, where necessary, those permitted under Articles XI, XII, XIII, XIV, XV and XX) are eliminated with respect to substantially all the trade between the constituent territories of the union or at least with respect to substantially all the trade in products originating in such territories, and, (ii) subject to the provisions of paragraph 9, substantially the same duties and other regulations of commerce are applied by each of the members of the union to the trade of territories not included in the union. *Source: WTO, n/d. User Guide. Available at: http://rtais.wto. org/UserGuide/User%20Guide_Eng.pdf.*

However, the WTO figures in Table 11.2 are based on notifications. It means that RTAs that cover trade in goods *and* trade in services are notified, and therefore counted, twice. Therefore, the 471 notifications collapse to 293 actual ('physical') agreements in force.

It should be noted also that the WTO definition covers any trade agreement that involves discriminatory trade liberalization, i.e. it is not limited to agreements among countries belonging to the same 'region' in the (usual) geographical sense of the word. Using a broad definition of regions,[5] the WTO finds that 129 agreements are intra-regional, while 182 are cross-regional (Table 11.3).[6]

Next to the elimination of trade barriers, the specification of the applicable rules of origin also incides in the regional value chain architecture. Of particular importance thereby are the cumulation provisions in inter-regional trade agreements that promote intra-regional sourcing by the trade partner (De Lombaerde and Garay 2005).

Services liberalization is sometimes a step towards the creation of a common market. The latter is not defined by the WTO but is generally understood as the integration of markets via the liberalization of trade in goods and services, the liberalization of flows of production factors

Table 11.2 Regional trade agreements in force, by type of agreement (as of 1 March 2019)

	Enabling clause	GATS Art. V	GATT Art. XXIV	Total
PSA	22	–	–	22
PSA – accession	2	–	–	2
FTA	16	–	239	255
FTA – accession	1	–	3	4
EIA	–	151	–	151
EIA – accession	–	7	–	7
CU	8	–	10	18
CU – accession	2	–	10	12
Total	51	158	262	471

Source: WTO (http://rtais.wto.org/UI/publicsummarytable.aspx, last accessed: 9 March 2019).

Table 11.3 Regional trade agreements in force, by geographical reach (as of 1 March 2019)

Geographical reach		Number of RTAs
Cross-regional		182
Intra-regional	North-America	1
	Central America	7
	Caribbean	0
	South America	6
	Europe	37
	CIS	33
	Africa	10
	Middle East	1
	East Asia	21
	West Asia	8
	Oceania	5
Total		311

Source: WTO, no date. *Regional Trade Agreements Information System (RTA-IS)* Available at: http://rtais.wto.org/UI/ PublicSearchByCr.aspx.

(labour and capital), together with the harmonization of rules and regulations. The European Union (EU) is the best example of such an integrated market. As common markets deepen the integration process and facilitate intra-regional business, they are conducive to the creation of RVCs because they minimize international transaction costs and create spaces with harmonized rules and institutional stability.

A crucial aspect of the RTA–RVC nexus is the stability of the rules. Instability or limited durations can lead to uncertainty and can lead to negative effects on the development of particular value chains and their related activities and employment. This has been illustrated, for example, in the case of Nicaragua's apparel industry, and more specifically with respect to the expiration of the tariff preference level (TPLs) under the Central America Free Trade Agreement (CAFTA) (Box 11.2).

Box 11.2 Conclusions of the Frederick *et al.* (2015) study on Nicaragua's apparel exports under CAFTA

The apparel industry in Nicaragua is a case that illustrates both the advantages and vulnerabilities created by export-oriented development that is dependent on specialised trade policies. Regional trade agreements like NAFTA or DR–CAFTA can be an asset to export growth and employment generation when they establish long-term economic relationships based on stable sources of comparative advantage for the signatories of these treaties. The less-developed countries in agreements such as NAFTA or DR–CAFTA seek to upgrade their industries over time in terms of the quality and value of their exports and the capabilities of exporting firms. When specific provisions of regional trade agreements are added that have a limited duration, like the ten-year TPL agreement with Nicaragua in CAFTA, then trade policies can become a liability because they create uncertainty among investors. This uncertainty is exacerbated in the absence of decisive steps by the government to strengthen or diversify the country's industrial base prior to the termination of these specific policies, and even then the success of such efforts is by no means guaranteed.

Perhaps more than anything, the TPLs provided Nicaragua with a window of opportunity to develop its export-oriented apparel industry in the context of heightened competition from low-cost Asian exporters. Over the last 5 years, the government has sought to exploit this window in a variety of ways, including by becoming one of only two countries in the Americas (along with Haiti) to participate in the Better Work programme, which is jointly sponsored by the International Labour Organization and the World Bank's International Finance Corporation to improve working conditions and increase competitiveness in the garment sectors of developing countries. In addition, Nicaragua has sought to differentiate itself from its competitors by emphasizing its relatively positive industrial relations environment. The country boasts an unusual degree of tripartite cooperation between the government, the private sector and the country's trade unions that represent garment workers in the free trade zones. A series of agreements negotiated and signed by representatives of these three parties are notable primarily for establishing multi-year schedules of predetermined minimum wage increases designed to provide stability to the industry by creating a predictable cost environment for manufacturers (Bair and Gereffi 2013). They also include a number of measures intended to benefit workers, including subsidised foodstuffs and a housing programme, although it is unclear how much progress is being made on the non-wage elements of the agreement. Whatever their achievements in practice, both Nicaragua's participation in Better Work and the Tripartite Agreement are intended to signal Nicaragua's status as a comparatively 'high road', if still low cost, sourcing destination.

Such efforts are critical for ensuring the future of the industry since the TPLs are not, in and of themselves, a source of long-term competitiveness for the industry in Nicaragua. Rather, they are (or could be) a means towards the end of building regionally integrated supply chains so that local manufacturers are able to use inputs that meet the CAFTA agreement's yarn-forward rules of origin once the TPLs expire. One scenario for achieving this objective is the expansion of Nicaragua's apparel industry to include fabric manufacturing alongside garment assembly. Developing countries such as Nicaragua confront a number of challenges in expanding beyond an assembly-based, export-processing garment industry, however. These include the availability and cost of electricity, which is a more important factor for textile manufacturing than labour costs. While government policies and investments can make a country a more attractive site for investment, such changes do not come quickly or easily. Moreover, because many importers have complex needs in terms of the range of inputs they require, it is not realistic that the future of Nicaragua's apparel industry can be fuelled entirely by this small country's domestic textile base. For this reason, the future viability of Nicaragua's apparel industry, and indeed the prospects for the rest of Central America more broadly, may well depend on the development and integration of a regional textile base.

The expansion of local yarn and fabric production on the scale that the region requires is most likely to come through foreign direct investment. [...] Nicaragua's apparel industry already has a diversified set of foreign investors; nine of the ten largest companies have parent firms based in Asia (Korea or Taiwan), while the remainder are based in North America. [...] All of the companies we identified as high risk for contraction or closure post-TPL are based in Asia. Among these firms are vertically integrated multinational manufacturers that are able to service their clients from a range of production sites. Under the TPL regime, these companies have been able to secure duty-free access to the US market for apparel assembled in Nicaragua from fabrics manufactured in their Asian facilities. The loss of this benefit may encourage such companies to shift their production from Nicaragua back to Asia.

Some of the Asian-based companies currently active in Nicaragua may choose to maintain a presence in the region, if not in Nicaragua, once the TPLs expire. For example, a large, Korean-owned manufacturer of knit apparel in Nicaragua is currently building a yarn-spinning mill in Costa Rica (Arias 2014). This company will be exporting the yarn spun in its Costa Rican facility to Guatemala, where it will be knitted into fabric, which will be cut and sewn into knit apparel in the same company's garment factories in Guatemala, Haiti and Nicaragua. As we learned from our interviews, decisions that producers make about aligning their global supply chains reflect, in large measure, the preference and strategies of the brands and retailers that ultimately drive the geography of the industry via their sourcing decisions. Lead firms are increasingly aware of the need to align value chains regionally. This imperative reflects not only regulatory factors, such as the rules of origin in preferential trade agreements, but also the reality of increasing production costs in Asia and the increased premium placed on flexibility and consumer responsiveness. Therefore, lead firms in the apparel value chain should be enlisted as partners to strengthen the regional capabilities needed to ensure the long-term viability of apparel production in the Americas, and Nicaragua's place within it.

RVCs as policy spaces and political spaces

The conceptualization of (regional and global) value chains, together with the growing empirical evidence thereon led policymakers to gradually consider them as relevant spaces for the formulation of policies and the 'insertion' or 'integration' in value chains has become an explicit objective of trade, investment or industrial policies. It has thereby been demonstrated that (liberal) foreign direct investment (FDI) policies, intellectual property rights (IPR) protection, and infrastructure and logistics policies impact GVC participation positively (Kowalski *et al.* 2015).

However, participating in GVCs does not necessarily mean that the participation in the total value added generated in the chain for each individual economy is considered as sufficient. Governments therefore pursue strategies and policies (or rather, policy mixes) for industrial/economic upgrading in order to upgrade their capacity to export more sophisticated goods or services (in the same or in related value chains) and/or to become more efficient in given production activities (Gereffi 1995; Gereffi *et al.* 2001). These policy mixes that are also multi-level and multi-actor have also been called 'value chain strengthening strategies' (Padilla Pérez 2014). Although such strategies are usually part of national development policies and targeting value chains that have mainly national geographical scopes, there are opportunities for regional cooperation and regional chain linkages, especially if the strategies receive support from regional integration organizations or regional development banks. The opportunity to expand intra-regional trade flows by strengthening value chains and capitalizing on economic complementarities has been observed, for example, in the case of agrifood products in Central America (Quiroz Estrada 2017: 46).

Value chain strengthening strategies can be considered as new industrial policies. They are different from earlier attempts to organize regional industrial cooperation in South America (Andrean Community, CAN), Southeast Asia (Association of Southeast Asian Nations, ASEAN) or even Eastern Europe (Council for Mutual Economic Assistance, COMECON) which were aiming at achieving economies of scale in emerging regions with relatively small domestic markets by physically concentrating production and agreeing on a regional division of labour, in accordance with comparative advantages or not (Moncayo *et al.* 2012; UNIDO 1983). At the same time, it should be noted that already in the early 1980s ASEAN e.g. launched its industrial complementation strategy which consisted in promoting and coordinating intra-regional special-isation in parts or production stages (ASEAN 1981; De Lombaerde 1994; UNIDO 1983). Although there were still no explicit references to the notion of 'regional value chains' then, RVCs as an idea was implicitly part of this strategic proposal. The results of these early regional industrial cooperation strategies have overall been 'mixed' and/or unsatisfactory in spite of initial optimism (UNIDO 1983). The rather complicated decision-making procedures were blamed for the lack of success of the ASEAN industrial complementation initiative, as in the case of the automotive industry (Solidum and Meow 1987).

The more recent value chain strengthening strategies differ from these earlier experiences because they are more specific and micro-level in nature, and aim at being more participatory. But as they imply governmental support for selected activities and companies, they have also clear political–economy implications. It is well known that they might attract private rent-seeking behaviour (Krueger 1974), but proponents of such strategies argue that if they consist of temporary support that tackle market imperfections (such as e.g. information asymmetries), if they are based on transparent chain selection criteria and if they are accompanied by indicator-based monitoring mechanisms, they can be welfare enhancing (Gomes Nogueira et al. 2017).

It has been noted also that the promotion of RVCs by governments is not always or not necessarily to be understood within a globalization logic. The promotion of RVCs, even if the wording is different, can also be a strategy to strengthen the (relative) regional autonomy (sover-eignty) and a response to the challenges of globalization. The South American case in the early 2000s is relevant here. The South American region (with connections to Central America and the Caribbean) has been used as a platform to contest neo-liberal and hegemonic globalization (Vivares 2014: 11). The region is thereby seen as a space where state and non-state actors interact in formal and informal institutions and shape a political project, which is again not uncontested. Regional schemes such as Union of South American Nations (UNASUR), Com-munity of Latin American and Caribbean States (CELAC) or Bolivarian Alliance of the People of our Americas (ALBA) have been the institutional vehicles for this/these alternative projects. Whereas CELAC and UNASUR were mainly foreign policy instruments and – in the case of UNASUR – a cooperation instrument in specific policy areas, ALBA included an economic agenda seeking to develop regional trade networks and production platforms, not via a market logic but via a logic of state-to-state cooperation. Initiatives were taken in sectors such as oil, communications and finance and included also the creation of (public) 'grand-national' com-panies and projects in the region. It has been shown that, next to oil trade, trade in intermediar-ies and agro-food trade have also significantly grown in the first ten years of ALBA (Aponte Garcia 2014).

But also in contexts where governments follow rather mainstream trade and investment pol-icies have value chains been discovered as relevant spaces for contestation, even if this is more so in the case of GVCs than in the case of RVCs. It is in the context of GVCs that the north–usouth dimension is visible and where NGOs and other stakeholders have scrutinized the behaviour of multinational companies when sourcing their inputs from the value chains they coordinate. More precisely, multinational companies are being scrutinized regarding their respect for human rights, labour rights, and the environment. There is indeed case study evid-ence that economic upgrading (see above) does not automatically lead to social upgrading (Bar-rientos et al. 2010: 7; Brown 2007). The latter can thereby be defined as the process of improvement in the rights and entitlements of workers as social actors, and enhances the quality of their employment (Barrientos et al. 2010: 7). But as this process is not automatic, a variety of social actors mobilize to put pressure on firms, governments and courts to act to protect the weak participants in (or victims of) the value chain activities, such as local populations, women, children, unskilled workers, farmers, etc. This way, it can be said that (G)VCs have been politicized.

Finally, recent work has shown that the geographical scope of the value chains to which firms belong also matters for the political economy of trade negotiations, in addition to the traditional distinction between export-oriented and import-competing industries, on the one hand, and the (more recent) distinction between high and low performing firms within industries (Melitz and Trefler 2012), on the other. Eckhardt and Lee (2018), for example, analysed the preferences and political behaviour of tobacco companies with respect to NAFTA negotiations. They confirm the general preference of high performing (i.e. highly productive) firms that integrate GVCs towards liberalizing trade agreements (such as NAFTA). However, they also find that within the group of high performing firms, those that are more regionally integrated (i.e. those that are sourcing most of their inputs intra-regionally) have a stronger preference for stricter rules of origin than firms that rely more on extra-regional sourcing. In other words, the design of trade agreements seems to be influenced by the way the leading (and politically influential) domestic firms are integrated in value chains: regional or global.

RVCs as spaces for re-regulation: the role of regional organizations

Although the development of value chains seems to have benefitted from worldwide deregulation since the 1990s, GVCs and RVCs are also becoming spaces of (re-)regulation, characterized by the existence of diverse value chain governance mechanisms and legal pluralism. Regulation is a key issue of value chain governance because it determines the interaction inside and among corporate groups and it influences behaviour and structure of these groups by means of binding and non-binding regulations (The IGLP Law and Global Production Working Group 2016: 62). Regulation can be approached from diverse perspectives, such as from the interaction between law and the geography of value chains, or the role of law in producing and distributing value and power in these chains (The IGLP Law and Global Production Working Group 2016: 58). In addition, value chains are not only externally regulated but, in many cases, value chain actors are also (auto-)regulators and this increases the legal pluralism within which value chains function (The IGLP Law and Global Production Working Group 2016: 62–63).

The interaction between law and geography as a dimension of value chain governance is strongly dependent on the regulatory entities involved, including the regional integration groupings. And the policy objective of upgrading (see above) in value chains is also influenced by the regulation of value chain activities and organization because the law and policy tools can influence the (re-)distribution of power along and across the chains (The IGLP Law and Global Production Working Group 2016: 73). The way profits are shared, the role of value chains in the development of the countries or regions where they operate and/or their potential negative impacts on people and the environment are central issues of value chains that are closely related with the regulatory design (Turner 2016: 381).

Besides the multiple levels of regulatory competences that apply to transnational activities of value chains, self-regulation inside and across chains is also relevant. This self-regulation is mainly identified with the corporate social responsibility (CSR) model, but refers also to other mechanisms to increase traceability (requested by regulations referring to audits or compliance mechanisms) (Turner 2016: 382–385). Many of these regulatory measures have a regional character.

Self-regulation can be complemented by voluntary standards that are proposed for making the goal of traceability possible and for implementing CSR models. These non-state regulations seek that corporate groups voluntarily comply with international environmental, human rights and governance standards. These standards are seen as complementary to the binding regulations that in many cases lack cross-border effects and, this way, they attempt to fill the gaps of international law regarding the accountability of corporate groups. Self-regulation is also a way used by corporate groups to establish their policies and to implement a managerial planning to comply with international standards. These compliance mechanisms also seek to increase quality, reputation, consumer acceptance, and serve as a response to global activism, without being legally constrained to comply with them (Gibbon *et al.* 2008; Henson and Humphrey 2010, quoted by Turner 2016: 386).

However, this does not fully address the general concerns about how to control value chain activities, how to make corporations accountable for their transnational operations (related to transnational issues such as environmental or human rights protection, the fight against corruption, responsive investment, technology transfer), and about the difficulties of lawmakers to regulate them with a transnational scope, basically because corporations are not accountable at the international level and the jurisdiction of states can hardly be extraterritorial (Turner 2016: 386–388).

The creation of such transnational law implies national and local regulations including non-state law related to gender or property regimes linked to social or religious norms. This is known as supply-chain legal pluralism, which involves state law as well (The IGLP Law and Global Production Working Group 2016: 76; Sarfaty 2015). In other words, chain law includes legal domains and regulations beyond the purely economic processes. The economic processes may also be influenced by plural legal orders related to resource allocation, negotiations around property rights or the availability of workforce. At the local level, international law and standards interact with plural local state and non-state norms, which complicates the understanding of the regulatory context (Turner 2016: 392–3).

Regional integration groupings can play an important role in shaping regulatory issues related to value chain governance. This is especially the case of the EU, but other groupings are also in a position to shape the governance of their value chains, including Mercosur or the Pacific Alliance. In addition, new generation FTAs and mega FTAs also contribute to building this regulatory environment. The latter include, for example, the Comprehensive and Progressive Agreement for Trans-Pacific Partnership (CPTPP) or the EU–Canada Comprehensive Economic and Trade Agreement (CETA). FTAs contain regulatory clauses, not only on market access, but also on public procurement regulations, intellectual property rights protection and investment, including investor–State dispute settlement (ISDS) mechanisms. The EU and the US are the main promotors of these new generation FTAs that go far beyond tariff liberalization. These agreements include so-called WTO+ and WTOx provisions. The former refer to clauses that deepen existing multilateral commitments in areas such as liberalization of trade in services, anti-dumping or government subsidies. The latter refer to clauses on regulatory domains that go beyond the current scope and mandate of the WTO. These include, for example, human rights, labour clauses and environmental clauses (Horn et al. 2009). NAFTA (1992) was a milestone in this development because next to the usual provisions (on tariffs, rules of origin, exclusions), this agreement included provisions on Sanitary and Phytosanitary Measures (SPS), technical barriers to trade (TBTs), investment and ISDS, services, temporary entry of business persons, public procurement, IPRs, anti-dumping, and side agreements on labour and the environment. NAFTA served as a catalyst for the negotiation of subsequent agreements that systematically included similar clauses (Table 11.4).

The EU-led FTAs cover similar issues but are – overall – characterized by more flexibility and somewhat less liberalization (Heydon and Woolcock 2009: 79). They include relatively more excluded agricultural tariff lines, more excluded sensitive services sectors, lay more focus

Table 11.4 Diffusion of the NAFTA model in the Americas

	NAFTA	Ecuador–Chile	G-3	Chile–Mercosur	Mexico–Nicaragua	Canada–Chile	Mexico–Northern Triangle	Bolivia–Mercosur	CARICOM–Dominican Rep.	Chile–Central America
Tariff elimination	X	X	X	X	X	X	X	X	X	X
HS-based rules of origin	X	–	X	–	X	X	X	–	X	X
ALADI-based rules of origin	–	X	–	X	–	–	–	X	–	–
Special rules–auto sector	X	X	X	X	–	X	–	–	–	–
Agriculture – separate chapter	X	–	X	–	X	–	X	–	X	–
SPS measures	X	X	X	X	X	–	X	X	X	X
Technical barriers to trade	X	X	X	X	X	X	X	–	X	X
Investment	X	X	X	–	X	X	X	–	X	X
Investor–state dispute settlement	X	X	X	–	X	X	X	–	–	–
Services	X	BE	X	–	X	X	X	BE	X	X
Temporary entry of business persons	X	–	X	–	X	–	X	–	X	X
Government procurement	X	BE	X	–	X	–	–	–	BE	X
Intellectual property	X	–	X	X	X	–	X	–	X	–
Anti-dumping/countervailing duties	X	X	–	X	X	X7	X	X	X	X
Competition policy	–	–	–	–	–	X	–	–	–	X
Dispute settlement	X	X	X	X	X	X	X	X	X	X
Labour/environment	SA	–	–	–	–	SA	–	–	–	–
Special and differential treatment	–	X	–	X	–	–	–	X	X	–

Source: IDB. 2002. Beyond Borders: The New Regionalism in Latin America. Washington: Inter-American Development Bank.

Notes

SA = side agreement; BE = best endeavour to define in the future: the parties shall explicitly seek to develop disciplines in these areas in the future; HS = harmonised system.

on agreed international standards in SPS and TBT, go less far on investment and public procure-ment provisions, and provide more scope for asymmetries. They also include human rights and sustainability clauses that seek to impose the European standards on their commercial partners.

Despite the dominance of national regulatory and legal environments, it should be observed, however, that value chain regulation is increasingly transnational. In addition, the home coun-tries of the parent corporations are expected to regulate their value chains and not only the corporate activities that occur in their territories. The Maastricht Principles on Extraterritorial Obligations of States in Economic, Social and Cultural Rights e.g. sought that states define accountability and provide legal remedies for the abuses perpetrated by businesses in their juris-diction but also in third states. The EU and the US have promoted the compliance of their value chains with international governance standards such as the Organisation for Economic Co-operation and Development (OECD) Guidelines for Multinationals or the United Nations (UN) Guiding Principles for Business and Human Rights.

At the regional level, the EU has developed a CSR, governance and business and human rights framework for EU value chains. The need to implement 'supply chain liability' to hold corporate groups accountable for their activities in the whole value chain and for the activities of their commercial partners has been a concern of EU policymakers. The need to develop transnational tort litigation and the adoption of codes of conduct are examples of this concern. EU states are increasingly pushing beyond the self-regulatory practices and try to make the pro-motion and protection of decent work conditions, the protection of consumers and/or local communities and environmental governance binding. The transnational regulation of GVCs seeks to fill the gap in international law by which corporations cannot be held accountable at the international level.

The EU has been highly active in regulating the activities of European value chains and some member states are seeking to increase the responsibility of corporate groups in the governance of value chains. The EU also seeks to enlarge the jurisdiction of home states by limiting the application of some fora (such as the *forum non conveniens* doctrine) and instead to promote the use of doctrines that support national judiciaries to accept cases weakly related with their country (Álvarez Rubio and Yiannibas 2017; Augenstein and Jägers 2017: 20; Pigrau Solé *et al.* 2016: 7).

Regarding the governance of corporate groups, the EU has also regulated the duty to report non-financial information that turns CSR practices into binding rules for European corporate groups, as well as for other corporate groups with activities in the EU. In addition, it promotes the subjection of corporations to the legal system where they have been incorporated to provide more legal certainty, transparency and ease for cross-border businesses. The EU also regulates the legal status of shareholders[8] such as the remuneration of directors, the identification of share-holders, and transparency for institutional investors, asset managers, etc. The EU has also regu-lated public procurement processes with extraterritorial effects in order to influence governance of value chains that do business with EU state agencies. Most of the EU countries have already adopted these directives as national legislation in order to address transparency and sustainable practices of value chains with activities in the EU (Corvaglia and Li 2019: 2; Lizarazo Rodríguez 2017). EU law has particularly regulated the timber and minerals value chains in order to avoid that subcontractors or commercial partners of EU corporate groups violate human rights or environmental standards in their chains. In addition, some countries such as France and the UK have legislated on the duty of their corporate groups to avoid modern slavery in their value chains and to evaluate the actual or potential risks for human rights of for the environment.[9]

The US has also adopted some regulations related to the governance of its value chains. These include, for example, the Foreign Corrupt Practices Act and the Lacey Act on wildlife protection, the obligation to disclose human rights risks in the conflict minerals value chains (section 1502 of the Dodd-Frank Financial Reform Act) and to avoid human trafficking (California Transparency in Supply Chains Act). These regulations also seek to adopt a transnational new governance of value chains by promoting CSR self-regulation and voluntary practices but also by imposing concrete duties by means of domestic law (Sarfaty 2015: 420). In addition, the US procurement regulation (The Federal Acquisition Regulation (FAR)) has also sought extraterritorial reach with respect to social and environmental compliance as it forbids that value chains of the commercial partners of state agencies be involved in forced or child labour, which has to be supported by certification schemes. The Federal Funding Accountability and Transparency Act obliges government agencies to publish (sub-)contractors as well as where the contracted has mainly taken place (Corvaglia and Li 2018: 7). However, in this case, there is no explicit link between these regulations and NAFTA/US Mexico Canada Agreement (USMCA) or other regional arrangement.

The Interamerican system, and particularly the Interamerican Court of Human Rights (IACtHR), requires member states to regulate corporate activities so that they respect the Interamerican Convention and protocols on human rights and international standards such as the ILO Convention 169 on the rights of indigenous populations (IACHR 2015: 17–18). As a result, the Interamerican System of Human Rights (IAHR) has held that states should: first, consult local populations on the signature of FTAs if the latter could affect their territories and natural resources; second, ensure the respect for human rights when implementing agreements with states, companies or other non-state entities; third, avoid commercial or investment legislation that weaken, undermine or deny their international human rights obligations (IACHR 2015: 44). However, not only multinational companies intervene, as investing states also play an active role (IACHR 2015: 69–70).[10] The Interamerican system formulated several recommendations but only a few targeted investing states of the Americas: these states should respect the international human rights legal framework when regulating and overseeing their businesses abroad and therefore, they should avoid public support to businesses involved in human rights abuses and policies that only pursue their economic interests. Moreover, they should provide effective mechanisms to grant access to justice for victims of businesses in their jurisdiction and conduct human rights impact assessments of FTAs to protect local communities (IACHR 2015: 179–180).

Conclusion

Value chains have emerged as very useful conceptual categories to understand the functioning of the international economy, especially the organization of production and the patterns of trade and investment. From an empirical point of view, many value chains are rather regional than global in scope, or they combine – at least – a regionally organized production platform with global sales of the final product of the value chain.

From an IPE perspective, one can observe various connections between RVCs, policies and politics at various governance levels. States respond to demands from international(-izing) companies and create regional economic spaces and larger markets through institutions like free trade areas, customs unions or common markets so that RVCs can be created. States also formulate development policies that consist of connecting local companies and workers to RVCs and GVCs. In turn, the actual functioning of these value chains leads them to either design specific policies for economic and social upgrading and/or to regulate the behaviour of companies in value chains. Regional organizations, such as the EU and the Inter-American Court of Human Rights, play a complementary role therein. Finally, RVCs and GVCs are increasingly seen as relevant contexts for local and trans-border political action for all involved stakeholders to defend their rights or interests. Stakeholders include those directly involved in the value chain (companies, workers, consumers) as well as those indirectly affected by the activities in the value chain.

Notes

1 See, Gereffi *et al.* (2005) for a typology of governance models of GVCs.
2 See, www.oecd.org/sti/ind/measuring-trade-in-value-added.htm#access.
3 See, www.wiod.org.
4 In September 2018, the three signatories announced that negotiations were concluded and an agreement reached to replace NAFTA by the US Mexico Canada Agreement (USMCA).
5 The WTO defines the following 'regions': North America, Caribbean, South America, Europe, Commonwealth of Independent States (CIS) (including associate and former member states), Africa, Middle East, East Asia, West Asia, and Oceania. See, http://rtais.wto.org/UserGuide/User%20Guide_Eng.pdf [last accessed: 11 February 2019].
6 See, http://rtais.wto.org/UI/PublicMaintainRTAHome.aspx [last accessed: 9 March 2019]. It should be observed, however, that the distinction between intra- and cross-regional agreements depends on the regional definitions used by the WTO. The Caribbean Community and Common Market (CARICOM) agreement, for example, is counted as a cross-regional agreement, involving countries from the Caribbean, Central America and South America.
7 The parties agreed to a reciprocal exemption from the application of anti-dumping.
8 Directive 2007/36/EC of the European Parliament and of the Council on the exercise of certain rights of shareholders in listed companies.
9 See, *Modern Slavery Act* of the UK or the *Loi sur le devoir de vigilance* of France.
10 E.g. Canadian Embassies are directly involved in procuring such investment, labelled economic diplomacy and therefore, foreign investment has also a relevant public law dimension that should be highlighted (IACHR 2015: 45–46).

Bibliography

Álvarez Rubio, J. J. and Yiannibas, K. (eds). 2017. Human Rights in Business: Removal of Barriers to Access to Justice in the European Union. Abingdon: Routledge.

Augenstein, D. and Jägers, N. 2017. Judicial remedies – the issue of jurisdiction. In: Álvarez Rubio, J. J. and Yiannibas, J. (eds) Human Rights in Business: Removal of Barriers to Access to Justice in the European Union. Abingdon: Routledge: 7–37.

Aponte Garcia, M. 2014 *El nuevo regionalismo estratégico: los primeros diez años del ALBA-TCP*, Buenos Aires: CLACSO.

Arias, L. 2014. South Korean company confirms opening of yearn spinning plant in Costa Rica. *The Tico Times*.

ASEAN. 1981. *Basic Agreement on ASEAN Industrial Complementation*, Manila: ASEAN.

Bair, J. and Gereffi, G. 2013. Towards better work in Central America: Nicaragua and the CAFTA context. In: Rossi, A., Luinstra, A. and Pickles, J. (eds) *Towards Better Work: Understanding Labour in Apparel Global Value Chains*, New York, NY: Palgrave Macmillan: 251–275.

Baldwin, R. 2012. Trade and industrialisation after globalisation's second unbundling: How building and joining a supply chain are different and why it matters. In: Feenstra, R. and Taylor, A. (eds.) *Globalization in an Age of Crisis: Multilateral Economic Cooperation in the Twenty-First Century*, Chicago, University of Chicago Press.

Baldwin, R. 2016. *The Great Convergence, Information Technology and the New Globalisation*, Harvard, Harvard University Press.

Baldwin, R. and López González, J. 2013. Supply-chain Trade: A Portrait of Global Patterns and Several Testable Hypotheses. *NBER Working Paper No. 18957*.

Baldwin, R. and Venables, A. 2013. Spiders and snakes: Offshoring and agglomeration in the global economy. *Journal of International Economics*, 90(2): 245–254.

Barrientos, S., Gereffi, G. and Rossi, A. 2010. Economic and Social Upgrading in Global Production Networks: Developing a Framework for Analysis. *Capturing the Gains Working Paper No. 03*.

Begg, R., Pickles, J. and Smith, A. 2003. Cutting it: European integration, trade regimes, and the recon-figuration of East-Central European apparel production. *Environment and Planning A*, 35(12): 2191–2207.

Brown, D. K. 2007. Globalization and employment conditions study. *Social Protection Discussion Paper No. 0708:* The World Bank.

Cadestin, C., De Backer, K., Desnoyers-James, I., Miroudot, S., Rigo, D. and Ming, Y. 2018. Multi-national enterprises and global value chains: The OECD analytical AMNE database. *OECD Trade Policy Papers No. 211.*

Cingolani, I., Iapadre, L. and Tajoli, L. 2018. International production networks and the world trade struc-ture. *International Economics*, 153: 11–33.

Cingolani, I., Panzarasa, P. and Tajoli, L. 2017. Countries' positions in the international global value net-works: Centrality and economic performance. *Applied Network Science* 2(21): 1–20.

Coe, N. M., Dicken, P. and Hess, M. 2008. Global production networks: Realizing the potential. *Journal of Economic Geography*, 8(3): 271–295.

Corvaglia, M. A. and Li, K. 2018. Extraterritoriality and public procurement regulation in the context of global supply chains' governance. *Europe and the World: A Law Review*, 2(1): 1–16.

Curran, L. 2015. The impact of trade policy on global production networks: The solar panel case. *Review of International Political Economy* 22(5): 1025–1054.

De Backer, K., De Lombaerde, P. and Iapadre, L. 2018. Analyzing global and regional value chains. *Inter-national Economics*, 153(May): 3–10.

De Lombaerde, P. 1994. ASEAN Industrial Joint-Ventures (AIJVs) in the light of the ASEAN Free Trade Agreement (AFTA). *Droit et Pratique du Commerce International*, 20(4): 675–680.

De Lombaerde, P. and Garay, L. 2005. Preferential rules of origin: EU and NAFTA regulatory models and the WTO. *Journal of World Investment and Trade*, 6(6): 953–994.

De Lombaerde, P., Iapadre, L., McCranie, A. and Tajoli, L. 2018. Using network analysis to study globali-zation, regionalization, and multi-polarity. *Network Science*, 6(4): 494–516.

Eckhardt, J. and Lee, K. 2018. Global value chains, firm preferences and the design of preferential trade agreements. *Global Policy*, 9(S2): 58–66.

Eckhardt, J. and Poletti, A. 2018. Introduction: Bringing institutions back in the study of global value chains. *Global Policy*, 9(S2): 5–11.

Frederick, S., Bair, J. and Gereffi, G. 2015. Regional trade agreements and export competitiveness: The uncertain path of Nicaragua's apparel exports under CAFTA. *Cambridge Journal of Regions, Economy and Society*, 8(3): 403–420.

Gereffi, G., 1994. The organization of buyer-driven global commodity chains: how US retailers shape overseas production networks. In: Gereffi, G. and Korzeniewicz, M. (eds.) *Commodity Chains and Global Capitalism*. Westport, CT: Praeger: 95–122.

Gereffi, G. 1995. State policies and industrial upgrading in East Asia. *Revue d'Économie Industrielle*, 71(1): 79–90.

Gereffi, G., Humphrey, J., Kaplinsky, R. and Sturgeon, T. 2001. Introduction: Globalisation, value chains and development. *IDS Bulletin*, 32(3): 1–8.

Gereffi, G., Humphrey, J. and Sturgeon, T. 2005. The governance of global value chains. *Review of Inter-national Political Economy*, 12(1): 78–104.

Gomes Nogueira, C., Padilla, R. and Villareal, F. 2017. Value chain selection and industrial policy. In: Padilla, R. (ed.) *Rural Industrial Policy and Strengthening Value Chains*. Santiago: ECLAC-IFAD: 147–166.

Guy, F. 2009. *The Global Environment of Business*, Oxford: Oxford University Press.

Guy, F. 2015. Globalization, regionalization and technological change. In: D. Archibugi and A. Filippetti (eds.) *The Handbook of Global Science, Technology and Innovation*. Hoboken, NJ: Wiley-Blackwell.

Henderson, J., Dicken, P., Hess, M., Coe, N. and Yeung, H. 2002. Global production networks and the analysis of economic development. *Review of International Political Economy*, 9(3): 436–464.

Heydon, K. and Woolcock, S. 2009. *The Rise of Bilateralism: Comparing American, European and Asian Approaches to Preferential Trade Agreements*. Tokyo: United Nations University Press.

Horn, H. Mavroidis P.C. and Sapir, A. 2009. *Beyond the WTO? An Anatomy of EU and US Preferential Trade Agreements*. Bruegel Blueprint Series, VII. Brussels: Bruegel.

IACHR. 2015. *Indigenous Peoples, Afro-descendent Cmmunities, and Natural Resources: Human Rights Protection In The Context Of Extraction, Exploitation, And Development Activities*, Washington: Inter-American Commission on Human Rights. Organisation of American States (OAS), (OEA/Ser.L OEA/Ser.L/V/II. Doc. 47/15).

Koopman, R., Wang, Z. and Wei, S. 2014. Tracing Value-added and Double Counting in Gross Exports. *The American Economic Review*, 104(2): 459–494.

Kowalski, P., Lopez, J., Ragoussis, A. and Ugarte, C. 2015. *Participation of Developing Countries in Global Value Chains: Implications for Trade and Trade-Related Policies*. OECD Trade Policy Papers.

Krueger, A. O. 1974. The Political Economy of the Rent-Seeking Society. *The American Economic Review*, 64(3): 291–303.

Lizarazo Rodriguez, L. 2017. Mapping Law and Development. *Indonesian Journal of International and Comparative Law*, 4: 761–895.

Melitz, M. J. and Trefler, D. 2012. Gains from Trade When Firms Matter. *Journal of Economic Perspectives*, 26(2): 91–118.

Miroudot, S. and Nordström, H. 2015. *Made in the World? EUI Working Paper*. (RSCAS 2015/60), European University Institute.

Miroudot, S., Rouzet, D. and Spinelli, F. 2013. Trade Policy Implications of Global Value Chains: Case Studies. *OECD Trade Policy Paper*, (161).

Moncayo, E., De Lombaerde, P. and Guinea, O. 2012. Latin American Regionalism and the Role of UN-ECLAC, 1948–2010. In: Auroi, C. and Helg, M. (eds) *Latin America 1810–2010. Dreams and Legacies*, London: Imperial College Press: 359–386.

OECD. 2013. *Interconnected Economies: Benefiting from Global Value Chains*, Paris: OECD Publishing.

Oh, C. H. and Rugman, A. 2014. The Dynamics of Regional and Global Multinationals, 1999–2008. *The Multinational Business Review*, 22(2): 108–117.

Padilla Pérez, R. (ed.). 2014. *Strengthening Value Chains As An Industrial Policy Instrument. Methodology And Experience Of ECLAC In Central America*, Santiago: ECLAC-GIZ.

Padilla Pérez, R. and Quiroz Estrada, V. 2017. Rural industrial policy. In: R. Padilla Pérez (ed.) *Rural Industrial Policy and Strengthening Value Chains*, Santiago: ECLAC-IFAD: 69–111.

Pigrau Solé, A., Álvarez Torné, M., Cardesa-Salzmann, A., Font i Mas, M., Iglesias Márquez, D. and Jaria i Manzano, J. 2016. *Human Rights in European Business: A Practical Handbook for Civil Society Organisations and Human Rights Defenders*. Tarragona: CEDAT.

Porter, M. E. 1985. *Competitive Advantage: Creating and Sustaining Superior Performance*. New York: Free Press.

Quiroz Estrada, V. 2017. Productive development challenges in the rural areas of Central America and the Dominican Republic. In: R. Padilla Pérez (ed.) *Rural Industrial Policy and Strengthening Value Chains*, Santiago: ECLAC-IFAD: 25–67.

Rugman, A. M. 2005. *The Regional Multinationals*, Cambridge, Cambridge University Press.

Rugman, A. M. 2008. Regional multinationals and the myth of globalization. In: Cooper, A., Hughes, C. and De Lombaerde, P. (eds) *Regionalisation and Global Governance. The Taming of Globalisation?* Abingdon and New York: Routledge: 99–117.

Rugman, A. M. and Verbeke, A. 2004. A Perspective on Regional and Global Strategies of Multinational Enterprises. *Journal of International Business Studies*, 35(1): 3–18.

Sarfaty, G. A. 2015. Shining Light on Global Supply Chains. *Harvard International Law Journal*, 56(2), 419.

Solidum, E. D. and Meow, S. 1987. Decision Making in an ASEAN Complementation Scheme. The Automotive Industry. *ISEAS Research Notes and Discussion Papers*, (60).

The IGLP Law and Global Production Working Group. 2016. The role of law in global value chains: a research manifesto. *London Review of International Law*, 4(1): 57–79.

Turner, B. 2016. Supply-chain Legal Pluralism: Normativity as Constitutive of Chain Infrastructure in the Moroccan Argan Oil Supply Chain. *The Journal of Legal Pluralism and Unofficial Law*, 48(3): 378–414.

UNIDO. 1983. *Regional Industrial Co-operation: Experiences and Perspective of ASEAN and the Andean Pact*, Vienna: UNIDO, (UNIDO/IS.401).

Vivares, E. 2014. Toward a political economy of the New South American regionalism. In: Vivares, E. (ed.) *Exploring the New South American Regionalism*, Farnham: Ashgate: 9–28.

12

Constructivist IPE

Stephen Nelson

Introduction

"Isms matter," as Jonathan Kirshner has recently observed (2015: 155). Isms – rationalism, realism, historical institutionalism, Marxism, feminism, social constructivism, post-structuralism, and other paradigmatic approaches to understanding the nature of social and political organiza-tion – are important because they distill the foundational analytical commitments that anchor scholars' theorizing about puzzling outcomes in world politics. Isms foreground some explan-atory factors and push others farther into the background. Isms also influence the kinds of out-comes that different scholars find puzzling in the very first place.

Clarifying and laying bare the foundational commitments associated with the different Isms we employ in the study of IR and IPE can help us, as Kirshner writes, "to understand the likely strengths, weaknesses, limitations, controversies, and specific attributes of the various theories" (2015: 155). Thus the move, advocated by some high-status senior IPE scholars (see Lake 2011 for a qualified endorsement) and accepted by a good deal of younger U.S.-based scholars in the field, to discard the Isms and head toward a post-paradigmatic model of issue-specific, middle-range theorizing and rigorous data analysis in which the outdated "battles" between various Isms simply don't matter, is misguided. But, once again with the aid of Kirshner's insights, we can go further: the "non-paradigmatic" approach preferred by many in what Cohen (2007) calls the "American school" of IPE is in fact itself a paradigm, built upon three core analytical commit-ments, which Kirshner (2009) labels "Hyperrationalism" (H), Individualism (I), and Materialism (M) (or HIM, for short).

By contrasting one Ism employed in the study of IPE – constructivism – with the near-hegemonic (in the United States, at least) HIM-style approach, I hope to clarify the key differ-ences between the approaches, and I attempt to highlight the contributions that the work associated with constructivist IPE has made (and continues to make) in deepening our under-standing of the politics of foreign economic policymaking and the nature of international eco-nomic relations.

The comparative strategy I pursue in this chapter differs from Rawi Abdelal's (2009) review of the constructivist approach in IPE in a previous edition of the *Routledge Handbook of International Political Economy*, which linked the rise of constructivist-inflected work in IPE to large-scale historical trends and episodes (such as the dismantling of the social welfare and developmental states in the 1980s and 1990s) that were difficult to explain with purely rational–materialist frameworks. In that chapter Abdelal also categorized constructivist work into four "pathways" (labeled "meaning," "cognition," "uncertainty," and "subjectivity"), a categorization schema that was explicated more fully in the groundbreaking 2010 volume *Constructing the International Economy*, which Abdelal co-edited alongside Mark Blyth and Craig Parsons. With the benefit of Abdelal's review, and with a decade of additional work to survey since Abdelal's chapter was published, I proceed by, first, contrasting the world assumed by what Kirshner calls the "HIM" approach with the world that constructivists tend to think many (if not most) economic actors and policymakers actually inhabit. I highlight three key dimensions of difference between these approaches: (1) whether actors' decisions are assumed to be primarily made under conditions of quantifiable *risk* or whether, instead, their choices are assumed to be primarily made in the face of radical *uncertainty* (see Box 12.1); (2) whether knowing the material conditions facing economic actors is sufficient to determine their interests and preferences or not; and (3) whether the behavior of a collective group can be reduced to the interests of its members. Each of these differences has important implications for whether scholars of IPE choose to foreground material rather than ideational factors as the key shapers of decision makers' preferences over economic policies – and for how strategic they think decision makers can be in trying to enact their preferences.

In the second part of the chapter I contrast empirical research in the HIM mode with findings from the constructivist vein of research in three of the bread-and-butter issue areas investigated by IPE scholars: the politics of international trade, money, and finance. This review shows that the constructivist approach has yielded a number of important insights that help us resolve research puzzles that are otherwise difficult to explain from the purely HIM perspective.

Comparing material–rationalist and constructivist approaches to IPE

"Constructivism," Abdelal writes,

> is analytical language composed primarily of the social facts of the world, those facts that exist only because they are collectively shared ideas. Such social facts influence patters of political economy directly as socially constructed coordination devices; they also influence how agents interpret the material reality around them.
>
> *(2009: 63)*

Applied to the domains of interest to scholars of IPE, this central constructivist claim contains an important implication: it cannot be assumed that decision makers, ranging from ordinary consumers to the highest-level economic policymakers, facing sufficiently similar "objective," material conditions (such as exposure to the same price changes for a bundle of goods or a change in an indicator of the direction of their country's macroeconomic performance), will converge in their expectations about what to do. For constructivists, shared beliefs, values, worldviews, and social conventions constitute the interpretive schemas that decision makers rely upon to make sense of the signals that they pick up from their environments. Material conditions on their own are not enough to drive actors that may have radically different belief systems to arrive at similar expectations and to follow similar strategies. "People can interpret their material environments in very different ways. Indeed, so many 'similar people' make so many 'dissimilar choices,'" according to Abdelal, Blyth, and Parsons, "that our mainstream theories correspond, at best, only to time- and space-specific subsets of the world economy" (2010: 2). And as much research in the constructivist vein has shown, because economic actors' "mental models" aren't easily discarded,

Box 12.1 Origins of the distinction between risk and uncertainty

The first person to introduce the conceptual distinction between risk and uncertainty was the economist Frank Knight. In *Risk, Uncertainty, and Profit* (1921), Knight tried to explain the puzzle of the existence of corporate profits: in a world of frictionless markets, new suppliers should enter markets until the marginal the price of good equaled the marginal cost to make the product. Knight's insight was that there are two different choice environments facing entrepreneurs: situations of *risk* (agents can calculate objectively correct probabilities for possible future states of the world) and *uncertainty* (there is no way for agents to attach probabilities to a set of possible future states of the world). He explained that successful entrepreneurs are willing to make investments with uncertain payoffs in the future.

In the same year that Knight published his book, John Maynard Keynes published *A Treatise on Probability*. The seeds of Keynes's future thinking about the dynamics of financial markets can be found in the book. In it, Keynes distinguished between three types of probabilities: *cardinal*, in which there are measurable, objective probabilities for risky events; *ordinal* probabilities where "we reason that some events, based on our evidence, are more likely to occur than others, but not how much more likely, because we don't have enough inferences to make a proper statistical inference" (Skidelsky 2009: 85); and *radical uncertainty*, which reigns when we have so little knowledge that the future course of events are simply unknown.

By 1937 Keynes was ready to sketch the behavioral implications of radical uncertainty. Keynes noted that for the classical economist theorists, Knight's distinction was unimportant: "the calculus of probability, tho mention of it was kept in the background, was supposed to be capable of reducing uncertainty to the same calculable status as that of certainty itself" (1937: 213). The classical assumption of decision-making on the basis of objective probabilities is only reasonable when goods are consumed "within a short interval of being produced" (1937: 213). Since production and pricing decisions are repetitive and provide quick feedback, the situation approximates Knight's view of decisions under risk (Gerrard 1994: 331).

But financial assets are different. We purchase stocks and bonds to trade in the future with no way of knowing what the future price of our assets will look like: "thus the fact that our knowledge of the future is fluctuating, vague, and uncertain, renders Wealth a peculiarly unsuitable subject for the methods of classical economic theory" (Keynes 1937: 123).

Practical men, in Keynes's view, have no choice but to rely on "conventions, stories, rules of thumb, habits, traditions in forming our expectations and deciding how to act." *Confidence* is an essential part of Keynes's view of decision-making under uncertainty. Our expectations about an uncertain future are shaped by the social factors that give us reason to have more credence that investments will yield our desired payoff. Confidence, for Keynes,

> is not a statement about the future to be checked against actual outcomes. The state of confidence is an epistemological phenomenon, a state of mind, a belief or feeling about the adequacy or otherwise of the knowledge base from which the forecasts of the future are derived.
>
> (Gerrard 1994: 332)

Consequently, for Keynes and his followers, financial markets are particularly prone to unpredictable bouts of euphoria and panic.

shared beliefs can guide action even when the strategy is, from a purely material self-interested perspective, costly, suboptimal, or otherwise just plain hard to understand.

The contrast between the underlying theoretical assumptions of constructivist IPE and its material–rationalist alternative is stark.[1] Unlike constructivists who see decision makers as falling back on beliefs and other non-material interpretive schemas to guide their choices in highly complex environments rife with uncertainty, rationalist explanations typically start by (implicitly or explicitly) assuming that individual agents in any choice setting seek to solve optimization problems. As Dani Rodrik (2014: 190) explains, an optimization problem involves three components: (1) the thing that the agent wants to maximize (an "objective function" – income, votes, power, and the like); (2) the constraints under which the agent operates (the "rules of the game," constituted by things like budgets, technologies, and formal political institutions); and (3) the set of possible choices available to the agent. Agents optimize by selecting the policy mix that maximizes an expected payoff function (Page 2008: 123). In this analytical mode, "people select certain actions as a rational response to their place in an environment implicitly characterized as an obstacle course, in which payoffs may be opaque, but they are knowable" (Abdelal, Blyth, and Parsons 2010: 3). Information is unevenly distributed among agents, but in the material–rationalist optic *all* decision makers have at least enough knowledge of their worlds to be able to attach payoffs to actions and to assign probability distributions over the states of the world that might be brought about by different choices.

One key dimension that differentiates constructivist from material–rationalist-style IPE, then, is whether choices are made primarily under conditions of *risk* or whether they are made primarily under conditions of *uncertainty* (Box 12.1). Decision makers live with risk – not uncertainty – in the rationalist approach. Betting on a coin flip is a risky decision: you can't be certain whether heads or tails will come up, but if the coin is a fair one you know the odds. Outside of casinos decision makers rarely know the objective probabilities in a given choice setting, but in the material–rationalist approach they behave *as if* they have a probability distribution in mind. In this analytical mode, as Kirshner observes, "if rational actors have access to the same information, they will reach the same conclusions about expected outcomes" (2009: 205). In the approach characterized by risky (again, *not* uncertain) decision settings and "hyperrational" expectations, people may have different objective functions they seek to maximize and different information, but they don't fundamentally disagree on what constitutes the objectively "correct" model of reality (Rodrik 2014: 193). The framework assumes "rational people responding to an obstacle course that any human being would perceive fairly similarly" (Abdelal, Blyth, and Parsons 2010: 4).

How do scholars working in the HIM mode of analysis justify the assumption that economic actors make rational decisions in environments characterized chiefly by risk? A line of thinking that grew out of work by economic theorists in the 1950s provides the key theoretical justification: the intense pressure of *competition* in the marketplace weeds out players with beliefs that fail to match the material facts of the settings in which they are embedded. As one of the theorists defending the assumption of strong rationality in the modeling of economic behavior wrote: "those who realize positive profits are the survivors; those who suffer losses disappear … individual random behavior does not eliminate the likelihood of observing 'appropriate' decisions" (Alchian 1950: 213–16). Financial economists later demonstrated that in economies with complete markets inconsistent

> beliefs are not sustainable, and market forces – namely arbitrageurs such as hedge funds and proprietary trading groups – will take advantage of these opportunities until they no longer exist, that is, until the odds are in line with the axioms of probability theory.
>
> *(Lo 2007: 12)*

In the rationalist mode of analysis, inconsistency is costly. The insight suggests that agents operating in hyper-competitive markets for goods and financial assets should, rationally, invest in gathering information to try to avoid making systematic mistakes. As Mark Blyth puts it: "since being deluded all the time is very expensive, especially when making margin calls, one would expect agents operating in such markets to correct these mistakes" (2003: 243). Over time, subjective probability estimates should converge on objective probabilities.

What David Lake calls the Open Economy Politics (OEP) approach to IPE adds another element to the analysis alongside the assumption of rational decision-making in risky, rather than fundamentally uncertain, choice settings: material self-interest (rather than collectively shared beliefs, values, worldviews, and conventions) underlies economic actors' policy preferences. Thus the mainstream approach to IPE that Lake calls OEP (and that Kirshner calls HIM) rests on two core assumptions: (1) *materialism*, in that foreign economic policies produce income effects that are driven by an agent's position in the domestic and international division of labor, which allows observers to infer the preferences of economic agents from the activity in which they earn the bulk of their income; (2) *rationalism*, in the sense that economic agents, once they know what they want, make rational decisions as if they know the relevant probability distributions.[2] For example, import-competing producers of tradable goods for the domestic markets will lobby for an undervalued currency and a flexible exchange rate, because they believe that there is a nearly 100 percent probability that these policies will yield better profits than the alternative policy scenarios (Frieden 1991). In most circumstances, according to scholars working in the OEP/HIM style of analysis, it is not particularly difficult for individuals and firms to deduce their preferences from their positions in the marketplace. Jeffry Frieden, for example, observes: "it is not hard to imagine how to derive a profit-maximizing firm's strategies toward price, quantity, and quality" (1999: 57). The approach assumes that there are relatively clear and knowable links connecting an actor's position in the domestic and international economy to the actor's identification of material self-interest and, further, that in the final step it is straightforward to map those interests onto the actor's articulable preferences over outcomes.

The OEP/HIM approach also has a staunchly individualist orientation, in the sense that theorizing begins by characterizing the interests of the lowest-level unit of analysis, the individual, before aggregating the interests shared by individuals who are similarly affected by economic policies into larger units (such as firms, sectors, or classes) (Lake 2009: 226). The collective interest of the group, it is assumed, reflects the interests of the average member. Scholars in this tradition, furthermore, tend to regard the political institutions through which organized groups seek to enact policy changes as primarily *regulative*, in the sense that the formal design of political institutions may give some groups advantages over others in shaping policy outputs – but the interests and preferences of the groups are *not* endogenously shaped by the rules, norms, and cultures of the institutions themselves.

Constructivists are skeptical of all three claims underlying the OEP/HIM variety of IPE. (Table 12.1, below, provides a concise comparison of some of the differing assumptions of constructivist IPE and the material–rationalist approach.) As noted above, constructivists by-and-large reject the blanket assumption that actors' preferences can be accurately deduced from the material conditions in which they are embedded. And, further, constructivist work in IPE tends to be skeptical of the assumption that economic decision-making is made in the presence of quantifiable risk rather than uncertainty. For many constructivists, economic actors' abilities to think probabilistically about economic problems are hampered by the incompleteness of our knowledge about the incredibly complex structure of the world (we cannot, in Mark Blyth's terms, always observe the "generators" that produce outcomes) and by large-scale transformations in the underlying economic structures (Blyth 2006). In these kinds of environments there

Table 12.1 Constructivist versus material–rationalist approaches in IPE

	Constructivist IPE	OEP/HIM-style IPE
Decision settings are (primarily) characterized by …	Unquantifiable uncertainty	Quantifiable risk
Knowledge about the material conditions in which actors operate is …	Insufficient for understanding why economic actors across different contexts want what they want	Sufficient to deduce actors' interests, which drive their preferences and inform their choices
The behavior of collectivities (unions, firms, classes, states, etc.) …	Is not reducible to the interests of the individual members of the collectivity, because organizational cultures and identities can drive the organization's behavior and shape its members' beliefs	Is reducible to the aggregated interests of individual members of the collectivity

is simply no basis for people to settle on what the "objective" probability distribution looks like. When faced with uncertainty people depend on shared beliefs and social conventions to guide their decisions (Goldstein and Keohane 1993: 13–17). Instead of following decision rules that maximize expected payoffs, actors fall back on social scripts to guide their choices. In environments characterized by "radical" uncertainty there is no reason why everyone's beliefs should converge on a single, shared model, and worldviews that are wrong "could remain so even in the face of new evidence if that evidence is just used to confirm past beliefs" (Rodrik 2014: 194).

Finally, constructivist research in IPE has often resisted the individualist bent observed in the OEP/HIM tradition; instead, constructivists have pointed out how meso-level forces can transform individuals' perceived interests and preferences.[3] Organizations, ranging from trade unions to national policymaking bureaucracies to international institutions like the International Monetary Fund (IMF), can develop cultures that are not reducible to the interests of the average member of the organization – and yet which powerfully shape the behavior of the organization as a collective and shape the beliefs of the individuals within it (Nelson and Weaver 2016). Ahlquist, Clayton, and Levi's (2014) study of the trade policy preferences of members of International Longshore and Warehouse Union (ILWU) illustrates the point: while material–rationalist theory predicts that US-based ILWU members should be strongly pro-trade (Ahlquist, Clayton, and Levi convincingly demonstrate that the increasing volume of cross-border commerce accompanying lower trade barriers increased these workers' incomes), the union and its members have consistently rejected trade openness and have supported tariffs and other protectionist policies. To resolve the puzzle the authors look to the union's culture, which confers a shared belief among members in international worker solidarity ("an injury to one is an injury to all"). The authors argue that the ILWU case "provides evidence that it is possible for organizations to encourage behavior that goes beyond myopic self-interest … [the organization's] members may come to reconsider their beliefs and preferences as a result of their organizational exposure and socialization" (Ahlquist, Clayton, and Levi 2014: 35–43).

Table 12.1 distills some of the key differences between the constructivist approach and the material–rationalist alternative to the study of IPE. In the next section of the chapter I move to a non-exhaustive review of the contributions that constructivist-inflected work has made in three areas of concern to IPE scholars (the politics of international trade, money, and finance). The "non-exhaustive" clause in the previous sentence denotes three limits of the chapter.

First, the vastness and diversity of existing IPE research in the constructivist mold cannot be fully surveyed in a short chapter. Second, the survey highlights more recent work in the constructivist strain of IPE that has emerged in the years since Abdelal's (2009) essay on the state of the field. And, finally, as in Abdelal's review, the overview of constructivism in IPE in this chapter draws mainly upon research that is broadly positivist in its aims – which is to say that the research strategies adopted by the many of authors of the work reviewed here start from the twin premises that (1) the direction and strength of relationships between variables can be assessed with quantitative and qualitative tests and (2) that *causal* relations between those variables can be discerned using conventional research methods. Not all self-identifying constructivists in IPE accept these premises; in particular, the scholars working in what Abdelal, Blyth, and Parsons (2010) call the "subjectivist" tradition, who more often employ interpretivist methods than quantitative tests using large-N datasets or qualitative small-N case comparisons – and who often approach their research topics with the more critical aim of unveiling the historically contingent (and deeply inequitable) nature of social relations (such as the debtor-creditor relationship) that are sometimes taken for granted by scholars more concerned with documenting causal connections between variables (e.g., De Goede 2005). Subjectivists are particularly attuned to the more insidious ways in which power relations structure social systems. While a material–rationalist might regard social norms and conventions as devices for managing coordination problems (such as the convention of driving on one side of the road rather than the other), and constructivists informed by economic sociology are more likely to argue that norms and conventions inform actors' role-identities and supply a "menu of means individuals can use to deal with a problem" (Seabrooke 2006: 46), many IPE scholars working in the subjectivist tradition view social norms, instead, as "objects of power that determine the boundaries of possible speech and action and operate by exclusion of alternatives as much as by constitution of identities" (Abdelal 2009: 75).

This divergence within constructivism over research orientations also springs from a difference in basic views of the nature of causality: for adherents to "constitutive" causal accounts, such as Alexander Wendt, claiming that the beliefs that an agent holds in her head explains variation in a behavioral outcome better than the materialist alternatives only captures part of the role of shared ideas in social life; in Wendt's view, "ideas also constitute social situations and the meaning of material forces" (1999: 78). Wendt's alternative "constitutive" model of causality fixes on how shared beliefs generate objects or subject-positions. However, this notion of causation is radically different from the standard "variable X preceded observed state Y, and a change in X produced a change in Y" formulation preferred by positivists. Moreover, sympathetic critics of Wendt's notion of "constitutive causality," like David Dessler and John Owen, suggest that constitutive explanation makes more sense as "constitutive analysis, or constitutive description" than as an alternative model of causality (Dessler and Owen 2005: 599).

Constructivism and the politics of international trade

The origin of the material–rationalist Open Economy Politics approach, as Lake notes (2009: 225), lies in political scientists' efforts to understand variation in countries' trade policies. Analysts in this research tradition started by assuming, in line with Becker's (1983) model of the "marketplace" for regulatory policymaking, that political influence was increasing in the level of material resources controlled by a particular interest group. Further, they assumed that societal groups would act rationally in calculating the costs and benefits of expending resources to try to push their country's trade orientation toward openness or closure: once the marginal costs of lobbying effort exceeds the marginal (material) benefits resulting from efforts to influence the government's policy agenda, the group would give up and let other groups steer the trade policy-making process. One avenue for research in the OEP tradition focuses on interest groups' varying capacities for engaging in costly collective action to sway trade policy in their favor (Alt and Gilligan 1994).

To answer the question of *why* some groups preferred trade openness rather than closure (and vice versa) researchers in the OEP tradition returned to economic theory. In Ronald Rogowski's (1987) classic analysis, variation in factor abundance predicts political coalition-formation and can account for variation in countries' trade policies. Building on Wolfgang Stolper and Paul Samuelson's foundational economic model, Rogowski argued that pro-trade coalitions would coalesce around the users of the relatively abundant factors of production within a country's borders, and anti-free trade sentiment would be strongest among the users of the country's relatively scarce resources; in settings where labor and land were abundant and capital was scarce, for example, one should observe a "red–green" coalition of urban industrial workers and rural farmers and peasants pushing in favor of openness, aligned against a protectionist bloc of (scarce-factor-owning) capitalists spanning different industries. Others built models of the trade policy-making process on different microeconomic foundations: the so-called Ricardo–Viner model assumes, *contra* Stolper–Samuelson, that the main factors of production could not be costlessly switched from their current usage to a different one (e.g., the workers and machines in a shoe factory could not quickly be retrained and redesigned to turn the factory into a production site for airplane tires), and thus the Ricardo–Viner model predicts not the cross-class coalitions of the Stolper–Samuelson model but rather within-class cleavages (capitalists and workers pitted against each other) based on sectors' proximity to the national comparative advantage. Hiscox's (2001) study found supportive evidence for both approaches, depending on the degree of factor mobility at a given point in time (when factors of production were highly mobile, trade politics looked like the Stolper–Samuelson world and when they were relatively fixed trade politics fell in line with the Ricardo–Viner model).

The politics of international trade looks very different when viewed through the constructivist lens, however. Preferences over an issue as complex as the government's international trade agenda are unlikely to be solely informed by self-interest rooted in the direct economic effects of the policy. Instead, constructivist-oriented scholars suggest, we need to look at how individuals come to understand what trade *means* for them and for the communities in which they are embedded – and this requires paying due attention to meaning-making forces in social and political life, such as shared belief systems and cultural frames. Indeed, a good deal of evidence has piled up in the last decade showing that individuals' attitudes toward trade do not seem to line up with the predictions from the material–rationalist approach to trade policy. For example, in Mansfield and Mutz's (2009) widely read study, Americans' attitudes toward trade were largely unrelated to indicators of their economic self-interest; instead, the strongest predictors of positions on trade were symbolic attachments and cultural values, such as partisan identity and, in particular, ethno-nationalist predispositions. "Trade preferences," Mansfield and Mutz conclude, "are driven less by economic considerations and more by an individual's psychological worldview" (2009: 451).

While much of the recent wave of survey-based research on trade policy attitudes has yielded findings that undermine the materialist bent of the OEP/HIM-style approach in IPE and fit better with the assumption that preferences over international economic policies are socially constructed, the new work in this vein has, with few exceptions, retained an individualist orientation. Another major contribution of the constructivist approach has thus been to connect the collective identities that develop in the context of an international system composed of nation-states to the question of how those collectivities make sense of and select from the menu of trade policy choices. Abdelal's (2001) *National Purpose in the World Economy* exemplifies this line of research. Motivated by the puzzling variation in how Central and Eastern European countries managed their trade relations after the collapse of the Soviet empire, Abdelal identifies the variants of nationalism that emerged in the post-communist environment as the key driver of countries' trade strategies with respect to Russia. Keith Darden (2009) pursues a similar puzzle in his study of post-communist countries' foreign economic policy choices: given that "the collapse of the USSR left 15 states with remarkable historical and institutional commonalities" (2009: 4), why did these countries take such different routes to membership in international trade-promoting institutions? (Some countries rapidly moved toward membership in the General Agreement on Tariffs and Trade (t) and its successor institution, the World Trade Organization (WTO), while others dragged their feet or resisted accession altogether.) Like Abdelal, Darden sees a large role for collective beliefs – though in Darden's case the animating beliefs are not strictly nationalist but rather are causal beliefs about the nature of trade relations and the likely effects of openness on national wealth (Darden identifies three main types of shared economic belief systems hewed to at different points in time by states in the region, which he calls Soviet integralist, liberal, and mercantilist beliefs).

Organizations, such as firms, trade unions, and consumer advocacy groups, lie at a level of aggregation below the nation-state but above the level of the average individual. Recall that the OEP tradition sees trade policy contests among groups as being fought purely along self-interested lines – the groups that expect to lose from a shift toward openness duke it out for control of the agenda with groups that expect to win from the trade policy change, and all the groups in the contest are reasonably predictable in their expectations and consistently rational in their strategies for winning the battle. The pressure imposed on profit-seeking firms in competitive marketplaces should, material–rationalists suggest, weed out aberrant beliefs and inefficient strategies that may be observed at the level of individual. But that perspective hinges, crucially, on the assumption that groups are formulating their strategies in decision environments characterized chiefly by risk.

Constructivists in IPE, like Cornelia Woll (2008), question that assumption: if firms are fundamentally uncertain about the distributional consequences of trade liberalization – that is to say, they have too few prior episodes upon which draw to be able to forecast with any degree of accuracy who will win and who will lose from the policy change – then they cannot rationally optimize. Instead, Woll suggests, "firms will rely on social devices to reduce uncertainty, such as traditions, networks, institutions, and the use of power" (2008: 12). Woll shows how the changing nature of production (shifting from primarily national to global, via supply chains that span many countries) and the changing nature of cross-border exchange (trading not just physical goods but also services) moved many firms out of the world of quantifiable risk and plunged them into the world of uncertainty. She asks: "How would we predict the policy preference of a large French textile company engaged in an integrated production chain beyond European borders or a small American software company with no international operations?" (Woll 2008: 29). Drawing on detailed case studies of American and Western European firms' lobbying activity on the issue of liberalizing trade in services, Woll convincingly shows that business' interests in this domain are not given by their material environment but rather are shaped by their perceived identities; and, further, she demonstrates that companies' strategies are shaped principally by what they learn from the national regulatory policymakers with whom they frequently interact.

The role of pervasive uncertainty – and the social strategies that actors adopt in order to cope with it – emerge as key themes in constructivist work on the design, behavior, and effects of international organizations (IOs) that write and enforce rules governing international trade.

S. Nelson

This is a distinctive contribution of the constructivist agenda, given that material–rationalist approaches tend to share some core assumptions regarding how IOs operate: actors within and outside of IOs are rational optimizers; formal "authoritative rule structures" are the key factors shaping agents' strategies (Nielson and Tierney 2003: 251); and the rule structures within which IO actors operate are strongly influenced by the distribution of material power among the members of the international system. Non-material factors like organizational cultures play a peripheral role in what Barnett and Finnemore (1999) call the "economistic" approach to the study of IOs. In this approach IOs are conceptualized as contractual arrangements among rational, materially oriented actors, varying in their capabilities, seeking to maximize their interests subject to the enduring environmental constraints and opportunities that inhere in their domains of operation.

Research focusing on "legalization" as the key form of variation of international rules illustrates how these material–rationalist assumptions have informed non-constructivist theorizing about the design of IOs. The "legalization" perspective focuses on three dimensions of international rules and rule-making bodies: obligation (the degree to which actors are legally bound to adhere to the rules), precision (the degree of ambiguity in the conduct specified by the international rules), and delegation (the degree to which authoritative interpretation and enforcement of the rules is delegated to third parties, such as an international court) (Abbott et al. 2000). Issue areas are subject to "hard law" when the legal institution governing that area features high values on all three dimensions (exemplified by the WTO's Dispute Settlement System). From the legalization perspective the most important issue is whether law in a given area is soft/weak or hard/strong. The actors that produce legal instruments, in this perspective, can (at least in principle) adjust the three dimensions to "produce an institution exactly suited to their specific needs" (Abbott et al. 2000: 404). International law is conceptualized as a problem-solving device, the terms of which are negotiated by materialist, rational actors. Variation in the strength/firmness of law in different issue areas in world politics is usually explained as an outcome of the struggle between states, whose interests and material capabilities vary, to extend or restrain the force of law, and the competing demands of domestic interest groups whose interests are affected by legalization (Kahler 2000). There's little scope, in this image of global rule-making, for the kinds of social norms and shared beliefs that, as in the constructivist perspective, are necessary for anchoring actors' expectations in the face of uncertainty.

The transformation of the GATT agreement during the Uruguay Round of multilateral trade negotiations (1986–1994), which gave birth to a successor agreement and its institutional embodiment, the WTO, marked a breakthrough for "hard" trade law at the international level. Through the material–rationalist lens it is "reasonable," writes Leslie Johns, to assume that the new WTO agreement and (in particular) "the resulting dispute settlement system was designed by mostly (if not completely) rational actors with an eye to the system's expected effect on international trade" (Johns 2015: 10). The international trade negotiators were operating rationally in the world of risk, in this view.

But the historical narratives of the Uruguay Round negotiations paint a very different picture: none of the key players in the discussions initially came to the bargaining table with clear, unambiguous interests related to the redesign of the system, nor did any of the negotiators expect that the end result would be a radically redesigned dispute settlement system involving an appellate body that could issue binding, enforceable judgments (Croome 1999; Preeg 1995). Manfred Elsig's interviews with trade negotiators suggest, "the ambitious outcomes [of the Uruguay Round negotiations] could not have been predicted at the outset of the process" (2017: 305). Rather, the "legalization leap" that produced the new WTO agreement and its strengthened adjudication system was a product of processes of mutual learning and trust building, conducted against the backdrop of pervasive uncertainty, that evolved over nearly a decade of negotiations.

Francesco Duina (2006) turns to the role that non-material cognitive schemas play in shaping another important set of rule-making bodies in trade – regional trade agreements. Duina focuses on variation in the design and functioning of three regional trade agreements (RTAs – the North American Free Trade Agreement (NAFTA), the EU, and Mercosur). His study identifies two major distinctions between RTAs: (1) the development of different legal systems to address harmonization among participants; (2) differences in the way in which interest groups responded to integration. Duina explains the emergences of these differences in two steps: first, he argues that the creation of RTA requires the construction of "cognitive guidebooks" to standardize disparate definitional and normative understandings of trade; second, the variation in the "cognitive guidebooks" designed by officials in each RTA is shaped by domestic legal institutions and customs (namely, common versus civil law traditions) and politics (the interplay of interest groups and elected officials in member countries of RTAs). The key point is that the beliefs underpinning these institutional arrangements – and the ways in which domestic groups and policymakers come to understand those arrangements – cannot be deduced from material conditions.

Beyond the design of international arrangements governing trade, there is a divide between the material–rationalist and constructivist perspectives over the putative effects of international rules and institutions. In the OEP tradition, the international rules and institutions structure the nature of bargaining between self-interested states and provide "credible commitments" to assure others (states and market players) that governments will follow through on their policy promises (to refrain from "defecting" from a codified agreement to refrain from raising tariffs, for example) (Lake 2009). States are strategic in designing international rules and the IOs that embody them, and they are strategic in using the rules – but the rules and rule-makers within IOs do not construct states' interests, preferences, or identities in a social learning process. States come to these interactions with their interests and strategies already determined by the rewards and punishments of the material environments in which they operate.

Michael Barnett and Martha Finnemore's (1999, 2004) constructivist-oriented work gives us a very different lens through which to view IOs. They point out that IO autonomy comes in different forms. IOs may have wide discretion when states are relatively indifferent to their activities, but they also exercise discretion when they avoid following states' directives, when they directly challenge powerful principals' interests, and when, crucially, they "change the broader normative environment and states' perceptions of their own preferences" (Barnett and Finnemore 2004: 27–9). The discretion of IOs like the WTO, in this perspective, is a function of the institution's dual roles: it is *in authority* because it has been formally delegated tasks by its members; it became *an authority* in world politics thanks to its rational–legal bureaucratic procedures and the specialized knowledge possessed by its staff and management. The constructivist lens allows us to see IOs as purposive actors in global governance using "their authority to expand their control over more and more of international life" (Barnett and Finnemore 2004: 44). IOs do more than just structuring the bargaining between states that have conflicting interests or supplying opportunities for states to credibly commit to a course of action (thus helping members realize their interests); they also work to construct boundaries between "legitimate" and "illegitimate" economic policies for their members. "In this sense," Abdelal observes, "international norms define the boundaries of choices. International organizations play an important role in fixing the meanings, thereby constituting the legitimate boundaries of policymaking" (Abdelal 2009: 72).

While constructivist-oriented research on the politics of international trade has not supplanted the material–rationalist perspective that continues to inform much empirical work in the field, the constructivist approach has generated important new insights. I highlighted three key constructivist claims in this brief overview: first, we need to look at how average individuals and elite policymakers alike come to understand what trade *means* for them and for the communities in which they are embedded (and over which they govern); second, the expectations of groups that are involved in trade policymaking may be formed in the presence of "radical" uncertainty, which requires an understanding of the socially constructed nature of those groups' interests and preferences; and finally, uncertainty shapes the design of international rules and institutions governing cross-border trade, and, further, those rule-making bodies, once in place, may produce the "scripts" that define how member states come to understand and internalize the boundaries between legitimate and illegitimate types of foreign economic policies.

Constructivism and the politics of international money and finance

Constructivists have also turned their attention to the politics of international money and finance – and, as was the case for international trade, their work has contributed to knowledge by identifying and explaining empirical puzzles that were difficult to understand through the material–rationalist lens (or were altogether off the material–rationalist radar).

One of the central themes in the IPE of money is the rise of a massive and highly mobile global pool of capital. The international market for capital and financial assets began to dramatically swell in the early 1960s, starting with the development of a large "offshore" pool of money lying beyond the reach of any country's regulatory authorities (the so-called Eurodollar market, housed in the financial hub of London but largely unregulated by the British (or any other) government) (Helleiner 1995). International economist Robert Mundell soon noted that in a world of global capital mobility governments had to navigate a new kind of macroeconomic policy tradeoff. If they hewed to fixed exchange rates and relinquished tight exchange controls sealing off their national financial system from the emerging global market, they had to ensure that their national interest rates did not deviate too far from the rates set by central banks in the financial centers in the international economy (namely, the U.S., UK, and Japan). If they did, the currency traders and international investors operating out of the Eurodollar market would move against them, putting either upward or downward pressure on the exchange rate. Faced with this tradeoff – currency stability at the cost of monetary policy independence – many states simply decided it was better to give up fixed exchange rates and to let the value of their currencies be set by market forces.

Scholars operating in the OEP/HIM mode invoked domestic interests to explain the politics of the tradeoff generated by large and unrestrained global capital flows. In Frieden's (1991) seminal contribution, domestic groups vary in their exposure to international market forces and in the degree to which the assets they hold are specific to their current uses – and it is these features that predict groups' preferences over the tradeoff in a world of unrestricted capital mobility. Others, like Verdier (1999), focus attention on different distributional fault lines in countries grappling with the consequences of international capital flows. One recent contribution, using survey experiments with a sample of ordinary Americans, suggests that self-interested preferences over the exchange rate stability versus monetary policy autonomy tradeoff can be induced by giving people relatively small amounts of contextual information, which helps average people connect the policy choice to their own personal financial circumstances (Bearce and Tuxhorn 2017). Regardless of how groups' and individuals' interests are characterized, all of this work depicts a structural feature of actors' material environments (the degree of capital mobility) as the determining factor in the construction of their policy preferences.

Kathleen McNamara (1998) directly targeted that assumption in her path-breaking constructivist work on the politics of European monetary cooperation in a post-global capital mobility world. Her case studies of episodes of policy coordination showed that fluctuations in European countries' positions on the tradeoff generated by capital mobility were *not* products of interest group politics. The world of capital mobility was not, *contra* the OEP view, one in which cleaner price signals and more intense competitive pressures clarified groups' self-interests; rather, firms and other organized groups were grappling with pervasive uncertainty, and "uncertainty creates highly fluid conceptions of interest" (McNamara 1998: 7).[4] Policymakers' shared beliefs, not societal groups' material interests, underpinned European governments' willingness to forego monetary policy autonomy in exchange for currency stability: the rise of the "neoliberal policy consensus that elevated the pursuit of low inflation over growth or employment," in McNamara's argument, turned high-level policymakers' preferences strongly toward a common European exchange rate system and, eventually, toward monetary unification on the continent (McNamara 1998: 3).

Other work in the constructivist mold questions the assumption that global capital mobility imposes, in law-like fashion, the strict policy choices identified by Mundell in the first place. Where OEP and other perspectives that take the tradeoff as a brute material fact of life in a world of capital mobility go wrong, some constructivists hold, is by assuming that capital mobility

> is a non-social machine that creates invariant and irresistible pressures for liberalization.... In this [constructivist] view, the effect of rising ICM [international capital mobility] may be mediated by intersubjective beliefs about 'appropriate policy'; that is, its impact on actor preferences for greater openness (or closure) may be conditional on variation in social facts.
>
> *(Chwieroth and Sinclair 2013: 472)*

Shared beliefs about what constitutes appropriate or acceptable deviations from disciplined (which is to say, austere) monetary and fiscal policy agendas provide the interpretive frames through which market players and policymakers understand the choices they face (Kirshner 2003: 14–15; Widmaier 2010).

Along these same lines, constructivists have provided rich empirical studies of the involvement of IOs in the production and dissemination of the "stigma" targeting capital controls (regulatory policies that restrict cross-border flows of money and financial assets) – a policy stigma that emerged and hardened in the 1980s and 1990s and has only eased in the wake of the 2008 financial crisis. Abdelal and Meunier (2010), for example, trace elite French policymakers' central roles in promoting regional and global rules that prohibited the use of capital controls. Chwieroth (2010) focuses on how a cohort of economic officials hewing to "neoliberal" economic beliefs promoted the norm of capital openness within the IMF.

One of the consequences of the drive toward capital decontrol and the unshackling of capital from within national borders is an increase in the proportion of countries experiencing serious financial crises (Reinhart and Rogoff 2009). In the OEP/HIM tradition financial crises have typically been treated as exogenous shocks that yield distributional effects or, in a move that partially endogenizes the conditions that give birth to financial market crises, as the suboptimal outcome of rational but myopic market players and market-captured regulators responding to incentives and seeking to maximize their short-term returns, with collectively disastrous results. Even before the 2008 eruption of the largest financial crisis in 70 years constructivists in IPE added a distinctive perspective on the nature of crises. Rather than assuming that crises bring with them self-evident features that do not require any kind of mediating interpretive frame-work, understanding how a particular crisis comes to be understood as type "X" rather than types "Y" or "Z" require understanding, first, that because crises are moments of radical uncertainty distributional consequences are unlikely to be clear and knowable, and, second, that vying epistemic communities composed of policy advocates are *always* involved in struggles over how to define and respond to a crisis (Farrell and Quiggin 2017; Widmaier, Blyth, and Seabrooke 2007).

Given that constructivists already had a keen interest in crisis episodes it is not surprising that the 2008 Global Financial Crisis (GFC) touched off a flurry of constructivist-influenced work in IPE. One theme loomed large in many of the discussions of the meaning and lessons of the 2008 crisis for the field of IPE: the failure of economists to recognize a looming crisis on the horizon and, once it had arrived, to say much of anything useful about it reflected the jettisoning of Knightian uncertainty from the analysis in favor of the assumption of a risk-only world, and IPE scholarship would do well not to make the same mistake as macroeconomists (Nelson and Katzenstein 2014). Some of the most prominent features of the 2008 GFC were difficult to understand without bringing in a role for radical uncertainty (see Box 12.1) and the social conventions that people rely upon to stabilize their expectations in the face of uncertainty. Why, for example, did well-informed market players with large stakes have such confidence in securitized assets that, in retrospect, were flimsily constructed? And why did confidence in the valuations of those assets erode so quickly?

The constructivist lens brought uncertainty into the center of the analysis of the run-up to the financial crisis of 2008 and its aftermath.[5] In this view, important decisions in and around financial markets are undertaken without precise knowledge about the probabilities of payoffs and the size of those payoffs. We simply don't know enough about the underlying process to reliably forecast future returns from past events.[6] Nonetheless, financial market actors still have to make choices – and they need to be confident that their decisions are the right ones; otherwise, they would be paralyzed by indecision. If financial markets resembled actuarial models of life and property insurance (where, thanks to good information and relatively stable parameters, risks can be reliably quantified), confidence would simply mirror past and current objective economic conditions (Skidelsky 2009: 41). The economic landscape, however, is more treacherous for investors in asset markets than insurance companies: financial market actors can win or lose big as massive, unpredicted swings in market sentiment render prior probability distributions poor guides to decision. Traders can sample the past to predict returns with some accuracy for some time, until catastrophic events that lurk in the far tails of the distribution "radically alter the distribution in ways that agents cannot calculate before the fact, irrespective of how much information they have" (Blyth 2006: 496). Crises occur with alarming frequency, and their causes are very difficult to diagnose, even years after they have passed.

Constructivist approaches informed by economic sociology recognize that financial markets are complex, deeply interdependent patterns of economic and social activity. Market actors, and the policymakers that observe and regulate financial markets, adopt social conventions to impose a sense of order and stability in their worlds, thereby allowing "exchange to take place according to expectations which define efficiency" (Storper and Salais 1997: 16). Conventions are not explicit agreements or formal institutions; rather, they are templates for understanding how to operate in contexts that are experienced as shared and common (Wagner 1994: 174). Conventions vary in their degree of materiality. They can take the form of public discourses and mental models, such as the "new era stories" that encouraged people to treat homes as assets that could not lose value, which anchored agents' expectations in uncertain environments (Akerlof and Shiller 2009). Conventions in financial markets also take material forms, such as risk management technologies (Biggart and Beamish 2003: 452–3). Social conventions can stabilize actors' expectations, but not permanently; Keynes, after all, argued that conventional expectations resting on a "flimsy foundation" are inherently unstable (Skidelsky 2009: 93). The conventions that inform market expectations do not mirror underlying economic fundamentals; rather, the partial and distorted views that market participants impose on the world shape the markets. And these views often evolve in a social environment in which "rumors, norms, and other features of social life are part of their understanding of finance" (Sinclair 2009: 451). In "reflexive feedback loops" these conventional views drive markets, which then subsequently shape beliefs and thus can generate far-from-equilibrium situations.

A distinctive contribution of constructivists studying the politics of finance has been to identify and investigate the purveyors of market-stabilizing conventions. By acknowledging the crucial role of uncertainty in finance and by looking for the conventions that become part of the deep structure of financial markets, constructivists were well placed to answer two fundamentally *political* questions: who governs, and how do they govern? An important governor in the realm of global finance has been the credit rating agencies (CRAs). The credit rating industry – with Moody's, S&P, and Fitch as the three largest firms – is indispensable for contemporary finance (Sinclair 2005). The CRAs' main purpose is to (illusorily) transform uncertainty into quantifiable risk (Abdelal and Blyth 2015; Carruthers 2013). The CRAs do this work by producing conventional judgments about borrowers' creditworthiness – judgments that are legible to participants in the markets. As Abdelal and Blyth observe, "contrary to what one would expect, rather than revealing new information, CRAs oftentimes codify what the market already knows: they become a part of the governance of markets by establishing 'the conventional judgment' regarding a borrower's creditworthiness" (2015: 40). Because they help establish market conventions (by codifying and signifying market sentiments ratings help drive upswings and downswings in asset prices), the CRAs' model-based judgments powerfully discipline many of their subjects; when they downgrade a sovereign state, for example, the CRAs reinforce what the market players already suspect (that the state is a high credit risk), and when the markets react accordingly, the subject of the rating starts to look more like it is indeed not creditworthy (Abdelal and Blyth 2015). And by describing "reality" through the use of ratings, the agencies' rating "makes that reality correspond more closely to the description" (Rona-Tas and Hiss 2010: 141).

Constructivism's contributions to the study of IPE

To conclude, this chapter has reviewed several key analytical commitments that distinguish the constructivist approach to IPE from the mainstream (in the United States, at least) rational–materialist perspective. I highlighted three main differences between these approaches: (1) whether actors' decisions are assumed to be primarily made under conditions of quantifiable *risk* or whether, instead, their choices are assumed to be primarily made in the face of radical *uncertainty* (see Box 12.1); (2) whether knowing the material conditions facing economic actors is sufficient to determine their interests and preferences or not; and (3) whether the behavior of a collective group can be reduced to the interests of its members. Reviewing well-established and more recent findings from studies spanning three central issue areas of concern to IPE scholars – the politics of international trade, money, and finance – shows that there are payoffs to broadening the scope of theorizing in IPE to bring in the concepts and empirical referents associated with the constructivist analytical style.

Echoing Abdelal's (2009) prior survey of the field, my efforts to highlight some of the distinctive contributions of constructivist-oriented work should not be taken as a repudiation of the

OEP/HIM-style research against which the constructive approach was compared. We simply don't know enough (and likely never will) to be able to confidently declare a champion in the grand battle between rival paradigms. Instead, we should seek to creatively combine insights from different approaches where appropriate, with an eye kept on the ultimate goal of creeping ever closer to solving the truly important research puzzles that we have yet to fully grasp.

Notes

1 This section draws from Nelson 2017.
2 At its core, OEP predicts that an agent would not switch her preferences if the material circumstances remain constant. The great strength of OEP as a research tradition in IPE, for Lake, is that it posits that interests emerge "from a prior, falsifiable, empirically robust theory … that both the relevant political actors and their interests are defined by their production profile or position in the international economy is the 'hard core' of the emergent paradigm" (2009: 227).
3 Meso-level phenomena sit at a level of granularity below the macro-level concepts and mechanisms that define the broadest contexts in which collective decisions are formulated (the anarchic international system of states or the system of global capitalism, for example) and at a level above the micro-mechanisms that focus on individual processes, attributes, and traits (be they emotional, cognitive, or genetic) (Hackman 2003).
4 Kinderman (2008), looking at German firms' exchange rate preferences and lobbying activities, found additional evidence that firms' preferences became more ambiguous as the complexity of their activities increased over time.
5 This section draws on Nelson and Katzenstein 2014.
6 Leamer (2010: 38–9) notes: "if we cannot reliably assess predictive means, variances, and covariances" for things like asset prices, "then we are in a world of Knightian uncertainty in which expected utility maximization doesn't produce a decision."

Bibliography

Abbott, K. W., Keohane, R.O., Moravcsik, A., Slaughter, A. M. and Snidal, D. 2000. The Concept of Legalization. *International Organization* 54, 3: 401–19.

Abdelal, R. 2001. *National Purpose in the World Economy: Post-Soviet States in Comparative Perspective.* Ithaca: Cornell University Press.

Abdelal, R. 2009. Constructivism as an approach to international political economy. In: Blyth, M. ed., *Routledge Handbook of IPE:* 62–76. New York: Routledge.

Abdelal, R. and Blyth, M. 2015. Just who put you in charge? We did: CRAs and the Politics of Ratings. In: Cooley, A. and Snyder, J. eds., *Ranking the World: Grading States as a Tool of Global Governance:* 39–59. New York: Cambridge University Press.

Abdelal, R., Blyth, M. and Parsons, C. 2010. Introduction: The case for constructivist political economy. In: Abdelal, R., Blyth, M. and Parsons, C. eds., *Constructing the International Economy:* 1–19. Ithaca: Cornell University Press.

Abdelal, R. and Meunier, S. 2010. Managed Globalization: Doctrine, Practice and Problem. *Journal of European Public Policy* 17, 3: 350–67.

Ahlquist, J. S., Clayton, A. B. and Levi, M. 2014. Provoking Preferences: Unionization, Trade Policy, and the ILWU Puzzle. *International Organization* 68 (Winter): 33–75.

Akerlof, G. and Shiller, R. 2009. *Animal Spirits: How Human Psychology Drives the Economy, and Why It Matters for Global Capitalism.* Princeton: Princeton University Press.

Alchian, A. 1950. Uncertainty, Evolution, and Economic Theory. *Journal of Political Economy* 58, 3: 211–21.

Alt, J. E. and Gilligan, M. 1994. The Political Economy of Trading States: Factor Specificity, Collective Action Problems and Domestic Political Institutions. *Journal of Political Philosophy* 2, 2: 165–92.

Barnett, M. N. and Finnemore, M. 1999. The Politics, Power, and Pathologies of International Organizations. *International Organization* 53, 4: 699–732.

Barnett, M. N. and Finnemore, M. 2004. *Rules for the World: International Organizations in Global Politics.* Ithaca: Cornell University Press.

Bearce, D. H. and Tuxhorn, K. L. 2017. When Are Monetary Policy Preferences Egocentric? Evidence from American Surveys and an Experiment. *American Journal of Political Science* 61, 1: 178–93.

Becker, G. S. 1983. A Theory of Competition among Pressure Groups for Political Influence. *Quarterly Journal of Economics* 98, 3: 371–400.

Biggart, N. and Beamish, T. 2003. The Economic Sociology of Conventions: Habit, Custom, Practice, and Routine in Market Order. *Annual Review of Sociology* 29: 443–64.

Blyth, M. 2003. The political power of financial ideas: Transparency, risk, and distribution in global finance. In: Kirshner, J. ed., *Monetary Orders: Ambiguous Economics, Ubiquitous Politics*: 239–59. Ithaca: Cornell University Press.

Blyth, M. 2006. Great Punctuations: Prediction, Randomness, and the Evolution of Comparative Political Science. *American Political Science Review* 100, 4: 493–8.

Carruthers, B. G. 2013. From Uncertainty toward Risk: The Case of Credit Ratings. *Socio-Economic Review* 11, 3: 525–51.

Chwieroth, J. M. 2010. *Capital Ideas: The IMF and the Rise of Financial Liberalization*. Princeton: Princeton University Press.

Chwieroth, J. M. and Sinclair, T. 2013. How You Stand Depends on How We See: International Capital Mobility as a Social Fact. *Review of International Political Economy* 20, 3: 457–85.

Cohen, B. J. 2007. The Transatlantic Divide: Why are American and British IPE So Different? *Review of International Political Economy* 14, 2: 197–219.

Croome, J. 1999. *Reshaping the World Trading System: A History of the Uruguay Round* (Second and Revised Edition). Geneva: World Trade Organization.

Darden, K. A. 2009. *Economic Liberalism and Its Rivals: The Formation of International Institutions among the Post-Soviet States*. New York: Cambridge University Press.

De Goede, M. 2005. *Virtue, Fortune, and Faith: A Genealogy of Finance*. Minneapolis: University of Minnesota Press.

Dessler, D. and Owen, J. 2005. Constructivism and the Problem of Explanation: A Review Article. *Perspectives on Politics* 3, 3: 597–610.

Duina, F. 2006. *The Social Construction of Free Trade: The European Union, NAFTA, and Mercosur*. Princeton: Princeton University Press.

Elsig, M. 2017. Legalization in Context: The Design of the WTO's Dispute Settlement System. *British Journal of Politics and International Relations* 19, 2: 304–19.

Farrell, H. and Quiggin, J. 2017. Consensus, Dissensus, and Economic Ideas: Economic Crisis and the Rise and Fall of Keynesianism. *International Studies Quarterly* 61, 2: 269–83.

Frieden, J. A. 1991. Invested Interests: The Politics of National Economic Policies in a World of Global Finance. *International Organization* 45, 4: 425–51.

Frieden, J. A. 1999. Actors and preferences in international relations. In Lake, D. and Powell, R. eds., *Strategic Choice and International Relations*: 39–76. Princeton: Princeton University Press.

Gerrard, B. 1994. Beyond Rational Expectations: A Constructive Interpretation of Keynes's Analysis of Behavior under Uncertainty. *The Economic Journal* 104, March: 327–37.

Goldstein, J. and Keohane, R. eds. 1993. *Ideas and Foreign Policy*. Ithaca: Cornell University Press.

Hackman, J. R. 2003. Learning More by Crossing Levels: Evidence from Airplanes, Hospitals, and Orchestras. *Journal of Organizational Behavior* 24, 8: 905–22.

Helleiner, E. 1995. Explaining the Globalization of Financial Markets: Bringing States Back. *Review of International Political Economy* 2, 2: 315–42.

Hiscox, M. 2001. Class versus Industry Cleavages: Inter-Industry Factor Mobility and the Politics of Trade. *International Organization* 55, 1: 1–46.

Johns, L. 2015. *Strengthening International Courts: The Hidden Costs of Legalization*. Ann Arbor: University of Michigan Press.

Kahler, M. 2000. Conclusion: The Causes and Consequences of Legalization. *International Organization* 54, 3: 661–83.

Keynes, J. M. 1937. The General Theory of Employment. *Quarterly Journal of Economics* 51, 2: 209–23.

Kinderman, D. 2008. The Political Economy of Sectoral Exchange Rate Preferences and Lobbying: Germany from 1960–2008, and beyond. *Review of International Political Economy* 15, 5: 851–80.

Kirshner, J. 2003. The Inescapable Politics of Money. In: Kirshner, J. ed., *Monetary Orders*: 3–24. Ithaca: Cornell University Press.

Kirshner, J. 2009. The second crisis in IPE theory. In Phillips, N. and Weaver, C. E. eds., *International Political Economy: Debating the Past, Present and Future*: 203–9. New York: Routledge.

Kirshner, J. 2015. The Economic Sins of Modern IR Theory and the Classical Realist Alternative. *World Politics* 67, 1: 155–83.

Lake, D. 2009. Open Economy Politics: A Critical Review. *Review of International Organizations* 4, 3: 219–44.

Lake, D. 2011. Why "isms" are Evil: Theory, Epistemology, and Academic Sects as Impediments to Understanding and Progress. *International Studies Quarterly* 55, 2: 465–80.

Leamer, E. 2010. Tantalus on the Road to Asymptopia. *Journal of Economic Perspectives* 24, 2 (Spring): 31–46.

Lo, A. 2007. Efficient Markets Hypothesis. In Blume, L. and Durlauf, S. eds., *The New Palgrave: A Dictionary of Economics*. New York: Palgrave McMillan.

Mansfield, E. D. and Mutz, D. C. 2009. Support for Free Trade: Self-Interest, Sociotropic Politics, and Out-Group Anxiety. *International Organization* 63, 3: 425–57.

McNamara, K. 1998. *The Currency of Ideas: Monetary Politics in the European Union*. Ithaca: Cornell University Press.

Nelson, S. C. 2017. *The Currency of Confidence: How Shared Beliefs Shape the IMF's Relationship with Its Borrowers*. Ithaca: Cornell University Press.

Nelson, S. C. and Katzenstein, P. 2014. Uncertainty, Risk, and the Financial Crisis of 2008. *International Organization* 68, 2: 361–92.

Nelson, S. C. and Weaver, C. 2016. Organizational Culture. In Cogan, J., Hurd, I. and Johnstone, I., eds., *The Oxford Handbook of International Organizations*: 920–39. New York: Oxford University Press.

Nielson, D. L. and Tierney, M. 2003. Delegation to International Organizations: Agency Theory and World Bank Environmental Reform. *International Organization* 57, 2: 241–76.

Page, S. 2008. Uncertainty, Difficulty, and Complexity. *Journal of Theoretical Politics* 20, 2: 115–49.

Preeg, E. 1995. *Traders in a Brave New World: The Uruguay Round and the Future of the International Trading System*. Chicago: The University of Chicago Press.

Reinhart, C. and Rogoff, K. 2009. *This Time is Different*. Princeton: Princeton University Press.

Rodrik, D. 2014. When Ideas Trump Interests: Preferences, Worldviews, and Policy Innovations. *Journal of Economic Perspectives* 28, 1: 189–208.

Rogowski, R. 1987. Political Cleavages and Changing Exposure to Trade. *The American Political Science Review* 81, 4: 1121–37.

Rona-Tas, A. and Hiss, S. 2010. The role of ratings in the subprime mortgage crisis: The art of corporate and the science of consumer credit rating. In Lounsbury, M. and Hirsch, P. eds., *Markets on Trial: The Economic Sociology of the U.S. Financial Crisis: Part A* (Research in the Sociology of Organizations, Volume 30): 115–55. Emerald Group Publishing Limited.

Seabrooke, L. 2006. *The Social Sources of Financial Power: Domestic Legitimacy and International Financial Orders*. Ithaca: Cornell University Press.

Sinclair, T. J. 2005. *The New Masters of Capital*. Ithaca: Cornell University Press.

Skidelsky, R. 2009. *Keynes: The Return of the Master*. New York: PublicAffairs.

Storper, M. and Salais, R. 1997. *Worlds of Production: The Action Framework of the Economy*. Cambridge, Mass.: Harvard University Press.

Verdier, D. 1999. Domestic Responses to Free Trade and Free Finance in OECD Countries. *Business and Politics* 1, 3: 279–316.

Wagner, P. 1994. Dispute, Uncertainty, and Institution in Recent French Debates. *Journal of Political Philosophy* 2, 3: 170–89.

Wendt, A. 1999. *Social Theory of International Politics*. New York: Cambridge University Press.

Widmaier, W. 2010. Trade-offs and trinities: Social forces and monetary cooperation. In: Abdelal, R., Blyth, M. and Parsons, C. eds., *Constructing the International Economy*: 155–72. Ithaca: Cornell University Press.

Widmaier, W., Blyth, M. and Seabrooke, L. 2007. Exogenous Shocks or Endogenous Constructions? The Meanings of Wars and Crises. *International Studies Quarterly* 51, 4: 747–59.

Woll, C. 2008. *Firm Interests: How Governments Shape Business Lobbying*. Ithaca: Cornell University Press.

13

World order

Perspectives on lines of transformation

Jens Mortensen

An age of uncertainty

Societal anxieties and political uncertainty related to globalizing economy are, together with global power-shifts, sweeping techno-economic changes, and new security concerns, reshaping the world, as we know it. Mainstream International Political Economy (IPE), understood as liberal and realist theorizing about the state–market relationship, frames this as a transformed world order. Liberals see an erosion of the US-led post-war liberal order, epitomized by Donald Trump's trade policy and the surge of economic populism from left and right. Realists see multipolarity as the key structural change underpinning a turn towards a harsher era of globalization. Critical IPE questions whether the world order has transformed at all.

On the concept of world order

The world order concept bridges the traditional focus of the IPE discipline, understood as the interaction between states and markets, to the contemporary IPE focus on the governance of the global economy. It can be defined, at its broadest, as "... the body of rules, norms, and institutions that govern relations among the key players in the international environment" (Mazarr et al. 2016). As such, the world order debate echoes the classic IPE debate of the 1980s on power and institutions, most notably on regimes (Keohane 1983; Krasner 1982), state-centric IPE realism (Gilpin 1987; 2001), non-statist structural IPE (Strange 1988; 1997), and the critical theory (Cox 1981). This 1980s debate propelled IPE as a distinct discipline on "states and markets", challenging the supremacy of economist thinking on the world economy, and the economic neglect of International Relations discipline. However, until recently, IPE have neglected the transformation of the world order. Liberal IPE depoliticized globalization by overemphasizing the power of interdependence. Liberal IPE was shocked by the financial crisis, however. Realist IPE ignored the transnational dynamics of globalization by maintaining its focus on national sources of economic power. Critical IPE tended to reduce both states and institutions to passive reproductions of transnational capitalist forces. It kept its political purpose intact, however. It kept a consistent focus on alternative visions of the liberal order, and how to promote it in global politics. The different theoretical lenses on globalization, power and institutions continue to see different lines of transformations in the world order.

The IPE disciplines have difficulties in agreeing on the exact composition of the world order. In order to address how to tackle the problems associated with globalization or engage in a debate on which direction to go, it is however necessary to specify what is meant by world order. IPE realism sees that the world economy rests on a political order, understood as the interactions of the political ambitions and rivalries of states, including their cooperative efforts, and creates the framework of political relations within which markets and economic forces operate (Gilpin 2001: 23).

IPE liberalism adds an ideational component to the political understanding of world order. For instance, liberal internationalism is "a vision of open and loosely rules-based order", and "a tradition of order-building that emerged with the rise and spread of liberal democracy, and its ideas and agendas have been shaped as these countries have confronted and struggled with the grand forces of modernity" (Ikenberry 2015: 8). Liberal IPE links the international political order of realist IPE to the liberal norms and to domestic politics. Liberals have also employed the term "the compromise of embedded liberalism" to capture how the post-war liberal economic orders represents as a fusion of international power and social purpose (Ruggie 1982). Both prioritize states in the making of the world order.

In contrast, critical IPE emphasizes the transnational sources of world orders. Robert Cox identified the historical transformations of the world economy as the interrelationship between "social forces", "forms of state" and "world orders" (Cox 1981: 137), the latter defined as particular configurations of forces, be that politically and socio-economic, that "define the problématique of war and peace for the ensemble of states" (Cox 1981: 138). States and their interrelationships are part of the world order, but not the defining components of the order.

Neglected concerns: shocks, agency and precision

This chapter tries to advance two arguments. First, it finds that IPE has neglected the shock-resistance of a liberal order. By extension, the role of agency in the transformation of a world order needs reconsideration (Acharya 2018). Did Donald Trump pull the liberal order apart alone? Part of the answer, this chapter argues, is to regain the original focus of the concept, and ask whether the social purpose is accepted, and openly supported, by the powerful actors. A world order is basically composed on power, interests and visions (Sørensen 2011). A stable world order thus represents a robust alignment between power, interests and ideas.

Box 13.1 Conceptual redefinition: towards a global order?

"[T]he foundations of global order include a set of ideas and norms pertaining to sovereignty, security, development, human rights, environmental protection, etc., that help to limit conflict, induce cooperation and stability, and expand legitimacy through representation and participation. And unlike some traditional conceptions of *international* order which see its creation mainly in terms of the role of a hegemonic power, or a select group of established powers and the institutions they have created and dominated, global order depends on the extent to which its core ideas, rules, and contexts are created and shared by the widest segment of humankind."

(Acharya 2018: 11)

Power-holders in the global economy support the order in practice, and invest in durable, effective institutions within which all relevant actors chose to cooperate, negotiate or compete. Actors comply with vaguely formulated rules because they share the underlying purpose of regulating the global economy in a particular manner. Businesses and states may free-ride within the order but only a minority actively try to dismantle the order. In contrast, a world disorder reflects a misalignment between power and underpinning visions about global market regulation. It produces either issue-specific fragmentation or full-scale forum shifting. It fosters conflictual competition beyond the rulebook rather than cooperation in accordance within the rulebook. Actors exhibit a disinterest in compliance of the foundational norms of the order.

Second, the chapter finds that if the world order concept is to be more useful for IPE research, it needs to be more precise. By focusing on how the rulebook is splintering in global trade, and in particular how the centrality of the World Trade Organization (WTO) in the trading order is challenged, the chapter tries to illustrate how the concept can enable us to pinpoint precisely how power transformations within the order and political contestations of the order produces a disorder. The world order remains a useful conceptual platform, the chapter argues, for a complex but necessary IPE discussion about the interplay between state, power and ideas in the globalizing economy. The concept needs precision, however.

The difficulty with the concept is that it points to the existence of the observable and unobservable foundation of the world "as we know it". However, it fails to provide the tool for identifying exactly what the order is. Its imprecision is a blessing and a curse. It enables IPE to ask cross-disciplinary questions about how security concerns of states influence the course of globalization, for instance, or how legitimacy concerns in and across societies affect the effectiveness of international organizations. It is however neither a theoretically coherent concept or a methodological consistent approach. It merely enables different types of theory-driven IPE analysis of current transformations. As such, it reflects the pluralism of the IPE discipline. It is enriching our understanding of how the global political economy is transformed. It enables a cross-disciplinary debate within IPE. It also reflects a fragmented discipline. It can be applied by realist, liberal and critical IPE but it has difficulties in presenting a stand-alone analysis in itself.

Box 13.2 A world order can be understood as …

- A world order can be understood as both the institutional framework that governs, but also a consequence of, policies and practices of states and non-state actors related to globalization, reflecting their strength, value-orientations and strategic calculations.
- Ideas, visions and shared understandings are embedded within a world order: World orders must be *legitimate* as well as *effective*, and are comprised by observable and unobservable components.
- Research on world orders requires precision and theoretical awareness.

Lines of transformation

Whereas the exact definition of a world order is absent, the issue of the future world order remains intensely debated in academia, in media and throughout policy circles. It is precisely the complexity of the transformations that defines the present disorderly "world order" of 2019. The world order is no longer a stabilizing framework for the interaction between states and markets. It is more accurate to speak of the transformative disorder rather than a world order.

Uncertainties have produced policy reorientations, ranging from anti-globalist to economic nationalist sentiments at the expense of what might be termed liberal internationalism. However, few expect a de-globalization of the global economy as such. The economic and political changes discussed within IPE under the heading of "globalization" in the past decades is perhaps about to slow down. Whereas globalization confronts new risks, policy uncertainties and market volatility, the world order is hit by power diffusion, policy reorientations and institutional fragility. By 2019, the world order underpinning the global economy, especially in trade, is being transformed at an astonishing pace. What seems certain is that the world order is less liberal today than previously, and that the year 2016 marks a turning point in the brief history of globalization. Yet, the liberal world order has not collapsed.

The economic transformations: inequality, technology and globalization

World orders are the product of intersecting lines of transformation. However, much of the debate is still about the state in the global market. IPE posed a similar question 30 years ago. Are states able to control the global market forces? The first IPE globalization debate of the 1990s ended somewhat inconclusively in the sense that globalization could not be reduced to either markets or states. A similar point is made today. *The Economist* (2019) has coined the term "slowbalization", arguing that globalization has gone from "light's speed to snail's speed". The global economy is a mix of hyper-globalization and de-globalization. The prediction is that future globalization will be dominated by geopolitical rivalry, especially on high tech, and a scaling back of transnational production and investments. Slowbalization fosters aggressive use of trade, tax and finance policy instruments to attract jobs and investments. Slowbalization has splintered the rulebook of the liberal order

Economic globalization transforms the liberal order. Two fundamental dynamics in globalization can be singled out; the rising inequality within societies and the pace of technological changes. Both have reformatted the order. First, economic globalization has created more inequality within societies. Inequality makes the order unstable. As globalization progressed, societal pressures have intensified for a reregulation of globalization. IPE broadly acknowledges today that the liberal order failed to do precisely that (Bourguignon 2015; Piketty 2014). Demands for a renegotiation of the order, and a search for alternatives to the order, are intensifying. Even the OECD (2019) is issuing dire warnings about the political casts created by rising inequality within countries. Critical IPE is not surprised, however. "What did you expect from Capitalism?" asks Varghese (2018).

Second, globalization is being transformed by technological changes, and vice versa. The rise of the knowledge economy, the digital economy and the transnational production put states under increasing competitive pressures. It gives rise to rivalry. Strategic industrial policies are proliferating. Rivalry is rooted in the quest for future competitiveness. Technological changes also threaten parts of the workforce, producing more inequality, and threatening the domestic stability of states. By extension, this erodes the legitimacy of the order. Furthermore, technological changes also threaten the operation of free markets in the future. Liberals are genuinely concerned about oligopolistic market structures of the future, in which a handful of high-tech corporations will dominate and consequently distort competition. This will lower economic growth in the future. Even the IMF warns about such market developments today (IMF 2019). Finally, as mentioned, the existing rulebook does not cover competition policies well, especially in these high-tech markets. Technological transformations thus accelerate the splintering of the rulebook, as no disciplines on fair competition in the strategic growth sectors like artificial intelligence and machine learning to the internet of things, genomics, robotics and big data exists.

The World Economic Forum has framed these developments as "Globalization 4.0". Technology changes fuel other ongoing geopolitical and social transformations. The previous world order, named "Globalization 3.0", was characterized by the internet, the WTO and the entry of China into the world economy, for instance. Globalization 3.0 was shaped by "critical improvements in information and communications technology as well as financial risk management tools combined with continued trade and capital liberalization" (World Economic Forum 2019: 5). This fostered global market integration and cross-border value chains. "Globalization 3.0" is, by shocks like Brexit and Trump, reflecting new concerns about immigration, data privacy and security. This made the World Economic Forum conclude that "we have entered a distinctly new era in which many of the assumptions of prior periods no longer hold" (World Economic Forum 2019: 6). Translated as, "the assumptions of prior periods", this is precisely what a world order is about.

Theoretical lines of transformation

The current turbulence of the liberal order has also forced IPE into critical self-reflection. The literature is vast. However, these transformations appear to validate a resurgence of realist-inspired, state-centric IPE at the expense of liberal and critical theorizing in IPE. Despite their obvious differences, both IPE liberalism and critical IPE shared the premise that states were no longer the primary vehicle of economic transformation. The trade war and the Brexit shock are paradox to IPE. The rise of a more illiberal world disorder heightens the risk of global economic disruption so unwanted by transnational business. Transnational business appears less powerful now than in 2015. A key question for IPE today is whether the realist IPE got it right. Both liberal IPE and critical IPE disagree.

The realist transformation: security, state power and multipolarity

Realists foresee the twilight of the liberal order (Kagan 2017). Realism has made a surprising return in IPE. State power is the focus of realist-inspired IPE, drawing on neorealism in International Relations (IR). Perhaps the distribution of power between states and the link between the economy and security has been a neglected line of transformation. Gilpin, often accredited as the founding scholar of state-centric IPE, operates with an understanding of a world order. "States, particularly large states, establish the rules that individual entrepreneurs and multinational firms must follow, and these rules generally reflect the political and economic interests of dominant states and their citizens" (Gilpin 2001: 23). The order is centred on states. The current disorder is created by states. A return to a stable order can be achieved by states only. International institutions are not important. What we are witnessing is re-assentation of state power over what proved to be an excessively globalized economy. The epicentre of the current disorder are the two great powers, the US and China. Whereas China is driven by the aspiration of benefitting from globalization, the US is driven by the fear of losing power over globalization. To the realist, states are worried about the distribution of the relative gains of globalization. States are not anti-globalist mercantilists. Protectionism is not an optimal policy response to uncontrollable globalization. It is about regaining control over globalization. Protectionism is at best a necessary reaction to disorderly multipolarity. Realists expect that "states will prefer, when possible, to enhance their relative economic autonomy, and remain skeptical that interdependence will inhibit conflict between states" (Kirshner 2009: 46). To realists, the renegotiation of a power-based order, in which the distribution of state power is multipolar, is difficult. It will inevitably produce clashes between positionalist-minded states.

Realists emphasize power *through* trade whereas liberal IPE emphasizes the power *of* trade. To realists, the market can be an effective instrument of power. Liberals are much more aware of the costs of using the market as a power instrument. Nor do realists accept any constraints on the use of national economic power in foreign policy; "the use of economic instruments to promote security goals was a matter of routine as the leading states sought to exploit asymmetries in their economic and strategic relationships with each other and lesser powers" (Mastanduno 1998: 829).

To contemporary realists, the true nature of the liberal order is now revealed. It was above all an American order. As a recent commentary suggested, the American order rested on "the humbling of organized labor" at home, and "on the collapse of Soviet Union and Bejing's strategic decision to integrate China into the global economy" abroad (Tooze 2019). IPE realism makes a simple argument. World orders cannot be isolated from great power politics. Similar to Cox's understanding, the realists trace world orders to a particular power configuration between states. Contrary to Cox, however, realist IPE focuses exclusively on state power. The current transformation is a mix of the internal dysfunction of the liberal order, the rise of contestations of that order within domestic politics of great powers and the geopolitical power shift of a multipolar system. Realists issue a warning. The West should not want the next world order to be strongly institutionalized: "If history is anything to go by, that new order will not emerge from an enlightened act of collective leadership. … What will resolve the current tension is a power grab by a new stakeholder determined to have its way" (Tooze 2019).

The liberal transformation: complexity and institutionalized compromises

To liberals, however, the realist framing of the transformed world order neglects the economic and regulatory complexity of the global economy. Globalization entailed a rise of international production, foreign investments, global trade and technology development. The world economy is transformed by global supply chains. It stands at the brink of a formidable technological transformation, ranging from the digital economy to automated production and artificial intelligence. This represents a regulatory challenge for states in the world order. The rulebook of the world economy is outdated and fragmented. Governments have difficulties in orientating themselves in such a transnationalized economy. To liberals, much of the current turbulence is caused by a clash between the national and transnational economy. This is perhaps most visible in the US, but the underlying tension between the territorialized and de-territorialized economy can be observed everywhere.

Liberals see the order as an institutionalized compromise between power and legitimate purpose. A stable order must also be accepted. Furthermore, it needs to be a balanced compromise on state sovereignty and market expansion in order to deliver economic growth. Leadership is required. Liberals are concerned, however. The existing compromise on globalization has lost its attraction. Liberals concede that it is in part a result of a dysfunctional liberal order itself. It has failed to fulfil on its promises. Liberals fear a disruption from below more than a great power challenge. Above all, IPE liberals located the prime vehicle of transformation in US domestic politics. The election of Trump initiated a retreat of the US from the liberal order. Liberals dread the consequences of this retreat. As Posen (2018: 14) writes, "[a] world in which the United States ceases to lead—or, worse still, attacks—the system it built will be poorer, nastier, less fair, and more dangerous for everyone".

Prior to Trump, Liberals were optimistic about the future of the order. Trade was seen as a solid stabilizer of the order (Guillén 2016; Ikenberry 2015). The world order may have transformed into one of multiplexity but it remains institutionalized and interdependent (Acharya 2014). Liberals expected a functional world order without a centre of gravity (Kupchan 2012).

Talk about a multipolar disorder is not so much a reflection of the decline of the US but really about the rise of other powers (Zakaria 2009). Instead, the current world disorder is character-ized by unexpected policy clashes and by frequent legitimacy struggles. No single vision of a new order exists. Liberals are also concerned with the retreat of democracy in the order. Even so, liberals remain hopeful that a loosely fragmented but rule-based liberal order will emerge (Deudney and Ikenberry 2018).

This is linked to the institutionalist literature on "regime complexes" (Drezner 2009; Meunier and Morin 2002; Orsini et al. 2013). A regime complex is a manifestation of the multi-scale transformation of the world order, understood as greater institutional, substantive and geograph-ical variation (Meunier and Morin 2002). A world order is more than a chess game dominated by states. It is also a web-like network of organizations, firms and networks (Slaughter 2016). This type of IPE liberalism represents a step away from thinking of world orders in terms of strictly state-controlled orders of realism. Each network of the global web, each component of the complex, brings something of its origins, resources and distinctive identity into a world order. Albeit fragmented, institutions constitute a whole within which different organizations and net-works communicate with each other, sometimes cooperatively, sometimes competitively.

Realist IPE criticizes institutionalist liberals for downplaying power while overstating the persistence of institutions. Drezner (2009: 66) pointed out that regime complexity dilutes regime "focal points", i.e. the norm, rule or procedure around which actors' expectations converge (recalling Krasner 1982). Overlapping legal mandates undermined the sense of legal obligation necessary for an institutional order. Critical IPE observes a spread of global networks techno-cracy. Cutler (2003) interprets these as parts of a transnational network of power (the "merca-tocracy") at work underneath and in-between the formal organizations, comprised of firms, private lawyers, trade professionals, government officials and representatives of international organizations. Critical IPE sees these actors as power-holders exercising "near-hegemonic influ-ence through its transnational capital and through its monopoly of expert knowledge, thought and institutional structures" (Culter 2003: 5).

The constructivist transformation: uncertainties, visions and values

In continuation of this, a deeper line of transformation stems from tensions between different sets of value-orientations and convictions held by different actors, organizations and segments of societies towards the global market. Constructivists see transformations driven by a possible disjuncture between transnationalist and nationalist visions, ideas and convictions about the appropriate world economic order. Constructivism in IPE can be traced in both realist, liberal or critical IPE. The constructivist turn in IPE, such as Blyth (2003), Abdelal et al. (2010), Broome and Seabrooke (2014) and Eagleton-Pierce (2013) reflects the pluralism of con-temporary IPE rather than a distinct IPE theory. IPE constructivism is used as an explanatory tool for liberals and realist IPE just as it is applied within a critical IPE perspective.

One constructivist line of inquiry into these transformations, here understood as liberal con-structivism, focuses on uncertainty and scope of agency. Multipolarity, paraphrasing Blyth (2003), does not come with an instruction sheet. It challenges the American liberal IPE explana-tion. A preference of trade liberalization within a state between competing interest groups is an insufficient explanation of what goes on in the trading order, for instance. No actors operate in a vacuum. Their "rational" calculation of future gains (and pains) from globalization is wracked by uncertainty. Complexity also complicates the conversion of preferences to acceptance of a particular world order. Actors tend to react on uncertainty by mirroring policies that are already in place. At the elite level, diplomats rely on experience-derived tools of interpretation in order to make sense of the world. A trade agreement is the end-product of specific frames, understood as cognitive filters through which decision-makers and diplomats interpret the world and employ as to solve specific problems encountered in the world, and following distinct policy scripts, understood as specific solutions to problems that reflect what is deemed as best or most appropriate policy choice (Duina 2010: 99–100). A realist order is constructed around national scripts and frames, reflecting perceptions about relative gain losses and emerging security concerns. A liberal order is sustained by actors' practices and convictions about the common good of market liberalization.

Liberal IPE constructivists tend to be more sensitive to the societal embeddedness of the world order. Ruggie (1982, see also Abdelal and Ruggie 2009; Carporaso and Tarrow 2009; Colgan and Keohane 2017) traces the transformation to the institutionalized compromise between ideas and interests struck by power-holders in the economy. Specifically, Ruggie argued that the General Agreement on Trade and Tariffs (GATT) represented a fusion of international power and domestic societal norms of the dominant states of the immediate post-war era, the US and the UK. Societal support is a vital component of a world order. Yet, the world order is also seen by Ruggie as an elite compromise between powerful states projecting their respective social purpose into the order. Recently, liberals openly acknowledged that the demise of the liberal order stems from the erosion within the order and the collapse of the social contract upon which embedded liberalism rested (Colgan and Keohane 2017; Rodrik 2017).

Box 13.3 Critical self-reflections in liberal IPE: erosion of "embedded liberalism" completed

"The problem with hyper-globalization is not just that it is an unachievable pipe dream susceptible to backlash—after all, the nation-state remains the only game in town when it comes to providing the regulatory and legitimizing arrangements on which markets rely. The deeper objection is that our elites' and technocrats' obsession with hyperglobalization makes it more difficult to achieve legitimate economic and social objectives at home—economic prosperity, financial stability, and social inclusion."

Rodrik (2017: 13)

"Some portion of the blame for the liberal order's woes lies with its advocates. Policymakers pursued a path of action favored by many academics, including us: building international institutions to promote cooperation. But they did so in a biased way—and, for the most part, we underestimated the risk that posed. Financial firms and major corporations enjoyed privileged status within the order's institutions, which paid little attention to the interests of workers. WTO rules emphasized openness and failed to encourage measures that would cushion globalization's effects on those disadvantaged by it, especially workers in the traditional manufacturing sectors in developed countries."

(Colgan and Keohane 2017: 39–40)

The liberal trading order has transformed into multipolar trading disorder.

The disorder cuts across the three domains of a world order: relative decline of the US and massive rise of China as a trade power, the institutional crisis of the WTO institutions and the eroding support for the free trade vision.

Ruggie focused on the domestic and diplomatic origins of the compromise. He excluded other potential sources of transformation. In this respect, Cox's understanding of a world order is different. The transnational line of transformation is the key driver of change. Cox is arguably also a critical constructivist in IPE, perhaps more so than a structuralist Marxist. The backlash of the liberal order makes good sense as a transnational societal reaction to the neoliberal, transnational capitalist world order. Yet, a genuine transformation of the order requires the articulation of a counterhegemonic vision, and subsequent acceptance of an alternative world order. If no alternative project to the liberal order has or is likely to acquire global societal support, a transformation towards an alternative world order is very difficult. The rise of economic nationalism is widely interpreted as an "economic populist" reaction created by the financial crisis (Rodrik 2017). Whereas critical IPE would see economic populism as the predictable societal reaction to the socio-economic injustices of globalization, it has problems explaining why growing segments in society primarily see globalization as a threat to sovereignty. Thus, economic populism does not represent a singular alternative to the liberal order. The contestation of the liberal order is the product of a simultaneous attack on the liberal order from sovereign-sensitive right-wing "nationalists" and from left-wing globalization critics.

A key driver for liberal and critical constructivist in IPE is that uncertainties, largely created by the financial crisis, paved the way for new value-orientations, which challenged the core of conventional liberal thinking about the economic order. The transformation of the liberal order has proven more difficult. No single alternative to the liberal order has acquired support within or across societies.

Box 13.4 Lines of transformation vary according to empirical focus and IPE theoretical orientation

- Realists focus on power, and ultimately warn about the security consequences of a multipolar disorder.
- Liberals focus on complexity of regulating the global market, and warn about the slowing down of globalization.
- Constructivists focuses on ideas, visions and values. Liberal constructivists warn about eroding support to the underlying social purpose and legitimacy of the order. Critical constructivists are challenged by the lack of an alternative vision of another world order among those who are contesting the liberal order.

The transformation of the trading order

The question is whether the current signs of world disorder represent a transformation of the world order. Do transformations represent changes *within* an order, or *of* an order? Is Donald Trump a temporary glitch in US trade policy? Does China represent a transformation within the order, meaning the slow inclusion of a statist economy in a liberal order, or does China represent a challenge of the order, meaning an illiberal, undemocratic, revisionist power? The study of world order transformation is difficult because of its temporal dimension. The illustration offered below of the multipolar trading disorder is limited to the period from 2016 to 2019. Nobody can predict the future. It is impossible to say whether the depth and direction of the current turbulence in trade indicate a transformed order. World orders transform by decades.

No conclusive analysis can be provided on the basis of a few months of disruptive signals. It is, however, important to think about what is being transformed in an order. What are its constituting components, and how can these be observed?

The crisis of the WTO

By 1990s, trade liberalization proved itself to be a powerful transformer of globalization. The creation of the WTO in 1994 marked a highpoint of liberal trading order. It is accredited for preventing a protectionist backlash after the financial crisis. However, the WTO was a focal point for anti-globalist sentiments. The secrecy of the process, exclusion of non-western powers, invisibility of its legal powers and neoliberal policy discourse galvanized fierce protests in the streets of Seattle in 1999 and the beaches of Cancun in 2003. By 2019, the liberal trading order appeared to be close to extinction. There is a certain irony in the situation. This is the 25th anniversary of the WTO. However, it may go down in the brief history of globalization as the year the WTO finally died, injured by decades of diplomatic deadlock in the Doha Round, and abandoned by old and new trade powers.

As argued, the liberal order is transformed by a rebalancing of economic state power, an unprecedented complexity of the globalizing world trade, and contestations of previously held policy visions on free trade. Institutionally, the trading order has move from an intergovernmental regime centered on the GATT/WTO, regional custom unions and bilateral trade agreements towards a more complex system incorporating inter-institutional regulatory arrangements and private market arrangements. What was formerly a simple system of intergovernmental treaties and organizations have turned into a dense network of interrelations between policy forums, hybrid forms of collaboration, hard governance and treaties, and soft governance, marked-based initiatives. Much of this happened prior to Trump. However, the resilience of the WTO order is challenged by Trump. Actors are reorienting themselves in a fragmenting world order. The "splintering of the rulebook" is shorthand for the decreasing relevance of the WTO. It is too early to tell whether the disinterest in the WTO represents a distinct line of transformation in itself, or whether it is a supplement to a more structural IPE analysis of the broader state power and socio-economic transformation. However, the interesting question is whether the apparent demise of the WTO is reduced to an agency-driven transformation, a Trump phenomenon, or whether the WTO crisis represents a deep-rooted order transformation.

Recalling the social purpose of the WTO

It is necessary to understand what the WTO does in context of the liberal order. It provides effective and legitimate regulation of international trade liberation. A crucial task is to determine precisely what the legitimate exceptions to free trade are, and how to assure actors that these exceptions remain within the confines of the order. One of the cornerstones of the WTO rulebook is GATT article III, known as the national treatment principle. Article III (1) establishes a general principle that internal taxes and regulations "should not be applied ... so to afford protection to domestic protection". The national treatment principle is a necessary supplement to the other liberal norm of the order, GATT article I, also known as the Most Favoured Nation clause (MFN). Any concession granted to a WTO member must be extended to all WTO members. However, exceptions exist. A bilateral trade agreement is permissible if approved by the other WTO members. The test is whether the arrangement furthers trade liberalization (Mortensen 2012). Another exception is GATT article IV, known as antidumping. WTO members may temporarily apply import duties in situations of unexpected and unforeseen surges of imports of a particular product, if the WTO is notified, certain procedures are respected during the investigations, the measure are temporary, if affected exports are consulted, and so forth. It does not allow permanent trade restrictions against structural trade imbalances. Finally, WTO members may also justify a MFN derogation by applying either the general exception rule (article XX, see Box 13.5) or the national security exception (article XXI, see Box 13.6).

Box 13.5 GATT Article XX: general exceptions

Subject to the requirement that such measures are not applied in a manner which would constitute a means of arbitrary or unjustifiable discrimination between countries where the same conditions prevail, or a disguised restriction on international trade, nothing in this Agreement shall be construed to prevent the adoption or enforcement by any contracting party of measures:

(a) necessary to protect public morals;

(b) necessary to protect human, animal or plant life or health;

(c) relating to the importations or exportations of gold or silver;

...

(e) relating to the products of prison labour;

(f) imposed for the protection of national treasures of artistic, historic or archaeological value;

(g) relating to the conservation of exhaustible natural resources if such measures are made effective in conjunction with restrictions on domestic production or consumption;

...

Box 13.6 GATT Article XXI: security exceptions

Nothing in this Agreement shall be construed

(a) to require any contracting party to furnish any information the disclosure of which it considers contrary to its essential security interests; or

(b) to prevent any contracting party from taking any action which it considers necessary for the protection of its essential security interests

  (i) relating to fissionable materials or the materials from which they are derived;

  (ii) relating to the traffic in arms, ammunition and implements of war and to such traffic in other goods and materials as is carried on directly or indirectly for the purpose of supplying a military establishment;

  (iii) taken in time of war or other emergency in international relations; or

(c) to prevent any contracting party from taking any action in pursuance of its obligations under the United Nations Charter for the maintenance of international peace and security.

How liberal is the trading order? Free trade supporters fear these WTO exceptions justify widespread neo-protectionist practices. Other liberals see them as essential safety valves in the trading order. By providing flexibility and by assuring sovereignty in the last resort, states are more willing to commit themselves to trade liberalization. These exceptions can be misused, however. States may circumvent their MFN concessions by using more subtle forms of "behind-the-border" discrimination, such as taxation or technical regulations. The WTO task in terms of the order is to assure that imported products are treated the same as domestically produced goods by impartial investigations. The WTO is not mandated to initiate its own investigations or independently file a case against a WTO member. Only states can initiate the WTO procedures against each other. The WTO is entitled to carry out non-enforceable policy surveillance reports, called trade policy reviews, and to facilitate continuous policy dialogues in the various intergovernmental WTO committees.

In the trading order, the devil is in the details. As mentioned, an important exception to national treatment is the "general exception" clause, GATT article XX. GATT art III (4) obliges members to treat "like products" alike in their domestic market. Article XX then determines how to separate legitimate domestic legislation or administrative practices from a disguised trade restriction. The social purpose of GATT article XX is to provide flexibility for state regulation without eroding the function of the trading order, namely to further trade liberalization. Disguised trade barriers are illegal. Yet, the WTO provides states with an explicit right to protect themselves in particular circumstances, a right to set the level of regulation irrespective of what other states do, as long as this does not function or motivated as protectionism.

The WTO agreements do not – and cannot – specify exactly what constitutes a legitimate concern. The trading order is designed to respect sovereignty. Consequently, exceptions are written in an ambiguous language. Not surprisingly, the interpretation of general exception in article XX has been a source of controversy. The precise meaning of article X is lost without extensive references to the GATT/WTO case law. For instance, the WTO requires trade-related environmental policies to be "necessary" for the policy objective, and not amount to arbitrary and unjustifiable discrimination. The WTO functions in this respect as an analytical institution (Mortensen 2012). It determines the meaning of words like "necessary" and "arbitrary and unjustifiable discrimination.

The exact meaning of this is hammered out in the WTO dispute settlement system on a case-by-case basis (on sustainable fishing of tuna and shrimps, on approvals and risk assessments, on hormone-treated beef or import bans on white asbestos[1]). The WTO dispute settlement signals what is permissible in the order. The predictability of its legal system and flexibility of the substantive rules are both sources of its robustness of the trading order. Its strength depends on whether it is able to contain exceptionalism within the order. In this manner, through decades of legal practice on GATT article XX in the dispute settlement system, the WTO legitimizes trade restrictions but requires states to demonstrate, for example, that a particular policy is necessary, impartially implemented and the least trade restrictive policy possible. However, GATT article XXI also provides a blanket exception to trade restrictions on the grounds of a vaguely worded clause on "national interest". In contrast, no member has ever used the exception (Yoo and Ahn 2016). The trading order has no experience with the security exception. It is "the nuclear option" of the WTO. If the US is permitted to justify its steel tariffs by article XXI, all WTO rules are meaningless. If the US is denied what it considers its right to defend its national interest in the steel sector, the US would exit the WTO. In any event, the WTO is in trouble.

Identifying the threats to the WTO order

Several fundamental threats exist today to the WTO order. The first is the paralysis of the WTO Appellate Body. The WTO will stop functioning as a legal system by December 2019 if the US continues to block the appointment of WTO judges. The second is a redefinition of the purpose of the WTO order implied by the national interest justification of article XXI in the current trade war of steel tariffs. The third threat concerns the outdated WTO rulebook on topics like investment, the digital economy, competition policy and state-owned enterprises. The US–China trade war was fuelled by accusations of unfair trade, technology theft and distorted competition. Not only is the rulebook slipping into irrelevance, the WTO has lost its centrality in the trading order.

Returning to the broader question, it is tempting to explain the WTO crisis as a direct consequence of President Trump taking office in 2016. After all, he declared even prior to his election that "the WTO doesn't matter … [W]e're going to renegotiate or we're going to pull out. These trade deals are a disaster, the World Trade Organization is a disaster" (quoted in *Financial Times* 2016). After taking office, the Trump administration acted on his promises. It took a year before his campaign rhetoric was translated into official policy. Furthermore, Trump appointed Robert Lighthizer as the US Trade Representative. Lighthizer explained in a 2010 Congressional hearing that "WTO commitments are not religious obligations", and that WTO violators "are not subject to coercion by some WTO police force" (Lighthizer 2010).

Assessing the threat to the trading order

A proper "theory test" of the explanatory power of realist, liberal, constructivist or critical IPE respectively warrants a more comprehensive analysis than offered below. This is merely an illustration of how to proceed with an inquiry about whether the WTO order is dismantled by Donald Trump. However, it is interesting to start by putting the present-day situation into a historical context. Is this crisis without precedence?

The US has been ambivalent towards multilateral organizations for decades. The first attempt to establish such an organization in the trading order, the International Trade Organisation in 1947, failed because of American resistance (Diebold 1952). Even the establishment of the WTO as an international organization, with recognized legal identity as opposed to its predecessor, the GATT, was not an American idea. The US demanded an automatic right to panel investigations, stricter time limits on investigations, and automatic retaliations if no consensus against it among WTO members. The US wanted effective enforcement of GATT rules, not an independent world trade court. However, the formal establishment of a WTO Appellate Body was a Canadian and European idea. The US negotiators reluctantly accepted it in the final endgame. The US even appointed a WTO committee in Congress to oversee whether the WTO was overstepping its powers when it ruled against the US (see Mortensen 2002).

Thus, it was a surprise but not entirely unexpected that the Obama administration decided to veto the reappointment of Seung Wha Chang, the South Korean member of the Appellate Body in May 2016. The United States Trade Representative (USTR) General Counsel Tim Reif explained that the US will not support any individual with a record of restricting trade agreement rights or expanding trade agreement obligations (Sarvarian and Fontanelli 2016). The US continues to veto new Appellate Body appointments; it is currently reduced to less than three, even if it paralyses the entire WTO legal system. The EU is openly discussing the prospect of a WTO without the US. This was unthinkable only a few years ago.

Seen in isolation, in the refusal to appoint WTO appellate judges, the enactment of unilateral tariffs on selected WTO members on grounds of the US national interest, and of restrictions in response to alleged technology theft and ineffective enforcement of WTO commitments by the Chinese, President Trump is delivering on his campaign promises to fight against unfair trade.

241

> ## Box 13.7 Quotes from "The President's 2019 Trade Policy Agenda"
>
> ### On rebalancing the global economy
>
> "For the past decade, the United States, the United Kingdom, France, Australia, New Zealand, Canada, Brazil, and Mexico, among others, have persistently run current account deficits. Meanwhile, countries including Germany, Switzerland, Denmark, Norway, The Netherlands, Japan, China, Korea, and Russia have consistently run current account surpluses over the past ten years. These persistent trends – which have led to tensions and instabilities throughout the world – demonstrate the significant imbalance in global trade that was in existence when President Trump took office.... Accordingly, in 2019, the United States will continue pressing our trading partners for policy changes that will address this imbalance and lead to a more balanced economy here and abroad. The United States looks forward to working with our trading partners to address these and other issues in the coming years."
>
> *(United States Trade Representative 2019: 30)*
>
> ### On the WTO Appellate Body
>
> "Following through on President Trump's promise to put America first, the Administration has also stood up to efforts by some at the WTO to infringe on national sovereignty.... The key point is that the WTO Appellate Body has repeatedly sought to create new obligations not covered in the WTO agreements. As made clear in the Statement of Administrative Action to the Uruguay Round Agreements Act, the United States is a sovereign country, and U.S. officials are responsible to the American people for their trade policy. The United States cannot be held responsible for obligations to which its elected officials never agreed. Thus, efforts by the Appellate Body to create new obligations are not legitimate."
>
> *(United States Trade Representative 2019: 25–26)*

Seen through the lenses of the trading order, however, the US has openly challenged the social purpose of the WTO order and the centrality of the WTO institution in the regulation of world trade and, by extension, is signalling a vision of a neo-protectionist trading order. Trump is an actor with the capacity to disrupt the liberal trading order.

A return to states or agency in IPE?

Perhaps trade is an exceptional field in the IPE discipline. The state controls borders. In principle it approves all products that cross the border. It has the authority to impose taxes, including tariffs. If the push for globalization in the 1980s to 1990s was characterized by a coordinated drive by dominant states and institutions towards liberal order, defined by openness towards incoming flows of goods, capital, knowledge and people, the retreat from globalization is marked by growing restrictions on access of goods, capital, knowledge and people. Sovereignty is seemingly easier "to reclaim" in trade than in other issue-areas of IPE.

The dominant transformation in the trading order appears to have returned to the state-level, perhaps even actor-level, whereas international institutions and transnational economy appears to be marginalized. China's Belt and Road initiative, the Trumpian trade wars and the Brexit saga points to a return of economic nationalism as a shared policy vision at odds with the liberal order. Still, economic nationalism does not necessarily oppose free trade or globalization (Helleiner and Pickel 2005). Perhaps unintendedly, however, economic nationalism points to a world economy marked by intense geo-economic and geopolitical rivalry, protectionist practices, aggressive export promotion, strategic competitiveness-enhancement, high-tech warfare and a hardening of economic borders. Yet, the lines of transformations are unsettled. The direction is uncertain. The liberal order may prove to be more resilient than expected. It remains populated by multilateral economic institutions, inhabited by organized and networked knowledge-holders, sustained by businesses and deep-rooted practices within states. Trump or Brexit may just represent a glitch in the economic history of globalization. Yet, the world order sustaining economic globalization, as we know it, also hinges on values and visions. These appear to have changed, unexpectedly and perhaps irreversibly.

However, the multipolar trade disorder does not necessarily produce a global economic disruption. Liberals fear an accidental, irresponsible and illogical disruption of globalization. The lack of leadership in the economic order is worrisome. Liberals accepts agency in the order. The US retreat from the order is dangerous and irrational. The realist is not concerned. It is a return of power politics. As globalization is about geopolitics, and as international relations is about state rivalry, the present trade war was predictable. Such a structural understanding leaves little room for agency in the realist order. The critics remain angry. The world order has not transformed. What it observed on trade is still in support of global capitalism until an alternative order replaces the capitalist order. The use of raw power is just more visible in a Trumpian world economy.

Box 13.8 Links and further reading

- United States Trade Representative: https://ustr.gov/
- Directorate-General for Trade (DG Trade), European Commission: http://ec.europa.eu/trade/
- World Trade Organization: www.wto.org/
- United Nations Conference on Trade and Development: https://unctad.org/en/Pages/Home.aspx
- The Council on Foreign Relations, the International Institutions and Global Governance Program on World Order: www.cfr.org/world-order
- The Observatory of Economic Complexity: https://atlas.media.mit.edu/en/

Abdelal, Rawi, Mark Blyth and Craig Parson (eds.) (2010): *Constructing the International Economy*, Cornell University Press.

Acharya, Amitav (2018). *Constructing Global Order: Agency and Change in World Politics*, Cambridge University Press.

Gilpin, Robert (2001): *Global Political Economy: Understanding the International Economic Order*, Princeton University Press.

Rodrik, Dani (2017): *Straight Talk on Trade Ideas for a Sane World Economy*, Princeton University Press.

Conclusions

A world order can be understood as the interrelationship between power, institutions and visions. The concept has something to do with pattered behaviour and regularized practices by state and market actors that are more or less consistent with, or embedded within, institutions. Orders can be consequential in terms of effects on actor behaviour, or constitutional in terms of expressing what is considered legitimate within the order. A world order is broadly – but not necessarily consensually – accepted as "the rulebook" by relevant actors. The concept reflects liberal, realist and critical thinking about effective and legitimate global institutions, and enables us to ask what, which and whose world order is in in the making, how world orders are transformed, and in particular whether orders represent a robust compromise between different ideas and interest of states, market actors and within societies.

World orders are not static. The lines of transformations are multiple. Globalization, power, institutions and ideas intersect and interfere with each other. IPE discipline offers a pluralistic, multiperspectual understanding of world order transformations. Yet, this is also a weakness. The lines of transformation have multiplied. Realist, liberal and critical IPE each present us with a distinct image of the world orders. The existence of different world orders contradicts the very notion of a world order. Is it accurate to portray the economic order as multipolar? This affirms the premises of IPE realism. Liberal and alternative IPE theories offer an entirely different set of lenses. The world order rests on the societal acceptance of the market. The rapid but uneven globalization of new technologies has enabled the expansion of markets for products; services and finance have complicated the regulation of globalization within the order. The rise of new value-orientations of everyday globalization, reflecting widespread concerns of climate change, social rights justice and gender equality, holds the potential of changing globalization.

The notion of a world order needs to be clarified. The components of an order need to be identified prior to an identification of how it is being transformed. In other words, in order to see which – and whose – world order is in the making today, we need to know what to look for, and we need to consider the substance of the order more carefully.

Note

1 See www.wto.org/english/tratop_e/envir_e/edis00_e.htm for case details.

Bibliography

Abdelal, R., Blyth, M. and Parson, C. (eds). 2010. *Constructing the International Economy*. Ithaca: Cornell University Press.

Abdelal, R. and Ruggie, J. 2009. The Principles of Embedded Liberalism: Social Legitimacy and Global Capitalism. In: Moss, D. and Cisternino, J. (eds.). *New Perspectives on Regulation*. Cambridge, MA: Tobin Project.

Acharya, A. 2014. *The End of American World Order*. Cambridge: Polity Press.

Acharya, A. 2018. *Constructing Global Order: Agency and Change in World Politics*. Cambridge: Cambridge University Press.

Blyth, M. 2003. Structures Do Not Come with an Instruction Sheet: Interests, Ideas and Progress in Political Science. *Perspectives on Politics* 1 (4): 695–706.

Bourguignon, F. 2015. *The Globalization of Inequality*, trans. Thomas Scott-Railton. Princeton: Princeton University Press.

Broome, A. and Seabrooke, L. (eds). 2014. *Seeing Like an International Organization*. London: Routledge.

Caporaso, J. and Tarrow, S. 2009. Polanyi in Brussels: Supranational Institutions and the Transnational Embedding of Markets. *International Organization* 63 (4): 593–620.

Colgan, J. D. and Keohane, R. O. 2017. Liberal Order Is Rigged. Fix It Now or Watch it Wither. *Foreign Affairs* 96.

Cox, R. 1981. Social Forces, States and World Orders: Beyond International Relations Theory. *Millennium: Journal of International Studies* 10 (2): 126–155.

Cutler, C. 2003. *Private Power and Global Authority – Transnational Mercant Law in the Global Political Economy*. Cambridge: Cambridge University Press.

Deudney, D. and Ikenberry, J. 2018. Liberal World: The Resilient Order. *Foreign Affairs*: 16–24.

Diebold, W. 1952. The End of the I.T.O. *Essays in International Finance*, no. 16, Princeton: 1–37.

Drezner, D. 2009. The Power and Peril of International Regime Complexity. *Perspectives on Politics* 7 (1): 65–70.

Duina, F. 2010. Frames, Scripts, and the Making of Regional Trade Areas. In: *Constructing the International Economy*. Abdelal, B. and Parson, C. (eds). Ithica: Cornell University Press: 93–113.

Eagleton-Pierce, M. 2013. *Symbolic Power in the World Trade Organization*. Oxford: Oxford University Press.

Financial Times. 2016. Donald Trump, interview. Available at: www.ft.com/content/d97b97ba-51d8-11e6-9664-e0bdc13c3bef.

Gilpin, R. 1987. *The Political Economy of International Relations*. Princeton: Princeton University Press.

Gilpin, R. 2001. *Global Political Economy: Understanding the International Economic Order*. Princeton: Princeton University Press.

Guillén, M. 2016. *The Architecture of Collapse: The Global System in the 21st Century*. Oxford: Oxford University Press.

Helleiner, E. and Pickel, A. (eds). 2005. *Economic Nationalism in a Globalizing World*. Cornell University Press.

Ikenberry, J. 2012. Liberal Leviathan: The Origins, Crisis, and Transformation of the American World Order. *Princeton Studies in International History and Politics*. Princeton: Princeton University Press.

Ikenberry, J. 2015. The Future of Multilateralism: Governing the World in a Post-Hegemonic Era. *Japanese Journal of Political Science* 16 (3): 399–413.

IMF. 2019. *World Economic Outlook*. Growth Slowdown, Precarious Recovery. Available at: www.imf.org/en/Publications/WEO/Issues/2019/03/28/world-economic-outlook-april-2019.

Kagan, R. 2017. The twilight of the liberal world order. Available at: www.brookings.edu/research/the-twilight-of-the-liberal-world-order/.

Keohane, R. 1983. The Demand for International Regimes. In: Krasner, S. (ed.). *International Regimes*. Ithaca; Cornell University Press.

Kirshner, J. 2009. Realist Political Economy. Traditional Themes and Contemporary Challenges, In: Blyth, M. (ed.). *Routledge Handbook of International Political Economy: IPE as a Global Conversation*. London: Routledge: 36–47.

Krasner, S. 1982. *International Regimes*. Ithaca: Cornell University Press.

Kupchan, C. 2012. *No One's World. The West, the Rising Rest, and the Coming Global Turn*. Oxford: Oxford University Press.

Lighthizer, R. 2010. Testimony before the U.S.–China Economic and Security Review Commission: Evaluating China's role in the World Trade Organization over the past decade. Available at: https://assets.documentcloud.org/documents/3259351/Lighthizer-2010-Testimony-on-China-Trade.txt.

Mastanduno, M. 1998. Economics and Security in Statecraft and Scholarship. *International Organization* 52 (4): 825–854.

Mazarr, M., Priebe, M., Radin, A. and Stuth, A. 2016. *Understanding the Current International Order*. Santa Monica: RAND Corporation. Available at: www.rand.org/pubs/research_reports/RR1598.html.

Meunier, S. and Morin, J. 2002. No Agreement is an Island: Negotiating TTIP in a Dense Regime Complex. In: Morin, J., Novotná, T., Ponjaert, F. and Telò, M. (eds). 2016. *The Politics of Transatlantic Trade Negotiations: TTIP in a Globalized World*. Aldershot: Ashgate.

Mortensen, J. 2002. *Multilateral Trade Governance in an Era of Globalization: WTO Legalism and its Limitations*. Ph.D. dissertation, Florence: European University Institute.

Mortensen, J. 2012. Seeing like the WTO: Numbers, Frames and Trade Law. *New Political Economy* 17 (1): 77–95.

OECD. 2019. In it together: Why less inequality benefits all. Available at: www.oecd.org/social/in-it-together-why-less-inequality-benefits-all-9789264235120-en.htm.

Orsini, A., Morin, J. and Young, O. 2013. Regime Complexes: A Buzz, a Boom, or a Boost for Global Governance? *Global Governance* 19 (1): 27–39.

Piketty, T. 2014. *Capital in the Twenty-first Century*. Cambridge, MA: Belknap Press: An Imprint of Harvard University Press.

Posen, A. 2018. The Post-American World Economy: Globalization in the Trump Era. *Foreign Affairs*: 28–38.

Rodrik, D. 2017. *Straight Talk on Trade – Ideas for a Sane World Economy*. Princeton: Princeton University Press.

Ruggie, J. 1982. International Regimes, Transactions and Change: Embedded Liberalism in the Postwar Economic Order. *International Organization* 36 (2): 379–416.

Sarvarian, A. and Fontanelli, F. 2016. The USA and re-appointment at the WTO: A legitimacy crisis? Comment on EJIL: Talk! Available at: www.ejiltalk.org/author/fontanelliandsarvarian/.

Slaughter, A. 2016. Global Complexity: Intersection of Chessboard and Web Trends. *Notes Internationals CIDOB*. Available at: www.cidob.org/publicaciones/serie_de_publicacion/notes_internacionals/n1_147_global_complexity_intersection_of_chessboard_and_web_trends/global_complexity_intersection_of_chessboard_and_web_trends.

Sørensen, G. 2011. *A Liberal World Order in Crisis. Choosing Between Imposition and Restraint*. Ithaca: Cornell University Press.

Strange, S. 1988. *States and Markets*. London: Pinter Publishers.

Strange, S. 1997. *The Retreat of the State*. Cambridge: Cambridge University Press.

The Economist. 2019. The steam has gone out of globalization. Available at: www.economist.com/leaders/2019/01/24/the-steam-has-gone-out-of-globalisation.

Tooze, A. 2019. Everything you know about global order is wrong. Available at https://foreignpolicy.com/2019/01/30/everything-you-know-about-global-order-is-wrong/).

United States Trade Representative. 2019. The President's 2019 Tradde Policy Agenda. Available at: https://ustr.gov/sites/default/files/files/Press/Reports/2018/AR/2018%20Annual%20Report%20I.pdf.

Varghese, R. 2018. Marxist World: What Did You Expect from Capitalism? *Foreign Affairs*: 34–42.

World Economic Forum. 2019. *The Global Risks Report*. 14th Edition. Available at: www3.weforum.org/docs/WEF_Global_Risks_Report_2019.pdf.

Yoo, J. and Ahn, D. 2016. Security Exceptions in the WTO System: Bridge or Bottle-Neck for Trade and Security? *Journal of International Economic Law* 19 (2): 417–444.

Zakaria, F. 2009. *The Post-American World and the Rise of the Rest*. London: Penguin.

14

From Marx to critical international political economy

Johannes Jäger

Introduction

Karl Marx was one of the most outstanding thinkers of the nineteenth century. He criticized dominant liberal perspectives and formulated a critique of political economy. This critical perspective is sill very relevant today. Marx was also the first thinker who systematically recognized the global nature of capitalism. It is, therefore, no surprise that his thinking has found its way into the field of international political economy (IPE). Moreover, because of the financial crisis of 2008, interest in his writings and in academic production in his tradition has increased. This chapter provides an overview of Marx's basic concepts and shows how and why they differ from other perspectives in IPE. Furthermore, Marx's specific mode of inquiry is discussed against the background of modern insights in the philosophy of science and methodological perspectives. Based on this, further developments and contemporary concepts in the tradition of Marx are presented. Perspectives in IPE, based on Marxist traditions, are often called structuralist perspectives. However, following Marx's own conceptualization in which he called his contribution a critique of political economy and building on recent trends in academic debate, the term, Critical (International) Political Economy (CIPE), is preferred instead. A reason for this is that 'structuralism' often mistakenly implies the importance of structures and, at least implicitly, tends to neglect the importance of agency. This chapter provides an overview of how critical political economy (CPE) approaches help us understand important current issues in political economy in general and in IPE in particular. CIPE is significantly different from other approaches in IPE and represents a very important, but often underestimated, perspective (see Box 14.1).

Karl Marx and critical international political economy

What is very relevant for IPE is that Karl Marx already conceived of capitalism as a world market, an emerging global system that is highly asymmetric, develops unevenly and depicts global relations of dependency. In this tradition, today CIPE shows that international developments have to be understood against the background of specific national and regional economic and political relations and processes. At the same time, it also analyses how international structures and processes affect the political economy at the local and national levels. Hence, it looks

> **Box 14.1 What can Marx and critical international political economy contribute?**
>
> - It explains why there are rich and poor people, how they relate to each other and why the world is divided into poor and rich countries, and how these relate to each other.
> - It helps to understand what drives global history and why there are always struggles and disputes, not only at the local or national levels, but also internationally.
> - It provides answers on how to improve the situation of exploited and oppressed groups and classes globally.

at complex interdependencies. However, local/national/regional/global levels are not conceived as given entities but as specific territorialities and spaces that emerge and change over time as an outcome of manifold economic processes and political struggles.

Marx ([1867] 2012), in his critique of political economy, referred to concepts introduced by classical authors in the tradition of political economy such as Adam Smith and David Ricardo but went considerably beyond them. He did, however, share some of their perspectives, such as the fact that different groups, respectively economic classes, have different roles and positions in the economy and in society and are related in a hierarchical structure. He also adopted some of the core concepts of the classical writers in political economy, such as the labour theory of value, but he argued against the 'naturalization' of capitalist economic relations. According to Marx, capitalism is not the natural endpoint of history but a transitory and constantly changing historical form of organizing the economy and society.

Like Smith and Ricardo, Marx insisted that capitalist economic relations of production tend to increase welfare in terms of profits for capitalists and land rents for the landed classes but do not necessarily improve the working and living conditions of the vast majority of the population, who are the workers in a capitalist system. This argument is based on the substance perspective on wages, which was shared by Smith, Ricardo and Marx. Workers, as a class, are a product of history. Historically, the enclosures of the commons in England deprived many people from their land and, therefore, their means of subsistence. As Marx put it drastically, workers were free in two ways: they were 'free' of their own means of production and they were free to sell their labour. In other words, they were forced to sell their labour power in order to receive means of subsistence. Given that historically, and today because of the introduction of labour-saving technology, there are usually more workers than jobs, workers must compete for the available jobs. In the absence of any institutions that allow for decent wages or other (public) sources that provide people with means of substance, workers are set in competition against each other. As there is no alternative, they will have to accept wages that are just high enough to ensure their reproduction, so-called subsistence wages. This implies that, despite the fact that that there tend to be technological improvements and overall production increases, the remuneration workers receive may remain broadly unchanged. The gains of improving technology and increasing production, therefore, do not benefit workers but lead to increased profits and rents. While Smith, Ricardo and Marx shared this perspective, the latter did not just accept the situation but accused it of being unfair, or as Marx called it, exploitation. Those who directly work – the workers – receive only a share, while other classes – capitalists and landlords – receive income, simply because they own the means of production. According to Marx, this is a situation which is undesirable for workers and which they tend not to be willing to accept.

Workers and marginalized people have always struggled for improving working and living conditions within the boundaries of a capitalist system. In many parts of the world this has led to the rise of trade unions, the implementation of minimum wages or collective bargaining systems, labour legislation which imposes limits on the exploitation, e.g. by reducing the maximum number of working hours and the implementation of social policies and a welfare systems which improve the living conditions of many workers. Many scholars of CPE in the tradition of Marx have supported those manifold struggles by providing a rationale for them and by providing an insight into how progress can be achieved collectively by the struggles of the working class, the exploited and oppressed people. Thereby, critical political economists have not focused only on class inequality but also on other types of inequality, such as gender and race inequalities, which are considered central and related forms of exploitation and oppression.

Marx and a significant number of academics working in his tradition have, however, also been very sceptical about the possibility of making capitalist societies fairer and less exploitative. They point, for example, to extreme poverty in the world, to huge and often increasing inequalities and the destructive tendencies of capitalism which often lead to economic crises but also to ecological crises (e.g. the depletion of natural resources, the disaster of global warming, etc.). In a historical perspective, workers have often struggled for a revolution and the implementation of a completely different economic and societal system. Marx had in mind a utopian idea of a classless society, which provides freedom to everyone. However, the experiences of real socialism have, thus far, been, at best, ambiguous. Although, in many cases of real socialism, the standard of living was increased substantially and quickly for the large majority of the population and, in particular for the poorer members of the working class, this often went hand in hand with repressive states which, of course, are not desirable in the perspective of Marx. Repressive forms of statehood are, however, not restricted to real socialist experiences; they are also very common in many capitalist societies.

In the tradition of critical political economy, both reformist and revolutionary perspectives are present today. Although they might appear contradictory and opposing views, one can argue that these two perspectives are complementary. In a radical reformist perspective, capitalism can be transformed by implementing successive and radical progressive reforms up to the point at which a new non-capitalist system emerges. Moreover, very different specific capitalist and non-capitalist (de-commodified) structures, as well as working and living conditions, exist in different regions and countries. This is due capitalist dynamics and specific class struggles at different (and linked) spatial levels. Due to the expansionary logic of capitalism, its global reach, and the fact that power resources tend to be concentrated in the hands of capitalists (and landlords), critical political economists consider that the workers' struggles are taking place on very uneven ground and they often only benefit a small part of the working class in selected areas or countries. Moreover, these struggles and developments are linked via the asymmetric structure of global capitalism.

Today, critical political economy analyses these developments and unveils underlying structures in order to contribute to progressive struggles against oppression, exploitation and poverty. These emancipatory struggles should lead to real freedom as the Frankfurt School argues in the tradition of critical political economy (Horkheimer 2002). This means that a rational society should end with oppression and lead to better and sustainable working and living conditions for all. Critical *international* political economy is based on this idea and focusses on the international and global dimension of capitalist development. CIPE thereby takes the class structure of capitalism as a starting point of analysis and focusses on the global dimension of capitalism and its underlying dynamics and the resulting implication for developments and progressive struggles at different, but linked, spatial levels. This includes the analysis of transforming geography and emerging new international structures. Hence, it differs substantially form prevailing liberal, realist as well as post-structuralist and other common approaches in IPE (see Box 14.2).

Box 14.2 Why is critical international political economy different from other approaches in IPE?

- It is different from *idealist approaches* because it shows that a liberal organization of the (international) economy is not beneficial for everyone but tends to benefit the wealthy in rich countries at the expense of working class people and poorer countries.
- It is different from *realist approaches* because it does not assume a national interest as given but shows that national interest is a product of power structures within a country that are based on the capitalist form of organizing the economy.
- It is different from *constructivist approaches* because it assumes that the power of discourses and ideas is limited and based on social relations of production. Hence, the material dimension of international production and distribution are decisive for the development of the international political economy.

Method of inquiry and goals

In the Introduction to *Grundrisse*, Marx ([1857] 2012) laid out his method of inquiry. His methodology stands in sharp contrast to mainstream approaches in social sciences and international relations in the tradition of the positivism of the nineteenth century, such as critical rationalism. This latter tradition was prominently criticized in philosophy of science by the influential work of Thomas Kuhn ([1962] 2012) and Paul Feyerabend ([1975] 2010). Marx's methodological approach is also different from increasingly more common approaches in a subjectivist, relativist and constructivist tradition. His approach goes beyond positivism and relativism and provides a kind of intermediate position between both poles. Marx's scientific method is based on dialectical reasoning and historical materialism. Marx started with Hegel's idealist philosophy but turned it upside down. It is not ideas but the materiality of life, which is the foundation that predominantly shapes the world. This does not mean that ideas, thinking and creativity do not play a role. As van der Pijl (2007: 13) points out:

> In Marx, there is no longer a functional mechanism in the discovery of a preordained, divine universe, but a historical force. Thinking is, so to speak, always trying to get ahead of things as they are. This puts Marxism on a different plane from naturalistic materialism and its empiricist method.

Today, many scholars in the tradition of critical political economy consider also Critical Realism, founded by Roy Bhaskar (1975), to be a proper meta-theoretical foundation. A reason for this is that Critical Realism can be understood as a further development of historical materialism (Jessop 2002). However, some argue that historical materialism is still a more adequate philosophical basis. In contrast to dominant critical rationalism, historical materialism and Critical Realism both assume that scientific practice is not independent of history, societal institutions and economic and political interests. Hence, a separation between the researcher (the subject) and society (the object) is not possible, but the researcher is part of society. This implies that there is no objective way of analysing phenomena of international political economy as analysis is inevitably related to different interest groups in society. According to Critical Realism this should be part of systematic reflection, and the positioning of the researcher in relation to different groups or classes should be made explicit. In addition, scientific practice is not an end in itself, as Marx puts it in one of his famous statements: 'Philosophers have hitherto only interpreted the world in various ways; the point is to *change* it.' (Marx and Engels [1845] 2011). Critical Realism, moreover, holds that the search for law-like regularities in mainstream scientific approaches is a misleading path to causalities:

> [Critical] Realism replaces the regularity model with one in which objects and social relations have causal powers which may or may not produce regularities, and which can be explained independently of them. In view of this, less weight is put on quantitative methods for discovering and assessing regularities and more on methods of establishing the qualitative nature of social objects and relations on which causal mechanisms depend. This in turn brings us back to the vital task of conceptualization.
>
> *(Sayer 1992: 2f)*

This implies that there is no direct access to reality, but our understanding of reality is mediated by abstract concepts. However, when using a specific concept, different people should make similar observations so that there is no judgemental relativism. Hence, '[o]bservation is neither theory-neutral nor theory-determined but theory-laden' (Sayer 1992: 83). The concepts, which are used to understand reality, stem from everyday life concepts as well as from scientific knowledge. Both forms of knowledge are considered to be historical social products. Different concepts about reality have different implications for different groups in society. It is, therefore, not surprising that there are disputes about which concepts should be used to understand reality. Scientific practice cannot consider only the 'empirics' but should also adopt theoretical views that are closer to the perspectives of certain groups in society than to others. While Critical Rationalism assumes that a scientific approach should be neutral, objective and free of value judgements, this is questioned by Critical Realism:

> Social scientists who treat 'data' literally as 'given things' (often those who feel most confident about the objectivity of their knowledge and the 'hardness' of their facts), therefore, unknowingly take on board and reproduce the interpretations implicit in the data: they think with these hidden concepts but not about them.
>
> *(Sayer 1992: 52)*

In line with this, Cox (1981) distinguished between problem solving and critical approaches in social sciences. While the former tend to contribute to the reproduction of a specific social order, the latter question it and aim at its transformation. According to Critical Realism, a commitment to emancipatory projects requires the researcher to be conscious of this problem and be careful in how they position themselves in the practice of social research. As neutrality or objectivity are considered impossible, researchers must select an ethical standpoint. In the tradition of critical international political economy, this standpoint should reflect the goals and needs of the oppressed and exploited groups in society in a global perspective. Critical political economy is, therefore, not more or less normative than other approaches in social sciences; it is, rather, more open and explicit with regard to methodological claims about values and the purpose of social research. This is because the theoretical possibility of value-free research postulated in positivist traditions such as Critical Rationalism is dismissed, and value claims are made explicit (Jäger et al. 2016: 113).

A central element of the methodological approach is the combining of abstract concepts at different levels of abstraction. Hence, the more specific approaches outlined in the section below should not be seen in competition with each other but as related by higher levels of abstraction such as social relations of production, superstructure, etc. These concepts are complementary and specifically relevant to understanding certain aspects of reality more precisely. Ideally, they are combined in order to analyse a situation in a holistic way, respectively in its totality. A specific method by which different abstractions can be combined is called *conjunctural analysis*. In this approach one focusses on the complex interplay between social forces and power relations, technological change, institutions and discourses and ideologies against the background of social processes in a specific historical moment in a specific place or geographical dimension. Hence, it is about studying a specific historical moment or conjuncture (Jessop 2008). It is necessary to adapt a conjunctural analysis to the specific situation under study. This implies that one must select adequate specific theories and use appropriate specific methods, whereby traditional quantitative and qualitative methods may be considered. In addition, in the research process one should, when necessary, also use insights that may stem from research in other perspectives or disciplines. This means that it might be desirable to include insights produced within mainstream perspectives in international political economy as well as within post-critical political economy or post-structuralist perspectives (Jäger et al. 2016). In a way, these perspectives can be seen as complementary to critical international political economy. Notwithstanding, post-critical perspectives tend to be problematic if not related systematically with critical political economy approaches as Browning and Kilmister (2006: 193f) point out. Post-structuralist approaches have their merits in pointing to the discursive dimension of social processes and the understanding of power in contemporary capitalism. However, rather than focussing on the deconstruction of discourses the material grounds of discourses should be investigated systematically. As Bieler and Morton (2008: 123) put it, they should 'address the question as to why a certain set of ideas, rooted within these material relations, dominates at a particular point in time'. Contrary to positivist approaches in social science typically applied in research in the tradition of critical political economy, the focus is on, not only the correct use of methods, but more so on the adequate combination of theories and abstractions which fits with the subject matter of the analysis. Moreover, it is necessary to consider the needs of the addressees of the results of the research process. In case of a conjunctural analysis, this should certainly not be exclusively researchers, but the focus should be on different emancipatory social agents who may use the findings in order to reflect on how to adapt and develop their strategies. Hence, a firm commitment to emancipatory agents and perspectives is an essential element of research in the tradition of critical political economy. The language applied should also reflect this. It should not hide problematic social facts or relations such as exploitation, repression, etc. but name them explicitly (Sayer 2005).

Key concepts in critical political economy

This section presents key concepts of Marx's approach and their relevance. It starts with an outline of the most important abstract concepts. The following chapter provides an overview of more specific concepts to understand today's challenges in international political economy. The starting point for inquiry is the material, transhistorical necessity of human beings to survive by having access to food, finding shelter, etc. They transform nature when obtaining and producing these goods. This material reproduction provides the basis for the production of sciences, art, etc. (Bruff 2011). The economy is based on social relations, which contribute to ensure the reproduction of human beings. These *social relations of production* are usually characterized by antagonistic classes. The term *class* is a relational concept that refers to the different positions or functions of different groups of people within a specific societal form of

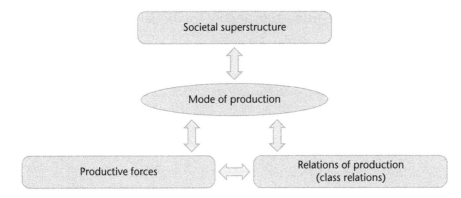

Figure 14.1 Mode of production

organizing production. As already described briefly above, taking economic *classes* as a starting point of analysis is essential in this approach. Classes do not stand for themselves but are a feature of a specific *mode of production*. The term *mode of production* refers to a societal form of producing and distributing the means of subsistence and wealth. It includes specific *class relations* and the existing form of domination of nature expressed by available *productive forces*. The term *productive forces* refers to the means of production and technologies available to transform nature. A mode of production and productive forces are dialectically related and, therefore, condition and influence each other. While social relations of production and productive forces are usually conceived as structures, a *mode of production* moreover includes a *superstructure*. The term *superstructure* refers to institutions such as norms, the state, ideas, beliefs, discourses, etc., which are considered important to stabilize specific social relations of production and productive forces. However, a superstructure is not completely determined by the structure but dialectically related to it. Hence, changes in the superstructure, e.g. on the level of discourses, may have an impact on social relations of production. As Marx ([1867] 2012: volume III) pointed out in his well-known trinity formula, bourgeois ideology which is present in the vulgar conceptualizations of economics (and today in mainstream neoclassical economics), veils the social relations of production and reifies them. However, according to Marx, the dominant ideology should be questioned, and the real structure of social relations should be unveiled.

Long-term history is conditioned by the further development of productive forces, which leads to changes in the social relations of production and the superstructures and the emergence of new modes of production. These changes are driven by disputes about its direction and, hence, by class struggles. Historically, different modes of production and, therefore, different class relations such as a hunter and gatherer society, feudalism, slavery, capitalism and planned economy, are distinguished. These different modes of production produce different territorialities and ways in which these territories relate to each other.

Within a given mode of production there are always changes and struggles over the specific configuration of the relations between different classes and, therefore, over the conditions of production and distribution. Antagonistic class interests encounter each other and struggle with one another. These class struggles modify modes of production and, thereby, drive human history. The struggles take place at different institutional or spatial levels: at the workplace, locally, nationally and internationally. These struggles may not just lead to changes within a given mode of production but also transform it and lead to the emergence of new historical modes of production.

The capitalist mode of production and international relations

Today, capitalist modes of production prevail. According to critical international political economy, it is necessary to understand this historically specific mode of production in order to analyse economic and political processes at the international level, the international political economy. Hence, in the following the characteristics of the capitalist mode of production are described. As Pradella (2015) shows, the global economy was at the core of Marx's inquiry. Following his tradition, general features, mechanisms, dynamics and tendencies of a capitalist mode of production can be singled out at the abstract level. However, concrete historical capitalist modes of production always have specific features that have to be analysed at lower levels of abstraction. This is reflected by the methodology of relating abstractions at different levels, which is required to systematically understand the international political economy as outlined above.

A capitalist mode of production is different to, for example, a feudal mode of production because it is based on the exploitation of free labour. On one hand there is a large mass of people, the working class, which possesses only labour power and has to sell this labour in order to obtain means of subsistence. On the other hand there are those who have the capacity, respectively the money capital, to purchase labour power and other means of production, the capitalists. Capitalists purchase means of production, organize production and sell the commodities that are produced. Beyond capitalists and workers other classes, such as a managerial class, fulfil an important function in capitalism (Duménil and Lévy 2018). This class has aligned with capitalists and together they are the decisive agents who exercise power. However, classes should not only be analysed at the national level but at the international level too. Some scholars in the tradition of critical political economy have even argued that a transnational capitalist class has emerged (Robinson 2004). Critical political economy points to the power of large transnational corporations. However, the driving forces are capitalists and the goal of a capitalist is to end up with more money capital. This is at the core of the process of capitalist accumulation, which Marx described with the formula M-C-M' which stands for money – commodity – more money. However, it is not the voluntary decision of the capitalists to make more money out of money. There is a structural pressure that forces the capitalist to make a profit in order to survive as a capitalist. In case capitalists are unsuccessful in making money they fail in competition because they lack money to purchase labour and other means of production. However, they must not just make a profit, but also invest the money and compete by cutting costs and/or by improving new technologies that allow them to stay competitive and even to escape competition to some degree by achieving monopoly power. This structural pressure is called *imperative to accumulate* and is a key reason why capitalism is so dynamic compared to other modes of production. It, therefore, explains why the means of production are constantly revolutionized by implementing new technologies and new forms of organizing work processes, and why modified and new products are developed. The currently ongoing process of digitalization of work and production is an example for this. A capitalist mode of production, hence, tends to be characterized by constantly and rapidly changing productive forces. The process of competition is embedded within historically specific frameworks such as rules of competition, state support, protectionism, etc. and it is a central issue, not just at the level of the nation state, but in the international political economy where it becomes manifest, e.g. in international trade and investment agreements.

Capitalist accumulation is, however, not smooth and steady process. It is, rather, characterized by frequent and often long-lasting *crises*. There are many different reasons for why crises occur. On a very abstract level, crises are a result of contradictions within the capitalist mode of production. These contradictions are intrinsic or structural problems of capitalism. For example, the imperative to accumulate capital may be in contradiction with the need to sell the commodities and realize the profit if the purchasing power of wages is too low because of cost cutting strategies. It is possible to deal with these contradictions for some time if an adequate institutional arrangement is found. *Regulation theory* stands in a Marxist tradition and provides a more specific framework to analyse these contradictions (Boyer 2018). Based on the work of Michel Aglietta ([1979] 2000), national developments and their relation to the international sphere, called international regime, are analysed. Thereby, this perspective insists that crises do not emerge only at the national level but are also caused or transmitted at the international level. International arrangements are often intended to deal with these contradictions. For example, such arrangements may allow for market access to other countries and corresponding credit flows in order to deal with capitalist contradictions temporarily and at least postpone a crisis – this was the case in the European Union prior to the crisis of 2008 (Becker and Jäger 2012).

At the core of the international political economy is international economic interaction, which is embedded into political and military institutions and structures. The world market, respectively the global economy, is marked by huge differences, asymmetries and dependencies. This is the reason why the international political economy is not a level playing field. On the surface, this becomes obvious when comparing the importance and power of some states relative to others. On an abstract level this is explained by the fact that capitalist forms of production develop unevenly. This means that advanced productive forces and corresponding social relations of production are located in specific places and territories while other places and territories are characterized by more traditional or less developed productive forces. Those places and territories that are more advanced tend to establish an asymmetric relationship with less advanced places and territories. In IPE terminology the former are called the core while the latter are called the periphery. This asymmetric relationship between core and periphery is based on market structures and military power and is embedded in international political institutions that tend to perpetuate this asymmetry.

The capitalist mode of production emerged in England during the eighteenth century and then expanded to other countries and world regions. It replaced previous modes of production like feudalism (and mercantilism). The emergence of capitalism in England, however, was not an isolated national issue but has to be understood against the background of the international insertion of England where colonies like India played an important role. Marx, in his reflections on the British colonial regime in India, pointed out its disastrous effects for India. The import of cotton from India to England, the production of cloth in England and its re-export to India was a central element in boosting the industrialization and capitalist development in England. The colonial trade regime, which prohibited the use of machines to weave cloth in India, protected the emerging industry in England and was important for this development. At the same time, Marx argued that the more developed capitalist country mirrors the future of the backward country, which means that productive forces and social relations of production are expected to undergo similar changes. Hence, the division into core and periphery is not an ironclad law. Historic economic and political processes have lead, and potentially may lead, to a (partial) inversion of this relationship.

In the tradition of critical international political economy, less abstract, i.e. more specific, approaches have been developed in order to deal with different aspects of the IPE. These are presented in the following subchapter.

Contemporary approaches in critical international political economy

The asymmetric character of global capitalism has important implications for the international political economy. Critical political economists have developed more specific theoretical perspectives in the tradition of Marx in order to analyse important aspects of the IPE (for an overview see Box 14.3). These perspectives provide frameworks at lower levels of abstraction to understand specific aspects of contemporary processes. In the methodological tradition of CPE they should not be understood as separated or opposing perspectives but as interrelated views, which highlight concrete specific aspects and together provide a more complete picture.

Box 14.3 Overview of important contemporary approaches in critical international political economy

- Theories of *imperialism* explain the international political economy of domination and war.
- Theories of *uneven and combined development* and *critical geography* explain global inequality structures and their implications.
- *(Neo-)Gramscianism* explains contested international institutions and political structures and shows possibilities for emancipatory strategies.
- *Dependency approaches* explain underdevelopment and analyse strategies to overcome it.
- The world systems approach shows how core and periphery historically emerge and how changes occur.
- *Political ecology* explains the uneven global use of resources and shows paths to environmental justice.
- *Critical feminist perspectives* are important to understand the complexities of IPE and show how gender-related forms of exploitation and suppression can be overcome.

Theories of imperialism have a long-standing tradition in critical international political economy. In the early twentieth century Rudolph Hilferding, Rosa Luxemburg and Vladimir Lenin provided a framework that allows understanding inter-imperial conflicts among the important powers. These rivalries and the historic configuration of the international political economy were understood against the background of the specific form of capitalist development. Inner limits of accumulation due to the suppression of wages led to crisis tendencies. This provided the background for aggressive military expansion to find markets abroad and to gain access to foreign resources required for national economic development. Although military intervention still happens, the period of classical imperialism is over. Nevertheless, authors in the tradition of critical political economy, such as Samir Amin (2017), James Petras and Henry Veltmeyer (2013) and David Harvey (2005), show how economically, politically and military powerful countries impose their interests on weaker peripheral countries. John Smith (2016), in his book on imperialism in the twenty-first century, analyses how the new international division of labour (Fröbels et al. 1980) characterized by outsourcing processes and global labour arbitrage, respectively the globalization of production, lead to super-exploitation in peripheral countries.

Perspectives on *uneven and combined development*, which are traced back to Leon Trotsky, are helpful for understanding crucial elements of international processes. Trotsky argued that capitalist development was uneven, i.e. different in different places. International processes are combined, which implies that the development in one country or region is influenced by the situation in other regions. Countries start to introduce capitalist modes of production from very different starting points and in differing international environments. Those which develop later may have advantages and could potentially leapfrog states that restarted earlier. However, there may also be disadvantages to being a late developer in that a subordinated economic position may lead to a distorted political structure, which implies limits to development and hence perpetuates a subordinated position (Callinicos and Rosenberg 2008). Today *critical geography* represents a somewhat similar perspective that is relevant for the analysis of global uneven capitalism. This approach explicitly deals with the question of the spatial dynamics of capitalist development and explains how capital produces spaces and places (Harvey 2006).

With the end of World War II, the following Cold War and the hegemony of the USA in the western world, the geopolitical constellation and the form of interaction changed. These changes were mirrored by the emergence of new theoretical perspectives in critical international political economy in the western hemisphere. Baran and Sweezy ([1966] 1989), in their work *Monopoly Capital*, laid the grounds for an understanding of a new form of capitalism and its international implications. Stabilizing the global economy and promoting growth and development became central concerns of the hegemonic USA. Changing labour relations, which led to increasing real wages, helped to boost the domestic economy. Notwithstanding this, a central concern of the USA was to support the expansion of its corporations abroad and find new markets. At the same time the promise of growth and development was aimed at winning the ideological battle with the Soviet Union. Against this background, in particular from the 1960s onwards, specific new theoretical concepts for understanding contemporary capitalism have been developed.

Starting with the work of Robert Cox (1987) a new tradition, inspired by Antonio Gramsci ([1971] 1999) emerged. Gramsci made important contributions to the theory of the state in the tradition of critical political economy. The *neo-Gramscian* approach deals with the role of international institutions and shows how global hegemony is reproduced. Critical media theory provides insights into the specific processes of how ideologies and discourses are produced by capitalist mass media to support capitalist's interests (Chomsky 1995). In contrast to mainstream theories, it is not the interest of the state that is taken as a starting point, but the underlying social relations of production. Hence, international hegemony is based on national hegemony, which is an expression of specific class relations in a concrete capitalist mode of production. Poulantzas ([1968] 1978: 129) considered the state as 'the specific material condensation of a relationship of forces among classes and class fractions'. Today, it is the hegemony of a capitalist class in the USA, which provides the basis for a specific historic form of US hegemony. Based on this approach, Leo Panitch and Sam Gindin (2012) showed the importance of the USA and their role in politically shaping the global economy in a way that facilitated the predominance of US capitalism. Like Petras and Veltmeyer (2001), they discarded the idea of globalization as a generative power and pointed to the ability of the USA to orchestrate global capitalism. In a neo-Gramscian tradition Magnus Ryner and Alan Cafruny (2017) show that the USA exercises power on not only developing countries but how it also conditions the European integration process. Critical political economists in this tradition also point to the importance of the global monetary regime (dominated by the US financial sector), US-dominated international financial institutions (e.g. the International Monetary Fund) and the US Dollar as the global currency for US hegemony. Peter Gowan (1999) coined the term 'Dollar-Wall Street Regime' to refer to this phenomenon. This global institutional structure has often contributed in peripheral countries to processes of financialization and subsequent crisis (Becker et al. 2010).

It was in peripheral countries, particularly in Latin America, that the contradictions of the capitalist mode of production proved to be highly problematic and contested in the second half of the twentieth century. Under the heading of *dependency approaches*, concepts for understanding why the post-war configuration of the international political economy made development in peripheral countries so difficult, if not impossible, emerged. Among others, Cardoso and Faletto ([1971] 1979) and Raul Marini ([1973] 1991) showed how specific contemporary capitalism led to dependent forms of capitalism in the periphery. While work based on Cardoso and Faletto tends to be more optimistic regarding possibilities of capitalist development in peripheral countries, traditions based on Marini are more pessimistic and see a need for revolution and socialist development. Dependency approaches explained how a dependent 'lumpen' bourgeoisie emerges and how this turns out to be an obstacle to the development of productive forces. Misleadingly, dependency approaches were often presented as exclusively focussing on external factors and negating any possibility of development (Kay 1989). This, however, is a reductionist interpretation which is not justified as already clarified in the classical work by Cardoso and Faletto ([1971] 1979: 28): 'analysis is complete only when the economic and the social have their reciprocal determinations defined at the internal and external levels'. Hence, processes and struggles at the national and international level are interrelated. More recently, dependency approaches have been rediscovered and adapted. Some follow the tradition of Marini for e.g. for the analysis of contemporary processes in Latin America (Katz 2018) Others, based on Cardoso and Faletto apply the analysis of core-periphery relations to the European Union and link it to other traditions in critical political economy such as regulation theory (Becker *et al.* 2015). Loosely related to this tradition are neo-colonial perspectives, such as Aníbal Quijano (2007), that emphasize the cultural dimension of domination and dependency in peripheral countries.

Dealing with questions of core and periphery in a global perspective, Immanuel Wallerstein (2004) developed the *world systems approach*. A central aim was to explain, in a long-run historical perspective, how a world system emerges and why some countries change their relative position in this system. Historically, from the sixteenth century onwards, Europe became the centre of the modern world system. This rise of Europe took place against the background of capitalist development in Europe and was based on the exploitation of former colonies in the global periphery. However, not just the concepts of core and periphery are used, but nation states may also have an intermediate function. These states are referred to as semi-periphery and, although dominated by core countries, they have their own industrial bases. The world systems approach explains which forces allow core countries to retain their position, and hence reinforce global inequality, as well as which historical processes in the changing mode of production allow for countries to move up or down in the global hierarchy. More recently, many scholars in this tradition (e.g. Giovanni Arrighi 2009) have focused on the rise of China and the causes and consequences of this rise.

The driver of capitalist accumulation is the unlimited search for increasing profits. According to critical political economy, labour and, hence, economic activity implies the transformation of nature. The use of nature depends on productive forces and the societal regulation of access to it. The unlimited strategy to increase profits stands in contrast to the fact that the earth and nature are limited. *Political ecology* is a critical perspective that deals explicitly with the environmental implications of capitalism. In a global perspective, the appropriation of nature (Zeller 2008) which often takes the form of accumulation by disposition (Harvey 2009) is accompanied by wars of plunder which often take place in the global periphery (Le Billon 2012). In general, the highly unequal use of natural resources in different countries and within different classes is stressed. These unequal patterns are also observed in the context of climate change. Ulrich Brand and Markus Wissen (2018) argue that the imperial lifestyle in core countries is a central problem and must be transformed by changing production and consumption patterns. However, given the expansive logic of capitalism and the (class) interests attached, there are serious obstacles under capitalist conditions. Hence, overcoming capitalism seems necessary in order to overcome the environmental crisis and overexploitation of nature and to achieve environmental justice.

Gender and feminist perspectives play an important role in critical international political economy, but they should be considered even more, as Anne E. Lacsamana (2016: 92) points out: 'feminists and Marxists must re-engage with one another to understand the centrality of gender and gender relations to more accurately capture the complexities of the IPE.' (Neo-)liberal forms of feminism are criticized because they tend to focus on a few elite women and do not question social class structures. While the intersectionality of gender, race and class is a frequently used concept in critical political economy, Meiksins Wood (1995) and Lacsamana (2016) have questioned this perspective. They argue that, in a critical political economy perspective, class has an ontologically different status because it is not possible to think of class as a category of identity that does not include exploitation and domination. While class is, by definition, a relationship of inequality and power, this is not the case for gender and race. In an international perspective, such critical feminist perspectives argue that the exploitation of women, in both core countries and peripheral countries, is an essential for sustaining current capitalist modes of production. This exploitation should be overcome.

Conclusions

In critical international political economy, based on the work of Marx, a broad variety of specific theories or abstractions exist which help to understand contemporary modes of production, struggles and processes in the international political economy. These different abstractions focus on different aspects and highlight certain aspects over others. Ideally, they are combined in the tradition of historical materialism and critical realism in order to analyse reality as a whole. However, the ultimate goal of critical international political economy is not only to understand reality, but also to contribute to overcoming exploitive and oppressive structures and social relations. This implies that CIPE should contribute to emancipatory processes and enter into conflict with dominant powers and the ruling classes and their ideas, theoretical concepts and discourses. These (class) struggles lead to reformist processes and, hence, to changes within the capitalist mode of production. Although this implies a perpetuation of power structures, the relative power of the working class together with material working and living conditions, may improve. Traditionally the struggles of the working class have always been about better working conditions (fewer working hours, less dangerous und unhealthy working conditions, etc.) and better payment, paid holidays and social security in case of old age or health problems. Additionally, other struggles for affordable housing, free education, childcare and so on have always been pivotal points of social (working class) struggles. Contrary to neo-liberal policies, this implies not privatization but a de-commodification respectively socialization of the provision of these elements that cover basic needs. Such reforms may lead to a radical transformation and a substantial cutback of capitalist elements and eventually contribute to overcoming a capitalist mode of production. Hitherto the central arena for these struggles has been the nation state. However, in the global economy these struggles develop unevenly and asymmetrically but are related to each other. The different specific concepts in the tradition of international political economy highlight this. International cooperation between different groups of oppressed and exploited people and international working class solidarity potentially contribute to emancipatory struggles being more successful. Although it is not very likely in the current conjuncture, it is possible that in the future, revolutionary movements may lead to the emergence of a new mode of production. However, it will be open to the specific struggles whether this will be a 'better' world or 'rational society'.

Bibliography

Aglietta, M. [1979] 2000. *A Theory of Capitalist Regulation. The US Experience*. London: Verso.

Amin, S. 2017. Contemporary Imperialism. In: *Mapping a New World Order. The Rest Beyond the West*. Popov, V. and Dutkiewicz, P. (ed.): 181–195. Cheltenham: Edward Elgar.

Arrighi, G. 2009. *Adam Smith in Beijing: Lineages of the 21st Century*. London: Verso.

Baran, P. A. and Paul M. Sweezy. [1966] 1989. *Monopoly Capital: An Essay on the American Economic and Social Order* New York: Monthly Review Press.

Becker, J. and Jäger, J. 2012. Integration in Crisis: A Regulationist Perspective on the Interaction of European Varieties of Capitalism. *Competition & Change* 16, no. 3: 169–187.

Becker, J., Jäger, J., Leubolt, B. and Weissenbacher, R. 2010. Peripheral Financialization and Vulnerability to Crisis: A Regulationist Perspective. *Competition & Change* 14, no. 3–4: 225–247.

Becker, J., Jäger, J. and Weissenbacher, R. 2015. Uneven and Dependent Development in Europe: The Crisis and Its Implications. In: *Asymmetric Crisis in Europe and Possible Futures. Critical Political Economy and Post-Keynesian Perspectives*. Jäger, J. and Springler, E. (ed.): 81–97. London: Routledge.

Bhaskar, R. 1975. *A Realist Theory of Science*. London: Verso.

Bieler, A. and Morton, A. D. 2008. The Deficits of Discourse in IPE: turning base metal into gold? *International Studies Quarterly* 21 no 1: 103–128.

Boyer, R. 2018. Marx's Legacy, Regulation Theory and Contemporary Capitalism. *Review of Political Economy* 30, no. 3: 284–316.

Brand, U. and Wissen, M. 2018. *The Limits to Capitalist Nature. Theorizing and Overcoming the Imperial Mode of Living*. London: Rowman & Littlefield.

Browning, G. and Kilmister, A. 2006. *Critical and Post-Critical Political Economy*. Basingstoke: Palgrave Macmillan.

Bruff, I. 2011. The Case for a Foundational Materialism: Going beyond Historical Materialist IPE in Order to Strengthen It. *Journal of International Relations and Development* 14, no. 4: 391–399.

Callinicos, A. and Rosenberg, J. 2008. Uneven and Combined Development: The Social-Relational Substratum of 'the International? An Exchange of Letters. *Cambridge Review of International Affairs* 21, no. 1: 77–112.

Cardoso, F. H. and Faletto, E. [1971] 1979. *Dependency and Development in Latin America*. Berkeley: University of California Press.

Chomsky, N. 1995. *Manufacturing Consent*. New York: Vintage.

Cox, R. 1981. Social Forces, States, and World Orders. *Millennium: Journal of International Studies* 10, no. 2: 126–155.

Cox, R. 1987. *Production, Power, and World Order. Social Forces in the Making of History*. New York: Columbia University Press.

Duménil, G. and Lévy, D. 2018. *Managerial Capitalism. Ownership, Management & the Coming New Mode of Production*. London: Pluto.

Feyerabend, P. [1975] 2010. *Against Method*. London: Verso.

Fröbel, F., Heinrichs, F. and Kreye, O. 1980. *The New International Division of Labour. Structural Unemployment in Industrialised Countries and Industrialisation in Developing Countries*. Cambridge: Cambridge University Press.

Gowan, P. 1999. *The Global Gamble. Washington's Faustian Bid for World Dominance*. London: Verso.

Gramsci, A. [1971] 1999. *Selections from the Prison Notebooks*. London: ElecBook.

Harvey, D. 2005. *A Brief History of Neoliberalism*. Oxford: Oxford University Press.

Harvey, D. 2006. *Spaces of Global Capitalism. Towards a Theory of Uneven Geographical Development*. London: Verso.

Harvey, D. 2009. The 'New' Imperialism: Accumulation by Dispossession. In: *The New Imperial Challenge. Socialist Register*. Panitch, L. and Leys, C. (ed.): 63–87. London: Merlin Press.

Horkheimer, M. 2002. *Critical Theory. Selected Essays*. New York: Continuum.

Jäger, J, Horn, L. and Becker, J. 2016. Critical International Political Economy and Method. In: *The Palgrave Handbook of Critical International Political Economy*. Cafruny, A., Talani, L. S. and Pozo, G. (ed.): 101–118. London: Palgrave Macmillan.

Jessop, B. 2002. Capitalism, the Regulation Approach, and Critical Realism. In: *Critical Realism and Marxism*. Brown, A., Fleetwood, S. and Roberts, J. (ed.): 88–115. London: Routledge.

Jessop, B. 2008. *State Power*. Cambridge: Polity Press.

Katz, C. 2018. *Imperialism Today: A Critical Assessment of Latin American Dependency Theory*. SP The Bullet March. Available at: https://socialistproject.ca/2018/03/imperialism-today-a-critical-assessment-of-latin-american-dependency-theory/.

Kay, C. 1989. *Latin American Theories of Development and Underdevelopment*. London: Routledge.

Kuhn, T. S. [1962] 2012. *The Structure of Scientific Revolutions*. Chicago: University of Chicago Press.

Lacsamana, A E. 2016. Feminism and Critical International Political Economy. In: *The Palgrave Handbook of Critical International Political Economy*. Cafruny, A., Talani, L. S. and Pozo, G. (ed.): 85–100. London: Palgrave.

Le Billon, P. 2012. *Wars of Plunder: Conflicts, Profits and the Politics of Resources*. New York: Columbia University Press.

Marini, R. M. [1973] 1991. *Dialéctica De La Dependencia*. Mexico DF: Ediciones Era.

Marx, K. [1857] 2012. *Grundrisse. Foundations of the Critique of Political Economy*. London: Penguin Classics.

Marx, K. [1867] 2012. *Capital. A Critique of Political Economy*. London: Penguin Classics.

Marx, K and Engels, F. [1845] 2011. *The German Ideology*. Eastford: Martino Publishing.

Meiksins Wood, E. 1995. *Democracy against Capitalism: Renewing Historical Materialism*. Cambridge: Cambridge University Press.

Panitch, L. and Gindin, S. 2012. *The Making of Global Capitalism. The Political Economy of American Empire*. London: Verso.

Petras, J. and Veltmeyer, H. 2001. *Globalization Unmasked: Imperialism in the 21st Century*. London: Zed Books.

Petras, J. and Veltmeyer, H. 2013. *Imperialism and Capitalism in the Twenty-First Century. A System in Crisis*. Farnham: Ashgate.

Poulantzas, N. [1968] 1978. *Political Power and Social Classes*. London: New Left Books.

Pradella, L. 2015. *Globalization and the Critique of Political Economy. New Insights from Marx's Writings*. London: Routledge.

Quijano, A. 2007. Coloniality and Modernity/Rationality. *Cultural Studies* 21, no. 2–3: 168–178.

Robinson, I. W. 2004. *A Theory of Global Capitalism: Production, Class, and State in a Transnational World*. Baltimore: Johns Hopkins University Press.

Ryner, M, and Cafruny, A. 2017. *The European Union and Global Capitalism. Origins, Development, Crisis*. London: Palgrave.

Sayer, A. 1992. *Method in Social Science. A Realist Approach*. 2nd ed. London: Routledge.

Sayer, A. 2005. *The Moral Significance of Class*. Cambridge: Cambridge University Press.

Smith, J. 2016. *Imperialism in the Twenty-First Century. Globalization, Super-Exploitation, and Capitalism's Final Crisis*. New York: Monthly Review Press.

Van der Pijl, K. 2007. Nomades, Empires, States. *Modes of Foreign Relations and Political Economy*, Volume I. London: Pluto Press.

Wallerstein, I. 2004. *World-Systems Analysis: An Introduction*. Durham: Duke University Press.

Zeller, C. 2008. From the Gene to the Globe: Extracting Rents Based on Intellectual Property Monopolies. *Review of International Political Economy* 15, no. 1: 78–96.

15
Gramscian IPE

Leonardo Ramos

Gramsci and IPE: planning a journey

Since the 1980s, Gramsci's ideas in the field of International Relations (IR) and International Political Economy (IPE) have resurfaced. Recent challenges to conventional IR worldviews have seen Gramscian thought pioneer new ontological, epistemological and theoretical reflections to cope with the new (and old) problems facing IR/IPE. For example, Constructivism(s), Post-Structuralism and new Marxist-inspired reflections, emerged in this fruitful critical context aggregated under the umbrella of "critical theory" or "post-positivism."[1] Such approaches, despite their differences, were very important toward destabilizing the status quo dominated by positivist approaches (Realism, Liberalism and their variations). In this context, contributions made by Robert W. Cox were important toward the development of a critical IPE and in particular a Gramscian-inspired IPE.[2]

Some scholars have criticized such Gramscian-inspired IPE, particularly the Coxian framework.[3] Such frameworks have been developed to advance Gramscian concepts and analysis to cope the breadth of IPE topics.[4] Robert W. Cox's work has been seen as critical in the development of neo-Gramscian studies on IR/IPE. For example, Adam Morton and Andreas Bieler point to Cox's "critical route to considering hegemony, world order, and historical change"[5] as the point of departure of the Gramscian perspectives in IPE (see Box 15.1). Such frameworks are a source of inspiration for a whole generation of Gramscian-inspired IPE analysis. Contrastingly, Owen Worth is critical of "Cox's Gramscian model of 'international' hegemony,"[6] and identifies two main "schools" or "routes."[7] These include the *Italian School*, mainly influenced by the Coxian concept of *world order* and the *Amsterdam School*, which focuses on the study of *transnational classes* – their impact on the construction of neoliberal hegemony.[8] Despite its followers and critics, the Coxian framework has an outstanding position on Gramscian IPE studies. This chapter intention is to present a contemporary, Gramscian-inspired IPE. To achieve this goal, this chapter will start with an explanation of the Coxian framework. It will be discussed with particular attention its dialogues with Gramsci on the concepts of internationalization and transnationalization of the state. Additionally, it will also present the debates between supporters and critics of Gramscian routes to IPE. To contextualize this debate, past, present and future routes of research of Gramscian IPE will be examined.

Box 15.1 Hegemony: from Gramsci to Cox

For Gramsci, "this is what hegemony is: to identify the peculiar features of a historical condition, of a process; to become the protagonist of the demands of other social strata, and of the solutions to these demands, uniting around oneself these strata, allying oneself with them in the struggle against capitalism, and thus isolating capitalism itself" (Gruppi 1972: 78). In this sense, "the battle of ideas – dialogue and cultural confrontation – assumes a decisive importance in the fight for hegemony" (Coutinho 2012: 45). Such aspects must be taken into account when attention is paid to Cox's Gramscian-inspired definition of hegemony at the international/world level: "Hegemony at the international level is thus not merely an order among states. It is an order within a world economy with a dominant mode of production which penetrates into all countries and links into other subordinate modes of production. It is also a complex of international social relationships which connect the social classes of the different countries. World hegemony is describable as a social structure, an economic structure, and a political structure; and it cannot be simply one of these things but must be all three. World hegemony, furthermore, is expressed in universal norms, institutions and mechanisms which lay down general rules of behaviour for states and for those forces of civil society that act across national boundaries – rules which support the dominant mode of production" (Cox 1994: 61–62).

Robert W. Cox: from historical structures and world hegemony to the internationalization of the state

According to Cox,[9] patterns of production relations are the point of departure for the analysis of how the mechanisms of hegemony work. Given the fundamental character of the relationship between production and power, Cox analyzes how power in the social relations of production gives rise to certain social forces. These social forces thus become the basis of power in state forms, which shapes the world order. Accordingly, there are three spheres of activity that can identify a historical structure: (1) the organization of production and the social forces engendered by the process of production; (2) state forms related to state/civil society complexes that are historically contingent; and (3) the world order, i.e., particular configuration of forces that successively define problems of war and peace.[10]

Stand out at this point the proximity between this view on power relations and those developed by Gramsci.[11] There is no unilateral relationship between the three spheres of activity, and they can have varying points of departure to explain the historical process.[12] Furthermore, in each sphere there are three other elements that may dialectically combine to constitute an historical structure: (1) ideas, understood as intersubjective meaning and collective images of the world order; (2) material capabilities, concerning accumulated resources; and (3) institutions, the amalgam between the two previous elements.

Using this framework, Cox analyzes the social structures that temporarily existed under the capitalist system of production, demonstrating the primary elements that form the social world. In this process Cox's point of departure is the world order and the Gramscian notion of hegemony began to develop a role, even if discreet, in Cox's theoretical framework.[13]

Returning to Gramsci, changes to the world order – like changes on the military–strategic and geopolitical equilibrium – resemble fundamental changes in social relationships. In addition, every hegemonic relation surpasses the limits of a nation, involving more complex relationships and having its foundations in the world beyond the state apparatus.[14] The state is still fundamental to international relations and the social relationship "through which capitalism and hegemony are expressed."[15] However, the state is understood in an extended sense that includes its own social basis and, for that reason, state centrism – or narrow understandings of the state that downsize it to its bureaucracy or its military capabilities – is set aside.[16]

In this process, the construction of a historical bloc has a "national moment" where a hegemonic class manifests itself as an international phenomenon as it develops a particular form of social relations of production (see Box 15.2). For Cox, once hegemony is established domestically, it may expand beyond a particular social order, on a world scale.[17] Thereby, the state condensates a hegemonic relationship between dominant classes and other class fractions, making its interests and aspirations compatible and coherent.[18] This relationship is also combined with social forces external to the state – on the transnational and global scales – which make the struggles over the construction of a hegemonic project even more complex. Hegemonies can operate on two scales or levels: the construction of a historical bloc and the establishment of social cohesion inside the state or the international expansion of a mode of production by its global projection throughout the world order. According to Cox, however, the "national moment" is the condition *sine qua non*: "a world hegemony is thus in its beginnings an outward expansion of internal (national) hegemony established by a dominant social class."[19]

Box 15.2 Historical bloc

Gramsci developed a crucial concept in order to cope with the dialectical relations between economics, politics and the social totality: the concept of historical bloc. According to him, "structures and superstructures forma an 'historical bloc.' That is to say the complex, contradictory and discordant ensemble of the superstructures is the reflection of the ensemble of the social relations of production" (Gramsci 2004: 250). In accordance with Stephen Gill, such concept "refers to a historical congruence between material forces, institutions and ideologies, or broadly, an alliance of different class forces politically organized around a set of hegemonic ideas that gave strategic direction and coherence to its constituent elements. For a new historic bloc to emerge, its leaders must engage in 'conscious, planned struggle' in both political and civil society, Any new historic bloc must have not only power within the civil society and economy but it also need persuasive ideas, arguments and initiatives that build one, catalyse and develop its political networks and organization" (Gill 2008: 60–61).

Yet, the "national moment" is not just the point of departure for the spatial expansion of capitalism,[20] but a "point of arrival." The hegemonic struggle involves transforming particular interests, related to a particular form of state, into something capable of being applied everywhere.[21] In sum, the failure in recognizing the spatial dimension of Gramscian thinking[22] may lead to an overestimation of what are the supposed national limits of this theory. This critique is explored by Randall Germain and Michael Kenny when they claim that "the historical nature of his [i.e., Gramsci's] concepts means that they receive their meaning and explanatory power primarily from their grounding in national social formations, and they were used exclusively by Gramsci in that capacity."[23] Likewise, Joseph Femia disregards the notion that states are only nodal points; in this regard, he affirms that for the Sardinian "the world is naturally divided into separate 'national units' and (...) these (...) are (and will remain) the main actors on the international stage."[24] Robbie Shilliam is also misguided when affirming that Gramsci does not concede constitutive status to the international sphere.[25] Conversely, in what concerns hegemony, "the restriction of its applicability exclusively to the 'national moment', if not make with care, can let to a wrong dissimulation (…) of the theoretical potential of the concept, of its sociological potentials."[26] To understand the relations between the state, in its extended sense, and the processes of globalization through the Coxian framework, it is necessary to contemplate the concept of internationalization of the state and its ramifications.

Gramsci addresses the concern over the articulation between national problems and the international context in which they exist. This is the case when Gramsci analyzes the United States' role in global politics and its relevance to the world economy and finance.[27] For example, voluntary associations and private and public associations operated "promoting American liberalism and supporting the universal projection of mass production."[28] Such associations include the Rotary Club, or the Young's Men Christian Association (YMCA) and Pan-Christians movements.[29] This is relevant as it helps to identify the shortfalls of critics whom emphasize the exclusive application of Gramscian categories to the national sphere or claim a denial, by Gramsci, of the international sphere as a causal factor for social transformations. We will return to this issue and its theoretical and methodological consequences further in the chapter. In truth, concepts like hegemony and passive revolution have a heuristic potential that goes beyond the national context, and points to the fact that "the perspective is international and cannot be otherwise." Accordingly, in Notebook 14 there is a fruitful line of thought dealing with the relationship between the global and the national:

> In reality, the internal relations of any nation are the result of a combination which is "original" and (in a certain sense) unique: these relations must be understood and conceived in their originality and uniqueness if one wishes to dominate them and direct them. To be sure, the line of development is towards internationalism, but the point of departure is "national" – and it is from this point of departure that one must begin. Yet the perspective is international and cannot be otherwise. Consequently, it is necessary to study accurately the combination of national forces which the international class will have to lead and develop, in accordance with the international perspective and directives.[30]

This topic must be seen in the light of Gramsci criticism of state centrism, which highlights the peculiar form which the author understands the "national moment." Gramsci argues against non-national concepts, namely against a cosmopolitism that sub estimates the necessity of nationalization of social classes, even if there is no restriction of hegemony to national political struggles. There is not a unilateral relationship between the three spheres proposed by Cox, and the point of departure to explain the historical process can vary. This is a crucial point, since it stresses the fact that, although it is possible to start from the "national," the "international" is also a nodal and non-dominant starting point, which is perfectly consistent with the spatial perception of Gramsci.[31]

Central to a Cox-inspired rereading of Gramsci to IPE is the perception of the impact of certain process of internationalization of production in the political sphere. The internationalization of the state is a process essential to understanding the mechanisms employed for the maintenance of hegemony under the *Pax Americana*, and the context that emerges from the intensification of globalization. The internationalization of the state is "the global process whereby national policies and practices have been adjusted to the exigencies of the world economy of international production."[32] The state has become part of a complex political structure that emerged on an international scale. This highlights two outcomes: (1) the state does not disappear in this process, but with the emergence of the "global," a new sphere of social interactions arises without causing the unimportance of other spheres;[33] (2) this is not a homogenous process. In truth, highlighting the national moment demonstrates the "interscalar articulation"[34] that exists between the international and national spheres. This is fundamental toward noticing the spatial dynamic of the dialectic of globalization.

It is possible to notice a process of change in the states' political structure caused by a new framework of power relations between domestic groups and those in other states toward a broader process of construction of historical blocs beyond the limits of the national state. Then, an interstate consensus is built related to the necessities of the world economy. Consequently, national structures are adjusted to translate the consensus into domestic public policies.

Since the emergence of Bretton Woods, the state occupied a role of mediator between the structures of international and world economy. During the *Pax Americana*, there was a prevalence of a world order, mainly driven by advanced industrial states, a form of the state apparatus that rendered account to both international economic institutions – such as the World Bank and the International Monetary Fund – and domestic public opinion. This is clearly expressed through the idea of "embedded liberalism"[35] or the possibility to combine free markets at the international sphere and state interventionism domestically to guarantee stability. In this process of change of gravitational center of national economies to the world economy, the state remained responsible for the stabilization of both spheres. It presupposes a structure of power where agencies of the United States government had a prominent position. However, this power structure did not operate exclusively through a top/bottom approach. Rather, it entails, as a process of hegemony construction, the identification of subordinate groups. Thus, processes of internationalization of the state must be understood in a dialectical perspective, generating contradictions and oppositional movements.

The hegemonic world order established by the *Pax Americana* "was founded by a country in which social hegemony has been established and in which that hegemony was sufficiently expansive to project itself onto the world scale."[36] Fordism as a model of production and a particular form of state became the standard and was exported globally. Behind the *Pax Americana*, there exists a hegemonic vision that is associated with an economic internationalism throughout social groups from the United States and prompts demands from mass consumption. This is a pertinent feature, as it reveals the importance of the spatial dimension of hegemony construction as: "the place that comes to exercise hegemony matters, therefore, in the content and form that hegemony takes." In the case of *Pax Americana*, "a spatial dialectic between the United States and the rest of the world rather than a conjunctural/universal historical dialectic with only incidental geographical features" is crucial toward understanding the contemporary global political economy.[37]

Such hegemony exhibits some particularities. Its power geography stems from a network power long established at "American marketplace society," which caused an internationalization of production and finance that generated significant consequences. It is the erosion of the same principles that guided the *Pax Americana* world order. In this process, "the United States and its hegemonic global position"[38] were crucial for the integration of production processes on a global scale through transnational corporations. It is possible to affirm that from a Gramscian-inspired perspective, "this organisation of production and finance on a transnational level fundamentally distinguishes globalization from the period of *Pax Americana*."[39]

Globalization processes and the route from internationalization to transnationalization of the state

Despite its relevance, the internationalization of the state was criticized given Cox's emphasis on the role of states in a neoliberal hegemony – the idea that state would be a transmission belt to neoliberalism, from the global to the local.[40] In this regard, Leo Panitch[41] affirmed the disproportionality of the top down aspect of power relations, understanding globalization as a unidirectional process, from the global to the national. Therefore, Cox would be neglecting the very fact that globalization is a states oeuvre. By the same token, L. H. M. Ling[42] and Andrew Baker[43] maintain that the concept of internationalization of the state is limited. It neglects the reciprocal interactions between the global and the local and how social relations are mutual reinforcing at the global political economy and disregard the role of class struggles within national social formations. Pinar Bedirhanoglu[44] also argues that Cox is misguided on the reading of the Marxian concept of "mode of production," which has resulted in a fetishized conception of the state and in the reproduction of (neo) liberal ideological practices. In sum, critics suggest that even if social forces may be integrated into transnational structures, the role of the state would still be determined by social struggles within national social formations.

Even Cox acknowledges the pertinence of criticisms concerning the "transmission belt" concept: such a metaphor led to a misinterpretation that external forces impact upon states and obscure "the role of the balance of social forces within the state and of the potential for resistance to globalization from hostile social forces." The idea of *nébuleuse* could assist to understand something incomplete and permeated by contradictions. Thus, in accordance with Cox,

> global capitalism is a multilevel process, determined at the national level by the balance of social forces within states, at the transnational level by an evolving ideology (neo-liberalism) (…), at the international level by those institutions that developed officially endorsed policy guidelines, and again at the national level by the translating of these guidelines into concrete measures of national fiscal and monetary policy.[45]

Second, Cox perceives the limits of the "transmission belt" metaphor in the explanation of how the state responds to external influences and how domestic class relations fit into this process.[46] In addition, the work of Morton[47] is essential as it shows the relationship between Cox and the work of Gramsci, contributing to dialectical materialism. It must be noticed that since 1981 – when the concept was developed – Cox warned about the necessity of more empirical research that would indicate how the internationalization of the state has occurred in IPE practices.

The incorporation of globalization as a category of analysis has led not only to the emergence of the concept of internationalization of the state, but its rigorous academic development. In this regard, Stephen Gill understands this process as a dissemination of hegemony centered on the United States, especially through the analysis of the Trilateral Commission.[48] Like Cox, Gill identifies the restructuring of global production through post-Fordism occurring in a context of structural change in the 1970s. This period is defined by the transition from an international to a liberal–transnational historical bloc.

From the end of World War II, there was a noticeable period of rapid internationalization of production and integration of capital and exchange markets on a global scale. In this context, national governments and workers were constrained by power resources and the mobility of transnational capital.[49] Fractions of the transnational capitalist class develop a sense of solidarity that is expressed, for example, within international organizations, financial international institutions and private councils on international relations.[50] Thus, a fraction of the capitalist class occupies the center of an emerging liberal–transnational historical bloc, which supports a wider transatlantic hegemony from a past historical period and a smaller incorporation of labor sectors. Gill further contributes to the Coxian thesis of internationalization through emphasizing the importance of transnational actors in the struggle over hegemony. Hence, the transnationalization of the state is:

a process whereby state policies and institutional arrangements are conditioned and changed by the power and mobility of transnational fractions of capital. In the 1970s and 1980s this gave increased weight to certain parts of government, notably finance and economic ministries relative to foreign and defence ministries, as well as the private offices of Prime Ministries or Presidents.[51]

According to Gill, supremacy is organized at the global sphere through two processes: new constitutionalism and disciplinary neoliberalism, concomitantly with the diffusion of a market civilization. Disciplinary neoliberalism is the expression during the 1990s of a capitalist counter-revolution on a world scale, responsible for reconstituting the state and intensifying social hierarchies associated with class, race and gender relations. Such a revolution involves the extension of "ease" and alienation based on the disciplinary effect of capital in social relations. It is a kind of structural power that combines both capital power with "panopticism" and a "capillary power." This disciplinary neoliberalism is institutionalized via the restructuration of the state and international institutions. It involves new legal structures and constitutional and quasi-constitutional arrangements, so-called "new constitutionalism, (...) the political project of attempting to make transnational liberalism, and if possible liberal democratic capitalism, the sole model for future development."[52] Related to this is the spread of a global market civilization based on an ideology of capitalist progress.

Likewise, William I. Robinson developed a theory of global capitalism. Robinson argues that globalization would represent "an *epochal shift*"[53] marked by the emergence of a capitalist transnational class and a transnational state. Given that the accumulation of power follows the accumulation of capital, from this new global configuration is the emergence of a transnational state within an interstate system. Once the material foundations of nation states are surpassed by globalization, it is necessary to reread the states process of social relations that take institutional forms that are historically determined.[54] In this regard, the nation-state would not be seen as a container of processes of capital accumulation, class formation and development, given that those are increasingly embedded in a globalized context.[55] The transnational state is defined in this sense as a particular constellation of class forces and relations bound up with capitalist globalization and the rise of a transnational capitalist class, embodied in a diverse set of political institutions. These institutions are transformed national states and diverse supranational institutions that serve to institutionalize the domination of this class as the hegemonic fraction of capital worldwide. The transnational state comprises those institutions and practices in global society that maintain, defend, and advance the emergent hegemony of a global bourgeoisie and its project of constructing a new global capitalist historical bloc.[56]

Such a coercive–regulatory apparatus is part of an emerging network without a centralized institutional design that comprehends national states as integrated with economic and political supranational forums. The transformation of national states and the birth of supranational institutions would not be, then, distinctive or mutually excluding aspects, but two dimensions of a same process of transnationalization of the state. Such supranational institutions are gradually supplanting domestic institutions in the formulation and development of policies and the management of the world economy. With this in mind, Robinson developed a rereading of the concept of transnationalization of the state: nation states are ceasing to be the formulators of national policies and are becoming the administrators of policies formulated previously by supranational institutions. In sum, it "becomes transformed with respect to its functions and becomes a functional component of a larger transnational state."[57]

The United States is exampled as a political institution of the supranational apparatus that exercises leadership on the development of policies and strategies on behalf of global capitalism.

This is a kind of "material condensation" of dominant groups' power worldwide to solve problems and ensure the reproduction of global capitalism. This is due to a series of reasons. Among all exceed the fact that the intensification of globalization processes occurred in a period where the United States exerted world dominance and because it concentrates its efforts into the military and financial resources so it can act on the behalf of the "globalizing elites." It must have a "political authority" capable to guarantee the necessary context to the amplified reproduction of capital on a global scale. American interventions may be seen as a commitment to the replacement of governing elites, where local and regional elites are replaced by those more favorable to the transnational project, as can be seen both in Latin America and Iraq, for example.[58]

Despite the merits of his analysis, previous critics of the original Coxian argument can be applied to Robinson, as he reproduces to some extent the "transmission belt" theory. This is problematic as it minimizes class struggles as a process of globalization. There are differences between the process of internationalization/transnationalization of the state, emphasizing the process of internalization of class interests, stressing the process of denationalization of the state and the metaphor of "transmission belt."

However, Robinson lacks a perception of a territorial and globalizing dialectic. Robinsons thesis that globalization, as an epoch change, leads to the emergence of a transnational state disregards the process of capitalist social relations that must be understood in association with the "(changing) role of the state in the spatial and social reproduction of capital."[59] There is an inherent contradiction between spaces of accumulation and spaces of governance in the development of social relations under capitalism.

In addition, according to Robinson "the material circumstances that gave rise to the nation-state are presently being superseded by globalization"; so, "this particular spatial form of the uneven development of capitalism is being overcome by the globalization of capital and markets and the gradual equalization of accumulation conditions this involves."[60] This assertion expresses the primary flaw in his transnational state thesis: namely, the idea of "homoficience of capitalism," which supposes that the diffusion and impact of capitalism worldwide occurs in a uniform manner. This is despite the "contradictions of uneven development expressed through the varied relations of capital in divergent state-formation processes."[61] However, as expressed in the concept of passive revolution, contradictions of unequal development are expressions of class struggles that occur on different spatial scales, from the local to the global, passing through the national.

This is clear when attentions are directed to economic crises' that have accumulated since the 1990s and the answers formulated by developed states to deal with them. Two responses deserve attention here, both directly associated with the Asian crisis (1997): first the absence of consensus over the model to be adopted to deal with the situation. In this case, there was a clear opposition between the models advocated by the United States and Japan, demonstrating the impossibility of a "homoficience of capitalism." This additionally demonstrated the role of states as actors during the reconfiguration of the process of capital accumulation on a global scale and, in this case, a regional scale. Second, beyond pinpointing the deterioration of the neoliberal model hitherto hegemonic, the crisis is originated on the G7, what would be later known as the G20. This may be seen as an attempt to restore the legitimacy that has been lost since the onset of the crisis. In other words, this is an element within a wider process of passive revolution on a global scale, expressing its own contradictions of unequal development and how the states are unequally incorporated into those processes.[62]

In sum, the "global processes and formations can be, and are, destabilizing the scalar hierarchy centered in the national state"[63] does not mean that new scales at the global level overpass old scales at the national level. In truth, aligning with the Coxian-inspired perspective, and the concept of internationalization/transnationalization of the state is essential toward avoiding the "territorial trap"[64] and globalism: both perspectives suffer from a flat ontology as they deny that the global and national are both relevant scales toward the process of capital accumulation. This helps to enlighten the understanding about the process of neo-liberalization presented from a systemic dimension[65] and is expressed historically in a discontinuous, unequal and contradictory reconstitution of relations between the global and the national. In other words, the processes of neo-liberalization has led to the expansion of neoliberalism worldwide and "*intensifying* the uneven development of regulatory forms across places, territories and scales," generating a "*systemic* production of geo-institutional differentiation."[66]

It must then be perceived how the process of capital accumulation occurs within multiscale social relationships to which the state is a nodal point, but a non-dominant one. The geographic space is an "undistinguishable set of systems of objects and systems of actions," which varies according to the epoch. If that is the case, "the objects that constitute the contemporary geographical space are intentionally conceived to the exercise of some ends, intentionally crafted and intentionally localized. *Hence, the resulting spatial order is an intentional one* (my emphasis)."[67] In this regard, it is possible to understand how globalization, pioneered by the influence of the United States, generates an ontological spatial transformation of world politics, opening new scale possibilities for political articulation and capital accumulation without denying the relevance of other scales.[68] This point is particularly pertinent when considering the example of Chinese international insertion processes in the last decade and its particularities. In fact, this can be seen specifically by looking toward strategies such as the *Go Global, China 2025* and the creation of new development banks, such as the Asian Infrastructure Investment Bank (AIIB) and the New Development Bank (NDB – so-called "BRICS Bank").[69] Such projects do not follow the neoliberal agenda and integrate some elements of the current economic world order. It is possible to talk about a new kind of globalization – or a "clash of globalizations" – in which the global, international and national scales operate in a new dialectical way, establishing perhaps new aspects for the contemporary internationalization/transnationalization of the state.

Dealing with the (neo)Gramscian IPE conundrum: past, present and future

After all, the big question that emerges is: what kind of relationship could be established between Gramsci's thought and the contemporary socio-economic issues, particularly the globalization processes?.[70] Hence, more than try to read Gramsci literally and apply his concepts to the international realm, the great question of Gramscian IPE is a methodological one. Looking again toward Worth's classification, it is possible to notice that both Italian and Amsterdam "schools" in some sense agree that Gramsci is a source of inspiration (and in many cases one source among others – Fernand Braudel and Giambattista Vico in Cox's case, or Fernand Braudel and Karl Polanyi in Gill's case, for example), and his thinking and concepts must be, in some sense, internationalized.[71] Once global capitalism has passed through an internationalization/transnationalization process, Gramsci's national concepts must be internationalized too.[72]

Regarding the Italian School, the Coxian conceptualization of world hegemony as a social, political and economic structure that expresses itself in local, national, international and global levels – even though it begins in the national level – is clear.[73] Cox's theoretical contributions to the idea of internationalization/transnationalization of the state and its relationship with the Gramscian concept of extended state is another example. In this case, such idea was central in Gill's or Robinson's attempts to transnationalize the concepts of domination and hegemony.

The Amsterdam School, for its side, places its focus on understanding capital as a transnational force and its consequences. As recognized by Henk Overbeek, Gramsci's influence came after almost a decade of debates, mainly focused on the "incorporation of the Marxian concept of *capital fractions* into the study of international politics."[74] To Amsterdam School scholars, Gramsci's conception of hegemony – particularly mediated by a dialogue with Robert Cox and Stephen Gill – seemed to be fruitful toward comprehending how fractions of the capitalist class propagate their particular worldview as a concept of control. In this sense, substantial contributions have been developed to understand the transition from corporate liberalism to systemic neoliberalism and nowadays to predatory neoliberalism.[75]

However, such internationalization attempts are not a consensus; some Gramscian IPE authors do not recognize them. For some – from the *Cultural* vein – the above-mentioned transition of hegemony, from national to the international level and the emphasis on capital fractions on the transnational scale, still reproduces structuralism. Hegemony should not be read in a linear way; the contradiction embedded in the relationship between culture and politics for Gramsci must be taken seriously[76] and hegemony must be seen as a "theory of the subaltern." In other words, there are "various cultural practices and processes used and articulated within the subaltern classes in order to achieve this hegemonic consent."[77] In this sense, Gramscian IPE should engage less with the Coxian framework and more with Ernesto Laclau, Raymond Williams and Stuart Hall's reading of Gramsci. Hence, it will be able to cope in a better way with culture, race and religion and their nexus with IPE in a critical vein.

Starting from the same macro-critique, other authors – from a *Philological* point of view – start from a textual analysis to understand how "Gramsci begins analytically from 'global' position focused on politics and political community in which the historical formation of the modern nation-state is theorised." Categories such as the state, the national–popular, the Southern Question and civil society would be very illustrative of the "interpenetration of 'national' and 'international' politics and context" in Gramsci's political theory.[78] Following such insights, the concept of passive revolution becomes central. Borrowing from Michael Burawoy's suggestion "where Trotsky's horizons stop, Gramsci's begin,"[79] some scholars relate the passive revolution concept as one closely related to the necessities that are brought about by the processes of uneven development of capitalism. Hence, as a condition, a concept and a theory, passive revolution would point to the state "as a social formation embedded in a global context of which it is both constitutive and constituted by."[80]

Once we take a close look at the four distinct perspectives – Italian, Amsterdam, Cultural and Philological – it is possible to notice that, in spite of their differences and distinctions, all present innovative ontological, epistemological and methodological perspectives to the IPE field.[81] Particularly, they provide important tools toward understanding the complexities of the transnationalization of capital and classes, the dialectic of globalization, the construction of hegemonic processes, passive revolutions and the role of culture in such broader process. As Craig Murphy affirmed once, Gramscian IPE shows that Gramsci concepts offer a rich methodological opportunity to IPE to understand shifting power relations at distinct levels or scales.[82] In other words, both contribute to the development of a "Gramscian way of thinking" about IPE. That is to incorporate the Gramscian method to analyze social and historical conditions that are different from those that called Gramsci's original attention.

Hence, a Gramscian-inspired analysis of globalization processes is able to integrate dialectically time and space, coping with "the contingent, historically constructed aspects of globalization, the agency of actors and the diversity of processes contained under the banner of globalization."[83] The globalization process does not mean the end or the retreat of the state, but instead a restructuration of different forms of state through the internalization, inside the states, "of new configurations of social forces expressed by class struggle between different (national and transnational) fractions of capital and labor."[84] In this context, concepts like transnationalization of the state, concept of control or passive revolution, for example, could help, from different perspectives, to understand *how* "the global can also be constituted inside the national" and *how* "the state have actually gained power because they have to do the work of implementing policies necessary for a global corporate economy."[85] That is, Gramsci concepts – as well as the Gramscian-inspired ones – can enrich our understanding about the complexities concerning the processes of denationalization.[86]

At the same time, Gramsci presents a critique of the state-centric analysis (criticized by him as a "statolatry").[87] In fact, it is quite the opposite: the state is seen as a form of social relations in which methodological – and not organic – distinctions concerning the scales and levels could be elaborated in order to better comprehend consensus and coercion. This is important because it opens new possibilities to think about contemporary changes in the world order. This can be understood in four parts: (i) the denationalization processes and their impacts in the north as well as in the Global South; (ii) the Global South current ethico-political, economic and social transformations and their relation with global capitalist transformations; (iii) the conservative turn in a global scale – and particularly in the US – its relation with the return of religion to international politics and its impact on the struggle over hegemony in national, international and global scale; and (iv) the political economy of China's rise and its impact on transnational class fractions relationship and interstate relations (north–north, north–south and south–south), as well as to global hegemony – just to name a few examples of the current international conjuncture.

Of course, Gramsci is not a kind of panacea that could resolve all contemporary problems IPE faces. Neither do these four perspectives present an exhaustive toolbox, which we should choose and use it uncritically. The above-mentioned topics are a clear example of it. Nevertheless, what must follow, for a Gramscian IPE, is not a mechanical and ahistorical use of Gramscian or Gramscian-inspired concepts, but to think of IPE – as a field and a realm – in a Gramscian way. In this process, attention must be paid to "translatability" – in the Gramscian sense of the concept: concerning the "translation" of Gramsci to the international reality, as well as the "translation" of other scholars and concepts to dialogue with Gramsci about such topics – in the same spirit that Gramsci had established fruitful and critical dialogues with Benedetto Georges Croce, Sorel and Vincenzo Cuoco, for example. In the end, the point of translatability is important once it calls attention to the methodological issue: in other words, to translate is to answer the question of *how* the Gramscian categories could be useful to IPE.[88] This seems to be the present and future research agenda for Gramscian IPE scholars to pursue.

Notes

1 Smith, Booth & Zalewski 1996.
2 Morton 2007; Leysens 2018. It is important to make clear, since the beginning, that wherever possible I will avoid the conventional term "neo-Gramscian" in this chapter. The reason is because, despite its popularity, the main intention here is to present contributions and debates around the uses and misuses of Gramsci in IPE study, and not enter in the conventional debate over *What does "neo" means in neo-Gramscianism?; or Are the neo-Gramscian real Gramscians?* – whatever that question means. In this sense, *Gramscian-inspired IPE* seems to me a more interesting definition, by which more scholars and contributions could be grasped.
3 See, for example, the contributors to the following works: Femia 2005; Ling 1996; Panitch 1997; Germain & Kenny 1998; Ayers, eds. 2008; Bieler et al., eds. 2006; Budd 2013; McNally & Schwarzmantel 2009; Worth 2009; Worth 2011. Some of them will be present in some detail in the course of the chapter.

4 See, for example, the work of Gill 1990, 2003; Gill & Law 1989; Rupert 1994; 1995, 2000, 2003; Robinson 1996, 2001, 2004, 2010. See also the work developed by the Amsterdam School (see Over-beek 2019, "Introduction," for a synthesis).
5 Morton 2007: 10.
6 Worth 2011: 21.
7 The term "school" used here by Worth calls attention to the fact that there is a rich debate over the Gramscian IPE and its classification: Adam Morton criticizes the idea of "school," choosing the notion of "perspectives" (Morton 2001); Henk Overbeek, in turn, prefers the notion of "school" (Overbeek 2019: "Introduction"). Despite the relevance of such debate to think about a sociology of knowledge of the Gramscian IPE, this chapter will not engage with it; actually, such terms will be presented here sometimes closely related to some scholar interpretation, or sometimes in a broader sense.
8 Worth 2008, 2009, 2011.
9 Cox 1987.
10 Cox (1981) 1996.
11 Morton 2007.
12 Cox (1981) 1996.
13 Cox 1987.
14 Gramsci 2002a, 2004.
15 Morton 2007.
16 Gramsci 2002a.
17 Cox 1987.
18 Morton 2007.
19 Cox 1994.
20 Agnew 2005; Morton 2001.
21 Gramsci 2002a.
22 Jessop 2005.
23 Germain & Kenny 1998.
24 Femia 2005: 345.
25 Shilliam 2004.
26 Mello 1996: 26.
27 Gramsci 2001a: 298–299, 2002a: 129–136.
28 Morton 2007: 100.
29 Gramsci 2001a, 2002a, 2002b.
30 Gramsci 2002a.
31 Morton 2007.
32 Cox 1987.
33 Cox 1987: 253.
34 Morton 2007: 138.
35 Ruggie 1982.
36 Cox 1987: 266.
37 Agnew 2005: 9.
38 Agnew 2005: 61.
39 Morton 2007: 124.
40 Cox (1992) 1996.
41 Panitch 1997: 89–96.
42 Ling 1996.
43 Baker 1999.
44 Bedirhanoglu 2008.
45 Cox 2002: 33.
46 Worth 2008, 2009.
47 Morton 2007.
48 Gill 1990.
49 Gill & Law 1989.
50 Ramos 2013.
51 Gill 1990: 94.
52 Gill 2003: 131–132.
53 Robinson 2004: 4.

54 Robinson 2001.
55 Robinson 2010.
56 Robinson 2001: 165–166.
57 Robinson 2004: 100.
58 Robinson 1996, 2004.
59 Lacher 2006: 12.
60 Robinson 2004: 98–99.
61 Morton 2007: 147.
62 Ramos 2013.
63 Sassen 2007: 14.
64 Agnew 2005.
65 Gill 2003.
66 Brenner et al. 2010: 184.
67 Santos 2004: 332.
68 Agnew 2005.
69 Overbeek & Yuan 2018.
70 Liguori 2007.
71 In a recent interview Robert W. Cox put this in a clear way:

> I don't like to say 'Gramscian' and especially 'neo-Gramscian', because I'm not quite sure what the 'neo' stands for. I've read Gramsci and derived certain ideas from that. Some people have criticized me in that what I've written is contestable in terms of Gramsci's work. Well, that may be true, but my point is that I'm not trying to repeat Gramsci, but I'm trying to use inspiration from Gramsci in order to develop my own thinking. So, I don't worry about that kind of criticism.
>
> *(Cox 2013: 306)*

72 Bieler et al. 2015.
73 Cox 1994.
74 Overbeek 2019.
75 Overbeek 1993; Overbeek & Von Apeldoorn 2012; Van Der Pijl 1998, 2019.
76 Pasha 2005, 2008.
77 Worth 2011: 382. See also Worth 2008, 2009.
78 See also McNally 2017. North–South relations in Italy, for example, a central condition to comprehend the "Southern Question," clearly express that, for Gramsci, "states are the product of *inter*national relations combining with *intra*national relations" (Bieler et al. 2015: 140; Gramsci 1987).
79 Burawoy 1989: 793.
80 Hesketh 2017: 389. See also Bieler, et al. 2015 and Roccu 2017. In other words, Gramsci "was not a 'methodological nationalist' who took the national scale for granted but typically analyzed any particular scale in terms of its connections with other scales" (Jessop 2008: 105). See also Jessop 2005.
81 Concerning such methodological issues, Jonathan Pass defends not only a philological engagement with Gramsci, but also an engagement with critical realist depth ontology, mainly in its emergentist form. In accordance with him, such engagement would contribute "to elaborate a more convincing (that is, structural) theory of hegemony, while shedding light on hegemonic transitions, the interstate system and the dynamics of the global capitalism in general" (Pass 2018: 618). For an overview about such dialogue between Gramsci, IPE and critical realism, see also the work of Jonathan Joseph and his materialist theory of hegemony (Joseph 2002; 2008).
82 Murphy 1998.
83 Oke 2009: 323.
84 Morton 2007: 133.
85 Sassen 2008: 63.
86 Sassen 2007.
87 Gramsci 2002a: 279–280, 332–333, 2002b: 349–351.
88 Ives & Lacorte 2010; Glasius 2012.

Bibliography

Agnew, J. 2005. *Hegemony: The New Shape of Global Power*. Philadelphia: Temple University Press.

Ayers, A., ed. Gramsci, A. 2008. *Political Economy and International Relations: Modern Princes and Naked Emperors*. Basingstoke: Palgrave.

Baker, A. 1999. Nébuleuse and the "Internationalisation of the State" in the UK? The Case of HM Treasury and the Bank of England. *Review of International Political Economy* 6, no. 1: 79–100.

Bedirhanoglu, P. 2008. The State in Neoliberal Globalization: The Merits and Limits of Coxian Conceptions. In: *Gramsci, Political Economy and International Relations: Modern Princes and Naked Emperors*. Ayers, A. (ed.) Basingstoke: Palgrave.

Bieler, A., Bonefeld, W., Burnham, P. & Morton, A. eds. 2006. *Global Restructuring, State, Capital and Labour: Contesting Neo-Gramscian Perspectives*. Basingstoke: Palgrave.

Bieler, A., Bruff, I. & Morton, A. 2015. Gramsci and "the International": Past, Present and Future. In: *Antonio Gramsci*. McNally, M. (ed.) Basingstoke: Palgrave.

Brenner, N., Peck, J. & Theodore, N. 2010. Variegated Neoliberalization: Geographies, Modalities, Pathways. *Global Networks* 10, no. 2: 182–222.

Budd, A. 2013. *Class, States and International Relations: A Critical Appraisal of Robert Cox and Neo-Gramscian Theory*. London: Routledge, 2013.

Burawoy, M. 1989. Two Methods in Social Science: Skocpol versus Trotsky. *Theory and Society* 18, no. 6: 759–805.

Coutinho, C. N. 2000. *Contra a corrente. Ensaios sobre democracia e socialismo*. Brasil: Cortez Editorial.

Cox, R. (1981) 1996. Social Forces, States and World Orders: Beyond International Relations Theory. In: *Approaches to World Order*. Cox, R. and Sinclair, T. (ed.) Cambridge: Cambridge University Press.

Cox, R. 1987. *Production, Power and World Order: Social Forces in the Making of History*. New York: Columbia University Press.

Cox, R. (1992) 1996. *Global Perestroika. Approaches to World Order*. Cox, R. and Sinclair, T. (ed.). Cambridge: Cambridge University Press.

Cox, R. 1994. Gramsci, Hegemony and International Relations: An Essay in Method. In: *Gramsci, Historical Materialism and International Relations*. Gill, S. (ed.) Cambridge: Cambridge University Press.

Cox, R. 2002. *The Political Economy of a Plural World: Critical Reflections on Power, Morals and Civilization*. London: Routledge.

Cox, R. 2013. Overcoming the Blockage: An Interview with Robert W. Cox. Interview by Garcia, A. S. & Borba de Sá, M. *Estudos Internacionais* 1, no. 2: 303–318.

Femia, J. V. 2005. *Gramsci, Machiavelli and International Relations*. Political Quarterly, 76, no. 3: 341–349.

Germain, R. & Kenny, M. 1998. Engaging Gramsci: International Relations Theory and the New Gramscians. *Review of International Studies* 24, no. 1: 3–21.

Gill, S. 1990. *American Hegemony and the Trilateral Commission*. Cambridge: Cambridge University Press.

Gill, S. 2003. *Power and Resistance in the New World Order*. New York: Palgrave Macmillan.

Gill, S. 2008. *Power and Resistance in the New World Order*. Second fully revised, updated & enlarged edition. London and New York: Macmillan-Palgrave.

Gill, S. & Law, D. 1989. Global Hegemony and the Structural Power of Capital. *International Studies Quarterly* 33, no. 4: 475–499.

Glasius, Marlies, ed. Gramsci, A. 2012. Twenty-First Century: Dialectics and Translatability. *International Studies Review* 14, no. 4: 666–686.

Gramsci, A. 1987. *A Questão Meridional*. Rio De Janeiro: Paz e Terra, 1987.

Gramsci, A. 2001a. Cadernos do Cárcere. *Civilização Brasileira* Vol. 4. Rio De Janeiro.

Gramsci, A. 2001b. Cadernos do Cárcere. 2ª Ed. *Civilização Brasileira*, Vol. 2. Rio De Janeiro.

Gramsci, A. 2002a. Cadernos do Cárcere. 3ª Ed. *Civilização Brasileira*, Vol. 3. Rio De Janeiro.

Gramsci, A. 2002b. *Cadernos do Cárcere*. Civilização Brasileira, Vol. 6. Rio De Janeiro.

Gramsci, A. 2004. *Cadernos do Cárcere*. 3ª Ed. Civilização Brasileira, Vol. 1. Rio De Janeiro.

Gruppi, L. 1972. *Il concetto di egemonia in Gramsci*. Roma: Editori Riuniti

Hesketh, C. 2017. Passive Revolution: A Universal Concept with Geographical Seats. *Review of International Studies* 43, no. 3: 389–408.

Ives, P. & Lacorte, R. eds. 2010. *Gramsci, Language and Translation*. Lanham, MD: Lexington.

Joseph, J. 2002. *Hegemony: A Realist Analysis*. London: Routledge.

Jessop, B. 2005. Gramsci as a Spatial Theorist. *Critical Review of International Social and Political Philosophy* 8, no. 4: 421–437.

Jessop, B. 2008. *State Power.* Cambridge: Polity.

Joseph, J. 2008. On The Limits of Neo-Gramscian International Relations. In: *Gramsci, Political Economy and International Relations: Modern Princes and Naked Emperors.* Ayers, A. (ed.) Basingstoke: Palgrave.

Lacher, H. 2006. *Beyond Globalization: Capitalism, Territoriality and International Relations of Modernity.* New York: Routledge.

Leysens, A. 2008. *The Critical Theory of Robert W. Cox: Fugitive or Guru?* Basingstoke: Palgrave.

Liguori, G. 2007. *Roteiros para Gramsci.* Rio de Janeiro: UFRJ.

Ling, L. H. 1996. Hegemony and the Internationalizing State: A Post-Colonial Analysis of China's Integration into Asian Corporatism. *Review of International Political Economy* 3, no. 1: 1–26.

McNally, M. 2017. The Neo-Gramscians in the Study of International Relations: An Appraisal. *Materialismo Storico* 1, no. 2: 12–32.

McNally, M. & Schwarzmantel, J., 2009. eds. *Gramsci and Global Politics: Hegemony and Resistance.* London: Routledge.

Mello, A. 1996. *Mundialização e Política em Gramsci.* São Paulo: Cortez.

Morton, A. 2001. The Sociology of Theorising and Neo-Gramscian Perspectives: The Problems of "School" Formation in IPE. In: *Social Forces in the Making of the "New Europe." The Restructuring of European Social Relations in the Global Political Economy.* Bieler, A. and Morton, A. (ed.) Basingstoke: Palgrave.

Morton, A. 2007. *Unravelling Gramsci: Hegemony and Passive Revolution in the Global Political Economy.* London: Pluto.

Murphy, C. 1998. Understanding IR: Understanding Gramsci. *Review of International Studies* 24, no. 3: 417–425.

Oke, N. 2009. Globalizing Time and Space: Temporal and Spatial Considerations in Discourses of Globalization. *International Political Sociology* 3 no. 3: 310–326.

Overbeek, H. ed. 1993. *Restructuring Hegemony in the Global Political Economy: The Rise of Transnational Neo-Liberalism in the 1980s.* London: Routledge.

Overbeek, H. 2019. Introduction – Political Economy, Capital Fractions, Transnational Class Formation: Revisiting the Amsterdam School. In: *Transnational Capital and Class Fractions: The Amsterdam School Perspective Reconsidered.* Jessop, B. and Overbeek, H. (ed.) London: Routledge.

Overbeek, H. & Von Apeldoorn, B. eds. 2012. *Neoliberalism in Crisis.* London: Palgrave.

Overbeek, H. & Yuan, M. 2018. Investimento Externo Direto Chinês na União Europeia. In: *A Expansão Econômica e Geopolítica da China no Século XXI: Diferentes Dimensões de um Mesmo Processo.* Vadell, J. (ed.) Belo Horizonte: Editora PUC Minas.

Panitch, L. 1997. Rethinking the Role of the State. In: *Globalization: Critical Reflections.* Mittelman, J. (ed.) London: Lynne Rienner Publishers.

Pasha, M. 2005. Islam, "Soft" Orientalism and Hegemony: A Gramscian Rereading. *Critical Review of International Social and Political Philosophy* 8, no. 4: 543–558.

Pasha, M. 2008. Return to the Source: Gramsci, Culture, and International Relations. In: *Gramsci, Political Economy and International Relations: Modern Princes and Naked Emperors.* Ayers, A. (ed.) Basingstoke: Palgrave.

Pass, J. 2018. Gramsci Meets Emergentist Materialism: Towards a Neo Neo-Gramscian Perspective on World Order. *Review of International Studies* 44, no. 4: 595–618.

Ramos, L. 2013. *Hegemonia, Revolução Passiva e Globalização: O Sistema G7/8.* Belo Horizonte: Editora PUC Minas.

Robinson, W. 1996. *Promoting Polyarchy: Globalization, US Intervention and Hegemony.* Cambridge: Cambridge University Press.

Robinson, W. 2001. Social Theory and Globalization: The Rise of a Transnational State. *Theory and Society* 30, no. 2: 157–200.

Robinson, W. 2004. *A Theory of Global Capitalism: Production, Class, and State in a Transnational World.* Baltimore: Johns Hopkins University Press.

Robinson, W. 2010. *Global Capitalism Theory and the Emergence of Transnational Elites.* United Nations University. World Institute for Development Economics Research, Working Paper. Available at: Www.Soc.Ucsb.Edu/Faculty/Robinson/Assets/Pdf/Wider.Pdf.

Roccu, R. 2017. Passive Revolution Revisited: From the Prison Notebooks to Our Great and Terrible World. *Capital & Class* 41, no. 3: 537–559.

Ruggie, J. 1982. International Regimes, Transactions and Change: Embedded Liberalism in the Postwar Economic Order. *International Organization* 36, no. 2: 379–415.

Rupert, M. 1994. Alienation, Capitalism and the Inter-State System: Toward a Marxian/Gramscian Critique. In: *Gramsci, Historical Materialism and International Relations*, Gill, S. (ed.) Cambridge: Cambridge University Press.

Rupert, M. 1995. *Producing Hegemony: The Politics of Mass Production and American Global Power*. Cambridge: Cambridge University Press.

Rupert, M. 2000. *Ideologies of Globalization: Contending Visions of a New World Order*. London: Routledge.

Rupert, M. 2003. Globalizing Common Sense: A Marxian-Gramscian (Re-)Vision of the Politics of Governance/Resistance. In: *Governance and Resistance in World Politics*. Armstrong, D. et al. (ed.) Cambridge: Cambridge University Press.

Santos, M. 2004. *A Natureza do Espaço: Técnica e Tempo, Razão e Emoção*. São Paulo: Edusp.

Sassen, S. 2007. *A Sociology of Globalization*. New York: W. W. Norton & Company.

Sassen, S. 2008. Neither Global nor National: Novel Assemblages of Territory, Authority and Rights. *Ethics & Global Politics* 1, no. 1–2: 61–79.

Shilliam, R. 2004. Hegemony and the Unfashionable Problematic of "Primitive Accumulation." *Millennium: Journal of International Studies* 33, no. 1: 59–88.

Smith, S., Booth, K. & Zalewski, M. eds. 1996. *International Theory: Positivism and Beyond*. Cambridge: Cambridge University Press.

Van Der Pijl, K. 1998. *Transnational Classes and International Relations*. London: Routledge.

Van Der Pijl, K. 2017. The BRICS: An Involuntary Contender Bloc under Attack. *Estudos Internacionais* 5, no. 1: 25–46.

Van Der Pijl, K. 2019. *A Transnational Class Analysis of the Current Crisis*. In: *Transnational Capital and Class Fractions: The Amsterdam School Perspective Reconsidered*. Jessop, B. and Overbeek, H. (ed.) London: Routledge.

Worth, O. 2008. The Poverty and Potential of Gramscian Thought in International Relations. *International Politics* 45, no. 6: 633–649.

Worth, O. 2009. Beyond World Order and Transnational Classes: The (Re)Application of Gramsci in Global Politics. In: *Gramsci and Global Politics: Hegemony and Resistance*. McNally, M. and Schwarzmantel, J. (ed.) London: Routledge.

Worth, O. 2011. Recasting Gramsci in International Politics. *Review of International Studies* 37, no. 1:373–392.

16
The concept(s) of hegemony in IPE

Owen Worth

Box 16.1 Hegemony: origins

- Thucydides used the term hegemony to show how a leading state (or in Ancient Greece, city) could control its authority over others. Hegemony was based on gaining the consent and recognition of their status in order to maintain control. This differed from a forceful, brutal form of rule, associated with the phrase 'arkhé' that, he believed, was ultimately flawed.
- Gramsci's use of the term was built on the debates that occurred within socialist circles during the Second International (1889–1916) where contributors such as Vladimir Lenin, Kaul Kautsky and Rosa Luxemburg would discuss how a socio-cultural order would develop under socialism – the hegemonic order. As with Thucydides, Gramsci's understanding of hegemony was one that showed how the gaining of consent from one class to another proved to provide a stable order.
- Thucydides and Gramsci come from different backgrounds with the former being associated with political realism and strategic International Relations and the latter with Marxist Social Science and with the politics of the left.
- Some have used the term in a way that reflects those within the more state-centric approaches to International Relations and others (within critical IPE) have used it in the more ideological sense associated with Gramsci.
- As a result hegemony is a contested concept.

Introduction

From the contemporary inception of International Political Economy (IPE), the notion of hegemony was a central concept in which claims and knowledge were derived and argued. Indeed, in the now common-read book dating the brief history of the subject by Benjamin Cohen, hegemony was the theoretical cornerstone in which both the American and the British

Schools were to draw their studies (Cohen 2008). 'Hegemonic Stability Theory' become the leading point of enquiry within American forms of IPE in the 1970 and 1980s and it was indeed Strange's interventions in criticising the nature of the theory, along with Robert Cox's own alternative interpretation of hegemony and world order that was to challenge its application within the discipline (Cox 1981; Strange 1987). Yet, the contested nature of the theory of hegemony is one that goes far beyond the realms of the short history of the study of IPE. As a term, hegemony has provided very different meanings across the social sciences and has equally differed depending how it has been methodologically applied. In addition, the study of hegemony in International Politics far outdates those within social and political studies that did not emerge as a theoretical vehicle until the nineteenth century. As a result, when we look at the concept in contemporary IPE, any analysis is highly dependent upon the theoretical and methodological manner in which it has been used and these tend to determine what claims are made.

This chapter seeks to illustrate these different theoretical departure points and then explain how we can understand hegemony in IPE in the current post-crisis era. In addition, it looks to show what sort of questions we should be posing about the role and the mechanism of hegemony. To some degree, we shall see that the questions that were initially asked back in the 1970s are still in some form or other being asked today. Namely whether the current 'hegemonic system', whether understood through US power or through the ideological remit of 'neoliberalism', is being contested. Consequently, if either another state – often understood as China – or competing ideology were to provide the basis for an alternative hegemonic economic system, what the character of such a system might be.

Two definitions of hegemony

The first common use of the term hegemony was seen in Thucydides' classic work *History of the Peloponnesian War* (1972). This fifth century BC book looked at the period of Athenian decline as the leader of the Greek city-state system that ended in war. The term hegemony or *hegemonia* is used in contrast with the term *arkhe*, with the former representing a form of legitimate and passive leadership and the latter representing empire or control (Lebow and Kelly 2001; Wickersham 1994). Thucydides illustrated that during the time when Athens relied upon *hegemonia* it appeared a more successful leader, but when it looked to the more coercive measures of force and control (*arkhe*) it descended into conflict and crisis. It this way, hegemony provides us with an entry to study the international system. The Hellas system of Greek city states fitting together as a microcosm of the international state-system that was to take shape in the aftermath of the Treaty of Westphalia.

In the post-war, Cold War-dominated era of International Politics, it was within IPE that the notion of hegemony was to thrive. Within the confines of realist and neo-realist International Relations, hegemony did not really play a role until after the Cold War. The preoccupation with balance of power and then later (through Waltz and neo-realism) with the notion of bipolarity made the idea of hegemony at the time redundant. It what thus after the Cold War when hegemony began to garner interest, particularly with neo-conservative circles, when hegemony appeared as a mechanism for the extension of US leadership (Ferguson 2003; Harries 2003; Ikenberry 2006; Kagan 2008).

Hegemonic Stability Theory, on the other-hand, was coined by Robert Keohane in 1980, largely reflecting on the work of Charles Kindleberger, whose work on the rise and decline of leadership in the international economy formed the basis for the hypothesis behind the concept. Namely, that the stability of an international system is dependent upon the strength of leadership by a dominant state (Keohane 1980; Kindleberger 1973, 1981, 1983). Both Kindleberger's

The World in Depression (1973) and Robert Gilpin's *War and Change in World Politics* (1981) argued that the international economy flourished when a dominant state had the capacity to lead and hold an economic system in place. This 'hegemony' was thus understood as a state that could serve a role that led and stabilised the international economy. When one was not apparent, the international economy appeared in flux and instability became common-place (Kindleberger 1983). The main illustrations of this were seen with the gradual decline of British leadership from the end of the nineteenth century and the resulting chaos that followed, followed by a post-war stability that was brought with the US-led dollar system that was constructed at Bretton-Woods. Thus written in the aftermath of the collapse of the Dollar system, Hegemonic Stability Theory affirmed the belief that the US was in decline and if there was to be new hegemon, then Japan seemed the most likely (Kindleberger 1983: 7–8). As it was, a system without the existence of such a hegemon would spiral towards instability.

Two responses were to emerge from Hegemonic Stability Theory. The first was from Robert Keohane in his book *After Hegemony*. While he accepted the general remit behind Hegemonic Stability Theory, he did not believe that a hegemon was necessarily required in order to facilitate a workable international economic system (Keohane 1984). Instead, he argued that leading states could work to co-ordinate policy to ensure that an institutional framework could be built, whereby the rules of such institutions would be adhered to. Obviously, the state that appeared to be dominant at the time would need to take the lead in order for this to be facilitated. This was Keohane's call for the US to look to take such a lead in building an institutional framework for economic action in light of its decline. The second response was far more poignant. It argued that the claim of American hegemonic decline was bogus. Bruce Russett argued from an empirical basis and suggested that the main indicators used for measuring the strength of a hegemon seemed to be manufacturing production, military expenditure and gross national product. These did not account for the strength of American-led capitalism, military expertise and the dominance of the nuclear industry (Russett 1985). For Strange, this pointed to a more significant claim. That the fall of the dollar system and relative decline of the US in the following decade and a half did not provide any justification in the claim that American hegemony had declined. Indeed, quite the reverse. As the US was still the clear leader in the realms of security, production, finance and knowledge, then its structural power and control over the international economic system was still very much evident.

In the aftermath of the collapse of the Soviet Union, the assertions made by Strange and Russett appeared vindicated as debate about US decline could not realistically be argued in a world where it was left as the only existing superpower (Cohen 2008: 77–79). This was not the end of the idea of the theory however. Indeed, as mentioned above, a version of Hegemonic Stability Theory now seemed to appear within the wider confines of International Relations theory itself. The emerging framework of 'unipolarity' suggested that the US was charged with leading the international political system as a whole. Therefore, US hegemony took on a new purpose. Back within IPE, the work of John Ikenberry has been notable. For Ikenberry, it was not 1944 or Bretton-Woods that was a mark of US hegemony but the end of the Cold War, which gave the US proportions of dominance not seen before in the modern state-system (Ikenberry 2004). Yet, as argued by Keohane before him, unless the US looked to use this dominance in order to build an international institutional system then it would struggle to maintain its supremacy. The various wars levelled by George W. Bush in the first decade of the twenty-first century might have appeared intended to stabilise potential hostilities within wider international society, but the rejection of institutional backing in favour of unilateral action in order to tackle such problems merely added to such struggles and put the unique American hegemonic position at risk (Ikenberry 2011).

The alternative understanding of hegemony was partly to emerge from the shortcoming evident within the positivism of Hegemonic Stability Theory. However, by the time Strange's criticisms appeared in the latter half of the 1980s, the foundations for such an alternative had already been made. Two highly influential pieces in the journal *Millennium* by Robert Cox in the early 1980s provide a new framework for understanding hegemony that drew in the Gramscian definition of the term. In responding to conventional readings within International Relations (IR), he argued that at the international level power structures are determined by a number of interrelated factors. Namely i) the organisation of production, ii) state formations and iii) the nature and for of social forces (Cox 1981: 137–142). These three factors define the character of world order at any one given historical time. Thus production defines which form of political economy is dominant at the international level; state formation determines what types of states exist within the state-system and social forces provide the ideological nature between and within states. These features would combine to form the basis of what we can term as a specific 'world order', which would be distinguished historically by their ruling characteristics. In this way, Cox appeared to draw heavily from Marx's classical understanding of historical materialism and also Gramsci's notion of historical blocs (Cox 1987).

Hegemony within Cox's understanding of world order was still reliant upon the nature of a leading state but the state in question looked to inspire a certain ideological framework rather than explicitly control it. Thus, the instabilities of the first half of the twentieth century that were illustrated by hegemonic stability theorists remain partly due to the lack of a leading state, but were more systematically down to the lack of a wider hegemonic framework evident at the international level (Cox 1983). The Gramscian understanding of hegemony was to become increasingly prominent with the end of the Cold War and with the emergence of the neoliberal world order and the manner in which neoliberal ideas were finding ascendency within institutional norms (Bieler and Morton 2001; Gill 1993, 2003; Murphy 1994; Rupert 1995, 2000). At the same time work was increasingly turning to Gramsci himself and Gramsci's own understand of the composition, manner and application of hegemony (Ayers 2008; Germain and Kenny 1997; McNally and Schwarzmantel 2009; Morton 2003, 2007; Worth 2011).

Gramsci's own use of hegemony was in relation to the use of the term developed within socialist theory that began in the nineteenth century (Worth 2015). In contrast to its use within the international state-system, here it referred to the revolutionary process required for socialist transformation. Hegemony therefore became both a strategy and a form of consciousness required to be developed within the wider process of socialism (Joseph 2002). Gramsci drew from these debates to build a theory of hegemony that unravelled the fortresses of civil society that he observed were strong in western forms of capitalism. In order to build a socialist hegemony, the many ideas, assumptions and forms of popular culture that facilitate capitalist society needed to be contested. Thus a 'war of position' was required in order for socialist ideas to win the hearts and minds of general society that would be geared around contesting what Gramsci referred to as the 'common-sense' of a specific hegemonic order (Gramsci 1971). In looking at the construction of hegemony, he also showed how class struggles between the dominant and subaltern classes develop whereby the former looks to maintain the character of such an order through the processes of coercion and – more favourably – consent. Thus for Gramscians the ways in which a hegemonic order is upheld and reproduced remains the main focus of study.

As has been oft-mentioned, Gramsci was largely – but not exclusively – commenting on the nation state as opposed to the international arena (Germain and Kenny 1997; Ives and Short 2013). Following Cox, the development of the neo-Gramscian accounts of hegemony has largely been focussed on looking at how the neoliberal post-Cold War order has been constructed and forged. Whether fused through institutional bodies that represent a form of neoliberal 'constitutionalism' (Gill 1995), or though transnational capital class formations (Van Der Pijl 1998) or from new forms of Imperialism (Harvey 2004), the emphasis for neo-Gramscians has been on how a specific form of capitalism in a specific period of history operates. Yet, at the same time, there does seem a certain amount of ambiguity in the way that hegemony at the international level is carried. Some see the process of hegemony largely being the result of a specific expression with the ruling classes, this neoliberalism being the 'ideological expression of the return of hegemony of the financial fraction of ruling classes' (Dumenil and Levy 2001). Others have focussed more upon the ideational manner in which hegemony has been fashioned – paying particular attention to the development of think tanks and organisations that have provided a platform for the construction and consolidation of norms (Cahill and Konings 2017; Peck 2010). Yet, the role of the US state still seems to play a significant position in the neo-Gramscian application of hegemony, yet at times, such a part is not fully defined (Worth 2015).

Box 16.2 Hegemony in the twenty-first century

- Hegemony can be understood in a number of different ways since the end of the Cold War.
- The US appeared to strengthen their influence on the international economy after the Cold War and so much attention is given to whether the US is strengthening its 'hegemony' over the international system or whether it appears to be waning.
- The rise of China as a contender state has taken considerable interest in the last two decade or so.
- Neoliberal hegemony has taken on increasingly important studies within the field of critical IPE since the end of the Cold War.
- In the aftermath of the global financial crisis, questions have been put to whether this form of neoliberal hegemony might be waning.

US hegemony or neoliberal hegemony?

As we have seen, the concept of hegemony in IPE has been a contested one in terms of meaning. In general we see one that refers to the US state and of state leadership and the other that tends to refer to the general workings of neoliberal capitalism. In the first case, as stated above, much work on hegemony in the decades that followed the end of the Cold War has moved towards the fields of strategic International Relations and towards those looking at conservative notions of hard power. As Cohen concedes in his study of the discipline, the idea of Hegemonic Stability Theory became marginalised after the Cold War due to the fact that the declinists were wrong (Cohen 2008: 78). Indeed, within the realm of journals such as *International Organizations*, discussions of hegemony have fallen from being at the heart of debate to being occasionally used as a term to describe dominant states asserting power in economic transactions over smaller states.[1] For Cohen, the decline of the centrality of hegemony was because the post-Cold War era of globalisation and international integration was 'not equated by hegemony but by market forces' (Cohen 2008: 79). The fact that such a development led to the very basis for the neo-Gramscian application of hegemony again shows the vastly different understandings adjacent perspectives have given to the term.

Despite these vast differences, the term, at least within IPE, has tended to be used in a manner that focusses on either US *or* neoliberal hegemony with often the two being interchangeable at the same time. Perhaps due to this imprecision, it has also been used within forms of constructivism in a manner that looks to provide an alternative model for the term (Hopf 2013). In the journal *Review of International Political Economy*, which was previously set up as a 'radical' outlet for critical or British forms of IPE in the 1990s, but has moved towards a more eclectic position since, hegemony has consistently provided a focal point in articles.[2] Again, while these appear inconsistent in terms of clarity and definition, there are synergies where certain examples can be used that bring together the notion of American and neoliberal hegemony. For example, the ideas and development of the so-called Washington Consensus provide us with an example whereby a mechanism was put in place that seemed to reflect both US and neoliberal forms of hegemony (Cerny 2008). Here, the US managed to use their majority voting rights at the World Bank to endorse a programme of loans to debt-torn countries dubbed 'structural adjustment programmes', which would see the World Bank write off a proposal of a state's debt on the condition that they facilitated fiscal discipline. In order for this to be met, states embarked upon radical liberalisation and privatisation policies, which led to them being compelled to open up their respective economies to international investors in order to meet the conditions of the loan (Gore 2000).

The case of the Washington Consensus provides us with an example where hegemony can be understood both ideologically and through state power leadership. Certainly in the 1990s, the Clinton administration embarked upon a number of initiatives that looked to forge US-inspired ideals within a number of international bodies. For example both the North American Free Trade Agreement (NAFTA) agreement and the World Trade Organization (WTO) all emerged during Clinton's period as President, alongside a doubling of United Nations (UN) Security Council resolutions and the re-orientation of the North Atlantic Treaty Organization (NATO). To return to Ikenberry, this strategy provides the most effective way of establishing US power within a hegemonic system. During that era, not only was the power of the US maintained and its position as the only superpower reinforced, but it looked towards international institutions to enshrine a new set of norms that would enhance the ideological underpinnings inherent within the traditions of the US state (Ikenberry 2006). For Ikenberry, who still regards himself as a 'hegemonic stability theorist', saw this as forming the basis of a 'liberal empire' whereby the US used the institutional apparatus to act against threats to a system as a whole, particular from states and actors that appeared to undermine its liberal character (Ikenberry 2011). As a result, while both Clinton and Obama have looked at institutionally forging such a system, the neo-Conservative approach taken by George W. Bush put it at risk.

If Ikenberry credits recent Democratic presidents for providing a framework for maintaining – or in the case of Obama to 'rehabilitate and adapt' US hegemony after the George W. Bush years (Ikenberry 2011: 309), then the same can be said for centre-left political parties outside the US when looking at the development of neoliberal hegemony. The endorsing of the so-called 'third way' approach to politics saw political parties such as the British Labour Party, the German SDP, the French Socialist Party and Presidents in Latin America such as Vicente Fox in Mexico and the former dependency theorist, Fernando Cardoso, all adopt a position that endorsed the principles of neoliberalism from a paradoxical position of social democracy. The 'third way' doctrine revised post-war principles of social democracy by arguing that its main objectives could be met by using and steering the market in a progressive manner. The inspiration for this came from the sociologist Anthony Giddens, whose *Third Way* manifesto argued that what should be considered as the main tenets of social democracy – full employment, greater inclusivity and welfare provision – which traditionally had been seen as needing the state in order to be facilitated, could be realised through the private sector in partnership with the state (Giddens 1998). Ultimately, this served to legitimise the principles of neoliberalism and strengthened its hegemony. By accepting the notion that market forces, as opposed to state intervention, provide the main premise for economic growth, both Keynesian understandings on economic intervention and socialist approaches to wealth redistribution were compromised (Worth 2015).

Thus the 1990s and 2000s saw the application of hegemony as an explanatory model within IPE played out alongside these different historical meanings of the term. Hegemony was also increasingly used consequentially, without reflecting upon the contested nature of the term itself. However, as we have seen in this section, there have been increasing synergies when looking at the term to explain US power/leadership and wider neoliberal ideology. Studies that have looked at the applications of hegemony have also suggested that while it is necessary to build upon the Gramscian understanding of hegemony, this does not mean that state leadership disappears into irrelevance (Worth 2015: 183–184). At the same time, the positivist methods used by hegemonic stability theorists in the 1970s and 1980s show us that any understanding of hegemony based solely upon the state is flawed. This is especially the case when crude forms of statistical evidence are used to substantiate such claims. It is also something that we need to be wary about when looking at any potential challenge to the contemporary hegemonic order.

The rise of China or counter-hegemony?

If the 1990s and the 2000s led to a number of studies about the development and sustainability of both US and neoliberal hegemony, then the last decade has led to a series of questions upon its fallibility. The global financial crisis that emerged in 2008 has led to a decade where the entire fabric of the neoliberal order has been contested. In the US, the commitment towards acting as a leader has become increasingly under threat from social developments within the country. This has been increasingly evident since the election of Donald Trump as leader. Indeed, if Ikenberry felt that George W. Bush up-picked the hegemonic position of the US by favouring state intervention over institutional procedure, then Trump threatens to tear it to shreds. Likewise, the austerity measures that were practiced across large parts of the world in light of the crisis has led to the fabric of neoliberal hegemony to be challenged in ways that it had not been before. Indeed, rather than look to expand and emphasise economic growth that had been the case previously, the ethos of neoliberalism seemed to go on the defensive (Worth 2013). While the previous two decades had to build upon assumptions that the global market provided wealth creation and productivity, governments now insisted that austerity was necessary in order to sustain economic life (Montgomerie 2016). Thus, when looking at the potential for hegemonic contestation and transformation it is useful to look at the arguments being forwarded both in terms of the emerging prominent states within the global economy and in terms of wider neoliberal ideology.

The rise of China has certainly led some to suggest that US hegemonic leadership might be on the wane. This has long been the observation and fear of post-Cold War neo-realist IR scholars, who have argued that China's role in challenging the US is inevitable (Kaplan 2005; Mearsheimer 2004). In terms of growth, China made significant economic gains during the 1990s and 2000s, leading it to become the second largest economy after the US and seeing it surpass the US in terms of foreign direct investment by 2012. In light of the financial crisis, China expanded its account surpluses and maintained an increase in its balance of trade, while advanced western capitalist states conversely continued to see an increase in deficits. In the aftermath of the financial crisis China became the leading foreign owner of US debt. Yet, these practices are hardly novel. Indeed, such transactions with dominant currencies are generally common-place in the international economy. Perhaps more significant has been in what some have seen as an alternative form of capitalism, which China has come to represent. Rather than pursue a neoliberal form, the Chinese model of capitalism appears to be one that is far more state-managed in its orientation (Arrighi 2007). Due to the increased influence Chinese investment has had in the developing world, such a model has been seen as one which is a viable alternative to the neoliberal economic model (Beeson 2010; Bisley 2011; Lampton 2008).

While China's economic model is still observed within the wider premise of socialism by the ruling Communist Party, its form of state-managed capitalism has been utilised in a manner that has been seen in developmental circles as challenging the market-led ideology inherent in the Washington Consensus. The 'Beijing Consensus' was a term that was characterised by the business executive Joshua Ramo while he was based in China in 2004 and has gained significance in recent years. Ramo argued that the Beijing alternative to economic growth was one that emphasised sustainability, a more even distribution of wealth and financial self-determinism as its wider philosophy (Ramo 2004). Writing as a retort after the financial crisis, John Williamson, the author of the Washington Consensus, suggested that the approach could be seen as favouring incremental reform, innovation, export-led growth, state capitalism and was authoritarian in nature (Williamson 2012). It was these main positions that differed from the free market conditionality of the neoliberal model. With China's influence growing and in light of Trump's retreat from trade negotiations such as the Trans-Pacific Partnership, the model has taken greater significance.

Yet, it can also be argued that China's entry into the global economy has merely served to add another clog to the neoliberal hegemonic regime. Rather than offering a firm alternative, the Chinese state has looked to provide cheap labour for the multinational firms that drive the global free market economy (Dirlik 2007). By retaining state control over such a labour force, firms have thus found China an attractive destination in which to invest. As a result, China's economy has become reliant upon foreign direct investment in order to develop. In this way they have merely residing within the wider market system. Indeed, some go further with this argument. David Harvey for example in his book *A Brief History of Neoliberalism* argues that the Chinese have explicitly pursued a neoliberal model in tandem with the west, describing it as 'neoliberalism with Chinese characteristics' (Harvey 2005: 120–152).

Ideological forms of contestation have conversely been understood at a wider level in terms of counter-hegemony. Although not a concept that Gramsci used himself, as his main focus was in building a hegemonic society for socialism to develop, 'counter-hegemony' has been commonly used across wider Gramscian subjects across the social sciences and indeed was the term favoured by Cox himself in his second *Millennium* piece (Carroll and Ratner 1994; Cox 1983). Here, a collection of social forces within state–societal complexes configure themselves to contest the fabric of the hegemonic order by constructing an oppositional position. While Cox himself was particularly interested in exploring this potential within the leading state (in other words the US), the growth of global civil society prompted Stephen Gill (possibly the most notable Gramscian after Cox in IPE and associated with the new constitutionalist literature) to suggest that, as Gramsci used the term 'modern Prince' to historicise Machiavelli's metaphorical Prince to twentieth-century socialism, then a 'post-modern Prince' could be used here (Gill 2000). The literature on resistance within IPE was apparent long before the financial crisis and had looked at how the era of neoliberal economic globalisation produced opportunities for transnational movements and campaigns to contest the dominant order (Amoore 2005; Chin and Mittelman 2000). This was even more evident with the advent of bodies such as the World Social Forum that was geared towards creating a space for such counter-hegemonic discourses to build (Fisher and Ponniah 2003).

After the financial crisis, the fabric of neoliberalism was immediately put under question with the general consensus across governments conceding that the crash had been brought about by too little regulation of the global market. Yet, a decade after the crisis, discontent has become more increasingly evident from those on the right of the political spectrum. The rise of populist right-wing parties, individuals and governments, emphasised right the way up to the pinnacle of global politics with the election of Donald Trump, has seen the neoliberal order not contested by any form of 'postmodern socialism' as such, but by a disjointed renewal of nationalism and populism (Worth 2019). Due to the ambiguous nature of such movements vis a vis free market economics, it remains difficult to suggest that this trend serves to strengthen the general position of the neoliberal order or places it under significant strain (Davidson and Saull 2017). In either case, the contradictions over the nature of the neoliberal order have been such that those who have looked to defend and deepen its hegemonic legacy have ended up opening up a set of nationalist forces capable of de-railing it. A good example here can be seen with the fallout of the Brexit referendum in the UK, where free marketers pushed for an exit in order to foresee an economy that appeared less regulated from the EU, but opened up and unleashed a set of nationalist social forces at the same time (Hopkin 2017). While this has brought greater instability, it has also seen oppositional forces on the left in retreat with social democratic parties fairing notably badly in elections across Europe. In South America, where the 'pink tide' ushered in a number of left-wing politicians a decade earlier, the right have also fought back and become more prominent; a position taken to the extreme with the election of Bolsonaro in Brazil.

The instabilities that have been evident since the financial crisis have therefore placed greater tension on the neoliberal hegemonic order and further questioned its legitimacy. While traditional political parties on the left have fared badly (with the notable exceptions of individuals within such parties such as with Jeremy Corbyn in the UK Labour Party and Bernie Sanders within the US democratic movement) the increase of resistance groups have become notable, particularly through anti-austerity protest movements within civil society that have explicitly contested austerity politics (Bailey, Clua-Losada, Huke and Ribera-Almandoz 2018; Fishwick and Connolly 2018). This has led to further questions over the longevity of neoliberalism in its present form and of whether the world order itself can be considered to be in a wider process of transformation. As with previous discussions, the prominence of China and the Beijing consensus is also relevant here and we can see how the rise of contender states alongside their interest in the state-management of capitalism can play further into the contestation of capitalism. From the Trump-led protectionists on the right to civil contestation on the left, instabilities have emerged to place strain on the neoliberal system in a manner that might complement the different approach to political economy emphasised by China and others and lead to wholescale systemic transformation. In considering this further, hegemony has increasingly had another dimension within the study of IPE in the sense that the emergence of regional arrangements have provided their own state leadership. This provides us with another avenue of contemplation when looking at the hegemonic longevity of the neoliberal global order itself (Destradi 2010).

Box 16.3 Regional hegemony

- The term regional hegemony applies to states that try to influence a specific region.
- Becoming increasingly significant as regions and regionalism become increasingly important in IPE.
- Often used to show how regional powerhouses such as China, Brazil, India and Russia assert their economic influence over a region.
- Has also been used in the case of the EU to account for German influence.

Regional hegemony or variegated neoliberalism?

The idea of regional hegemony can also, to a degree, be separated into the different meanings of state and ideology. Are regional entities being increasing led by one particular state or have such influence states within a specific region looked to create a counter-hegemonic construct that seeks to contest the wider dynamics of neoliberalism? The BRICS (Brazil, Russia, India, China, South Africa) have been institutionally considered to be respective 'spokespersons' and leaders of their respective regions, but how valid are they as potential hegemonic game changers as such? The role of China was discussed above, but East Asia itself has provided an environment in the past where hegemonic conditions have been build and contested (Beeson 2009). The Cold War saw a number of Communist states set up, with the Association of Southeast Asian Nations (ASEAN) being constructed as an anti-Communist body that resisted its spread. The influence of China saw ASEAN emerge as a post-Cold War body that looked to check the power of China, yet greater free trade agreements in recent years have seen closer relations between the two. Indeed, the authoritarian-led forms of capitalism implicit within many ASEAN members is strongly compatible with the Beijing consensus that suggests an ideological convergence as opposed to one that contests Chinese influence.

Russia and India have perhaps stronger claims to assert economic dominance over a specific region, yet in the case of the latter, profound instability with its neighbours has left any claims towards regional hegemony redundant. The pink tide in South America might have looked towards Brazil as an inspiration leader at some level. The rise of the Worker's Party, the setting up of the WTO and Brazilian's representation at BRIC(S)[3] summits might reinforce this view. Yet, if it does, the election of Bolsonaro has put pay to the notion that Brazil might maintain a counter-hegemony attack on the contours of US-inspired neoliberalism. Yet, the importance of Brazil in the South American region is such that it would suggest that while the election of Bolsonaro certainly did not start the reversal of pink tide within the region, his increased prominence has seemingly certainly led to its eradication as a potential form of regional opposition (Gonzalez 2018). This brings us to another question. Whether the different forms of regional-led projects actually seem to provide us with different models of neoliberalism as opposed to different models of capitalism along the lines of the Beijing consensus. This is turn would suggest that while contestation remains significant, in light of the recent developments in world politics, the idea that competing models from forms of regionalism might result in some form of hegemonic challenge might not necessarily be apparent.

The idea of variated neoliberalism is one that draws partly from the variety of capitalism literature (Hall and Soskice 2001). Used to make sense of the different spatial levels that exist within the international capitalist system, essentially it suggests that neoliberalism has been developed through a number of waves and applied unevenly (Brenner et al. 2010). The geographical dimension of space is one that sees the understanding of free market hegemony not being reinforced at either the global or the national level, but at different spatial levels of society. The post-crisis move to reconstruct and defend neoliberalism has been testament to this as some states and areas have seen institutions appear more interventionist as a means to protect the market system while others have adopted a more ideological laissez-faire position (Jessop 2012; Macartney 2010). Regionally this explains the seemingly different approaches to the global economy. For example, while the state-managed Chinese system of capitalism might appear to offer an alternative to neoliberalism, it can also be understood as another variant. For the Chinese state might look to interfere in the economy in a manner that is fundamentally at odds with the 'invisible hand' approach to the market, yet it appears to do this in order to gain wider dividends from the global neoliberal system itself (Birch and Mykhnenko 2010). The state and other regulatory financial bodies thus provide different forms of means in order to facilitate the wider neoliberal market place.

The concept of variegated neoliberalism appears to suggest that hegemony is forged at different levels and through different means in order to gain the same neoliberal results. But that does not mean that it is in any way less contested. Indeed, as Stuart Hall once observed, the contours of hegemony are consistently shifting and need continual work in order to sustain consent and legitimacy (Hall 1988). Therefore, different forms of contestation can be seen at different spatial levels in global society, resulting in different conclusions. It also explains that how in the instability of the post-crisis atmosphere, populism and authoritarianism have emerged, some of which rely on coercive means for support (Bruff 2014). Again, as we have seen, while hegemony in its different interpretations does inhibit certain forms of coercion any reliance upon it, as we saw from Thucydides, often leads to chaos. This only adds to the levels of contestation.

Questions around regional forms of hegemony can thus be understood in a number of ways within IPE. First, it can refer to how specific regions rely upon one leading state in order to function coherently. In this sense, regions can be viewed almost as regional versions of hegemonic stability system. Second, they can be seen at the wider global level as a form of challenge to the hegemonic practices inherent within the current world order. Finally, we can see how different regions and states in the world can adopt different political strategies in order to forge variants of neoliberalism. As a result, neoliberalism both retains its position as a hegemonic process, but metaphases itself in different forms that in turn can open up contrasting forms of contestation. Studies into regional forms of hegemonic expression provide avenues that both add to and provide new areas for the focus of hegemony in IPE.

Conclusion

This chapter has looked to outline the various ways hegemony has been applied and understood within IPE. It suggests that the concept has been central to both debates and the general understanding of explaining how the International Political Economy functions. Increasingly the term has been used in a manner that does not often explain how it is intended. As we have seen here, IPE as it emerged in the 1970s placed the notion of hegemony at its heart. The question and debates around Hegemonic Stability Theory dominated what is now referred to in light of Cohen's history of the discipline as the American School (Cohen 2008). Yet, conversely, it has largely been from the so-called British School where hegemony as a concept has been developed. As the end of the Cold War seemed to suggest that the arguments that US economic hegemony was in decline were premature, few of its proponents continued to use the logistics that it set up. With certain exceptions (for example John Ikenberry), few looked to revisit the main claim of Hegemonic Stability Theory itself – that an economic system is more stable when one state leads or dominates over others.

The main feature of hegemony in IPE is that it remains a contested term. In general, when the term is used in contemporary debate it either refers to the prominence of the US state or the ideology of the neoliberal system (Worth 2015). As I have explained here at the beginning of the chapter, both of these have different historical roots and emerged for different reasons. Increasingly, a form of convergence, particularly in the more critical understanding of the term within the British School, has generally understood hegemony in IPE to be a US-inspired system geared around the ideology of neoliberalism. In the area of regionalism, it has also been used within regional sub-systems, which again looks at both dominant states and/or ideologies and whether these are in allegiance with the dominant practices at the wider global level. As a result, hegemony remains a key concept within IPE, particularly in looking at the systemic development and transformative of its workings as a whole.

Starting from a position where hegemony was a central mechanism that showed how international economy worked and functioned, the concept has developed towards one that provides new avenues for understanding the way power is formed, produced and contested in the global political economy. It provides us, no matter how it has been applied, with a useful framework of how world order transforms over time. As a concept is thus remains very important to the study of IPE and will continue to stimulate new studies and debates.

Notes

1 Indeed a simple word search of the term on the *International Organizations* website shows how it dominated debate in the 1970s and 1980s but diminished as a 'key word' within articles after that.
2 A similar search on the RIPE website provides over 250 articles where hegemony was a key word. Here, while there are numerous articles in the radical early years of the journal that focus on ideological forms of hegemony, there has been a steady and consistent set of articles since that seem to use the term both primarily as a term of American power, neoliberal power and regionally.
3 The first BRIC summit was held in 2009 and it did not become the BRICS until South Africa was added for the 2011 summit.

Bibliography

Amoore, L. *Globalisation and the Politics of Resistance*. London: Routledge.

Arrighi, G. 2007. *Adam Smith in Beijing: Lineages of the Twenty-First Century*. London: Verso.

Ayers, A. (ed.). 2008. *Gramsci, Political Economy and International Relations Theory.* , Basingstoke: Palgrave.

Bailey, D., Clua-Losada, M., Huke, N. and Ribera-Almandoz, O. 2018. *Beyond Defeat and Austerity*. London: Routledge.

Beeson, M. 2009. Hegemonic Transition in East Asia? The Dynamics of Chinese and American Power. *Review of International Studies* 35 (1): 95–112.

Beeson, M. 2010. There are alternatives: The Washington Consensus vs State Capitalism. In M. Beeson and N. Bisley (eds) *Issues in 21st Century World Politics*. Basingstoke: Palgrave.

Bieler, A. and Morton, A. (eds). 2001. *Social Forces in the Making of the New Europe*. Basingstoke: Palgrave.

Birch, K. and Mykhnenko, V. (eds). 2010. *The Rise and Fall of Neoliberalism: The Collapse of an Economic Crisis?* London: Zed Books.

Bisley, N. 2011 Biding and Hiding No Longer: A More Assertive China Rattles the Region. *Global Asia* 6 (4): 62–73.

Brenner, N., Peck, J. and Theodore, N. 2010. Variegated Neoliberalisation: Geographies, Modalities, Pathways. *Global Networks* 10 (2): 182–222.

Bruff, I. 2014. The Rise of Authoritarian Neoliberalism. *Rethinking Marxism* 26 (1): 113–129.

Cahill, D. and Konings, A. 2017. *Neoliberalism*. Cambridge: Cambridge University Press.

Carroll, W. and Ratner, R. 1994 Between Leninism and Radical Pluralism: Gramscian Reflections on Counter-Hegemony and the New Social Movements. *Critical Sociology* 20 (2): 3–26.

Cerny, P. 2008. Embedding Neoliberalism: The Evolution of a Hegemonic Paradigm. *The Journal of International Trade and Diplomacy* 2 (1): 1–46.

Chin, C. and Mittelman, J. 2000. Conceptualising resistance to globalization. In: B. Gills (ed.) *Globalization and the Politics of Resistance*. Basingstoke: Palgrave: 29–47.

Cohen, B. 2008. *International Political Economy: An Intellectual History*. New York: Princeton University Press.

Cox, R. 1981. Social Forces, States and World Order: Beyond International Relations Theory. *Millennium* 10 (2): 126–155.

Cox, R. 1983. Gramsci, Hegemony and International Relations: An Essay in Method. *Millennium* 12 (2): 162–175.

Cox, R. 1987. *Power, Production and World Order: Social Forces in the Making of History*. New York: Columbia University Press.

Davidson, N. and Saull, R. 2017. Neoliberalism: A Contradictory Embrace. *Critical Sociology* 43: 4–5, 707–724.

Destradi, S. 2010. Regional Powers and Their Strategies: Empire, Hegemony and Leadership. *Review of International Studies* 36 (4): 903–930.

Dirlik, A. 2007. *Global Modernity: Modernity in the Age of Capitalism*. Boulder: Paradigm Press.

Dumenil, G. and Levy, D. 2001 Costs and Benefits of Neoliberalism: A Class Analysis. *Review of International Political Economy* 8 (4): 578–607.

Ferguson, N. 2003. Hegemony or Empire. *Foreign Affairs* 82 (5): 154–161.

Fisher, W. and Ponniah, T. (eds). 2003. *Another World is Possible: Popular Alternatives to Globalization at the World Social Forum*. London: Zed Books.

Fishwick, A. and Connolly, H. (eds). 2018. *Austerity and Working Class Resistance*. London: Rowman & Littlefield.

Germain, R. and Kenny, M. 1997. Engaging Gramsci: International Relations Theory and the New Gramscians. *Review of International Studies* 24 (1): 3–21.

Giddens, A. 1998. *The Third Way: The Renewal of Social Democracy*. Cambridge: Polity Press.

Gill, S. (ed.). 1993. *Gramsci, Historical Materialism and International Relations*. Cambridge: Cambridge University Press.

Gill, S. 1995. Globalisation, Market Civilisation and Disciplinary Neoliberalism. *Millennium* 24 (3): 399–423.

Gill, S. 2000. Towards a Post-Modern Prince? The Battle in Seattle as a Moment in the New Politics of Globalisation. *Millennium: Journal of International Studies* 29 (1): 131–140.

Gill, S. 2003. *Power and Resistance in the New World Order*. Basingstoke: Palgrave.

Gilpin, R. 1981. *War and Change in World Politics*. Cambridge: Cambridge University Press.

Gonzalez, M. 2018. *The Ebb of the Pink Tide: The Decline of the Left in Latin American*. London: Pluto Press.

Gore, C. 2000. The Rise and Fall of the Washington Consensus as a Paradigm for Developing Countries. *World Development* 28 (5): 789–804.

Gramsci, A. 1971. *Selections from the Prison Notebooks*. London: Lawrence and Wishart.

Hall, P. and Soskice, D. 2001. *Varieties of Capitalism: The Institutional Foundations of Comparative Advantage*. Oxford: Oxford University Press.

Hall, S. 1988. *The Hard Road to Renewal*. London: Verso.

Harries, O. 2003. *Benign or Imperial? Reflections on American Hegemony*. Sydney: ABC Books.

Harvey, D. 2004. *The New Imperialism*. Oxford: Oxford University Press.

Harvey, D. 2005. *A Brief History of Neoliberalism*. Oxford: Oxford University Press.

Hopf, T. 2013. Common-Sense Constructivism and Hegemony in World Politics. *International Organizations* 67 (2): 317–354.

Hopkin, J. 2017. When Polanyi met Farage: Market Fundamentalism, Economic Nationalism and Britain's Exit from the European Union. *British Journal of Politics and International Relations* 19 (3): 465–478.

Ikenberry, J. 2004. Liberalism and Empire: Logics of Order in the American Unipolar Age'. *Review of International Studies* 30 (4): 609–630.

Ikenberry, J. 2006. *Liberal Order and Imperial Ambition: Essays on American Power and International Order*. Cambridge: Polity.

Ikenberry, J. 2011. *Liberal Leviathan: The Origins, Crisis and Transformation of the America World Order*. Princeton: Princeton University Press.

Ives, P. and Short, N. 2013. On Gramsci and the International. *Review of International Studies* 39 (3): 621–642.

Jessop, B. 2012. The world market, variegated capitalism and the crisis of European integration. In: P. Nousios, H. Overbeek and A. Tsolakis (eds) *Globalization and European Integration: Critical Approaches to Regional Order and International Relations*. London: Routledge.

Joseph, J. 2002. *Hegemony: A Realist Analysis*. London: Routledge

Kagan, R. 2008. *The Return to History and the End of Dreams*. New York: Vintage.

Kaplan, R. 2005. Why Would We Fight China? *The Atlantic Monthly* June.

Keohane, R. 1984. *After Hegemony: Cooperation and Discord in the World Political Economy*. Princeton: Princeton University Press.

Kindleberger, C. 1973. *The World in Depression 1929–1939*. Berkeley: University of California Press.

Kindleberger, C. 1981. Dominance and Leadership in the International Economy. *International Studies Quarterly* 25: 242–254.

Kindleberger, C. 1983. On the Rise and Decline of Nations. *International Studies Quarterly* 27: 5–10.

Lampton, D. 2008. *The Three Faces of Chinese Power: Money, Might and Minds*. Berkeley: University of California Press

Lebow, R. and Kelly, R. 2001. Thucydides and Hegemony: Athens and the United States. *Review of International Studies* 27 (4): 593–609.

Macartney, H. 2010. *Variegated Neoliberalism: EU Varieties of Capitalism and International Political Economy*. London: Routledge.

McNally, M. and Schwarzmantel, J. (eds) 2009. *Gramsci and Global Politics: Hegemony and Resistance*. London: Routledge.

Mearsheimer, J. 2004. The Rise of China will not be Peaceful at All. *The Australian* November 18.

Montgomerie, J. 2016. Austerity and the Household: The Politics of Economic Storytelling. *British Politics* 11 (4): 418–437.

Morton, A. 2003. Historizing Gramsci: Situating Ideas in and beyond Their Context. *Review of International Political Economy* 10 (1): 118–146.

Morton, A. 2007. *Unravelling Gramsci: Hegemony and Passive Revolution in the Global Economy*. London: Pluto Press.

Murphy, C. 1994. *International Organization and Industrial Change*. Cambridge: Polity Press.

Peck, J. 2010. *Constructions of Neoliberal Reason*. Oxford: Oxford University Press.

Pijl, van der, K. 1998. *Transnational Classes and International Relations*. London: Routledge.

Ramo, J. 2004. *The Beijing Consensus*. London: Foreign Policy Centre.

Rupert, M. 1995. *Producing Hegemony: The Politics of Mass Production and AmericanGlobal Power*. New York: Cambridge University Press.

Rupert, M. 2000. *Ideologies of Globalization*. London: Routledge.

Russett, B. 1985. The Mysterious Case of Vanishing Hegemony; or, is Mark Twain Really Dead? *International Organizations* 39 (2): 207–231.

Strange, S. 1987. The Persistent Myth of Lost Hegemony. *International Organizations* 41 (4): 551–274.

Thucydides. 1972. *History of the Peloponnesian War*. London: Penguin.

Wickersham, J. 1994. *Hegemony and Greek Historians*. London: Rowman & Littlefield.

Williamson, J. 2012. Is the "Beijing Consensus" Now Dominant? *Asia Policy* 13: 1–16.

Worth, O. 2011. Recasting Gramsci in International Politics. *Review of International Studies* 37 (1): 373–393.

Worth, O. 2013. *Resistance in the era of Austerity: Nationalism, the Failure of the Left and the Return of God*. London: Zed Books.

Worth, O. 2015. *Rethinking Hegemony*. Basingstoke: Palgrave.

Worth, O. 2019. *Morbid Symptoms: The Global Rise of the Far-Right*. London: Zed Books.

17

Ghosts, pluriverse and hopes

From "development" to post-development

Alberto Acosta and John Cajas-Guijarro

Introduction: the relevance of post-development

The world lives a systemic, multiple and asymmetrical crisis. That crisis is induced mostly by the contradictions coming from the capitalist logic of permanent accumulation of economic value and power; a process sustained through exploitation of human and natural life and, consequently, through continuous violations of social and environmental bounds. Although those contradictions have created a "global crisis not manageable within existing institutional frameworks" (Kothari et al. 2019: xxiii), capitalist civilization has achieved the capacity – almost in a hegemonic sense – to present capital accumulation as a good-in-itself, as a synonymous of "development" (see Acosta and Cajas-Guijarro 2015: 133–134).

Such a role given to the term "development" – as part of the glorification of accumulation – makes it understandable why it is usually reduced to "economic growth" (a process needed to guarantee the expanded reproduction of capital). Thus, the conception of "development" as "linear, unidirectional, material, and financial growth, driven by commodification and capitalists' markets" is not accidental but a legitimizing device of the "modern colonial capitalist patriarchal world system" (Kothari et al. 2019: xxii–xxiii).

Given this origin, it is crucial to abandon "development" and its reformist policies impregned by a seductive rhetoric – sometimes named as "developmentality" or "developmentalism" (see Deb 2009; Kothari et al. 2019: xxi) – if we want to prevent a social and natural collapse. To achieve this, "development as a regime of representation" and "the Western economy as a system of production, power and signification" must be replaced by "different subjectivities" and "hybrid, creative, autonomous alternatives to it," alternatives grouped by the broad name of *post-development* (Escobar 2012: 216–221, cited by Asher and Wainwright 2019: 30)[1] and focused on the transition toward post-capitalism through the construction of a *pluriverse*: "a world where many worlds fit" as the Zapatistas of Chiapas clearly propose; a "transition toward plural ways of making the world" (Escobar 2018: 7) in a complete *relational*[2] *harmony* among human beings and between them and Nature.

Post-development is a position in permanent construction and rethinking, and because of that, it has received some critiques.[3] Nonetheless, its main objective of building a pluriverse in relational social and natural harmony feeds the hope to find alternatives against the rhetoric

---

Box 17.1 Post-development

A broad term that groups different subjectivities and hybrid, creative, autonomous *alternatives to "development,"* focused in the construction of a post-capitalist *pluriverse* (a world where many worlds fit, that is, a transition toward plural ways of making the world) in a complete relational harmony among human beings and between them and Nature.

---

of "development" and, more important, against the ghosts and death coming from the dynamics of the capitalist accumulation. Those alternatives may come from all the theoretical and concrete experiences (marxism, feminism, anticolonialism, ecologism and so on) which try to create a new *bio-centric* socio-natural system where all living beings, human or not human, have the same ontological value and the same right to live in dignity and without suffering any kind of exploitation to feed capital and power. Thus, post-development not only overcomes "development" but also questions the entire capitalist civilization that suffocates life and everything to do with it, as the Ecuadorian philosopher Bolívar Echeverría (2010) affirmed.

The understanding of the relevance of post-development in the prevention of the collapse seeded by the contradictions of – capitalist – "development" is urgent. A first step in this sense is to get a clear idea of why "development" is just an unreachable ghost, why it is just a *myth* (as many other myths created by the economic and social thinking dominated by capital, like the myth of *free market*[4]).

Development, an unreachable ghost with a "developmentalist reason"

Since the mid-twentieth century a ghost has traversed the world … that ghost is "development." Without denying the validity of a long-standing process by which human beings have attempted to satisfy their needs in the best way, we accept that the global mandate of "developmentalism" was institutionalized on January 20, 1949. Then, the President of the United States, Harry Truman, in the inaugural speech of his second term of office to Congress, defined the greater part of the world as "*underdeveloped areas.*" In "point four" of his address[5] he affirmed that

> we must embark on a bold new program for making the benefits of our scientific advances and industrial progress available for the improvement and growth of underdeveloped areas. More than half the people of the world are living in conditions approaching misery. Their food is inadequate. They are victims of disease. Their economic life is primitive and stagnant. Their poverty is a handicap and a threat both to them and to more prosperous areas. For the first time in history, humanity possesses the knowledge and skill to relieve the suffering of these people.

In a few words Truman set down a powerful ideological mandate:

> Our aim should be to help the free peoples of the world, through their own efforts, to produce more food, more clothing, more materials for housing, and more mechanical power to lighten their burdens. It must be a worldwide effort for the achievement of peace,

plenty, and freedom. With the cooperation of business, private capital, agriculture, and labour in this country, this program can greatly increase the industrial activity in other nations and can raise substantially their standards of living.

The old imperialism – exploitation for foreign profit – has no place in our plans. What we envisage is a program of development based on the concepts of democratic fair-dealing.

Thus, the head of state of the world's most powerful country – conscious that especially the United States and other industrialized nations were "at the top of the evolutionary social ladder" (Sachs 1996) – announced that all societies would have to walk the same path (which would serve as the basis for Walt Whitman Rostow's (1959) stages theory) and aspire to a single goal that, incidentally, became also the conceptual basis for another form of imperialism: "development."

The metaphor of "development," appropriated from the natural world, acquired a rare vigour. It transformed into a goal to be achieved by all Humanity. It became a global mandate that involved the spread of the North American model of society, heir of many European values (although Truman was assuredly not fully aware of the transcendence of his speech). Here it is worth remembering, following Koldo Unceta (2014), that

> when Adam Smith wrote The Wealth of Nations, the debate on development that is today ongoing was in some way "inaugurated".[6] Prior to that, other thinkers – from Kautilya in ancient India, to Aristotle in Classical Greece, or Saint Augustine in medieval Europe – had theorized about the chances, or lack thereof, of certain actions or decisions when it came to achieving greater prosperity for citizens, countries, and kingdoms, and for their inhabitants. However, it would not be until the eighteenth century when, at the hands of enlightened thinking, a rational and universal perspective on these issues would begin to clear a path.
>
> With it, a development of knowledge would prevail that was increasingly emancipated from religion, as would a global understanding that was capable of going beyond the particular views influenced by local beliefs.[7]

After World War II, when the Cold War was getting under way – and during the rise of the nuclear threat and terror – the debate on "development" consolidated a structure of dichotomous domination: "developed," "underdeveloped," rich–poor, advanced–backward, civilized–savage. Even from critical positions that duality became indisputable: core-periphery.

A result of this process can be named as "developmentalist reason": the use of reason and any other means – in an instrumental sense[8] – to become "developed" at any cost (in a reductionist version the main focus is given to "economic growth"). As a result of this "developmentalist reason" flourished plans, programs, projects, theories, "development" manuals and methodologies, as well as banks specialized to finance "development," "development" aid, "development" training and education, communication for "development" and so on.

Box 17.2 Developmentalist reason

A form of instrumental reasoning focused to achieve "development" (a global mandate) at any cost (in a reductionist version the main focus is given to "economic growth").

At the height of the Cold War, around "development" evolved the confrontation between "capitalism" and "communism." The Third World was invented. And its members became pawns of the international geopolitical chess. Both sides, the left and the right, establishing specificities and differences, get trapped in the "developmentalist reason." Across the globe, communities and societies were – and continue to be – reordered under the myth of "development." This became the common fate of Humanity, a non-negotiable obligation, almost a global religion.

But, behind the scenes, and in the name of "development," central or developed countries continued with their various interventions and operations that interfered in the internal affairs of the peripheral, "underdeveloped" or poor countries. Even "development aid policies" were a sort of continuance of former colonial policies. For instance, in recent times we have seen recurrent economic interventions by the International Monetary Fund (IMF) and the World Bank, and even military actions legitimized by the rhetoric of bringing "development" (freedom, democracy and so on) to "backward" countries, when actually those actions only try to protect those countries from the influence of any rival power.

Meanwhile, the poor countries, in an act of generalized subordination and submission, accepted this as long as they were considered "developing countries." In the exclusive circles of diplomacy and international institutions it is not common to speak of "underdeveloped" countries, and less common to accept that they are poor or peripheral, even in the quest for "development." This has sense since the term "underdeveloped" gained a peculiar sense especially when people like André Gunder Frank (1970; 1979) (German economist–sociologist and relevant thinker of the dependency theories) proposed the idea that "underdevelopment" of some countries would be the result of the "development" of others (*"development of underdevelopment"*); a process sustained, for instance, through mechanisms like *unequal exchange* (see Amín 1970; Emmanuel 1969).

Box 17.3 Development of underdevelopment

Idea (proposed by people like André Gunder Frank) that "underdevelopment" of some countries would be the result of the "development" of others.

Putting away the idea of "development of underdevelopment," countries deemed as "backward" accepted the application of multiple policies, instruments and indicators in order to break out their "backwardness" and become "developed." Thus, many countries accepted – and keep accepting – the "developmentalist reason" and try to follow an imaginary path mapped out by already "developed" countries. How many have achieved it? Very few if we accept that what they achieved was indeed "development" (because even the term – until now – has no clear definition).

When problems began to undermine the faith in "development" and its "grand theory" began to leak on all sides, descriptions or names were added to the term, trying to create differentiations which improve the legitimizing role of the term: "economic development," "social development," "local development," "global development," "rural development," "sustainable development," "eco-development," "ethno-development," "human scale development," "endogenous development," "development with gender equality," "co-development," "transformative development" ...

It is worth pointing out that Latin America was relevant in generating controversial revisions to "development," such as *structuralism*, the different *dependency theories*, and other more recent

positions. These unorthodox positions and critiques have great importance, but also have limitations. On the one hand, their proposals did not seriously question the conceptual core intuition
behind "development": the western notion of *progress* generally perceived as an – almost monotonous – ascension of mankind toward perfection (see Nisbet 2009); and when they questioned
it they could not abandon *anthropocentrism* (Acosta 2013a). On the other hand, each of these
questionings generated a wave of revisions that could not come together and link up with each
other. In some cases, they generated a peak in the critiques and even in the proposals, but soon
after, these efforts languished.

Box 17.4 Progress

Western notion generally perceived as an – almost monotonous – ascension of mankind toward
perfection.

It took time to realize that the big issue is not about accepting one or other path toward "development." The difficulty stems from the concept. "Development," as a global and unifying proposal – moved by the western notion of progress – is utterly unaware of the dreams and struggles
of those condemned to "underdevelopment." The – sometimes even brutal – denial of this was
often the result of direct or indirect action by the "developed" nations; clear examples are the
destructive activities of colonization or which have the IMF policies as modern representants.

"Development," insofar as reproducing the lifestyles of "core" countries, is unrepeatable on
a global scale. Moreover, that consumerist and predatory way of life threatens global ecological
balances and increasingly marginalizes masses of human beings from the (supposed) advantages
of the – never attainable – "development." Despite undeniable technological advances, not
even hunger has been eradicated from the world and the problem is not a lack of food production: according to Food and Agriculture Organization (FAO), in a world where obesity and
hunger coexist, each year more than 1.3 billion tonnes of perfectly edible food, that could feed
3 billion people, are wasted (670 million in the Global North and 630 million in the Global
South, including the poorest countries on the planet).[9] 70 percent of cereals traded in the world
are under speculative logics. Food is produced for cars (agrofuel or biofuel). Only as an example,
profit interests, deficiencies of infrastructure and even mistaken public policy, seem to cause that
in India a third of food goes bad before it reaches the consumer; this happens although there is
an important program to provide food for the poor within the country (see Basu 2018).

Increasingly, land mass is dedicated to monocultures causing a rapid loss of biodiversity.
Genetically modified organisms and their technologies do their own thing. Since the beginning
of the twentieth century this situation has led to the loss of 75 percent of vegetable genetic
diversity. According to the German Ministry of Agriculture, 30 percent of seeds are in danger
of extinction. While 75 percent of the world's food comes from 12 species of plants and five
species of animals, just three species – rice, corn and wheat – contribute about 60 percent of the
calories and proteins obtained by humans from plants. Barely 4 percent of the 250,000 or
300,000 species of known plants is used by human beings. According to Maristella Svampa
(Brand 2016), in Argentina 22 of the 33 million hectares available for agriculture were con-
verted into transgenic soybean crops. And in this scenario, when hunger assails more than a
billion people in the world, we see how large transnational food conglomerates – such as Mon-
santo – use the control of seed to concentrate their power. Water is another resource at risk,
presenting enormous inequality in its distribution and its increasingly unjustifiable use.

Although "development" has in the notion of progress its main *raison d'être*, in reality it seems the world undergoes a generalized *"bad development"* (including those countries considered "developed"). José María Tortosa (2011) points out that:

> The functioning of the contemporary world system is "bad development" (…). The reason is easy to understand: it is a system based on an efficiency that tries to maximize results, reduce costs and achieve an incessant accumulation of capital (…). If "anything goes", the problem is not who is playing or why, the problem is the rules of the game itself. In other words, the world system has been badly developed as a result of its own logic and it is to this logic that we must look.

Now, as multiple simultaneous crises (distributional, financial, alimentary, migratory, environmental and so on) swamp the world, we discover that the ghost of "development" has provoked and continues to provoke disastrous consequences. "Developmentalist reason" may have no real content, but it can justify the means and even the failures. To get "developed" most of the globe has accepted the rules of *"anything goes."*[10] All is tolerated in the name of eschewing "underdevelopment" and all is tolerated in the name of progress. All is sanctified in the name of such a lofty and promising goal: "to be like them" (Galeano 1997), to be like the "developed" – our superiors – we must accept that *"any sacrifice goes."* This is exactly what makes the "developmentalist reason" a kind of *instrumental reason* where the efficiency to achieve an – impossible – end can become even more important than the life of those who are supposed to be "saved" …

Box 17.5 Bad development

Term used to denote that the path toward "development" has created a situation where multiple crises (distributional, financial, alimentary, migratory, environmental and so on) swamp the world.

Thus, environmental and social devastation are accepted in exchange for achieving "development." One terrible example is the acceptance of the grievous social and ecological destruction caused by mega-mining even when it strengthens the system of extractivist accumulation (inherited from colonial times), and when it reinforces "underdevelopment."

Also, historical and cultural roots are neglected in the emulation of "modern" countries, resulting in "underdeveloped" societies rejecting the search for what could be their own path toward a life in relational harmony. The "underdeveloped" economy is dominated by the logic of global capital accumulation. Imported science and technology almost rule the organization of "backward" societies. Commodification becomes the main power: everything is up for grabs when "development" is the objective. The rich have determined that the poor must pay to escape from poverty; they must imitate them buying their knowledge, and marginalizing and rejecting their own knowledge, their own ancestral practices and even their own life.

In summary, the path followed since the post-war years and up to these days has been complex. The results have not been satisfactory. "Development," in terms of global impact, as the great Peruvian thinker Aníbal Quijano (2000) noted, became

> a term of random biography. (…) Since the Second World War it has changed identity and name many times, a tug of war between a constant economistic reductionism and the

insistent calls of all the other dimensions of social existence. That is, between very different power interests. And it has been greeted very unevenly from one time to another in our changing history. At the beginning it was without doubt one of the most mobilizing propositions of this half of the century that is now approaching its end. Its promises swept along all sectors of society and somehow ignited one of the most bemusing and vibrant debates in history, but they slipped out of sight over an increasingly elusive horizon and their standard bearers and followers were caged by disillusionment.

Wolfgang Sachs (1996) was already conclusive in that respect:

> The last forty years can be called the development era. That era is reaching its end. The time has come to write its obituary.

> Like a majestic lighthouse that guides the sailors towards the coast, "development" was the idea that guided the emerging nations on their journey through post-war history. Independently of whether they were democracies or dictatorships, having been liberated from their colonial subjugation, the Southern countries declared development to be their primary aspiration. Four decades later, governments and citizens still have their eyes fixed on that light, twinkling now as far away as ever: every effort and every sacrifice is justified to achieve that goal, but the light continues to fade into the darkness.

> (...) the idea of development rises like a ruin in the intellectual landscape, (...) deception and disillusionment, failures and crimes have been permanent companions of development and all tell the same tale: it didn't work. Moreover, the historical conditions that catapulted the idea to prominence have disappeared: development has become antiquated. But above all, the hopes and desires that gave wings to the idea are now spent: development has come to be obsolete.

When it is understood that "development" is a *ghost* used only to legitimize a civilization where the power of capital is fed by the exploitation – and sacrifice – of human and natural life, the search for alternatives to "development" emerges forcefully: it urges the search of new ways to organize our life outside and beyond "development." This compels us to reject the conceptual kernels of "development," to reject the *Leviathan par excellence*: the very notion of progress, which emerged forcefully 500 years ago in Europe and was imposed to most of the world trying to legitimize the European colonialist expansion. The fundamental elements of the dominant view imposed by "development" are nourished by the values imposed by the progress of the European civilization. An extremely expansionist and influential process that was also destructive.[11]

To leave the western notion of progress seems the essential step if we want to end capitalism and its logic of social and environmental devastation before capital and power make life unbearable. For the many, capitalism does not represent a promise or a dream to be fulfilled but it is a nightmare made reality.

However, as Wolfgang Sachs indicated, it has taken time to begin to bid "farewell to the defunct idea in order to clear our minds for new discoveries." Despite the failure of the fundamental ideas of "development," there are still those who believe that it is possible "to return to development" (Ornelas 2012), attempting, of course, a critical revision of what "development" means as a proposition with colonial origins.

Simply put, even though we know "development" is dead, its influence will weigh upon us for quite some time. We should accept that we will escape "development" – and capitalism –

while dragging many of its imperfections with us during a long and tortuous journey, with advances and setbacks (Marx 1875). When understanding this, it becomes clear how crucial it is to gain political clarity, strength and even self-control and self-consciousness to take on the challenge and do not end cooptated by capital and power. The road is dark, but there is hope: within capitalism itself alternatives are emerging to overcome it, alternatives that could be the germs for a new *post-capitalist* civilization. Post-development is one place where we can search for those germs.

Post-development, principles for a hope

As mentioned before, *post-development* is a broad term that tries to englobe alternatives to development looking for the constructions of a pluriverse. One of the main sources from which the notion of pluriverse is particularly inspired comes from the *Zapatista Autonomy* that "comprises modes, processes, and networks of struggle, government, and rebel life that together constitute a radical alternative to the established system and its institutions" (Leyva-Solano 2019: 335). This autonomic process represents one example of how – through the resistance against government, from the bottom and the local organization – it is possible to connect the "spheres of everyday life" with a "glocal planetary consciousness" focused on defeating the capitalist system (Leyva-Solano 2019: 337–338); a struggle that necessarily implies the search for a *post-capitalist* civilization.[12]

To build a post-capitalist civilization it is required to rethink the interaction between economy, politics, ecology and many other branches of human thinking. In the specific case of economy, as far as economics turned into one of the predilect instruments to legitimate capitalist accumulation (similarly to what happens with the term "development"), it is urgent to propose an alternative capable of going beyond both orthodox and heterodox economic approaches. In that sense, within the alternatives grouped by post-development we can include *post-oikonomics*, a term we use for a transitory social thinking focused to a profound criticism of the so-called "economic sciences" and their *imperial pretensions* over other social sciences (Acosta 2015) while – at the same time and through transdisciplinarity (advancing beyond interdisciplinarity and multidisciplinarity, accepting and studying the world as a diverse unit) – contributes in the construction of a pluriverse and a post-capitalist civilization (see Acosta 2019; Acosta and Cajas-Guijarro 2018a).[13]

Box 17.6 Post-oikonomics

A transitory social thinking focused to a profound criticism of the so-called "economic sciences" and their imperial pretensions over other social sciences which – at the same time and through transdisciplinarity – contributes to the construction of a pluriverse and a post-capitalist civilization.

Between the main demands coming from *post-oikonomics* we can mention (cf. Acosta 2019: 282):

- de-commodification of Nature and common goods, looking for a reengagement with Nature, ensuring its capacity for regeneration, based on respect, responsibility and reciprocity;[14]

- recognition of rights and harmonious relations among all living beings, where *Human Rights* and the *Rights of Nature*[15] become elements of a broad system of *Universal Rights*;
- community-based criteria of evaluation of economic and social relations;
- elimination of any form of exploitation over humans and Nature, with the objective to stop feeding the concentration of power in the few through the sacrifice of the many;
- decentralized and deconcentrated production;
- a profound change in patterns of consumption;
- a radical redistribution of wealth and power.

To accomplish with these and other demands, post-oikonomics criticizes the global unviability of the dominant lifestyle, based on premises of *anthropocentric* exclusion and exploitation. On a global scale the *fetish* of economic growth, based on inexhaustible natural resources and a market that pretends to absorb everything produced, is unsustainable in natural (remember, for instance, climate change) and social levels (remember, for instance, the increase in inequality registered by Piketty 2014). Also, growth widens the cracks in society: wealth and power of the few is almost always based on the exploitation and sacrifice of the many. Even when poverty falls, it does not affect capitalist logics and structures, particularly the tendencies toward concentration of wealth, financialization dominated by speculation, crisis and structural violence caused by the expansion of economic activities typical of capitalist modernity.

In this sense, post-development presents a proposal for the reorganization of international economic relations. It asks to stop – and even to push back – economic growth; that is, it asks for *degrowth*[16] especially in the Global North. In a broad sense, degrowth can be understood as a project that "challenges economic growth and calls for a democratically led redistributive down-scaling of production and consumption in industrialized countries as a means to achieve environmental sustainability, social justice, and well-being" (see Demaria and Latouche 2019: 148).

Box 17.7 Degrowth

A project, mostly focused on the Global North, which challenges economic growth and calls for a democratically led redistributive downscaling of production and consumption in industrialized countries as a means to achieve environmental sustainability, social justice, and well-being.

Therefore, degrowth does not involve only the physically slowing of the "economic metabolism." The economy must be subordinated to the mandates of the Earth and the demands of Humanity, which is Nature itself. This requires a socio-environmental rationality that deconstructs the current logic of production, distribution, circulation and consumption, and uncouples these processes from the perversity of global capitalism and its speculative nature.[17] Such a deconstruction implies to stop the expanded reproduction of a civilization where profits are based on the exploitation of human beings and Nature. That civilization, which reproduces the utilitarianism and anthropocentrism of Modernity, should be replaced by an alternative that accepts that all beings (human or not human) have the same *ontological value*, even when they have no use value in human terms (our original conception of *value* should also be questioned).

From a *post-oikonomic* perspective, while the Global North should focus on degrowth, in the Global South the most appropriate response may be the consolidation of *post-extractivism*.[18] This term refers to a "dynamic socio-economic and political" critique of extractivism[19] as a "development model" (Acosta 2016) In other words, post-extractivism calls to stop with the massive removal and extraction of natural resources – almost without any processing – focused entirely to the global market through exports and replace this "primary exports-led model" with endogenous processes socially and ecologically harmonious and sustainable (based, for instance, on agriculture and agrarian reforms combined with productive technologies adapted to local conditions[20]) (Acosta 2013b; Acosta and Brand 2017; Gudynas 2009).

Box 17.8 Post-extractivism

A term, mostly focused on the Global South, which calls to stop the massive removal and extraction of natural resources – almost without any processing – focused entirely on the global market through exports – and replace this "primary exports-led model" with endogenous processes socially and ecologically harmonious and sustainable.

The combination of degrowth in the Global North and post-extractivism in the Global South, as part of a global *post-oikonomic* alternative, implies a new form of international economic relations and international political economy.[21] Particularly, it implies the refusal of the contemporaneous rules given by the international division of labor, where peripheral and dependent countries are assigned the role of providing natural resources to core capitalist countries which keep growing – and accumulating – as if environmental boundaries do not exist. Of course, there are transnational groups with big interests which mean that such a change may never occur, such as large extractive firms and conglomerates (in oil, large-scale mining, fishing, farming, forestry and so on) as well as large high-tech companies whose production is fed by extractivism jointly with labor overexploitation (like the assembly of high-tech products).

Against those interests, it is crucial that the reinforcement of local and decentralized productive activities from communities which, at the same time, can gain political autonomy (here the Zapatistas may be an interesting starting point), avoid any kind of highly centralized government that can be coopted for the benefit of particular interests. Therefore, an international post-oikonomic alternative toward the consolidation of post-development necessarily needs to think also of how the notion of "state" relates to the economy (particularly with the processes of production–distribution–circulation–consumption–reproduction).

Therefore, it should be stressed that, for post-development, the starting point is not in the states, nor in the governments and less still in the markets. An authentic democratization of power requires the social control and participation of the bases of rural and urban society, of the neighborhoods and the communities on economic, political and all other social processes. Social movements and new political parties may play a central role during the transition toward the empowerment of those that today are powerless. The objective is to consolidate flat power structures, real democracy and direct action as well as self-management, where top-down leadership and individual leaders, autocrats or visionaries are unacceptable. Such a reorganization of economic and political power may require also the reorganization of many other forms of power like: new ways to manage and spread information and education; breaking the contemporaneous utilitarist, consumerist and alienating cultural structures; promoting the use of technology in a democratic way while breaking the capitalist tendency to make humans mere tools for machines as Ivan Illich recommended;[22] liberating scientific knowledge[23] and motivating a respectful dialogue with ancestral wisdom; and so on.

In this collective search for multiple alternatives, above all in the community spaces, the current global challenges cannot be ignored. For instance, it is broadly accepted that the speculative structures of the international financial system must be dismantled, as well as the financial links with organized crime, terrorism and even war. The existence of diverse financial institutions that serve as tools of political pressure is also questionable, so that a large state or an authority controlled by a few powerful states can impose conditions (typically unsustainable) on weaker countries; one example is external debt, almost always used as a tool of political domination.[24] It is equally necessary to encourage world peace through a massive disarmament and using those resources to meet the most pressing needs of Humanity (deactivating many violent processes).

Building blocks for a post-capitalist pluriverse

A post-development process like the one presented here implies many complex issues, including the problem of how agency and social structures may interact in this new type of society. In other words, which kind of new forms of relatively stable social interaction (structures) may rise and how they can promote or limit the capacity of individuals to act, to behave and even to think? A final answer to this issue seems unavailable from post-development proposals (at least for the moment[25]). However, there are multiple experiences of life, knowledge and *resistance* (coming from communities that have not been totally absorbed by capitalist modernity or that have stayed on the periphery) that bring insights about how, from post-development, it is possible to propose concrete forms of social organization that can overcome the civilization of capital and can be useful in the building of a pluriverse.

Buen Vivir – good living – is one crucial example. Originally coming from what could be understood as an indigenous philosophy of life,[26] ("indigeneity" in the terms of Aníbal Quijano 2014b), today Buen Vivir represents "an ensemble of South American perspectives which share a radical questioning of development" that "hybridizes [Andean and Amazonian] indigenous elements with internal critiques of modernity" coming both from indigenous and non-indigenous thinkers, without being a backward concept or a romantic view of the indigenous and nationalities' reality (Chuji et al. 2019; see also Acosta 2013a; Gudynas and Acosta 2011).

Such a hybrid proposal is fed by notions of Buen Vivir from Ecuador, Vivir Bien – from Bolivia[27] among other analogous indigenous concepts from South America, traditionally marginalized, but not vanished, such as *sumak kawsay* (in kichwa), *suma qamaña* (in aymara), *ñande reko* or *tekó porã* (in guaraní), *pénker pujústin* (shuar) and *shiir waras* (ashuar) *inter alia*. There are similar notions in other indigenous groups, for instance *kyme mogen* (Mapuche of Chile), *balu wala* (Kuna of Panama) and *laman laka* (Miskito in Nicaragua), but also in the Mayan tradition of Guatemala and in the Chiapas of Mexico (see Acosta 2018).[28] In the Ecuadorian case, Buen Vivir can be seen as "the art of good and harmonious living in a community, although defined in social and ecological dimensions at the same time" (Chuji et al. 2019: 112). However, since one homogeneous meaning of the term does not exist, when speaking about Buen Vivir it is best to think always in plural terms, i.e., Buenos Convivires (Albó 2009; see also Acosta 2017).

To understand Buen Vivir some observations about indigenous wisdom are useful. First, an idea analogous to "development" does not exist for some indigenous worldviews. Likewise, for indigenous perspectives the concept of a linear life-process that establishes a previous and subsequent state (e.g., "underdevelopment" and "development") has no sense. For them historical processes are multiple, parallel, non-linear and even circular. Also, concepts like "wealth" and "poverty" seen as accumulation or lack of material goods are not accepted; instead, relevance is focused on an adequate distribution of income and redistribution of wealth for all members of a community (where community becomes central as well as plurality and diversity).

In general, the indigenous philosophy sees the world based mainly on the principles of relationality (everything is related with everything else), correspondence (everything corresponds to everything else in harmony), complementarity (everything co-exists with its specific complement) and reciprocity (to each action corresponds a reciprocal action) (see Estermann 1998; 2014). Some implications of those principles are the calling, from indigenous movements, to the building of *plurinationality* (to build a state that accepts the co-existence of multiple peoples and nationalities seen as economically, politically, culturally and historically differentiated)[29] and *interculturality* (all these peoples and nations should have cultural co-existence and interchange without any possibility for one group to impose its culture on others).

Considering all this background, Buen Vivir becomes a term that, in general, calls for the construction of a philosophy of life alternative to "development" and where human beings (through communitarian and holistic interactions, recovering many principles from the indigenous wisdom) engage in a relational harmony between themselves and with Nature (breaking any anthropocentric logic). This philosophy of life includes many proposals: construction of a "full life" beyond material consumption, calling for austerity and recovering affective and spiritual dimension; at the same time, promotion of individual freedom and consolidation of a collective-being that englobes humans and Nature; dominance of use value over exchange value (and over any other economic value in general); deconstruction of patriarchal, colonial and any other form of structures built for social domination (including the division of society between exploiter and exploited social classes) (Acosta 2018; Acosta and Cajas-Guijarro 2015).

Box 17.9 Buen Vivir

A term that, in general, calls for the construction of a philosophy of life alternative to "development" and where human beings (through communitarian and holistic interactions, recovering many principles from the indigenous wisdom) engage in a relational harmony between themselves and with Nature (breaking any anthropocentric logic).

Apart from Buen Vivir, there are many examples of concrete experiences with the potential to be incorporated in the construction of a pluriverse. Some of them are:

- *Agaciro* ("worth," "dignity," "self-respect"): a cultural attitude, coming originally from Rwanda, and which focuses on dignity looking to enable people to project themselves as principal agents of social processes instead of being passive recipients (Ndushabandi and Rutazibwa 2019: 79).
- *Agdals*: a term from the North of Africa (originally from the Amazigh/Berber language) which refers to a "type of communal resource management in which there is a temporary restriction on the use of specific natural resources within a defined territory, with the intention of maximizing their availability in critical periods of need" (Dominguez and Martin 2019: 82).
- *Hurai* ("all the best things"): a term coming from the Chines Tuvan's people's cosmology (that originally expresses "the logic of transforming from nature to animals and then to human beings") which sustains the belief that human beings are capable of continuously receiving the blessing from Nature (Hou 2019: 203); to obtain that blessing, "humans need to devote activities to safeguarding well-being as a whole [Nature], not only in rituals but in a daily basis" (Hou 2019: 204).
- *Ibadism*: an ancient – and little known – school within Islam (which emerged before the Sunni versus Shia divide) characterized by "a community-driven mode of governance, asceticism as a way of life, and cultural pluralism" (M'Barek 2019: 206).

- *Shohoj*: a term grounded in the spiritual tradition of Bengal, "generally meaning an intuitively simple but transparent way of being in the universe" which implies "learning to relate with internal and external realities with all our human faculties in a unity, allowing no hierarchy between our sensuous, intellectual or imaginative faculties." Its main objective is to "transcend an oppressive, painful, and dehumanized existence" (Mazhar 2019: 247).
- *Swaraj* ("self-rule"): Indian term that calls for "finite, face-to-face neighbourhood assemblies," "a community in which the individual can come into her own through filial, cultural, social, political, economic and ecological relationships with those including sentient beings other than the humans around her," "individual's [and] community's autonomy to 'create' their choices, rather than passively accepting the menu from which they must 'choose'" (see Shrivastava 2019: 284–285). As an extension of this notion has emerged, also from India, the term *eco-swaraj* which focuses on a *Radical Ecological Democracy*[30] respecting "the limits of the Earth and the rights of other species, while pursuing the core values of social justice and equity," putting "collectives and communities at the centre of governance and economy" (Kothari 2019: 289).[31]
- *Ubuntu*: term coming from southern Africa, which means "humanness" and "concerns the unfolding of the human being in relation to other human beings and the more-than-human world of non-human nature." Particularly, this term "suggests that our moral obligation is to care for others, because when they are harmed, we are harmed. This obligation extends to all of life, since everything in the cosmos is related: when I harm nature, I am harmed." In this sense, "Ubuntu is the manifestation of the power within all beings that serves to enhance life, and not thwart it" (Le Grange 2019: 323–325).[32]

All these proposals – and many others – demonstrate that the "building blocks" for a postcapitalist pluriverse exist. This feeds the hope of reencountering the "utopian dimension," as the Peruvian Alberto Flores Galindo (n.d.) proposed in the 1980s. Intuitively or explicitly, many voices around the globe demand for alternatives against the barbarism of capitalism and its legitimizing tools (like the notions of "development" and its father, progress). If we want to save our world from the collapse coming with the crisis of the capitalist civilization, we must build a new world where many worlds fit through relation harmony, dignity and freedom.

Notes

1 It seems the first time the word "post-development" appeared was at the beginning of the 1990s precisely "to take into account the practices and thoughts that [...] [are] shaping the period following the demise of the development ideology" (Rahnema 1997: xi).
2 "Relational" in the sense that "everything is connected with everything else" (Kothari et al. 2019: xxix).
3 For a review of some critiques to post-development see Asher and Wainwright (2019).
4 For a brief discussion of why the notion of "free market" may be a myth, see Cajas-Guijarro (2018: 13–19).
5 See Truman (1949).
6 It is even possible to find in Smith's *Wealth of Nations* some concrete observations on what today could be assumed as "stages of development" (from agriculture to manufacture and international trade) (see Bell 1992).
7 To track the origins of this debate on development one should go back to the works of Adam Smith, Karl Marx or especially Friedrich List (1789–1846), who, with his book *Das nationale System der Politischen Ökonomie* (1841), can be considered a pioneer in the field of "development." More recently we have the contribution of Joseph Schumpeter, with his book *The Theory of Economic Development*, published in 1912; he maintained that development is an economic fact, rather than a social one. The list of authors who tackled this topic after 1949 is long and diverse in focus and contributions: Arthur

Lewis, Gunnar Myrdal, Walt Whitman Rostow, Nicholas Kaldor among many others. Of course, one would also have to include dependentistas and structuralists, highlighting Raúl Prebisch, Celso Furtado, Aníbal Quijano, Ruy Mauro Marini, Agustín Cueva, André Gunder Frank, Samir Amín, Theotonio dos Santos, among others, to complete a long list of people who have participated in one of the richest and most intense debates in the history of Humanity. A recommended read on this subject is that by Jürgen Schuldt (2012).

8 That is, a reasoning focused mainly on finding effective ways to achieve an end, forgetting the legitimacy of the means and considering as irrelevant any type of critical reasoning (see Horkheimer 1967).

9 Cited by Jürgen Schuldt (2013). This Peruvian economist is another of the most prominent researchers on the subject of development and its criticism.

10 In the form of combat known as "Anything Goes" the fighters may use any martial art or contact sport, as the rules allow any technique and type of fighting.

11 From 1492, when Spain invaded Abya Yala (America) with a strategy of domination for exploitation, Europe imposed its imagination to legitimize the superiority of the European, the "civilized," and the inferiority of the other, the "primitive." At this point the coloniality of power, the coloniality of knowledge and the coloniality of the being emerged. These colonialities remain valid until today. And it has in the idea of race the most effective instrument of social domination for the last 500 years. It is not a memento of the past. Coloniality explains the current organization of the world in its entirety, in that fundamental point in the agenda of Modernity. Among the critics of coloniality we highlight Aníbal Quijano, Arturo Escobar, Boaventura Souza Santos, José de Souza Santos, Enrique Dussel, Edgardo Lander, Enrique Leff, Alejandro Moreano, *inter alia*. Above all we recommend from among these various authors the contributions of Aníbal Quijano; his most outstanding works are contained in *Cuestiones y Horizontes – Antología Esencial – De la dependencia histórica-estructural a la colonialidad/decolonialidad del poder*, CLACSO, Buenos Aires (2014a).

12 For more reflections on autonomy, see Esteva (2019).

13 Originally, we presented this term as "post-economía" (in Spanish) (Acosta and Cajas-Guijarro 2018a; Acosta 2019) but here we try to bring it a more general connotation.

14 Here it is worth highlighting the valuable reflections of Vandana Shiva (1996) in this respect in the *Diccionario del desarrollo – Una guía del conocimiento como poder*, edited by Wolfgang Sachs (1996).

15 An important contribution to this discussion is the book by Eduardo Gudynas; *Los Derechos de la Naturaleza – Respuestas y aportes desde la ecología política* (2016).

16 Texts on this issue are increasingly numerous. It is interesting to note the contribution by various authors in the book by Giacomo D'Alisa, Frederico Demaria and Giorgios Kallis (2015).

17 See the proposals summarized by Alberto Acosta and John Cajas-Guijarro (2015).

18 Alberto Acosta and Ulrich Brand (2017).

19 A recommended study on extractive activities is offered by Eduardo Gudynas (2015).

20 For a discussion of some possible alternatives in this sense see Chaves (2019) and Mazhar (2019).

21 For a brief literature review on how degrowth and post-extractivism may be joined see Brand et al. (2017).

22 See the compilation of the main texts by Ivan Illich (2015). This author is regaining renewed strength in the framework of the debates on degrowth and in the search for profoundly transformative alternatives.

23 On this subject one may consult, for example, the book *Flok Society – Buen Conocer, Modelos sostenibles y políticas públicas para una economía del conocimiento común y abierto en Ecuador*, Instituto de Altos Estudios Nacionales, Quito (Vila-Viñas and Barandiaran 2015).

24 The proposal to form an International Tribunal for Arbitration of Sovereign Debt by Oscar Ugarteche and Alberto Acosta (2006). The convincing elements of this initiative have already been debated and approved in the core of the United Nations, although with the expected rejection by the great powers that benefit from these inequitable structures in the international financial sector.

25 One example is the absence, in much of the post-development literature, of a profound discussion of the concrete social structures created by the capitalist civilization that are crucial to sustain processes like *hegemony*. About this discussion see Asher and Wainwright (2019).

26 Normally in the indigenous world there are few written texts. As they are oral cultures this is understandable. A text that contributed, in Ecuador, to spreading these ideas was that by Carlos Viteri Gualinga (2000). Someone who has worked on the origin of Buen Vivir, above all in Ecuador is David Cortéz.

27 The list of texts that tackle this subject is ever longer. It is worth noting the contributions of Atawallpa Oviedo (2011), Fernando Huanacuni (2010), Omar Felipe Giraldo (2014), Eduardo Gudynas (2009, 2014), Josef Estermann (1998, 2014), Pablo Solón (2016), , *inter alia*; one could even retrieve the approaches to the common good of Humanity by Francois Houtart (2011).

28 Other experiences come from the constitutions of Ecuador (2008) and Bolivia (2009); however, in practice, governments of these countries drained the conceptual content of Buen Vivir and transformed it into a power mechanism to consolidate authoritarian regimes (in the Ecuadorian case, see Acosta and Cajas-Guijarro 2018b: 32–34).

29 Discussions on plurinationality and the contributions of the indigenous world in this sense are extremely broad in Bolivia and to a lesser degree in Ecuador. From a very long list, one can recommend German texts by Isabella Radhuber (2014), Philipp Altmann (2013), Boaventura de Souza Santos (2010), Aníbal Quijano (2014a) and Raúl Prada Alcoreza (2010)*inter alia*.

30 This kind of democracy is based on five interlocking spheres: ecological wisdom and resilience; social well-being and justice; direct or radical political democracy; economic democracy; cultural and knowledge plurality (see Kothari 2019: 290–291).

31 Can be consulted in Kothari et al. 2015.

32 A brief approximation to the subject is available in the book by Giacomo D'Alisa, Federico Demaria and Giorgios Kallis (2015).

Bibliography

Acosta, A. 2013a. *El Buen Vivir Sumak Kawsay, una oportunidad para imaginar otros mundos.* Barcelona: ICARIA.

Acosta, A. 2013b. Extractivism and neoextractivism: two sides of the same curse. Chapter 4 In: Lang, M. and Mokrani, D. (Eds) *Beyond Development. Alternative Visions from Latin America:* 61–86. Quito: Fundación Rosa Luxemburg.

Acosta, A. 2015. Las ciencias sociales en el laberinto de la economía. *POLIS Revista Latinoamericana* 41. Available at http://journals.openedition.org/polis/10917.

Acosta, A. 2016. Las dependencias del extractivismo. Aporte para un debate incompleto. Magazine Aktuel Marx Intervenciones 20. Available at www.biodiversidadla.org/Objetos_Relacionados/Las_dependencias_del_extractivismo._Aporte_para_un_debate_incompleto.

Acosta, A. 2017. Los buenos convivires: Filosofías sin filósofos, prácticas sin teorías. *Trilhas Filosóficas* 10(1): 205–245.

Acosta, A. 2018. From the ghost of development to Buen Vivir. Chapter 22 In: Fagan, H. and Munck, R. (Eds) *Handbook on Development and Social Change:* 433–454. Cheltenham: Edward Elgar.

Acosta, A. 2019. Post-Economía. In: Kothari, A., Salleh, A., Escobar, A., Demaria, F. and Acosta, A. (Eds) *Pluriverse: A Post-development Dictionary:* 280–283. New Delhi: Tulika Books.

Acosta, A. and Brand, U. 2017. *Salidas del laberinto capitalista – Decrecimiento y Postextractivismo.* Quito: Fundación Rosa Luxembrug.

Acosta, A. and Cajas-Guijarro, J. 2015. Instituciones transformadoras para la economía global – Pensando caminos para dejar atrás el capitalismo. Chapter 4 In: Lang, M., Cevallos, B, and López, C. (Eds) *La osadía de lo nuevo – Alternativas de política económica.* Quito: Fundación Rosa Luxemburg and Abya Yala.

Acosta, A. and Cajas-Guijarro, J. 2018a. De las "ciencias económicas" a la posteconomía: Reflexiones sobre el sin-rumbo de la economía. *Ecuador Debate* 103: 37–59.

Acosta, A. and Cajas-Guijarro, J. 2018b. *Una década desperdiciada. Las sombras del correísmo.* Quito: Centro Andino de Acción Popular.

Albó, X. 2009. Suma qamaña = el buen convivir. *Revista Obets* 4: 25–40.

Altmann, P. 2013. El Sumak Kawsay en el discurso del movimiento indígena ecuatoriano. *Indiana* 30: 283–299.

Amín, S. 1970. *La Accumulation a l'echelle mondiale.* Paris: Anthropos.

Asher, K. and Wainwright, J. 2019. After Post-development: On Capitalism, Difference, and Representation. *Antipode* 51(1): 25–44.

Basu, K. 2018. *The Republic of Beliefs.* Princeton: Princeton University Press.

Bell, J. 1992. Adam Smith's Theory of Economic Development: 'Of the Natural Progress of Opulence'. *Journal of Economics and Finance* 16(1): 137–145.

Brand, U. 2016. *Lateinamerikas Linke – Ende des progressiven Zyklus.* Hamburg: VSA.

Brand, U., Boos, T. and Brad, A. 2017. Degrowth and Post-extractivism: Two Debates with Suggestions for the Inclusive Development Framework. *Current Opinion in Environmental Sustainability* 24: 36–41.

Cajas-Guijarro, J. 2018. *Los capos del comercio. Concentración, poder y acuerdos comerciales en el Ecuador: un preludio.* Quito: Plataforma por el Derecho a la Salud/Fundación Donum/FOS.

Chaves, M. 2019. Ecovillages. In Kothari, A., Salleh, A., Escobar, A., Demaria, F. Acosta, A. (Eds) *Pluriverse: A Post-development Dictionary:* 175–178. New Delhi: Tulika Books.

Chuji, M., Rengifo, G. and Gudynas, E. 2019. Buen Vivir. In Kothari, A., Salleh, A., Escobar, A., Demaria, F. Acosta, A. (Eds) *Pluriverse: A Post-development Dictionary:* 111–114. New Delhi: Tulika Books.

D'Alisa, G., Demaria, F. and Kallis, G. (Eds) 2015. *Decrecimiento. Vocabulario para una nueva era.* Barcelona: ICARIA.

De Souza Santos, B. 2010. *Refundación del Estado en América latina – Perspectivas desde una epistemología del Sur.* Lima: Instituto Internacional de Derecho y Sociedad.

Deb, D. 2009. *Beyond Developmentality.* Delhi: Daanish Books.

Demaria, F. and Latouche, S. 2019. Degrowth. In Kothari, A., Salleh, A., Escobar, A., Demaria, F. and Acosta, A. (Eds) *Pluriverse: A Post-development Dictionary:* 148–151. New Delhi: Tulika Books.

Dominguez, P. and Martin, J. 2019. Agdals. In: Kothari, A., Salleh, A., Escobar, A., Demaria, F. and Acosta, A. (Eds) *Pluriverse: A Post-development Dictionary:* 82–85. New Delhi: Tulika Books.

Echeverría, B. 2010. *Modernidad y blanquitud.* Mexico: Editorial ERA.

Emmanuel, A. 1969. *Unequal Exchange: A Study of the Imperialism of Trade.* New York: Monthly Review Press.

Escobar, A. 2012. *Encountering Development: The Making and Unmaking of the Third World.* Princeton: Princeton University Press.

Escobar, A. 2018. *Designs for the Pluriverse. Radical Interdependence, Autonomy, and the Making of Worlds.* Durham and London: Duke University Press.

Estermann, J. 1998. *Filosofía andina. Estudio intelectual de la sabiduría autóctona andina.* Quito: Abya-Yala.

Estermann, J. 2014. Ecosofía andina – Un paradigma alternativo de convivencia cósmica y de vida plena. In: Oviedo, A. (Ed.) *Bifurcación del Buen Vivir y el sumak kawsay:* 23–45. Quito: Ediciones SUMAK.

Esteva, G. 2019. Autonomy. In Kothari, A., Salleh, A., Escobar, A., Demaria, F. and Acosta, A. (Eds) *Pluriverse: A Post-development Dictionary:* 99–101. New Delhi: Tulika Books.

Flores Galindo, A. (n.d.) *Reencontremos la dimensión utópica.* Lima: Instituto de Apoyo Agrario and El Caballo Rojo.

Frank, A. 1970. *Capitalismo y subdesarrollo en América Latina.* Buenos Aires: Siglo XXI.

Frank, A. 1979. *Lumpenburguesía y lumpendesarrollo.* Barcelona: Laia.

Galeano, E. 1997. To be like them. Chapter 21 In: Rahnema, M. and Bawtree, V. (Eds) *The Post-development Reader:* 214–222. London and New Jersey: Zed Books.

Giraldo, O. 2014. *Utopías en la era de la supervivencia – Una interpretación del Buen Vivir.* Mexico: ITACA.

Gudynas, E. 2009. Diez tesis urgentes sobre el nuevo extractivismo. In *Extractivismo, política y sociedad:* 187–225. Quito: Centro Andino de Acción Popular and CLAES.

Gudynas, E. 2014. Buen Vivir: sobre secuestros, domesticaciones, rescates y alternativas. In Oviedo, A. (Ed.) *Bifurcación del Buen Vivir y el sumak kawsay:* 23–45. Quito: Ediciones SUMAK.

Gudynas, E. 2015. *Extractivismos – Ecología, economía y política de un modo de entender desarrollo y la Naturaleza.* La Paz: CLAES – CEDIB.

Gudynas, E. 2016. *Los Derechos de la Naturaleza – Respuestas y aportes desde la ecología política.* Quito: Abya Yala.

Gudynas, E. and Acosta, A. 2011. La renovación de la crítica al desarrollo y el buen vivir como alternativa. *Revista Utopía y Praxis Latinoamericana* 16(53): 71–83.

Horkheimer, M. 1967. *Crítica de la razón instrumental.* Buenos Aires: Sur.

Hou, Y. 2019. Hurai. In: Kothari, A., Salleh, A., Escobar, A., Demaria, F. and Acosta, A. (Eds) *Pluriverse: A post-development Dictionary:* 203–205. New Delhi: Tulika Books.

Houtart, F. 2011. El concepto del sumak kawsay (Buen Vivir) y su correspondencia con el bien común de la humanidad. *Ecuador Debate* 84: 57–76.

Huanacuni, F. 2010. *Vivir Bien/Buen Vivir Filosofía, políticas, estrategias y experiencias regionales.* La Paz: Convenio Andrés Bello, Instituto Internacional de Investigación y CAOI.

Illich, I. 2015. *Obras Reunidas.* Mexico: Fondo de Cultura Económica.

Kothari, A. 2019. Radical ecological democracy. In Kothari, A., Salleh, A., Escobar, A., Demaria, F. and Acosta, A. (Eds) *Pluriverse: A Post-development Dictionary:* 289–292. New Delhi: Tulika Books.

Kothari, A., Demaria, F. and Acosta, A. 2015. Buen Vivir, Degrowth and Ecological Swaraj: Alternatives to Sustainable Development and the Green Economy. *Development* 57(3–4): 362–375.

Kothari, A., Salleh, A., Escobar, A., Demaria, F. and Acosta, A. (Eds). 2019. *Pluriverse: A Post-development Dictionary*. New Delhi: Tulika Books.

Le Grange, L. 2019. Ubuntu. In Kothari, A., Salleh, A., Escobar, A., Demaria, F. and Acosta, A. (Eds) *Pluriverse: A Post-development Dictionary*: 323–326. New Delhi: Tulika Books.

Leyva-Solano, X. 2019. Zapatista autonomy. In Kothari, A., Salleh, A., Escobar, A., Demaria, F. and Acosta, A. (Eds) *Pluriverse: A Post-development Dictionary*: 335–338. New Delhi: Tulika Books.

List, F. 1841. *Sistema nacional de economía política*. Madrid: Aguilar.

Marx, K. 1875. Critique of the Gotha program. In: *Marx and Engels Collected Works Vol. 24*: 75–99. London: Lawrence and Wishart.

Mazhar, F. 2019. Nayakrishi Andolon. In: Kothari, A., Salleh, A., Escobar, A., Demaria, F. and Acosta, A. (Eds) *Pluriverse: A Post-development Dictionary*: 247–250. New Delhi: Tulika Books.

M'Barek, M. 2019. Ibadism. In: A Kothari, A., Salleh, A., Escobar, A., Demaria, F. and Acosta, A. (Eds) *Pluriverse: A Post-development Dictionary*: 205–208. New Delhi: Tulika Books.

Ndushabandi, E. and Rutazibwa, O. 2019. Agaciro. In: Kothari, A., Salleh, A., Escobar, A., Demaria, F. and Acosta, A. (Eds) *Pluriverse: A Post-development Dictionary*: 79–82. New Delhi: Tulika Books.

Nisbet, R. 2009. *The Idea of Progress: A Bibliographical Essay*. New Brunswick, NJ: Transaction Publishers.

Ornelas, J. 2012. Volver al desarrollo. *Problemas del Desarrollo*, 168(43): 7–35.

Oviedo, A. 2011. *Qué es el sumak kawsay – Más allá del socialismo y capitalismo*. Quito: Ediciones SUMAK.

Piketty, T. 2014. *Capital in the Twenty-First Century*. Cambridge, Mass.: Belknap Press of Harvard University Press.

Prada Alcoreza, R. 2010. Umbrales y horizontes de la descolonización. Chapter 2 In: Sader, E. (Ed.) *El Estado – Campo de Lucha*: 43–96. La Paz: CLACSO Ediciones, Muela del Diablo Editores, Comuna.

Quijano, A. 2000. El fantasma desarrollo en América Latina. In: Acosta, A. (Ed) *El Desarrollo en la globalización. El reto de América Latina*: 11–27. Caracas: Nueva Sociedad e ILDIS.

Quijano, A. 2014a. *Cuestiones y Horizontes – Antología Esencial – De la dependencia histórica-estructural a la colonialidad/decolonialidad del poder*. Buenos Aires: CLACSO.

Quijano, A. (Ed.) 2014b. *Descolonialidad y bien vivir – Un nuevo debate en América Latina, Cátedra América Latina y la Colonialidad del Poder*. Lima: Universidad Ricardo Palma.

Radhuber, I. 2014. *Recursos naturales y finanzas públicas. La base material del Estado plurinacional de Bolivia*. La Paz: Plural Editores.

Rahnema, M. 1997. Introduction. In: Rahnema, M. and Bawtree, V. (Eds) *The Post-development Reader*: ix–xix. London and New Jersey: Zed Books.

Rostow, W. 1959. The Stages of Economic Growth. *The Economic History Review*, 12(1): 1–16.

Sachs, W. 1996. *Diccionario del desarrollo – Una guía del conocimiento como poder*. Lima: PRATEC.

Schuldt, J. 2012. *Desarrollo a escala humana y de la Naturaleza*. Lima: Universidad del Pacífico.

Schuldt, J. 2013. *Civilización del desperdicio – Psicoeconomía del consumidor*. Lima: Universidad del Pacífico.

Schumpeter, J. 1912. The Theory of Economic Development. In: Backhaus, J (Ed.) *Joseph Alois Schumpeter. The European Heritage in Economics and the Social Sciences*: 61–116. London: Kluwer Academic.

Shiva, V. 1996. Recursos. In: Sachs, W. *Diccionario del desarrollo. Una guía del conocimiento como poder*. Lima: PRATEC.

Shrivastava, A. 2019. Prakitik Swaraj. In: Kothari, A., Salleh, A., Escobar, A., Demaria, F. and Acosta, A. (Eds) *Pluriverse: A Post-development Dictionary*: 283–286. New Delhi: Tulika Books.

Solón, P. 2016 *¿Es posible el Buen Vivir?, Reflexiones a Quema Ropa sobre Alternativas Sistémicas*. La Paz: Fundación Solón.

Tortosa, J. 2011. *Mal desarrollo y mal vivir – Pobreza y violencia escala mundial*. Quito: Abya–Yala.

Truman, H. 1949. Truman's Inauguration Address. Available at https://avalon.law.yale.edu/20th_century/truman.asp

Ugarteche, O. and Acosta, A. 2006. Los problemas de la economía global y el tribunal internacional de arbitraje de deuda soberana. *POLIS Revista Latinoamericana* 13. Available at https://journals.openedition.org/polis/5393.

Unceta, K. 2014. *Desarrollo, postcrecimiento y Buen Vivir – Debates e interrogantes*. Quito: Abya-Yala.

Vila-Viñas, D. and Barandiaran, X. (Eds) 2015. *Flok Society – Buen Conocer, Modelos sostenibles y políticas públicas para una economía del conocimiento común y abierto en Ecuador*. Quito: Instituto de Altos Estudios Nacionales.

Viteri Gualinga, C. 2002. Visión indígena del desarrollo en la Amazonía, *POLIS Revista Latinoamericana* 3. Avilable at https://journals.openedition.org/polis/7678.

Part III
Beyond traditional perspectives

18

The BRICS initiative as a challenge to contemporary IPE

Javier A. Vadell

Introduction

In times of social and economic transformations, the theoretical and conceptual tools that were used to understand social phenomena are challenged. New configurations, new sceneries and surprising changes question the existing epistemological, theoretical and methodological apparatuses. The interregnum, paraphrasing Antonio Gramsci, as an uncertainty interval, is presented as an opportunity of curios cognitive flexibility to interpret new phenomena.

In the fields of International Relations (IR) and International Political Economy (IPE), there is a remarkably similar process. The modern field of IPE was born in the 1970s (Cohen 2014) in a context of economic and capitalist governance crisis, which questioned the economic primacy of the United States of America (USA) before the challenge posed by the economic emergence of its European allies and Japan. The interstate system known as bipolar was reconfigured with the approach of the People's Republic of China (PRC) to the USA and the effort to isolate the Union of Soviet Socialist Republics (USSR).

In this sense, we can observe a tacit division of labour in mainstream international studies. While the research focus of IR was interstate relations – in an effort to understand the bipolar system and the historical balance of power configurations – IPE projected, since the publication of Susan Strange's (1970) fundamental work, to bring international economy closer to international politics in order to understand the shifts in the international scene during the 1970s. The post-war Latin American thinking was not indifferent to Strange's concern. However, the 1950s Economic Commission for Latin America and the Caribbean (ECLAC) prominent intellectuals, like Raúl Prebisch, Celso Furtado or Osvaldo Sunkel (Bielschowsky 2000) and moreover, the Dependence theory (or theories) were never included in the debate of IR and IPE mainstream thinking. The historical–structural method and the ontological presuppositions of a hierarchic international system based on the core/periphery dichotomy contrast with the mainstream presuppositions: anarchic order, rational agents, liberal evolutionism from the economic viewpoint (Rostow 1960) and from the political viewpoint (Huntington 1968), both of which became popular prescriptions for periphery countries under the auspices of the Trilateral Commission (Gill 1990) and afterwards, of the Washington Consensus (Williamson 1990).

Starting from this premise, the aim of this chapter is to analyse the BRICS phenomenon from an intellectual proposal made by Vivares in his opportune work about the development of IPE in South America and its contemporary challenges (Vivares 2018). This chapter is an invitation to open new ontological and epistemological paths in a transition period marked by movements of plate tectonics in the unequal and unstable social structures of the periphery countries' development trajectory.

The leading problem of our chapter is to explore how the mainstream IR and IPE interpret the emergence of BRICS as an "economic and political formation" (Nayyar 2016) of the international system. In other words, we intend to question the contemporary debate of the mainstream IR currents of thought that pose the questions: to which extent do the BRICS challenge the liberal Western order? And, how does this change affect the development and global insertion of periphery countries?

Box 18.1 What is BRICS?

BRICS is an acronym created for a group of five emerging or re-emerging countries. Originally, it was Jim O'Neall, the Goldman Sachs executive, who coined BRIC to refer to four promising emerging markets: Brazil, Russia, India and China. The first Summit was in June 2009, in Yekaterinburg, Russia and reflecting the group's commitment to claim about the importance of reforming financial institutions to increase the participation of emerging middle powers in the international order. Since 2009, the BRICS nations have met annually at formal summits. In 2010, South Africa was invited to participate as a full member consolidating the label BRICS. In the global and international reordering process, the BRICS group (Brazil, Russia, India, China and South Africa) becomes an important actor of the international political scene. The constitution and evolution of the BRICS should be analysed taking into account that the emerging middle powers did not participate in an active way in the institutions of global economic governance until the creation of the G20, as a summit of heads of state and governments, in 2008. The BRICS emerged in a multipolar international political system in a world capitalist system as a mutual claim for a more participation into the international institutions of Governance.

On that ground, this matter methodologically introduces us, in the first place, to the theoretical debate on "emergence" within international relations and, in the second place, to analyse the relevance of the BRICS in the "emergence" process. In this respect, BRICS phenomenon is important in the sense that its institutional evolution (Vadell and Ramos 2019), founded on the collective financial statecraft (Roberts et al. 2018), supports a set of demands regarding institutional reforms of the liberal Western order. Moreover, it promotes a new normative order led by the PRC, based on regulatory principles and South–South Cooperation (SSC), which challenge neoliberal grounds.

Our hypothesis is that this process of the BRICS' institutional strengthening and its potential to expand as BRICS Plus (BRICS 2017) is not an isolated process. Hence, it cannot be studied without taking into consideration China's leading role in the establishment of a set of minilateral institutions (Wang 2014) and a multilateral one, the Asian Infrastructure Investment Bank (AIIB). These institutions paradoxically contribute to the BRICS' subsumption into a myriad of parallel institutions created and stimulated by China.

Following this objective, the chapter presents an introduction, three main parts and the conclusions. The second section is focused on the theoretical considerations about the emergence phenomenon, starting from the mainstream interpretations and concluding with the IPE critical theory, with the purpose of analysing BRICS phenomenon. The third part presents the BRICS emergence, its evolution and future challenges in a greater institutional frame led by China.

Theoretical considerations

Mainstream IPE and IR theory and the question of emergence

In the twenty-first century, the rise of "emerging powers" and "emerging markets" has questioned the existing distribution of power and it has stimulated a debate about which is the type of emergence or "re-emergence" that is observed in the contemporary international system and which will be the consequences of these transformations. This debate entails a theoretical and methodological challenge for traditional IPE and international relations theory. In this sense, how do mainstream IR and IPE theories interpret the evolution of the BRICS, their institutionalisation and the role of "emerging countries"?

The emergence issue is present in the mainstream theories. For realist thinkers, who conceive the international system within an anarchical context and international relations as a zero-sum game where relative gains among actors prevail, the possibility of conflict between emerging countries and the hegemonic power is expected (Layne 2018; Mearsheimer 2001, 2006, 2010). For these scholars, the rise of emerging powers, especially of China, will imply changes in the distribution of power in view of a probable outbreak of conflict – inevitable, from the radicals' perspective. In this direction, somehow moderating the deterministic position, Graham Allison warns us about Thucydides Trap. The starting point is ancient Greece, where "It was the rise of Athens and the fear that this instilled in Sparta that made war inevitable" (Allison 2017). According to the author, in the last 500 years there were 16 cases of emerging powers trying to get their fair share and posing a threat to the dominant power. The result is that in 12 of those cases there was a military conflict. The imminence of conflict is tempered by the possibility of a course of action taken by state actors before the system's constraints.

In this regard, in addition to the spectre of China's rise during the last years, there is an intense debate over the American decline. Christopher Layne (2018) asserts the most rigid realist postulates in relation to the threats faced by the *Pax Americana*. For Layne, "The fate of international orders is closely linked to power transition dynamics" (2018: 104). Supposing that the liberal ruled-based international order (LRBIO) is intrinsically related to the *Pax Americana*, if this regulatory order decays "the decline of United State will follow the same fate". According to Layne's perspective, in view of the deep changes in the geopolitical status of the American hegemony, alongside the rise of emerging powers, especially of China, there are no possibilities of preserving the *Pax Americana* status quo and its LRBIO.

However, realism is nourished by other influential current of the IR and IPE theory that acknowledges the existence of hierarchy among states and it even asserts that a dominant power is necessary to keep the political and economic international system stable. It is not the balance of power but rather a leader's preponderance of power what ensures stability.

> We are now in position to understand more clearly why the usual distribution of power in the world has not been a balance but rather a preponderance of power in the hands of one nation and its allies. And we can understand why world peace has coincided with periods of unchallenged supremacy of power, whereas the periods of approximate balance have been the periods of war.
>
> *(Organski 1968: 363)*

According to this approach, the transition period from one hegemonic power to another is historically marked by conflict and war, saving rare exceptions. As Organski (1968: 362) features, the peaceful transfer of power from the United Kingdom to the United States was the highlight exception. This brings him closer to Allison's (2017) hypothesis, the previously mentioned Thucydides Trap. As Kim and Gates stated:

> Organski's power transition theory rests on two fundamental observations. The first is that a country's power stems from internal development. Since development occurs at different rates, nations will rise and fall relative to one another. The second fundamental for power transition theory is that the international system is decisively shaped by the dominant nation, the hegemon. Those occasions in which a rising power overtakes the dominant power are called power transitions.
>
> *(Kim and Gates 2015: 220)*

In line with the power transition theory, there are requirements, or external and domestic determinants, which are essential for a nation to be or to aspire to be hegemonic; for instance, national character, population, territory and economic and technological development of a country. In this direction, the feature that is related to one of the most popular theories of IPE – that is, the Hegemonic Stability Theory (HST) – is the nature of systemic stability. According to Organski (1968), instability occurs when the hegemon is challenged. For the Hegemonic Stability theorists, instability takes place when the hegemon does not assume the responsibility of providing international public goods, because of either negligence or material incompetence (Gilpin 1987, 2001; Kindleberger 1973, 1981). The HST links political and economic issues to the post-world LRBIO.

The international economic and liberal order cannot be self-regulated because its outcome would be chaos or entropy, paraphrasing Schweller (2014). Just as in national domestic spheres there are institutions to regulate currency, transactions, security, etc., in the global scene, the presence of a hegemonic leader is imperative. With time and in consonance with post-Cold War changes, authors such as Gilpin acknowledged the possibility of a governing authority that included more actors, like the G-7 or the G-8 (Gilpin 2000, 2001).

Furthermore, the liberal institutional perspective, despite conceiving the international system as anarchic, highlights the regulatory structure and the interdependence of state actors in this shared institutional framework of liberal values. The "liberal" representative of the HST, Robert Keohane (Keohane 1984), was the creator of the label HST in a lively debate with Gilpin during the 1980s. When there is a hegemonic decline, Keohane places trust in a strong and consolidated liberal institutional framework to manage global economy. Nevertheless, after the end of the Soviet Union and the beginning of a unipolar stage, the mainstream IR and IPE had to face the intellectual challenge posed by the political and economic changes produced in the global capitalist system, the neoliberal model crisis and the rise of emergent countries, some of them Asian, oriented by planned economy models. For these liberal institutional academics, the (re) emerging powers have great possibilities of occupying spaces in the LRBIO by promoting the incorporation of their states to the international regulations, a duty which the Western powers and the United States should also fulfil. The heir to Keohane's (1984) legacy, John Ikenberry (2018), states that the emerging powers like China have risen within the liberal international regulations and governance which they are therefore committed to observe. In line with this idea, there are scholars that advert the possibility that the United States can employ a lock-in strategy. This strategy assumes that if the institutions of the *Pax Americana* are reformed, Beijing (and other non-Western emerging powers) will find it more attractive to remain in the post-1945 international order than to overturn it (Brooks et al. 2012/2013).

From middle to emerging powers: stabilisers versus destabilising countries?

From the emerging countries' point of view, it was since the mid-twentieth century that the first theoretical debates regarding middle and emerging powers started to arise. They began in the Canadian academy (Cooper et al. 1993; Cooper and Higgott 1990; Huelsz 2009) and they were further developed in the late 1990s and mainly during the twenty-first century. A shared feature in the new millennium debate is the distinction between traditional middle powers and emerging powers (Huelsz 2009; Nolte 2007). The latter are typically big states with vast territories and large populations, which despite being considered "developing" countries, show a surprising economic growth and potential. This is the case of the BRICS.

In a research work about the BRICS and multilateral institutions, Gregory Chin identifies three stages. The first one is focussed "on how the contemporary group of rising states positioned themselves in relation to the established multilateral arrangements and the global order more broadly" (Chin 2015: 19). We can set as examples the issues on niche diplomacy of traditional middle powers (Gilley and O'Neil 2014), the role of middle powers in the institutions of Western "liberal governance" and their foreign policies (Cooper 1997) and the concept of "middlepowermanship" (Alexandroff and Cooper 2010; Cooper 2013; Cox 1989; Hurrell 2000).

The second stage highlights the behavioural aspect of emerging countries in order to learn to which extent they were incorporated or not to multilateral institutions. In other words, "Whether the rising powers were behaving as 'status quo or revisionist' powers, the issue of their socialization into the existing multilateral arrangements" (Chin 2015: 19). The third stage is more interesting for the sake of this chapter and it is about the role of the BRICS in the existing institutions, that is to say, "whether the rising powers are trying to (re)shape some global norms and rules even while they selectively internalise some of the established global rules" (Chin 2015: 19).

Thereby, the question whether the rising powers are promoting alternative multilateral arrangement is related to Eduard Jordaan's contribution about the relevance of the "emerging middle power concept" (Jordaan 2017). This current debate incorporates earlier discussions of middle powers and specially, the expectations about the rise of China.

Questioning the concept of middle powers and its usefulness in the contemporary world, Jordaan turns to the classification of "middle powers" in terms of behaviour and hegemony. For Jordaan, the middle power concept is "too elusive" as a useful category. The proper concept is "mid-range states", not as counter hegemonic tendencies, but as supporters of a liberal hegemonic project. Nevertheless, there is no clear answer about what factors (gross national product, regional significance, leadership, internal cohesion, diplomatic skills or moral behavioural-based activities) should be measured and how to weigh the various components of state powers (Jordaan 2017: 2).

In terms of hegemony and in consonance with our discussion about the BRICS, the concept brings up the debate about whether middle powers are stabilisers or destabilisers. Jordaan's perspective emphasises agent-oriented positions and behaviour in international politics, consequently distinguishing three kinds of middle powers.

The first type is middle powers as stabilisers. In fact, they are "supporters of the hegemony" (Cooper 1997; Jordaan 2017) with a pro status quo position. In the Cold War era, Robert Cox had pointed out that the task of the middle power – Japan in this case – was to support and to legitimise the prevailing international order (Jordaan 2017: 5). Nevertheless, the context of Cold War, the defeat of Japan in the Second World War and the hegemonic position of the United States in the capitalist system were the main factors that determined the behaviour of middle powers in this period.

The second approach to middle power has an ambivalent position towards the US hegemony or primacy in global capitalism and international institutional governance. The preference for adherence to status quo rules and institutions has varied from country to country since the Cold War ended, and especially in the new millennium. Some contemporary emerging middle powers, for example, are dissatisfied with certain norms and rules of the current institutional governance system, but not necessarily with the existing international organisations that embody these norms and rules. A good example is the International Monetary Fund (IMF) and the World Bank reform debate (Cox 1989: 826).

The third approach to middle power "sees middle power interest as 'countering great power hegemony'. In this view, middle powers prefer a multipolar international order because it translates into more states having an influence on specific issues" (Ramos et al. 2012). The problem with this fixed model is the impossibility of using it to comprehend the current complex dynamics of global economy and the rise of China in the "Trump era". In the present age of "switching roles", when "following the United States" does not necessarily mean following a "liberal international order", the scenario becomes more complex. In other words, we have to pay attention to the changing structural economic and geopolitical order and incorporate it into the analysis in order to understand the processes of emergence and hegemony building in the capitalist system.

Critical IPE and the subsumed BRICS

In order to understand the importance of the BRICS in the current transformation process of the global capitalist system, in the first place, we must go beyond the (state) agent-oriented rational action processes, which are estimated according to capacity quantification. In the second place, as a methodological guideline, agents should be understood from a comprehensive approach that considers structural transformations including economy, politics, history, ideas, culture and values.

The economic relevance of the BRICS and its members' economic rise, especially of China and India, is part of the persistently historical process of capitalist global expansion. As Li stated:

> The premise of IPE shows that all states and markets are connected in global systems of production, exchange and distribution, and IPE investigates the ways in which states and markets of the world are connected to one another and the arrangements or structures that have evolved to connect them. The rise of China and other emerging powers have indeed "disturbed" the conventional distribution of power and the ways in which states and markets are interrelated with each other.
>
> *(Li 2019a: 4)*

Therefore, the world system theory and the IPE neo-Gramscian approach provide a holistic historical perspective to understand emerging countries and the possibilities of upward or downward mobility in the global system hierarchy.

Changes in the capitalist economy and in the geopolitical game played by the great powers could alter the motivations of a semiperipheral political and economic formation, individually or collectively, to try to change the rules. Nonetheless, as noted above, emerging countries may want to change some rules without wanting to change the organisations. Emerging countries can perceive the system and its rules as unfair, rules that do not reflect the new multipolar political equation. Thus, as Wallerstein states, the role of the semi-periphery, as the realm of "middle powers", is crucial to understand the possibility of changing the global power balance. The semiperipheral countries:

> must choose their alliances and their economic opportunities carefully and swiftly. For semiperipheral states are primarily in competition with each other. If, for example, during a Kondratieff B-phase there is significant relocation of an erstwhile leading industry, it will usually go to semiperipheral countries. But not, however, to all of them; perhaps only to one or two of them. There is not enough space in the production structure of the whole system to permit this kind of relocation (called "development") simultaneously in too many countries. Which one of perhaps fifteen countries will be the locus of such relocation is not easy to determine in advance or even to explain in retrospect. What is easy to grasp is that not every country can be so favoured, or profits would plummet downward too rapidly and too steeply. The competition between strong states and the efforts of semiperipheral states to increase their status and their power result in an ongoing interstate rivalry which normally takes the form of a so-called balance of power, by which one means a situation in which no single state can automatically get its way in the interstate arena.
>
> *(Wallerstein 2004: 57)*

This approach helps us to cope with the (re)emerging countries' current role as well as their structural position, which will be essential in order to analyse the BRICS and the role of China in the global system as well within BRICS. A favourable conjuncture could offer opportunities to countries in a critical interstate conflict scenario, but it could also generate rivalry among emerging countries. In fact, in this context, promotion by invitation is possible. According to Wallerstein:

> "Promotion by invitation" refers to the upward mobility path enjoyed by a semi-periphery or periphery country, whose geopolitical position is vital during the period of global power struggles, or whose internal condition is favourable to global capital mobility and production relocation. This upward mobility is stimulated by the favourable external environment created by the promotion and invitation of the existing hegemon, or by a group of core nations, for the sake of their own geopolitical and geo-economic interests.
>
> *(Wallerstein 2004: 57)*

The dilemma is not promotion by invitation, but who, how and under what circumstances an actor is invited. Li Xing (2017: 4) highlights the example of China entering into the capitalist system in the 1970s and 1980s through the consolidation of Deng Xiaoping's system of "socialism with Chinese characteristics". In this historically critical period, China benefited from the geopolitical anti-USSR scenario as well as the possibility of "promotion by invitation". After the Cold War, and particularly in the twenty-first century, emerging powers acquired a strong international identity "based on a clear view of world order and an understanding of the country's actual and potential position within this order" (2017). Furthermore, unlike traditional middle powers, (re)emerging countries are also regional powers and tend to influence some issue areas of the global agenda. In this context, the 1990s economic crisis helped to catalyse and put forward the demands of emerging countries for a "reforming" agenda in global governance institutions.

Furthermore, Robert Cox's (Cox 1981; 1987) contribution is important to organically understand the links between hegemony, social forces and historical change. Cox reinterprets Gramsci's concept of hegemony within the international scene, that is to say, how domestic hegemony directed by a dominant class or class segment, as a hegemonic social force, is projected and expands geographically at a global scale. This expansion is at the same time geographic and trans-territorial (Scholte 2000); and it includes ideas, material forces and institutions, the latter being a binding agent for the first two (Bieler and Morton 2003; Li 2019a).

The creation of the BRICS alongside China's rise reveals the structural and dialectical liaisons between material capacities, ideas (conceptions of social/world order) and institutions, which constitute the Coxian triadic process of hegemonic reproduction. In these dynamics, change can come from any of the three spheres. In the example of the creation and institutional evolution of the BRICS, we can see this complex transformation, which will be developed in the following section.

The BRICS origins and purpose

Since the new millennium, there was an enhancement of a transformation dynamics in the international system: a gradual "reordering process" (Li 2014) that challenges not only the mainstream theories, as it was previously explained, but also the critical international political economy. In this reordering process, the BRICS group (Brazil, Russia, India, China and South Africa) becomes an important actor of the international political scene.

In hindsight, the constitution and evolution of the BRICS should be analysed taking into account that the emerging middle powers did not participate in an active way in the institutions of global economic governance until the creation of the G20 as a ministerial summit, after the Asian economic crisis in the late 1990s. But it was not until 2008 that it included a summit of heads of state and governments. In the early 2000s, Brazil, India, China, South Africa and Mexico were gradually invited to participate as G8 observers (G8 + 5). Nevertheless, as it was pointed out (Ramos et al. 2012), the five emerging countries did not take part in the debates about the direction of the world economy. In 2003, IBSA (India, Brazil and South Africa) was created (Giaccaglia 2013), and in 2006 the first meeting of Brazil, Russia, India and China's foreign ministers took place (Vadell and Ramos 2019). This concatenation of events and demands for reforms of the liberal Western order fertilised the ground for the first BRIC summit, in June 2009, in Yekaterinburg, Russia (BRICS 2009).

On that account, what is the significance of the BRICS for the world order? Could the BRICS propose a new development paradigm? We cannot assert that the BRICS propose a new development paradigm but rather that their constitution and institutional consolidation through the New Development Bank (NDB) is associated with the transformations of the global economic and political system and that it is linked to China's rise.

The starting point of this work differs from other studies that attribute the origin of the BRICS to an aversion to the unipolar system, which is reinforced in the post-Cold War period. The BRICS emerged not in a unipolar era "after the collapse of the Soviet Union in the early 1990s", as Roberts et al. stated (Roberts et al. 2018: 5), but in a multipolar one, between the 2001 and 2008 economic crises and it became institutionalised after the latter. Therefore, the "common aversions" cannot be pictured as the necessary focal point (Roberts et al. 2018: 8) for the BRICS' collaboration and cooperation. The assumption of this work is close to a common claim in a multipolar era. The diagnosis of a multipolar system and the demand for a more balanced one is found in countless official documents of China for the Global South (China 2008, 2011, 2015; China–SCPRC 2011).

In this direction, the chapter is based on three presuppositions, which stimulated the constitution of common purposes for the creation of the BRICS. They can be categorised as follows:

1   *The crisis of global neoliberalism paradigm*: it implies a neoliberal globalisation crisis and the resultant questioning of the role of the transnational financial class (Jessop and Overbeek 2019), espe-

cially after the 2008 crisis (Costa Vazquez 2018). In the political–institutional field, the developing and emerging countries questioned how the national crises were managed through the World Bank (WB) and the International Monetary Fund (IMF) by means of imposing predetermined prescriptions stated in the Washington Consensus. In the 2010 G20 Seoul summit, the countries reached an agreement that was being discussed since the Toronto summit, in June 2010. The "Seoul Consensus" highlights the importance of sustainable and inclusive economic growth to reduce poverty, as well as the inexistence of a unique formula for development. That leadership also agreed to change the quota and voting shares in the IMF.

2   *Mutual claim for more participation in the global institutions*: BRICS members present an increasing demand for greater participation of the emerging powers in global economic governance institutions: the WB and the IMF. As Christensen and Li stated, "we are witnessing movements toward new patterns of IPE in terms of new alliance formations resulting from global responses to the new situations" (Christensen and Li 2016), as well as from a "new type of hegemonic relations between the existing and the emerging powers" (Li 2016). The BRICS, the "Second World", the Belt and Road Initiative (BRI), the New Silk Road, the NDB or "BRICS Bank", the Silk Road Fund, and the AIIB are now important institutions of international relations and international political economy governance, "symbolizing a growing phenomenon of the changing world order in which the system is no longer ruled and governed by the US-led post-war treaties" (BRI 2015).

3   *Growing and central role of China in global governance, from rule shaper to rule maker* (Li 2019a; Wang 2018): this process entails a new type of leadership in IPE issues, in global governance and in interstate relations. The rise of the PRC and Xi Jinping's 2013 new administration promoted a series of changes in foreign policy, which some authors consider as a substantial change with a more assertive and expansive purpose (Yan 2014). This change has had a correlation with the creation of financial mini-lateral institutions (Wang 2014), a multilateral one, the AIIB, the consolidation of international trade and a greater encouragement of foreign investments. This Chinese strengthening and expansion process outlined what is known as fusion and subsumption of BRICS institution (NDB) into the broad Chinese embedded parallel institutional proposals.

Starting from these three factors, the following section presents a retrospective outline of the BRICS evolution from their constitution as an "economic and political formation" (Wang 2018) until the NDB institutionalisation and the Chinese proposal of the BRICS Plus. Together with this narrative, there will be an analysis based on the critical IPE, showing the process, in view of the three mentioned factors.

Since the first summit in 2009 (Nayyar 2016), the BRICS main objective has been to cooperate in the framework of the G20 summits and to emphasise the importance of reforming financial institutions to increase the participation of emerging middle powers in the international order (BRICS 2009). In their second summit, the BRIC members highlighted the crisis of legitimacy of international institutions – particularly the United Nations (UN) and the IMF – and they claimed for a reform of both institutions (Vadell and Ramos 2019).

The third BRICS summit took place in Sanya in 2011. Two highlights of this summit were (i) the inclusion of South Africa in the bloc and (ii) the fact that, at the time, all countries participating in the BRICS were also on the UN Security Council, which made the summit especially important for security issues, such as the events following the Arab Spring. For the first time, there was an explicit reference to the UN reform in the final declaration resulting from the summit (BRICS 2010). It also reaffirmed the importance of the G20 in the international financial architecture and the need to complete the Doha Round (BRICS 2011: §8).

The fourth BRICS summit was held in New Delhi in 2012 and it was characterised by a joint and more proactive position, apart from advocating reforms in governance institutions. For the first time, it was discussed the possibility to create the BRICS New Development Bank. The resulting compromise committed the finance ministers of each BRICS country to an examination of the feasibility of such a bank (BRICS 2011).

The progression in the number of members (from four to five) and the institutional evolution is observed in the fifth 2013 BRICS summit in Durban. It was also a landmark in the South African quest for greater international presence and geopolitical relevance in order to open the African countries to cooperation for development. As in previous summits, the BRICS reaffirmed its commitment to multilateralism and to the quest for more democratic global governance through the reform of international financial institutions in general and more specifically, of the IMF quota system, as it had been agreed in 2010 (BRICS 2012). Moreover, the BRICS re-emphasised its commitment to the conclusion of the Doha Round: it would support the attempts to give Brazil, India and South Africa a more prominent role in the UN. Finally, the BRICS countries expressed their support for Brazilian Roberto Azevedo as World Trade Organization (WTO) Director-General. These demands express the will for greater participation in the economic governance institutions led by Western powers. However, the BRICS announced the creation of a New Development Bank, with the purpose of seeking "resources for infrastructure and sustainable development projects in BRICS and other emerging economies and developing countries to complement the existing efforts of multilateral financial institutions and regional partnerships for global growth and development" (BRICS 2013: §13). Then, a US$100 billion reserve fund was also created to "help the BRICS countries to avoid short-term liquidity pressures" (BRICS 2013: §9).

The 2014 sixth BRICS summit in Fortaleza launched a new era of meetings where the importance of proposals probably exceeded the importance of demands. The topic was "Inclusive Growth: Sustainable Solutions" and it was one of the most important events in the BRICS process of institutional consolidation and financial cooperation. The "Agreement establishing the New Development Bank (NDB) was signed, with the purpose of mobilizing resources for infrastructure projects and sustainable development in BRICS and other emerging and developing economies" (BRICS 2013: §10). The NDB authorised an initial capital of US$100 billion with a subscribed initial capital of $50 billion, "divided equally among founding members" (BRICS 2014: §11). Additionally, participants signed the BRICS–Contingent Reserve Arrangement (CRA) (with $100 billion capital), the Memorandum of Understanding for Technical Cooperation between Credit Agencies, and a number of export guarantees. The former would "have a positive effect in terms of precaution" and would "help countries counteract short-term liquidity pressures", while the latter would "improve the enabling environment for increased trade opportunities" among the BRICS countries (BRICS 2014: §12).

There were high expectations for the seventh BRICS summit, held in Ufa in 2015. Some advancement was made on intra-BRICS trade and on financial and investment cooperation by deepening the dialogue among the "BRICS Export Credit Agencies", on the one hand, and with the "BRICS Interbank implementation of the BRICS Framework for Trade and Investment Cooperation", on the other hand (BRICS 2015).

2015 was the most clear meeting point between the BRICS' institutional proposal – the NDB–CRA – and the greatest multilateral financial initiative led by China – the AIIB, which would be important to finance the infrastructure projects and the Belt & Road Initiative (BRICS 2014: §13–§14). The participants discussed the details of these new institutional arrangements and there are already indications of how the NDB will function. Moreover, they presented a proposal of cooperation between the NDB and the AIIB (BRI 2015).

The claims for a fairer world order that allows greater participation of the BRICS in the international institutions were reaffirmed in the Goa summit, with emphasis on a "multipolar international order" (BRICS 2016) with a "concerted and determined global approach" based on mutual trust, equity and cooperation.

Alongside the diagnosis of a multipolar system and the demands for a more democratic multilateralism in international relations, the topics on international security were expressly stated in the declarations: Syria's conflict, the need for a two-state solution to the Israel–Palestinian conflict and the challenges posed to the promotion of peace in Afghanistan while combating terrorism and drug trafficking.

Nevertheless, the process of institutional strengthening responds to financial issues, specifically to the NDB. The most remarkable topics are: (i) the proposal to create a BRICS rating agency (BRICS 2015: §15); (ii) the creation of a joint discussion platform for the BRICS Export Credit Agencies to work on trade cooperation among the BRICS countries (BRICS 2016: §44) and (iii) the establishment of the BRICS Customs Cooperation Committee within the framework of the BRICS Strategy for Economic Partnership.

The ninth BRICS summit was held in Xiamen, China. Three relevant documents on institutional financial strengthening were signed at the summit: (i) the action plan for innovation and cooperation (2017–2020); (ii) the strategic framework for BRICS customs cooperation; and (iii) the Memorandum of Understanding on Cooperation (MOU) between the BRICS Business Council and the NDB. The summit also contributed to launch the initiative to develop the BRICS Local Currency Bond Markets and to establish a future BRICS Local Currency Bond Fund (BRICS 2016: §13), highlighting "the progress in concluding the MOU among national development banks of BRICS countries on interbank local currency credit line and on interbank cooperation in relation to credit rating" (BRICS 2017: §10); iv. It was agreed that the NDB African Regional Centre in South Africa would become the first NDB regional office (BRICS 2017: §11); v. Finally, the CRA System of Exchange in Macroeconomic Information was established (BRICS 2017: §31).

The main subject that was debated during the 2018 BRICS Summit, held in Johannesburg, was the 4th Industrial Revolution or the Industry 4.0 (BRICS 2017: §31). The principal objectives are strongly related to China's economic expansion: i) the consolidation of economic cooperation among member countries, which aims at an inclusive growth in the context of the 4th Industrial Revolution; ii) the institutional expansion of the NDB with an office in Sao Paulo, Brazil and iii) the constitution of BRICS Plus, which means the possibility to expand the BRICS' economic and political formation towards a format that is not yet determined.

The BRICS expansion, as a Chinese initiative, was a subject that was present in the Xiamen summit agenda. The State Councillor Wang Yi even suggested the incorporation of Mexico, Pakistan and Sri Lanka with the purpose of creating a wider society of developing countries as a more active SSC platform.

Understanding the BRICS subsumption process

The rise and institutional evolution of the BRICS economic and political formation, composed of five emerging and regional powers, presents an interesting paradox. As the BRICS moved forward in its institutional consolidation and showed evidence of a future increase in the number of members, this evolution has undergone a subsumption process, within a structural transformation of global scope led by the PRC. This process can be analysed following Robert Cox's (1981) model of tripartite hegemony (see Figure 18.1). It is applied to the case of the rise of China to illustrate the BRICS subsuming process.

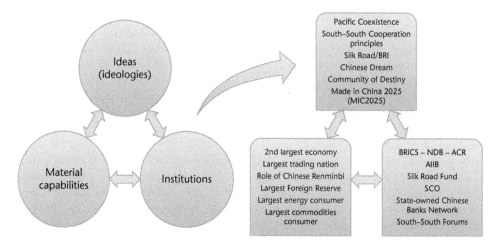

Figure 18.1   Dialectical model of hegemony in relation to the Chinese expansion process based on Li Xing's figure (2019)

Robert Cox's historical and dialectical model of hegemony

The BRICS group, as a political, economic and institutional formation, constitutes the binding agent and the means through which a changing global order is perpetuated. This order, in accordance with Cox's theory, as a "particular configuration of forces which successively define the problematic of war and peace for the ensemble of the states" (Cox 1981: 138), can be understood following the structural connections of the tripartite dialectic model: the "ideas", that is, the collective images of the global social order; the material capabilities; and the specific regulations and institutions that the PRC has been developing during the twenty-first century. China's role has been highlighted and analysed by Li Xing in his outline on BRI (Li 2019b), nevertheless this work will focus on the BRICS paradox.

The BRICS institutional evolution does not evidence a decline, which could be simply interpreted as ineffectiveness, a fall in the members' participation or institutional extinction. Despite the fact that two of its members are suffering economic and political crises (Brazil and South Africa), the BRICS has not diverted from its course. After the admission of South Africa, there were sceptic analysts, like the acronym's creator, Jim O'Neall, who have marked inconsistencies in the BRICS (Naidoo 2012; Vadell and Ramos 2019). Some analysts stress the incongruity of Russia being a member (Cooper 2006; Khalid 2014; Macfarlane 2006). Other criticisms to the BRICS belong to Kiely (2016), who has recently questioned the decline of the United States and has presented a sceptical scenario for the rising BRICS arguing that "there are good reasons why this supposed rise was based on a one-sided discourse, and even more, that we are now moving into a news period where we can talk less about the rise of emerging powers, and more about an emerging market crisis" (Kiely 2016: 3).

The above critical remarks are inconsistent with the institutional improvements of the BRICS and with its outreach process (Vadell and Ramos 2019). Nevertheless, the paradox is that the BRICS political and economic formation, in its process of institutional strengthening, has gradually been incorporated to another regulatory–institutional body led by the PRC, which stimulated the creation of other institutions that complement the NDB and the BRICS Plus (see Figure 18.1). Those institutions are: the AIIB, the Shanghai Cooperation Organization (SCO), the Silk Road Fund (SRF), the State-Owned Chinese Banks Network – of which we can highlight the China Development Bank (CDB) and the Export–Import Bank of China; and the important South–South Forums: the Forum on China–Africa Cooperation (FOCAC), created in 2000; the China–Caribbean Economic and Trade Cooperation Forum (CCETCF), created in 2003; the Forum for Economic and Trade Co-operation between China and Portuguese-Speaking Countries (FETCCPC), created in 2003; the China Arab-States Cooperation Forum (CASCF), created in 2004; the China–Pacific Island Countries Forum (CPICF), created in 2006; and the China–CELAC Forum, officially created in the first Ministerial Meeting, in 2015.

The theoretical basis stems from the South–South Cooperation principles of China's foreign policy, which date back to the 1955 Bandung conference and Zhou Enlai's speech in Senegal in 1964 (Domínguez 2016, 2018; Hong 2017; Vadell 2019). The five principles of pacific coexistence and mutual benefits have been the main guidance of China's foreign policy since the 1949 Revolution. Even in the twenty-first century, the PRC presents and identifies itself before the world as a "great developing nation", as it is stated in official documents (China 2011; China–SCPRC 2011, 2014). Xi Jiping's administration has given a new turn to foreign policy without resigning the mentioned principles. The Chinese Dream (Li 2015; Li and Shaw 2014) and the launch of the New Silk Road or BRI introduced an original ideological impulse to China's expansion.

In this respect, the Chinese President Xi Jinping indicated that the BRI is inspired in the ancient Silk Road, but it does not intend to repeat its geographical trade scope; it rather aims at expanding to the entire world and be open to every country, promoting cooperation and mutual benefits:

> The Belt and Road Initiative is rooted in the ancient Silk Road. It focuses on the Asian, European and African continents, but is also open to all other countries. All countries, from either Asia, Europe, Africa or the Americas, can be international cooperation partners of the Belt and Road Initiative. The pursuit of this initiative is based on extensive consultation and its benefits will be shared by us all.
>
> *(Xi 2017)*

The 2015 Chinese governmental document "Vision and Actions" underlines that the PRC does not aim to restore the ancient Silk Road but to appeal to the metaphor of "the Silk Road spirit", which is an allusion to the past, as a cultural significance to stimulate international cooperation (Liu and Dunford 2016: 4).

Even if it is not possible to make an in-depth analysis of China's official foreign policy under Xi Jinping's administration, it is worth emphasising its assertive feature, which did not imply the resignation of the principles inherited from Den Xiaoping regarding the low profile to foster national development (Qin 2014).

Final considerations

The IPE and IR meet a new challenge to understand the economic transformations and the movements of plate tectonics in international politics, before the emergence of new actors. Some expressions, like "new cold war" attempt to draw inspiration from the past to understand the present; others make allusion to physics and the concept of "entropy" (Schweller 2014), which is an analogy of chaos as the result of an USA post-hegemonic world. Re-establishing the idea of a multipolar world generally comes together with fears regarding cultural issues that stem from the increasingly important role of countries like China and India in global economy.

Before these transformations and the uncertainty caused by this process, the BRICS phenomenon is only a sign, an important symptom of these changes.

This work intended to interpret the BRICS and the challenging to the liberal Western order and whether this change would affect the global insertion of periphery countries. Furthermore, our conclusions reveal a paradox. Although we cannot assert that the BRICS proposes a new development paradigm, there is a gradual and consistent institutional consolidation process through the NDB, as well as a high possibility of increasing the group's members by virtue of the BRICS Plus proposal. However, this institutionalisation process is not detached from greater transformations related to the rise of the PRC and its increasingly important role within the group and in global political economy. The NDB or BRICS' Bank cannot be separated from the Chinese approach to South–South cooperation in consonance with China's power regarding the financial cooperation network process, which is increasingly intertwined with the BRI. Acharya's concept of "multiplex world" helps to reinforce the idea of this work in the sense that it identifies a feature of the current international system "in which elements of the liberal order survive, but are subsumed in a complex of multiple, crosscutting international orders" (Acharya 2017: 272).

This "metamorphosis" of the Western liberal order into a kind of multiplex order has specific features dialectically linked to China's rising process and its ambitious proposal of an embedded Chinese liberal order, which could be analysed in a further research project. To conclude, Figure 18.1, which details this process according to Cox's model of hegemony, includes the material forces that attribute meaning to the dialectic triad. China became the second largest world economy in 2010 and this is a growing tendency (Moore 2011). In 2013, the PRC became the largest trading nation, surpassing the US (Monaghan 2014). As regards currency issues, despite the US dollar's pre-eminence and the fact that the Renminbi is below the American and European currencies in international payments, the growing role of the Chinese Renminbi is a strong tendency with concrete steps to become a vehicle currency for trade facilitation, through the conclusion of bilateral currency swap deals with more than 30 countries. In this direction, in October 2016, the IMF included the Chinese currency in its Special Drawing Rights basket. In 2008, China held the largest foreign currency reserves in the world. In addition, the Asian giant is the largest energy consumer and the largest commodities consumer.

The BRICS continues its course and its agenda will agree with the imperatives of China's expansion in the contemporary capitalist system. The stimulation of intra-group trade and a more balanced economic cooperation could be of mutual benefit, since the current commercial focal point of the BRICS is oriented towards China. During the twenty-first century, the PRC has become the first trading partner of the rest of the BRICS members (Brazil, Russia, India and South Africa), with remarkable trade surplus for China. Furthermore, there is an institutional strengthening of the NDB, which will open an office in Brazil. Finally, BRICS Plus, in whichever format it adopts, and Industry 4.0 are a priority in the PRC's global initiative of a New Silk Road, known as the Belt & Road Initiative.

Bibliography

Acharya, A. 2017. After Liberal Hegemony: The Advent of a Multiplex World Order. *Ethics & International Affairs* 31 no. 3: 271–285.

Alexandroff, A. S. and Cooper, A. F. 2010. *Rising States, Rising Institutions: Challenges for Global Governance.* Waterloo, Ont./Washington, DC: Brookings Institution Press.

Allison, G. 2017. *The Thucydides Trap.* Foreign Policy. Available at: https://foreignpolicy.com/2017/06/09/the-thucydides-trap/.

Bieler, A. and Morton, D. A. 2003. Theoretical and Methodological Challenges of Neo-Gramscian Perspectives in International Political Economy. *International Gramsci Society*. Available at: www.international gramscisociety.org/resources/online_articles/main/main.html.

Bielschowsky, R. 2000. *Cinqüenta Anos De Pensamento Na Cepal*. Sao Paulo: Record, CEPAL.

BRI. 2015. *Full Text: Action Plan on the Belt and Road Initiative*. Available at: http://english.gov.cn/archive/publications/2015/03/30/content_281475080249035.htm.

BRICS. 2009. *First Summit: Joint Statement of the Bric Countries Leaders*. Available at: http://brics.itamaraty.gov.br/pt_br/categoria-portugues/20-documentos/73-primeiro-declaracao.

BRICS. 2010. *Second Summit: Joint Statement*. Available at: http://brics.itamaraty.gov.br/category-english/21-documents/66-second-summit.

BRICS. 2011. *Third Summit: Sanya Declaration and Action Plan*. Available at: http://brics.itamaraty.gov.br/category-english/21-documents/67-third-summit.

BRICS. 2012. *Fourth Summit: Delhi Declaration and Action Plan*. Available at: http://brics.itamaraty.gov.br/category-english/21-documents/68-fourth-summit.

BRICS. 2013. *Fifth Summit: Ethekwini Declaration and Action Plan*. Available at: http://brics.itamaraty.gov.br/category-english/21-documents/69-fifth-summit.

BRICS. 2014. *Sixth Summit: Fortaleza Declaration and Action Plan*. *Available at:* http://brics.itamaraty.gov.br/category-english/21-documents/223-sixth-summit-declaration-and-action-plan.

BRICS. 2015. *Vii Brics Summit – Ufa Declaration*. Available at: http://brics.itamaraty.gov.br/category-english/21-documents/253-vii-brics-summit-ufa-declaration.

BRICS. 2016. *8th Brics Summit Goa Declaration*. Available at: http://brics.itamaraty.gov.br/images/pdf/GoaDeclarationandActionPlan.pdf.

BRICS. 2017. *Brics Leaders Xiamen Declaration*. Available at: www.brics.utoronto.ca/docs/170904-xiamen.pdf.

Brooks, S. G., Ikenberry, J. and Wohlforth, W. (2012/2013). Don't Come Home, America. The Case against Retrenchment. *International Security* 37, no. 3: 7–51.

Chin, G. T. 2015. The State of the Art: Trends in the Study of the Brics and Multilateral Organizations. In: *Rising Powers and Multilateral Institutions*. Lesage, D. and Van de Graaf, T. (ed.) Basingstoke/New York: Palgrave Macmillan.

China. 2008. *China's Policy Paper on Latin America and the Caribbean*. Available at: www.gov.cn/english/official/2008-11/05/content_1140347.htm.

China. 2011. *White Paper on China's Peaceful Development*. Available at: www.china.org.cn/government/whitepaper/node_7126562.htm.

China. 2015. *China's Second Africa Policy Paper*. Xinhua.

China–SCPRC. 2011. *White Paper China's Foreign Aid*. Available at: http://english.gov.cn/archive/white_paper/2014/09/09/content_281474986284620.htm.

China–SCPRC. 2014. *White Paper China's Foreign Aid*. Available at: http://english.gov.cn/archive/white_paper/2014/08/23/content_281474982986592.htm.

Christensen, S. F. and Li, X. 2016. The Emerging Powers and the Emerging World Order: Back to the Future? In: *Emerging Powers, Emerging Markets, Emerging Societies*. Christensen, S and Xing Li. New York: Palgrave Macmillan.

Cohen, B. J. 2014. *Advanced Introduction to International Political Economy*. Northampton: Edward Elgar Publishing.

Cooper, A. F. 1997. Niche Diplomacy: Middle Powers after the Cold War. *Studies in Diplomacy*. , Basingstoke; New York: Macmillan; St. Martin's Press.

Cooper, A. F. 2013. Squeezed or Revitalised? Middle Powers, the G20 and the Evolution of Global Governance. *Third World Quarterly* 34, no. 6: 963–984.

Cooper, A. F. and Higgott, R. A. 1990. *Middle Power Leadership and Coalition Building: The Cairns Group and the Uruguay Round, March 1990. Working Paper*. Canberra: Research School of Pacific Studies. Australian National University.

Cooper, A. F., Higgott, R. A. and Nossal, K. R. 1993. Relocating Middle Powers: Australia and Canada in a Changing World Order. *Canada and International Relations*. Vancouver: UBC Press.

Cooper, J. M. 2006. Russia as a BRIC: Only a Dream? In: *European Research Working Paper Series* No 13. Available at: www.download.bham.ac.uk/govsoc/eri/working-papers/wp13-cooper.pdf.

Costa Vazquez, K. 2018. *Can the Brics Propose a New Development Paradigm? Aljazeera*. Available at: www.aljazeera.com/indepth/opinion/brics-propose-development-paradigm-180718121646771.html.

Cox, R. W. 1981. Social Forces, States and World Orders: Beyond International Relations Theory. *Millennium – Journal of International Studies* 10, no. 2: 126–155.

Cox, R. W. 1987. *Production, Power, and World Order: Social Forces in the Making of History*. New York: Columbia University Press.

Cox, R. 1989. Middlepowermanship, Japan, and Future World Order. *International Journal* 44, no. 4: 823–862.

Domínguez, M. R. 2016. En Los Pliegues De La Historia: Cooperación Sur-Sur Y Procesos De Integración En América Latina Y El Caribe. *Estudos Internacionais 4*, no. 2: 57–77.

Domínguez, M. R. 2018. China Y El Renacimiento De África. In: *A Expansão Econômica E Geopolítica Da China No Século Xxi*. Vadell, J. (ed.): 300. Belo Horizonte: Editora PUC Minas.

Giaccaglia, C. 2013. Estrategias De «Quodlíbet» En El Escenario Internacional Contemporáneo: Las Acciones De India, Brasil Y Sudáfrica (Ibsa) En Los Ámbitos Multilaterales. *Revista Brasileira de Política Internacional* 55, no. 2: 90–108.

Gill, S. 1990. American Hegemony and the Trilateral Commission. *Cambridge Studies in International Relations*. Cambridge; New York: Cambridge University Press.

Gilley, B, and O'Neil, A. 2014. *Middle Powers and the Rise of China*. Washington, DC: Georgetown University Press.

Gilpin, R. 1987. *The Political Economy of International Relations*. Princeton: Princeton University Press.

Gilpin, R. 2000. *The Challenge of Global Capitalism: The World Economy in the 21st Century*. Princeton: Princeton University Press.

Gilpin, R. 2001. *Global Political Economy: Understanding the International Economic Order*. Princeton: Princeton University Press.

Hong, Z. (ed.) 2017. *China's Foreign Aid: 60 Years in Retrospect*. Singapore: Springer.

Huelsz, C. 2009. *Middle Power Theories and Emerging Powers in International Political Economy: A Case Study of Brazil*. PhD Thesis, University of Manchester: Faculty of Humanities.

Huntington, S. P. 1968. *Political Order in Changing Societies*. New Haven; London: Yale University Press.

Hurrell, A. 2000. *Paths to Power: Foreign Policy Strategies of Intermediate States in Some reflections on the role of intermediate powers in international institutions*. Hurrell, A., Cooper, A. F., González, G., Ubiraci, R. and Sitaraman, S. (eds). Washington, DC: *Latin American Program*. Washington DC: Woodrow Wilson International Centre.

Ikenberry, J. G. 2018. Why the Liberal World Order Will Survive. *Ethics & International Affairs 32*, no. 1: 17–29.

Jessop, B. and Overbeek, H. 2019. *Transnational Capital and Class Fractions. The Amsterdam School Perspective Reconsidered*. Ripe Series in Global Political Economy. Brassett, J., Tsingou, E. and Soederberg, S. New York: Routledge.

Jordaan, E. 2017. The Emerging Middle Power Concept: Time to Say Goodbye? *South African Journal of International Affairs* 24, no. 3: 1–18.

Keohane, R. O. 1984. *After Hegemony: Cooperation and Discord in the World Political Economy*. Princeton: Princeton University Press.

Khalid, A. 2014. The Power of the Brics in World Trade and Growth, Analysing the Macroeconomic Impacts within and across the Bloc. In: *The Rise of the Brics in the Global Political Economy: Changing Paradigms?* Io Lo, V. and Hiscock, M. (ed.) Cheltenham: Edward Elgar.

Kiely. 2016. *The Rise and Fall of Emerging Powers*. London: Palgrave Macmillan.

Kim, W. and Gates, S. 2015. Power Transition Theory and the Rise of China. *International Area Studies Review* 18, no. 3: 219–226.

Kindleberger, C. 1973. The World in Depression, *1929–1939. History of the World Economy in the Twentieth Century*. Berkeley: University of California Press.

Kindleberger, C. 1981. Dominance and Leadership in International Economy. *International Studies Quarterly* 25, no. 2: 242–254.

Layne, C. 2018. The US–Chinese Power Shift and the End of the Pax Americana. *International Affairs 94*, no. 1: 89–111.

Li, X. 2014. *The Brics and Beyond: The International Political Economy of the Emergence of a New World Order*. Farnham: Ashgate.

Li, X. 2015. Interpreting and Understanding "the Chinese Dream" in a Holistic Nexus. *Fudan J. Hum. Socials Science 8*, no. 4: 505–520.

Li, X. 2016. The Expansion of China's Global Hegemonic Strategy: Implications for Latin America. *Journal of China and International Relations 4*, no. Special Issue: 1–26.

Li, X. 2017. The Rise of Emerging Powers & China and the Enlargement of "Room for Maneuver" and "Upward Mobility". *Rising Powers in Global Governance*. Available at: http://risingpowersproject.com/

the-rise-of-emerging-powers-china-and-the-enlargement-of-room-for-maneuver-and-upward-mobility/.

Li, X. 2019a. Mapping China's "One Belt One Road" Initiative. In: *International Political Economy Series*. Shaw, T. (ed.) London/New York: Palgrave Macmillan.

Li, X. 2019b. Understanding the Multiple Facets of China's: One Belt One Road Initiative. In: *Mapping China's "One Belt One Road" Initiative*. Li, X. (ed.) London/New York: Palgrave Macmillan.

Li, X. and Shaw, T. M. 2014. Same Bed, Different Dreams and Riding Tiger Dilemmas: China's Rise and International Relations/Political Economy. *Journal of Chinese Political Science* 19, no. 1: 69–93.

Liu, W. and Dunford, M. 2016. Inclusive Globalization: Unpacking China's Belt and Road Initiative. *Area Development and Policy* 1, no. 3: 1–18.

Macfarlane, N. S. 2006. The "R" in Brics: Is Russia An Emerging Power? *International Affairs* 82, no. 2: 41–57.

Mearsheimer, J. J. 2001. *The Tragedy of Great Power Politics*. New York; London: W.W. Norton.

Mearsheimer, J. 2006. China's Unpeaceful Rise. *Current History* 105, no. 690: 160–162.

Mearsheimer, J. 2010. The Gathering Storm: China's Challenge to Us Power in Asia. Chinese *Journal of International Politics* 3, no. 4: 381–396.

Monaghan, A. 2014. China Surpasses Us as World's Largest Trading Nation. *The Guardian*. Available at: www.theguardian.com/business/2014/jan/10/china-surpasses-us-world-largest-trading-nation.

Moore, M. 2014. China Is the World's Second Largest Economy. *The Telegraph*. Available at: www.telegraph.co.uk/finance/economics/8322550/China-is-the-worlds-second-largest-economy.html.

Naidoo, S. 2012. South Africa's Presence "Drags Down Brics". *Mail & Guardian*.

Nayyar, D. 2016. Brics, Developing Countries and Global Governance. *Third World Quarterly* 37, no. 4: 575–591.

Nolte, D. 2007. How to Compare Regional Powers: Analytical Concepts and Research Topics. *ECPR Joint Session Workshops*. Helsinki.

Organski, A. F. K. 1968. *World Politics*. Second Edition ed. New York: Alfred A. Knopf.

Qin, Y. 2014. Continuity through Change: Background   Knowledge and China's International Strategy. *The Chinese Journal of International Politics* 7, no. 3: 285–314.

Ramos, L., Vadell, J., Saggioro, A. and Fernandes, M. 2012. A Governança Econômica Global E Os Desafios Do G-20 Pós-Crise Financeira: Análise Das Posições De Estados Unidos, China, Alemanha E Brasil. *Revista Brasileira de Política Internacional* 55, no. 2: 10–27.

Roberts, C., Armijo, L. and Katada, S. 2018. *The Brics and Collective Financial Statecraft (Kindle Edition)*. Oxford: Oxford University Press.

Rostow, W. W. 1960. *The Stages of Economic Growth, a Non-Communist Manifesto*. Cambridge Eng.: University Press.

Scholte, J. A. 2000. *Globalization: A Critical Introduction*. New York: St. Martin's Press.

Schweller, R. 2014. The Age of Entropy, or Why the New World Order Won't Be Orderly. *Foreign Affairs*. Available at: www.foreignaffairs.com/articles/united-states/2014-06-16/age-entropy.

Strange, S. 1970. International Economics and International Relations: A Case of Mutual Neglect. *International Affairs (Royal Institute of International Affairs 1944-)* 46, no. 2; 304–315.

Vadell, J. A. 2019. China in Latin America: South-South Cooperation with Chinese Characteristics. *Latin American Perspectives* 46, no. 2: 107–125.

Vadell, J. and Ramos, L. 2019. The Role of Declining Brazil and Ascending China into the Brics Initiative. In: *The International Political Economy of the Brics*. Li, X. (ed.). London: Routledge.

Vivares, E. 2018. Regionalism, Development and the Post-Commodities Boom in South America. In: *International Political Economy Series*. Shaw, T. (ed.) London: Palgrave Macmillan.

Wallerstein, I. 2004. *World-Systems Analysis. An Introduction*. Durham and London: Duke University Press.

Wang, H. 2014. *From "Taoguang Yanghui" to "Yousuo Zouwei": China's Engagement in Financial Minilateralism*. CIGI Papers no. 52. Available at: www.cigionline.org/sites/default/files/cigi_paper_no52.pdf.

Wang, H. 2018. *China and International Financial Standards: From "Rule Taker" to "Rule Maker"? CIGI Papers*. Available at: www.cigionline.org/sites/default/files/documents/Paper no. 182_0.pdf.

Williamson, J. 1990. *What Washington Means by Policy Reform. Latin American Adjustment: How Much Has Happened?*. Williamson, J. (ed.) Washington: Institute for International Economics.

Xi, J. 2017. *Full Text of President Xi's Speech at Opening of Belt and Road Forum*. Xinhuanet. Available at: www.xinhuanet.com/english/2017-05/14/c_136282982.htm.

Yan, X. 2014. From Keeping a Low Profile to Striving for Achievement. *The Chinese Journal of International Politics* 7, no. 2: 153–184.

19
The long battle for global governance continued

Stephen Buzdugan and Anthony Payne

Introduction

We published a book with Routledge in 2016 entitled *The Long Battle for Global Governance* in which we self-consciously sought to open up the way that research on the subject of global governance was conventionally conducted within IPE. We think that the arguments we made in that book remain valid – indeed, the sense that global governance is something that is being battled over has only increased in the last couple of years – and so we make no apology for reprising here the essential features of the 'contested' re-interpretation of the evolution of global governance over the last seven decades since the mid-1940s that we set out in much greater detail in our book.

We needed then, and similarly need now, to begin with some clarification of our approach and use of key terms. We generally take it for granted these days that we live in some kind of global order, characterised by an ongoing process variously described from different conceptual positions as globalisation, interdependence or growing interconnectedness. It is therefore hardly surprising that IPE as a field has devoted more and more time to the study of the governance of this new global order. Although it arguably overstates the coherence of what has actually been put in place as yet on this front, the term that is now most frequently used to open up discussion of how the world is governed is global governance. As Timothy Sinclair noted at the beginning of his account of the extensive contemporary use of this concept, it is 'a difficult idea to get away from these days', not least because it also 'seems to capture something very important about our world in the second decade of the twenty-first century' (Sinclair 2012: 1). We agree and deploy the term global governance as a short-hand for what might otherwise be more clumsily described as the governance of a globalising, and thus over time increasingly globalised, world political economy.

But such a declaration, although useful, does not resolve all of the issues that need to be resolved in order to establish the broad conceptual and historical framing of this research arena. There is no doubt that the literature on global governance from within IPE has unquestionably grown hugely in volume over the last few years. But, for all that, it remains embryonic and still lacks an accepted conceptual shape. As has already been implied, the field's preoccupation has instead been with the concept and process of globalisation itself. Fortuitously, this is actually the right place from which to begin the analysis of global governance. Put differently, the political economy (structure) must be understood before the politics (agency) can be grasped. This notion of a necessary link between political economy context and associated pattern of governance runs through the one outstanding historical study that has been written about the early phases of the emergence of governance at the global level, namely, Craig Murphy's (1994) account of international organisation and industrial change since 1850. He shows in this work that the world organisations that first emerged in this modern period derived most of their effectiveness from the fact that transnational coalitions of liberal social forces invested them with the task of promoting the leading sectors of each successive phase of industrialism. The method used by Murphy, with its emphasis on the necessary interaction between developments in the superstructure and substructure of global affairs, has much merit and, in that spirit, the analytical task confronting us can be expressed as that of mapping and understanding the interaction of changing modes of governance and a changing global political economy.

However, we must still clarify our usage of the concept of governance in this context. The beginning of the debate about this can be traced explicitly to the publication in the early 1990s of *Governance without Government: Order and Change in World Politics*, jointly edited by James Rosenau and Ernst-Otto Czempiel (1992). Prior to this moment most attempts to understand 'government at the global level' had been made via rationalist studies of regime formation mostly inspired by the work of Robert Keohane (1984). The central insight of this school was that, over time, states could learn to cooperate in non-zero-sum ways if they formed intergovernmental institutions, or regimes, in particular policy areas. Rosenau, who wrote the extended introductory chapter in *Governance without Government*, was clearly influenced by regime theorising, although in this work he sought deliberately and successfully to move the discussion forward. He set out the idea of governance as a set of 'regulatory mechanisms in a sphere of activity which function effectively even though they are not endowed with formal authority' (Rosenau 1992: 5). Governance thus differs from government in that 'it refers to activities backed by shared goals that may or may not derive from legal and formally prescribed responsibilities and that do not necessarily rely on police powers to overcome defiance and attain compliance'. It is, in other words, 'a more encompassing phenomenon' which 'embraces governmental institutions, but ... also subsumes informal, non-governmental mechanisms' (Rosenau 1992: 4). Here lay the similarity with the conventional notion of regimes, except that regimes had generally been seen to exist in certain defined issue areas (Krasner 1983) and governance was used here by Rosenau in a manner which clearly tied the concept to the whole global order. In a later article in the first issue of the journal *Global Governance*, Rosenau (1995: 13) returned to these questions, defining global governance as 'systems of rule at all levels of human activity ... in which the pursuit of goals through the exercise of control has transnational repercussions'. Finally, by the time this piece had been edited to reappear in his book, *Along the Domestic-Foreign Frontier*, the ultimate Rosenau definition of governance had been refined as: 'spheres of authority ... at all levels of human activity ... that amount to systems of rule in which goals are pursued through the exercise of control' (Rosenau 1997: 145).

Many thought, and no doubt still think, that this was a very loose way of conceiving of governance at the global level. But the appeal of Rosenau's working approach was precisely its breadth. It was not at all, as sometimes alleged (Finkelstein 1995), a matter of bringing together different types of actor in some great 'spaghetti bowl', but rather of sensitising analysts of the changing patterns of post-Cold War international relations to the extent of the mix of actors – governmental and non-governmental, public and private, legitimate and illegitimate – which had come to participate in the shaping of systems of global rule. Rosenau captured this very effectively. The problem with his analysis was rather different: it was, as Murphy (2000: 796)

Box 19.1 What is global governance?

Although there is no agreed definition of global governance within the field of IPE, some of its key features can nonetheless be distilled from the various debates. The first point, which sets global governance apart from other phenomena in IPE, is that it requires the existence of a multilateral regulatory function in a variety of issue areas that may, *inter alia*, be economic, environmental, political and/or social in nature. Next, 'governance' implies the exercise of control at various levels, in which power in its structural and agential forms influences the shaping of agendas; the development and enforcement of policies; and the inclusion or exclusion of governmental and non-governmental actors in the process. Understanding the nexus of power between the ideas, institutions and actors involved in any particular form of global governance is the key to making sense of its nature and dynamics over time. Finally, global governance may have varying degrees of formality and informality and thus includes, but does not necessitate, formal treaties, agreements and multilateral organisations, such as the IMF, the World Bank and the WTO.

---

himself noted, that he was 'less capable of explaining why so much of this creative movement in world politics seems to have added up to the supremacy of the neoliberal agenda both within and across states'. Yet this lacuna can easily enough be filled by the incorporation of some of the insights of constructivist thinking in political analysis. As is well known now, these suggest that all actors within international relations have the capacity in their exchanges to influence each other's understanding of their own interests, which means that the norms of those exchanges, the manner of the communication, matters. To follow Murphy again (2000: 797), in the contemporary era 'liberal norms ... exert power not due to their inherent validity or rightness, but because they are regularly enacted within certain realms, because some international actors have become convinced of their rightness and validity'.

As ever, though, theoretical constructs grounded in the primacy of agency generally do not fully grasp the constraints which systematically bear upon the freedom of manoeuvre of the actors they identify and address. It is certainly important that this focus on agency is not lost in too severe an embrace of structuralism, but the argument must nevertheless be made that it needs to be more astutely related to an awareness of structural power and an exploration of structural context than has generally been the norm in mainstream international relations theorising. In sum, Rosenau, combined with a measure of constructivism, both suitably embedded within a sense of the limits and opportunities provided by the existence of a set of structures called the global political economy, constitutes the best conceptual basis on which to conduct research into global governance.

We have also seen that discussion of global governance per se did not really begin until the 1990s. This is problematic, because it makes no sense to think of global governance as actually beginning in that decade. If it is the case, as we have argued, that it seeks to describe a process of governing an emerging global political economy, then one might suppose that its advent would more accurately coincide with the beginnings of a widespread realisation that such a global order needed some sort of governance for its survival and functionality. Immanuel Wallerstein (2004) and associated world-system theorists date that process as beginning somewhere around 1450 with the development at that time of a major economic crisis at the heart of European feudalism. Many others point plausibly to the emerging imperial rivalries of the first decade of the twentieth century and the first significant attempt in 1918 to create a genuinely global organisation, the League of Nations, by which to bind the world together in peace and liberalism. However, we prefer, as is generally the norm, to date the beginning of global governance to that extended moment – which ran roughly from the planning and eventual holding of the Bretton Woods Conference in the United States (US) in July 1944 through to the ratification of the United Nations in October 1945 – when the Second World War was brought to an end and all of the major institutions of the modern post-war era, including the International Monetary Fund (IMF), the World Bank and then the General Agreement on Tariffs and Trade (GATT), came into existence one after the other. This process was also accompanied by a widespread sense across many parts of the globe that a new beginning was being made in global affairs. A global framework was self-consciously designed and created to allow much of the world to emerge both from war and colonialism and to advance together towards prosperity. It also in time permitted the process that we have come to know as globalisation to break out and also flourish. In short, it is not difficult to argue that 1944–1945 marks the real start of the modern period of global governance.

The final preliminary question that needs to be discussed in the introductory section of this chapter concerns the emphasis that we think it is important to place on the politics of the process by which global governance has been shaped from 1944–1945 onwards. It is often said that winners write their own histories; even more truly, they shape the nature of the settlements that follow long periods of conflict. Global governance did not just appear at the end of the Second World War, as if generated miraculously out of the exhaustion of all the combatants. It was, to all intents and purposes, imposed by the power of the victors, principally the United States, supported by Britain, and was honed in accordance with the dominant ideas held by the elites of these two states, an amalgam of views and values best summarised as Anglo-American liberalism. At that particular historical moment several other key states in the world languished in defeat and many others remained caught as colonies in the trap of empire. In other words, it was far from the case that all countries and peoples of the world were consulted about this new global deal and the reality is that the settlement that was reached was not liked in many quarters. Although opposition to its main elements has often been ignored in histories of the Bretton Woods settlement (for an exception, see Helleiner 2014), that does not mean that it did not exist or was not openly articulated both at the time and afterwards.

This fact exposes the key point that we want to emphasise in our proposed reframing of the study of global governance. The point is that over the subsequent 60–70 years, many critiques were mounted of this emergent mode of global governance, accompanied often by fierce challenges to the status quo and passionate calls for the implementation of a new and different world order. We are thinking here in particular of the rise of so-called 'North/South' tensions in global politics in the 1970s. These have been widely studied, but they have not generally been seen as part of the history of global governance. Yet it is actually very helpful in analytical terms to locate this history in such a context. Global governance has always been a contested process. In particular, we see when we look more closely that poor and middle-income countries have repeatedly challenged a whole range of policy orthodoxies. They have done so by organising politically into a variety of different alliances from which to articulate their demands and then respond to the way those demands have either been met or not met. In so doing, they have in effect been seeking to re-shape many of the familiar contours of global governance laid down in that highly creative, extended moment of 1944–1945.

From our perspective this is a critical consideration, because it addresses directly the question of who global governance works for – of what ideas it mainly promotes, of how genuinely representative of the globe as a whole it is, of how much it has always been, and perhaps still remains, a vehicle for the assertion of power by minority interests in global politics and global political economy. Indeed, the novelty of the research agenda that we propose is that it invites extended and ongoing exploration of the origins and validity of these key contentions about the nature of contemporary global governance. We argue, in fact, that there has taken place over a period of many years what we call a 'long battle' for global governance, a battle that is far from over and bound, by definition almost, to continue into the foreseeable future. We suggest that such a focus acts as an important corrective to conventional understandings of the modern history of global governance, precisely because it highlights the sometimes hidden, sometimes challenging, but nearly always critical, voices of the huge majority of non-dominant countries that were always part of and subject to the workings of the emergent post-1945 global order.

The 'long battle' in its historical phases

Our book aimed to tell, or perhaps more accurately re-tell, the story of this battle, bringing forward the under-noticed and under-researched roles played and perspectives taken by those countries of the world that have been variously described over the past 70 years or so as 'poorer', 'ex-colonial', 'Third World', 'underdeveloped', 'less developed', 'developing' and lately 'emerging'. The next section of this chapter, supported by a number of boxes drawing attention to key episodes, identifies briefly the key features of the six historical phases into we divided this story.

Box 19.2 Global governance as a "long battle"

Global governance is the result of a long, contested, historical process that can be traced back to the earliest developments of capitalism in Western Europe. However, its modern form is firmly rooted in the negotiations between the Allied nations prior to the end of the Second World War, which gave rise to the GATT, the IMF, the World Bank and the UN. With only few exceptions, dominant accounts of the evolution of modern global governance tend to neglect the presence, interests and activities of the so-called 'developing' countries, whereas, for example, nearly half of the countries which attended Bretton Woods were 'developing' countries. Thus, from the start, the modern institutions of global governance were forged within an environment of unequal relationships between groups of countries, resulting in a governance framework that reflected the most powerful interests and reinforced the positions of the dominant countries in the world order. From their inception, these institutions accommodated only the minimum demands of the 'poorer' countries in order to secure their acceptance and participation in the system. The 'long battle' derives, therefore, from the strategies and efforts of the more 'marginalised' countries to transform or develop alternatives to the modern institutions of global governance that better met their long-held demands.

Bretton Woods and the foundations of modern global governance

The foundations of modern global governance were indeed laid down at the Bretton Woods Conference and subsequent meetings about trade, but they cannot be properly explained by reference to the dominant narrative in the IPE literature. This derives principally from John Gerard Ruggie's highly influential article (1982), which introduced and rendered orthodox the concept of 'embedded liberalism'. In it Ruggie portrayed the process of arriving at the compromise of a multilateral, liberal economic order with a permitted measure of domestic intervention as a negotiation, and ultimately a creative synthesis, between the ambitions of the US and Britain. At no point did Ruggie refer to the fact that 42 other countries attended Bretton Woods, or even mention what they had hoped to achieve by attending. Instead, the multilateral system that emerged was generally described quite wrongly as something based on a consensus. Although there is no doubt that the US and Britain led these initiatives and framed what it was possible to agree, the other participants, particularly the Latin American countries, Australia, India and the Soviet Union, were not silent or necessarily supportive.

Several issues show this. At the conference countries such as India and Mexico presented the case for giving a greater developmental focus to both the IMF and the World Bank. Some compromises were achieved, in which developmental aims became incorporated into the two institutions (more so in the World Bank than the IMF), although these were not enough to shift the general view among these and other poorer countries that these two new institutions were aligned more with the interests and requirements of the industrialised countries than those of the poor and 'less developed'. Additionally, in the negotiations for a trade institution to parallel the Fund and the Bank, countries such as Australia, India, Brazil and Chile mounted a persistent effort to divert the Anglo-American proposals away from a global free trade agenda to one that offered a degree of protection to more vulnerable economies. But again these objectives were only partially realised, with the interim GATT agreement meeting most of the immediate trading needs of the major industrialised countries.

In sum, countries beyond the US, Britain and their industrialised partners did at least succeed in placing their demands on the table of the new emerging mode of global governance. It is striking, to say the least, that issues which two or three decades later came angrily to the fore in global politics can often be seen to have been articulated at the very inception of the system.

The United Nations and the emergence of the 'Third World'

Possessing few options in the immediate post-war years to force the Fund, the Bank and the GATT to rethink their initial mandates, most other countries moved instead to seek out alternatives within the United Nations (UN), formed in parallel with Bretton Woods in 1945. It was not only that the UN operated in accordance with a more equal 'one-country, one-vote' system, but also that it responded to pressure from the growing number of newly independent countries in the world to set up new bodies that spread its economic remit. The most important was the UN Conference on Trade and Development (UNCTAD) which met initially in Geneva in 1964. Seeing the opportunity, many so-called 'developing' countries moved enthusiastically to organise themselves into a new bloc, the Group of 77 (G77), as the basis from which to bargain for the significant changes in global governance that they had long desired.

Yet, even by 1966, 'there was a general feeling among the developing countries that UNCTAD was not making much progress' (Toye and Toye 2004: 223). The industrialised countries, which at first had suffered a 'collective fright induced by the emergence of the Group of 77', began to regain their own self-confidence and embarked on a number of effective stalling tactics in relation to the implementation of decisions taken at UNCTAD. These frustrations set the tone for the G77's official meeting in Algiers, in October 1967, in preparation for the follow-up UNCTAD II conference the following year. It produced in the Algiers Charter 'a comprehensive document which straightaway became the foremost authentic and authoritative expression of the G77's collective endeavours and aspirations' (Geldart and Lyon 1980: 90). These included commodity agreements, supplementary financing, trade preferences for manufactured products, international shipping reforms and a target of 1 per cent of Gross Domestic Product for international aid. But, again, in all but minor respects, UNCTAD II was another failure, marked by a stubborn refusal to engage by the 'developed' countries.

> ## Box 19.3 The rise in 'Third World' demands for change: UNCTAD 1 and 2
>
> Amid disappointment and frustration with the de facto global governance of trade through the GATT, 'developing' countries from Africa, Asia and Latin America, which collectively held a majority at the UN after their acquisition of political independence in the post-colonial era, sought the creation of a new institution in the 1960s to govern global trade on more equal terms. Following from a UN General Assembly proposal by these countries in 1961, the United Nations Conference on Trade and Development ('UNCTAD I') was convened in Geneva in 1964 with the reluctant support of the 'developed' countries. On the insistence of the 'developing' countries, Dr Raúl Prebisch, an influential Argentinian economist, was installed as its Secretary-General. Under his leadership at UNCTAD I, and then at UNCTAD II in 1968, the 'developing countries' asserted that deteriorating terms of trade for their primary exports held back their development. They called for the 'developed' countries to redress this imbalance through commodity agreements, supplementary financing, trade preferences for manufactured products, international shipping reforms and a target of 1 per cent of GDP for international aid. Although ultimately they failed to persuade the 'developed' countries to accept these demands, UNCTAD I & II were nonetheless highly significant events in the 'long battle' for global governance. They facilitated the organisation of the 'developing' countries into a 'Group of 77' (G77) and produced the first formal consensus on the G77's demands. For a time thereafter the G77 was viewed by the 'developed' countries as a threat to their dominant position in global governance.

The lines had in effect been drawn for the next phase of the battle over the structure of the global economy and its governance. By the end of the 1960s, the G77 countries were increasingly being described as *a* 'Third Force', more as *the* 'Third World'. They became ever more 'fretful and demanding' (Toye and Toye 2004: 229) in the face of this stalling and steadily came to realise that they had again to rethink their strategy and tactics.

The 'Third World' challenge

For a brief period in the 1970s, it appeared as if the global economic order and the institutions supporting its governance were about to witness a fundamental change from the patterns established at Bretton Woods. In particular, the forced devaluation of the US dollar in 1971 suggested that a 'fundamental disequilibrium' (Baldwin 1978: 505–506) had occurred and that the US could no longer act as the world's monetary and economic leader. In combination with the simultaneous questioning of US hegemony at the political level as well, occasioned by its defeat in Vietnam, it appeared that a genuine and far-reaching moment of change in the Western-dominated global order had perhaps been reached.

The 'developing' countries were certainly presented with a new opportunity to present even more vociferously their case for a 'New International Economic Order (NIEO)'. They benefited from the existence of institutions within which they could make their demands (the G77 and UNCTAD) or take concerted action directed at the 'developed' countries (as, for example, the Organization of Petroleum Exporting Countries (OPEC) did in 1973–1974); a set of ideas deriving from dependency theory that attributed the problems of development to the structure of the global political economy; and, critically, the seemingly weakened economic condition of the dominant 'developed' countries. For a period, at UNCTAD III in 1972 and the Sixth Special Session of the UN General Assembly in 1974, it appeared as if these factors were going to be sufficient to reconfigure the rules of the global economy, granting more advantages to at least some groups of 'developing' countries.

Box 19.4 The New International Economic Order (NIEO)

In the early 1970s the G77 benefited from a unique political opportunity to express its demands, generating a palpable sense that the 'developed' countries could no longer ignore them outright. The leading capitalist economies (known collectively as the Group of Ten (G10) countries) were embroiled in a severe monetary crisis that resulted in the end of fixed exchange rates, one of the key features of the Bretton Woods system. In addition, OPEC simultaneously increased the price of oil and instituted an embargo directed mainly at the US, but causing immediate economic hardship among all oil-dependent 'industrialised' countries – a tactic that became known as 'the oil weapon'. The arresting effects of the 'oil weapon' led the 'developed' countries to agree to a Sixth Special Session of the UN General Assembly to discuss not only OPEC's actions but also, at Algeria's insistence as an OPEC member, wider matters related to primary production and development generally that were of concern to the whole G77. The key outcomes of the Session were the 'Declaration on the Establishment of a New International Economic Order' (Resolution 3201) and the 'Programme of Action on the Establishment of a New International Economic Order' (Resolution 3202). The latter set out a full list of demands to change fundamentally the structure of global economic governance. Because of its link with the OPEC crisis, the NIEO fully caught the attention of the 'developed' countries. However, by the end of the 1970s they had managed systematically to diffuse the 'oil weapon', allowing them thereafter to ignore and subvert the demand for an NIEO.

However, these hopes were again dashed, blocked by the continuing intransigence of the key beneficiaries of global governance. By the end of the 1970s, especially after the anti-climax of the 'North–South' conference in Paris, it was once more apparent that the 'developing' countries had neither fundamentally altered the existing Bretton Woods institutions in their favour, nor fully succeeded in bringing forward other institutions as viable alternatives. What is more, they had also lost much of the voice they had painstakingly acquired in global negotiations over the course of an even longer period. In particular, with the decoupling of development issues from the threat of further oil price increases, G77 countries no longer possessed a powerful instrument with which to press their demands. What was left was only the option of appealing for concessions from the 'developed' countries based on arguments of 'reason' and 'morality'.

The neoliberal turn

The 1980s began with the final defeat of the 'Third World' challenge to the existing structure of the world economy and the institutions of global economic governance. The Independent Commission on International Development Issues, better known as the 'Brandt Commission', named after its chairman, the former West German Chancellor Will Brandt, had sought to set out a compromise 'programme for survival' on all of the issues that had dominated the politics of global governance during the 1970s. However, by the time of the Cancún Summit, which met in October 1981, the conditions which had seemed to present the 'developing' countries with a real opportunity to challenge the dominant 'advanced' countries and the rules of international trade, finance and development they favoured had disappeared and any prospect of significant change had petered out. Cancún in effect closed the door on the G77's attempts to transform the world economic order in its preferred fashion.

Confronted by a weakened 'Third World', a neoliberal 'counterrevolution', with its epicentres in the Ronald Reagan and Margaret Thatcher administrations in the US and Britain respectively, moved to reorient the main ideas around which the strategies and policies of the World Bank and IMF were based. By means of various mixtures of coercion and consent, various aspects of the neoliberal policy paradigm, which was often called accurately enough the 'Washington Consensus', were increasingly adopted by countries at all levels of development across the entirety of the world, shaping new patterns of cooperation *and* division between the 'developing' and 'developed' worlds. At the same time, as a consequence of the 'end of the Cold War' and the reforms that were getting underway in the Soviet Union from the late 1980s onwards, the most significant, even if deeply flawed, alternative to the Western-dominated institutions of global economic governance and the liberal ideas embedded within them was effectively withdrawn from the global stage.

Box 19.5 The 'Washington Consensus'

The Keynesian ideas that had underpinned the modern system of global governance since Bretton Woods began to lose their dominance during the prolonged international economic recession of the 1970s as a neoliberal 'counterrevolution' gained ground. These ideas emanated mainly from elite US economics departments, most famously at the University of Chicago, and came to underpin the economic doctrines of the Reagan administration in the US and the Thatcher government in the UK, in particular. The influence of such neoliberal ideas also grew within the IMF, as newly minted PhDs in economics from US universities joined the organisation. Within the World Bank, however, the installation of neoliberal ideology occurred principally through appointments made to its presidency and research department by the Reagan administration. In its cumulative form the 'Washington Consensus' – a term coined in 1989 by John Williamson, an English economist working at a think-tank in Washington, DC – was a set of ten neoliberal policy instruments that became focal points for the pursuit of development policy as envisaged by the US government, the IMF and the World Bank collectively. Among the key instruments promoted by this consensus were reductions in state spending, trade and exchange rate liberalisation, deregulation and privatisation.

In this changed geopolitical context, serious questions were raised as to how far the apparent triumph of liberalism would spread among all countries and what role the institutions of what was now *truly global* economic governance would play in the reshaping of a world order characterised by the new ascendancy of the 'First World' and the concomitant breakdown of the 'Second' and 'Third Worlds'. The US-based intellectual and writer, Francis Fukuyama, captured the flavour of the moment by arguing that the world was witnessing 'the universalization of Western liberal democracy as the final form of human government'. As such, this denoted 'the end of history' (Fukuyama 1989: 4).

The proclaimed new world order

In a deliberate effort to seize and shape the moment created by the so-called 'fall of communism', US President George H. W. Bush used a series of speeches at the beginning of the 1990s to articulate his administration's vision of a 'New World Order'. This envisioned an arrangement in which US power was unchallenged and yet could be negotiated through multilateral institutions to the benefit of subscribing countries. Unsurprisingly, this idea did not generate consensus across a world in which other countries were keen to flex their muscles and assert their autonomy freed of fear of the 'communist threat'. In retrospect, it was obvious that the 'unipolar moment' presented to the US in the wake of the Soviet Union's collapse was fleeting at best and illusory at worst.

As Held and McGrew (1998) rightly observed, the spread of liberal, democratic principles across the world, the increasing meaninglessness of categorising the world economy in terms of 'North' and 'South' and the growing range of issues touched by the institutions of global economic governance (particularly after the completion of the missing third pillar with the formation of the new World Trade Organization (WTO) in 1995) did not mean of themselves that there had been engineered a successful shift to a new neoliberal order. In fact, the sudden emergence in 1997 of a damaging financial crisis in East Asia, a region that had for many years experienced 'miraculous' growth, showed the existence of real frailties within the global economic system as a whole. Subsequent attempts to reform the global economic institutions along the lines of a 'post-Washington Consensus', thereby bolstering their effectiveness and legitimacy, were not that successful and they did not create a re-stabilised world order along these softer ideological lines.

What had, nevertheless, occurred was an important shift from 'a purely state-centric politics to a more complex form of multilayered global governance' (Held and McGrew 1998: 242), in which the major institutions of global economic governance featured more prominently than ever before. Yet, given the persistence of global inequality, the resulting divisions and clashes

---

Box 19.6 East Asian financial crisis

It was not long after the publication of a World Bank report heralding the growth of the newly industrialising countries of East Asia as a 'Miracle' that a financial crisis emanating initially from Thailand in 1997 plunged the world into what then US Treasury Secretary Robert Rubin declared was the 'the most serious financial crisis of the last 50 years'. This implicit comparison to the Great Depression was important for global governance, now reoriented along neoliberal lines, because it was the type of event modern global governance was intended to prevent and/or remedy effectively. The IMF responded to the crisis with the largest bailout in its history, targeted at Thailand, Indonesia and South Korea, but with strict insistence that these countries implemented 'Washington Consensus' reform policies. These policies failed to have an early positive effect on these economies and the resultant spread of the crisis, prompting strong criticism from the chief economist of the World Bank, Joseph Stiglitz. Still open to at least some Keynesian ideas, Stiglitz offered a vision of a 'post-Washington Consensus', which called for a greater role for the state and international institutions to address 'market failures' of the type that precipitated the crisis. However, with its focus on the necessity of 'good institutions' to ensure adequately functioning markets, the 'post-Washington Consensus' augmented, rather than radically challenged, dominant neoliberal ideas, thereby again reinforcing the primacy of Washington-based institutions in the governance of the world order.

witnessed within the newly formed WTO and the obvious capacity of financial liberalisation to decimate whole regions of the world economy, as cruelly experienced by East Asia in the late 1990s, the underlying stability of this new mode of global governance was far from certain.

Towards global crisis

The start of a new millennium in 2000 inevitably inspired a further bout of stock-taking regarding the condition of global governance. It was apparent that neoliberalism remained dominant as an overarching governing ideology, but also that it had yet to be grounded politically in a stable way across much of the world. After the East Asian crisis there was much talk of the need for a 'new international financial architecture'. This was not engineered, although some reforms were made to draw 'emerging economies' a little more closely into the inner decision-making apparatus around the IMF. Within the WTO the series of biennial ministerial conferences that started in Singapore in 1996 served initially to reveal the major clashes of position that had come to exist by then between different groups of trading countries, until, in the unique circumstance created by 9/11, agreement was reached in Doha in November 2001 to embark upon the negotiation of a full new trade round. By this time just about every state in the world had come to be involved in global trade governance, creating a diverse array of intricate and changing coalitions. It had come to be realised too that climate change had the capacity to penetrate every aspect of global economic management, which meant that the series of 'conferences of the parties' initiated under the auspices of the UN Framework Convention on Climate Change (UNFCCC) from the mid-1990s onwards came more and more to be considered as a core part of the system of global governance. The Kyoto Protocol (to the UNFCCC), although agreed in late 1997, only came into force as a legal entity in early 2005, by which time meetings, also exposing a bewildering variety of new coalitions of states on climate issues, had started on the next stage in the process of states agreeing voluntarily to cut their greenhouse gas emissions.

Box 19.7 The G20

The frequency and severity of the financial crises that occurred in the 'developing' countries in the 1990s had serious economic consequences for the 'developed' countries as a result of deepening financial globalisation. In 1999 this motivated the G7 countries (Canada, France, Germany, Italy, Japan, the UK and the US) to invite a number of 'emerging' countries (Argentina, Australia, Brazil, China, India, Indonesia, Mexico, Russia, Saudi Arabia, South Africa, South Korea and Turkey) to join them, with additional representation from the European Union, in a new body known as the Group of 20 which would meet at Minister of Finance level. Together, these countries represented 87 per cent of the world's GDP and some 65 per cent of its population. Although seen by some as evidence of a shift in the locus of power to 'developing' regions of the world, the establishment of the G20 is better understood as a move by the G7 countries to bring 'emerging' countries into their sphere of governance in order to monitor and influence the latter's financial policies and activities more directly. Nevertheless, the G20 was on hand when the 2008–2009 global financial crisis struck and it rose to critical importance in global governance when US President George W. Bush called a meeting of G20 Leaders in Washington, DC in November 2008 to organise a global response to the crisis. The G20's response to the crisis was Keynesian at the moment of the crisis, initiating significant stimulus packages for the affected countries at first, but it fell back into conventional neoliberal austerity programmes thereafter.

It was into this scene of complex, contested global governance that there suddenly exploded the global financial crisis, characterised most strikingly by the enforced bankruptcy in September 2008 of Lehman Brothers, the huge US investment bank. The crisis was a seismic moment in the modern history of the global political economy, at the same time utterly unexpected and yet completely predictable. It generated a major reform of global governance in the creation of a new Group of 20 (G20) gathering of world leaders to act as the 'premier forum for our international economic cooperation', as the leaders themselves proclaimed at their third meeting in Pittsburgh in the US in September 2009. In a very meaningful sense, a new and even more uncertain chapter in the 'long battle' for global governance began with the onset of the crisis in 2008 and continues to this day.

Conclusion

It is possible in looking back over all the battles summarised in the preceding section of the chapter to insist that little, in essence, has changed. It is an obvious reality that the Bretton Woods institutions still exist; indeed, they have arguably been completed in respect of the original design by the eventual establishment in 1995 of the WTO. Global economic governance began, of course, as we saw, as an 'embedded liberal' form of political economy and, although the extent of its embeddedness in society has undoubtedly lessened since this formative phase, it is the case that what exists today remains at heart and despite threats a liberal international order As Andrew Gamble (2014: 28) has argued, neoliberalism is best understood as

> the latest version of economic liberalism which seeks to find ways to police the boundaries between the public and the private, between the state and the market, and to ensure that in moments of crisis these fundamental relations are not breached.

Moreover, and notwithstanding much discussion of its decline, the United States still sits at the apex of global economic governance, although it is also clear that President Trump is uncomfortable with this inheritance and seemingly willing to treat it recklessly. It is true too that US power within and over the global political economy is not as all-encompassing as it was in that early post-1945 foundational period, but no single country matters more in contemporary global governance than the United States and this will change any time soon. Truly could a *Financial Times* (2009) editorial written in late 2009 amid global financial crisis have noted that global governance is 'still lost in the old Bretton Woods'!

If this is so, what must we conclude happened to the challenge to the Bretton Woods mode of global governance mounted so aggressively and repeatedly by various coalitions of (relatively speaking) excluded countries from the time of those important early meetings in New Hampshire in 1944? Has it failed or succeeded? The honest answer is that it has done both. Manifestly, these countries have not overturned the Bretton Woods system, as once, especially in the 1970s, they thought they wanted to do, but they have now entered much more fully into it and operate within it more effectively than before. This is the symbolic significance of the elevation of the G20 to a leaders' forum in November 2008 and the series of important G20 summits that have taken place since then. We see the change too in the new activism of many former 'Southern' countries in the politics of the WTO; we see their engagement with the climate change issue; and we see new initiatives that challenge the financial primacy of the IMF and the World Bank emerging from China and other emerging so-called BRICS countries (Brazil, Russia, India, China, South Africa). These include, notably, the creation of the New Development Bank by the BRICS and the Asian Infrastructure Investment Bank by China, which have jointly been seen as a 'distinct threat to the World Bank' (Güven 2017: 1155). And yet: for there is a powerful qualification to be made to the rather exaggerated claim advanced by some analysts that 'the "global South" is restructuring world capitalism from within' (Golub 2013: 1000). It is that, thus far, China, India, Brazil, South Africa and the other leading countries of the old 'Third World' have behaved within the councils of global governance in a surprisingly orthodox fashion. They have joined the club and have flexed their muscles occasionally and to effect, most frequently to block initiatives to which they are hostile. They have also provoked traditional bodies to make a response: the World Bank has, for example, responded to the appearance of new financial institutions by increasing its development budget by nearly US$40 billion in the period up to 2013, precisely in order to secure its place as 'the only truly global multilateral finance institution' (Linn 2018). Manifestly, what the BRICS and others have not done is disrupt the rules of the game in any significant way and, indeed, they no longer make vociferous demands for their comprehensive rewriting. At the same time they have not yet generally sought to lead affairs and there is the danger that their fuller insertion into the system serves only to limit the capacity to lead of the long dominant countries without necessarily bringing forward new and different sources of global strategy (Pieterse 2011).

In reflecting on this concern, which has been expressed by some keen journalistic observers of global affairs (Schneider 2013), we need to confront the possibility that the G20's emerging leadership of what is still a recognisably post-Bretton Woods system of global governance masks in a potentially dangerous way the sheer extent, depth and complexity of the crisis that hit the global political economy and its associated institutions of global governance in 2008. The key point here is that the way we choose to conceptualise this crisis is critical to how we assess the success of the efforts that have been made to deal with it and restabilise the global order. On this key question, it is possible to take very different views. For example, it was widely proclaimed in some quarters that all that was needed was to fix a few faults in the governance of the system, thereby enabling the neoliberal world order to get quickly back on the road and resume its position in the fast lane (Ostry et al. 2016). In this case, we know, as it were, what the G20 and its agents were expected to do and can judge them accordingly. But it has also been argued that the crisis actually connoted something much more serious – that it was in effect an existential challenge for neoliberalism, at least as it had come to operate in increasingly unregulated fashion by late 2008 (Önis and Güven 2011) – and therefore put on the table nothing less than the design of a new world order grounded in a new model, or models, of global capitalism. Needless to say, in this reading the task that faces the G20, the IMF, the World Bank and the WTO, not to mention all the economic and other institutions of the United Nations, is of a completely different nature and scale, with associated and very different implications, of course, for evaluation of their performance.

Box 19.8 'The Great Uncertainty'

The prolonged nature of the global financial crisis that began in 2008–2009 has exposed the presence of three major processes of global structural change that are occurring simultaneously and interacting in complex ways and have been said to generate 'The Great Uncertainty' (Hay and Payne 2013). First, a largely Western financial crisis brought about by neoliberal excesses reveals the power of financial markets and the ease with which vast quantities of money can move around the world. These flows contribute to the instability of the system, reinforcing the likelihood of future crises and posing a challenge for every government seeking to adopt a viable growth model that delivers economic and social benefits to their citizens. Second, a gradual but inexorable shift in the locus of economic power in the world highlights the disparity between the rise in economic power of countries such as the BRICS and their relative lack of concomitant political power. For example, China's new economic might has not been accompanied by a consequential rise in its economic and political leadership on the world stage, even though it has recently made US policy-makers think by creating an Asian Infrastructure Investment Bank (AIIB), with 87 members across the 'developed' and 'developing' countries. Finally, an environmental threat exhibited by, but not limited to, climate change expresses the mounting evidence of the vast environmental damage that global economic activity has cumulatively caused, especially since industrialisation. The recent unilateral decision by the Trump administration in the US to withdraw from the Paris Agreement on climate change serves only to undermine the only structure of global governance that exists to address this grave issue. The political challenges within and across 'developed' and 'developing' countries that are involved in tackling each of these three issues are as enormous as they are complex, and it is therefore extremely difficult at this point to predict the path this crisis may take.

We take the latter perspective and offer a brief schematic overview of what sort of crisis we think the world currently faces. We do so alert to the destructive side of the current Trump administration, but mindful also of the existence of deeper, even more intractable, structural changes that are occurring simultaneously and interacting in all manner of complicated ways. In a previous publication Hay and Payne (2013) labelled the current era 'The Great Uncertainty' and drew our attention the contemporary coalescence of the following three key issues: unresolved financial crisis; shifting economic power; and grave environment threat. To put it at its mildest, all of this constitutes an enormous set of governance challenges that have to be confronted and overcome urgently. The solution – the only available solution – is to start from where we are now, which means taking up, working with and intensively researching the system of global governance that has been honed and shaped by the 'long battle' fought for control of its means and mechanisms by so many countries since the mid-1940s. *A luta continua!*

Bibliography

Baldwin, D. A. 1978. International political economy and the international monetary system. *International Organization*, 32(2), 497–512.

Financial Times. 2009. Editorial: Still Lost in the Old Bretton Woods, 28 December.

Finkelstein, L. S. 1995. What is global governance? *Global Governance*, 1(3), 367–372.

Fukuyama, F. 1989. The End of History. *The National Interest*, Summer, 3–18.

Gamble, A. 2014. Ideologies of governance, in Payne, A. and Phillips, N., eds., *Handbook of the International Political Economy of Governance*, Edward Elgar Publishing: Cheltenham.

Geldart, C., Lyon, P. 1980. The Group of 77: A perspective view. *International Affairs*. Royal Institute of International Affairs 1944: 57(1), 79–101.

Golub, P. S. 2013. *From the New International Economic Order to the G20: How the 'Global South' is Restructuring World Capitalism from Within*. London: Taylor and Francis.

Güven, A. B. 2017. Defending supremacy: how the IMF and the World Bank navigate the challenge of rising powers. *International Affairs*, 93(5), 1149–1166.

Hay, C., Payne, A. 2013. *The Great Uncertainty* [online], Sheffield Political Economy Research Institute: Sheffield, available: http://speri.dept.shef.ac.uk/papers/.

Held, D., McGrew, A. 1998. The end of the old order? Globalization and the prospects for world order. *Review of International Studies*, 24(5): 219–245.

Helleiner, E. 2014. *Forgotten Foundations of Bretton Woods: International Development and the Making of the Postwar Order*, Cornell University Press: Ithaca, NY.

Keohane, R. O. 1984. *After Hegemony: Cooperation and Discord in the World Political Economy*, Princeton University Press: Princeton, NJ.

Krasner, S. D. 1983. *International Regimes*, Cornell University Press: Ithaca, NY.

Linn, J. F. 2018. *Will a Capital Increase Mean a Greater Global Role for the World Bank?* [online]. Brookings Institution Future Development Blog, available: www.brookings.edu/blog/future-development/2018/05/14/will-a-capital-increase-mean-a-greater-global-role-for-the-world-bank/ [accessed 14 Aug 2018].

Murphy, C. N. 1994. *International Organization and Industrial Change: Global Governance Since 1850*, Polity Press: Cambridge.

Murphy, C. N. 2000. Global governance: poorly done and poorly understood. *International Affairs*, 76(4): 789–804.

Öniş, Z., Güven, A. B. 2011. The Global Economic Crisis and the future of neoliberal globalization: Rupture versus continuity. *Global Governance*, 17(4): 469–488.

Ostry, J. D., Loungani, P., Furceri, D. 2016. Neoliberalism: oversold? *Finance and Development: A Quarterly Magazine of the IMF.*

Pieterse, J. N. 2011. Global Rebalancing: Crisis and the East-South Turn. *Development and Change*, 42(1): 22–48.

Rosenau, J. N. 1992. Governance, order, and changes in world politics. *Governance Without Government: Order and Change in World Politics*, Cambridge University Press: Cambridge.

Rosenau, J. N. 1995. Governance in the twenty-first century. *Global Governance*, 1(1): 13–43.

Rosenau, J. N. 1997. *Along the Domestic-Foreign Frontier: Exploring Governance in a Turbulent World*, Cambridge University Press: Cambridge; New York.

Rosenau, J. N., Czempiel, E.-O. 1992. *Governance Without Government: Order and Change in World Politics*, Cambridge University Press: Cambridge.

Ruggie, J. G. 1982. International regimes, transactions, and change: Embedded liberalism and the post-war economic regimes. *International Organization*, 36, 195–232.

Schneider, H. 2013. In a Muddled World Economy, the Great Stalemate Baffles Policymakers, *Washington Post.*

Sinclair, T. J. 2012. *Global Governance*, Polity Press: Cambridge.

Toye, J., Toye, R. 2004. *The UN and Global Political Economy: Trade, Finance, and Development*, Indiana University Press: Bloomington, IN.

Wallerstein, I. M. 2004. *World-Systems Analysis: an Introduction*, Duke University Press: Durham.

20

The global political economy of regionalism

Beyond European and North American conceptual cages

Ernesto Vivares and Cheryl Martens

Introduction: debates and methodological orientations

The debate concerning the political and economic nature of regionalism is extensive. Supporters and detractors of both progressive and neoliberal approaches to regionalism have long based their arguments on underlying assumptions about the outcomes of the reciprocal and dynamic interactions between world order, regionalisms, and development. For some, this is a matter of which theoretical perspectives are right or wrong. For others, it is a problem of methodology. Indeed, the academic discussion crosses disciplinary boundaries and theoretical perspectives, reframing, from different angles, the form in which the research is done, in what Burgess resumes as the role of the theory in research (1982).

Few scholars would deny that social knowledge production in the International Political Economy research interconnects with existent power relations. Several authors argue that differences and struggles are inherent to the field of International Political Economy (IPE), and that diversity for the basis of its growth (Cox and Schechter 2002; Dunne, Hansen, and Wight 2013: 406). Hence, while some theorists emphasize hypothesis testing, covariation and causality as key to academic knowledge in the fields of IPE and regionalism, others argue that it is only via critical reflection and developing better interpretations of reality that we can have a better understanding of the political economy of regionalism.

These contrasting epistemological approaches, however, share similar historical roots regarding the production of knowledge, beyond the variety of parameters that make up their conceptual frameworks, based on the British/Pluralist, and mainstream North American IPE. For scholars in the field of IPE and regionalism, social scientific knowledge consists of a range of theoretical sources, research formats, a plurality of ideas, and any attempt to eliminate this diversity would reduce the essence of knowledge production and difference. The academic question is thus how scholars situate themselves concerning their definitions of "knowledge" and methodologies concerning regionalism, the role of theory in research and the use of certain concepts that in turn bring specific formats of academic production (Jackson 2011). In other words, we need to evaluate whether the IPE of regionalism should focus on testing hypotheses and running correlations or also should examine the assumptions and premises that underlie the

343

perspectives that nurture such hypotheses, to build knowledge and produce refined concepts (Dunne, Hansen, and Wight 2013).

Some main problems with the conceptual frameworks underlying dominant paradigms in the IPE of regionalism lay on their assumptions regarding the political and economic dynamics between regionalism and development in a changing the world order, as well as particular unrevised ontologies, concepts, or standard methodologies. These frameworks are often adopted and used without reviewing, analyzing, or debating their validity. However, the crises of the last 10 years have impacted on the dominant, neoliberal, and positivist models within academia. Moreover, that compels scholars to rethink the role of theory in research and how to grasp the rise of new regionalism, either benning and malign, forms of governance, and the inseperable relationship between conflicts and developments.

This chapter is concerned with identifying the dominant political and economic views behind the leading positions about regionalism, in terms of how regional development is conceived and how these theoretical perspectives define the relationship between ideas, politics, and economics as a frame of development. Working along these lines makes it possible to identify a broader range and more eclectic approaches that can logically grasp and integrate diverse dimensions of development and regionalism. It also facilitates the contextual comprehension of divergent regionalist projects, modes, and levels of integration, as well as cooperation looking at a broader range of aspects, such as agency–structure, formal- and informal development, conflict and well-being, (Dunne, Hansen, and Wight 2013; Lake 2013; Payne and Phillips 2010; Sil and Katzenstein 2010). These lines broaden the vision concerning what we understand by critical political economy and the study of how reality is produced and how it has come to be so.

What we understand as "development," for example, can thus be analyzed as based on normative and socio-historical and geographical assumptions, configurations of inseparable dynamic among ideas, politics, and economics, where integral issues, such as well-being and conflict, can be understood as taking place in a given historical context within a specific world order and geographical configurations. Yes, there is much that can be said in support of, or against the intellectual history of IPE, as outlined by Eric Helleiner in this handbook.

What leads our discussion is a critical and pragmatic analytical search for interpretations and approaches that allow us to bridge the gap between theories and methodology, and between mainstream IPE perspectives and regionalist research approaches. Therefore, we aim to examine how we might approach IPE regionalism research, ontologically and epistemologically, in a way that avoids the bias of the dominant Anglo-Saxon and Western mainstream approaches (Acharya 2011; Dunne, Hansen, and Wight 2013; Jackson 2011)

We contend that dominant regionalist approaches to rest, by and large, upon theoretical–methodological positions of different academic networks concerning definitions of world order, regionalism, and development. This chapter argues in favor of the concept that diversity, differences, and even confusion are part and parcel of analyzing the relationship between regionalism and the whole, and how the role of theory in research is defined (Burgess 1982; Jackson 2011).

IPE and regionalism

Some scholars in IPE argue that new regional configurations rising in different parts of the world in the last two decades, including South America, have to be understood as "new regionalisms." These regionalisms are defined by their relations with the world order and development orientations. They represent struggles between different kind of political projects, driven either by states and non-state actors, and can be formal and informal such as organized crime or terrorism. These new regionalisms have ascended within the frame of the new, post-Cold War order, the global crisis of neoliberalism, the exhaustion of the Bretton Woods institutions, the incapacity of the United Nations to handle international conflicts and, above all, the rise of China and the BRICs (Brazil, Russia, India, China and South Africa) (Breslin et al. 2002; De Lombaerde and Söderbaum 2014; Higgott 2003; Payne 2004). These new egionalisms have progressively come onto the scene as reactions and responses to an order characterized by several worlds – such as the Westphalian system of states, multilateral institutions, regions, business global networks, informal, organized crime, etcetera. This scenario challenges us to rethink different assumptions/directions/implications about conflict and development, and above all, the place of regions and regionalism (Shaw 2000). Thus, there is a wide variety of theoretical viewpoints stemming from the dominant IPE perspectives regarding how to approach research on regionalism, regionalization, and regions, although all differentiated by how the role of theory in research is defined methodologically (Burgess 1982; Dunne, Hansen, and Wight 2013).

Analytically, we have a wide range of criteria and types of classifications to work with, however, that each one of them is associated with specific understandings of the existent international order, emerging powers, and concepts such as development, since they are products of different and even opposing epistemic communities and networks of production of knowledge (Acharya 2011; Dunne, Hansen, and Wight 2013; Söderbaum and Shaw 2003). The major approaches, which will be discussed here, are based on distinctions between orthodox and heterodox methodologies, between rationalist and reflectivist approaches, or interdisciplinary and disciplinary perspectives.

Given the necessity of using a criterion capable of delimiting present and dominant IPE perspectives, we adopt a line based on the relation between knowledge and power manifested in epistemic networks. The approach taken here views social knowledge as aligned with particular projects of development and responding to existent pursuits of wealth and power of someone (Cox and Schechter 2002). Indeed, knowledge has emerged, is bound to or responding to different civilizatory powers (Acharya 2011: 624–25), which takes us to the question of whether North American and European centrism will eventually contend with another centrism (Chinese, Indian, or South American). Moreover, yes, it is an endless historical game that challenges the academy to respond via research.

These classifications of the world order and its changing can be adjusted, modified, or enlarged, but, without a doubt, if we want to examine these approaches with their application to South American regionalism, it is strategic to maintain the criteria concerning the role that these dominant schools play in our research. So far, the North American and British schools have been playing a central role in the comprehension of political economy in the academic history of the complex configuration and reconfiguration of other regions, producing hybrids or different conversations as Tussie shows (see the chapter in this Handbook). In this regard, we adopt and adapt Benjamin Cohen's distinction between two major IPE perspectives defined by the power and networks of these, by adding the South American perspective, which has reemerged as a growing epistemic network in the region (Acharya 2011; Cohen 2008).

Other scholars in the field have compared North American and British schools. According to Viotti and Kauppi, it can be traced to the first decade after World War II, as "British scholars did not embrace the behavioral movement that came to dominate political sciences in North America in the 1950s and 1960s" (2012: 243).[1] Hence, three main IPE perspectives and networks can be identified as useful for our regional case: The North American, the British and, after more than two decades of rejection and systematic degradation, the revitalization of Latin and South American IPE. Cohen adopts the Coxian distinction between problem-solving theories, namely those that take "the world as it finds it, with the prevailing social and power relationships and the institutions into which they are organized, as the given framework for action" (Cox 1981: 88). On the other hand, critical theories address change and transformation in historical perspective, which stand "apart from the prevailing order and asks how the order came about" (Cox 1986: 88).

This distinction is politically pragmatic, with a regional basis, and it does not hide its political orientation, but openly views that North American and British perspectives are dominant academic schools produced by the North trans-Atlantic world order more than a geographical–national locus. There are scholars on both sides of the debate whose work does not fall within the geographic limits, namely Gilpin (2001) and Katzenstein (2000). Here we identify negative and positive elements of the diverse theoretical perspectives on regionalism anchored to the main IPE perspectives as an initial step to build research agendas for IPE regionally, drawing on New South American Regionalism as a case study. As Sautú (2003) points out, all research is theoretically constructed, assumed or explained, and the theoretical formulation of a problem, at all times, defines the research approaches and methodologies adopted by scholars.

North American and British IPE

This section will consider the North American and British/Pluralist IPE perspectives, before examining how regionalism is demarcated within these perspectives and concerning South American regionalism. The first school of theory–methodology is North American IPE (NAIPE) (Cohen 2008; Cox 2009), based on the contributions of scholars such as Krasner (2000), Keohane (2002), Nye (2002), Frieden and Lake (2000), most of whom are former high-level US diplomats. The central concern of NAIPE is the stability and security of the international system. There the underlying assumptions are that universal and ahistorical market dynamics, as well as the institutionality, determine the international system and regional projects. The epistemology is a mix between neo-classical economics and actor-oriented positivist perspectives where the system lays on their universal rationalities, and always tends toward equilibrium. Scholars from this perspective view politics and state intervention in the economy as distorting market equilibrium, and see political regulation as reducing rather than promoting globalization.

The primary concern of mainstream NAIPE is to explain how economic policies affect politics and vice versa, conceives as a problem of articulation between two independent realms of development, governed by two different logics, and explained by two different sciences. These are political and economic sciences, each one defined by its ontology, epistemology, methodology, and way to conduct research (Frieden and Lake 2000; Waltz 2001). Their creeds are based on realism and neoliberal institutionalism, both claiming the inexorable globalizing destiny of free trade and finance based on the historical economic, political, and institutional experience of Great Britain and the United States (Keohane 2002; Waltz 1979). Accordingly, positivist, empirical research frameworks are the only scientific tool to reach objectivity, precision, and capacity to answer clear and direct research questions. A central academic focus is on the prescription of the solution with the view of improving the functions and effectivity of international, regional, and national systems. NAIPE focuses mainly on the political behavior of states, institutions, and governments, assuming that these, like humans, are oriented continuously to self-maximization. Therefore, that means studying the actor's actions, whereby it is possible to gain understanding and knowledge of the international system.

Ontologically, regionalism is thus based on formal organizations and formal integration, as the result of what governments and states do, while regional institutions are structures as well as trade and financial agreements, namely the factual outcomes of regionalism. However, three significant weaknesses characterize this perspective: the limitations of institutional neoliberalism in grasping the dimensions of conflict and power in regional development; the limited range of elements that the view can deal with; and, finally, the belief that economics work under universal laws.

The second mainstream IPE school is somewhat misleadingly called "the British School," and its lesser-known name, "Pluralist IPE" given the multiple perspectives that have contributed to it (Cohen 2008; Cox 2009) Among its leading scholars are Susan Strange (1986, 1988) and Robert Cox (1981, 2009). Many of its adherents are educated in the intellectual traditions of economic history, critical realism, and Gramscian thought, as well as the ideas of Karl Polanyi (2001). Perhaps its central feature is that it does not account for an organized body of theories and concepts, let alone a standard or unique methodology. A fundamental characteristic of the Pluralist IPE (PIPE) is its openness to different theoretical perspectives and mixed methods to explain the change, conflict, and development. The PIPE of development represents an intellectual space of critical reflection focused on research and comprehension of the new complex process, agency and social structures of change in historical and geographical contexts (Cox and Schechter 2002: 76).

A significant concern of PIPE is the creation of social reality, in terms of how specific power relations produce realities and forms of governance, within a given historical period. It lays on the notion that the sum of the parts represents the whole, and that the whole constitutes more than the sum of parts. In this sense, international order is conceived as historical, where social and economic structures are stable, framing, and shaping development or how the reality is produced in one way and not in another. Its primary strength is the richness of its conceptual devices to understand the complex relations of structure–agency, international–domestic, state–markets, and conflict–development. Its significant weaknesses lie in the limited amount of empirical research, given the emphasis on conceptualization to understand change and conflict, as well as its lack of conceptualizations upon the complex relations between informal and formal development and regionalism, borderless states, ecology, and new wars.

Accordingly, agency and structure must be integrated into PIPE analysis, where regionalism constitutes another dimension of development, something key to grasping the IPE nature of conflict and development (Payne 2005). The research within PIPE is eclectic and seeks to bridge gaps between theories and research, thus creating a multidisciplinary dialogue through different approaches and methods. In many ways, the PIPE school is a heterodox relative of mainstream North American IPE, critical about the latter but also reflects in essential ways the trans-Atlantic focus of the world order in recent centuries. However, it remains highly based on Eurocentric centers and concepts (see Berry in this handbook).

These two schools represent the two dominant sides of the historical production of knowledge post-WWII, and their networks and research at times have been interlinked without clear limits between the two (see Berry in this handbook). There is a wide range of ontological, epistemological and methodological spaces of eclectic integration between the two perspectives in what Lake (2013) defines as the debate about the role of theory and the use of middle range theories in an eclectic and integrated form (2013: 572). Having outlined these two major academic schools in IPE, the following questions emerge: How have the North American and British schools developed different and even opposing views regarding regionalism? Also, what is the relationship between these perspectives and research concerning the regional dynamics of other regions such as Latin America? In the following section, we will explore the complex relationship between IPE and regionalism.

IPE and theories of regionalism

While the debates concerning the political and economic nature of regionalism range widely, scholarly discussions on regional dynamics in regions such as South America has, until recently, been dominated by NAIPE and Eurocentric conceptions of regionalism (Riggirozzi 2010). The large volume of regionalist research in Latin/South America rests upon an IPE that can be identified by four markers. First, the notion that the study of the agency of regionalism, focuses on governmental leadership, inter-governmental agreements, and formal integration processes in trade and customs, explains the nature of it. In this sense, it takes for granted that regionalism is built "from above," by which it is always formal and institutional, and therefore it is a matter of international organizations rather than political economy of conflict and development.

Second, there is a strong tendency toward a biased interpretation of European regionalist experience, as a point of reference in scholarly research and the desired endpoint of development, a conceptual and epistemological position driven more by the influence of specific academic institutions and regional powers than its scientific weight. Third, there is a conviction in some academic circles, inherited from and bound to the North American political sciences, that economics and politics are an independent dimension ruled by its logic. There the economic nature is always market-based, and politics underpin it, both solely explicable through the scientific neo-positivist and institutionalist political methods. Fourth, and finally, these regional studies of South America rest upon a research format that negatively predefines its outcomes, since these are based on unrevised theories or rationalizations of historical process alien to the region (e.g., the Industrial Revolution, the Cold War, European economic integration, regional institutions, and populism). This particular mode of production of knowledge is usually grounded on hypothesis testing or correlation studies based on macro theories to which is applied the orthodox protocol Durkheim and King, Keohane, and Verba (named KKV), without recognizing that there is neither more than one methodological inference system nor macro theories to review and consider (Jackson 2011; Lake 2013).

However, there is a good deal of research on regionalism that does not present the limitations mentioned above or biases. Much of this research is critical as it does not take the reality only as given but wonders how that has come to be like this and not in another way, where it goes, who wins, as well as who lost and how. Those approaches do not deny the academic gains of decades of contributions from the Global North, which are adopted by many, and they do not take as unquestionable some macro theories, dominant concepts, or methodologies. A proper strategy to avoid these theoretical limitations, barriers, or conceptual cages and methodologies is to focus the analysis in the dimensions logically articulated in all substantive, eclectic, and integral research: ontology, epistemology, and methodology (Acharya 2011; Burgess 1982; Dunne, Hansen, and Wight 2013; Lake 2013; Jackson 2011; Sil and Katzenstein 2010). Different scholars have already worked along these lines of research such as Fredrik Söderbaum (2003, 2012, 2013, 2015); Adrian Bonilla and Long (2010); Björn Hettne (1997, 2003, 2006, 2008); Timothy Shaw (1988; 2000); Anthony Payne (1996, 2004, 2005) and Philippe de Lombaerde and Garay (2006). These scholars represent a wide range of regionalist theoretical approaches, which is open and eclectic in its theoretical and methodological approaches. These scholars have thus been able to find methodological lines that extend and carry out more wide-ranging and integrated research concerning the relations between regionalism and development.

Despite these accomplishments, there remain significant areas that require further research. For example, since each scholar builds and follows their own approach, according to Söderbaum, the first step is to shift the research agenda of regionalism from its limited, Eurocentric focus, and analytically differentiate the theoretical meanings of region, regionalism, and region-alization to organize and comprehend the broad and heterogeneous field of research, namely new regionalism from the Global South (2005, 2012). Thus, we can distinguish between approaches that limit or bias the research and those that open it up. There is general agreement that a region is a conjunction of states with close interrelations, given that their geography allows for a significant level of interdependence (Nye 1965). However, today, this definition is unable to adequately theorize the link between regions and world order, or the dynamics between state and non-state actors. A different approach is to assume that all regions are always socially and historically constructed within a political and economic context of development and politically disputed regarding identifies, boundaries and external relations by state and non-state actors (Riggirozzi 2010). Therefore, all regions keep a vital level of heterogeneity, with dynamic geographic margins moving continually, by which no homogenous regions can exist without different and opposing internal orientations concerning development. It follows that convergence and homogeneity is not the *sine qua non* of regionalization and that, therefore, it is crucial to capture and understand how the dynamics between regionalism and regionalization constituted different regions (Söderbaum 2012). To better understand the dominant notions of regionalism and their limitations, the following section will explore some of the conceptual shortcomings of the main theories of regionalism.

Successful ideas at one point in time can turn into "conceptual cages" in another

The idea that IPE is biased toward certain preconceived notions, conceptual frameworks, and research practices is not new, as numerous scholars point out how misleading concepts and research practices implicit in Eurocentric regionalism, North American actor-oriented, or liberal economic integration perspectives, have contributed to their failure to grasp new regional pro-cesses and outcomes elsewhere (Acharya 2011; Jackson 2011; Riggirozzi 2012; Söderbaum 2013; Torrent 2003). According to Söderbaum, the problem inherent in these approaches is their assumption that puts the European experience "as the foundation for conceptual develop-ment, theory building, and comparison," thus leading to a "false universalism" based on a "Eurocentric" reading of regional integration in the past (2013: 1).

This point is theoretically and methodologically central since the study and evaluation of the new regionalisms, such as South American regionalism, require an eclectic and critical integ-rated research agenda in international relations (IR) and IPE to better grasp other realities, beyond mainstream ideas. South American regionalism, however, keeps a strong bond with both North American–European influence in the academic fields of International Relations and Political Economy and above all, concerning regionalism, globalization, and development. There is relatively little research on Latin American or South American contributions to IR, IPE, and regionalism beyond the umbrella of the Eurocentric and North American market-led perspectives of integration. Different historical and academic factors have contributed to this, but yes, the dominant theoretical views in the region rest on neo-functionalism, institutionalist Eurocentric and North American perspectives, somehow limit the research (Söderbaum 2012: 5).

In *The Protestant Ethic and the Spirit of Capitalism*, Max Weber warned how the successful ideas and projects of one era could become into the political *iron cages* of another (2001). Accord-ing to Weber (2001), the use of certain concepts for current research, removed from their ori-ginal meaning and the political purposes, usually justify the survival and expansion of existing powers rather than explaining social changes. Weber calls such historical ideas, namely those with a strong political orientation within their development and conceptualization, "long-lasting iron cages." These iron cages are ideas based on rationalized forms of how reality functions within a given historical context (ibid.). The Weberian metaphor is a potentially useful concept to identify and analyze the theoretical and methodological elements that are key to avoiding the biases of Eurocentric, North American actor-oriented, or liberal economic integration perspectives on regionalism.

The main problem with Eurocentric regionalism and the North American actor-oriented or liberal economic integration lies in the architecture of their paradigms that rest on reductionist assumptions concerning the role of theory in research on regionalism and IR, the base of its "false universalism." The problem is not (necessarily) with the theories and their important uses, but with the dominant and unquestioned epistemic assumptions on which they rest. Conceptual cages can be identified as framing issues of development, setting hierarchical assumptions, thus limiting the paradigms of research and the production of knowledge. In other words, they constitute epistemic practices that distort, depoliticize, and then turn them into technical concepts concerning specific projects of development (Bøås and McNeill 2004: 1–4). Their epistemic power, as theoretical and methodological lenses, ends in a transformative logic that takes research generally toward a focus on ahistorical, top-down and liberal–institutionalist analyses and assessments of other regionalist experiences (Bøås and McNeill 2004; Söderbaum 2013).

These conceptual cages are thus marked by an excluding tendency to block other agency – structure dynamics out of the formal regional processes such as informal processes, conflict, and development (Shaw, Marchand, and Bøås 2005; Taylor 2010). Conceptual cages function as consensual epistemic devices and depend and extend according to the power of epistemic communities. They legitimize and operationalize a specific ontological hierarchy of assumptions. This work is done in stages, first depoliticizing historical or contextual concepts of development; then to operationalizing them through technical means; and in the last step, to produce conceptual technical frameworks to measure or assess the extent to which other realities fit the mold (Bøås and McNeill 2004). In the following section, we will consider Eurocentric, Liberal Economic Integration, Actor-oriented North American Regional Perspectives, and Neoliberal Institutionalism and the limitations of these frameworks, concerning South American regionalism.

Eurocentric regionalism

Eurocentric regionalism is a conceptual cage subordinating any regional research framework to a rationalization of the European experience. It explicitly or implicitly sets a hierarchy of legitimate knowledge based upon a depoliticized reading of European regionalism, hiding the complex, contradictory, and conflicting political and economic processes behind its historical construction. The central assumption of the Eurocentric regionalism is its conditions *sine qua non* for the existence of regionalism: a) economic convergence; b) the transfer of sovereignty from national powers to supra-regional institutions; c) reduction state powers. As Söderbaum (2013) notes, this assumption is deeply associated with the first theoretical debates concerning the nature of European regionalism as the response to great wars. Nonetheless, here history diverges with theory, and in that sense, the ontological nature of the dominant approach can invert the reading of reality.

Indeed, the successful creation of the European Union (EU) is, to an extent, indebted to the historical purpose of ending centuries of horrific wars between neighboring authoritarian empires and nationalistic movements, which, counting only the two world wars, resulted in nearly 90 million deaths in the region (Leitenberg 2006). In the case of South American regionalism, there is no comparative example. Moreover, the notion of sovereignty transfer to supranational structures represents a political concept derived and sponsored by the United States, based on its insistence on the creation of superregional institutions to diminish nationalist conflicts – in contrast, the United Kingdom (UK) feared and opposed a deeper integrated Europe (Carolan 2008). The complex epistemic process of rationalization, starting with Mitrany's functionalism and subsequently Haas' neo-functionalism, were theoretical responses to rationalize European regionalism under a pragmatic, technocratic, and institutional system based on the utilitarian calculus of individual actors (Haas 1975: 12).

Following Malamud (2011a), we can identify that three other theoretically and methodologically central sub-elements are of the concept of Eurocentrism. First are Mitrany and Hass' functionalist and neo-functionalism paradigms, which associate regionalism with institutional integration and, in the end, with the idea that this implies a cession of state authority (Malamud 2011a: 222). Mitrany believed in the historical challenge to overcome the problem of European nationalism and the competence between political units by learning from the experience of the North American *New Deal* (Mitrany 1966). This functionalist concept rests upon institutional and liberal perspectives, and it claims that the existence of regionalism and integration depends on institutions and the deconcentration of power from states (Haas 1975).

The second element is the subordinate relation of politics to a particular understanding of economic development. Followers of this idea generally assert that economic integration follows from economic expansion through logical and linear stages, a concept formulated initially by Bela Balassa (1961), the year of the construction of the Berlin Wall at the peak of the Cold War. Finally, there is the existence of the third element, that of the extended and unrevised notion of "convergence" and "homogeneity" within and of a region (Dabène 2012: 5; Malamud 2011b). Accordingly, countries in a given area are said to give up their sovereignty "voluntarily" and converge around common and concentric regional projects (Malamud 2011b). There, shared projects of region, common regional structures, and lack of national differences drive the regionalism. Along these lines, Portugal, Greece, Germany, France, or Poland, would be all under the same conditions of political power within the EU.

Liberal economic integration

Perhaps the most used and dominant conceptual cage concerning South American regionalism is the Inter-American System and its academic networks for understanding regional integration and regionalism. The liberal economic integration approach commonly cements the relation between – and is the basis of – the economic assumptions upon which neorealism and neoliberal institutionalism are conceptually integrated. Accordingly, regional economic integration is the foundation and objective of any regional project, a process that develops from the bottom up through a logical and linear sequence of market integration stages (e.g., free trade areas, customs unions, common markets, monetary unions, and economic integration).

Ironically, such a *logical sequence of economic integration stages* has never occurred in any significant historical case of regionalization, in particular, the EU (Torrent 2003). Liberal economic integration (LEI) is probably the most academic construction of all conceptual cages, developed by economists seeking to depoliticize the nature of regional integration based on liberal institutional assumptions. The epistemic device rests upon an extensive network of scholars on both sides of the Atlantic who frequently connect with Bretton Woods institutions (i.e., Estevadeordal and Suominen 2007). As mentioned, the construction of LEI based on liberal institutional assumptions was unfolded by economists who positioned a particular perspective about integration.

Consequently, LEI is an epistemic device of research that frames alternative policies of development, via depoliticization and technification of alternatives of integration based on assumptions of free trade.

One of the most important exponents of liberal economic institutionalism is the Hungarian-born economist Bela Balassa, professor at Johns Hopkins University and a consultant for the World Bank, renowned for his theory of regional economic integration (1961). Marked by the concerns of the Cold War, Balassa embraced free markets and concerns with the re-establishment of Western Europe as a world power based on liberal institutional and free-market developments decontaminated from politics as an idealist framework (Machlup 1977). At the time, European scholars were deeply concerned about the prospect of European disintegration due to rivaling nationalisms, thus the focus of their views on models and abstract rationalization on pure economic regional integration without politics. Remarkably, the condition for that was not set by European states but by the sponsorship of the United States. It is the administrator of the Marshall Plan and US director of the Economic Cooperation Administration (ECA), Paul Hoffman, who used first the concept of regional economic integration in 1949 as a way to create a single European market (Machlup 1977: 11).

LEI rests on the idea of a linear progression from preferential trade areas to free trade areas, with customs unions, common markets, and monetary unions, and ending in a complete economic regional integrated area. It is generally the basis of most of the research on regionalism in regional development banks. These theories are concerned principally with the possible welfare effects stemming from trade creation, diversion, and integration (Cable and Henderson 1994), although they present rigid limitations to explain development given their disciplinary economist boundaries integrally.

Liberal regional economic integration approaches work in combination with actor-oriented theories to generate models to predict and enhance paths of interstate cooperation and measure liberal economic integration (Estevadeordal and Suominen 2007: 4). In this sense, there are two different lines of economic integration research. The first line of study concentrates on whether the impact of economic regionalism contributes to the world trading system. The second line of research, also created to explain economic integration in Europe, distances itself from orthodox economics by focusing more on investment, employment, infrastructure, and structural transformations, as well as market and government failures (Robson 1993).

The advantage of this second approach is that it provides the conceptual grounds to explore regionalism in developing regions. Its primary disadvantage is the absence of research regarding heterodox experiences and politico-economic processes of regionalization, such as those seen in South America. Indeed, liberal regional economic integration still offers a vast and rich field of research that can integrate more heterodox perspectives on the impact of alternative strategies of growth based on the experiences of developing regions. The key in this regard is to bridge economics and politics by transcending the rigid disciplinary boundaries and unrealistic assumptions of problem-solving or actor-oriented approaches (Söderbaum 2005: 231).

Actor-oriented North American Regional Perspectives

To a large extent, the conceptual limitations of North American Regional Perspectives (NARP) are linked theoretically and methodologically to mainstream North American IPE and draw on rational choice, neorealism, and neoliberal institutionalism. NARP epistemologies are defined by its methods and positivist approach to scientific procedures rather than based on an ontology of the reality (Lake 2011) when it comes to regionalism.

Actor-oriented NARP share common ontological and epistemological premises with the Eurocentric school and mainstream IR theory as the result of the behavioralist research and theories of modernization that embraced, in the decades after the end of WWII, North America, Europe, and Japan (Viotti and Kauppi 2012). The development and focus of NARP is rooted in the conservative branch of traditional North American political sciences' school, unfolded today in what is termed as Open Economy Politics (OEP), a sort of subfield of the Strategic Choice approach in North American IR (Lake 2011). NARP examines South American regionalism from the perspective of its institutional degree and trade variation vis-à-vis specific "standards" based in Europe, North America, and Asia-Pacific.

Two elements define NARP as this relies on implausible theoretical assumptions that claim its methodology and procedures are the only ones scientifically acceptable for producing knowledge in IR (Hay 2002: 9; Jackson 2011: 43). However, this does not mean that in specific cases, neo-positivist methods may be the most appropriate to find answers to central research questions on integration and regional institutions.

The main issue with NARP is how it utilizes the classic hypothetical deductive method, where science is limited to testable hypotheses, under *ceteris paribus* conditions for all contexts. Its methodology isolates objects in order to define variables (e.g., Y and X) the dependent and independent variables, under a universal and unique inference model. The conceptual cage is, thus, how this framework produces knowledge via a limited methodological approach. In other words, the KKV model, regarded as the only scientific method based on universal rules of scientific inference in IR (Jackson 2011; King, Keohane, and Verba 1994). This model rests the rational choice assumption that agency (actor interests and decisions) from above produce regional development and that in order to understand them, it is necessary to bracket preference actors over economic development. The second central assumption is its basic political economy definition concerning economic openness or closure, based on trade, a paradigm inherited from trade policy and later extended to regional monetary and financial relations (Lake 2011: 48). A neoliberal view of development thus defines regional outcomes from this perspective, and economic free trade integration rationalized in the analytical labyrinth of formal actors and economic assumptions.

A second conceptual cage of NARP pertains to the neorealist, unrevised, and extended idea of Hegemonic Stability Theory (HST). According to this theory, a region is dependent on the existence of a hegemon, or a large state willing to provide stability and economic growth through free trade and open markets. The main argument from this perspective applied to South America is that, without Brazil or Mexico assuming the hegemonic role to provide the regional leadership and necessary security, South America regionalism is just a collection of different regional projects. Indeed, the assertion clashes with the complex process of the regional multilateralism and different projects shaping the New South American Regionalism (Vivares 2018). For example, although the weight of Brazil and Mexico has been relevant in terms of political and economic influence, these countries have not necessarily assumed a hegemonic role in shaping regional processes. Neither have they assumed the leadership to provide stability in aspects of inter-regional security and development.

This neorealist regionalism focuses on the hegemon in pursuit of free trade and open markets, on the struggle and distribution of power within a particular region as the result of the links between security and growing economic interdependence (Gomez-Mera 2008). From this view, regionalism is seen to arise whenever cooperation is necessary for geopolitical reasons, following open economic tendencies, in order to counter the power of rising regional power or to restrict the behavior of conflictive small state members in the region (Grieco 1997). Regional hegemonic power is a necessary condition for regionalism to promote regional cooperation and institutionalization (Hurrell 1995).

Neoliberal institutionalism

Finally, neoliberal institutionalism brings together functionalist and institutionalist approaches, emphasizing the importance of institutionalizing regional integration. Based on the central premise that regionalism is the rational response of governmental cooperation for solving the problems of an increased regional interdependence, such as the European experience (Deutsch, Burrell, and Kann 1968; Haas 1958; Mitrany 1966). Neoliberal institutionalism is one of the most dominant approaches to regionalism, marrying epistemologically neorealism and neo-liberalism (Keohane 1984; Mansfield and Helen 1997). Neoliberal institutionalism is stronger in its explanation of the relationship between politics and economics than NARP. From the neo-liberal institutionalism perspective, politics is shaped and limited by the allegedly "universal" laws of neo-classical economics. Market power thus constrains states, where a globalized economy, dominated by trade and finance, limit development. States thus respond to these challenges through regional trade agreements (trade regionalization), as global and regional economic integration is unstoppable, giving rise to the importance of institutions and regimes (Keohane 1984). Therefore, regional trade agreements constitute the cornerstone of regional public goods as they are part of an incremental problem-solving process, defined by the level of institutionalization and trade complementarity (Söderbaum 2005: 227).

However, three elements mark the central weaknesses of neoliberal institutionalism. The first is the idea that institutionalization subordinated to the dynamics of trade defines regionalism, based on the regional experiences of the EU, North American Free Trade Agreement (NAFTA), and Asian Pacific Economic Community (APEC). Second, the identification of regionalism as a formal state-led project of integration, which confines the concept of regionalism and its research to states and governmental agencies, leaving our non-state actors and informal regional powers. Finally, it reduces regionalism to a trade phenomenon where institutions only play a role in creating incentives and constraints to given processes (Söderbaum 2005).

Conclusions

This chapter has questioned how mainstream regionalism theories have limited the development of other research agendas. The analysis of three perspectives such as Eurocentric regionalism, liberal integration theory, and the actor-oriented North American regional perspective, the adaptation of the Weberian concept "conceptual cages," demonstrates that such political economy perspectives concerning regionalism and development limit the diversity of concepts and methodological formats that skew the comprehension of other regionalism, such as New South American Regionalism.

One of the main "conceptual cages" of Eurocentric regionalism is the premise that a successful integration process demands the cession of the sovereignty of the states to that of a supra-regional instance. This vision depoliticizes the historical construction of European regionalism, also concealing political–economic processes inherent in its consolidation. Its limitations are linked to the idea that regionalism should be assimilated and applied as a project based on a state-centric experience in the specific world order. However, this vision does not necessarily fit with other experiences of regionalism, such as that of South America, where integrationist and regionalist projects have failed in their attempts to achieve a high degree of institutionalization and assignment of sovereignty.

Regarding liberal integration theory, it contains a linear approach that understands integration as a process that takes place in stages of economic growth. Its limitations are linked both to the universalist postulates and the notion of development based on economic neoliberalism.

That is the only formula for regional integration, which has not proven sufficient in the case of South America.

In the case of actor-oriented North American Perspectives to regionalism, they rest on an empiricist epistemology about scientific knowledge, aligned with theories that situate within rationalist understandings of international relations. From this view, a hegemon is required to maintain the status quo and provide for the economic growth of other actors in the international system, and are necessary conditions for the existence of regionalism and greater cooperation. However, this perspective does not explain the dynamics of New South American Regionalism, its actors, and the endogenous and structural factors that characterize the region.

In the case of institutional neoliberalism, its central premise rests on the importance of institutions and, therefore, on the need to achieve high levels of institutionalization in regional integration processes. Three elements constitute the central weaknesses of neoliberal institutionalism. The first is the idea that regionalism is defined by its level of institutionalization subordinated to the dynamics of trade, and based on the regional experiences of the EU, NAFTA, and APEC. Second, that regionalism is a state-led project of integration, which confines the concept of regionalism and its research to states and governmental agencies, leaving out not only strategic areas of analysis but also questions of conflict and well-being. Finally, the reduction of regionalism to a trade phenomenon where institutions only play a role in creating incentives and constraints to given processes (Söderbaum 2005). Regionalism as a political–economic concept is more comprehensive than regional economic integration, these can be different and even complementary avenues of research.

In conclusion, the main issue with the four dominant paradigms discussed here is how they epistemologically, methodologically, and theoretically limit the generation new concepts, perspectives, and methodologies applicable to the domestic and structural dynamics of specific regions. Because they have become widely accepted as hierarchical assumptions, they constrain not only research but also the redefinition of the notions of development in regions, such as South America. These assumptions thus need to be reviewed from a critical perspective in order to better analyze regional configurations, characterized by a context of intensification of globalization processes, trans-nationalization of investments, finance, trade, and the presence of new state and non-state actors in the global arena.

Note

1 See also Bull (1966).

Bibliography

Acharya, A. 2011. Dialogue and Discovery: In Search of International Relations Theories Beyond the West. *Millennium: Journal of International Studies* 39 (3): 619–637. Available at: https://doi.org/10.1177/0305829811406574.

Balassa, B. 1961. *The Theory of Economic Integration*. London: Routledge.

Bøås, M. and McNeill, D. eds. 2004. *Global Institutions & Development: Framing the world?* New York: Routledge.

Bonilla, A. and Long, G. 2010. Un nuevo regionalismo sudamericano. *Íconos: revista de Ciencias Sociales* 38: 23–28.

Breslin, S., Hughes, C., Phillips, N. and Rosamond, B. eds. 2002. *New Regionalisms in the Global Political Economy: Theory and Cases*. London: Routledge.

Bull, H. 1966. International Theory: The Case for a Classical Approach. *World Politics* 18 (3): 361–377.

Burgess, R. (ed.) 1982. The role of theory in field research. In *Field Research: A Sourcebook and Field Manual*: 209–212. London: Routledge Curzon.

Cable, V. and Henderson, D. 1994. *Trade Blocs? The Future of Regional Integration*. London: Royal Institute of International Affairs.

Carolan, B. 2009. The Birth of the European Union: US and UK Roles in the Creation of a Unified European community. *Tulsa Journal of Comparative & International Law* 16 (1).

Cohen, B. 2008. *International Political Economy: An Intellectual History*. Princeton: Princeton University Press.

Cox, R. 1981. Social Forces, States and World Orders: Beyond International Relations Theory. *Millennium: Journal of International Studies* 10 (2): 126–155. Available at: https://doi.org/10.1177/030582988 10100020501.

Cox, R. 2009. The "British School" in the Global Context. *New Political Economy* 14 (3): 315–328. Available at: https://doi.org/10.1080/13563460903087441.

Cox, R. and Schechter, M. eds. 2002. *The Political Economy of a Plural World: Critical Reflections on Power, Morals and Civilizations*. London: Routledge.

Dabène, O. 2012. Consistency and resilience through cycles of repolitization." In *Rise of Post – Hegemonic Regionalism: The Case of Latin America*. Riggirozzi, P. and Tussie, D. (ed.): 41–64. London: Springer.

De Lombaerde, P. and Garay, L. 2006. *The New Regionalism in Latin America and the Role of the US. OBREAL/EULARO*. Tokyo: Sophia University and the Japan Center for Area Studies.

De Lombaerde, P. and Söderbaum, F. (eds.) 2014. *Regionalism*. Belgium: SAGE-UN.

Deutsch, K., Burrell, S., and Kann, R. (eds.) 1968. *Political Community in the North Atlantic*. Princeton: Princeton University Press.

Dunne, T., Hansen, L., and Wight, C. 2013. The End of International Relations Theory? *European Journal of International Relations* 19 (3): 405–425. Available at: https://doi.org/10.1177/1354066113495485.

Estevadeordal, A. and Suominen, K. 2007. *Sequencing Regional Trade Integration and Cooperation Agreements: Describing a Dataset for a New Research Agenda*. Washington, DC: Inter-American Development Bank.

Frieden, J. and Lake, D. (eds.) 2000. *International Political Economy: Perspectives on Global Power and Wealth*. New York: St. Martin's Press.

Gilpin, R. 2001. *Global Political Economy: Understanding the International Political Economy*. Princeton: Princeton University Press.

Gomez-Mera, L. 2008. How "New" is the "New Regionalism" in the Americas? The Case of Mercosur. *Journal of International Relations and Development* 11 (3): 279–308. Available at: https://doi.org/10.1057/jird.2008.14.

Grieco, J. 1997. Systemic Sources of Variation in Regional Institutionalization in Western Europe, East Asia and the Americas. In *The Political Economy of Regionalism*, Mansfield, E. and Milner, H. (eds.): 164–188. New York: Colombia University Press.

Haas, E. 1958. *The Uniting of Europe: Political, Social and International Organization*. Stanford: Stanford University Press.

Haas, E. 1975. *The Obsolescence of Regional Integration Theory*. California: Institute of International Studies, University of California.

Hay, C. 2002. Divided by a Common Language? Conceptualising Power. In: *Political Analysis: A Critical Introduction*, Hay, C. (ed.). Estados Unidos: Palgrave Macmillan.

Hettne, B. 1997. The Double Movement: Global Market versus Regionalism. In: *The New Realism: Perspectives on Multilateralism and World Order*, Cox, R (ed.): 223–244. Tokyo: United Nations University Press.

Hettne, B. 2003. The New Regionalism Revisited. In: *Theories of New Regionalism*. Söderbaum, F. and Shaw, T. (eds.): 22–42. Basingstoke: Palgrave MacMillan.

Hettne, B. 2006. Beyond the "New" Regionalism. In: *Key Debates in Political Economy*. Payne, A. (ed.). London: Taylor & Francis.

Hettne, B. 2008. *Regional Actorship and Regional Agency: Comparative Perspective*. Brussels, 9–13 June.

Higgott, R. 2003. Alternative Theories of Economic Regionalism: Trade and Finance in Asian Cooperation. *Review of International Political Economy* 10 (3): 430–454.

Hurrell, A. 1995. Regionalism in Theoretical Perspective. In: *Regionalism in World Politics: Regional Organization and International Order*. Fawcett, L. and Hurrell, A. (ed.): 9–73. Oxford: Oxford University Press.

Jackson, P. 2011. *The Conduct of Inquiry in International Relations: Philosophy of Science and its Implications for the Study of World Politics*. New York: Routledge.

Katzenstein, P. 2000. *Asian Regionalism*. New York: Cornell University Press.

Keohane, R. 1984. *After Hegemony: Cooperation and Discord in the World Political Economy*. Princeton: Princeton University Press.

Keohane, R. 2002. *Power and Governance in a Partially Globalized World*. London: Routledge.

King, G., Keohane, R., and Verba, S. 1994. *Designing in Social Inquiry: Scientific Inference in Qualitative Research*. Princeton: Princeton University Press.

Krasner, S. 2000. State Power and the Structure of International Trade. In: *International Political Economy: Perspectives on Global Power and Wealth*. Frieden, J. and Lake, D. (eds.) 4th. Edition: 19–36. Boston: Routledge.

Lake, D. 2011. TRIPS across the Atlantic: Theory and Epistemology in IPE. In: *International Political Economy: Debating the Past, Present and Future*. Phillips, N. and Weaver, C. (eds.): 45–52. New York: Routledge.

Lake, D. 2013. Theory is Dead, Long Live Theory: The End of the Great Debates and the Rise of Eclecticism in International Theory. *European Journal of International Relations* 19 (3): 567–587.

Leitenberg, M. 2006. Deaths in War and Conflicts in the 20 Century. Cornell University. *Peace Studies Program*. Occasional Paper 29.

Machlup, F. 1977. *A History of Thought on Economic Integration*. London: Macmillan Press.

Malamud, A. 2011a. A Leader without Followers? The Growing Divergence Between the Regional and Global Performance of Brazilian Foreign Policy. *Latin American Politics and Society* 53 (3): 1–24.

Malamud, A. 2011b. Conceptos, teorías y debates sobre la integración regional. *Norteamerica* 6 (2).

Malamud, A. and Gardini, G. 2012. Has Regionalism Peaked? The Latin American Quagmire and Its Lessons. *The International Spectator* 47 (1): 116–133. Available at: https://doi.org/10.1080/03932729.2012.655013.

Mansfield, E. and Helen, M. (eds.) 1997. *The Political Economy of Regionalism*. New York: Columbia University Press.

Mitrany, D. 1966. *A Working Peace System*. London: Royal Institute of International Affairs.

Nye, J. 1965. *Pan Africanism and East African Integration*. Cambridge: Harvard University Press.

Nye, J. 2002. *The Paradox of American Power: Why the World's Only Superpower Can't Go It Alone*. New York: Oxford University Press.

Payne, A. 1996. The United States and its Enterprise for the Americas. In: *Regionalism and World Order*. Gamble, A. and Payne, A. (ed.): 93–129. London: Macmillan.

Payne, A. 2004. *The New Regional Politics of Development*. New York: Palgrave.

Payne, A. 2005. *The Global Politics of Unequal Development*. London: Palgrave.

Payne, A. and Phillips, N. 2010. *Development*. London: Polity.

Polanyi, K. 2001. *The Great Transformation: The Political and Economic Origins of Our Time*. Boston: Beacon Press.

Riggirozzi, P. 2010. Region, Regionness and Regionalism in Latin America: Towards a New Synthesis. *Latin American Trade Network*. Available at: http://latn.org.ar/wp-content/uploads/2014/09/WP_130_RegionRegioness_Riggirozzi.pdf.

Riggirozzi, P. 2012. Region, Regionness, and Regionalism: Towards a New Synthesis. *New Political Economy* 17 (4): 1–23.

Robson, P. 1993. The New Regionalism and Developing Countries. *Journal of Common Market Studies* 31 (3): 329–384. Available at: https://doi.org/10.1111/j.1468-5965.1993.tb00467.x.

Sautú, R. 2003. *Todo es teoría: objetivos y métodos de investigación*. Buenos Aires: Ediciones Lumiere.

Shaw, T. 1988. Africa Renaissance/African Alliance: Towards New Regionalism and New Realism in the Great Lakes the Start of the Twenty-first Century. *Politeia* 17 (3): 60–74.

Shaw, T. 2000. New Regionalism in Africa in the New Millennium: Comparative Perspectives on Renaissance, Realism and/or Regressions. *New Political Economy* 5 (3): 399–414.

Shaw, T., Marchand, M., and Bøås, M. (eds.) 2005. *The Political Economy of Regions and Regionalism*. London: Palgrave Macmillan.

Sil, R. and Katzenstein, P. (eds.) 2010. *Beyond Paradigms: Analytic Eclecticism in the Study of World Politics*. New York: Palgrave Macmillan.

Söderbaum, F. 2003. Introduction: Theories of New Regionalism. In: *Theories of New Regionalism*. Söderbaum, F. and Shaw, T. (ed.): 1–21. Basingstoke: Palgrave Macmillan.

Söderbaum, F. 2005. The International Political Economy of Regionalism. In: *Globalizing International Political Economy*. Phillips, N. (ed.). London: Palgrave MacMillan.

Söderbaum, F. 2012. Conceptualizing Region, Regionalism and Regionalization. *Georgetown Journal of International Affairs, Summer*.

Söderbaum, F. 2013. What's Wrong with Regional Integration? The Problem of Eurocentrism. Working Papers N64: RSCAS.

357

Söderbaum, F. 2015. *Rethinking Regionalism*. Basingstoke: Palgrave Macmillan.

Söderbaum, F. and Shaw, T. 2003. *Theories of New Regionalism*. Basingstoke: Palgrave MacMillan.

Strange, S. 1986. *Casino Capitalism*. New York: Manchester University Press.

Strange, S. 1988. *States and Markets*. New York: Continuum.

Taylor, I. 2010. *China's New Role in Africa*. New York: Lynne Rienner Publishers.

Torrent, R. 2003. Regional Integration Instruments and Dimensions: An Analytical Framework. In: *Bridges for Development: Policies and Institutions for Trade and Integration*. Devlin, R. and Estevadeordal, A. (eds.): 119–135. Washington, DC: Inter-American Development Bank.

Viotti, P. and Kauppi, M. 2012. *International Relations Theory*. United States: Pearson.

Vivares, E. (ed.). 2018. *Regionalism, Development and the Post-Commodity Boom in South America*. London: Palgrave Macmillan.

Waltz, K. 1979. *Theory of International Politics*. United States: Addison-Wesley.

Waltz, K. 2001. *Man, the State and War*. New York: Columbia University Press.

Weber, M. 2001. *The Protestant Ethic and the Spirit of Capitalism*. London: Routledge.

21

The IPE of transnational class and contemporary capitalism

Shawn Nichols

Transnational capitalism: an introduction

Vigorous debates have been waged over the concept of *globalization*, with the term becoming popularized in the 1990s, following the neoliberal restructuring of the 1980s. Indeed, it is one of the most debated subjects of the late twentieth to early twenty-first century, with academics, politicians, and casual observers advancing a multitude of divergent and often contradictory claims. One set of questions, in particular, lies at the heart of scholarly disagreement, namely those focusing on whether or not the processes associated with economic globalization are novel. For example, is it a new phenomenon that began to take shape in the latter part of the twentieth century – or simply the continuation of historical processes associated with centuries of capitalist development? While a lack of consensus exists over the answers to these questions, it is clear to at least most critical observers that the nature of the global economy has evolved significantly from the era when capitalist production processes were largely confined within single jurisdictions to the current era in which production is organized transnationally.

To this end, a number of different critical approaches have been advanced to provide an analytical framework for explaining how transformations in the organization of production processes have impacted the relationship between social groups, the state, and global institutions. While differing on several points, these critical theorists all reject the tendency of conventional international political economy approaches to take the world, with its existing power relations, as it is. To this end, they point out that adopting the assumption that power relations are fixed reflects an ideological bias that is driven by the problem-solving goal of identifying sources of destabilization in order to maintain the existing power hierarchy. The starting point for critical theory is thus that power relations must not be taken for granted. Instead, their origins must be traced, and potential moments of destabilization identified. Such an exercise is not merely academic but is driven by the normative goal of contesting the power structure and transforming the current order to one that is more socially and politically just. In this way, these perspectives reflect the understanding that only through historicizing the existing power relationships can moments of historical discontinuity be identified and harnessed for emancipatory change (Cox 1987).

Box 21.1 Hegemony through the lens of historical materialism

While conventional approaches explain hegemony in terms of the military and economic power held by states, it is conceptualized in far broader terms by neo-Gramscian analyses. These perspectives consider the operation of, and interaction between, ideology, institutions, and material interests in generating consent for the existing political and economic system. In this sense, political coercion is rendered unnecessary by making the interest of the powerful appear to be the same as the general interest. This is accomplished through developing a dominant discourse that limits the scope of ideas that might arise in response to political, economic, and social questions. Related to this, material structures are also created that tie the interests of the many to the interest of the few. It is worth considering, for example, the fact that a working class individual identifies their interests as tied to Wall Street if their retirement portfolio depends on investment performance. Each of these components is also reinforced through institutionalizing and, thus, locking in the prerogatives of powerful groups, severely circumscribing the range of options available to both political leaders and regular citizens.

Narrowing the scope to focus on a particular subset of critical political economy perspectives, this chapter illuminates a body of scholarship that draws on the insights of Italian Marxist Antonio Gramsci in considering hegemony, world order, and historical change. The first section provides the contours of the ontological assumptions broadly shared by these neo-Gramscian approaches, with particular focus on the *global capitalism* thesis and its emphasis on transnational social forces. The next section applies the analytical framework, sketching the historical events that drove the shift under consideration, beginning with the economic crisis of the 1970s and the breakdown of the Bretton Woods System of fixed exchange rates. The following section explores the consequences of these developments and the new accumulation strategies that have reinforced the power of the dominant transnational social forces that have emerged from the crisis. The chapter concludes by highlighting a number of questions that require consideration in the current context.

Neo-Gramscian perspectives and the global capitalism thesis

Nation states are not the only source of power impacting global relations, nor are interactions between them necessarily the most important processes to analyze. This recognition, among other conceptual departures, drove a group of theorists led by Robert Cox in the 1980s to break from the dominant mainstream international relations approaches and shift the analytical focus beyond the logic of the nation state to probe social forces, structures, and social relations. Drawing on Gramsci's insights, these scholars revived the historical materialist methodological approach to analyze the evolution of production structures driving the global division of labor and the transformation of social relations accompanying these processes (Cox 1981; Gramsci 1967). They sought to historicize the concepts taken for granted as universally valid by conventional approaches and render the analytical focal points specific to time and place. While a diversity of neo-Gramscian perspectives exist, they share in common several goals and assumptions.

Box 21.2 The global capitalism thesis

An influential set of perspectives, referred to as the global capitalism school, challenge the notion that the current era of neoliberal capitalism is simply an extension of imperial processes. Instead, this thesis posits that a historical rupture took place following the crisis of Keynesianism and the abandonment of the Bretton Woods system of fixed exchange rates. The subsequent adoption of policies of deregulation and liberalization that abolished barriers to capital flows led to the transformation of the social relations of production as corporations took advantage of the cost savings associated with spreading the production process across multiple national jurisdictions. In contrast to the previous era in which corporations mostly produced goods within the borders of one country to sell to consumers both at home and abroad, the transnational supply chain model engendered the rise of a new dominant set of social forces and transformed the state. The removal of barriers to capital flows increased the structural power of mobile capital, the exit option of which served as a disciplining mechanism to governments. Whereas in the earlier nation-state era of capitalism the state was called upon both to mediate class conflict by serving a social welfare function and to defend the interests of capital rooted within its borders, this state form came to serve as an impediment to accumulation in the neoliberal era. It is in this context that a dominant transnational capitalist class (TCC) emerged, transforming the state along neoliberal lines and bringing about epochal change.

First, they recognize that both structure and agency must be considered to understand the dialectic between the enduring patterns and the forces of transformation. The processes under consideration are thus analyzed in terms of both conjunctural events and structural constants. In other words, while specific events performed by actors with agency matter, the social structures that endure, including patterning habits, institutional forms, expectations, and philosophical systems, must also be taken seriously. Fernand Braudel referred to these long-lasting social patterns, including the "mentalities that prevail in a given era," as the "long durée" (Braudel 1969; Gill and Mittelman 1997: 5).

A second shared assumption is the understanding that capitalist development has evolved through several distinct phases, or world orders, each of which has been associated with different social relations of production. The social relations of production correspond to three dialectically related components that govern the way work is done. The first component concerns the power relations governing production. In other words, the decisions over *what* will be produced are exercised by those with accumulated social power who have the ability to determine such priorities. A second component pertains to the organization of the production process or, as described by Robert Cox, the process through which a "division complementarity of roles," is "bound together by a structure of authority that governs the production process" (Cox 1987: 12). The third component arises in the distribution of benefits that are derived from the production process, a distribution that reflects the outcome of social struggles over time. Crucially, the structure of the production process emerges from a pre-existing class structure, but it also generates a particular set of social forces, with individuals developing intersubjective meaning with respect to their relationship to the modes of production and others in their own – and other – social classes. In this way, the class structure crystalizes as people engage in the production of goods and services that form the basis of a society's wealth and its ability to mobilize power (Cox 1981: 135, 1987: 51). The social relations of production that emerge are thus understood to be "the totality of social relations in material, institutional, and discursive forms" (Bieler and Morton 2004: 87). They operate across each of these three spheres, the persistence of which provides coherence to the world order that exists in a given era (Gill 1997).

Third, the notion is shared that each transformation in the social relations of production is linked to the exercise of state power. Crucially, however, the form taken by the state depends upon the particular configuration of social forces and the social struggles playing out between them. As noted by William Robinson, "the nation state is not transhistorical" (2004: 89) and therefore should not be understood as fixed, but rather as a political form that reflects a historically specific relationship between modes of production, class, and, territoriality. Moreover, the interplay between an existing set of social forces and state form arise dialectically to produce a particular *world order*, which may be characterized by either stability or conflict.

Finally, a broadened conception of hegemony separates neo-Gramscian approaches from conventional international relations, and even some Marxist, perspectives, which limit the scope to the military capabilities and economic power wielded by states. Expanding the analytical lens to explain the relationship between the state and society, sources of power and political action are understood as not reducible to material interests and capabilities. These perspectives thus focus on the means through which power and domination are exercised through the combined mechanisms of ideas, material resources, and both national and supranational institutions to generate broad-based consent. It is here that Gramsci's concept of *historical blocs* is deployed (Gramsci 1967). When a particular constellation of dominant social forces, engendered by the social relations of production, has achieved a sufficient degree of broad-based consent to render the world order sufficiently stable, an historical bloc is said to have formed. The existence of an historical bloc implies that it is capable of articulating the economic, political, moral, and intellectual unity necessary to generate consent, or hegemony, as a form of class rule (Overbeek 1993). This historical bloc thus gives meaning to the political community through both coercion and the generation of consent, providing the class structure that defines the state's nature and function. This is not to suggest that the state is directly instrumentalized by the dominant groups, but rather that the range of possibilities available to state agents are constrained by their

---

Box 21.3 The fourth epoch in the development of capitalism

The birth of capitalism emerged from the decay of the feudal order approximately five centuries ago. Unlike feudalism and social systems before it, capitalism was the first to require constant accumulation and expansion in order to survive. This requirement has driven a variety of strategies in order to secure the land, labor, resources, and markets necessary to maintain this dynamism. The current, or fourth, epoch is understood by the global capitalism school to correspond to processes that are qualitatively different from the previous periods, which were characterized by the spatial enlargement of capitalism, or the bringing into the capitalist logic areas that were previously outside of it. By the end of the twentieth century, capitalism's processes of geographical expansion were mostly complete, with few parts of the world remaining outside of the capitalist logic following decolonization and the collapse of the socialist alternative. The fourth epoch has thus made way for processes that intensify the commodification of spheres of social life in ways that were formally outside of the logic of the market. This has included everything from health care and education to the creation of new commodities by way of such schemes as carbon trading and innovative financial products.

general understanding of the class structure and the limits associated with it. As described by Dutch political economist, Kees Van der Pijl, the struggles involved in "reinforcing the capacity of the ruling class to expand its mode of production to global dimensions … determine the priorities of a broad range of actors" (1997: 9). Indeed, the historical bloc "becomes part and parcel of the state itself" (Cox 1987: 5).

While neo-Gramscian perspectives share in common many assumptions, they are not monolithic and therefore do not speak with one voice. Indeed, a variety of diverse, but related, perspectives building on Cox's, and Gramsci's ideas before him, emerged in the decades that followed to further theorize hegemony, world order, and historical change. One point of departure, in particular, crystallized between different schools of thought, an analytical disagreement centering on the question of the novelty of the processes associated with neoliberal globalization. The question became: Do the observed processes represent the continuation of earlier historical processes in a manner that reflects only quantitative changes? Or, do they represent a discontinuity that is different in a qualitative sense? In other words, do these processes actually represent epochal change?

On one side of this debate is a group of scholars who argue that the processes we are witnessing in the current period merely reflect the intensification, or a quantitative increase, of historical patterns playing out across national boundaries (Hirst, Thompson and Bromley 1996; Weiss 1998; Wood 1999). Emphasizing that power relations among national states are of primary concern for understanding the existing social conditions, Leo Panitch and Sam Gindin, for example, argue that core capitalist states, particularly the United States, remain highly implicated in directing these processes, which should be thought of as *international* and analyzed in terms of interactions between nation states (McMichael 2001: 203; Panitch and Gindin 2005: 102). Deploying a state-centered or geographically discrete understanding, others similarly focus their analyses on structures and processes that they view as an extension of imperialism (Chase-Dunn 1998; Panitch and Gindin 2005, 2014; Wallerstein 1974).

On the other side of this debate, an increasingly influential set of perspectives referred to as the *global capitalism school* has emerged, which conceptualizes the processes associated with neoliberal globalization as representing epochal change. Given the transformations in the global system of production in the 1980s and 1990s, the current order is understood as irreducible to the extension of pre-existing historical processes. Instead, it is understood as a set of qualitatively different processes driven by changes in the social relations of production that have transformed the state and, ultimately, world order. Eschewing nation-state centered accounts, transnational class relations are thus taken seriously. Van der Pijl, for example, provided early analysis of the class consequences of the transnationalization of capitalist production (Van Der Pijl 1984, 1989). Others, too, sought to analyze class formation beyond the nation state logic (Gill 1990; Overbeek 2001; Sklair 1995, 2002). Importantly, these perspectives are predicated on the notion that the nation state and social forces exist in non-dualistic terms. In this way, the state is understood as constituted by the prevailing social forces, rather than sitting apart from them in a "state-society complex" (Cox 1987: 205; Gramsci 1967). The attention to transnational social forces thus takes the focus beyond the nation state, while not denying its continuing relevance.

The implication of these conclusions is that the political, economic, and social processes that have emerged in the current epoch are not mediated by fixed geopolitical dynamics as in past eras. They should therefore not be understood in terms of *international* transactions taking place across discrete national borders, but rather as *global* processes that are decentered, reflecting the new production model that has emerged with its historically distinct set of imperatives. More concretely, the transnational capitalist production model simply does not resemble the

Atlantic Fordist production model of the early to mid-twentieth century with its concomitant requirements for nation state-directed processes of accumulation and welfare state policies designed to mitigate class conflict. This is not meant to imply that the state is no longer necessary for capitalist accumulation, however. On the contrary, the state is heavily implicated in establishing the conditions necessary for accumulation, both in the articulation of national policies and through global institutions. As noted by Robinson, however, the state does not play a passive role, but functions as a "proactive instrument for advancing the agenda of global capitalism" (Robinson 2004: 109).

A key contribution offered by global capitalism perspectives is the observation that a capitalist group has risen to dominance, the members of which share a common interest in global, rather than national, circuits of capital. Specifically, a dominant transnational capitalist class (TCC) is understood to have emerged in the current era. As described by Robinson, this group "constitutes the commanding heights of the global economy," and is "represented by a class conscious transnational elite made up of an inner circle of transnational capitalists, along with transnational managers, bureaucrats, technicians, and leading ideologues and intellectuals in the service of the TCC" (Robinson 2004: 47–48). While the TCC is understood to be dominant, its supremacy is by no means guaranteed in the long-term, however, as class struggle continues, albeit beyond the bounds of the nation state.

Box 21.4 The transnationalization of the economy at a glance

The degree to which the global economy has become transnationalized can be measured according to three specific metrics, among others. First, foreign direct investment (FDI), or investments that provide some control over a given entity and thus represent a longer-term interest in its economic operations, has grown approximately 18 percent each year since 1990, from a level of $409 billion (U.S.) to $1.8 trillion (U.S.) in 2015 (UNCTAD World Investment Report). Dramatically outpacing the growth in world production, these figures underestimate the degree of transnationalization since they do not include outsourcing and subcontracting. A second indicator is the growth in foreign portfolio investment (investments that do not constitute a controlling interest in a firm). Following the deregulation of the 1970s and 1980s, the volume of cross-border flows of portfolio investment grew from $120 billion (U.S.) in 1980 to more than $1.5 trillion (U.S.) by 2014 (UNCTAD World Investment Report). A third measure, the growth in the value of the trade of goods and services across borders, until the last couple of years, increased at a far greater rate than the growth in world production (UNCTAD World Economic Situation and Prospects), signaling that a larger percentage of output is consumed outside of the jurisdiction in which it was produced. Moreover, intrafirm trade (the purchase of goods and services between branches of the same firm in different countries) accounts for approximately two-thirds of global trade (UNCTAD; World Bank).

If the state reflects the dominant set of social forces, as noted earlier, understanding the implications of the rise of a transnational capitalism class requires reconceptualizing the nature and role of the state. The global capitalism school directs attention to the construction of a transnational state apparatus that includes not only national states, but also private networks, and supranational institutions, all of which serve to regulate global circuits of capital and institutionalize the domination of the TCC globally. In this way, global financial institutions, such as the International Monetary Fund (IMF), World Bank, regional development banks, and the World Trade Organization, together with other supranational institutions, such as the United Nations, the G-8, the Organization for Economic Cooperation and Development (OECD), and regional associations including the European Union, the North American Free Trade Agreement (NAFTA), and the Asian Pacific Economic Community (APEC) function to codify the most favorable conditions for capital accumulation wherever capital may flow. These institutions provide the organizational structure that was primarily provided in the previous era by dominant capitalist nation states.

The transition from the nation state as the primary organizing entity to that of transnational institutions and networks remains incomplete, however, as capitalist development is an open-ended, dynamic process that is rife with contradictions. Struggles continue to emerge between competing social forces in response, providing the logic driving a series of sustained efforts to discipline would-be government reformers who might adopt policies that limit accumulation. These strategies, referred to by Stephen Gill as "new constitutionalism" (Gill and Cutler 2014) have served to lock in neoliberal policies, insulating them from popular pressure. These strategies are discussed later in more detail. First, however, it is necessary to outline the processes through which transnational class formation has unfolded in order to understand the global capitalism school's thesis that neoliberal globalization represents epochal change, rather than simply a quantitative intensification of processes from previous eras.

Class formation in historical perspective: the rise of a transnational capitalist class

We have entered the fourth epoch in the historical development of capitalism. This is a central claim of the global capitalism thesis. Having moved from a capitalist era that developed around national circuits of accumulation linked to other nationally articulated economies into an era driven by globalized circuits of accumulation, a dominant transnational capitalist class (TCC) has emerged and transformed the nation state (Hardt and Negri 2000; Robinson 2004; Sklair 2002). Differing from other critical perspectives that view the state form as remaining essentially unchanged and as acting on behest of capitalists within its borders, global capitalism adherents reject the notion that the state is permanent and immutable. Instead, they argue, it should be thought of as a state-society complex that has been transformed into a component of a larger transnational state apparatus (TNS) that includes both national states and supranational organizations through which the TCC articulates its agenda. Directing attention to the dominant social forces that emerged in the wake of the capitalist restructuring of the late 1970s, these inquiries apply historical inquiry to investigate the structures and processes through which social groups have sought to establish hegemony. Such processes involve struggles over knowledge production and the construction of broad-based consent, noted earlier, through the exercise, or threat of, material capabilities, but also, crucially, through ideology and institutions.

A brief survey of earlier capitalist epochs, particularly the previous one, is illustrative for what it reveals about the current era. The first epoch, spanning from the late fifteenth to the late eighteenth century, commenced in the context of a decaying feudal order in Europe and was characterized by violent processes of primitive accumulation carried out through extermination, subjugation, and conquest. This mercantilist period was constituted by a set of production relations that embody the most extreme form of exploitation. The struggles that arose around exploitation determined groups' priorities, the outcome of which defined the limits of the politically possible. When the Glorious Revolution replaced the previous state form with one that guaranteed "the self-regulation of property-owning civil society" and separated "its public functions from the private sphere" (Van Der Pijl 1997), social forces realigned. As described by

365

Box 21.5 The investor–state dispute settlement (ISDS) regime as an instrument of neoliberal discipline

Included in many new free trade and investment agreements, ISDS enables individuals and corporations to seek compensation from taxpayers for new policies adopted by governments that negatively impact future profitability by classifying such measures as acts of expropriation. Based on the American legal concept of eminent domain, this new regime expands the boundaries of property rights to cover future market share and profitability, providing another example of the intensive commodification of social relations. Moreover, this new strategy of accumulation dispossesses citizens of the ability to successfully translate popular demands for protection into laws and regulations when such measures negatively impact corporate profitability. A wide range of disputes have been brought against governments around the world for policies designed to protect the environment, health, or accomplish other social goals.

Kees Van der Pijl in his description of class formation, if the ascendant bourgeoisie was to rise to dominance, it required developing a new identity to be able to benefit from the exploitation of local labor. This priority, which emerged through struggles around exploitation, eventually gave rise to the rupture that would follow as social forces realigned and the gap was bridged "between the cosmopolitan aristocracy and counter-revolutionary Catholics." The alliance of these groups created the distance between the bourgeoisie and the labor available in their communities necessary to generate consent and render labor exploitable (Van der Pijl 1997).

The second epoch, that of competitive capitalism, spanned from the late eighteenth to the late nineteenth century and unfolded amid the Industrial Revolution and the consolidation of the nation state (Hobsbawm 1994), which saw an alliance formed between European rulers and haute financiers. As capitalist social relations deepened in England, however, new ideological claims advanced by Adam Smith and David Ricardo, among others, reinforced the growing dominance of merchant capital, which, copying patterns of mass production and adopting the rules of international commerce established earlier by the British, was able to construct hegemony (Gill 1997: 9–17). The expansion of the market economy during this period relied on the establishment of a strong liberal state, which functioned to roll back mercantilist regulations, enabling merchant capital to generate its dominance. By the late nineteenth century, hegemony was eroded by crises stemming both from imperial rivalry and contradictions generated within capitalist states (Van der Pijl 1997: 123). Inside the nation state, the widening of political rule, required of the liberal state, led to the inclusion of new social groups, including skilled workers, who eventually revolted "against the discipline of market forces" (Gill 1997: 12). The interaction between these structures and events led to the emergence of a new constellation of social forces that engendered another historical rupture.

The third epoch that followed is particularly illustrative for what it reveals about the emergence of the dominant transnational capitalist class and the world order of the fourth epoch under analysis by the global capitalism school. Spanning from the late nineteenth century until the 1970s, and including the Great Depression, two world wars, and the emergence of an ideological challenge by way of the socialist bloc, the third epoch saw the growth of monopoly capitalism and the beginning of the organization of world capitalism. At this point, a new model of production relations emerged, referred to as *Fordism* for Henry Ford's assembly line. Organized vertically, this mode of production had workers performing fixed, standardized processes in centralized locations. The entire production process would take place within one national jurisdiction, with products being sold domestically and internationally. This nation state-centered model of production relations placed demands on the state that included defending the interests of capital rooted within its borders. It was also called upon, domestically, to mediate relations – and struggles – between capitalists and workers, including regulating capitalist competition and serving basic welfare functions based on Keynesian principles. Moreover, this era saw the deepening of integration of societies in Asia, Africa, and Latin America into global capitalism through policies of development advanced by core capitalist countries. The tenuous class compromise that developed during this period would come to be challenged, however, as Keynesian principles lost widespread support in the wake of the 1970s economic crisis, the culmination of a crisis of accumulation that ended in stagflation.

It is not enough for a dominant knowledge framework to be discredited, however. Ruling classes do not establish relative cohesion in short order. A new framework must emerge to replace it. Social formations arise from processes that are uniquely historical and that unfold through a series of cumulative, contingent episodes over a considerable period of time (Thompson [1968] 1980; Gill 1997; Van der Pijl 1997). Indeed, the social forces that emerged dominant in this period had been organizing for several decades, both in the United States and in Europe. It was at this pivotal moment that the ideas and prescriptions based on the teachings of Milton Friedman and Friedrich Hayek were advanced, ideas that provided the interpretive lens through which political elites evaluated the crisis and considered the range of possible responses. Explaining the crisis as the failure of the Keynesian model to maintain capitalist growth, these ideas served to provide a scientific explanation of the crisis and prescriptive measures for establishing a new regime of accumulation (Cox 1987: 279–285).

Aggressively articulating these ideas was a network of increasingly influential policy groups that served to advance the interests of an emerging transnationally oriented capitalist class. Concretely, they sought to translate ideas into political action by providing the intellectual justification required to generate consent for a set of policies that would come to be institutionalized around the world (Harvey 2005; Smith 1991; Strange 1994). The earliest roots of this transnational network are traceable back to the establishment of the Mont Pèlerin Society in 1947, a group founded by Friedrich Hayek, which was linked to dozens of smaller organizations in Europe and the United States that were created to serve as part of a global knowledge structure for advancing neoliberal policies globally (Carroll and Carson 2006; Desai 1994). Among other prominent organizations, the Bilderberg Group, from which the Trilateral Commission was spawned, served as one of the primary policy coordinating bodies for international capital (Carroll and Carson 2006). The World Chambers Federation and the World Economic Forum similarly played an integral role in linking transatlantic capitalist interests and forging a global strategy, as did a number of other notable organizations, including the Commission of the European Community, the International Chamber of Commerce, the Business Roundtable, and the Heritage Foundation, which were established with heavy backing from the transnationally oriented business community (Carroll and Carson 2006; Desai 2006; Harvey 2005; Van Apeldoorn 1998). Sympathetic scholars in a number of prestigious economic departments, for their part, provided ideological support, advocating for the removal of restrictions on the movement of capital adopted as part of the New Deal (Harvey 2005; Smith 1991: Van der Pijl 1998). Smaller, issue-focused groups also complemented these efforts, conducting studies and circulating philosophical arguments that justified the adoption of neoliberal policies (Harvey 2005). The ideas and proposals that were disseminated for popular consumption under the guise of scientific certainty served to "stretch the bounds of credulity" and render neoliberal ideas "fit to be hegemonic" (Desai 1994: 28–31). Indeed, the dominant set of ideas advanced reflected the "changing balance of political forces mobilized for a specific interpretation of the crisis ... and the appropriate solutions" (Jessop 2002: 94).

It was thus in the context of widespread disillusionment over Keynesian policies in both the United States and Europe that the opportunity existed for a new set of ideas to become dominant, ideas emphasizing market liberalization, deregulation, and a shift from public to private forms of governance. Given the United States' position in the world order, it played the dominant role in reestablishing the conditions for accumulation. However, differing from realist, and even World Systems and classical Marxist, analyses, the global capitalism thesis posits that the hegemonic configuration that existed under the Pax Americana was replaced by the emergence of a transnational capitalist class whose rise benefited from U.S. leadership. With the Bretton Woods system severely weakened by President Nixon's decision to abandon the dollar-gold standard, and in light of the dramatic growth of the Eurodollar market, political and economic elites began advocating for the removal of the restraints placed on capital after World War II.

The institutionalization of neoliberal ideology thus began in earnest, with elites in the U.S. undertaking a series of reforms that dramatically altered the social mode of production, reinforcing the dominance of these emerging transnational social forces. Among other measures, financial markets were liberalized and other deregulatory measures dismantling barriers to cross-border capital flows were undertaken, as were policies protecting the rights of workers. These initiatives enabled corporations to arbitrage, or take advantage of the cost savings associated with decentralizing the production process across multiple jurisdictions. In the United States, the neoliberal turn was first institutionalized by a group of prominent political elites influenced by Hayek and his protégées, including Milton Friedman, at the University of Chicago, and, later, U.S. Treasury Secretary George Shultz, and Federal Reserve Chairman, Paul Volcker (Nichols 2016).

In Europe, too, political and economic elites similarly interpreted the 1970s economic crisis as a failure of the Keynesian model, an interpretation that ultimately influenced the direction of European integration. While competing visions existed between a "Europeanist" group that sought to focus on unifying Europe and the competitiveness of firms based in Europe relative to those located abroad and a "globalist" fraction constituted by firms with transnational interests, after a series of political struggles, the globalists emerged as the more dominant group (Van Apeldoorn 1998: 14–20). The strategy then became focused on how to steer the European Union as an active vehicle for transnational flows of capital, rather than simply serving to remove internal borders within the continent. The prevailing sentiment was articulated by the European Round Table, which noted, "governments must recognize that every economic social system in the world is competing with all others to attract footloose businesses" (ERT 1996: 15).

Industry groups with transnational interests were by this point steering the policy direction on both sides of the Atlantic. These developments strengthened the relative structural power of transnational capital, as the existence of the jurisdictional exist option served as a disciplining mechanism vis-à-vis the state, further transforming it along neoliberal lines. The new configuration of social forces that emerged corresponded to a capitalist rationality that was historically specific in its material foundations (Van der Pijl 1998: 27). Specifically, the shift from a capitalist system based on trade and financial flows between discrete nation states to a global economy constituted by a system of globalized financial flows and production systems redefined the relationship between production and territoriality, the logic of which defines the interests of the TCC.

These developments have direct implications for the nature and role of the state. Global capitalism scholars observe that the state has been *transformed* in a way that reflects the dominance of the dominant social forces. Given that the state mediates the class relations between capital and other social groups, in the current era it advances the interests of the newly dominant

TCC (see Robinson 2004). Moreover, in so doing, it has become a component of a larger transnational state (TNS) apparatus that also includes supranational organizations. It is through these institutions that neoliberal ideology is institutionalized, globally, reinforcing the power of the dominant groups and generating broad-based consent, or hegemony. The structural transformation engendered by the emergence of this historical bloc thus represents a rupture from the previous world order that ushered in the fourth epoch of global capitalism.

The rise in transnational production and financial flows

The degree to which the capitalist system has been globalized is measurable according to a number of indicators that, if anything, underestimate the degree to which transnational processes have intensified in recent decades. The process of selling goods and services across borders is not new, nor is the phenomenon of portfolio capital flowing across borders. In the past, however, commodities were generally produced within one country and sold on the market to consumers in other jurisdictions, with the profits flowing back to the company producing the goods in the home jurisdiction. In the current epoch, both production and profits have been restructured, with decentralized global supply chains extending horizontally across borders. Policies of liberalization and deregulation, combined with new technologies and improvements in transportation and communication, drove new forms of workplace organization and techniques, such as "just-in-time," outsourcing, subcontracting, and corporate alliances, enabling the production process to be broken into different components that could be spread across territories, globally (Robinson 2004: 17). This phenomenon, which has made possible the division and specialization of labor across borders, has consequently fragmented the working class and decreased its power vis-à-vis transnational capital, which is increasingly centralized as an organizing force.

While global trade has often been the focus of much analysis of economic globalization, the production relations stemming from the transnationalization of supply chains is perhaps of greatest consequence. The growth in foreign direct investment (FDI) is one of the most significant measures of this phenomenon, albeit one that underestimates it since transnational production also takes place through outsourcing and subcontracting. Foreign direct investment is defined as investment that involves a long-term interest, relationship, and control by an entity in one economy in an enterprise in an economy different from its own (UNCTAD 2017: 3). It is revealing that FDI flows have significantly outpaced the growth in world production (Robinson 2004). By the beginning of the twenty-first century, FDI was growing approximately 18 percent a year. By 2015, global FDI had increased from a 1990 level of $409 billion (US) to $1.8 trillion, not including outsourcing and subcontracting (UNCTAD: iii). As an additional measure, production by firms with processes spanning multiple jurisdictions rose to a value of approximately $8 trillion (US) by 2015. Crucially, both the assets and sales of these transnational firms' foreign affiliates have grown much faster their counterparts confined to national jurisdictions (UNCTAD 2016: 9). Further demonstrating the degree of transnationality of the modern corporation is the fact that more than 40 percent of foreign subsidiaries and affiliates possess multiple passports, with 60 percent of them having multiple cross-border ownership linkages to the parent corporation (UNCTAD 2016: x). Even more revealing, the largest of these corporations each possess more than 500 affiliates spanning more than fifty countries. As noted by a revealing UNCTAD World report, "the nationality of investors in, and owners of, foreign affiliates is becoming increasingly blurred" (2016: x; see also Nichols 2016).

Another measure of the transnationalization of the economy is the growth of foreign portfolio investment (FPI) flows, the profitability of which is highly dependent on risk reduction through geographic diversification. These investments primarily involve stock brokerage firms and mutual funds and differ from FDI in that the investors do not possess a controlling interest in the associated firms. Including a multitude of foreign investments, such as bank lending, bonds, equities below a certain percentage ownership threshold, money market instruments, derivatives and other securities, these cross-border financial flows represent one component of the dramatic integration of the financial system. Moreover, these flows amounted to more than $1.5 trillion (US) by 2014 (UNCTAD 2015). Spurred by the deregulation of the 1970s and 1980s, the volume of cross-border equity transactions "grew at a rate of 28% per year, from $120 billion (US) in 1980 to $1.4 trillion (US) in 1990" (Robinson 2004: 26). During the same period, cross-border bank lending grew from $324 billion (US) to $7.5 trillion (US), while offshore bond markets grew from $259 billion (US) to $1.6 trillion (US) (Robinson 2004: 26).

These trends underscore the transformation from an international economy based on flows of goods and capital between discrete countries to one characterized by a global system of transnational production and financial flows. The boundary between FDI and portfolio investment has been eroded in this transformation since the modern corporation is invested globally. As noted by a senior U.S. Treasury Department official, "The two forms of investment are no longer mutually exclusive … companies with FDI also have portfolio investments … they have both categories of interests" (Nichols 2016: 10). The implications of these developments cannot be overstated, as the fusion of these categories, or *fractions*, of capital, combined with the decentering of production, has contributed heavily to transnational class formation in the era of neoliberalism.

The rapid growth in the trade of goods and services across borders since the 1970s is another indicator of the transnationalization of the global economy, as it has far outpaced the growth in world production and GDP, signaling that a larger percentage of output has been consumed outside the jurisdiction in which it was produced (UNCTAD 2018). Here, too, the distinction is made between *international* trade and *transnational* transactions, with other forms of trade than simply purchases on the open market (arm's length trade) constituting an increasing percentage of these cross-border exchanges. Among other strategies, corporations engage in both outsourcing and subcontracting from other firms. If, for example, a company purchases the labor of a subcontractor, provides the raw goods to be processed and then pays for the finished good, this is a form of "non-arm's-length" trade (Robinson 2004: 28). Intrafirm trade, transactions that occur between different branches of the same entity located in different jurisdictions, has also significantly increased in recent decades. These latter two categories of trade already constituted the majority of global trade by the close of the twentieth century (Ietto-Gillies 2002: 19). One might consider the growth in these forms of trade and the transnational supply chain as two sides of the same coin. It is thus the qualitative difference in the flows of capital, goods, and services across borders that represents a departure from the previous epoch.

A final point is that the transnational corporation (TNC), defined as a firm with headquarters in four or more countries, plays a key institutional role in the dispersal of production and exchange processes, globally. It is the embodiment of these transnational processes, functioning as the primary institutional form through which transnational capitalist accumulation is organized and around which transnational social structures and, transnational class formation, specifically, are generated. In the two decades following the onset of neoliberalization, the number of TNCs increased from approximately 7,000 to more than 60,000, producing more than $15.7 trillion (US) in goods and services (UNCTAD 2001: 1). Local firms, too, have become incorporated into the transnational structure through outsourcing, subcontracting, licensing, mergers and acquisitions, strategic alliances, and other arrangements, resulting in the transnationalization of the national bourgeoisies. Consequently, the cleavages that historically existed between nationally oriented capitalists and those with interests predominantly abroad have largely been resolved. The resulting configuration thus affords transnational capitalists a structure of accumulation characterized by greater control over production and labor, both of which are highly fragmented. What this means for global class formation is that the power of transnational capitalists is significantly strengthened vis-à-vis other social groups.

Returning to Gramsci's insights, we can observe that a transnational structure of accumulation has been created that is constituted by mutually reinforcing ideological norms and institutions. While the nation-state era of capitalism was characterized by a strong welfare state and a centralized, vertical mode of production based on a logic of class compromise that incorporated popular classes into a historical bloc, the neoliberal regime of accumulation that has followed reflects the new alignment of social forces that has arisen in light of the transnationalization of production and financial flows. As national barriers to capital were removed, power relations shifted and the nation state was transformed into part of a larger transnational state apparatus that includes supranational organizations, such as the World Trade Organization, World Bank, and International Monetary Fund, among many others (Robinson 2004: 76). Together, these institutions have functioned to reinforce the power of the transnational capitalist class, which maneuvered to establish hegemony. Buffered by a professional managerial class, the interests of which have been incorporated and channeled into this political project, the historical bloc must consistently work to maintain broad-based consent. In order to do so, it seeks to lock in neoliberal discipline through a variety of institutional and ideological structures, the topic to which we now turn.

Instituting neoliberal discipline

In order to bring about the most advantageous conditions for accumulation wherever capital flows, a multitude of institutions of the transnational state apparatus have articulated the interests of the TCC, instilling neoliberal discipline through a variety of mechanisms. The neoliberal state, for its part, provides the basic infrastructure for the global economy, including adopting fiscal and monetary policies designed to ensure macroeconomic stability, codifying trade and investment policies, and providing basic social order, albeit through increasingly militaristic means. Stephen Gill has provided excellent analyses of the mechanisms through which discipline has been institutionalized and maintained, a set of processes that correspond to what he refers to as *new constitutionalism* (Gill 1995; 2002). Such discipline is essential to preventing ideological and institutional retreat, Gill observes, given the inequality generated by neoliberal policies globally. In essence, new constitutionalism includes not only constitutions, but also "laws, property rights and various institutional arrangements, designed to have quasi-permanent status" (Gill 2002: 48). In essence, these mechanisms function to lock in neoliberal policies, insulating them from popular contestation and severely circumscribing the limits of political possibility.

Such observations raise a variety of questions, which lie at the heart of vigorous academic analyses and debates. For example, through which institutional and ideological means does new constitutionalism operate? The answer to this question directs attention to opportunities for contestation. In terms of the means, one prominent strategy undertaken at the level of the nation state has involved insulating monetary policy from popular decision-making and contestation by rendering central banks "independent" from the policy making state apparatuses. This has enabled elites from the financial community to prioritize the goal of maintaining macroeconomic stability and a low rate of inflation, often at the expense of higher levels of domestic employment and spending on social welfare.

Another set of vehicles through which neoliberal discipline has been instilled are supranational institutions, such as the International Monetary Fund, World Bank, and other global financial institutions, whose "assistance" in debt crises brought about by the TCC itself have provided the opportunity to require state actors to restructure their economies along neoliberal lines through structural adjustment programs. In doing so, they have forced governments around the world to slash social programs, devalue currencies, liberalize trade and financial markets, and prioritize export industries over production for national consumption. The social consequences of these imposed policies have been acute, sparking protests, riots, and electoral upheavals around the world. The devastating inequality that has resulted has forced further institutional forms of discipline to be demanded by the TCC and its agents in the TNS.

One of the more consequential means of instilling neoliberal discipline in more recent decades has been through the use of free trade agreements. From the North American Free Trade Agreement to the hundreds of bilateral and multilateral trade and investment agreements, an extensive list of requirements and prohibitions have been adopted that limit the ability of elected officials to adopt policies and regulations when they conflict with the profit maximization goals of investors (Nichols 2018: 4). Efforts by the TCC to broaden and codify new sets of property rights, in particular, lie at the heart of the neoliberal political project. Given that private property rights constitute a social relation enforced by the capitalist state, the state is heavily implicated in this class struggle, adopting trade agreements that contain provisions broadly defining intellectual property rights, as well as the investor–state dispute settlement (ISDS) regime. Empowering foreign investors to bring disputes against governments for adopting new regulations that threaten future profitability and seek compensation based on potential future earnings that might have been earned in the absence of such measures, ISDS provisions reinforce the dominance of the transnational capitalist bloc vis-à-vis other social groups. It does so by dispossessing citizens of the ability to translate popularly demanded initiatives into laws and regulations when such measures conflict with corporate profit maximization goals. In doing so, the regime both relies on and reinforces the notion that the neoliberal goal of economic growth is sacrosanct, foreign investment is an essential ingredient, and all measures must be taken in order to "protect it."

Conclusion: discontinuity and the contestation of hegemony

The events of the past several years have led many to question the longevity of the world order characterized by the dominance of a transnationalist bloc. From Brexit to the election of Donald Trump in the U.S. and the increasing number of candidates from the extreme right gaining popularity around the world, the stability of the global neoliberal project is in question. These developments seem to suggest that the contradictions generated by neoliberal policies are challenging the ideological hegemony that has been constructed since the 1970s. Indeed, the national and supranational institutions codifying neoliberal discipline are facing severe challenges from both sides of the political spectrum. Whether or not the current world order will erode in light of the deterioration of the global institutions created since World War II and the ideology that has been articulated through them will depend on the outcome of the vigorous struggles between social forces that are currently unfolding. Will the current world order be stabilized by the transnational capitalist class and its agents of the TNS? Or, will reactionary forces of the right once again provide the impetus that led to the rupture in the early part of the twentieth century? Alternatively, will this moment of transformation be seized by progressive forces harnessing the insights offered by critical perspectives that reveal the mechanism through which domination is exercised? Certainly, the goal of global capitalism scholars is to provide the intellectual landscape from which to build an effective emancipatory response when the opportunity avails itself.

Bibliography

Bieler, A. and Morton, A. D. 2004. A Critical Theory Route to Hegemony, World Order and Historical Change: Neo-Gramscian Perspectives in International Relations. *Capital & Class* 28 No. 1: 85–113.

Braudel, F. [1969] 1980. *On History* (Matthews, S. trans). Chicago: University of Chicago Press.

Carroll, W. and Carson, C. 2006. Neoliberalism, Capitalist Class Formation and the Global Network of Corporations and Policy Groups. In: *Neoliberal Hegemony: A Global Critique*. Plehwe, D., Walpen, B. and Neunhöffer, G. (ed.): 51–69. Routledge: New York.

Chase-Dunn, C. 1998. *Global Formation: Structures of the World-Economy*. Lanham: MD: Rowman & Littlefield.

Cox, R. 1981. Social Forces, States, and World Orders: Beyond International Relations Theory. *Millennium: Journal of International Studies* 10, no. 2: 126–155.

Cox, R. 1987. *Production, Power, and World Order*. New York: Columbia University Press.

Desai, R. 1994. Second-hand Dealers in Ideas: Think-Tanks and Thatcherite Hegemony. *New Left Review*, I, no. 203: 27–64.

Desai, R. 2006. Neoliberalism and Cultural Nationalism: A Danse Macabre. In: *Neoliberal Hegemony: A Global Critique*. Plehwe, D., Walpen, B. and Neunhöffer, G. (ed.): 225–235. Routledge: New York.

European Round Table. 1996. Benchmarking for Policy-Makers: The Way to Competitiveness, Growth and Job Creation. Brussels: *European Roundtable of Industrialists*. Available at: www.ert.eu/document/benchmarking-policy-makers.

Gill, S. 1990. *American Hegemony and the Trilateral Commission*, Cambridge: Cambridge University Press.

Gill, S. 1995. Globalization, Market Civilization, and Disciplinary Neoliberalism. *Millennium* 23, no. 3: 399–423.

Gill, S. 1997. Transformation and Innovation in the Study of World Order. In: *Innovation and Transformation in International Studies*. Gill, S. and Mittelman, J. (ed.): 5–24, Cambridge: Cambridge University Press.

Gill, S. 2002. Institutionalizing Inequality and the Clash of Globalizations. *International Studies Review* 4, no. 2: 47–65.

Gill, S. and Cutler, A. 2014. New Constitutionalism and World Order. In: *New Constitutionalism and World Order*. Gill, S. and Cutler, C. (ed.): 1–22, Cambridge: Cambridge University Press.

Gill, S. and Mittelmann, J. 1997. *Innovation and Transformation in International Studies*, Cambridge: Cambridge University Press.

Gramsci, A. 1967. *Selections from the Prison Notebooks*, New York: International Publishers.

Hardt, M. and Negri, A. 2000. *Empire*, Cambridge: MIT Press.

Harvey, D. 2005. *A Brief History of Neoliberalism*. Oxford: Oxford University Press.

Hirst, P., Thompson, G. and Bromley, S. 1996. *Globalization in Question*, Cambridge: Polity Press.

Hobsbawm, E. 1994. *The Age of Extremes*. London: Michael Joseph.

Ietto-Gillies, G. 2002. *Transnational Corporations: Fragmentation amidst Integration*. Routledge: London.

Jessop, B. 2002. *The Future of the Capitalist State*. Malden, MA: Blackwell.

McMichael, P. 2001. Revisiting the Question of the Transnational State. *Theory and Society* 30, no. 2: 201–210.

Overbeek, H. 1993. *Restructuring Hegemony in the Global Political Economy: The Rise of Transnational Liberalism in the 1980s*. London: Routledge.

Overbeek, H. 2001. Transnational Historical Mechanism: Theories of Transnational Class Formation and World Order. In: *Global Political Economy: Contemporary Theories*. Palan, R. (ed.): 168–183, London: Routledge.

Nichols, S. 2016. Transnational Capital and the Transformation of the State: Investor-State Dispute Settlement (ISDS) in the Transatlantic Trade and Investment Partnership (TTIP). *Critical Sociology*, 45, no. 1: 137–157.

Nichols, S. 2018. Expanding Property Rights under Investor-state Dispute Settlement (ISDS): Class Struggle in the Era of Transnational Capital. *Review of International Political Economy* 25, no. 2: 243–269.

Panitch, L. and Gindin, S. 2005. Superintending Global Capital. *New Left Review*, 35: 101–123.

Panitch, L. and Gindin, S. 2014. *The Making of Global Capitalism*. London: Verso.

Robinson, W. 2004. *A Theory of Global Capitalism*. Baltimore, MD: Johns Hopkins University Press.

Robinson, W. 2011. Global Capitalism Theory and the Emergence of Transnational Elites. *Critical Sociology 38*, no. 3: 349–363.

Sklair, L. 1995. *Sociology of the Global System*. Baltimore, MD: Johns Hopkins University Press.

Sklair, L. 2002. *Globalization: Capitalism and Its Alternatives*. New York: Oxford University Press.

Smith, J. 1991. *The Idea Brokers*. New York: The Free Press.

Strange, S. 1994. *States and Markets*. London: Pinter Press.

Thompson, E. P. [1968] 1980. *The Making of the English Working Class*. Harmondsworth: Penguin Press.

United Nations Conference on Trade and Development. 2001. *World Investment Report*. Available at: http://unctad.org/en/pages/PublicationArchive.aspx?publicationid=656.

United Nations Conference on Trade and Development (UNCTAD) 2015. *World Investment Report*. New York: United Nations. Available at: https://unctad.org/en/PublicationsLibrary/wir2015_en.pdf.

United Nations Conference on Trade and Development (UNCTAD). 2016. *World Investment Report*. New York: United Nations. Available at: http://unctad.org/en/PublicationsLibrary/wir2016_Overview_en.pdf.

United Nations Conference on Trade and Development (UNCTAD). 2017. *World Investment Report*. New York: United Nations. Available at: http://unctad.org/en/PublicationsLibrary/wir2016_Overview_en.pdf.

United Nations Conference on Trade and Development (UNCAD). 2018. World Economic Situation and Prospects. Available at: www.un.org/development/desa/dpad/wpcontent/uploads/sites/45/publication/WESP2018_Full_Web-1.pdf.

Van Apeldoorn, B. 1998. Transnationalization and the Restructuring of Europe's Socioeconomic Order. *International Journal of Political Economy* 28, no 1: 12–53.

Van der Pijl, K. 1984. *The Making of an Atlantic Ruling Class*. London: Verso.

Van der Pijl, K. 1989. Ruling Classes, Hegemony, and the State System. *International Journal Political Economy* 19, no. 3: 7–35.

Van der Pijl, K. 1997. Transnational Class Formation. In: *Innovation and Transformation in International Studies*. Gill, S. and Mittelmann, J. (ed.): 118–134, Cambridge: Cambridge University Press.

Van der Pijl, K. 1998. *Transnational Classes and International Relations*, London: Routledge.

Wallerstein, I. 1974. *The Modern World System*. New York: Academic Press.

Weiss, L. 1998. *The Myth of the Powerless State*. Ithaca: Cornell University Press.

Wood, E. M. 1999. Unhappy Families: Global Capitalism in a World of Nation-States. *Monthly Review* 51, no. 3: 1.

22

The IPE of degrowth and sustainable welfare

Max Koch and Hubert Buch-Hansen

Introduction

Thresholds for specific biophysical processes such as climate, biodiversity and the nitrogen cycle are being approached or crossed (Steffen et al. 2015). In the case of climate change, the natural sciences agree that the increases in average global temperatures over the past century are due in large part to the emission of greenhouse gases, primarily stemming from fossil fuel consumption and land-use changes such as deforestation. In its Fifth Assessment Report on the Physical Science Basis for Climate Change, the Intergovernmental Panel on Climate Change (IPCC 2014) highlights that concentrations of CO_2 and other greenhouse gases in the atmosphere have risen to levels that are unprecedented in at least the last 800,000 years, with the burning of fossil fuels being the main reason behind the 40 per cent increase in CO_2 concentrations since the Industrial Revolution. By the end of the twenty-first century, the IPCC projects the global surface temperature increase to exceed 1.5°C relative to the period 1850–1900 in all but the lowest and most optimistic scenarios considered. Exceeding this threshold, beyond which uncontrollable climate change with frequent droughts, floods and storms plus largely unpredictable climate feedback effects is expected, is increasingly likely. Other scenarios predict global temperatures to rise by as much as 4.8°C. The higher end of this range – and in particular the unprecedented speed of the temperature rise – is far outside the experience of human civilization. Warming of 4°C or more would expose more than 70 per cent of the world's population to deadly heat stress, while 3°C is regarded as a crucial factor for the extinction of more than 50 per cent of species (Ramanathan et al. 2017). Beyond 2100, the IPCC expects warming to continue, the Arctic sea ice cover to shrink and thin and the Northern Hemisphere spring snow cover as well as the global glacier volume to decrease further.

The mainstream policy response, which has been actively promoted by the Organization of Economic Cooperation and Development (OECD), the World Bank, the United Nations (UN) Environment Programme as well as the European Union (EU), is to promote 'green growth' or 'ecological modernization'. According to the proponents of green growth, the pursuit of environmental goals including climate change mitigation will require a much more active state than in the previous decades, to set goals and targets, manage risks, promote industrial policy, realign prices and counter negative business interests. By reducing energy and material costs and the reliance on the fragile geopolitics of energy supply, providing jobs in the expanding 'green' sector and meeting carbon emission reduction targets, the intention is to achieve synergy between economic, ecological and also welfare goals. Central to any evaluation of the feasibility of green growth strategies is the distinction between 'absolute' and 'relative' decoupling of Gross Domestic Product (GDP) growth from carbon emissions and resource use. Here it can be noted that while resource impacts have declined relative to GDP in a range of developed countries, they have either not done so in absolute terms at all or not to the extent that climate scientists regard as necessary (Antal and Van Den Bergh 2014). Not only have improvements in energy efficiency been offset by increases in the overall scale of economic activity, but the prospects of achieving this in the future to the required extent are very low indeed. In contrast, comparative research (Fritz and Koch 2016; O'Neill et al. 2018) continues to indicate a strong link between the level of economic development measured in GDP per capita, on the one hand, and carbon emissions and ecological footprints of production and consumption, on the other.

It is not least due to the lack of evidence for absolute decoupling of GDP growth, material resource use and carbon emissions that an alternative scenario has been tabled: that of 'no-', 'post-' or 'degrowth'. There are now a range of heterogeneous approaches that have in common the questioning of what some describe as capitalism's structural 'growth imperative' (Speth 2008; see also Daly and Farley 2011) and a joint search for ecologically and socially sustainable alternatives. All growth-critical perspectives have a common starting point: that the ecological crisis and the increase in social inequality are basic features of an increasingly deregulated capitalism and of its extension from North America and Europe to the rest of the world. A common goal is to re-embed production and consumption patterns into planetary limits through a decrease of matter and energy throughputs, particularly in the rich countries.

In International Political Economy (IPE) scholarship there has been limited engagement with such growth-critical perspectives. While IPE research has dealt with environmental policy issues, the major theoretical perspectives and debates defining the field are not oriented towards the impact of economic processes on the environment. To contribute to fill this gap in existing research, in this chapter we in various ways link growth-critical perspectives to political economy, mainly but not exclusively political economy in the historical materialist tradition. We start out by discussing tensions between the reproduction principles of nature and of the capitalist mode of production as highlighted by Marx. Moving from the abstract to the concrete we then consider the institutional variety of real-existing capitalisms and the ecological performance of different welfare regimes. Next we identify various streams of research that question whether economic growth and environmental sustainability can be reconciled. This brings us to the post-growth vision of sustainable welfare, which integrates social inequality and welfare with environmental sustainability research. Sustainable welfare involves various eco-social policies of which we give particular focus to wealth and income caps. The final section before the conclusion utilizes insights from the strand of IPE research known as transnational historical materialism to reflect upon some of the main obstacles to and possibilities for a transition towards a smaller and more socially equitable global political economy.

Capitalism and nature

Far from disregarding natural laws Marx made the pivot (*Springpunkt* in the German original) of his critique of political economy the dual nature of commodities as constituting both exchange value and use value and of work as producing both abstract value and concrete products through the transformation of raw materials and energy. Understanding this 'double character' provides insight not only into further economic categories, associated social relations and modes of consciousness but also into the corresponding tensions between the capitalist economy and the ecological system that amplify the greenhouse effect (Koch 2012, 2018). Exchange value refers to the commodity's monetary value for the seller, while use value is concerned with the material and/or symbolical usefulness for the purchaser. However, under the imperative of valourization, the concrete and material aspect of labour, which is reflected in use values of commodities, is subordinated to abstract labour and exchange value and, hence, somewhat sidelined. Use values, matter and energy are not of primary interest on capitalist markets but instead their form as values, that is, repositories of abstract, socially necessary labour. Ecological goals such as sustainable land-use practices, the preservation of species diversity, and, in the sphere of consumption, clean air and water as well as non-congested transport networks are governed by the need to produce exchange value, that is, their societal handling has to respect the priority of valourization.

A further tension between the monetary form of values and the principles of natural reproduction is that the former is completely divisible from monetary quota, while the natural world, of which the work process is composed, represents 'highly interconnected and interdependent material, biological and thermodynamic systems of varying entropy levels.' (Burkett 2005: 144) Furthermore, monetary claims on wealth in the forms of bank accounts, stocks or bonds are highly mobile, and this often contradicts the locational fixedness and specificities of ecosystems. Finally, while money and valourization are quantitatively unlimited and, hence, reversible, low-entropy matter and energy are not. The earth's stock of fossil fuels, in particular, is confined, and the existing stock can only be burnt once. In other words, it is irreversible. There is a structural tension between the value and money form of societal wealth and its material and energy substance.

Profit production is possible due to the fact that a commodity is available for sale that has the use value of creating exchange value and which can be used longer than that which represents the cost of its own reproduction: labour power. Capitalism is characterized as being a mode of production where producers – as wage-earners – are largely separated from their means of subsistence and production and have no alternative but to offer the only commodity at their disposal on 'labour markets'. The other 'factors of production' – land, raw materials, fuels, auxiliaries etc. – can be purchased on separate markets, and it is only through the intermediation of employers, who hold the necessary capital, that the former comes in contact with the latter. This implies that capitalism's reproduction requirements are distinct from the material and ecological preconditions for the reproduction of labour power and the other factors of production. For capitalist production, all that matters are that these factors and the ingredients of material production are separately available for purchase, and in forms that can be combined in the production process of capital. Given this precondition, capitalist reproduction tends to disrespect the imperatives of natural reproduction such as the preservation of the fossil fuel stocks due to its inherent tendency to expand the scale of production.

In the chapters of *Capital* on cooperation, the manufactory and 'machinery and modern industry', Marx (1961: Part IV) discusses the advancement of the division of labour and how the work process became independent from the subjective limitations of individual workers through the systematic application of natural forces and the natural sciences. The Industrial Revolution introduced tools and machinery that reduced the role of many individual workers to that of an 'appendage'. When the work process had an industrial foundation, then the subjugation of nature under capital became more complete. Now nature was for the first time … purely an object for humankind, purely matter of utility; ceases to be recognized as a power to itself; and the theoretical discovery of its autonomous laws appears merely as a ruse so as to subjugate it under human needs, whether as an object of consumption or as a means of production.

(Marx 1973: 409)

Marx also shows that expanding scales of production, which are a corollary from the valourization logic of capitalist production, normally coincide with greater amounts of throughput of raw materials and auxiliary substances, especially in the form of fossil fuels, as well as available energy. All other things being equal, an increase in productivity means that a given work force processes a larger quantity of raw materials and consumes more energy. Rising demand for raw materials and available energy normally leads to rising prices, for example, for crude oil, creating incentives for individual companies to recycle and to use a given quantity of materials or fuels in more efficient ways. Marx (2006: Chapter 5) described this as a long-term trend towards a greater 'economy in the employment of constant capital'. Yet progress in the efficiency of raw and auxiliary materials does not fundamentally alter the link between the expansion of the scale of production and the increase in the material and energy throughput, a phenomenon that had been observed by the British economist William Stanley Jevons in the 1860s (Jevons 1865). According to the 'Jevons paradox', greater efficiency in the use of a fossil energy source such as coal or oil leads to an increase in demand – not to a decrease. On the contrary, this increase becomes the precondition for further capital expansion and economic growth.

In summary, an analysis of the ecological crisis, and climate change in particular, that takes the double nature of the commodity and work as both value in motion and a concrete stock of invested time- and place-specific assets of matter and energy as point of departure is able to demonstrate that the capitalist mode of production is oriented towards unlimited and short-term valourization, quantitative and geographic expansion, circularity and reversibility, while the principles that guide the ecological system involve stable and sustainable matter and energy transformations and throughputs as well as irreversibility (Koch 2012). Capital's 'expansionism' tends to be accompanied by the degradation of the environmental conditions of production and especially reductions in their ability to act as sources and sinks for the permanently increasing flow and throughput of matter and energy (Clark and York 2005). When these sources and sinks cease to function, their decelerating impact on the greenhouse effect is nullified, thus increasing the risk of negative feedback mechanisms within the climate system.

The diversity of real-existing capitalism

It is important to remember that the contradictions and tensions identified in the previous section are located at a relatively high level of abstraction: Marx's 'mode of production' where abstraction is made from institutional regulation and individual actors are reduced to their role of economic 'character mask', that is, to the roles they play in the production process. Though this level of analysis allows for insights into the general tensions between economy and ecology that characterize *all* capitalist societies, it does not sufficiently consider how these structural tensions are articulated in actual societies and institutional circumstances. General tensions and tendencies do not only manifest themselves directly in different 'Varieties of Capitalism' (Hall and Soskice 2001) but are also temporarily arrested under particular regulatory preconditions. With regard to climate change, the level of abstraction of the capitalist mode of production allows for the important hypothesis that rising CO_2 emissions are caused by the long-term trend under the capitalist mode of production of the expansion of the scale of production and the

Table 22.1 Tensions between capitalist development and nature

Form	Exchange-value moment	Use-value moment
Commodity and production • Commodity's double character serves as 'pivotal point' for the critique of political economy (and ecology)	• Exchange value reduces concrete works as well as matter and energy to repositories of abstract labour	• Use value and work process moments allow for a consideration of ecological parameters in economic analysis, which are sidelined both in the exchange side of the commodity and in neoclassical reasoning
Money and valorization (capital)	• General expression of societal wealth • Profit and interest-bearing capital • Qualitatively homogenous, quantitatively unlimited, divisible, mobile, reversible	• Measure and store of value, legal tender • Energy and matter side of valorization are associated with qualitative heterogeneousness, quantitative limitations, indivisibility, locational uniqueness, irreversibility
Labour power and conditions of production	• Abstract labour as sole source of surplus value and substitutable condition of production • Land, raw materials fuels and other uncultivated resources are used as 'free gifts' from nature and sources of rents	• Labour power as bearer of concrete skills and specific knowledge • Reproduction of conditions of production as 'fictitious commodities' dependent on the (increasingly undermined and expensive) preservation of natural scarcities
Productive (industrial) capital	• Profit production especially through relative surplus • Contradiction of relative surplus production counteracted by the expansion of the scale of production (accumulation) • Increasing efficiency in the use of constant capital overcompensated by rising demands for natural resources	• Production of use values through the rearrangement of matter and energy • Expansion of production scale translates into increasing throughputs of raw materials, auxiliaries etc. especially as fossil fuels and advances exploitation of the natural conditions of production • Greater fossil fuel consumption disrupts the carbon cycle, triggering climate change
Accumulation and turnover of capital	• Valorization logic forces entrepreneurs to reduce the non-productive stages of the capital cycle and to speed up turnover • Tendency towards overcoming distances in time and space or 'simultaneity'	• Production takes place under specific temporal and local conditions • Consumption of matter and energy is always linear and irreversible • Capital's 'expansionism' is accompanied by the degradation in the environment and increase in the greenhouse effect

Source: Elaborated from Koch 2012.

associated increase in material and energy throughput. But this perspective is too abstract and general to explain why CO_2 outputs per economic unit differ between Fordist and post-Fordist growth strategies or why one capitalist country (say Sweden) presents considerably lower CO_2 outputs per capita than another country (say the USA). Since certain institutional particulars of a growth strategy will amplify the general tendency towards increasing CO_2 emissions, while others will modify or decelerate it, these will have to be considered more systematically.

Institutional theories hitherto deployed in research on environmental regulation and climate performance include both perspectives originating in the historical materialist traditions, such as regulation theory, and other perspectives such as Varieties of Capitalism theory (Mikler and Harrison 2012) and applications of the welfare regimes approach. For instance, core concepts of regulation theory such as 'accumulation regime' including operationalization of production and consumption norms, 'mode of regulation' and 'institutional forms' have been complemented by the notion of 'energy regimes' and environmental regulation, which allowed for an empirical and comparative analysis of CO_2 emissions in accordance with the production and consumption patterns in the two main post-war capitalist growth strategies: Fordism and finance-driven capitalism (Koch 2012). The regulation of nature often proceeds in different ways that must themselves be understood as the temporary results of social struggles between various social actors. Consumption, for example, is then not viewed as an isolated or behavioural phenomenon, as the result of autonomous individual choices, but within its social genesis and context (Aglietta 1987: 154).

Seen from a historical materialist perspective, the choice of certain environmental policies or of a particular policy instrument over others is not in the first place a matter of having the 'better argument' but reflects wider societal power relations and asymmetries, including divisions within the capitalist class as well as in the institutional traditions of different countries. Indeed, without an adequate concept of financialization (and also of transnationalization) of investment and capital accumulation and the corresponding transnational actors much of the current attempts to regulate CC in the form of commodification and carbon markets could not be fully understood (Lohmann 2010). In relation to greenhouse gas emissions, Christoff and Eckersley (2011) found that domestic political institutions (proportional representation versus first-past-the-post electoral systems and the presence of green parties in parliament and government) and corporatist systems that include business and labour have a statistically relevant impact. The study pointed out that while national vulnerability to climate change is a poor indicator, both reliance on fossil fuel extraction and energy-intensive industry heighten opposition to carbon reduction. Meanwhile, hopes that social democratic welfare regimes, which are least unequal in socio-economic terms, would also perform best in ecological and climate terms and gradually turn into 'eco-social states' (Gough et al. 2008) could not be verified in comparative empirical research (Koch and Fritz 2014). The dialectics of the Western welfare state appears to lie in the fact that the same mechanism that defuses the socio-economic inequalities inherent in capitalist development ensures the inclusion of an increasing amount of people in environmentally problematic production and consumption practices. Overall, a clear pattern between ecological performance and environmental regulation, on the one hand, and welfare and other institutional features, on the other, has as yet not been established. Conversely, what *has* been confirmed in a range of studies since Jackson's *Prosperity without Growth* (Jackson 2009) is the close connection between economic development measured in GDP, material resource use and environmental stress such as climate change (Fritz and Koch 2016; O'Neill et al. 2018). While there is some evidence for the relative decoupling of GDP growth, material resource use and CO_2 emissions per unit of economic output in OECD countries, there is no evidence whatsoever for an absolute decoupling of these parameters which would be necessary to meet the climate targets issued by the IPCC (2014) that would make a temperature increase of below two degrees by the end of the century a realistic possibility. This seems to confirm the 'Jevons' paradox' once again: that increased efficiency in the use of fossil fuels results in an increase in demand for them.

Degrowth and sustainable welfare

If environmental sustainability and endless economic growth (be it green or some other colour) are irreconcilable, the question becomes whether a non-growing economy is at all a possibility. These years a growing number of scholars and activists argue that indeed it is a possibility. They envision scenarios that go under labels such as 'post-growth', 'degrowth' and 'a steady-state economy'. The steady-state economy (SSE) vision emerged in 1970s in the works of one of the fathers of ecological economics, Herman Daly. The SSE is an environmentally and socially sustainable economic system that does not grow in the sense that it keeps two factors at a constant level: the population of artefacts (stocks of physical wealth) and the number of people. The goal is to keep the level of *throughput* as low as possible, with throughput denoting 'flows of matter and energy from the first stage of production (depletion of low-entropy materials from the environment) to the last stage of consumption (pollution of the environment with high-entropy wastes and exotic materials)' (Daly 1991: 17).

Daly (1991: 50–76) proposes that three institutions are crucial for maintaining an SSE. First, a system of government-auctioned physical depletion permits that keeps the stock of physical artefacts constant and matter–energy throughput at sustainable levels. Second, a population stabilization institution that serves to keep the 'stock of people' within ecological limits. This could involve the more or less controversial ideas of 'transferable birth licences', economic incentives in the form of tax breaks to families with few children as well as immigration reforms (Dietz and O'Neill 2013: 81–83). Third, a distributist institution aiming to reduce inequality. Indeed, the legitimacy and long-term maintenance of all social orders requires that structural inequalities are held within certain acceptable limits. Daly (1991: 53–56) explicitly proposes an arrangement of setting maximum limits on income and wealth and minimum limits on income. Many scholars see the SSE as the endpoint of degrowth transitions, whereas many others do not.

Like the SSE notion, the concept of 'degrowth' has also been around since the early 1970s where it was first used by left-wing intellectual André Gorz. Yet it is only over the past decade or so that a large number of scholars, activists and others have embraced it. In its contemporary usage, degrowth

> is on the one hand a keyword that has a scientific basis on the recognition that continuous economic growth is not only unsustainable but also undesirable, and on the other, a keyword that aspires to mobilize a social movement, a "movement of movements", that will act politically to stop the self-destructive path of growth economies, creating a better society along the way.
>
> *(Petridis et al. 2015: 176).*

The overall degrowth vision involves the societies of the world's rich countries to follow trajectories leading to socio-economic systems that, while being socially equitable, are much smaller in terms of their material and energy throughput. Importantly, this does not entail that all dimensions of all economic spaces have to shrink. Rather the idea is that 'some sectors, such as education, medical care, or renewable energy, will need to flourish in the future, while others, such as dirty industries or the financial sector shrink' (Kallis et al. 2015: 5). Moreover, whereas material sacrifices in the rich parts of the world are deemed necessary in order to bring about sustainable low-carbon economies, degrowth proponents acknowledge the need for poor countries to develop economically (Demaria et al. 2013; Kallis et al. 2015). Kallis et al. (2015: 4) envisage a socially equitable 'degrowth society' with a smaller metabolism, in which 'everything will be different: different activities, different forms and uses of energy, different relations, different gender roles, different allocations of time between paid and non-paid work, different relations with the non-human world'.

Serge Latouche – a leading intellectual in the de-growth movement – writes that '[a] generalized capitalism cannot but destroy the planet in the same way that it is destroying society and anything else that is collective' (2009: 91). It follows that degrowth is 'fundamentally anti-capitalist' (ibid.). Degrowth is thus not to be thought of merely as capitalism without growth. Even if a non-growing capitalism could be well-functioning – and little in the history of capitalism suggests that this is the case – this would not in itself make it compatible with the degrowth project. The degrowth vision of socially equitable societies is directly at odds with capitalism, which is an economic system that is premised on exploitation and which produces inequality (Harvey 2014). Certainly, the extent to which capitalism is exploitative and entails inequality varies in time and space. For instance, the social democratic welfare regimes that emerged – as a result of working-class pressure – in some of the world's rich countries in the post-World War Two decades served to reduce inequalities (Esping-Andersen 1990; Lipietz 1992). Yet, these welfare regimes, while facilitating high economic growth rates, were still premised on exploitation (Offe 1984) and unsustainable consumption of natural resources (Brand and Wissen 2012; Koch 2012). These regimes, which were subsequently transformed into neoliberal 'competition states' (Cerny 1997), do thus not resonate well with the degrowth vision of an equitable and environmentally sustainable economic system (Koch and Buch-Hansen 2016).

This brings us neatly to a concept that is central in some growth-critical research, namely 'sustainable welfare' (Koch and Mont 2016). The concept has emerged as a response to the lack of interest in the intersection of, on the one hand, inequality and social welfare research and, on the other, environmental sustainability research. Although recent comparative research suggests that Western production and consumption standards cannot be generalized to the rest of the world due to ecological and planetary limits (Fritz and Koch 2016; O'Neill et al. 2018), neither policy-makers nor welfare scholars have paid much attention to the relevance and potential implications of ecological sustainability issues and climate change, in particular with regard to social policy and welfare theory. Conversely, however, sustainability researchers have not paid much interest to issues of inequality and welfare. 'Sustainable welfare' recognizes the long-term implications of contemporary production and consumption patterns, and, accordingly, raises normative questions such as whose welfare should be represented in current welfare societies.

Brandstedt and Emmelin (2016) argue that the distributive principles underlying existing welfare systems would need to be extended to include those affected in other countries and in the future. Current welfare provision would need to consider that satisfying present welfare demands should not undermine the ability of future generations to meet their welfare needs. This includes the recognition of critical thresholds and limitations, and also of the fact that needs, aspirations and wants must be reviewed – and possibly restrained. Hence, the understanding of climate change as a devastating threat, in particular, and the very idea of environmental sustainability, in general, constitute a challenge to 'business as usual' in policy-making and have significant implications for the scope and direction of welfare policies, which need to give greater weight to distribution and justice across nations and generations. Within the concept of 'sustainable welfare', the key welfare concern is not the provision and distribution of material riches to the 'happy few' in Western societies, but rather the satisfaction of basic needs for all humans now and in the future (Koch et al. 2017). In his recent work, Ian Gough (2017) addresses issues of intergenerational concerns and universality in the context of climate change. Underlining the necessity to tackle climate change, he suggests 'policy auditing', a principle under which critical thresholds for a 'minimally decent life' are constantly (re-)defined in light of the advancement of academic and practical knowledge. While it is, in principle, possible to satisfy basic human needs on a global scale, the degree to which more than basic needs can be provided on a planet with finite resources remains subject to scientific inquiry. The sustainable welfare perspective may also constitute a theoretical and normative framework for redesigning existing policies in an 'eco-social' direction.

Eco-social policies: caps on wealth and income

Advocates of degrowth and sustainable welfare have identified a range of eco-social policy instruments that could aid transitions to just and environmentally sustainable societies. These for instance include work sharing, minimum income schemes, caps on wealth and income, time-banks, job guarantees, complementary currencies and debt auditing (for more details, see e.g. D'Alisa et al. 2015). These and other policy instruments are intensely debated among degrowth scholars and activists. In the present section we will focus on the policy instruments of wealth and income caps. While some growth-critical scholars argue in favour of such instruments (e.g. Daly 1991), wealth and income caps also have advocates among scholars who are not against economic growth (the policy instruments have, to the best of our knowledge, received next to no attention in IPE scholarship). *Wealth caps* involve that a maximum limit is placed on how much wealth an individual is allowed to possess – with wealth being defined as everything owned by a person that either has monetary or exchange value, minus any debts. In a similar vein, *income caps* entail that a maximum limit is placed on income, i.e. the flow of earnings a person receives from working, investments and land.

Why are such caps potentially relevant to degrowth? First of all, they are relevant because they are instruments that can be used to promote social equity. As noted above, a very large number of people live in poverty. Under the growth paradigm, the solution to this problem is economic growth. Historically, growth has indeed lifted many people out of poverty. Yet as there are ecological limits as to how big the economic system can become, limits that have already been exceeded, continued growth in the rich countries of the world is not, according to growth-critical scholars, a viable way forward. A key alternative to growth is redistribution, meaning that resources are transferred from the wealthiest and/or those with the largest incomes to those at the bottom of the income distribution.

Outside degrowth circles, scholars have made the argument that poverty is morally unacceptable: that for moral reasons it is wrong for economic resources to be spent on luxury items (mansions, yachts, private jets etc.) when the same resources could prevent people from living in poverty (Medeiros 2006; Robeyns 2017). Daly (1991: 53) argues that 'private property and the whole market economy lose their moral basis' if no limits are placed on incomes and wealth. He notes that classical (liberal) political economists John Stuart Mill and John Locke believed that private property ceases to be legitimate beyond a certain point and observes that wealth becomes an instrument of exploitation if it is not curbed (Daly 1991: 54–55). There are also environmental reasons for imposing limits on wealth and income. While being wealthy or having a high income does not necessarily involve leading an environmentally unsustainable lifestyle, certainly there is a tendency for the rich to have a bigger ecological footprint than others. According to Oxfam (2015: 4), 'the richest 1% may emit 30 times more than the poorest 50%, and 175 times more than the poorest 10%'. Imposing limits on wealth and income is a means to limit the excesses of the rich.

> **Box 22.1 Emissions of the rich and the poor (excerpts from the summary of the 2015 Oxfam *Extreme Carbon Inequality* briefing)**
>
> - Climate change is inextricably linked to economic inequality: it is a crisis that is driven by the greenhouse gas emissions of the 'haves' that hits the 'have-nots' the hardest.
> - [T]he poorest half of the global population – around 3.5 billion people – are responsible for only around 10% of total global emissions attributed to individual consumption yet live overwhelmingly in the countries most vulnerable to climate change.
> - Around 50% of these emissions meanwhile can be attributed to the richest 10% of people around the world, who have average carbon footprints 11 times as high as the poorest half of the population, and 60 times as high as the poorest 10%. The average footprint of the richest 1% of people globally could be 175 times that of the poorest 10%.

The liberal argument against caps on wealth and income is that the market is the best judge of what an individual's contribution is worth (monetarily speaking) and that people are wealthy because they deserve it. On this view, then, limits on wealth and income are illegitimate and detrimental to the operation of the free market. Against this view, advocates of caps argue that 'free markets' are incapable of setting salaries in a fair way, i.e. in a way that reflects the actual value created by their recipients. The escalation of CEO pay is frequently used to illustrate this point (e.g. Daly 1996: 203; Pizzigati 2018). The size of CEO pay is typically contingent upon the financial performance of the company. Yet this performance is never solely the product of one individual's contributions. To the contrary, it will to a large extent be the outcome of a multitude of circumstances (such as market fluctuations, the macroeconomic climate and technological developments) and of the contributions of employees as well as past executives (Ramsay 2005: 204–205). In other words, 'the market can undervalue a person's contribution and fail to provide a living wage. But the market can also overvalue a person's contribution' (Ramsay 2005: 204).

How, then, could caps on wealth and income concretely be designed? In the literature, a variety of answers to this question can be identified. Here we will briefly outline two income cap proposals, both of which have been developed outside degrowth scholarship. These proposals tackle the issue of how to determine the maximum income level rather differently. One proposal involves the *introduction of an income cap tied to an income floor*. The leading advocate of this proposal is Sam Pizzigati (2018) who advocates a 'Ten Times Rule' system under which income ten times bigger than the income floor is taxed 100 per cent. Pizzigati highlights as an advantage of this system that it – once it is in place – gives wealthy individuals a certain incentive to operate within it. Specifically, it gives them an interest in persuading policy-makers to raise the minimum wage so as to raise the maximum ceiling. In this way he expects the system to raise the living standard of those worst off.

Another proposal is to introduce an 'affluence line' above which all income is transferred to those economically worst off. The satisfaction of human needs is central to this approach. Jan Drewnowski, the father of the affluence line concept, writes that it represents an absolute threshold 'the level above which consumption need not and should not rise' (1978: 264) because 'the satisfaction of needs above these standards is not reasonable and has no merits for the individual and is unacceptable from the point of view of the society' (1978: 271). It has been suggested that the affluence line is defined in relation to a 'needs satisfaction line' which represents the minimum income needed for an individual to participate in society (Concialdi 2018). Empirically, this line is established based on the so-called 'reference budgets' that have first been developed in the UK with the purpose of establishing a minimum income standard required for a full participation in society (Bradshaw et al. 2008; see Davis et al. 2008). An advantage of reference budgets is that they are socially grounded by drawing on inputs from both citizens and experts (Concialdi 2018: 11), whereas a drawback is that the budgets have not yet been developed for many countries.

Compared to imposing higher taxes on wealth and/or income, placing a cap on them is a far-reaching step to take. Yet seen from a degrowth perspective, standard taxation is likely to be insufficient. Thomas Piketty and others have proposed to impose a global wealth tax of 80 or 90 per cent on the wealthiest individuals. Yet even such a tax would not prevent the rich from leading ecologically harmful lifestyles as it would still allow for extraordinary extents in private wealth in absolute terms. It is evident that proposals to cap income wealth and/or income are not popular among those who have the most to lose from them (the wealthiest and those with the highest incomes). Seen from a degrowth perspective, imposing caps on wealth and/or income is not entirely unproblematic either. For example, the implementation of caps requires the existence of active and 'interventionist' states and international organizations. Yet in the growth-critical mainstream state policies are not particularly popular. In fact, much degrowth thought has tended to view states as part of the problem rather than as the solution (Cosme et al. 2017). Yet Cosme et al. also demonstrate that most concrete policy proposals tabled by growth-critical scholars are rather traditional 'top-down' and state-led than 'bottom up' and community-led. Hence, there is a necessity to both theoretically and practically address the contradiction between conceptualizing the state as an external power, incapable of initiating change in an ecological and social direction, and politically appealing to it to do precisely this. Certainly, if caps on wealth and/or income are to resonate with degrowth values they cannot be dictated as a top-down measure. Instead, they need to be developed and deliberated in democratic forums where experts, citizens and policy-makers come together. Moreover, if caps are to have the desired effects, close transnational cooperation is undoubtedly required.

The political economy of a degrowth paradigm shift

It goes without saying that planned degrowth transitions to non-growing economies and sustainable welfare are, at the time of writing, very far from being a reality. Existing welfare states are part of a transnational capitalist system that is firmly committed to economic growth. Currently, degrowth is politically marginalized: while a growing number of people shares its vision of a profoundly different society and while countless initiatives emerging at the local level resonate with this vision, overall the societies of the rich world are not heading in the direction of planned degrowth. In the literature there has been little discussion of why degrowth (and sustainable welfare) remains at the margins let alone of what it would take to change this situation. One way of addressing this matter could be to utilize insights from IPE perspectives on institutional/socio-economic 'paradigm shifts'. In the following we will illustrate this by distilling four preconditions for socio-economic change identified in the IPE tradition of 'transnational historical materialism' (THM) (Cox 1987; Robinson 2014; Van Apeldoorn and Overbeek 2012) and then, in turn, relating these to degrowth.

The first precondition for socio-economic paradigm shifts identified in THM research is a deep crisis that cannot be solved within the framework of existing institutional arrangements (e.g. Van Apeldoorn and Overbeek 2012). These years there is, unfortunately, no shortage of crises. According to Max-Neef (2014: 17), 'never before in human history have so many crises converged simultaneously to reach their maximum level of tension'. The economic and social scars left by 2008 financial crisis continue to be deep, and a new financial crisis is already looming (IMF 2016: 1). Massive and growing inequality (OECD 2015) has resulted in a social crisis. The environmental crisis described above undermine current and future living conditions for human beings and other species (Speth 2008). Several other actual or impending crises can be mentioned (see, e.g. Brand and Wissen 2012; Robinson 2014). Overall, it seems highly unlikely that these crises – which can also be thought of as one *multidimensional crisis* – could be resolved under the institutional arrangements of neoliberal capitalism.

A second precondition for socio-economic paradigm shifts is the existence of one or more political projects that show the ways out of the crisis (Van Apeldoorn 2002). Is degrowth such a project? Typically, degrowth is not conceptualized as a political project. More frequently it is seen as an emerging intellectual paradigm (Martínez-Alier et al. 2010) or as a social movement (Demaria et al. 2013). Still, degrowth arguably does have key attributes of a political project. That is, aside from addressing the problems of economic and social injustice and the environmentally unsustainable nature of an economic system that needs to grow endlessly, degrowth presents a general vision of a different form of society as a solution to the current crises. As noted above, various eco-social policies – including caps on wealth and/or income – that could make degrowth work in practice are identified. Certainly, degrowth is still 'under development' and it is impossible to know how well its policies actually work on a societal level until they have been implemented (this goes for the policies of all new political projects).

Third, for a political project to come to deeply shape socio-economic developments, core ideas underpinning it have to become hegemonic (e.g. Cox 1987). That is, key ideas it incorporates need to be widely perceived as 'common sense', thus 'bringing about not only a unison of economic and political aims, but also intellectual and moral unity' (Gramsci 1971: 181). Both the Keynesian and the more recent neoliberal project are premised on the idea that GDP growth is fundamentally desirable. That this idea has become hegemonic is evidenced in the widely held assumption that the growth paradigm is the natural – and only – way of steering the economy and society (Koch 2018). A precondition for a political project to become hegemonic is that a constellation of social forces with sufficient power and resources to implement it then needs to find it appealing and struggle for it. In this context, it is worth noting that degrowth, as a social movement, has been gaining momentum for some time, not least in Southern Europe. Countless grassroots' initiatives (e.g. D'Alisa et al. 2013) are the most visible manifestations that degrowth is on the rise. A growing interest in degrowth in academia also indicate that an increasing number of people embrace such ideas. Still, the degrowth project is nowhere near enjoying the degree and type of support it needs if its policies are to be implemented through democratic processes. The number of political parties, labour unions, business associations and international organizations that have so far embraced degrowth is modest to say the least. Economic and political elites, including social democratic parties and most of the trade union movement, are united in the belief that economic growth is necessary and desirable. This consensus finds support in the prevailing type of economic theory and underpins the main contenders in the neoliberal project, such as Centre-left and nationalist projects.

The final precondition for socio-economic paradigm shifts identified in THM scholarship is broad-based consent, or at least passive consent, for the political project (Van Apeldoorn and Overbeek 2012: 5–6). It is safe to say that degrowth enjoys no such consent from the majority of the population. For the time being, degrowth remains unknown to most people. Yet, if it were to become generally known, most people would probably not be attracted to the vision of a smaller economic system. Degrowth is incompatible with the lifestyles to which many of us who live in rich countries have become accustomed. Economic growth in the Western world is, to no small extent, premised on the existence of consumer societies and an associated consumer culture most of us find it difficult to completely escape. In this culture, social status, happiness, well-being and identity are linked to consumption (Jackson 2009). If degrowth were to be institutionalized, many citizens in the rich countries would have to adapt to a materially lower standard of living.

In the above, four preconditions for deep socio-economic change were distilled from THM scholarship and related to degrowth. The first is a deep crisis of the existing system and of the prevailing paradigm. The second is an alternative political project. The third is a comprehensive coalition of social forces waging political struggles with a view of making the project hegemonic. The fourth is consent, at least passive consent, in the population. In particular, the two latter preconditions for a degrowth paradigm shift are currently missing: the degrowth project does not enjoy support from a sufficiently comprehensive coalition of social forces or from the public at large. Against this background, a degrowth paradigm shift does not currently appear to be in the cards.

It is also significant that degrowth transitions would begin in societies that are, to a very large extent, transnationally integrated, which could well mean that an additional precondition for a paradigm shift is international coordination. Moreover, many obstacles to and opportunities for change differ from one context to the next. Political economy scholarship on capitalist diversity and institutional change tells us that even radical political change does not entail a clean break with the past. Rather than being written on a blank slate, new policies are always shaped by the context into which they are introduced, not least by existing ideational legacies, socio-economic circumstances, institutional arrangements and political power relations. In other words, if degrowth transitions were to actually take place, they would have to begin from the diverse institutional arrangements characterizing contemporary capitalist societies (Buch-Hansen 2014). To some extent, these institutions would – as a result of ideational and material path dependencies – shape the institutions that succeed them.

Conclusion

The ecological footprint of the contemporary global political economy far exceeds the carrying capacity of the planet, resulting in environmental degradation and climate change. The tensions between the reproduction principles of nature and of the capitalist mode of production were already highlighted by Marx. When considering the variety of forms actually existing capitalism takes, it becomes clear that these tensions come in different guises. Yet while some countries emit far less CO_2 per capita than do other countries, all varieties of contemporary capitalism are environmentally unsustainable. Moreover, today's global political economy is marked by vast economic inequalities: on one hand unfathomable wealth is concentrated on the hands of a small group of individuals, on the other hand millions of people live in poverty and do not have the resources to satisfy even their basic human needs. Against this background various movements and strands of research call for a profoundly different type of socio-economic system: one that is not primarily premised on accumulation and growth but that rather functions within ecological boundaries and is socially equitable. For the post-growth vision of sustainable welfare to come into existence and function, a variety of eco-social policies and institutions are needed. One of these could be caps on wealth and income so as to redistribute resources from the wealthiest individuals to those most in needs, while reducing the environmental damage caused by the lifestyles of the rich. There are many obstacles to shift towards degrowth and sustainable welfare in the global political economy. Drawing on insights from transnational historical materialism, we in particular highlighted the lack of a sufficiently powerful and comprehensive coalition of social forces behind the degrowth 'project' and a lack of (passive) consent in the populations of rich countries for political initiatives pointing in the direction of less or no growth.

Bibliography

Aglietta, M. 1987. *A Theory of Capitalist Regulation: The US Experience*, 2nd edition. London: Verso.

Antal, M. and Van Den Bergh, J. 2014. Green Growth and Climate Change: Conceptual and Empirical Considerations. *Climate Policy* 16(2): 165–177.

Bradshaw, J., Middleton, S, Davis, A. Oldfield, N., Smith, N., Cusworth, L. and Williams, J. 2008. *A minimum income standard for Britain. What people think*. London: Joseph Rowntree Foundation.

Brand, U. and Wissen, M. 2012. Global Environmental Politics and the Imperial Mode of Living: Articulations of State–Capital Relations in the Multiple Crisis. *Globalizations* 9(4): 547–560.

Brandstedt, E. and Emmelin, M. 2016. The concept of sustainable welfare. In: Koch, M. and Mont, O. (eds) *Sustainability and the Political Economy of Welfare*. London: Routledge: 15–28.

Buch-Hansen, H. 2014. Capitalist diversity and de-growth trajectories to steady-state economies. *Ecological Economics* 106: 173–179.

Burkett, P. 2005. Entropy in Ecological Economics: A Marxist Intervention. *Historical Materialism* 13(1): 117–152.

Cerny, P. G. 1997. Paradoxes of the Competition State: The Dynamics of Political Globalization. *Government and Opposition* 32(2): 251–274.

Christoff, P. and Eckersley, R. 2011. Comparing state responses. In Dryzek, J., Norgaard, R. and Schlosberg, D. (eds) *Oxford Handbook of Climate Change and Society*. Oxford: Oxford University Press.

Clark, B. and York, R. 2005. Carbon Metabolism: Global Capitalism, Climate Change, and the Biospheric Rift. *Theory and Society* 34(4): 391–428.

Concialdi, P. 2018. What Does it Mean to be Rich? Some Conceptual and Empirical Issues. *European Journal of Social Security* 20(1): 3–20.

Cosme, I., Santos, R. and O'Neill, D. 2017. Assessing the Degrowth Discourse: A Review and Analysis of Academic Degrowth Policy Proposals. *Journal of Cleaner Production* 149: 321–334.

Cox, R. W. 1987. *Production, Power and World Order*. New York: Columbia University Press.

D'Alisa, G., Demaria, F. and Cattaneo, C. 2013. Civil and Uncivil Actors for a Degrowth Society. *Journal of Civil Society* 9(2): 212–224.

D'Alisa, G., Demaria, F. and Kallis, G. 2015 (eds) *Degrowth. A Vocabulary for a New Era*. London and New York: Routledge.

Daly, H. E. 1991. *Steady-state Economics*. Washington: Island Press.

Daly, H. E. 1996. *Beyond Growth*. Boston: Beacon Press.

Daly, H. E. and Farley, J. 2011. *Ecological Economics. Principles and Applications*. Washington: Island Press.

Davis, A., Hirsch, D., Pedley, M. and Stephered, C. 2008. *A Minimum Income Standard for the UK 2008–2018: Continuity and Change*. London: Joseph Rowntree Foundation.

Demaria, F., Schneider, F., Sekulova, F. and Martinez-Alier, J. 2013. What is Degrowth? From an Activist Slogan to a Social Movement. *Environmental Values* 22(2): 191–215.

Dietz, R, and O'Neill, D. 2013. *Enough Is Enough. Building a Sustainable Economy in a World of Finite Resources*. San Francisco: Berrett-Koehler Publishers.

Drewnowski, J. 1978. The Affluence Line. *Social Indicators Research* 5: 263–278.

Esping-Andersen, G. 1990. *The Three Worlds of Welfare Capitalism*. Cambridge: Polity Press.

Fritz, M. and Koch, M. 2016. Economic Development and Prosperity Patterns around the World: Structural Challenges for a Global Steady-state Economy. *Global Environmental Change* 38: 41–48.

Gough, I. 2017. *Heat, Greed and Human Need: Climate Change, Capitalism and Sustainable Wellbeing*. Cheltenham: Edward Elgar.

Gough, I., Meadowcroft, J., Dryzek, J., Gerhards, J., Lengfield, H., Markandya, A. and Ortiz, R. 2008. JESP Symposium: Climate Change and Social Policy. *Journal of European Social Policy* 18(4): 25–44.

Gramsci, A. 1971. *Selections from Prison Notebooks*. London: Lawrence and Wishart.

Hall, P. A. and Soskice, D. W. 2001. *Varieties of Capitalism. The Institutional Foundations of Comparative Advantage*. Oxford: Oxford University Press.

Harvey, D. 2014. *Seventeen Contradictions and the End of Capitalism*. London: Profile Books.

IMF. 2016. *Fiscal Monitor*. Washington, DC: International Monetary Fund.

Intergovernmental Panel on Climate Change (IPCC). 2014. *Climate Change 2014: Synthesis Report. Summary for Policymakers*, Geneva; available at: www.ipcc.ch/report/ar5/syr/.

Jackson, T. 2009. *Prosperity without Growth: Economics for a Finite Planet*. London: Earthscan.

Jevons, W. S. 1865. *The Coal Question. An Inquiry Concerning the Progress of the Nation, and the Probable Exhaustion of Our Coal-Mines*. London: Macmillan and Co.

Kallis, G., Demaria, F. and D'Alisa, G. 2015. Introduction: Degrowth. In: G. D'Alisa, F. Demaria, and G. Kallis (eds) *Degrowth. A Vocabulary for a New Era*. London and New York: Routledge: 1–17.

Koch, M. 2012. *Capitalism and Climate Change. Theoretical Discussion, Historical Development and Policy Responses*. Basingstoke: Palgrave Macmillan.

Koch, M. 2018. The Naturalisation of Growth: Marx, the Regulation Approach and Bourdieu. *Environmental Values* 27(1): 9–27.

Koch, M. and Buch-Hansen, H. 2016. Human needs, steady-state economics and sustainable welfare. In: M. Koch and O. Mont (eds) *Sustainability and the Political Economy of Welfare*. London and New York: Routledge.

Koch, M., Buch-Hansen, H. and Fritz, M. 2017. Shifting Priorities in Degrowth Research: An Argument for the Centrality of Human Needs. *Ecological Economics* 138: 74–81.

Koch, M. and Fritz, M. 2014. Building the Eco-social State: Do Welfare Regimes Matter? *Journal of Social Policy* 43(4): 679–703.

Koch, M. and Mont, O. 2016. *Sustainability and the Political Economy of Welfare*. London and New York: Routledge.

Latouche, S. 2009. *Farewell to Growth*. Cambridge: Polity Press.

Lipietz, A. 1992. *Towards a New Economic Order. Postfordism, Ecology and Democracy*. Cambridge: Polity Press.

Lohmann, L. 2010. Uncertainty Markets and Carbon Markets: Variations on Polanyian Themes. *New Political Economy* 15(2): 225–254.

Martínez-Alier, J., Pascual, U., Vivien, F.-D. and Zaccai, E. 2010. Sustainable De-growth: Mapping the Context, Criticisms and Future Prospects of an Emergent Paradigm. *Ecological Economics* 69(9): 1741–1747.

Marx, K. 1961. *Capital: A Critique of Political Economy, Vol. 1*. Moscow: Foreign Languages Publishing House.

Marx, K. 1973. *Grundrisse: Foundations of the Critique of Political Economy*. Harmondsworth: Penguin.

Marx, K. 2006. *Capital: A Critique of Political Economy. Vol. 3*. London: Penguin Classics.

Max-Neef, M. 2014. The world on a collision course and the need for a new economy. In: S. Novkovic and T. Webb (eds) *Co-Operatives in a Post-Growth Era*. London: Zed Books.

Medeiros, M. 2006. The Rich and the Poor: The Construction of an Affluence Line from the Poverty Line. *Social Indicators Research* 78(1): 1–18.

Mikler, J. and Harrison, N. E. 2012. Varieties of Capitalism and Technological Innovation for Climate Change Mitigation. *New Political Economy* 17(2): 37–41.

OECD. 2015. *In It Together: Why Less Inequality Benefits All*. Paris: OECD Publishing.

Offe, C. 1984. *Contradictions of the Welfare State*. London: Hutchinson.

O'Neill, D., Fanning, A. L. Lamb, W. F. and Steinberger, J. K. 2018. A Good Life for All within Planetary Boundaries. *Nature Sustainability* 1: 88–95.

Oxfam. 2015. *Extreme Carbon Inequality*, Oxfam Media Briefing, 2 December.

Petridis, P., Muraca, B. and Kallis, G. 2015. Degrowth: between a scientific concept and a slogan for a social movement. In: J. Martínez-Alier and Muradian, R. (eds) *Handbook of Ecological Economics*. Cheltenham: Edward Elgar Publishing.

Pizzigati, S. 2018. *The Case for a Maximum Wage*. Cambridge: Polity.

Ramanathan, V., Molina, L., Zaelke, D. 2017. *Well under 2 Degrees Celsius: Fast Action Policies to Protect People and the Planet from Extreme Climate Change*. Available at: www.igsd.org/wp-content/uploads/2017/09/Well-Under-2-Degrees-Celsius-Report-2017.pdf.

Ramsay, M. 2005. A Modest Proposal: The Case for a Maximum Wage. *Contemporary Politics* 11(4): 201–216.

Robeyns, I. 2017. Having too much. In: J. Knight and M. Schwartzberg (eds) *NOMOS LVI: Wealth. Yearbook of the American Society for Political and Legal Philosophy*. New York University Press.

Robinson, W. I. 2014. *Global Capitalism and the Crisis of Humanity*. Cambridge: Cambridge University Press.

Speth, G. 2008. *The Bridge at the Edge of the World*. New Haven and London: Yale University Press.

Steffen, W., Richardson, K., Rockström, J. Cornell, S. E., Fetzer, I., Bennett, E. M., Biggs, R., Carpenter, S. R., de Vries, W., de Wit, C., Folke, C., Gerten, D., Heinke, J., Mace, G. M., Persson, L. M., Ramanathan, V., Reyers, B. and Sörlin, S. 2015. Planetary Boundaries: Guiding Human Development on a Changing Planet. *Science* 347: 6223.

Van Apeldoorn, B. 2002. *Transnational Capitalism and the Struggle Over European Integration*. London and New York: Routledge.

Van Apeldoorn, B. and Overbeek, H. 2012. Introduction: The life course of the neoliberal project and the global crisis. In: B. van Apeldoorn and H. Overbeek (eds) *Neoliberalism in Crisis*. New York: Palgrave: 1–20.

23
Extractivism
The curse of plenty

Alberto Acosta

"That is the never-ending paradox – the poor live in nations that are rich from the generosity of nature"

José Cecilio del Valle, 1830

Introduction

Countries that specialize in exporting primary goods as the main source of revenue for their economies are apparently doomed to poverty – precisely because they are "rich" in natural resources (Schuldt 2005). Their economies and indeed their societies are trapped in a pernicious mindset known as the "paradox of plenty" or the "resource curse" – stated in more inflammatory terms, the "curse of plenty" (Acosta 2009).

Since the early days of colonization, many of these economies exporting primary goods have been linked to global markets. This linkage immediately resulted in countries rich in natural resources taking passive and submissive positions in the international division of labor since they were obliged to acquiesce to global market demands. This pattern has stymied the efforts of these countries to achieve the chimera called "development."

Although at first it does not seem very likely, recent evidence and much experience have supported the assertion that the economic difficulties of these countries are in some way related to natural resource wealth (Schuldt and Acosta 2006), leading to the conclusion that countries rich in natural resources, with economies mostly based on the extraction and export of these resources, find it more difficult to ensure the well-being of their citizens. In particular, countries that are well endowed with one or a few primary products seem to be doomed to *under-development* (as opposed to *development*).

The high availability of natural resources, especially minerals and oil, tends to exacerbate already distorted economic structures and the allocation of productive factors within countries. Consequently, it is common to see regressive distribution of national income and greater concentration of wealth in a few hands, while at the same time, economic value is being drawn from the peripheries toward the capitalist centers. Further, out of extractivism comes authoritarianism, with its inseparable companion: corruption (Gudynas 2017; Acosta and Cajas-Guijarro

2017). This situation is further aggravated by a series of endogenous "pathological" processes that accompany this abundance of natural resources.

Despite much evidence for the above, one of the basic tenets of free markets, considered the end-all and be-all of the (orthodox) economy and beyond, is the frequent repetition of the old argument of comparative advantage, that is, to intensify extractivism. Free trade advocates preach that we must be consistent in how the advantages provided by nature are exploited and how to make the most of them. This list of doctrines can include several others that accompany extractivism: globalization as an indisputable option; the market as supreme regulator; privatization as the only path; and competitiveness as a virtue *par excellence*.

At this point, it should be noted that the concept of extractivism is relatively new. It emerged in the mid-twentieth century as "extractive industries," becoming very popular due to the promotional activities of international organizations such as the World Bank and even the United Nations, but its most significant symbolism has emerged from the resistance to these "industries" (Gudynas 2015).[1] Theories about "curses" are the outcome of much deliberation that was first based on dependency theories (Acosta 2016). The combination of these inputs leads to interpretations that are both powerful and profound due to their mobilizing capacity and the opportunity to better understand the sociopolitical phenomena caused by extractivism.

Box 23.1 Extractivism: a definition

Extractivism, in general and throughout history, refers to activities that remove (almost always intensively) large volumes of natural resources (minerals or oil) and that grow food crops for export using agroindustrial methods with minimal processing; since they are intended for export, these products are deemed commodities. Normally (but not always, as in some gold mining activities), these extractive activities require large investments and have significant macroeconomic effects, as well as serious social, environmental, and cultural impacts in the affected areas. Extractivism is not limited to minerals or oil. Other forms exist, such as extractivist agriculture, forestry, and fishing and even extractivist tourism. Thus, in accordance with Eduardo Gudynas (2015), one of the authors who has delved deeply into this subject, it is more accurate to discuss extractivisms. However, we must be very precise in definitions because an overly broad approach would lead to misunderstandings and limit the ability to identify suitable alternatives.

The curse of alarmist literature

Overcoming their state of underdevelopment seems to be a difficult challenge for these types of economies. For example, the Inter-American Development Bank (IDB) has even expressed a certain geographical determinism: the countries richest in natural resources and closest to the Equator (tropical countries) are fated to be more backward and poorer. Their environmental and geographical conditions determine their state of "underdevelopment" (Gudynas 2009). According to this narrative, the situation is even more serious for inland countries, such as landlocked Bolivia and Paraguay.[2]

In contrast with these alarmists are those that contend that countries are successful because they are forced to be competitive and more efficient due to their limited natural resources and because of the effects of more temperate and even cold climates.[3] This interpretation is definitely simplistic because severe climates are not exclusive to the tropics.

Those who express these theories clearly ignore (or attempt to hide) that the primary-product exporting economies have colonial origins. Even the system that concentrates land ownership (even more concentrated today) largely dates from this period. Those who espouse these alarmist views do not understand that the unrelenting processes of conquest and colonization not only have impacts today, but they also replicate in bad ways. The free traders do not consider the demographic, social, and cultural hecatomb that resulted from the arrival of Europeans in the Americas. They are not concerned with the inequalities and structural inequities that abound in this type of primary-product exporting economy but are instead interested in a socioeconomic reality that is definitely much more complex than "climate" and "geography" can explain.

Here, we must highlight the historical role that colonialist labor and wealth extraction played (and still plays) in contributing to the "success" of the economies considered to be "developed." It suffices to mention the processes of accumulation by dispossession as presented by David Harvey (2004) and even the sort of original, worldwide accumulation described by Karl Marx, in which transnational corporations and metropolitan countries actively participate. Similarly, extractivism uses "land grabs" (*Landnahme*, as expressed by Rosa Luxemburg) and "extrahection" – violent appropriations of natural resources (Eduardo Gudynas). All of these concepts contribute to an understanding of modern capitalism but especially to how "development" and "underdevelopment" are two sides of the same process. Without these types of approaches, it is impossible to understand that extractivism is an essentially violent act against nature and human beings themselves.

Box 23.2 Potential of the "extractivism" concept

Extractivism is a concept that helps to explain the colonial and neocolonial looting, accumulation, concentration, and devastation, as well as the evolution of modern capitalism and even the ideas of "development" and "underdevelopment," as two sides of the same process. In fact, extractivism was forged more than 500 years ago with the conquest and colonization of the Americas and did not end with their eventual domination by Europe.

Throughout the region, whether in countries with neoliberal or "progressive" governments, extractivism is expanding rapidly while colonial practices persist. One of the great contributions of this concept, which has been solidified by the struggles of those resisting extractivism, is that it helps to overcome the traditional understanding of primary-product exporting economies that demand nationalist responses and focus on government action – a clearly inadequate approach.

It is interesting to note that conventional interpretations do not consider the aberrations resulting from economies historically tied to an unfair and inequitable foreign trade regime, even environmental regimes. They are even less interested in the harmful impacts of the extractive policies of neoliberalism or neo-developmentalism that further increase the dependence of the primary-product exporting countries. In short, they do not incorporate the still-present, destructive effect of the "coloniality of power."[4]

This lack of incorporation is why they make no mention of the historical and ecological debts that should be attributed to imperialist nations. In addition to these debts is the biopiracy committed by several transnational corporations that obtain patents in their home countries for a range of indigenous plants and knowledge. In short, we could assert that not only is there a commercial and financially inequitable exchange, as suggested by dependency theories, but there is also an ecologically unbalanced and destabilizing exchange.

A look at what underlies this age-old curse

At first glance, the starting point for answering this question seems to be to examine how natural resources are extracted and used, as well as how the proceeds of the extraction are distributed. There has also been much ink spilled on attributing existing problems to the presence of trans-national interests that affect the operation and even the existence of state entities. However, the problem is much more profound, as shown below.

We must ask ourselves why the massive extraction of natural resources for export in these countries has not stopped the spread of poverty, nor has it prevented recurring economic crises. Instead, it seems to have solidified "rentier" mentalities (another addiction to overcome). We know from experience that all of these factors further weaken already fragile and inadequate institutions, encourage corruption, and degrade the environment. Complicating this situation are the clientelist and paternalistic practices that are employed and that hinder the development of citizenship. When viewed in this light, the "the curse of plenty" issue surrounds all of society, including its political and cultural life, and extractivism triggers a number of "spillovers" (Gudynas 2015) that ultimately encompass entire countries and even extend beyond their borders.

As Gudynas noted, these "spillover effects" extend far beyond the precise locations of each extractive activity. They include impacts on many other areas and environments and affect the comprehension and meaning of various public policies (such as environmental, social, or economic policies), as well as the way in which politics, justice, democracy, the environment, and nature are understood. They have an impact on property relationships and sovereignty within countries, as well as on their connections to the rest of the world. Even various perspectives on development are influenced by extractivism, which in one way or another encourages the pursuit of a phantom: the development and progress that are directed by global markets from beginning to end.

Thus, the reality of a primary-product exporting economy (that is, an exporter of nature) is also manifested in a lack of interest in investing in the domestic market, which constrains the export sector's integration with domestic production. There are no incentives to develop and diversify domestic production or to link it to export processes, which in turn should transform natural resources into goods with higher added value. As confirmed on a daily basis, these societies have for decades preferred products "made elsewhere" over domestic products and solutions. It would seem that there is a curse that prevents us from even discovering our potential.

This situation can be explained by the relative ease of securing income from a bountiful natural environment and inexpensive labor. The benefit from these activities goes to wealthy economies – the resource importers that later earn even higher profits by processing the primary-products and selling finished goods – while the primary-product exporting countries, which earn minimal income from nature (or Ricardian income), bear the burden of environmental and social liabilities.

If one accounted for all of the economic costs of the social, environmental, and productive impacts of oil or mineral extraction, as well as the hidden subsidies from these activities, many of their potential economic benefits would disappear. However, our leaders never venture this far since they are mired in free trade beliefs or trapped in development sects that have extractivist parentage.

Added to this situation is the massive concentration of nature's income in a few powerful groups, mostly transnationals. These extractivist groups and broad business sectors, obsessed with rent seeking, do not find or create incentives for investments in domestic markets. They prefer to encourage the consumption of imported goods. They often remove their profits from the country and manage their businesses through companies incorporated in "tax havens."

There is also no incentive or pressure to invest the income from primary-product exports in the export activity itself since the comparative advantage lies in the generosity of nature, rather than in the innovative efforts of human beings. For example, the oil industry – which should not be confused with oil extraction activities – has developed almost exclusively in the industrialized countries that import oil and not in the countries that extract and export it, with the exception of Norway.[5]

If we accept for now that things have an economic value because of the average "work" or "effort" that society requires for their extraction, then that primary-product exports depend more on the generosity of nature than on human effort raises the question of how much extractivist activities actually create value or whether they are truly only rent-seeking activities that suck the value out of productive activities through speculation (e.g., speculation on raw material prices in international markets). Therefore, if extractive activities are rent seeking (even speculative) and nonvalue creating, it is easier to understand why the income from such activities is highly volatile and unstable and further distorts the underdeveloped capitalist economies that depend on it.

These economies are, as has been demonstrated throughout history, closely linked to global markets. These markets are the source of the motivation to expand (or not) the extractivist activities and the economy itself. Further, when the reserves of a product decline or are affected by technological changes, governments focus their attention on other natural resources.

Dependence on foreign markets, although paradoxical, is even more pronounced in times of crisis, especially in the event of generalized government blockades. Most economies dependent on primary resource exports fall into the trap of forcing up extraction rates when prices drop. They seek to sustain, by any means possible, the revenues generated by primary exports. This policy can prove beneficial: a larger supply of raw materials – oil, minerals or food – in times of depressed prices creates a surplus, which reduces prices even further, thus generating "impoverishing growth" (Bhagwati 1958).

It is also important to consider the link between primary-product export prices and the major cycles of the global capitalist economy identified, for example, by Nikolai Kondratieff (1935). Similarly, it would be useful to review the link between these cycles and those that specifically influence extractivist economies, which in one way or another play minor roles in these profound technological transformations, although their undervalued raw materials help to finance these changes.

In extractivist economies with high demand for capital and technology that function as enclaves (they do not integrate the primary-product export activities with the rest of the economy and society), the productive apparatus is subject to the vicissitudes of the global market. In particular, it is vulnerable to competition from other countries in similar positions, which seek to sustain their income levels without paying sufficient attention to adequate price management. Opportunities for regional integration, which are indispensable if domestic markets are to expand, disappear if neighboring countries produce similar raw materials, compete with one another, and suppress export prices instead of working together in regional blocks that expand their markets and increase the complexity of their productive apparatuses.

Furthermore, by applying simple logic, it is impossible to accept that all countries producing similar primary goods (which are many) will grow with the expectation that international demand will be sustained at sufficiently high levels over time to guarantee the satisfactory performance of their economies.

A core point must be made here. Actual control of national exports depends on certain key countries, even if significant foreign investment has not been made in extractive activities. Even many state enterprises of primary-product exporting economies (with the consent of their respective governments) seem to be programmed to react only to foreign stimulus. Moreover, because their operations often have socio-environmental impacts that are equal to or greater than those caused by transnational corporations, sometimes these state entities raise the flag of nationalism to defeat resistance by communities in areas of oil or mining expansion. It is the activities of the transnational and state companies, both motivated by external demand, that decisively influence the primary-product exporting economies.

Somewhat complementing the above are the few (or nonexistent) linkages that enable new lines of production, even from the extractive activities themselves. There are few to no productive conglomerates, either for the domestic market or for expanding and diversifying the range of export products. Distribution of income is inadequate, and ultimately the required tax revenue falls short because these economies are always overwhelmed by repressed or fictitious demands. Furthermore, because this form of (capitalist) accumulation is so severely focused outward, it strengthens a cultural scheme dependent on the outside, which minimizes or thoroughly marginalizes local cultures. Thus, an "imperial way of life" (Brand and Wissen 2017) takes root among the elites and middle classes and even has a demonstration effect on the working class and the poor.

Due to these conditions and the technological characteristics of extractivist activities, such as oil, mining, or monocultures, there is no massive and direct generation of employment. The highest demand for labor comes from the processing of these raw materials in the industrialized countries and not from their extraction. This fact also explains the contradiction of countries that are rich in raw materials but where most of the population is unemployed or underemployed and is consequently impoverished. While production in wealthy countries is oriented toward mass consumption, production in poor countries is almost always aimed at consumption by elites, who also consume large quantities of imported products.

This type of accumulation does not require an internal market and can even function under decreasing wages. There is no social pressure to reinvest in productivity improvements or to respect nature. Moreover, the income from nature, as the main source of financing for these economies, determines the productive activity and the rest of the social relationships. To make matters worse, extractivism – especially oil and mining – fosters social relationships. For example, if we examine the pernicious effects of the community relationships and investments of these companies that ultimately replace the state itself in the provision of social services, although it is not their function.

Moreover, the rentier states build legal frameworks that favor extractive companies, which have sometimes embedded their own officials or intermediaries in government positions. In fact, there is a whole apparatus of lawyers and technicians who not only pursue foreign investment in the country but also monitor legal reforms to ensure that they are advantageous to foreign investment.

This interference, encouraged by multilateral organizations, is seen again and again in the oil and mining sectors, in which the same company managers or their lawyers take management jobs in state regulatory agencies or in the extraction companies: the revolving door is the order of the day. Another twisted situation occurs when inexperienced people manage these companies, which soon deteriorate and create the conditions for transnationals to come and save the day at the last minute.

Box 23.3 Violence – a necessary condition

Violence is a consubstantial element of extractivism – a "biocidal model." Examining only the violence unleashed by the extractive companies themselves, there are various levels: state repression; criminalization of the defenders of life; civil war; open warfare between countries; and imperial aggression by some powers committed to securing natural resources by force (especially hydrocarbons and minerals, in recent times).

This point is essential. Violence for appropriating natural resources that are extracted by trampling human rights and the rights of nature "is not a consequence of a certain type of extraction but a necessary condition for appropriating natural resources," as Eduardo Gudynas (2013) rightly pointed out. This appropriation is perpetrated regardless of the harmful social, environmental, and even economic impacts of extractive projects. In fact, the complete depletion of resources and its consequences are often not even considered.

Let us go one step further. In the words of Michael J. Watts (1999), we can conclude that "the entire history of oil is replete with criminality, corruption, the raw exercise of power, and the worst aspects of frontier capitalism." This statement is fully applicable to all types of extractivism.

A culture of miracles threatens democracy

Everything mentioned in the previous point weakens democratic governance because it establishes or facilitates permanent governments, which must be authoritarian and clientelistic, as well as voracious companies that are also clientelistic. The often-wasteful management of the income from massive exportation of raw materials and the absence of forward-looking policies end up weakening the existing institutions or preventing their development. In effect, these extractive countries are not held up as examples of democracy but quite the opposite.

Latin America has extensive experience in this area. Venezuela has been a paradigmatic example since the beginning of the twentieth century. Other Latin American countries have also undergone authoritarian periods spawned by the primary-product export accumulation modality, propped up by only a few mineral resources. The same could be said for other oil-exporting countries, such as Nigeria. Similarly, Saudi Arabia and the United Arab Emirates, along with other countries in their region, are very wealthy, with enormous financial resources and high levels of per capita income. However, they cannot be included in the ranks of the "developed" countries due to the many areas of intolerable inequality (such as gender and ethnic inequality). Additionally, their governments are not only undemocratic but are characterized by profoundly authoritarian practices. The situation in many countries that depend on mineral exports (like many African countries) is even more drastic.

Regarding Latin America, in recent years, we have seen how governments, progressive and neoliberal alike, pursue more revenue by expanding extractivism to promote ambitious "development" projects and sustain broad welfare programs for a society with many needs and ever-increasing demands. In fact, social demands are one of the main reasons for maintaining and supporting primary-product export activities. Governments hope to finance action on these long-delayed social demands through these efforts, and as we saw earlier, this level of extractivist pressure is sustained even when the prices of raw materials are in crisis.

During boom times, several governments with economies rich in natural resources have even predicted the impending "defeat of underdevelopment." In recent history, Iran is one of the most often-evoked examples of this phenomenon. Shah Mohammad Reza Pahlavi, one of the United States' closest allies in the Middle East, encouraged by the country's lofty oil revenues in the 1970s, claimed that his country would be among the five wealthiest and most powerful nations on the planet before 2000. This dream did not last long because his government was overthrown a few years later by a broad popular movement led by the ayatollahs.

As Fernando Coronil (2002) stated regarding Venezuela (a situation that can be extrapolated to other countries), a "magical state" flourishes in these types of economies, with the ability to deploy the "culture of the miracle." Thanks to the considerable revenue generated by oil and mineral exports, the rulers of this type of state often presume to be the bearers of the collective will and attempt to accelerate the leap toward coveted western (capitalist) modernity. This process is how short-lived miracle models emerge, as was seen in Ecuador's commodities boom during President Rafael Correa's administration.

The exploitation of nonrenewable natural resources on a massive scale in these countries has led to the emergence of paternalist states, the influencing capacity of which is tied to their political capacity to negotiate a greater or lesser share of the rents from mining or the oil industry. These states have added a monopoly on political violence to the monopoly on natural resources (Coronil 2002). Although it might seem paradoxical, a state of this type, which often delegates a substantial part of its social obligations to the oil or mining companies, abandons vast regions in development terms, and under these conditions of state "deterritorialization," they become police states that repress victims of the system while refusing to meet their social and economic obligations.

In these oil and mining enclave economies, the political structures and dynamics that have taken shape are not only authoritarian but also greedy. During the boom years in particular, this greed took the form of an often-disproportionate increase in public spending and, above all, discretionary distribution of public funds. This type of political practice (especially during export booms) is also explained by the determination of governments to remain in power and/or by their intent to accelerate a series of structural reforms that seem essential to them to transform atavistic societies (from the still dominant perspective of coloniality, which marginalizes and represses ancestral knowledge and practices). This increase in public spending and investment is also the result of the growing conflict over distribution that breaks out between the most disparate groups with power. As noted by Jürgen Schuldt (2005), "it is thus a dynamic and neverending power play that arises endogenously from the boom. And the discretionary public spending increases more than the revenue attributable to the economic boom (pro-cyclical fiscal policy)."

This "greed effect" leads to desperate pursuit and abusive appropriation of a significant proportion of the surplus generated in the primary-product export sector. In the absence of a broad national agreement about how to manage these natural resources, without solid democratic institutions (which can only be built with widespread and sustained citizen participation), and without respect for the rights of humans and nature, various uncooperative powerful groups appear on the scene, desperate to obtain a share of mining or oil rents. In addition, as large forested areas are opened up as a result of mining or oil activities, other extractive activities are undertaken that themselves cause serious environmental and social problems, such as logging and monoculture plantations.

Those embroiled in this dispute over natural resource rents are, above all, the transnational corporations directly or indirectly involved in these activities and their local allies, international banks, broad business and financial sectors and even the armed forces and some politically influential sectors of society. Trade union groups linked to this type of extractive activity, known as the "labor aristocracy," also obtain significant benefits. Understandably, this struggle over the distribution of rents, which can be conflict ridden, provokes new political tensions that facilitate authoritarian governments.

In many countries that export primary-products, the governments and the ruling elites, the "new corporate class," not only control the state (without major checks and balances) but have also co-opted important media outlets, pollsters, business consultants, universities, foundations, and law firms. Thus, things such as privatization and the increasing commodification of knowledge are the order of the day. Undoubtedly, even "science" is ever more dependent on the hegemonic powers that have fixed their sights on the systematic appropriation of nature and the control of strategic territories.

With this focus, the large extractivist transnationals have become a "privileged political actor" by having "levels of access and influence the likes of which no other interest group, stratum, or social class enjoys", which enable them to "push for the reconfiguration of the rest of the social pyramid [...] it is an invisible hand of the state that grants favors and privileges, and once obtained, tends to hold onto them at any cost", considering them to be "acquired rights" (Durand 2006).

This reality entails multiple economic costs: the undervaluation of foreign sales or the overvaluation of costs to reduce taxes or tariffs; temporary and surprising reductions in extraction rates to generate higher profits; the growing presence of all types of intermediaries that hinder production and add costs to transactions; and even the reduction of sectoral investments, at least by the most serious companies. Furthermore, so much reliance on the generosity of nature marginalizes productive innovation and even marketing efforts.

Walking hand in hand with the "curse of plenty" is the "everlasting debt" resulting from external credit (Acosta 1994). In the midst of an economic boom, public debt (especially external) grows in greater proportion than the boom itself (it is also true that it increases due to external conditions produced by capital accumulation). Here, again, the "greed effect" appears, driven by the appetite to feast on the enormous influx of income from international banks (private and multilateral) or from countries (such as China today), which are jointly responsible with the multilateral organizations for the external debt processes.

As a result of the high tax collection from the exploitation of natural resources, governments tend to stop collecting other taxes, such as income tax. In reality, they apply minimal tax pressure. This laxity, as Schuldt (2005) pointed out, allows citizens to develop "bad habits." Even worse, "what this means is that the public does not demand government transparency, fairness, representativeness, and efficiency in spending": it is often heard that it is not so bad when a public official steal if he or she is "getting things done." This lack of attention is concerning since the demand for democratic representation in government, as Schuldt reminded us, usually arose as a consequence of tax increases, for example, more than 400 years ago in Great Britain and in France at the beginning of the nineteenth century.

Rentierism and clientelism mindsets and even consumerism are quite different from citizenship and can even impede its development. Further, these clientelist practices, by encouraging individualism, can counteract communal proposals and actions, affecting social organizations and, even worse, the sense of community. These governments attempt to repress social movements, and if they fail to do so, they impose parallel structures controlled by the state itself.

Without minimizing the importance of providing for the consumption levels needed by the traditionally marginalized population, there will surely be some who (ingenuously) see democratizing elements in consumerism. They often do so without considering the imported goods consumption patterns that emerge and without considering that growing demand is almost always fulfilled by the supply from large economic groups and even by imported goods. The upsurge in consumerism, which can last as long as the boom itself, is nothing less than a psychological issue, in political terms. This increase in material consumption is confused with an improvement in the quality of life, which is clearly consistent with the fetishist nature of the exchange of goods. Thus, governments can gain legitimacy from the consumerism mindset, which is not environmentally or socially sustainable.

In these economies, an inhibiting "one-track export mentality" is exhibited that stifles the creativity of and incentives for local entrepreneurs, who might have been willing to invest in economic activities with high added value and returns. This almost pathological "pro-export mentality" also extends to the heart of government and even spreads to the citizenry. All of this change leads to a denigration of the country's human, communal, and cultural capabilities and potential. It injects a type of extractivist DNA into the entire society, starting with its leaders, and of all this transformation does not go unnoticed in the political arena.

The governments of these primary-product exporting economies not only have significant resources (especially in boom times) to undertake the necessary public works, but they can also afford to implement measures and actions aimed at co-opting the public to ensure a level of "governability" that enables them to introduce the reforms and changes that they consider necessary. However, good intentions frequently lead to authoritarian and messianic government practices that, at best, disguise themselves as "delegative democracies."

In addition, spending more public money on clientelist activities reduces the latent pressure for greater democratization. It is a sort of "fiscal pacification" (Schuldt 2005), aimed at tamping down social protest. Here, we see the various types of financial bonds used to alleviate extreme poverty, especially those framed in a pure and hard clientelism that rewards the most submissive.

The government's considerable revenues enable it to oust or prevent the formation of opposition or independent groups and factions of power that would be able to demand political and other rights (human rights, justice, shared government, etc.). Considerable resources have even been expended to persecute opponents, such as those who do not understand the "indisputable benefits" of extractivism. The government can allocate large sums of money to the reinforcement of its internal controls, including the repression of opponents. In addition, without effective citizen participation, democracy becomes hollow regardless of how much the public is consulted at the ballot box.

Box 23.4 Hyperpresidentialism hand in hand with hyperextractivism

Dependence on nonrenewable natural resources often consolidates authoritarian governments due to the following factors:

- state institutions that are too weak to enforce laws and control government activities;
- an absence of rules and transparency that encourages discretionality in the use of public funds and communal property;
- conflict over the distribution of rents among powerful groups that, by consolidating rentierism and patrimonialism, reduces investment and economic growth over the long term; and
- short-term and poorly planned government policies.

In addition, these presidentialist governments that serve clientelist social demands are the breeding ground for new forms of sociopolitical conflict because the causes of poverty and marginality are not structurally addressed. Similarly, the significant environmental and social impacts typical of these large-scale extractive activities reduce governability, in turn leading to new repressive action.

As long as inadequate institutional frameworks persist, the environmental, social, political, and even economic costs (related to the use of public power) of containing the confrontations incited by large-scale mining or oil activities (for example) will not be negligible. In addition, the effect of this almost planned social instability on other productive activities in mining regions must be expected. All of these factors require extractivist governments, regardless of their stated ideological affiliations, to respond with authoritarian measures to repress any dissidence.

The effects of these conflicts and violence also impact regional and municipal governments, for example. These bodies can be attracted by the siren songs of companies dedicated to mass extractivism, offering financial contributions. However, sooner or later, these states will have to bear the costs of this complex and conflictive relationship among communities, businesses, and government. Local "development" plans will be jeopardized since mining or oil activities reign supreme, even over justice at times. Thus, it is not surprising that this activity could end up demolishing plans developed by local inhabitants in a participatory and purposeful manner. This issue cannot go unnoticed.

To conclude this point on the impact of the primary-product export mindset on the political life of a country, we should recall that extractivist economies usually severely and irreversibly degrade the natural and social environments in which they function. In the long run, this

---

Box 23.5 Aggression – the umbrella for all extractivism

In Colombia, President Juan Manuel Santos used the figurative "mining locomotive" to symbolize his country's mining-driven journey to the coveted state of "development," attacking any attempt at criticism (in our understanding). Bolivia's Vice President Álvaro García Linera gave a speech laced with attacks and insults but without substantiation, and he did not hesitate to label the critics of extractivism "green Trotskyites." Something similar occurred with Ecuadoran President Rafael Correa, who described opponents of extractive activities as "childish ecologists or indigenists." Correa said, "we have lost too much time for development; we don't have a second to lose […] those who delay us are the same demagogues that say no to mining, no to oil; we waste all our time discussing nonsense. Listen, in the United States, they'd say get out of here with that nonsense; in Japan, they'd put them in an insane asylum."

The truth is that these government leaders, who assume the role of the Holy Inquisition to protect the extractivist faith (propped up by the infallible experts of the extractivist inner sanctum), have no credible arguments when they attack the heretics (the theologians who defend "the true religion") but instead use caricatures, threats, and dismissive rhetoric against opponents, thus preventing a more insightful debate.

In short, the neoliberal rulers and the "progressives" cling similar to castaways to a single lifeline: comparative advantage as a basic reference point for all economies specializing in producing and exporting raw materials. In fact, they adopt this ideological vision similar to a theology, regardless of its predatory consequences for human beings and nature. They defend a consumerist ideology, with the market as the sole regulatory instrument of socioeconomic relationships, with exploitation and domination as their *raison d'être*. In addition, "progressive," or neoliberal governments, with their various formal nuances, are both fervent believers in the religion of economic growth (which has capitalist accumulation as its foundation). All of these issues poison the environment and somehow obscure a clearer vision of the path to follow to attain a dignified and harmonious life for all human beings and for human beings with nature.

degradation can generate economic, social, and environmental problems that can cause irreversible problems if a new export product is not found that can replace the products in crisis. These problems range from the depletion of several nonrenewable resources (and even renewable ones) to declines in public welfare, and all these issues lead to various types of violence.

Understanding the main pathologies of these curses

To address so many curses, one must fully understand the problems to be solved and the capabilities available to tackle them. Let us seek to understand, then, the pathologies of the economies upon which their governments and dominant elites have laid their bets; these wagers prioritize the extraction and export of natural resources – an option that has become practically indisputable.

To remain grounded in reality with some key points, noted here are several of these pathologies that are the outcomes of this accumulation scheme, which feeds and empowers itself in vicious circles that are progressively more pernicious. This interpretation is complemented by the approach offered by Gudynas (2015) on "extractivism spill-over," which is sometimes confused with oil spills or mining effluent, for example.

- It is normal for these economies to experience a series of "diseases," particularly "Dutch disease" (Schuldt 1994). The abrupt and massive influx of foreign currency overvalues the exchange rate, and the local currency loses competitiveness, with adverse effects on the manufacturing and agricultural export sectors. When the real exchange rate appreciates, resources shift from the secondary sector to nontradable segments and to the booming primary-product export activities or areas affected by the boom. This movement distorts the economy by reducing investment funds that could be directed toward the very sectors that provide the greatest added value, more employment, greater technical progress, and linkage effects.
- In the long term, specialization in the export of primary goods has been a negative strategy due to the trend of declining terms of trade. This decline positively affects imports of industrial goods and negatively affects exports of primary goods. The reasons for this decline include that primary goods have low income elasticity, they can be substituted by synthetics, they do not have any monopoly power due to their low technological contribution and level of innovation (they are commodities – their prices are established mainly by market perception), the trends of reduced raw material content of manufactured products, etc. These trends prevent any widespread sharing in the rewards provided by worldwide economic growth and technical progress by countries specializing in the export of highly homogeneous goods.
- The high profitability of primary goods, due to the substantial differential or Ricardian rents (derived from nature's bounty rather than human effort), leads to their overproduction, which can even result in "impoverishing growth," as previously mentioned. In addition, these rents – when the corresponding royalties or taxes are not collected – lead to excess profits that further distort the country's resource allocations, hence the importance of "nationalizing oil," at least when it is intended as a redistribution of the extraordinary profits and oil revenues acquired by these companies.
- The volatility of raw materials prices in global markets has caused the primary-product exporting economies to suffer recurring problems with the balance of payments and fiscal accounts, resulting in heavy dependence on external financing and causing unpredictable fluctuations in domestic economic and sociopolitical activities. All of these factors are

aggravated when prices fall in international markets, and the balance of payments crisis deepens. This critical situation is exacerbated by the massive flight of foreign capital that entered the country to profit from the boom years, along with the flight of local capital, intensifying external constraints and the pressure to resort to debt.

- The boom in primary exports also attracts the ever-vigilant international banks, which freely disburse loans during the boom years as if it were a sustainable process. This financing has been received with open arms by government leaders and businessmen, who believe in permanent miracles. In such circumstances, the overproduction of primary resources accelerates, increasing the distortions in economic sectors. However, most importantly, as past experience has shown, the future of the economy is mortgaged when the inevitable time comes to start repaying the massive amounts of external debt contracted during the export euphoria, and logically, this debt service becomes even more onerous when export prices fall.

- Several times, the abundance of external resources fueled by the flow of oil or mineral exports created a boom in consumerism with the aforementioned impacts. Resources were then wasted when domestically produced products were substituted by imported products, driven by the exchange overvaluation resulting from the massive influx of foreign currency. If appropriate measures are not undertaken, more investment and higher public spending encourage imports instead of domestic production. In the end, experience has taught us that there is no suitable use for the abundant resources that have been made available.

- This experience also shows us and confirms that extractivism does not generate the dynamic linkages necessary for the proper functioning of the economy. No reliable forward or backward integrating and synergistic links are established, and final demand (consumption and fiscal) cannot be assured. Even less likely is the facilitated and guaranteed transfer of technology and the distribution of externalities to benefit other branches of the country's economy. This failure produces the classic feature of our primary-product exporting economies, even during colonial times: its enclave characteristics, with extractivism usually segregated from the rest of the economy.

- Closely related to the above, the companies that control the exploitation of nonrenewable natural resources as enclaves become powerful (parastatal) business entities within relatively weak nation states due to their location and methods of exploitation. As soon as the nation-state model weakens, the "deterritorialization" of the state begins. The state neglects the oil or mining enclaves, leaving (for example) the fulfillment of social demands by the extraction companies, which leads to disorganized and unplanned management of these regions, which often even operate outside the reach of the laws of the country. All of these factors establish an atmosphere of widespread violence and growing marginality that leads to short-sighted and clumsy responses from a police state that does not fulfill its social and economic obligations.

- The low demand for labor and the inequitable distribution of income and assets lead to an apparent dead end on both sides: the marginal sectors, with higher capital productivity than modern sectors, do not grow because they lack the resources to invest; and the modern sectors, with higher labor productivity, do not invest because they lack the domestic markets that can ensure attractive returns. In turn, these conditions diminish the availability of technical resources, a skilled workforce, infrastructure, and foreign currency, thereby discouraging investors and so on. In other words, the structural heterogeneity of these productive apparatuses becomes more pronounced (Pinto 1970).

- Added to these factors is the quite obvious fact (unfortunately necessary for reasons other than technological ones) that, unlike other economic sectors, extractive activity (particularly mining and oil) uses little (although well paid) direct and indirect labor. It is also intensive in capital and imports, hires highly qualified (often foreign) managers, uses foreign inputs and technology almost exclusively, etc. Therefore, the "internal value of the return" (equal to the added value that is retained in country) of the primary-product export activity is laughable. This fact generates new social tensions, in which these natural resources are extracted since there are usually very few people in these areas who can join the workforces of mining and oil companies. Further, in monocultures, in which much labor is still used, labor relations are very unsteady and even have practices with semislavery characteristics.

- The increasing concentration and centralization of income and wealth, in addition to political power, in the hands of a few, are byproducts of primary-product exports. Transnational companies benefit the most from these activities, and they attain "merit" for assuming the risk that accompanies the exploration and exploitation of these resources. There is no mention of how this process leads to a greater "denationalization" of the economy, partly due to the financing needed to reach the point of resource exploitation, partly due to the lack of an established domestic entrepreneurial sector, and to no less extent, partly due to the government's unwillingness to form strategic alliances with local entrepreneurs. Moreover, some transnational corporations have unfortunately taken advantage of their contributions to the balance of trade by attempting to influence the balance of power in the country, constantly threatening governments that dare to swim against the tide.

- In these enclave economies, the political structure and dynamics are characterized by "rentierism," greed, and authoritarianism of decisions made in the oil business. Greed pushes public spending to disproportionate heights through discretionary fiscal management practices. This "greed effect" is seen in the desperate pursuit and abusive appropriation of significant portions of the surpluses generated by the export sector or by the state providing compensation. The politically powerful plunder these surpluses, even resorting to corrupt means, all to remain in power.

- This type of extractivist economy degrades the natural and social environment in which it operates, despite some company efforts to minimize pollution, as well as the efforts of the sociologists and anthropologists that they hire to establish "friendly" relationships with the communities. This process provokes increasing reactions from the affected communities, which are increasingly repressed by governments and extractivist companies.

Although these pathologies are well known after so many decades of dependence on this type of extractive activity, there remain very few effective responses. Perhaps the most noteworthy thing to emerge in recent years is the creation of some stabilization funds, the effectiveness of which depends on the persistence of low raw material prices in the global market. What is absolutely clear is that dependence on extractivism has increased, in countries with both neoliberal and "progressive" governments. All of these governments have embarked upon a new crusade of development and extractivism.

However, that is not all; there is more going on in the background. With extractivism comes serious socio-environmental impacts. A mining pit, for example, has serious impacts on nature since it is a figurative, forcible amputation that prevents the reproduction and realization of life itself. In most cases, these extractive activities completely disregard the existence, sustenance, and renewal of nature's life cycles, structures, functions, and evolutionary processes. They deny nature's right of renewal and restoration. As we know so well, all of these activities can lead to the extinction of species, the destruction of ecosystems, or the permanent alteration of natural cycles.

Nevertheless, despite the enormous weight of the arguments against primary-product export accumulation, there is a new positioning of this activity that could be the real curse. The curse might be the inability to face the challenge of developing alternatives to the primary-product export accumulation, which seems to persist despite its unmistakable failures.

New horizons of freedom for overcoming so many curses

Someone – whether in bad faith or in ignorance – might be captivated by the following hallucinatory idea: if the primary-product export economy generates and perpetuates "underdevelopment", the solution would be to halt natural resource exploitation. Obviously, this idea is a fallacy. In the words of Joseph Stiglitz, "the natural resource curse is not a matter of fate but a matter of choice" (2006). This curse should be, at very least, a democratic choice that establishes the bases to drive transition processes that free us from the bonds of extractivism without risk to life, regardless of the reason.

There are powerful interests that want to remain us on this dead-end road, and the challenge lies precisely in promoting change in new directions, with concrete solutions that are not mere copies of other situations that might have been successful.

To achieve this, we need alliances and consensus that provide answers from the inside out, taking greater advantage of local and national capacities, including those that offer regional integration based on a vision inspired by autonomous regionalism and not by the open regionalism proposed by neo-liberals. While it is not the focus of this chapter, especially because of space, it remains necessary to encourage discussions about the *democratic construction* of solutions that transform important natural resources into levers for greater well-being, overcoming the "curse of plenty" that repeatedly produces underdevelopment.

Overcoming these curses will not occur overnight. Transition strategies are needed that can be implemented even while natural resources continue to be extracted – resources that in some way bring about this "curse of plenty." During this transition, there will still be latent risks of dependence on these activities, perpetuating the colonial features of raw material exporters (when emerging from extractivism, we will have to bear its shortcomings for a while longer).

Successful emergence from extractivism will depend on the consistency of the alternative strategy that challenges extractivism and other curses that have kept us wandering around the capitalist labyrinth (Acosta and Brand 2017). Success will depend on the degree of societal support for these strategies, especially those inspired by visions of a civilizing change that compels us to seek alternatives to development, such as those proposed in *Buen Vivir* (Acosta 2017).

These factors demand a sweeping, comprehensive transformation, conceived and executed based on the protection of human rights and the rights of nature.

Notes

1 This term can cause confusion in Brazil since it is often used to describe conservation activities, such as the sustainable extraction of the Amazonian Brazil nut.
2 There are several writers who have developed this "tropical fatalism", such as: Michel Gabin and Ricardo Hausmann (1998); Michel L. Ross (1999) and (2001), whose works are considered classics in the field; Jeffrey Sachs (2000), who is key to understanding geographical determinism; Ricardo Hausmann and Roberto Rigobon (2002), who made a theoretical contribution on the curse of natural resources.
3 There is no shortage of people who contend that underdevelopment is caused by racial, religious, or demographic factors. These arguments do not hold up under serious scrutiny.

4 For a better understanding of the historical background of the underdevelopment that is the foundation of world power, consider Aníbal Quijano (2001), who asserted that

> the current pattern of world power consists of the articulation between: 1) the coloniality of power – the idea of 'race' as the foundation of the universal pattern of basic social classification and social domination; 2) capitalism, as a universal pattern of social exploitation; 3) the state as a universal and central form of control of collective authority, and the modern nation-state as its hegemonic variant; and 4) Eurocentrism as the main form of subjectivity/inter-subjectivity, particularly in generating knowledge.

5 Norway was already a "developed" capitalist country when it began to export oil and had the socio-economic conditions and robust democratic institutions to manage substantial revenue sustainably. It is clear that the "responsible" management of hydrocarbon-related activity in this country does not eliminate the impacts on nature. However, an important industry for manufacturing the equipment used in extractive activities has indeed developed.

Bibliography

Acosta, A. 1994. *La deuda eterna – Una historia de la deuda externa ecuatoriana.* Colección Ensayo, Libresa, Quito.

Acosta, A. 2009. *La maldición de la abundancia.* CEP, Swissaid y Abya–Yala. Quito.

Acosta, A. 2016. Las dependencias del extractivismo – Aporte para un debate incompleto. *Revista Aktuel Marx* No. 20. Nuestra América y la Naturaleza, Santiago de Chile.

Acosta, A. 2017. *El Buen Vivir Sumak Kawsay, una oportunidad para imaginar otros mundos,* ICARIA, Barelona.

Acosta, A. and Brand, U. (2017). *Salidas del laberinto capitalisa – Decrecimiento Postextractivismo,* ICARIA, Barcelona.

Acosta, A. and Cajas-Guijarro, J. 2017. *Cruda realidad – Corrupción, extractivismos, autoritarismo.* Available at: www.rebelion.org/docs/230588.pdf.

Bhagwati, J. 1958. Immiserizing growth: A geometrical note. *Review of Economic Studies,* Vol. 25, No. 3: 201–205.

Brand, U. and Wissen, M. 2017. *Imperiale Lebensweise – Zur Ausbeutung von Mensch und Natur in Zeiten des globalen Kapitalismus,* Oekom Verlag, München.

Coronil, F. 2002. *El Estado mágico. Naturaleza, dinero y modernidad en Venezuela,* Consejo de Desarrollo Científico y Humanístico de la Universidad Central de Venezuela-Nueva Sociedad, Caracas.

Durand, F. 2006. *La mano invisible en el Estado. Efectos del neoliberalismo en el empresariado y la política,* Desco/FES, Lima.

Gabin, M. and Hausmann, R. 1998. *Nature, development and distributions in Latin America – Evidence on the role of geography, climate and natural resources.* Working Paper No 378, Washington: IDB..

Gudynas, E. 2009. La ecología política del giro biocéntrico en la nueva Constitución del Ecuador. *Revista de Estudios Sociales,* No. 32, Bogotá.

Gudynas, E. 2013. Extracciones, extractivismos y extrahecciones – Un marco conceptual sobre la apropiación de recursos naturales. *Observatorio del desarrollo,* No. 18. Available at: www.extractivismo.com/documentos/GudynasApropiacionExtractivismoExtraheccionesOdeD2013.pdf.

Gudynas, E. 2015. *Extractivismos – Ecología, economía y política de un modo de entender el desarrollo y la Naturaleza,* Claes y CEDIB, Cochabamba.

Gudynas, E. 2017. *Naturaleza, extractivismos y corrupción. Anatomía de una íntima relación,* La Libre, Cochabamba.

Harvey, D. 2004. The "new" imperialism: accumulation by dispossession. *Socialist Register.* Vol. 40: 63–87. Available at: http://socialistregister.com/index.php/srv/article/view/5811/2707#.VigHeyswCfU.

Hausmann, R. and Rigobon, R. 2002. *An alternative interpretation of the "resource curse". Theory and policy implications,* National Bureau of Economic Research, Cambridge.

Kondratieff, N. 1935. The long waves in economic life. *The Review of Economic Statistics,* Vol. XVII, No. 6.

Pinto, A. 1970. Naturaleza e implicaciones de la "heterogeneidad estructural" de la América Latina. *El Trimestre Económico,* Vol. 37, No. 145.

Ross, M. L. 1999. The political economy of the resource curse. *World Politics,* Vol. 51, No. 2.

Ross, M. L. 2001. Does oil hinder democracy? *World Politics*, Vol. 53, No. 3.

Quijano, A. 2001. *Colonialidad del Poder, Globalización y Democracia*. In Tendencias básicas de nuestra era. Instituto de Estudios Internacionales Pedro Gual. Caracas.

Sachs, J. 2000. *Tropical underdevelopment*. CID Working Papers No. 57, Center for International Development at Harvard University.

Schuldt, J. 1994. *La enfermedad holandesa y otros virus de la economía peruana*, Universidad del Pacífico, Lima.

Schuldt, J. 2005. *¿Somos pobres porque somos ricos? Recursos naturales, tecnología y globalización*, Fondo Editorial del Congreso del Perú, Lima.

Schuldt, J. and Alberto, A. 2006. *Petróleo, rentismo y subdesarrollo: ¿Una maldición sin solución?* Nueva Sociedad, No. 204, Buenos Aires.

Stiglitz, J. 2006. *Cómo hacer que funcione la globalización*, Taurus. Madrid.

Watts, M. J. 1999. *Petro-violence. Some thoughts on community, extraction, and political ecology*. Working Papers, Institute of International Studies, University of California, Berkeley.

24
IPE of borders
Between formal and informal regionalisms

Gustavo Matiuzzi de Souza

Introduction

This chapter explores the International Political Economy (IPE) of borders from experiences of the Global South. The dominance of Anglo-Saxon perspectives in the study of IPE has not permitted more nuanced views on its rapport to (inter)national borders. Rationalist accounts on interstate politico-economic relationships, such as realisms and neoliberal institutionalisms, have pervaded the lenses through which one understands borders and borderlands – simply as nation-state fixtures – which entails a limited comprehension of the significant role of borders in the current global order. The prevailing (mis)conception of borders and borderlands as mere politico-geographical components of the intricate interrelations between state and non-state actors can also diminish (or even ignore) the relevance of the multilevel and multifaceted character of such a reality.

Global South, sui-generis regionalisms experiences can contribute to a more comprehensive IPE vis-à-vis the dynamics involving borders and borderlands. Regionalisms of the Global South can confront analytical premises and standpoints not only in traditional social sciences but also in interdisciplinary fields (Shaw et al. 2011) such as IPE. They can present 'specificities, dilemmas, paradoxes, and contradictions of development' (Vivares 2018: 1) that require an attentive eye to data originated from such idiosyncrasies, which recurrently beget diverse outcomes of IPE. In other words, studying the IPE of borders and borderlands of the Global South can demonstrate how multiple facets of the political and economic relations take place within different, yet interconnected, global systems.

Among many peculiarities of borders and borderlands of the Global South, the conspicuousness of informal regionalisms is at the centre stage. Organised crime and the illicit activities across borders, the (mis)use of natural resources and its transnational impacts, and networks of migration and refugee movements are some of the cross-border flows operating within informal grids of the global systems. To do so, informal regionalisms utilise these global spaces of ambiguous complementarity (i.e. borders and borderlands) to function and expand their networks. They exist within and beyond the formal international structures and are manifested in diversified ways at borders.

Söderbaum (2010), by analysing micro-regional dynamics in borderlands of Southern Africa, recognises connections between formal policies and informal economies, in which corruption, financial and structural state deficiencies, as well as the institutional deficit of the state substantiated the existence of a 'shadow regionalism', one that permitted the spread of informal networks and illegal ventures across borders. By revealing a looser distinction between formal and informal systems, shadow regionalism also shows the connections between local and transnational realities and a less optimistic understanding on the nature of regionalisms (generally displayed by mainstream scholarship as positive).

Formal strategies concerning borders and borderlands of the Global South mainly focus on development, security, and defence. Constructed as local, national, or regional projects, states engender border policies to maintain a degree of control over cross-border flows while producing conditions to achieve practical objectives within their territory. As public policies, formal plans are, in most cases, top-down strategies with little or no connections to local realities of borders and borderlands. On the other hand, Global South borders and borderlands present specificities of their own that are exploited by a myriad of informal exchanges that are only visible from a bottom-up perspective. Such informal cross-border dynamics, besides providing sustenance for underprivileged local populations – also connect to segments of the international systems, not rarely by illegal networks.

Box 24.1 Formal and informal relationships in Global South borders and borderlands

Borders are central elements of the current global order. Their porosity reveals connections between formal and informal actors, networks, and processes. The local level of borderlands uncovers global systems of cross-border flows. Shadow regionalism shows the connections among state and non-state actors operating cross-border networks.

Corruption opens state boundaries, allowing the movement of illegal and/or irregular goods and persons transnationally. Transnational crime spreads using corruption and bribery, weakening state capabilities of securing and controlling territory.

The role of kinship in forming hard-to-trace networks across borders is key in the spread of transnational crime. Family, ethnic, and amicable ties connect bordering countries as well as local populations to high-level officials.

The misuse of natural resources reveals the disregard of their cross-border nature and impacts local relations, producing conflicts across borderlands with limited resources. The institutional and governance vacuum in providing public services are also a conflict factor.

An idea of industrialisation and development that neglect local realities is evident in national and regional projects that aim at increasing agricultural and electricity production in borderlands without delivering basic public needs and destroying the environment.

Market demands for cheap labour and access to natural resources has been responded by state actors with deregulation and lenience, affecting the quality of life of workers, damaging the environment, and producing masses of illegal immigrants.

Domestic and international conflicts have generated flows of forced migrants and refugees, which flee to border departments of adjacent countries. The proximity to the border is usually followed by cross-border conflicts, terrorist activities and profound social and economic difficulties within and without refugee camps.

(Matiuzzi De Souza 2018a)

Regionalisms and borders are social constructs interwoven in functional and conceptual realities, both elements of the same multiescalar global systems and spatial components in which and through which actors interrelate 'in a much more complex, multi-layered, interconnected system of manifold networks' (Matiuzzi de Souza 2018b: 256). The IPE of borders from experiences of the Global South entails a global understanding of the multifaceted nature of regionalisms; a wider view on the exchanges, actors, and processes – beyond and/or behind the formal structures of power, of the state, and of the organisations; an emphasis on the relationship between the formal and informal structures and actors operating at the borders and/or border regions; a multilevel perspective with a bottom-up approach.

This chapter provides a brief exploration on the nodes between formal and informal regionalisms at borders and within borderlands by analysing how these two distinct modi operandi interact. Three types of cross-border flows are here investigated: transnational crime; the (mis)use of natural resources; and the movements of migrants and refugees. The first section of the chapter develops on the role of borders and borderlands in the global order. The second part analyses the importance of the local level for the formal–informal relationship in borderlands. The third section develops on the relationship nodes that function as bridges between formal and informal regionalisms concerning the three types of cross-border flows. Among many observable nodes, this chapter explores, by examining some cases, the role of corruption and kinship relations vis-à-vis the spreading of transnational crime, the effects of institutional vacuum and an idea of development and industrialisation on cross-border natural resources, and the influence of market demands and conflict on international migratory flows. Final remarks conclude this chapter.

Borders in the global order

In the history of Global South regionalism (particularly the 1945–1990 period) nations aimed, among other things, at reaching development and autonomy in the international system (Matiuzzi de Souza 2018a). States were commonly arranged in regional organisations, while still attempting to regulate their land – and their borders – to their own preservation. Territoriality, a spatial approach in which a state attempts to control and govern people and resources by ruling area through a rationale of geographic space, was applied to categorise social phenomena, to manifest boundaries, and to govern over resources, ideas, people, symbols, and exchanges, always generating borders in terms of boundaries and limits. Vice-versa, borders became mechanisms of territoriality, essential components of the territorial nation-state (Anderson and O'Dowd 1999).

The formal(ising) practices of the state (public policies, agreements, and treaties) produced certain politics embedded in a diverse set of regionalisms. Most of regional cooperation or integration processes had the goal of maintaining the status-quo of the state, being complementary to the boundary function of borders by raising control and power of the state (Malamud 2011). International and regional politics have been playing a significant role in deciding what, for whom, and in which cases and places are transnational movements accepted within state agendas. However, the current global order has been witnessing the continuing upsurge of global flows with speeds and volumes too high to be controlled by state systems once created with this very purpose.

Since the turn of the century, uncertainty and volatility gradually permeated the political and economic interrelations around the globe as well as the traditional mechanisms used by states to control the effects of the deepening of global interdependence. The unavoidable globalisation and the rise of actors and phenomena of global scale evinced the contradictions of this new world order and the fragility of the state system and of its ability to deal with the consequent negative impacts on (inter)national (social, political, and economic) stability (Matiuzzi de Souza 2018b; Sørensen 2016). Borders and borderlands displayed the uncertainties begot by the rise of global exchanges and deep interconnectedness and the concomitant (and persisting) territoriality of the traditional nation-state as well as by the swift modifications in the politico-economic relations within the international systems. Such deepening changes in the global structures of power and production revealed an alteration in the spatial logics of the IPE of borders.

The rapid increase of flows of goods, capital, workforce, and technology, while providing social and economic development, also created the necessity of new regulations and new forms of governance. Global economy began to organise itself in dissimilar (bigger and/or smaller) scales according to the requirements of capital circulation, triggered by recurrent crises and the subsequent search for new spatial substitutes. Borders and borderlands have been thus peripheralised (Sparke 2002: 205–206). The marginal position of the Global South in the production system as supplier of raw materials and provider of low-skilled workers exacerbated the marginalised function of borders and borderlands of underdeveloped countries. In the mid-1990s, the functional role of borders and borderlands within the global production system was restricted to facilitating infrastructure development and providing local action to solve transboundary issues, particularly by state actors but also by market and societal players. On the other hand, the increasing interdependence of global transactions made economic flows operate simultaneously in small and global scales, which consolidated borders and borderlands as sub-systems of the global production and/or as hubs or corridors to exploit jurisdictional differences and economic complementarity.

The transfer of state power to different scales (trans/subnational), and the integrative movement of global systems promoted the development of many types of cross-border regions all around the world. Some borderlands emerged as scalar articulations, some as discourse and/or identity hubs, and some as (formal or informal) governance settings (Perkmann and Sum 2002). Progressively, borders and borderlands evolved into a *complex of connexions between global contexts and local realities* – spatial components of international flows and core mechanisms of global networks. The local level of cross-border exchanges became increasingly germane to the construction of the (current) global order as well as the multilevel actors and connections that produced such indispensable microregions.

For this reason, when looking at the local level of borders and borderlands, the global is unfolded. Hence, these cross-border regionalisms cannot be considered solely politico-economic practices within marginalised spaces. Mattheis, Raineri, and Russo (2018: 2) call attention to the fact that the location of borders 'at the fringes of formal constructions such as nation states, regional organisations or jurisdictions enable these borderlands to establish their own economic, social and political realities' that reveal the intricate societal tissue of a global order, in which 'the cross-border practices of non-state actors, informal institutions rooted in states' peripheries, and alternative, overlapping sources of legitimacy and identity' (ibid: 2) not only build regions but are key processes of the global reality. Local, national, and transnational (formal and informal) politico-economic processes and actors, their relations, and their functioning roles vis-à-vis cross-border flows and mechanisms need to be at the heart of any analysis concerning the IPE of borders of the present global order.

The importance of local level

Two opposite spatial processes are manifest when investigating cross-border flows. On the one hand, economic and populational movements trying to surpass borders; on the other hand, (inter) state politics attempting to secure them. As Van Schendel (2005: 40) has put it, 'If flows stand for the fluid, the spatially elusive, the underworld, then the border symbolises the solid, the territorial, the ordered, the rule of law'. The escalation of cross-border flows (and the inefficient responses used by states to fight them) undermined the hard notion of border as separation and control, rendered space to the filtering capabilities of the border, and can be understood as components of multi-layered, intricate systems (Matiuzzi de Souza 2018b). The paramount reality of borders and borderlands – multilevel, interconnected, and integral parts of a complex macrosystem – suggests that the current global order has become much less territorial than what states (and mainstream scholarship) tend to believe. As Vivares (2018: 337) recognises, in the current 'globalised neoliberal economy and institutional order, regions have become less attached to [traditional, statist] spaces and more to cross-border institutional settings, underground work, and virtual networks'.

The coexistence of formal and informal networks that are integral parts of both bigger systems and local realities is the main characteristic of Global South borders and borderlands. Informality, besides being the most common modus vivendi of border communities to circumvent economic and social limitations (frequent condition at local-level realities), can also be understood as a countermovement in response to the inability of the state system to deal with the challenges of a global international economy and its socio-political corollaries (Hart 2006). The co-occurrence of the two types of exchange is not only a visible feature in borderlands, but also a requirement for them to exist and to be functionally useful within the global economic grids, being sui-generis global spaces, in which transnational flows are both products of local and global interactions and of formal and informal regionalisms.

However, understanding the complexities of the IPE of borders involves more than the mere recognition of the coexistence and complementation of formal and informal regionalisms. Although it may appear, prima facie, that both systems constantly dispute political and economic power in a transnational space, understanding formal–informal relationship only as a dichotomy offers the risk of oversimplification. The empirical observation of Global South borders and borderlands indicates that such relational nodes are much more intricate, and the differences between formal and informal regionalisms are not as clear as one can imagine, as the limits between their structures and relations are blurred. As previously seen, the study of micro-regional processes in borderlands of Southern Africa by Söderbaum (2010: 9), identifies the relationship between formal policies and informal economies, recurrently linked by government officials through a myriad of corruption mechanisms. In his 'shadow regionalism', financial and structural state deficiencies (as well as its power deficit, i.e. 'failed states') alongside a corrupted framework, facilitated and frequently sponsored the advance of informal exchanges and networks, fostering illegalities.

Box 24.2 Defining formal, informal, and shadow regionalisms

Formal regionalisms are state-driven processes focused on institution-building and following a politico-economic outline. Regional organisations, international agencies, bilateral/trilateral agreements, non-governmental organisations (NGOs), national legislations and state policies are part of formal structures of power and production.

Informal regionalisms are created within, beyond, despite or because of the state. They can be spontaneous or organised, local, regional or global. They are frequently illegal and function as a parallel system made possible by the connections established with formal actors.

Shadow regionalism is the rapport between formal and informal regionalism, a complex of nodes formed by a corrupted framework and exploiting local and regional underdevelopment as well as state financial, material and institutional limitations.

(De Lombaerde et al. 2010; Matiuzzi De Souza 2018a; Söderbaum 2010; 2011)

Formal regionalisms represent state-driven processes, focused on institution-building and following a politico-economic agenda; informal regionalisms, on the other hand, are developed beyond, despite or because of the state and its regulations, independent of international organisations, spontaneous or organised, and recurrently illegal (De Lombaerde et al. 2010; Matiuzzi de Souza 2018a; Söderbaum 2011). Shadow regionalism (and its simultaneously micro- and multilevel approach) reveals the once unobtrusive connections among formal and informal actors and processes, the nodes by which borders and borderlands are socially constructed. Formal–informal nodes are multilevel, interconnected, and overlapping, pervading all areas of socio-economic and political relations among states and domestically, affecting regional settings and global systems. They are transnational social constructions that link formal and informal actors and networks, which execute and manage cross-border flows, policies, and processes. By providing alternative, informal paths for cross-border exchanges, such nodes are also the breaches in the limitation and regulation mechanisms of the state, being one of the main causes for the porosity of borders and for political instability and persisting social hardship of borderlands' populations. The focus on shadow regionalism, that is, on the nodes between formal and informal international political economies, allows us to see borders and borderlands of the Global South as significant micro-representations of the ambiguous complementarity between innumerable informal and formal arrangements of the global politico-economic systems.

The rapid increase of the global drug trade and of organised crime and other illicit cross-border activities, of the (trans)national (mis)use of natural resources and its outcomes, and of the macroscale migration and refugee flows are some of the developments that (not solely) Global South states are required to manage in terms of territory and consequently of borders. These experiences figure as negative aspects of regionalisms (usually presented as naturally positive by prevailing literature). Present processes and updated figures demonstrate that state control of territory and spatial dynamics is/has always been very limited in the face of informal transnational exchanges and networks, affecting governance in local, national, regional, and global scales. Inadequate material and institutional capacities make Global South states more vulnerable as institutions and less powerful to regulate and control transnational fluxes, either by means of domestic policymaking or by engendering regional arrangements.

This indicates that the current global order entails that borders and borderlands remain fluid insofar as it has been constructed on a basis of transnational exchanges and cross-border flows using relational nodes between formal and informal regionalisms. Studying the IPE of borders from experiences of the Global South requires, therefore, decentralising the analytical emphasis from strictly formal, state-led region-building processes (in which states are at the centre and borders occupy the periphery) to a more embracing framework that allows the analysis on the linkages between the formal and the informal, on regionalisms that stem outside of the traditional centres of political and economic power and are constructed by entangled webs of cross-border activities. It is necessary to look at borders and borderlands, to understand them as spaces in which the formal and informal coexist – sometimes embracing and making use of formal(ising) practices, sometimes fighting state structural power (and not rarely using state fragilities), and sometimes complementing each other's necessities.

Formal–informal nodes

Borders and borderlands of the Global South are subject to many institutional agendas that attempt to regulate and control informal flows and networks as well as suppress illegalities and criminal activities. Most policies, regional plans, and/or formal networks are, nevertheless, built more in response to contingent domestic and/or global pressures rather than as a proactive governance strategy. Common to all current political projects is the fact that cross-border dynamics cannot be neglected, as they have been in the history of formal interrelations. Another recurrent strategy is the attempt to deal with informal flows by means of building regional cooperation to achieve security, development, and a more effective governance.

Regional policy-building is thus among the major approaches by which formal actors, institutions and processes relate to cross-border dynamics. Several groups have been experimenting with regional and international cooperation concerning borders and borderlands. In Asia, the Central Asia Regional Economic Cooperation Program (CAREC), the Association of South East Asian Nations (ASEAN), and the South Asian Association for Regional Cooperation (SAARC) engendered dozens of programmes and agreements on cross-border crime and terrorism, labour, electricity, human security, and many other themes (Gordon 2009; Singh et al. 2018). In Latin America, the Southern Common Market (MERCOSUR), the Andean Community, and the Central American Integration System (CAIS) signed arrangements on health, security, education, labour, and other areas of development to concomitantly foster regional cooperation in borderlands (Oddone and Matiuzzi de Souza 2017; Rhi-Sausi and Oddone 2013). In Africa, the African Union (AU), the Economic Community of West African States (ECOWAS), and the West African Economic and Monetary Union (UEMOA) constructed programmes to fight drug routes expansion, terrorist activities, and social and economic underdevelopment both inter-regionally and within each organisation, promoting and regulating cross-border exchanges (OECD/SWAC 2017). Bilateral and trilateral agreements and or/ agendas are too numerous to be listed but are significant political concertations that reveal the growing importance of borders and borderlands in the regional and global scenes.

Nevertheless, the effectiveness of such regional policies is to be contested, to say the least. Borders and borderlands of the Global South remain vulnerable in political, economic, human, and security terms. Border populations live in poor conditions. Poverty indeed plays a crucial role in furthering informality and shady activities at the local level of borderlands. States continue failing in offering public services and goods. Illegal flows persist on increasing. Material, institutional, and political limitations are key factors that encourage the creation of links between formal and informal networks that allow cross-borders networks based on informal flows and relationships and on socio-economic (and sometimes political) webs to thrive.

Such connections, this chapter will demonstrate, are entwined with locals' necessities of survival and state weaknesses. The examples are multiple. The Karakoro Basin, in the Malian–Mauritanian borderlands, holds substantial cross-border informal trade of cattle, cereal, hand-crafted products, and medical supplies, with strong social interaction between local communities. The Malian and Mauritanian governments, the ECOWAS, the Sahel and West Africa Club (SWAC) of the OECD, and the GRDR Africa (a local NGO) launched the Karakoro Initiative, a joint programme created to regulate such cross-border activities (Bolouvi and Trémolières 2009), with virtually no success. Without such exchanges, given the low social and economic conditions of both countries, local populations at the Karakoro Basin would struggle even more to survive. Both national economies rely on such informal flows, which represent a substantial share of the commerce within and between the two countries. More importantly, the borderlands also form an important corridor for food security and the most important local resource for poverty reduction. Although formal institutions attempt to regulate and control such flows, they also depend on informal exchanges to maintain a level of social cohesion at the local and regional levels. Any disruption on the informal processes can potentially undermine the national governments and the regional stability.

The Argentina–Brazil–Paraguay tri-border area (the most populous borderland of South America) is a complex of interwoven social and commercial networks among local and transnational populations that extrapolate the limits of the border area. The informal flows for subsistence include small-scale smuggling and the commerce of non-durable goods. Such cross-border movements, however, are also used by individuals and local criminal syndicates to implements illegal routes of tobacco and agrochemicals (contraband), and arms and narcotics (drug trafficking and terrorism), among other products (electronics, car parts, etc.). The three neighbouring countries have responded with security and integration policies concomitantly (mainly through MERCOSUR), attempting to foster regional commerce and political ties by investing in cross-border infrastructure and education and culture policies while keeping control over their territories and suppressing violence escalation with the use of the military and ad hoc joint forces (Renoldi 2015), which were proven to be ineffective in face of such illicit ventures. The informal and illegal exchanges were estimated to represent almost half of Paraguayan gross domestic product (GDP) in 2010 (Pinheiro-Machado 2011) and were the basis of the structural organisation of the towns within the borderlands, including subsistence of local populations, concentration of front companies, transportation infrastructure, populational gathering, and land use.

These anecdotes describe how informal networks and formal structures of power and production are intertwined within the countries of the Global South insofar as they depend upon each other to keep running, at the local, national, and regional levels. In the examples, regional security and national economies depend heavily on informal systems and cross-border networks to remain at minimum requirements, indicating the weight of state deficiency on the prevalence of shadow regionalism in the Global South. The formal–informal nodes are social mechanisms that both (re)produce this dependence and respond to the needs of populations and state itself. Among many observable nodes, this chapter will explore the role of corruption and kinship relations vis-à-vis the spreading of transnational crime, the effects of institutional vacuum and the search for development and industrialisation on cross-border natural resources, and the influence of market demands and conflict on international migratory flows.

Transnational crime: corruption and kinship

Organised crime is a reality in all regions of the globe. It is a compound of enterprises concentrated in illegal activities that can range from theft, fraud, drug trade, prostitution, to loan-sharking, gambling, smuggling, money-laundering and human-trafficking, among many other unlawful practices (Augustyn et al. 2019). Increasingly transnational, criminal syndicates and flows concentrate much of its activities and resources within borderlands with the objective of crossing state boundaries towards a worldwide market. The unique combination of structural and geopolitical elements makes most Global South borders and borderlands vulnerable in two correlated aspects: borderlands (and national territories, for that matter) are typically vast and borders are extremely permeable (Grant 2008; Moulaye 2014). For example, the lack of institutional power and consequently of control and security in borderlands of Guinea-Bissau, Kenya, and Nigeria (to the extent of being called 'ungoverned spaces') made such regions easy targets for drug traders and other organised illicit activities (Klantschnig, Dimova, and Cross 2016).

Global South borders and borderlands are indeed used by criminal groups as a key spatial resource. Prabhakar (2012) demonstrates how the organised crime employ borders and borderlands to finance, expand, and manage illegal activities. She describes, for instance, the process of smuggling of goods and persons across borders as an important source of income for the Federally Administered Tribal Areas (FATA) in the border of Pakistan and Afghanistan. This borderland has become a central harbour for al-Qaida fugitives and Taliban forces. The (originally) US-based criminal organisation MS-13 also raised funds by escorting persons across US borders, making connections with other organised groups in Mexico and in the Gulf. Investigations show how drug lords and Hezbollah members used the free-trade zone in the Argentina–Brazil–Paraguay tri-border region to raise and launder money by smuggling stolen and falsified products into Paraguay and selling them in their shops. The collecting of 'taxes' from other smugglers by such groups is also an important source of revenue.

Another example is the Maputo Corridor, linking Southern Mozambique with Eastern South Africa – a primarily informal cross-border region, in which migration flows and informal trading are widespread as are socio-ethnic relations. The exchange of illegal armaments is usual and is part of a booming market in the region, making criminality rates and the presence of organised criminal groups escalate. Smuggling of many types, theft, drug trafficking, money forgery, and cattle raiding are among the main criminal practices of such syndicates. The Maputo Corridor rapidly became an important narcotics route, making the region prosper and bringing investment to the Mozambican economy by the spending of drug money. Collusion between state officials and criminal groups through many forms of corruption and bribery involve policing agencies, border officers, high state representatives, and politicians (Söderbaum and Taylor 2008).

Simply put, [c]orrupt countries tend to have porous borders' (Warf 2019: 5). Less corrupt countries also have problems in securing and controlling their borders, but nations in which corruption is widespread are likely to have very permeable borders, which facilitates and encourages the expansion of informal exchanges. The 'contagion effect' is also an issue. Matters related to crime and corruption may expand to neighbouring countries as illegal networks increase in the direction of consumer markets for their illicit products (Samir Kassab and Rosen 2019). This is typically the case when borderlands become transnational corridors and in regions where countries suffer from weak institutions.

The payment of bribery by criminal syndicates at borderlands are key to creating and maintaining transnational corridors of illicit goods. In the Maputo Corridor, bribery habitually assumes the form of 'informal duties', with lower rates than official customs obligations. The use of falsified documents with the connivance of customs bureaucrats help shipments be exempted from duty, as if they were in transit to Zambia or Zimbabwe was also frequent. Large-scale customs schemes revealed connections between important Mozambican enterprises and high-level politicians, which would involve nearly half of the country's imports in the 1990s (Harrison 1999). In US–Mexico borderlands, police officers with large drug apprehensions were given lucrative positions along border corridors of narcotics. In key postings, they remained confiscating drugs to keep successful records while regulating the volume of seizures that occurred under their responsibility, 'enough to make it look like they are accomplishing something, but not enough to eat into the drug traffickers' profit margins' (Nagle 2010: 102).

The complicit relations between criminal organisations and state officials fuelled by corruption and bribery produces a parallel power that weakens state capabilities in fighting illegal networks. It connects shadowy business to formal institutions and promotes non-orthodox regionalisation processes. The presence of organised syndicates and wide-spread corruption in transnational corridors indicates that besides actors and groups created originally to practice criminal activities, other actors with formal functions of order and control (as the state or security agencies) are used for illicit endeavours. Truth is, transnational crime cannot happen on such a magnitude without the involvement of corrupt bureaucrats.

Besides corruption, the role of kin-like relationships in the criminal cross-border activities deserves attention, as it lies in the construction of production and power (local) networks and in the creation of small and medium family enterprises engaged in crossing illegal products and/or committing other transnational offences. In the Brazil–Bolivia borderlands, drug trafficking initiated as small family businesses that participated in retail and wholesale of narcotics by a dis-tribution system across neighbourhoods, with little dispute over territories. Brazilian family groups were shown to have easier access to Bolivian drug producers through amicable relations and to be harder to detect, as they operated in ordinary family homes. With the arrival of large drug syndicates (such as the PCC), these organisations have extensively become branches of a larger structure (Oliveira and Villela Lima da Costa 2012). Nowadays, the transnational links of the PCC is known to reach the most important Italian mafia ('Ndrangheta), being responsible for a network that feeds the drug market of Africa, Asia, and Europe with Colombian and Bolivian narcotics (Anesi et al. 2018).

Kinship organisations also have worked as facilitators within exchange networks, building trust among cautious participants and providing a more fluid system for transnational crime (Kenney 2007). On the Chinese–Burman borderlands, family ties were important for leasing land that were extensively used to cultivate opium and for controlling certain areas close to the borderline (Chin and Zhang 2015). In the illegal timber trade system in Vietnamese–Lao bor-derlands, corruption mechanisms and the organisation of the whole commercial structure depended heavily on 'kin-like relationships, friendships, and the maintenance of trust through social rituals and tributes' (To et al. 2014: 171) to the extent that financial transactions alone were not enough to make it work.

In most cases, such familial criminal syndicates were dispersed along the border, utilising the vastness of territory to avoid law enforcement. Effective suppression has been unfeasible, par-ticularly because of strong bonds among members and the well-scattered nuclei that composed the larger power and production systems that go all the way up to high-level politicians and entrepreneurs. The poor social conditions of local populations also guarantee that, even if certain families and small groups were dismantled, new actors rose due to the financial opportunities that such activities offer. As Bergman (2018) also recognises, the lack of proper border control in Global South countries lowers the price of illegal goods considerably and involves less soph-istication to trafficking, making Latin American, Asian and African countries important prolif-eration hubs of illegal actors.

Natural resources: institutional vacuum and development

Natural resources are essentially cross-border. Boundaries-forming rivers, wildlife migration, and human activities straddle international borders and affect multiple countries. Resource scarcity, populational growth, persistent poverty, and (global) macroeconomic changes are major influen-cing factors in Global South countries that require cross-border collaboration in dealing with the management of natural resources. Studies (Cooley et al. 2014; Guo 2015) indicate, however, that cross-border resource management involves a high number of actors with little interest on pursu-ing or providing means to cooperation. The existence of two or more political regimes (and environmental legislations) and short-term national/local policymaking strategies convolute the creation of policies that involve neighbouring countries. Although natural resources are shared transnationally, they are not managed cooperatively. Fall (2011) reminds that the power game of the management of transboundary resources is not confined within the limits of the international political arena. Private interests are also part of the environmental equation, by which the global capital has increasingly been exploiting spaces to profit from what once were of exclusive state administration. It is not uncommon that local populations lose control of or access to resources in face of state and capital interests over transnational resources.

Water management (or the lack thereof) is among the most important issues regarding the use of transnational natural resources. The inability to conduct negotiations towards joint water management from state actors is visible. National governments do not have the institutional and/or material means to engender and implement water management strategies; the political pressure to respond to subnational demands for development gets in the way of international/ regional concertation; the political costs for water management policies are higher than short-term political returns, which weakens political will; third-party involvement (i.e. multilateral organisations, NGOs) is a delicate matter in (failed) countries where sovereignty is already in jeopardy; the inexistence of previous cooperation on the matter is also a hindering factor. All of which are requirements for proper construction of cross-border water management (Albrecht et al. 2017).

The absence of state strategies, the disregard by government authorities, and/or the obliviousness towards resources that are both local and transnational creates an institutional vacuum that generates a volatile space, particularly where few natural resources are available. As a result, water conflicts have risen. According to the Pacific Institute (2019) report, from 2000 to 2018, 442 water conflicts took place in the Global South. Most of them were developments of political, ideological, or territorial confrontations with historical roots and not rarely with armed disputes involving militia, paramilitary, formal armies, and terrorist groups. This is mainly the case in the Middle East and North Africa region (MENA) and Sub-Saharan Africa. However, such disputes seldom took place at the fringes of national territories but have a direct impact on water supplies across borders by constructing watercourse blockages, cutting irrigation systems, and destroying water sources. In Central Asia, where most of the major rivers cross international borders, the water conflict has escalated due to the planning, in the beginning of 2010, to build hydropower plants that will affect the water supplies of former Soviet republics of Tajikistan, Kyrgyzstan, Turkmenistan, Kazakhstan, and Uzbekistan. Gas distribution is used as counter-movement by exporting countries to assure their access to water (Gleick and Heberger 2013).

In the study of transboundary aquifers in the Global South, the lack of durable commitment by states, caused by tensions between bordering countries, failed to produce lasting effect at the local level access to water (Nijsten et al. 2018). Groundwater is one of the most important sources of water supply in arid regions. With no 'vertical integration' (i.e. between local and national levels), borderlands suffer from the lack of formal projects able to build institutional capacity to foster equitable resource governance (Albrecht et al. 2017). However, when analysing water conflicts happening exclusively within borderlands, one finds that such clashes involve solely local populations for subsistence. Since the beginning of the century, 13 local water conflicts occurred, usually in borderlands still in dispute and with poor access to streams, wells, or irrigation systems. Six of these conflicts were disputes for water and pasture in the Sub-Saharan Africa involving herders from rival tribes (Pacific Institute 2019). Local water conflicts in borderlands thus indicate a dual-source of confrontation: on the one hand, the lack of an effective state agenda for water security (institutional vacuum); on the other hand, the harsh social and economic conditions of communities of Global South borderlands.

The links between environmental degradation and population displacement are numerous: droughts, floods, water pollution, scarcity – all of them connected to institutional or political instabilities. Again, poverty continues to play a key role in the flows of the so-called environmental refugees. Other factors have been under study in the last decades. With the advance of economic powers into the markets of poor states to exploit or produce, the weight of foreign capital on environmental degradation (and subsequent migratory flows) is becoming more visible. Jorgenson (2006) demonstrates that foreign direct investment (FDI) in manufacturing has a direct effect on environment degradation in less-developed countries. The dependence of poor states on transnational corporations is usually followed by lower environmental standards and laxer regulatory systems, with strong impact on green-house gas emissions and organic water pollution. Tax incentives and a low-paying labour market complement the welcoming package to FDI in Global South countries. The empirical analysis evinces the fact that foreign capital is prone to disregard environmental issues for profits and legislation of Global South countries still lacks accountability mechanisms.

Not surprisingly, industrialisation and the search for development have also become major sources of mishandling of cross-border natural resources. In Bangladesh, the increasing demand for non-agricultural use of land has provoked rural exodus caused by landlessness, unemployment, and falling income. Combined with the misuse of groundwater and rivers, as well as with bad distributive policies (for irrigation) and natural disasters (cyclones, floods), rural populations have sought moving to India, by legal or clandestine means (Alam 2003). On the other hand, the effects of this crisis are originated in India, which, despite pressing demands for environmental regulation aware of the regional ecosystem, particularly in the Indian border state of West Bengal, has not been prone to apply policies that hinder water use by farmers, whose lobbies are politically strong (Mukherji 2006). Almost all Bangladeshi rivers have their springs in India, where they have been diverted or dammed upstream in Indian territory, causing important changes in their hydraulic capacity and in the ecology of the Ganges–Brahmaputra–Meghna Basin, one of the most populated basins in the world (Kawser and Samad 2016).

The Yadana gas pipeline in the borderlands of Burma and Thailand did not provide local villages power supply (despite the promises of government officials), heavy militarisation repressed ethnic populations, damaged locals' land use and degraded the environment – forest areas were devastated, the clearing of vegetation caused erosion and floods. In Laos–Thailand borderlands, the construction of the Nam Theum 2 mega-dam had ignored indigenous voices with a project that affected cross-border environment and local access to fish and agriculture. The dams of the Salween river in Burma–Thailand borderlands were projected with the objective of exporting energy to Thailand despite the risks of destructing the ecological balance of the region, once again overlooking local contexts and needs (Simpson 2007). Energy security as a development strategy commonly disregard the environment as well as the socio-economic necessities of local communities while state actors and business elites take the benefits. A fuzzy idea of development translated into big projects that affect the ecosystems activates cross-border natural disasters and subsequent migratory flows.

Migration and refuge: market demands and conflict

Market demands in more developed countries and poverty/social stagnation in poorer countries fuel labour migration. They also create a node of formal and informal regionalisms within borderlands. The increase of South–South labour migration is made possible by a set of facilitators, agents that profit from migrant flows by helping them cross international borders in legal and illegal ways. These 'merchants of labour' are important intermediaries who shape the movements of migration through the creation of transnational networks. Although formal institutions do provide migration services within legal systems, the significance of informal networks in South–South labour migration is still key in understanding cross-border recruitment processes (Rahman 2017: 81–82).

In Southeast-Asian borderlands (Burma–Thailand, Thailand–Cambodia), capital investments and outsource contracts are numerous due to abundant natural resources and lenient regulations of local governments, which often allow legal and illegal crossing of labourers. Working conditions in most cases are detrimental, with human rights violations and environmental irregularities. Deregulation is the tool local policymakers utilise to sanction the entrance and the stay of a priori illegal (at national level) labour immigrants (Pangsapa and Smith 2008). In China–Vietnam borderlands, Chinese agriculture demands for cheap labour and the pauper conditions of Vietnamese populations have propelled illegal crossings (almost 20,000 in 2016 in the province of Cao Bang alone) despite the danger of such initiatives and of working conditions. Lax control and extensive border provided opportunities to border crossing (*Vietnam News* 2017). In the borderlands of Brazil and Uruguay, even with agreements enabling cross-border citizens to work, study, and reside legally on either side of the border, it is customary to employ labourers 'off the book'. Construction industry, local commerce, and agriculture absorb most irregular workers, which do not receive social security and minimum wages, working in substandard circumstances (Matiuzzi de Souza 2018a). Authorities do not have enough human resources to supervise the hiring of workers, only doing scarce incursions into the main streets and commercial chains.

Borderlands, as subjects of local practices by private-sector, local governments, and community actors, function more as bridges than barriers in response to manufacture and agriculture pressure groups. The power of capital and of market interests over local border policies and cross-border flows opens international borders to labour migration, be it legal or illegal. Lobby, corruption and lack of human and material resources of Global South states are followed by local governments' (or state officials') leniency as well as deregulation of migration laws, working conditions, and border controls.

Domestic and/or international conflicts are also an important source of cross-border flows, particularly of refugees and of forced migrants. Local, national and even transnational actors fight over ethnicity, nationality, religion, political opinion or any type of association to certain groups – conflicts in which social groupings become targets of persecution, flee, and are unable to return (UNHCR 2018b). 'Conflict zones often result in the destruction of markets, habitats, seizure of land and other forms of property, the forced relocations of minority populations (ethnic cleansing) and genocide' (Pangsapa and Smith, 2008: 509). The human impact of some disputes is staggering. In 2017, conflicts in Syria, Afghanistan, South Sudan, Myanmar, and Somalia alone – only five countries – were responsible for two-thirds of all refugees worldwide (roughly 13.5 million). Diseases, malnourishment, and violent regimes accelerated the search for haven. Bordering states (Turkey, Pakistan, Uganda, Lebanon, Iran, Bangladesh, Sudan, Ethiopia, and Jordan) were among the countries that received the greatest number of refugees (Germany was an exception). As the efforts of the UN and other international organisations continued to fail to respond to the increasing demand for shelter (UNHCR 2018b), neighbouring countries faced humanitarian crises and socio-economic challenges in managing such growing flows of refugees.

Borderlands are among the most impacted areas. In Turkish border provinces, what was initiated as the activation of cross-border kinship networks in the beginning of the turmoil escalated in the same proportion of the Syrian conflict. In 2013, an estimate number of 100,000 refugees were living outside of camps. Conditions in these camps remained problematic, but refugees did receive attention by Turkish government, which was not the case elsewhere. This represented a problem not only for refugees, but for local populations and governments, which struggled to provide assistance and integration (Özden 2013). This is the case for all countries bordering Syria. The UN estimates that 'over 70 percent of Syrian refugees who cross international borders self-settle in cities, towns and villages where they have long-established social networks' (Chatty 2016: 21). Aid agencies and the UN are not aware of the arrival of such groups, as many refuse to enter as refugees.

Following the developments of the refugee crisis in the Tanzanian Kagera region, bordering Rwanda and Burundi, Baez (2011) finds that the closer the recipient villages were to the border, the larger the contingent of refugees and more serious the health and economic implications due to the proximity of the conflict and to deteriorated social conditions of the borderland. Camarena (2017) shows how the presence of refugee camps often triggered cross-border assaults, helped in recruiting soldiers, facilitated environmental degradation and the spreading of diseases and other public health crises. However, in East Africa, it has been the most applied strategy by national governments to contain refugees' populations or limit their transit. The creation of economies of scale seems to weight on the decision-making processes of the state in favour of border camps, despite the high implementation costs (compared to low cost of allowing refugees to scatter and the possible advantages from international reputation).

Conclusion

Shadow regionalism blurs the lines between formal and informal networks and flows. It allows one to question to what extent the state really fights illegalities and seek to regulate cross-border flows. The formal, institutional objectives of control and regulation of cross-border flows are less evident when analysing the interactions among local-level state officials with individuals and syndicates in borderlands of the Global South. Corruption is the first node by which irregular and illegal ventures find breaches in the borderline. The absence of state institutions and policies in borderlands (legislation, physical presence, material/financial aid), caused by lack of resources or simply by ignoring local realities, produces a vacuum that is occupied by informal networks of commerce, illicit flows, and other criminal enterprises. Such cross-border grids allow local populations to survive and feed parallel global systems of production and power. An idea of development and industrialisation by national governments and/or regional organisations have been fostering agriculture, electricity, and manufacture projects that are not rarely indifferent to cross-border dynamics, such as natural resources, immigration, and basic needs of border communities. Connected to this process of disregard to borderlands' socio-economic necessities, the global market demands for facilitated access and use of natural resources and for low-paid labour have been responded to with deregulation and complicity to human and environmental violations by state authorities.

The six nodes of formal–informal relationship explored in this chapter (corruption, kinship, institutional and governance vacuum, an idea of industrialisation and development, market demands and the global capital, and conflict) were shown not to be circumscribed in specific flows or networks, but as integral parts of all cross-border movements, they exert more or less influence depending on the cases studied, revealing their overlapping character. Poverty and underdevelopment are found to be the leitmotif of the engagement of locals in such cross-border networks, maintaining the flows in and out of state territories according to their own needs. The exploitation of this condition by state and non-state actors, in illegal or illegitimate schemes of cross-border nature, plays a role in all formal–informal nodes. Corruption and bribery are found to boost not only transnational crime, but also cross-border conflicts, institutional vacuum, development plans, deregulation, and other forms of relationship between formal and informal ventures. Domestic and international conflicts are, in some cases, triggered by scarcity of natural resources; on other occasions they are the result of political turbulence. All in all, conflicts are at the core of numerous cross-border currents, from transnational crime, to destruction of environment and migratory flows.

The nodes between formal and informal regionalisms of Global South borders are also integral parts of global systems as socio-political and economic articulations for capital, drugs, commodities, manufactures, workers, technologies, and ideas. They are essential elements of regional and global flows, to which borders and borderlands offer spatial resources for their operation. The cases analysed suggest a position of borders and borderlands in the global systems that reinforces the functional value of state boundaries but undermines their original purpose of regulation and control.

Bibliography

Alam, S. 2003. Environmentally induced migration from Bangladesh to India. *Strategic Analysis* 27 no. 3: 422–438.

Albrecht, T. R., Varady, R., Zuniga-Teran, R., Gerlak, A. and Staddon, C. 2017. Governing a shared hidden resource: A review of governance mechanisms for transboundary groundwater security. *Water Security* 2: 43–56.

Anderson, J. and O'Dowd, L. 1999. Borders, border regions and territoriality: Contradictory meanings, changing significance. *Regional Studies* 33, no. 7: 593–604.

Anesi, C., Rubino, G. and Adorno, L. 2018. *O PCC e a máfia italiana*. UOL Notícias. Available at: https://noticias.uol.com.br/reportagens-especiais/os-negocios-do-pcc-com-a-mafia-italiana/index.htm.

Augustyn, A., Bauer, P., Duignan, B., Eldridge, A., Gregersen, E., Luebering, J. E., McKenna, A., Petruzzello, M., Rafferty, J. P., Ray, M., Rogers, K., Tikkanen, A., Wallenfeldt, J., Zeidan, A. and Zelazko, A. 2019. *Organized crime. Encyclopedia Britannica*. Available at: www.britannica.com/topic/organized-crime.

Baez, J. E. 2011. Civil wars beyond their borders: The human capital and health consequences of hosting refugees. *Journal of Development Economics* 96, no. 2: 391–408.

Bergman, M. 2018. *Illegal Drugs, Drug Trafficking and Violence in Latin America*. Cham: Springer.

Bolouvi, G. M. and Trémolières, M. 2009. *Cross-Border Diaries: Bulletin on West African Local-Regional Realities 10*. Fada N'gourma, Burkina Faso: OECD.

Camarena, K. R. 2017. *Location Matters: The Politics of Refugee Camp Placement. Working Paper*. Available at: www.researchgate.net/publication/320255741.

Chatty, D. 2016. The Syrian humanitarian disaster: Disparities in perceptions, aspirations, and behaviour in Jordan, Lebanon and Turkey. *IDS Bulletin* 47, no. 3: 19–34. Available at: https://bulletin.ids.ac.uk/idsbo/article/view/2728/10.19088/1968-2016.142.

Chin, K. L. and Zhang, S. 2015. *The Chinese Heroin Trade: Cross-Border Drug Trafficking in Southeast Asia and Beyond*. New York: New York University Press.

Cooley, H., Ajami, N., Ha, M. L., Srinivasan, V., Morrison, J., Donnelly, K. and Smith, J. 2014. Global water governance in the twenty-first century. In: *The World's Water: The Biennial Report on Freshwater Resources*. Gleick, P. (ed.): 1–18. Washington and London: Island Press.

De Lombaerde, P., Söderbaum, F. and Van Langenhove, L. 2010. The problem of comparison in comparative regionalism. *Review of International Studies* 36, no. 3: 731–753.

Fall, J. 2011. Natural resources and transnational governance. In: *The Ashgate Research Companion to Border Studies*. Wastl-Walter, D. (ed.): 627–641. Aldershot: Ashgate.

Gleick, P. H. and Heberger, M. 2013. Water and conflict events, trends, and analysis (2011–2012). In: *The World's Water: The Biennial Report on Freshwater Resources*. Gleick, P. (ed.): 159–172. Washington and London: Island Press.

Gordon, S. 2009. Regionalism and cross-border cooperation against crime and terrorism in the Asia-Pacific. *Security Challenges* 5, no. 4: 75–102. Available at: www.jstor.org/stable/26460070.

Grant, J. A. 2008. Informal cross-border micro-regionalism in West Africa: The case of the Parrot's Beak. In: *Afro-regions: The Dynamics of Cross-Border Micro-Regionalism in Africa*. Fredrik, S. and Ian Taylor (ed.): 105–120. Stockholm: Nordiska Afrikainstitutet.

Guo, R. 2015. *Cross-Border Management: Theory, Method and Application*. Berlin: Springer-Verlag.

Harrison, G. 1999. Corruption as 'boundary politics': The state, democratisation, and Mozambique's unstable liberalisation. *Third World Quarterly* 20, no. 3: 537–550. Available at: www.jstor.org/stable/3993320.

Hart, K. 2006. Bureaucratic form and the informal economy. In: *Linking the Formal and Informal Economy: Concepts and Policies*. Guha-Khasnobis, B., Kanbur, R. and Ostrom, E. (ed.): 21–35. Oxford, New York: Oxford University Press.

Jorgenson, A. 2006. The transnational organization of production and environmental degradation: A cross-national study of the effects of foreign capital penetration on water pollution intensity, 1980–1995. *Social Science Quarterly* 87, no. 3: 711–730. Available at: https://doi.org/10.1111/j.1540-6237.2006.00405.x.

Kawser, M. and Samad, A. 2006. Political history of Farakka Barrage and its effects on environment in Bangladesh. Bandung. *Journal of the Global South* 3, no. 16: 1–14.

Kenney, M. 2007. The architecture of drug trafficking: Network forms of organisation in the Colombian cocaine trade. *Global Crime* 8, no. 3: 233–259.

Klantschnig, G., Dimova, M. and Cross, H. 2016. Africa and the drugs trade revisited. *Review of African Political Economy* 43, no. 148: 167–173.

Malamud, A. 2011. Conceptos, teorías y debates sobre la integración regional. *Norteamérica* 6, no. 2: 219–249.

Matiuzzi de Souza, G. 2018a. *Local Perceptions on the New Agenda for Cooperation and Border Development in the Brazilian-Uruguayan Cross-Border Region.* PhD thesis, University of Liège and Pontifical Catholic University of Rio Grande do Sul.

Matiuzzi de Souza, G. 2018b. Notions of border in regionalism theory and praxis: A critical overview. *Civitas. Revista de Ciências Sociais* 18, no. 2: 245–256.

Mattheis, F., Raineri, L. and Russo, A. 2018. *Fringe Regionalism: When Peripheries Become Regions.* Cham, Palgrave Macmillan.

Moulaye, Z. 2014. *La problématique de la criminalité transnationale et le contrôle démocratique du secteur de la sécurité.* Bamako, Mali: Friedrich-Ebert-Stiftung.

Mukherji, A. 2006. Political ecology of groundwater: The contrasting case of water-abundant West Bengal and water-scarce Gujarat, India. *Hydrogeology Journal* 14, no. 3: 392–406.

Nagle, L. 2010. Corruption of politicians, law enforcement, and the judiciary in Mexico and complicity across the border. *Small Wars & Insurgencies* 21, no. 1: 95–122.

Nijsten, G., Christelis, G., Villholth, K., Braune, E. and Bécaye, C. 2018. Transboundary aquifers of Africa: Review of the current state of knowledge and progress towards sustainable development and management. *Journal of Hydrology: Regional Studies* 20: 21–34.

Oddone, N. and Matiuzzi de Souza, G. 2017. Cross-border paradiplomacy in Mercosur: A critical overview. *Monções. Revista de Relações Internacionais da UFGD* 6, no. 12: 199–216.

OECD/SWAC. 2017. *Cross-border Co-operation and Policy Networks in West Africa.* West African Studies. Paris: OECD Publishing. Available at: www.oecd.org/publications/cross-border-co-operation-and-policy-networks-in-west-africa-9789264265875-en.htm.

Oliveira, G. and Villela Lima da Costa, G. 2012. Redes Ilegais e Trabalho Ilícito: Comércio de Drogas na Região de Fronteira de Corumbá/Brasil – Puerto Quijarro/Bolívia. *Boletim Gaúcho de Geografia* 38: 137–156. Available at: https://seer.ufrgs.br/bgg/article/view/37323.

Özden, S. 2013. *Syrian Refugees in Turkey. Migration Policy Centre Research Report.* Robert Schuman Centre for Advanced Studies. San Domenico di Fiesole (FI): European University Institute. Available at: http://cadmus.eui.eu/handle/1814/29455.

Pacific Institute for Studies in Development, Environment, and Security. 2019. *Water Conflict Chronology Timeline List.* Worldwater. Available at: www.worldwater.org/conflict/list/.

Pangsapa, P. and Smith, M. 2008. Political economy of Southeast Asian borderlands: Migration, environment, and developing country firms. *Journal of Contemporary Asia* 38, no. 4: 485–514.

Perkmann, M. and Sum, N. 2002. *Globalization, Regionalization and Cross-Border Regions.* New York: Palgrave Macmillan.

Prabhakar, H. 2012. *Black Market Billions: How Organized Retail Crime Funds Global Terrorists.* New Jersey: FT Press.

Pinheiro-Machado, R. 2011. Caminhos do descaminho: etnografia da fiscalização na Ponte da Amizade e seus efeitos no cotidiano da Tríplice Fronteira. In: *A Tríplice Fronteira: espaços e dinâmicas locais.* Macagno, L., Montenegro, S. and Béliveau, V. (ed.): 127–145. Curitiba: Editora UFPR.

Rahman, M. 2017. *Bangladeshi Migration to Singapore: A Process-Oriented Approach.* Singapore: Springer.

Renoldi, B. 2015. Estados posibles: travesías, ilegalismos y controles en la Triple Frontera. *Etnografica* 19, no. 3: 417–440.

Rhi-Sausi, J. and Oddone, N. 2013. Integración Regional Y Cooperación Transfronteriza En Los Nuevos Escenarios De América Latina. *Investigación y Desarrollo* 21, no. 1: 260–285. Available at: http://rcientificas.uninorte.edu.co/index.php/investigacion/article/viewArticle/5005.

Samir Kassab, H. and Rosen, J. 2019. *Corruption, Institutions, and Fragile States.* Cham: Palgrave Macmillan.

Shaw, T., Grant, A. and Cornelissen, S. 2011. *The Ashgate Research Companion to Regionalisms (International Political Economy of New Regionalisms Series).* Farnham and Burlington: Ashgate Publishing Group.

Simpson, A. 2007. The environment-Energy security nexus: Critical analysis of an energy 'love triangle' in Southeast Asia. *Third World Quarterly* 28, no. 3: 539–554.

Singh, A., Jamasb, T., Nepal, R. and Toman, M. 2018. Electricity cooperation in South Asia: Barriers to cross-border trade. *Energy Policy* 120, no. C: 741–748.

Söderbaum, F. 2010. 'With a little help from my friends': How regional organizations in Africa sustain clientelism, corruption and discrimination. *Paper presented at the Statsvetenskapliga förbundets årsmöte i Göteborg* at Gothenburg University, Gothenburg, Sweden.

Söderbaum, F. 2011. Comparing regionalisms: Methodological aspects and considerations. In: *The Ashgate Research Companion to Regionalisms*. Shaw, T., Grant, A. and Cornelissen, S. (ed.): 31–50. Farnham and Burlington: Ashgate Publishing Group.

Söderbaum, F. and Taylor, I. 2008. Competing region-building in the Maputo development corridor. In: *Afro-regions: The Dynamics of Cross-Border Micro-Regionalism in Africa*. Söderbaum, F. and Taylor, I. (ed.): 35–52. Stockholm: Nordiska Afrikainstitutet.

Sørensen, G. 2016. *Rethinking the New World Order*. London: Palgrave Macmillan.

Sparke, M. 2002. Between post-colonialism and cross-border regionalism. *Space and Polity* 6, no. 2: 203–213.

To, P. X., Mahanty, S. and Dressler, W. 2014. Social networks of corruption in the Vietnamese and Lao cross-border timber trade. *Anthropological Forum: A Journal of Social Anthropology and Comparative Sociology* 24, no. 2: 154–174.

UNHCR, The United Nations High Commissioner for Refugees. 2018b. *The New York Declaration for Refugees and Migrants: Answers to Frequently Asked Questions*. New York: UNHCR. Available at: www.unhcr.org/584689257.pdf.

Van Schendel, W. 2005. Spaces of engagement: How borderlands, illicit flows, and territorial states interlock. In: *Illicit Flows and Criminal Things: States, Borders, and the Other Side of Globalization*. Van Schendel, W. and Itty Abraham (ed.): 38–68. Bloomington and Indianapolis: Indiana University Press.

Vietnam News. 2017. *Illegal Labour Migration to China Rising in North Việt Nam*. Available at: https://vietnamnews.vn/society/379835/illegal-labour-migration-to-china-rising-in-north-viet-nam.html.

Vivares, E. 2018. *Regionalism, Development and the Post-commodities Boom in South America*. London: Palgrave Macmillan.

Warf, B. 2019. *Global Corruption from a Geographic Perspective*. Cham: Springer.

25

The international political economy of war and liberal peace

Michael Pugh

Introduction

The purpose of this chapter is to introduce key issues that researchers have investigated in the economics of war and peace. Their encounters provide insights into a wide range of contentious issues: the transformative dynamics of war; the costs of intervention in troubled areas; motivations for resorting to violence; the economics of how wars are fought and how people survive; the economic significance of cross-border economics; and the prescriptions for economic recovery. An important question in the following discussion is how organised violence and the aftermaths relate to power in the global economy. International policy makers and commentators have tended to fix on the conditions of violent unrest *in situ* while largely ignoring the external economic policies and developments that frame those situations. War has been deemed the responsibility of those who fight in states inscribed as 'failed'. A prime example was a glossy World Bank book (2003) on civil war and development policy which offered a mere paragraph on the social stress of externally-induced structural reforms.

By contrast this discussion has a materialist and structural bias because peace and violent conflict are inseparable from the socio-economic structures and needs of human existence. Identity, reasoning, passion, superstition and social relations are important determinants of action and policy, but these depend ultimately on securing the basic needs that enable existence. War and peace condition transformative phases in the struggle to continue the right to exist. A critical approach to theories and analysis of the political economy of actions and policy further requires interrogation of who foment theories and decide policy, and for what purpose.

The central theme is the attention paid to war and peace in liberal economic thought and practice, and the claim since the last quarter of the twentieth century that neoliberalism was a solution to problems of economic security. In practice, however, the neoliberal project from the 1970s undercut social solidarities and created grotesque inequalities that, for many scholars and some policy makers, contributed to generating conflict in the developing world and re-asserted fragmentation *post-bellum*.

The chapter begins with a brief note on transformations related to war. The second part deals with the costing of conflict in the context of regime change wars conducted by external military powers. The next part examines the nature of war economies in so-called civil wars (though

425

these are also internationalised in some form). The subsequent section interrogates the claims of peacebuilding economies as vehicles for pacification and stabilisation by interventionists.

Economic transformations, war and peace

Community, national, regional and global economies are motors of, and subject to, historical transformations, that may be exerted over a long period of time. Such were the transformations that marked the decline of European feudalism, the displacing of mercantilism by capitalism and the advent of industrialisation. As elaborated at a century apart in their singular fashions by Karl Marx (1857–58) and Karl Polanyi (1944), transformation in capitalism raised major problems for social relations, but were considered revolutionary stages in political economy on which to build a classless society. However, the Karls were also attuned to sudden, extreme crises: for Marx the Napoleonic wars, the 1848 revolutions and the Paris Commune; for Polanyi the two world wars and great depression. Debate about the role of war and peace in economic change has never been exhausted.

A widespread liberal view in the nineteenth century, associated with the classical British economists, notably Smith and Ricardo, proposed that international trade without government obstacles worked to exercise comparative advantage. In Marxian terms, capital 'must nestle everywhere'. It was a logical step for liberals to argue that peace and free trade were symbiotic because international markets needed stability, trust and reliability. Liberal theory posited that war entailed protectionism, and disrupted patterns of production, free trade and social reproduction (not only through war deaths but labour market distortions). Further, war production represented high opportunity costs (a bridge produced transfer savings, a tank destroyed assets). Taking this as axiomatic Norman Angell (1909), eventually a Nobel Laureate, argued that violent conflict made no sense for a capitalist system. Trade and indebtedness in the global economy were interlinked. Demonstrating this truth, John Maynard Keynes (1920), having attended the Versailles Conference and subsequent meetings on German reparations after the War, strongly objected not only to the punitive treatment of Germany, but also to the devastating consequences for the victors.

Actually, however, periods of peace were often outcomes of asymmetric power and imposition: Britain's naval enforcement of free trade when it commanded the seas; the post-1918 disarmament of Germany; the post-1945 division of Germany; the US role in the Oslo process in the Israel–Palestine conflict; the North Atlantic Treaty Organization's (NATO) enforcement of regime change in Kosovo. In addition, after the two world wars liberal internationalists made some headway in a quest to manage world peace through international diplomatic institutions and not solely through military power. Remarkably, liberal attempts to manage conflict, through the League of Nations and United Nations (UN), persisted in international politics after the massive political and economic shocks to the system in the twentieth century. Nevertheless, the designs for achieving international harmony were in large part an Atlanticist, mainly Anglophone conceptualisation, though US economic power would be used against allies (see Mazower 2009). Pragmatic ideas for managing ceasefires with peacekeeping, for example, came from a Canadian Foreign Minister and Norwegian UN Secretary-General in the 1950s. Theorising order after civil wars in the 1990s (still known as 'peacebuilding'), was dominated by US academics and think tanks, mainly on the East Coast, and in concert with their conceptions of US interests (Pugh 2019). However, another significant, incremental transformation as a consequence of neoliberalism and changes in international power relations corroded the foundations of what became widely known among academics as the Liberal Peace. Derived from theoretical strands in Rousseau, Paine, Cobden, Kant and Wilson among others, in post-Cold

War peace discourse it represented policies of free trade, human security and development, human rights and rule of law, democracy and good governance (Richmond 2006, 2011). However, wired-in biases of internationalism allowed liberal and governments to continue pursuing interests with violence, appealing to Just War theory, rather than hewing to peace ideals they had promoted.

Nevertheless, the accountancy of war and its social impacts continued to agitate the minds of rulers, administrators, political economists and scholars as it had done since Herodotus and Thucydides in the fifth century BC. War produced winners and losers, within as well as between states. Modern research embraced a rich and varied field in financial policy, food supplies, population management and trade (e.g. Milward 1977; Tooze 2008; Winter 1975). Casualties, disruption and destruction occurred of course, but private companies supplying war materiel made gains and a combination of shortages of goods and regulatory regimes stimulated black markets. Employment opportunities arose, often for women, albeit on a temporary basis until male combatants returned to reclaim job privileges. All this facilitated the accumulation of capital. Werner Sombart (1913) had earlier argued that war stimulated scientific and industrial advances – a theory rejected by John U. Nef (1950) who showed that innovation emerged from political stability, and that military applications were by-products of peace. Subsequently Charles Tilly (1985) highlighted the role of crime and violence in state formation and capital accumulation. Yet the association of liberalism with peace provided a power of privileged knowledge about why and how violence occurs. As Christopher Cramer further argues (2006a: 286–287), 'Liberal amnesia about the often-brutal foundations of democratic, capitalist modernity is just one example of a tendency to cover up … foundational violence'.

Regime change wars: costing conflict

Ancient empires did not rely on slaves and dutiful wealthy adherents to support the burden of war, but also on mercenaries and regulars who had to be paid and sustained. Persian kings were acutely aware of potential costs of military expansion if not recovered by tribute and economic growth. Through to the present-day treasurers and financial advisers have exercised prominent roles in the governance of war. It was commonly argued, though perhaps in exaggeration, that the Soviet Union collapsed because of costs of defence. The difficulties of measuring costs and benefits are immense, and contingent, not least on the time-scale used to estimate consequences. For example, Oliver Nachtwey (2018) argues that the Vietnam War was a turning point in the global economy because it caused the US to leave the gold standard in 1971. This launched financial deregulation and a global boom that eventually fomented increasingly outlandish social inequalities, suppression of upward mobility and, by 2015, political instability in neoliberal economies themselves. When national survival is at stake financial burdens get pushed to the background, but when threats are indirect and, a matter of revenge, ideology, prestige, interpreting conflicting intelligence or a diversion from political trouble at home, the alleged benefits of war agitate democracies. Such was the case with liberal democracies participating in conflicts to change regimes.

Refinements in metric calculus became particularly important for governments engaged in liberal imperialism and regime change wars. Non-military interventions or economic punishment, such as support for Allende's overthrow in Chile and withdrawal of aid from Yemen, posed lower costs to perpetrators. But an expert industry, notably in the US, engaged in calculating the costs of international interventions, often with a view to exposing potential opportunity costs for social development. A team at the Institute for Policy Studies in Washington, DC estimated Congressional spending in 2004 on the regime change war in Iraq at above

US$151 billion, corresponding to US$3,415 per US household, even with allied burden-sharing. Corruption and war profiteering took a further toll in the aftermath as corporations took advantage of the US$18 billion reconstruction funds (Bennis 2004: 22–23, 27–28). For Iraq, the deleterious impact of neoliberal policies included the doubling of pre-war unemployment and attendant increases in criminality (Dodge 2010; Herring 2011). A wider-ranging paper for the Watson Institute of International and Public Affairs at Brown University, Rhode Island, estimated that between 2001 and 2018 the regime change wars in (Iraq, Afghanistan, Pakistan and Syria), caused the US Federal Government to spend, or was obligated to spend (on veterans' care and homeland security, for instance) US$5.6 trillion, almost entirely financed by borrowing (Crawford 2017). For Syria, the cumulative costs of conflict from 2011 to the end of 2016 were estimated by the World Bank (2017) at four times greater than the state's pre-conflict GDP, a case of de-development.

In the neoliberal economic contexts marked by quests to reduce state and international expenditures, balance sheets mattered as much as domestic political support and international reputation. By the mid-2010s, the costs of UN humanitarian aid, peacekeeping and peace-building (governance reforms and reconstruction) were running out of control and considered unsustainable. The UN's authorised peacekeeping budget alone increased from US$6.8 billion in FY 2007–2008 to $8 billion for FY 2017–2018 (though a mere 0.5 percent of global military spending and a tiny fraction of $611 billion spent by the US on defence). International enthusiasm for conflict prevention intensified, as evidenced by a comprehensive joint study published in 2018 by the UN and World Bank with academic inputs, *Pathways for Peace*. It stressed the financial benefits of conflict prevention measures. Expenditures on dealing with violence reached almost US$10 trillion or 11 per cent of world GDP in 2012 whereas prevention costs were estimated at only a half to a third of that. For the report, Hannes Müller made a 'business case' based on prevention versus intervention modelling. Müller calculated assumed net savings in peacekeeping and humanitarian aid after deduction of estimated prevention costs. Savings could range from about US$0.5 billion a year for expensive conflict prevention interventions, weak conflict avoidance and high GDP losses, rising to 1.5 billion a year for lower prevention costs, conflict prevention successes, avoidance of high GDP losses (UN and World Bank 2018: 2018: 3–4). Thus, while decisions about intervention reflected many concerns, security obviously, it could also be constructed as a business matter in line with managerial discourse. Perhaps unsurprisingly, concepts of entrepreneurialism and profit maximising infiltrated debates about motivations for combat and how civil wars were resourced.

Civil war economies

So-called internal conflicts or civil wars, mainly in former colonial territories with mixed ethnic populations, featured strongly in violent conflict after 1945. Tracked by Uppsala University Conflict Data Programme, civil wars (including those with international involvement), predominated over inter-state wars by some margin. In the period 1992 to 2017, no year had more than two state-versus-state conflicts, whereas there were 51 internal ones in 2017, a post-Cold War high. Both low and high intensity conflicts grew. From 2005 to 2017 a ten-fold increase in internationalised civil wars produced a commensurate increase in battle-related deaths, 76 per cent of which occurred in Afghanistan, Iraq and Syria – with Yemen in fourth place (Allansson, Melander and Themnér 2017).

It should be recognised that the term 'civil war', used here, is slightly misleading, given the involvement of external powers and their allies. US and UK material support for Saudi Arabia, which led a campaign against Houthi areas in Yemen (2014–) was a case in point. Moreover, such wars could spill throughout a region as evidenced in the Sahel where Tuaregs sought a homeland and jihadists conducted raids, and in East Africa where the al-Shabaab Islamic insurgency in the 2010s ignored state frontiers. The Kivus in the Democratic Republic of Congo and the Pakistan–Afghanistan borders exemplified networks where state straddling occurred. Indeed, the cartography of borderlands repays examination. Not only fought over, they are sites of trafficking, trade and exchange, sanctuary and training. They sheltered elements of economic development beyond government control (Conciliation Resources 2018; Goodhand 2011). Internal borderlands, created to anaesthetise security problems, also signified a mapping of identity and allegiance, as in Sri Lanka to pick out a Tamil area from the dominant Celanese. In Bosnia and Herzegovina, and Kosovo, externally-induced peace processes intensified difference on the basis of ethnicity but extended political–economy relations to neighbouring patron states. For example, Western Herzegovina grew as a tax haven and investment hub for Croatia, and Northern Mitrovica remained economically dependent on Serbia – further weakening central state control from Sarajevo and Prština respectively.

The term 'network wars' suggests how wars were conducted: with no hard and fast lines of separation, non-state militaries and the use of IT to organise operations, funding and logistic support, sometimes with global reach. Fluid networks of social and economic relations could be more reliable than using official systems, and combatants traded with the enemy, as a Croat mafia did in Central Bosnia (Goodhand 2004: 68–69; Silber and Little 1996: 296). Even so, it was important to capture and guard territory and assets, and defend the porous and fluid borders that were necessary to tax trade. Finally, the appellation 'ethnic wars' applied to these conflicts is also problematic. It ignores rivalries and violence among same ethnicities as in north-west Bosnia and Herzegovina where Bosniaks fought other Bosniaks, or where mixed ethnic communities continued solidarity practices as in the city of Tuzla.

From the 1990s a new literature arose on economic inequalities and marginalisation as drivers of conflict (Nafziger and Auvinen 2003; Stewart and FitzGerald 2001). This gave rise to labels to categorise economic systems in war: shadow, parallel, unofficial, illegal, criminal for instance. These could infer flawed assumptions, such as inscribing a trade as 'illegal' though legal systems had broken down. Warlords leveraged official facilitation and officials participated in illegal business (Reno 1999). War entrepreneurs might enter politics to protect private wealth, a strategy not unknown in peacetime democracies.

Cutting through the semantic maze, Jonathan Goodhand suggests the categories – combat, shadow and coping economies – while recognising that they overlap (see Box 25.1). Peace-building economies are a logical addition to the categories, and discussed below.

Box 25.1 Economic features of civil wars

- *War economies.* Activities conducted for resourcing combat. They include the capture of assets and the mobilisation and reallocation of economic resources to sustain conflict and disruption and destruction of opponent's resources. Economic agents are combatant parties (state and non-state), with leaders sometimes referred to as conflict entrepreneurs.
- *Economies of accumulation.* Economic activities conducted outside, and unaudited by, state-regulated frameworks (as also in peace economies). In conflict areas, objectives are less military than either: (a) profit-seeking from new war-time opportunities for production and trade; or (b) necessity-driven participation to cope and survive, with a greater interest in peace.

- *Coping and survival economies.* Groups cope by using social networks and assets to maintain basic living standards. Surviving without assets at minimum or below minimum standards entails high risk strategies such as of begging, theft, smuggling, prostitution and other casual work.
- *Peacebuilding economies.* The purpose of peacebuilding is to assist adjustment to post-war conditions. It comprises part humanitarian aid, e.g. for refugees, but is mainly related to rebuilding state capacity to pave the way for neoliberalism at the behest of donors and bodies that provide funds and 'expertise' for demilitarisation, reconstruction and democracy. Peacebuilding tends to be co-constituted with former war leaders and oligarchs who confuse politics with their own prosperity.

    Source: Based on categories expounded by Jonathan Goodhand, with thanks for permission to include them. He is not responsible for the descriptors and the peacebuilding category.

Greed, grievance and funding

In the research community of the 1990s scholars reappraised the issue of incentives for violent conflict, in the footsteps of earlier analysts. Ted Gurr 1970 had already used correlation coefficients to examine over a thousand occasions between 1961 and the end of 1965 in over a hundred sites. His theory postulated that the motives of individuals operating had psychosocial impetuses that required examination. His concept of relative deprivation, that is the discrepancy between what people thought of as their just deserts and what they actually got, created frustrations that could lead to aggression, albeit basic needs were satisfied. On the other hand, people commonly endured hardship and suffering without resort to violence. Certain other variables might favour action, such as leadership competence and the level of repression by authorities. Democracies were more likely to listen to grievances. Picking up on the measurement of incentives and pursuing metric analysis of motivations, Paul Collier and Anke Höffler (2001; 2004) concluded, on the basis of what Collier referred to as 'hard science', that in the period 1966 to 1999 the traditional ethnic hatred explanations and inter-group grievances were unsound. Unlike Gurr they posited a materialist and rational basis for unrest, though Gurr (2011) later change his mind about rationality. Employing a binary division of motives as either 'greed' or 'grievance', the 'scientists' proposed a stronger correlation between violence and incentives to grab resources and milk rents than with grievances. They had to use statistically susceptible proxies. Representing 'greed', they measured the share of a state's primary produce as a percentage of exports (exports cast as incentives for violent competition); the proportion of young men in a populace (as potential combatants); and low literacy rates (for ease of mobilisation). They represented grievance by levels of ethnic and religious fragmentation and economic inequality; levels of political rights; and level of per capita GDP growth over the five years prior to outbreaks of violence (as an indicator of state competence). In tune with theories of individuals maximising self-interest, greed motivations won the contest – explained speculatively as a consequence of people readily enduring grievances.

The findings unleashed critiques, partly questioning the relevance of the proxies, partly on grounds of sampling, partly for ignoring state violence and partly since state-based data evaded regional cross-border operations. Further, David Keen (2008: 25–31) criticises the paucity of social, political and cultural motives; the notion that grievances masked greed; and the ellipsis of domestic and international elite responsibilities for stressful structural adjustment. As Cramer argues (2006b) various economic purposes and rationalities were in play; it was fallacious to adopt reductionist analysis based on the maximum utility of violence to individuals. Political economy involves social, organised conflict over the distribution of accumulation. Self-enrichment opportunities certainly arose in war, but it is also worth asking what underpinned core greediness. After the invasion of Iraq in 2003 some US$12 billion in cash went missing that had been sent to US contractors and Iraqi ministries, paid out of Iraq's assets, oil revenues and UN oil-for-food surpluses. An estimated 120 billion euros a year in the European Union vanishes in corruption, money laundering and tax dodging – in peacetime (EU Commission 2014).

Nevertheless, examining the resourcing of civil wars is a valid empirical research issue (see Berdal and Malone 2000). Wars are not fought entirely on enthusiastic volunteering or coercion, hate speech and mobile phone networking. Inevitably, the economic grounding of combat required various modes of operation, from formal and informal taxation to looting, predation, trafficking, and exploitation of labour and material resources. In other words, primitive accumulation contended with and overlapped official systems. Opportunities arose from cross-border trafficking and windfall rents, from control of transport and other assets, from humanitarian aid and diaspora remittances.

Lucrative exportable resources as well as income from them were seen as a variant of 'resource curse' theory (a correlation of abundant mineral wealth and poor economic growth). Valued resources facilitated conflict, so the argument went (Angoustures and Pascal 1995: 36–42; Ballentine and Sherman 2003; De Soysa 2000; Global Witness 2002). Government combatants were likely to benefit from state control of regular taxation and centralised control over exports. Partly because a dominant asset in many conflict situations was agriculture, insurgents needed access to high value, easily looted and transported goods, such as diamonds, drugs and counterfeit cigarettes (Le Billon 2001; Ross 2006). Resources could explain the *longevity* of conflict though not its onset. Noting that affordability affects sustainability, Achim Wennmann (2007: 372–376) hazards a model of low intensity conflict that required about US$2 to $11 million a year per thousand soldiers. For high intensity conflict requiring between US$4.5 and $34.8, predation and diaspora remittances were of limited value and unreliable. Both levels might benefit from heavyweight external military assistance. Furthermore, financial assets and exports could be subject to sanctions and blockade. Drug running and human trafficking was clearly a risky business, but the returns reflected this. Trading in diamonds from war economies (such as 'blood diamonds' from Sierra Leone) became subject to the 2003 Kimberly Certification Scheme. However, adherence to self-regulation by companies supplying value-added centres such as Antwerp was voluntary, and the regulations did not cover governments at war (Ballentine and Nitzschke 2005; Cooper 2006).

In coping and survival economies people explore new opportunities for income generation. Farmers in Afghanistan could switch to growing opium poppy for example. Civilian and military interventionists needed local services: drivers, translators, accommodation and entertainment. Contingent on such factors as the size of the local economy, the extent and longevity of an intervention, and the degree of interventionist self-sufficiency (as in Baghdad's Green Zone), the direct economic impacts of an intervention could be boosted by as much as 10 per cent of GDP for a time (Pugh 2012), though not without social costs as well. Such development entailed social costs as well: rent increases, racketeering and sex industries (Jennings 2010).

Non-combatants, usually women and older children, had to generate household subsistence, to manage social relations, child care and care of the elderly. Women caught up in conflict were often singled out for vile abuse and bore the brunt of household deprivation. Scholars have somewhat neglected the economic role of women in civil wars, though giving greater recognition to their organisation of peace lobbies and participation in mediation efforts (O'Reilly 2013). Beyond seeking out existing assets and receiving humanitarian aid they tended and marketed agricultural produce or found part-time work. They also used traditional social networks or organised new ones for welfare provision. Where available, microfinance might assist,

431

though as Milford Bateman (2010) explains, it was not generally a transformative avenue to sustainable income and often a path to indebtedness. In general, however, women's resource strategies enabled households to cope and survive.

Political economy of peace missions

Humanitarian crises and intra-state violence in the 1990s was not a new phenomenon and had been marked in the Cold War by 'proxy wars' in former colonies. But they seemed out of place in the post-colonial, post-Cold War era. In part the liberal ideal of a social contract with the state had limited relevance for former colonies whose elites struggled to integrate or replace patronage and clientelism with Weberian institutions and legal frameworks for providing equitable allocation of resources and welfare (including famine relief for instance). Additionally, the stresses of losing international patrons and markets, such as the USSR, increased reception to capital mobility, western-dominated IFIs and structural adjustment programmes. Other exogenous factors, including oil price shocks, were also difficult for some states to manage. The capacity and legitimacy for maintaining central state authority, the loosening of nationalist and class framing of politics in multi-religious and multi-ethnic communities also became unmanageable in some states in the 1990s. Disintegration of authority in Somalia, Haiti, former Yugoslavia, Rwanda and West Africa, all with distinctive economies and routes to conflict, fostered a sense of international crisis that spurred international liberalism to launch interventions. Whether in the form of diplomacy, peacekeeping, NGO humanitarianism, debt relief, sanctions or bombing, it is arguable that this activism had a positive effect in reducing the incidence of conflict. Indeed, in the late 1990s the Bretton Woods institutions and other fonts of capitalism extolled the benefits of political economies that brought social justice for averting violence (e.g. World Bank 1997). Yet it took Bosnia and Herzegovina approximately 10 years to reach its pre-secession GDP in spite of approximately US$5 billion in aid, and more from the foreign presence. Unlike recoveries in Europe after 1945, governments lacked an ability to dragoon populations into reconstruction efforts through a sense of mass solidarity and combinations of austerity and welfare. Since the 1970s and 1980s, the citizen's social contract with state appears to have fragmented. The problem of recovery from war exposed the global power structure at a transformative point.

The riches of the global economy were such that advances in infrastructure, communications and consumerism, for example, were unparalleled. However, just as finance capitalism itself failed in a morass of feckless banking and high levels of private debt in 2007–2008, a new surge of violence was underway. The number of violent deaths, average conflict duration, armed groups participating and the internationalisation of conflicts, especially in Africa and the Middle East correlated with increased economic inequalities within and between states, and decreasing labour shares of income UNCTAD (2004, 2018). In Africa a conflict-poverty trap could be linked to 'multilateral global political and economic governance' (Salih 2009). Large and rapid increases in GDP growth rates after civil wars had certainly occurred, but this often reflected low start points, injections of aid and an unbalanced growth of big cities. After more than 15 years of international administration and peacebuilding in Bosnia and Herzegovina, the World Bank estimated that 20 per cent of the population lived below the national poverty line in 2011. In 2017 almost 40 per cent of the work force had registered as unemployed (20 per cent actually jobless according to the household interviewing methodology of a Labour Force Survey) (Pugh 2018). Loss of population to migration *after* the conflict reached levels that suggest a desperate escape from deprivation and lack of hope. 'You cannot blame people because they are going in search of a better life when you have not done anything to offer them better conditions to stay here', said a Bosnian economist (Kovačević 2018).

Box 25.2 Rudiments of liberal peacebuilding economies

- Capital for reconstruction includes diaspora remittances and returns from primitive accumulation, but weak state capacity and shortage of capital requires international intervention. The World Bank organises donor conferences; promised funds can take 3 or more years to dispense. 'Toxic' debts may have to be repaid, unless the state qualifies for debt reduction. International agencies exert macroeconomic leverage through loan conditionalities. Attracting FDI needs low-level regulation.

- Continuation of war-time primitive accumulation under new or crony management. War entrepreneurs acquire privatised state assets, engage in asset stripping and employ workers in unregulated as well as formal labour markets. Rentierism provides quicker and higher returns than industrial or agricultural production; it is also incubating financial fraud and continued corruption. Criminal asset acquisition and war crime allegations are no obstacle to power.

- Elite bargains for the economy involve a co-constitution of clientelistic neoliberalism. Domestic elites are wary of regulated competition but have commonalty with internationals in: (a) promoting private capital accumulation; (b) sustaining a low wage, biddable labour force weakened by legislation, unemployment and poverty; (c) evading strong state development.

- Internationals prioritise open economies for global integration, mediated by foreign policy and geo-strategic goals. Resource extraction for external value added exacerbates dependency. Balance of payments deficits add pressure on budgets, furthering state shrinkage. Poverty is moderated by clientelism and network welfare. Social and economic stability often achieved by authoritarian politics and crude appeals to identity markers. Spatial differences grow, migration continues, liberalism wilts.

Political economies of peacebuilding mirrored neoliberal policies of core capitalism, with consequential increased inequalities and social stress (see Box 25.2). Susan L. Woodward (2017: 41–43) shows that in dealing with so-called 'fragile states' international institutions prioritised 'good governance', which entailed neoliberal economic discipline of the kind previously employed in Russia and eastern Europe after authoritarian communist regimes collapsed. In referring to 'crises faced by our *clients*' (my italics), the World Bank Group asserted that 'preventing fragility and conflict and violence is central to reducing poverty and achieving shared prosperity' – a switch in the emphasis on reducing poverty and inequalities to prevent violent conflict (UN and World Bank 2018: xi–xii, xvii, 11). Developmental narratives now inscribed the poor as sources of violence, masking the sources of violence in capital's restructuring of social relations. The new model was to '[b]uild resilience of the most vulnerable people, reduce poverty, enhance food security, and sustain peace' (UNs and World Bank 2017). As decoded by Mark Duffield (2007: 228–230) however, 'resilience of the most vulnerable people' meant isolating a category rather than making universal provision. It emphasised self-insurance against risks, rather than employment contributions towards welfare. Self-help, he argues, paradoxically generated shadow economies, network welfare, and spatial and social discriminations that weaken state performance.

Discourses of helping the poor did not, however, disrupt the mandates, ideas and practices of peacebuilding agencies. In supporting social resilience, the Bretton Woods and other institutions could sustain the goal of 'leaving no one behind' in the neoliberal globalisation project and to define good governance according to structural adjustment benchmarks (see Woodward 2017: 57). In Bosnia and Herzegovina for instance, the Office of the High Representative, European Bank of Reconstruction and Development, World Bank, and vigorously backed by the US, ordained the privatisation of state enterprises. Together with the IMF, and EU, the World Bank, determined macroeconomic policy and state budgets (Grabovac 2015). Likewise, a UN mission established the Kosovo Trust Agency in 2002 to privatise socially owned property. Run by the EU, operations were temporarily suspended when they were deemed illegal in an international court. Before handing over to Kosovan control in 2008 (with a new name) the Agency destroyed records, perhaps because of evident corruption by officials (Lemay-Hébert and Murshed 2016: 520; Pugh 2013). Recovery planning also stressed the importance of phasing international assistance 'within political and investment cycles' (UN and World Bank 2018: 276). Since good governance implicated capital mobility in general and Foreign Direct Investment (FDI) in particular, peacebuilding management kept faith with capitalism's corporate, investment-friendly globalisation. Thus, assessment missions surveying the needs of war-affected societies advocated the removal of obstacles to private capital accumulation and international economic integration as essential to the process. In practice, this could mean governments offering potential investors 'sweeteners', such as 100 per cent profit repatriation, low taxation or low regulation standards, such as weak environmental controls (see Hoenke 2014). Moreover, corporate power and decision-making on investment sites required no exercise of democracy.

By 2010, peace missions had become less about peace than asserting stability. Human rights, social justice, even democracy and rule of law had been stripped out. In the assessments of John Karlsrud (2019) and this author, peacekeeping and peacebuilding had adopted aggressive postures. In part this reflected a move towards counter-terrorism and counter-insurgency. It also suggested that peacebuilding operations were co-constituted with domestic bosses. Both international authorities and local power-holders adopted security stabilisation at the expense of democratic governance. Specific implementations of stability management varied according to host resistances and bargains with local power-holders. Leaders in post-conflict countries negotiated assistance and signed up to 'good governance' formulae without relaxing their grip on political systems or control of capital, including privatisation processes (Donais 2005; Pospisil and Kühn 2016, Wennmann 2010). Elites accommodated external impositions, such as the Governance and Economic Assistance Program in Liberia, in order to secure international funding. For war entrepreneurs, opportunity costs of peace encouraged them to deal, provided they had a domestic following to offer incentives to peacemakers and could sustain bargaining power into the transition. The UN and World Bank (2018: 190) recommended designing incentives for leaders to adopt peace policies. External peacemakers regarded some as allies and others as 'spoilers' but made plenty of room for rentier entrepreneurs with or without serious war-time abuses in their profiles. Kosovo became a rentier state, deeply corrupt (Lemay-Hébert and Murshed 2016). Policies for supporting private accumulation and docile labour forces imbued the mutually constitutive processes of neoliberal transformation. From El Salvador to Rwanda, from Yemen to Mali and former Yugoslav states, post-conflict elite bargains also facilitated the installation of elected authoritarian regimes and oligarchs who combined business and politics, rentierism and repression (see Bliesemann de Guevara and Kühn 2014; HRW 2014; Lewis, Heathershaw and Megoran 2018). The Liberal Peace had been hoist on the petard of neoliberal contradictions.

Conclusion

War and peace, as Tolstoy revealed, extends searchlights on domestic political economies and social relations. Studies of conflicts and their aftermath probe international political economy in revealing ways. But without taking into account the context of global economic power, including for the past half century the ideology and authority of neoliberalism, such studies lack a structural dimension to analysis. Indeed, the ontology of war and peace is forged on the fierce foundations of primitive capital accumulation and its history of ascendance. It is not simply that international agencies failed to encourage civil society support for peace or had imperfect understanding of the social roles and epistemologies of war-affected societies, which Donais argues (2005). The model was inherently flawed. Legitimising intervention on humanitarian grounds lost traction in Iraq, Afghanistan and Libya with civilian deaths from military operations (38,000 in Afghanistan alone). Nor could justification reside in the myth of assisting war-affected countries to rebuild for a process of convergence with western standards of living. Fall-out from the economics of peace missions exposed, what Ha-Joon Chang (2002) referred to as 'kicking away the ladder' of development.

In fact, a UN Secretary-General's agenda for *Sustaining Peace* in 2018 had linked the notion of peace to the *Agenda for Sustainable Development 2030* of 2015, stressing the need to tackle structural inequalities and also advocated labour rights and 'decent work' (UN 2015: Goal 8, 2018: 5). The OECD (2018) repeated the lesson, warning that 'inequality puts our world at risk' in direct economic and social consequences. Yet the foundations rested on policies that promoted competitive states and individuals as the mechanism for irrigating economic development and wealth distribution – a Darwinian process for achieving international harmony. The contradiction for social stability was inherent in this principle, destroying social solidarities, intensifying spatial discrimination, strengthening inequalities, injustices and authoritarian forms of stability. Neoliberal policies have been particularly injurious for people on the lower parts of the supposed ladder of development. An economic rulebook that by 2019 had placed about 50 per cent of the world's wealth in the hands of 26 individuals may be hard to sustain without social unrest and violence (Oxfam 2019). If further global transformation is underway, perhaps steered by corporate monetisation of personal data (dubbed 'surveillance capitalism'), this will also fashion modes of passivity and resistance for scholars to study. In studying war and peace economies, it is valid to focus on how people interpret the economic structures that frame their lives. Indeed, such variables as beliefs, culture and governance shape the possibilities of unrest, and can help explain why violence occurs in particular environments at particular times. But without examining the structural components of economic transformations that bring about social stress, including policies of discrimination and inequitable distribution, the picture will be incomplete. Researchers should bear in mind the contradictions that are integral to driving capital accumulation along. Development is not solely dependent on peace, as evident from liberalism's ruthless and violent pursuit of accumulation. And who can say that human rights, even the right to existence, would have been achieved without struggle, sometimes violent?

Bibliography

Allansson, M., Melander, E. and Themnér, L. 2017. Organized Violence, 1989–2016. *Journal of Peace Research* 54(4): 574–587.

Angell, N. 1909. *Europe's Optical Illusion*, London: Simpkin, Marshall, Hamilton, Kent.

Angoustures, A. and Pascal, V. 1995. Diasporas et Financement des Conflits. In Jean, F. and Rufin, J. C. (eds), *Economie des Guerres Civiles*. Paris: Hachette: 36–42.

Ballantine, K. and Nitzschke, H. 2003. *The Political Economy of Civil War and Conflict Transformation*. Berlin: Berghof Research Center.

Ballantine, K. and Sherman, J. (eds). 2003. *The Political Economy of Armed Conflict: Beyond Greed and Grievance*. Boulder, CO: Lynne Rienner.

Bateman, M. 2010. *Why Doesn't Microfinance Work? The Destructive Rise of Local Neoliberalism*. London: Zed Books.

Bennis, P. 2004. *Paying the Price: The Mounting Costs of the Iraq War, Study for the Institute for Policy Studies and Foreign Policy in Focus*. Washington, DC: IPS. Available at: www.ips-dc.org/iraq/costsofwar/.

Berdal, M. and Malone, D. (eds). 2000. *Greed and Grievance: Economic Agendas in Civil Wars*. Boulder, CO: Lynne Rienner.

Bliesemann de Guevara, B. and Kühn, F. P. 2014. The Political Economy of Statebuilding: Rents, Taxes and Perpetual Dependency. In Chandler, D. and Sisk, T. D. (eds), *Routledge Handbook of International Statebuilding*. Abingdon: Routledge: 219–230.

Chang, H.-J. 2002. *Kicking Away the Ladder: Development Strategy in Historical Perspective*. London: Anthem Press.

Collier, P. and Höffler, A. 2001. *Greed and Grievance in Civil War*. World Bank paper. Available at: www.worldbank.org/research/onflict/papers/greedandgrievance.htm.

Collier, P. and Höffler, A. 2004. Greed and Grievance in Civil War. *Oxford Economic Papers* 56(4): 563–595.

Conciliation Resources. 2018. Borderlands and Peacebuilding: A View from the Margins. *Accord Insight 4, Conciliation Resources*.

Cooper, N. 2006. Chimeric Governance and the Extension of Resource Regulation. *Conflict Security and Development* 6(3): 315–335.

Cramer, C. 2003. Does Inequality Cause Conflict? *Journal of International Development* 15(4): 397–412.

Cramer, C. 2006a. *The Sense that War Makes*. OpenDemocracy. Available at: www.opendemocracy.net/theme_7-vision_reflections/war_sense_3970.jsp.

Cramer, C. 2006b. *Civil War is Not a Stupid Thing: Accounting for Violence in Developing Countries*, London: Hurst.

Crawford, N. C. 2017. *United States Budgetary Costs of Post–9/11 Wars Through FY2018 Costs of War Project Report*. Watson Institute of International and Public Affairs. Brown University, Providence, RI. Available at: https://watson.brown.edu/costsofwar/costs/economic.

De Soysa, I. 2000. The Resource Curse: Are Civil Wars Driven by Rapacity or Paucity? In Berdal, M. and Malone, D. (eds), *Greed and Grievance: Economic Agendas in Civil Wars*. Boulder, CO: Lynne Rienner: 113–135.

Dodge, T. 2010. The Ideological Roots of Failure: The Application of Kinetic Neo-Liberalism to Iraq. *International Affairs* 86(6): 1269–1286.

Donais, T. 2005. *The Political Economy of Peacebuilding in Post-Dayton Bosnia*. London: Routledge.

Duffield, M. 2007. *Development, Security and Unending War: Governing the World of Peoples*. Cambridge: Polity.

EU Commission. 2014. *Anti-Corruption Report to the Council and European Parliament COM (2014)38*. Brussels. Available at: http://ec.europa.eu/transparency/regdoc/rep/1/2014/EN/1-2014-38-EN-F1-1.Pdf.

Global Witness. 2002. *All The President's Men: The Devastating Story of Oil and Banking in Angola's Privatised War*. Available at: www.oneworld.org/globalwitness.

Goodhand, J. 2004. Afghanistan in Central Asia. In Pugh, M., Cooper, N. and Goodhand, J. (eds), *War Economies in a Regional Context: Challenges of Transformation*. Boulder, CO: Lynne Rienner.

Goodhand, J. 2011. War, Peace and the Places in Between: Why Borderlands are Central. In: Pugh, M., Cooper, N. and Turner, M. (eds), *Whose Peace? Critical Perspectives on the Political Economy of Peacebuilding*. Basingstoke: Palgrave Macmillan: 227–246.

Grabovac, N. 2015. *Privreda Bosne i Hercegovine pred kolapsom: zbirka eseja i drughi dokumenata [BiH Economy Brought to Collapse: essays and documents]*. Fojnica: Štamparija Fojnica.

Gurr, T. R. 1970. *Relative Deprivation and the Impetus to Violence. Why men rebel*. Princeton, NJ: Princeton University Press.

Gurr, T. R. 2011. Why Men Rebel Redux: How Valid are its Arguments 40 Years On? *E-International Relations*. Available at: www.e-ir.info/2011/11/17/why-men-rebel-how-valid-are-its-arguments-40-years-on.

Herring, E. 2011. Neoliberalism versus Peacebuilding in Iraq. In Pugh, M., Cooper, N., Turner, M. (eds), *Whose Peace? Critical Perspectives on the Political Economy of Peacebuilding*. Basingstoke: Palgrave Macmillan: 49–66.

Hoenke, J. 2014. Business for Peace the Role of 'Ethical' Mining Companies. *Peacebuilding* 2(2): 172–189.

HRW (Human Rights Watch). 2014. *World Report 2014: Rwanda*. Available at: www.hrw.org/world-report/2014/country-chapters/rwanda.

Jennings, K. 2010. Unintended Consequences of Intimacy: Political Economies of Peacekeeping and Sex Tourism. *International Peacekeeping*, 17(2): 229–243.

Karlsrud, J. 2019. From Liberal Peacebuilding to Stabilization and Counterterrorism. *International Peacekeeping* 26(1):1–21.

Keen, D. 2008. *Complex Emergencies*. Cambridge: Polity.

Keynes, J. M. 1920. *The Economic Consequences of the Peace*. London: Macmillan.

Kovačević, D. 2018. *Emigration Damages Bosnia's Long-term Growth*. Balkan Insight. Available at: www.imf-reduced-bosnian-growth-forecast-due-to-population-migration-20-02-18.

Le Billon, P. 2001. The Political Ecology of War: Natural Resources and Armed Conflicts. *Political Geography* 20(5): 561–584.

Lemay-Hébert, N. and Murshed, S. M. 2016. Rentier Statebuilding in a Post-conflict Economy: The Case of Kosovo. *Development and Change* 47(3): 517–541.

Lewis, D., Heathershaw, J. and Megoran, N. 2018. Liberal Peace? Authoritarian Modes of Conflict Management. *Co-operation and Conflict* 53(4).

Marx, K. [1973] 1857–1858. *Grundrisse: Foundations of the Critique of Political Economy*. London: Penguin Books.

Mazower, M. 2009. *No Enchanted Palace: The End of Empire and the Ideological Origins of the United Nations*. Princeton, NJ: Princeton UP.

Milward, A. 1977. *War, Economy and Society 1939–45*. London: Allen Lane.

Nachtwey, O. 2018. *Germany's Hidden Crisis: Social Decline in the Heart of Europe*. London: Verso.

Nafziger, E. and Auvinen, J. 2003. *Economic Development, Inequality and War. Humanitarian Emergencies in Developing Countries*. Basingstoke: Palgrave Macmillan.

Nef, J. U. 1950. *War and Human Progress: An Essay on the Rise of Industrial Civilization*. New York: Norton.

OECD. 2018. *A Broken Social Elevator? How to Promote Social Mobility*. Paris: OECD Publishing.

O'Reilly, M. 2013. Gender and Peacebuilding. In Mac Ginty, R. (ed.), *Routledge Handbook of Peacebuilding*. Abingdon: Routledge: 57–68.

Oxfam. 2019. An Economy for the 1%. *Oxfam Briefing Paper*. Available at: www.oxfam.org/en/research/economy-1.

Polanyi, K. 1944. *The Great Transformation: The Political and Economic Origins of Our Time*. New York, Farrar & Rinehart.

Pospisil, J. and Kühn, F. 2016. The Resilient State: New Regulatory Modes in International Approaches to Statebuilding. *Third World Quarterly* 37(1): 1–16.

Pugh, M. 2012. The Political Economy of Exit. In Caplan, R. (ed.), *Exit Strategies and State Building*. New York: Oxford University Press: 276–292.

Pugh, M. 2013. Statebuilding and Corruption. In: Berdal, M. and Zaum, D. (eds), *Political Economy of Statebuilding: Power After Peace*. Abingdon: Routledge: 79–93.

Pugh, M. 2018. Precarity in Post-Conflict Yugoslavia: What About the Workers? *Civil Wars* 20(2): 151–170.

Pugh, M. 2019. *Peacebuilding's Origins and History*. Paper at Peacebuilding Workshop. University Centre Saint-Ignatius Antwerp: 1–7.

Reno, W. 1999. *Warlord Politics and African States*. Boulder, CO: Lynne Rienner.

Richmond, O. P. 2006. The Problem of Peace: Understanding the 'Liberal Peace'. *Conflict Security and Development* 6(3): 291–314.

Richmond, O. P. 2011. *A Post-Liberal Peace*. Abingdon: Routledge.

Ross, M. 2006. A Closer Look at Oil, Diamonds and Civil War. *Annual Review of Political Science* 9(1): 265–230.

Salih, M. A. 2009. A Critique of the Political Economy of the Liberal Peace: Elements of an African Experience. In: Newman, E., Paris, R. and Richmond, O. (eds), *New Perspective on Liberal Peacebuilding*. Tokyo: United Nations University Press: 133–158.

Silber, L. and Little, A. 1996. *The Death of Yugoslavia*. London: Penguin.

Sombart, W. 1913. *Krieg und Kapitalismus*. Munich: Duncker & Humblot.

Stewart, F. and FitzGerald, V. (eds). 2001. *War and Underdevelopment*, 2 vols. Oxford: Oxford University Press.

Tilly, C. 1985. *Coercion, Capital, and European States* AD *990–1990*. Oxford: Wiley–Blackwell.

Tooze, A. 2008. *Wages of Destruction: The Making and Breaking of the Nazi Economy*. London: Penguin.

UNCTAD. 2004. *Least Developed Countries Report 2004: Linking International Trade and Poverty Reduction*. No. E.04 11.0.0.27, Geneva.

UNCTAD. 2018. *Trade and Development Report: Power, platforms and the free trade delusion (Overview)*. Geneva: UNCTAD: 5, 27.

United Nations. 2015. *Transforming Our World: Agenda for Sustainable Development 2030*, UN doc. A/Res/70/1.

United Nations. 2018. *Peacebuilding and Sustaining Peace, Report of the Secretary-General*. UN doc. A/72/707.

United Nations and World Bank. 2017. *Partnership Framework for Crisis-Affected Situations*.

United Nations and World Bank. 2018. *Pathways for Peace: Inclusive approaches for preventing violent conflict*. Washington, DC: World Bank.

Wennmann, A. 2007. *Conflict Financing and the Recurrence of Intra-state Conflict: What Can be Done from the Perspective of Conflict Financing to Prevent the Recurrence of Intra-state Conflict?* PhD thesis, Institute Universitaire de Hautes Études Internationales, University of Geneva.

Wennmann, A. 2010. *The Political Economy of Peacemaking*. Abingdon: Routledge.

Winter, J. M. ed. 1975. *War and Economic Development*. Cambridge: Cambridge University Press.

Woodward, S. L. 2017. *The Ideology of Failed States: Why Interventions Fail*. New York: Cambridge University Press.

World Bank, 1997. *World Development Report, 1997: The State in a Changing World*. New York: Oxford University Press. Available at: https://openknowledge.worldbank.org/handle/10986/5980.

World Bank. 2003. *Breaking the Conflict Trap – Civil War and Development Policy, A World Bank Report*. Washington, DC: World Bank/Oxford University Press.

World Bank. 2017. *The Toll of War: The Economic and Social Consequences of the Conflict in Syria*, Washington, DC: World Bank.

26

Transnational organized crime and political economy

Daniel Pontón

Introduction

Transnational organized crime (TOC) broke abruptly into the political agenda of international security by the end of the 1980s (Vlassis 2005). This phenomenon, which is considered among the "new threats" to the liberal world peace, has shifted the traditional points of International Studies after the Cold War sovereignty, territory and military power, to new themes (García 2005; Lupsha 1996). Since then, the police and judicial-related aspects have acquired a critical importance in international affairs, becoming the new high-priority diplomatic topics for different governments around the world (Andreas and Nadelmann 2005). This subject has given rise to the use of a new glossary of words to define threat (asymmetric war) and to new forms of managing the countries' security under the criteria of "cooperative security" (Kahhat 2003).

The extent of organized crime's power comes, without any doubt, from the control of highly profitable illegal markets, which empower its finances through a wide international connection (Fernández 2008). This fact has attracted the attention of one of the areas of criminology known as "economic criminology," which emphasizes the origin and approach of the kind of crime that results in financial loss, fraud, corruption, tax evasion, and above all, illicit enrichment through illegal and semi-illegal and completely illegal activities (Valer 2018). And certainly, the understanding of these practices implies the development of a complex mixture of global and local logic to approach economic crime and its organization.

Academically, the matter demands the building of research connections between economic criminology and certain aspects of concern of the International Political Economy (IPE). IPE is considered to be the field that deals with the understanding of the globalization phenomenon (Payne 2005), which envisages the economic factors as the cause or consequence of an important fact that takes place in society and in the world. Therefore, issues like international commerce, international finances, multinational enterprises, global governance and economic integration, among others (Bustelos 2003: 157), start to be seen as the central pieces in the comprehension of a complex undercover world (Cox 2002) known as "the dark side" or "the unwanted effects of globalization" (Andreas and Nadelmann 2005). However, little has been said about the theoretic articulation between political–economic and criminology, as well as how to approach them.

Therefore, the objective of this chapter is to raise the various politic and cognitive dilemmas of the interdisciplinary dialogue between IPE and economic criminality around TOC. The central assumption is that that the articulation of these two disciplines must be understood within the framework of a complex web where old theoretical and epistemological problems of criminology overlap in a dynamic international political context. To reach that, we will first analyze the emergence of the concept of organized crime within the framework of social and economic transformations of capitalist societies. In the second and third part of the chapter, we will explore and discuss the contributions of the different criminology schools for the understanding of TOC under abrupt social and cultural changes of capitalist societies. Finally, the chapter will examine the contribution of the IPE discipline and its relationship with old premises arising from the sociological debate on economic criminology.

The concept

The term "organized crime" appeared in the framework of the Americas of the 1920s as a product of the language of police and judicial operators. The intent was to define a new criminal modus operandi of certain groups of people with worldwide connections who benefited from the control of highly profitable banned services and products (prostitution, alcohol, games) that established marked informal segmentations. They were hierarchical organizations with ethical codes, a sense of belonging to a community and relative job stability (Arroyo 2007; Fernández 2008). The under cover nature of these organizations and operations meant that this concept attracted the attention of public opinion from the very beginning, as it became the central topic of various literary works, and politics, where the economic, migratory (xenophobia) and police matters remained trapped in complex trilogies.

A prevailing topic in the criminological debate was the idea that certain criminal organized practices were ascribable to certain traditional communities as piracy and banditry. True as this may be, there was not be a discussion on the historic etiology of crime, but on the proliferation of these crime practices and on the social and political context that set out to establish a criminal modus operandi with its own characteristics and dynamics. For many authors, the transformation of the industrial capitalistic societies is where proliferation of these ways of living in illegality take place, due to the remaining tension between the traditional institutions (many of them gangster related) and the modern ones. An example of this is the criminal Italian diaspora after the expulsion impended by Benito Mussolini of mafia groups from the country. As a result of this measure, a complex criminal web, known as "La Cosa Nostra" was established in the United States; this led to the fact that the problem of the Italian mafia was no longer seen as a local issue, but as an international issue (Dickie 2006). Because of that, the appearance of this concept is tracked to the framework of deep social transformations of American society at the beginning of the twentieth century. And it is precisely in this nation where these matters start to become a core issue of concern to scholars. In other words, the context was nourished by various kinds of general knowledge that originated to become a new purely sociological lexicon related to criminal matters, which are far from the biological and psychological traditional explanations that appeared in Europe at the end of the nineteenth century.

The contribution of the American schools

In the history of criminological studies there are several schools of thought that in one way or another nurtured the communication between what we know nowadays as organized crime and the political economy. While the advent of those schools address crime in general terms, somehow, they focused on crime motivated by economic factors (minor offenses and organized crime) compared to other forms of crime. This strengthening of thought was originated as a product of the social impact that these crimes started to have (in terms of frequency) in social life, which was in some way concatenated with social, political and economic transformations of the contemporary world.

The first sociological current that clearly emphasizes the appearance of this form of crime was known as the "School of Chicago." According to this school, the emergence of these conducts and criminal organizations, that controlled high-profit illicit activities, were the product of the demographic transformation in industrial cities in the United States. Cities were characterized by aggressive processes of internal and external migration and changes in the organization of family and traditional social institutions. In this scenario, the city was an explosive mosaic of multiple urban contexts, many of them immersed in conflict and tension. As a result, the concept of social disruption emerged, which explained how certain poverty-stricken areas of the city known as "concentric areas" were spontaneously created in a breeding ground of gangster and deviant behavior. These pathological communities imply a gradual breaking of relations with the social ties of the traditional way of living and the beginning of the transformation of urban life and its opportunities (Downes and Rock 2011: 85–120). A famous book written as a product of this tradition during the 1940s was *The Street Corner Connection* by William Foote Whyte (1971). Its contribution beyond its richness and methodological innovation was to unveil the process of formation, organization and operating mode of organized gangs and mafias in American neighborhoods with a large Italian–American population. Therefore, its connection with IPE provides a theoretical framework that allows an understanding of the creation of certain forms of organized crime in an accelerated process of urban development at a global scale.

A second key moment in the sociological tradition about the criminal affairs was the contribution of Robert Merton (Harvard School) and his macro-social explanation of crime and deviance in the 1940s. Actually, Merton reiterated Emile Durkheim's concept of anomia, which refers to the lack of regulatory frames in developed societies. According to this School, anomia was a structural problem of new capitalist societies that created multiple adaptive options such as innovation, withdrawal, insurgency and ritualism. Therefore, criminality was the expression of these multiple structural options that strain two large systems: the cultural system (the American dream, easy money) and the social system (institutions that ensure equal access to all these cultural aspirations). It is noteworthy that, for Merton, criminality was conceived as a type of social innovation considered "normal" when the tension between social and cultural systems is present in developed societies.

Even though Merton does not specifically refer to organized crime, the contribution of his theory is fundamental in order to understand the kind of crime related to economy per se in which the theory of tension is the center of the explanation for the expansion process of TOC on a global scale (Downes and Rock 2011: 151–204; Merton 2002: 209–274). In this sense, the process of globalization has been denounced as a contradictory and conflictive process of inclusion and homogenization of values (culture of success, unlimited lucrative purposes) among widening inequalities and social asymmetries (relative deprivation) (Castell 2000). However, as well as the Chicago School, there is a fixed approach regarding the criminology of poverty-stricken societies, which is one of the main epistemological problems of criminology as the cognitive instrument of social reality.

Almost at the same time, the contribution of Edwin Sutherland in the 1930s and 1940s is an important milestone in the understanding of economic crime. Trained in the Chicago School, Sutherland sought to separate it from urban criminal and deviation studies to focus on the development of a criminology theory that exceeds the social bias of his predecessors. The fundamental contribution of Sutherland to the economic criminology consists of his unprecedented research into the powerful and wealthier classes in 1939, known as The White-Collar Criminal, which caused rejection, turmoil and even censorship among the academic atmosphere at that time. With his contribution, Sutherland (2009) pretended to put an end to the criminological focalization of the crime of the poor and call attention to the crime carried out by businessmen, and high social status and prestigious people. The work consisted of the statistical analysis of civil and administrative offenses in the business world that were not formally addressed by criminal legislations (until nowadays) as crime; even though its potential consequences create as much or more damage than common crimes in society. Therefore, they follow the generic pattern of criminal behavior. The objective of his study was to reveal how society sternly treats certain criminal behavior in poverty-stricken communities through criminal legislation, while, on the other hand, society tolerates and overlooks certain behavior and activities of those with high-class status even when they know the social harm it generates.

Through this study, Sutherland defined the nature of enterprise work as organized crime. The research carried out in 1937, known as "the professional thief," was relevant to fully understand this concept, in which the sense of professionalism and the system of organization of criminal communities in low social classes are highlighted. These organizations are actually closed cycles marked by inclusion and exclusion mechanisms, a sense of distinction and group identity. An interesting aspect of this approach is that the characteristics of professional crime are also deep-rooted in white-collar crime. For Sutherland, "White collar crime illustrates the culture of business world, in the same way as the professional criminal exemplifies the culture of the marginal world" (Sutherland 2009: 334). The behavior of the white-collar criminal is permanent as is the professional thieves' conduct, and it is marked by a high sense of status and respectability according to the social class where these people operate.

According to Sutherland:

> Businessmen generally feel rejection towards the law. In this sense, they are alike professional thieves, who despite the law, policemen, prosecutors and judges. Usually, businessmen see bureaucrats and politicians as authorized intruders that investigate commercial activities. They believe that the least governance the better, except when they need favors from it, sometimes they consider the enactment of a law as a felony, instead of judging the breaking of the law as a crime. The despite of the law by businessmen, as well as by the professional thief, arises from the fact that the law prevents their behavior.
>
> *(Sutherland 2009: 336)*

Sutherland's theory has been the key for the creation of the concept of criminal subculture developed during the 1950s in the Anglo-Saxon context (Cloward 2008). The subculture concept was initially influenced by Sutherland's theory known as "differential association," which consists of a communicative process of socialization of negative values and techniques (abilities and criminal methods) that prevail in certain spaces or social groups in an iterative approach rather than other positive values (Pires et al. 2014). The theory originated in the understanding not only of white-collar crime but also of organized crime in the lower classes. Thus, the "differential association" is the social process that emerged in the closest context of the criminal (close circle of friends, professional groups, enterprises, family groups, neighborhoods). For this reason, according to the theoreticians of criminal subculture such as Albert Cohen and David Matza (quoted by Downes and Rock 2011), the criminal subcultures were new ways of social organization that generated as an adaptive response to the social disruption of transitional capitalistic societies. However, these subcultures entered into a permanent conflict with social life values that are not criminal (Downes and Rock 2011: 205–260).

The theory of subculture has also received criticism. The problem with the theory of differential organization (subculture) and conflict is that it underestimates the importance of the general values that motivate this kind of high socio-economic class to justify and learn from illicit activities. Under this concept, a plural dimension of society will recognize that there is as many values as social groups. Hence, when white-collar crime takes place, there are two macro-values in conflict and permanent tension that rule the dilemmas of capitalistic global societies: free accumulation and state regulation.

Another contribution to this dilemma is proposed by Matza and Sykes (2014) to whom the criminal subcultures values are not very distinct from the bulk of the conventional values of capitalistic society. That is the reason why they use the concept of "underground values." The criminal identity, therefore, is a process by which a series of "underground values" (leisure, entertainment, easy money, malignancy, violence, negativity, hedonism) are considered as the center of a group identity; these are not considered as central values by society although they are present in daily life. Matza and Sykes (2014) recognize these values as conflictive in relation to societies in general, although these are practiced and recognized in one way or another by non-criminal groups. Despite that, the problem arises when the idea of "underground values" gives a clandestine, close and not conventional nature to the values of white-collar criminal organizations, and meanwhile these organizations are widely disseminated in the social system. It means that this conflict is far from the asymmetric game of "puritans against bandits."

To deny the asymmetric idea of the value conflict will result in taking up the old theory of systemic tension proposed by Merton (2002). According to this theory, criminality is the way social innovation takes place due to the tension that exists between the cultural objectives of capitalism (success and lucrative purposes) and illicit social abilities (privation). Unlike Merton, Sutherland beliefs will not comprehend the problem as a tension between culture and privation, but as a cultural issue and as an excess of regulation. The problem of the "economic crime," therefore, is that there is an insolvable tension between an individual cultural lucrative goal and the imposed collective state regulations. A clear example of this is the value placed on state regulation by certain elites where "the social planning for a more inclusive society is criticized by businessmen, like bureaucracy, utopia or communism" (Sutherland 2009: 369).

As well as the Merton School, Sutherland understands that the social context that takes account of this value conflict is originated under the anomia context or social disruption. However, this idea must not be understood as a product of the change of a traditional society to a modern or industrial one (in the Durkheimian and Mertonian tradition), but as the change of deep-rooted values of a free competition society (capitalistic folklore) from the end of nineteenth century against the new society of regulative capitalism, the product of the American New Deal after 1930. This tension points to the center of the existential dilemma of the economic individual of global societies: the virtuous innovative businessmen (Thomas Schumpeter's model) who is idealized by neoclassical economists, according to Sutherland, and at the same time is a transgressor of the social organization. What is an empire of fair laws for some people are to others the "tax hells," and what for certain people is a "tax heavens," for others means a hiding place for modern piracy.

As can be seen, Sutherland's contribution generates an epistemological leap on the topics related to crime and control, which has been a referent to economic criminology studies, and, as will be seen later, as the beginning of critic criminology. The goal of this author was to create a conscience about legislation to broaden the perspective toward a not very frequent series of behavior and activities that cause the same or even more damage to society. It also shares with other American schools a tacit allusion of capitalism and its demographic, cultural and social effects as factors that encourage crime, even though its objective was to give an account of the motivations of individual behavior from a micro-social perspective. For Sutherland and the other schools, crime is an autonomous, positive and tangible category that could arise from social issues, which somehow triggers a mechanical response to the problem. In other words, it presupposes the existence of an autonomous penal law that expresses a "social discomfort" toward the act of individual responsibility.

An important and revolutionary leap in the history of criminal thought was taken by the second School of Chicago in the 1960s, which became known as "labeling approach." Actually, this school was not considered as a monolithic contribution, but as the product of several contributions of different authors, successors of the symbolic interactionism of Hebert Mead from which there are some prominent names such as Edwin Lemert, Irwin Hoffman and Howard Becker. The focus of this thought was to give deserved importance to the effect of social reaction in the creation of the concept of what is known as deviation. In other words, besides the importance of the primary nature of deviant behavior (etiology), the social process of "labeling" is considered to be influential over certain conducts as well as the role of social stigma and stereotypes in the replication of criminal careers. Consequently, the crime is not an autonomous unit with its own life but a negotiated construct, fitted with specified and socially defined meanings and roles (Larrauri 1991).

The fundamental contribution of this School of economic criminology is based on the understanding of the role that morality plays in the penal configuration of the well-known "prohibition" concept (drugs, prostitution, games, weapons) that, through certain activities, is traditionally related to the appearance of international organized crime and gang culture around the world. Likewise, it contributes to the comprehension of specialized bureaucracy (justice and police operators) on the selective actions taken by these groups toward certain behavior or activities of some social groups. The statistic production, therefore, is not a quantitative reproduction of reality, but the epistemological process of construction of the social senses that produce and make sense to the ones that society knows as "deviant" and his/her treatment (Becker 2009; Downes and Rock 2011; Larrauri 1991). The deviation sociology proposed by this second School of Chicago has been the key for the emergence of critical criminology. Its contribution lies in the assertion and criticism of the principles of labeling theory, which are the base from which criminology and the political international economy are linked.

The Marxist theories

The National Deviance Conference took place in 1968 and gathered several criminologists, scholars, government officials and social activists that refuted the conventional ideas of positivist criminology, the cultural monism and the pathological nature of criminal behavior. They agreed on the labeling approach theory of the deviating, which was considered to be a social construct, as well as the importance of social reaction in order to understand the deviant process. However, they criticized the labeling approach theory due to its liberal ideas and its lack of comprehension of the historical perspective of power relationships (Larrauri 1991). The result of this conference was not homogeneous, but its core ideas contributed to the establishment of certain criminological premises with the traditional ideas of Karl Marx starting what is known as "critical criminology" with different views and extents (Downes and Rock 2011). From then on, the criminological topics, which were focused on micro-social themes, started to link with the macro-social transformation of classic Marxism; in other words, a complex connection between traditional political economy and criminology was created.

A basic principle of the critical perspective is to understand criminal law and the law enforcement agencies within the wide range of international capitalist interests. According to this perspective, the relationship between the economic structure and the criminal system varied among deterministic and less deterministic approaches (with a wide range of disputes). Likewise, it involved several Marxists views where the structural ideas of Louis Althusser were prominent, as were the cultural and historic views of Eric Hobsbawn, Antonio Gramsci's hegemony concept and the central ideas of the School of Frankfurt. For the different Marxist views, the deviant as a social construction is a political and contentious act that links the macro-social and micro-social level (Larrauri 1991; Taylor, Walton and Young 1977).

There are different positions about the social reaction toward crime in general (organized crime for the purposes of this chapter). The first and most remarkable has labeled social reaction as an ideological institution related to the maintenance and refinement of the repressive state structure and the authority symbols with the established authority justification. The ideas of Rushe and Kirchheimer in 1968 (quoted by Garland 2007) about "punishment and social structure" have been important to this matter. This theory suggests understanding the reaction or the punishment toward crime outside of its instrumental value. The shape and objective of criminal policy must be considered within an analytical framework, conditioned by high-level economic and political interests. Regarding these ideas, the old Durkheimian idea about crime and punishment is picked up as a "scape goat" to reinforce the symbol of social power and cohesion (Garland 2007). Other views understand the social reaction to crime as a way of control that falls on the poverty-stricken social classes, the role of which is to neutralize social mobilization, the implementation of discipline and the maintenance of the "reserve army of labor." Stanley Cohen's concept of "moral panic" (2011) was created under this theory, and refers to the oversized and idealistic character of the crime as a product of the expansion of the media. The political effects of this phenomenon are considered to be a distractor and obstacle to social action toward the systematic capitalistic crisis.

This political–economic dimension has ensured that Edwin Sutherland's ideas take on a very important value in the analysis of contemporary criminal politics. On one side, the predatory and savage nature of the cultural folklore of capitalism is accepted as a triggering factor of the emergence of economic crime. From this perspectives, it is assumed that networks of organized delinquency are inevitable in the reproduction of capitalism. Permissiveness toward abusive behaviors and activities are linked to powerful business interests. On the other hand, the understanding of Sutherland from a dimension of power would explain the selective character of the reaction of the state and justice operators toward the restraining of certain focalized behavior (generally located in low social contexts). In other words, since the critical discussion on Edwin Sutherland's theory, this permissiveness/selectivity game is a criminogenic element per se and at the same time is a control and dominance instrument that allows the capital reproduction process (Downes and Rock 2011; Larrauri 1991; Taylor, Walton and Young 1977). Both are ways of government based on the interests of dominant social classes (Baratta 1986). Because of this premise, Andreas (2013) states that the dynamics of the criminal webs of global capitalism bring a sophisticated bureaucracy of international control over the problem.

However, a weakness in this approach has been its inability to comprehend the impact of organized crime because of its frequent trivialization. Within the criminological subject there have been other critical approaches of realistic foundations that have understood the acute social effects of organized crime in certain territories. These perspectives have criticized the Marxist currents as radical theories that contribute little to the social, political and economic understanding of the problem and its neutralization. The effect of organized crime is not a problem of the rich against the poor, but a problem that affects the intraclass and interethnic groups

(Downes and Rock 2011; Young and Mathews 1993). In the same way, the criminal webs reproduce the most hide-bounded dimensions of society and are far from being an idyllic idea of the Robin Hood figure in certain communities. This matches the conservative view that the problem of organized crime must be dealt with seriously, but the difference lies in the fact that these show the deep structural causes of organized crime as a result of the economic, social and cultural contradictions of capitalism. This awareness not only considers underclass crime, but also is critical of the social wounds of white-collar crime. Because of this, it has also contributed to the consolidation and strengthening of an extensive international economic crime control system that combines punitive as well as non-punitive strategies.

To sum up, the various sociological traditions present different scenarios and theoretical, methodological and epistemological options that indirectly contribute to the understanding of the incidence of social transformations of capitalistic societies (demographic, social, economic and cultural aspects) in the nature of the rise of economic crime. Despite this, the development of the international political economy as a discipline for the understanding of "globalization" provides its own elements for the comprehension of the complex cognitive dynamic of international organized crime.

IPE and TOC

During the past years, IPE studies have shown noticeable interest in understanding the complex aspects of transnational organized crime and its global impact. Generally, the interest has been focused on the comprehension of the causes and consequences of the expansion of this problem at a global level and the understanding of the different local, national and global dynamics that articulate this problem. There are three substantive issues that contribute to IPE in the comprehension of TOC. The international system, the debate about the state and its role, and the criminal agency's rationale. All these areas are closely interrelated with one another. However, if the old argument already installed in the criminological approach from long time ago is not taken into an account, these debates appear unidirectional. There are two criminological dimensions that are implicit in the articulation between IPE and TOC: the positivist dimension that understands TOC as an autonomous analytic category; and the critical dimension that sees TOC as a social construct of the power with broad geopolitical dimensions. Only through the articulation of these analytic areas can the configuration of organized crime be understood by a complex relationship (sometimes conflictive and explosive) among the economy, politics and culture that is aggravated in global contexts (Andreas 2013: 3).

Within the positivist line of IPE there are two visions: the conservative and the liberal view. The conservative view tries to place TOC as the central point of the debate; however, it has a decontextualized understanding of the deep causes of this problem (structural). The understanding of TOC turns into what Pavarini (2005) calls a "abject art" that promotes an international crusade against "social demons" that aim to subvert the order and liberal world peace (Mathews 2014: 38–41). This ideological vision has largely worsened since 9/11 when TOC became widely related to the emergence and growth of "international terrorism."

On the other hand, the liberal dimension does not talk about motivations of criminal conduct, but talks about the elements that facilitate this behavior. In this regard, there is a tacit knowledge of globalization and its effects as criminogenic elements that promote the expansion of this problem as the economic, commercial and financial liberation of the countries (Levi 2005); the technological development of media and the industry of transportation and distribution (Simons and Tucker 2007); transboundary foreign migration (Sansó 2011); and the universalization of punitive policies on a global scales (Andreas 2013; Serrano and Toro 2005). There are other positions that maintain that TOC is the result of the conflict or chaos produced for exclusion and underdevelopment in the framework of sprawling and disorganized processes of urbanization; also, because of the lack of stability in public, economic and social institutions in certain countries or regions of the world (Cox 2002). There are also mixed approaches that admit that this economy takes place with more emphasis as a product of the gap generated between the sudden growing process and capitalistic expansion of a territory, with weak processes of modernization and state institutionalization of control (Gambetta 2007). In general, it could be said that this liberal posture understands TOC as one of the unintended consequences of "globalization" (Andreas and Nadelmann 2005; Levi 2005), for which it is necessary to search the instruments and international inputs and outputs for its control and neutralization.

Apart from that there is the critical discussion. For this approach, TOC is the result of certain hegemonic geopolitical interests. The use of this concept has been permanently nurtured by the security agendas of the United States (the country of origin of this concept) since the Cold War. From this point of view, there are opinions that encourage the use of the term "organized crime" as the representation of the binary demarcation of the world and society (good/bad; legal/illegal) that originates a new classification of a high geopolitical spectrum of the world (safe world, developed/dangerous world/underdeveloped) depending on determined geopolitical interests. There are also studies concerning the political use of "organized crime" in the internal security policy of that country. The basic idea of this approach has been to highlight the image of the external enemy (foreigner) who breaks the deepest conservative and puritan values of American society founded at the beginning of the last century and that expresses the ideal life of American society (Fernández 2008). These studies are not free of ethnic and racist prejudice attributed to the historic migrations to this country during the 1920s and 1930s (Italian American gangs) (Arroyo 2007; De León and Silva 2004: 6). All these values are the factors that have permeated the view of the political class and dominate public opinion at an international level through the ideological process of colonization and which have far-reaching consequences in the design of public policies from the countries at an internal and external level.

Box 26.1 The trial of alias "Chapo Guzman" and his declarations[1]

At the beginning of 2019, a jury of the United States found the leader of the Sinaloa Cartel, El Chapo Guzman Loera, guilty of all ten charges against him, and sentenced him to life in prison. The jury took place at the Federal Court of District in Brooklyn, it lasted 3 months in which the evidence was presented against the defendant, and there was a cooperation of 56 witnesses, including a former Mexican deputy, who was a lover of Chapo.

Chapo was one of the most important drug lords in Mexican cartel history. He was a very popular man and was appreciated by the lower strata of society. His smuggling tactics were a product of his wit and the current technological facilities, plus a great deal of violence and the capacity to corrupt the political system to get into its structure, making it possible for him to escape justice a couple of times.

During the trial there were important declarations about actors, governmental infiltrations (Mexican, American and from other Latin American countries), corruption of high authorities, procedures, financial aids, logistics and bloody tactics used to reach certain objectives. This showed the fragile capacity of control of the states in which territories the criminal actions were perpetrated; he was accused of having generated 14,000 million of dollars as a product of illicit transactions of the transportation of more than 200 tons of narcotic drugs. During the trial, it was heard from several witnesses that bribe payments were made to politicians and to security forces members, including the police and armed forces. It became public knowledge that a presumed illegal payment was made to the former Mexican President Enrique Peña Nieto for about 100 million dollars when he was a candidate for the presidency, as well as other payments to a secretary of state and high-ranking officials.

Vast amounts of marijuana, cocaine, heroin and synthetic drugs were trafficked from Mexico and exchanged for large sums of money. It was also known that the Mexican territory needed money laundry. All of these contributed to a wave of violence unleashed by the disputes in the smuggling territories and routes, which included murders, rapes and cremations, among other crimes. According to the Drug Enforcement Administration (DEA), the Sinaloa Cartel strengthened its operations in spite of the capture of its criminal leader in January 2016, increasing its production of heroin by 37 percent. Likewise, the confiscation of fentanyle (an opioid used in drug manufacturing) doubled on the Mexican–American border.[2] This case reveals the strength of the connection of TOC at the international and local scale, and its complex web of politic, economic and social interrelations.

Notes

1 The investigation for this case was possible due to Francisco Chamorro's help. He is a Professor at Instituto de Altos Estudios Nacionales.
2 Information obtained from *The New York Times* (2019) Available at: www.nytimes.com/es/2019/02/12/chapo-guzman-culpable/?rref=collection%2Fsectioncollection%2Fnyt-es.

Regarding the state and its role, IPE is very important in the comprehension of TOC. After the decline of the state-centered approach in the analysis of international studies at the end of the 1960s, the state's position once again became important precisely because of its role between global and local dynamics of globalization. Castel (2010) named this phenomenon "glocalization"; a new way of understanding how the states deal with the complex problems of the globalized world in specific places instead of using the classic route of military intervention (Keohane and Nye 1988).

This realignment of the state in the global context gives it a central role in the reproduction of organized crime. From the conservative perspective, this role of the state takes up the classic realistic debates that urge the states to bring order against a chaotic scenario of exogenous threats in the national context. The ultimate duty of a state is to protect its population and available resources (security and defense strategy). In this scenario, the state is a determinant variable that explains the cause and the remedy of the problem. From this viewpoint, the conservative explanation originated around the "failed state" arising from 9/11, which classifies the countries within the international community in relation to its vulnerability or fragility (economic, social, politic and institutional) (Rotberg 2003; Santos 2009). Weak and failed states allow to organized crime and international terrorism to operate; therefore strengthening the state is the main strategy employed to improve international security.

On the contrary, from the liberal viewpoint, the response of the state is explained by a process of adaptive response that consists of the control capacity of the effect of the deregulation of commerce and the financial and technological relocation. In the words of Duffield (2007: 14),

> this has led to the proliferation of new form of authority, protection and legitimacy emerged from this undiscovered criminal world essentially not liberal … and they could be developed as a not territorial web that work through and around the United States.

Therefore, the liberal vision assumes the moderate role of the state as a regulatory agency of the infiltration of TOC at an international level. Likewise, the dependence and mobility of this economy and its webs of actors is admitted at a transnational scale. What a state does or does not do at an international scale necessarily affects other states. To address this scenario, it is necessary to create a high level of local and global governance that implies joint efforts to focalize, dismember and neutralize illicit economic activities.

Despite this, from the conservative and liberal viewpoints there is no historic evidence to prove that the more open a state is, the greater the infiltration of organized crime. Moreover, affirming this could result in a "double standard" political contradiction of those liberal groups that promote the economic openness of the state, while the free movement of people is restricted as a control strategy or as an inhibition of transnational organized crime through greater control from the state (Berdal and Serrano 2005). Likewise, the use of the category "weakness of the state" generates a relatively high margin of error in comparative politics. First of all, because the countries with institutional weakness or with little consolidation of democracy do not always show a higher incidence of this type of criminality; and second, because it is not known if the incidence of the organized crime per se could be an important trigger for the consolidation of the institutions and the democracy of a country, or if it is precisely this lack of consolidation that impacts on the presence of the organized crime (Ávila 2010). Without discrediting the importance that the states have on the control of these activities, to place the state as the center of gravity of the problem generates incorrect interpretations since, in general, the variable "state" has little capacity for geographic predictability that allows us to know its dynamics and development.

The "state" variable, on the other hand, does not explain the complex geopolitical relationship of the supply and demand of illegal services or products, and its way of operating within the globalization that works at an independent level of development, control and/or state openness. This is most likely due to the fact that, within globalization, TOC operates without localization; in other words, an illegal organized operation can be simultaneously planned in a country while it is perpetrated in another place ,and its financial gains are hidden in a tax haven (Sansó 2011). There are often several errors of interpretation on the problem of the influence of criminal economies. In general, the weight of these criminal economies is oversized in countries with high levels of informal economy. This approach, however, hides the strong relationship between the supply and demand of illicit products worldwide and the trajectory of resources in developed countries and tax havens (Fernández 2008).

The lack of a specific geography is where the critical view takes shape again. That crime or deviation are social constructs of power becomes more evident in the practice of TOC. In general, the measurement of the true incidence of TOC is clouded by the clandestine and informal nature of its activities, moving away from the classical system of formal measurements of the legal world. This causes serious problems of application and factual veracity in the measurement of this criminal world (Fernández 2008). This situation has resulted in the generation of a highly speculative factor in the valuation of this problem, although not without individual, corporate and political interests in its insights. The activity of measuring these types of economies uses indirect methodologies (statistical estimates). Sometimes, these mechanisms are expensive and apply different methodologies, and they also show significant variations in the results and interpretation of them. The management and financing of these epistemic communities of measurement, therefore, is a fundamental piece of the dominant geopolitical interpretation of this topic. In the tradition of Howard Becker and the second School of Chicago, the appreciation of the incidence, operation and the penetration of conventional organized crime ends up reflecting the point of view and bias of a series of operators that build a reality and nurture various political operators, public opinion and media about this clandestine world. Therefore, the geographic dimension of TOC turns into a social construct parceled out according to a broad spectrum of institutional and geopolitical rationales and interests.

Another IPE dimension in the understanding of TOC is the criminal agency. Addressing this issue, the interest has centered on the understanding of the behavior of the agency at the organizational and group level, and not at the individual level. At this level, the criminological theories of David Matza and Albert Cohen regarding criminal subcultures have played a fundamental role in analyzing the transmission of values, rationale and criminal methods. This also shows the social construct of the sense of belonging, identification and ways of organization of the criminal groups. A more contemporaneous contribution to this level comes from the theory of the modern organizations, which provide several elements for the classification in different ways (Fernández 2008).

The business views on the organizational perspective of these groups is highlighted. On one side, there are views that the criminal organizations resemble the organization and rationality of the legal transnational enterprises (Abadinsky 1990/2010; Ruggiero 1996). Other people look at criminal organizations as a way of creating a certain order within the anomic and clandestine world of illegal transactions (De León and Silva 2004: 7). There, hierarchical and stable organizations are involved in the establishment of a protection system against public control through corruption and extortion (Gambetta 2007; Gilinskiy 2006; Resa 2005).

Despite this, certain dimensions that avoid placing this analysis at the organizational level have appeared, due to the fact that, in practice, these are seen more as a product of the labeling of the language of the police, which lack verifiable sources to prove the existence of these organizations. To focus on the organization as an element of analysis would generate a confusing field for the understanding of the criminal phenomenon. In general, the organizational field is always ambiguous because these criminal ways operate in most cases in a short-term context, precisely because of a lack of confidence among the agents and the lack of predictability and stability in the transactions (Fernández 2008). For this reason, for Gambetta (2007), the organization is an "attribute" and is not the center of these criminal enterprises.

For this reason, some liberal contributions suggest paying attention to the criminal agents as economic subjects instead of focusing on the groups. This supports the contributions of Gary Becker (2009), who views the criminal as a rational being, adverse to risk, that behaves on an encouragement and reward scheme basis. From these points of view, the criminal markets are a consequence of a type of economy built around illegality. Criminal actors converge with internalized rules that in some way ensure their sustainability through time (Gambetta 2007); in other words, the criminal business is somehow supported by certain micro-economic assumptions, such as risk aversion, protection and the profit motive (Albanese 2010). Violence, corruption and social and political corruption are shaped in the instrumental rationale of reproduction and expansion of TOC, based on these assumptions. The criticism for this dimension is based on the fact that it locates the professional criminal as a *homo-economicus* who is individualist and universal and underestimates the influence of the different social and cultural contexts. In the same way, it places the crime in an ambiguous moral logic where one can not differentiate what is right or wrong in a society.

But beyond criticism, the contribution of localizing the criminal agency in terms of business rationality is that they state things as they are. It is in this sense that the contribution of Edwin Sutherland is relevant to IPE. For this author, society is not a harmonious cohesive entity, but a place of conflicts and disagreements. For this reason, these similarities and the low level of differentiation between the legal and the illegal world could only be explained by a power scheme that ends up criminalizing and stigmatizing certain behaviors (generally behaviors from underprivileged social sectors) and rewarding or stimulating other conducts based on the system operation. In this way, the present problem of tax havens would be explained as well as the Panama Papers, which from the criminological dimension have seized or avoided the advantages or risk factors of globalization (according to how it is seen) based on the pathological tendency of money gain and on selfish and anti-social individualism.

Box 26.2 Panama Papers – Mossack Fonseca

In April 2016, the Consorcio Internacional de Periodistas de Investigación disclosed several documents related to enterprises in tax havens that involved political leaders and famous people around the world, who through offshore financial systems, known as offshore enterprises, had hidden thousands of millions of dollars. This unfolded a worldwide scandal that ended up with the involvement of such prominent people as Mauricio Macri, people close to Vladimir Putin and FIFA members, to cite some examples.

Mossack Fonseca is a firm of lawyers, legally based in Panama, with branch offices in 40 countries, and which had the main objective of creating a number of facades and hidden accounts for approximately 14,000 clients around the world. While in Panama the functioning of offshore enterprises to avoid the payment of taxes is legal, the problem has an impact in the way of managing of these entities, an extreme secrecy that covers up the origin and the purpose of the transactions, as well as to whom they belong. Therefore, there was a complete ignorance about the financial transactions made by these types of companies. What exacerbated the problem even more is that, according to the investigative consortium, people and companies that are involved in this activity are on the "black list" of the United States as a result of their relationship with drug trafficking, terrorism and money laundry.

Since these facts came to light, a series of political actions and trials against offshore enterprises have been generated in several countries. For example, in Ecuador, in February 2017, there was a referendum with the objective to establish the illegality of politicians and public officials that were owners or shareholders of offshore enterprises in tax havens. Likewise, in the United States, in December 2018, four business leaders linked to the investigation of the Panama Papers were formally accused of defrauding the government of the United States through money laundry and electronic fraud in association with a Panamanian firm called Mossack Fonseca.

According to the Center of Public Integrity, a non-profit journalism organization, since this scandal, there have been at least 150 investigations into money laundry and tax evasion in more than 70 countries. This is a relevant case since it shows the complexity and highly sophisticated way economic crimes of fraud and tax evasion are carried out that in many countries are judged as organized crime. It also openly shows the cognitive criminal dilemma of "white-collar crime" demonstrated by Sutherland. It is remarkable that the presence of American citizens and celebrities was excluded in this list, which shows evidence of the use of information about this problem on the basis of geopolitical interests.

Conclusion

In general terms, there has been very little communication between the political economy and the economic criminology. While the control of the criminal affairs has been an area of practical relevance for criminological sciences at a local level, the themes related to international politics have worked little on the dynamics for the control and criminalization within societies and its relationship with power. Therefore, this chapter proposes a dialogue between these two disciplines in order to have a better view of the complexity of TOC at an international level.

The criminological view contributes with the updating of the old debate of academic traditions and the different sociological schools. However, this thought is a product of the rise of capitalism as an economic system of the world, and the placing of the United States of America as a global power. Consequently, the demographic, cultural and social topics of the societies undergoing a transition to capitalism generate an epistemological framework as a base for the articulation between organized crime and the political economy. Despite this, the Marxist theories and its approach of power and the social reaction are the ones that contribute to a complex connection between these two dimensions.

The IPE as a discipline of globalization generates its own elements in the scale of this phenomenon at a global level. Taking up the epistemological dilemma of the classic economic criminology, IPE also contributes with an insight into the complex dimension of TOC in global societies. This dimension is expressed as a multifaceted interrelation at the global, national and subnational level that overlaps political, cultural, moral and economic agendas in the international system. However, this complexity is highlighted in the understanding of global capitalism in two dimensions that, rather than antagonist, are complementary in global contexts: capitalism as a system of control and as a system of economic reproduction. In other words, it is a system that infringes upon the "good liberal government" but at the same time is a product of capitalistic structures and its transformations. Under this logic, the problem of TOC as the "dark side of the globalization" is of a systematic nature, which appears as an adaptive response to a political scheme that the same system produces and rejects. A social system that is afraid of itself!

Bibliography

Abadinsky, H. 1990/2010. *Organized Crime*, 9th ed. Belmont, CA: Wadsworth.

Albanese, J. 2010. Assessing Risk, Harm, and Threat to Target Resources against Organized Crime: A Method to Identify the Nature and Severity of the Professional Activity of Organized Crime and its Impacts (Economic, Social, Political). *Working Papers Series, No. 12. Global Consortium on Security Transformation (GCST)*. Available at: www.securitytransformation.org/gc_publications.php.

Andreas, P. 2013. *Smuggler Nation: How Illicit Trade Made America*. New York: Oxford University Press.

Andreas, P. and Nadelmann, E. 2005. *Policing the Globe. Criminalization and Crime Control in International Relations*. New York: Oxford University Press.

Arroyo, C. 2007. *Una revisión conceptual del crimen organizado y sus tendencias en América Latina*. Nicaragua: Instituto de Estudios Estratégicos y Políticas Públicas, Mirador de Seguridad.

Ávila, A. 2010. Injerencia política de los grupos armados ilegales. In: López, C. *Refundaron la patria: De cómo mafiosos y políticos reconfiguraron el Estado colombiano. Corporación Nuevo Arco Iris*. Bogotá, Colombia: Corporación Nuevo Arco Iris.

Baratta, A. 1986. *Criminología crítica y crítica del derecho penal*. México: Siglo XXI.

Becker, H. 2009. *Outsiders. Hacia una sociología de la desviación*. Buenos Aires: Siglo XXI.

Berdal, M. and Serrano, M. 2005. Crimen transnacional organizado y seguridad internacional: Un breve panorama. In Berdal, M. and Serrano, M. (eds) *Crimen transnacional organizado y seguridad internacional. Cambio y continuidad*: 13–26. México: D.F. Fondo de Cultura Económica.

Bustelos, P. 2003. El enfoque de regulación económica y economía política internacional. ¿Paradigmas convergentes? *Revista de Economía Mundial* No 8. 143–173. Madrid. Available at: www.ucm.es/info/eid/pb/Bustelo%20-%20REM03.pdf.

Castel, R. 2010. *El ascenso de las incertidumbres. Trabajo, protección del estatuto del individuo*. Buenos Aires: Fondo de Cultura Económica: 15–55.

Castell, M. 2000. *Globalización, sociedad y política en la era de la Información. Bitacora 4-i*. Available at: https://dialnet.unirioja.es/descarga/articulo/4008342.pdf.

Cloward, R. 2008. Medios ilegítimos, anomia y comportamiento desviado. In: *Delito y Sociedad*. Santa Fé: UNL Ediciones.

Cohen, S. 2011. *Folk Devils and Moral Panics: The Creation of the Mods and Rockers*. London: Routledge Classics.

Cox, R. 2002. The Covert World. In Cox, R. and Schechter, M. (eds.) *The Political Economy of a Plural World: Critical Reflections on Power, Morals and Civilization*. London: Routledge: 118–138.

De León, I. and Silva, G. 2004. Problemas sociológicos y de tipificación penal relacionados con el crimen organizado. *Borradores de Método Área de Crimen y Conflicto: Documento 25*.

Dickie, J. 2006. *Cosa Nostra. La historia de la mafia siciliana*. Barcelona: Debate.

Downes, D. and Rock, P. 2011. *Sociología de la desviación*. México: Gedisa.

Duffield, M. 2007. *Global Governance and the New Wars: The Merging of Development and Security*. London: Zed Books.

Fernández, A. 2008. *Las Pistas Falsas del Crimen Organizado. Finanzas Paralelas y Orden Internacional*. Madrid: Catarata.

Gambetta, D. 2007. *La mafia siciliana. El negocio de la protección privada*. México D.F: Fondo de Cultura Económica.

García, J. 2005. *Nuevas amenazas y trasformación de la defensa: el caso de Latinoamérica*. Available at: www.ieepp.org/documentos/cdi/sectordefensa/reforma_Transformacion_de_fuerzas_armadas.pdf.

Garland, D. 2007. *Crimen y castigo en la modernidad tardía*. Universidad de los Andes, Pontificia Universidad Javeriana – Instituto Pensar, Colombia: Siglo del Hombre Editores.

Gilinskiy, Y. 2006. Crime in Contemporary Russia. *European Journal of Criminology*, 3(3): 259–292.

Kahhat, F. 2003. *Los estudios de seguridad tras el fin de la Guerra Fría*. México: CIDE.

Keohane, R. and Nye, J. 1988. *Poder e Interdependencia. La Política mundial en transición*. Buenos Aires: Grupo Editor Latinoamericano.

Larrauri, E. 1991. *La herencia de la criminología crítica*. Madrid: Siglo XXI.

Levi, M. 2005. Liberalización y crimen financiero transnacional. In Berdal, M. and Serrano, M. (eds) *Crimen transnacional organizado y seguridad internacional. Cambio y continuidad*. México D.F.: Fondo de Cultura Económica: 86–107.

Lupsha, P. 1996. Transnational Organized Crime versus the Nation-state. *Transnational Organized Crime*, No. 1: 21–48.

Mathews, R. 2015. *Criminología Realista*. Buenos Aires: Didot.

Matza, D. and Sykes, G. 2014. Delincuencia juvenil y valores subterráneo. In: *Revista Delito y Sociedad*. Santa Fé: UNL Ediciones.

Merton, R. 2002. *Teoría y estructura sociales*. México D.F.: Fondo de Cultura Económica.

Pavarini, M. 2005. *Un arte abyecto. Ensayo sobre el gobierno de la penalidad*. Buenos Aires: Ad-hoc.

Payne, A. 2005. The Study of Governance in Global Political Economy. In: Phillips, N. (ed.) *Globalization International Political Economy*. London: Palgrave Macmillan: 55–81.

Pires, A., Debuyst, C. and Digneffe, F. 2014. Elementos para una relectura de la teoría del delito de Edwin Sutherland. In: *Revista Delito y Sociedad*, No 37. Santa Fé: UNL Ediciones: 9–40.

Resa, C. 2005. *Crimen Organizado Transnacional: Definición, Causas Y Consecuencias*. Madrid: Editorial Astrea.

Rotberg, R. 2003. *When States Fail*. Princeton, NJ: Princeton University Press. Available at: http://press.princeton.edu/chapters/s7666.pdf.

Ruggiero, V. 1996. *Organized Crime in Europe: Offers That Can't be Refused*. Aldershot: Dartmouth Publishing Company.

Sansó, D. 2011. Inteligencia criminal: una lección estratégica en clave de seguridad frente a la iniciativa de la delincuencia organizada. In: Rivera, F. (ed.) *Inteligencia estratégica prospectiva*. Quito: FLACSO-SENAIN, AECID.

Santos, G. 2009. *Estados fallidos: definiciones conceptuales*. Centro de Documentación, Investigación y Análisis, Subdirección de Política Exterior, Cámara de Diputados, México D.F. Available at: www.diputados.gob.mx/cedia/sia/spe/SPE-ISS-07-09.pdf.

Serrano, M. and Toro, M. 2005. Del narcotráfico al crimen organizado en América Latina. In: Berdal, M. and Serrano, M. (eds) *Crimen transnacional organizado y seguridad internacional*: 233–274. *Cambio y continuidad*. México D.F.: Fondo de Cultura Económica.

Simons, A. and Tucker, D. 2007. The Misleading Problem of Failed States: A 'Socio-Geography' of Terrorism in the Post-9/11 Era. *Third World Quarterly* 28(2): 387–401. Available at: http://faculty.nps.edu/asimons/docs/CTWQ_A_215315_O.pdf.

Sutherland, E. 2009. *El delito de cuello blanco*. Buenos Aires: Bfd.

Taylor, I., Walton, P. and Young, J. 1977. *La nueva criminología. Contribución a una teoría social de la conducta desviada*. Buenos Aires: Amorrortu.

Valer, D. 2018. *Criminología de la delincuencia organizada. Partheneon*. Available at: www.parthenon.pe/publico/criminologia-de-la-delincuencia-economica-un-breve-repaso-a-la-teoria-de-sutherland-a-proposito-del-fenomeno-de-la-criminalidad-economica-y-su-conexion-con-la-corrupcion-en-el-peru/.

Vlassis, D. 2005. La Convención de Naciones Unidas contra el crimen transnacional organizado. In: Berdal, M. and Serrano, M. (eds). *Crimen transnacional organizado y seguridad internacional. Cambio y continuidad*. México D.F.: Fondo de Cultura Económica: 131–148.

Whyte, W. F. 1971. *The Street Corner Connection*, Ed. Diana. México.

Young, J. and Mathews, R. 1993. Reflexiones sobre el "realismo" criminológico. In: *Revista Delito y Sociedad* No. 3. Santa Fé, UNL Ediciones: 13-35.

Part IV

Regional perspectives and inquiries

27

IPE beyond Western paradigms

China, Africa, and Latin America in comparative perspective

Melisa Deciancio and Cintia Quiliconi

Introduction

Political economy is about the sources of political power and its uses for economic ends. As power distribution varies around the globe, so does economic development and its approach to it. As Benjamin Cohen puts it, "the field of International Political Economy (IPE) teaches us how to think about the connections between economics and politics beyond the confines of a single state" (Cohen 2008: 1). However, not all the states look alike. When Cohen proposed a global conversation within the field of IPE he centered on American and British IPE, and in English spoken authors and approaches he only explored the construction of IPE in the Anglo-Saxon world. In the same line, in the last decades several authors started to reflect about academic fields like International Relations (IR) and IPE, in close connection with the growing development that the field has had around the globe. This development has spurred a number of critical approaches about Western approaches in both IR (Eagleton-Pierce 2009; Schmidt 1998; Tickner 2003) and IPE but in this field more incipient (Chin, Pearson, and Yong 2013; Tussie 2015) that strive to develop new lines of research that bring other perspectives to the center of the scene, constructing alternative contributions to those imposed or disseminated from the centers of world power. Thus, lately, some relevant studies have emerged on the place that national and regional schools occupy within social sciences and the work of numerous scholars has aimed at making them more "global" (Acharya 2014; Cohen 2008; Helleiner 2014; Phillips and Weaver 2011; Tussie 2015).

As ideas and knowledge travel, so do disciplines. The way IPE developed in the Anglo-Saxon world had set the main bases to its study in other regions of the world centering the attention on the way markets and power operate worldwide. However, when approaching the way IPE developed "outside the mainstream" particularities emerge, and a whole set of conceptualizations and questions arose that differ in a great manner from those in the developed world. Markets and power are both main concerns in the capitalist world we live in but the way we think about that interaction changes if we are on one side of the globe or the other(s). Inquiries, ideas, and analysis in the Global South are proof of that. Thinking capitalism from the core – namely Europe and the US – has a completely different approach than thinking it from the South. Problems and approaches vary if you are from developed countries or if you are from developing or emerging countries, if you are a rule maker or a rule taker, if you are a creditor or a debtor, if you are inserted in the global economy as a producer of manufactures or a commodity exporter.

This led us to another question. In this framework, should IPE be global? Can IPE be global? Do we need it to be global? Globalizing fields of research can also be a trap. As globalization itself became a way of homogenization and Westernization of the rest of the world, making disciplines more global (although it has good intentions) could also be, on one hand, the way the mainstream comprises concepts and ideas from other regions of the world but does nothing with them. On the other hand, it could also be the way the mainstream embrace concepts and ideas from other regions of the world but do nothing with them. In this vein, we can think of IPE as being global in its subject study, but we can question its globalizing scope showing the risk that it has for the field and the way different parts of the world approach it. Making it global can also mean making the Global South problems more diffuse, blurry, and imperceptible, which can imply that the only ones capable of thinking about and developing solutions to those problems are the same ones that cause them.

In this chapter we will address the way IPE developed outside the mainstream, in the Global South, focusing on the case studies of Africa, Asia, and particularly China and South America. Bringing into light the way IPE has been approached in these regions of the world will allow us to identify problems, ideas, and concerns different from those in the North and that also place attention on the necessity of conscious reading of these works in order to find suitable solutions to the market–,power dynamics affecting "the rest of the world." It seeks to resume the contributions made by IPE in the Global South to the construction of a research agenda on IPE beyond the West (and North). First, we will discuss the aim of making IPE a global field and the limits of the global conversation. Afterwards, we will approach the way IPE developed in Africa, China and South America. Finally, conclusions based on a comparison of these diverged approaches will follow.

In methodological terms, for the analysis we will focus on the agents of knowledge production (academics and specialists) as well as the spaces (institutions, networks, publications) where the specialized knowledge about IPE was developed in the Global South. It seeks to identify institutions, networks, people, and knowledge that influenced the formulation of new approaches to IPE. Among the spaces studied, we will consider first topics and main debates in IPE for each region; then universities, as areas of training and dissemination of knowledge; public and private institutions of knowledge production; and networks that stimulated the proliferation of international studies at the national level (Altamirano and Sarlo 1997; Buchbinder 2005; Clark 1997). Finally, the agents considered will be intellectuals specialized in the production of knowledge, both for academic debate and for the state (Altamirano and Sarlo 1997; Plotkin and Zimmermann 2012).

IPE and the limits of the global conversation

Political economy has always been part of IR (Cohen 2008) and, as such, IPE (and IR in general) has been considered a discipline designed by and especially outlined by the experiences and problems of the US and European central countries. This determined not only who dominated the field but also with which tools. In recent years, this deep and ponderous intellectual dominance led several academics from different parts of the world to the task of developing their own approaches or recovering local and regional ones to offer a broader vision of the discipline alerted by its narrowness and the denial of the existence of other voices, experiences, knowledge, and perspectives from outside the centers. Thus, it has exposed the limitations of theories and approaches developed by the centers to explain – and especially to modify – the realities of the periphery. Therefore, the reflection has focused on the circulation of knowledge between center and periphery and how that circulation has marked the form IPE has developed in other parts of the world.

It is known that IPE has achieved its greatest development in the English-speaking world, both in methodological and theoretical terms. As Benjamin Cohen (2008) points out, "globally, the dominant version of IPE (we might even say the hegemonic version) is one that has developed in the United States, where most scholarship tends to hew close to the norms of conventional social science" (Cohen 2008: 3) and where "the other" is British IPE (Blyth 2009; Phillips and Weaver 2011). As a result, geographically, on one hand, Anglo-Saxon academia became the reference point for the development of IPE in the world, while on the other hand, the study of "the other" has been focused on the transatlantic dialogue and British IPE. Theoretically, the conversation tends to leave behind Marxism, critical IPE studies, and many idiosyncratic views that neither dialogue with the North nor incorporate their methodological standards.

To make this scenario even more complex, in the Global South the adoption of theories and ideas from the centers were largely adopted indiscriminately without taking into account the structural differences between the two spaces. However, even when compared with what happened in Anglo-Saxon countries, the study of IPE in the Global South may seem relatively recent, it is certainly not absent or completely new. While the development of IPE in Anglo-Saxon countries was due to challenges arising from the dynamics between markets and power, in the other regions of the world the field and its main formulations developed associated to the emergence of real challenges from both the international economic scenario and the different strategies of insertion in the global economy developed by those regions. IPE in the South has been marked by the struggle for economic development, access to credit, debt payment, regional integration to access a better international insertion, and adding value to its exports. These concerns put the focus on different necessities and required different approaches from those of developed countries to understand their realities.

Box 27.1 IPE in Anglo-Saxon countries

While the development of IPE in Anglo-Saxon countries was due to challenges arising from the dynamics between markets and power, in the other regions of the world the field and its main formulations developed associated to the emergence of real challenges from both the international economic scenario and the different strategies of insertion in the global economy developed by those regions. IPE in the South has been marked by the struggle for economic development, access to credit, debt payment, regional integration to access a better international insertion, and adding value to its exports.

The discussion on the place that the Global South plays in mainstream debates has been mainly addressed by IR scholars. Several authors have pointed out the narrowness of IR theory that has arisen from the Western world centers that does not serve to explain the reality of those located in the periphery because they left aside voices, experiences, knowledge, and perspectives from outside of the centers (Acharya 2014; Acharya and Buzan 2010; Bilgin 2008; Thomas and Wilkin 2004; Tickner 2003; Tickner and Wæver 2009). For this reason, in recent years we have witnessed a great reflexivity among IR scholars in an attempt to incorporate a new agenda for research or to bring other IR perspectives to the center of the stage, different from those imposed from the Anglo-Saxon world. Thus, many scholars gathered around the need to outline a global agenda centered on the place regional and national schools have within the IR field (Deciancio 2016a).

This attempt has barely occurred within IPE (Lavelle 2005; Shaw 1975). However, some efforts have been made among scholars in the Global South to think IPE differently and bring into light the specificity of the field to think their own realities, understand them, and design their own solutions to them. The following sections are an attempt to summarize the main characteristics of IPE in Africa, China, and Latin America.

IPE in Africa

Box 27.2 African IPE

Although African IPE is quite new, going back into the roots of IR ideas and concepts allows to trace many African contributions to IPE from the Global South ignored by mainstream Western IPE. Contributions on decolonization, development, and the political economy of foreign aid brings into the discussion how the relation between markets and politics operate from the perspective of debtors instead of creditors, and the implications that has for the insertion of Global South economies into the world.

African IPE has been almost unexamined and disciplinary reflections are mostly invisible. Although IPE as a field of research – as considered in Western universities – is quite new in African research institutions, studies on development and political and economic relations date to the 1960s when International Relations was institutionalized as a discipline. In fact, development studies pioneered the studies of IR along with debates on decolonization. As it takes place in the Latin American case, in Development Studies a political economy dimension was present from the beginning but not considered within Western/mainstream IPE as part of the field. Structural and institutional factors were assigned a key role in the development process. As Ohiorhenuan and Keeler (2015) pointed out, in the initial phase of the field, the state was also assigned a large role in promoting development almost as a historical imperative. Dependency theorists of the 1960s and 1970s explicitly introduced an international political dimension to analyses of the asymmetric relationships between the industrial primary producing countries (Ohiorhenuan and Keeler 2015). As such, Development Studies considered within the wider definition of IPE have a long tradition in Africa. Questions of poverty, development, and underdevelopment have always been central in the debates concerning IPE in Africa (Nkiwane 2001).

Addressing the African case brings us a big challenge. First of all, we are aware that the first problem to analyze the development of IPE in Africa is the sole idea of taking the continent as a whole. Doing this leaves aside the particularities of each country and the way knowledge developed in each place. However, it is difficult for those studying individual African countries to separate their analyses from wider circumstances on the continent. In order to have a more comprehensive approach to our subject, we will address African IPE as a case taking into account the general common ground where the field is grounded. The study of political issues cannot be separated from the examination of economic issues, and vice versa. Also, as it has been said before, an IPE approach cannot leave aside the local, the national, the regional, and the international levels of analysis. Second, African IPE has been analyzed more from outside the continent (Beckman and Adeoti 2006; Shaw 1975; Smith 2009) than from within, often defined and oriented by the dominant international and geopolitical agendas of the day (Taylor and Williams 2004).

African involvement in world economy has been addressed from multiple perspectives within the Western IR, especially considering its relevance in terms of political and economic stability and access to natural resources (Geldenhuys 2015; Lavelle 2005). In Western IR, although they haven't been completely absent, African states have not constituted the core theoretical concern of either IR or IPE. The lack of attention of the IR field is still surprising. Where there have been attempts at bringing Africa into the fold, it has been done from the perspective of "what can Western IR do to incorporate Africa," rather than "what can we learn from Africa" (Smith 2009). In this sense, as Nkiwane (2001) pointed out, exploring IR – and IPE – contributions from Africa offers a powerful understanding of the functioning of states and markets, as well as the potential for their failure. In fact, the literature on colonialism and imperialism in Africa existed parallel to the development of mainstream Western IR but left aside by it.

Africa needs the world economy due to the nature of the aid regime, which requires African states to engage in world markets; while the world economy does not need African production, which remains mainly agricultural. At the same time, as Shaw (1975) pointed out, while colonization made Africa part of the global economy; we cannot understand its political economy or its political (lack of) development without reference to the strategies of collaboration or confrontation adopted by African regimes to their situation. Reliance on external associations and support may bring short-term gains but it replaces reliance on a domestic constituency with dependence on foreign interests (Shaw 1975). At present, "neocolonialism" in its modern and changing forms continues to determine Africa's development and underdevelopment, leading to increased inequalities on the continent. The African debate has been best exemplified by the question of structural adjustment programs (SAPs), as advocated by the International Monetary Fund (IMF) and the World Bank, and whether Africa has reached a "post-adjustment" period (Nkiwane 2001).

In 1975, Tim Shaw lamented himself for the state of IPE field in Africa, by then, he was concern about:

> i) the relative inattention afforded to the impact of international politics on the rate and direction of social change in African states; ii) the need for a new conceptual framework to advance our understanding of the linkage politics between African elites and external interests; and iii) the related growth and international inequalities on the continent.
>
> *(Shaw 1975: 29)*

Almost 50 years from then little has changed. One of the most problematic aspects of the position of Western IR theorists from the point of view of a variety of African scholars is with regard to the marriage of the propagation of democracy to foreign economic and political penetration. The debate on structural adjustment in Africa has outlined this concern most clearly. The hostility with which international financial institutions have approached the question of state intervention in Africa has been the subject of much discussion, particularly with respect to the economic, social, and political effects of structural adjustment on the continent (Nkiwane 2001).

The main change was during the postwar and postcolonial era, when world systems theory and "development studies" considered Africa as part of the debate. These investigations acknowledged that the economic governance structures of the former colonial metropole directed the postcolonial economies (Lavelle 2005). However, development studies have always been separated from IPE, and African countries were only included in the analysis as "case studies" but not as agents of knowledge production. After political independence, the preoccupation was the search for economic and social independence. To escape from underdevelopment, African regimes need increased domestic control to advance their strategy of international confrontation (Shaw 1975). During the 1970s, debates within African IPE were mainly focused on inequalities but the orthodox paradigm were more preoccupied with notions of modernization, political capacity, and political responsiveness, and with concepts of development, adaptation, integration, and unity.

In the 1990s, the centrality of the neoliberal economic argument has been challenged from African IPE with a pragmatic perspective, after over two decades of liberal market reform throughout much of Africa. The belief in the positive power and effects of markets alleviating the African economic condition is open to empirical contestation. There is no firm consensus on the effects of liberal market reforms in Africa, but a powerful and growing African perspective argues that these reforms have not only failed to improve the African condition, but they made it worse (Ake 1995; Amin 1996). The importance of this perspective as a criticism of the liberal paradigm cannot be overstated, because if true the liberal assumption in IR of open markets offering opportunities for mutual gain will of necessity be open to question (Nkiwane 2001).

In the last decades, African IPE responded to the specificity of African economies, marked by the participation of foreign actors in their economic structure. Foreign aid marked a strong part of African IPE in the last decades. It is a significantly higher ratio of foreign capital inflows to Africa than any other region: 87 percent compared to an average of 54 percent for all developing countries, and it is also a significantly higher ratio of GDP: 19 percent compared to an average of 3 percent for all developing countries (Ohiorhenuan and Keeler 2015). The three main focus of analysis have been, in the first place, the political and economic implications of foreign aid specially focused on the administration of these funds and the political and economic implications they have in the continent (Goldsmith 2001). On the other hand, the actors involved in the administration of the funds also differs from other regions of the world. Compared to Latina America or Asia, a big percentage of capital entering and exiting African economies either is mediated by public-sector organizations and/or non-governmetal organizatins (NGOs), or is not captured in official statistics at all (Lavelle 2005).

Although African IPE is quite new, going back into the roots of IR's ideas and concepts allows to trace many African contributions to IPE from the Global South ignored by mainstream Western IPE. Contributions on decolonization, development, and the political economy of foreign aid brings into the discussion how the relation between markets and politics operate from the perspective of debtors instead of creditors, and the implications that has for the insertion of Global South economies into the world. Political stability has been one of the main concerns of African countries since decolonization, strongly bound to the effects of economic development and the need for financial support to gain this goal.

IPE in China

Box 27.3 IPE in China

Looking within China there is a diversity of IPE views, but three concepts have been key in Chinese IPE: development, hegemony, and globalization. Those concepts are related to the Chinese need to respond to changes in official policy and the norms of the governing Chinese Communist Party (CCP).

As China's influence in the world is increasingly important, it is central to understand the underpinnings of its International Political Economy. Though the IPE field started to develop in the 1970s and took off in the mid-1980s it was not until the 1990s that it got around in China. Song (2001) attributed the neglect of IPE in China to the following reasons: mutual isolation of universities from research institutions in a situation in which scholars studying international politics knew little about international economy and vice versa, and an approach based on policy-oriented research and applied studies given that academic research in China has a close link with national policies. In this sense, the Marxian theoretical approach was central until the 1990s when Western IPE as a set of concepts caught up quickly among Chinese scholars.

There was a level of academic insularity in China that was understandable, given the relative and limited involvement in international markets that the country experienced in the 1970s and 1980s (Zweig and Zhimin 2007). In this sense, according to Breslin (2007) the dominant approaches to studying China's international relations overemphasize the national level of analysis and build on statist and realist notions of international relations that also reflected in the way in which IPE has emerged as a field of enquiry within China itself. Most academic explanations of China's reforms, and even its foreign policy, have been based on domestic politics. Song (2001) argues that "the divides which separate disciplines and institutions are still very deep in China." This is a consequence of the social setting in which the study of IR and IPE in China takes place – namely, the dominance of policy-related research, the residual ideology, and the fact that the state remains a very powerful force in contemporary China. In combination, these factors reinforce the separation of disciplines and have obstructed the emergence of an IPE that considers the importance of non-state actors and economics in general (Breslin 2007).

Nonetheless, some ideas have gained traction and influence, but there are also important differences in the basic assumptions of IPE in the West. Particularly, the roots in Marxian thinking as the official doctrine since 1949 and China's socialist economy were simply too powerful, preventing changes in global prices or international economic forces from affecting domestic prices, domestic supply, and demand. In fact, due to China's fixed currency and even the East Asian Financial Crisis, which toppled leaders across Southeast Asia and triggered structural economic reforms, had a limited impact on China's economic development (Zweig and Zhimin 2007). According to Chin, Pearson, and Yong (2013) the enduring influence of Marxian political economy was related to the fact that the approach dominated the analysis of all major social sciences and that the think tanks that have a Marxian approach, such as the Institute for Marxism at Chinese Academy of Social Sciences (CASS), receive privileged funding from the state.

The global rise of China and particularly China's "open policy," and its deeper engagement with the global economy allowed a more suitable environment for Western IPE to become known by Chinese scholars. In the 1990s a new momentum, triggered by the new promotion to a higher level of the open-door policy supported by Deng Xiaoping in order to open up

China to foreign investments vis-á-vis a high speed economic growth, allowed the opportunity to introduce IPE. Concepts such as globalization and interdependence were widely discussed in China and given its more open strategy, and IPE escaped the typical fate of Western international relations theories that usually were suspected, selectively introduced, criticized, and modified (Wenli 2001).

In general, the development of IPE in China is divided into three phases: the first one that lasted until the 1990s, in which a Marxist view and structuralist ideas dominated the field. A second stage started in the 1990s in which the field was institutionalized when the Ministry of Education recognized IPE as one of the subjects to study within international politics and diplomacy (Cohen 2019). Although the first texts on IPE lean on a classical Marxist view (Song and Yue 1999), the following ones began to incorporate Western ideas (Chen, Angling, and Yugui 2001; Fan 2001) as the IPE field blossomed in many universities. A third stage began in the 2000s when Western IPE was fully incorporated into Chinese academia that shares similarities with the Global North debates.

Looking within China there is a diversity of IPE views, but three concepts have been key in Chinese IPE: development, hegemony, and globalization. Those concepts have been related to the Chinese need to respond to changes in official policy and the norms of the governing CCP. In this sense, we agree with Chin, Pearson, and Yong (2013) that Chinese IPE is powerfully induced by political power and the role of the CCP defining the parameters of the policy and academic debate that are closely intertwined and that set ideas as the dominant and correct approach.

Chinese IPE has been reluctant to a benevolent view of hegemony, according to Wenli (2001) this resistance is based on various idiosyncratic factors that are key in China. First, in Chinese cultural values hegemony is always related to oppression and selfishness and it is usually assessed in a coercive fashion. Second, China did not suffer the same experience as Western countries in terms of a hegemonic power providing public goods and win–win competition for the world system; given that Chinese enterprises joined the world economic system in the 1980s raising protectionism and trade barriers were common in world trade. Third, when the United States had the chance to adjust the international economic system after the end of the Cold War, it rarely acted as a benign hegemon eager to sustain free trade. Given this experience, Chinese academia was reluctant to address a benevolent view of hegemony. Nonetheless, the view of hegemony has evolved from a critical view that analyzed this concept as imperialism-based on Marxist ideas to a more power politics concept in the 1990s, reaching a more recent benevolent view in the 2000s (Chin, Pearson, and Yong 2013).

The key role that political power played in shaping Chinese IPE is reflected in the way that the term globalization was addressed in academia. This concept appeared in the 1990s since the introduction of China's "open policy," and its deeper engagement with the global economy. Since this term started to be used by official authorities in the mid-1990s, scholars of Chinese IR and IPE began to analyze the challenges and opportunities presented by economic globalization.

International forces strengthened the local state in the 1980s and 1990s, while the remarkable opening following China's World Trade Organization accession undermined state power at all levels of the system (Zweig and Zhimin 2007). Chinese admit globalization of economic activities, environmental issues, and information techniques but are reluctant to political, cultural, and social dimensions of globalization. Since the state is still at the center of Chinese IPE they reject the idea that that national frontiers have weakened and that national governments and nation states have lost control of the political economic life (Wenli 2001).

Breslin (2007) argues that, on one hand, nationalism was at the heart of the reform process initiated by Deng Xiaoping, legitimized by the need to build a strong China that could resist and oppose the existing hegemonic global order. On the other hand, the resurgence of nationalism in China is partly explained by a new sense of pride in China's economic successes and a feeling that key external groups have been trying to prevent China's development and threaten Chinese interests.

In terms of modes of development, Chinese IPE discusses whether external forces will drive China's regime, or whether the CCP and China's bureaucrats will shape these external forces. State-led development models, particularly in East Asia, suggest that bureaucrats can manage the external environment and control the direction of economic development (Breslin 2007). According to Wenli (2001), when China began its economic reform in the 1980s there were already three dominant modes of development: The Anglo-Saxon dominated by Great Britain and the US, The West European exemplified by France and Scandinavian countries, and the Asian mode represented by Japan. The Asian mode became the most popular with Chinese intellectuals, particularly because Western countries completed industrialization under favorable geographical and historical conditions that could not be replicated. Conversely, the East Asia experience offered a more suitable way to catch up in terms of modernization. This triggered a rich debate among Chinese scholars and the Asian mode assumed considerable importance to address Chinese economic reform at least until the Asian financial crisis.

In sum, Chinese IPE presents three main characteristics. First, a close link between Chinese IPE and the statist view of the CCP, there is a strong policy orientation in which IPE is not only a field of study but also a normative and practical ground similar to dependency theory in Latin America. Second, in the case of China, ongoing integration of global and Western IPE theory may well involve a deep questioning of the most fundamental categories assumed in Western IR and IPE such as state, market, and civil society (Hurrell 2016). In this sense, Chinese response and critique to Western IPE is the main way to develop the Chinese IPE field. Third, this debate allows a significant diversity in current Chinese IPE that ranges from Marxian political economy to more mainstream perspectives that address IPE in Western terms.

IPE in South America

> ### Box 27.4 Until the 1980s, IPE has been marked by …
>
> Until the 1980s, IPE has been marked by the studies on regional integration and regionalism, constituting also one of the main contributions of Latin America to global IR and with a clear Southern perspective.

Diana Tussie (2015) points out that, in Argentina and South America, IPE had two strong pushes: the first, initiatory, marked by the impulse of the Dependency theory; and another more recent, in the 1990s, with the creation of Mercosur and regional blocs. This second stimulus gave a less deterministic tone to academic research that at the same time approached a dialogue and a more intimate interaction with public policy. Both show the great amount of changes that have marked the development of the studies, granting them their own characteristics and altering their course (Tussie 2015). This approach to IPE and theoretical developments transcended national borders to become a phenomenon of regional scale. That is why it wouldn't be accurate to address these contributions as exclusively of one nation, although much of the debate was driven by Raúl Prebisch, an Argentine intellectual. Though, since its beginnings, Latin American IPE has been a phenomenon that developed at the regional level and that stimulated studies on this and other branches of the discipline in many of the Latin American countries. Within this framework, the study of regions and regionalism acquired special relevance. This does not imply that this has been the only contribution of Latin American IPE but it has been the one that emerged as one of the most relevant research issues within IR discipline, along with the more preponderant studies of foreign policy and international security (Deciancio 2018). Latin American versions of Developmental Sociology and Developmental Economics, based on structuralism, critical sociology, and dependency theory, were expressions of the ability of social scientists in the region to confront dominant ideas in the international debate questioning conventional wisdom and transforming it to reinvent it (Tussie 2015).

Since the late nineteenth century, Social Sciences have been influenced by the region's structural conditions such as resources, political instability, and economic crisis. Since the economic crisis that affected South American countries at the end of the nineteenth century, a body of specialists in Economics was consolidated, and institutions dedicated to the teaching of Economics emerged. As a result of these events, economists occupied the center of the scene when both the state and society began to demand tighter, expert knowledge able to identify what was happening, while at the same time they increasingly gained more legitimacy (Plotkin 2010).

In the Latin American IR field, attention has mainly been centered on such issues as the Cold War, Defense, and Security, and national and regional Foreign Policies with indifference and even denial about the gravity of economic forces and market operators. It is in part for this reason that IPE constantly puts into question the analyses that presume an excessive autonomy of economics over politics (Tussie 2015). For Guzzini, for example, IPE emerged as a reaction, partly in favor and partly against, the much more systemic – but restricted – neorealist IR theory proposed by Kenneth Waltz (Guzzini 1998). From Adam Smith, John Stuart Mill, and Karl Marx, Economics is considered eminently political, while at the same time politics is tied to economic phenomena. But IR did not make the factors and economic actors its center of attention until the fall of the Bretton Woods system and the devaluation of the dollar in 1973. The oil crisis contributed and brought into light the limitations of and started questioning the foundations – until then invisible – of the Western economic system. Concerns with economic decline and its debates opened the path for a greater confluence between IR and IPE in Latin America.

By the end of the 1970s, political economy gained strength from the discomfort of scholars with the distance between abstract models of political and economic behavior and what was really happening in Latin American economies and politics. At the same time, economic crises increasingly politicized Economics while concerns of political systems on economic factors started to increase (Frieden and Lake 2000).

In Latin America, Economics and Economic Sociology contributed to the development of an approach to IR where new actors and processes were included in a field that, as noted earlier, was traditionally centered on the state as the main actor and producer of international relations. The inclusion of economic variables and forces into the dynamics of foreign relations was mainly motivated, in its beginnings, by the regional integrationist proposals when the peripheral place of the region in international economic relations was assumed. As a result, from the first works of Argentine engineer Alejandro Bunge and his proposal to create a Southern Customs Union, to the integrationist project of the 1960s, led by Raúl Prebisch, a Latin American developmentalist, studies on regional integration have marked and promoted IPE in Latin America. As a result, by the middle of the twentieth century, center-periphery tensions established a new understanding of international politics. At the same time, the IR field started to be recognized as an autonomous discipline in the hands of its institutionalization in universities and a growing sense of urgency regarding the political and economic dependence of the region emerged (Tickner 2003).

Until the 1980s, IPE has been marked by the studies on regional integration and regionalism, constituting also one of the main contributions of Latin America to global IR (Acharya 2011, 2014; Deciancio 2016b) and with a clear Southern perspective. In a way, to make a parallel with the European process, while the theory of European regional integration had its roots in Social Sciences, Latin American regional integration has its roots in Latin American political economy (Perrotta 2018) and more specifically, in a regional vision of IPE (Tussie 2015).

Perrotta (2018) argues that three schools are key in the development of IPE in South America – structuralism, dependency, and autonomy – and they have a close link when analyzing the practical problems that the region was experiencing. In this sense, the South American school of IPE developed particularly around practical topics (Ramos and Scotelaro 2018; Tickner 2008) and with an emphasis first on development and, since the 1980s, with a focus on regional integration given the failure of the Latin American Free Trade Association (ALALC) and its reconversion to the Latin American Integration Association (ALADI).

In the 2000s, new agendas and approaches to South American regionalism emerged, accompanying the creation of new regional organizations such as the Bolivarian Alliance of the People of Our Americas (ALBA), the Union of South American Nations (UNASUR), and the Community of Latina American and Caribbean States (CELAC). These regional groupings are characterized as "regionalism with adjectives" (Perrotta 2018) since the main labels that appeared are: postliberal (Chodor and McCarthy 2013; Sanahuja 2012), posthegemonic (Riggirozzi and Tussie 2012; Schulz, Söderbaum, and Ojen 2001), and post-trade (Dabène 2012). These approaches delineated a new set of conceptualizations to explain the turn in policy. Since UNASUR and CELAC had a rich agenda of functional cooperation it opened up the studies of sectoral agendas of cooperation in regionalism, ranging from defense, drugs ,and security (Battaglino 2012; Quiliconi and Rivera 2019), health (Herrero and Tussie 2015; Riggirozzi 2017), migration (Montenegro 2017), to infrastructure, energy, and environment (Dabène 2012; Palestini and Agostinis 2015). This new set of regional arrangements and the variety of issues and overlapping agendas led to a rich debate that addresses the kind of regionalism the region is experiencing (Gómez 2015; Nolte 2018; Quiliconi 2014; Quiliconi and Salgado 2017; Vadell 2018; Vivares 2014).

Latin American regionalism has been strongly linked to the economic and political cycles of the region. Likewise, and as Perrotta (2018) points out, the waves or cycles of this regionalism have been strongly linked to the organizations that have emerged alongside each of these moments. In this sense, the crisis and loss of dynamism of both the UNASUR, CELAC, and ALBA and their agendas based on premises of recovery of autonomy and the margins of South American development (Deciancio 2016b) give way to a moment where the most traditional agendas of trade integration will prevail with new regulatory elements that have already been incorporated by the countries that signed asymmetric Free Trade Agreements (FTAs) and belong to the Pacific Alliance. Here, the IPE literature is opening a new debate about regulatory adjustments and deep integration in organizations with light or no institutional structures (Legler, Garelli-Ríos, and González 2018).

Conclusions

Robert Cox (1981: 128) pointed out that "theory is always for someone and for some purpose." In the case of the regions addressed in this chapter we have demonstrated that IPE's locally grounded theory has sought to speak for excluded and marginalized groups in the case of Africa,

Marxism and the state in the case of China, and development and the public sector for Latin America. The main issue is that traditional IPE grounded in the North does not consider this type of debate as part of the IPE field. Given that mercantilism, liberalism, and Marxism have been considered as the underpinning of current IPE, and most of the Global South ideas have been neglected in IPE debates. For this reason, reflections like this chapter are encouraging a great reflexivity among IPE scholars in an attempt to incorporate a new agenda for research or to bring other IPE perspectives from the Global South to light. Thus, many scholars gathered around the need to outline a global agenda centered on the place regional and national schools have within the IR and IPE fields (Deciancio 2016a).

Proof of the lack of recognition of alternatives tradition is that Cohen (2019), in his recent reedition of the book *Advanced Introduction to International Political Economy*, diagnoses that the Latin American state of IPE is unproductive, fragile, and anemic, only citing a few academics in that tradition that have recently published on IPE and selecting most of the ones that lived and worked in the Global North. In the case of China, Cohen (2019) recognizes that even though the field is thriving, the field has not managed to provide any transformational contribution. Unfortunately, he does not address at all the state of the field in Africa. In our view his assessment of IPE has a bias toward recognizing theories that come from the North and neglects the contribution of IPE from the Global South due to little knowledge of how the field is developing in those regions.

Particularly, in the case of Latin America, the IPE field is prospering with a new generation of scholars that have finished their PhDs in the Global North and have returned to the region to work in local universities, propelling a thriving debate particularly in issues such as regionalism, development, and finance and also creating new PhDs programs that are producing new generations of scholars entirely educated in the region with high standards. Just a few countries that are examples of this trend are Argentina, Brazil, Chile, Colombia, Ecuador, and Mexico. Similar trends are taking place in China and Africa even though in Africa the development of the field is still incipient. Table 27.1 compares the main characteristics of non-Western IPE in the regions addressed in this chapter.

Table 27.1 Non-Western IPE in comparison

Regions/dimensions	Topics	Methodology	Theoretical approaches
Africa	Decolonization, Foreign aid	Policy-oriented, qualitative	Marxism, decolonial studies, mainstream IPE (specially from studies made from abroad)
China	Hegemony, globalization, development	Policy-oriented, qualitative	Marxism, and recently mainstream IPE
Latin America	Development and regionalism	Policy-oriented, qualitative	Marxism, structuralism, recently new eclectic approaches

Source: Authors' own elaboration.

Bibliography

Acharya, A. 2011. Dialogue and Discovery: In Search of International Relations Theories Beyond the West. *Millennium: Journal of International Studies* 39 (3): 619–637.

Acharya, A. 2014. Global International Relations (IR) and Regional Worlds. A New Agenda for International Studies. *International Studies Quarterly* 58 (4): 647–659.

Acharya, A. and Buzan, B., eds. 2010. *Non-Western International Relations Theory: Perspectives On and Beyond Asia*. London: Routledge.

Ake, Claude. 1995. The New World Order: A View from Africa. In: *Whose World Order? Uneven Globalization and the End of the Cold War*. Holm, H. and Sorensen, G. (ed.):19–42. Boulder: Westview Press.

Altamirano, C. and Sarlo, B. 1997. *Ensayos argentinos. De Sarmiento a la vanguardia*. Buenos Aires: Ariel.

Amin, S. 1996. The Challenge of Globalization. *Review of International Political Economy* 3 (2): 216–259.

Battaglino, J. 2012. Política de defensa y política militar durante el kirchnerismo. In: *La política en tiempos de los Kirchner*. Malamud, A. and De Luca, M. (ed.): 241–250. Buenos Aires: Eudeba.

Beckman, B. and Adeoti, G. eds. 2006. *Intellectuals and African Development: Pretension and Resistance in African Politics*. London: Zed Books.

Bilgin, P. (2008). Thinking Past 'Western'IR?. *Third World Quarterly* 29 (1), 5–23.

Blyth, M. 2009. Torn between Two Lovers? Caught in the Middle of British and American IPE. *New Political Economy* 14 (3): 329–336.

Breslin, S. 2007. Beyond the Disciplinary Heartlands: Studying China's International Political Economy. In: *China's Reform and International Political Economy*. Zweig, D. and Zhimin, C. (ed.): 21–41. London: Routledge.

Buchbinder, P. 2005. *Historia de las universidades argentinas*. Buenos Aires: Editorial Sudamericana.

Chen, Y., Angling, X., and Yugui, H. eds. 2001. *Introduction to International Economics and Politics*. Beijing: High Education Press.

Chin, G., Pearson, M., and Yong, W. 2013. Introduction. IPE with China's Characteristics. *Review of International Political Economy* 20 (6): 1145–1164.

Chodor, T, and McCarthy, A. 2013. Post-Liberal Regionalism in Latin America and the Influence of Hugo Chavez. *Journal of Iberian and Latin American Research* 19 (2): 211–223.

Clark, I. 1997. *Globalization and Fragmentation: International Relations in the Twentieth Century*. New York: Oxford University Press.

Cohen, B. 2008. *International Political Economy: An Intellectual History*. Princeton: Princeton University Press.

Cohen, B. 2019. *Advanced International Political Economy*. Cheltenham: Edward Elgar Publishing.

Cox, R. 1981. Social Forces, States and World Orders: Beyond International Relations Theory. *Millennium: Journal of International Studies* 10 (2): 126–155.

Dabène, O. 2012. *Explaining Latin America's Fourth Wave of Regionalism: Regional Integration of a Third Kind*. Paper presented at the Congress of the Latin American Studies Association (LASA). *Panel: Waves of change in Latin America. History and Politics*. San Francisco, CA, May 25.

Deciancio, M. 2016a. *Historia de la construcción del campo de las Relaciones Internacionales en la Argentina*. Doctoral thesis, FLACSO Ecuador.

Deciancio, M. 2016b. International Relations from the South: A Regional Research Agenda for Global IR. *International Studies Review* 18 (1): 1–13.

Deciancio, M. 2018. La Economía Política Internacional en el campo de las Relaciones Internacionales argentinas. *Desafíos* 30 (2): 15–42.

Eagleton-Pierce, M. 2009. Examining the Case for Reflexivity in International Relations: Insights from Bourdieu. *Journal of Critical Globalisation Studies* 1 (1): 111–123.

Fan, Y. 2001. *Western International Political Economy*. Shanghai: Shanghai Renmin Press.

Frieden, J. and Lake, D. 2000. *International Political Economy. Perspectives on Global Power and Wealth*. London: Routledge.

Geldenhuys, D. 2015. South Africa's World: Perspectives on Diplomacy, International Political Economy, and International Law. *South African Journal of International Affairs* 22 (4): 407–409.

Goldsmith, A. 2001. Foreign Aid and Statehood in Africa. *International Organization* 55 (1): 123–148.

Gómez, L. 2015. International Regime Complexity and Regional Governance: Evidence from the Americas. *Global Governance* 20 (1): 19–42.

Guzzini, S. 1998. *Realism in International Relations and International Political Economy. The Continuing Story of the Death Foretold*. London: Routledge.

Helleiner, E. ed. 2014. Principles from the Periphery: The Neglected Southern Sources of Global Norms. *Special Section of Global Governance* 20 (3): 359–418.

Herrero, M. and Tussie, D. 2015. UNASUR Health: A Quiet Revolution in Health Diplomacy in South America. *Global Social Policy Journal* 15 (3): 261–277.

Hurrell, A. 2016. Towards the Global Study of International Relations. *Revista Brasilera de Politica Internacional* 59 (2): e008.

Lavelle, K. 2005. Moving in from the Periphery: Africa and the Study of International Political Economy. *Review of International Political Economy* 12 (2): 364–379.

Legler, T. 2013. Post-hegemonic Regionalism and Sovereignty in Latin America: Optimists, Skeptics, and an Emerging Research Agenda. *Contexto Internacional* 35 (2): 325–352.

Legler, T., Garelli-Ríos, O., and González, P. 2018. La Alianza del Pacífico: un actor regional en construcción. In: *La Alianza del Pacífico: ¿atrapada entre el péndulo del regionalismo y del interregionalismo?* Pastrana, E. and Blomeier, H. (ed.): 143–172. Ciudad de México: Konrad Adenauer Stiftung (KAS).

Montenegro, A. 2017. Migration Governance in South America: The Bottom-up Diffusion of the Residence Agreement of Mercosur. *Revista Brasileira de Administração Pública de la Fundación Getulio Vargas* 52 (2): 303–320.

Nkiwane, T. 2001. Africa and International Relations: Regional Lessons for a Global Discourse. *International Political Science Review* 22 (3): 279–290.

Nolte, D. 2018. Costs and Benefits of Overlapping Regional Organizations in Latin America: The Case of the OAS and UNASUR. *Latin American Politics and Society* 60 (1): 128–153.

Ohiorhenuan, J. and Keeler, Z. 2015. International Political Economy and African Economic Development: A Survey of Issues and Research Agenda. *Journal of African Economies* 17, Issue supplement 1.

Palestini, S. and Agostinis, G. 2015. Constructing Regionalism in South America: The Cases of Transport Infrastructure and Energy within UNASUR. *EUI Working Paper RSCAS 2014/73*, Robert Schuman Centre for Advanced Studies, Global Governance Programme 117.

Perrotta, D. 2018. El campo de estudios de la integración regional y su aporte a las Relaciones Internacionales: una mirada desde América Latina. *Relaciones Internacionales* 38: 9–39.

Phillips, N. and Weaver, C. eds. 2011. *International Political Economy: Debating the Past, Present and Future.* London: Routledge.

Plotkin, M. 2010. *La recepción y circulación de ideas económicas en la Argentina y las crisis de la segunda mitad del siglo xx.* Paper presented at the Primer Simposio Internacional Interdisciplinario Aduanas del conocimiento: *La traducción y la constitución de las disciplinas entre el centenario y el bicentenario*, Buenos Aires.

Plotkin, M. and Zimmermann, E. eds. 2012. *Los saberes del Estado.* Buenos Aires: Edhasa.

Quiliconi, C. 2014. Competitive Diffusion of Trade Agreements in Latin America. *International Studies Review* 16 (2): 240–251.

Quiliconi, C. and Rivera, R. 2019. Ideology and Leadership in Regional Cooperation: The Cases of Defense and the World Against Drugs Councils in UNASUR. *Revista Uruguaya de Ciencia Política.*

Quiliconi, C. and Salgado, R. 2017. Latin American Integration: Regionalism à la Carte in a Multipolar World? *Colombia Internacional* 92: 15–41.

Ramos, L. and Scotelaro, M. 2018. O estado da arte da Economía Política Internacional no Brasil: Possibilidades para pensar (e practicar) una EPI a partir de baixo. *Desafíos* 30 (2): 127–157.

Riggirozzi, P. 2017. Regional Integration and Welfare: Framing and Advocating Pro-Poor Norms through Southern Regionalisms. *New Political Economy* 22 (6) 661–675.

Riggirozzi, P. and Tussie, D. eds. 2012. *The Rise of Post-Hegemonic Regionalism.* Dordrecht: Springer.

Sanahuja, J. 2012. Post-liberal Regionalism in South America: The Case of UNASUR. *EUI Working Paper RSCAS 2012/05*, Global Governance Programme 13, Transnational and Global Governance.

Schmidt, B. 1998. *The Political Discourse of Anarchy: A Disciplinary History of International Relations.* Albany: State University of New York Press.

Schulz, M., Söderbaum, F., and Ojen, J. 2001. *Regionalization in a Globalizing World: A Comparative Perspective on Forms, Actors and Processes.* London: Zed Books.

Shaw, T. 1975. The Political Economy of African International Relations. Issue: *A Journal of Opinion* 5 (4): 29–38.

Smith, K. 2009. Has Africa Got Anything to Say? African Contributions to the Theoretical Development of International Relations. *The Round Table: The Commonwealth Journal of International Affairs* 98 (402): 269–284.

Song, X. 2001. Building International Relations. Theory with Chinese Characteristics. *Journal of Contemporary China* 10 (26): 61–74.

Song, X. and Yue, C. 1999. *Introduction to International Political Economy*. 2th ed. Beijing: Renmin University Press.

Taylor, I. and Williams, P. 2004. Introduction: Understanding Africa's place in world politics. In: *Africa in International Politics. External Involvement on the Continent*. Taylor. I and Williams, P. (eds): 1–23. London and New York: Routledge.

Thomas, C. and Wilkin, P. 2004. Still Waiting After all these Years: "The Third World" on the Periphery of International Relations. *British Journal of Politics & International Relations* 6 (2): 241–258.

Tickner, A. 2003. Hearing Latin American Voices in International Relations Studies. *International Studies Perspectives* 4 (4): 325–350.

Tickner, A. 2008. Latin American IR and the Primacy of Lo Práctico. *International Studies Review*,10: 735–748.

Tickner, A. and Wæver, O. 2009. *International Relations Scholarship Around the World*. New York: Routledge.

Tussie, D. 2015. Relaciones internacionales y economía política internacional: notas para el debate. *Relaciones Internacionales* 24 (48): 155–175.

Vadell, J. 2018. El Foro China-CELAC y el nuevo regionalismo para un mundo multipolar: desafíos para la Cooperación "Sur-Sur." *Revista Carta Internacional* 13 (1): 6–37.

Vivares, E. 2014. Toward a Political Economy of the New South American Regionalism. In: *Exploring the New South American Regionalism*. Vivares, E. (ed.): 9–28. Surrey: Ashgate.

Wenli, Z. 2001. International Political Economy from a Chinese Angle. *Journal of Contemporary China* 10 (26): 45–54.

Zweig, D. and Zhimin, C. 2007. *Introduction: International Political Economy and Explanations of China's Globalization*. In: *China's Reform and International Political Economy*: 204–221. London: Routledge.

28

The political economy of the European Union
Between national and supranational politics

Johannes Karremans and Zoe Lefkofridi

Introduction

In June 2016 the citizens of the United Kingdom (UK) voted on whether their country should remain in or withdraw from the European Union (EU). The referendum – which became famous with the name of 'Brexit' – resulted in a tight victory of the 'leave' vote (51.89 per cent versus 48.11 per cent), implying that since 31 January 2020 the UK is no longer be part of the EU. This means that the UK will withdraw from the rights and obligations that are tied to EU membership, regaining autonomy on a broad sphere of policies, which will, in turn, have important political and economic implications, both within the UK and internationally (Menon and Salter 2016). Membership to the EU, in fact, provides access to one of the world's largest markets (see Box 28.1), creating a tight interdependence between member states. At the same time, the UK's withdrawal from the Union alters the EU borders, entailing that where now goods, services and people are passing freely, tariffs and controls typical of national borders will be (re)installed.

The negotiations between the UK and the EU on the terms of this divorce have been far from easy as they need to confront a wide range of legal and political questions, such as the rights of (non-British) EU citizens currently residing in the UK, or the problem of the historically disputed border between Ireland and Northern Ireland. In addition, Brexit also poses important international economic uncertainties, particularly in the financial sector: with London being one of the world's largest financial centres – and transnational financial markets being one of the most important components of the EU's economy – Brexit raises high levels of uncertainty for market operators. One of the main functions of the EU Single Market is, in fact, to facilitate financial transactions across borders and to create common rules for market competition. The EU, thereby, provides a vast jurisdiction for market operators to trade on the basis of a common set of rules. With the withdrawal of the UK, from 1 February 2020 onwards the financial centres based in London will suddenly be located outside of this jurisdiction.

The Brexit episode is instructive of the political economy of the EU, which consists different national political economies that are not yet fully integrated. The political aspect of the EU's economy, therefore, plays a key role in defining its size and its jurisdictional borders. In parallel, it is again politics that ensures that the integration of the various national economies works

472

smoothly. The Brexit episode is the first important setback to a decennia-long process of integration and also symbolizes the political challenges that the EU is currently facing. The integration of different national economies requires in fact also coordination in an ever-growing sphere of policy areas. The main challenge that European integration is confronted with today, consequently, is the 'dissensus' of national electorates: as they become increasingly aware of the reach of decisions taken at the EU level their voices of concern become increasingly louder.

In this chapter, we highlight the tension between supranational economic policy-coordination and national political demands, which risks becoming an increasingly significant factor in the future development of the EU's political economy. This is particularly true in the aftermath of the recent Eurozone crisis (Box 28.2), during which international financial speculation made apparent not only the interdependence of European national economies, but also the contradictions in the current allocation of supranational and national policy-competences (Scharpf 2011). Consequently, the EU and its policies gained unprecedented salience in national electoral campaigns; moreover, political competition has shifted from the traditional left–right dimension towards a pro/anti-EU dimension, which concerns preferences for different levels of political and economic integration (Hobolt 2016; Hutter and Kriesi 2019; Lefkofridi and Katsanidou 2018; Otjes and Katsanidou 2017). This development, which is progressively altering traditional patterns of electoral coalitions (Beramendi et al. 2015), is likely to change the political alliances that drive policy-making in the near future.

In this chapter, we aim to provide a comprehensive overview of the background of these developments. We begin by explaining why the EU is a unique actor in both the world of states as well as in that of international organizations. Subsequently, we will zoom into one of the key aspects of the EU – namely the European monetary union (EMU) – to highlight how the tensions between national and supranational levels of policy-coordination render it a non-optimal currency area. We then proceed by identifying the causes of these tensions, which essentially consist in the difficulties of integrating different national political economies. Subsequently, we look at how integration of one policy area results in the need for integrating other policy areas as well, creating uncertainties about the distinction between national and supranational spheres of competence. Finally, we illustrate how these disputes between national and supranational levels of policy-competence are increasingly being politicized, and are becoming an important motive in electoral campaigns. We conclude this chapter by reflecting on the implications of this development for the future of the EU and its political economy.

Box 28.1 The European Single Market

The European Single Market was officially established in 1993 and guarantees the free movements of goods, capital, services and labour across the EU's member states. According to the European Commission, the Single Market is one of the EU's biggest achievements as, by promoting competition and improving the efficiency of the allocation of resources, it has stimulated economic growth and improved the living environment for both citizens and businesses. The Single Market is also one of the world's biggest economies, producing a yearly GDP of about €15 trillion (European Commission, 2017 figures).

Box 28.2 The Eurozone crisis

In the EU, the global financial crisis of 2008 quickly spread into a sovereign debt of various member states of the so-called Eurozone, i.e. the countries having adopted the European common currency. As a result, five Eurozone countries needed a European bail-out to finance their current expenses and to save their national banks: Greece, Ireland, Spain, Cyprus and Portugal. Towards the end of 2009, the governments of these countries started to be unable to pay their debts and to bail-out their national banks. Consequently, financial assistance was provided by fellow EU member states, the European Central Bank and the International Monetary Fund. Because of the high costs of this assistance, these sovereign debt crises gradually became a threat to the resilience of the EU's common currency. This threat was addressed through severe austerity measures in all EU member states. The crisis also triggered important institutional responses that uploaded political authority from the national to the supranational level.

Trapped in an international political trilemma

The institutional framework of the EU resembles in many aspects that of a nation-state, featuring legislative, executive and – within certain boundaries – judiciary powers (Box 28.3). Compared to nation-states, however, these powers are much more dispersed across different institutions, and in some cases are far less effective than the powers of national institutions. Legislative power and executive powers, in fact, are shared by supranational and national institutions, and competence over certain policy areas is regularly a matter of dispute between the two levels of governance. The institutional configuration of the EU, in turn, is also in a continuous evolution, reflecting the fact that the European multilevel polity remains for a large extent still in-the-making (e.g. Beetz et al. 2016; Héritier 2007; Hooghe and Marks 1999). The most recent institutional changes have in fact largely been a power struggle between the strengthening of supranational authority and the intergovernmental method for decision-making (Bickerton et al. 2015).

This power struggle is also visibly present in the EU's legislative process, which is distributed among three institutions: two are supranational and one is intergovernmental. Legislation is initiated at the supranational level by the European Commission, which is often regarded as the EU's executive as it is responsible for managing the day-to-day business of the EU (Wille 2013). Once a new legislative initiative has been proposed by the Commission, it is discussed in both the European Parliament (EP) and the Council of the EU. The former is the only directly elected EU institution, and represents EU citizens at the supranational level. The latter, instead, represents the executive governments of the member states and is thus the symbol of intergovernmental policy-making within the EU.

In various aspects, the current state of affairs in the distribution of power-competences between the EU and its member states strongly evokes the international political trilemma theorized by Rodrik (2000). The logic behind Rodrik's political trilemma is that full economic integration imposes a choice between either national sovereignty or mass democracy: as economic integration requires countries to conform their fiscal, economic and social policies to a common set of rules, relevant political decisions are made at the supranational level. Therefore, in order to be effective, democracy must be expressed at the supranational level, rendering thereby the territorial division in sovereign legal jurisdictions obsolete. If national governments wish to maintain their national jurisdictions, instead, this comes at the cost of suffocating democracy, because regulating the common market requires political agreements at the international level, and national electoral preferences may not always be in line with the needs of an economic union.

During the last decades Europeans witnessed an alternation of the strengthening of supranational institutions on the one hand and the affirmation of the intergovernmental method for decision-making on the other. Consequently, in the current institutional configuration of the EU it is not always clear where the locus of political power actually is. The EP for instance, between the 1990s and 2000s progressively succeeded in increasing its involvement in the EU's decision-making process, strengthening thereby the relevance of supranational democratic representation. In the years following the Eurozone crisis, however, the EP's political authority often ended up being overshadowed by the Council of the EU, i.e. the body representing the national governments (Lefkofridi and Schmitter 2015; Niemann et al. 2018). In parallel, the European Commission has seen its political authority grow in some areas and remain limited in others, and generally as a result of intergovernmental agreements (Bickerton et al. 2015; Rittberger 2014).

This power struggle between the national and supranational political spheres stands at the heart of scholarly disputes about how to explain the process of European integration (see Wiener et al. 2019), i.e. the process whereby – since the signing of the Treaty of Rome in 1957 – European states have gradually transferred their powers from the national to the European level. The key controversy has been between the neo-functionalist and inter-governmentalist approaches (for a detailed discussion of each approach, see Niemann et al. 2018; and Moravcsik and Schimmelfennig 2019 respectively).

For intergovernmentalists, the EU is a 'successful intergovernmental regime designed to manage economic interdependence through negotiated policy coordination' (Moravcsik 1993: 474). Its formation and development are the result of the relative power capabilities of self-interested member states, whose preferences are shaped by domestic economic interests. Neofunctionalists, in turn, assume that regional integration is transformative in that it changes the nature of its participants, activities, institutions and objectives over time. They view the formation and development of the EU as the result of activities of *both* governmental and non-governmental actors (e.g. interest associations, social movements, political parties, firms). While acknowledging the interdependence of actors at different levels (subnational, national, supranational), neofunctionalists focus on the ability of supranational actors such as the European Commission or the European Central Bank (ECB) in exploiting the interconnection between different economic sectors, to expand the scope of political integration from one policy-sphere to the other.

As we shall see in the following pages, both perspectives need to be taken into account when trying to understand the past and current stages of European integration. The intergovernmental perspective, in fact, allows to grasp a deeper understanding of how key decisions taken at the EU level are sometimes the result of the dispute between competing national interests. On the other hand, one of the most relevant insights from neofunctionalism is the idea that the process of European integration has at least partially been driven by *spill-over* effects, in the sense that integration in one sector 'spills over' into pressure for integration in another sector. It is this effect – we argue – that has inevitably triggered the current tensions between the national and supranational levels of policy-making, particularly after the establishment of the European Monetary Union (EMU) in the 1990s.

Box 28.3 The institutions of the EU

The European Commission is the executive arm of the EU, the guardian of the EU treaties, and the institution responsible for their successful implementation. It drafts and proposes legislation.

The European Parliament is the only directly elected body of the EU. Besides sharing legislative power with the Council, it also co-decides on the EU's budget.

The Council of the EU, also known as the Council of Ministers, represents the national governments. It has both legislative and executive powers and is arguably the most powerful institution of the EU. It is similar but distinct from the European Council.

The European Council is the group of the heads of state or government. Even though it has no legislative power, it helps defining the EU's long-term policy direction.

The European Central Bank is responsible of the Eurozone's monetary policy. It has the aim of maintaining price stability and is politically independent.

The Court of Justice is the judiciary arm of the EU. In case of disputes, it interprets EU laws and treaties.

The Court of Auditors is a body with no formal powers that makes an annual report about the implementation of the EU's budget. These reports are often used by the Parliament when holding the Commission accountable on the budget.

The European Monetary Union and the Eurozone crisis

The gradual transfers of authority from the national to the supranational level reached a defining moment with the establishment of EMU in 1993 and the consequent entry into force of the Euro in 1999 as the official common currency. Countries adopting the common currency gave up their monetary sovereignty. For these countries, monetary policies were no longer under the control of a national central bank, but became instead competence of the ECB. At the same time, however, the Euro was not backed by a fiscal union, and featured many internal imbalances, as the Eurozone crisis made clear. EMU is therefore the case in point for understanding how the process of EU polity formation has remained stuck between the national and supranational level.

The case of EMU is also an example of how both intergovernmentalism and neofunctionalism are useful for understanding the process of European integration. On the one hand, the establishment of EMU has been driven by national interests: as a response to German reunification, many member states, most notably France, acting on the basis of calculations of relative power and national interest, insisted on an enlarged Germany giving up the Deutschemark, as a sign of commitment to the integration process (Niemann et al. 2018). Though the intention was to prevent German hegemony in Europe, it ended up increasing its relative power (Schmitter and Lefkofridi 2016). On the other hand, EMU has also triggered various *spill-over* effects, as – particularly in the aftermath of the Eurozone crisis – it has driven a banking union and a fiscal union on the political agenda (Howarth and Quaglia 2014; Niemann et a. 2018).

The Eurozone crisis has uncovered the lack of clarity regarding the locus of political authority in governing the European economy. Particularly significant was the initiative taken by the ECB in 2012 to extensively buy national bonds of EU member states, whereby large amounts of liquidity were injected in the European economy. This action was the direct result of the plan of the ECB President Mario Draghi to 'do whatever it takes' to save the common European currency.[1] This action raised more than one eyebrow, particularly among European constitutionalists and legal scholars, who observed that by injecting practically an unlimited amount of liquidity in the economy, the ECB was in direct contrast with some of the foundational rules of the EU, namely that capital should be allocated through competitive markets (Menéndez 2017: 58; Scicluna 2017). At the same time, Draghi's action was also praised because it helped prevent the European common currency from collapsing. This episode is significant because it taps into the main peculiarities of the EU's political economy, namely the existence of a monetary union without a fiscal union, and a currency that is not shared by all EU member states.

Currently, only 19 of the 28 EU member states share the common currency and are thus part of the 'Eurozone'. Most of the non-Eurozone members are countries that joined the EU in the latest rounds of the enlargement process (see Box 28.4) and are obliged to join EMU once they meet the eligibility criteria, which essentially consist of macroeconomic indicators, including price stability, sustainable public finances, exchange-rate stability and long-term interest rates. Other EU member states – such as Denmark and the UK – instead, have maintained their monetary sovereignty. These peculiarities make the EU in various respects a non-optimal currency area (Scharpf 2011) as, particularly in times of crisis, they appear rather as imperfections. Some scholars, for instance, argue that during the global financial crisis of 2008–2009, the Bank of England was able to prevent an outflow of capital in the financial markets because of its monetary autonomy, that allowed to print and inject British money in the national economy (De Grauwe 2017: 118–122).

Outflows of capital, instead, were much easier in those countries adopting the common currency, and happened in large magnitudes to those countries that were most severely hit by the crisis (see Box 28.2). As markets started to lose confidence in the ability of countries such as Spain or Portugal to pay back their debts, bond-holders started to sell these bonds and buying bonds of countries that were perceived as having more solid public finances, such as for example Germany (De Grauwe 2017: 118–122). This practice was facilitated by the fact that the various countries had the same currency. Consequently, large amounts of capital flowed from (mainly) Southern European countries towards (mainly) Northern European countries. This mechanism pushed various European countries (mostly in Southern Europe) towards a sovereign debt crisis.

These imbalances within the Eurozone – and the relative facility through which markets can push states towards a sovereign debt crisis – had two main consequences. First, they unveiled a vacuum of political authority that, as mentioned above, induced the ECB to arguably move beyond its institutional mandate and to buy Southern European sovereign bonds. Second, they co-caused a vast redistribution of public money, signifying essentially that the Northern European governments had to bail-out their Southern partners under very strict conditions; consequently, through the bail-outs, Northern EU governments became more involved and had more direct interests in seeking to influence long-term economic policy in the Southern European countries. As a result, the bail-outs not only fuelled high political tensions among member states – rendering intergovernmental cooperation more difficult – but also triggered the start of a wave of austerity measures throughout the whole Eurozone (advocated by elected governments in the North).

Box 28.4 The enlargement of the EU, 1957–2018

The EU currently counts 27 member states, excluding the UK, which left on 31 January 2020. The various member states joined the EU at different points in time:

Founding members (1957)

Belgium, France, (West) Germany, Italy, Netherlands and Luxemburg.

1973 enlargement

Denmark and the UK

Mediterranean enlargement (1981–1986)

1981: Greece
1986: Portugal and Spain

1990s enlargement

1995: Austria, Finland and Sweden

Eastern and Central European enlargement (2004–2007)

2004: Czech Republic, Estonia, Hungary, Latvia, Lithuania, Poland, Slovakia and Slovenia
2007: Bulgaria and Romania

Western Balkan enlargement (2013)

Croatia

The European constraints on national budgets

When – in the aftermath of the Eurozone crisis – negotiations were initiated to reform EMU, a contraposition emerged around two different conceptions for the further development of the monetary union: one based on fiscal discipline and one based on fiscal solidarity (Wasserfallen and Lehner 2017). This contraposition coalesced on the one hand mainly Northern European creditor countries, and on the other mainly Southern European debtor countries. The two coalitions – led respectively by Germany and France – largely reflected the conflicting interests in the aftermath of the Eurozone crisis, with the creditor countries advocating more common rules for ensuring fiscal discipline, and with countries who received bail-outs advocating for rules ensuring solidarity among member states. This contraposition, however, is not only reflective of a situation that emerged during the Eurozone crisis, but also highlights the difference between different economic models, with Northern European economies being more reliant on exports, and Southern economies being traditionally more reliant on domestic consumption.

More importantly, the tension that emerged in the post-Eurozone crisis negotiations is a manifestation of the strain between the *spill-over* effects of EMU and the historical inheritances of different national economic trajectories.

Even though EMU has not (yet) *spilled-over* into a fiscal union, since its establishment member states are required to fulfil to the EU-criteria of sound public finances, which mainly consist in public debt not exceeding 60 per cent of the country's gross domestic product (GDP) and public deficits not exceeding 3 per cent of national GDP. These rules were introduced with the Treaty of Maastricht in 1993 (see Box 28.5) and were strengthened between 2011 and 2012 by giving sanctioning powers to the Commission, in order to ensure stricter adherence to these rules (Laffan 2014). The strengthening of European budgetary rules, in turn, was accompanied by a wave of austerity measures across all Eurozone countries. Even though formally the EU rules leave member states free to design national taxation and expenditure policies within the given limits, the combination of budgetary thresholds and competition in a common market forms a substantial constraint on the extent to which national governments can tax and spend (Karremans and Damhuis 2018).

As a consequence of the provisions set in the Treaty of Maatstricht and of the strengthening of budgetary rules between 2011 and 2012, between the 1990s and today the national parliaments of the various member states have been introducing new national legislation imposing strict budgetary discipline to the executive (Doray-Demers and Foucault 2017). Such laws serve as the extended arm of the European agreements and restrict the fiscal policy space available to governments. Even though the European brakes on governments' debt and deficit levels are in theory not a direct constraint on the ways in which governments shape their taxation and spending policies, in practice – because of the functioning of the common market – they work as a straitjacket for national fiscal policies. In other words, while the functioning of the Single Market represents a sort of an informal brake on governments' taxation policies, the European budgetary rules work as formal constraints on the governments' expenditure policies.

As the Single Market facilitates the movement of business across the EU jurisdiction, excessive taxation in one member state brings the risk of triggering de-location of enterprises to other EU member states (Genschel and Schwarz 2013). Against the background of the European budgetary rules and the loss of national monetary sovereignty, in turn, this disincentive to increase taxation puts great constraints on governments' expenditure policies. Thereby, governments are *de-facto* no longer fully autonomous in pursuing economic and social policies, as the room-for-manoeuvre is restricted by their European commitments. These commitments, in turn, are often criticized for being more functional to the development of some economies rather than others (Johnston and Regan 2016).

According to some authors (e.g. Regan 2017), in fact, the European budgetary rules are particularly constraining for the economies of the South, whose growth has historically relied on national consumption, and which – before the establishment of EMU – have been accustomed to respond to economic downturns by devaluing their currencies. Under EMU, they have thus lost the capacity to devalue their currency and – because of the budgetary restrictions – they are no longer free to stimulate national consumption by increasing expenditure. Northern European economies, by contrast – like for example the Netherlands and Germany – base their growth more on exports. Having an interest in containing the cost of labour in order to facilitate exports, for these countries the EU's budgetary rules tend to be more in line with their national strategies for economic growth. This imbalance became clearly visible in the years following the Eurozone crisis, as Northern European countries such as Germany and (since 2016) the Netherlands started to perform budgetary surpluses, while Southern European countries like Italy continued to struggle with high public debt and government deficits.

The formation and functioning of the European Single Market – and in particular of EMU – has puzzled political economists in Europe and outside, pointing in particular to the difficulty (or impossibility) of reforming the diverse patterns of state intervention in the economy (e.g. Truchlewski 2018). Reforming the patterns whereby national governments tax and spend, in fact, requires a reform of national welfare states, which in most EU member states represent the main category of running expenditures. The reform of national social security provisions has thus been a recurrent theme in the various stages of European integration.

Box 28.5 The Treaties establishing the EEC, EC and EU

The EU does not feature a constitution in the traditional sense, but lays its foundations in a succession of Treaties:

1957 (1958) – The Treaty of Rome: established the European Economic Community and the customs union; proposed a common market.
1986 (1987) – The Single European Act: set the objective of establishing the Single Market by 1992.
1992 (1993) – The Treaty of Maastricht: officially known as the Treaty on the European Union, it expanded the competences of European institutions and laid the foundations for the European Monetary Union.
2007 (2009) – The Treaty of Lisbon: the latest amendment to the constitutional basis of the EU. It strengthened the role of the European Parliament in the EU's legislative process; it further strengthened and formalized political authority at the European level.

The European social agenda *versus* national social pacts

The European Economic Community (EEC) – established in 1957 with the Treaty of Rome – started as a project to create a common market and a customs union among its members. With the completion of the single internal market in 1993, the EEC was renamed 'European Community', reflecting the fact that by then its scope was no longer solely limited to economic policy, but was gradually developing towards a monetary union, which would in turn require cooperation on a broad range of other policy areas as well. If there is one lesson to draw from the experience of European integration, it is that policy areas do not have clear-cut borders. Integration in one area creates imbalances in other policy areas that were not initially part of the scope of integration. The best example is how the creation of the monetary union gradually *spilled over* into debates about integrating the member states' fiscal and social policies, which in turn stumbled both on the political question about the extent to which political authority should remain at the member state level or be fully transposed to the supranational level, as well as on the practical problem of dealing with different fiscal and social security systems.

As already anticipated, Europe comprises great sub-regional variation in the organization of capitalism and the provision of social security. Since the advent of the modern market economy, Europe has been home to different modalities through which public authorities tried to regulate free markets. Much of how scholars think about political economy, in fact, largely comes from comparisons of how capitalism is organized in different parts of Europe. The heterogeneity of the European market economies has for example inspired much of the variety of capitalism literature (Hall and Soskice 2001), and the different national social protection systems have been famously labelled as the 'three worlds of welfare capitalism' (Esping-Andersen 1990). As has been laid out in Esping-Andersen's pioneering classification, post-war European welfare states have developed different levels of de-commodification of citizens from markets. These different developments can be clustered on the basis of sub-regional differences, with Scandinavian countries presenting the highest levels of social protection, continental and Mediterranean featuring intermediate levels of social protection and the UK having an overall more passive social policy.[2]

Despite the fact that upon its establishment the activities of the EEC were explicitly restricted to the development and implementation of the common market – and that member states were determined to maintain their social sovereignty (Ferrera 2005) – the Treaty of Rome in some ways already anticipated the issues that would emerge in the following decades, explicitly referring to the potential problems of having different levels of social security in different member states. Consequently, with the view of the possible scenarios that could evolve with the free movement of people, it introduced the aim of establishing cooperation among member states in the field of labour market law and working conditions (Caune et al. 2011: 21). In the 1980s, this initial aim was expanded and centralized at the European level. Following the accession of Greece, Spain and Portugal (Box 28.4), in fact, the EEC had started comprising even more variety in social security provisions, particularly in terms of family and unemployment policies, which in three Mediterranean newcomers were scarcely developed. As a response to this imbalance, the European social fund was established, to foster and harmonize social progress.

Building up on this aim, from the Treaty of Maastricht onwards the EU started becoming the most important driver of change in national systems of welfare provisions (Graziano et al. 2011). In 2000, member states agreed on a common social policy agenda that – besides aiming for harmonizing the quality of employment, industrial relations and social protection – also identified social policy as a means of production (O'Connor 2005). The European social agenda thereby largely adopted the social investment strategy, wherein social policy is not merely understood as a means of sheltering people from market mechanisms, but rather as a means to help people participating in and benefiting from the market economy (Hemerijck 2017). This understanding of social policy, however, also entails flexible labour market laws that – rather than protecting employees from redundancies – facilitate the transition from job to job. This entails that rather than providing unemployment benefits, social security should instead be about investing in the reintegration in the labour market of people who have lost their job.

These reforms of the welfare state proved to be highly successful first in Scandinavia, in the Netherlands and during the 2000s also in Germany. In France and Southern European countries, however, the attempts to reform the labour market stumbled against the opposition of social partners (Bonoli and Emmenegger 2010). This difference in the reform of national social security systems is again narrowly linked to different national economic trajectories. In parallel to the varieties of the organization of capitalism and the provision of social security, sub-regional differences can also be found in the ways in which industry groups, trade unions and governments have interacted over the course of the decades and have installed different institutional frameworks.

The various European national political economies have in fact largely resulted from different pacts about how to combine national economic industrial growth with social welfare (Rhodes 2001). Compared to countries like the Netherlands or Sweden, in France and Italy industrial relations have historically been much more conflictual. In Southern Europe, thus, the efforts to Europeanize the national welfare systems stumbled on more than one occasion against these hard-won agreements between governments, employers and labour-organizations. While it is beyond the scope of this chapter to delve into the specifics of these national socio-economic trajectories, it is important to understand that much of each country's fiscal and government spending policies are strongly tied to this historical heritage of different social pacts.

This difficulty of integrating different market economies, in turn, seems to be increasingly stumbling upon the dissensus of parts of national electorates. The pressures for reforming existing pension systems are increasingly getting to the attention of electorates across Europe. As in general such reforms tend to render existing social provisions less generous – with for example increases of the retirement age – the agreements that governments make at the European level are increasingly becoming object of electoral contestation (Hutter and Kriesi 2019). While until the 2000s European integration proceeded in a de-politicized manner, thus, since the outbreak of the Eurozone crisis and the subsequent wave of austerity policies, questions about the future of the EU are increasingly structuring political competition and thus the formation of governing coalitions.

The challenge of the politicization of the EU

Following the principle that collective binding decisions need to be backed by democratic legitimacy, the need for democratic representation at the supranational level increases when decisions taken at the supranational level become more binding and wider in scope. The expansion of EU policy-competences during the 1990s has therefore inevitably opened the premises for a debate about the democratic legitimacy of the decisions taken at the European level. In academic circles, this debate has seen a lengthy exchange of views between on the one hand the proponents of the democratic deficit argument and on the other scholars highlighting the democratic qualities of the EU. In the former (e.g. Hix and Hoyland 2011), emphasis is being given to the perceived distance between EU policy-makers and citizens. In the latter (e.g. Moravcsik 2008), by contrast, emphasis is placed on the multiple mechanisms of accountability that characterize EU policy-making.

The growth of powers of the EP can in many ways be interpreted as an institutional response to this debate and relates also to the Rodrik's (2000) political trilemma discussed above, as it can be considered as an attempt to move democracy at the supranational level. Being the only directly elected EU polity, its growing involvement in the EU legislative process and its growing grip over the activities of the European Commission have established a closer link between the votes of EU citizens and political decisions taken at the European level, substantially improving the democratic accountability of EU policy-makers.

However – notwithstanding the need for more democracy at the supranational level, the obvious policy benefits of transnational cooperation and the fertile soil (coherence within supranational party formations in the EP) – transnational parties remain weak and a strong transnational party system has not yet emerged; key obstacles are first, the lack of a 'government in waiting' at the EU level (Follesdal and Hix 2006) and second, the weight of national political settings on party organization strategy and style of competition style in European elections (Bardi et al. 2010). Neither national nor European elections had, prior to the crisis, been about Europe and its policies (e.g. Lefkofridi and Kritzinger 2008) – a key impediment in familiarizing Europeans with the proceedings of their common polity. Not surprisingly, European voters were largely ignorant of both the opportunities (e.g. their rights as EU citizens) and the constraints derived by EU – and Eurozone – memberships and electoral turnout at European elections has been typically low. Crucially, as long as Europe and its policies were not important in domestic or European contests, governments did not risk punishment for their performance at the EU level. Hence, Europe's politicization was portrayed as a 'sleeping' (Van der Eijk and Franklin 2004) or even a 'sedated' (Mair 2007) giant.

The EU's depoliticization reinforced negative incentives for organizational adaptation to the EU polity and policy environment, which includes many more actors (EU institutions and other member states) compared to the domestic arena. Our own data,[3] in fact, suggest that only the party officials that have been exposed to the EU level (e.g. by serving a term in the European Parliament) are more knowledgeable and sophisticated in their discourse about the EU. The rest tends to have a harder time talking about the specifics of complex EU decision-making procedures, i.e. the 'rules of the game' of the European decision-making process. This is because, despite ever closer integration, national party organizations did not shift their loyalties towards the supranational political centre, as neofunctionalism would expect (Lefkofridi and Schmitter 2015). However, lack of party adaptation to an ever-changing EU environment results in parties' declining capacity to shape policy, which renders policy differences between national parties meaningless (Lefkofridi 2014).

In this context of lethargy and depoliticization, the 'eruption' of the Eurozone crisis brought EU-affairs directly onto the national political agenda, changing the patterns of political competition in Europe substantially. While up until the crisis the EU had been largely absent from the national and EP election campaigns (e.g. Lefkofridi and Kritzinger 2008; Pennings 2006) and EP elections functioned as 'second-order elections' (Reif and Schmitt 1980), during the last decade the issue of European integration has become clearly prominent in political competition (Lefkofridi and Katsanidou 2018). Recent national elections across the continent have seen an impressive growth of Eurosceptic forces, at the expense of the Europe's traditional party-families, namely Christian-democrats, Social-democrats and liberals.

The growth of the Eurosceptic electoral force has gone hand in hand with a change in the structure of political competition (Hutter and Kriesi 2019). While for the last few decades Europe's traditional party-families have been competing on the political left–right dimension, today electoral competition seems to become increasingly shaped by the positions that parties have with respect to European integration. As recent research has shown, this development is strongly linked to the growing perception of citizens about economic policy remaining unaltered irrespective of who governs, i.e. centre-right or centre-left parties (Alonso and Ruiz-Rufino 2018). This effect appears to be even stronger when citizens perceive that their government's policies are imposed by supranational actors (Ruiz-Rufino and Alonso 2018).

Recent national elections across the continent have registered remarkable successes of Eurosceptic parties – i.e. parties that are sceptical towards the process of European integration. In Austria and Italy, for example, Eurosceptic parties have even come to gain leading positions in national governments. The success of these parties, many authors argue (e.g. Alonso and Rui-Rufino 2018), is strongly related to the popular discontent that emerged in the aftermath of the global financial crisis of 2008 and the following Eurozone crisis (Box 28.2). This popular discontent, in turn, is argued to be strongly related to the distance that has grown between policy-makers focused on the functioning of the global market economy and daily lives of ordinary citizens (Mair 2014).

Consequently, commentators and observers of European politics are becoming increasingly concerned with the possibility that current and future elections (e.g. Jones 2018) will produce yet another increase of Eurosceptic forces within European institutions. In the meantime, across Europe Eurosceptic parties are increasingly entering relevant political positions. In Austria and Italy, for instance, Eurosceptic parties such as the Austrian Freedom Party (FPÖ) and the Italian Northern League (*Lega Nord*) have come to occupy important ministries in their respective national governments. On average, Eurosceptic parties rely on the support of at least 20 per cent of the electorate (Taggart and Sczerbiak 2018).

The future development – and the fate – of the EU's political economy is inevitably linked to the Eurosceptic challenge. As anticipated in the Introduction, the economy of the EU is largely dependent on political decisions. The entry in leading decision-making positions of either pro- or anti-EU actors can have highly divergent consequences on the EU's economy, affecting its jurisdictional size and the scope of political coordination it can rely upon.

Conclusion

This tension between supra- and national policy-coordination has opened a challenging phase in the history of European integration, that has historically been characterized by a 'permissive consensus' from European electorates, and that now is increasingly faced with a 'constraining dissensus' (Hooghe and Marks 2009; Jones 2018). The question of whether the EU should move forwards towards becoming an 'ever closer Union' or instead be rolled back in order to give more space for national decision-making autonomy, is in fact becoming the main political dispute in European politics (Hobolt 2016). Despite being largely an electoral and sociological phenomenon (Hobolt 2016; Hutter and Kriesi 2014), the outcome is likely to have lasting economic consequences, as it will inevitably touch upon the extent to which Europe will develop into a unified political power, or whether instead it will fragment into diverse (small) (semi)-sovereign states.

The tension between European-level and national politics became inevitably salient during the recent Eurozone crisis (Box 28.2). While on the one hand requiring effective supranational crisis management, in fact, the Eurozone crisis also uncovered many imperfections of EMU (see Box 28.3), which subjects countries with diverse fiscal regimes to a common set of fiscal rules (Scharpf 2011). Attempts to reform EMU between 2010 and 2012, consequently, saw the contraposition of countries favouring more fiscal solidarity vis a vis countries favouring more fiscal discipline (Wasserfallen and Lehner 2017). These contrapositions, in turn, are indicative of different national political economies.

The functioning of the EU, thereby, needs to be understood in light of some contradictions at its very foundational elements. Being more than an international organization but not yet a state, the EU is itself a unique institutional entity, having supranational powers that are however still limited by the sovereignty of its member states. The tension between such supranational powers and national sovereignty was not only at the heart of the political disputes that emerged in the aftermath of the Eurozone crisis, but is arguably at the heart of the main political questions that Europeans are facing today. To understand the political economy of the EU, therefore, it is crucial to map how – and to what extent – the shifting of policy-competences from the national to the supranational level challenges the political autonomy of national governments, and in particular in the field of fiscal policy. At the same time, it is equally important to trace how the re-claiming of national spheres of competences not only may stand in contrast with existing European rules but may also have direct consequences on the economies of other member states.

In this chapter we have provided an overview of the problems related to coordinating different national economies in the European polity. In particular, we have devoted our attention towards how the needs related to the completion of the European Single Market may sometimes stand in contrast with national political demands that are often related to distinct political trajectories.

Notes

1 Speech by Mario Draghi, ECB President at the Global Investment Conference in London 26 July 2012.
2 A more complicated story needs to be told about the welfare states of Central and Eastern Europe, which until the beginning of the 1990s were subjected to the Soviet Union. For an analysis of the development of these welfare states, please see Deacon (2000).
3 Prior to the crisis, Zoe Lefkofridi conducted qualitative fieldwork in Greece, including semi-structured interviews with Greek members of the party in public office (PASOK, ND and SYNASPISMOS, which was core component of SYRIZA coalition) in Athens, May–June 2006.

Bibliography

Alonso, S. and Ruiz-Rufino, R. 2018. The costs of responsibility for the political establishment of the Eurozone (1999–2015). *Party Politics*. Published Online.
Bardi, L., Bressanelli, E., Calossi, E., Gagatek, W., Mair, P. and Pizzimenti, E. 2010. *How to Create a Transnational Party System*. Brussels: European Parliament.
Beetz, J. P., Corrias, L. and Crum, B. 2017. We the people (s) of Europe: Polity-making and democracy in the EU. *European Law Journal*, 23(6): 432–440.
Beramendi, P., Hausermann, S., Kitschelt, H. and Kriesi, H. (Eds) 2015. *The Politics of Advanced Capitalism*, New York: Cambridge University Press.
Bickerton, C. J., Hodson, D. and Puetter, U. 2015. The new intergovernmentalism: European integration in the post-Maastricht era. *JCMS: Journal of Common Market Studies*, 53(4): 703–722.
Bonoli, G. and Emmenegger, P. 2010. State-society relationships, social trust and the development of labour market policies in Italy and Sweden. *West European Politics*, 33(4):830–850.
Caune, H., Jacquot, S. and Palier, B. 2011. Social Europe in action: The evolution of EU policies and resources. In: Graziano, P., Jacquot, S. and Palier, B. (Eds) *The EU and the Domestic Politics of Welfare State Reforms: Europa, Europae*, Basingstoke and New York: Palgrave Macmillan: 1–18.
Deacon, B. 2000. Eastern European welfare states: The impact of the politics of globalization. *Journal of European Social Policy*, 10(2): 146–161.
De Grauwe, P. 2017. *The Limits of the Market. The Pendulum Between Government and Market*, Oxford: Oxford University Press.
Doray-Demers, P. and Foucault, M. 2017. The politics of fiscal rules within the European Union: a dynamic analysis of fiscal rules stringency. *Journal of European Public Policy*, 24(6): 852–870.
Esping-Andersen, G. 1990. *The Three Worlds of Welfare Capitalism*, Cambridge: Polity Press.
Ferrera, M. (Ed.) 2005. *Welfare State Reform in Southern Europe*, London: Routledge.
Follesdal, A. and Hix, S. 2006. Why there is a democratic deficit in the EU: A response to Majone and Moravcsik. *JCMS: Journal of Common Market Studies*, 44(3): 533–562.
Genschel, P. and Schwarz, P. 2013. Tax competition and fiscal democracy. In: Schäfer, A. and Streeck, W. (Eds) *Politics in the Age of Austerity*, Cambridge: Polity Press: 59–83.
Graziano, P., Jacquot, S. and Palier, B. 2001. The usages of Europe in national employment-friendly welfare state reforms. In: Graziano, P., Jacquot, S. and Palier, B. (Eds) *The EU and the Domestic Politics of Welfare State Reforms: Europa, Europae*, Basingstoke and New York: Palgrave Macmillan: 1–18.
Hall, P. A. and Soskice, D. (eds) 2001. *Varieties of Capitalism. The Institutional Foundations of Comparative Advantage*, Oxford: Oxford University Press.
Hemerijck, A. (ed.). 2017. *The Uses of Social Investment*, Oxford: Oxford University Press.
Héritier, A. 2007. *Explaining Institutional Change in Europe*, Oxford: Oxford University Press.
Hix, S. and Hoyland, B. 2011. *The Political System of the European Union*, Basingstoke: Palgrave Macmillan.
Hobolt, S. B. 2016. The Brexit vote: A divided nation, a divided continent. *Journal of European Public Policy*, 23(9): 1259–1277.
Hooghe, L. and Marks, G. 1999. The making of a polity: The struggle over European integration. In: Kitschelt, H., Lange, P., Marks, G. and Stephens, J. D. (eds) *Continuity and Change in Contemporary Capitalism*. Cambridge: Cambridge University Press: 70–98.
Hooghe, L. and Marks, G. 2009. A postfunctionalist theory of European integration: From permissive consensus to constraining dissensus. *British Journal of Political Science*, 39(1): 1–23.
Howarth, D. and Quaglia, L. 2014. The steep road to European banking union: Constructing the single resolution mechanism. *JCMS: Journal of Common Market Studies*, 52: 125–140.

Hutter, S. and Kriesi, H. (Eds) 2019. *European Party Politics in Times of Crisis*, Cambridge: Cambridge University Press.

Johnston, A. and Regan, A. 2016. European monetary integration and the incompatibility of national varieties of capitalism. *JCMS: Journal of Common Market Studies*, 54(2): 318–336.

Jones, E. 2018. Towards a theory of disintegration. *Journal of European Public Policy*, 25(3): 440–451.

Karremans, J. and Damhuis, K. 2018. The *changing face of responsibility: A cross-time comparison of French social democratic executives*. *Party Politics*. Online First: https://doi.org/10.1177/1354068818761197.

Laffan, B. 2014. Testing times: The growing primacy of responsibility in the Euro area. *West European Politics*, 37(2): 270–287.

Lefkofridi, Z. 2014. National political parties and EU Policy developments: The case of Greece prior to the crisis. *Journal of Modern Greek Studies*, 32(2): 287–311.

Lefkofridi, Z. and Katsanidou, A. 2018. A step closer to a transnational party system? Competition and coherence in the 2009 and 2014 European Parliament. *JCMS: Journal of Common Market Studies*, 56(6): 1462–1482.

Lefkofridi, Z. and Kritzinger, S. 2008. Battles fought in the EP arena: Developments in national parties' Euromanifestos. *Österreichische Zeitschrift für Politikwissenschaft*, 37(3): 273–296.

Lefkofridi, Z. and Schmitter, P. C. 2015. Transcending or descending? European integration in times of crisis. *European Political Science Review*, 7(1): 3–22.

Mair, P. 2007. Political opposition and the European Union. *Government and Opposition*, 42(1): 1–17.

Mair, P. 2014. Representative versus responsible government. In Mair, P. *On Parties, Party Systems and Democracy*, Colchester: ECPR Press: 581–596.

Menéndez, A. J. 2017. The crisis of law and the European crises: From the social and democratic rechtsstaat to the consolidating state of (pseudo-) technocratic governance. *Journal of Law and Society*, 44(1): 56–78.

Menon, A. and Salter, J. P. 2016. Brexit: Initial reflections. *International Affairs*, 92(6): 1297–1318.

Moravcsik, A. 1993. Preferences and power in the European Community: A liberal intergovernmentalist approach. *JCMS: Journal of Common Market Studies*, 31(4): 473–524.

Moravcsik, A. 2008. The myth of Europe's democratic deficit. *Intereconomic: Journal of European Economic Policy*, 43(6): 331–340.

Moravcsik, A. and Schmimelfennig, F. 2019. Liberal intergovernmentalism. In Wiener, A., Börzel, T. and Risse, T. *European Integration Theories*, Oxford: Oxford University Press.

Niemann, A. Lefkofridi, Z. and Schmitter, P. C. 2018. Neofunctionalism. In Wiener, A., Börzel, T. and Risse, T. *European Integration Theories,* Oxford: Oxford University Press: 43–63.

O'Connor, J. S. 2005. Policy coordination, social indicators and the social-policy agenda in the European Union. *Journal of European Social Policy*, 15(4): 345–361.

Otjes, S. and Katsanidou, A. 2017. Beyond Kriesiland: EU integration as a super issue after the Eurocrisis. *European Journal of Political Research*, 56(2): 301–319.

Pennings, P. 2006. An empirical analysis of the Europeanization of national party manifestos, 1960–2003. *European Union Politics*, 7(2): 257–270.

Regan, A. 2017. The imbalance of capitalisms in the Eurozone: Can the north and south of Europe converge? *Comparative European Politics*, 15(6): 969–990.

Reif, K. and Schmitt, H. 1980. Nine second-order national elections – a conceptual framework for the analysis of European Election results. *European Journal of Political Research*, 8(1), 3–44.

Rhodes, M. 2001. The political economy of social pacts: 'Competitive corporatism' and European welfare reform . In: Pierson, P. (Ed). *The New Politics of the Welfare State*. Oxford: Oxford University Press 165–194.

Rittberger, B. 2014. Integration without representation? The European Parliament and the reform of economic governance in the EU. *JCMS: Journal of Common Market Studies*, 52(6): 1174–1183.

Rodrik, D. 2000. How far will international economic integration go? *Journal of Economic Perspectives*, 14(1), 177–186.

Ruiz-Rufino, R. and Alonso, S. 2018. Democracy without choice: Citizens' perceptions of government's autonomy during the Eurozone Crisis. In: Merkel, W. and Kneip, S. (Eds) *Democracy and Crisis,* Springer, Cham: 197–226.

Scharpf, F. 2011. Monetary union, fiscal crisis and the pre-emption of democracy. *Zeitschrift für Staats-und Europawissenschaften (ZSE)/Journal for Comparative Government and European Policy*, 9(2): 163–198.

Schmitter, P. C. and Lefkofridi, Z. 2016. Neo-functionalism as a theory of disintegration. *Chinese Political Science Review*, 1(1): 1–29.

Scicluna, N. 2017. Integration through the disintegration of law? The ECB and EU constitutionalism in the crisis. *Journal of European Public Policy*, 25(12): 1–18.

Taggart, P. and Szczerbiak, A. 2018. Putting Brexit into perspective: The effect of the Eurozone and migration crises and Brexit on Euroscepticism in European states. *Journal of European Public Policy*, 25(8): 1–21.

Truchlewski, Z. 2018. Oh, what a tangled web we weave': How tax linkages shape responsiveness in the United Kingdom and France, *Party Politics*. Online First: https://journals.sagepub.com/doi/full/10.1177/1354068818764017.

Van der Eijk, C. and Franklin, M. N. 2004. Potential for contestation on European matters at national elections in Europe. In: Marls, G. and Steenbergen, M. (Eds) *European Integration and Political Conflict*, Cambridge: Cambridge University Press: 32–50.

Wasserfallen, F. and Lehner, T. 2017. Mapping contestation on economic and fiscal integration: Evidence from new data. *EMU Choices Working Paper 2017*, University of Salzburg.

Wiener, A., Börzel, T. and Risse, T. 2019. *European Integration Theories*, Oxford: Oxford University Press.

Wille, A. 2013. *The Normalization of the European Commission: Politics and Bureaucracy in the EU Executive*, Oxford, Oxford University Press.

29

IPE scholarship about Southeast Asia

Theories of development and state–market–society relations

Bonn Juego

Introduction

Southeast Asia is one of the most puzzling regions in the world for students of international political economy (IPE) because of its sheer diversity and heterogeneity. The region is composed of eleven countries with different histories, languages, social and cultural characteristics, racial and ethnic composition, economic development, and political regimes—namely: Brunei, Cambodia, East Timor, Indonesia, Laos, Malaysia, Myanmar, the Philippines, Singapore, Thailand, and Vietnam. With the exception of East Timor, the ten member states belong to the Association of Southeast Asian Nations (ASEAN) regional bloc. Thus, doing an intensive comparative approach is indispensable to understand the region as a whole and achieve a deeper understanding of the dynamics of societies. While being sensitive to the peculiar characteristics of each society in Southeast Asia, research on IPE needs to capture developments they share and locate these in specific ways global processes have unfolded not only at the traditional geographical scales defined by regions and nation-states, but also at the levels of local grassroots communities, family households, and the human person.

This chapter highlights key contributions to the study of Southeast Asia within the field of IPE. Its flow of discussion shows that, since the 1950s, IPE scholarship on and about Southeast Asia has developed and evolved into three main theoretical themes:

1   development theory;
2   state theory; and
3   theories of state–market–society relations.

The first and second themes regarded societies in the region as "new independent nations" during the post-colonial period, or as part of the "Third World" during the Cold War. While theories of development have identified factors and provided explanations on the mechanisms that cause poverty and instability in the former colonies, theories of the state have described the characteristics of state institutions (notably, their governance processes and capacities) in the developing world. The third theme offers interpretations of the nature of social embeddedness of state–market relations in the context of capitalist globalization, especially under conditions of its "neoliberal" phase which started to intensify in the early 1990s.

Though not exhaustive, the literatures—and the theories associated with them—that are reviewed in this chapter are considered classic, state-of-the-art, or seminal works in their respective areas of inquiry. Their contents are understood within specific contexts. And the critiques on them point to issues that may contribute to efforts at improving on, if not formulating an alternative to, existing analytical frameworks for the study of Southeast Asian political economy.

Development theory

Earlier literatures on the political economy of Southeast Asia dealt with the classic debates in Third World development theories—which provided explanations of the structure of underdevelopment in peripheral countries of the Global South due to their dependent relationship with core capitalist centers in the Global North, offered policy prescriptions for developing economies to catch up with industrialization processes, and proposed strategies to overcome the general conditions of mal-development. In these debates, the plight of Southeast Asia was understood through modernization theory, dependency school or world-systems theory.

Modernization theory and the doctrine for political development

The original versions of modernization theory described post-colonial countries in Southeast Asia as traditional societies, which are "pre-state, pre-rational and pre-industrial" and whose backwardness was a result of varying cultural, psychological, and socio-economic factors (Higgott and Robison 1985a: 17–18). They prescribed a process of "Westernization" to modernize primitive and backward societies. By this it meant that Asian states and economies should institute similar political and economic model of "the West" (i.e., democracy and capitalism), including the emulation of the development strategies pursued by advanced capitalist countries when they were still developing (i.e., industrialization).

The most recognized proponents of modernization theory today were part of an interdisciplinary group of scholars that emerged around the early 1950s from the Harvard University's Department of Social Relations, the US Social Science Research Council (SSRC), and the Massachusetts Institute of Technology's Center for International Studies – notably, the sociologists Talcott Parsons, Edward Shils, and James Coleman; the economists Paul Rosenstein-Rodan and Walt W. Rostow; the communication scientist Daniel Lerner; the anthropologist Clifford Geertz; and the political scientists Gabriel Almond and Ithiel Pool. In the mid-1950s, the Ford Foundation supported the SSRC to create a Committee on Research in Comparative Politics whose main objective was to generate theories of modernization to guide public policy and create stable institutions in transition societies. Well-known scholars of Southeast Asia were appointed as key members of this committee: George Kahin, Guy Pauker, and Lucien Pye. The initiative led to a series of publication in the 1960s called *Studies in Political Development* (for a comprehensive account of US government's interests in Southeast Asian politics research program, see Latham 2000; Kahin 2003, Klinger 2016).

Seminal articles on Southeast Asian politics by the doctrinaires of modernization and democratization pointed to the particular condition of the Third World undergoing a process of decolonization in a broad global context. They problematized the cultural traditions and the socio-political features of a village society where governmental activity was limited to traditional autocratic rulers or the elite few practitioners, and where public participation in decision-making of issues above—yet with direct impact on—the village level was also restricted (Kahin, Pauker and Pye 1955). Southeast Asian societies like Malaya, Indonesia, and the Philippines were characterized by "non-Western" political process and value systems. Whereas politics in non-Western countries was based on communal and personal interests, politics in the West was organized around interest groups, political parties, class interests, and policy objectives. Thus, the political process in Southeast Asia was viewed as irrational, expedient, communalistic and personalistic (Pye 1967). This description of Third World social structure had found resonance in a number of political studies on Southeast Asia during the 1960s that used the once predominant "patron–client model," in which social relations were based on personal exchange of loyalties and favors and political competition was perceived as non-ideological and non-programmatic (e.g., Lande 1965; Riggs 1966; Scott 1972).

With the publication of Samuel Huntington's (1968) *Political Order in Changing Societies*, the objective of the modernization project moved from the process of democratization to social stabilization. At the heart of this was the emphasis on the "reason of the state" to realize societal order and protect its political authority, rather than to embody the will of the people. This agenda to "revise" modernization theory was due to the "crises of development" and new concern for public policy (Huntington 1971; Higgott 1983; Cammack 1997). The ideology about the necessity of social order as precondition for political modernization and economic development seemed to have provided the intellectual rationale for the authoritarian regimes that emerged in Southeast Asia during the 1970s and the 1980s—specifically, the "New Society" of Ferdinand Marcos in the Philippines (Agpalo 1992) and the "New Order" of Suharto in Indonesia (Vatikiotis 1998). The modernization paradigm on the relationship between political development and economic growth was also influential in Malaysian studies on politics and social change from the 1960s to the 1980s (Nair 2005).

On the economic sphere, a variety of interpretations had been offered between the late 1980s and mid-1990s to explain the process of capitalist modernization in Southeast Asian economies. A notable study by Yoshihara Kunio (1988) described the "ersatz capitalism" in Thailand, Malaysia, the Philippines, Indonesia, and Singapore since the 1960s. Kunio argued that the social and political environment in these economies made their respective "indigenous capital" conducive to rent-seeking activities, where connections to government officials and resources generate business advantages. The region's industrialization, in particular, had been "ersatz" in the sense that its indigenous capitalists were technologically dependent on Japanese and other foreign companies (cf. McVey 1992). Kunio then suggested modernizing Southeast Asia's capitalism through progress in science and technology, efficient government intervention in the economy, and a liberal policy toward foreign direct investments.

In the academic and policy communities, the developing countries in Southeast Asia had been analyzed in relation with their more advanced neighboring economies in Northeast Asia—specifically Japan, South Korea, Hong Kong, and Taiwan. The theory of the "flying geese" pattern of development elicited debates about a region-wide modernization process led by Japan and the prospects for Southeast Asian countries to catch up with techno-economic and socio-cultural modernity (Cumings 1984; Korhonen 1994; UNCTAD 1993; Hart-Landsberg and Burkett 1998). First proposed by the Japanese economist Kaname Akamatsu in the 1930s, it became more accessible to the English-speaking world since the 1960s and later on adopted to explain general development trajectories and specific industrialization processes of Asian countries during the 1980s–1990s. Akamatsu (1962) argued that "economic growth in the Asian area was brought about by the eastward advance of Western European capitalism" (p. 3). Following the theory's stages of industrial development (i.e., from importation to production and exportation), the suggestion is that individual countries in Southeast Asia should start with importing the needed machineries and raw materials from technologically advanced countries to build their domestic productive capacities in order to produce competitive manufactured goods for both their home and international markets. Gradually, as lesser developed countries repeatedly and increasingly upgrade their production techniques and skilled labor, technological diffusion would take place across economies in the region. Eventually, the leading Japanese industrial structure is replicated by the follower countries. The formerly underdeveloped countries of Southeast Asia would then be capable of producing sophisticated products, which could even be exported to the mother country Japan and the Western industrialized countries.

Within Southeast Asian studies, there are two main criticisms that have emerged against the ideas of political and economic modernization. The first is the critique that views these modernizing ideas as resembling of the colonial ideology of "orientalism," which distorts the existence of many realities in the historical evolution of diverse societies in "the East" and which normatively attempts to create an "ideal other" patterned after the image of so-called "advanced" social system of the West (Said 1978). Along this critical theme, the classic study of Syed Hussein Alatas (1977) unpacked the ideological mystification of the colonialist ideological project that propagated "the myth of the lazy native," which presented Malays, Indonesians, and Filipinos as indolent, dull, primitive, and treacherous so as to justify their colonization. The second set of critical literature has offered expositions of the vested interests behind the discourse on modernization and the doctrine of political development, specifically the agenda to impose the hegemonic policy of the West on the region of Southeast Asia. For example, the research of Walden Bello, David Kinley, and Elaine Elinson (1982) exposed leaked World Bank documents and dissected its former president Robert McNamara's Vietnam War policy and the "relief for the poor" campaign—which all showed the primary agenda to protect and promote the material and ideological interests of the US.

Dependency school

Literature reviews on Southeast Asian political economy often pit modernization theory against dependency theory (e.g., Rodan, Hewison and Robison 2006a; Rasiah and Schmidt 2010a). However, there is a tendency in this way of presentation to gloss over the diversity in the "school of dependency" and its origins from the traditions of Marxism and Latin American structuralism, both of which predate the introduction of modernization theory (Palma 1978; Higgott 1981). Some of the classic reviews on the evolving discourses on dependency analysis include Gabriel Palma's (1978) work that situates dependency as an aspect of Marxist theory on "capitalist development in backward nations" in the context of global imperialism, and Joseph Love's (1980) account of the structuralist influences on dependency which developed out of the works of Raúl Prebisch and the UN Economic Commission for Latin America in the late 1940s that led to the formulation of the "theory of unequal exchange" in center–periphery relations.

The dependency school came out within the debates on theories of capitalism and imperialism, particularly about the relationship between core and peripheral countries in the world capitalist system, as well as the development of capitalism in pre-capitalist societies. Broadly speaking, these debates had evolved into three phases (Palma 1978). The first phase was from the argument of Marx and Engels (1848) that capitalism is a "historically progressive system" which can "draw all, even the most barbarian, nations into civilization" because of its capability to improve a country's means of production. This is possible despite or because of the mechanisms of "primitive accumulation" such as colonialism and free trade (Marx 1859 [1973]). The second phase came from theorists of the "classics of imperialism"—namely, Rudolf Hilferding, Rosa Luxemburg, Nikolai Bukharin, and Vladimir Lenin—that understood the structural constraints of backward economies to become modern industrial nations due to the renewed imperatives for dominance of advanced countries at the "monopolistic" stage of global capitalist development. Their analyses inquired into the economic possibilities of late industrialization and the political prospects of bourgeois revolutions in post-colonial nations.

It was in the third phase of the debate that the dependency school emerged as an attempt to theorize "underdevelopment" in the context of Latin America's position in the world economy. Paul Baran's (1957 [1962]) *The Political Economy of Growth* put forward the thesis that: "What is decisive is that the economic development in underdeveloped countries is profoundly inimical to the dominant interests in the advanced capitalist countries" (pp. 11–12). Central to the strategy of core countries is to form an alliance among pre-capitalistic domestic elites in poor, but resource-rich, countries. This is to perpetuate foreign capital's expropriation activities to extract surplus from the natural and human resources of the peripheral countries. In effect, the core countries get richer, while the periphery remains economically stagnant. The only way out of this process and relations of dependency is found in the realm of the political. Against this background, Andre Gunder Frank (1967) argued for the necessity of a socialist revolution as the only alternative to break away from the "metropolis–satellite" chain, which is the kind of relations that made the capitalist economies of Latin American countries as they got incorporated into the world economy. Frank's concept of the "development of underdevelopment" basically means that the cause of wealth of the center and the poverty of the periphery was the exploitative relations between them. In particular, the development of the center depends on the underdevelopment of the periphery.

There are differences among the *dependentistas*; thus it is important not to oversimplify their respective analytical nuances. Since Baran and Frank laid the theory's general concept of the development of underdevelopment, dependency analyses were revised in more sophisticated fashion by various critical scholars both theoretically and empirically. Yet, dependentistas share a number of notable ideas: (a) the level of analysis in the international division labor in the world capitalist economy is between states in the core and states in the periphery; (b) the development of the core capitalist states is dependent on the underdevelopment of the peripheral Third World states; (c) the overarching cause of underdevelopment in the peripheral states is the structure of the geopolitical economy that is external, rather than internal, to them; and (d) the only political solution left to peripheral countries is to be self-reliant by delinking from the system of capitalist imperialism in the world economy so as to unshackle the metropolis–satellite chain and put an end to the vicious center–periphery dependent relationship.

The dependency school has contributed a great deal to studies on the global political economy of development by, among other things, opening up a compelling problematique about the dynamics of underdevelopment and mal-development in the Third World. As Palma (1978) noted in his comprehensive review of the school:

> the most successful analyses are those which resist the temptation to build a formal theory, and focus on 'concrete situations of dependency'; in general terms ... the contribution of dependency has been ... more a critique of development strategies in general than an attempt to make practical contributions to them (882).

In the Southeast Asian region, the dependency approach, though most popular during the 1970s–1980s, continues to hold sway over the language and concepts of several critical political economists and scholar-activists (Hewison 2001; see, e.g., Bello 2002).

Interestingly, the major criticisms hurled on dependency theory are based on empirical case studies that show the relative success stories of some Asian economies since the 1970s. Critics of dependency argue that it puts much emphasis on external forces (i.e., colonialism) at the expense of domestic political, economic, and cultural factors that constitute social change. As a response to critiques, proponents of the dependency school had introduced a series of theoretical improvisations. One is the "unequal exchange" thesis that provides a certain degree of agency to analyze the internal mechanisms within the ambit of the national state in its relations with the global economy (Amin 1976). And the other is the "world-systems theory," which accounts for the existence of the "semi-periphery" between core and peripheral countries to explain the possibility of economic development under conditions of US imperialism as shown in the successful experience of a few Asian countries like Japan, South Korea, Taiwan, Hong Kong, and Singapore (Wallerstein 1979). Moreover, these critiques have been used as the basis of prescriptions for peripheral states in Latin America to emulate national industrialization projects in the Asia Pacific (e.g., Evans 1987; Abbot 2003). Peter Evans (1987), for instance, proposed the extension of dependency's thinking on the role of the state to forge a "triple alliance" behind dependent capitalist development in which transnational and local private capital (as the essential actors in Latin America) are in partnership with a relatively autonomous state (as the dominant partner in East Asia).

The dependency debates triggered a revival of interests through the 1980s, when the related issue of imperialism was particularly examined with reference to the interaction of local social forces with the international structure. For example, Bill Warren (1980) argued for the crucial role of domestic factors in peripheral industrialization, and James Petras (1980) pointed out the emergence of "neo-fascism" in the Third World in which a common external factor of global imperialist capital accumulation operates alongside internal processes. During this period, the dependency theory was criticized for its flaws as an analytical tool to understand the dynamics in the Third World, especially the Asia Pacific. In empirical and theoretical terms, the dependency approach has been critiqued for its inadequacy to comprehend the process of "late development" in parts of East and Southeast Asia where states played a strategic role in industrialization projects by creating a development coalition with domestic and international market forces— either to pursue their respective national economic interests (Amsden 1989), or to respond more to the needs of global, rather than national, capital (Robinson 1985).

The development experience of the Asia Pacific induced a major rethinking of the relationship between global capitalism and the Third World. Notably, the so-called "Murdoch School" then led by Richard Higgott and Richard Robison from the Asia Research Centre, Murdoch University in Perth, Australia proposed an alternative approach—the "post-dependency radical theory"—which can be regarded as the first major academic and theoretical attempt at understanding capitalist development in Southeast Asia in terms of the complex relationship between the structure of capital and the dominant class. This alternative theory offers a framework that explains capitalist transformations in specific countries by utilizing the concept of the "international division of labour." Its foci are on production rather than exchange, on accumulation rather than unequal exchange, and on specific dynamic of capital–state relations and decision-making in all nations rather than on the static relationship of exploitation between central and peripheral countries (Higgott and Robison 1985a).

Contemporary studies on the political economy of Southeast Asia, especially those influenced by the Murdoch School, have criticized dependency theory for what they interpret as its static approach, resulting in its inability to explain processes of social change and to take into account the specific dynamics in different national situations within the region (e.g., Rodan, Hewison and Robison 2006a; Rasiah and Schmidt 2010a). These criticisms have been made along theoretical, methodological, empirical, and analytical terms. Theoretically, the dependency approach is seen as inadequate in explaining the mutations in the system of global, regional, and national capital accumulation since the 1970s and how this has impacted on capitalist development across Southeast Asia. Methodologically, its emphases on market determination in exchange relations (instead of class relations in the mode of production) and on dominance/ dependence dichotomy (rather than on the dialectics of conflicts and change) are perceived as a perspective that is based on an unhistorical and undialectical understanding of structural transformation, class relations, state character, and capital accumulation processes. Empirically, it is often viewed for being unable to anticipate the remarkable economic success stories in parts of Asia and appreciate the economic mechanisms underpinning their industrialization processes since the 1960s. And analytically, it is regarded as incapable of accounting for the changing configuration of new class relationships in Southeast Asia, the changing role of governments, and the increasing complexity of state–society linkages—particularly the emergence of national bourgeoisies in the region who confront as well as coalesce with states and foreign capital.

State theory

In the 1980s, controversies on Southeast Asian political economy shifted from a focus on predominantly external determinants of development (modernization versus dependency theories) to a consideration on the problem of the internal processes of the state. Marxist and Weberian contributions—especially Higgott and Robison (1985b) and Evans (1989), respectively—have become particularly influential in characterizing capitalist states in the region. Relative development and underdevelopment in specific countries embody distinct state forms that have been characterized as "corporatist," "predatory," or "developmental."

The changing forms of state power in Southeast Asia in the 1980s and the 1990s was a consequence of, as well as a response to, the changes brought about by the global crisis of the 1970s that ushered in the neoliberal phase of capitalist development. During these transitional decades, the Marxist political economy perspective of the Murdoch School observed the increasing attraction of developing countries for "corporatism" as a state form in which attempts at market-oriented principles were accommodated to elite interests in regime security, order and stability (Higgott and Robison 1985a; Robison, Hewison and Higgott 1987; Hewison, Robison and Rodan 1993). Here, following the definition of Ray Pahl and Jack Winkler, corporatism is understood as "an economic system in which the state predominantly directs and controls privately owned business towards four goals: unity, order, nationalism and success" (Pahl and Winkler 1976: 7; for a critical review of the material and social bases of corporatism, see Jessop 1990: 110–143). Since means of production is privately owned but publicly controlled in a corporatist state form (Jessop 1990), there is "a tendency to *over*control at the political level and *under*control at the economic level" (Higgott and Robison 1985a: 43). This structural contradiction in corporatism among private actors and public institutions, and between the political and the economic, in the context of Southeast Asian capitalist societies had been manifested in the corporatism projects and experiments in Indonesia, Malaysia, the Philippines, Thailand, and Singapore—namely, the Singapore model of "tripartism" developed by Lee Kuan Yew since the mid-1960s (Rodan 1989), the "New Order" under Suharto during 1966–1998 (MacIntyre 1999), the "New Economic Policy" (NEP) initiated under the government of Tun Abdul Razak in the 1970s which were carried on in the "Privatization Programmes" and "Malaysia Incorporated" of Mahathir since the 1980s (Jomo 1995), the "New Society" of Ferdinand Marcos from the 1970s to mid-1980s (Stauffer 1985); and the "CEO state" of Thaksin Shinawatra in the early 2000s (Pasuk and Baker 2004).

Weberian statist–institutionalist approaches also emerged as a theoretical and analytical response to the rise of neoliberalism, which was seen as a political project concerned with institutional changes on a scale not seen since the immediate aftermath of the postwar (Campbell and Pedersen 2001). It was the seminal work of Peter Evans (1989) entitled "Predatory, Developmental, and Other Apparatuses: A Comparative Political Economy Perspective on the Third World State" which influenced mainstream characterization of Southeast Asian states from the 1990s on. Evans (1989) examined the connection of different state performance to different state structure. In particular, he contrasted two polar types of states—the "klepto-patrimonial state" of Zaire and the "developmental states" of East Asia—and also analyzed the internal and external dynamics of the "intermediate state" of Brazil. He provided a taxonomy between "predatory states" and "developmental states." Predatory states like Zaire "may extract such large amounts of otherwise investable surplus and provide so little in the way of 'collective goods' in return that they do indeed impede economic transformation" (ibid.: 562). On the other hand, developmental states such as Japan are

> able to foster long-term entrepreneurial perspectives among private elites by increasing incentives to engage in transformative investments and lowering the risks involved in such investments. They may not be immune to 'rent seeking' or to using some of the social surplus for the ends of incumbents and their friends rather that those of the citizenry as a whole, but on balance, the consequences of their actions promote rather than impede transformation.
>
> *(Ibid.: 563)*

A distinctive feature of developmental states is their "embedded autonomy," understood as the state's capacity to combine two apparently contradictory features: "a Weberian bureaucratic insulation with intense immersion in the surrounding social structure" (ibid.: 574).

Evans (1995) elaborated on the concept of embedded autonomy as a critique of neo-utilitarian "state-versus-market" dichotomy in economics (Buchanan, Tollison and Tullock 1980) and as a revision of the "state-versus-society" contribution to political science (Migdal 1988) by characterizing differences in state structure and state–society relations. Predatory states are characterized by a dearth of the ideal–typical Weberian bureaucracy and as such incumbent government officials are individualistic whose ties to the society are personalistic. On the other hand, developmental states have a Weberian rational and meritocratic bureaucracy, which is *autonomous* (from particular vested interests of private elites due to their strong sense of corporate coherence), yet *embedded* (in concrete set of social ties through negotiations of collective goals and action). The virtues of embeddedness and autonomy, joined together, are peculiar and indispensable to developmental states (Evans 1995).

Arguably, Weberian-inspired statist–institutionalist studies have been more influential than the Marxist approach of the Murdoch School among researchers of Southeast Asia's political economy. To a large extent, this is due to the former's concepts that evoke normative connotation and utility for policy-making. Chalmers Johnson (1982) was the first to observe the idiosyncrasies of the developmental state in his study of Japan—characterized by an autonomous bureaucracy, state planned and coordinated public–private cooperation, and substantial investment in education for the training of labor. This was then adopted or modified in several conceptualizations like "governed markets" (Wade 1990) and "governed interdependence" (Weiss and Hobson 1995). Yet, it was the taxonomy and typology provided by Evans (1989, 1995) on state performance and structure that have significantly defined a number of conceptual frameworks on Southeast Asian studies since the 1990s. For example, several scholars have characterized the Philippines as a "predatory state" (Rivera 1994), Malaysia as an "intermediate state" (Abrami and Doner 2008), and Singapore as a "developmental state" (Huff 1995).

In the same vein in state theory, the dynamics in Southeast Asia have contributed to researches that examine the relationship between regime type and economic performance. The variations of regimes within the region—ranging from democratic to authoritarian systems—have been an intriguing phenomenon in the study of political economy. Some assume the conduciveness of democracy for economic growth because of the institutional guarantee for individual property rights, free market competition, and protection against arbitrary authoritarianism. Others posit that authoritarian regimes can offer strong institutions which provide a certain degree of predictability for the business operations of capitalists. However, empirical studies of single-country cases in Southeast Asia suggest that there is an indeterminate relationship between type of regime and rate of growth (e.g., Przeworski, Alvarez, Cheibub and Limongi 2000), and that, in examining economic outcomes, the more appropriate foci of analysis are the relationships between elites, domestic coalitions and institutions, rather than the mere descriptive features of particular regimes (e.g., Bertrand 1998).

One of the main criticisms against traditional Weberian statist–institutionalism is its typological approach. As a result, when applied to studying Southeast Asia's political economy, it either excludes or trivializes the very important questions of history and politics in theorizing processes of capitalist transformation and societal change in the region. For instance, numerous scholarships on the evolution of late industrialization in East Asia like the most cited case of South Korea (e.g., Chibber 1999) have taken too lightly the essential role of the history of colonialism under Japanese rule and the authoritarian politics behind the economic development strategy instituted in the early 1960s in creating a "capitalist" developmental state through the establishment of a repressive labor regime (Pirie 2008).

Furthermore, the state–institutionalist debates on "models of capitalism" in developed and developing countries are criticized for paying little attention to social change and the conflicts or class struggle it entails. The critique stems from their inadequate theory of states in capitalist societies. First, by treating the state as a single entity, they fail to recognize different forms of state, which are constituted within their respective complex historical social relations and are also embedded in broader political–economic systems with particular social formations (Jessop 2008). Second, by falling into the state–capital instrumentalist trap, they downplay the reality of conflicts in social change where states do not always act in the interest of capital, as well as the issues of class struggle where there are links between the processes of exploitation, accumulation and legitimation in capitalism (Cammack 2007; Juego 2015a).

Theories of state–market–society relations

In essence, studies on the political economy of contemporary Southeast Asia are attempts at explaining the nature of capitalist development in the region. Their concern is to provide theoretical and empirical explanation on the dynamics and processes involved in the relationship between market, state, and society against the background of globalizing capitalism (Robison, Hewison and Higgott 1987; Rodan, Hewison and Robison 1997, 2001a, 2006a; Rasiah and Schmidt 2010b). Three competing approaches have defined the terms of debate in this research area, namely: (a) neoclassical economics; (b) Weberian historical institutionalism; and (c) Marxist social conflict theory.

The first two opposing approaches provide different explanations of the remarkable economic performance of East and Southeast Asian countries since the postwar and even during the global crisis of the 1970s. On the one hand, the free market camp of neoclassical economists argues that the success was due to market-driven liberalized production and finance (e.g., Bowie and Unger 1997). On the other hand, the developmental state camp of the historical institutionalists argues that the region's high growth record with equity was due to state's planning and active intervention in the sphere of economic development through policies of industrial protection and regulation (e.g., Wade 1990). An alternative to this state-versus-market debate is the social conflict theory of the Murdoch School, which critiques mainstream approaches that essentialize or abstract the state and the market. Social conflict theory delineates the power structures in the origin and reproduction of state institutions and markets, alongside the intrinsic conflicts in the process of societal change (e.g., Rodan, Hewison and Robison 2006a).

Neoclassical economics and neoliberalism

Neoclassical economics has its ideological roots from the classical political economy of Adam Smith and David Ricardo, both of whom believed in the so-called "invisible hand" of market forces that maintains the equilibrium of the economy. Its philosophy is associated with the libertarian tradition, which underpins the ethos of methodological individualism (i.e., the perspective that the decisions and actions of individual human beings shape social phenomena) and the doctrine of market fundamentalism (i.e., the idea that the free market is efficient, whereas the state is inefficient, in allocating scarce resources). It is an approach that explains how individuals and firms should behave in order to maximize utility and profits, respectively. Its concerns revolve around the operations of the market economy at the micro and macro levels–including issues of allocative efficiency (i.e., the measurement of utility in the distribution of resources), behavior and choices of economic agents (i.e., the decision-making of individuals as rational actors), the determinants of supply and demand (i.e., the production and consumption of goods and services), and price formation (i.e., reflected by the cost of production and the law of supply and demand).

For neoclassical economists, the capitalist market economy is the best possible system. It is where "the market" takes precedence over other social variables; as such, it is the means and ends of socio-economic and human development. The market is regarded as a realm of individual freedom, choice and progress; a society is no more than a tapestry of individuals; and the state is best kept limited to a minimal function (Friedman and Friedman 1979). Hence, the market, the state, and the society are separate entities which must mind their respective businesses so as to achieve harmony within the economy and between individuals. Neoclassical economics argues that the internal mechanisms of the free market under laissez-faire capitalism, where states abstain from interfering in the workings of the economy, shall generate economic growth that will trickle-down for the benefit of the society as a whole. It got into the mainstream as the theoretical foundation of "neoliberalism," which is the ideology and set of economic policies promoted by international financial institutions (IFIs) such as the International Monetary Fund (IMF), the World Bank and other multilateral development banks. Neoclassical economists and policy advisers blamed the state as the culprit for underdevelopment and put their faith in the market as prime development agent. Within this framework, an efficient economy requires a state whose role is limited and restricted to the protection of individual rights and the enforcement of private property rights.

The 1970s recession and its attendant global crises paved the way to the epoch of neoliberalism, marked by a paradigm shift from state-managed to market-oriented development policy and from import-substitution to export-oriented industrialization strategies. This general change in the focus and priorities in governance and economic policy-making was adopted in distinct forms in specific Southeast Asian economies (Hart-Landsberg and Burkett 1998). The IFIs, particularly the IMF and the World Bank, subjected the Philippines and Indonesia to neoliberal policy discipline in the 1990s through a comprehensive set of structural adjustment programs of privatization, liberalization, deregulation, and fiscal austerity as conditionalities upon the enormous sovereign debts that their governments incurred during the Marcos and Suharto regimes in the 1970s–1980s (Bello 2004; Hadiz and Robison 2005). Thailand also entered into the IMF–World Bank structural adjustment programs since the early 1980s to address problems of inflation, current account deficit and external debt (Robinson, Byeon, Teja and Tseng 1991). In the case of Malaysia, which was one of the recipients of the massive inflow of Japanese direct investment into Southeast Asia as a result of the Plaza Accord of 1985, the government of Mahathir "voluntarily" introduced neoliberal economic policies, notably privatization and selective liberalization, without direct imposition from the IFIs, while pursuing its national industrialization plans (Juego 2018a).

Policy recommendations of neoclassical economists for state governance and regulation in Southeast Asia, particularly for an enabling legal environment, are oriented toward correcting market imperfections and thus ensuring efficient functioning of markets (cf. Ito and Krueger 2004). A key objective is to depoliticize the economy, in which the market is emancipated from the presumed inefficiencies of the state, specifically from the rent-seeking, corrupt, or predatory tendencies of self-interested politicians and government functionaries. In this socio-economic system and institutional set-up where the market would be dis-embedded from the society, the business operations and other appropriation activities by the private sector are provided considerable immunity from democratic accountability and public responsibility.

There are diverse schools within neoclassical economic theory; yet a common analytical theme in their practical conclusions and normative prescriptions is their abstract assumptions on the concept of "the market," which is viewed independent of social context and questions of political power. Here then lies a fundamental blind spot of this mainstream theory of neoclassical economics in analyzing capitalist development in Southeast Asia. First, its fetishism for the market systematically excludes other relevant social and non-market factors in the system of capitalism. Second, its programmatic separation of the economic from the political fails to recognize the social and power relations embedded, as well as constituted, in the formation and operations of the market. And third, its focus on market abstractions inadvertently neglects the concrete competing interests among political and economic agents—hence, the conflictual nature within the structure of capitalism.

Weberian historical institutionalism, Keynesian economics, and the developmental state

Historical institutionalism has evolved from the traditions of Weberian historical sociology in the study of the modern state. Since the 1980s, there has been growing attention to sociological theorization of the state as a response to the claims of mainstream neoclassical economics about the discursive ascendancy of the market during the era of neoliberal capitalism. This historical sociology perspective attempts to provide a "state–institutionalist" theory of change. It does so by describing and explaining the origins, powers, and changing configurations of specific states, and by examining the internal and external dimensions of state power (Hobden and Hobson 2002).

Weberian historical sociology offers an alternative theoretical framework to hard core realist conception of the state in international relations (e.g., Gilpin 1984), and a critique of the "bringing the state back in" and the "strong society, weak state" theses in political science (Migdal 1988). This is done in two major ways: (i) by pointing out state agential power in the international system, instead of reifying the international structure at the expense of state-agency; and (ii) by stressing on the state as embedded in domestic social relations as well as international relations (Evans 1995; Weiss 1998). The latter suggests that the depth of state's embeddedness within society determines its strength and capacity for effective governance. Hence, state–society relations is not a zero-sum game because strong social forces do not merely constrain domestic state power, but may also enable and enhance the governing capacity of the state. In locating the "social sources" of state power, Weberian historical sociology brings both the state and the society (and international society) back in the analysis of capitalist development (Hobson 2000).

The amalgamation of state-centered (e.g., Johnson 1982; Amsden 1989) and society-centered (e.g., Doner 1992) historical institutionalisms constitute the statist–institutionalist approach to the study of IPE. This new institutionalist perspective was reinvigorated in the 1980s as the rise of neoliberalism induced tremendous institutional changes, not least in relation to market deregulation, the decentralization of governance, and a significantly reduced state intervention into economic affairs (Campbell and Pedersen 2001a). Its object of inquiry was the intricacies of institutions in determining political and economic performance of states and societies. It was an alternative theory to that of the mainstream neo-utilitarian paradigm in the 1970s, which associated Third World states with rent-seeking and cronyism (e.g., Krueger 1974).

While the classic Weberian institutionalist school has evolved into different strands over the years under the rubric "new institutionalisms" in the study of European and North American political economy (Campbell and Pedersen 2001), the most controversial case studies of institutionalist analysis were the newly industrialized countries or the so-called "developmental states" in Northeast Asia, whose analytical framework was later on applied to the examination of the relationship between state structure and economic performance in Southeast Asian countries (Woo-Cumings 1999). The concept of the developmental state has been referred to as "the distinctive East Asian contribution to international political economy" (Bello 2009). It is anchored to the policies and principles of Keynesian economics which, *inter alia*, proposes a proactive role of the state in national development planning, strategic investments for industrialization, policy coordination, and crisis management of the market economy. The developmental state is often typified as possessing at least three main features: (i) an insulated and autonomous set of government agencies with a strong capacity to implement economic policies and programs; (ii) an activist industrial policy to build export-oriented industries that are globally competitive; and (iii) a governance principle that emphasizes the indispensable function of the state in securing socio-economic development goals (Weiss and Hobson 1995; Chibber 1999).

Taking a cue from Johnson's (1982) study of the peculiarity of the Japanese development experience, a number of scholars on the political economy of Southeast Asia have presented the developmental state as an alternative development framework to neoliberal capitalism (e.g., Beeson 2006). Yet, it must be recalled that the developmental states of Japan and South Korea were a capitalist and authoritarian project (Johnson 1987). In fact, Asia has long been a showcase for "repressive-development regimes" (Feith 1981). In Japanese economic history, an absolutist state combined with a capitalist economy from 1889 to 1947 (Taira 1983). In South Korea, an oppressive and exploitative political and labor regime especially under General Park Chung-hee, trained by the Japanese Imperial Army, was central to industrialization strategy during the 1960s–1970s (Cumings 1984; Deyo 1987; Haggard, Kang and Moon 1997). As Johnson (1982) had indicated, it is more appropriate to conceive of a *capitalist* developmental state that blends capitalism with authoritarianism (see Box 29.1).

Box 29.1 The capitalist developmental state

Often missed out in typological accounts of the developmental state are the significance of colonial history and social relations within which the accumulation process in capitalism is embedded. If history and social relations were to be considered, then several important characteristics of the regime of accumulation under conditions and governance of the *capitalist* developmental state could be identified:

a   a state with long-term development agenda in alliance with key industrial business elites and does not make compromises with vested interest groups (Johnson 1982);

b   a state-guided capitalist system that has a plan-rational economy with market-rational political institutions (Johnson 1995);

c   authoritarian and paternalistic government able to mobilize economic and political resources (Taira 1983; Johnson 1987);

d   embedded autonomy institutionalized in state–business relations (Evans 1995);

e   state–society relations as an effective countervailing force to preserve the institutions of embedded autonomy; and

f   a political–economic framework that amalgamates capitalism with authoritarianism (Taira 1983; Johnson 1987; Cammack 2007; Pirie 2008).

Government–business partnership, state–capital relations, and politics–business interaction are recurring themes in the political economy of Southeast Asia (McVey 1992; Robison, Hewison and Rodan 1993; Gomez 2002). The influential report of the World Bank (1993) on *The East Asian Miracle*, in particular, greatly framed the development narrative among policymakers, academics, and journalists about government–business relationship, not least in the aftermath of the 1997–1998 Asian currency and financial crisis (Stiglitz and Yusuf 2001; Jomo 2003). The authors of the report noted the ASEAN countries of Singapore, Malaysia, Thailand, and Indonesia as part of the "high-performing Asian economies" (HPAEs) together with Japan, South Korea, Taiwan, and Hong Kong. Between 1960 and 1990, these HPAEs had attained "rapid growth with equity" as shown in their unusually high rates of private investments, efficient allocation, and rising endowments for the education of human capital, and superior productivity performance through technological catch-up. While the authors acknowledged that these impressive results were made possible through a range of market-oriented and state-led policies deployed by specific HPAE over time, they recommended selective government policy interventions only for purposes of correcting market failures, addressing coordination problems, and achieving the economic fundamentals of macroeconomic stability, rapid export growth, and high savings. Furthermore, the authors criticized the "developmental state models" of some economists and political scientists which "overlook the central role of government-private sector cooperation" (World Bank 1993: 13). They posited that:

> While leaders of the HPAEs have tended to be authoritarian or paternalistic, they have also been willing to grant a voice and genuine authority to a technocratic elite and key leaders of the private sector. Unlike authoritarian leaders in many other economies, leaders in the HPAEs realized that economic development was impossible without cooperation.
>
> *(Ibid.; cf. Juego 2018b)*

In answer to the flaws of the original formulation of the developmental state, historical institutionalists have developed far less statist conceptualization of East and Southeast Asian political economy – notably, the concept of "governed interdependence" which emphasizes the importance of establishing institutional structures in rethinking government–business relationship "where both strong state and strong industry go hand-in-hand" (Weiss 1995: 592), and the concept of "inclusionary institutionalism" in which there is "less domination and more cooperation between state and business and within the business world itself" as necessary precondition for building complex institutional capacity (Doner 1991: 819). Historical institutionalism is concerned with the problem of how variations in political and other social institutions shape the capacities of actors for action, policy-making, and institution-building (Campbell and Pedersen 2001). It argues that change and institutional evolution are "path-dependent"—in other words, historical and past experiences have enduring impact on the understanding of the origins and development processes of particular institutions. Pre-existing arrangements influence options and preferences, and outcomes may be contingent and full of unintended consequences (Thelen 1999). Moreover, social norms and cultural identities, alongside political conflicts and unequal power relations, can all be mechanisms of institutional change (Abrami and Doner 2008). These theoretical improvements, therefore, draw attention beyond the state and the market so as to include non-state and non-market institutions as salient variables in explaining the political economy of development.

However, despite the advances made in its theoretical framework and even though Southeast Asianists have increasingly demonstrated its utility both in practical policy advice and in academic explanation of economic change, historical institutionalism has been criticized for its weaknesses and limitations in at least three important analytical issues in studying capitalist development. First, the priority given to institutions as "intermediate" variables between state and society tends to discount an appreciation of the "organic" relationship between social, economic and political power relations, processes and actors within the larger system of capitalism (Katznelson 1998). Second, there is little analysis of the class composition and dynamics in institutions—particularly on the question how social forces and whose class interests are articulated, resisted, negotiated, or mediated within institutions (Hawes and Liu 1993). And third, there is a normative preference for order and stability in governance by proposing the insulation of institutions from vested interests; hence, there is the tendency to miss out the analytical point that conflicts constitute, as well as induce, processes of institutional and social change (Peters 1999; Rodan, Hewison and Robison 2006a).

Marxist social conflict theory and the Murdoch School

While the so-called "Cornell School" and the "Singapore School" of Southeast Asian Studies have contributed to the issue areas in history, politics, culture, anthropology, geopolitics, and security across countries in the region (Siegel and Kahin 2003; McCargo 2006), the Murdoch School can be said to have pioneered the social conflict approach to the political economy of Southeast Asia. Marxist critical political economy has been the analytical lodestar of the Murdoch School's research program to explain Southeast Asian political and economic development through an examination of state–capital interrelations against the background of the international capitalist economy. Since the mid-1980s, the Murdoch School—especially represented by the works of Richard Robison, Richard Higgott, Garry Rodan, Kevin Hewison, and Kanishka Jayasuriya—have published six major co-edited books on the political economy of Southeast Asia. The analyses in these book anthologies are consistently informed by social conflict theory using class analysis in a historical perspective, and most of the article contributions in them discuss specific country case studies (see Box 29.2).

Box 29.2 Social conflict theory

The process of historical change is a central theme in social conflict theory. The Murdoch School introduced this theoretical framework in the 1980s, initially as an alternative to what they considered as static and ideological postwar orthodoxies—specifically, growth theory, political order theory, political development theory, modernization theory, and dependency theory (Higgott and Robison 1985a). Then at the turn of the twenty-first century, in the context of post-1997 Asian financial crisis, social conflict theory has been presented as a critique of neoclassical economics' reification of the market and the Weberian-inspired historical institutionalism's understanding of reform and change as a simple problem of institutions and capacity building (Rodan, Hewison and Robison 1997, 2001a, 2006a).

The Murdoch School particularly introduced and utilized "social conflict theory" in the context of post-1997 crisis Southeast Asia (Rodan, Hewison and Robison 2001a, 2006a). The theory attempts to provide crucial linkages between the processes of crisis, state restructuring, and social change. It was proposed as an alternative reading to established theories from neoclassical economics and Weberian/Keynesian-inspired institutionalist approaches that have provided their respective analyses of the causes and effects of the 1997 crisis.

Essential assumptions and claims of the social conflict approach include:

a   the proposition that social conflicts drive institutional change;
b   the understanding of the class-based nature of institutions and their function as mechanisms for the allocation of power;
c   the fundamental point that crisis reshapes class relations; and
d   the analytical objective to unpack power relations and the shape of political–economic regimes.

The first book in the series was published in 1985—*Southeast Asia: Essays in the Political Economy of Structural Change*—which was a pioneering attempt at theorizing capitalist development in Southeast Asia (Higgott and Robison 1985b). It proposed a "post-dependency radical theory" as a critique of mainstream theories in development studies and political science, placing internal dynamics of specific countries in the region within changes in the broader international division of labor. Beyond dependency theory, Higgott and Robison (1985a) proposed a focus on the logic of state–capital relations in the systems of production and accumulation to understand capitalist transformation at both the domestic and international scales. This is an alternative to dependency theory's seemingly mechanical processes of circulation and unequal exchange between the core and periphery.

The second book published was *Southeast Asia in the 1980s: The Politics of Economic Crisis*, which analyzed processes of structural change as elicited from the interaction between international political economy and domestic political–economic interests in policy-making (Robison, Hewison and Higgott 1987). Its focus was on the politics of crisis-induced economic transformation from import-substitution industrialization projects that dominated development policy in the 1950s–1960s to export-oriented industrialization from the 1970s on. In terms of theory, this anthology critiqued neoclassical economics' free market-centric interpretation of structural change and questioned dependency theory's limitations. It proposed an alternative reading of economic crisis, and highlighted conflicts over policy, by examining the interaction between the spheres of production and circulation at both the international and local levels. Within this framework, the politics of the economic crises of the 1970s and the 1980s was observed to have involved

> at one level, disruptions to existing patterns of domestic capital accumulation and fiscal systems engendered by changes in international terms of trade. At another level they involve intense political and social conflict between forces representing class, political and ideological interests for whom changes in economic strategies and policies hold fundamental consequences.
>
> *(Robison, Hewison and Higgott 1987: 15)*

This observation, which was validated in the empirical cases of several country studies in the volume, exhibited some of the key theoretical underpinnings of the social conflict approach. Specifically, the arguments and research findings suggested the inextricable link between social, economic and political factors, and the inherent conflicts in policy formulation (i.e., international versus national capital, manufacturers versus mineral exporters or bankers, and state capital versus private capital).

The third was *Southeast Asia in the 1990s: Authoritarianism, Democracy and Capitalism* that focused on the political aspect of the region's political economy. Amid the rapid changes in social, economic, and political dynamics brought about by the end of the Cold War and the wave of democratization from Eastern Europe and Latin America to Southeast Asia, the country case studies in this anthology particularly examined the different impacts of capitalist development on varying political regimes of democracy and authoritarianism within the region (Hewison, Robison and Rodan 1993). Based on a critique of "modernization theory, dependency theory, and post-dependency empiricism," as well as the voluntarist interpretations of the transitions literature, it offered a "social structural explanation" of the historical development of state power and social formations in the process of social change (Robison, Hewison and Rodan 1993: 11-12). Following the concept introduced by Ralph Miliband (1965, 1983) on the "partnership" between the state and dominant class, it explains state–society–regime relationships "in terms of all three dynamics—instrumental, structural and state-centred—according to the specific historical factors that prevail" (Robison, Hewison and Rodan 1993: 31). This state–class partnership, however, also entails tensions. While states may work for the short-term interests of a fraction of capital, they operate under certain structural constraints when it comes to the goal of protecting the long-term and general interest of the capitalist system.

These two latter publications have sketched out key theses of social conflict theory on the process of political and economic change: (i) that economic, political and social factors are inseparable; (ii) that policy formation and economic strategies encompass specific vested interests; (iii) that "not only is determination of policy a consequence of the balance of power and the outcome of conflict between competing elements within, and between, capital and labour and the state, but also that it is a consequence of these conflicts at both a national and an international level as well" (Robison, Higgott and Hewison 1987: 12); and (d) that political outcomes "reflect the balance of social forces and the nature of political struggle" (Robison, Hewison and Rodan 1993: 29).

Succeeding publications of the Murdoch School from the mid-1990s have been a series of editions of *The Political Economy of Southeast Asia*, each of which addresses a specific theme in a particular historical juncture in Southeast Asian development experience. Its first edition was published just before the 1997 Asian financial crisis when observers had the penchant for explaining "Asian economic miracles" and comparing Asian models of development stimulated by a remarkable economic boom and industrial transformation in the region during the last quarter of the twentieth century. Contributors to this issue with six country case studies (Indonesia, the Philippines, Thailand, Malaysia, Singapore, and Vietnam) and three thematic chapters (on labor, regional economic integration, and sub-regional growth zones) have derived their respective analyses from various elements of "new institutionalist," "pluralist," and "Marxist-derived political economy" approaches—all of which are outside the mainstream neoclassical economics framework. These approaches, especially Marxist political economy, that dissect the social and political dimensions of economic development can be considered the intellectual antecedents to the social conflict approach to Southeast Asian studies (Rodan, Hewison and Robison 1997).

It was in the second edition where the Murdoch School categorically stated "social conflict theory" as the most illuminating theoretical framework—distinct from neoclassical political economy and historical institutionalism—for understanding periods of economic boom in Southeast Asia especially since the mid-1980s, as well as the causes of the 1997 Asia crisis and its impact on social formation, economic restructuring and political dynamics in the region (see Box 29.3). In contrast to the first edition, which was primarily concerned with explaining capitalist successes in the region, the second edition asked broader questions on whether the capitalist crisis had put an end to Asian "illiberal" mode of capitalism and paved the way for the inexorable convergence towards liberal politics and free markets (Rodan, Hewison and Robison 2001a, 2001b).

Box 29.3 Interpretations of the 1997 Asian financial crisis

Highly nuanced analyses have been provided to explain the nature and causes of the 1997 Asian financial crisis, yet these may possibly be categorized into two opposing schools of thought along the state-versus-market debate. The first and most influential came from the neoliberals, who provided the mainstream neoclassical economics account of the crisis. They basically believed in the efficiency of the market in creating stability in the economy and harmony in the society. The international financial institutions—such as the IMF, World Bank, and the Asian Development Bank—argued that the crisis resulted from market-distorting practices in Asian countries, notably: selective state intervention in economic affairs, illiberal non-market-based controls, and government failure to construct proper market-based regulatory systems.

The second were the so-called historical institutionalists and heterodox/post-Keynesian economists, who championed the developmental states. They argued that the crisis was a result of the compromised or weakened capacity of the state to govern markets due to externally promoted economic policies of liberalization and deregulation. They proposed that a strong state is essential, rather than antithetical, to integration in the global economy. They perceived of social change as a process involving complex questions of power, class interests, and the relationships between these societal structures and the international economy.

In the third edition, the same social conflict theory has been adopted in understanding the intricacies of power and contestation in the relationship between markets and politics in the international and domestic contexts. Southeast Asian countries found themselves structurally entangled in the rapidly changing global economic environment and geopolitical turn spurred by the aftermath of the 1997 crisis, the global war on terror, and the rise of China. Viewed at the system level, markets and market institutions are delineated as products of wider and deeper processes of social and political conflicts (Rodan, Hewison and Robison 2006a, 2006b).

Although these major books of the Murdoch School can be said to be single-country case studies and thus defeating the object of comparative study (Rasiah and Schmidt 2010a;), the theoretical and analytical tools of social conflict theory that they have outlined over the years encourage a comparative political economy perspective (Hameiri and Jones 2014). The approach would be able to demonstrate the social relations and disposition of power in capitalism, specifically the embedded relationships between market, state, and society at national and international levels. At the same time, it can unpack social change as a dynamic and systemic process of contestation involving conflicting interests.

Southeast Asia at the turn of the twenty-first century

The discussions in this chapter suggest that the scholarship about Southeast Asia, informed by theories on development and capitalism, have been responsive to changes and crises in world historical moments since the 1950s: that is, from the post-colonial and Cold War periods, to the neoliberal phase of capitalist globalization. In the same way, the dynamics of countries and human conditions in Southeast Asia are to be analyzed in their particular contexts against the background of the evolving geopolitical economy during the first quarter of the twenty-first century—thus far, marked by the US-led war on terrorism after the 9/11 attacks, the 2008 North Atlantic economic crises, the rise of anti-democratic politics of populism, and the re-emergence of China as a powerful regional and global actor, among others (Carroll, Hameiri and Jones 2020). To this end, there emerge a few remarkable IPE research endeavors on the political economy of Southeast Asia.

One thematic study contributes to the characterization and explanation of distinctive types of political and economic regime in contemporary Southeast Asia. For example, the concept of "authoritarian neoliberalism" describes how a neoliberal market economy is embedded in an autocratic strong state, and explains why the relationship between political authoritarianism and economic capitalism are organic rather than accidental (Juego 2018a, 2018b). This is likewise exemplified in the logic of the ASEAN Economic Community agenda whereby the principle of state sovereignty (i.e., non-interference in domestic affairs) is linked to the idea of market sovereignty (i.e., non-intervention of the government in economy) (Juego 2014; cf. Jones 2012, 2016). Thus, diversity of national political regimes and socio-cultural orientations is observed, while economic convergence toward an open regional competitive capitalism is enforced. This means that neoliberal capitalism can be made to operate in a variety of political regimes, even in a non-democratic or authoritarian political framework (Juego 2015b).

Another emerging academic agenda introduces the concept of "deep marketization," which is the phenomenon in twenty-first century capitalism where the politics of global competitiveness and the ethos of capitalism itself are universally embedded practically everywhere, from the policies of international organizations and states to daily lives of households, families, and the real individuals. With the development of the "world market" as the unit of analysis, this research aims to examine how the imperatives of "competitive capitalist social relations" are embodied in, or refracted into, countries across Southeast Asia and all spheres of social life (Cammack 2012; Carroll 2012; Carroll and Jarvis 2015). Its key objective is to investigate the extent to which the logic of marketization is accepted, adapted, or resisted as manifested in the policy choices of governments, the material conditions of workers, the behavior of businesses and other economic agents, and the conduct of citizens and ordinary people.

The research theme on the marketization is also closely related to the growing interest in "Everyday IPE," which has been recently adopted in the study of Southeast Asia as an alternative to elite-centric studies of capitalist relations, processes and institutions (Elias and Rethel

2016a). Part of the aim of this "Everyday Political Economy" approach is to contribute to efforts at bringing in non-elite and non-Western perspectives in the study of IPE (Hobson and Seabrooke 2007). Its central analytical concern in rethinking Southeast Asian political economy includes the examination of "how the developmental ambitions of elites intersect with local social relations of gender, race, class and even age, producing distinctive political–economic outcomes, and how capitalist processes of marketization intersect with everyday lived experiences on the ground" (Elias and Rethel 2016b: 6).

Indeed, through the years, the objects and subjects in the study of Southeast Asian political economy are becoming more comprehensive and inclusive, ranging from the analyses of world-systemic structure and inter-state relations to researches about state restructuring, social change, and the everyday activities of the human person. Yet, theories of development and state–market–society relations remain the overarching theme in understanding the political economy of capitalism in Southeast Asia.

Bibliography

Abbot, J. 2003. *Developmentalism and Dependency in Southeast Asia: The Case of the Automotive Industry.* London: Routledge Curzon.

Abrami, R. and Doner, R. 2008. Southeast Asia and the Political Economy of Development. In Martinez, E., Slater, D. and Vu, T. (eds) *Southeast Asia in Political Science: Theory, Region, and Qualitative Analysis:* 252–273. Stanford, CA: Stanford University Press.

Agpalo, R. 1992. Modernization, Development, and Civilization: Reflections on the Prospects of Political Systems in the First, Second, and Third Worlds. In: Bauzon, K. (ed.) *Development and Democratization in the Third World: Myths, Hopes, and Realities:* 81–98. London: Taylor & Francis.

Akamatsu, K. 1962. A Historical Pattern of Economic Growth in Developing Countries. *The Developing Economies* 1(1): 3–25.

Alatas, S. 1977. *The Myth of the Lazy Native: A Study of the Image of the Malays, Filipinos and Javanese from the 16th to the 20th Century and Its Function in the Ideology of Colonial Capitalism.* London: Frank Cass.

Amin, S. 1976. *Unequal Development: An Essay on the Social Formation of Peripheral Capitalism.* Sussex: Harvester Press.

Amsden, A. 1989. *Asia's Next Giant: South Korea and Late Industrialization.* Oxford: Oxford University Press.

Baran, P. 1957 [1962]. *The Political Economy of Growth.* New York: Monthly Review Press.

Beeson, M. 2006. Politics and Markets in East Asia: Is the Developmental State Compatible with Globalization?. In: Stubbs, R. and Underhill, G. (eds) *Political Economy and the Changing Global Order:* 443–453. Ontario: Oxford University Press.

Bello, W. 2002. *Deglobalization: Ideas for a New World Economy.* London: Zed Books.

Bello, W. 2004. *The Anti-Development State: The Political Economy of Permanent Crisis in the Philippines.* Manila: Anvil.

Bello, W. 2009. States and Markets, States versus Markets: The Developmental State Debate as the Distinctive East Asian Contribution to International Political Economy. In: Blyth, M. (ed.) *Routledge Handbook of International Political Economy (IPE): IPE as a global conversation:* 180–200. New York: Routledge.

Bello, W., Kinley, D. and Elinson, E. 1982. *Development Debacle: The World Bank in the Philippines.* San Francisco, CA: Institute for Food and Development Policy.

Bernard, M. and Ravenhill, J. 1995. Beyond Product Cycles and Flying Geese: Regionalization, Hierarchy, and the Industrialization of East Asia. *World Politics* 47(2): 171–209.

Bertrand, J. 1998. Growth and Democracy in Southeast Asia. *Comparative Politics* 30(3): 355–375.

Bowie, A. and Unger, D. 1997. *The Politics of Open Economies: Indonesia, Malaysia, the Philippines, and Thailand.* Cambridge: Cambridge University Press.

Buchanan, J., Tollison, R. and Tullock, G. (eds). 1980. *Toward a Theory of the Rent-Seeking Society.* College Station, TX: Texas A & M University Press.

Cammack, P. 1997. *Capitalism and Democracy in the Third World: The Doctrine for Political Development.* London: Leicester University Press.

Cammack, P. 2007. Class Politics, Competitiveness and the Developmental State. *Papers in the Politics of Global Competitiveness*, No. 4. UK: Manchester Metropolitan University.

Cammack, P. 2012. Risk, Social Protection and the World Market. *Journal of Contemporary Asia* 42(3): 359–377.

Campbell, J. and Pedersen, O. 2001. The Rise of Neoliberalism and Institutional Analysis. In: Campbell, J. and Pedersen, O. (eds) *The Rise of Neoliberalism and Institutional Analysis:* 1–23. Princeton, NJ: Princeton University Press.

Carroll, T. 2012. Working On, Through and Around the State: The Deep Marketisation of Development in the Asia-Pacific. *Journal of Contemporary Asia* 42(3): 378–404.

Carroll, T. and Jarvis, D. 2015. The New Politics of Development: Citizens, Civil Society, and the Evolution of Neoliberal Development Policy. *Globalizations* 12(3): 281–304.

Carroll, T., Hameiri, S. and Jones, L. (eds). 2020. *The Political Economy of Southeast Asia: Politics and Uneven Development under Hyperglobalisation*. Cham, Switzerland: Palgrave Macmillan.

Chibber, V. 1999. Building a Developmental State: The Korean Case Reconsidered. *Politics & Society* 27(3): 309–346.

Cumings, B. 1984. The Origins and Development of the Northeast Asian Political Economy: Industrial Sectors, Product Cycles, and Political Consequences. *International Organization* 38(1): 1–40.

Deyo, F. (ed.). 1987. *The Political Economy of the New Asian Industrialism*. Ithaca, NY: Cornell University Press.

Doner, R. 1991. Approaches to the Politics of Economic Growth in Southeast Asia. *The Journal of Asian Studies* 50(4): 818–849.

Doner, R. 1992. *Limits of State Strength: Toward an Institutionalist View of Economic Development. World Politics* 44(3): 398–431.

Elias, J. and Rethel, L. (eds). 2016a. *The Everyday Political Economy of Southeast Asia*. Cambridge: Cambridge University Press.

Elias, J. and Rethel, L. 2016b. Southeast Asia and Everyday Political Economy. In: *The Everyday Political Economy of Southeast Asia:* 3–24. Cambridge: Cambridge University Press.

Evans, P. 1987. Class, State and Dependence in East Asia: Lessons for Latin Americanists. In: Frederic C. Deyo (ed.) *The Political Economy of the New Asian Industrialism:* 203–226. Ithaca, NY: Cornell University Press.

Evans, P. 1989. Predatory, Developmental, and Other Apparatuses: A Comparative Political Economy Perspective on the Third World State. *Sociological Forum* 4(4): 561–587.

Evans, P. 1995. *Embedded Autonomy: States and Industrial Transformation*. Princeton: Princeton University Press.

Evans, P. and Gereffi, G. 1981. Transnational Corporations, Dependent Development, and State Policy in the Semi-Periphery: A Comparison of Brazil and Mexico. *Latin American Research Review* 16(3): 31–64.

Feith, H. 1981. Repressive-Development Regimes in Asia. *Alternatives: Global, Local, Political* 7(4): 491–506.

Frank, A. 1967. *Capitalism and Underdevelopment in Latin America: Historical Studies of Chile and Brasil*. New York: Monthly Review Press.

Friedman, M. and Friedman, R. 1979. *Free to Choose: A Personal Statement*. New York: Harcourt Brace Jovanovich.

Gilpin, R. 1984. The Richness of the Tradition of Political Realism. *International Organization* 38(2): 287–304.

Gomez, E. (ed.). 2002. *Political Business in East Asia*. London: Routledge.

Hadiz, V. and Robison, R. 2005. Neo-liberal Reforms and Illiberal Consolidations: The Indonesian Paradox. *Journal of Development Studies* 41(2): 220–241.

Haggard, S., Kang, D. and Moon, C. 1997. Japanese Colonialism and Korean Development: A Critique. *World Development* 25(6): 867–881.

Hameiri, S. and Jones, L. 2014. Murdoch International: The Murdoch School in International Relations. *Working Paper No. 178*. Perth, Western Australia: Asia Research Centre, Murdoch University.

Hart-Landsberg, M. and Burkett, P. 1998. Contradictions of Capitalist Industrialization in East Asia: A Critique of "Flying Geese" Theories of Development. *Economic Geography* 74(2): 87–110.

Hawes, G. and Liu, H. 1993. Explaining the Dynamics of the Southeast Asian Political Economy: State, Society, and the Search for Economic Growth. *World Politics* 45(4): 629–660.

Hewison, K. 2001. Nationalism, Populism, Dependency: Southeast Asia and Responses to the Asian Crisis. *Singapore Journal of Tropical Geography* 22(3): 219–236.

Hewison, K., Robison, R. and Rodan, G. (eds). 1993. *Southeast Asia in the 1990s: Authoritarianism, Democracy and Capitalism*. Sydney: Allen & Unwin.

Higgottt, R. 1981. Beyond the Sociology of Underdevelopment: An Historiographical Analysis of Dependencia and Marxist Theories of Underdevelopment. *Social Analysis* (7): 72–98.

Higgott, R. 1983. *Political Development Theory: The Contemporary Debate*. London: Croom Helm.

Higgott, R. and Robison, R., with Hewison, K. and Rodan, G. 1985a. Theories of Development and Underdevelopment: Implications for the Study of Southeast Asia. In: Higgott, R. and Robison, R. (eds) *Southeast Asia: Essays in the Political Economy of Structural Change*: 16–62. London: Routledge and Kegan Paul.

Higgot, R. and Robison, R. (eds). 1985b. *Southeast Asia: Essays in the Political Economy of Structural Change*: 16–62. London: Routledge and Kegan Paul.

Hobden, S. and Hobson, J. (eds). 2002. *Historical Sociology of International Relations*. Cambridge: Cambridge University Press.

Hobson, J. 2000. *The State and International Relations*. Cambridge: Cambridge University Press.

Hobson, J. and Seabrooke, L. (eds). 2007. *Everyday Politics of the World Economy*. Cambridge: Cambridge University Press.

Huff, W. 1995. The Developmental State, Government, and Singapore's Economic Development Since 1960. *World Development* 23(8): 1421–1438.

Huntington, S. 1968. *Political Order in Changing Societies*. New Haven, CT: Yale University Press.

Huntington, S. 1971. The Change to Change: Modernization, Development, and Politics. *Comparative Politics* 3(3): 283–322.

Ikeda, S. 1996. The History of the Capitalist World-System vs. the History of East-Southeast Asia. *Review (Fernand Braudel Center)* 19(1): 49–77.

Ito, T. and Krueger, A. (eds). 2004. *Governance, Regulation, and Privatization in the Asia-Pacific Region*. Chicago: Chicago University Press.

Jessop, B. 1990. *State Theory: Putting Capitalist States in their Place*. University Park, PA: Pennsylvania State University Press.

Jessop, B. 2008. *State Power: A Strategic-Relational Approach*. Cambridge: Polity Press.

Johnson, C. 1982. *MITI and the Japanese Miracle: The Growth of Industrial Policy, 1925–1975*. Stanford, CA: Stanford University Press.

Johnson, C. 1987. Political Institutions and Economic Performance: The Government-Business Relationship in Japan, South Korea, and Taiwan. In: Deyo, F. (ed.) *The Political Economy of the New Asian Industrialism*: 136– 164. Ithaca, NY: Cornell University Press.

Johnson, C. 1995. *Japan: Who Governs? The Rise of the Developmental State*. New York: W.W. Norton.

Jomo, K. (ed.) 2003. *Southeast Asian Paper Tigers? From Miracle to Debacle and beyond*. London: RoutledgeCurzon.

Jones, L. 2012. *ASEAN, Sovereignty and Intervention in Southeast Asia*. Basingstoke, UK: Palgrave Macmillan.

Jones, L. 2016. Explaining the Failure of the ASEAN Economic Community: The Primacy of Domestic Political Economy. *The Pacific Review* 29(5): 647–670.

Juego, B. 2014. The ASEAN Economic Community Project: Accumulating Capital, Dispossessing the Commons. In: *Perspectives Asia 2/13: More or Less? Growth and Development Debates in Asia*: 12–19. Berlin: Heinrich Böll Stiftung.

Juego, B. 2015a. Elite Capture and Elite Conflicts in Southeast Asian Neoliberalization Processes. In: South-South Tricontinental Collaborative Programme (eds) *Inequality, Democracy and Development under Neoliberalism and Beyond*: 68–93. New Delhi: IDEAs, CLACSO, and CODESRIA.

Juego, B. 2015b. The Political Economy of the ASEAN Regionalisation Process. In: *Dossier: Understanding Southeast Asia*. Berlin: Heinrich Böll Stiftung. Available at: www.boell.de/en/2015/10/28/political-economy-asean-regionalisation-process.

Juego, B. 2018a. The Institutions of Authoritarian Neoliberalism in Malaysia: A Critical Review of the Development Agendas Under the Regimes of Mahathir, Abdullah, and Najib. *Austrian Journal of South-East Asian Studies* 11(1): 53–79.

Juego, B. 2018b. Authoritarian Neoliberalism: Its Ideological Antecedents and Policy Manifestations from Carl Schmitt's Political Economy of Governance. *Administrative Culture* 19(1): 105–136.

Kahin, G. 2003. *Southeast Asia: A Testament*. London: RoutledgeCurzon.

Kahin, G., Pauker, G. and Pye, L. 1955. Comparative Politics of Non-Western Countries. *The American Political Science Review* 49(4): 1022–1041.

Katznelson, I. 1998. The Doleful Dance of Politics and Policy: Can Historical Institutionalism Make a Difference?. *The American Political Science Review* 92(1): 191–197.

Klinger, J. 2016. A Sympathetic Appraisal of Cold War Modernization Theory. *The International History Review* 39(4): 691–712.

Korhonen, P. 1994. The Theory of the Flying Geese Pattern of Development and Its Interpretations. *Journal of Peace Research* 31(1): 93–108.

Krueger, A. 1974. The Political Economy of the Rent-Seeking Society. *The American Economic Review* 64(3): 291–303.

Kunio, Y. 1988. *The Rise of Ersatz Capitalism in South-East Asia*. Oxford: Oxford University Press.

Lande, C. H. 1965. *Leaders, Factions, and Parties: The Structure of Philippine Politics*. New Haven: Yale University Press.

Latham, M. 2000. *Modernization as Ideology: American Social Science and "Nation Building" in the Kennedy Era*. Chapel Hill, NC: The University of North Carolina Press.

Love, J. 1980. Raúl Prebisch and the Origins of the Doctrine of Unequal Exchange. *Latin American Research Review* 15(3): 45–72.

MacIntyre, A. 1991. *Business and Politics in Indonesia*. Sydney: Allen & Unwin.

Marx, K. 1859 [1973]. *Grundrisse: Foundations of the Critique of Political Economy*. Harmondsworth, UK: Penguin.

Marx, K. and Engels, F. 1848. *The Communist Manifesto*. London: Electric Book Company.

McCargo, D. 2006. Rethinking Southeast Asian Politics. In: Chou, C. and Houben, V. (eds) *Southeast Asian Studies: Debates and New Directions*: 102 -122. Singapore: ISEAS -Yusof Ishak Institute.

McVey, R. 1992. The Materialization of the Southeast Asian Entrepreneur. In: McVey, R. (ed.) *Southeast Asian Capitalists*: 7–34. Ithaca, NY: Cornell Southeast Asia Program Publications.

Migdal, J. 1988. *Strong Societies and Weak States: State-Society Relations and State Capabilities in the Third World*. Princeton, NJ: Princeton University Press.

Miliband, R. 1965. Marx and the State. In: Miliband, R. and Saville, J. (eds) *Socialist Register 1965*: 278–296. London: Merlin Press.

Miliband, R. 1983. State Power and Class Interests. *New Left Review* 138: 57–68.

Nair, S. 2005. The State of Malaysian Studies. *Critical Asian Studies* 37(1): 161–175.

Pahl, R. and Winkler, J. 1976. Corporatism in Britain. In Timothy Raison (ed.) *The Corporate State – Reality or Myth?*: 5–24. London: Centre for Studies in Public Policy.

Palma, G. 1978. Dependency: A Formal Theory of Underdevelopment or a Methodology for the Analysis of Concrete Situations of Underdevelopment? *World Development* 6 (7–8): 881–924.

Pasuk, P. and Baker, C. 2004. *Thaksin: The Business of Politics in Thailand*. Copenhagen: Nordic Institute of Asian Studies.

Peters, B. 1999. *Institutional Theory in Political Science: The 'New Institutionalism'*. London: Pinter.

Petras, J. 1980. Neo-Fascism: Capital Accumulation and Class Struggle in the Third World. *Journal of Contemporary Asia* 10(1–2): 119–129.

Pirie, I. 2008. *The Korean Developmental State: From Dirigisme to Neo-liberalism*. London: Routledge.

Przeworski, A., Alvarez, M., Cheibub, J. and Limongi, F. 2000. *Democracy and Development: Political Institutions and Well-Being in the World, 1950–1990*. New York: Cambridge University Press.

Pye, L. 1967. *Southeast Asia's Political Systems*. Englewood Cliffs, NJ: Prentice Hall.

Rasiah, R. and Schmidt, J. 2010a. Introduction. In: Rasiah, R. and Schmidt, J. (eds) *The New Political Economy of Southeast Asia*: 1–43. Cheltenham, UK: Edward Elgar.

Rasiah, R. and Schmidt, J. (eds). 2010b. *The New Political Economy of Southeast Asia*. Cheltenham, UK: Edward Elgar.

Riggs, F. 1966. *Thailand: The Modernization of a Bureaucratic Polity*. Honolulu: East-West Center Press.

Rivera, T. 1994. *Landlords and Capitalists: Class, Family, and the State in Philippine Manufacturing*. Quezon City: University of the Philippines Press.

Robison, R., Hewison, K. and Higgott, R. (eds). 1987. *Southeast Asia in the 1980s: The Politics of Economic Crisis*. Sydney: Allen & Unwin.

Robison, R., Hewison, K. and Rodan, G. 1993. Political Power in Industrialising Capitalist Societies: Theoretical Approaches. In: Hewison, K., Robison, R. and Rodan, G. (eds) *Southeast Asia in the 1990s: Authoritarianism, Democracy and Capitalism*: 9–38. Sydney: Allen & Unwin.

Robinson, D., Byeon, Y., Teja, R. and Tseng, W. 1991. Thailand: Adjusting to Success – Current Policy Issues. *Occasional Papers* 85. Washington, DC: International Monetary Fund.

Robison, R., Higgott, R. and Hewison, K. 1987. Crisis in Economic Strategy in 1980s: The Factors at Work. In: Robison, R., Hewison, K. and Higgott, R. (eds) *Southeast Asia in the 1980s: The Politics of Economic Crisis:* 1–15. Sydney: Allen & Unwin.

Robinson, W. 1985. Imperialism, Dependency and Peripheral Industrialization: The Case of Japan in Indonesia. In: Higgott, R. and Robison, R. (eds) *Southeast Asia: Essays in the Political Economy of Structural Change:* 195–225. London: Routledge and Kegan Paul.

Rodan, G. 1989. *The Political Economy of Singapore's Industrialization: National State and International Capital.* London: Macmillan.

Rodan, G., Hewison, K. and Robison, R. (eds). 1997. *The Political Economy of South-East Asia: An Introduction,* Oxford, UK: Oxford University Press.

Rodan, G., Hewison, K. and Robison, R. 2001a. Theorising South-East Asia's Boom, Bust, and Recovery. In Garry Rodan, Kevin Hewison and Richard Robison (eds) *The Political Economy of South-East Asia: Conflicts, Crises, and Change* 1–41. Oxford: Oxford University Press.

Rodan, G., Hewison, K. and Robison, R. (eds). 2001b. *The Political Economy of South-East Asia: Conflicts, Crises, and Change.* Oxford: Oxford University Press.

Rodan, G., Hewison, K. and Robison, R. 2006a. Theorising Markets in South-East Asia: Power and Contestation. In: *The Political Economy of South-East Asia: Markets, Power and Contestation:* 1–38. Oxford: Oxford University Press.

Rodan, G., Hewison, K. and Robison, R. (eds). 2006b. *The Political Economy of South-East Asia: Markets, Power and Contestation.* Oxford: Oxford University Press.

Said, E. 1978. *Orientalism: Western Conceptions of the Orient.* London: Routledge and Kegan Paul.

Scott, J. 1972. Patron-Client Politics and Political Change in Southeast Asia. *American Political Science Review* 66(1): 91–113.

Siegel, J., and Kahin, A. (eds). 2003. *Southeast Asia over Three Generations: Essays Presented to Benedict R. O'G. Anderson.* Ithaca, NY: Cornell University Press.

Skocpol, T. 1985. Bringing the State Back In: Strategies of Analysis in Current Research. In: Evans, P., Rueschemeyer, D. and Skocpol, T. (eds) *Bringing the State Back In: 3–42.* Cambridge: Cambridge University Press.

Stauffer, R. 1985. The Philippine Political Economy: (Dependent) State Capitalism in the Corporatist Mode. In: Higgott, R. and Robison, R. (eds) Southeast Asia: Essays in the Political Economy of Structural Change: 241–265. London: Routledge and Kegan Paul.

Stiglitz, J. and Yusuf, S. (eds). 2001. *Rethinking the East Asian Miracle.* Washington, DC: World Bank and Oxford University Press.

Taira, K. 1983. Japan's Modern Economic Growth: Capitalist Development Under Absolutism. In: Wray, H. and Conroy, H. (eds) *Japan Examined: Perspectives on Modern Japan History:* 34–41. Honolulu: University of Hawaii Press.

Thelen, K. 1999. Historical Institutionalism in Comparative Politics. *Annual Review of Political Science* 2(1): 369–404.

UNCTAD. 1993. *Trade and Development Report, 1993.* New York: United Nations Conference on Trade and Development.

Vatikiotis, M. 1998. *Indonesian Politics under Suharto: The Rise and Fall of the New Order,* Third edition. London: Routledge.

Wade, R. 1990. *Governing the Market: Economic Theory and Role of Government in East Asian Industrialization.* Princeton, NJ: Princeton University Press.

Wallerstein, I. 1979. *The Capitalist World Economy.* Cambridge: Cambridge University Press.

Warren, B. 1980. *Imperialism: Pioneer of Capitalism.* London: New Left Books and Verso.

Weiss, L. 1995. Governed Interdependence: Rethinking the Government-Business Relationship in East Asia. *The Pacific Review* 8(4): 589–616.

Weiss, L. 1998. *The Myth of the Powerless State.* Ithaca, NY: Cornell University Press.

Weiss, L. and Hobson, J. 1995. *States and Economic Development: A Comparative Historical Analysis.* Oxford: Polity Press.

Woo-Cumings, M. (ed.). 1999. *The Developmental State.* Ithaca, NY: Cornell University Press.

World Bank. 1993. *The East Asian Miracle: Economic Growth and Public Policy.* Oxford: Oxford University Press.

30

East Asia's developmental states in evolution

The challenge of sustaining national competitiveness at the technological frontier

Sung-Young Kim

Introduction

The dramatic industrial transformation of East Asia, which includes Japan, Korea, Taiwan and Singapore (and now, China) has gained wide attention over the last five decades. From the perspective of one of the leading authorities in the field, Keun Lee, the scale of this development cannot be underestimated, holding special historical significance (Lee 2013: 131). By the 1980s, Korea's and Taiwan's individual per capita gross domestic product (GDP) had not only caught up with the Latin American countries but, from 1980s to 2000, while Latin America stood still, Korea and Taiwan more than tripled their per capita real incomes. East Asia's economic rise is all the more fascinating when contrasted against the continuing economic backwardness of today's least developed countries (LDCs). African countries like Ghana or Mozambique exhibited greater economic promise than Korea and Taiwan in the 1950s as Ha-Joon Chang's (2008) seminal book on economic development, *Bad Samaritans*, reminded us. Yet, the contrast in development outcomes today is striking.

Identifying the causes of economic success of the 'miracle economies' became an enormous academic industry in itself with many (especially international development agencies) emphasizing the role of free markets while some drew links with pre-modern features of a 'national culture' (Song 1990). Others were uncompromising in their view of the classical tiger economies as the beneficiaries of US support during the geo-politics of the Cold War (Cumings 1998). All these factors undoubtedly mattered (to varying extents) but, in the search for an explanation, the state's activist role in the economy came to be seen as the defining element – from critics and protagonists alike. This did not mean any type of interventionist government but, a state capable of pursuing and executing *strategic industry policy* or 'developmental states' – a concept coined by the late Chalmers Johnson (1982) in his seminal study of Japan.

States with strategic industry development objectives in East Asian countries climbed the ladder of economic development through establishing labour-intensive industries such as textiles, then more capital-intensive industries like shipbuilding and automobiles. In the mid-1980s/1990s onwards, these firms moved into ever more rapidly changing, technology-intensive industries such as digital televisions, semiconductors and telecommunications. This transition is what Lee refers to as specializing in *higher-tech* 'short-cycle technologies' after first pursuing *lower-tech* 'long-cycle technologies' (Lee 2013: 19). Today, firms such as Korea's Samsung and Taiwan's AU Optronics (ACER) operate at the cutting edge of advanced technologies. Their successful rise in global markets have helped enrich the countries from which they emanate. East Asia has now successfully caught up (as China is currently emulating) with the advanced industrial countries, facing many of the same challenges as those of other industrially mature economies competing at the technological frontier.

Developmental states may have facilitated the rapid rise of high-technology firms, but to what extent is this form of state-guided industrialization still useful as innovation-led development takes precedence over imitation-led development? In this chapter, I cannot hope to provide conclusive answers to this big question. My more modest aim is to highlight the ideational, institutional and political sources of the state's capacity to drive technological catch-up, and their *evolution*, as countries compete at or close to the technology frontier in a globalized economy. However, the extent to which developmental states can sustain their relentless drive for national techno-economic competitiveness at the technological frontier remains deeply contested. There are four key issues at stake in the debate, which I discuss in sequential order in this chapter.

The first issue concerns the ability of governments to strategize for competing at the technological frontier. The second relates to the existence of wide political support for sustaining high-risk innovation and/or uncertainty. The third is on the organizational features of the state, specifically on the utility of centralized or decentralized structures. The fourth concerns the relationship between large transnational corporations and the state in driving technological innovation. I conclude with the observation that the developmental state debate is far from settled, not least because of the state's propensity to adapt to new challenges in unexpected and creative ways. Before delving into these issues in more depth, let us begin with a brief overview of the role of the developmental state in facilitating East Asia's economic catch-up and the sources of the state's capacity to do so.

East Asia's developmental states and economic catch-up

The single most important work on the 'developmental state' was Chalmers Johnson's (1982) *MITI and the Japanese Miracle*. His work was the first to detail an institutional basis for Japan's postwar economic transformation. Various writers applied the developmental state idea to explain the high-growth economies of Korea (Woo 1991), Taiwan (Wade 1990/2004) and Singapore (Deyo (ed.) 1987). Notwithstanding important differences from country to country, these studies brought to light the role of governments in their pursuit of national industrial transformation.

Box 30.1 Market-led accounts of the East Asian miracle economies

Market-led accounts flatly denied or at best underplayed the activist role of governments. Governments, according to views of international development bodies such as the World Bank and International Monetary Fund, were hopelessly prone to 'rent-seeking' from special interests. This supported – and – continues to support – their default policy position that 'government failure' is generally worse than 'market failure' thereby, justifying the virtues of free markets encompassed in the ideals of the 'Washington Consensus' (Wade 2010:150). While many in the economics profession may continue to embrace this view, it is fair to say that the empirical evidence presented by studies of the developmental state made it difficult to deny that states played an activist role in the East Asian miracle.

In doing so, their key aim was to challenge market-led accounts (the 'Washington Consensus' view) of East Asia's industrialization (Box 30.1). On this front, it is fair to say the jury is still out on how effective governments were in 'governing the market' (Box 30.2).

Box 30.2 Measuring the impact of industry policies

For Robert Wade, the Taiwan government *governed the market* by allocating resources 'so as to produce different production and investment outcomes than would have occurred with either free market or simulated free market policies' (Wade 1990/2004: 26, 27). Of course, the effectiveness of industry policy is another matter altogether. On this front, it is clear that the jury is still out on how *effective or ineffective* industry policies are, especially those of the more informal 'nudging' kind exercised by bureaucratic official (Wade 1990/2004: xxii), which even the best econometric modelling has had difficulties showing conclusively (Rodrik 2008: 14).

Paralleling but remaining separate from the work of political scientists were writers in management schools who sought to explain how 'latecomer firms' could close the technology gap with the advanced industrial (e.g. Amsden 1989; Lee 2013; Mathews 1997). In this regard, East Asian firms seemed to defy all expectations over the futility of being little more than low-cost subcontractors for advanced country firms in a globalized world economy. South Korea's Samsung, Japanese firms such as Toshiba and Taiwanese firms such as ACER/AU Optronics did not seek begin their journeys by emulating frontier innovators who focused on highly original technologies. These companies forged a different path. They grew by reaping the advantages of being 'second movers', which can be contrasted with frontier innovators or 'first-mover' firms. Being a second-mover meant perfecting a new model of development based on technological followership or what the groundbreaking work of John Mathews referred to as 'technology leveraging' strategies (Mathews 1997; Mathews and Cho 2000). This refers to a process, which involves sourcing the most advanced technologies from around the world, rapidly diffusing and mastering them with the purpose of developing mass manufactured products from this new process of learning (Mathews 1997: 27). Followership initially took the form of technological imitation (via reverse engineering) and later involved faster-followership such as 'technological leapfrogging' – a situation where 'latecomer' firms bet on an alternative technological path to the incumbents and surpass the original frontier innovators (Lee and Lim 2001: 482). The rise of an increasingly interdependent and competitive global economy was not so much an obstacle for latecomers, but an opportunity to exploit new market opportunities through a 'linkage, leverage and learning' (Mathews 2002) (Box 30.3).

The studies above helped rethink what 'innovation' means, which at the time had been dominated by narrow conceptions of what counted as 'real' innovation i.e. limited to highly original technological development being undertaken in the advanced industrial countries (e.g. Malerba and Orsenigo 1996). As Mathews notes, this perception was derived from Joseph Schumpeter's own ideas about 'innovation' and 'creative destruction' in the advanced industrial countries and his dismissal of followership as little more than 'imitation' (Lee 2013: xiii). While this type of Western-dominated thinking continues even today, there is growing recognition among experts in the field of the significance of East Asia's technology catch-up for studies of technology and innovation management. It is noteworthy that the International Joseph Schumpeter Society awarded the prestigious 2014 Schumpeter Prize to Keun Lee and in 2018, to John Mathews – two leading authorities on economic catch-up.[1]

Box 30.3 The strategy of latecomer firms: 'linkage, leverage and learning'

In *Dragon Multilnational*, John Mathews (2002: 323–324) argues that latecomer firms from the developing world (such as East Asia) are not doomed for failure in a world of powerful and more advanced incumbents. They can rapidly catch-up and surpass with the industrial leaders by *linking* up with sources of knowledge, skills and technology available in the global economy. If a consensus over catch-up exists, these firms (and their governments) can the exploit these connections through *leveraging* advanced technologies to builds their own internal capabilities. By repeating the process of linkage and learning, groups of firms engage in *learning* how to accelerate the development process.

Where the work of political scientists and management scholars met at a cross roads was in their shared interest in understanding the *conditions* for why governments in the region seemed to execute industry policies relatively more effectively (for political scientists) and why firms throughout the region had so rapidly become major players in industry after industry (for management specialists). These research agendas sought to uncover the *underlying system* behind the formulation and implementation of industry policies, identifying and understanding what features of the domestic *institutional* context mattered and why.

To understand the relationship between government and business actors, Peter Evans (1995) advanced the notion of 'embedded autonomy' (in developing contexts). For Linda Weiss (1998), the challenge was how to conceptualize institutionalized relationships of *genuine negotiation* between the state and industry (guided by broader goals set and monitored by the state) of which the outcome according to Weiss was 'governed interdependence'. Industry policies in East Asia's miracle economies worked relatively well due to the presence of governed interdependence whereas cases of developmental failure (in so many other national contexts) exhibited the polar opposite of *ungoverned interdependence* or *statism*. For the late Alice Amsden (1989), the state's use of 'monitorable performance outcomes' (rather than giving out support freely) in interactions with the private sector helped drive industrial transformation.

There are similarities and differences between these concepts, but all of the writers above are likely to agree on the following ideational, institutional and political features of developmental states listed in Box 30.4.

Box 30.4 Core elements of 'developmental states'

- A strategic, goal-oriented, outlook among elite economic bureaucrats.
- An insulated 'pilot agency'.
- Institutionalized mechanism for negotiation between state and industry.
- Highly organized private sector actors.
- Existence of 'political space' for the economic bureaucracy.

A strategic, goal-oriented, outlook

Johnson's (1982) book on Japan may have intrigued analysts for his final chapter on the core institutional features of a developmental state. But, he made it explicitly clear from the outset of that study that the key difference between the developmental state and other state types was at its core, the state's *commitment* to the pursuit of long-term focused goals for enhancing the techno-economic competitiveness of the nation (Johnson 1982: 305). In a more recent study of Korea, Elizabeth Thurbon (2014) views the existence of a 'developmental mindset' as the core, defining feature of the developmental state model. Japanese economic bureaucrats shared the same level of seriousness, urgency and mission-oriented outlook one might find in national defence agencies. This type of strategic thinking was also evident in Korean, Taiwanese and Singaporean government officials in their efforts to catch-up in high-technology sectors such as semiconductors (Mathews and Cho 2000).

The origins of these developmental worldviews was a matter of great interest throughout the 1990s. Meredith Woo highlighted the role of war and colonialism in moulding *nationalism* as the binding glue for an entire generation of peoples (Woo-Cumings 1999: 9–11). A more specific type of nationalism – economic nationalism – emerged as a means to correct a perception of 'status inconsistency' with the Western powers. The geo-politics of the Cold War also ensured that a deep and persistent perception of an external threat created the conditions for a *crisis mentality* among elite policymakers throughout the classical East Asian developmental states (Zhu 2002).

Insulated pilot agencies

One organizational feature common to the East Asian four was the existence of technocratic elites who were committed to strategic goals and responsible for formulating and monitoring the implementation of industry policies. During the catch-up era of the 1960s to 1990s 'central pilot agencies', which sat atop all other organs of the bureaucracy assumed such roles. These include Japan's Ministry of International Trade and Industry (MITI), Korea's Economic Planning Board (EPB), Taiwan's Council for Economic Planning and Development (CEPD) and Singapore's Economic Development Board (EDB). While not widely known, Korean policymakers themselves have long referred to this type of body as a 'control tower' (Larson and Park 2014: 346). Central pilot agencies had two core functions: first, identifying new 'sunrise' sectors for targeting and deselecting 'sunset' sectors as part of what Johnson referred to as 'industrial structure policy'. Second, to plan the most effective way to pursue the development of promising new industries through 'industrial rationalization policy' (Johnson 1982: 27–28; Pekkanen 2003).

While pilot agencies fascinated analysts, the more important point was their *insulation* from special interests in the private sector – enabling the pursuit of long-term focused strategic goals. Various studies including the now widely publicized report from the World Bank detailed various ways such bodies equipped themselves with high levels of information gathering and analysis capabilities (Johnson 1982: 315–320; Weiss 1998: 49–54; World Bank 1993: 17–18). The holding of rigorous national civil service examinations also created a common mechanism to recruit the nation's best and brightest into the ranks of the central government ministries, conferring enormous prestige upon successful candidates. One way to understand the importance of such agencies is by noting their absence in the 'crony-capitalist' states of Southeast Asia (e.g. Thailand, the Philippines, Indonesia) characterized by highly interventionist, but weakly insulated, governments.

Institutionalized mechanisms for negotiation between state and industry

The existence of an elite insulated economic bureaucracy may be important, but without 'state-industry linkages' (Weiss 1998: 55) governmental actors would possess little more than high levels of autonomy, which can heighten developmental failure. East Asian governments created extensive and *regularized* formal and informal links with the private sector. Institutionalized mechanisms for negotiation and information-sharing between government and business helped minimize public policies being short-sighted and simply reactive to new crises when they occur. Rather than meeting on an ad-hoc basis or left to chance, governments created a network of forums for industrial actors to provide input into the design and implementation of industry policies, helping to provide a means for conflict resolution, building trust and consensus between government and business.

Perhaps one of the most famous countries known for its extensive state–industry linkages is Japan through the use of 'deliberation councils'. As detailed in the World Bank's (1993: 181–189) *The East Asian Miracle* – one of the rare occasions, which departed from the principles of the Washington Consensus – MITI created an elaborate complex of horizontal (e.g. over tax policy) and vertical (e.g. specific sectors like automobiles) deliberation councils. These venues invited input from business, labour, academia and other interested parties into the policymaking process. Similar bodies were evident in South Korea until the 1980s where the President himself chaired Monthly Export Promotion Meetings attended by all the ministers of the government and were held to account on meeting performance targets at the follow-up meetings. In Singapore too, government officials regularly consulted the private sector through government advisory committees and government statutory boards.

The creation of vast networks of state–industry linkages was most visible in Taiwan through the country's creation of industrial parks of which the most well-known is the Hsinchu Science Park. Brought to the world's attention vividly by Mathews (1997) in a seminal essay on Taiwan's integrated circuit industry, that study traced the mechanisms for technological diffusion, collaboration and learning between government research institutes such as the Industrial Technology Research Institute (ITRI) and small and medium enterprises (SMEs). These mechanisms for public–private exchange were the main ways to help accelerate Taiwan's technological catch-up in high-technology fields like semiconductors.

Highly organized private sector actors

The organization of the private sector is important to the extent that widely encompassing industrial associations or trade bodies can help facilitate collaboration between governments and business (Weiss 1998: 60–62). To be effective in providing input into public policies, such bodies must be capable of achieving consensus within their members. In the case of Taiwan's electronics sector, private sector bodies such as the Taiwan Electrical and Electronic Manufacturers Association (TEEMA) helped organize technological upgrading in partnership with larger firms all under the auspices of the state's goals to accelerate technological upgrading (Kuo 1998; Mathews 1997: 44). In Korea, at least until the mid-1980s, national peak bodies such as the Federation of Korean Industries and sectoral industrial associations such as the 'Promotion Association for the Korea Electronics Industry' were central forums for business actors to formulate development plans and work as partners with industrial bureaucrats (Amsden and Cho 2003: 92).

Existence of 'political space' for the economic bureaucracy

The final feature widely seen to have facilitated the pursuit of strategic industry policies was a supportive political environment (Pempel and Muramatsu 1995; Woo-Cumings 1995). In Johnson's (1982; 1999) works, he made clear that in order for the economic bureaucracy to play a strategic role in the economy, they must enjoy sufficiently high levels of 'political space' akin to the type of discretionary powers foreign trade negotiators enjoyed. Bureaucrats were provided with such space through long-term political leadership provided by the Liberal Democratic Party in Japan, Singapore's People's Action Party (PAP) headed by Prime Minister Lee Kuan Yew. In Korea, successive military leaders (President Park Chung-hee, Chun Doo-hwan, Roh Tae-woo) and in Taiwan, the *Kuomintang* (KMT) (Chiang Kai-shek, Chiang Ching-kuo) provided political space for the economic bureaucracy to play a guiding role in the economy.

There was much discussion over how such political systems came into being. While it may have been tempting to attribute causation to the legacies of neo-Confucian statecraft, Johnson instead highlighted the role of nationalism. Governing elites in East Asia were not of an everyday kind but were 'quasi-revolutionary' regimes, whose legitimacy to govern was derived from a profound sense of nationalism (Johnson 1999: 52–53). In a 'developmental citizenry' such as Korea's (Chang 2007: 68), society placed their trust and respect in the nation's merit-based economic bureaucracy to deliver on the promise of economic growth with equity. Of course, this is not to suggest that societal actors *also* accepted the simultaneously authoritarian nature of the revolutionary regime, which in fact, was quite the opposite as the vibrant pro-democracy struggles in Taiwan and Korea demonstrated (Kim 2018: 462).

The point is that developmentalism *resonated* with wide segments of societies throughout East Asia. In order for political leaders to deliver on society's expectations of national economic transformation, technocratic elites were charged to fulfill their missions as a matter of the highest national priority.

This section has outlined the ideational, institutional and political features of a developmental state, which were seen to facilitate the pursuit of strategic industrial goals up until the early 1990s. East Asian governments may have been highly effective in catching-up with the more advanced industrial countries but there are now serious questions over the utility of developmental states for promoting competitiveness at or close to the technological frontier in a globalized world economy. As I will show below, the answer to this question is far from straightforward. In the sections below, I discuss four key issues, which lie at the heart of the debate (summarized in Box 30.5).

Box 30.5 Four key issues in the debate over East Asia's developmental states beyond catch-up

- Strategizing for competing at the technological frontier.
- The political appetite for higher risk innovation and uncertainty.
- The organization of innovation: centralized vs. decentralized state structures.
- The structural power of globalized corporations and the transformative capacity of states.

Strategizing for competing at the technological frontier

Catching-up involved closing the technology gap with clearly defined targets such as companies or countries at an advanced level of development. However, the logic of keeping-up or staying ahead of competitors involves a different set of competitive challenges, which require coping with less predictable technological targets. Reminiscent of the arguments advanced by some American sceptics of the Japanese government's ability to promote frontier innovation in the ICT sector (Anchordoguy 2005; Callon 1995), some writers have recently cast doubt on the ability of East Asian governments to continue to be effective in 'picking winners' in such an advanced stage of development. The broader issue at stake is whether governments can *strategize* (just as they did for technological catch-up) under conditions of high-risk and/or uncertainty – one of the defining features of frontier innovation.

In science-intensive sectors such as biotechnology – widely seen as a major new technological growth industry – Joseph Wong's (2011) important book, *Betting on Biotech*, demonstrates the significant difficulties faced by policymakers in Korea, Taiwan and Singapore. The biotechnology sector is different from the 'high-risk' nature of development in traditional manufacturing such as semiconductors or shipbuilding. Biotechnology research and development (R&D) involves 'uncertainty' over what fundamental technologies should be and their development, the economic pay-offs of new breakthroughs, and when new advances will be of relevance (Wong 2011: 182). While Wong does not question the state's continuing activism, he argues that policymakers have been unable to pick winners, instead shifting focus to nurturing processes to develop *potentialities* of innovation. The implication is that developmental states simply no longer have the capacity to strategize for promoting knowledge-intensive development, retreating from their former mission-oriented roles.

This a thought-provoking proposition and one part of his broader argument over the erosion of the developmental project in East Asia (more below); he is by no means alone (e.g. Ó Riain 2004; Yeung 2016). However, there are several counter arguments that need to be considered before rushing to such a conclusion.

First, the very nature of basic science involves trials and tests of potentially new breakthroughs in which development failure is the norm (Thurbon 2014: 14). The difficulties faced by policymakers in managing technological and economic uncertainty is hardly unique to East Asia but one of the defining characteristics of the global biotech sector. This sector is also dominated by a handful of powerful firms (in Japan, Europe and the US) who enjoy monopoly protection for their patents through an international intellectual property rights system (e.g. TRIPs Agreement), which many have come to view as obstructive of genuine innovation and national competitiveness (Mathews 2012). For both reasons, the biotechnology sector is a weak test of the state's capacity to guide knowledge-intensive development.

Second, while picking winners may be significantly more challenging than in traditional manufacturing sectors, strategically oriented governments do much more than making bets on winning technologies. As my work on the Korean government's promotion of mobile platform software in the early 2000s has shown, the former Ministry of Information and Communications helped nurture research and development alliances with the private sector, secure an initial market for domestic firms and coordinate domestic and international standardization (Kim 2012b). Of course, as Korean firms are now competing at the very frontier of cutting-edge technologies in a variety of fields such as fifth-generation mobile communication technologies and smart microgrids (Kim and Mathews 2016: 8), public and private efforts have shifted focus to developing fundamental technologies, which can be aligned with any *defacto* international standard that may emerge in the future. Outside of the Korean setting, Jenn-hwan Wang's study of Taiwan's biotechnology sector has argued that the state's strategy for managing technological uncertainty has been to re-work itself as a 'platform builder', which undertakes four key actions (Wang 2016: 111). These include benchmarking 'best practice' in R&D development (especially US innovation agencies), providing seed funding and other financial mechanisms to stimulate private sector investment, creating networks between domestic and global networks, and securing export markets for domestic firms (especially mainland China).

Third, the term 'picking winners' misleadingly gives the impression that government officials alone, without any need for consultation with the private sector, identify promising new sunrise industries. Yet, nothing could be further from reality. If South Korea's processes involved in identifying strategic technological growth areas under its 'IT839 Strategy' (2003–2007) in the telecommunications sector, provides any guide the government utilized a vast complex of public and private networks for the formulation and implementation of industry policies (Kim 2012a: 156–158). The creation of such public–private mechanisms for negotiation and information-sharing was also evident in Taiwan's drive to promote its photovoltaic (PV) industry (Mathews et al. 2011: 195). Government research institutes such ITRI, SMEs and large firms such as TSMC and AU Optronics collaborated through the CIGS (copper, indium, gallium and selenium) Alliance. These types of institutionalized public–private exchanges have taken on even deeper meaning in driving smart grids initiatives in Korea and Taiwan's green energy sector (Kim 2019). The point is that picking promising technologies is challenging for both governments *and companies*. The solution for coping with such higher levels of risk has been to fuse public and private actors more deeply as these examples above suggest.

Lastly, irrespective of where one chooses to stand in this debate, it would be helpful to adopt a broader view of what constitutes 'policy success'. The ability to pick a winning technology in global markets can have immense economic benefits but surely, it should not be the only or even the main measure of success. In a study of China's technological standardization strategy, Dieter Ernst (2011) argues that success needs to be defined by more than simply whether the market adopts a preferred technology standard or not. The promotion of domestic technology standards can create immeasurable learning opportunities about effective standardization especially in international bodies, create bargaining chips in dealings with foreign companies who hold influential patents thereby reducing licensing fees and avoiding what is widely known as the 'galapagos' effect on innovation (Ernst 2011: 17–18). Nowhere were such benefits more evident than in the widely studied example of China's TD-SCDMA 3G mobile communications standard (Murphree and Breznitz 2018: 247). South Korea's attempts to globalize the 4G Mobile Wimax standard also provides an interesting example whereby the standard failed to reach meaningful domestic and international adoption yet, provided Samsung Electronics with a competitive advantage in the core technology, orthogonal frequency-division multiple access (OFDMA), which underpinned the competing long-term evolution (LTE) standard (Kim 2012c).

Understanding the extent to which developmental states remain relevant in frontier innovation is also dependent on a closely related but separate issue from the state's ability to continue picking winners, namely, whether the political appetite exists for pursuing higher levels of technological risk.

Political appetite for higher risk innovation

One of the major premises upon which Wong's overall argument rests is that the political costs involved in making large losing bets are simply too great for government officials whose very legitimacy relies on the expectation that they deliver speedy and substantial success (Wong 2011: 182). Bureaucrats have focused not on picking winners but *mitigating political risks* involved in the biotech sector given the long development cycles involved in scientific discoveries, the high failure rate and large investments required. As a result, East Asia's developmental states have simply 'chosen to be less developmental' (Wong 2011: 181). For Wong, East Asia's losing bets in the biotech sector is part of a longer-term process of state decline since the 1990s, which revealed a mismatch between technonationalist strategies and a globalizing world economy (Wong 2011: 180). Even if one accepts that states such as Korea can still play an activist (although less strategic) role in enhancing the techno-economic competitiveness of national firms, liberalizing reforms to the economy (after the 1997 financial crisis) have undermined political support for the state's guiding role (Kalinowski 2008: 460). As Kyung-sup Chang's authoritative work has shown, liberal reforms marked the end of the era of high growth with equity and the beginning of jobless economic growth and increasing levels of economic inequality (Chang 2007: 69–70).

Somewhat similar arguments have been made for Japan's lacklustre performance in other technology-intensive sectors such as telecommunications where many East Asian firms hold leading positions – Samsung being the stand out. For Steven Vogel, an influential writer on Japanese political economy, this can be attributed to various reasons of which one major factor is the economic bureaucracy's 'profound loss of prestige, confidence, and power' (Vogel 2013: 364). As Vogel notes, this is in no small part due to the politicization of the bureaucracy by the short-lived Democratic Party of Japan (DPJ) in their efforts to take control of the policy process. The bureaucracy's maligned role in the Japanese political scene is also due to the Liberal Democratic Party's (LDP) 'bureaucrat bashing' in an effort to preserve its domestic power base and the Japanese–American Security Treaty (Johnson 2001).

These are stimulating arguments. However, the proposition that states have suffered an irretrievable loss of political support for playing a guiding role over industrial governance deserves greater scrutiny. Various studies have shown that the unprecedented levels of economic inequality have renewed, rather than squeezing out the political space for the state to play a developmental role. My study of the Korean government's efforts to carve out a market for domestic semiconductor chip manufacturers by launching (formally and informally) a publicity campaign against Qualcomm who had dominated the domestic market provides one example of this logic (Kim 2012b).

Perhaps the clearest illustration of the renewed role of developmental states is in the addressing what is arguably the greatest challenge facing East Asian governments i.e. greening the economy. As various studies have shown, over the past decade we have witnessed the rise of coordinated national efforts to build renewable energy technology industries such as electric vehicles, green power generators and smart grids throughout East Asia (Dent 2014; Mathews 2017). The embrace of green growth as a new way of growing and greening the economy has been conceptualized as the rise of 'developmental environmentalism' (as an extension of the developmental state) (Kim and Thurbon 2015) and 'new developmentalism' (Dent 2014).

Therefore, even if one accepts that economic bureaucrats in East Asia have experienced a significant loss of political space to play a developmental role, it is also entirely possible that the state can *re-galvanize* political support to pursue strategic goals. Let us now turn to the third key issue in the debate over the utility of the developmental state at the technological frontier: the organization of innovation.

The organization of innovation

In recent years, several groundbreaking studies have challenged the 'state-less' portrayal of the American political economy, showing that frontier innovation requires a *different* kind of state-guidance, *not less*, compared to promoting technological catch-up (Block 2008; Block and Keller 2011; Weiss 2014). In this body of work, there is growing recognition that coping with the challenges of frontier innovation is best met by decentralized governance structures. There are striking parallels in other national contexts. Seán Ó Riain's (2004) study of the Irish 'developmental network state' (DNS) and Breznitz and Ornston's (2013) examination of 'Schumpeterian Development Agencies' in Finland and Israel, both emphasize the utility of decentralized government agencies for promoting innovation.

These features pose a problem for East Asian governments, which have been cast as 'developmental bureaucratic states' (DBS) by recent proponents of the DNS idea (Block 2008; Ó Riain 2004). Under the DBS framework, the structure of the state in the classical examples of Japan and Korea is hopelessly centralized, inflexible and characterized by top-down governance, which are seen as impediments to competing in the rapid innovation-based sectors. In contrast to these views, Wong's work clearly demonstrates that governments in Korea, Taiwan and Singapore have decentralized the governance of industry policy (at least in the promotion of biotech) to cope with the challenges of technological uncertainty (Wong 2011). However, his ultimate conclusion shares common ground with the authors above. Decentralization has dispersed expertise among competing state actors, eroding away the state's capacity to target winning technologies throughout East Asia (Wong 2011: 180–181). These authors are not alone in holding such views.

One recent study argues that the imperative to drive large-scale initiatives to promote high-tech start-ups (modelled after the example of Silicon Valley) such as the Korean government's 2013–2017 'Creative Economy' strategy has created a mismatch in organizational coherence (Debanes 2018). Governmental organizations designed to promote *horizontal innovation* support have 'diluted' the very rationale for the existence of older structures established for *targeted technological catch-up* associated with the developmental state (Debanes 2018: 20). The dismantling of pilot agencies and/or decentralization of governance over strategic industry policy have only compounded the challenges faced by East Asian developmental states in coordinating development in a world of globalized innovation and production networks (Yeung 2016: 5, 36).

The writers mentioned above treat decentralization as a symptom of the state's decaying capacity to promote frontier innovation throughout East Asia (oddly in stark contrast to the American setting where decentralized state agencies are seen as a strategic strength (Block 2008)). However, as I will discuss below, the decentralization of governance over strategic industry policy is far from being a developmental liability as studies of East Asia have shown.

One clear example is the role played by the former Korean Ministry of Information and Communications, which coordinated Korea's drive to prominence in manufacturing code-division multiple access (CDMA)-based mobile communications technologies after the abolishment of Korea's former central pilot agency, the EPB. The MIC's role was also critical in guiding the country's leadership of third- and fourth-generation technologies – prior to its dismantling in 2008 and absorption into different ministries/agencies (Kim 2012a: 155). In 2013, the Ministry of Science, ICT and Future Planning (MSIP) emerged as the leading government agency charged with jurisdiction over the ICT sector (Larson and Park 2014: 356).

Also in Korea, the Ministry of Trade, Industry and Energy (MOTIE) has long held jurisdiction over 'traditional' or 'core' sectors like automobiles and shipbuilding and its role as a specialized pilot agency has become more prominent in recent years. The financial crisis of

1997 served as a turning point for MOTIE officials in doubling efforts targeted at building technological upgrading alliances between conglomerates and SMEs (parts and components suppliers). The idea was not only to close the technology gap with foreign suppliers but also to become leading exporters through their ties with *chaebol* in foreign markets (Kim and Kwon 2017: 520).

Singapore's rapid progression into increasingly higher-technology sectors provides another interesting example. An array of governmental agencies (affiliated with the central ministries) have orchestrated national efforts to turn the country into an innovation leader in greener and smarter city technologies. This includes the Centre for Liveable Cities (affiliated with the Ministry of National Development) and government-linked companies such as the Jurong Town Corporation (spun out of the Economic Development Board), which have led technological partnerships with foreign companies such as Panasonic (Miao and Phelps 2019: 327–328). The idea is to draw foreign companies into technological alliances with domestic companies and government agencies to acquire, co-develop and test new eco-city technologies as part of a broader export strategy. This reflects the continuity of a 'linkage, leverage and learning' strategy discussed earlier (Lall 2002: 53–54; Mathews 2002) with decentralized state agencies at the helm of such efforts in a completely new sector.

The studies above suggest that decentralized state agencies have posed no obstacle to driving strategic industry policies. Furthermore, it is arguable that while a centralized pilot agency may be useful for coordinating technological catch-up as part of nation-building efforts, decentralized and more technologically specialized 'quasi-pilot agencies' appear to have greater effectiveness as a country competes close or at the technological frontier (Kim 2012a: 155). The key similarities and differences between centralized pilot agencies on the one hand, which have responsibility for overall economic management and budget allocation and on the other hand, specialized quasi-pilot agencies, which hold jurisdiction over a specific technological sector, are summarized in Table 30.1.

At the same time, a note of caution in emphasizing the utility of decentralized state agencies is necessary as their effectiveness depends on factors beyond technology type or complexity. It is widely accepted among South Korea's policymaking elite that the most important organizational pillar of the country's pursuit of green growth was the 'Presidential Committee on Green Growth' (PCGG) (Kim and Thurbon 2015: 227–228). While falling short of being a full

Table 30.1 Key differences between a central pilot agency and a quasi-pilot agency

Functions/organization	Centralized pilot agency	Technoloigcally specialized quasi-pilot agency
Policy Focus	• Industrial Rationalization • Industrial Structure	• Technological Growth Areas • Technological Value Chains
Recruitment	Mostly generalists, but engineers also recruited into the sectoral planning divisions	Predominantly experts in specific technological fields
Insulation Mechanisms	Negotiations with firms undertaken by working-level ministries	Negotiations with firms undertaken by affiliated governmental agencies
Information-Gathering Infrastructure	Affiliated think-tanks and working-level ministries	Affiliated think-tanks, governmental agencies and research institutes

Source: Kim 2012a: 153.

ministry like the former EPB, the PCGG exhibited the authority and capabilities to formulate long-term focused industry policies via the participation of the central ministries in its deliberation meetings. It's presence in the Korean political economy (prior to its 'downgrading' to the Prime-Ministerial 'Committee on Green Growth' in 2013) represented the *recentralization* of governance over strategic industry policy as it related to driving a *whole-economy* approach to greening.

The key point is that decentralized and more centralized forms of governance can *both* drive innovation programmes. This displays a remarkable ability to 'recombine' core institutional strengths to meet ever-changing new industrial challenges (Kim 2012a). In some sectors, this involves a complex of various governmental organs to develop a coordinated approach; in others, a more centralized type of pilot agency may be beneficial in organizing development efforts.

I now turn to the final issue in the debate over the utility of developmental states at the technology frontier: the rise of big business and their transnational operations.

Growth of global production and innovation networks

For one of the most prolific writers in this field, Henry Yeung, as domestic firms become increasingly engaged in 'strategic coupling' with globalized firms, developmental states simply become less effective in guiding industrial governance (Yeung 2016: 4–6). It is not states but the decisions made by leading firms of global production and innovation networks that have the greatest impact on national development. In such an environment, developmental states simply become less effective or 'downgraded' as one writer puts it (Hundt 2014: 511).

Of course, it has long been recognized that large corporations wield 'structural power' (Lindblom 1977) or the power to resist any reforms, which may threaten their interests given their structurally privileged positions within society. The structural power of transnational corporations has taken on even greater significance with the rise of a more open and interdependent world economy and one in which science and technology has taken on special importance in sustaining economic development (Dicken 2015: 164). John Mikler interprets these globalizing processes as culminating in the growth of *The Political Power of Global Corporations* (2018).

There is little argument that the fortunes of domestic firms are increasingly tied to lead firms of global production networks (GPNs) or global value chains (GVCs). However, the assertion that these processes are occurring at the *expense* of the developmental role of their home governments throughout East Asia suffers from two major shortcomings. First, even the most globalized firms are still highly dependent on their home governments for sustaining technological competitiveness. As various studies have shown, knowledge-intensive competition involves high levels of risk, which in turn tends to deepen (not reduce) the need for the state's involvement in high-technology promotion (Warwick and Nolan 2014; Weiss 2005: 744). Perhaps the clearest illustration of mutual dependence between public and private actors is in the gritty world of technological standards-setting especially in inter-governmental standards development organizations such as the International Telecommunications Union (ITU). The enormous success of firms such as Samsung in transitioning into technological leadership simply could not have been possible without the coordinative role of government agencies in getting national technology standards (e.g. CDMA) recognized by the ITU and other standards development organizations (Kim 2013: 189).

The second limitation is that claims of the developmental state's downgrading provide a lopsided view from the perspective of globally leading firms while underplaying the activist role of governments. In Japan, while policymakers are shy to admit as such, the Ministry of Economy, Trade and Industry's (METI) 'Japan Smart Community Alliance' has a membership of 255 firms (including large firms such as Toyota) whose core goal is to drive the development of energy resilient smart microgrids (DeWit 2018). Parallel efforts in Korea and Taiwan also provide interesting examples (Kim 2019). In 2014, the MOTIE established the Korea Micro Energy Grid (K-MEG) Consortium and Korea Smart Grid Association (KSGA) to coordinate the creation, testing and export of smart microgrids for a variety of settings. The MOTIE delegated large conglomerates such as Samsung C&T to exert project leadership of networks composed of other public and private actors including large firms and SMEs. Their Taiwanese counterparts include the Taiwan Smart Grid Industry Association (TSGIA) and Taiwan Smart Grid General Projects, led by government agencies such as ITRI. As I have argued, these bodies reflect the Korean and Taiwan states' efforts to build 'hybridized industrial ecosystems' as a means to spearhead the global market for smart grids (Kim 2019). As a number of other studies (of Korea) have shown, the idea behind linking SMEs with large firms in development alliances was to create new sources of competitive advantage for *both* Korea's leading *chaebol* and their suppliers (Kim 2012a: 157–158; Kim and Kwon 2017).

The main point is that while many domestic firms have globalized their operations and become more technologically sophisticated (which provides one measure of their independence), they continue to depend on the transformative capacity of their home governments. Nowhere is this becoming more apparent than in sharing the risks involved in developing new technologies in promising growth sectors such as green energy.

Conclusion

To what extent are East Asia's developmental states still useful as innovation-led development as the technological frontier takes precedence over imitation-led, technology followership? I have discussed four issues at stake in the debate: strategizing for competing at the technological frontier; the political appetite for sustaining support for high-risk and/or uncertain technologies; the organization of the state in promoting innovation; and growth of global production and innovation networks. If my discussion of these issues tells us anything, it is that the debate over East Asia's developmental state is far from settled, not least because of the state's propensity to evolve in unexpected and creative ways. This is a reality often underplayed by developmental state sceptics in their haste to reach (premature) conclusions over the erosion of the state's power to guide industrial development. Interest in East Asia's economic transformation and the idea of the developmental state is therefore likely to remain a vibrant research agenda in studies of IPE in the years ahead.

Note

1 www.issevec.uni-jena.de/Schumpeter+prize.html (Accessed 27 February 2019).

Bibliography

Amsden, A. 1989. *Asia's Next Giant: South Korea and Late Industrialization.* Oxford: Oxford University Press.

Amsden, A. and Cho, H. 2003. Appendix: Differences in National R&D Systems Between Early and Late Industrializers. In: *Innovation and Catching-Up: Content, Theory, and Policy Analysis for Korea, Science & Technology Policy Institute (STEPI) Report 2003–19.* Cho, H., Amsden, A., Kwak, J. and Kang, M. (eds): 77–117. Seoul: STEPI.

Anchordoguy, M. 2005. *Reprogramming Japan: The High-Tech Crisis under Communitarian Capitalism.* Ithaca, NY: Cornell University Press.

Block, F. 2008. Swimming Against the Current: The Rise of a Hidden Developmental State in the United States. *Politics and Society 36*, no. 2: 169–206.

Block, F. and Keller, M. (eds). 2011. *State of Innovation: The U.S. Government's Role in Technology Development*. Boulder, CO: Paradigm Publishers.

Breznitz, D. and Ornston, D. 2013. The Revolutionary Power of Peripheral Agencies: Explaining Radical Policy Innovation in Finland and Israel. *Comparative Political Studies 46*, no. 10: 1219–1245.

Callon, S. 1995. *Divided Sun: MITI and the Breakdown of Japanese High-Tech Industrial Policy, 1975–1993*. Stanford, CA: Stanford University Press.

Chang, K. 2007. The End of Developmental Citizenship? Restructuring and Social Displacement in Post-Crisis South Korea. *Economic and Political Weekly 15*: 67–72.

Chang, H. 2008. *Bad Samaritans: The Myth of Free Trade and the Secret History of Capitalism*. New York: Bloomsbury Press.

Cumings, B. 1998. The Korean Crisis and the End of 'Late' Development. *New Left Review 231*: 43–72.

Debanes, P. 2018. Layering the developmental state away? The knock-on effect of startup promotion policies on the innovation bureaucracy in South Korea. *INCAS Discussion Paper Series*. Available at: https://halshs.archives-ouvertes.fr/halshs-01800489/document.

Dent, C. 2014. *Renewable Energy in East Asia: Towards a New Developmentalism*. London: Routledge.

DeWit, A. 2018. Japanese Smart Communities as Industrial Policy. In: *Sustainable Cities and Communities Design Handbook (Second Edition)*. Clark, W. (ed.): 421–452. Burlington, MA: Butterworth-Heinemann Inc.

Deyo, F. (ed.). 1987. *The Political Economy of the New Asian Industrialism*. Ithaca, NY: Cornell University Press.

Dicken, P. 2015. *Global Shift: Mapping the Changing Contours of the World Economy* (7th Ed). New York: Guilford Press.

Evans, P. 1995. *Embedded Autonomy: States and Industrial Transformation*. Princeton, NJ: Princeton University Press.

Ernst, D. 2011. *Indigenous Innovation and Globalization: The Challenge for China's Standardization Strategy*. La Jolla, CA: UC Institute on Global Conflict and Cooperation; Honolulu: East-West Center.

Hundt, D. 2014. Economic Crisis in Korea and the Degraded Developmental State. *Australian Journal of International Affairs 68*, no. 5: 499–514.

Johnson, C. 1982. *MITI and the Japanese Miracle: The Growth of Industrial Policy, 1925–1975*. Stanford, CA: Stanford University Press.

Johnson, C. 1999. The Developmental State: Odyssey of a Concept. In: *The Developmental State*. Woo-Cumings, M. (ed.): 32–60. Ithaca, NY: Cornell University Press.

Johnson, C. 2001. Japanese 'Capitalism' Revisited. *Thesis Eleven 66, no. 1*: 57–78.

Kalinowski, T. 2008. *Korea's Recovery since the 1997/98 Financial Crisis: The Last Stage of the Developmental State*. New Political Economy 13, no. 4: 447–462.

Kim, K. and Kwon, H. 2017. The State's Role in Globalization: Korea's Experience from a Comparative Perspective. *Politics & Society 45*, no. 4: 505–531.

Kim, S. 2012a. Transitioning from Fast-Follower to Innovator: The Institutional Foundations of the Korean Telecommunications Sector. *Review of International Political Economy 19*, no. 1: 140–168.

Kim, S. 2012b. The Politics of Technological Upgrading in South Korea: How Government and Business Challenged the Might of Qualcomm. *New Political Economy 17*, no. 3: 293–312.

Kim, S. 2012c. Sorry, Apple: Samsung is winning the war on 4G platform. *The Conversation*. Available at: https://theconversation.com/sorry-apple-samsung-is-winning-the-war-on-4g-platforms-9256.

Kim, S. 2013. The Rise of East Asia's Global Companies. *Global Policy 4*, no. 2: 184–193.

Kim, S. 2018. Wither Developmentalism After Democratisation? In: *Routledge Handbook on Democratization in East Asia*. Cheng, T. and Chu, Y. (ed.): 457–470. London: Routledge.

Kim, S. 2019. Hybridized Industrial Ecosystems and the Makings of a New Developmental Infrastructure in East Asia's Green Energy Sector. *Review of International Political Economy 26*, no. 1: 158–182.

Kim, S. and Mathews, J. 2016. Korea's Greening Strategy: The Role of Smart Microgrids. *The Asia-Pacific Journal: Japan Focus 14*, no. 24: 1–19. Available at: https://apjjf.org/2016/24/Kim.html.

Kim, S. and Thurbon, E. 2015. Developmental Environmentalism: Explaining South Korea's Ambitious Pursuit of Green Growth. *Politics & Society 43*, no. 2: 213–240.

Kuo, C. 1998. Private Governance in Taiwan. In: *Beyond the Developmental State: East Asia's Political Economies Reconsidered*. Chan, S., Lutz, H., Lam, D. and Clark, C. (ed.): 84–95. London: Palgrave Macmillan.

Lall, S. 2002. Linking FDI, Technology Development for Capacity Building and Strategic Competitiveness. *Transnational Corporations 11*, no. 3: 39–88.

Larson, J. and Park, J. 2014. From Developmental to Network State: Government Restructuring and ICT-led Innovation in Korea. *Telecommunications Policy 38*, no. 4: 344–359.

Lee, K. 2013. *Schumpeterian Analysis of Economic Catch-up: Knowledge, Path-Creation and Middle-Income Trap*. Cambridge: Cambridge University Press.

Lee, K. and Lim, C. 2001. Technological Regimes, Catching-up and Leapfrogging: Findings from the Korean Industries. *Research Policy 30*, no. 3: 459–483.

Lindblom, C. 1977. *Politics and Markets: the World's Political-Economic Systems*. New York: Basic Books.

Malerba, F. and Orsenigo, L. 1996. Schumpeterian Patterns of Innovation. *Cambridge Journal of Economics 19*, no. 1: 49–65.

Mathews, J. 1997. A Silicon Valley of the East: Creating Taiwan's Semiconductor Industry. *California Management Review 39*, no. 4: 26–54.

Mathews, J. 2002. *Dragon Multinational: A New Model of Global Growth*. Oxford: Oxford University Press.

Mathews, J. 2012. Reforming the International Patent System. *Review of International Political Economy 19*, no. 1: 169–180.

Mathews, J. 2017. *Global Green Shift: When Ceres Meets Gaia*. London: Anthem Press.

Mathews, J. and Cho, D. 2000. *Tiger Technology: The Creation of a Semiconductor Industry in East Asia*. Cambridge: Cambridge University Press.

Mathews, J., Hu, M. and Wu, C. 2011. Fast-Follower Industrial Dynamics: The Case of Taiwan's Emergent Solar Photovoltaic Industry. *Industry and Innovation 18*, no. 2: 177–202.

Miao, J. and Phelps, N. 2019. The Intrapreneurial State: Singapore's Emergence in the Smart and Sustainable Urban Solutions Field. *Territory, Politics, Governance 7*, no. 3: 316–335.

Mikler, J. 2018. *The Political Power of Global Corporations*. Cambridge: Polity Press.

Murphree, M. and Breznitz, D. 2018. Indigenous Digital Technology Standards for Development: The Case of China. *Journal of International Business Policy*: 234–252.

Ó Riain, S. 2004. *The Politics of High-Tech Growth: Developmental Network States in the Global Economy*. Cambridge: Cambridge University Press.

Pekkanen, S. 2003. *Picking Winners? From Technology Catch-up to the Space Race in Japan*. Stanford, CA: Stanford University Press.

Pempel, T. J. and Muramatsu, M. 1995. The Japanese Bureaucracy and Economic Development: Structuring a Proactive Civil Service. In: *The Japanese Civil Service and Economic Development: Catalysts of Change*. Kim, H., Muramatsu, M. and Pempel, T. J.: 19–76. New York: Oxford University Press.

Rodrik, D. 2008. Normalizing Industry Policy. *Commission on Growth and Development Working Paper No. 3*. Washington, D.C.: World Bank. Available at: https://siteresources.worldbank.org/EXTPREMNET/Resources/489960-1338997241035/Growth_Commission_Working_Paper_3_Normalizing_Industrial_Policy.pdf.

Song, B. 1990. *The Rise of the Korean Economy*. New York: Oxford University Press.

Thurbon, E. 2014. The Resurgence of the Developmental State: A Conceptual Defence. *Critique Internationale 63*, no. 2: 59–75.

Thurbon, E. 2016. *Developmental mindset: The revival of financial activism in South Korea*. Ithaca, NY: Cornell University Press.

Vogel, S. 2013. Japan's Information Technology Challenge. In: *The Third Globalization: Can Wealthy Nations Stay Rich in the Twenty-First Century?* Breznitz, D. and Zysman, J. (eds.): 350–372. Oxford: Oxford University Press.

Wade, R. 1990/2004. *Governing the Market: Economic Theory and the Role of Government in East Asian Industrialization*. Princeton, NJ: Princeton University Press.

Wade, R. 2010. After the Crisis: Industrial Policy and the Developmental State in Low-Income Countries. *Global Policy 1*, no. 2: 150–161.

Wang, J. 2016. Toward a Platform Builder: The State's Role in Taiwan's Biopharmaceutical Industry. In: *The Asian Developmental State: Reexaminations and New Departures*. Chu, Y. (ed.) 97–115. London: Palgrave Macmillan.

Warwick, K. and Nolan, A. 2014. Evaluation of Industrial Policy: Methodological Issues and Policy Lessons. *OECD Science, Technology and Industry Policy Papers No. 16*. Paris: OECD.

Weiss, L. 1998. *The Myth of the Powerless State: Governing the Economy in a Global Era*. Ithaca, NY: Cornell University Press.

Weiss, L. 2005. State-Augmenting Effects of Globalisation. *New Political Economy 10*, no. 3: 345–353.

Weiss, L. 2014. *America Inc.?: Innovation and Enterprise in the National Security State*. Ithaca, NY: Cornell University Press.

Wong, J. 2011. *Betting on Biotech: Innovation and the Limits of Asia's Developmental State*. Ithaca, NY: Cornell University Press.

Woo, J. 1991. *Race to the Swift: State and Finance in Korean Industrialization*. New York: Columbia University Press.

Woo-Cumings, M. 1995. Developmental Bureaucracy in Comparative Perspective: The Evolution of the Korean Civil Service. In: *The Japanese Civil Service and Economic Development: Catalysts of Change*. Kim, H., Muramatsu, M. and Pempel, T. J. (ed.): 431–458. New York: Oxford University Press.

Woo-Cumings, M. 1999. Introduction: Chalmers Johnson and the Politics of Nationalism and Development. In: *The Developmental State*. Woo-Cumings, M. (ed.): 1–31. Ithaca, NY: Cornell University Press.

World Bank. 1993. *The East Asian Miracle: Economic Growth and Public Policy*. Washington, DC: World Bank.

Yeung, H. 2016. *Strategic Coupling: East Asian Industrial Transformation in the New Global Economy*. Ithaca, NY: Cornell University Press.

Zhu, T. 2002: Developmental states and threat perceptions in East Asia. *Conflict, Security & Development:* 2(1): 5–29.

31
Building an interdependence framework for the IPE of a rising India

Aseema Sinha

Introduction

The scholarship on India's economic trajectory has focused largely on domestic political economy, developing varied theoretical models to understand slow and incremental policy change, and the evolving alliances between state and capital. Policy change in 1985 and 1991 led to a growth spurt and opening up of the economy. Scholars have begun to think about global–domestic interactions, and changes in India's place in the world. The strengths of the Indian scholarship on comparative political economy could be joined with new concepts and approaches to usher in a new international political economy (IPE) of a rising India. This nascent literature on India's international political economy would be well served to engage with studies of Indian foreign policy to furnish accounts of the economic foundations of change and continuity in India's foreign policy behavior. Moreover, rather than let international relations (IR) scholars build theories about the nature of the global level, an IPE of India should also develop a theory of the global level and attempt to develop an interactive theory of domestic–global interactions. In this quest, new approaches in the American tradition of IPE, such as the interdependence approach, could be combined with a theory of linkage politics to lay out the mechanisms that affect how the global and domestic levels overlap and interact. This chapter reviews a wide-ranging set of literatures that relate to India's political economy and foreign policy and offers a linkage politics and interdependence framework that synthesizes ideas and concepts from IPE with insights from diverse approaches on India's domestic political economy.

In 2009, the *Routledge Handbook of International Political Economy*, aimed to outline the geographic origins of "multiple traditions of IPE" had no chapter on India with four chapters on "IPE in Asia," which comprised different perspectives about East Asia, China, and Australia (Blyth 2009). This absence reflects the recent and slow rise of India but also the difficulty of integrating India into larger comparative political economy (CPE) and IPE debates. India's late trajectory of reforms within a democratic context has made it difficult to integrate India into the larger debates. India's economic reform program started in mid 1980s, but then reversed and only re-started in a more comprehensive manner in 1991. By then, China was galloping ahead in terms of growth rates and reduction in poverty. Growth picked up in India after 1992 but was not spectacular until 2003 or so when India began to see growth rates of 8 percent per annum and above. Then, around 2008–2009, growth slowed again to 5 percent per annum. The period from 2011 to 2018 has seen growth rates ranging from 6.6 percent to 8.2 percent per annum making India to be the second-fastest growing economy (See Figure 31.2). By 2019 a structural crisis has begun to pull down India's growth to 4–5 percent per annum even as China's also faced a slowdown.

Furthermore, India's rising power has taken place in a democratic context and during a coalition era (1990s), when it is difficult to attribute unilateral credit to the government of the day. The realist focus on states is not easy to fit onto India with the complexity of its multiple parties and contested democratic practice. Coalition governments have facilitated growth, a puzzle for IR theories (Nooruddin 2011) and difficult to fit into the prevailing models. Overall, the developmental state debates, and attention of IPE analyses largely bypassed an analysis of India with some notable exceptions (Chibber 2006; Echeverri-Gent 2007; Evans 1995; Herring 1999; Sinha 2005). In these accounts, India was characterized as an intermediate state with some embeddedness and some autonomy (Evans 1995) but not enough to characterize India as a successful developmental state. The dominant understanding was that India was a failed developmental state (Herring 1999). Even when scholars identified subnational developmental states (Kohli 2012; Sinha 2005), the larger developmental state literature, used to small states in East Asia and South East Asia, did not know what to make of regional diversity and the re-location of analysis to infranational levels. Moreover, the bifurcation of mass politics and elite politics in our theoretical models and the idea that insulated autonomy was crucial to economic policy sidelined the politics around economic policy pervasive in India (Echeverri-Gent 2015). In essence, it was difficult to integrate democratic practice of India into the larger IR and IPE debates, which privileged state autonomy.

This global invisibility to India was mirrored by choices made by scholars of India. Scholars of India largely focused on ethnic politics and the vicissitudes of party politics and electoral dynamics—mass politics—with less attention to political economy, especially international political economy, although this has changed in recent years. Importantly, if IPE is the "the interplay of economics and politics in the world arena" (Frieden and Lake 2000: 1), scholars of India have not developed theories of the world economy while developing complex analyses of the domestic political economy. India's insular economic policies, and closed nature of its economy from 1950s to the 1980s made this analytical choice sound. The idea of a locked-in political economy (Chibber 2006) and the "Bardhan trap" (Mitra 2019) to understand the political economy of India has been the dominant frame of analysis. A weaker tradition of thinking of IPE in India with a focus on comparative or domestically oriented political economy reinforced these real-world developments. This scholarship has made significant gains in our understanding of class dynamics, state's role, and policy changes, while the global level of analysis has been deployed as an exogenous context, creating incentives for domestic actors (Echeverri-Gent 2004: 306–307). This resonates with the "open economy politics" approach in IPE even though IPE as an autonomous field of study is largely absent in the Indian scholarship; scholars of India have not built and created concepts about the international political economy until recently.

While it has been difficult to fit Indian trajectory into larger theories and debates, the strength of the Indian scholarship has been a focus on diverse ways of approaching the internal political economy of India, which could make the boundary between international political economy and comparative political economy more permeable, a valuable goal demanded by many IR scholars and especially the open economy approach in IPE. The large Indian political economy scholarship can provide the tools to open up the black box of domestic politics. Specifically, the

---

Box 31.1 Timeline of India's rise

1947: India emerges as an independence and post-colonial state;
Partition of British India and the creation of India and Pakistan
India a member of the General Agreement on Tariffs and Trade (GATT)

1947, 1965, and 1971: Three wars with Pakistan

1962: Border conflict with China

1971: India helps Bangladesh become a nation; signs a friendship treaty with the Soviet Union

1947–onwards: Non-alignment replaced by Strategic Autonomy

1955–1991: Planned Economy

1985: A new government (Rajiv Gandhi) starts a modest reform program

1991: a new minority government (Narasimha Rao) starts a reform program that is substantial and path-breaking

1995: World Trade Organization (WTO) comes into being

1998: India nests nuclear weapons;
Loses three cases at the WTO

2005: Bush administration conducts a reassessment of India. The administration pursues a civil nuclear deal with India. WTO comes into full force in India

---

scholarship on Indian political economy allows us to trace the domestic determinants of growing global and regional power, providing better sense of the contested politics of economic policy and of its international actions. Integrating these insights about the nature of domestic politics into an analysis of India's foreign policy behavior or of India's behavior in global alliances presents an important and much-needed corrective to the current bodies of scholarship that stand apart. If done self-consciously, the strengths of the Indian political economy will allow us to build a domestic and micro political economy of foreign policies and actions in global forums, advancing both theoretical and empirical debates across subfields.

As India slowly but surely integrated into the global supply chains, world of ideas, markets, finance and institutions in the 1990s and 2000s, new and recent research on changing political economy of India emerged (Echeverri-Gent 2004; 2007, 2015; Jaffrelot et al. 2019; Kohli 2012; Mukherji 2013, 2014; Naseemullah 2017; Sinha 2016). Trade in goods started increasing slowly in the 1990s but accelerated after 2000 despite the uncertainties of the global economy (see Figure 31.1).[1]

These real-world and scholarly developments offer a new opportunity to build a new research program on international political economy of a rising India. This chapter offers elements of such a framework by synthesizing concepts and ideas from an interdependence framework (Farrell and Newman 2016; Sinha 2017b), a dynamic open economy model that takes domestic interests and contested elite politics seriously (Echeverri-Gent 2015; Sinha 2016), and diverse models of comparative political economy about continuity and change in India (Jenkins 1999; Kohli 2012; Mukherji 2014). Such a framework would help us think about foreign–domestic politics of contemporary India in a more theoretically conscious way, but do so by inserting an analysis of the micro-foundations of internal political economy into models of the world economy and India's foreign policies. In such an integration, conscious attention needs to be paid to how domestic and global levels interact and how linkage mechanisms travel and create overlap or conflict among actors that span those levels.

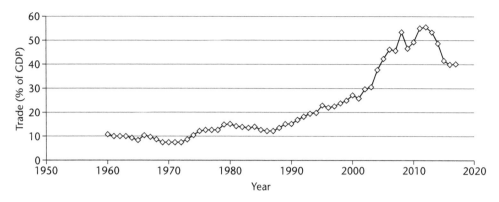

Figure 31.1   India's trade in goods as a % of GDP

Source: Author's calculations from World Development Indicators.

The argument and approach adopted in this chapter

In order to build an interdependence approach for understanding India's rise, I draw insights and concepts from a wide array of literature focusing on India's rising power and changing political economy. The study of a rising India has appeared in three distinct and parallel bodies of literature spanning: political economy of policy change, comparative political economy, and foreign policy of a rising power, making for a rich set of approaches and findings. In order to articulate an IPE of India, I highlight what we have learnt from this disparate scholarship about three distinct questions of interest to international political economy.

1   What are the domestic and international sources of India's rise?
2   What is the nature of India's political economy?
3   What strategies does India adopt?

The scholarship on these three questions have generated important empirical findings and new concepts regarding the domestic side of the causal sequence and should be combined or made compatible with various strands of IPE scholarship in the US, notably, open economy politics, constructivism, realism and an interdependence framework. I, thus, lay out the basic elements of traditional (realism and constructivism) and new IPE approaches (open economy politics (OEP) and interdependence) that can be used to develop elements of a new framework of IPE of India. A more conscious engagement with the larger theoretical debates in IPE would enhance both the Indian scholarship and integrate India into the dominant theoretical frameworks. In this section I outline the key ideas of the IPE debates that could be integrated into an IPE framework of India. The second half of this chapter reviews the recent literature that has begun to integrate these concepts and levels of analysis.

Realist political economy rests on the three elements: "the role of the state, that pursues the national interest in an anarchic international system" (Kirshner 2009: 36). The state is an autonomous state with ideas about the national interest; it seeks both power and plenty and goes beyond the sum of existing interests in society to carve out an independent economic policy. Realists are skeptical about peace and cooperation enjoined by global interdependence or liberal ideas; rather they see the possibility of power-seeking states pursuing war or military enhancement to gain power in an anarchic international system. Realists, then, are wary of the idea of commercial peace, the idea that trade and economic interchange could prevent wars and conflict. The realist emphasis on a state-centered political economy resonates strongly with the scholarship on India even when the diversity of domestic interests common in India complicates the analysis.

In contrast to realists, constructivists bring in new tools of analysis, notably collective ideas and shared beliefs, identities and norms arguing that how material facts are interpreted and framed through the lens of cognitive ideas and beliefs have economic and political consequences (Abdelal 2009; Blyth 2002). States' perceptions and ideas about the economy become important in this approach. Constructivists also argue that facts about the world market and rules were social constructs, and markets or globalization were constituted by politics and the interpretations that state and private actors bring forth. The Indian literature's emphasis on ideas as a source of policy change has strong resonances with this approach (see below). Future work on this strand of analysis should aim toward tying the ideas and concepts from a constructivist political economy with Indian examples and contribute to that theoretical program more directly.

Beyond traditional debates in IR and IPE, new approaches have emerged that seek to modify the existing frames of analysis: Open economy politics and interdependence approach. OEP emerged in the late 1990s and the interdependence approach has been recently articulated as a partial critique of OEP in 2018.[2] OEP is interested in two salient questions: Why do countries open their economies, making economic liberalization a dependent variable? And, how does integration affect the interests, sectors, factors of production, or national policies? (Lake 2009). These questions and new research led to the development of a common set of assumptions. As described by Lake:

> OEP begins with individuals, sectors or factors of production as units of analysis and derives their interests over economic policy from each unit's position in the international economy. It conceives of domestic political institutions as mechanisms that aggregate interests (with more or less bias) and structure the bargaining of competing social groups. Finally, it introduces, when necessary, bargaining between states with different interests. Analysis within OEP proceeds from the most macro-to the most macro-level in a linear and orderly fashion, reflecting a unidirectional conception of politics as flowing up from individuals to interstate bargaining.
>
> *(Lake 2009: 225)*

The scholarship of India's changing political economy is compatible with the OEP approach with a focus on the domestic process to explicate where interests come from and a bracketing of how the international economy affects those interests. Naseemullah (2017), Kohli (2012), and Jenkins (1999) are part of this research program, even though they do not link themselves directly to its assumptions and ideas. Lake calls this strategy, "a partial equilibrium or comparative statics approach to theory and knowledge" (Lake 2009: 225).

A new approach in IPE calls itself the "interdependence approach" and posits that rule overlap rather than anarchy is the defining characteristic of the global system. Building on the idea of "complex interdependence" outlined by Keohane and Nye (2001), they argue that OEP conceptualizes globalization as an exogenous shock that needs to be replaced by the idea that there is significant overlapping of domestic–global authorities across issue areas and state systems—rule overlap; they, then, argue for building truly interactive theories rather than the one-way causal accounts found in OEP. Sinha builds upon these recent debates to develop a dynamic open economy model combining OEP with a second image reversed analysis that resonates with the interdependence approach in opening up the blackbox of both domestic and international levels (Sinha 2016). Thus, the scholarship on India has clear overlaps and cognitive resonances with different strands of the IPE theories; these should be developed theoretically, contributing to the larger research programs more directly. In the rest of the chapter I review the scholarship on and from India and outline what we have learnt that could deployed to build an IPE of India.

Mapping India's rise with both domestic and international concerns in mind

India's unexpected economic rise and turnaround in the 2000s has attracted much international attention and scholarly analysis.[3] The International Monetary Fund's (IMF) analysis of the ten largest economies finds that India is the fifth largest by the size of its nominal gross domestic product (GDP) in 2019. According to various estimates, by 2030 the size of the Indian economy would be 46.3 trillion, reaching second place in terms of overall size of the GDP, after China's.[4]

Many popular books resonate with a euphoric, somewhat overstated, assessment of India.[5] In 2003 these assessments about India's rise were strengthened when Goldman Sachs published a report about emerging powers that it labeled BRICs (Brazil, Russia, India, and China).[6] Subsequently, the Goldman Sachs research team has suggested a more positive outlook for India.[7] Newspapers and business magazines are awash with stories of India's capabilities. Simultaneously, scholarly research has struggled to analyze the potential and the reality of India's promise, documenting the endemic problems familiar to India watchers and the gap between potential and promise.[8] India's large population means that that growth has to be shared among its 1.35 billion people creating many challenges. At any rate, economic changes led to these revised assessments and are worth tracing briefly.

The economic crisis between 1989 and 1991 led to an IMF structural adjustment loan, which was used by the then Finance Minister, Manmohan Singh, to introduce extensive domestic liberalization unleashing competition and private sector de-regulation (Ahmad and Varshney

Table 31.1 GDP, Current prices

Country	Value of GDP (trillion US$)
United States	21.34
China	14.22
Japan	5.18
Germany	3.96
India	2.97
France	2.76
United Kingdom	2.83
Italy	2.03
Brazil	1.96
Canada	1.74
South Korea	1.66
Russia	1.61
Indonesia	1.1
Mexico	1.24
Turkey	0.7

Source: IMF. 2019. World Economic Outlook. Available at: www.imf.org/external/datamapper/NGDPD@WEO/OEMDC/ADVEC/WEOWORLD.

2012). India grew rapidly in the 2000s earning it the title of the "second-fastest growing economy in the world." The financial crisis of 2008–2010 slowed India's growth but did not reverse its growth momentum (Echeverri-Gent 2015). More recently, India's growth has slowed, such as between 2011 to 2014, and from 2017–2020; this slowdown creates a gap between the potential and promise of India's global growth and its realization. Figure 31.2 presents the picture since 1990.

The largely domestic orientation of India's economy as evident by the low trade to GDP ratio for much of its post-independence history allowed it to ride the storm easier than many countries of the world. Such rapid economic change transformed India's global profile, as more and more countries and investors began paying attention to changes within India. Simultaneously, in the early 1990s, India began changing its foreign policies and relations toward East Asia, Israel, and the United States and by the 2000s debate about India's place in the world led observers to re-think the nature of power in the global realm.[9] India's performance in economic multilateral regimes and diplomacy improved and its ability to negotiate became more skillful and effective.[10] This review of Indian developmental history raises an interesting empirical and analytical puzzle relevant to an IPE of India: What are the domestic and international sources of India's economic rise and entry onto the global economic stage? It is worth reviewing the Indian scholarship on these questions.

What are the sources of India's rise?

Domestic policy changes, acceleration of growth rate in the 1990s, as well as changes in the global economy are responsible for India's rise in power and status. Scholars of India have developed complex models of policy changes and economic changes with a focus on domestic levers of change. Given the preeminent role of the state and the closed nature of the Indian economy (high tariffs and low trade intensity), many analyses of the Indian economy are domestically oriented. I interrogate this scholarship about the role of global economic and political changes to develop the contours of an IPE of India.

First, India's rising growth rates in the early 2000s (2003–2009) brought India to the world's attention but the foundations of this modest but significant acceleration were laid in the 1980s and 1990s. Economic change in India has been incremental yet consequential. Since changes in India's political economy took place without massive political change, the pre-1991 political

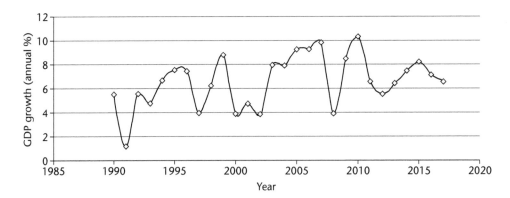

Figure 31.2 India's growth since 1990

Source: World Bank, World Development Indicators, 2019.

economy continues to shape the nature of the transition. In fact, India's inward-looking era—1947–1990—when the growth rate was described as an indifferent "Hindu rate of growth" laid the groundwork of a diversified economy and human capital that was ready to take advantage when policy change did occur. As an example, the success of India's pharma and software success can be attributed to the 1970s Patent Act, and an educational infrastructure set in the 1960s and 1970s. Both state policy change and market actions and response were key to this acceleration.

Second, the balance of class forces internal to the country provide a drag on India's growth and serve as a force mitigating radical change. Bardhan's analysis (1999) of the distribution of conflict between the three propertied classes—big business, landowning classes, and professional and organized working classes—continues to hold sway although the emergence of "complex interdependence" urges us to refine and modify our theoretical constructs. It accounts for the state as a powerful third actor that manages the conflict between diverse propertied fractions and provides a multitude of subsidies (Bardhan 1999). In a similar vein, Rudolph and Rudolph (1987) called it "involuted pluralism" to argue that the diverse demand groups shape economic policy. Writing in 1993 and then again in 1999, Bardhan argued that the lack of collective action on behalf of each class group and the continued proliferation of subsidies confirmed his analysis. When growth happens, it must satisfy and provide support to these propertied classes rather than being pro-market (Kohli 2012). If this analysis continued to hold true after India was liberalized, what factors, then, led to India's increasing growth rate in the 1990s and the subsequent rise in power, status, and recognition? This question has led scholars both to changing internal economic foundations and policy changes such as the 1991 reforms. I go deeper into the insights for an IPE of India by dividing the scholarship on India into two distinct themes: Policy change, and the nature of the emerging political economy. Each of these questions reveal different approaches and outline diverse mechanisms of understanding international–domestic interactions.

What do theories of policy change tell us about the factors that led to change in India?

Scholars are united in noting that the 1985 reforms, followed by the 1991 reforms constituted a paradigm shift in the rate of growth and also set the Indian economy on to a new path (Jenkins 1999; Kohli 2006a, 2006b; Rodrik and Subramanian 2004). We also have well-developed theories of the origins of the 1985 reform and the 1991 reforms (Harriss 1987; Jenkins 1999; Kohli 1989; Mukherji 2014; Shastri 1995). What do these accounts tell us about the domestic and international sources of change? What role do they accord to state-initiated change? It is useful to divide the literature into three distinct approaches:

a   ideas-based arguments;
b   state autonomy arguments; and
c   interest and institution-based arguments.

Technocratic ideas as a driving force

Vanita Shastri focused on the 1985 and the 1991 reform and argued that policy entrepreneurs and "change teams" comprising of technocrats and political leadership were key to why the reform occurred in 1991. She notes: "In India between 1985 and 1989, the new ideas that were introduced into policy discourse played an important role in the resultant policy reform and continued to be instrumental in *institutionalizing … these ideas into norms of policymaking"* (1995: 10; italics added). She notes that the Rajiv Gandhi's reforms represented a "shift in discourse and the introduction of new ideas," which "resulted in actual policy changes as well" (Shastri 1995: 27).

How does Shastri deal with international-level variables? She conceptualizes them as external pressure in response to crisis (1995: 13–14) but also acknowledges the role of "international socialization that make possible the transmission of policy relevant knowledge," (Shastri 1995: 13) through foreign advisors and technocrats who may have worked in international institutions and foreign universities. She, thus, implicitly challenges a pure "foreign pressure" thesis arguing that the World Bank and IMF had been recommending similar reforms for almost two decades, but it was only when local policy teams transmitted these ideas that they became the foundations of Indian policy reforms. In Shastri's account we see the beginnings of the idea that ideas of reforms may "have their origins in international sources but had been internalized by the reformers" (1995: 32). In doing so, Shastri explicitly addresses the issue of where policy ideas come from. Sengupta (2009) and Sinha (2016) take up these ideas further, arguing for broadening of the mechanisms through which the global factors work domestically, outlining a clearer global–domestic link that was raised by Shastri's arguments. Notably, these ideas were generated within the state and therefore state-centric explanations and ideas-based explanations can be combined for Shastri (Shastri 1995: 9).

Mukherji's analysis carried this further, arguing that the reforms of 1991 were driven, through a tipping point process, by policy ideas generated in the 1980s. Mukherji argues: "The cases in this book demonstrate that economic change in India after 1991 emerged because the technocratic elite and the political leadership had become disillusioned with import substitution, which had produced fiscally unsustainable growth" (2014: 33). Mukherji brings in some international-level variables in his analysis when he notes that:

> Transformative change in 1991 occurred at the time of a severe balance of payments crisis and when the Soviet Union—India's trusted friend for more than four decades—had collapsed. At this critical juncture, India's policymakers viewed the alignment with the globalizing international economic system to be superior to the continuation of an import-substituting regime.
>
> *(2014: 33)*

Mukherji accords more analytical weight to the ideas of technocrats and bureaucrats, and undertakes a careful analysis of policy ideas generated by various government report in the 1970s, as well as the "political and technocratic team" (76–82), that took shape in the 1980s noting: "the 1980s had generated a critical mass of reforming technocrats in India." Although Mukherji does not give analytical weight to international factors in his causal theory, his empirical analysis finds, similar to Shastri, that many of the reformist ideas germinated when economists placed aboard interacted with policy elites, who had begun to identify serious problems with India's economic model. His account, it could be argued, identifies a complementary role of ideas generated by internationally placed economists in interaction with policy studies of failures created from within the government. He observes:

> The interaction between Indian economists and technocrats occurred at a time when the Indian government had begun noting its policy failures in various reports that had appeared in the 1990s. The reformers had developed a sophisticated and homegrown reform agenda because they had confronted India's peculiar problems in a substantial way. They were able

to engage the IMF and the World Bank and move towards a policy consensus in 1991. India's reforms would not have been successful had it not been for the research on policy problems and limited experiments carried out in India before the balance of payments crisis of 1991.

(2014: 81)

Echeverri-Gent's analysis of monetary policy and "fiscal politics" advances this debate offering a new perspective on the role of ideas and technocratic politics of economic policy. He argues that the assumed dichotomy between elites and popular support, common in the Indian literature, is misleading. He observes:

Dichotomizing India's political economy [between elite and mass politics] obscures important political dynamics that underpin policy change. Technocratic policymakers often advocate disparate solution to policy challenges, and contestation between elite policymakers creates a dynamic that shapes the reform process. Government ministers supervise policymaking, and their actions are shaped by broader political considerations. Finally, fiscal politics is a domain, in which mass politics shapes technocratic politics and technocratic decisions affect mass politics.

(2015: 88–89)

This body of scholarship has confronted the changing role of ideas in shaping India's trajectory of policy reform. Yet, many scholars also note that the ideas to reform were located within a larger commitment to Nehruvian policies and support of state as a leading actor. Miller's (2013) analysis of post-imperial ideology located in collective trauma may help us understand this paradox of new ideas framed in historically meaningful sensibilities. She shows how colonialism's framing continue to shape ideas and framings. The role of ideas is emphasized in this literature with some exploration of the route through which ideas work. These ideas have strong resonances with the constructivist program in international relations. If one had to build a new international political economy of India, it would be important to focus attention on how the visions of diverse set of actors have evolved to accommodate India's rising power and status focusing on both change and discursive continuities.

Political strategy and state autonomy

In contrast to an emphasis on ideas, both Atul Kohli and Rob Jenkins accord more agency to the political actors and see the reforms as a "political process." Kohli's analysis of the early attempts at reforms under Indira Gandhi notes: "The economic policy shift under Indira Gandhi is thus best understood as an integral aspect of her overall political strategy" (Kohli 1989: 310). In doing so, Kohli accords greater initiative to the state and political actors. It's worth noting that Kohli gives short shrift to the role of advisors arguing that what had changed was "the nature of the political leadership and the sense of who—the leaders or the advisors—are really in charge of economic policy making" (1989: 312). Both Kohli and Jenkins argue for the need to focus on the political management of reforms and how the political actors used diverse tactics to prevent political opposition form bubbling over. Jenkins elaborates this into a sophisticated argument of "reform by stealth" stressing the role of democratic actors in a contested polity. In doing so, Jenkins arguments synthesize diverse variables and spans both state-centric arguments, subject to the institutional and political logic of democracies.

Interest-driven and institutional arguments for policy change

Jenkins develops a complex argument about democracy's contributions to the durability of India's reform program positing that democratic institutions make it possible for political actors to initiate reforms but to do so in a paradoxical way, by obfuscating and using the reform process to serve their political ends. Thus, contrary to the democracy-skeptics, Indian democracy facilitated the reform process but did so, not by declaring an unapologetic vision of reforms, but through negotiation, and deploying skills of compromise, manipulation, and stealth. Political actors use the economic reform to seek "new sources of patronage" and rewrite the rules and script of the reform process (Jenkins 1999: 5) by compensating narrowly defined social groups and thus lessening the "perceived political cost" of reform (1999: 5). Importantly, formal and informal institutions, especially the federal system, absorb the strain by "quarantining" political resistance to state level arenas even as the unleashing of competition among state actors created new supporters, and losers were fragmented. Political management of reforms—what Jenkins calls "skills"—include, in addition to outright pilfering: shifting unpleasant responsibilities and blame onto political opponents, surreptitiously compensating selected interests, concealing intentions, re-assuring and then abusing the trust of longtime of political allies, and obscuring policy change by emphasizing essential continuity" (1999: 7). In essence, political actors adapt and their interests shift and their skills became more diverse as policies changes and as the federal structure shapes and regulates the reform process.

The scholarship on policy change in India has developed a variety of theoretical approaches to understand India's peculiar trajectory of policy change, finding answers to the challenge posed by Haggard and Webb squarely: "If interest groups determine policy, and interests in the period before reform tend to favor the status-quo, how is reform ever possible?" (Haggard and Webb 1994: 5) In so doing, we have a complex analysis of diverse actors, such as state elites, technocrats, and how institutions of democracy facilitate reforms by being adaptive, flexible, and capable of introducing new ideas, i.e. technocratic ideas, as well as political skills of managing the transition. This complexity of India's transition to a "pro-business" economy modifies the aggregate nature of variables generated in the larger political economy of reform literature. Rather than a broad focus on ideas, scholars showed that technocratic ideas created a tipping point in India's locked-in political economy (Mukherji 2013). Rather than assume that democracies predispose against change and international integration, scholars identified the adaptive strategies adopted by politicians, and the role of institutions in fragmenting collective action against reforms (Jenkins 1999). In the field of monetary and fiscal policy, an innovative argument showed how diverse approaches existed within policy and technical elites which had policy consequences (Echeverri-Gent 2015). The larger CPE and IPE scholarship needs to integrate the insight generated in the Indian literature that economic reforms emerge as a product of a contested political process in contrast to the conventional idea that state autonomy is good for industrial transformation and policy change.

What is the nature of the emerging political economy in India?

What picture of the new political economy is evident in the scholarship on India? Naseemullah (2017) argues for a focus on the institutional micro-foundations of manufacturing suggesting the renewal of manufacturing across diverse sectors such as automobiles, pharma, and textiles. He argues that two different patterns of "industrial governance" combining different ways in which firms mobilize capital and manage workers have taken shape as India liberalized its economy. Kohli (2012) reframes Indian reforms as being pro-big business rather than pro-market. Kohli argues that a narrow ruling alliance between the state and big business groups has taken shape in the last few decades. This narrow alliance has to be managed politically. Kohli argues that a two-track policy has emerged, "one an electoral track and an economic governance track: mass participation is encouraged—nay, deliberately mobilized—in the electoral arena, but efforts are then made to insulate key decisions from mass pressure" (Kohli 2012: 65). Sinha's analysis of a Janus-faced state, a state that pursues both development and crony capitalism, is also relevant here (2019). Agarwala's work complements this analysis by suggesting that the Indian state has developed "a two-track strategy" of weakening laws protecting formal labor and benefitting big business but also creating a "new political class of informal and contract and self-employed labour" (2019: 101–106). The nature and effects of such an alliance are demonstrated across a wide variety of public institutions (Sinha 2019), policy and issue areas—labor, land, media—and across states and cities in a recent volume co-edited by Jaffrelot, Kohli, and Murali (2019). The new data and analysis point to new instrumental strategies used by business actors even as the indirect, structural power of business has increased. Chandra argues that patronage has been re-located to new areas of the economy, creating new "structural opportunities for patronage" (2015: 47).

Newer research complicates the picture of a narrow but unified ruling alliance by showing that the diversity and variation across sectors (Hsueh 2012; Sinha 2016) and issue areas and the emergence of diverse industrial orders and governance patterns at the firm level across manufacturing (Naseemullah 2017). What is common and different across different regimes—Nehruvian and the post-1991 reform polity— if both are defined by patronage and corruption? Naseemullah in *Development after Statism* focuses on how capital and labor are managing and creating new forms of governance after economic reforms. Naseemullah's approach adds a valuable perspective by focusing on firms and micro (workplace) and meso level (financial institutions) governance orders. Notably, performance-oriented sectors jostle with rent-seeking sectors but diverse institutional patterns co-exist and find ways of adjustment (Naseemullah 2017; Sinha 2016). Sinha finds that textile and garment sectors and pharmaceutical have revived and there is evidence of innovative technological upgrading shaped by their exposure to the rules of the global order. Sinha's (2016) analysis of pharma also adds to the innovative ways in which some firms and sectors have adapted to the global onslaught of rules and supply chains. Naseemullah argues that some firms across both formal and informal governance orders manage to do well, capitalizing on their strengths and specific skills in managing the challenges of the new economy. Resonating with these ideas, studies from business schools speak of the emerging multinationals from India (Ramamurthi and Singh 2009). Echeverri-Gent's research shows that some subsectors such as equity markets have reformed dramatically shaped by economic incentives, institutional leverage, and global norms (2004).

Overall, these new findings give us a sense of how the dominant proprietary classes are becoming fragmented and following different trajectories shaped by nature of the issue area (finance vs. trade for example) (Echeverri-Gent 2004), global linkages (Sinha 2016), sectors (Hsueh 2012) and firm-level industrial patterns (Nasseemullah 2017). They also resonate with the idea that the emerging political economy of India is a hybrid market economy combining diverse market instruments and public-private partnerships (Saez and Chang 2009). The new Indian political economy is much more diverse and differentiated than our existing models. What does globalization do? How do these accounts theorize the role of international factors, an issue of concern to the larger IPE scholarship?

One way to connect the different arenas—domestic and international—is to assess how the domestic political economy is changing to support a more proactive global ambition. Another is to focus on the recursive feedback loops that allow a linkage between domestic and global levels. India's actions at the global level in bilateral or multilateral relations need to be supported by or at the very least made consistent with domestic actor's interests and actions. It is here that the dense contributions of India's comparative political economy scholarship can offer many clues and linkages. The balance of class forces, a dominant theme of India's domestic political economy, predisposes India to concerns about stability and continuity in economic policy and foreign policy. "The lack of a well-articulated IR network" (Mohan 2009) that might push for new ideas and new foreign and economic policies has historically created a hesitant effect in India's foreign policy and economic policy actions. Non-alignment and a post-colonial imagination are the dominant motifs guiding strategic culture and strategic policy. Yet, in Mohan's view, A new nascent "vanguard" is emerging in India. He notes:

> Nor can there be any doubt that Indian diplomacy demonstrated significant strategic imagination in recent decades. There have been many achievements on the foreign policy front. Some of them are: the 'Look East' policy (launched in the early 1990s), the post-Pokhran diplomacy that limited the costs of India's nuclear defiance in 1998, the negotiation of the civil nuclear initiative with the US and the mobilization of international support for it during 2005–2008, and the attempts, which are not entirely successful, to restructure relations with both China and Pakistan. With neither the benefit of distilled academic wisdom nor an insightful policy road map, India has constantly surprised itself and the world with its capacity for thinking on the run and generating major unexpected breakthroughs. I would argue that this was possible because of the existence of tiny, informal and consequential networks spanning the full spectrum of the Indian elite opinion and acting as the vanguard of India's new foreign policy.
>
> *(2009: 158)*

In a parallel way, new research could explore if Sinha and Naseemullah's actors—firms from the globally connected and performance-oriented manufacturing sectors—have become part of this informal network or "woodwork reformers" (Sinha 2016), creating a push for domestic changes as well as for renewed focus on economic aspects of foreign policies. Thus, we need new research on how these new actors, emboldened by economic changes, act both at the global and national level and shape foreign and domestic policies.

India's international political economy

While most studies of Indian political economy and developmental trajectories neglect the external sources of change in India, recently, new political economy analysis has sought to bring in the international or external level of analysis in a more explicit and theoretically conscious way (Echeverri-Gent 2004; Hopewell 2016; Kapur 2010; Sinha 2016; Ye 2014). The theoretical ideas include, linkage politics (Olsen and Sinha 2013), transaction costs and information effects (Sinha 2016), persuasion as well as pressure (Sengupta 2009), and social networks (Ye 2014). Echeverri-Gent elaborates the effect of diverse mechanisms such as opportunity costs of market flows, leverage of international institutions, and global norms (2004) in an analysis of reform of Indian equity markets. Lim and Mukherjee (2017) also argue for a theory of mechanisms such as trade, capital, and soft power, linking economic statecraft and foreign policies of emerging powers. This new nascent literature, I would argue, represents an *emerging subfield of international political economy on India.*

Sinha analyzes the role of the WTO in catalyzing change within India (Sinha 2016), and Kapur focuses on the Indian diaspora as the third triad of the globalization triangle (Kapur 2010).

Min Ye's comparative work on Indian and Chinese diaspora offers a rare comparative analysis of diverse forms of diaspora and their effects. Thus, we have learnt about not only state agency but also the actions of diasporas, diverse kinds of firms, production networks, and middle classes in transforming India's goals, markets, capacities, and ideas and in shaping the nature and pattern of India's journey. These authors analyze domestic–international interactions explicitly. Kapur focuses on the domestic impact of the Indian diaspora. Min Ye analyzes differential foreign direct investment (FDI) inflows in China and India, and attributes that to the role played by India's and China's diasporas. Sengupta analyzes the 1991 reforms and argues that the IMF reforms succeeded because the IMF took a softer approach that considered domestic compulsions of elites. Each of these authors find that international-level variables and actors have definite causal effects on changing India's political economy.

Min Ye's book (2014) argues that diaspora networks play very different roles, leading to variable effects on the flow of FDI into India and China. For her, the nature of diaspora networks—a relational variable—is the key. She argues that entrepreneurial diasporas—from China—are very different from the professional diasporas from India. While diasporas from China bring in investment, Indian diasporas bring new policy ideas. This circulation of different kinds of elites provides a more fine-grained analysis of India and China than blunt regime-based (democracy vs. one-party state) arguments. She analyzes the interactions between levels of analysis explicitly and explores the sources of differences in FDI across two major powers.

Devesh Kapur analyzes the economic, social, and political effects of Indian diasporas on India. He argues that diasporas' financial remittances have changed consumption patterns in India, and "also enhanced the Indian state's ability to withstand sanctions imposed in the aftermath of the nuclear tests" (Kapur 2010: 18). They have also created new inequalities across India's regions and households. Kapur also finds that the Indian diaspora has positively affected India's reputation at the global level.

Sengupta proposes an intriguing analysis of the IMF reforms. She argues that most scholars of the 1991 reforms focus on domestic level changes without analyzing the role played by the IMF. In her argument the IMF was not an agent of coercion, but a powerful mediator with a soft touch. The IMF gave India enough autonomy to design what appeared to be a homegrown program, because the IMF chose to do so. In very similar ways to other writings, this account theorizes that IMF's role is much too complex to be encapsulated in terms of pressure or coercion, a tendency found in much of the literature on India's political economy. Sengupta's analysis allows us to construct different faces of an international organization and confirm that global forces work in more subtle and indirect manners than commonly assumed. She gives powerful intentionality to the IMF, though, while Sinha argues that the effect of the international organization analyzed—the WTO—was unintended.

Resonating with these claims Sinha (2016) argues that we must broaden the way we analyze at the international level to encompass not only threats or pressure but also sovereignty costs, information revelation, and transaction costs. International organizations unleash powerful changes in many domestic contexts, not through pressure, but more indirectly by creating the conditions for changing the domestic balance of power. In doing so, Sinha (2016) examines the effect of trade-related global organizations in changing the logic of collective action within sectors (pharmaceuticals and textiles) and among India's policy making elite. In a similar vein, Olsen and Sinha (2013) offer a theory of linkage politics to understand the variation in Brazil's and India responses. They argue that different linkages across India and Brazil's private and social movement sectors shaped the state's responses. Global level linkages (markets, rules, or networks) are the important mechanisms through which domestic state autonomy is enforced and sustained. Their theory of linkage politics posits that global or systemic variables such as global rules, global supply chains and global networks reach into the domestic political economy – even in strong and self-regarding powers – to change the fundamental interests, and the capabilities, of domestic actors.

(2013: 3)

Each of these authors offer some clues about the international and domestic mechanisms that impact India. Kapur's analysis of the four channels through which migration affects countries— prospect, absence, diaspora, and return— is important and illuminating in disaggregating different types of effects and mechanisms (Kapur 2010: Ch 2). For Sengupta, the IMF works through soft power, not hard coercion, while for Ye, the class composition of the diasporas in question (China vs. India) has differential effects (Sengupta 2009; Ye 2014). In a similar vein, Sinha (2016) builds a theory of different mechanisms that undergird trade reform in India focusing on transaction costs, sovereignty costs, and information effects. Many of these mechanisms originate in global markets and global organizations but each of these has a domestic logic, allowing us to build a truly integrated international political economy of India. Now, these insights from India's political economy and international political economy need to be combined and integrated with studies of Indian foreign policy, which constitutes a distinct and separate scholarship from studies of Indian political economy.

An inside out perspective: what strategies does India adopt?

What is the relationship between economic change and foreign policy in India, a question of relevance to an IPE approach. A nascent literature has emerged to examine this complex issue.[11] Compared with many other large developing economies, India's economic reforms came late and in a diffident manner. India continues to be self-absorbed and inward directed (Malone 2011: 3). Most scholars and observers see India's changing foreign economic orientations to be somewhat delayed, insufficient, and not deep enough. But India's changing economic fortunes and the rise of China and geo-political alignments caught the eyes of the US President Bush and his team, who signaled a change in US alignments and position toward India, unleashing the incorporation of India into international regimes. Thus, India's so-called "rise" was accelerated by responses of a dominant power, the US, and facilitated by a changing international context, initially the fall of the Soviet Union, and then with the emergence of China. Hopewell (2016; 78) suggests that Brazil and India's "mobilization and leadership of developing country coalitions" allowed them to exercise power and influence at the WTO. Within India, new economic policies not only affected domestic support but also began to shape the conduct of Indian foreign policy even if the exact translation of that has been less than perfect. India's usually skeptical public came to support India's great power aspirations and a pro-US tilt in foreign policy. A survey noted that 79 percent of India's public believes that India will become a great power by 2020.[12] Simultaneously, scholars of Indian foreign policy have noted a transformation in India's bilateral and multilateral foreign policies partly due to the changes in its economic policies, the resultant rise in growth rates, and the changing global system. A large literature on India's bilateral and multilateral foreign policies documents the changes and continuities of India's foreign policies (Bajpai and Pant 2013; Hall 2014; Malone et al. 2015). India seems to have moved away from domestic stability concerns to attempting to domestic growth; global trade and global statecraft has become crucial to India's foreign policies.

Now, we need to integrate the two bodies of literature as the changing economic strength and economic diversity is affecting India's foreign policies, actions, and statecraft. As noted by

Ahuja and Kapur: "Changes in India's economy are creating new economic interdependencies that are washing over into its security and foreign policy and are revising core tenets of India's external relations" (2018: 77). These developments call out for the need to build a theory of mechanisms that link economic changes with foreign policies and statecraft, feedback loops that connect political economy support with foreign and security policies, linkage politics that ensures overlap with domestic and global levels, and an interdependence framework that theorizes the nature of the global system.

Building an interdependence framework: thinking about linkages of actors, ideas, and interests

In order to build a framework for thinking about India's international political economy, we need to connect changes in India's domestic economy with its foreign policy stances. The recent scholarship has started to make some connections between India's rising growth rates and economic prosperity and its changing foreign policy stances at the global level. However, we need an explicit theory of linkages and mechanisms between the domestic and international levels that go between economic and policy stances with security policies. In what exact way and through what mechanisms does domestic economic growth contribute toward changing security policies? How do changing security relationships generate "security externalities" (Lim and Mukerjee 2017). Ahuja and Kapur (2018) suggest that in India instruments of economic statecraft have come into "sharp focus" and India has begun to deploy a geo-economic strategy through trade, investment and financial assistance to accomplish geo-political objectives. Sinha (2016) argues that global markets and rules have disrupted the domestic political economy as well as creating new global motivations and institutional capacities; the effect of these combined changes has been a discernable shift in how domestic actors view the global political economy— as an opportunity and not merely as a threat. Domestic economic changes have created new tools of global statecraft and tradecraft. Many observers have observed that Indian security actors within India "see an open global economic order vital for its economic growth and a key component of its grad strategy" (Ahuja and Kapur 2018: 83.). Economic diplomacy and tradecraft have become an important element of India's foreign strategies making the linkages between economic and security policies a tighter one. We also need an account of how these vary across different systems. As Narang and Staniland (2018) argue the accountability environments vary creating diverse incentives for different foreign policy choices.

Therefore, we need a more explicit theory of linkages, mechanisms, and institutional variations that outlines how sub-state actors as well as state actors think about and act upon rule overlap and multiple levels of authority and jurisdictions that globalization entails. Such a theory of linkage and feedback loops should outline how material and ideological interests of domestic actors are affected by global linkages, and how the circulation of markets, ideas, and elites across global and domestic levels creates new channels of national and global interest formation. If India's domestic political economy is becoming more differentiated and complex, then their linkages with the global worlds are being shaped by new interests, ideas, and institutional overlaps. Such a theory of linkages will complement the interdependence framework outlined in IPE and help us understand how interests and ideas change or adapt faced with new configuration of global forces.

Conclusion

If IPE is, as Blyth observed, "a broad and evolving global conversation," (Blyth 2009) then, in 2019, new traditions have joined the conversation. The Indian debates bring something new to the table but also resonate with larger IPE debates. This chapter aimed to build a framework by laying out the disparate building blocks of research on India's political economy, India's rising power and foreign relations, and connecting them together in service of an IPE of India. Analysis of policy reforms of India reveal many competing perspectives about the sources of economic reforms giving much depth to the domestic logic of India's place in the world. Simultaneously, India's rise also offers an opportunity to develop new concepts, re-frame existing theories and insert India in diverse literatures. The insights from the Indian scholarship create the need to add a theory of linkage politics to open economy politics (OEP) as practiced in American IPE. For example, the Indian experience may enable us to explore the linkages between economics and security, as suggested by Echeverri-Gent, and the links and interactions between elite and mass politics (2015). It is, thus, also important to consider new concepts and theories and aim toward theory development in IR and IPE of India. This synthesizing of the literature and teasing out the conceptual innovations relevant to the rise of India creates an opportunity to outline what we don't know as yet, and open new research questions.

I argue that we know a lot about India's history and agency (culture, etc.) in crafting its foreign policies and global presence; we now need to focus more on the changing linkages of India with the world at large and how to theorize about both foreign and domestic political economy (Sinha 2017a). It may be time to develop more integrated theories that can help us understand India's changing interactions with an inter-dependent world and the churning within the domestic political economy unleashed by foreign policies, domestic aspirations, and external forces. Importantly, studies of India need to bring in the distinctly international and transnational processes that are creating new pressures, channels of diffusion, and new ideas for domestic actors. Precisely, because domestic–global interactions have become more intense and complex, domestic state and non-state actors seek to use global changes to their benefit, ride the waves of globalization, and adopt global and domestic strategies to manage its effects. While great progress has been made in the sprawling literatures, what we now need is theoretical integration and self-conscious engagement with international relations theory in service of an interactive framework to understand interdependence and India. IR theory also needs to pay attention to the varied theoretical mechanisms found in the Indian tradition of CPE and emerging IPE.

Notes

1 This data underestimates India's total trade as the data on services is not part of this calculation.
2 The OEP research program is large and voluminous. See Lake (2009) and Keohane (2009) for a review. See, for a critique, Oatley (2011).
3 An analysis of India's rising power include Ganguly (2003, 2008), Mohan (2004), Chiriyankandath (2004) among many others. A recent popular assessment is by Ayres (2018).
4 Digg, "The Predictions for the World 10 Largest Economies in 20130 are Quite Surprising," Digg. com at: http://digg.com/2019/largest-ten-economies-2030.
5 Ayres (2018); Kamdar (2007).
6 Wilson and Purushothaman (2003: 1–22). In 2012, South Africa was added to the group making it BRICS.
7 Poddar and Yi (2007: 1–33). Also, see www.goldmansachs.com/insights/archive/archive-pdfs/brics-dream.pdf.
8 Pekrovich (2003–2004), Sinha and Dorscher (2010), Jaffrelot (2009); Malone (2011), and Bardhan (2010).

9 This debate has created the need to think about geo-economic factors that shape a country's rise and changing international behaviors. Geo-economics is emerging as a distinct set of questions and issues that need to be thought of in analyzing a country's place in the world apart from geo-politics. See, columns by G. Bhatia and M. Asher, "Establishing IAPD is consistent with geo-economic initiatives," August 31, 2011, accessed at: www.dnaindia.com/money/comment_establishing-iapd-is-consistent-with-geo-economic-initiatives_1581787; and M. Asher, "Growing Importance of geo-economic approach for India," March 2, 2011, accessed at: www.dnaindia.com/money/comment_growing-importance-of-geo-economics-approach-for-india_1514295.

10 My interviews with negotiators from a wide array of countries confirm India's rising negotiating capacity. Malone (2011) also notes this point.

11 An excellent study of this topic is Sridharan (2002). Also, see Sinha and Dorschner (2010), Timberg (1998), Denoon (2009), Ahuja and Kapur (2018), and Mohan (2012).

12 Cited in Mohan (2008).

Bibliography

Abdelal, R. 2009. Constructivism as an Approach to International Political Economy. In *Routledge Handbook of International Political Economy* (IPE). Blyth, M. (ed.) 62–76. London: Routledge.

Agarwala, R. 2019. The Politics of India's Reformed Labour Model. In *Business and Politics in India*. Jaffrelot, C., Kohli, A. and Murali, K. (eds): 95–123 New York: Oxford University Press.

Ahmed, S. and Varshney, A. 2012. Battles Half Won: Political Economy of India's Growth and Economic Policy Since Independence. In *Oxford Handbook of the Indian Economy*. Ghate, C. (ed.). 56–104. Oxford: Oxford University Press.

Ahuja, A. and Kapur, D. 2018. India's Geo-Economics Strategy. *India Review* 17 (1): 76–99.

Ayres, A. 2018. *Our Time Has Come: How India is Making Its Place in the World*. Oxford and New York: Oxford University Press.

Bajpai, K. and Pant, H. V. 2013. *India's Foreign Policy: A Reader*. New Delhi: Oxford University Press.

Bardhan, P. 1999. *The Political Economy of Development in India*. Expanded Edition with an epilogue on the political economy of reform in India. Oxford: Oxford University Press.

Bardhan, P. 2010. *Awakening Giants, Feet of Clay: Assessing the Economic Rise of China and India*. Princeton: Princeton University Press.

Blyth, M. 2002. *Great Transformations: Economic Ideas and Institutional Change in the 20th Century*. Cambridge: Cambridge University Press.

Blyth, M. 2009. *Routledge Handbook of International Political Economy (IPE)*. Blyth, M. (ed.) London: Routledge.

Chandra, K. 2015. The New Indian State: The Relocation of Patronage in the Post-Liberalization Economy. *Economic and Political Weekly* 50 (41): 46–58.

Chibber, V. 2006. *Locked in Place: State-Building and Late Industrialization in India*. Princeton: Princeton University Press.

Chiriyankandath, J. 2004. Realigning India: Indian Foreign Policy After the Cold War. *The Roundtable* 93 (374): 199–211.

Denoon, D. 2009. *The Economic and Strategic Rise of China and India; Asian Realignments After the 1997 Financial Crisis*. New York: Palgrave Macmillan.

Echeverri-Gent, J. 2004. Financial Globalization and India's Equity Market Reform. *India Review* 3 (4): 306–332.

Echeverri-Gent, J. 2007. Politics of Market Micro Structure: Towards a New Political Economy of India's Equity Market Reform. In *India's Economic Reforms*. Mukherji, R. (ed.): 328–58. Delhi: Oxford University Press.

Echeverri-Gent, J. 2015. India's Response to the Global Financial Crisis: From Quick Rebound to Protracted Slowdown? In *Unexpected Outcomes: How Emerging Economies Survived the Global Financial Slowdown*. Wise, C., Armijio, L. and Katada, S.: 74–101. Washington, DC: Brookings.

Evans, P. 1995. *Embedded Autonomy*. Princeton: Princeton University Press.

Farrell, H. and Newman, A. 2016. The New Interdependence Approach: Theoretical Development and Empirical Demonstration. *Review of International Political Economy* 23 (5): 713–736.

Frieden, J. and Lake, D. 2001. *International Political Economy: Perspectives on Global Power and Wealth*. London: Routledge.

Ganguly, S. (ed.) 2003. *India as an Emerging Power*. London: Frank Cass.

Ganguly, S. 2008. The Rise of India in Asia. *In International Relations of Asia.* Shambaugh, D. and Yahuda, M. (eds): 150–170, Lanham: Rowman and Littlefield Publishers Inc.

Haggard, S. and Webb, S. 1994. *Voting for Reform: Democracy, Political Liberalization, and Economic Adjustment.* Cambridge University Press.

Hall, I. (ed.) 2014. *The Engagement of India: Strategies and Responses.* Washington, DC: Georgetown University Press.

Harriss, J. 1987. The State in Retreat: Why Has India Experienced Such Half Hearted Liberalization in the 1980s? *IDS Bulletin* 18 (4): 31–38.

Herring, R. 1999. Embedded Particularism: India's Failed Developmental State. In *The Developmental State.* Woo-Cumings, M. (ed.): 306–334. Ithaca: Cornell University Press.

Hopewell, K. 2016. *Breaking the WTO: How Emerging Powers Disrupted the Neo-liberal Project.* Stanford: Stanford University Press.

Hsueh, R. 2012. China and India in the Age of Globalization: Sectoral Variation in Postliberalization Reregulation. *Comparative Political Studies* 45 (1): 32–61.

International Monetary Fund, 2018. *World Economic Outlook,* IMF.

Jaffrelot, C. 2009. India, An Emerging Power, But How Far? In: *Emerging States: The Wellspring of a New World Order.* Jaffrelot, C. (ed.): 76–89. New York: Columbia University Press.

Jaffrelot, C., Kohli, A. and Murali, K. (eds.). 2019. *Business and Politics in India.* Oxford: Oxford University Press.

Jenkins, R. 1999. *Democratic Politics and Economic Reform in India.* Cambridge: Cambridge University Press.

Kamdar, M. 2007. *Planet India: How the Fastest-Growing Democracy is Transforming the World.* New York: Scribner.

Kapur, D. 2010. *Diaspora, Development, and Democracy: The Domestic Impact of International Migration from India.* Princeton: Princeton University Press.

Keohane, R. 2009. The Old IPE and the New. *Review of International Political Economy* 16 (1): 34–46.

Keohane, R. and Nye, J. 2001. *Power and Interdependence.* 3rd Edition. London: Longman.

Kirshner, J. 2009. Realist Political Economy: Traditional Themes and Contemporary Challenges. In: *Routledge Handbook of International Political Economy (IPE).* Blyth, M. (ed.): 36–47. London: Routledge.

Kohli, A. 1989. Politics of Economic Liberalization in India. *World Development* 17 (3): 305–328.

Kohli, A. 2006a. Politics of Economic Growth in India, 1980–2005, Part I: The 1980s. *Economic and Political Weekly* 41 (3): 1251–1259.

Kohli, A. 2006b. Politics of Economic Growth in India, 1980–2005, Part II: The 1990s and Beyond. *Economic and Political Weekly* 41 (3): 1361–1369.

Kohli, A. 2012. *Poverty amid Plenty in the New India.* New York: Cambridge University Press.

Lake, D. 2009. Open Economy Politics: A Critical Review. *The Review of International Organizations* 4 (3): 219–244.

Lim, D. J. and Mukherjee, R. 2017. What Money Can't Buy: The Security Externalities of Chinese Economic statecraft in Post War Sri Lanka. *Asian Security.*15 (2): 73–92.

Malone, D. 2011. *Does the Elephant Dance: Contemporary Indian Foreign Policy.* Oxford: Oxford University Press.

Malone, D., Mohan, C. R. and Raghavan, S. (eds.). 2015. *The Oxford Handbook of Indian Foreign Policy.* Oxford: Oxford University Press.

Miller, M. 2013. *Wronged by Empire: Post-Imperial Ideology and Foreign policy in India and China.* Stanford: Stanford University Press.

Mitra, S. 2019. Uncertain India? Deepening Globalization, Unanticipated Consequences and the Challenge of Sustainability. *India Review* 18 (1):112–123.

Mohan, C. R. 2004. *Crossing the Rubicon: The Shaping of India's New Foreign Policy.* New Delhi: Palgrave Macmillian.

Mohan, C. R. 2008. India's Great Power Burdens. *Seminar.* 581 (January 2008).

Mohan, C. R. 2009. The Remaking of Indian Foreign Policy: Ending the Marginalization of International Relations Community. *International Studies:* 46 (2): 147–63.

Mohan, C. R. 2012. *India's Foreign Policy Transformation.* Asia Policy 14: 108–110.

Mukherji, R. 2013. Ideas, Interests, and the Tipping Point: Economic Change in India. *Review of International Political Economy* 20 (2): 363–389.

Mukherji, R. 2014. *Globalization and Deregulation: Ideas, Interests, and Institutional Change in India.* New Delhi: Oxford University Press.

Narang, V. and Staniland, P. 2018. Democratic Accountability and Foreign Security Policy: Theory and Evidence from India. *Security Studies* 27 (3): 410–447.

Naseemullah, A. 2017. *Development After Statism*. Cambridge: Cambridge University Press.

Nooruddin, I. 2011. *Coalition Politics and Economic Development: Credibility and the Strength of Weak Governments*. Cambridge: Cambridge University Press.

Oatley, T. 2011. The Reductionist Gamble: Open Economy Politics in a Global Economy. *International Organization* 65 (2): 311–341.

Olsen, T. and Sinha, A. 2013. Linkage Politics and the Persistence of National Policy Autonomy in Emerging Powers: Patents, Profits, and Patients in the Context of TRIPS Compliance. *Business and Politics* 15 (3): 323–356.

Pekrovich, G. 2003–2004. Is India a Major Power? *Washington Quarterly* 27(1): 129–144.

Poddar, T. and Yi, E. 2007. India's Rising Growth Potential. Goldman Sachs. *Global Economics Paper* No: 152: 1–33.

Ramamurthi, R. and Singh, J. (eds.) 2009. *Emerging Multinationals in Emerging Markets*. Cambridge: Cambridge University Press.

Rodrik, D. and Subramanian, A. 2004. From "Hindu Growth" to Productivity Surge: The Mystery of the Indian Growth Transition. *IMF Working Paper, WP/04/77*: 1–42.

Rudolph, L. and Rudolph, S. 1987. *In Pursuit of Lakshmi: The Political Economy of the Indian State*. Chicago: The University of Chicago Press.

Saez, L. and Chang, C. 2009. The Political Economy of Global Firms from India and China. *Contemporary Politics* 15 (3): 265–286.

Sengupta, M. 2009. Making the State Change its Mind: The IMF, World Bank and the Politics of India's Market Reforms. *New Political Economy* 14 (2): 181–207.

Shastri, V. 1995. *The Political Economy of Policy Formation in India: The Case of Industrial Policy, 1948–1994*. PhD dissertation, Cornell University.

Sinha, A. 2005. *The Regional Roots of Developmental Politics in India*. Bloomington: Indiana University Press.

Sinha, A. 2016. *Globalizing India: How Global Rules and Markets are Shaping India's Rise to Power*. New York: Cambridge University Press.

Sinha, A. 2017a. Understanding Change and Continuity in India's Foreign Policy. *International Affairs* 93 (1): 189–198.

Sinha, A. 2017b. Understanding India as a Rising Power: An Open Economy and Interdependence Framework. *The World Financial Review*, February 15, 2017.

Sinha, A. 2019. India's Porous State: Blurred Boundaries and the Evolving Business-State Relationship. In: *Business and Politics in India*. Jaffrelot, C., Kohli, A. and Murali, K. (eds.): 50–87. New York: Oxford University Press.

Sinha, A. and Dorschner, J. 2010. India: Rising Power or a Mere Revolution of Rising Expectations? *Polity* 42 (1): 74–100.

Sridharan, K. 2002. Commercial Diplomacy and Statecraft in the Context of Economic Reform: The Indian Experience. *Diplomacy and Statecraft* 13 (2): 57–82.

Timberg, T. 1998. The Impact of Indian Economic Liberalization on US-India Relations. *SAIS Review* 18 (1): 123–136.

Wilson, D. and Purushothaman, R. 2003. Dreaming With BRICs: The Path to 2050. Goldman Sachs. *Global Economics Paper* No: 99: 1–22.

World Bank, 2018. *World Development Indicators*, World Bank.

Ye, M. 2014. *Diasporas and Foreign Direct Investment in China and India*. Cambridge and New York: Cambridge University Press.

32

The international political economy of human security in Africa

Abigail Kabandula

Introduction

Following the Cold War, the world changed in unprecedented ways. Economically, it became more interdependent with the intensification of globalization. However, inequality among and within states also grew as the world became more connected. The shift in the security referent object coupled with the effects of globalization promoted more global approaches to addressing insecurity. Human security has emerged as a more comprehensive approach to secure people across the world. However, in the African context, human security has proved difficult to realize in the wake of interconnectedness through information technologies that have exacerbated contemporary security challenges like civil war, state fragility, terrorism, poverty, and human trafficking. While a few gains can be noticed in human rights, overall, Africa's connection to the global economy seems to have worsened human insecurity on the continent. This chapter examines the international political economy (IPE) of human security in contemporary Africa. The chapter begins with a brief section on theories of IPE and how they relate to security. The section that follows defines human security. Thereafter, the chapter critically examines the application of theories of IPE to human security in Africa. Selected issues in IPE and human security in Africa are discussed in the last section. The chapter concludes that contemporary international political economy poses a threat on human security in Africa and that a human security perspective allows for such challenges to be observed and responded to by both academics and policymakers.

International political economy approaches and security

There are many approaches and paradigms to the study of the international political economy (IPE) or global political economy. Initial chapters in this edition explicate this issue in more detail. Nonetheless, in this chapter, it is vital to briefly highlight the three main approaches to situate a discussion on security more broadly and human security more specifically. The most well-known approaches are the economic nationalist, liberal economist, and critical (radical) approaches. The link between the economy or development and security is increasingly acknowledged and appreciated in the post-Cold War era due to changes in the global economic and security landscape. Africa like other parts of the world has undergone enormous changes that have allowed for a general appreciation of the connection between the security and economy – national, and human (citizen) security. However, different IPE approaches have varying ways in which they acknowledge or dismiss the connection as sections below elucidate.

The economic nationalist approach

Economic nationalists are sometimes referred to as "mercantilist," "neo-mercantilist," or "statist." They are the equivalent of realist approaches in international relations (IR). They emphasize the role of the state and the significance of power in shaping outcomes in the international political economy (O'Brien and Williams 2016). Like realists, their theories focus on the protection of the state and its interests in the global economy. For economic nationalists, the state comes before the market, while market relations are shaped by political power. As such, IPE is perceived as a struggle for power and wealth, and the survival of the state is determined by its ability to ensure that its citizens benefit from international production and exchange (Cohn 2016). Further, economic nationalists assume that the goal of economic policy is to build a more powerful state (Balaam and Dillman 2015). In this vein, the global political economy configuration reflects the interests of powerful states because they wield a lot of power. The central unit of analysis and focus is the state or nation, and not individuals. As such, the state is the main actor in the global political economy. Even though the economic power of contemporary actors such as Transnational Corporations (TNCs) is acknowledged, economic nationalists argue that their power is subordinate to that of the state thus continues to be limited. Nonetheless, liberals criticize nationalist policies for promoting conflict among states because of competition for absolute power (O'Brien and Williams 2016).

Economic nationalist approaches to security

Economic nationalists acknowledge the link between economics and security. For them, economics and security mutually influence each other even though economic interests are subservient to the economy (O'Brien and Williams 2016). Economic nationalists thought tends to stress economic power as a prerequisite for military power. They argue that military power is dependent on the economic resources that a state possesses (Cohn 2016). Therefore, the link between the domestic economy and national security continues to inform foreign and security policy. Like realists, economic nationalists see security mainly in terms of military security since the unit of analysis, also the object of security, is the state.

The liberal economic approach

Liberal thinking informs much of economic thought in the contemporary global political and economic order. Unlike nationalist economic thought, liberal economic theory focuses on the individual and other varied actors such as interest groups, transnational corporations, and the state to study the economy (O'Brien and Williams 2016). Consequently, liberal economic theory and analysis starts with the individual, his or her needs and choices to understand, and to predict behaviour. The individual and not the state is the main economic actor. Therefore, the behaviour of individuals, firms, and states constitute an essential aspect of liberal analysis. The assumption is that when individuals are left to participate in the economy freely – production, exchange, and consumption – the broader society will benefit (Patomäki 2016). Thus, liberals tend to be unreceptive towards state (or political) involvement in the economy. They argue that state involvement removes the benefits accrued from the economic activities and increases the cost of participating in the market (Balaam and Dillman 2015). The market is the centre of economic life in liberal thought, and economic development is a result of the interaction of varied individuals and actors including the state, pursuing their interests. Therefore, TNCs are considered a positive force in the economy even though liberals are criticized for underrating the power some of TNCs and powerful states espouse to influence markets (Dunn 2009).

Unlike economic nationalists who see the inevitability of conflict between and among states in the global system, liberals suggest a link between liberal economic policies and peace (Kant 1917). Supporters of market liberalism argue that economic exchange reduces the possibility of war among states (liberal peace theory) (Doyle 1986). Instead, states see opportunities for mutual benefit through economic cooperation. Therefore, interdependence and not anarchy characterizes the international system (Keohane and Nye 1977). Thus, the international political economy is fundamentally cooperative based on the assumption that market relations will lead to positive outcomes for all who participate (comparative advantage theory) (Hunt and Morgan 1995). This logic negates the need for conflict, and favours cooperation and peace among countries through interdependence and increased interaction (globalization).

Liberal economic approaches to security

Even though liberal economic thinkers reject the inevitability of conflict between states and advocate for mutual state benefits in the global economy, liberal thinkers in IPE modulate the link between the political economy and security. They are reluctant to connect the political and economic realms because they think different rules and behaviour govern the two worlds. For liberals, the economic realm operates on a set of economic laws, whereas the political is marred with emotions. Actors in the economy make rational economic choices, whereas actors in the political arena make emotional and irrational choices (O'Brien and Williams 2016). For this reason, liberal thinkers in the global political economy are reluctant to link the political economy and security.

The critical approach

Critical approaches in IPE take a radical approach against traditional thinking such as nationalist or liberals. They move beyond the state and individuals as units of analysis. They consider other aspects of human life such as class, gender, and the environment. Marxist theories are the most prominent in this approach. Feminists, environmentalists, poststructuralist, and cultural political economy theories also make up the field. Nonetheless, this chapter will briefly highlight the Marxist and feminist approaches. Critical theory expands the unit of analysis beyond state and individuals as well as actors and agencies in the international political economy and security. The notion of security that centres on the state is thus challenged.

Marxist theories

Marxist theories emphasize class and the plight of workers rather than state interests in their analysis. Marxists see class as the main actor in the global political economy (Balaam and Dillman 2015). Unlike liberals who focus on individuals, Marxists embrace a communal approach to organizing and studying the economy, similar to nationalist economic perspectives. However, the state represents class interests rather than cohesive communal interests suggested by economic nationalists (O'Brien and Williams 2016). Dominance and exploitation among and within classes in societies form the basis for Marxist theories. Contrasting liberal approaches, Marxists argue that market relations are inherently exploitative because, in capitalism, workers do not get good remunerations due to surplus value because capitalists pay workers less than their labour is worth (Cohn 2016). As such, Marxists view international economic relations as innately unbalanced and conflictual. In the global economic system, conflict is inevitable as various capitalists seek profits as well as to protect their state interests, causing them to undermine other capitalist interests, which often leads to conflict (O'Brien and Williams 2016). Given Marxists' heavy criticisms of the organization of the national, and the global economies, they generally tend to oppose globalization.

Feminist theories

Feminist theories highlight the plight of a specific group of people – women. Feminist IPE scholars focus their analysis on the unequal gender (power) relations between women and men. Gender, in this case, does not mean sex – female and male, rather the social construction of feminine and masculine identities and subsequent power relations and hierarchies within and between them (Beckwith 2005). Conceiving gender in this sense has allowed feminist scholars and some policymakers to delineate specific contexts in which feminine and masculine behaviours, actions, attitudes, and preferences result in particular outcomes (Beckwith 2005). Using gender, feminists can study and analyse the different effects of specific social, political, economic, societal structures, and policies on women and men. For instance, feminist studies in economics and security show that defined gender roles and social structures can lead to economic disempowerment and insecurity for women (Boserup et al. 2007). In conflict situations, Cohn (2013) notes how women experience conflict differently from men. Key to their experiences is how a gendered division of labour creates conditions of insecurity. In rural areas particularly, gathering firewood requires women to go far away in the bush which puts them at risk of rape, capture or murder.

Critical approaches to security

Like economic nationalists, critical approaches acknowledge the mutual influence of economics and security, although in varying ways. For many critical scholars including Marxists, security matters are heavily dictated by economic interests, while the exact opposite is true for economic nationalists (O'Brien and Williams 2016). Critical thinkers have been a significant factor in expanding the field of critical security studies. Unlike economic nationalists and liberals who are state-centred and individual-focused respectively, critical security scholars such as the Welsh, Paris, and Copenhagen schools expand the objects, actors, and agencies of security as well as sources of threats. The object of security can be the state, a person, a group of people (women, men, girls, race, ethnicity), the environment, and the earth, while actors and agencies range from states, non-governmetnal organizations (NGOs), civil society to prominent individuals in society. Security threats could emanate from states, ethnic groups, the economy, and the environment (water–energy–food–climate nexus). Variations in critical scholars also mean disparities in referent objects, actors, and threats thereby complicating questions about who/what is secured, by whom, and how is it secured? Along with the goals, and methods of security analysis (Peoples and Vaughan-Williams 2015). Liberal and critical theories inform contemporary individual-focused or human-centred forms of security widely known as human security (citizen security) which will be explored in detail below.

Human security

Human security is possibly one of the most debated concepts in security and development studies. This section of the chapter locates the origins of the concept in the changes that took place in the global political economy, and security order towards the end of the twentieth century. It shows how these changes influenced a paradigm shift in the security unit of analysis (referent object), from the state to individuals within the state.

Why human security?

Human security as a policy framework emerged primarily out of need by the international community (United Nations) to respond to challenges towards the end of the twentieth century caused by global reconfiguration following the end of the Cold War (Besada et al. 2010), and adverse environmental and economic impacts. In the 1990s, myriad problems beset Africa. Deadly civil wars, genocide, poverty, drought, diseases, inequality, and poor economic development become rampant. These challenges could not be understood within established state-centric and economic growth-focused theories of the economic nationalists and liberal economic approaches. The "new" challenges especially civil war or "new wars" (Kaldor 2012) threatened the security of the state and people from within, and not necessary from outside the state as initially conceived (Karns and Mingst 2010; Waltz 2010). The new challenges had transnational implications for other countries in the region and the globe. Diseases like HIV/AIDS and Ebola, or civil war, were not confined to, nor could they be considered a problem of, one country. Therefore, the new challenges promoted a reassessment of security and insecurity from state-centred to individual-centred conceptions given that people within states were most affected by the new problems.

The post-Cold War era posed both conceptual and policy challenges for security experts. Conceptually, questions about what is meant by security, who is secured, and by whom begun to arise. The United Nations (UN) was particularly instrumental in this endeavour. In 1994, a Pakistani economist Mahbub-ul-Haq (Haq) articulated the concept of human security in that year's United Nations Development Programme (UNDP) *Human Development Report* entitled a "Secure Human Development." The report interrogated the economic, social, and political conditions of the time and articulated a new security framework that reflected the realities that the world especially less developed countries were facing. It noted:

> For most people, a feeling of insecurity arises more from worries about daily life than from the dread of a cataclysmic world event. Will they and their families have enough to eat? Will they lose their jobs? Will their streets and neighbourhoods be safe from crime? Will they be tortured by a repressive state? Will they become a victim of violence because of their gender? Will their religion or ethnic origin target them for persecution?
>
> *(UNDP 1994: 22)*

Thus, the report put forward a new form of security that endeavoured to address the challenges of the time by focusing on the wellbeing of the individual within the state. A human-centred or citizen security was thus articulated. Human security broadly was defined as "safety from the constant threats of hunger, disease, crime and repression … and protection from sudden and hurtful disruptions in the pattern of our daily lives – whether in our homes, in our jobs, in our communities or in our environment" (UNDP 1994: 3). The central argument was that the individual within the state should be free from want and fear.

The idea of human security aimed to change the focus of security from national security to people's security, from military security to sustainable human development. The seven main categories of human security were listed as: economic security, food security, health security, environmental security, personal security, community security, and political security (UNDP 1994: 24–25).

Box 32.1 Characteristics of human security

- Human security is a *universal* concern. It is relevant to people everywhere, in rich nations and poor. Many threats are common to all people such as unemployment, drugs, crime, pollution, and human rights violations. Their intensity may differ from one part of the world to another, but all these threats to human security are real and growing.
- The components of human security are *interdependent*. When the security of people is endangered anywhere in the world, all nations are likely to get involved. Famine, disease, pollution, drug trafficking, terrorism, ethnic disputes, and social disintegration are no longer isolated events, confined within national borders. Their consequences travel the globe.
- Human security is *easier to ensure through early prevention* than later intervention. It is less costly to meet these threats upstream than downstream (UNDP 1994: 22).

The 1994 UNDP report is a milestone in security studies because it linked development (economy) to security and broadened the possible threats and actors responsible for producing and resolving insecurity. It stresses the rights of the individual to realize their full capabilities economically, politically, and socially to be secure (Sen 2001). In this sense, human security takes a neo-liberal approach to security. Further, the report recognizes the transnational nature of the threats, as well as the multiplicity of actors involved. As such, it broadens the notion of security, threats, and actors responsible for producing and resolving insecurity, and in this sense takes a critical approach to analyse security.

Further, the report presents human security as a global issue which requires global cooperation from all actors both state and non-state actors. It postulates that human security is relevant to people everywhere, in rich as well as developing nations. While the threats to security may differ from country to country, there are some which are common among nations such as job insecurity and environmental threats. Because of the interdependence and interconnectedness among states, insecurity of people in one nation affects people in other states. For instance, in cases of ethnic conflicts, social disintegration, terrorism, pollution, and drug trafficking, other nations are likely to be affected hence the need for global cooperation to resolve the challenges. Therefore, the report argues that threats to human security were no longer personal or local or national, they were becoming global (UNDP 1994: 4).

More importantly, human security represents a fundamental shift in the security referent object (unit of analysis), from state to the individual. It also broadens the types of threats and actors that perpetuate and address insecurity. It challenges the notion of the state as the leading player or provider of security. At the same time, it presents a paradigm shift from the traditional view of state security informed by the possibility for conflict between states to that shaped by daily challenges faced by individuals in life.

Narrow versus broad conceptions of human security

Even though the broad conception of human security is generally used and advocated for by many policymakers, most academics criticize it heavily. Many academics find the broad view a conceptual and analytical nightmare. As outlined above, the broad view of human security encompasses all aspects of human life that affect the individual such as rights, governance, development, the environment, and health. The broad view is mostly accepted in the policy world with many countries devising national, regional and global mechanisms to tackle various aspects of human security.

Writing from experience in the policy world, former Canadian Foreign Minister Lloyd Axworthy (2004: 349) supports the broad conception of human security, arguing that "national and human security are really two sides of the same coin." Therefore, "both policy-makers and academics must dramatically recalibrate in order to address the much broader range of harms now falling under the security rubric." Acharya (2004) agrees with Axworthy. Acharya claims human security is a "rational response to the 'globalizing' of international policy. Governments at various scales must take on a wider mandate than simply economic growth, political stability, and invasion by foreign armies" (2004: 355). Speaking to academics directly, he asserts:

> the need for human security is evident if academic debates are to meet pressing challenges in the policy arena. Human security reflects new forces and trends in international relations.... Human security challenges the academic community to transcend the so-called inter-paradigm debate ... in itself a holistic paradigm; at least, it offers opportunities for creative synthesis and theoretical eclecticism.
>
> *(2004: 355–356)*

Acharya raises important points on the need for security theory and academic debates to be multidisciplinary in order to meet the demands of the contemporary security world.

However, in academia, conceptual thinking on human security has been slow. Debates on the definition and analytical frameworks continue to divide academics as Paris (2004) aptly summarizes:

> Human security seems to encompass everything from substance abuse to genocide. This definitional expansiveness serves the political purpose of enticing the broadest possible coalition of actors and interests to unite under the human security banner, but it simultaneously complicates matters for academic researchers.... Because the concept encompasses both physical security and more general notions of economic and social well-being, it is impractical to talk about certain socioeconomic factors "causing" an increase or decline in human security, given that these factors are themselves part of the definition of human security.
>
> *(2004: 371)*

Therefore, some scholars in security studies tend to narrow the focus of human security. The narrow view focuses on the protection of individuals from violence or physical harm. Most scholars who support this view do so for conceptual precision, and analytical rigor and practicality (policy implications). Most critics point to challenges for policy creation and implementation and academic theorization due to everything being a security issue. Policy-wise, many feel it makes it difficult to conceive precisely what aspects of the individual's life create insecurity.

MacFarlane (2004: 369) argues that a broad conception of human security is not useful to policy because it "makes establishment of priorities in human security policy difficult." However, Hubert (2004) disagrees and contends that human security has policy relevance. He asserts that it is not a question of relevance but rather conceptualization that has led to a divergence in international policy approaches to human security.

Conversely, divergence in conceptions of security has not hindered international action on many threats that undermine the security of people in the world. Hubert (2004) points to the banning of landmines and the establishment of an International Criminal Court (ICC) as crucial human security policy impacts. Perhaps for its policy impact, Newman (2010: 77) sees human security arguments as "problem-solving," that do not engage in epistemological, ontological, or methodological debates thus considered unsophisticated for critical security scholars.

Nonetheless, MacFarlane (2004: 368–369) remarks that "it is unclear what additional analytical or normative traction one gets from relabeling sustainable human development, for example, as human security." On the contrary, he notes

> the narrower focus on protection has stimulated significant normative change (e.g. the attenuation of state sovereignty implicit in UN Security Council resolutions 1265 and 1296), which is to a degree reflected in practice (for example in the inclusion of civilian protection in peacekeeping mandates).

Krause (2004) agrees with MacFarlane, and notes that

> Human security ought to be about 'freedom from fear,' and not about the broad vision of 'freedom from want' … the broad vision of human security is ultimately nothing more than a shopping list; it involves slapping the label of human security on a wide range of issues that have no necessary link. At a certain point, human security becomes a loose synonym for 'bad things that can happen,' and it then loses all utility to policymakers – and incidentally to analysts.…
>
> *(2004: 367–369)*

Others, such as Thakur (2004), contribute to the discussion by attempting to point to specific aspects of human security in question. Thakur focuses on personal safety and threats deemed a crisis. For him, human security entails "the security of people against threats to personal safety and life expectancy" and should be limited to threats that constitute a crisis. However, "personal safety," or "crises" vary from one individual to another, and from regional to regional, hence his conception does not overcome the broadness problem, nor does it narrow the threats to be considered.

North-East Asian countries have rejected the concept of human security as articulated in the UNDP report, particularly its focus on individuals. Societies in these countries tend to focus on the wellbeing of the community as a whole or the collective good as opposed to the individual. Consequently, human security is not widely accepted for this reason, and it is often regarded as a Western imposition on Asian societies. Most countries in the region have developed alternative concepts of security such as human security suited to their contexts which focus more on the collective and freedom from want than fear (Acharya 2001).

Buzan does not see the relevance of human security as a concept altogether. For him, the unit of analysis of security – the individual – is already covered under human rights or traditional security. He remarks,

If the referent object of human security is the individual, or humankind as a whole, then little if anything differentiates its agenda from that of human rights. All that is gained is the possibility of allowing human rights to be discussed in places where that term causes political difficulties.…

(Buzan 2004: 369)

To bridge the divide between those that advocate for a narrow and broad view, Owen (2004) proposes a threshold-based conceptualization of human security. Threshold-based human security entails picking threats that are severe in any aspect of human life, be it social, economic, or political. For Owen, threats should not be included based on a specific category, such as violence, rather on their actual severity. Therefore, threshold-based human security is not defined by an arbitrary list, rather by threats that severely impact people.

Therefore, what emerges is a proliferation of conceptions, definitions, and frameworks of human security depending on unit of analysis of security or the goal of a specific policy matter. Human security both as an academic concept and policy framework is dependent on scholars or policymakers engaging with it, which has led to further fragmentation and variations across disciplines, countries, and regions.

Responsibility to protect (R2P)

Another notable, yet controversial variation of human security is the responsibility to protect (R2P) promoted by the Canadian government. Initially a supporter of the broad view of human security, Canada subsequently focused on "freedom from fear" embodied in the R2P concept. At the start of the twenty-first century, Canada led efforts to create a mechanism for the international community to protect civilian within a sovereign state from gross human rights violations and genocide. The movement was partly born out of the failure by the international community to respond to the Rwandan Genocide in 1994 and the Srebrenica massacre in 1995. It was also partly due to a call by then, and now deceased, UN Secretary-General Kofi Annan to the international community to reconcile the complex problem of state sovereignty and humanitarian intervention in the wake of gross human rights violations and genocide (Annan 2000).

Canada took on the challenge, devoted resources, and created a platform to engage with the issue. At the UN Millennium Summit in 2000, then Canadian Prime Minister Jean Chrétien announced the creation of the International Commission on Intervention and State Sovereignty (ICISS). The Commission's first report entitled *The Responsibility to Protect* in 2001 laid a foundation for how states were to conduct humanitarian interventions within states and the use of force to prevent genocide and other mass atrocities. Nonetheless, it was only towards the end of 2005 at the UN World Summit that all member states accepted the responsibility to protect their people from genocide, war crimes, ethnic cleansing, and crimes against humanity. States also pledged to act under provisions of R2P to prevent and not to incitement gross human rights violations and crimes against humanity (General Assembly 2005).

The concept of R2P was first articulated in a report by ICISS in 2001. The report aimed to establish rules, procedures, and parameters for humanitarian interventions in sovereign states. See Box 32.2 for the core principle of R2P. The report emphasized the responsibilities and rights of the state to protect its citizens. Thus, if the state failed in its obligation to protect its citizens, the international community had the responsibility to protect the people of that country from possible atrocities that could lead to massive loss of life such as genocide and ethnic cleansing. Thus, sovereignty was no longer a right, but rather a responsibility. Responsibility defined in threefold:

> First, it implies that the state authorities are responsible for the functions of protecting the safety and lives of citizens and the promotion of their welfare. Secondly, it suggests that the national political authorities are responsible to the citizens internally and the international community through the UN. And thirdly, it means that the agents of the state are responsible for their actions; that is to say, they are accountable for their acts of commission and omission.
>
> *(ICISS 2001: 13)*

Hence, the report introduced a new concept of sovereignty conditional on the responsibility to protect people, and at the same time signified a significant change in the Westphalian concept of non-intervention in internal matters of another state.

While R2P is well-meaning, especially in the wake of gross human rights violations and genocide prevention, most state actors, mainly from non-Western countries, Africans included, did not welcome the concept with open arms. Critics argue that it does not adequately address who has the right to military intervene, and when and how the intervention should occur (Pattison 2010). Nevertheless, in 2002, when the African Union came into being, its Constitutive Act echoed R2P sentiments. Under Articles 4h and 4j of the Act, the AU has the "right to intervene" in a member state in grave circumstances such as war crimes, genocide, and crimes against humanity (African Union 2000). However, implementation of these articles remains a challenge (Kuwali 2009).

Box 32.2 The responsibility to protect: core principles

1 Basic principles

A   State sovereignty implies responsibility, and the primary responsibility for the protection of its people lies with the state itself.

B   Where a population is suffering serious harm, as a result of internal war, insurgency, repression or state failure, and the state in question is unwilling or unable to halt or avert it, the principle of non-intervention yields to the international responsibility to protect.

2 Foundations

The foundations of the responsibility to protect, as a guiding principle for the international community of states, lie in:

A   obligations inherent in the concept of sovereignty;

B   the responsibility of the Security Council, under Article 24 of the UN Charter, for the maintenance of international peace and security;

C   specific legal obligations under human rights and human protection declarations, covenants and treaties, international humanitarian law and national law;

D   the developing practice of states, regional organizations and the Security Council itself.

---

3 Elements

The responsibility to protect embraces three specific responsibilities:

A   The responsibility to prevent: to address both the root causes and direct causes of internal conflict and other man-made crises putting populations at risk.

B   The responsibility to react: to respond to situations of compelling human need with appropriate measures, which may include coercive measures like sanctions and international prosecution, and in extreme cases military intervention.

C   The responsibility to rebuild: to provide, particularly after a military intervention, full assistance with recovery, reconstruction and reconciliation, addressing the causes of the harm the intervention was designed to halt or avert.

4 Priorities

A   Prevention is the single most important dimension of the responsibility to protect: prevention options should always be exhausted before intervention is contemplated, and more commitment and resources must be devoted to it.

B   The exercise of the responsibility to both prevent and react should always involve less intrusive and coercive measures being considered before more coercive and intrusive ones are applied.

Source: International Commission on Intervention and State Sovereignty 2001.
The Responsibility to Protect.

International political economy and human security

Above, we discussed how the three main IPE theoretical approaches view security and the economy. This section locates human security in IPE theories. We discussed economic nationalists' thought on security and the economy – the strengthening of the economy influences military power. Consequently, their focus is state security. Intrinsically, economic nationalists ignore human security because their conception of security is at state level while the idea of human security focuses on individuals within the state. To economic nationalists, threats within the country such as civil wars are not considered threats to national security even though they pose a threat to individuals. In their view, the state structures are not threatened as they are concerned with inter-state threats.

Whereas liberals do not appreciate linking the economy and security, their ideas about empowering individuals and global interconnection have been central to human security conceptually and practically. Nonetheless, it is the ideas of critical scholars that significantly inform human security conceptually. Given their focus on non-traditional security, critical scholars have advanced theorization of individual-focused security in the contemporary world. Critical theory expands the concept of security beyond the state and individuals to other aspects of human existence and the earth and its biosphere. For instance, the Paris School analyses practices and processes that occur beyond the confines of the official discourse to determine what constitutes threats and security in contemporary times (Bigo 2006). The Welsh School analysis does not only look at what affects the individual's security, it also comprises emancipation and creating consciousness among people of their insecurity (Booth 2005). The Copenhagen School focus on existential threats through securitization (speech act) theory. Securitization entails looking at the way something (the environment or race) or someone becomes a security issue (Buzan 2009). Therefore, critical thinkers have been instrumental in articulating and actualizing human-centred security.

Contemporary issues in international political economy and human security in Africa

At the dawn of the new millennium, UN Secretary-General Kofi Annan voiced his concerns about the uneven distribution of the benefits of globalization and how billions of people across the globe were left to live in squalor (Annan 2000). His sentiments resonated with many academics and policymakers across the world. The negative impacts of globalization were already apparent across Africa from the implementation of Structural Adjustment Programs (SAPs) (Muyeba 2008). Bergamaschi and Tickner (2017) suggest a combination of growing frustrations with North–South relations, and unpopularity of SAPs revived South to South cooperation in the 2000s. Developing countries began to form forums and coalitions through multilateral organizations such as AU and forums such as BRICS (Brazil, Russia, India, China and South Africa) to promote their interests, agendas, and visions for global governance and international development. While South to South development cooperation is still evolving, Van der Merwe (2016) cautions of exploitative potential as well as developmental opportunities that come with emerging powers' political and economic engagement with Africa. Chinese and Turkish competing interests in the Horn of Africa for instance have disrupted development, as well as peace and security. Djibouti is highly indebted to China. Thus, China has leveraged debt to take control of Djibouti's lucrative strategic Port of Doraleh as debt repayment. Several African countries risk falling into a similar debt trap. The rest of the Horn of Africa countries are at risk of militarization following Turkey and the Gulf States' military engagement in the region (Kabandula and Shaw 2018a). Nonetheless, the effects of globalization on Africa are not only economic and political but social and cultural as well (Harrison 2010). However, this section focuses on the economic and political effects of various aspects of globalization on human security.

Digital economies and human security in Africa

The development of information communication technologies (ICTs) has endlessly connected the continent – governments, societies, economies, security, and cultures – in an incredible and perhaps unprecedented manner. Predominantly in the economic sector, Kshetri (2013) notes that advancement and reduced costs of ICTs have encouraged rapid digitization of economies in sub-Saharan Africa. Unlike a decade and a half ago, sending or receiving money within the country was done mainly through the local post office or national bank. Those closer to cities took a couple of days, while those in remote places could take up to two weeks to receive money. With the coming of foreign banks, and other financial services such as Western Union, sending and receiving money within and outside the country has become instant. The availability of cheaper mobile phones and internet services especially among the middle class have encouraged rapid money transfers. Today, over 80 per cent of adults in some sub-Saharan Africa own a smartphone (Poushter and Oates 2015). Cell phones are used to receive or send money via text messages without a bank account. While only 35 per cent of Africans have access to the internet, compared to the global average of 54 per cent (Internet World Stats 2017), many Africans in cities have internet service which has allowed them to participate in regional and global economies through trade and investment. People can access goods and services within the country, region and abroad. Travel within and out of the continent is easier, faster, and safer with the development of safer and faster modes of transportation.

Millions of African diasporas across the globe have also taken advantage of the revolution in information technologies and digitization of African economies to engage in the continent economically, politically, and socially. Globalization in information technologies has enabled diasporas to remit money and make investments easily. Despite having the highest cost of remitting money in the world, at 9.1 per cent compared to the global average of 7.2 per cent of sending US$200 (World Bank Group 2017), the World Bank projected an increase in 2017 from US$34 billion in 2016 to US$38 billion of formal remittance flows to sub-Saharan Africa (World Bank Group 2017). The sum comprises both global and intra-regional remittances – those sent from regions within the continent. However, informal remittances are not captured in formal transactions because of the difficulties in determining them since they do not go through the formal banking and money transfer channels. Given the significance of remittances in African economies, formal and informal, the African Union recognizes the unique contribution of diasporas to the overall development of Africa, therefore designating them a sixth region of the continent (African Union 2016).

Many diasporas are viewed as the life support for their families, villages, and towns. In fragile states and countries experiencing protracted conflict like Somalia, diaspora finances contribute substantially to the economic, political, and social life of the country. Remittances have been a significant source of income for the general Somali population given the raging conflict and terrorism in the southern part of the country. About US$500 million to US$800 million per year in remittances are sent to Somalia (Kambere 2012). Further, Somalia has significant diaspora investments in the banking, telecommunications, and livestock sectors which have contributed to job creation for Somali youths and economic growth for the country. Even though minimal, remittances have been effective in addressing human security issues on the continent because they are often given directly to people who need them most thereby addressing specific needs like food, shelter, health, and education.

Further globalization in information can be seen to contribute to advancing of human rights in Africa. A multiplicity of actors – individuals, Non-Governmental Organizations (NGOs), Intergovernmental Organizations (INGOs), and the private sector have been able to respond to and prevent human rights violations, particularly those that concern women. Ordinary people are more conscious of human rights violations and can efficiently mobilize through local networks and new technology on social media like Facebook, Twitter, and WhatsApp as part of social movements for human security. Movements against girl child marriages and female genital mutilation (FGM) have been partly successful because actors can communicate quickly and across borders (Equality Now 2017). Consequently, globalization in information and communication technologies has had a positive impact in promoting human security on the continent.

State fragility, civil war, and insecurity in Africa

Africa's engagement in the global economy is seen to exacerbate specific human security threats and sometimes render measures to address insecurity ineffective. Particularly in conflict and fragile states, globalization seems to prolong civil war as well as support insurgents, terrorist groups, and organized crimes nationally and across borders (Kabandula and Shaw 2018b).

Civil war and state fragility are prevalent in Africa. They pose the highest trans-border security threat given their connection to terrorism and organized crime. While state fragility is highly controversial, African countries rank highest in fragility susceptibility (or state failure) due to the pervasiveness of civil war, a significant indicator of state fragility or failure. The World Bank and Fund for Peace (FFP) indexes show more African countries characterized as fragile (World Bank 2018). The Fund for Peace 2018 Fragile States Index puts the continent fragility as either warning or on high alert (Fund for Peace 2018).

Information technologies have necessitated the growth of spaces where states have limited, weak, contested or absent control or authority. These could be social, political (fragile states), and economic spaces (Clunan and Trinkunas 2010). In particular cyberspace, offshore banking institutions have been most challenging for African states to exert control over because of the rise of powerful non-state actors that contest and undermine state authority and legitimacy. The state has little control over cyberspace, which is used to undermine human security mainly using online banking activities. In this sense, globalization has disaggregated state authority among a range of non-state actors including transnational corporations, NGOs and INGOs, and terrorist groups (Clunan and Trinkunas 2010). As a result, the state is no longer the sole custodian of security, law, justice, or order. Thus, the role of the state as a security actor is reduced, bringing to question the legitimacy of the state and its ability to provide security for its citizenry.

Due to global interconnectedness, fragile states as "ungoverned spaces" are increasingly seen to contribute to global insecurity and negatively impact the global political economy. A state is considered fragile, weak, or failing if it does not guarantee public order (through legitimate use of force) within its borders and fails to support the international system and global order (Schneckener 2006). Fragile states are seen to harbour security threats with national, regional, and international implications including terrorism, nuclear proliferation, human rights violations, poverty, armed conflict, and refugee flows (Cook and Downie 2015). However, Menkhaus (2004) and Mantzikos (2011) dispute these claims by suggesting that fragile states like Somalia are unfriendly to foreign terrorist who prefer a complacent central government for their own security.

Information technologies have been found to prolong and intensify civil wars, and encourage state failure. McRae (2001) shows how information technologies such as the internet and offshore banking institutions enable non-state actors to acquire resources to continue the war and make it difficult to protect civilians. Non-state actors with illegal control of local resources such as gold and diamonds can trade on the international black markets and use the money to pay for guns. They are also able to keep and access their funds in international banks. The conflicts in Sierra Leone (1991–2002), Somalia (2006 to present), and Nigeria (2009 to present) are cases in point.

Information technologies and terrorism in Africa

Parts of East Africa, North Africa, West Africa, and the Sahel region are the new terrorism and extremism epicentres (Aning and Abdallah 2016). Notable groups include Al-Shabaab, Boko Haram, AQIM (al-Qaeda in Islamic Maghreb) (North Africa), Ansar Dine, and the Movement for Oneness and Jihad in West Africa (MUJAO) (US Department of State 2016). Contemporary terrorism is distinct in the sense that it is mostly perpetrated by non-state actors motivated by religious, political, and economic reasons. Terrorist activities in Africa transcend borders, are well organized, deadly, and ever adaptive.

Terrorist groups such as Al-Shabaab and Boko Haram have benefited from the revolution in information technology to strengthen, expand, and sustain their insurgency. For instance, Al-Shabaab today is a fundamentally different group from that of 2006. Despite the AU multinational peace operation (African Union Mission in Somalia, AMISOM), the group has become transnational and has extended its reach to most countries in East Africa and some parts of Southern Africa (Mozambique), and established transnational networks with Al-Qaeda and the Islamic State in Iraq and Syria (ISIS) (IGAD 2016). Al-Shabaab has survived and sustained its activities by utilizing readily available and sophisticated information technologies for recruitment and financing. The group uses many social media avenues such as YouTube, Twitter, and Facebook to recruit followers and fighters, and for fundraising.

Al-Shabaab has adopted many ways of financing its activities. Locally, it is mainly through kidnapping, illegal sales of ivory, extorting local businesses through illegal taxes, and investing in businesses. Al-Shabaab invests in local business big and small in Somalia and Kenya. They allegedly own substantial shares in one of Somalia's telecommuting company – Hormuud Telecom (Sperber 2018). Nonetheless, a substantial share of their finances come from sympathetic foreign governments, charities, and Somali diaspora (Masters and Sergie 2018). The group was forced to look for outside funding after it lost control of its major local trade at Kismayo and Bakara market in Mogadishu and suffered a disruption of its charcoal trade by AMISOM and Somali forces (Kambere 2012).

As already mentioned in the section on digital economies and human security in Africa, diaspora finances have been a significant source of funding for the general Somali population. However, it is almost impossible to determine how much of these of finances goes to funding Al-Shabaab. Since the US Department of Justice crackdown on Al-Shabaab financiers in 2012, there are fewer to none cases of Al-Shabaab fundraising reported in the recent past. However, it does not mean that Al-Shabaab has stopped receiving transnational finances, it could mean that people have found other ways of evading authorities or detection. Shadow banking – another aspect of globalization and information technology offers money transferring services without detection.

Shadow banking can be defined as full or partial credit intermediate entities and activities outside the regular banking system (Claessens and Ratnovski 2012). It enables organized crime networks such as terrorist organizations and money laundering syndicates to move money without detection. Minimally or fully regulated facilities such as a pre-paid store, debit cards, mobile phone money transfers, and virtual currencies like Bitcoin and cryptocurrencies can be used without any documentation or identification to move small and large sums of money across borders without detection. The lack of documentation when loading or acquiring the money makes it almost impossible for authorities to track such transactions. Although Western Union and VISA have put a limit on the amount of money an individual can send, or load on a card respectively. Both companies have developed anti-money laundering and anti-terrorist financing (AML/ATF) standards to curb money laundering or financing terrorism through their services (VISA 2015; Western Union 2014).

Depite many anti-terrorist financing regimes, terrorist groups in Africa and the world continue to access global finances. In 2016, European Union's law enforcement agency (Europol) reported over 3,000 individuals identified in the Panama Papers (individuals with offshore accounts) as credible matches for suspected terrorists and cybercriminals (Pegg 2016). Further, legal experts have shown the possibility of financing terrorism through offshore accounts and shell companies. The uncomplicated process of creating shell companies and the secrecy associated with offshore bank accounts enable terrorists to mask their true identities from law enforcement (Baughman 2016), and so gain access to the global finances to further their cause.

Therefore, it should not be a surprise that Al-Shabaab's overseas financing seems untraceable. Al-Shabaab allegedly receives financial and military support from foreign governments such as Eritrea, Iran, Saudi Arabia, Syria, Qatar, and Yemen. In 2012, a UN report from the Monitoring Group on Somalia and Eritrea (SEM) said Eritrea through its embassy in Nairobi was giving about $80,000 per month for 10 years to members of Al-Shabaab. Further, Gulf States were accused by the Somali Federal government of providing funds and weapons to Al-Shabaab. The Gulf States also continued trading with Al-Shabaab despite the charcoal ban and arms embargo sanctioned by the UNSC (SEM 2012). However, all the states denied any involvement, financial or otherwise, with Al-Shabaab, proving the point about the difficulty of tracking finances meant for illegal or criminal activities, in this case, terrorism. The impact of continued terrorist activities in East Africa, West Africa, and the Sahel region is devastating human insecurity.

Transnational organized crime

Transnational organized crimes (TOC) are among the most daunting security challenges in Africa today. They include but are not limited to human and drug trafficking, money laundering, piracy, and small arms proliferation (Aning and Abdallah 2016). Information technology aids criminal activities in fragile states as it enables the export of local or regional conflict and insecurity to the global level. Improved communication makes it possible for entrepreneurs of violence to link and mobilize through the internet, radio, and cell phones.

Transnational organized crimes seem to flourish in fragile states and conflict situations because of generalized insecurity. This insecurity threatens the security of neighbouring states and other regions as refugee flows and criminal networks linked to belligerents enter and establish networks. Eastern Congo is an example. There are over ten rebel groups from Rwanda, Uganda, and the Congo (IRIN 2010), all with different grievances and goals hence the continuance of the war in that part of the state and persistent state and human insecurity for the country, its neighbours, the region, and the globe.

The United Nations Office on Drugs and Crimes (UNODC) Transnational Organized Crime in Eastern Africa threat assessment report notes that conflict and poverty have contributed to increase in human smuggling across the Gulf of Aden and the Red Sea to Yemen (UNODC 2013). In 2015, the United Nations High Commission for Refugees (UNHCR) reported an increase in refugees arriving in Yemen via the Horn of Africa from 65,000 in 2013 to over 82,000 (Al Batati 2015). At the same time, there is an increase in heroin and ivory trafficking on the continent to the Middle East and Asia. More than 22 tons of heroin is estimated to be transported through East Africa by year (UNODC 2013). While piracy seems to be under control since 2012, the threat has not been eliminated entirely. Pirates continue to threaten maritime security in East Africa and more recently in West Africa. Therefore, piracy remains a lucrative venture for Al-Shabaab and Boko Haram in tough economic times.

The conflict, transnational organized crime and terrorism nexus

The most distinct feature about the aforementioned effects of aspects of globalization on human security is their complex interlinkage creating a conflict–TOC–terrorism nexus. A conflict–TOC–terrorism nexus strains and sometimes renders state-centric (military) efforts to promote peace and security ineffective as has been the case in Somalia and Democratic Republic of Congo. As alluded to in the section on civil war and fragile states, criminal activities and networks including terrorism, drug, and human trafficking thrive in conflict situations. Globalization in information technologies has entrenched organized crimes. Increasingly, armed groups like Al-Shabaab and Boko Haram are engaging in TOC to raise funds to further their insurgence. Al-Shabaab in Somalia exemplifies this situation. After losing control of major local trade at the port of Kismayo and Bakara market in Mogadishu, Al-Shabaab's local revenues declined significantly forcing the group to turn TOC in heroin trafficking to Tanzania and ivory poaching in Kenya (UNODC 2013). The complex linkage among these contemporary security threats in Africa has made it problematic to promote human security on the continent.

Multinational corporations and human security

Multinational Corporations (MNCs) or Transnational Corporations (TNCs) are the main agents of globalization. MNCs are firms that own or control the production of goods or services in one or more countries outside their home country. MNCs vary in size, ownership, strategy, management, and structure (Cohn 2016). Microsoft, Exon Mobile, Beyond Petroleum (BP, formerly British Petroleum), Philips, and Shell are examples. Most TNCs have been American or European until about a decade ago when MNCs from BRICS countries and other emerging powers seemed to overshadow their Western counterparts. China has paved the way for non-Western investments in developing countries. Chinese multinational corporations are very competitive and often supported by the state. They have invested in critical resources and market share across many developing countries especially Africa (Alden and Davies 2006). Therefore, TNCs of all types and sizes are ubiquitous in the contemporary global economy more especially in developing countries. Baregu (1977), when discussing the impact of Western MNCs in Africa, argues that they are both agents of modernization and instruments of American and European finance capital. Indeed, the adverse effects of MNCs on the developing world have been a subject of many academic scholarship as a simple Google Scholar search reveals. MNCs seem to magnify social, development, and political problems relating to worth creation, alienation, domination, and the interface between corporations and national states (Hymer 1970). Other scholars perceive MNCs, especially those from Western countries, as the new form of imperialism which also reinforce underdevelopment (Fieldhouse 2002).

In (physical) security, MNCs manifest as Private Security Companies (PSCs) and Private Military Companies (PMCs). PSCs and PMCs can be both large and small, some of the most common PSCs and PMCs include G4S PLC, ADT Inc., and Securitas AB, and Control Risks, AirScan, and Academi (formerly Blackwater) respectively. Even though a common feature of contemporary security, their use in conflict and fragile states is contentious because of their business with armed non-state actors. The distinction between the PSCs and PMCs is debatable, given some of the security companies like G4S also provide military-related services. Nonetheless, PMCs provide offensive services with a military impact, while PSCs offer defensive services intended to protect people and property (Holmqvist 2005).

PSCs and PMCs are among the most powerful actors in international security given that the state no longer holds a monopoly of force. The commercialization of security is associated with a shift of public-private relations resulting from globalization (Bryden 2006). In Africa, the prevalence of armed conflict, fragile states, and corruption have rendered public security institutions non-functional thus creating a market for PSCs and PMCs. From ordinary citizens, government officials, diplomats, and international staff; basic security facilities like having a guard at the gate of a home or workplace are an everyday necessity. Their affiliation with MNCs gives PSCs and PMCs the ability, capacity, and flexibility to provide security services such as operational support in combat, military advice, training, arms procurement, housing, communications services, intelligence gathering, and crime prevention (Holmqvist 2005). However, PSCs and PMCs are driven by capital and profit, which makes them open for business to whoever can pay for their services, including non-state actors like Al-Shabaab.

The profit motive together with the ability to provide services quickly across borders makes PMCs and PMCs essential players in transnational organized crime. For instance, in Somalia,

Sterling Corporate Services was reported to supply weapons to armed non-state actors including Al-Shabaab. The action made it difficult for the UN arms embargo to be effective (SEM 2012), thereby perpetuating fighting and compromising human security in the country.

Conclusion

This chapter has explored IPE and human security in Africa. It has shown how the main IPE approaches theorize security. The chapter notes a fundamental conceptual shift in security theory and practice following the Cold War. As the world changed in unprecedented ways with globalization, so did the security of the people within the state. The intensification of globalization led to inequality among and within states promoting a paradigm shift in security analysis (referent object). The change in security referent object coupled with the effects of globalization promoted a global approach to addressing insecurity. Human security emerged as an inclusive approach to secure people across the world. However, in the African context, human security has proved difficult to realize in the wake of globalization in ICTs. While ICTs have connected the continent endlessly, encouraged digital economies to flourish, and advanced women and children's rights, ICTs have adversely impacted human security on the continent.

The chapter argues that Africa's engagement in the global economy through ICTs has exacerbated specific human security threats. Particularly in conflict and fragile states, globalization has prolonged conflict/civil war, supported insurgents and terrorist groups, encouraged transnational organized crime, and state failure. Therefore, the chapter concludes that contemporary international political economy poses a threat to human security in Africa and that a human security view allows for contemporary security challenges to be observed and responded to by academics and policymakers alike. As such, IPE could be more beneficial to Africa if non-traditional security-related problems such civil war, TOC, water, energy, and food (WEF–climate nexus) and terrorism are highlighted as well as given due priority in policy making and implementation. Prioritizing people-centred problems in turn serves to address security, economic, and development challenges resulting from the unintended effects of ICTs, consequently improving the prospects of Africa achieving the Sustainable Development Goals.

Bibliography

Acharya, A. 2001. Human Security: East Versus West. *International Journal*, 56(3): 442–460.

Acharya, A. 2004. A Holistic Paradigm. *Security Dialogue*, 35(3): 355–356.

Africa Union. 2000. *The Constitutive Act*. Addis Ababa: African Union.

African Union. 2016. *AU Sixth Region*. Available at: http://auads-nl.org/au-sixth-region/.

Al Batati, S. 2015. *African Migrants Face Death at Sea in Yemen*. Sanaa: Al Jazeera.

Alden, C. and Davies, M. 2006. *Chinese Multinational Corporations in Africa*. Pretoria: Africa Institute of South Africa.

Aning, K. and Abdallah, M. 2016. Confronting Hybrid Threats in Africa: Improving Multidimensional Responses. In: De Coning, C., Gelot., L, and Karlsrud, J. (eds.) *The Future of African Peace Operations: From Janjaweed to Boko Haram*. London: Zed Books: 20–37.

Annan, K. A. 2000. *We the Peoples: The Role of the United Nations in the 21st Century*. New York: United Nations Department of Public Information.

Axworthy, L. 2004. A New Scientific Field and Policy Lens. *Security Dialogue*, 35(3): 348–349.

Balaam, D. and Dillman, B. 2015. *Introduction to International Political Economy*. 6th ed. London: Routledge.

Baregu, M. 1977. Multinational Corporations in Africa. *Taamuli: A Political Science Forum*, 7(2): 10–31.

Baughman, S. 2016. *Panama Papers Show How Easy it is to Finance Terror Using U.S. Shell Companies*. Boston: The Conversation.

Beckwith, K. 2005. A Common Language of Gender? *Politics & Gender*, 1(1): 128–137.

Bergamaschi, I. and Tickner, A. B. 2017. Introduction: South-South Cooperation Beyond the Myths – A Critical Analysis. In: Bergamaschi, I., Moore, P. and Tickner, A. (eds.) *South-South Cooperation Beyond the Myths: Rising Donors, New Aid Practices?* London: Springer Nature: 1–28.

Besada, H., Goetz, A. and Werner, K. 2010. African Solutions for African Problems and Shared R2P. In: Besada, H. (ed.) *Crafting an African Security Architecture: Addressing Regional Peace and Conflict in the 21st Century*. Burlington: Ashgate Publishing Company: 1–15.

Bigo, D. 2006. Internal and External Aspects of Security. *European Security*, 15(4): 385–407.

Booth, K. 2005. *Beyond Critical Security Studies. Critical Studies and World Politics*. Boulder: Lynne Rienner.

Boserup, E., Tan, S. and Toulmin, C. 2007. *Woman's Role in Economic Development. Routledge*. 1st ed. London: Routledge.

Bryden, A. 2006. Approaching the Privatisation of Security from a Security Governance Perspective. In: Bryden, A. and M. Caparini, M. (eds.) *Private Actors and Security Governance*. Geneva: LIT & DCAF: 3–22.

Buzan, B. 2004. A Reductionist, Idealistic Notion That Adds Little Analytical Value. *Security Dialogue*, 35(3): 369–370.

Buzan, B. 2009. *People, States & Fear: An Agenda for International Security Studies in the Post-Cold War Era*. 2nd ed. Colchester: ECPR Press.

Claessens, S. and Ratnovski, L. 2012. What is Shadow Banking. *Economics and Policy*, 12(12): 1–36.

Clunan, A. and Trinkunas, H. 2010. Conceptualizing Ungoverned Spaces: Territorial Statehood, Contested Authority, and Sovereignty. In: *Ungoverned Spaces: Alternatives to State Authority in an Era of Soften Sovereignty*. Stanford: Stanford University Press: 17–33.

Cohn, C. 2013. Women and Wars: Towards a Conceptual Framework. In: C. Cohn, ed. *Women and Wars: Contested Histories, Uncertain Futures*. Cambridge: Polity Press: 1–35.

Cohn, T. H. 2016. *Global Political Economy: Theory and Practice*. 6th ed. London: Routledge.

Cook, J. and Downie, R. 2015. *Rethinking Engagement in Fragile States*, Washington, DC: CSIS Africa Program.

Doyle, M. 1986. Liberalism and World Politics. *American Political Science Review*, 80(4): 1151–1169.

Dunn, B. 2009. *Global Political Economy: A Marxist Critique*. London: Pluto Press.

Equality Now. 2017. *End FGM*. Available at: www.equalitynow.org/end_fgm.

Fieldhouse, D. 2002. A New Imperial System? The Role of the Multinational Corporations Reconsidered. In: Frieden, J. and Lake, D. (eds.) *International Political Economy: Perspectives on Global Power and Wealth*. London: Routledge: 177–189.

Fund for Peace. 2018. *Fragile States Index*. Available at: http://fundforpeace.org/fsi/.

General Assembly. 2005. Resolution adopted by the General Assembly on 16 September 2005 A/RES/60/1. 2005 World Summit Outcome . New York: United Nations General Assembly.

Harrison, G. 2010. *Neoliberal Africa: The Impact of Global Social Engineering*. London: Zed Books.

Holmqvist, C. 2005. *Private Security Companies: The Case for Regulation*. Stockholm: Stockholm International Peace Research Institute.

Hubert, D. 2004. An Idea that Works in Practice. *Security Dialogue*, 35(3): 351–352.

Hunt, S, and Morgan, R. 1995. The Comparative Advantage Theory of Competition. *The Journal of Marketing*, 59(2): 1–15.

Hymer, S. 1970. The Efficiency (Contradictions) of Multinational Corporations. *The American Economic Review*, 60(2): 441–448.

ICISS. 2001. *The Responsibility to Protect: Report of the International Commission on Intervention and State Sovereignty*. Ottawa: International Development Research Centre.

IGAD. 2016. *Al-Shabaab as a Transnational Security Threat*. Addis Ababa: Intergovernmental Authority on Development.

Internet World Stats. 2017. *Internet World Stats*. Available at: https://internetworldstats.com/stats1.htm.

IRIN. 2010. *Who's Who Among Armed Groups in the East*. Available at: www.irinnews.org/report/89494/drc-who's-who-among-armed-groups-east.

Kabandula, A. and Shaw, T. 2018a. Rising Powers and the Horn of Africa: Conflicting Regionalisms. *Third World Quarterly*.

Kabandula, A. and Shaw, T. 2018b. *Security and Development in the Horn of Africa: Emerging Powers, and Competing Regionalisms*. 11(11): 1–9. Institute for Peace and Security Studies Policy Brief.

Kaldor, M. 2012. *New and Old Wars: Organized Violence in a Global Era*. Cambridge: Polity Press.

Kambere, G. 2012. Financing Al Shabaab: The Vital Port of Kismayo. *Combatting Terrorism Exchange (CTX)*, 2(3): 40–48.

Kant, I. 1917. *Perpetual Peace: A Philosophical Essay*. London: G. Allen & Unwin Limited.

Karns, M. and Mingst, K. 2010. *International Organizations: The Politics and Processes of Global Governance*. 2nd ed. Boulder: Lynne Rienner Publishers.

Keohane, R. and Nye, J. 1977. *Power and Interdependence*. 2nd ed. Boston: Scott, Foresman & Company.

Krause, K. 2004. The Key to a Powerful Agenda, If Properly Delimited. *Security Dialogue*, 35(3): 367–368.

Kshetri, N. 2013. *Cybercrime and Cybersecurity in the Global South*. London: Palgrave Macmillan.

Kuwali, D. 2009. The End of Humanitarian Intervention: Evaluation of the African Union's Right of Intervention. *African Journal on Conflict Resolution* 9(1): 41–61.

MacFarlane, S. 2004. A Useful Concept that Risks Losing Its Political Salience. *Security Dialogue*, 35(3): 368–369.

Mantzikos, I. 2011. Somalia and Yemen: The Links between Terrorism and State Failure. *Digest of Middle East Studies*, 20(2): 242–260.

Masters, J. and Sergie, M. 2018. *Al-Shabab*. Available at: www.cfr.org/backgrounder/al-shabab.

McRae, R. 2001. Human Security in a Globalized World. In: R. McRae, D. Hubert, R. McRae and D. Hubert (eds.) *Human Security and the New Diplomacy: Protecting People, Promoting Peace*. London: McGill-Queen's University Press: 14–27.

Menkhaus, K. 2004. *Somalia: State Collapse and the Threat of Terrorism*. London: Routledge.

Muyeba, S. 2008. *Globalization and Africa in the Twenty-First Century: A Zambian Perspective*. Bloomington: Author House.

Newman, E. 2004. A Normatively Attractive but Analytically Weak Concept. *Security Dialogue*, 35(3): 358–359.

O'Brien, R. and Williams, M. 2016. *Global Political Economy: Evolution & Dynamics*. 5th ed. London: Macmillan International Higher Education.

Owen, T. 2004. Human Security-Conflict, Critique and Consensus: Colloquium Remarks and a Proposal for a Threshold-based Definition. *Security Dialogue*, 35(3): 373–387.

Paris, R. 2004. Still an Inscrutable Concept. *Security Dialogue*, 35(3): 370–372.

Pattison, J. 2010. *Humanitarian Intervention and the Responsibility to Protect: Who Should Intervene*. Oxford: Oxford University Press.

Patomäki, H. 2016. International Political Economy and Security. In Cavelty, M. and Balzacq, T. (eds.) *Routledge Handbook of Security Studies*. 2nd ed. London: Routledge: 32–42.

Pegg, D. 2016. Panama Papers: Europol Links 3,500 Names to Suspected Criminals. *The Guardian*.

Peoples, C. and Vaughan-Williams, N. 2015. *Critical Security Studies: An Introduction*. 2nd ed. London: Routledge.

Poushter, J. and Oates, R. 2015. *Cell Phones in Africa: Communication Lifeline*. Washington, DC: Pew Research Centre.

Schneckener, U. 2006. Fragile Statehood, Armed Non-State Actors. In: Bryden, A. and Caparini, M. (eds.) *Private Actors and Security Governance*. Geneva: LIT & DCAF: 23–40.

SEM. 2012. *Letter Dated 27 June 2012 from the Members of the Monitoring Group on Somalia and Eritrea addressed to the Chairman of the Security Council Committee Pursuant to Resolutions 751 (1992) and 1907 (2009) Concerning Somalia and Eritrea*, New York: United Nations.

Sen, K. 2001. *Development as Freedom*. 2nd ed. New York: Oxford University Press.

Sperber, A. 2018. Somalia is a Country Without an Army. *Foreign Policy*. https://foreignpolicy.com/2018/08/07/somalia-is-a-country-without-an-army-al-shabab-terrorism-horn-africa-amisom.

Thakur, R. 2004. A Political Worldview. *Security Dialogue*, 35(3): 347–348.

UNDP. 1994. *Human Development Report*. New York: Oxford Press.

UNODC. 2013. *Transnational Organized Crime in Eastern Africa: A Threat Assessment*. Vienna: United Nations Office on Drugs and Crime.

US Department of State. 2016. *Foreign Terrorist Organizations*. Available at: www.state.gov/j/ct/rls/other/des/123085.htm.

Van der Merwe, J. 2016. Seeing Through the Mist: New Contenders for the African Space? In: Van Der Merwe, J. and Arkhangelskaya, A. (eds.) *Emerging Powers in Africa: A New Wave in the Relationship?* London: Springer Nature: 1–14.

VISA. 2015. *Anti-Money Laundering/Anti-Terrorist Financing (AML/ATF) and Sanctions Compliance Program Questionnaire*. Available at: http://catalystcorp.org/docs/default-source/default-document-library/visa-amlq.pdf?sfvrsn=2.

Waltz, K. 2010. *Theory of International Politics*. 2nd ed. Long Grove: Waveland Press.

Western Union. 2014. *Agent Anti-Money Laundering*. Denver: Western Union.

World Bank Group. 2017. *Migration and Development Brief 28*. Washington, DC: World Bank Group.

World Bank. 2018. *Harmonized List of Fragile Situations*. Available at: www.worldbank.org/en/topic/fragilityconflictviolence/brief/harmonized-list-of-fragile-situations.

33
Regionalism in the Middle East
Turkish case in perspective

Mustafa Kutlay and Hüseyin Emrah Karaoğuz

Introduction

This chapter discusses regionalism in the Middle East with particular reference to the Turkish case. The current international order is passing through major transformations, characterized by two interconnected trends. First, the US-led unipolar system gradually gives way to a multi-polar world. The unipolar moment emerged with the collapse of the Soviet Union and has gradually waned in 2000s. The re-emergence of non-western great powers, China in particular, has been reshaping the international system by undermining hegemonic control mechanisms at the global level. Second, regions have become the main level of analysis at which power con-stellations are being shaped in a post-hegemonic era. Regionalism is now considered as one of the key trends in contemporary international relations (Acharya 2007; Katzenstein 2005) and regional powers are becoming more important actors in shaping alternative orders in their respective regions (Flockhart 2016; Nolte 2010).

This chapter focuses on the recent regionalism attempts in the Middle East with particular reference to the Turkish case. Turkey has pursued proactive policies over the last two decades in the Middle East towards a more integrated regional order. The regional policies pursued by the Turkish ruling elite are illustrative in terms of the potentials and limits of middle power activism in an unstable regional environment. The rest of the chapter proceeds as follows: The second section provides an overview of the dynamics of regionalism. The third section applies the framework to the Turkish case by questioning the rise and fall of the Turkish trading state. The fourth section concludes the chapter.

Regionalism: a framework for analysis

Region and regionalism are elusive concepts (Breslin et al. 2002). As Buzan (1998: 68) states, 'the concept of region is frequently used but rarely described openly'. Despite the ambiguity surrounding the concept, Thompson (1973: 101) specifies 'necessary and sufficient conditions' for a regional sub-system: (i) geographical proximity, (ii) the density of interactions between regional actors 'to the extent that a change at one point in the subsystem affects other points', and (iii) the internal and external recognition of the subsystem as 'a distinctive area'. Regional integration is defined as the process of developing common rules, functioning institutions and regulatory standards to foster formal economic, political and security linkages between states located within a regional subsystem. The key puzzle about regionalism, as Mattli (1999) points out, is that most attempts fail and only a few of them succeed. When and how will regional integration schemes function as envisaged? What explains the key differences between failures and successful attempts? Following Mattli (1999) we can suggest that supply and demand conditions inform the outcomes of regional integration attempts.

On the demand side, the market conditions must be favourable for regional integration to yield concrete results. The expected gains from market integration in the form of trade, investments and labour mobility must be significant enough to motivate actors pursuing regional rather than extra-regional economic transactions.[1] On that note, not only the economies of scale, market proximity and market size but also the economic complementarity within a region determines the demand conditions whether regional integration succeeds or fails (Mattli 1999: 42, 47; also see Haggard 1995). On the supply side as well, there must be a set of political factors that supplement regionalism. First, as regionalism is basically a political process, political leaders of the regional states must demonstrate a certain level of willingness to deepen regional integration process. The ideological factors, regimes types and/or economic drivers play their roles that shape the preferences of ruling elites. The willingness of the leaders of key regional powers, in this context, appear crucial as those actors provide public goods and invest in the supply of 'commitment institutions' that help overcoming collective action problems and facilitate political integration (Mattli 1999: 43).[2] On the other hand, Schirm (2010: 199) underlines the importance of the eagerness of other regional actors to cooperate with the regional leaders as 'successful leadership depends not only on resources and ambition but also crucially upon the support of followers'.

One of the defining characteristics of the Middle East regionalism is the intensity of regional rivalries under heavy involvement of external actors. As Fawcett and Gandois (2010: 623) underline, 'regional leadership and institution building are decidedly lacking' in the Middle East. In terms of the distribution of power capabilities several states assume a key role in the region but none of the regional actors are in a position to play hegemonic roles. Furthermore, the long shadow of history and the deeply embedded legacies of the historical conflicts among regional actors still haunt the current political arrangements. Several regional integration attempts during the Cold War era and the post-1990s failed in the Middle East due to wars, foreign intervention, regime insecurity and incompatible visions of regional actors (Fawcett and Gandois 2010). Therefore, the supply of regional institutions proves a challenging task for Middle Eastern regional actors attempting to play a regional leadership role.

Box 33.1 Regionalism in the Middle East

In the Middle East, many regionalism attempts have been launched in the twentieth century. However, these attempts largely failed. In 1945, the League of Arab States (AL) was created. The aim to establish AL was to promote ëpan-Arabismí among Arab states. However, the growing emphasis put on sovereignty by the Arab states curbed the attempts to establish well functioning regional organizations. Therefore, ambitious projects such as the Arab Common Market (in 1964) remained heavily under-institutionalized. By the 1970s, an Islamic version of the AL, the Organization of the Islamic Conference (1969) was created. Gulf Cooperation Council established in 1981 is another notable regional integration project in the Middle East. United Arab Emirates,

Bahrain, Kingdom of Saudi Arabia, Oman, Qatar, Kuwait are the members of Gulf Cooperation Council. The final regional institution is the Arab Maghreb Union, which was established in 1989. The aim of the Arab Maghreb Union was to establish deep economic integration within Middle Eastern states. However, it proved one of the least successful attempts (also see Owen 1999).

In short, the regions with market potential for integration and political leaders willing to deepen regional integration process are more likely to succeed (Mattli 1999). The Middle East is a useful case to assess the scope conditions of regionalism. Although regionalism in the Middle East has a long history, most initiatives failed due to unfavourable supply and demand conditions. Supply-side factors such as under-institutionalization and lack of a regional leader 'in search of followers' undermined regionalism attempts. Demand-side factors, such as weak economic complementarity and deep-seated rivalries also hampered regional integration in the Middle East. The following part discusses potentials and pitfalls of regional integration in the Middle East with reference to Turkey's attempts as a key actor in the region.

The rise and fall of the 'Turkish trading state'

The Turkish case, more specifically the debate on the rise and fall of the 'Turkish trading state', is illustrative as it exemplifies many of the above dynamics.[3] While the first decade of the new millennium witnessed the rise of Turkey's enthusiastic attempts at fostering regionalism by way of economic integration, the following years witnessed the opposite trend – Turkey's endeavour in the Middle East to deepen regionalism through economic integration and cultural affinity were replaced with traditional security concerns in foreign policy-making. This section examines this process with its effects on Middle East regionalism.

2002–2010: the rise of the Turkish trading state

What accounts for Turkey's reinvigorated interest in deepening regional integration in the Middle East? Many factors and conditions are said to influence Turkish foreign policy over the last two decades, including Turkey's Europeanization process (Aydın and Açıkmeşe 2007; Öniş 2003), redefinition of its state identity (Bozdağlıoğlu 2003; Cizre 2003; Dağı 2005), domestic political developments (Bilgin 2008) and geopolitical factors (Karaosmanoğlu 2000; Sayarı, 2000). All these are derived from different International Relations theories and approaches to foreign policy, including variants of constructivism (Bozdağlıoğlu 2003; Cizre 2003; Dağı 2005). Among many contributions that shed light on different dimensions of the issue, only a few systematically attempted to explain the motives of Turkey's regional policies with reference to economic elements, as many attributed only secondary importance to such dynamics. However, economic calculations had also become relevant in foreign policy-making in Turkey especially in the first decade of the 2000s.

Box 33.2 The original formulation of the 'trading state'

In his book *Rise of the Trading State: Commerce and Conquest in the Modern World* published in 1986, Richard Rosecrance introduced the concept 'trading state' to the literature. In essence, Rosecrance claimed that states can either become a 'trading state' or a 'territorial state', and this is partly conditioned by the international or global environment in which the states operate. Whereas a 'trading state' specializes in commerce and aims at economic integration to foster trade and wealth accumulation, a 'territorial state' prioritizes military expansion to maximize wealth through its control over new territories. One of the main claims of Rosecrance is that current circumstances force states to choose and embrace trading strategies over military expansion since, while the marginal benefit expected from military expansion has decreased in time, trade has become more appealing to all actors in an interdependent world. In other words, the increasing volume of trade and networks have constrained state aggression, since key decision makers have searched for and found new opportunities to enhance wealth and prosperity via commerce. This latter claim is also one of the main assertions of interdependence perspective (Keohane 1984; Keohane and Nye 1972).

Kirişçi (2009) arguably captures this idea best in an oft-cited article on the 'Turkish trading state'. In a nutshell, the story goes as follows (Kirişçi 2009; Kirişçi 2013; Kirişçi and Kaptanoğlu 2011): In comparison to the pre-1980 period, the volume of foreign trade increased dramatically in Turkey in the 2000s. While the volume of total exports increased from US$1.4 billion in 1975 to US$113.9 billion in 2010, total imports likewise increased from US$4.7 billion to US$185.5 in the same period (Table 33.1). Whereas the weight of total trade in gross domestic product (GDP) was 13.8 per cent in 1975, it was recorded as 38.8 per cent in 2010 (Table 33.1). The structural transformation in the 1980s through which import–substitution–industrialization was replaced with the neoliberal-guided export-oriented industrialization in Turkey (Kirişçi 2009: 43–45). Turgut Özal's initiatives, one of the key political actors at the time as being the leading figure of the neoliberal restructuring as the Prime Minister (1983–1989) and the President of Turkey (1989–1993), sow the seeds of the 'Turkish trading trade'. Regarding the structural transformation, the period between 1983 and 1989 witnessed Turkish economy's rapid liberalization and integration into the world economy. Trade was liberalized in a step-by-step manner in the 1980s, and then a big step was undertaken with capital account liberalization in 1989.

Özal himself encouraged several economic activities that aimed to increase interdependency in the Middle East and thereby promote peace in the region (Atlı 2011). Even though some failed, such as the water pipeline project of 1986 with which Turkish water was to be carried to the Gulf countries and Israel, many others were successful (Kirişçi 2009: 44). In order to symbolize Turkey's economic-oriented approach to foreign policy and to support Turkish firms' attempts to secure shares in foreign markets, Özal took a very high number of business people

Table 33.1 Turkey's foreign trade performance in selected years (US$ billion)

	1975	1985	1995	2000	2005	2010	2011	2012	2013	2015	2016	2017
GDP	44.6	67.2	169.5	273.0	501.4	771.9	832.5	874.0	950.6	859.8	863.7	851.5
Total export	1.4	8.0	21.6	27.8	73.5	113.9	134.9	152.5	151.8	143.8	142.5	157.0
Total import	4.7	11.3	35.7	54.5	116.8	185.5	240.8	236.5	251.7	207.2	198.6	233.8
Overall trade	6.1	19.3	57.3	82.3	190.3	299.4	375.7	389.0	403.5	351.1	341.1	390.8
Overall trade (% of GDP)	13.8	28.7	33.8	30.1	37.9	38.8	45.1	44.5	42.4	40.8	39.5	45.9

Source: TÜİK and Work Bank Indicators (only GDP figures).

with him to state visits (Atlı 2011; Buğra 1994). Özal also tried to attract more foreign tourists by relaxing the Turkish visa regime since greater mobility meant deepened interdependence and a chance of achieving peace in the Middle East via the trade, human interaction and investments.

Examples can be proliferated to illustrate Turkish economy's neoliberal transformation and economic integration to the global markets in the 1980s. In any case, the key point is that the change in perspective in the early 1980s, whereby the leading cadre in Turkey embraced the Washington consensus, laid the groundwork for the rise of the Turkish trading state in the 2000s. As the turbulent 1990s had come to an end by the end of that decade (Öniş and Rubin 2003), trade once again surfaced as an important dimension thanks to the efforts of influential state officials such as İsmail Cem, the Minister of Foreign Affairs from 1997 to 2002, and the continuing increase in the volume of foreign trade (Table 33.1). After the Justice and Development Party (AKP in Turkish acronym) had come to power in November 2002, it inherited Özal and his followers' economic-oriented foreign policy strategy. On top of this, relieved from the systemic constraints of the Cold War era, the AKP government crafted a much more proactive strategy regarding the Middle East regionalism by capitalizing on the religious and cultural affinity (Öniş 2011; Öniş and Kutlay 2017). As a result, the supply-side conditions gained momentum as the AKP government has become more willing to increase Turkey's role as a region-building actor in the Middle East.

On the demand-side, the non-state actors such as economic interest groups also perceived the growing market size and demand in the Middle East as an opportunity for Turkish firms. The business associations, for instance, started to play a more pronounced role in further consolidation of the trading state mentality in Turkey. As rightly noted, the Independent Industrialists and Businessmen's Association (MÜSİAD), the Turkish Industry and Business Association (TÜSİAD), the Turkish Union of Chambers and Commodity Exchanges (TOBB), the Turkish Exporters Assembly (TİM), the Foreign Economic Relations Board (DEİK), the International Transporters Association (UND) and the Turkish Contractors Association (TMD) had been among the dominant associations (Atlı 2011; Kirişci and Kaptanoğlu 2011; Öniş 2011). In the words of Kirişci (2009: 49), 'these interest groups not only interact[ed] with various government agencies, but also [had] direct access to the government itself and [were] capable of shaping public opinion [in the Middle East]'. As a result, the balance was tilted in favour of trade-friendly foreign policy rather than a security-based approach. The trade-friendly approach was utilized within the context of 'zero-problems with neighbors policy' of the AKP, which was most ambitiously promoted by Ahmet Davutoğlu (former Minister of Foreign Affairs and Prime Minister) especially until the beginning of Arab upheavals in 2011. In a nutshell, zero-problem policy reflected Turkey's willingness to rely on its soft power and regional institution-building attempts in the Middle East by using geopolitical advantages, market proximity and strong cultural ties to the region.

As Kirişci (2009: 48–49) argued, even though the causes of the zero-problem approach can be explained in different ways, one possible line of explanation is related to economic dynamics, mainly Turkish businesses' willingness to find new export markets. For instance, different business associations' lobbying efforts both in Turkey and Iraq influenced the Turkish military intervention into Northern Iraq in 2008 (to reduce the potential harm to trade and the construction market in Northern Iraq), the Turkish–Armenian Business Development Council played a role in Abdullah Gül's, the then President of Turkey, momentous visit to Armenia in 2008, and TOBB's active involvement partly enabled Shimon Peres and Mahmud Abbas' visit to Turkey in 2007 (see Altunisik and Martin 2011). In particular, as a key regional actor in the Middle East and a gateway for Turkish exporters, Syria occupied the centre stage in Turkey's regional policies. The Turkish policy-makers pursued active diplomacy to liberalize the Syrian political and economic system. The attempts paved the way for partial economic integration just before the Syrian civil war as visa requirements were lifted between the two countries. Furthermore, in June 2010, Turkey, Syria, Jordan and Lebanon established the Quadripartite High Level Strategic Cooperation Council that aimed to create an economic zone for free movement of goods and people among the four countries.

The regional breakdown of Turkish foreign trade in the 2000s indicates that economic ties with the Middle East were intensified in absolute and relative terms. For instance, while the volume of the Turkish trade with the region was US$5.9 billion in 1996, this increased to US$36.3 billion in 2010. The share of foreign trade with the Middle East in Turkey's total foreign trade also increased from 8 per cent to 12 per cent in the same period. Likewise, there had been an increase in Turkish exports to many countries in the region, including Syria, Iraq, Iran, Israel, Algeria, Tunisia, Libya and Egypt (Table 33.2). Between 2000 and 2010, Turkey signed free trade agreements with key Middle Eastern countries, introduced visa-free travel, and created joint inter-ministerial councils to overcome commitment and collective action problems (Kutlay 2011). As a result, between 2000 and 2010, overall exports to these countries increased from US$2.1 billion to US$19.4 billion – with the share of total exports to the region in Turkey's overall exports increasing from 7.5 per cent to 17 per cent.[4]

To sum up, as the policy-making elite in Turkey embraced neoliberal restructuring in the 1980s, the sheer volume of foreign trade increased tremendously in the following decades. With the emergence of new and powerful actors who had a stake in trade, there occurred a shift in the Turkish foreign policy towards the late 1990s from the security-based understanding to a more economy-oriented perspective. The AKP government, especially until Arab upheavals, strove to deepen regionalism in the Middle East by placing Turkey as a key regional actor through economy and soft power instruments. As a result, Turkey's trading state strategy encouraged regionalism in the Middle East by promoting economic interdependence.

Post-2010: the fall of the Turkish trading state

The trading state concept captures the driving economic logic behind Turkey's regional integration policies in the Middle East in the first decade of the twenty-first century. By prioritizing the economic incentives over regional security concerns, Turkish policy-makers introduced a

Table 33.2 Turkey's exports to selected Middle East countries in the 2000s (US$ billion)

	2000	2005	2007	2010	2011	2012	2013	2014	2015	2016	2017
Syria	0.2	0.6	0.8	1.8	1.6	0.5	1.0	1.8	1.5	1.3	1.4
Iraq	0.0	2.8	2.8	6.0	8.3	10.8	11.9	10.9	8.5	7.6	9.1
Iran	0.2	0.9	1.4	3.0	3.6	9.9	4.2	3.9	3.7	5.0	3.3
Israel	0.7	1.5	1.7	2.1	2.4	2.3	2.6	3.0	2.7	3.0	3.4
Algeria	0.4	0.8	1.2	1.5	1.5	1.8	2.0	2.1	1.8	1.7	1.7
Tunisia	0.2	0.3	0.5	0.7	0.8	0.8	0.9	0.9	0.8	0.9	0.9
Libya	0.1	0.4	0.6	1.9	0.7	2.1	2.8	2.1	1.4	0.9	0.9
Egypt	0.4	0.7	0.9	2.3	2.8	3.7	3.2	3.3	3.1	2.7	2.4
Total	2.1	7.9	10.0	19.4	21.7	32.0	28.7	27.9	23.6	23.2	23.0
Overall exports	27.8	73.5	107.3	113.9	134.9	152.5	151.8	157.6	143.8	142.5	157.0
% in overall exports	7.5	10.7	9.4	17.0	16.1	21.0	18.9	17.7	16.4	16.3	14.6

Source: TÜİK.

paradigmatic change regarding the collective imagination of the Middle East in Turkish foreign policy discourse. However, the Turkish trading state reached its limits after 2010 and Turkey's regional integration strategy faced a strong backlash. Several factors that led to Ankara's contribution to Middle East regionalism virtually faded away. The supply and demand factors, again, account for the retreat in question and its causes.

The first goal is to document the regression of the Turkish trading state. As a matter of fact, there was virtually no increase between 2011 and 2017 (Table 33.1). While the share of total trade in GDP was 45.1 per cent in 2011, this only increased to 45.9 per cent in 2017. Likewise, while the Turkish foreign trade was worth US$134.9 billion in 2011, it reached US$157 billion in 2017.[5] Regarding the Middle East, Turkish foreign trade with the region actually decreased from US$48.4 billion to US$47.3 billion between 2011 and 2018. The regional composition of Turkish foreign trade did not change dramatically to alter calculations in the Middle East (Figure 33.1). For instance, while Iraq was the fourth country that Turkey exported most in 2018, 5 per cent of Turkey's total exports, this weight remained the same in 2009. While there was optimism regarding the diversification of the Turkish foreign trade composition, for instance the EU's weight in Turkish total exports decreased from 56 per cent in 2002 to 38 percent in 2012, this optimism does not have a basis now as EU's weight once again increased to 50 per cent in 2018. There has not been a major change in the foreign trade composition of Turkey (Figure 33.1).

The same inference can be drawn in the field of investments as well. The increase in Turkish foreign direct investment abroad was noted as both a cause and consequence of the Turkish trading state (Kirişçi 2009: 52). Indeed, in comparison to 1987, Turkish foreign direct investments abroad (as a percentage of GDP) increased from 0.01 per cent to 0.28 per cent in 2010 (Table 33.3). However, there has been stagnation since then. A quick look at Turkey's foreign

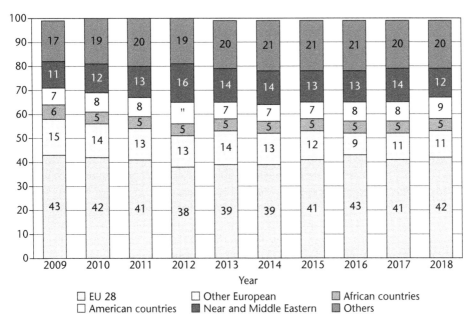

Figure 33.1 Regional breakdown of Turkish foreign trade (% in total trade)
Source: TÜİK (prepared by the authors).

Table 33.3 Foreign direct investment (outflows/inflows) of Turkey

	1987	1995	2000	2005	2010	2011	2012	2013	2014	2015	2016	2017
FDI, net outflows (% of GDP)	0.01	0.07	0.32	0.21	0.19	0.28	0.47	0.38	0.75	0.59	0.36	0.32
FDI, net inflows (% of GDP)	0.13	0.52	0.36	2.00	1.18	1.94	1.57	1.43	1.40	2.09	1.54	1.28

Source: World Bank Indicators.

trade record reveals that in comparison to the 1970s and the 1980s, the volume and weight of foreign trade increased dramatically in the country in the 2000s. Likewise, economic relations with the Middle East gained momentum. The Turkish trading state concept is still valid if only judged by foreign trade statistics and compared with the 1970s. However, the data also reflect a slowdown in pace, including the economic relations with the Middle East. We can therefore claim that the Turkish trading state has at least been stagnant in the second decade of the new millennium.

The stagnation in Turkey's regionalization policies and the stalemate in its attempt at nurturing economic interdependence in the Middle East are closely associated with the stateness problems that emerged in post-2010. First, many states faced major political turmoil in the post-Arab spring, which immediately affected their economies, trade relations and foreign policies. Many states had significantly lost their ability to secure and control their borders, which led to the proliferation of the 'weak' or 'failed' states in the region. Turkey had to adjust to the new atmosphere of chaos and volatility in a severely changed regional security environment. The Syrian state's collapse amid a shattering civil war; emergence of violent non-state actors and the power vacuum in Iraq; Turkey's worsening relations with Egypt – the only remaining viable trade route to the Middle East and North Africa region after Syria and Iraq, and worsening relations with Libya, hindered the economy-driven integration strategies (Kutlay 2016).

The demand-side factors, however, constitute one part of the changing dynamics of Ankara's regionalism policies. On the supply-side, domestic and external developments jointly undermined the Turkish regional leadership role. The Turkish government had to face many challenges, including the then ambiguous consequences of the 2008 global economic crisis, domestic political instability and its souring relations with the West. The 2008 global economic crisis hit Turkish economy, but recovery was relatively quick and robust, thus the crisis did not have a significant impact on the country. Be that as it may, the other concerns did have significant impacts via different channels. A series of major political unrest shook the country, including the Gezi Park protests between May and June 2013, '17–25 December operations' in 2013,[6] failure to establish a coalitional government in June 2015 that led to the controversial elections in November 2015, and, finally, the failed coup attempt in July 2016. Turkey switched to a presidential system from an almost century-long parliamentary one in April 2017 with a referendum won by a small margin – 51.4 per cent to 48.6 per cent. These developments altogether had adverse consequences in terms of the quality of the already fragile democratic environment. Many authors observed a backsliding of democracy in Turkey, as the ruling elite exclusively relied on the majority rule at the expense of political rights and civil liberties, freedom of speech, media freedom, minority rights, etc. (Esen and Gumuscu 2017a, 2017b).

The adverse political developments also affected state–business relations in Turkey by hampering the synergy among the political elite and different business groups. Arguably being one of the most important rifts, the governments' sharp political criticisms against TÜSİAD, the biggest business association in Turkey representing the mainstream capitalist establishment, caused a new source of instability in the domestic political economy. Furthermore, some business organizations that had become influential in the 2000s were shut down or became dysfunctional as they were claimed to be a part of a network that orchestrated the failed coup attempt. Thus, state–business relations became more polarized and politicized in a way that contradicted with, and weakened, the underlying dynamics of the trading state. In addition, after the '17–25 December operations' in 2013, and especially after the failed coup attempt in July 2016, there had been large-scale dismissals in the Turkish bureaucracy. Likewise, more than 125,000 civil servants were dismissed from various governmental bodies after the failed coup attempt (Cakir 2018). One example illustrates the immediate effects of the massive layoffs. In 2015, the Scientific and Technological Research Council of Turkey (TÜBİTAK), the brain-trust of the country and the leading organization of the Turkish innovation system, had to reject a local court's request for evidence analysis since there were no qualified specialists at the organization because of layoffs (Kutlay and Karaoğuz 2018). The deterioration in Turkish democracy, in combination with the EU-related factors, deteriorated bilateral relations between Turkey and the EU (Aydın-Düzgit and Kaliber 2016).

In conclusion, the rise of the Turkish trading state in the first decade of the 2000s led to a wave of optimism in the nurturing of Middle East regionalism. However, internal and external challenges undermined both the Turkish leadership and the regional integration prospects. In Turkey, and in several countries in the region, security-based concerns once again dominated foreign policy agenda at the expense of much-needed economic and institutional interdependence.

Domestic sources of regional powerhood

The Turkish case raises a set of important questions with regards to regional activism under heavy external great power involvement: To what extent can a middle-power pursue an assertive regional foreign policy when global players are also heavily involved in that region? More specifically, what are the boundaries of Turkey's influence in the Middle East given that the US and Russia are highly active and visible in the region? These broad questions can be elaborated in different ways. Here, we would like to briefly examine the second question by sticking to the core analytical argumentation of the trading state. We claim that a thorough analysis of the Turkish state's internal and external capacities in relation to technological upgrading and policy-making is one possible way to augment the trading state perspective, and better examine the causes that limit Middle East regionalism.

To begin with, Öniş and Kutlay (2013) noted that Turkey faced two proximate and two structural challenges in its quest for regional power influence, which also tested the Turkish trading state's capacity and longevity. While the proximate challenges were chronic current account deficit and excessive reliance on energy imports, the structural ones were the middle-income trap and the problematic transition from a 'procedural' to a 'substantive democracy'. First, low domestic saving rates, overdependence on foreign capital and the resultant chronic current account deficit were said to create a 'crisis–growth–current account deficit–crisis circle', and hence put a strain on Turkey's regional power strategy (also see Güven 2016). Second, low-technological capacity and challenges to establishing inclusive institutions were said to undermine the state capacity in Turkey. In fact, all these drawbacks are still relevant today – arguably much more pronounced than before. Turkey is still struggling with a serious current account deficit problem, the Turkish lira hit an all-time low versus the US dollar in late 2018, and high inflation – around 15 per cent – has once again become a major concern. The heavy dependence on energy remains a structural problem despite diversification efforts.

Many drawbacks associated with the Turkish state's low capacity in nurturing pro-development institutions constrain its attempts to assume a leading role in its region. To exemplify, Turkish governments took several steps to launch a new wave of neo-developmentalism in the aftermath of the 2008 global economic crisis (Öniş and Kutlay 2013: 1420–1422), and this was especially the case in the research and development (R&D) sector (Kutlay and Karaoğuz 2018: 298–299). Turkish state officials were aware of the fact that the question was one of technological upgrading and structural transformation in state–market relations if the eventual goal was to ensure strategic autonomy of the country in the Middle East as a more influential regional actor. However, the attempts were only partially successful (Kutlay and Karaoğuz 2018). We suggest that all these issues are relevant to the Turkish trading state discussions and influence the fate of Middle East regionalism.

Conclusion

This chapter discussed economic regionalism attempts in the Middle East with reference to the Turkish case. The regional integration must meet both demand and supply conditions. The Turkish case, in this context, provides an illustrative example to test the limits of the economic-driven integration policies. The Turkish ruling elite and non-state actors adopted avowedly pro-integration policies in the Middle East during the first decade of the twenty-first century. The growing market opportunities in the region and the willingness of domestic stakeholders to capitalize on the new markets undergird Turkish trading state policies. However, the regional security environment changed dramatically in the post-Arab upheavals. On the demand side, the collapse of state structures undermined market opportunities in the Middle East and jeopardized trade linkages among key regional states including Turkey. On the supply side, the deterioration of the Turkish state capacity – in terms of political institutions and stagnation in domestic economy – undermined the regional integration attempts of the Turkish policy-makers. This chapter, as a result, argued that Turkish case is illustrative because of the achievements and inherent limitations.

Notes

1 The importance of 'transaction costs' and the role of international and regional regimes to reduce these costs is widely discussed in the literature. For a classical analysis, see Keohane (1984).
2 Following Haas (1958: 16), we define political integration as 'the process whereby political actors in several distinct national settings are persuaded to shift their loyalties, expectations and political activities toward a new centre, whose institutions possess or demand jurisdiction over the pre-existing national states'.
3 Some of the key arguments in this chapter are first developed in Kutlay and Karaoğuz (2019).
4 One point that is worth mentioning is that despite recurring political tensions with Israel, especially after 2010, there had been a steady increase in the volume of foreign trade between Turkey and Israel.
5 We should note, however, that the degree of openness in Turkish economy remains low in comparison to several developing countries. Therefore it is difficult to claim that the Turkish trading state had reached its natural limits.
6 BBC, 'Turkey ministers Caglayan, Guler and Bayraktar Resign amid Scandal', www.bbc.com/news/world-europe-25514579 (accessed on 9 April 2019).

Bibliography

Acharya, A. 2007. The Emerging Regional Architecture of World Politics. *World Politics* 59(4): 629–652.

Altunisik, M. and Martin, L. 2011. Making Sense of Turkish Foreign Policy in the Middle East under AKP. *Turkish Studies* 12(4): 569–587.

Atlı, A. 2011. Businessmen as Diplomats: The Role of Business Associations in Turkey's Foreign Economic Policy. *Insight Turkey* 13(1): 109–128.

Aydın, M. and Açıkmeşe, S. 2007. Europeanization through EU Conditionality: Understanding the New Era in Turkish Foreign Policy. *Journal of Southeastern European and Black Sea Studies* 9(3): 263–274.

Aydın-Düzgit, S. and Kaliber, A. 2016. Encounters with Europe in an Era of Domestic and International Turmoil: Is Turkey a De-Europeanising Candidate Country? *South European Society and Politics* 21(1): 1–14.

Biddle, J. and Milor, V. 1997. Economic Governance in Turkey: Bureaucratic Capacity, Policy Networks, and Business Associations. In Maxfield, S. and Schneider, B. R. (eds), *Business and the State in Developing Countries*: 277–309. Ithaca, NY: Cornell University Press.

Bilgin, H. 2008. Foreign Policy Orientation of Turkey's Pro-Islamist Parties: A Comparative Study of the AKP and Refah. *Turkish Studies* 9(3): 407–421.

Bozdağlıoğlu, Y. 2003. *Turkish Foreign Policy and Turkish Identity: A Constructivist Approach.* London: Routledge.

Breslin, S., Hughes, C., Phillips, N. and Rosamond, B. 2002. *New Regionalisms in the Global Political Economy.* London: Routledge.

Buğra, A. 1994. *State and Business in Modern Turkey: A Comparative Study.* Albany: State University of New York Press.

Buğra, A. and Savaskan, O. 2014. *New Capitalism in Turkey: The Relationship between Politics, Religion and Business.* Cheltenham: Edward Elgar.

Buzan, B. 1998. The Asia-Pacific: What Sort of Region in What Sort of World? In Brook, C. and McGrew, A. (ed.), *Asia-Pacific in the New World Order.* London: Routledge.

Cakir, F. 2018. 2 Yil Suren Ohalin Bilancosu. *Haberturk.* July 17.

Cizre, U. 2003. Demythologizing the National Security Concept: The Case of Turkey. *Middle East Journal* 57(2): 213–229.

Dağı, Z. 2005. Ulusal Kimliğin İnşası ve Dış Politika. *Demokrasi Platformu* 2(5): 57–71.

Esen, B. and Gumuscu, S. 2017a. Turkey: How the Coup Failed. *Journal of Democracy* 28(1): 59–73.

Esen, B. and Gumuscu, S. 2017b. A Small Yes for Presidentialism: The Turkish Constitutional Referendum of April 2017. *South European Society and Politics* 22(3): 303–326.

Fawcett, L. and Gandois, H. 2010. Regionalism in Africa and the Middle East: Implications for EU Studies. *European Integration* 32(6): 617–636.

Flockhart, T, 2016. The Coming Multi-order World. *Contemporary Security Policy* 37(1): 3–30.

Güven, A. 2016. Rethinking Development Space in Emerging Countries: Turkey's Conservative Countermovement. *Development and Change* 47(5): 995–1024.

Haas, E. 1958. *The Uniting of Europe: Political, Social, and Economic Forces 1950–1957.* Stanford: Stanford University Press.

Haggard, S. 1995. *Developing Nations and the Politics of Global Integration.* Washington, DC: Brookings Institution.

Karaoğuz, H. 2018. The Political Dynamics of R&D Policy in Turkey: Party Differences and Executive Interference during the AKP Period. *Journal of Balkan and Near Eastern Studies* 20(4): 388–404.

Karaosmanoğlu, A. 2000. The Evolution of the National Security Culture and the Military in Turkey. *Journal of International Affairs* 54(1): 199–216.

Katzenstein, P. 2005. *A World of Regions: Asia and Europe in American the Imperium.* Ithaca: Cornell University Press.

Keohane, R. 1984. *After Hegemony: Cooperation and Discord in the World Political Economy.* Princeton: Princeton University Press.

Keohane, R. and Nye, J. 1972. *Transnational Relations and World Politics.* Massachusetts: Harvard University Press.

Kirişçi, K. 2009. The Transformation of Turkish Foreign Policy: The Rise of the Trading State. *New Perspectives on Turkey* 40 (Spring): 29–57.

Kirişçi, K. 2013. *Turkey and the Transatlantic Trade and Investment Partnership: Boosting the Model Partnership with the United States.* Brookings Turkey Project Paper, No. 2: 20.

Kirişçi, K. and Kaptanoğlu, N. 2011. The Politics of Trade and Turkish Foreign Policy, Middle Eastern Studies. *Middle Eastern Studies* 47(5): 705–724.

Kutlay, M. 2011. Economy as the 'Practical Hand' of New Turkish Foreign Policy: A Political Economy Explanation. *Insight Turkey* 13(1): 67–89.

Kutlay, M. 2016. Whither the Turkish Trading State? A Question of State Capacity. *The GMFUS on Turkey Series*.

Kutlay, M. and Karaoğuz, H. 2018. Neo-developmentalist Turn in the Global Political Economy? The Turkish Case. *Turkish Studies* 19(2): 289–316.

Kutlay, M. and Karaoğuz, H. 2019. The Ties that Don't Bind: Interdependence, Trading States, and State Capacity (under review).

Mattli, W. 1999. *The Logic of Regional Integration: Europe and Beyond*. Cambridge: Cambridge University Press.

Nolte, D. 2010. How to Compare Regional Powers: Analytical Concepts and Research Questions. *Review of International Studies* 36(4): 881–901.

Öniş, Z. 2003. Turkey and the Middle East after September 11: The Importance of the EU Dimension. *Turkish Policy Quarterly* 2(4): 84–95.

Öniş, Z. 2006. Globalization and Party Transformation: Turkey's Justice and Development Party in Perspective. In Burnell, E. (ed.), *Globalizing Politics, Party Politics in Emerging Democracies*: 1–27. London: Routledge.

Öniş, Z. 2011. Multiple Faces of the 'New' Turkish Foreign Policy: Underlying Dynamics and a Critique. *Insight Turkey* 13(1): 47–65.

Öniş, Z. and Kutlay, M. 2013. Rising Powers in a Changing Global Order: The Political Economy of Turkey in the Age of BRICS. *Third World Quarterly* 34(8): 1409–1426.

Öniş, Z. and Kutlay, M. 2017. The Dynamics of Emerging Middle Power Influence in Regional and Global Governance: The Paradoxical Case of Turkey. *Australian Journal of International Affairs* 71(2): 164–183.

Öniş, Z. and Rubin, B. (eds) 2003. *Turkish Economy in Crisis*. London: Frank Cass.

Owen, R. 1999. Inter-Arab Economic Relations during the 20th Century: World Market vs. Regional Market. In Hudson, M. (ed.), *The Middle East Dilemma: The Politics and Economics of Arab Integration*: 215–232. London: I.B. Taurus.

Rosecrance, R. 1986. *The Rise of the Trading State: Commerce and Conquest in the Modern World*. New York: Basic Books.

Sayarı, S. 2000. Turkish Foreign Policy in the Post-Cold War Era: The Challenges of Multi-Regionalism. *Journal of International Affairs* 54(1): 169–182.

Schirm, S. 2010. Leaders in Need of Followers: Emerging Powers in Global Governance. *European Journal of International Relations* 16(2): 199.

Thompson, W. 1973. The Regional Subsystem: A Conceptual Explanation and a Propositional Inventory. *International Studies Quarterly* 17(1): 89–117.

34

The IPE of development finance in Latin America

Leonardo Stanley

Introduction

In order to evaluate the international political economy of development finance in Latin America (IPE–DFLA), the chapter asks three essential, interrelated questions:

1   What is development all about?
2   Which are the leading financial institutions, who the key actors?
3   Who is responsible for what and with what consequences for whom? Do governments compensate losers – including those belonging to future generations?

The first section evaluates the evolution of development ideas, including a brief reference to some of its theoretical foundations – the second reviews both traditional and new sources of funding. Then, we introduce the main social and environmental flaws of actual sources of funding, including the challenges climate change is imposing to the region and the funds associated to mitigate it.

The idea of development: a brief historical analysis

The idea of development remains controversial, and even its origin remains under discussion, but most authors trace its roots from laggard countries; efforts to emulate the British industrial revolution (O'Brien and Williams 2016). From the start, industrialization became synonymous with development, but funds were coming from internal sources. As the idea became associated with poorer countries' industrialization, development implied the arrival of external funds.

Latin America developmental ideas emerged in the 1930s, as the financial crisis came to highlight the drawbacks of the neoclassic macro approach and the social limitations of the export-led growth model. Both US and Latin American leaders were seeing industrialization as synonymous with development (Helleiner 2014). In order to install the import substitution industrialization (ISI) model, both the state sector initiative and development funds were highly relevant. By this time, international financial markets were under suspicion: Keynesianism economics was now ruling the world. Suddenly enthusiasm over the ISI path vanished, paving the way for the implementation of a new (more micro-oriented) generation of development models. For those at the academy, Latin America policy failure became associated with price distortions, high effective rates of protection, and rent-seeking conducts. Consequently, mainstream economists arrived with their magic advice: to put the prices right: "to move from inward-looking strategies toward liberalization of the foreign trade regime and export promotion, to submit to stabilization programs, to privatize state-owned enterprises; and to follow the dictates of the market price system" (Meier 2000). Briefly, a new development consensus centred on Neoliberalism began to dominate.

Meanwhile, environmental non-governmental organizations (NGOs) began to plead with international organizations to change toward a more holistic perspective on growth: development should be socially inclusive and environmentally sustainable. Therein, poverty alleviation would become central on global forums and on the agenda of multilateral development banks (MDBs). The environmental issue would be included in *Our Common Future* agenda (WCED 1987), and further elaborated in the 1992 Earth Summit at Rio. The social dimension remained absent from the debate until the World Summit on Social Development, Copenhagen (1995), to be finally included after the World Summit on Sustainable Development, Johannesburg (2002). Last but not least, at the UN Conference on Sustainable Development (Rio + 20), global leaders agreed to a green economy in the context of sustainable development and eradication of poverty (*The Future We Want*). Around the same time, indigenous peoples' rights irrupted in the development agenda,[1] leading to a series of legal amendments directed to empower them (including the bypassing of the International Labor Organization 169 Declaration on Indigenous and Tribal Peoples).[2] Minority rights would become further enhanced by the (2007) UN Declaration on the Rights of Indigenous Peoples as by the (2015) Montevideo Consensus on Population and Development Rights. To sum up, the multilateralism that characterized the postwar liberal order has produced a substantial advance in recognition of social and environmental rights. As an illustration, consider the shift in the scope of United Nations Social Development Goals (UN–SDG) "from a micro-level focus to more ambitious economy-wide goals in terms of infrastructure provision, climate change, and social inclusion" (Kring and Gallagher 2019).

New theoretical insights were undoubtedly crucial, but how economic theory has influenced the idea of development remains a daunting intellectual task beyond the scope of these notes. We instead have chosen to pick a couple of issues which would be valuable for answering the chapter questions knowing that some traditional topics are left behind, as the debate concerning the roles of the state and the market in promoting economic development.

First, the finance–development link, which nowadays observes necessary changes. Developmental funds were initially raised to industrialize the country, as envisioned by policymakers in the postwar world. As development moves from a narrow economic toward a more holistic vision, a new vision is required for installing a sustainable finance–development model. Schoenmaker's (2017) idea of sustainable finance looks at how investing and lending actions interact with economic, social and environmental issues. In order to account for those new issues, we need to move from the traditional gross domestic product (GDP) measure of human progress. Another issue relates to how to bypass all these challenges observed when trying to install a finance scheme for the long-run future – what Mark Carney (2015) describes as the "tragedy of the horizon."

On the one hand is the measurement issue. In the early 1970s, Nordhaus and Tobin (1973) declared the inadequacy of the GDP indicator as it confused growth with social progress. Simultaneously, a group of authors would put in doubt the idea of unlimited growth (Meadows et al. 1972). After that, the academy started to install an alternative measure, and more complexes indexes considering social issues (to consider inequality), as well as environmental topics (the crisis of the biosphere–climate change), began to be drafted. Elinor Ostrom and Alan Boyce would become pioneers in linking both issue and the Brundtland Report the first to include the justice-sustainability nexus.[3] The recent UN Sustainable Development Goals (SDGs) describe a series of interrelated economic, societal and environmental objectives to obtain sustainability. From a social perspective, new indicators are aiming to recognize the fundamental human rights, including the rights of people to be involved in decisions that affect them (see below). Minorities living in poor and unequal societies are certainly more prone to suffer from environmental-related catastrophes. At the 2015 United Nations–Intergo (UN–ICCP) Paris Summit, scientific experts made an urgent call to world leaders to realize how close humankind is to affecting the earth's boundaries definitively.

On the other hand is the long-term finance issue. Traditional development finance does not price environmental or social problems, it priortizes shareholder value and maintains a short-term bias. It looks after an optimal combination of return and risk, disregarding both issues. Henceforth, it might admit investing in "sin industries" such as coal (see below). A further step would be to internalize social and environmental costs, including both concepts into the corporate decision-making process which now involves new stakeholders. The inclusion of a broader set of participants might lead to properly price natural capital depletion, which, for instance, might permit beneficiaries to augment human capital. Indirect stakeholders, however, might be deeply affected if the investment (for example) increases climate change risks. What is needed is a new idea of finance; it should move toward long-term value creation (to answer the question of how to finance the common good value) (Schoenmaker 2017). The transition to a low-carbon economy, as implied in the Paris Agreement, has potentially far-reaching consequences for the financial system. Unfortunately, whereas actions should be initiated in the short run to mitigate climate change adversely, the adverse effects would be stronger only in the second half of the present century (ECLAC 2015) – the "tragedy of the horizon" paradox. Additionally, the transition toward the new "sustainable finance" framework should be carefully designed, as "a rapid move towards a low-carbon economy could materially damage [the actual financial system] stability" or a climate Minsky moment according to Carney (Bank of England 2018).[4] Beyond paradoxes and risks, action is needed to prevent the likelihood of a significant economic crisis. A climate change-related crisis does not just affect people's current incomes and productivity, but also put their assets at risk. As the issue mainly affects more minorities and the destitute, government action is not only needed but should be mandatory.

A second topic relates to the property issue. Traditionally evaluated under a binary categorization (either private or public), private ownership is considered the only option feasible for economic development. Moreover, then an article arrived at the environmental debate: "The Tragedy of the Commons" (Hardyn 1968). According to it, given the non-cooperative character of the economic agents, a common property would dissipate agents' conservational efforts: a call for privatization. Elinor Ostrom would come to challenge this, showing how community lands remain a possible arrangement if agents could maintain a cooperative outcome (Ostrom 1990). Hereupon, the concept moves from a narrow definition of property (either individual or collective) to include a continuous one which assumes the possibility of collective goods property. To govern the use of commons by coalitions is both feasible and efficient, as exemplified by indigenous people groups in the Amazon, whose presence is highly effective in preventing deforestation in particularly vulnerable areas (Nogueira et al. 2018).

A final and highly contemporary issue is associated with the interaction between development and democracy, which mainly explores the final beneficiaries of the development process. Initially, growth was seen as benefiting the elites (under the first globalization). After 1930, the national interest was at the centre (of economic growth). The elite decided to extend the franchise. In Latin America, a highly repressive and closed financial system permitted governments to finance the industrialization process but punished the elites. Once the economies became financially open, the art of development finance became more problematic: elites were now able to leave their capitals abroad. Additionally, the return of democracy pushed newly elected governments with the challenging task to simultaneously ensure elites' property rights and to ensure the social demands of the majority. The solution to this tension was associated with an unstable political cycle from neoliberal (prioritizing property rights and capital accumulation) to populism (by prioritizing political rights and income redistribution) governments.[5] As a long-term agreement proved unfeasible, the provision of public goods became unviable for the many and almost absent for those excluded from the bargaining table (Noboa and Upham 2018)

The modern idea of development remarks on the need to guarantee the voice of all a country's inhabitants, otherwise the democracy catalogues is classed as "illiberal" (Zakaria 1997). There are several alternatives when the time of chosing the (political regime) arrives (Mukand and Rodrik 2015). To put it briefly, we could set a continuum of political choices, qualified according to the set of rights recognized by each of them: from property or illiberal democracies in one extreme, to pass through mass or majority ruling democracies, to finally place participatory or liberal regimes at the other extreme of the spectrum. Democracy might be in place, but nothing guarantees its liberal credentials if minorities are left behind. Liberal democracies, on the other hand, could turn back to an illiberal regime – the reversal does not circumscribe to underdeveloped nations (Rodrik 2018), but it might also affect mature Western democracies (Laurent 2019).

Development discussions, however, have historically and still follow a hierarchal, top to bottom approach, with the voice of minorities often left aside. Unfortunately, discussions continue to concentrate at the central government level and are (often) subject to the veto of the elites. Despite this, once democracy returned, and civil society demands began to expand, governments all around the region were ready to recognize new rights, for example, by granting constitutional character to one of its most representative minority groups: the indigenous people. A similar remark could be made on the environmental front, with governments complaining about introducing new institutions and practices. In both cases, however, the old paradigm came under challenge. The wording if ILO 169 remains vague and incomplete, leaving some black holes available for governments and firms to bypass indigenous and tribal people's opinions and the powerful right to associate their "free, prior and informed consent" was terminated as an empty slogan. A similar statement might be appropriate for environmental regulation, where most governments just watered down the enforcement. To address this government should be able to tax[6] and regulate, otherwise, democratic societies will become illiberal. Henceforth, in the design of a sustainable development agenda, the functioning of a pluralistic and democratic society becomes a necessary condition. The dismissal of local necessities alongside the rise of environmental and social costs led the population to distrust democracy.

Development finance: from the North hegemony to Southern sources

In order to answer the second question, we first explore traditional sources. Development finance was at the very beginning an affair of Western powers trying to emulate industrial Great Britain and, henceforth, internally funded. After the 1930s, industrialization ideas expanded among the least developed, but capital scarce, countries. Henceforth, funding became mainly associated with a repressed financial model. Often portrayed as a victim, the scheme has, however, also permitted the export-led growth model in Asia. Since the late 1970s, however,

Latin America structural transformation became exogenously financed: originally from trans-national banks, and later through the capital market. A series of financial crises starting in the mid-1990s somehow showed its limits and, then, China arrived.

From Bretton Woods to Washington consensus

Two new multilateral institutions resulted from the Bretton Woods Conferences: the International Monetary Fund (IMF) and the Bank for International Reconstruction and Development (as the original name of the World Bank Group, WBG).[7] The former oriented to solve the balance of payments (short-term) imbalances, whereas the latter envisioned to deal with (long-term) developmental issues. The WBG involve a series of institutions,[8] mainly directed to support financial assistance but also associated with the development of norms and guidance, and (indirectly) to solve disputes (throughout the International Centre for Settlement of Investment Disputes (ICSID) tribunals).

Postwar development finance geography largely reflected a North–South pattern, with the former providing the funds, and the latter receipting and accepting donors' conditions. Projects were often responding to transnational firms' interest in the host country industry or directed to natural resource projects associated with local elites, both highly dependent on foreign technology (Sanahuja 2001). Years later the enthusiasm for development reduced, and poverty reduction became the Bank mantra under the McNamara administration (1968–1981) (although funding for infrastructure projects remained). By the late 1970s, Latin American financial markets started to deregulate and internationalize. According to the neoliberal discourse, this would undoubtedly benefit capital-dependent countries: as investors in the North realized the opportunity to obtain better yields, and capital would flow into South.

The arrival of Margaret Thatcher in the UK (1979) and Ronald Reagan to the US (1981) implied not just the defeat of Keynesianism, but it also initiated a period of pessimism regarding the developmental ideal. Under the Clausen administration (1981–1986), the neoliberal ideological shock finally colonized the Bank: poverty reduction lost weight and conditionality became king. The so-called structural adjustment loans (SAL) would be touching all missions,[9] helping the Bank to install its new agenda for putting the "prices right."[10] Henceforth, and in order to access new funds, the beneficiary country was committed to complaining about some specific conditions favoring the needed structural change. Financial retrenchment, however, did not impact Multilateral Financial Institution's (MFI) influence as rule makers.

The debt crisis became the first but not the last one affecting LDCs. Nonetheless, the Bank persisted in viewing the crisis as reflecting a problem of liquidity (instead of one of solvency). Henceforth, by reorienting the economies toward external markets (external gap) and reducing public expenditures (fiscal gap), indebted Latin American countries would overcome the situation. Although aimed to transform the economic structure, SAL ended up pushing local economies into recession and mainly affecting regional economies and more deprived groups. As the crisis deepened, more voices were ready to recognize the crisis as expressing a solvency problem than recognizing the adverse effects the adjustment had on the most impoverished.[11]

Despite the political failure, the Bank neoliberal discourse deepened and spread extensively over the institution. The public sector was then blamed as the primary cause of macroeconomic deterioration: the state presence has not just crowded out private investments but (mainly) affected entrepreneurs' innovative skills. Privatization would get market dynamism back. The influence of the message went beyond the economic realm to reach the institutional setting. For example, take the mining industry, whose legislation would radically transform during the 1990s under the World Bank (WB) endorsement. The new mining laws privileged the entry of foreign firms over sovereign returns and, despite the rhetoric, disregarded both social rights and environmental issues. Bank pressure was also evident in the diffusion of the bilateral investment treaty (BITs), as well as in the inclusion of the investor–state dispute settlement (ISDS) scheme.

Financial globalization further transformed development finance, and sovereigns began to endorse capital markets for funds (instead of transnational banks). The new funding source installed somewhat atypical legislation, placing New York tribunals as the new arbitrator for sovereign debt disputes – at least for bonds issued by Latin American countries. However, market participants' over-optimism pushed capitals in, and something unexpected made investors undo their positions and leave the problem behind. Following the Tequila crisis, a series of financial crises began to hit emerging economies elsewhere. Two points are relevant here. The first relates to the causes of the crisis, and the second looks at the responses to it.

For mainstream economists, like those at the World Bank, the crisis was unrelated to cross-border funding and unregulated financial markets effects but signaled internal incoherences. The South Korea crisis, for example, was explained by the presence of Chaebols and its effect on the local economy. The sudden reversal of fortune would be avoided if sovereigns kept the (neoliberal) agenda in place, that is placing the appropriate institutions. Aware of the substantial costs imposed by IMF treatment and aiming to avoid a new financial crisis, Asian countries entered into a cooperative game.[12] Likewise, most emerging market economies (EMEs) began to accumulate international reserves and (at least, an essential group among them) decided to follow heterodox exchange rate policies in order to avoid becoming constrained by the dictates of the monetary trilemma. The Global Financial Crisis would shock the faith of those still believing in the neoliberal credo, with the IMF staff reinstalling the capital controls issue in the debate. The crisis also came to demonstrate the relevance of macro coordination as well as Southern liquidity provisions schemes.

The financial crises have also given an invigorating impulse to development banking ideas (Kring and Gallagher 2019),[13] not just in EMEs but also among developed countries (DCs) (Griffith-Jones 2016). However, instead of discussing financial issues in isolation (credit repayment), the debate now included governance or sustainability topics. In terms of governance, the new landscape demonstrates how different (development finance) institutions may behave if creditors or debtors rule (Ray and Kamal 2019). One of the advantages of creditor participation relates to credit rating, as banks are often profiting from AAA scores. Furthermore, theoretically, the bank remains autonomous under both situations. In practice, however, creditor vision often prevails. EME share of international capital flows has become significant, and a greater institutional influence should be expected. However, as traditional donors are still debating the importance of development banks, China and other emerging economies are advancing with new structures (Abdenur 2015; Humphrey 2015b).

The rise of the rest: development finance, an Asian approach

Development finance shows now EME roots, representing 80 percent of all development bank assistance (Kring and Gallagher 2019). The Asian region shows a long and rich tradition in development finance, the relevance of which was recently rediscovered by mainstream economists since China decide to lead the cause in Africa. The Chinese approach to development finance, however, did not arise from scratch but followed the postwar Japanese experience.

China

Whereas China's role as a donor country is not novel, the level of development-related funds has significantly increased for a country that, until 2007, remained a net recipient country. Beyond similarities and legacy, according to Wen Jiabao (ex-China premier), the success is a response to unique Chinese characteristics (Kondoh 2015: 38).

Box 34.1 Japan's approach to finance development

Japan learned from the war how costly an unequal relation might be (Fukuda-Parr and Shiga 2016). At the San Francisco Conference (1951), which fixed the terms to restoring sovereignty, the government agreed to assist a group of Asian nations (Burma, Philippines, Indonesia and Vietnam) in postwar reconstruction. The resulting Colombo Plan came to signal the start of a new developmental approach, distant primarily to the traditional paternalistic aid focus prevalent among Western donors: for Japanese authorities, assistance development resembles a bilateral relationship between equals, which should be mutually beneficial for both parts (Fukuda-Parr and Shiga 2016; Ohno 2014). Authorities were also aware of the financial needs in order to transform traditional economic structures, but also of the importance not to be involved in their neighbor's policies or in its political orientation (non-interference principle). The fundamental task of structural transformation proves difficult for Least Developed Countries (LDCs), given their low savings ratio as well as the reduced capacity to generate hard currency gains. Development assistance might help to overcome both (saving and external) gaps and, henceforth, permit the assisted to advance with industrialization. Japanese developmental funding was aimed to fulfill three different objectives: aid, trade and investments (Fukuda-Parr and Shiga 2016; Kondoh 2015; Ohno 2014; Saidi and Wolf 2011). It first brings aid assistance, primarily directed to infrastructure building in recipient countries, whose construction will seduce Japanese firms to entry. Japanese regional real (trade) and financial (aid and investment) flows were also reflected the flying geese pattern of economic development in Asia. Japanese development programs were also pioneers in tying loans to public work contracts (tied procurement), as in using concessional lines for technology diffusion purposes (technological lock-in) – both practices directed to boost local firms' globalization. Last, but not least, Japan was also the first to install particular lines of credit, being China being among the earliest beneficiaries of the commodity back loans (CBLs) scheme (Bräutigam 2010; Saidi and Wolf 2011; Xu and Carey 2015). From an economic perspective, the Japanese approach has always recognized the existence of market failures as well the critical role played by the state in economic development and social transformation. During the 1990s, this heterodox view clashed with the US and the World Bank orthodox perspective. Sixty years after its irruption the developmental ideal still underpins aid and financial assistance from Japan, as testified a recent position paper (GoJ 2015). The abovementioned paper restates the old framework, now aiming to help local firms to go global and now confronting Chinese competition (Ohno 2014).

The bilateral movement

External assistance is associated with the publication of Mao Tse-dong and Zhou Enlai leading principles, a position still guiding the country development finance agenda[14] (Bräutigam 2010; Chin and Frolic 2007). Geopolitics issues initially dictated the agenda (to contain Taiwan and declare the PRC as the legitimate representative in all international forums), and African countries were among the first to benefit from Beijing's assistance (Bräutigam 2010; Ling and Wang 2014). Geopolitical reasons were also behind China's financial assistance for Cuba and the fact that it still funds a group of Central American and Caribbean countries (Stallings 2016). Once recognition of the PRC expanded, economic goals started to complement political objectives and, once again, Africans were among those reaping the benefits from the start. Nowadays, Chinese assistance is everywhere, reaching 161 countries and benefiting more than 30 multilateral agencies (Tseng and Krog 2014).

In formal terms, China's official position is laid out in the Foreign Aid White Paper, which states the complementary role of the bilateral assistance (Abdenur 2015; Humphrey 2015b; Xu and Carey 2015). So, in a broad sense, this is what authorities do: direct funds toward poverty reduction through multilateral (traditional) channels, while using bilateral (Asian) lending to finance development-related projects. China donor policy is used to access markets either to obtain natural resources (Bräutigam 2010) or, increasingly, to finance local firms going global (Sanderson and Forsythe 2013; Sato et al. 2010; Stallings 2016; Tseng and Krog 2014; Wang 2016; Xu and Carey 2015).

China's development finance regime is constructed around four different types of assistance (aid, concessional loans, preferential interest rate loans and below-market interest rate) and three different sources (Ministry of Commerce (MOFCON), China Export–Import Bank (CHEXIM) and China Development Bank (CDB)). Aid and concessional loans are supervised by both MOFCON and the Ministry of International Relations. CDB, on the other hand, offer sovereigns a preferential (slightly above London Inter-Bank Offered Rate (LIBOR)) interest rate, backing repayment with commodities of any sort (including oil). The practice is expansively used by local and regional authorities eager to expand infrastructure works at home, encouraging the infrastructure-related industry boom (Wang 2016), and CDB assistance compels the global expansion of the phenomenon (Provaggi 2013; Sanderson and Forsythe 2013).

In Latin America, the arrival of Chinese policy banks proved determinant for a group of outsider countries (Argentina, Ecuador and Venezuela) with no access to international financial markets. Adding Brazil to this group, we have explained 91 percent of all credits made by the two political banks in the region (with a majority of them from the CDB). Loans were, financially, highly beneficial. CDB charged a below-market interest rate and did not place any conditionality at all (Gallagher et al. 2012). Chinese financial agents often used the commodity-backed loan scheme and tied procurement contracts to loan disbursement (Maggiorelli 2017). Between 2005 and 2017, Latin America received loans for US$150 billion, which placed Chinese banks among the region's leading financial institutions (Andean Financial Corporation either the InterAmerican Bank) (China–Latin America Finance Database). Currently, China builds and finances more emerging market infrastructure than all multilateral development banks and the Organisation for Economic Co-operation and Development (OECD) countries combined, according to the Brookings Institution. Besides traditional funding, China has also offered a series of cooperative agreements to (financially) assist governments (throughout bilateral swap agreements) and regional organizations (as the funding offer to the Latin America and the Caribbean Community (CELAC)).

To sum up, the rise of China has come to dispute the hierarchy relationship imposed by traditional donors (Stuenkel 2013). Beijing offers a cooperative relationship (Ling and Wang 2014), free from political conditionality (Kondoh 2015; Ohno 2014). Chinese development assistance, however, presents some flaws. Among other criticisms, two have become recurrent: lack of transparency and tied procurement. The new multilateral institutions being proposed by Beijing overcomes both shortcomings; this is why they have a positive reception (Biswas 2015; Humphrey 2015b).

China goes multilateral

Chinese authorities have recently decided to advance with the creation of the Asian Investment and Infrastructure Bank (AIIB), in whose directory China maintains a majority stake (although authorities compromised to dilute its veto power) (Humphrey 2015b: 26). The political challenge, if successful, might permit the recognition of a new (pro-developmental) leadership (Xu and Carey 2015). The new entity has also advanced in the social and environmental realm, installing new guidelines whose consideration would be mandatory at the loan evaluation process. Institutional progress implies dismissing all tying practices, as the bank has compromised to install a more open and transparent agenda. All these changes have enlarged the list of potential interested, developed or least developed countries, in the new bank (see: www.aiib.org/en/about-aiib/governance/members-of-bank/index.html). Seven countries of the region (Argentina, Bolivia, Brazil, Chile, Peru, Panama and Venezuela) are part of the bank.

In company with Brazil, Russia, India and South Africa, China decided to introduce the New Bank of Development or BRICS Bank. In contrast to the AIIB, and despite the open-door policy toward new members, the five original members will retain the majority and habilitated to participate in the directory. Despite differences, all partners share (or used to share) some universal principles (Stuenkel 2013). On the one hand, politically, all of them agree on the non-interference principle. On the other hand, a pro-active ideal of development is also evident among members. Additionally, the new bank might play an essential role in financing the infrastructure gap (Stuenkel 2013; Stern et al. 2013).

Brazil, Russia, India, China and South Africa (BRICS) nations have also installed a US$100 billion contingent reserve agreement, where China has compromised to contribute US$40 billion. The primary agreement objective is to bring financial assistance to LDCs, particularly those confronting a balance of payments crisis. In contrast to the Chiang Mai Initiative, the scope of the contingent reserve agreement assistance is more substantial − at least, in theory (Stuenkel 2013). As observed in the past (CMI), both emerging economies' disconformity with the Fund and IFIs' refusal to recognize them have been present at the time the agreement was discussed by the BRICS (Biswas 2015).

Last but not least comes the multilateral belt and road initiative fund (BRI Fund), on which Beijing compromised with US 40 billion. The BRI is a large and ambitious infrastructure program, aimed to boost China's connection with the rest of Asia, Africa and Europe. Latin American participation, initially disregarded, was the motive of Xi Jinping announcements at CELAC – China forum, in Santiago de Chile, January 2018. As the infrastructure deficit remains large, countries in Latin America (but also all around the world) are, one after another, hopefully expecting to be included in the list. For those who adopted Xi Jinping free market discourse, participating at BRI helps to signal them as true globalizers.

Development finance: a short reading list

Latin America: the need for a new developmental vision

There is now a global consensus on the need for strong climate actions, a challenge conveying an invaluable investment effort in sustainable infrastructure. Beyond the discourse, however, there stands a developmental institution fundamental contradiction: in order to maintain its reputation (financial soundness and pro-investor climate) it needs to simultaneously try to obtain its ambitious objectives on poverty reduction, social inclusion and environmental goals (Sanahuja 2001). Critics might trace the origin to financial short-term bias, which prevents to pursue viable long-term, sustainable projects. Development finance, henceforth, might help in perpetuating a growth path that tends to affect the country social cohesion and its environment. In order to accomplish long-run SDGs, financial institutions and policymakers alike should ideally place common goods at the center (Schoenmaker 2017). Next comes the evaluation of the social and environmental dimension of economic development, whose main questions were posed at the beginning of this chapter: Who is responsible for what and with what consequences for whom? Do governments compensate losers – including those belonging to future generations? Questions like those center the analysis of the conflict in a new political dimension: social–environmental link.

A brave new world, new actors, new challenges, old shortcomings

After years of pledging technological progress at any cost, the idea of development was suddenly put on trial. This led the Bank to introduce social costs and environmental concerns to its political toolkit while remaining set on internal reorganization and discourses (Wade 1997; 2016). The WBG continued to finance non-sustainable export-oriented projects in non-renewable energy, mining and agribusiness.

Latin America brings an extensive list of debatable loans, which markedly affected the environment and minority groups. The Polonoroeso Road Project in Brazil intended to pave 1,500 km in a sparsely populated area of the Amazon, and initiates an iconic list (Rich 1994)[15] that resulted in a high reputation cost for the institution (Wade 1997; 2016). Years later, the International Finance Corporation (IFC) decided to fund the Yanacoa, a large gold mine project in Cajamarca, Peru. Mining operations, however, were initiated without the consent of the local (indigenous) population – despite this being mandatory according to ILO 169 legislation recognized by Peru.[16] Mine operations created "many devastating environmental and social problems ranging from severe water contamination and a major mercury spill to an upsurge in prostitution, alcoholism and domestic violence" (Bretton Woods Project 2004). Following years of mobilizations and social unrest, the government finally decided to retire the permission. The IFC was also involved in the Marlin mine project in Guatemala Highlands, which became the object of local conflict and international scrutiny for nearly a decade (Zarsky and Stanley 2011). In mid-2010, in order to protect the health, environment and human rights of local indigenous communities, the Inter-American Commission on Human Rights of the Organization of American States issued precautionary measures, calling on the Guatemalan government to suspend operations at the Marlin mine.

The social achievements are also highly adverse for the Bank, as almost all funds were directed to finance large projects benefiting a few. Consider the US$30 billion IFC loan to Dinant Corporation in Honduras, which has faced an allegation of backing violence against local farmers. Recently, a class action was filed by a group of farmers accusing the International Finance Corporation of the murder of several peasants (*Financial Times* 2017). Alternatively, in 2013 the IFC made a US$85 million loan to financially support the international expansion of (Brazilian giant, beef processing firm) Minerva in the Paraguayan Chaco, one of the most extensive dry forests in the Americas, mostly rich in providing water and carbon sequestration (US–AID 2017). The rapid expansion of the cattle industry is reporting to increase deforestation and to violate fundamental human rights, including child and forced labor (Bretton Woods Project 2018).

The InterAmerican Development Bank's (IDB) role in the development of the Camisea Gas Project (Peru), shows how double discourses are expanded. Peruvian authorities refused to recognize the rights of the isolated indigenous groups living in the area, even though the project was mainly located within the Nahua–Kugapakori Territorial Reserve for isolated indigenous people (Bast et al. 2015). Environmental critics were also fierce but not confined to environmental NGOs: Citigroup and other large financial institutions such as the US's Export–Import Bank or the US Government's Overseas Private Investment Corporation (OPIC), refused to get involved in the project funding.

China's regional involvement has also raised concerns all over the region, as a result of their social and environmental records (Ray et al. 2017). Indeed, the commodity boom has placed " heavy strain on water supplies, and increased deforestation and greenhouse gas emissions (GHGs). Shougang Group Co, a state-owned iron producer, was the first mover in Latin America (1992 – Peru). After gaining the concession for the Marcona mine, it sparkled the area with low wages, environmental pollution and conflicts with residents (Sanbord and Chonn 2017). The second wave of Chinese overseas foreign direct investment (OFDI) began to arrive in the mid-2000s,[17] including NMG Mining Ltd, the recent acquisition of La Bamba to First Quantum (Canada). Once exploitation began (then the world largest open-pit copper mine in operation), conflicts start to rise. The Mirador Cooper Mine Project is another example of Chinese involvement. Located in the Ecuadorian Amazon, the Project is situated in a remote area in the East of the country, traditionally one of the most biodiverse regions in the world and is inhabited by the Shuar community – an ancient ethnic group (Chicaiza 2010; Sanchez-Vazquez et al. 2016). So, when the Correa government decided to grant the concession to Corriente Resources,[18] an environmental conflict ensued – including a lawsuit against the government for violating the Rights of Nature. Chinese influence in Amazon deforestation is highly controversial and fundamentally driven by agribusiness development (cattle herd, soybean production, logging and agro-industrial expansion), as well by infrastructure projects (roads and dams) (Fearnside 2005; Fearnside and Figuereido 2017; Ritter et al. 2017).

Independently of the origin of the investor, all mentioned projects share a typical pattern: investments increase environmental costs and affect the country's more impoverished, particularly the indigenous people. When conservational topics are included (conditioning the loan), it just estimates the opportunity costs of forgone economic activities (as agriculture), basically omitting "the cost not only of maintaining indigenous territories and protected natural areas but also of creating the necessary development opportunities for their resident population" (Walker et al. 2014). Socio-environmental conflicts might be a natural response to these omissions, explaining why activists confront a hard and dangerous present.[19] Mexico, Colombia and Brazil are among the most lethal places for those advocating defense of the earth or indigenous tribes (Front Line Reporters 2018),[20] although a few Latin American countries are absent from the list, as shown by the murder of high-profile environmental activist Berta Cáceres. If extractive industries are often among the usual suspects, for the first time in 2017 the agribusiness industry surpassed mining as the most dangerous sector.[21] Socio-environmental-related conflicts (often associated with extreme weather and climate change), are helpful in explaining the present Central American migration trend (*Financial Times* 2019; Raleigh et al. 2008; Reuveny 2007).[22]

Sustainable development, finance and climate change

In March 1987, Gro Harlem Brundtland (former Norwegian Prime Minister), coordinated a UN Commission on World Commission on Environment and Development, which later edited the *Our Common Future* report and instilled the idea of sustainable development.[23] (Almost) thirty years later, world leaders made an urgent call to UN members to act: "the increase in the global average temperature to well below 2°C above pre-industrial levels and pursuing efforts to limit the temperature increase to 1.5°C above pre-industrial levels, recognizing that this would significantly reduce the risks and impacts of climate change" (UN 2015).[24] Hence-forth, "if we intend to stay within the 1.5-degree carbon budget, no new fields, gas fields, or coal mines should be developed anywhere in the world, beyond those that are already in use or under construction" (Oil Change International 2016). Risks would certainly be higher among those socially excluded, with millions potentially pushed deeper into poverty (Stern 2007). Extreme climate events might additionally induce "conflict over natural resources, population displacement and migration as the result of sea-level rise or other large-scale biophysical, eco-logical or social disruptions, and the prospect of increasingly frequent humanitarian disasters" (O'Brien et al. 2008). Extreme weather events, causing droughts or floods, are now regular and, indeed, have started to affect several Latin American economies, mainly affecting their agri-culture, water, biodiversity and forests. Climate change is also altering precipitation patterns, soil humidity and runoff, and accelerates glacier melt, therefore affecting agriculture and related activities. The tourism industry also suffers adverse effects, a fate particularly severe for Central American and Caribbean countries. Paradoxically, the region contribution to total greenhouse gas emission is reduced, producing a tiny fraction of it (ECLAC 2014), a fact explained by the global character of the issue. In other words, for Latin America and the Caribbean, climate change is associated with a negative externality whose mitigation costs might, unfortunately, be redressed by a few.

The climate change issue led Robert Zoellick (by the time, the Bank President) to promise a large amount of money through the Climate Investment Fund. Alas, a different picture emerged from its loan statistics: between 2007 and 2009 the Bank lent nearly US\$2.2 billion in fossil fuel project (*The Ecologist* 2009). Twelve years later, at the *One Planet Summit*, Jim Young Kim (WBG President 2018) announced that the Bank "will cease project lending for upstream oil and gas projects after 2019,"[25] but began channeling funding to developing countries to help them to cope with global warming. In order to align with the Paris Agreement on climate change, the Bank committed to allocate their funds better to finance the transition toward a green economy. Beyond its proposals and discourses, the WBG continued to finance non-renewable energy sources and even favored the high pollutant coal industry with loans (*The Ecologist* 2009; EDF 2009; Oil Change International 2016; Wright et al. 2017). This explains why the Bank still ranks as the main contributor to fossil fuels' financing in developing coun-tries, with the IFC playing a pivotal role concerning volume but also compared to the funds the same entity gives to energy-related climate finance (Wright et al. 2017).[26] As a result, the Bank loans lock in the sovereign into a particular energy source, explaining why existing investment might have long-term consequences.

The environmental issue has also become relevant for Chinese leaders, as observed during the 19th National Party Congress when Xi Jinping "explicitly recognized the importance of China's leadership in tackling climate change and the importance of sustainable development for ensuring equitable improvements in people's lives" (quoted in Ahmad et al. 2018). Despite the decreasing reliance on coal supplies and the significant investments made in the green energy industry, China continues to finance coal and fossil fuel projects all around the world. CDB and the CHEMIX still fund vast numbers of fossil fuel projects (Ahmad et al. 2018; Zhou et al. 2018), whereas eleven of the world's biggest twenty coal plan developers are Chinese (Ahmad et al. 2018). Until now Chinese investments have certainly encouraged Latin America onto high-carbon pathways (Edwards and Roberts 2014). China's investments, therefore, might lock the region into an unsustainable growth model that would make the management of climate change more difficult and the sovereign more vulnerable to environmental-related risks. Options, however, are available as the region is bringing Chinese clean energy firms a golden opportunity (Edwards and Roberts 2014, Gallagher 2018).

On a periodical basis, ECLAC provides information on expected GDP losses due to climate change, disaggregated by region and country (ECLAC 2014; 2015). Remarkably, an importune asymmetry characterizes the distribution of losses among countries in the region: whereas the estimated average costs for the more extensive and wealthiest countries of the region range between 1.0 to 1.5 percent of GDP (ECLAC 2014), a reduced group of small and poorer countries have confronted costs above 20 percent of GDP.[27] As previously mentioned, asymmetry is large among Central American countries, which explains between 0.3 to 0.8 percent of global greenhouse gas emissions and confronts substantial mitigation costs (ECLAC 2015). The infrastructure deficit of Latin America has traditionally been significant, and now extra funds are increasingly needed to mitigate climate change effects (Bhattacharya and Holt 2015; Bhattacharya et al. 2015; ECLAC 2015; Meltzer 2016; Smallridge et al. 2013; Stern et al. 2013). MDBs might help fund the necessary infrastructure investments (Studart and Gallagher 2016). Room for development finance might also be found among private sources, as the financial system keeps internalizing the relevance of environmental and social issues. Financial regulators are rapidly becoming aware of the challenges climate change-related risks place on the system, and are beginning to talk about the introduction of specific prudential rules.[28] Above all, however, remains the national state.

Conclusions

The IPE of development finance has undergone an impressive transformation, particularly after Southern actors began to challenge the traditional (Western) ideal of development assistance. The Asian response to the financial crisis of the late 1990s could qualify as a starting date for this transformation, and China is becoming the leading actor in the actual institutional strengthening. Developmental ideas have also passed through a transcendental conversion, which helps to explain the advancements in rights as observed at the UN's SDGs. Unfortunately, progress at the multilateral level is now contested and basically Western powers. The liberal view, as well as its accompanying technical ideal of poverty reduction, is rapidly left behind, and the geopolitical view has once again returned to shape the development finance agenda. The Trump administration has recently sounded sirens, warning Western allies that "the World Bank and other bastions of the US-led international economic order are at risk of being captured by Chinese influence" (*Financial Times* 2018).

Latin America still needs large sums of money to eliminate extreme poverty, but mainly to reduce inequalities and mitigate climate change. The region could undoubtedly benefit from factors such as a large pool of funds as well by the new geopolitical perspective. Latin America's stock of natural resources remains a potent lighthouse for foreign investors. Foreign direct investments and local capitalists both keep funding the mining, non-renewable energy or agribusiness industries. Both factors, however, could also lock the region into a long-term unsustainable development path. Besides funds, what the region still miss is a democratically discussed and carefully planned program of inclusive and sustainable development. Latin American global insertion proved incapable of reducing social tensions in order to guarantee a sustainable path. So, the question of who is funding development might be indistinct (as the developmental path being followed continues to be socially inequitative and environmental harmful).

A political economy vision helps us to disentangle the different sets of actors, institutions, and policies behind the development finance issue. The sort of questions left would relate to: How developmental funds are being directed, and to which sectors? Why are some projects being undertaken, despite their negative social and environmental impacts? Who do the projects benefit? How could development finance help in overcoming the illiberal dilemma?

Notes

1 Indigenous exploitation traces its roots to the conqueror's *terra nulis* doctrine, which would remain practically untouched for centuries – think about their status during the Amazon colonization rush during the 1950s.
2 The following Latin American countries have constitutionally recognized the validity of ILO 169: Argentina (1994); Plurinational State of Bolivia (1994, 2004, 2009); Brazil (1988/2005); Colombia (1991, 2003); Costa Rica (1999); Ecuador (1996, 1998, 2008); El Salvador (1983/2000); Guatemala (1985/1998); Honduras (1982/2005); Mexico (1992, 1994/1995, 2001), Nicaragua (1987, 1995, 2005); Panama (1972, 1983, 1994); Peru (1993, 2005); Paraguay (1992); and the Bolivarian Republic of Venezuela (1999).
3 The nexus is also observable at the UN Millennium Development Goals (MDGs) (2000) (www.un.org/millenniumgoals/). Signed by 189 UN Member States, the UN Millennium Declaration committed world leaders to combat poverty, hunger, disease, illiteracy, environmental degradation and discrimination against women.
4 As stated in the Bank report, the impact of the transition on carbon-intensive sectors could affect energy and commodity prices, corporate bonds, equities and certain derivatives contracts, all of which, naturally, increase the likelihood of financial risk.
5 Instability, in particular, relates to the impossibility to settle an agreement among leading actors. When cooperation is not feasible, an unstable growth path follows (from neoliberalism to populism and back). In Acemoglu and Robinson parlance, traditional Latin American elites have never accepted to extend the franchise and, consequently, a democratic equilibrium (even in its most reduced version) proves difficult to sustain.
6 Mukand and Rodrik (2015) left us with the following questions: "which determines the taxes, who pays the taxes and how the public good is targeted." Laurent's (2019) explanation of the *Gilet Jaunes* crisis goes in this direction: the proposal of the Macron administration to introduce a fossil fuel tax, which was levied without any social consideration.
7 The Inter-American Development Bank (IADB) funded a couple of years later and became a leading actor. The Development Bank of Latin America (CAF, for its original Spanish name, Corporación Andina de Fomento) is another highly relevant actor.
8 The WBG is conformed by i) the International Bank for Reconstruction and Development (IBRD); ii) the International Development Association (IDA); iii) the International Finance Corporation (IFC); iv) the Multilateral Investment Guarantee Agency (MIGA) ICSID; and, v) The International Centre for Settlement of Investment Disputes (ICSID) (more information at www.worldbank.org/en/about).
9 The signature of a stabilization program with the IMF (May 1979), Turkey became the first country to use the SAL device. Two years later the structural adjustment issue would be included in the World Development Report (WDR).
10 Conditionality clauses were also included in bilateral loan packages, such as those originated in the US, UK or France.
11 World Bank experience in Bolivia would become crucial for the new approach, particularly after UNICEF publication of *Adjustment with a Human Face*, document that was highly critical of World Bank performance.
12 Japanese financial authorities proposed the creation of an Asian Monetary Fund in the fall of 1997 – although the proposal was later abandoned. Three years later, Association of East Asian Nations (ASEAN) leaders plus financial authorities from the PRC, Japan and South Korea decided to establish a network of bilateral swaps agreement: The Chiang-Mai Initiative (*New York Times* "East Asia Unites to Fight Speculators" May 8, 2000).
13 Kring and Gallagher found that a significant portion, more than 60 percent of US$6 trillion, in short-term liquidity assistance has been raised in the South (Kring and Gallagher 2019).
14 Chinese principles of foreign assistance are: equal treatment and mutual benefits, non-interference, external assistance to boost local capacities and sharing knowledge, as to recognize the existence of a variety of development paths.
15 The Bank would become an important financial source for the project, the only one coming from abroad.
16 Seven months after the approval; however, the Alberto Fujimori administration decided to introduce new legislation to promote private investments, in all the national jurisdiction and indigenous and peasants territories (Law N° 26505). Although un-constitutional, the new legal framework prevailed.

17 The entry of Chinese firms intensified during 2007–2010 when it paid US$1.750 million for a group of (foreign) private junior companies. In 2007 Zijin Consortium acquired Rio Blanco Cooper mine from a UK junior firm (US$186m). After that, all the targets companies were Canadians (Sanbord and Chonn Ching 2015).

18 In 2010 the company was bought by two state-owned, Chinese firms: China Railway Construction Company (CRCC) and Tongling Nonferrous. Two years later the Correa administration granted them the environmental license, allowing Ecuacorriente to begin open-pit exploration and exploitation.

19 For more information: Observatorio de conflictos mineros en América Latina, www.ocmal. org/environmental justice atlas, https://ejatlas.org/environmental law alliance worldwide, www.elaw. org).

20　　I have reported on the impact of these killings, and the 'criminalization' that often precedes them, throughout my travels on behalf of the UN, to Honduras, Brazil, Mexico, and many other countries. I have seen the scars left by bullets and the graves of murdered leaders. the killings make news, but hidden behind these headlines is something even more insidious: the silencing of entire communities.

(Victoria Tauli – Corpuz, UN Special Rapporteur on the Rights of Indigenous People)

21 The dismal record counted 46 defenders who protested against palm oil, coffee, tropical fruit and sugar cane plantations, as well as cattle ranching, were murdered in 2017 (At What Cost?).

22 As described by the notes posted by Judde Webber "Honduran Farmers Flee Effects of Climate Change" (*Financial Times* 2018) or the one signed by Jeff Abbott and Sandra Cuffe (*Al-Jazzera News* 2019).

23 For the Brundtland Report, ecological sustainability means "at a minimum sustainable development must not endanger the natural systems that support life on Earth: the atmosphere, the waters, the soils, and the living beings" (WCED 1987: 44).

24 During 2015, the UN Summit adopted the Sustainable Development Goals and the 2030 development agenda.

25 He also declared that the Bank was starting to apply a shadow price on carbon in the economic analysis overall projects in key high emissions sectors (Bretton Woods Project 2018).

26 Fossil fuels and coal are also being funded by other MDBs as well by private entities – particularly active are the Swiss (Greenpeace Switzerland 2018), US and Canadian banks (FT–Environment 2018). Local governments and national development banks are also highly active in the field, particularly among emerging G20 members (Oil Change International–Friends of the Earth–WWF–Sierra Club 2018). Asian practice remains highly controversial: Japan, South Korea and China are among the leaders of fossil fuel funding (Wright et al. 2017).

27 Charveriat notes the cases of Barbados (20 percent), Nicaragua (32 percent) and St. Kitts & Nevis (85 percent) (quoted by Ibararran et al. 2007). Central America and the Caribbean are mainly affected by major extreme weather-related events, whereas their economies are among the continent's poorest (ECLAC 2015).

28 A Network for Greening the Financial System (NGFS) was also created, with the participation of 18 central banks and financial supervisors (FT Special Report 2018).

Bibliography

Abdenur, A. 2015. *The New Multilateral Development Banks and the Future of Development: What Role for the UN?* United Nations University. Centre for Policy Research (UNU-CPR).

Ahmad, E., Neuweg, I. and Stern, N. 2018. *China, the World and the Next Decade: Better Growth, Better Climate*. London: Grantham Research Institute on Climate Change and the Environment and Centre for Climate Change Economics and Policy, London School of Economics and Political Science.

Al-Jazzera News. 2019. Palm Oil Industry Expansion Spurs Guatemala Indigenous Migration, February.

Bank of England. 2018. *Transition in Thinking: The Impact of Climate Change on the UK Banking Sector*. Prudential Regulation Authority.

Bast, E., Doukas, A., Pickard, S., Van Der Burg, L. and Whitley, S. 2015. Empty Promises: G20 Subsidies to Oil, Gas and Coal Production. *A Report by Overseas Development Institute and Oil Change*.

Bhattacharya, A. and Holt, R. 2015. Assessing the Changing Infrastructure Needs in Emerging Markets and Developing Countries. *G-24/GGGI Paper Series*.

Bhattacharya, A., Openheim, J. and Stern, N. 2015. Driving Sustainable Development Through Better Infrastructure: Key Elements of a Transformation Program. *Global Development and Economy at Brookings: The New Climate Economy. Global Economic & Development Working Paper 91*. Gratham Research Institute on Climate Change and the Environment.

Biswas, R. 2015. Reshaping the Financial Architecture for Development Finance: The New Development Banks. *LSE Global South Unit, Working Paper Series 2*.

Bräutigram, D. 2010. *The Dragon's Gift: The Real Story of China in Africa*. Oxford University Press.

Bretton Woods Project. 2004. IFC-funded Goldmine Shut Down by Local Protest, 22 November.

Bretton Woods Project. 2018. World Bank Investment in Paraguayan Cattle Industry Linked to Human Rights Violations and Environmental Harm. *Bretton Woods Observer*, Autumn.

Carney, M. 2015. *Breaking the Tragedy of the Horizon – Climate Change and Financial Stability*. Speech at Lloyd's of London.

Chicaiza, G. 2010. The Mining Enclave of the Cordillera del Cóndor. *Acción Ecológica*. Ecuador.

Chin, G. T. and Frolic, M. B. 2007. *Emerging Donors in International Development Assistance: The China Case*. Report. Partnership & Business Development Division. IDRC-CRDI CANADA.

Devesh Kapur, J., Lewis, P. and Webb, R. 2016. Boulevard to Broken Dreams, Part 1: The Polo Noroeste Road Project in the Brazilian Amazon, and the World Bank's Environmental and Indigenous Peoples' Norms. *Revista de Economia Política* 36(1).

ECLAC. 2014. The Economics of Climate Change in Latin America and the Caribbean: Paradoxes and Challenges. *Sustainable Development and Human Settlements Division of the Economic Commission for Latin America and the Caribbean (ECLAC)* Report Galindo, L. and Samaniego, J. (Coor.).

ECLAC. 2015. The Economics of Climate Change in Latin America and the Caribbean: Paradoxes and Challenges of Sustainable Development. *Sustainable Development and Human Settlements Division of the Economic Commission for Latin America and the Caribbean (ECLAC)* Report Galindo, L. and Samaniego, J. (Coor.).

EDF. 2009. Foreclosing the Future: Coal, Climate and Public International Finance. Environmental Defense Fund – Report by Bruce Rich. Available at: www.edf.org.

Edwards, G. and Roberts, T. 2014. *A High-Carbon Partnership? Chinese-Latin American Relations in a Carbon-Constrained World*. Global Development and Development at Brookings. Available at: www.brookings.edu/research/a-high-carbon-partnership-chinese-latin-american-relations-in-a-carbon-constrained-world/.

Fearnside, M. P. 2005. Deforestation in Brazilian Amazonia: History, Rates, and Consequences. *Conservation Biology* 19 (3): 680–688.

Fearnside, M. P. and Figuereido, A. 2017. China's Influence on Deforestation in Brazilian Amazon: A Growing Force in the State of Matto Grosso. In Ray, R., Gallagher, K., López, A. and Sanborn, C. ed.: *China and Sustainable Development in Latin America: The Social and Environmental Dimension*. Anthem Press.

Financial Times. 2017. Honduran Farmers Accuse World Bank Arm of "Profiting from Murder." March 8.

Financial Times. 2018. US Warns of Chinese Influence at Multilateral Lenders. December 20.

Financial Times. 2019. Honduran Farmers Flee Effects of Climate Change, December 31.

Front Line Reporters (ed.) 2018. Stop the Killings. Available at: www.frontlinedefenders.org/sites/default/files/stop_the_killings_report_as_revised_04_july1.pdf).

FT-Environment. 2018. Banks Boost Lending to Environmental Damaging Energy Projects. March 28.

FT Special Report. 2018. Sustainable Finance: Central Banks Test Water on Climate Risks, Sustainability Finance.

Fukuda-Parr, S. and Shiga, H. 2016. Normative Framing of Development Cooperation: Japanese Bilateral Aid between the DAC and Southern Donors. *JICA Research Institute, Working Paper 130*.

Gallagher, K. 2018. China Must Calibrate Overseas Lending Towards Paris Climate Goals. *FT–Beyondbrics*, December 10.

Gallagher, K. P., Irwin, A. and Koleski, K. 2012. *New Banks in Town: Chinese Finance in Latin America*. Washington, DC: Inter-American Dialogue.

Global Witness. 2018. Available at: www.globalwitness.org/en/campaigns/environmental-activists/at-what-cost/.

Greenpeace Switzerland. 2018. Swiss Banks in the End of the Fossil Fuel Age.

Griffith-Jones, S. 2016. National Development Banks and Sustainable Infrastructure; The Case of KfW. BU. *Global Economic Governance Initiative, GEGI Working Paper 006–07*.

GoJ. 2015. *White Paper on Development Cooperation.*

Hardyn, G. 1968. The Tragedy of the Commons. *Science* 162(3859): 1243–1248.

Helleiner, E. 2014. *Forgotten Foundations of Bretton Woods: International Development and the Making of the Postwar Order.* Cornell University Press.

Humphrey, C. 2015a. Challenges and Opportunities for Multilateral Development Banks in 21st Century Infrastructure Finance. *Inter-Governmental Group of Twenty-Four and the Global Green Growth Institute, Working Paper Series.*

Humphrey, R. 2015b. Developmental Revolution or Bretton Woods Revisited? Overseas Development Institute. *ODI Working Paper 418.*

Ibarrán, M. E., Ruth, M., Ahmad, S. and London, M. 2007. Climate Change and Natural Disasters: Macroeconomic Performance and Distributional Impacts. *Environment, Development and Sustainability: A Multidisciplinary Approach to the Theory and Practice of Sustainable Development* 11(3): 549–569.

Kondoh, H. 2015. Convergence of Aid Models in Emerging Donors? Learning Processes, Norms and Identities, and Recipients. *Comparative Study on Development. Cooperation Strategies. JICA-RI Research Institute Focusing on G20 Emerging Economies. JICA Research Paper N 106.*

Kring, W. and Gallagher, K. 2019. Strengthening the Foundations? Alternative Institutions for Finance and Development. *Development and Change* 50(1).

Laurent, E. 2019. From the 'Yellow Vests' to the Social-Ecological State. *Social Europe,* January.

Ling J. Y. and Wang, Y. 2014. China-Africa Co-operation in Structural Transformation: Ideas, Opportunities, and Finances. *World Institute for Development Economics Research - WIDER Working Paper N 046.*

Maggiorelli, L. 2017. Chinese Aid to Latin America and the Caribbean: Evolution and Prospects. *Revista Internacional de Cooperación y Desarrollo* 4(2).

Meadows, D., Meadows, D., Randers, J. and Behrens, W. 1972. *The Limits to Growth: A Report to The Club of Rome.* Nebraska: Potomac Books.

Meier, G. M. 2000. Introduction: Ideas for Development. In Meier, G. and Stiglitz, J. eds.: *Frontiers of Development Economics: The Future in Perspective.* Oxford: Oxford University Press.

Meltzer, J. 2016. Financing Low Carbon, Climate Resilient Infrastructure: The Role of Climate Finance and Green Financial Systems. *Global Economy and Development at Brookings.*

Mukand, S. and Rodrik, D. 2015. The Political Economy of Liberal Democracy. *National Bureau of Economic Research: NBER Working Paper 21540.*

Noboa, E. and Upham, P. 2018. Energy Policy and Transdisciplinary Transition Management Arenas in Illiberal Democracies: A Conceptual framework. *Energy Research & Social Science* 46: 114–124.

Nogueira, E., Yanai, A., Vasconcelos, Alencastro, P. and Fearnside, P. 2018. Carbon Stocks and Losses to Deforestation in Protected Areas in Brazilian Amazonia. *Regional Environmental Change* 18(1): 261–270.

Nordhaus, W. and Tobin, J. 1973. Is Growth Obsolete? In Moss, M. ed., *The Measurement of Economic and Social Performance.* National Bureau for Economic Research.

O'Brien, R. and Williams, M. 2016. *Global Political Economy: Evolution and Dynamics.* Palgrave McMillan.

O'Brien K., Sygna, L., Leichenko, R., Adger, W. N., Barnett, J., Mitchell, T., Schipper, L., Tanner, T., Vogel, C. and Mortreux, C. 2008. Disaster Risk Reduction, Climate Change Adaptation and Human Security – A Commissioned Report for the Norwegian Ministry of Foreign Affairs. University of Oslo.

Oil Change International. 2016. The Sky's Limit. Why the Paris Climate Goals Required a Managed Decline of Fossil Fuel Production. Available at: http://priceofoil.org/content/uploads/2016/09/OCI_the_skys_limit_2016_FINAL_2.pdf.

Oil Change International–Friends of the Earth–WWF–Sierra Club. 2017. Talk is Cheap: How G20 Governments are Financing Climate Disaster.

Ohno, I. 2014. Japanese Development Cooperation in a New Era: Recommendations for Network-Based Cooperation. *National Graduate Institute for Policy Studies. GRIPS Discussion Paper 15.*

Ostrom, E. 1990. *Governing the Commons: The Evolution of Institutions for Collective Action.* Cambridge University Press: 280.

Provaggi, A. 2013. *China Development Bank's Financing Mechanisms: Focus on Foreign Investments.* Global Project Center at Stanford University.

Raleigh, C., Jordan, L. and Salehyan, I. 2008. Assessing the Impact of Climate Change on Migration and Conflict. The Social Development Department – The World Bank Group.

Ray, R., Gallagher, K., López, A. and Sanborn, C. 2017. *China and Sustainable Development in Latin America: The Social and Environmental Dimension.* Anthem Frontiers on Global Political Economy. Anthem Press.

Ray, R. and Kamal, R. 2019. Can South–South Cooperation Compete? The Development Bank of Latin America and the Islamic Development Bank. *Development and Change* 50(1): 191–220.

Reuveny, R. 2007. Climate Change-induced Migration and Violent Conflict. *Political Geography* 26: 656–673.

Rich, B. 1994. *Mortgaging the Earth: World Bank, Environmental Impoverishment and the Crisis of Development.* Routledge.

Ritter, C., McCrate, G., Nilsson, H., Fearnside, P., Palme, U. and Antonelli, A. 2017. Environmental Impact Assessment in Brazilian Amazonia: Challenges and Prospects to Assess Biodiversity. *Biological Conservation* 206: 161–168.

Rodrik, D. 2018. *Straight Talk on Trade: Ideas for a Sane World Economy.* Princeton University Press.

Saidi, M. D. and Wolf, C. 2011. Recalibrating Development Co-operation: How can African Countries Benefit from Emerging Partners? *Working Paper No. 302.* Paris: OECD Development Centre

Sanahuja, J. 2001. *Altruismo, Mercado y Poder: El Banco Mundial y la lucha contra la pobreza.* INTERMON-OXFAM.

Sanbord, C. and Chonn Ching, V. 2015. Chinese Investment in Peru's Mining Industry: Blessing or Curse? Boston University. *Global Economic Governance Initiative, Discussion Paper 8.*

Sanchez-Vazquez, L., Espinosa, M. G. and Eguiguren, M. B. (2016). Perception of Socio-Environmental Conflicts in Mining Areas: The Case of the Mirador Project in Ecuador. *Ambiente & Sociedade, São Paulo* 19(2): 23–44.

Sanderson, H. and Forsythe, M. 2013. *China's Superbank: Debt, Oil and Influence – How China Development Bank is Rewriting the Rules of Finance.* Wiley-Bloomberg Press.

Sato, J., Shiga, H., Kovayashi, T. and Kondoh, H. 2010. How do "Emerging" Donors Differ from "Traditional" Donors? An Institutional Analysis of Foreign Aid in Cambodia. *KIJCA Research Institute. JICA Working Paper N 2.*

Schoenmaker, D. 2017. *Investing for the Common Good: A Sustainable Finance Framework.* Bruegel Essays and Lectures Series.

Smallridge, D., Buchner, B., Trabacchi, C., Netto, M., Gomes, J. and Serra, L. 2013. *The Role of National Development Banks in Catalyzing International Climate Finance.* IADB – InterAmerican Development Bank.

Stallings, B. 2016. Chinese Foreign Aid to Latin America: Trying to Win Friends and Influence People. Chapter 4 in Myers, T. and Wise, C. ed.: *The Political Economy of China–Latin America Relations in the New Millenium.* Taylor & Francis Group.

Stern, N. 2007. *The Economics of Climate Change. The Stern Review.* Cambridge University Press.

Stern, N., Bhattacharya, A., Stiglitz, J. and Romani, M. 2013. *A New World's New Development Bank.* Project Syndicate.

Studart, R. and Gallagher, K. 2016. Infrastructure for Sustainable Development: The Role of National Development Banks. Boston University. *Global Economic Governance Initiative. GEGI Policy Brief.*

Stuenkel, O. 2013. Institutionalizing South-South Cooperation: Towards a New Paradigm? *Submitted to the High-Level Panel on the Post-2015 Development Agenda.*

The Ecologist. 2009. World Bank Shackling Developing World to High-carbon Future, October 6.

Tseng, H.-K. and Krog, R. 2014. *No Strings Attached: Chinese Foreign Aid and Regime Stability in Resource-Rich Recipient Countries.* Manuscript.

UN. 2015. Paris Agreement. Available at: https://unfccc.int/files/essential_background/convention/application/pdf/english_paris_agreement.pdf.

US–AID. 2017. Land Rights, Beef Commodity Chains, and Deforestation Dynamics in The Paraguayan Chaco Tenure and Global Climate Change (Tgcc) Program. This publication was produced for review by the United States Agency for International Development by Tetra Tech, through the Tenure and Global Climate Change Project, Contract No: AID-OAA-TO-13-00016.

Wade, R. 1997. *Greening the Bank:* The Struggle over the Environment, 1970–1995. In Devesh Kapur, J., Lewis, P. and Webb, R. ed.: *The World Bank: Its First Half Century, Vol. 2.* Brookings Institution Press.

Walker, W., Baccini, A., Schwartzman, S., Ríos, S., Oliveira-Miranda, M., Augusto, C., Romero Ruiz, M., Soria Arrasco, C., Ricardo, B., Smith, R., Meyer, C., Jintiach, J.C. and Vasquez Campos, E. 2014. Forest Carbon in Amazonia: The Unrecognized Contribution of Indigenous Territories and Protected Natural Areas. *Carbon Management* 5(5–6): 479–485.

Wang, Y. 2016. The Sustainable Infrastructure Finance of China Development Bank: Composition, Experience and Policy Implications. Boston University. *Global Economic Governance Initiative. GEGI Policy Brief 05.07.*

WCED. 1987. *Our Common Future*. Oxford: World Commission on Environment and Development, published by the United Nations through the Oxford University Press.

Wright, H., Holmes, I., Barbe, R. and Hawkins, J. 2017. Greening Financial Flows: What Progress Has Been Made in the Development Banks? *E3G: Briefing Paper*.

Xu, J. and Carey, R. 2015. China's International Development Finance: Past, Present, and Future. *UNU-WIDER. Wider Working Paper 130*.

Zakaria, F. 1997. The Rise of Illiberal Democracy. *Foreign Affairs* November–December.

Zarsky, L. and Stanley, L. 2011. Searching for Gold in the Highlands of Guatemala: Economic Benefits and Environmental Risks of the Marlin Mine. *Global Development and the Environment Institute at TUFTS University*.

Zhou, L., Gilbert, S., Wang, Y., Muñoz Cabre, M. and Gallagher, K. P. 2018. Moving the Green Belt and Road Initiative: From Words to Actions. *Working Paper*. Washington, DC: World Resources Institute. Available at: www.wri.org/publication/moving-the-green-belt.

35

The constructivist IPE of regionalism in South America

Germán C. Prieto

Introduction – a constructivist framework for the study of regionalism

From a constructivist standpoint, regions are, like everything else in social life, social constructions. This means that regions are not fixed, neither defined *a priori* before actors start interacting in ways that increasingly define a regional space, and further, to paraphrase Alex Wendt's famous statement, it means that regions become 'what actors make of them'. But specifically, what a constructivist analysis of the IPE of regionalism contributes to the understanding of the social construction of regions is the assessment of the relationship between material incentives – benefits and costs – and ideational structures, like identity, institutions, knowledge and culture, in orienting actors' interactions that bring forward the process of a geographic space becoming a region 'more or less'.[1]

Constructivism defines a region as an imagined space, though always geographically delimited, where actors' activities are more or less determined by what happens in such region, either because

Table 35.1 Theoretical perspectives on the unfolding of regionalism

Approach	Core explanation
Realism	Regionalism unfolds as long as it increases material capabilities for states.
Liberalism	Regionalism unfolds as long as regional cooperation provides material benefits for states dealing with interdependence.
Marxism	Regionalism unfolds as long as it allows centre states to maintain their dominant position, or periphery states to improve their exchange terms with the centre.
Neo-Gramscian Critical Theory	Regionalism unfolds as long as it serves hegemonic of counter-hegemonic projects for states.
Constructivism	Regionalism unfolds as long as there are ideational structures of regional identity and regional institutions mutually constituting each other and constituting states' interests.
Poststructuralism	Regionalism unfolds as long as there are discourses legitimating state action towards regionalism.

they willingly procure for the region to play a role in their actions, or because some of the region's social structures – like collective identity and regional institutions – compel agents to account for the region in a greater or lesser extent to develop their actions.[2] As a social construction, thus, the region may be a means for procuring certain goals, but it can also be a structure that conditions actors' actions. A region is both imagined and geographically located because regional structures are socially shared 'mental models' for action, but always referred to a geographical space that has physical boundaries (not necessarily much static) and that eventually adjoins other regions.

The constructivist literature on regionalism and region-building has focused on identity and institutions as the two most important ideational structures orienting the pursuit of regionalism,[3] fundamentally for two reasons: on the one hand, organising a region along certain political and economic lines – as regionalism is broadly defined[4] – entails agreeing on a model containing the guidelines and aims of regionalism. For this, constructivists contemplate different sources of states' identification with one another, like culture, common past, interdependence (economic or otherwise), common fate (including common aims and/or threats), ideology, political and economic homogeneity (regarding problems and resources) and also, eventually, a tradition of self-restraint (avoiding aggression on one another), which generates trust to cooperate.[5] On the other hand, organising a region along a certain type of political and economic model requires building some sort of institutional framework that allows states to coordinate their actions, make decisions and implement policies, and eventually managing common resources they allocate for achieving their regionalist aims.[6] Constructivism acknowledges a relationship of mutual constitution (co-constitution) between identity and institutions, for it is expected that institutions are built because actors identify with one another and design institutions to pursue common aims. Yet, institutions may also be spontaneously created in the absence of previous significant collective identification, and once they start operating they can make actors identify with one another because they see themselves as reproducing – or acting along the lines of – those institutions, which in turn also make actors identify with the institutions they reproduce.[7] Hence, the analysis of the relationships between collective identity and regional institutions, considering their sources and process of formation, and their interplay with material conditions and incentives, will be the focus of the constructivist analysis of the IPE of regionalism here developed.

Box 35.1 Approaching regionalism from constructivism

- For constructivism, regions are social constructions, produced through actors' interaction in geographically limited spaces, but which acquire meaning in actors' mindsets due to the importance regions have for defining actors' interests.
- A constructivist analysis of the IPE of regionalism assesses the relationship between material incentives – benefits and costs – and ideational structures, like identity, institutions, knowledge and culture, in orienting actors' interactions in the process of constructing a region.
- Constructivists focus on collective identity and regional institutions as the two main ideational structures orienting the unfolding of regionalism.

In what follows, the chapter will address the two main regionalist projects that have taken place in South America since its countries' independence from Spain and Portugal, namely the Andean Community (AC) and the Common Market of the South (Mercosur).[8] By focusing on a number of case studies for each regionalist project, it will be argued that collective identity and regional institutions played an important role in orienting state action towards regionalism, for they significantly shifted state action that could have taken another direction facing the presence or absence of certain material incentives. In the case of the AC, it will be shown that cultural, ideological and intergroup collective identities were determinant for the unfolding of regionalism in the three case studies observed, where regional institutions operated also as powerful sources of state identification with one another, and as pushers for bringing cooperation forward. In the case of the Mercosur, it will be contended that in the absence of strong regional institutions, and of a cultural and an intergroup identity, the ideological dimension of collective identity was the main driver of regionalism in the two case studies addressed. But before proceeding with this analysis, a word must be said about South America as a region and South American regionalism as distinct from a broader Latin American one.

While the noun 'Latin America' to denominate Hispanic America and Brazil became fully accepted in international official discourse after the Second World War,[9] the first employments of the noun 'South America' to distinguish this region from broader Latin America in international official discourse are more difficult to trace. A turning point could be set at Brazilian president Itamar Franco's proposal of constituting a South America Free Trade Area in 1993, after which presidents Cardoso and Lula adopted South America as one main target of Brazilian foreign policy, something that had not ever occurred in the past.[10]

The fact that regions were not named as such before – particularly in official discourse – does not mean they did not exist. On the contrary, if they are first named it might be because those who name them have been acknowledging their existence for some time. Yet, once they are named, regions begin to operate as new referents for – say – political talking, surely both in official and intellectual/academic affairs. The question of major concern at this point is whether regionalism can take place without referring to a distinctive 'named' region. From a broad, and not only a constructivist perspective, the answer is no, since to organise a region under certain political and economic lines requires defining clearly enough what is the regional space that is going to be organised. In this sense, those regionalist projects that take place within a region that is not recognised as such, can hardly account as regionalisms for that region. However, there can be regionalist projects aiming at organising a region within a region, also known as 'subregionalist projects', that even though do not aim at organising the broader or macro-region, they take the broader region as a reference point, and in this fashion may yield certain outputs for the organisation of the macro-region, as in a form of regionalism-by-default.

In the case of South America, the first (sub)regionalist project that emerged in this region was the Andean Pact (later on the Andean Community) in 1969,[11] aimed at organising the so-called 'Andean region' and with no particular reference to South America, but instead, to Latin America.[12] In the same vein, when the Mercosur was created in 1991, the Treaty of Asuncion's preamble stated that the project should be considered as an advance towards Latin American integration, and there was no explicit reference to South America. Thirteen years after the Mercosur's creation, the Community of South American Nations (later on UNASUR) was founded, then becoming the first South American organisation to include the twelve countries located in this subcontinent, as the single other regional organisation, the CONMEBOL, only included ten of them.[13] However, although UNASUR has been broadly recognised as a regionalist project, its type of regionalism differs from the one of the AC and Mercosur, for the political and economic lines engaged by this body to organise the South American region are not as clear and homogenous. On the one hand, UNASUR does not address trade and economic issues,[14] like the AC and Mercosur do, and therefore lacks specific economic lineaments, at least in relation to a particular economic model. On the other, while UNASUR intends to ensure a peace zone in South America, and to constitute a forum for political dialogue and cooperation among member states, there isn't either a concrete political model to follow, besides one of dialogue and peace,[15] which resembles more a kind of regional fora like the Rio Group (now CELAC),[16] or the Organization of American States (OAS), that correspond more to international organisations than to regionalist projects as such. In any case, and though the AC and Mercosur are more suitable for comparison and analysis of regionalism in South America, some reflections will be made about UNASUR in the concluding remarks of the present chapter.

The Andean Community

The Andean Community (AC) is a regionalist project that started in 1969 (then named the Andean Pact) including Colombia, Bolivia, Ecuador, Peru and Chile, as countries sharing a common geographic feature, being that having portions of their territory in the Andes mountain range. However, besides geography, there was also an ethnic and cultural feature that excluded Argentina (which also has territory on the Andes), as it was the Inca heritage that permeated most pre-Columbian indigenous groups inhabiting these lands before the Spanish conquest in the sixteenth century. This cultural heritage defined 'the Andean', a concept attached to the Andes Mountains as the Inca's motherland – the *Tiwantinsuyu*.[17] Subsequently, Venezuela joined the Andean group in 1973 and Chile withdrew in 1976, once the dictator Pinochet chose to pursue a development strategy that clashed against the import substitution model engaged by the Andean Pact since 1969. In these terms, not only a discourse about 'the Andean' (*lo andino*) had evolved in the so-called Andean countries, referring to music, handcrafts, traditions, indigenous peoples and culture in general, but also the AC official discourse began reproducing this concept of the 'Andean' since its creation, in an effort to build a regional identity that justified the pursuit of Andean regionalism as distinct from other regionalisms and regions.

A previous work of mine[18] identified this concept of the 'Andean' as a main component of what I established as the cultural dimension of the AC's collective identity, which also entailed a component of political homogeneity, consisting of a common history as republics that were liberated by Simón Bolívar (not much shared by Peru and much less by Chile), and sharing political features in their political regime type, namely, underdevelopment, poverty, *caudillismo*, corruption and inequality.[19] As a result, not only Andean regionalism became a political object and the target of several academic approaches, but also a whole field of Andean studies emerged as a distinctive area for the social sciences in Andean countries. The Andean region surely existed before the AC, but this regionalist project just rounded up the definition of a region where political and economic processes of its own took place, and mostly, concrete policies were being made for addressing them, in the form of Andean regionalism.

Box 35.2 The cultural dimension of collective identity in the Andean community

- The cultural dimension of collective identity in the AC corresponds to those ideas about a common past and political history that have provided a sense of cultural and political homogeneity to Andean countries.
- Culturally, 'the Andean' (*lo andino*) refers to the cultural heritage of the Inca Empire that has been preserved by good portions of indigenous peoples in Andean countries and has eventually become part of their national culture.
- Politically, Andean countries share a common history as countries liberated by Simón Bolívar (though less for Peru and Chile), and have maintained common type-features regarding poverty, underdevelopment, *caudillismo* and corruption.

The other two dimensions of collective identity that I was able to distinguish were the ideological and intergroup ones. The ideological dimension refers to the consensus on the economic model chosen to pursue developmental goals, whereas the intergroup dimension refers to the sense of belonging to a group that emerges among national officials, and also between them and regional bureaucrats, which considerably affects their actions working in both domestic and regional affairs.[20] These three dimensions of collective identity will be employed to analyse the IPE of the AC and Mercosur's regionalisms, altogether with regional institutions like regional norms and regional organisations.

The AC emerged in 1969 as a project fully committed with the developmental goal of industrialisation through import substitution, all-fashioned by the so-called ECLAC[21] thinking of the mid-twentieth century. The ECLAC conceived development as the process of industrialisation, where the productive structure of Latin American countries, traditionally based on commodities or primary goods, should become based on manufactured goods with greater added value. It was expected that the manufacturing sector would attract more workers from the rural sector, which meant they would be paid higher wages, and their greater purchasing power would expand the domestic market and consolidate it as the driver for economic growth, thus reducing the commodity-export dependency that had characterised these countries since their times of independence. While the Latin American Free Trade Association (LAFTA) was created in 1960 to foster manufacturing trade among the largest Latin American economies, slow progress and several failures to fulfil tariff reduction schedules shown by LAFTA members motivated Andean countries to create a regional scheme of their own, which ensured them a larger market and incentives to develop certain industrial sectors, in an effort to follow their Central American neighbours who had launched the Central American Common Market also in 1960, after having been excluded from LAFTA (for reasons of least relative development).

So, in this scenario, the economic–material incentive for the AC creation was clear: Andean countries needed a regional market to increase their manufacturing trade and support their domestic industrialisation policies. In these terms, where do ideational structures like collective identity and regional institutions fit in, considered from an IPE perspective? While the analysis of the AC offered in this section will focus in the 1990s and the 2000s, two things are worth mentioning here regarding this question. First, the criteria for defining the geographic scope of the Andean regionalist project at its foundation – that is, membership – corresponded to a conception of identity referring to 'being Andean', and not to economic criteria like GDP, trade balancing or the size of countries' industrial sectors. Second, the institutional framework designed for developing the regionalist project was a complex one that entailed a certain degree of sovereignty cession: a free trade area, a customs union and a set of Sectoral Plans for Industrial Development (SPIDs), all governed by an intergovernmental body, the Andean Commission (composed of Ministers of Trade), which could make decisions based on a majority (two-thirds of member states); and by a more supranational one, the *Junta* (composed by three delegates chosen by the Andean Commission). This type of institutional organisation very much resembled the one of the European Economic Community, which was taken as a model for Andean regional integration, and in this line decisions made by the Andean Commission became part of member countries' national legal bodies without needing the approval of their national parliaments, despite the fact that they were made by a majority vote and not by consensus. Sovereignty cession, at least on those areas where the Commission and the *Junta* intervened (namely trade and customs ones) was at play, and thus formal regional integration was taking place in the Andean region. As will be further argued, this type of institutional framework contributed very much to the consolidation of collective identity, particularly in its intergroup dimension, and this crucially determined the progress and maintenance of Andean regionalism.

During the 1970s intra-regional trade multiplied ten times, and though SPIDs did not prosper, several member countries' manufacturing industries, particularly in the foods and beverages, textiles, plastics, chemicals and metal–mechanic sectors grew substantially thanks to the preferential trade and customs agreements that fostered import substitution in the Andean regional market. The growing pace of intra-regional trade faced a dramatic fall in the 1980s, mainly due to the decreasing demand for imports caused by the debt crisis that affected most Latin American countries. But in the meantime, the institutional structure of the Andean Group had proved suitable for coordinating trade and customs policies, and Andean collective identity had strengthened along all its three dimensions, particularly in the intergroup one, as the events of the 1990s would later show.

In 1989, at the Galapagos Summit, AC member countries' presidents decided to re-launch the Andean integration process under the orientations of so-called 'open regionalism', which dictated organising a regional market with enough protection to foster national producers' competitiveness, but as much open as possible to trade with third partners, so the region would serve as a platform for international economic insertion. For this effort, a regional free trade zone and a customs union were needed, but AC member countries were not in the same material conditions to adopt these trade schemes. On the one hand, Venezuela and Colombia had been less impacted by the debt crisis of the previous years, while Peru had suffered major economic damage. On the other hand, Bolivia and Ecuador were still economies with a lesser relative level of development, and thus needed special and differential treatment. Hence, Peruvian authorities were reluctant to grant greater market access to Colombian and Venezuelan exports, and to adopt a scaled common tariff as Colombia and Venezuela wanted. They were also jealous that special and differential treatment was given to Ecuador and Bolivia, given that Peru's economic situation was also critical at the time. But since the Andean free trade zone (FTZ) and the Andean common external tariff (CET) were crucial tools for the success of open regionalism and the consolidation of an Andean common market – namely the ultimate goal of Andean integration at the time – the other member countries reached the point to compel Peru to choose between adopting both trade schemes, or to quit AC membership. These negotiations, which took place between 1990 and 1997, showed the importance of collective identity and regional institutions for explaining Peru and the other members' decision to preserve Peru's full AC membership without adopting the FTZ and the CET, at least not in the same fashion as the other members.[22]

Despite the material incentives Peru had for not adopting these trade schemes, Peru chose to remain an AC member and ask for a waiver to adopt the FTZ and the CET, and after tough negotiations Peruvian delegates finally convinced the other AC members to obtain it. A constructivist IPE analysis of the role of collective identity and regional institutions significantly contributes to explain this outcome. Hyperinflation and the strong supply contraction of the Peruvian industrial sector made Peruvian authorities prefer a flat tariff instead of a scaled one, as the one adopted by the other AC members. And the lower competitiveness of Peruvian manufacturing industries vis-à-vis Colombian and Venezuela ones made them reluctant to grant freer access to Colombian and Venezuelan exports. Hence, from a materialist calculation point of view, Peru had enough incentives not to adopt both trade schemes and quit AC membership, as the other members were asking it to do. However, interviews with national officials and AC regional bureaucrats, contrasted with press reports and official documents of the time, pointed to certain ideas about an Andean collective identity that motivated Peru to remain an AC member and the other member countries to ease the pressure on Peru and accept its permanence in the regional bloc without adopting the FTZ and the CET. These ideas had to do with two main identity issues. First, the political cost that the Peruvian government did not want to pay for leaving the AC. Interviewees, official documents and press reports associated this political cost with a Peruvian identity as an integrationist country, and as an AC member that had long benefited from its membership to the Andean group since the 1970s. Second, a conception of fraternity – pointed out by interviewees – that member countries had about themselves as being 'naturally Andean', and thus unable to escape an Andean identity that led countries to keep negotiating despite their harsh differences.

Interestingly, these identity issues were tightly related to regional institutions, mainly Andean norms and the Andean General Secretariat (AGS – then corresponding to the *Junta*[23]) as the organisation in charge of elaborating the agendas and schedules for negotiations. On the one hand, Peruvian authorities benefited from the existence of Andean norms that significantly helped the making of their trade policies. On the other, the AGS having a supranational character, in terms of their bureaucrats representing the whole group of states and not each of them individually – and the autonomy this implied – which enabled it to mediate between member countries, provided technical support to convince Peru about the benefits of remaining an AC member, and even pressured Peru not to leave the regional scheme despite the material costs this could imply for its economic policy (though there could be material benefits as well, derived from greater market access to the other AC members). As a result, both norms and the AGS reinforced Peru's Andean identity and its government's perception that leaving the AC would imply a too high political cost that it was not ready to pay, neither facing the domestic public nor at the regional and international arenas.

Box 35.3 Collective identity and regional institutions explaining Peru remaining an AC member

- The political cost that, according to interviewees and press reports of the time, the Peruvian government did not want to pay for abandoning the AC, is related to Peru's identity as an integrationist country that belonged to the Andean integration process since 1969.
- There was also a conception of fraternity between AC members that gave account of states' identification with each other, which motivated Peru to maintain full membership to the regionalist project despite its perception of inconvenience towards the free trade area and the common external tariff.
- Peru also identified with Andean norms as they provided benefits for Peru's trade policymaking.
- The Andean General Secretariat (then called the *Junta*) provided technical support and mediated among AC members for solving their differences with Peru.

The other two case studies of my analysis showed something similar. In the case of the AC collective negotiation of a FTA with the EU between 2008 and 2010, Andean collective identity proved determinant for engaging negotiations in a collective fashion and for their unfolding, which ended in Bolivia and Ecuador dropping off negotiations and Colombia and Peru signing a multi-party agreement with the EU. According to interviewees, AC member countries decided to collectively negotiate the FTA with the EU, not so much because this was a EU condition for negotiating, but rather because Andean countries saw in collective negotiation an opportunity to reinforce the AC integration process, which had severely weakened with

Venezuela's withdrawal from the AC in 2006 due to Colombia and Peru's signing of FTAs with the US. Such motivation indicated a strong sense of member countries' identification with the AC, which corresponded to an issue of collective identity. On the other hand, interviewees highlighted the benefits they obtained from Andean norms for negotiating with the EU, particularly in issues related to non-tariff barriers, and also the identity that Andean norms provided to them for negotiating as a group, helping each other and learning from each other for defining their negotiating positions and strategies.

Furthermore, the ideological dimension of collective identity played an important role in the unfolding of negotiations with the EU, for interviewees pointed to ideological differences as the main cause for Ecuador and Bolivia's decision to withdraw from these negotiations, after being unable to agree with Colombia and Peru on intellectual property and environmental issues. The ideological shift that both the new Ecuadorian and Bolivian governments made regarding their development model (with the arrival to power of Rafael Correa and Evo Morales, respectively), opposing neoliberalism and free trade, broke the ideological consensus that AC member countries had kept for the last 18 years around open regionalism and trade liberalisation, and the breaking-off of this ideological dimension of collective identity crumbled the bloc's last bet on trade integration as the main driver of Andean regionalism.

Box 35.4 Identity and institutions in AC collective negotiations with the EU

- Member states' interest in reinforcing the Andean integration process through collective negotiations of a FTA with the EU demonstrated strong identification with the regionalist project.
- Member states' identification with the AC was also explained by the benefits they obtained from Andean norms for trade policy and bargaining with third parties.
- The breaking-off of the ideological consensus around free trade and market economics led Bolivia and Ecuador to abandon collective negotiations with the EU, which showed the importance of collective identity for the AC acting as a bloc.

In the case of the implementation of the Integrated Plan for Social Development (PIDS, in Spanish), interviewees stressed the group feeling that emerged when, at the beginning of the 2000s, and facing a decrease in the pace of intra-regional trade growth, AC authorities decided to advance a social integration agenda, and national officials began talking about their social problems and policies, finding they had many things in common and a lot to learn from each other. This group feeling grew as new institutional bodies were created for formulating and implementing the PIDS, and with time a process of mutual learning developed particularly in the areas of socio-labour and environmental standards that very much helped the making of national legislation for AC member countries. In a time where trade integration was facing stagnation and the political and security issues included in the AC agenda during the 1990s had lost momentum, the PIDS and cooperation in the social area became an important driver of Andean regionalism, mostly led by issues of collective identity in turn fostered by regional institutions. These ideational structures were more important for the pursuit of regionalism than material incentives, mainly because material benefits from such cooperation, in the form of accessing significant amounts of financial resources or getting to attend domestic social needs in a large scale, were lowly expected.

Box 35.5 Identity and institutions in the implementation of the integrated plan for social development

- Facing the stagnation of the trade area, AC member countries' decision to foster cooperation around social issues denoted their identification with the regionalist project.
- A group feeling emerged among national and regional officials meeting at institutional spaces where they found they had many social problems to share and a lot to learn from each other.
- AC member states also developed strong identification in the social area as their regional agreements became sources for their national legislations in labour, environmental and health issues.

The analysis of the importance of collective identity and regional institutions, through their contrast with the significance of material incentives in orienting state action towards regionalism, constituted a constructivist IPE analysis that yielded some relevant conclusions about the factors that explain the progress and maintenance of Andean regionalism, and that may well be applied to the analysis of other regionalist projects, as will be done in the next section: first, the importance of pursuing regionalism for preserving a regionalist state identity, that is, an image of a state/government fully committed to the pursuit of regionalism as an Andean/Latin American state that sees regional cooperation as a must. This is tightly related to the political cost that states do not want to pay for leaving a regionalist project. Second, institutional flexibility as a source of

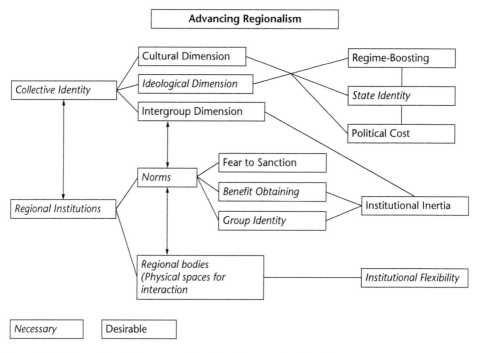

Figure 35.1 A constructivist approach to the advance of regionalism

Source: Own authorship.

state identification with the regional scheme, inasmuch as such flexibility makes states comfortable enough to engage what they want and marginalise from what they consider harmful, and keep negotiating until a good deal is achieved. And third, the institutional inertia that is generated inasmuch as national officials and regional bureaucrats get used to working with each other on both regional and domestic affairs, which reinforces the intergroup dimension of collective identity and makes it harder for governments and states to get rid of regional cooperation even if they have strong reasons to do so. These factors guarantee neither the maintenance nor the progress of regionalism; instead, they help to explain its pace, and its preservation in times of decline. As a conclusion, contrasting ideational structures like collective identity and regional institutions with material incentives for pursuing regionalism facilitates understanding the unfolding of regionalism, and so this same exercise will be made in what follows for the case of Mercosur.

Mercosur

To start with, the Southern Cone has not had a source of regional collective identity based on a shared history and culture, like the Andean region has, at least not one referring to a common pre-Columbian indigenous heritage, or a shared history of independence.[24] This could, in principle, discard the cultural dimension of collective identity as a significant factor orienting Mercosur regionalism. In its beginnings, the ideological dimension seems to have been the main dimension of collective identity explaining the creation of Mercosur. Several works[25] show that the ideological consensus on the belief that economic liberalisation was key to achieving democratisation and vice versa, mainly between Argentina and Brazil, emerged as a fundamental source of member countries' identification with the Mercosur project, which altogether with other sources of collective identity like economic interdependence, homogeneity in the type of political regime and self-restraint,[26] ensured the prosperous first stage of Mercosur between 1991 and 1999. Yet, because this chapter's emphasis is on the relationships between collective identity and regional institutions, going over the times of Mercosur creation does not seem very sound, because the project's institutional framework had just began to be designed. Nonetheless, it is worth noting that, in contrast to the AC, Mercosur's original institutional framework did not get any close to a supranational one, as the leading bodies – the Common Market Council (composed by Ministers of Trade and Finance) and the Common Market Group (composed by ministerial representatives) – were merely intergovernmental and made decisions only by consensus, and further, these decisions needed (and still do) approval from national parliaments for them to be incorporated into member states' national legislations. This lack of interest in sovereignty cession could be initially explained precisely because of the lack of other sources of state identification with one another, like culture and a common past, though this is not the focus of the analysis here.

Box 35.6 Collective identity in Mercosur

- The lack of a common past and history initially rule out the relevance of a cultural dimension of collective identity in Mercosur.
- The consensus on neoliberalism, and the belief that economic liberalisation would foster democratisation in the Southern Cone, showed the relevance of the ideological dimension of collective identity for the creation of Mercosur.
- The lack of a strong institutional framework (also without involving sovereignty cessions) made it difficult for the intergroup dimension of collective identity to develop in Mercosur.

Instead, and considering that detailed case studies cannot be addressed here due to the lack of fieldwork involving semi-structured interviews (as could be done in the previous section regarding the AC),[27] two cases can be illustrative for the analysis of collective identity and regional institutions in the Mercosur's unfolding: one, maintaining the Mercosur during the economic crisis that struck member countries at the millennium's turn, and two, developing cooperation in the social area in the first half of the 2000s. These two cases are chosen for two reasons: first, the fact that the economic crisis Mercosur faced at the end of the twentieth century threw the project's maintenance into doubt, and after, the hope that member countries placed on social issues to re-launch the regionalist project; and second, the possibility of accessing some thorough literature that provides relevant information to analyse identity and institutional issues in both cases.[28]

After a prosper decade in terms of increasing trade flows and forwarding institutional agreements, the Mercosur faced a strong halt first in 1999 and then in 2000–2001, when both Brazil and Argentina devalued their currencies and created a trade and macroeconomic conflict that led authorities from both countries to question the convenience of their membership to the regionalist project.[29] Between 1991 and 1998 Mercosur's exports to the world almost doubled, going from US$45.9 billion to US$82.3 billion, falling to US$74.3 billion in 1999, but recovering again to US$84.6 billion in 2000 and US$87.9 billion in 2001. In turn, in the same period intra-Mercosur exports quadrupled, going from US$5.1 billion in 1991 to US$20.3 billion in 1998, though not showing the same recovery pattern of total exports after the fall to US$15.2 billion in 1999, since intra-regional exports went only up to US$17.7 billion and US$15.2 billion in 2000 and 2001 respectively. Hence as a share of total exports, intra-Mercosur exports went from 8.9 per cent in 1990 to 25 per cent in 1998.[30] Additionally, after the signing of the Treaty of Asuncion, foundational of Mercosur in 1991, the Ouro Preto Protocol established the customs union in 1994, and in 1998 the Ushuaia Protocol was signed establishing Mercosur as a democratic space. Approaching the end of the twentieth century, the Mercosur was thus posited as a successful example of the open regionalism strategy promoted by neo-liberalism believers, and surely the most successful one in Latin America, despite the fact that the customs union had plenty of exceptions, and very little progress had been made regarding non-tariff barriers reduction, as well as defining common rules for commercial defence mechanisms, and dispute settlement in trade issues among member countries.[31]

In the first months of 1999, and after a period of severe contraction in net inflows of foreign capital, Brazil completed a total devaluation of 40 per cent of the *real*, which severely impacted the exports and competitiveness of the other Mercosur members.[32] In the following months and during 2000, Argentina proceeded to apply a wide range of safeguards and other trade protective measures, as well as increasing tariffs and thus failing to fulfil Mercosur's CET, with Paraguay and Uruguay proceeding in similar fashion. Facing this cascade of unilateral action, both Argentinian and Brazilian authorities began to question the viability and utility of Mercosur, as reported in both countries' main media press. These positions, added to public and private manifestations of Argentinian and Uruguayan officials declaring their interest in negotiating FTAs with the US,[33] brought the Mercosur into its first serious critical moment. However, despite the press reporting that both Brazilian and Argentinian authorities tabled the possibility of abandoning the regionalist project in the first half of 2000, and even after the Argentinian devaluation that reached nearly 140 per cent by the end of 2002 – with its respective serious impacts over the other members' exports[34] – the Mercosur was preserved.

Phillips points to three factors that may explain Mercosur's maintenance.[35] First, the bloc's external negotiations; second, developments in institutionalisation; and third, incipient policy harmonisation processes, particularly in the macroeconomic and social areas. The task of the constructivist IPE approach proposed in this chapter thus consists of analysing the role of collective identity and regional institutions in the unfolding of these three factors. However, before we start, it must be clarified that from a constructivist perspective, only the first factor pointed out by Phillips may soundly account as an explanation for Mercosur's maintenance, for it was something that had been taking place before the crisis; in contrast, the other two rather correspond to actions that followed authorities' decision to make efforts for preserving the regionalist project, namely, developing further institutionalisation and policy coordination. However, since both factors are tightly related to institutional issues, and since Phillips provides great detail about their unfolding process, they account as fertile material to develop the analysis here proposed.

Starting with bloc external negotiations,[36] Phillips asserts that the Free Trade Area of the Americas (FTAA) negotiating process that had been taking place since the second half of the 1990s was seen by Mercosur members as something they should address together in order to gain greater bargaining power, particularly in issues regarding market access and agriculture (what was then called the WTO-plus agenda).[37] But while this sounds perfectly reasonable, we have already observed that the only cornerstone that Mercosur members could be ready to defend as a bloc achievement was the customs union, as they had left their differences almost untouched regarding the reduction of non-tariff barriers, namely a key issue in hemispheric trade negotiations with the US. Furthermore, while there was an official position towards addressing WTO negotiations as a bloc, in practice Mercosur members, particularly Brazil and Argentina, held contrasting positions towards a wide range of issues (including sugar, intellectual property, pharmaceuticals and services), and were even bringing their trade disputes into the WTO,[38] which didn't quite match their intentions to participate in WTO negotiations as a unified bloc. Could it thus be possible that Mercosur members wanted to collectively address FTAA negotiations because of a certain degree of identification with the regionalist process, and not only because together they would have greater bargaining power, just as AC members did with the EU[39] as showed in the previous section?

Increasing bargaining power is closely related to Phillips's observation that Brazil was particularly interested in obtaining its Mercosur partners' support for its positions to gain leverage facing the US's, in an attempt to build a South American pole within FTAA negotiations.[40] Furthermore, Phillips suggests that another reason why Mercosur countries wanted to collectively address FTAA negotiations was their fear that, because the regionalist project was mainly a trade agreement (involving a customs union), it would be absorbed by the hemispheric agreement once the latter was completed.[41] What could these aspects be, besides material benefits obtained from the first years of intra-regional trade, which made member states identify with the Mercosur project to the point of preserving it vis-à-vis the FTAA?

Although there is enough evidence showing that the ideological consensus (ideological dimension of collective identity) around neoliberalism and open regionalism among Mercosur countries remained solid by the end of the 1990s, Phillips does not provide any evidence about other sources of members' identification with the regionalist project, at least not of the type showed in the previous section regarding cultural aspects – like states' 'integrationist' or 'fraternal' identities – or institutional aspects – like identification with regional norms/institutions or the emergence of an intergroup identity among members' national officials. On the contrary, Phillips questions the strength of such ideological consensus, arguing that the four member countries had different visions of regionalism: the Brazilian vision envisaged regionalism as a tool for promoting industrialisation, while Argentina saw it as tool for promoting trade; on their part, Uruguay and Paraguay saw regionalism as a matter of economic necessity because their inferior size compelled them to secure access to their two biggest regional partners' markets.[42] Moreover,

Phillips points to particular issues that hampered Mercosur's bloc bargaining at the time, like the lack of bargaining expertise in the FTAA negotiating areas (except market access and agriculture, more developed at WTO stances), and a tendency to bilateralism that could be observed in both Argentina's and Uruguay's moves to seek FTAs with the US.[43] Other issues like interdependence and common fate may also explain Mercosur members' decision to collectively engage FTAA (and other) negotiations, but because these issues are clearer to observe in the other two factors suggested by Phillips, the analysis will now move to address them.

Although Mercosur members held differing positions towards institutionalisation during the 1990s, concerns about strengthening the project's institutional structure increased due to the economic crises suffered at the turn of the century, particularly after Argentina's financial difficulties that appeared to convene the other members' solidarity and support to face the pressures of the IMF and international creditors.[44] According to Phillips, while Brazil and Argentina had favoured a 'light' intergovernmental institutional framework, Uruguay and Paraguay desired a more rule-based and stronger institutional design that could protect their special treatment from the unilateralism – and at times bilateralism – showed by their larger Mercosur partners.[45] But facing Argentinian devaluation, and the following reaction of both Uruguayan and Brazilian authorities of breaching the customs union to protect from lower Argentinian prices, different sectors began to call for designing a dispute settlement mechanism, developing a 'Mercosur jurisprudence' and even creating a parliamentary commission.[46] Hence, in 2002 the Olivos Protocol was signed, establishing a Permanent Review Tribunal, consisting of five judges whose judgements were not open to appeal and could not be taken to the dispute settlement system of the WTO. Also in 2002, the Mercosur Secretariat was created, after Uruguay and Paraguay had pushed for the conversion of the Permanent Secretariat into a more technical institution, transcending the administrative character it had until then.[47] And in 2003 Argentina and Brazil proposed the creation of a Mercosur Parliament, which was finally created in 2005.

On its part, the core of the discussion about macroeconomic policy coordination revolved around the monetary union, which was first formally proposed by Argentinian authorities in 1998 but rapidly dismissed by Brazilian ones. In contrast, Brazil agreed with Argentina to table the proposal once again in 2003.[48] Crucially, what Phillips underscores about this new process of policy coordination is not the viability of the monetary union as such – which at the time she (correctly) found impossible – but rather the fact that this idealist goal motivated economic authorities from all member countries to gather and attempt to coordinate fiscal and monetary issues, under a common consciousness that measures should be taken to protect as a group from future economic critical moments like the ones suffered at the turn of the millennium.[49] Hence, in the first years of the 2000s, policy measures and adjustments were made regarding issues like lowering inflation to international levels through ensuring Central Banks' independence, fixing debt limits for financial self-sufficiency, fostering the free movement of factors of production (especially labour) and ensuring greater flexibility in prices and wages, and harmonising exchange rate policies.[50] In these terms, from Phillips's account it can be inferred that there was a strong identification of member states with the Mercosur as an institutional framework to handle macroeconomic issues, despite the fact that the regionalist project had proven incapable of providing the tools for collectively managing economic crises and, on the contrary, operating as a means of contagion.

To this point, therefore, it is not possible to establish that the interest in bringing forward greater institutionalisation and macroeconomic policy coordination in Mercosur was triggered by institutional benefits obtained in the past, or by an intergroup dimension of collective identity, since what had been missing was precisely an institutional framework that enabled those. The creation of the Permanent Review Tribunal and the transformation of the Mercosur

Secretariat may be explained by Mercosur authorities' conviction about their necessity, after having witnessed increasing unilateral action during economic crisis, and facing the lack of instruments to countervail contagion effects derived from economic interdependence. Likewise, the issues of collective identity that could explain the renewed interest in macroeconomic policy coordination may have been a common consciousness about the risks of macroeconomic damage, and the recognition of a strong interdependence among Mercosur members – mostly Argentina and Brazil – which derived from deep trade liberalisation pursued during the 1990s. Eventually, this consciousness about the significance of economic interdependence and the belief that the Mercosur should serve to deal with it in times of crisis (common fate), may well also explain member states' interests in collectively engaging external negotiations, as suggested above. These ideas, in any case, would correspond to an ideological dimension of collective identity, alien to a cultural or an intergroup dimension. Indeed, it is the ideological shift in Mercosur leadership that can complement the understanding of the relationship between identity and institutions in Mercosur's ability to overcome its critical stage at the millennium turn.

Box 35.7 Collective identity explaining Mercosur's institutional developments

- Economic interdependence and ideological consensus over the need for macroeconomic stability explain states' identification with the Mercosur to the point of preserving it despite member states' unilateral actions and contagion effects during the macroeconomic crisis of the millennium's turn.
- Ideological consensus also explains Mercosur's shift towards cooperation in the social area in an effort to reinforce the regionalist project, which in turn was used as a tool for regime-boosting used by the new left-progressive governments that arrived to power in the region.

Proposing the creation of a Mercosur Parliament is indeed more related to an interest in democratising the regionalist project and opening spaces for greater social participation that was shared by the new political faces that arrived to office in both Brazil and Argentina, namely, Lula Da Silva (2003) and Eduardo Duhalde (2002, succeeded by Néstor Kirchner in 2003), respectively. These new leaders held a more leftist-progressive ideology and favoured greater state intervention in the economy, and thus, this new interest in deepening institutionalisation could be explained by these leaders' ideological identification and their interest in turning the Mercosur into a more controlled process that should harness the negative repercussions of the market instead of facilitating them. Effectively, both Lula and Kirchner arrived to power with the promise to back off neoliberalism and put social welfare at the front of the political agenda. In their need to boost their political legitimacy, the Mercosur was a fertile ground, for it had shown the perversities of letting the market – and the project – to run free from state control, as economic crises had hit the two largest economies and the regionalist project had proven incapable of restraining their effects on the other two smaller members. It was in this shifting political environment that policy coordination in the social arena became the main content of the Mercosur's re-launching in the following years in the form of the 'Mercosur Social', as will be analysed in what follows.

Amid the economic crisis that was severely impacting Brazil and Argentina in the early 2000s, and consequently the other two smaller Mercosur partners, voices began to emerge calling for a greater focus in developing a social agenda that could transcend the project's commercial focus and expand social benefits beyond the ones coming directly from trade, which were of course decreasing in a time of crisis (particularly regarding intra-regional trade, as shown above). Hence, in 2000 the Buenos Aires Charter about Mercosur's Social Commitment was signed, where authorities emphasised the state's responsibility of formulating policies aimed at combating poverty, and instructed countries to take coordinated action in order to overcome social problems.[51] And in December that year, the Mercosur Meeting of Ministers and Authorities for Social Development was created, whose task should be to propose the Mercosur executive authorities measures for undertaking joint actions for social development. After their first meeting in March 2001, a technical group was created for policy, programmes and project coordination in the areas of extreme poverty and child labour, employment, basic social services, human resources training, and strengthening citizen participation.[52]

The social dimension of integration in Mercosur had been traditionally associated with parliamentary and municipal authorities' representation,[53] and with developing labour issues.[54] But in the early 2000s, the way was paved for more left-oriented progressive governments to take power, with programmes that not only criticised free-market economics, but also the regionalist project as a tool at the service of economic liberalisation. Geneyro and Vázquez argue that the arrival to power of Brazilian president Lula da Silva (in 2002), Argentinian Néstor Kirchner (in 2003) and Uruguayan Tabaré Vázquez (in 2004) marked the turning point for giving Mercosur an impetus on the social dimension of integration, since these presidents identified with each other on ideological issues like implementing a new economic development model that could seek international economic insertion without taking the risks implied by broad economic liberalisation.[55] Hence, once in office, presidents Lula and Kirchner signed the Buenos Aires Consensus in October 2003, where both declared their intentions to foster 'social integration' in Mercosur, and included as regional aims the consolidation of political democracy, fighting against poverty and inequality, unemployment, hunger, illiteracy and disease.[56] Besides these issues, and according to Caetano, both presidents also coincided in this document around the strategic and productive role of the state, and around the will to deepen the regional integration process as a main aim of their foreign policies.[57] Later on, in 2004 the programme 'Mercosur Social' was created, with the aim of gathering joint strategies for addressing social issues related to poverty, education, labour, health, and strengthening citizen participation in the Mercosur.[58] In general terms, Phillips recognises that despite the dismissive perspective that Mercosur had held towards social issues in its initial years, in the first years of the twenty-first century the social policy area became much more embedded in the regionalist project's negotiation agenda and in the visions that its political leaders had about it.[59]

Besides identification on the ideological dimension, constituted by the new leftist-progressive presidents that arrived to power in all member countries but Paraguay,[60] and on major concerns about the impacts of economic crisis, a constructivist IPE approach may also point to 'regime-boosting' as another identity-based explanation for the emerging interest in developing the Mercosur area of social integration. According to Söderbaum, regime-boosting refers to the practice that governments engage for promoting their political legitimacy through regionalism, both at the domestic and international levels.[61] From this perspective, the pursuit of regionalism functions as a 'symbolic game' that raises rulers' profiles and images. This is even more understandable when states and/or political regimes are seen as weak and illegitimate, both by the domestic and the international public, and thus regionalism serves as a promotion tool for those leaders trying to show they will do all they can for solving their countries' problems. This could surely be the case of the leftist-progressive presidents who arrived to power in the early 2000s in Brazil, Argentina and Uruguay. Not only did they identify with one another on ideological stances, but were also interested in legitimating their coming into office through promoting regionalism, and gaining peoples' support by showing they would work together, simultaneously sending a powerful message to the international community that they would work as a team whose benchmark would be prioritising social issues over free trade and market economics. While regime-boosting could also be present as a driver to preserve Mercosur in relation to bloc bargaining and macroeconomic policy coordination, its role is easier to observe in social policy coordination, for this was the 'promise' that the new leftist-progressive leaders made in their run for power and about regionalism once they took office.

In synthesis, the ideological dimension seems to have been the most salient element of collective identity explaining both the maintenance of Mercosur in times of economic crisis and the choosing of the social area as the new driver for revitalizing the regionalist project. None of the literature engaged for this analysis showed any signs of a cultural dimension of identity at work, neither of an intergroup one, for the project lacked an institutional framework strong enough to develop it. On this latter point, the absence of strong regional institutions can hardly explain what occurred in the two case studies addressed, and instead it is the ideological dimension of collective identity, consisting of (shifting) agreement on the economic model and a consciousness of common fate derived from economic interdependence – and also from a shared interest in regime-boosting – that may have motivated member states to bring forward greater institutionalisation and policy coordination in macroeconomics and in the area of social integration. Hence, although institutional inertia cannot be clearly observed in the Mercosur due to the lack of strong institutionalisation and member countries benefiting from regional norms, institutional flexibility might have been at play in the form of a light institutional framework that admitted non-compliance regarding the customs union, and maintaining the pace of intergovernmental meetings at different levels where crucial decisions were not made, but the talking continued. This latter point could have motivated member states to preserve their identity as Mercosur members, ones that did not make much progress in deepening regional integration but were nonetheless committed to regionalism and to finding new pathways for regional cooperation.

Box 35.8 State identity, institutional flexibility and institutional inertia

- Preserving membership to a regionalist project may benefit state identity inasmuch as the state shows itself as a 'modern one' committed with regionalism and international cooperation.
- Institutional flexibility motivates states to maintain their regional membership, as they feel confident enough to fulfil what is in their interest and to reject what is not.
- Institutional inertia operates as a useful mechanism for preserving regionalism, but its emergence depends on the existence of institutional spaces for bureaucrats' interaction, and of benefits obtained from institutional bodies and regional norms.

Lastly, what can be further learned from a constructivist IPE approach is that neither in the maintenance of Mercosur, nor in the promotion of the 'Mercosur social', were there clear material incentives for member states to proceed the way they did. In the first case, incentives were operating in the opposite direction, as the dismantling of Mercosur seemed more reasonable facing its incapability to countervail the economic crisis and rather operating as a means for contagion. In the second case, besides political legitimacy, Mercosur authorities had nothing to gain in terms of material benefits derived from cooperation in the social area, as granting access to material resources for social intervention was not contemplated.[62]

Conclusion

This chapter offered a constructivist IPE analysis of regionalism consisting of contrasting ideational structures like collective identity and regional institutions with material incentives for explaining state action in some case studies of the AC and Mercosur. Based on previous works on both schemes, it was shown that the cultural and intergroup dimensions of collective identity were more important in the AC than in the Mercosur, mainly because the latter project lacks a common past and a cultural referent spinning a cultural identity, and its institutional and normative developments have been scarce, thus impeding the development of strong identification among national bureaucracies (more the less with regional ones). In contrast, the ideological dimension of collective identity was shown determinant in both regionalist projects, even more in the Mercosur, where the consensus on the economic model and its political contingencies not only motivated its foundation, but also fostered the project's maintenance and its relaunching after the economic crisis suffered at the millennium's turn.

Although material incentives were also present in all case studies, the analysis of the relationships between collective identity and regional institutions significantly complemented the understanding of state action in the unfolding of both regionalist projects. Concretely, institutional flexibility proved significant for motivating member states to keep talking and negotiating over issues that caused discord, but that nevertheless were of common interest, and states never felt uncomfortable enough to leave the regionalist project because of dissent. Institutional inertia was of course more present in the AC due to the existence of more institutionalised spaces for bureaucratic interaction, and to greater benefits derived from a common normative that helped member states to develop their internal legislation and to better negotiate with third parties. Finally, it was seen how important regionalism is for preserving state identity, where the political cost of abandoning regionalism is much greater than the usefulness of the regionalist for boosting state leaders' political legitimacy.

To present, and regarding the construction of South America as a region, it is not possible to observe a particular type of South American regionalism, at least not one different from UNASUR, which has only provided a space for political dialogue and for ministerial cooperation in several policy areas – particularly defence, infrastructure and health – but has not revolved around a particular economic model, as it has let trade and economic issues out of its scope. This is surely due to the fact that South American countries have split into two regionalist projects (the AC and Mercosur) to organise their sub-regions along particular economic and political lines, in an effort to reinforce their development strategies with regionalism. Although both AC and Mercosur member states are associate members of each other, and since 2004 there is a free trade agreement between the two blocs (plus Chile), there has never been an integral initiative to merge them, besides the formalist mandate received from UNASUR in the mid-2000s to work for their rapprochement and eventual integration in the future – but no formal institutional effort has been made in this direction. Today, facing the AC decline and the emergence of the Pacific Alliance as the new liberal regionalist alternative in the region (and in Latin America), some actors in Mercosur have rather called for an association with this new bloc, but no voices have demanded a single regionalist project for South America, at least not an economic one, even less facing the questioning of UNASUR as a true form of regionalism capable of transcending its focus on political dialogue, which has in turn raised significant doubts facing its lack of action towards the Venezuelan political crisis in the last years. As a region, South America has been rather constructed as two sub-regions, which have been the product of complex regionalist projects where collective identity and regional institutions have marked their progress and setbacks, but where identification around a South American region and institutionalisation for organising it along particular economic and political lines seem still far from germination.

Notes

1 Hettne and Söderbaum 2000.
2 Hurrell 1995.
3 Some salient works are Hettne and Söderbaum 2000; Checkel 2001, 2016; Herrmann, Risse and Brewer 2004; Söderbaum 2004; Risse 2009; Van Langenhove 2011.
4 Payne and Gamble 1996.
5 Wendt 1999.
6 Checkel 2016.
7 Checkel 2001.
8 The Pacific Alliance and the ALBA also include non-South American countries, and thus they are not considered South American as such. The Union of South American Nations (UNASUR) may be considered another South American regionalist project, but for reasons that will be further provided, it will not be a core part of the present analysis, though some words will be addressed to it in the conclusion.
9 Bethell 2010: 478–479. There is broad consensus among authors that the first one to refer to an America that was 'Latin' was the French intellectual Michel Chevalier, back in 1835, but the first political speeches in the subcontinent to use the term 'Latin America' are located in the 1850s in the works of the Colombian intellectual José María Torres Caicedo and the Chilean intellectual Francisco de Bilbao (Quijada 1998; Bethell 2010; Ayala 2013). While some newspapers and other types of intellectual writings began using the term 'Latin America' since the 1860s (Gobat 2013, *The Invention*), until the Second World War most intellectuals and politicians in Latin America, Brazil and the US excluded Brazil from the 'Hispanic' America that Latin America usually referred to (Bethell 2010).
10 Gomes 2010.
11 There had been, of course, other regional agreements in South America in the past after its countries' independence, like the Great Colombia (Colombia, Ecuador and Venezuela, between 1821 and 1831) and the ABC Pact (Argentina, Brazil and Chile between 1915–1930), but the former was indeed a single country (one single state with one central government), and the latter was more of a non-aggression agreement, thus, not regionalists projects according to the definition here deployed.
12 In the Cartagena Agreement, namely the AC foundational treaty, Article 1 states that one of the project's aims is to facilitate its member countries' participation in the integration process advanced by the Latin American Free Trade Association (ALALC, in Spanish), which existed since 1960.
13 CONMEBOL, the South American Football Confederation (founded in 1916), includes Argentina, Bolivia Brazil, Chile, Colombia, Ecuador, Paraguay, Peru, Uruguay and Venezuela. UNASUR (Union of South American Nations) includes these ten countries plus Guyana and Surinam, whose national football federations belong to CONCACAF (Confederation of North, Central American and Caribbean Association Football).
14 The South American Free Trade Area (SAFTA) was completed in 2004, after the AC and Mercosur members, plus Chile, reached an agreement on how to harmonise the existing free trade agreements among them, and taking measures to further deepen trade liberalisation in the future. However, since this was mainly a bloc-to bloc agreement (plus Chile), the then-called Community of South American Nations, neither later the UNASUR, incorporated the SAFTA into its institutional structure.
15 UNASUR also has a democratic charter, by which any member state that does not preserve a democratic regime will be expelled from the organisation. However, the poor reaction of UNASUR towards the Venezuelan political crisis that has been taking place in the past years, has made some member states question the validity of this charter.
16 In Spanish, *Comunidad de Estados Latinoamericanos y del Caribe*, created in 2010, including all Latin American and Caribbean states.
17 Murra 1975.
18 Prieto 2016.

19 See also Prieto 2003.

20 Prieto 2016.

21 Economic Commission for Latin America and the Caribbean.

22 This analysis and the remaining portions of this section are more broadly developed in my book on the AC (Prieto 2016).

23 The AGS was officially created in 1996.

24 In the book *El Cono Sur. Una historia común* (Rapoport and Cervo 2001), contributors include Chile and Bolivia in the Southern Cone region, besides Brazil, Argentina, Uruguay and Paraguay, and they show that the 'common history' among these countries is one of regional interactions, but not one of a common culture, past or political history. While Argentina and Paraguay obtained their independence in the early 1820s, Uruguay as an autonomous republic did in 1828. José de San Martín was the main liberating figure for Argentina, and also for Paraguay and Uruguay if we acknowledge that these countries were then united under the state called 'Provincias Unidas del Río de la Plata'. But Paraguay pursued its independency also from Argentina since 1810, and Uruguay did along the 1810s and 1820s, until Argentina recognised its independence in 1828 (which only did with Paraguay until 1850). Hence, other figures like José Artigas for Uruguay and José Rodríguez de Francia for Paraguay are more emblematic for their independencies. For its part, Brazil declared its independence also in the early 1820s, but its 'independent' governor – Pedro I – happened to be the son of the Portuguese king, and thus the other Southern Cone countries did not see it as an independent free country as the others, for the monarchic regime – under the rule of Emperor Pedro II – prevailed until 1889, when Brazil became a Republic.

25 Cammack 1999; Hirst 1999; Prieto 2003; Phillips 2004; Gardini 2010; among others.

26 Wendt 1999.

27 As shown in Prieto 2016.

28 In what follows, the work of Phillips (2004) will be used as a main source to pursue the analysis, for it provides substantial detail on both cases (though much more on the first one), which allows observing relevant issues of collective identity and regional institutions, even though it does not engage a constructivist perspective.

29 Phillips 2004: 95–96.

30 Ibid., 90.

31 Ibid., 89.

32 Ibid., 93–94.

33 Ibid., 95–96.

34 Ibid.

35 Ibid., chapter 6.

36 Between 2000 and 2004 Mercosur also advanced bloc negotiations with the EU and with the AC member countries (mainly for FTAs, but also both involving some political aspects) but these bargaining processes are not addressed here for they entailed far less problematic issues for internal coordination between Mercosur members than did FTAA and WTO negotiations (see Phillips 2004: 124–127). Less problematic issues meant agreement was easier to reach, and thus less room for assessing the significance of collective identity, apart from identification based on common (or simply not confronting) interests.

37 Phillips 2004: 116–121.

38 Ibid.: 115–119.

39 By the time of FTAA negotiations, AC member countries had also agreed to engage this bargaining process as a bloc.

40 Phillips: 120-127. Such attempt resulted in success at the end, when FTAA negotiations were definitely cancelled in 2005 mainly because of Brazil and Argentina's rejection of US conditions.

41 Ibid.: 120.

42 Ibid.: 100–106.

43 Ibid.: 119–124.

44 Ibid.: 115.

45 Ibid.: 103–104. Brazil and Argentina's reasons for this were different, though: Phillips (Ibid.: 103) contends that while Brazil wanted to preserve its political autonomy, Argentina followed a political conviction about the inconvenience of state intervention in economic matters, which would be favoured by greater institutionalisation within the regional bloc.

46 Ibid.: 128.

47 Ibid.: 129.
48 Ibid.: 130.
49 Ibid.: 131.
50 Ibid.
51 Vázquez 2011: 173.
52 Ibid.
53 Geneyro and Vázquez 2006.
54 Ermida 2003.
55 Geneyro and Vázquez 2006.
56 Ibid.: 8.
57 Caetano 2011: 47.
58 Vázquez 2011: 173–175.
59 Phillips 2004: 140.
60 Between 2003 and 2008, Paraguayan president Nicanor Duarte did not share these ideological standpoints with his Mercosur presidential counterparts. This radically changed in 2008 with the arrival of Fernando Lugo to the Paraguayan presidency, who completed Mercosur's 'left-turn' that characterised it between 2003 and 2015, when the new Argentinian and Brazilian presidents showed a new ideological shift to the right, once again backing free-market economics and relegating Mercosur to a lesser priority level.
61 Söderbaum 2004: 96–98.
62 Arguably, Mercosur's Fund for Structural Convergence was created in 2004 with the aim of reducing the asymmetries between the bloc members, and though issues of social development are included as funding targets, its creation derived from the process of developing the social area that began in the early 2000s, instead of having inspired it.

Bibliography

Ayala, E. 2013. El origen del nombre América Latina y la tradición católica del siglo XIX. *Anuario Colombiano de Historia Social y de la Cultura* 40, no. 1: 213–241.

Bethell, L. 2010. Brazil and 'Latin America'. *Journal of Latin American Studies* 42, no. 3: 457–485.

Caetano, G. 2011. Breve historia del MERCOSUR en sus 20 años. Coyunturas e instituciones (1991–2011). In: *Mercosur: 20 años.* Caetano, G. (coord.) Ch. 1. Montevideo: Centro de Formación para la Integración Regional.

Cammack, Paul. 1999. Mercosur: From Domestic Concerns to Regional Influence. In: *Sub-regionalism and World Order.* Hook, G. and Kearns, I. (eds) Ch 5. Basingstoke: Palgrave Macmillan.

Checkel, J. 2001. Why Comply? Social Learning and European Identity Change. *International Organization* 55, no. 3: 553–588.

Checkel, J. 2016. Regional Identities and Communities. In: *The Oxford Handbook of Comparative Regionalism.* Börzel, T. and Risse, T. (eds) Ch 24. Oxford: Oxford University Press.

Ermida, O. 2003. *La dimensión social de Mercosur.* Derecho y Sociedad 21: 127–153.

Gardini, G. 2010. *The Origins of Mercosur. Democracy and Regionalization in South America.* New York: Palgrave Macmillan.

Geneyro, R. and Vázquez, M. 2006. La ampliación de la agenda política y social para el Mercosur actual. *Aldea Mundo* 11, no. 20: 7–18.

Gobat, M. 2013. The Invention of Latin America: A Transnational History of Anti-Imperialism, Democracy, and Race. *The American Historical Review* 118, no. 5: 1345–1375.

Gomes, M. 2010. Política externa brasileira para os países sulamericanos e os processos de integraçao na regiao: Crenças na formulçao e pragmtismo na prática. In Martínez, L., Ramanzini, H. and Vázquez, M. (coord.) *Anuario de la Integración Regional de América Latina y el Gran Caribe*: 77–92. Buenos Aires: Coordinadora Regional de Investigaciones Económicas y Sociales.

Herrmann, R., Risse, T. and Brewer, M. (eds) 2004. *Transnational Identities. Becoming European in the EU.* Lanham: Rowman and Littlefield Publishers.

Hettne, B. and Söderbaum, F. 2000. Theorising the Rise of Regionness. *New Political Economy* 5, no. 3: 457–473.

Hirst, M. 1999. Mercosur's Complex Political Agenda. In *Mercosur: Regional Integration, World Markets.* Roett, R. (ed.) Ch. 3. Boulder: Lynne Rienner Publishers.

Hurrell, Andrew. 1995. Explaining the Resurgence of Regionalism in World Politics. *Review of International Studies* 21, no. 4: 331–58.

Murra, J. 1975. *Formaciones económicas y políticas del mundo andino*. Lima: Instituto de Estudios Peruanos.

Payne, A. and Gamble, A. 1996. Introduction: The Political Economy of Regionalism and World Order. In: *Regionalism and World Order*. Gamble, A. and Payne, A. (eds): 1–20. Basingstoke: Palgrave Macmillan.

Phillips, N. 2004. *The Southern Cone Model. The political economy of regional capitalist development in Latin America*. London: Routledge.

Prieto, G. 2003. Constructing Regionalism in South America: The Role of Ideas in the Andean Community and Mercosur Projects. *Colombian Economic Journal* 1 no. 1: 268–303.

Prieto, G. 2016. *Identidad Colectiva e Instituciones Regionales en la Comunidad Andina. Un análisis constructivista*. Bogotá: Editorial Javeriana.

Quijada, Mónica. 1998. Sobre el origen y difusión del nombre 'América Latina' (o una variación heterodoxa en torno al tema de la construcción social de la verdad). *Revista de Indias LVIII* no. 214: 595–615.

Rapoport, M. and Cervo, A. (comps.) 2001. *El Cono Sur. Una historia común*. Buenos Aires: Fondo de Cultura Económica.

Risse, T. 2009. Social Constructivism and European Integration. In: *European Integration Theory*. Wiener, A. and Diez, T. (2nd. ed.) Ch 8. Oxford: Oxford University Press.

Söderbaum, F. 2004. *The Political Economy of Regionalism: The Case of Southern Africa*. Basingstoke: Palgrave Macmillan.

Van Langenhove, L. 2011. *Building Regions. The Regionalization of the World Order*. Farnham: Ashgate.

Vázquez, M. 2011. El MERCOSUR social: Cambio político y nueva identidad para el proceso de integración regional en América del Sur. In *Mercosur: 20 años*. Caetano, G. (coord.) Ch. 5. Montevideo. Centro de Formación para la Integración Regional.

Wendt, A. 1999. *Social Theory of International Politics*. Cambridge: Cambridge University Press.

36

The IPE of Caribbean development

Matthew Louis Bishop and Merisa S. Thompson

Introduction

The Caribbean rarely appears in the major IPE journals or, indeed, books like this. Why might this be so? An intuitive explanation could be that the region is peripheral to the major transformations in the GPE, its constituent territories are small, and the ideas that underpin the field do not emanate from such places. Yet such an explanation would be deeply problematic. The Caribbean was once the very core of global capitalism: for almost half a millennium, sugar slavery generated inordinate amounts of wealth and misery, and it financed and shaped an international order in which plantocrats were the 'masters of the universe' (Burnard 2012). This left longstanding legacies of class, race and gender stratification that still structure society today. Moreover, smallness is a questionable reason for (not) researching something: the obsession with 'gigantism' in much of IPE (and IR) is belied by the fact that small countries and institutions are the norm, not the exception (Sharman 2011; Veenendaal and Corbett 2015). There is, therefore, no intrinsic reason why studying the US and China, the IMF or the EU is intellectually preferable to, or any less 'parochial' than, examining the political economy of Jamaica or Barbados, the lending practices of the Caribbean Development Bank (CDB), or regional integration via the Caribbean Community (CARICOM). The tiny island of St Lucia (population: *c.*165,000) has produced *two* Nobel prizewinners – the poet Derek Walcott and the economist W. Arthur Lewis – so the Caribbean does not lack ideas, either.

Fortunately, a welcome recent trend in 'critical' or 'heterodox' IPE has been to champion the 'bringing in' of marginalised places and their thinkers, and to take questions of race, ethnicity and gender more seriously (as well as citing more systematically women and people of colour). By 'decolonising' what we study and how we study it, we can offer a counterpoint to dominant approaches that do not illuminate fully the distinctive postcolonial reality of much of the world (which, for the Caribbean, was forged by its particular history of sugar and slavery). Indeed, today, the wider theme of 'modern slavery' – to give one example – can be poorly served even by critical, materialist IPE literatures that struggle to grasp the implications of *unwaged* forms of 'unfree' labour (LeBaron and Phillips 2019: 2). Such a decolonial endeavour is, then, long overdue in a field with 'global' pretensions. However, this process potentially carries with it an unwitting neo-colonial logic: the very notion of broadening horizons to include the 'left out' can (again) undermine their agency and elide the initial act of ignoring when IPE's blind-spots were produced by conscious decisions made to *not* focus on certain things. It is also potentially in tension with the deeply political, emancipatory and decolonising drive of Caribbean scholarship.

There have, in fact, always existed rich political economy traditions beyond the West: many have produced scholarship of astonishing breadth and depth on places like the Caribbean and its thinkers; they just have not often done it in the major contemporary IPE journals or with reference to the debates that animate them. Volumes as diverse as Eric Williams' (1944) *Capitalism and Slavery*, C. L. R James' (1938) *Black Jacobins*, Aimé Césaire's (1989 [1950]) *Discours sur le Colonialisme*, and Frantz Fanon's (1961) *Les Damnés de la Terre* are considered canonical in disciplines like history or black and postcolonial studies. But they have also extended our comprehension of the GPE's evolution in ways that would have been unimaginable had we relied solely on prominent eighteenth-century European theorists, and they predate the establishment of IPE as a formal field of study in the 1970s by decades. So, why are they not automatically viewed as foundational texts, in the same way as *The Wealth of Nations* (Smith 1974 [1776]), *Das Kapital* (Marx 1867) or *The Great Transformation* (Polanyi 2001 [1944])?

The book by a West Indian that is found most often on IPE reading lists – usually in the week on 'dependency theory' if there happens to be one – is by Walter Rodney. Yet this exception proves the point: *How Europe Underdeveloped Africa* (Rodney 1972) was neither about his native Guyana nor the wider Caribbean and is discussed primarily in terms of whether or not Latin American ideas can travel to Africa. The Caribbean is left out of this story and its own variants *of* dependency theory are rarely analysed in their own right, so students are familiar with Prebisch, Cardoso, Faletto, Gunder Frank and Dos Santos but not their West Indian counterparts (see Bishop 2013). In this chapter, we argue that the region, its thinkers and those that write about them need to be taken seriously, on their own terms. We demonstrate their importance, first, by tracing how the distinctive political economy of the (English-speaking) Caribbean rose and ultimately declined alongside the prevailing development debates of the immediate postcolonial period, and, second, by suggesting how contemporary currents in both real-world Caribbean development and new trends on the critical margins of IPE offer potential for reinvigorating these kinds of ideas.

Arthur Lewis and Caribbean 'modernisation'

The developmental problématique inherited by the small, mainly island territories of the West Indies from the colonial era was – and remains – distinguished by three interlinked conditions: atrophied economies designed to serve extractive interests; a marked vulnerability to external shocks; and dependence on more powerful extra-regional forces. Caribbean islands are geographically small, insular and remote, have little in the way of natural resource endowments, and have historically relied on the export of cash crops like sugar while importing food to eat (see Thompson 2019a). Such dependence has long accentuated the region's extreme vulnerability to outside pressure, with its intellectuals acutely aware of this. Consequently, after World War Two, indigenous approaches to grappling with these structural constraints – emanating primarily from the University of the West Indies (UWI) – were preoccupied with how to engender development by exploiting the limited resources at hand.

West Indian political economy was politically engaged and emancipatory: it saw economic development as a right alongside political and civil progress (Bernal, Figueroa and Witter 1984). Those in the vibrant ideas factory that was the UWI of the 1960s and 1970s attempted to understand Caribbean reality on its own terms and challenge what Norman Girvan (1973: 24) once disparagingly called 'the metropolitan economic models then in vogue'. Part of the target of this critique was the dominance, during the 1950s and early 1960s, of the 'modernisation' school of development theory, which – put crudely – held that the challenges faced by societies at the dawn of independence were fundamentally endogenous. That is, a series of 'primitive' or 'traditional' religious norms, tribal identities, 'backward' institutions and practices represented internal barriers that prevented largely-rural places in the Global South from enjoying the high levels of growth that would lead to them becoming secular 'modern' or 'advanced' urban societies. It was only by aping the already-rich countries that they could, in effect, 'catch up' to enjoy high levels of industrialisation and consumption (see Payne and Phillips 2010, for a good critique).

From a contemporary vantage point, this binary way of thinking seems, at best, essentialist. However, when judged on its own terms, modernisation had much to offer, including its Caribbean variant. This was strongly associated with the aforementioned Arthur Lewis, who did not actually spend much of his career in the Caribbean, but rather worked at the LSE, Manchester and Princeton (where he won the Nobel Prize for economics in 1979). He was thus never truly considered a Caribbean radical, even though his later critics revered him as an outstanding intellectual (Best 1992). His work, though, was genuinely ground-breaking, and it represented the 'first cogent statement on the British West Indies as a unit of analysis by a Caribbean thinker' (Bernal, Figueroa and Witter 1984: 10). He took inspiration from John Maynard Keynes' work on the laissez-faire failure to resolve the Great Depression during the 1930s by asking similar questions about the endemic stagnation in Caribbean economies before and after the war, and operated at the cutting-edge of the 'nascent field of development economics' (Payne and Phillips 2010: 61).

As he saw it, the primary problem was limited economic growth, itself a consequence of widespread *under*employment in agriculture. Farms had too little land, too much labour and not enough work, meaning that 'the marginal productivity of labour is negligible, zero, or even negative' (Lewis 1954: 189). Since workers only earned enough to subsist, it was impossible to raise the overall savings level sufficiently to stimulate the capital investment and growth that might lead to diversification: the 'central problem in the theory of economic development', he argued, is to work out how savings rates could increase from low-single to double-digit levels and underpin 'rapid capital accumulation' (Lewis 1954: 155). This was, broadly speaking, the fundamental challenge faced by many societies on the cusp of decolonisation. But the Caribbean was distinctive: its tiny islands experienced *both* underemployment *and* a chronic lack of savings (and therefore capital, of all kinds). Moreover, these problems existed in a circular relationship: greater agricultural productivity required investment and diversification, but those things could only be achieved – from within, at least – with greater productivity. Land was limited, which inhibited agricultural expansion, and the unique colonial history of the region – typified by the extractive dominance of the plantocracy and rentier merchant capital – meant that there was no local bourgeois-industrial class with the inclination to invest locally in real productive activity.

For Lewis, the solution was industrialisation, which, at the time, was not unreasonably viewed by the growth theorists as the path to modernity. In a paper entitled 'The Industrialisation of the British West Indies' (Lewis 1950), he argued for a process of 'rapid industrialisation' which would, over time, lead to the export of manufactures, the generation of new sources of capital and better jobs for more people. However, while he reasoned that industrialisation would reflect productivity growth, ultimately generating greater financial, human and technological capital – and therefore a positive cycle of more growth – the initial capital input still needed to be found from somewhere. Given the prevailing constraints, money, equipment and expertise could only be found was outside, so Lewis demanded large increases in foreign investment to provide the necessary inflows of them. His ideas had both practical import and appeared to make sense in a 1950s context. As Dennis Conway (1997: 5) once noted, Lewis's approach was, 'in its full theoretical formulation, a thoughtful and progressive model to follow'.

Unfortunately, though, his industrialisation experiment is generally regarded as a failure. On the positive side of the ledger, it did stimulate investment and much of the region enjoyed strong, but not spectacular, growth of around 5 per cent annually from the late 1950s to the early 1970s. Moreover, its eventual unravelling was arguably not due to any inherent failing: rather, the enduring reality of dependence meant that, once the global economy experienced the upheavals of the 1970s, with terms of trade for developing countries as a whole collapsing, the Caribbean was precipitously exposed. It was by now even-more dependent on external capital and had failed to diversify or alleviate its dependence on primary commodities, the value of which was still being largely extracted along 'neo-colonial' lines (see Levitt 1996). Industrialisation had also failed to assuage the chronically high levels of unemployment and underemployment which underpinned its original rationale (Sutton 2006). In sum, for its critics, the industrialisation policy had utterly failed to internalise the growth dynamic, and the use of foreign capital to initiate 'autocentric' forms of development had effectively further entrenched the dominance of that capital (Girvan 1973).

The New World Group and West Indian *'dependencia'*

The backlash to Lewis came from an authentic Caribbean brand of dependency theory, the key thesis of which is that the underdevelopment of the 'periphery' is inextricably linked to its colonial – and neo-colonial – exploitation by the 'core'. Its adherents in the *New World Group* coalesced around visions of alternative development and regional integration, and included, among others, Lloyd Best, Kari Polanyi Levitt, Norman Girvan, Owen Jefferson, George Beckford and George Lamming, and neo-Marxist thinkers – or those with more radical materialist tendencies – such as Clive Thomas, Trevor Munroe and the aforementioned Rodney. Their work differed to Latin American *dependencia* in certain respects, and they explicitly refuted the label, emphasising instead their eclecticism, lack of doctrinal commitment to either a rigid methodology or disciplinary orientation, the indigenous nature of their theorising, and how this changed over approximately two decades (Best 1992; Girvan 2010). But such comparisons were inevitable: these scholars undeniably took inspiration from the intellectual ferment elsewhere in the hemisphere (see Tussie, this volume) and their analysis was strikingly similar: it postulated, from a distinctively West Indian vantage point, a core-periphery critique of modernisation. It was also distinguished by two intellectual tendencies, as in Latin America: a 'historical–structural' approach that evoked the 'dependent development' favoured by Cardoso and Faletto, and a more explicitly Marxian 'historical–materialist' variant *à la* Gunder Frank (see Bishop 2013).

Drawing further inspiration from the work of historians like Williams and James, these thinkers embarked upon historical and institutional analyses of the development of Caribbean economies from the seventeenth to twentieth century. In recognition of the region's unique experience, Best and Levitt (1968) developed the concept of the 'plantation economy' and this remains relevant for understanding social, cultural, political and economic processes today (see also: Best 1968; Best and Levitt 2009). George Beckford (1972) also built on this in his book *Persistent Poverty* to explain why colonial legacies endured. For Best, the 'fundamental difference' between Lewis and those that came later was not that 'he saw imperialism as part of the solution while we saw it as part of the problem', but rather that 'we saw an underlying organisation of the world economy which led to this persistent poverty in countries like our own' (Best 1992: 11).

From this perspective, pervasive neo-colonial economic structures continually undermined attempts to stimulate meaningful development. In an influential paper entitled 'The Economics of Development in Small Countries', William Demas (1965) had argued that the failure of industrialisation resulted from the natural geographic and demographic constraints of the Caribbean, which, along with the limited internal market, made import substitution extremely difficult. Although this argument made sense, it was also partial: Best and Levitt later subjected it to a fierce critique, coining the derisive term 'industrialisation by invitation' to pour scorn on Lewis's earlier invocation of foreign capital (which, by implication, had been accumulated in the colonial era and was to be put, as they saw it, once again to neo-colonial ends).

With that in mind, they emphasised the region's enduring 'metropolitan dependence and the economic and social legacy of the plantation system' (Levitt 2005: 35). The theory of plantation economy was, as Levitt (2005: 13) has since discussed, an attempt to 'produce a stylised model of a typical (generic) Caribbean economy' and move beyond approaches which stressed primarily the 'natural' obstacles to growth rather than the economic, social and historical. In short, it was colonially constituted external dependence that had produced '*under*development' (see: Dos Santos 1970; Cardoso and Faletto 1979; Frank 1966) in the region, and this was subtly different to its Latin American manifestation due to the distinctive social structures that had been laid down and institutionalised by the dominant mode of production, the extractive sugar plantation. It cannot be overstated how important this analysis was: the Caribbean colonial experience differed to other developing regions in that its pre-colonial population had essentially been wiped out almost *entirely*, and a completely new society had been grafted onto it, with *whole islands* serving no other purpose than to produce sugar (see, inter alia: Lewis 1968; Williams 1970; Mintz 1974).

Best and Levitt's theory identified four phases of historical development and transition. The 'pure plantation economy' (1600–1838), based primarily on slave labour, was brought into existence purely to produce exports and profits for the metropole. It is a one-sector economy, with plantation production as the single economic activity. For the slave, the plantation is a 'total' institution encompassing all areas of social and economic life. The planter class governs, but is subordinate to the enterprising merchant class, both in terms of decision-making and price-taking. The transition to the 'plantation economy modified' (1838–1938) was characterised by emancipation and the introduction of first indentured, and then wage labour, the adoption of free trade with Britain and the emergence of both a national economy and a 'residentiary sector' of non-plantation peasant production by freed slaves. The next transition, to 'plantation economy further modified' (1938–1970s) heralds the onset of industrialisation, characterised by the industrialising state. In this phase, plantocrats turned, depending on the territory in question, to new activities like bauxite and petroleum, and new crops like bananas and rice. This period also saw increased foreign direct investment (FDI) and the rise of the multi-national corporation (MNC). Ultimately, the final and longed-for transition was for the 'anti-model' of social and economic transformation where the plantation legacy would finally be extinguished, and the locus of decision-making would shift from external to local agents. Such emancipatory thinking was central to New World thinking: as Girvan (2002) later suggested, their key motivation was to discover 'the features of a self-reliant, self-sustaining Caribbean economy' to distil them and put them into practice 'in the interests of the majority of the population'.

The central thesis underpinning the plantation economy notion was that the Caribbean 'has undergone little structural change since the establishment of the slave plantation over 300 years ago' and that 'the economy remains, as it always has been, passively responsive to external demand and external investment, almost exclusively from metropolitan sources' (Best and Levitt 2009: 13). Therefore, despite the modifications at each stage, each new manifestation replicated the divisions and ownership structure of the previous incarnation. It continued to be structurally aligned to serving the commercial needs of external – meaning European and, later, American – capital, rather than those of its own population. The key features of a plantation economy are that it is established, owned and controlled by foreign actors, it is export-oriented, and profits accrue to the metropole. This in turn is facilitated by the intermediary merchant classes, who – playing an analogous role to the 'comprador elite' in Latin American dependency theory (see Frank 1967) – are generally the white Creole descendants of the original plantocracy (Thomas 1974). Caribbean economies and societies were, therefore, in effect '*created by* Western European enterprise as an appendage of the Metropolitan Economy, passive and lacking in internal dynamic from the start' (Girvan 2009: xiv, emphasis added). The enduring dominance of rentier import–export activity in small territories with captive populations has perpetuated this subsequently, since elites have little incentive to stimulate risky, but genuinely productive development (Marshall 2002). Whether in terms of patterns of production, control of finance, or stratified relations of power, wealth, race, class and gender, Caribbean societies still reflect this inheritance to a staggering degree (Bishop 2013).

The Best–Levitt model successfully challenged the inadequacy of imported paradigms that attempted to apply universalised and general theory to the specificity of the Caribbean experience. However, it also came under critical scrutiny, particularly on account of its dualistic conception of the peasant–planter and hinterland–metropole dichotomies, and its narrow focus on the formal economy. Additionally, Marxist critiques highlighted the limited reference to class, class conflict and the state, and made accusations of elitism due to New World's implied commitment to bourgeois-capitalist development (Sudama 1979). On this reading, it seemed that non-Marxist variants of Caribbean radical thought – like dependency theory more broadly – actually shared rather a lot with modernisation in terms of end-goals; they simply differed on the reasons why growth was proving so difficult to realise. As the intellectual divide between the historical–structuralists and the historical–materialists intensified, the latter increasingly emphasised the essential impossibility of liberating the region from its position as a peripheral provider of raw materials at the bottom of the international division of labour. Only one conclusion could be drawn: if Caribbean dependency is a dynamic, yet inescapable phenomenon, meaningful reform within the capitalist system was impossible and nothing less than 'a comprehensive strategy for transforming the productive forces and liberating the political and social order' would suffice (Thomas 1974: 59).

Yet the historical–materialist account itself was problematic, too. It was unable to gain a foothold in the region due to the limited Marxist tradition in British colonial education, and it lost much of its lustre in the wake of the Grenadian revolution (Payne 1984). It was also theoretically questionable. As Best (1971) himself insisted, although Marxism had provided much inspiration for plantation theory, its conception of class was distilled from the particular experience of nineteenth century Europe, and did not fully capture relations of dependency in a region where ethnic cleavages (among others) were considerably more pronounced. The plantation way of thinking also could not fully account for diversity within the Caribbean, since some societies, such as Trinidad, appeared to approximate the model less than others (Sudama 1979). As Williams (1964: 81) asserts, 'Trinidad in 1833 was not a plantation society … it was a society of small estates operated by a few slaves'. Sudama (1979) also argued that, by focusing on the continuity of structural constraints, the plantation literature may also obscure change (and especially so in its Marxian variant) rendering it deterministic. Although after decolonisation the Caribbean state was certainly 'patronage-based' with elites eschewing locally-productive investment in order to 'safeguard vestigial colonial interests', for Don Marshall (1998: 43) the right kind of state action *could have* brought about a substantial overhaul of these structures. To suggest that 'the post-1960 era was marked', he argues, 'by a smooth transition from plantation colony to neocolony is to deny the greater capacity for manoeuvrability that decolonisation brought' (Marshall 1998: 64).

The complexity of social relations, especially in terms of gender, were also insufficiently problematised. As Green (2001: 42) contends, 'political-economic relations are, or were, seen to be about the business of class, race and colonial or nation-state relations: gender was never seriously factored in as part of the equation'. Moreover, the focus on the plantation mode of production and transnational capital ignores the human subjects that actually 'people' these institutions: such invisibility is particularly harsh to women. Green instead put forward 'modes of re/production' as 'a feminist-materialist improvement upon the old mode-of-production formulation with its exclusive attention to class (between male antagonists) and goods-production' (Green 2001: 65). This reformulation, therefore, immediately presumed a historically specific articulation between production and social reproduction (we return to such feminist themes in the next section).

By the 1980s, the global dialogue between modernisation and dependency had withered away, culminating in the 'impasse' in development theory identified by David Booth (1985). These tendencies were reflected in the West Indies, too, where the radical era of political economy had also come to an end. Beset by internal battles, New World had fragmented: its members generally went into consultancy or government work and those who remained in the critical parts of academia often took up posts overseas (Payne and Sutton 2001). They had rapidly become overwhelmed by the crises into which many Caribbean countries had fallen, and the dramatic impact of the Washington Consensus. Structural adjustment policy and neoliberal ideas were disseminated throughout the region by international agencies which effectively took over responsibility for the conception and programming of development policy from national governments. According to Anthony Payne and Paul Sutton (2001; 2007), the 'politicos' had been replaced by the 'técnicos'. From now on, development was to be an 'offthe-shelf' endeavour: it would no longer be characterised by discussions 'of grand design developed within the region for the region' but would rather become 'about how best to administer the programmes that were designed elsewhere under the neo-liberal paradigm' (Sutton 2006: 59).

After the impasse: new directions for Caribbean political economy

The ensuing stranglehold of neoliberalism has been remarkable. Partly, this reflects the influence of the international financial institutions and development agencies that provide much of the funding underpinning the research and consultancy activity of Caribbean academics – as well as project-based support for governments – and the instinctively narrow, metric-driven ways of thinking which inherently circumscribe the intellectual boundaries of that work. This is a longstanding issue: Marshall (2014: 119) recounts how, towards the end, Best admonished his New World compatriots for their 'fatal attraction for governments, and a tendency to substitute policy-oriented research for contemplative scholarship'.

Neoliberal hegemony also reflects the professional socialisation of subsequent regional technocratic elites: they emerged *after* the independence-generation of political leaders and their intellectual vanguard, and many were trained as orthodox positivist economists, often outside the region. Moreover, the major challenges of the 1990s and 2000s were fundamentally trade-related: governments were preoccupied with developing the requisite technical capacity to participate in the newly-established World Trade Organization (WTO) and coping with the looming end of EU trade preferences and the shift towards reciprocity (see Bishop, Heron and

Payne 2013). It is not surprising, then, that the flagship social sciences MSc established at UWI in this period was in *International Trade Policy*. This practical degree was generally taught by the region's corpus of trade lawyers and economists, and was – at least in part – geared towards equipping the region with more negotiating capacity to carry out the daunting and highly technical task of global trade diplomacy.

As such, there is relatively little *political* economy left, and certainly not much heterodox IPE as readers of this book would comprehend it. Reflecting on this state of affairs, Girvan (2009: xvii) himself noted that, not only did New World become 'one of the many casualties of the neoliberal counter-revolution in economics', but also that 'younger economists *hardly know of its existence*' (emphasis added). So, even in the Caribbean itself, this brilliant indigenous tradition of genuinely 'critical' political economy is only taught patchily at UWI, rarely by its economists, and survives mainly in a handful of courses on Caribbean thought in spaces such as the Sir Arthur Lewis Institute of Social and Economic Studies (SALISES) and the remaining social science departments. Marshall is one of these. He recently argued that West Indian academics are caught in a double-bind: even those with radical intentions are exhorted to constantly give policy advice to, and undertake technical work for governments and other actors, and 'the university's struggle for relevance and its sensitivity to budget efficiency do make for a climate where conformity to the prevailing common sense seems the best course for research programming' (Marshall 2014: 120). There is now relatively little meaningful dialogue between more orthodox and heterodox scholarly opinion in the Caribbean: neither group really understands each other; they come from very different places intellectually; and this continues to inhibit the regional development debate (see Bishop 2015).

So, where are the interesting sites of analysis today? In the remainder of this section, we look at four trends in political economy analysis – as very broadly conceived, to the extent that some of the work we discuss may not be viewed at all in those terms by its authors – that represent potential reinvigorations of the kinds of critical themes we have already discussed. The first is the limited tendency within IPE in general (and very occasionally in IR, as also loosely understood) to address issues in which Caribbean territories, or other small island states and regions, play some kind of role. Sometimes this is tangential, in the sense that the region or countries under the microscope represent little more than convenient case studies, but it can be more systematic. This includes work on: micro-state sovereignty, offshore finance and gambling (e.g. Cooper 2011; Sharman 2017; Vlcek 2014); the contemporary production and trade of colonial commodities and other cash crops, as well as the travails of Caribbean agriculture (e.g. Payne 2006; Richardson 2009; Thompson 2019a); and the implications of service sectors such as tourism (e.g. Bishop 2010; Ferguson 2011; Lee, Hampton and Jeyacheya 2015).

This leads us to the second point, which is that much of the best critical research on the development of Caribbean economies – how they function, patterns of state-society contestation, who wins and loses from structural change – is undertaken by anthropologists, sociologists, human geographers and feminists. Indeed, just taking tourism as one example from above: feminists have written brilliant accounts of the many pathologies that afflict the sector, including the prevalence of abusive forms of sex work and trafficking, cultural stereotyping and the exoticisation of Caribbean peoples and places, the destruction of natural patrimony and other forms of environmental degradation, and so on (e.g. Kempadoo 2004; Nixon 2015). Overall, by far the most exciting contemporary scholarship emanating from the Caribbean comes from feminist scholars and activists. The formation of Women and Development Studies groups at UWI in 1982, and the Centre for Gender Studies in 1993 – later designated the Institute for Gender and Development Studies (IGDS) – marked significant turning points in research, teaching and advocacy. Consciously established as an independent institute, rather than incorporated into existing faculty, IGDS has proactively adopted an interdisciplinary stance aimed at challenging the basis of all disciplinary knowledge (Reddock 1994).

By applying feminist analytical tools and concepts to all aspects of Caribbean society, the ultimate aim is to achieve meaningful gender equality and social transformation. To do this, feminists today explore how gender, sexuality, race, ethnicity, class, religion and nation intersect with political and socio-economic colonial legacies as well as contemporary dynamics (see: Bailey and Leo-Rhynie 2004; Barriteau 2003; Hosein and Outar 2016; Mohammed 2002; Thompson 2019b). A significant body of related literature has also looked at the impact of global processes of transformation, industrialisation and structural adjustment on women in the Caribbean (see, inter alia: Antrobus 1993; Freeman 2000; Momsen 1993; Peake and Trotz 1999; Senior 1991). Women's subordination has deep colonial roots: the Caribbean is unique because it has high numbers of female-headed households, a legacy of the sexual division of labour established under slavery (Barrow 1996). Although it has made significant gains in terms of women's education and participation in the workforce, significant economic hardship remains, which disproportionately affects women and children. These challenges have been intensified by global restructuring: some women – e.g. those with 'white collar' skills (Freeman 2014) – have benefitted in some ways, while others, especially in rural, marginalised areas have suffered due to collapses in export agriculture and depression of wages. Furthermore, as a highly patriarchal space, the Caribbean continues to face high levels of domestic violence and struggles over the rights and citizenship of LGBTQ populations.

Eudine Barriteau – the first head of IGDS at the UWI Cave Hill campus in Barbados – is the leading feminist political economist in the region, and possibly one of very few who conceives of her work in those explicit disciplinary terms. Her theorising of gender systems of power in the Caribbean centres both the material *and* ideological relations of gender (Barriteau 1998; 2003). This is particularly useful, because she places emphasis on how 'gender and gender systems … operate within the political, social, and cultural economy of states' (Barriteau 1998: 187). Therefore, her analytical framework emphasises the 'interaction of political, economic and cultural dimensions of gender in the public domain … an area that is largely under-theorized' in recognition that gender does not just take place in the private sphere (Barriteau 1998: 189). Thinking in this way helps us to understand changing gender systems over time and how they interact with the 'project of modernity' through the transitions from colonial to postcolonial Caribbean societies. It has also become central to work that analyses the negotiation of gender relations with the state (Hosein and Parpart 2016; Thompson 2019b).

The third site of interesting intellectual activity also stresses colonial legacies. There is, as we suggested in the introduction to the chapter, an extremely rich history of postcolonial thought that was, in the mid-twentieth century, led by Caribbean thinkers like Frantz Fanon, Aimé Césaire, Marcus Garvey and others, and this intersected with wider trends in 'Black Atlantic' critical theory that later came to typify the work of people like Paul Gilroy (1995) and Stuart Hall (2017). In Caribbean critical studies in general – especially at the intersection of social theory, history, anthropology and literary studies – there has always existed a marked trend in theorising the acts of forgetting, especially around slavery and the early colonial experience, that have predominated in a western-centric academy that frequently suffers from historical amnesia (see: Scott 2004; Trouillot 1995). More recently, scholars who work more explicitly in or around IR and IPE have sought to re-emphasise both the enduring importance of such thinking *and* the necessity of remembering the enduring effects of colonialism. The most striking strand of this work – from the perspective of IPE – owes much to the efforts of Robbie Shilliam. Rather than applying the hegemonic tools and concepts distilled from the work of centuries-dead European thinkers *to* the problems that conventionally animate (even critical parts of) the field, he has instead deployed insights *from* the Caribbean and other postcolonial intellectual spaces to interrogate the very assumptions that underpin prevailing knowledge.

For example, Shilliam (2012) has drawn on Césaire's thought to juxtapose eighteenth-century liberal justifications for the commodification of labour under slavery with contemporary forms of liberalism which have failed to truly emancipate humans under capitalism. He has also applied the ideas and concepts of various Caribbean thinkers – including genuinely subaltern ones such as the Rastafari of Jamaica – to debates about abolition, development and so on that are normally dominated by intellectual elites (Shilliam 2014). More broadly, there is a thriving postcolonial community posing an ever-greater challenge to the assumptions of the critical mainstream, and making rapid inroads into challenging IPE to think more systematically about imperial legacies (see Narayan, this volume). This kind of research is invaluable because it actively traverses – and frequently rejects – disciplinary boundaries to locate the postcolonial experience in every area of social and political life (e.g. Narayan 2019; Pugh 2017). Shilliam's latest work, generally with Lisa Tilley, has also opened up a pressing new line of analysis *within* IPE: that is, exhorting the field to take more seriously the profoundly 'raced' dimensions of market and other transactions which cannot be understood solely on the basis of conventional class-based analyses (see Shilliam 2018; Tilley and Shilliam 2018). All of this contributes to a wider trend in IPE and IR to 'decolonise' the Eurocentric assumptions, concepts and ideas underpinning what we study, how and why (Hobson 2013a, 2013b).

Why does all of this matter for Caribbean development, specifically? Our final argument here is that it is absolutely crucial. The world of today is quite different to the one inherited at independence by the New World Group: the region faces a daunting set of challenges, in an extremely unkind global context, and remains mired in conventional ways of thinking when it comes to addressing them (Bishop 2015). Before his untimely passing, Girvan asked whether this situation had become so dire as to be characterised by truly 'existential threats' that pose fundamental 'systemic challenges to the viability of our states as functioning socio-economic-ecological-political systems' (see Bishop 2013: 51–53). These include: economic stagnation and flatlining levels of growth; high and growing debt burdens, and an inability to access concessional development financing; deteriorating governance; rising crime and violence associated with the hemispheric drug and weapons trade; extremely high levels of out-migration, especially of the most educated; a looming environmental challenge linked to climate change; and so on.

Critical analysis of these issues matters: they are not simply technical problems to be solved by externally driven, neoliberal interventions; they are profoundly *political*; they intersect deeply with each other and exclusionary colonial legacies; and they are both constituted by, and constitutive of the contemporary GPE. For example, climate change does not just require money for adaptation, it needs to be understood as reflective of longstanding neo-colonial patterns of inequality that require much more fundamental ideational and political change (Sealey-Huggins 2017). The same is true of modern patterns of debt: these reflect profoundly unequal global patterns of development inherited from the colonial era, for which claims for reparations are growing ever-louder (see Beckles 2013). The chronically high level of out-migration in the region is not just a monetary problem hitting national balance-sheets, it represents a much bigger set of logics linked to 'dispossession' of those with limited economic power (Phillips 2009). Why does the Caribbean suffer so much violence? Because drug prohibition has unfortunately placed it directly on the transit route between the producer countries of Latin America and consumers further north. In short, it is only by grasping the deeper underpinnings of the development problems that apparently face these small islands and territories that we can genuinely understand them and re-envision meaningful solutions.

Conclusion

We opened this chapter by claiming that the Caribbean rarely features in conventional analysis in IPE. Even on its own terms this state of affairs is indefensible: the region once had its own variants of the classical 'modernisation vs dependency' debates which were equally as vibrant as those going on elsewhere; it has produced a staggering number of the world's foremost intellectuals of all kinds, and their ideas clearly have relevance for modern political economy. Some of the most exciting trends in the field are today being driven by feminist and postcolonial scholars, and they consistently point out the value of utilising these ideas, concepts and framings to better-comprehend the reality faced by people, groups and societies whose experience is poorly served by existing hegemonic tendencies. This is, we suggest, not really about 'bringing in' marginalised voices from outside, but rather excavating what is already there and giving it proper recognition. On this reading, IPE as a field should be less an analysis *of* the global economy – as understood in the classic 'big picture' terms of looking at trade, finance and production in the supposedly 'core' institutions and 'systemically important' spaces – and more a genuinely 'global' analysis of the varied phenomena that comprise the often-ignored and obscured economic and social reality of large parts of the world.

Indigenous theorising, ways of thinking and modes of meaning are, therefore, crucial to such an endeavour. The Caribbean – like other under-researched regions of the world – has a distinct intellectual richness which has been, at times, undermined by neoliberalism and the technification of development policy. Three broad implications follow from these insights. First, the pressing development challenges facing the region can only be resolved in any substantive way from a serious re-engagement with those literatures on the part of academic and policy elites, and with it an attempt to re-envision new kinds of development. Second, the work of New World needs to be brought up to date: their analysis of the 'plantation' economy still describes in some measure the fundamental basis of the social settlement in many small, tropical island societies, and has a key role to play in the rejuvenation of a critical Caribbean form of political economy. Third, these ideas should not just be confined to describing the places from which they emerged. The liberal, realist and constructivist mainstream are rarely shy about describing large swathes of the world in their favoured terms; why should peripheral ideas – which are only so because of relations of power, not their relative ability to say something useful or interesting – be any different? The emerging postcolonial turn in IPE has shown us that, if we look hard enough, we can certainly find examples of phenomena in the GPE that would be illuminated by an updated twenty-first century New World treatment.

Bibliography

Antrobus, P. 1993. Structural Adjustment: Cure or Curse? Implications for Caribbean Development. *Gender & Development*, 1(3): 13–18.

Bailey, B. and Leo-Rhynie, E. 2004. *Gender in the 21st Century: Caribbean Perspectives, Visions and Possibilities*. Jamaica: Ian Randle.

Barriteau, E. 1998. Theorizing Gender Systems and the Project of Modernity in the Twentieth-Century Caribbean. *Feminist Review*, 59: 186–210.

Barriteau, E. 2003. *Confronting Power, Theorizing Gender: Interdisciplinary Perspectives in the Caribbean*. Kingston, Jamaica: UWI Press: 27–45.

Barrow, C. 1996. *Family in the Caribbean: Themes and Perspectives*. Princeton, NJ: Markus Wiener.

Beckford, G. 1972. *Persistent Poverty: Underdevelopment in Plantation Economies of the Third World*. Oxford: Oxford University Press.

Beckles, H. 2013. *Britain's Black Debt: Reparations for Caribbean Slavery and Native Genocide*. Mona, Jamaica: UWI Press.

Bernal, R., Figueroa, J. and Witter, M. 1984. Caribbean Economic Thought: The Critical Tradition. *Social and Economic Studies*, 33(2): 5–96.

Best, L. 1968. Outlines of a Model of Pure Plantation Economy. *Social and Economic Studies*, 17(3): 283–323.

Best, L. 1971. Independent Thought and Caribbean Freedom. In: Girvan, N. and Jefferson, O. (eds) *Readings in the Political Economy of the Caribbean*. Mona, Jamaica: New World Group: 7–28.

Best, L. 1992. The Contribution of George Beckford. *Social and Economic Studies*, 41(3): 5–23.

Best, L. and Levitt, K. 1968. *Externally Propelled Industrialisation and Growth in the Caribbean*. Montreal: McGill Centre for Developing Area Studies.

Best, L. and Levitt, K. 2009. *Essays on the Theory of Plantation Economy: A Historical and Institutional Approach to Caribbean Economic Development*. Kingston, Jamaica: UWI Press.

Bishop, M. 2010. Tourism as a Small State Development Strategy: Pier Pressure in the Eastern Caribbean? *Progress in Development Studies*, 10(2): 99–114.

Bishop, M. 2012. The Political Economy of Small States: Enduring Vulnerability? *Review of International Political Economy*, 19(5): 942–960.

Bishop, M. 2013. *The Political Economy of Caribbean Development*. Basingstoke: Palgrave Macmillan.

Bishop, M. 2015. *Caribbean Development in the Midst of New Regional and Global Dynamics*. Paper prepared for the Forum on the Future of the Caribbean, Port of Spain, Trinidad. Available at: https://bit.ly/2HCXsUq.

Bishop, M., Heron, T. and Payne, A. 2013. Caribbean Development Alternatives and the CARIFORUM-European Union Economic Partnership Agreement. *Journal of International Relations and Development*, 16(1): 82–110.

Booth, D. 1985. Marxism and Development Sociology: Interpreting the Impasse. *World Development*, 13(7): 761–787.

Burnard, T. 2012. Et in Arcadia ego: West Indian Planters in Glory, 1674–1784. *Atlantic Studies*, 9(1): 19–40.

Cardoso, F. and Faletto, E. 1979. *Dependency and Development in Latin America*. London: University of California Press.

Césaire, A. 1989 [1950]. *Discours Sur le Colonialisme*. Paris: Présence Africaine.

Conway, D. 1997. Pursuing an Appropriate Development Model for Caribbean Small Islands: Can Past Experience help Subvert the Neo-Liberal Agenda. In *The Latin American Studies Association XX International Congress: Neoliberal Theory and Practice in Latin America*. Guadalajara, Mexico.

Cooper, A. 2011. *Internet Gambling Offshore: Caribbean Struggles Over Casino Capitalism*. Basingstoke: Palgrave Macmillan.

Demas, W. 1965. *The Economics of Development in Small Countries with Special Reference to the Caribbean*. Montréal: McGill University Press.

Fanon, F. 1961. *Les damnés de la terre*. Paris: François Maspero.

Ferguson, L. 2011. Tourism, Consumption and Inequality in Central America. *New Political Economy*, 16(3): 347–371.

Frank, A. 1966. The Development of Underdevelopment. *Monthly Review*, 18(4): 17–31.

Frank, A. 1967. *Capitalism and Underdevelopment in Latin America*. New York: Monthly Review Press.

Freeman, C. 2000. *High Tech and High Heels in the Global Economy: Women, Work, and Pink-collar Identities in the Caribbean*. Durham, NC: Duke University Press.

Freeman, C. 2014. *Entrepreneurial Selves: Neoliberal Respectability and the Making of a Caribbean Middle Class*. Durham, NC: Duke University Press.

Gilroy, P. 1995. *The Black Atlantic: Modernity and Double Consciousness*. Cambridge, MA: Harvard University Press.

Girvan, N. 1973. The Development of Dependency Economics in the Caribbean and Latin America: Review and Comparison. *Social and Economic Studies*, 22(1): 1–33.

Girvan, N. 2002. *Notes for a Retrospective on the Theory of Plantation Economy of Lloyd Best and Kari Polanyi Levitt*. Working Paper. Available at: www.normangirvan.info.

Girvan, N. 2009. Foreword Plantation Economy in the Age of Globalization. In Best, L. and Levitt, K. (eds) *Essays on the Theory of Plantation Economy: An Institutional and Historical Approach to Caribbean Economic Development*. Kingston, Jamaica: UWI Press.

Girvan, N. 2010. New World and Its Critics. In Meeks, B. and Girvan, N. (eds) *The Thought of the New World: The Quest for Decolonisation*. Kingston, Jamaica: Ian Randle: 3–29.

Green, C. 2001. Caribbean Dependency Theory of the 1970s: A Historical-Materialist-Feminist Revision. In Meeks, B. and Lindahl, F. (eds) *New Caribbean Thought: A Reader*. Kingston, Jamaica: UWI Press: 40–72.

Hall, S. 2017. *Familiar Stranger: A Life between Two Islands*. Durham, NC: Duke University Press.

Hobson, J. 2013a. Part 1 – Revealing the Eurocentric Foundations of IPE: A Critical Historiography of the Discipline from the Classical to the Modern Era. *Review of International Political Economy*, 20(5): 1024–1054.

Hobson, J. 2013b. Part 2 – Reconstructing the non-Eurocentric Foundations of IPE: From Eurocentric 'Open Economy Politics' to Inter-Civilizational Political Economy. *Review of International Political Economy*, 20(5): 1025–1081.

Hosein, G. and Outar, L. 2016. *Indo-Caribbean Feminist Thought: Genealogies, Theories, Enactments*. London: Palgrave Macmillan.

Hosein, G. and Parpart, J. 2016. *Negotiating Gender, Policy and Politics in the Caribbean*. London: Rowman & Littlefield.

James, C. 1938. *The Black Jacobins*. London: Secker and Warburg.

Kempadoo, K. 2004. *Sexing the Caribbean: Gender, Race, and Sexual Labor*. London: Routledge.

LeBaron, G. and Phillips, N. 2019. States and the Political Economy of Unfree Labour. *New Political Economy*, 24(1): 1–21.

Lee, D., Hampton, M. and Jeyacheya, J. 2015. The Political Economy of Precarious Work in the Tourism Industry in Small Island Developing States. *Review of International Political Economy*, 22(1): 194–223.

Levitt, K. 1996. From Decolonisation to Neoliberalism: What Have We Learned About Development? In: Levitt, K. and Witter, M. (eds) *The Critical Tradition of Caribbean Political Economy: The Legacy of George Beckford*. Kingston: Ian Randle: 201–221.

Levitt, K. 2005. *Reclaiming Development: Independent Thought and Caribbean Community*. Kingston: Ian Randle.

Lewis, G. K. 1968. *The Growth of the Modern West Indies*. New York: Monthly Review Press.

Lewis, W. 1950. The Industralization of the British West Indies. *Caribbean Economic Review*, 2(1): 1–39.

Lewis, W. 1954. Economic Development with Unlimited Supply of Labour. *Manchester School of Social and Economic Studies*, 22(2): 139–191.

Marshall, D. 1998. *Caribbean Political Economy at the Crossroads: NAFTA and Regional Developmentalism*. Basingstoke: Macmillan.

Marshall, D. 2002. At Whose Service? Caribbean State Posture, Merchant Capital and the Export Services Option. *Third World Quarterly*, 23(4): 725–751.

Marshall, D. 2014. The New World Group: Reflections of a Caribbean Avant-garde Movement. In Desai, V. and Potter, R. (eds) *The Companion to Development Studies*. 3rd Edition. London: Routledge: 116–121.

Marx, K. 1867. *Das Kapital*. Hamburg: Otto Meissner.

Mintz, S. 1974. *The Caribbean Region*. Daedalus. The MIT Press, 103(2): 45–71.

Mohammed, P. 2002. *Gendered Realities: Essays in Caribbean Feminist Thought*. Mona, Jamaica: UWI Press.

Momsen, J. 1993. *Women & Change in the Caribbean: a Pan-Caribbean Perspective*. Bloomington, IN: Indiana University Press.

Narayan, J. 2019. *British Black Power: The Anti-imperialism of Political Blackness and the Problem of Nativist Socialism*. The Sociological Review, FirstView.

Nixon, A. V. 2015. *Resisting Paradise: Tourism, Diaspora, and Sexuality in Caribbean Culture*. Jackson, MS: University of Mississippi Press.

Payne, A. 1984. Introduction: Dependency Theory and the Commonwealth Caribbean. In: Payne, A. and Sutton, P. (eds) *Dependency Under Challenge: The Political Economy of the Commonwealth Caribbean*. Manchester: Manchester University Press: 1–11.

Payne, A. 2006. The End of Green Gold? Comparative Development Options and Strategies in the Eastern Caribbean Banana-producing Islands. *Studies in Comparative International Development*, 41(3): 25–46.

Payne, A. and Phillips, N. 2010. *Development*. Cambridge: Polity Press.

Payne, A. and Sutton, P. 2001. *Charting Caribbean Development*. Florida: University Press of Florida.

Payne, A. and Sutton, P. 2007. *Repositioning the Caribbean within Globalisation*. Waterloo, Ontario: Centre for International Governance Innovation (CIGI) Caribbean Paper No. 1.

Peake, L. and Trotz, D. 1999. *Gender, Ethnicity and Place: Women and Identities in Guyana*. London: Routledge.

Phillips, N. 2009. Migration as Development Strategy? The New Political Economy of Dispossession and Inequality in the Americas. *Review of International Political Economy*, 16(2): 231–259.

Polanyi, K. 2001 [1944]. *The Great Transformation: the Political and Economic Origins of Our Time*. Boston, MA: Beacon Press.

Pugh, J. 2017. Postcolonial Development, (Non)Sovereignty and Affect: Living On in the Wake of Caribbean Political Independence. *Antipode*, 49(4): 867–882.

Reddock, R. 1994. Women's Studies at the University of the West Indies: A Decade of Feminist Education? *Women's Studies Quarterly*, 22(3&4): 103–115.

Richardson, B. 2009. *Sugar: Refined Power in a Global Regime*. London: Palgrave MacMillan.

Rodney, W. 1972. *How Europe Underdeveloped Africa*. London: Bogle-L'Ouverture.

Santos, T. Dos. 1970. The Structure of Dependence. *The American Economic Review*, 60(2): 231–236.

Scott, D. 2004. *Conscripts of Modernity: The Tragedy of Colonial Enlightenment*. Durham, NC: Duke University Press.

Sealey-Huggins, L. 2017. '1.5°C to Stay Alive': Climate Change, Imperialism and Justice for the Caribbean. *Third World Quarterly*, 38(11): 2444–2463.

Senior, O. 1991. *Working Miracles: Women's Lives in the English-speaking Caribbean*. Indiana, IN: Indiana University Press.

Sharman, J. 2011. *Small is Beautiful: The Perils of Gigantism and the Pay-offs of Studying Small International Organisations*. Paper Presented at the AGORA Workshop on Institutional Diversity in the Governance of the Global Economy, Griffith University, Queensland, Australia, January 11–12. Available at: www.griffith.edu.au/__data/assets/pdf_file/0014/293000/Sharman.pdf.

Sharman, J. 2017. Illicit Global Wealth Chains after the Financial Crisis: Micro-states and an Unusual Suspect. *Review of International Political Economy*, 24(1): 30–55.

Shilliam, R. 2012. Forget English Freedom, Remember Atlantic Slavery: Common Law, Commercial Law and the Significance of Slavery for Classical Political Economy. *New Political Economy*, 17(5): 591–609.

Shilliam, R. 2014. Open the Gates Mek We Repatriate: Caribbean Slavery, Constructivism, and Hermeneutic Tensions. *International Theory*, 6(2): 349–372.

Shilliam, R. 2018. *Race and the Undeserving Poor: From Abolition to Brexit*. Newcastle: Agenda.

Smith, A. 1974 [1776]. *An Enquiry Into the Nature and Causes of the Wealth of Nations (Abbreviated Edition)*. New York: Penguin Books.

Sudama, T. 1979. The Model of the Plantation Economy: The Case of Trinidad and Tobago. *Latin American Perspectives*, 6(1): 65–83.

Sutton, P. 2006. Caribbean Development: An Overview. *New West Indian Guide*, 80(1&2): 45–62.

Thomas, C. 1974. *Dependence and Transformation: The Economics of the Transition to Socialism*. New York: Monthly Review Press.

Thompson, M. S. 2019a. Still Searching for (Food) Sovereignty: Why are Radical Discourses Only Partially Mobilised in the Independent Anglo-Caribbean? *Geoforum*, 101: 90–99.

Thompson, M. S. 2019b. Cultivating 'New' Gendered Food Producers: Intersections of Power and Identity in the Postcolonial Nation of Trinidad. *Review of International Political Economy*, iFirst.

Tilley, L. and Shilliam, R. 2018. Raced Markets: An Introduction. *New Political Economy*, 23(5): 534–543.

Trouillot, M. 1995. *Silencing the Past: Power and the Production of History*. Boston, MA: Beacon Press.

Veenendaal, W. and Corbett, J. 2015. Why Small States Offer Important Answers to Large Questions. *Comparative Political Studies*, 48(4): 527–549.

Vlcek, W. 2014. From Road Town to Shanghai: Situating the Caribbean in Global Capital Flows to China. *The British Journal of Politics & International Relations*, 16(3): 534–553.

Williams, E. 1944. *Capitalism and Slavery*. Chapel Hill, NC: University of North Carolina Press.

Williams, E. 1964. *History of the People of Trinidad and Tobago*. New York: Praeger.

Williams, E. 1970. *From Columbus to Castro: The History of the Caribbean 1492–1969*. London: André Deutsch.

Part V
New research arenas

37

The IPE of global social policy governance

Andrea Bianculli and Andrea Ribeiro Hoffmann

Introduction

Social policy has been studied mostly at the national level as nation-states have been the focus of social policy making since the creation and spread of the notion of a welfare state in the nineteenth century. The idea of social policy making beyond nation-states flourished much later, and was consolidated in the 1990s, following the discussion on the (negative) effects of globalisation and the need for 'global governance' (Goodin & Mitchell 2000; Rosenau & Czempiel 1992). The discussion of policy making at the global level covers several issue areas from security, to trade and social policies. This chapter explores global policy governance in the issue area of social policy. Moreover, the chapter investigates global social policy governance from an international political economy (IPE) perspective, in other words, it addresses the relations between politics and economics, between states and markets (Strange 1994). In doing so, it also highlights the role of state and non-state actors such as private companies, non-governmental organisations (NGOs), networks, social movements and think tanks, and the multi-level nature of policy making in the national, regional and global levels. We advance that the regional level has become a key locus of social policy making and therefore explore this level in depth.

The definition of social policy is not straightforward (Bianculli & Ribeiro Hoffmann 2016a). Hall and Midgley conceptualise social policy as the 'measures that affect people's well-being, whether through the provision of welfare services or by means of policies that impact upon livelihoods more generally' (2004: XIV). From a more general approach, Mkandawire argues that social policy

> should be conceived of as involving overall and prior concerns with social development, and as a key instrument that works in tandem with economic policy to ensure equitable and socially sustainable development (...) as collective interventions directly affecting transformation in social welfare, social institutions and social relations.
>
> *(2001: 1)*

These attempts to define social policy emphasise objectives, instruments and mechanisms that work at the collective level rather than at the level of the individual. Indeed, it is contended that

637

the most important component of social policies relates to the promotion of the integration process by paying attention to social development, what in turn would lead to the construction of a 'communitarian identity' (Bizzozzero 2000). Thus, changes in the level where social policies are addressed could lead to the transformation of identities. We deem the relation between social policies and identities a key issue in the literature as it mobilises deep expectations of citizens about the political entities they belong to, especially at national and regional levels, as explored below.

Box 37.1 Definition of social policy

The 'measures that affect people's well-being, whether through the provision of welfare services or by means of policies that impact upon livelihoods more generally' (Hall & Midgley 2004: XIV).

This chapter proceeds by addressing first the global, and then the regional level of social policy making. In so doing, the objective is twofold. First, to revise how the literature has evolved, key authors in the field, and the main topics addressed; second, to provide an IPE perspective. This implies examining the profound interconnections between politics and economics, i.e. states and markets, but also an increasing array of civil society actors, on the one hand, and across levels, i.e. the national, the regional and the international, on the other. We also explore the drivers and mechanisms of global social policies in case studies; labour policy and the International Labour Organization (ILO) on the global level, and the case of the European Union (EU) and comparative regionalism studies, on the regional level.

Studying social policy from a global perspective

Social policy is traditionally studied at the national level, with a focus on single countries or comparative studies (Kennett 2013; Surender & Walker 2013). During the 1990s a new sub-field was developed by scholars advancing the necessity to develop social policies at the global level to counteract the negative impacts of economic globalisation, namely, Global Social Policy (GSP). A key scholar to the consolidation of this research agenda was Bob Deacon, who died in 2017, and was Professor of International Social Policy at the University of Sheffield, directed the Globalism and Social Policy Program at this institution, and was the founding editor of the journals *Critical Social Policy* (1980) and *Journal of Global Social Policy* (2001). Deacon also acted as advisor and consultant on aspects of international social policy to many international organisations such as the ILO, the United Nations Development Programme (UNDP) and the Council of Europe. Deacon's place in the GSP is summarised by Stubbs when he argues that 'his trilogy of books "Global Social Policy" (1997), "Global Social Policy and Governance" (2007), and "Global Social Policy in the Making" (2013) will define the discipline for years to come.' The context of these books structured the agenda of GSP, i.e. how globalisation influences social policy, the actors involved in global social policy making (such as think tanks, global policy advocacy coalitions, global social movements, knowledge networks, epistemic communities), and their role in the promotion of regulation, rights and redistribution, referred to in Deacon's work as the '3 Rs'. Moreover, in his work, global social policy 'builds on a tradition of critical development theory which has sought a broader understanding of human development and addresses the social impacts of an international political economy through the lens of whether or not they meet basic human needs' (Deacon & Stubbs 2013: 7).

More recently, Seckinelgin (2014) has claimed that the work by Deacon and his colleagues, such as Paul Stubbs and Alexandra Kaash, has developed at least two central orientations:

(a) considerations of the role played by international organisations within globalisation pro- cesses that impact peoples' wellbeing in different contexts and (b) normative considerations based on the possibilities of thinking of alternative roles for international organisations to address commonly observed global wellbeing problems.

(2014: 589)

Throughout his work, Deacon has advanced a critical approach to globalisation and an activist dimension to academic concerns. The impact of globalisation on the making and context of social policy was summarised by him as (a) setting welfare states in competition with each other, (b) bringing new (international) players into the making of social policy, (c) raising the issues with which social policy is concerned to supranational level, (d) creating a global private market in social provision, and (e) encouraging 'a global movement of peoples that challenges territorial- based structures and assumptions of welfare obligation and entitlement' (Deacon 2007: 9–10). Despite being a declared Marxist, he advanced a reformist approach to counter globalisation, while being aware of the limits:

One problem identified by Paul Stubbs and I (Deacon and Stubbs 2007) is that the very processes of consultancy-driven international development has captured and de-radicalized a whole generation in many countries that might otherwise have played such a radical role. Not only have governments become agencies for the realization of neo-liberal goals, as Cohen and Baumann identified, but so have many of those who would have been activists in an earlier era been bought off by and bought into the existing form of development politics.

(Deacon 2014: 211)

Holden has also criticised the rather conservative turn of GSP to the extent that 'the dominant forms taken by GSP will continue to be piecemeal, minimalist and essentially neoliberal for as long as an effective global political movement in favour of a more extensive GSP is absent' (2018: 1).

In addressing some of these criticisms, Yeates (2008), for instance, took a more bottom–up approach in the discussion of GSP, exploring the historical and geographical contexts of social policy as well as the phenomena of global migration flows and the challenges thus posed to GSP. The questions of gender, race, intersectionality as well as 'post-colonial issues' also only gained prominence in the literature (Deacon 2014; Razavi & Hassim 2006; True 2003). In all, gender governance, and therefore gender (global) policy, can be seen as a 'specific dimension of social governance, covering regulation aiming to achieve equal opportunities and equal treatment, and measures aiming to redistribute benefits between women and men' (Van der Vleuten 2016: 406). Yet, it is far more comprehensive: 'Achieving gender equality in politics, economy, and society constitutes a cross–cutting aim, which is reflected by gender mainstreaming as a trans- formative strategy to achieving gender equality by incorporating a gender perspective in all policies (…). Finally, gender is not only a variable but also a perspective' (idem), and it is pos- sible to study governance and (global) social policies from a gender perspective. Differently from studying gender as a policy area or a mainstreaming agenda, which is more present in the liter- ature, a gender perspective on (global) social policy would ask 'where are the women in global social policy making?' Building on Van der Vleuten, this implies 'looking for "femocrats" (feminist bureaucrats) and openings for feminist alliances, analysing gender relations at summits, the construction of power, masculinity and femininity, and the processes of socialization' (2016: 420).

More recently, in a provocative article, Steffek and Holthaus (2017) argued that the sources for what they refer to as 'welfare internationalism' are not 'domestic analogies', or the transposal of welfare ideas and institutions from national to the global level after the Second World War, but rather they stem from four different origins:

> One was a transfer of notions of professional colonial administration to the international sphere: expert-driven, rationalist in a utilitarian way and openly paternalistic. The second was a cosmopolitan interpretation of 19th century public unions as caretakers of global public interests, understood as the interest of individuals rather than states. The third ingredient was European reform-oriented socialist traditions that had found an international institutional home in the ILO, guided by its charismatic founding director Albert Thomas. Fourth, welfare internationalism was influenced by forms of imperial humanitarianism – the belief that Western societies ought to limit the suffering of distant strangers.
>
> *(2017: 108)*

In this light, the domestic welfare state and welfare internationalism developed at the same time; and the origins of the latter are less virtuous than often portrayed in the literature, exposing 'paternalistic, technocratic and racist traits' (Steffek & Holthaus 2017: 108). The authors also advance that

> the assumption that IOs should be responsible for individual welfare raises some thorny issues of the practical-political kind. The material resources of IOs are notoriously limited and often insufficient to live up to the promises made in their mission statements. What is more, in practice, welfare internationalism often implies a redistribution of resources across borders. Such redistribution from wealthier to poorer areas of the globe is regularly called for – on moral, legal and political grounds – but proved hard to achieve in the past. The long-standing controversy over the size of official development assistance (ODA) can illustrate the point. At an aggregate level, it never even came close to the mark of 0.7% of developed countries' gross domestic product (GDP) that was first envisaged in 1970.
>
> *(2017: 107)*

Steffek and Holthaus's call for a critical view on GSP, questioning its origins and the possibilities under which it could play a positive role in the well-being of individuals is certainly much more radical than the more traditional questioning of the limits of global social policy under neo-liberalism (Haarstad & St Clair 2011), and require a deeper thinking about the way ahead, in light of the increasing concentration of wealth and democratic crisis worldwide.

From a less radical perspective, some particularities of GSP and the developing countries such as informality, conditionality and the role of South–South cooperation have been underscored (Surender & Walker 2013). South–South cooperation has provoked a discussion about the content and mechanisms of policy diffusion, and therefore, how it has affected global social policy making. The High-Level United Nations Conference on South–South Cooperation (SSC) held in Nairobi in 2009, acknowledged SSC as an important element of international development cooperation, distinguishing it from official development assistance (ODA). The Nairobi Outcome Document adopted by the United Nations General Assembly established six principles of South–South cooperation: Respect for national sovereignty, national ownership and independence; equality (horizontality); non-conditionality; non-interference in domestic affairs; mutual benefits. It also established the elements that should inform SSC practices: common objectives and solidarity; multi-stakeholder approach; national well-being; promotion of national and collective self-reliance; internationally agreed development goals; alignment to national development; priorities at the request of developing countries; capacity development.

(BRICS Policy Center & South–South Cooperation Research and Policy Centre 2017: 16)

These practices have spread in bilateral, triangular and multilateral cooperation and therefore, global social policy making.

The role of knowledge, policy networks and the so-called 'turn of think tanks' have also been discussed in the GSP literature (Reinicke 1999; Stone 2013; Williams 2016; Witte et al. 2005). Stone's study on how 'knowledge organizations deliver conceptual understanding of policy problems, how networks set policy agendas and the effectiveness and legitimacy (or not) with which they implement and monitor (non) governmental public action' (2013: 2) calls attention to the changing nature of GSP and the powerful role of policy research institutes. The concept of policy network has been used extensively in the literature on regulation, norms diffusion and even world order (Bianculli et al. 2015; Börzel 1998; Castells & Cardoso 2005; Jordana 2017; Slaughter 2004). Similar developments are still missing in social policy. As Stone argued:

> In classical political science, public policy occurs inside nation-states. In the field of international relations, a 'realist' perspective would also hold that states are the dominant actor in the international system and that international policies are made between states. With its strong tendency to 'methodological nationalism' (Wimmer & Schiller 2002), traditional comparative public policy has compounded this standpoint. Scholars in the field usually compare policy development within and between states where states remain the key policymaking unit'
>
> *(Stone 2008: 23)*

In other words, the double state-centrism of international relations and of social policy has led to the downplay of the relevance of policy networks in the study of global social policy. Finally, the role of political parties has been addressed in a study on the responses to the 2008 crisis, where the authors concluded that 'in welfare states with relatively low benefits and therefore small automatic stabilizers, crisis responses are indeed shaped by partisan politics' (Starke et al. 2014: 228). While partisan politics plays a less relevant role in GSP, it is also a crucial element at the regional level. Next, the case study of labour policy and ILO is discussed.

Case study: the International Labour Organization

The ILO is one of the world's oldest international organisations and has just turned its centenary. It was created in 1919 as a functional organisation to the League of Nations at the Versailles Treaty, with the main aim of promoting social justice through international labour standards. While it is a precursor of the idea of GSP, it drew on earlier movements and initiatives, such as the International Association for Labour Legislations. ILO's unique 'corporatist tripartite' structure, which includes representatives from its member states governments as well as from organised labour and employers in decision-making bodies, is seen as an answer within capitalist countries to the spread of communism. The ILO has adopted almost 200 conventions and 200 recommendations, ranging from basic human rights charters to detailed regulatory codes for specific industries, but the gap between treaty adoption and ratification has increased over the years, leading to a current discredit of its capacity to influence societies (Helfer 2006: 653). In a study about ILO's law making and monitoring of labour standards, it is argued that the organisation was quite successful during its first decades, establishing close relations with national trade unions. Yet, in the post-war period its attempt to expand its mandate was frustrated, and ILO remained stagnated until the 1990s, when it entered a new phase to respond to the changes triggered by economic globalisation and the transformations in labour markets.

Robert Cox, a leading international relations and IPE scholar who worked at the ILO for about twenty-five years, has elaborated about the role of international institutions and the ILO in his 'critical theory' approach (Cox 1977; Cox & Jacobson 1973; Moolakkattu 2009). In an interview in 2009, he summarised his view on ILO in the following terms:

> I left the ILO in the 1970s for personal reasons. But I also had the feeling that the organization was moving towards the side-lines of the world. Subsequently, any international issues involving labour, which used to be dealt with by the ILO, were increasingly being dealt with by the WTO or OCDE. In other words, those organizations that deal directly with economic issues were the ones that were decisive. The ILO continued to exist because it has a constituency, but like most bureaucratic organizations, you can create them, but you can't kill them (…) I doubt that it is likely to be a forum for any significant activity in the international field. That function was important in the period between the two World Wars and the years immediately following, when welfare states were building up. The ILO rules and regulations had a certain influence on countries, being incorporated into their laws. The ILO helped the labour movements in those countries by giving them a model that they could follow when they were strong enough politically within a country to influence and enforce something. In that period the ILO played an important role, I am not sure it has continued to play that sort of role. Even in the period of the independence of the African countries, for example, some of the ILO rules were contrary to the interests of development, because they represented a way of making the organized worker into a kind privileged person, as a minority within society; and there were those in the ILO who began to be interested much more in spreading employment than protecting the position of employed workers. Spreading employment was the way to help those societies develop, and that became sort of conflictual within the ILO. The traditionalists said 'no, we can't do that, our role is to promote standards'; but to promote standards in countries whose economies which were not in the shape that standards meant something for the general good was not a very useful activity. (…) they didn't take much of an interest for a while in the phenomenon of multinational corporations, in the way that corporations were operating in a number of different countries and how that created differences within countries. I didn't want to say anything negative about the ILO, but I don't see it as something that has a great future. The social movements will not be much interested in using the ILO as they are in perhaps in getting more publicity through other organizations, such as the United Nations, or other organizations that have an impact on opinion in some countries (…). What is happening now is that they [labour standards] are negotiated as part of trade agreements. The values and interests are different there, the interests of trade are preeminent. The United States, for example, with its strong movement to prevent the exporting of jobs, leads towards a form of protectionism. So, workers' organizations are making themselves felt in different ways, but not through the ILO.
>
> *(Saggioro Garcia & Borba de Sá 2013)*

Whitworth (1994) explores the role of the ILO in the agenda of gender, and shares the current negative assessment of the ILO, without, however, undermining its historical role. She argues that ILO's treatment of gender was influenced by women's movements and changing under-standings of gender relations, and 'has revolved around the perennial debate between what they call the protectionists and the equal righters' over its history, i.e. between the idea that women required special protection because of their physical differences and role in childbearing, and the idea that this kind of legislation would make them less employable and therefore hinder women's equality on the labour market (Whitworth 1994: 8). Boris et al. (2018) analyse the role of women's transnational networks in shaping ILO's debates and policies, and what were the gen-dered meanings of international labour law in a world of uneven and unequal development at the turn of the organisation's 100th anniversary. They, thus, called attention for the need of further research into gender politics and the ILO.

The regional as a *meso* level for social policy

As argued above, social policy has been mainly tackled – both from a policy and academic per-spective – at the domestic and global levels. Social policies have thus been studied either in (domestic) comparative perspective or from a global approach. On the contrary, the regional level has remained underexplored (Deacon 2011). Consequently, social policy regionalism (Bianculli & Ribeiro Hoffmann 2016a) has not been given appropriate attention in the social policy literature until more recently, despite the resurgence of regionalism and interregional relations since the late 1980s. Moreover, and rather paradoxically, whereas there is an extensive literature on the creation and development of regional organisations and regionalism initiatives, including comparative approaches, studies on the expansion, diffusion and impact of regional social policies and regulations remain rather minimal.

Box 37.2 Definition of regional organisations

The international relations scholarship has defined organisations as formal institutions with 'pre-scribed hierarchies and capacity for purposive action' as opposed to looser international regimes with 'complexes of rules and organisations, the core elements of which have been negotiated and explicitly agreed upon by states' (Keohane 1988: 384). Regional organisations thus refer to formal institutions involving members based on their geographical delimitation: they are composed of states that belong to or perceive themselves as belonging to a region (Hurrell 1995). Despite differences in their institutional design, and especially on the question of supranational decision-making, regional organisations share common characteristics, i.e. territoriality, identity and scope.

This section explores the region as a unit to mitigate the negative effects of market instability and the challenges to domestic welfare systems (Beeson 2007; Telò 2001), but also as a develop-ment space for managing uncertainties through social regulation (Deacon 2010; Kaasch & Stubbs 2014; Yeates & Deacon 2006), and thus responding to global challenges and opportunities. In other terms, it investigates regionalism and regional organisations as providers of social policies and regulations.

Exploring the drivers and mechanisms of social policy regionalism

Explaining policy dynamics and change in regional integration and cooperation is certainly a challenging task (Caporaso 1998). Relevant theoretical accounts have been proposed to explain processes of institutional, policy and norm transformation. Drawing on earlier work (Bianculli & Ribeiro Hoffmann 2016b), we address and assess the multiplicity of possible drivers of regional social policies and regulations to enlighten the empirical analysis of the complex reality of regional policy dynamics. A wide variety of actors can act as drivers of regional institutional, norm and policy change. These range from international organisations, 'peer' regional organisations, institutions and bodies within regional organisations, governments of member states, labour and business representatives, and civil society organisations (CSOs) including NGOs and social movements.

International organisations are depicted as relevant drivers of social policies at the regional level. Regional development banks, regional economic commissions and regional branches of the UN social agencies, i.e. ILO, United Nations Educational, Scientific and Cultural Organization (UNESCO), the UNDP, and United Nations International Children's Emergency Fund (UNICEF), have promoted 'regional social policy from above' (Deacon & Macovei 2010). Yet, their strategy focuses mainly on countries pertaining to regions, thus overlooking regional organisations and associations. Furthermore, when targeting regional organisations, these global entrepreneurs tend to neglect the social dimension of regionalism and regional cooperation. Despite its limitations, the role of international organisations is fundamental as drivers of social policy regionalism since they support lesson learning across countries, thus promoting capacity building in regional organisations, in fields such as labour migration, communicable diseases monitoring, and social protection and social security, among others. (Deacon & Macovei 2010: 61). Scholars have found similar empirical support for a positive dynamic between international and regional organisations, mainly through capacity building and coordinating or monitoring activities in policy fields related to cross-border employment and health problems (Lavenex et al. 2016). UN regional commissions, as in the case of the Economic Commission for Latin America and the Caribbean (ECLAC), their discourse and policy recommendations had a strong development component in the post-war era, which was then rather neglected under the years of neoliberal trade liberalisation and regional integration. Yet, social policy came into the organisation's policy as a means to respond to the failures of import substitution industrialisation, and later on of neoliberalism (Mahon 2015). Thus, starting in the mid-1990s, but especially with the turn of the century, ECLAC called for more active social policies, thus moving towards a rights approach (Ocampo 1998).

If we accept that regions are constructed, then states and state-led organisations are not to be taken as the sole drivers of regionalism. Alternatively, different non-state actors, including firms, transnational corporations, NGOs, and other types of social networks and social movements are relevant actors in regionalism and the broadening of scope and depth of regional integration and cooperation. From a bottom-up perspective, studies have delved into the role of social movements and CSOs, i.e. 'regional social policy from below' (Brennan & Olivet 2007; Olivet & Brennan 2010). Civil society and social movements are portrayed as counter-hegemonic actors, resisting neoliberal reforms and promoting alternative, progressive policies and instruments at various levels. From a regional perspective, the expansion of free trade negotiations created an opportunity to discuss the relation between regional organisations and the provision and regulation of social policy. In Latin America, for example, negotiations for the Free Trade Area of the Americas (FTAA) generated contestation and protests about the negative effects of (regional) trade liberalisation, as illustrated by the creation of the Hemispheric Social Alliance (HSA) in

Table 37.1 Drivers of institutional, norm and policy change at the regional level

Actors	International organisations/ UN system	'Peer' ROs	ROS and regional institutions (from the RO under consideration)	Member-state governments	Business	Labour	CSOs, NGOs, social movements
Mechanisms							
Diffusion (direct and indirect influence)	X (top down)	X (horizontal, interregional)	–	X (bottom up)	–	–	–
Judicial power	–	–	X	X	–	–	–
Legislative power	–	–	X	X	–	–	–
Pressure, contestation	–	–	–	–	X	X	X

Source: Bianculli & Ribeiro Hoffman (2016a).

645

1997 and the demonstrations during the Third Summit of the Americas in 2001 (Briceño-Ruiz 2007; Tussie & Botto 2003; Von Bülow 2010). Yet, similar developments abound in other world regions, as in the case of the Southern African People's Solidarity Network (SAPSN), ASEAN Civil Society Conference/ASEAN Peoples' Forum (ACSC/APF), People's SAARC (South Asia), and Civil Society Europe (CSE). These networks bring together CSOs and social movements, and through their collective action they underpin the creation of transnational political spaces, where politics are discussed and deliberated beyond borders, and at the regional level.

Relations between regions and regional organisations is another relevant driver of institutional and norm change in social policy regionalism. Portrayed as the process of dialogue and relations between two regional organisations, interregionalism and transregionalism have gained increasing significance in international political economy starting in the 1990s and as repercussion of the new or open regionalism (Doctor 2007; Rüland 2010). Taken as 'region-to-region relations', interregionalism operates as a horizontal driver, and can assume at least three forms (Hänggi 2006). Whereas the first category refers to institutionalised relations between regional groupings (e.g. EU–Common Market of the South (MERCOSUR)), the second category relates to relations between regional groupings and third states (e.g. EU–China). Finally, the third category, loosely referred to as 'other interregional or transregional mechanisms', includes relations between a regional organisation and a more or less coordinated group of states in different regions (e.g. the Asia–Europe Meeting/ASEM), relations between two more or less coordinated groups of states in different regions (e.g. the Forum for East Asia–Latin America Cooperation/FEALAC) and relations among states, groups of states and regional organisations from different regions (e.g. Asia–Pacific Economic Cooperation/APEC). In all, interregionalism and transregionalism have proved to be useful tools to push for regional integration worldwide. They are portrayed as playing a fundamental role in promoting norm and capacity building through the engagement of formal regional organisations (i.e. interregionalism) and through less formalised relations between regions as well as non-state actors (Ribeiro Hoffmann 2016). Furthermore, whereas the literature has emphasised the qualitatively asymmetric profile of the regions involved in (Doidge 2007), as focus has been mostly on EU's interregionalism vis-à-vis regions and sub-regions in Africa, Asia and Latin America, inter and transregionalism have increasingly bridged South–South regions, organisations and actors, i.e. MERCOSUR–Southern African Development Community (SADC), SADC–ASEAN, and Forum on China–Africa Cooperation (FOCAC).

Certainly, explaining the transformation of regional integration processes remains a difficult task (Caporaso 1998). Yet, the legislative or regulatory power of regional institutions and member states has been extensively analysed in the more traditional theories of regional cooperation and integration. Though an important building block of regional integration theories, neofunctionalism primarily focuses on how integration evolves through functional spillover and institutional activism, i.e. supranationality, all of which is expected to lead to more integration, yet, many questions remain unanswered (Haas 1958; Niemann & Schmitter 2009). Among others, these include the (non-technocratic) role of policymakers, societal actors and even external and international variables, all of which could be explaining the process of regional integration. Liberal intergovernmentalism has thus attempted to bring together 'a liberal theory of preference formation with an intergovernmental focus on power-bargaining among states' (Caporaso 1998: 9). Nevertheless, two factors remain still neglected: first, the relevance of transnational linkages and society in further promoting regional integration, and second, the capacity of supranational organisations to promote policy outcomes that contradict the preferences of dominant states (Mattli & Stone Sweet 2012).

More recently, new regionalism theories assumed a critical engagement with the international relations and IPE literatures and have addressed the relevance of civil society actors, thus showing that regional integration processes involve continuing linkages between state and non-state actors and across levels – the international, the regional, and the domestic (Söderbaum 2016). As regionalism and regions advance and mature, pressure and contestation from below may emerge. In other words, as 'their powers and prerogatives increase (…) so does public scrutiny' (Fioramonti 2013), being this exacerbated during periods of crisis. This brings us then to the role of non-state actors and civil society.

Whereas the notion of civil society is no longer confined to the borders of the territorial state (Kaldor 2003), the emergence of regional and international governance structures does not indicate the demise of the state and national patterns of social organisation (Price 2003). However, the regional arena as a meso level between the national and the international offers a new space for dialogue and contestation, and one where civil society, taken as a large and heterogeneous group, deploys diverse preferences and collective action strategies that relate to three broad types: conformist, moderate and radical (Korseniewicz & Smith 2001; Scholte et al. 1999). In terms of their role, civil society, i.e. mainly business associations, NGOs and think tanks, can have three roles: legitimisation, manipulation and contestation (Fioramonti 2013). First, they can act as 'legitimisers' of the regional status quo when accepting to participate in formal and institutionalised mechanisms, thus having voice and influence without actually questioning the policy process. Second, civil society can 'manipulate' standing participatory mechanisms to promote reforms in regionalism and regional organisations from within. Finally, 'contestation' occurs when civil society 'provides a counter-hegemonic challenge to mainstream regional institutions, especially market-driven regional integration processes' (Fioramonti 2013). In any case, these categorisations can be taken as 'ideal types' as the actor constellation, their collective action strategies, role and effectiveness in (re)shaping regions and regionalism change in line with their respective capabilities and the changing patterns of regional governance. Therefore, the extent to which these dialogues and mobilisations can turn into direct influence or impact on regional social policies remains contested and requires further scrutiny. In all, their effectiveness is varied. Certainly, the role and effects of social actors depends on the political opportunity structure, which shapes patterns of inclusion/exclusion, and thus affect the collective action strategies of these groups. Thus, whereas studies have found empirical evidence pointing to civil society as being mainly engaged in service provision and legitimisation of regional policies (Godsäter & Söderbaum 2017), scholars have also argued that even if the participation of civil society is still a challenge in this regional policy area, the emergence of policy networks and epistemic communities certainly contributes to the diffusion of ideas and standards (Herrero & Loza 2018). Diffusion is precisely the last mechanism through which norms, policies and institutions in the area of social policy can spread over time and across space (Gilardi 2012). The literature has identified different diffusion mechanisms (Marsh & Sharman 2009). From a comparative regionalism perspective, direct and indirect mechanisms have been identified (Börzel & Risse 2012). Focused on the diffusion process as initiated by the sender, direct mechanisms include coercion, manipulation of utility calculations, socialisation and persuasion. Indirect mechanisms, on the contrary, investigate the diffusion process from the recipient perspective and involve competition, lesson-drawing and normative emulation. Furthermore, whereas these various mechanisms are not mutually exclusive (T. A. Börzel & Risse 2012), in practice, the distinction between indirect and direct mechanisms may become blurred (Lenz 2012). Based on this analytical categorisation, when examining social policy regionalism in Europe and Latin America, diffusion processes are underscored as playing a role in the ways in which norms, policies and institutions diffuse in this policy area. Yet, these more intensely operate indirectly, through competition, lesson-drawing and normative emulation (Bianculli & Ribeiro Hoffmann 2016). As an interdependent process, diffusion can lead to particular patterns of policy adoption (Elkins & Simmons 2005; Risse 2016). Comparative studies across regions and regionalism have shown that whereas 'full-scale adoption or convergence around specific models of regional cooperation and integration' are rare, diffusion is most likely to lead to selective adoption, adaptation and transformation (Risse 2016: 88).

Regional organisations and the practices of social policy regionalism

Regional organisations exhibit interesting variation in the ways in which they deal with social problems, leading thus to different practices or models of social policy regionalism. For reasons of scope and size of this chapter, it has been decided to investigate the development of a social agenda and social policy governance in the EU in more detail, being this followed by a more succinct description of social policy regionalism across different regional organisations and regions.

Case study: the EU

The EU stands out as a pioneer in the implementation of social policy regionalism, even if this agenda came at a later stage in the regional integration process. Certainly, the EU's strategy followed the policy guidelines of international organisations, i.e. Organisation for Economic Cooperation and Development (OCDE) and UN institutions. In time, EU norms, instruments and practices served as an inspirational model, resulting in emulation by other regional projects. The EU's delay in implementing a social policy agenda is explained by policymakers' reluctance given the peculiarities of the national social protection systems, and the well-developed public health and education services already in place in 1957, which added to these countries' strong commitment to expenditure on social benefits (Threlfall 2010). Yet, the EU would gradually incorporate social policy elements. Thus, and especially after the adoption of the Social Charter in 1989, the EU was perceived as a relevant actor in this policy area (Leibfried & Pierson 1995). Since then, an EU social acquis Communautaire has progressively developed, including binding and non-binding agreements, i.e. treaties, directives, regulations, declarations, recommendations and guidelines. Regarding the mechanisms and instruments in place, Structural Funds are key. These include the European Regional Development Fund (ERDF) established in 1975 to support the creation of infrastructure and jobs, and the European Social Fund (ESF) created in 1958 under the Treaty of Rome to promote the integration of the unemployed and disadvantaged social groups into the labour market through training. In 1994, the EU launched the Cohesion Fund with the aim of financing large infrastructure projects in the fields of environmental protection and transport. In all, both the Structural and Cohesion Funds aim to reduce economic and social disparities between member states and regions. Furthermore, in 1992, the Maastricht Treaty on the European Union (TEU) incorporated relevant social policy areas as part of the tasks conferred to the EU, including education, youth policy and public health, while also expanding the scope of existing funds support. However, EU competences in this domain remained limited. Having been unable to reach a unanimous agreement, 11 Member States decided to move ahead by concluding an Agreement on Social Policy, which was included as an appendix. The United Kingdom (UK), who had vetoed the agreement, was thus exempted. Despite these shortcomings, the TEU was a breakthrough in the area of social policy due to the creation of a European citizenship, which led the EU to take up many issues such as the rights of intra-community migrants. Additionally, important regulations were issued in the area of gender equality in the 2000s, even if most social regulations have not followed the supranational path. On the contrary, these remain as non-binding initiatives.

In 1997, the Treaty of Amsterdam (ToA) incorporated the Agreement on Social Policy into the text, which included a co-decision to replace cooperation, extended the provisions related to ESF, and the free movement of workers and social security for EU migrant workers. The ToA made the European Commission (EC) responsible for the implementation of the European Employment Strategy (EES) through a coordinated strategy with member states, based on the Open Method of Coordination (OMC). In all, the European Social Model gained full recognition in 1997, and Social Dialogue is a fundamental component: business and labour representatives can contribute to the design of EU social policies. Three years later, the Lisbon Strategy extended the OMC to pensions, health and long-term care as part of the 'social OMC'. As the objective set for the EU was 'to become the most competitive and dynamic knowledge-based economy in the world capable of sustainable economic growth with more and better jobs and greater social cohesion,' the Lisbon Strategy and later revisions embraced overarching social policy aims, including social cohesion, equality between men and women, and effective social protection systems, among others. The Lisbon Treaty, signed in 2007, took a step forward by incorporating a 'social clause' that requires the EU's policies to consider social requirements, while recognising and emphasising the role of social partners at the regional level to acknowledge diversity across national systems. Despite existing limitations, the EU increasingly projected itself both as the institution where discussion of common problems should take place and as the venue where solutions should be found – through the reform of the European Social Model and through streamlining and consolidating social policies into the heart of integration policy (Threlfall 2010: 85).

However, starting with the international financial markets' crises, and its quick spread to the region's economy and social and political institutions, the European Social Model came under pressure. Against this background the EU adopted the Europe 2020 Strategy, which prioritised inclusive growth through high employment, social and territorial cohesion, while also prioritising pensions, health and social care. These were followed by the establishment of the European Semester in 2011, which included Country Specific Recommendations to member states in areas of perceived weakness, the Fund for European Aid to the Most Deprived (FEAD) in 2014, and the EC Communication on the European Pillar of Social Rights (EPSR) intended to support a transformed process of convergence towards better living and working conditions in Europe. However, while the EU continued to put forward austerity as a crucial policy to overcome the crisis (Hyman 2015) and evidenced a 'balanced budget fundamentalism' (De Grauwe 2011), member states were not affected in the same way. Recent studies have shown that the EU 'has failed to rebalance the social and economic dimensions of its governance, while fiscal consolidation measures have put the so-called European Social Model under strain' (Vanhercke et al. 2017: 201). Moreover, and based on an analysis of CSRs, evidence has shown that since 2010, progress in EU social policy has been dominated by 'powerful political and anti-welfare state tendencies', thus more strongly supporting market development, and delegitimising a market-correcting model of social policy at the EU level (Copeland & Daly 2018: 1015).

Moving beyond the EU, and from a comparative regionalism perspective, different models have been proposed to assess the various practices in which regional organisations have enacted social policy regionalism. A first categorisation has reflected on regional social policies across four axes: regional redistribution mechanisms, social regulations, social rights and social intergovernmental cooperation (Deacon et al. 2007; Deacon 2010; Yeates 2014). In addition to the so-called 3Rs – redistribution, regulation and rights – intergovernmental cooperation is also depicted as a looser form of instrument for social policy regionalism. First, regional social redistribution mechanisms involve regional banks and funds and aid from third parties. Second, regional regulations can include the setting of standards to avoid a race to the bottom and the regulation of private social services. Third, regional treaties and legal systems, such as the European Union Court of Justice and the Council of Europe's Court of Human Rights, can raise awareness and assure access to social rights. Finally, regional intergovernmental cooperation includes several instruments, i.e. technical cooperation, capacity building, harmonisation of domestic policies and regulations, and the mutual recognition of education degrees and social security entitlements.

A second categorisation distinguishes four social governance regimes. Based on their specific logics, regional organisations can thus promote an individual rights regime, a market-led regulatory regime, a state-led developmental regime and a state-led conservative regime (Van der Vleuten 2016). The individual rights regime relies mainly on social standard setting, solid monitoring commissions and courts, and is mainly found in regional organisations that do not pursue market integration. Present in regional organisations whose main objective is market integration; market-led regulatory regimes more strongly involve the elimination of obstacles to unfair competition. The third type, the state-led developmental regime, aims to promote social policy as part of an alternative and transformative project to overcome structural inequality and exclusion. Finally, state-led conservative regimes promote social policies through lax declarations and statements, thus refusing to establish standard-setting instruments and bodies.

In all, from a comparative regionalism perspective, different institutions and decision-making mechanisms may be created or charged with the responsibility of dealing with social policy problems or challenges, whereas the number and type of policy instruments adopted to implement and translate the policy problems into effective action may also vary. Moreover, empirical evidence suggests that this variation may be explained by the specific ways in which social issues are defined and framed as regional problems, all of which may lead to different patterns of social policies and regulations across regional organisations, and even across policy areas within the same organisation (Bianculli 2018).

The complexity and challenges of the IPE of global social policy

The broad purpose of this chapter was to discuss how the literature on global social policy has evolved, the key authors and main topics addressed, and to assess the achievements on global social policy making beyond nation-states. We explored the relations between politics and economics, states and markets in the development of global and regional social policy governance.

We argued that the theoretical debates on GSP need to incorporate broader perspectives, moving further beyond traditional comparative and state-based tools given the increased multidimensional characteristics of contemporary public policy and decision-making processes, which more and more operate above and beyond the state.

At the empirical level, we analysed how global social policy making has evolved from the nineteenth century to current times, and how international and regional organisations designed and addressed social policies beyond the states, thus contributing to the provision of welfare policies and services. We discussed the paradigmatic case of ILO showing that despite its key role at the beginning of the twentieth century, it has become increasingly challenged by the increasing marketisation of society and neoliberalism in the global political economy. We have also contended that regional organisations, given their deeper claims to collective identities, presented themselves as a possible *meso* level of governance to fill the gap between national and global social policy making. Yet, evidence showed mixed results regarding the role of the EU and other regional organisations in the context of comparative regionalism studies.

Challenges and prospects to effective delivery of social justice ahead vary across levels – global, regional and domestic – as the effects and consequences of global social policy and social policy regionalism remain contested. We conclude with a call for more research in this area in order to contribute to the alternative responses to the ever-increasing inequalities among and within societies worldwide.

Bibliography

Beeson, M. 2007. *Regionalism and Globalization in East Asia: Politics, Security and Economic Development.* Basingstoke: Palgrave.

Bianculli, A. 2018. From free market to social policies? Mapping regulatory cooperation in education and health in MERCOSUR. *Global Social Policy* 18 (3): 249–266.

Bianculli, A. & Ribeiro Hoffmann, A. 2016. Regional Organizations and Social Policy in Comparative Perspective. *Regional Organizations and Social Policy in Europe and Latin America:* 291–307. London: Palgrave Macmillan.

Bianculli, A., Jordana, J. & Juanatey, A. 2015. International Networks as Drivers of Agency Independence: The Case of the Spanish Nuclear Safety Council. *Administration & Society* 49 (9): 1246–1271.

Bianculli, A. & Ribeiro Hoffmann, A. 2016a. Regional Organizations and Social Policy: The Missing Link. In: *Regional Organizations and Social Policy in Europe and Latin America A Space for Social Citizenship?.* Basingstoke: Palgrave Macmillan: 1–22.

Bianculli, A. & Ribeiro Hoffman, A. 2016b. *Regional Organizations and Social Policy in Europe and Latin America: A Space for Social Citizenship?* Basingstoke: Palgrave Macmillan.

Bizzozzero, L. 2000. La construcción de la dimensión social en los nuevos regionalismos. El caso del MERCOSUR. In: *Aspectos sociales de la integración de América Latina y el Caribe.* Caracas: Sistema Económico Latinoamericano y del Caribe.

Boris, E., Hoehtker, D. & Zimmermann, S. 2018. *Women's ILO: Transnational Networks, Global Labour Standards and Gender Equity, 1919 to Present.* Leiden: Brill Academic Publishers.

Börzel, T. 1998. Organizing Babylon – On the Different Conceptions of Policy Networks. *Public Administration* 76 (2): 253–273.

Börzel, T. & Risse, T. 2012. When Europeanisation Meets Diffusion: Exploring New Territory. *West European Politics* 35 (1): 192–207.

Brennan, B. & Olivet, C. 2007. Regionalisms Futures: The Challenges for Civil Society. *Global Social Policy* 7 (3): 267–270.

Briceño-Ruiz, J. 2007. Strategic Regionalism and Regional Social Policy in the FTAA Process. *Global Social Policy* 7 (3): 294–315.

BRICS Policy Center & South-South Cooperation Research and Policy Centre. 2017. *Paths for Developing South-South Cooperation Monitoring and Evaluation System.* Brasília.

Caporaso, J. 1998. Regional Integration Theory: Understanding Our Past and Anticipating Our Future. *Journal of European Public Policy* 5 (1): 1–16.

Castells, M. & Cardoso, G. 2005. *The Network Society: From Knowledge to Policy.* Washington, DC: Johns Hopkins Center for Transatlantic Relations.

Copeland, P. & Daly, M. 2018. The European Semester and EU Social Policy. *JCMS: Journal of Common Market Studies* 56 (5): 1001–1018. DOI: 10.1111/jcms.12703. Available at: https://onlinelibrary.wiley.com/doi/abs/10.1111/jcms.12703.

Cox, R. & Jacobson, H. K. 1973. *The Anatomy of Influence: Decision-Making in International Organization.* New Haven: Yale University Press.

Cox, R. 1977. Labor and Hegemony. *International Organization* 31 (3): 385–424. Available at: www.cambridge.org/core/article/labor-and-hegemony/F2FCD4CBC111EBCDF64211F2E9F142C8.

Deacon, B. 2007. *Global Social Policy and Governance.* London: SAGE Publications.

Deacon, B. 2010. World-Regional Social Policy and Global Governance. In: *New Research and Policy Agendas in Africa, Asia, Europe and Latin America.* London: Routledge.

Deacon, B. 2011. Globalization and the Emerging Regional Governance of Labour Rights. *International Journal of Manpower* 32 (3): 334–365.

Deacon, B. 2014. Toward a Transformative Global Social Policy. In: Kaasch, A. & Stubbs, P.: *Transformations in Global and Regional Social Policies:* 201–217. London and New York: Palgrave Macmillan.

Deacon, B. & Macovei, M. 2010. Regional Social Policy from Above: International Organizations and Regional Social Policy. *World-Regional Social Policy and Global Governance: New Research and Policy Agendas in Africa, Asia, Europe and Latin America*: 40–62. Routledge Taylor & Francis Group.

Deacon, B., Ortiz, I. & Zelenev, S. 2007. *Regional Social Policy*. DESA Working Paper.

Deacon, B. & Stubbs, P. (Eds.). (2007). *Social Policy and International Interventions in South East Europe*. Cheltenham: Edward Elgar Publishing.

Deacon, B. & Stubbs, P. 2013. Global Social Policy Studies: Conceptual and Analytical Reflections. *Global Social Policy* 13 (1): 5–23.

Doctor, M. 2007. Why Bother With Inter-Regionalism? Negotiations for a European Union-Mercosur Agreement. *Journal of Common Market Studies* 45 (2): 281–314.

Doidge, M. 2007. Joined at the Hip: Regionalism and Interregionalism. *Journal of European Integration* 29 (2): 229–248.

Elkins, Z. & Simmons, B. 2005. On Waves, Clusters, and Diffusion: A Conceptual Framework. *Annals of the American Academy of Political and Social Sciences* 598: 33–51.

Fioramonti, L. 2013. The Role of Civil Society in (Re)Shaping World Regions. In: Fioramonti, L.: *Civil Society and World Regions. How Citizens are Reshaping Regional Governance in Times of Crisis*. Lanham: Lexington Books.

Gilardi, F. 2012. Transnational Diffusion: Norms, Ideas, and Policies. In: Carlsnaes, W., Risse, T. & Simmons, B. A. (Eds.). *Handbook of International Relations*. London: SAGE.

Godsäter, A. & Söderbaum, F. 2017. Civil Society Participation in Regional Social Policy: The Case of HIV/ AIDS in the Southern African Development Community (SADC). *Global Social Policy* 17 (2): 119–136.

Goodin, R. & Mitchell, D. 2000. *The Foundations of the Welfare State*. Cheltenham: Edward Elgar Publishing.

De Grauwe, P. 2011. *Balanced Budget Fundamentalism*. Brussels. Available at: www.ceps.eu/publications/ balanced-budget-fundamentalism.

Haarstad, H. & St Clair, A. 2011. Social Policy and Global Poverty: Beyond the Residual Paradigm? *Global Social Policy* 11 (2–3): 214–219.

Haas, E. 1958. *The Uniting of Europe*. Stanford: Stanford University Press.

Hall, A. & Midgley, J. 2004. *Social Policy for Development*. Thousands Oak, CA: SAGE Publications.

Hänggi, H. 2006. Interregionalism as a Multifaceted Phenomenon: In Search of a Typology. In: Hänggi, H., Roloff, R. & Rüland, J. (Eds.). *Interregionalism and International Relations A Stepping Stone to Global Governance?*: 31–62. London and New York: Routledge.

Helfer, L. 2006. Understanding Change in International Organizations: Globalization and Innovation in the ILO. *Vanderbilt Law Review* 59 (3): 649–726.

Herrero, M. & Loza, J. 2018. Building a Regional Health Agenda: A Rights-based Approach to Health in South America. *Global Public Health* 13 (9): 1179–1191.

Holden, C. 2018. Global Social Policy: An Application of Welfare State Theory. *Journal of International and Comparative Social Policy* 34 (1): 40–57.

Hurrell, A. 1995. Regionalism in Theoretical Perspective. In: Fawn, R. & Hurrell, A. (Eds.). *Regionalism in World Politics: Regional Organization and International Order*: 37–73. Oxford: Oxford University Press.

Hyman, R. 2015. Austeritarianism in Europe: What Options for Resistance? In: Natali, D. & Vanhercke, B. (Eds.). *Social Policy in the European Union: State of Play*: 97–126. Brussels: European Trade Union Institute (ETUI) and European Social Observatory (OSE).

Jordana, J. 2017. Transnational Policy Networks and Regional Public Goods in Latin America. In: Estevadeordal, A. & Goodman, L. (Eds.). *21st Century Cooperation. Regional Public Goods, Global Governance, and Sustainable Development*: 55–72. London: Routledge.

Kaasch, A. & Stubbs, P. 2014. *Transformations in Global and Regional Social Policies*. Basingstoke: Palgrave MacMillan.

Kaldor, M. 2003. The Idea of Global Civil Society. *International Affairs* 79 (3): 583–593.

Kennett, P. 2013. *A Handbook of Comparative Social Policy*. Cheltenham: Edward Elgar Publishing.

Keohane, R. 1988. International Institutions: Two Approaches. *International Studies Quarterly* 32 (4): 379–396.

Korseniewicz, R. & Smith, W. 2001. *Regional Networks in the Process of Hemispheric Integration*. Buenos Aires: FLACSO-Argentina.

Lavenex, S., Givens, T. E., Jurge, F. & Buchanan, R. 2016. Regional Migration Governance. In: Börzel, T. & Risse, T. (Eds.). *The Oxford Handbook of Comparative Regionalism*: 457–485. Oxford: Oxford University Press.

Leibfried, S. & Pierson, P. 1995. *European Social Policy: Between Fragmentation and Integration*. Washington, DC: Brookings Publications.

Lenz, T. 2012. Spurred Emulation: The EU and Regional Integration in Mercosur and SADC. *West European Politics* 35 (1): 155–173.

Mahon, R. 2015. Integrating the Social into CEPAL's Neo-structuralist Discourse. *Global Social Policy* 15 (1): 3–22.

Marsh, D. & Sharman, J. 2009. Policy Diffusion and Policy Transfer. *Policy Studies* 30 (3): 269–288.

Mattli, W. & Stone Sweet, A. 2012. Regional Integration and the Evolution of the European Polity: On the Fiftieth Anniversary of the Journal of Common Market Studies. *Journal of Common Market Studies* 50 (s1): 1–17.

Mkandawire, T. 2001. *Social Policy in a Development Context*. Geneva: UNRSID.

Moolakkattu, J. 2009. Robert W. Cox and Critical Theory of International Relations. *International Studies* 46 (4): 439–456.

Niemann, A. & Schmitter, P. 2009. Neofunctionalism. In: Wiener, A. & Diez, T. (Eds.). *European Integration Theory*: 45–66. Oxford: Oxford University Press.

Ocampo, J. 1998. Más allá del Consenso de Washington: una visión desde la CEPAL. *Revista de la CEPAL* 66: 7–28.

Olivet, C. & Brennan, B. 2010. Regional Social Policy from Below: Reclaiming Regional Integration: Social Movements and Civil Society Organizations as Key Protagonists. In: Deacon, B., Macovei, M.C., Van Langenhove, L & Yeates, N. (Eds.). *World-Regional Social Policy and Global Governance: New research and policy agendas in Africa, Asia, Europe and Latin America*: 63–81. London: Routledge Taylor & Francis Group.

Price, R. 2003. Review Article: Transnational Civil Society and Advocacy in World Politics. *World Politics* 55 (4): 579–606. Available at: http://muse.jhu.edu/journals/world_politics/v055/55.4price.html.

Razavi, S. & Hassim, S. 2006. *Gender and Social Policy in a Global Context. Uncovering the Gendered Structure of 'the Social'*. London: Palgrave Macmillan.

Reinicke, W. 1999. The Other World Wide Web: Global Public Policy Networks. *Foreign Policy* (117): 44–57. Available at: www.jstor.org/stable/1149561.

Ribeiro Hoffman, A. 2016. Inter- and Transregionalism. In: Börzel, T. & Risse, T. (Eds.). *The Oxford Handbook of Comparative Regionalism*: 600–621. Oxford: Oxford University Press.

Risse, T. 2016. The Diffusion of Regionalism. In: Börzel, T. & Risse, T. (Eds.). *The Oxford Handbook of Comparative Regionalism*: 87–108. Oxford: Oxford University Press. Available at: http://oxford handbooks.com/view/10.1093/oxfordhb/9780199682300.001.0001/oxfordhb-9780199682300-e-6.

Rosenau, J. & Czempiel, E. 1992. *Governance without Government: Order and Change in World Politics*. Cambridge: Cambridge University Press.

Rüland, J. 2010. Balancers, Multilateral Utilities or Regional Identity Builders? International Relations and the Study of Interregionalism. *Journal of European Public Policy* 17 (8): 1271–1283.

Saggioro Garcia, A. & Borba de Sá, M. 2013. Interview: 'Overcoming the Blockage': An interview with Robert W. Cox. *Estudos Internacionais. Revista De relações Internacionais Da PUC Minas* 1 (2): 303–318.

Scholte, J., O' Brien, R. & Williams, M. 1999. The WTO and Civil Society. *Journal of World Trade* 33 (1): 107–124.

Seckinelgin, H. 2014. Review of Bob Deacon (2013), Global Policy in the Making: The Foundations of the Social Protection Floor. Bristol: Policy Press. *Journal of Social Policy* 43 (4): 859–860. Available at: www.cambridge.org/core/product/identifier/S004727941400049X/type/journal_article.

Slaughter, A. 2004. *A New World Order*. Princeton: Princeton University Press.

Söderbaum, F. 2016. Old, New, and Comparative Regionalism: The History and Scholarly Development in the Field. In: *The Oxford Handbook of Comparative Regionalism*: 16–37. Oxford: Oxford University Press.

Starke, P., Kaasch, A. & Van Hooren, F. 2014. Political Parties and Social Policy Responses to Global Economic Crises: Constrained Partisanship in Mature Welfare States. *Journal of Social Policy* 43 (2): 225–246. Available at: www.cambridge.org/core/product/identifier/S0047279413000986/type/journal_article.

Steffek, J. & Holthaus, L. 2017. The Social-Democratic Roots of Global Governance: Welfare Internationalism from the 19th Century to the United Nations. *European Journal of International Relations* 24 (1): 106–129.

Stone, D. 2008. Global Public Policy, Transnational Policy Communities, and Their Networks. *Policy Studies Journal* 36 (1): 19–38.

Stone, D. 2013. *Knowledge Actors and Transnational Governance. The Private-Public Policy Nexus in the Global Agora*. London: Palgrave Macmillan.

Strange, S. 1994. *States and Markets*. London: Pinter Publishers. Available at: https://upfinder.upf.edu/.

Surender, R. & Walker, R. 2013. *Social Policy in a Developing World*. Cheltenham: Edward Elgar Publishing.

Telò, M. 2001. European Union and New Regionalism. Regional Actors and Global Governance in a Post-Hegemonic Era. In: *The International Political Economy of New Regionalisms Series*. Aldershot: Ashgate Publishing.

Threlfall, M. 2010. Social Policies and Rights in the European Union and the Council of Europe: Exhortation, Regulation and Enforcement. In: Deacon, B., Macovei, M.C., Van Langenhove, L. & Yeates, N. (Eds.). *World-regional Social Policy and Global Governance: New Research and Policy Agendas in Africa, Asia, Europe and Latin America*: 85–107. London: Routledge.

True, Jacqui. 2003. Mainstreaming Gender in Global Public Policy. *International Feminist Journal of Politics* 5 (3): 368–396.

Tussie, D. & Botto, M. 2003. *El ALCA y las Cumbres de las Américas: ¿una nueva dialéctica público-privada?* Buenos Aires: FLACSO-Argentina and Editorial Biblos.

Vanhercke, B., Sabato, S. & Bouget, D. 2017. Conclusions. Social Policy in the EU: High Hopes but Low Yields. In: Vanhercke, B., Ghailani, D. & Sabato, S. (Eds.). *Social Policy in the European Union: State of Play 2017*: 201–215. European Trade Union Institute (ETUI) and European Social Observatory (OSE).

Van der Vleuten, A. 2016. Regional Social and Gender Governance. In: Börzel, T. & Risse, T. (arg.).: *The Oxford Handbook of Comparative Regionalism*: 405–429. Oxford: Oxford University Press.

Von Bülow, M. 2010. *Building Transnational Networks. Civil Society and the Politics of Trade in the Americas*. Cambridge: Cambridge University Press.

Whitworth, S. 1994. Gender, International Relations and the Case of the ILO. *Review of International Studies* 20 (4): 389. www.journals.cambridge.org/abstract_S0260210500118182.

Williams, F. 2016. Critical Thinking in Social Policy: The Challenges of Past, Present and Future. *Social Policy & Administration* 50 (6): 628–647.

Witte, J., Reinicke, W. & Benner, T. 2005. Beyond Multilateralism: Global Public Policy Networks. In: Pfaller, A. & Lerch, M. (Eds.). *Challenges of Globalisation: New Trends in International Politics and Society*: 109–131. New York: Routledge.

Yeates, N. 2008. *Understanding Global Social Policy*. Bristol: Policy Press.

Yeates, N. 2014. The Socialization of Regionalism and the Regionalization of Social Policy. In: Kaasch, A. & Stubbs, P. (Eds.). *Transformations in Global and Regional Social Policies*: 17–43. Basingstoke: Palgrave Macmillan.

Yeates, N. & Deacon, B. 2006. Globalism, Regionalism and Social Policy: Framing the debate. *UNU-CRIS Occasional Papers*. Brugge: United Nations University Institute on Comparative Regional Integration Studies.

38
Globalization and global production networks

Syed Javed Maswood

Introduction

Economic globalization is a process that can be traced back to the 1980s. One major development associated with globalization is the progressive transformation of manufacturing, away from in-house to where it is increasingly globally networked. If the process continues, it may, at some point in time in the future, lead to a single and unified global economy, a "borderless world" (Ohmae 1999), or a "world without walls" (Moore 2003), with or without formal political integration. Globalization has deepened trade linkages between countries as a result of trade liberalization, and according to Moore and Lewis, is marked by the dominating presence of multinational enterprises, just-in-time (JIT) delivery of parts from a network of suppliers that are geographically dispersed, and advanced communications technology (2009: 209). The attraction of a JIT inventory control system is its cost-effectiveness, because parts and components are delivered to end-users only as needed rather than held in costly inventory. Advances in communications technology have made it possible to coordinate activity throughout the network of dispersed production units in real time, and reduction of transportation costs have made this, as mentioned above, a cost-effective production strategy. These global production networks (GPNs), also known as global value chains (GVCs), a broader concept that incorporates not only producer-initiated networks but also networks initiated by retail groups, have become "the world economy's backbone and central nervous system" (Cattaneo, Gereffi and Staritz 2010: 7).

As for consequences, most analysts agree that globalization underpinned the vast expansion of global economic growth and prosperity, at least until the financial and economic crisis of 2008. That was true not only for most developed countries, but global economic engagement also helped lift some developing countries out of their poverty trap. Particularly in China, but also in India and elsewhere, globalization was a catalyst for industrial deepening through increased involvement in global production networks. On a less positive note, even if not causative, globalization correlated with economic and income inequality in both developed and developing countries. For example, the *World Inequality Report 2018*, prepared by Alvaredo et al. (2017: 10), observed that the share of income going to the top 1 percent of the population in the US had increased from around 11 percent to around 20 percent between 1980 and 2015, whereas the share of the bottom 50 percent had dropped from around 21 percent to about 11 percent in the same time period. Inequality increased also in emerging markets such as India and China but remained relatively stable in European countries. Overall, data suggested a progressive and significant worsening of income distribution. At a rhetorical level, many governments and international agencies acknowledged this as a matter for concern, but did little to correct the failings, even after such highly visible protests as the Occupy Wall Street movement that began in late 2011. The "yellow vest" protest movement in France was similarly motivated by growing inequalities and, according to Cole Stangler (2018), French President Macron "exemplified the state's abdication of responsibility toward the least well-off." In his first budget, he had removed the wealth tax that applied to the rich, and then proceeded to remove subsidies and increase the fuel tax that disproportionately hurt the poor and the disadvantaged members of French society. The protest movement was triggered by a fuel tax hike, and no amount of dressing it up as necessary to mitigating climate change was able to placate the protestors who were angry about the general direction of Macron's economic policies.

To remedy the growing income gap, Nobel laureate Eric Maskin proposed some form of training and re-skilling for those who had been marginalized by loss of job opportunities in the globalizing economy (see: www.worldbank.org/en/news/feature/2014/06/23/theorist-eric-maskin-globalization-is-increasing-inequality). As simple as the suggestion appears to be, existing re-skilling strategies, such as the Trade Adjustment Assistance that was introduced in the US in 1962, have generally failed to retrain displaced workers, becoming instead another unemployment benefit. In a digital economy, there is even less certainty that displaced factory workers can be retrained for employment in more demanding technology sectors. Continual life-long learning may be an imperative in the digital economy, but re-skilling from factory work to the technology sector is an entirely different proposition.

An alternative is income redistribution and progressive taxation. The World Inequality Report 2018 underscored the importance and effectiveness of progressive taxation and noted that tackling "global income and wealth inequality requires important shifts in national and global tax policies" (Alvaredo et al. 2017: 19) Instead, in practice, progressivity of taxation dropped sharply between 1970 and mid-2000s. The returns from globalization and increased overall prosperity could have been used to compensate those who had been displaced in the transition to globalization but, "the benefits [were] rarely … redistributed, and [consequently] the communities and workers harmed by globalization … turned to populism and protectionism" (Lund and Tyson 2018: 136). The backlash culminated in the election of President Trump in the US, an avowed anti-globalist. In the absence of policies to create a more broad-based economic system, there has been an assault on globalization. Trump presented himself to voters as an economic nationalist who would restore jobs and reverse a perceived hollowing-out of American industry. The UK had its own anti-globalization moment in the summer of 2016, when a referendum on withdrawal from European Union was approved by a narrow majority of British voters. These events raised the specter of a reversal of the globalist momentum, as had happened in earlier periods of liberal trade and interdependence.

In this chapter, I will develop a more benign perspective on the question of reversal and de-globalization. That requires, first, to analyze circumstances that led to the emergence of economic globalization. I will show that global production networks (GPNs) that occupy a central position in globalization today can be causally traced to a surge in protectionism in the early 1980s and not, as is widely accepted, to progressive trade and economic liberalization after the Second World War. Advances in communications technology that allowed real time coordination of spatially dispersed production units, as well as inexpensive and rapid transportation played a facilitative, yet important, role in the spread of GPNs.

Another common orthodoxy about globalization is that it is the continuation of a long, even if interrupted, march of economic liberalization that began in the mid-nineteenth century. Instead, I will suggest that contemporary economic globalization is a unique and unprecedented phase of capitalist evolution. In regard to prospective de-globalization, it is important to consider whether globalization can, indeed, be rolled back, as was the case with earlier periods of liberalization, or primitive globalization. This will help us understand the consequences of globalization for trade stability. My central argument is that globalization, as constituted by global production networks, has strengthened the foundations of liberal international trade in ways that deny the possibility of a wholesale reversal.

Representative of the orthodoxy, Moore and Lewis (2009) assert that many aspects of economic globalization can be found not only in recent past but in antiquity. In addition to three recent periods of globalization identified by Thomas Friedman (2000), they find parallels also in the distant past. They (Moore and Lewis 2009: 210–211) identify the following four periods of economic globalization.

Globalization v. 0.5   27 BCE– AD 200 (Moore and Lewis 2009; Frankopan 2017: 13)
Globalization v. 1.0   1492–1800 (Friedman 2000)
Globalization v. 2.0   1800–2000 (Friedman 2000)
Globalization v. 3.0   2001–future (Friedman 2000)

Like Moore and Lewis, Peter Frankopan (2017: 13), in his history of the silk roads that spanned across Europe and Asia, writes, "We think of globalization as a uniquely modern phenomenon; yet 2000 years ago too, it was a fact of life, one that presented opportunities, created problems and prompted technological advance." The presumed "commonness" of globalization is the orthodoxy. Paul Krugman (2013) insists that only our conceit explains why some continue to insist that contemporary economic realities are unparalleled. Others, like Hirst and Thompson (1996), Rodrik (1997: 71), Gilpin (2000: 18–19) and Keohane and Nye (2000: 7) all agree that contemporary globalization has parallels to at least nineteenth-century trade interdependence and perhaps to earlier times as well. In this rendition, economic globalization is typically attributed to trade liberalization policies after the Second World War, and to technological advances in transport and communications, especially after the 1980s.

Moore and Lewis (2009) are technically correct to note that quite a few of the business forms and business cultures that we associate with globalization also existed in the past. Thus, it is true that GPNs, a core component of globalization, is bed rocked on the principle of a division of labor, a principle that Adam Smith had formulated in the late eighteenth century. Adam Smith, however, associated division of labor to the factory floor but the factory floor today comprises the global space, an extension of an established principle rather than a revolutionary break from the past.

However, even with the past as prologue, history is not necessarily a seamless evolution, but contains sharp breaks that define distinctive epochs. According to Finley, developments since 1800s, industrialization and management strategies and techniques etc. have "rendered parallels with the ancient world invalid" (cited in Moore and Lewis 2009: xii). Actually, contemporary economic globalization has rendered many of the basic principles of traditional economics, management and international trade obsolete. Disagreement between the two schools cannot be readily written off as a case of whether the glass is half-full or half-empty because if we accept the orthodoxy, it essentially distracts us from the true roots of contemporary globalization and important corollaries. An evolutionary perspective leads to a conclusion that it is possible to trace a long continuity from liberal trade after the Second World War, through to economic interdependence in the 1970s (Keohane and Nye 1989), and to contemporary economic globalization. This, however, obscures the significance of a critical disruptive force that intervened to initiative a new trajectory leading to contemporary economic globalization and globalized production. If we assume that trade liberalization produced economic globalization, it gives credence to the argument that, "just as protectionism led to de-globalization" in earlier times, that same path of de-globalization remains a possibility for the current state of global integration. The reality, however, is that with the spread of global production networks, a return to rampant protectionism, and its consequent de-globalization, is no longer a credible possibility. In industries that are highly networked, whether regional or global, any return to protectionism will be a sub-optimal outcome. It is in that context that we can make some sense of higher US tariffs on steel and aluminum, imposed in June 2018. These are not globally integrated industries. Similarly, Chinese retaliation honed in on products that were largely beyond the scope of globalized production, such as soy beans, bourbon and orange juice.

As mentioned above, contemporary globalization is embedded in the well-established principle of division of labor, but its global adaptation as geographically dispersed production was driven not by the efficiency gains of liberal trade but as a result of a short interregnum of neo-protectionism in US–Japan economic relations in the early 1980s. Globalization is not underpinned by trade liberalization but its precise opposite. It is possible that in an alternative reality, globalization might have evolved in some ways out of trade integration and advances in communications technologies, but that can only be a matter for conjecture. Contemporary globalization has its roots in trade protectionism. Moreover, it was an unintended consequence, not willed by strategic considerations on the part of advocates of protectionism. Technology, of course, played an important part in real-time coordination of geographically dispersed production networks but in this chapter, I question the dominant narrative and argue that it was not trade liberalization that brought us economic globalization but its precise opposite, neo-protectionism.

In the 1970s and 1980s, neo-protectionist measures, inconsistent with General Agreement on Tariffs and Trade (GATT) preference for tariff-based and non-discriminatory trade policies, became an important feature of US–Japan trade relations and affected trade in steel, electronics and automobiles. In particular, quantitative restrictions placed on Japanese export of cars to the US was instrumental in the spread of networked manufacturing strategies from Japan to other western countries. As Japanese manufacturers established production facilities in the US, to escape export restrictions, they replicated in these production facilities their own networked production model as practiced in Japan. American auto manufacturers, in turn, were quick to adopt the principle, and the end result was a global spread of manufacturing based on a network of geographically dispersed suppliers of parts and components. This is the single most defining characteristic of contemporary globalization and its roots lie in neo-protectionism, not as the orthodoxy will have it, in trade and economic liberalization.

In restricting Japan's exports of cars, the US government wanted to encourage Japanese car makers to establish manufacturing facilities in the US, rather than rely solely on exports to service US demand. That it did, but in the process had the unintended consequences of transforming manufacturing processes in a more general sense. A country that had borrowed and learned from the West for centuries, including even the networked manufacturing process, had become a source of learning for western manufacturers in the 1980s.

To begin, the next section will show how American neo-protectionist policies in the early 1980s led ultimately to the contemporary ubiquity of global production networks, and to the on-going process of economic globalization. In a sense these neo-protectionist measures became, strangely enough, the building blocks of contemporary globalization. In the final section, I will explain how the logic of globally networked manufacturing has rendered obsolete some of the old ideas behind protectionism and economic nationalism, leading to greater trade stability, at least in networked industries. In this section, I will consider also prospects for de-globalization amid a resurgence of populist economic nationalism in the UK and US.

Globalization as an unintended consequence of neo-protectionism

Capitalism is a system of market-based exchange of goods and service in which economic activity is determined by levels of consumption (demand) and production (supply). Contemporary economic globalization is unique in its impact on each of the two dimensions of a market economy. Globalization of consumption today, as in its presumed earlier manifestations, has been driven by trade liberalization after the Second World War. Globalization of production, however, is a shift in production technique that has no historical parallel. It has transformed Adam Smith's division of labor from its application on the factory floor to a global level. Smith could not have envisaged this as necessary as long as there was unfettered free trade and given, of course, the existing state of communications and transportation technologies.

Contemporary globalization, a combination of both consumption and production, is historically unique and its spread cannot be attributed to trade liberalization or to technological advancements. The latter facilitated it, but the true catalyst was a "global" adaptation of Japanese networked manufacturing, after Japanese car manufacturers began foreign investments and foreign manufacturing in the early 1980s. Until that time, Japanese car manufacturers had relied on exports to meet foreign demand but were forced to start foreign manufacturing, in order to protect market shares, when the US, in 1981, imposed import quotas on Japanese cars, in the guise of Japan's voluntary export restraint.

There is nothing heroic about protectionism, but globalized production was a response to American neo-protectionism in the 1980s. The target was Japan which had large and growing trade surplus against the US, and many other advanced industrial countries. The negotiated neo-protectionist measures included the Trigger Price Mechanism (TPM) on steel, Orderly Marketing Agreement (OMA) on color television sets, and Voluntary Export Restraint (VER) on automobiles. It was the last of the three policy instruments that had the greatest trade-disruptive effect and became also the trigger for the spread of networked manufacturing and global production networks.

American car manufacturers lobbied for relief from imports through some protective action although, as recently as 1980, the US International Trade Commission had ruled that imports had not increased so substantially as to cause US manufacturers "serious injury" (Nelson 1996: 37) Notwithstanding that, a new government in the US pushed for some negotiated agreement to reduce the volume of Japanese car exports. Japanese car companies were initially opposed to any form of export restrictions but ultimately caved to US pressure, when the lead Japanese negotiator, Amaya Naohiro Vice-Minister of the Ministry of International Trade and Industry, impressed upon them the imperative for concessions given Japan's dependence on the US for its security. The VER agreement, signed in 1981, placed an annual ceiling on Japanese exports of cars to the US. Compared to Japanese exports of 1.82 million cars to the US in 1980, the VER restricted total Japanese car exports to 1.68 million units in the first year (April 1981–March 1982), and a slightly higher quota for the next two years of a three-year export restraint agreement. In the absence of a VER, Japanese exports might have exceeded two million cars, based on average growth rates of Japanese exports in the previous two years, slightly above 13.5 percent (Maswood 1989: 62ff.) With the VER in place, American car manufacturers were allowed a respite and breathing space to restructure production, innovate, recapture market share and return to profitability.

Even if Japanese manufacturers were cognizant that export restrictions would allow them to capture protectionist rent and demand a premium on prices, their immediate concern was the implicit threat to market share in the US. The potential loss of hard-won market share in the US was the main reason they abandoned an export-only marketing strategy for a combination of exports and local production in the US. In turn, local production based on their established network manufacturing process became the catalyst for the emergence of global and disaggregated manufacturing processes as western car manufacturers, in a "structural adjustment" mode, began to emulate Japanese manufacturing strategies.

The flow of Japanese FDI was something that US negotiators had hoped to encourage with restrictions on export sales. The US government understood that Japanese manufacturing in the US would add value to the US economy and generate employment in an industry that had lost its luster. Indeed, this was part of the US government calculus, that Japanese firms might be induced to set up production facilities in the US and contribute to American industrial renaissance. In this, neo-protectionism did not disappoint. This is precisely what happened. In the years following the VER, Japanese car manufacturers began to invest in manufacturing in the US and other important export markets.

Honda was the first of the Japanese manufacturers to set up production in the US in 1982 partly because with a smaller share of the Japanese domestic market, it required access to foreign markets and could not afford to lose market share in the US. Other Japanese car manufacturers followed and as these ventured overseas, they took their own manufacturing networks with them to respective host locations. Over time, the balance between export and local production has shifted markedly. In the early 2000s, foreign production of Japanese car manufacturers was close to 50 per cent of all production by Japanese car companies and, in 2012, J.P. Morgan forecast that by 2014 foreign manufacturing would likely reach 76 percent of the total (*Economist* 2012). The goal was to protect foreign market shares but Japanese FDI also became the first step toward contemporary globalization. Global production networks modeled on Japanese networked production, *keiretsu*, have spread globally, but nowhere "in the world is production fragmentation quite as much … or as fast growing, as in Asia" (Ferrarini and Hummels 2014: 1). It was easy to see also that networked manufacturing was, in many ways, superior to in-house manufacturing.

Export restrictions prompted Nissan, Toyota and other Japanese car manufacturers to establish production facilities in the US. But it did much more than that because alongside the car manufacturers, came also their many subcontractors and with that a replication of Japanese manufacturing processes on US soil. Thus, as parent companies set up factories so did their subcontractors, which also established factories in the US to manufacture and supply parts for final car assembly. FDI by Toyota brought in additional foreign investments so that its suppliers could continue their long-term relationship which was essential to maintenance of JIT (Just in Time) manufacturing. In the JIT system, manufacturers receive parts from subcontractors just when these are needed, obviating the need for large and expensive inventories. With long-established relationships between manufacturers and subcontractors it was easy to replicate the same practices that had worked so well in Japan, such as the JIT inventory control system. In the end, Japanese car manufacturers in the US relied parts and components produced in the US by their Japanese subsidiaries and imported others from Japan.

Production can be organized either in-house from start to finish or based on parts and components sourced from either independent external producers or subsidiaries, or as some combination of the two. Typically, Japanese manufacturers relied on networked manufacturing among firms that were part of a large conglomerate or *keiretsu*. Production networks involved a parent company (*honsha*), such as Toyota, and its many independent but affiliated subcontractors (*shitauke*). In Japanese manufacturing, networks were long-term relationships and a survey in the mid-1980s revealed that two-thirds of small subcontracting firms had never changed their relationships with the parent *honsha* and that 97 percent of relationships had been in place for more than 5 years (Whittaker 1997: 88). As long-term partners, subsidiaries were fully integrated and involved in the manufacturing process, providing creative input and design ideas. Often these long-term networked relationships were consolidated with cross-holding of shares, sometimes exceeding 70 percent of outstanding shares in a company which, according to Dore, explained why corporate executives in Japan did not turn first to the stock market reports in newspapers (Dore 1997: 24; Sheard 1994). Company directors did not have to be excessively sensitive to shareholder concerns since retail shareholders were a relatively small minority. Iwao Nakatani, for example, made a distinction between Japanese "network capitalism" and American "market capitalism" (see Bergsten and Noland 1993: 7). This system of networked manufacturing was very different from western in-house manufacturing practices. As an illustration of networked manufacturing, within the Toyota Group there were a small number of lead companies and more than 200 parts suppliers that participated in Toyota's networked production process, whereas General Motors (GM), for example, did much of its automotive car manufacturing in-house, rather than rely on extensive subcontracting arrangements. Moreover, when parts were subcontracted to other firms, it was without any long-term association or loyalty commitments.

An advantage of network manufacturing, as practiced and perfected in Japan, was that it kept manufacturing costs down and added to a firm's international competitiveness. Subcontractors with long-term loyalty agreements manufactured and delivered parts and components on a JIT basis that obviated the need for costly stockpiles of inventory. For example, an engine block might get manufactured in the morning and fitted to an automobile in the evening, without having to be stored for an extended period, as was common in the West and which incurred storage costs (Pegels 1984: 97). Equally important was that JIT forced subcontractors to ensure quality and fault-free deliveries without which production might be disrupted at the main plant. Higher coordination and transactions costs associated with network manufacturing were kept low with long-term loyalty arrangements and long-term supply arrangements also enabled technology transfer between parent firms and subcontractors without any risk of technological innovations flowing through to competitors.

In the absence of JIT and quality-controlled deliveries, western car manufacturers carried large inventories to allow for a high proportion of defective parts. This resulted in additional costs to manufacturers (Koichi 1992: 153). In western and American manufacturing, even if there was extensive reliance on subcontractors, all engineering decisions were largely controlled in-house and subcontractors manufactured parts according to a final design. Chrysler in the US, for instance, had many more suppliers of parts than Toyota in Japan, but these only supplied parts according to Chrysler's design, with little input in the engineering of components (Dyer 2000). Moreover, Chrysler did not foster long-term relational arrangements but rather procured parts only on cost considerations and from the cheapest supplier. GM, too, had subcontractors that supplied parts and components, but the main procurement criterion was cost that was determined by a bidding system and without the establishment of long-standing networks. Even if Japanese suppliers were lower in the organizational hierarchy, the relationship was long term, based on loyalty and partnership, whereas western parts manufacturers were always under constant pressure to lower production costs. Thus, whereas Japanese producers procured parts from 100–300 tightly linked subcontractors, Chrysler had subcontracting arrangements with 3,000–4,000 companies. GM relied on supplies from more than 10,000 companies, but its finished products still had a much higher in-house content than was the case for Japanese companies (Monden 1993: 337–339). Later, however, as they embraced Japanese-style supply management, they rationalized and reduced the number of subcontractors and formed long-term contractual arrangements.

As the benefits of Japanese network manufacturing became obvious and better understood, because of their close proximity to US manufacturers, emulation by US firms did not take long. Xerox was among the first to embrace it for its own manufacturing at its manufacturing facility in Webster, New York in 1984. Based on information from 1,400 deliveries in the first year of its new manufacturing process, the transition was a clear success as it delivered impressive results with "zero late deliveries, zero early deliveries and zero defects" (Lubben 1988: 158) Chrysler was among the first movers in the automotive sector in the late 1980s and results quickly flowed through to its profit margins per vehicle that increased from US$250 in 1980 to US$2110 in 1994. This was due largely to savings from inventory and quality control processes.

Initially, the seemingly closed nature of Japanese manufacturing in the US and the reliance of Toyota and Nissan, for example, on their pre-existing network forms, which also established manufacturing in the US, alongside their parent firms was met with some concern because American parts manufacturers felt left-out and excluded. In the early years, this was perhaps inevitable. Since then, however, Japanese manufacturers have established long-term network relationships with non-Japanese firms in host locations. Because of greater reliance on local production, in 2014, of all the Japanese-branded vehicles sold in the United States, more than 70 percent were of North American manufacture, a remarkable shift from the early 1980s (JAMA 2014). Moreover, Japanese factories in the US also emerged as exporters in their own right. Essentially, the set of forces unleashed by Japanese investments in western countries had important global consequences. The existing literature has largely overlooked this process of Japanization, its emulation, and its culmination ultimately in globalized production. The initial stimulus for this came not from trade liberalization but from precisely the opposite forces.

In the initial years, network manufacturing was essentially nationally based but that changed with exchange rate movements in the late 1980s that prompted Japanese firms to secure supplies from cheaper production locations to compensate for a higher exchange value of the Japanese Yen. This led to inclusion of suppliers based in China and other East Asian countries, a practice that was again emulated by western manufacturers and became the basis for region al and global production networks.

At its core, global production networks began as a defense against the rising tide of protectionism, and Japanese firms spearheaded the drive toward networked production, forcing industries in the United States and elsewhere to emulate the Japanese model. Thus, as observed by Douglas Nelson, "One of the striking things about the auto story is that, while the [US] auto industry got more or less what it wanted from the state [i.e. protection from Japanese imports], it was the U.S. industry, not the Japanese industry, that did the adjusting" (Nelson 1996: 42). One hundred years after the Japanese had embarked on a massive campaign to learn from the West in order to achieve rapid industrialization and modernization, it was now the turn of Japan to emerge as a model for others to follow.

In the next stage, networked manufacturing became a globalized system led, again, by Japan following the 1985 Plaza Accord that revalued the Japanese Yen. The revaluation of the Yen, and of the German Mark, was designed to slow both Japanese exports and Japan's growing trade surpluses. By the end of 1986, the Japanese Yen had appreciated about 30 percent in real terms against the Dollar and significantly eroded Japan's export competitiveness. As exports from Japan suffered, manufacturers ventured out to cheaper production platforms, in China and other Asian countries, to lower their cost structure. The attraction of China was proximity, cultural affinity and its transition to a more open economic system. Earlier in the decade, the Chinese leader Deng Xiaoping had relaxed socialist controls and opened the country to foreign trade and investments. Japanese investments in China expanded rapidly after 1985 as manufacturers set up factories for parts and components and integrated those facilities into their existing production networks. This system was replicated also by western firms in competition with Japanese manufacturing and the two events, neo-protectionism and currency revaluation, became the main sources of global production networks that are such a ubiquitous and important feature of manufacturing today. In contemporary economic globalization, it is the addition of globalization of production that makes it unprecedented and unique compared to earlier periods of trade interdependence that involved at best globalization of consumption based only on trade liberalization. The catalyst for globalization of production was targeted protectionism and the Japanese response to it, and emulation of Japanese manufacturing processes by western companies.

One consequence is that globalized manufacturing today stands as a robust firewall against major trade restrictive practices. Logic suggests that no government in countries that are globally integrated will engage in practices that might disrupt network linkages, for the damage that such actions might inflict on domestic industries.

The distinction between contemporary and nineteenth-century economic integration is that globalization today combines both functions, consumption and production, of the capitalist market system, whereas nineteenth-century interdependence only integrated "world" economies at the level of consumption. Each form of globalization is the derivate of a different dynamic although, other things being equal, it is not impossible that technological advances would have eventually created a global division of labor. The uniqueness of contemporary globalization can be depicted as in Figure 38.1.

While there are similarities between the two periods, only contemporary globalization combines both aspects of market capitalism, production and consumption. The orthodox view, that of Hirst and Thompson (2002), Rodrik (1997), Keohane and Nye (2000), Gilpin (2000) and Sachs (2005) among many others, however, is to postulate a basic continuity that implies that if nineteenth-century "globalization; could be reversed, de-globalization was a possibility for its current iteration."

Second, the relative stability of liberal trade and globalization, and by contrast the impracticality of using protectionism in the pursuit of national economic goals in times of cyclical downturns, stems first, from producers' interests in protecting the integrity of international supply chains from myopic protectionist policies and, second, producers' capacity to influence and shape foreign trade policymaking.

In addition to its efficiency and productivity gains, trade in the contemporary period has transformed manufacturers and producers as *consumers* of intermediate goods. A large portion of international trade today is in components and parts, for use as inputs in disaggregated production processes and, according to estimates, approximately 80 percent of global trade is linked to

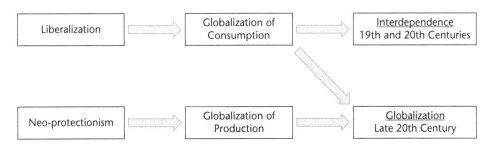

Figure 38.1 A schematic representation of interdependence and globalization

global production networks (Phillip 2017: 430–431). There are, in effect, two categories of consumers, those of manufactured parts and intermediate goods, and those of finished consumer products or individual consumers. To some extent, manufacturers always were consumers, but of industrial raw materials, but have now also emerged as important consumers of machined products, produced both domestically and abroad. Increasingly, and in many sectors of the economy, manufacturing has become part of a global value chain. This development has both positive and negative consequences. On the downside, production everywhere is much more vulnerable to disruptions along the supply chain, whether as a result of natural disasters like tsunami and earthquakes, or deliberate actions like political and economic conflict. For example, flooding in Bangkok and surrounding regions in 2011 disrupted manufacturing in Japan, as did popular unrest and agitation against Japanese interests in China during the Sino-Japanese conflict of 2012. This negative aspect of GPNs is balanced, first, by the spread of industrialization to developing countries through their participation in production networks and, second, by the positive effects on the stability of international trade. In this section, I will explain this with reference to the origins of GPNs.

Technological advances were, of course, an important factor, without which geographically dispersed production could not be coordinated, as these are in in real time, but technology was an enabling condition and not a causal variable. The dominant narrative has causally attributed GPNs to trade liberalization after the Second World War but, as argued above, there is more reason to trace their lineage to protectionism in the 1980s. Liberal trade did not *cause* the shift to globalized production but, instead, globalization has had the *effect* of strengthening the foundations of liberal trade. This is because the production efficiency of GPNs depend on preservation of open trade. Nineteenth-century interdependence originated in trade liberalization but collapsed as a result of creeping illiberal trade practices that led to the First World War. It is a moot point whether protectionism can force a retreat from globalization, or even whether protectionism is a viable policy option in the age of globalization. In capitalist economies, governments cannot be blind to interests of the business community and the new reality is that businesses that engage in globalized production have no interest in protectionism that could disrupt their supply chain activities. Ironically however, events in 2016, seemed to foreshadow just such an outcome.

De-globalization

Leaving aside arguments for infant industry protection, the ebb and flow of liberal trade has historically been associated with the business cycle, liberal trade in times of economic expansion, and followed by protection for domestic producers to shield them from foreign competition in times of economic downturns. Protectionism may also, alternatively, follow from some recessive appeal to mercantilist ideas. Contemporary globalization, and globalization of production, in particular, is however predicated on the preservation of liberal trade, and according to the United Nations Conference on Trade and Development (UNCTAD), about 80 percent of global trade takes place through global value chains. Recent events in US, UK and elsewhere have, nonetheless, shaken the foundations of liberal trade (see: https://unctad.org/en/pages/PressRelease.aspx?OriginalVersionID=113). These events compel us to consider the likelihood that globalization may also, like earlier periods of liberal trade and interdependence, be wound back through a return to protectionism. However, for reasons detailed above, even if this is a possibility, whole sale de-globalization is improbable. Nonetheless, trade stability cannot be stated in absolutist terms yet, given that globalization is itself in an early evolutionary stage. Nonetheless, industries that are globally networked, generally large corporations, can be assumed to have little to gain from protectionist policies, even in times of crises, when they remained committed to liberal trade rather than lobby for protection. Given that size of an industry and of its major firms has an impact on policy outcomes, it is not surprising therefore that during the first major economic crisis of the globalization era in 2008, there was no significant jump in protectionism. Globally networked production has made it harder for businesses to advocate, or for states to pursue narrow self-interest through, protectionist policies.

With the transformation of producers also as consumers of intermediate goods, they have acquired a new-found commitment to liberal trade, regardless of economic cycles. Thus, globally networked firms have advanced Adam Smith's prediction of free trade on the basis that free trade is in the interest of consumers. Adam Smith may have anticipated that consumers of finished products, beneficiaries of liberal trade, would eventually prevail over mercantilist practices, but it appears that it will be producers, as consumers of parts, components and intermediate goods, that will stabilize liberal trade and contain threats of protectionism. The contrast in firm behavior to earlier times is salient. In the early 1980s, the US auto industry was at the forefront of attempts to secure protection from Japanese imports, but in a replay of similar circumstances in 2008, there was no clamor for protection from imports. As Richard Baldwin and Simon Evenett (2009: 3) observe, in a world of supply-chain connectedness, raising "tariffs on manufactured imports … does not protect domestic manufacturing jobs, it destroys them." The 2008 financial crisis did have an impact on global trade but not necessarily because of protectionism, rather because of a range of other factors, including a drop in consumption demand and credit constraints. A Trade Monitoring Report of the World Trade Organization (WTO) in 2016 noted that in the first two years of the financial crisis, in 2009 and 2010, there were a total of twenty-seven new trade restrictive and twenty-nine new trade facilitative measures introduced by WTO members (see: www.wto.org/english/news_e/news16_e/trdev_22Jul16_e.htm). Even if the trade impact of these measures is unclear, there was no singular trend toward protectionism.

Systemic de-globalization has become less likely even if, by some quirk of fate, some countries chose a more self-reliant path, notwithstanding the economic costs. In the more likely scenario, the cost of de-globalization coupled with lobbying by globally networked producers will contain the possibility of nationalistic tendencies. Globalization is its own defense against protectionism and against any policy program that includes protection for domestic industries from import competition.

While it is true that Adam Smith, in the eighteenth century, had discredited the national interest argument for protectionism, it must still be acknowledged that there can never be any fool-proof defense against ill-conceived national economic policies. There may be some legitimate national interest reasons for protecting strategic and defense-related industries, but there are other more spurious reasons why states often resort to protectionism. These include balance of payment deficits, employment protection or a stated desire to create a level playing field. All of these, including accusation that China was engaged in unfair trade practices that extended to theft of intellectual property, were part of the broad justification given by the US, in 2018, to restrict Chinese imports. Against this, it should be noted that trade theory, both classical and neo-classical, maintains that unilateral free trade is superior to protectionism. Based on that, it must follow that attempts to de-globalize also inflict self-harm. Still, protectionism can happen, and it can happen either for purely partisan political reasons or from attempts to deflect popular attention away from domestic political failures to imagined external threats.

There is no denying that there has been a backlash against globalization led, to a large extent, by the iniquitous distribution of the gains from global engagement. In some western countries, while globalization has been beneficial in macro terms, there are many who feel disenfranchised and disempowered as a result of globalization. As leading corporate executives amassed enormous wealth in this globalization period, their employees, in the thousands, were paid low, or minimum, wage and were forced to supplement their incomes with government handout and welfare. Fifty of the wealthiest individual globally had more wealth than 50 percent of the global population. In was only in October 2018 that Jeff Bezos, founder of Amazon and perhaps the richest person in the world, agreed to pay his more than half a million employees a wage of $15 an hour, still low but an improvement over existing hourly wage.

It was this distributional flaw that led to popular unrest in developed countries, symbolized by the "Wall Street Movement" and the "We are the 99 per cent" movement. The alarm was sounded but political leaders, everywhere, continued in their quiescent ways rather than take heed of the looming threats. Ultimately, 2016 ushered in two massive, and totally unpredictable, shifts that shook the foundations of globalization. These were, first, the British decision to leave the European Union, and second, the election of Donald Trump to the presidency in the United States, on a pledge disengage from globalization and to put "America First."

In the summer of 2016, British voters narrowly approved a referendum for Britain to exit the European Union, a symbol of Britain's external engagement. This referendum was an affirmation of British desire to protect national identity and sovereignty from the globalist trajectory of the past few decades. Proponents of Brexit, however, did not position themselves as against globalization but argued, instead, that freed from shackles of the EU, Britain could pursue more profitable and broader global engagement, without any loss of sovereignty. As such, even if Brexit was not sold as de-globalization, it was de-globalization to the extent that it implied re-erecting new walls where none had existed before.

At the least, Brexit meant a different vision of globalization for Britain, one in which Britain could decide on its own trade future, do trade deals with other countries unencumbered by EU rule and continue trade relations with EU, either on a free trade basis or under the World Trade Organization's MFN (Most Favored Nation) rules. Since Brexiteers decried unrestricted labor mobility across EU borders, their goal was a new vision both of "globalization without labor" and of secure borders. They urged a step back to the type of globalization that was the norm for most other, non-EU, globally networked economies. If that was the ultimate dream, the immediate reality of Brexit, depending on the final version of exit agreement, would leave Britain without access to a large market at its doorstep for the unknown potential that British industry, and the financial services sector in London, could easily and quickly replace EU networks with links to the rest of the world. It should be noted as well, that most of the "globally" networked activities are actually concentrated around particular regions. The three regional hubs are the EU, East Asia and North America, and for Britain to exit the EU, its biggest trading partner, in order to pursue broader global connections defied the logic of "natural" network connectivity. British and European manufacturing are intricately linked through production networks and any Brexit agreement short of a customs union arrangement will result in chaotic transition for both.

In any event, negotiating the terms of British departure became a vexing issue, both for Brexiteers who wanted a clean break from the EU, and for the British government under Prime Minister May, which insisted on a customs union arrangement to protect access to its largest export market. The government position was essentially to engineer a "leave" option without actually "leaving" the European market and was supported neither by Brexiteers nor "remainers." Its main support came from business groups, which ideally wanted to remain within the EU or at least retain full access to EU on a customs union basis.

In the lead up to the Brexit referendum, Airbus Industries, with its production network extending to England, had cautioned that leaving the EU Common Market would be detrimental to its operating future in the UK. In June 2018, it added a cautionary warning that if Britain left the EU without some customs union arrangement, it might pull out of UK and relocate its British manufacturing elsewhere, risking the livelihood of 14,000 employees of Airbus and as many as 100,000 employees throughout its British supply chain. If Airbus were indeed to pull out of Britain, it would create a short-term problem for the aircraft manufacturer as it reworked its production network, *sans* Britain, but it would not necessarily lead to de-globalized aircraft manufacturing. Britain will, however, have disconnected from global manufacturing and at a tremendous cost to its economy. At the same time as the Airbus announced its cautionary note, the EU also urged member states to draw up contingency plans for the worst-case scenario of a hard Brexit. This was in light of negotiations that had stalled between the UK and EU and Michel Barnier, chief negotiator for the EU, warned Britain that it could not continue to blame EU for "the consequences of their [British] choice" (*Financial Times* 2018: 2). Shortly after Airbus' warning to the British government, Garman car manufacturer BMW also issued a statement that a hard Brexit would compel it to review its operations in the UK.

By late 2018, the EU and Britain had reached agreement on a transitional customs union arrangement until a more lasting framework could be worked out. This did not please either the remainers or the Brexiteers because, first, it meant that Britain would be forced to follow EU rules without having any say in them, and second, because it meant no real Brexit that would allow Britain the policy autonomy to negotiate separate trade deals with other countries. Prime Minister May's government came under intense pressure from not only the opposition political parties but also from members of her own Conservative Party. With uncertainty surrounding the final Brexit outcome, there was growing support for a "people's vote", a second referendum that could include even a "no Brexit" option.

If Brexit complicated the globalist agenda, the election of Donald Trump to the US presidency a few months after the Brexit vote, added to the level of uncertainty. The election of Trump was an unequivocal message of discontent with globalization and a commitment to put "America First." Early in his presidency, Trump pulled the US out of both the Trans-Pacific Partnership (TPP) that was in its final stages of negotiations, and an ambitious new Transatlantic Trade and Investment Partnership (TTIP) that would have brought US and EU closer together.

Brexit and an America First political agenda together constituted major setbacks for the future of globalization. These were two large economies that had seemingly declared a readiness to pull back from their existing level of engagement with economic globalization, and their global economic weight would clearly have systemic consequences. If, on the other hand, relatively small economies disengage from the global economy, there might be economic costs to those countries but unlikely to have any major systemic fallout. Events in the UK and the US inevitably lead us to questions about the future of the globalizing economy. In assessing that future, we can focus on developments in the US because of its vastly greater systemic consequence. We can begin with an initial observation that the genie of economic globalization will not be easily returned to the bottle, and in-house manufacturing is not likely to return and replace networked production.

The American decision to pull out of TPP and TTIP may have been early knee-jerk reactions but this and other actions taken thus far suggested that the new US administration was driven by three inter-related main concerns.

1   Unfair trade practices and trade imbalance.
2   US manufacturing and jobs creation.
3   Renegotiating trade deals.

President Trump brought to the White House a skepticism for all existing, and under negotiation, trade agreements as detrimental to American national interests. His essential argument was that the US had, for too long, allowed other countries to free ride on US openness and generosity. From that premise, it was relatively easy to exit trade agreements that had not yet concluded, such as the TPP and TTIP, and after that, focus shifted to creating a system of fair trade.

As a presidential candidate, he had frequently voiced his conviction that China's growing surplus in trade with the US, $223 billion in 2015 and $375 billion in 2017, was a result of unfair trade practices, exporting surplus production to the US while denying access to its market for foreign companies. To end this presumed free ride, the President, in 2018, announced two separate packages of higher tariff on Chinese imports in 2018 to force the Chinese government to provide equal access to US producers and to eliminate the trade imbalance. In April 2018, the US imposed higher tariffs on $50 billion worth of Chinese imports, and later that same year, higher tariffs on an additional $200 billion worth of Chinese imports. Following each of these two episodes the Chinese retaliated with their own tariffs on $110 billion worth of US exports to China. If the tariff war continues, it will lead to trade realignment and trade diversion that will harm both countries. For example, it could benefit some specific countries that are able to capture the trade diversionary effects. Selective trade protection against China, for example, could also result in trade diversion and trade creation for other countries, such as India and Bangladesh in South Asia. However, a broader concern, at this stage, is that a trade war will hurt global economic prosperity. Certainly, growth slowed significantly in China following the onset of trade conflict with US, and, yet, there appears to be no early Chinese capitulation to US pressures. Slower growth will have general systemic consequences and an early indication of this, in October 2018, was acute instability and turmoil in global capital markets.

Just as was the case with VERs on Japanese auto exports, higher tariffs on Chinese exports were designed, in part at least, to compel Chinese exporters to rely less on exports and invest in manufacturing in the US. This was even more directly the case with actions taken against imported washing machines and solar panels from South Korea and China. In January 2018, the Trump administration announced steep tariffs on imported solar panels and washing machines. The higher tariffs on solar panels was in response to complaints by two Chinese manufacturers of solar panels in the US and the end goal appeared to be to encourage "more manufacturing of solar panels [by foreign manufacturers and exporters] in the United States" (*The Straits Times* 2018) Similarly, the new tariffs on washing machines seem to be part of a cat and mouse game between the US on the one hand, and the two Korean manufacturers, Samsung and LG, on the other. The US had imposed tariffs on South Korean exports of washing machines, which had prompted Samsung and LG to shift some of their manufacturing to China. When, in 2017, the US announced tariffs on exports from China, LG and Samsung shifted production to Thailand and Vietnam. Sensing the likelihood of additional action by the US, the two manufacturers announced plans, in 2017, to open factories in the US. Samsung's factory in South Carolina has already commenced production and the LG plant in Tennessee will start production in 2019. The latest tariff measures seem to be an attempt to force these companies to shift more of their manufacturing to the US. As and when that happens, it will deepen production linkages and networks that exist at present and will serve to strengthen the foundations of globalization of production, rather than lead to de-globalization.

The North American Free Trade Agreement (NAFTA) was also in Trump's sights as a trade agreement that had allowed Mexico and Canada to prosper at the expense of the US. He opened fresh negotiations to create a more "balanced" trade agreement and, again, in 2018, the US, Canada and Mexico agreed to a new free trade deal that revised some of the provisions of

NAFTA, including increasing the North American local content of cars from 62.5 percent to 75 percent in order to qualify for zero tariffs. Important also was a provision that required up to 45 percent of components to be manufactured by employees earning at least the US minimum wage of $16 an hour. This is expected to either raise wages in Mexico, or stimulate manufacturing in US and Canada, or at least stem the flow of manufacturing jobs out of the United States.

Whether influenced by the more protectionist stance of the US government, a number of car manufacturers, such as Toyota, Mazda, Volvo and Mercedes-Benz, announced major new investments in the US to boost production and create new jobs. The largest new investment decision was that of Toyota and Mazda to set up a $1.6 billion joint production facility in Alabama to produce Toyota Corollas and Mazda SUVs. This particular investment will create 4,000 new jobs, but not necessarily make cars disconnected from global supply chains. Instead, these new investments will ultimately bind the US further in global production networks and globalization. In-house manufacturing has, in many industries, given way to networked manufacturing and this shift is not a passing phenomenon. Targeted protectionism in the 1980s began the process of globalization of production and a return of those protectionist policies may not only not unravel, but even advance, the globalist agenda.

If there is any uncertainty, it is whether America First policies will lead to global leadership vacuum and systemic instability. Adam Posen says that the premise that the other countries have taken an unfair advantage of the US in the postwar period is patently false and that it is the US that has benefitted from a free ride on other countries' efforts in providing development assistance (ODA), supporting global multilateralism and the UN, and combatting climate change. However, regardless of whether the starting premise is valid, he was confident that the system will survive even if the US decides to disengage from globalization, just as the international trading system survived Chinese abandonment of trade engagement in between the fifteenth and eighteenth century, and likewise Japan's withdrawal and isolationism (*sakoku*) during the Tokugawa period, from early seventeenth century to the mid-nineteenth century (Posen 2018: 36). Of course, as argued here, present circumstances have no parallels in history, but there is also little reason to worry that America will descend to its own version of *sakoku* in the future, even with news commentaries that suggest that the US is abdicating its global leadership role.

At the same time, potential threats to globalization, presumed or real exit strategies of Britain and the US, are mitigated, as observed by Posen, by greater global engagement of the European Union and countries of the Pacific. The European Union has extended free trade agreement with several major countries and is in the process of negotiating new free trade agreements, while in the Pacific Japan and Australia, as they have often partnered in other regional initiatives in the past, have pushed TPP forward without American participation. In March 2018, eleven Asia–Pacific countries agreed to a Comprehensive and Progressive Agreement for Trans-Pacific Partnership (CPTPP). Once it is ratified and becomes effective, it will lock in preferential trade among the member countries. Earlier in January 2018, at the Davos World Economic Forum, President Trump appeared to relax his opposition to TPP and suggest that the US might be prepared to join with some revisions to the previous agreement. In the end however, CPTPP excluded the US and the remaining participants were able to avoid thorny and complicated issues of interest to the US, such as investments and intellectual property rights. Even if the CPTPP does not live up to the potential of the TPP, it is an important trade agreement from which the US has been completely sidelined. The US is the loser with no major scaling back of globalization. Separately, as Lund and Tyson (2018: 130) point out, globalization will march ahead, even with contemporary challenges, with the growth in digital technology and e-commerce, in which China has emerged as a key player.

Ultimately, Posen's "post-American world economy" is not a future that can be extrapolated from actions taken thus far by the US government. As well, it should be noted that US leadership is not the bedrock of global capitalism, which is instead dependent on support from leading manufacturers that are invested in global supply chain activities. The most important trade stabilizing factor is globalization itself in which businesses, as consumers, have become the main bulwarks against protectionism that might undermine their commercial interests. As Cattaneo, Gereffi and Staritz (2010: 6) point out, GVCs/GPNs have proved resilient and become "crucial and enduring structural features of the world economy." It is worth noting that President Trump's economic policies have been, so far, comparatively more circumspect than his inflammatory rhetoric. In the on-going trade conflict with China, the US government excised particular commodities of interest to major American corporations. Business groups have consistently advised caution and their voice cannot be completely ignored as the new US government contemplates its trade strategy. There may be some fraying of the structure of globalization at the margins, but a complete reversal is implausible. This is because, even the President has to take in the big picture.

Conclusion

Globalization is the third iteration in the evolution of capitalism. Like monopoly capitalism before, there is no assumption that globalized manufacturing will encompass all manufacturing activity. There are industries that are not a good fit for networked manufacturing. At the same time, it is also clear that international trade is increasingly in parts and components linked to networked production processes. This has brought stability not only to trade but to globalization as well. Globalization is here to stay and is, in that respect, unlike any earlier period of economic integration. Globalization is unique and not a restoration of, say, the nineteenth-century period of economic interdependence that followed Britain's repeal of the Corn Laws. Trade is on a more stable footing and protectionism less likely to be a viable response to changes in the economic cycle.

These two developments cannot be stated in absolutist terms yet, given that globalization is an evolutionary process. De-globalization may have caught the peoples' fancy, but it is not a realistic future scenario. Discontent with globalization may have propelled Trump to the US Presidency and led to the rise of nationalist political parties in several western countries but is not enough to dissolve practical links forged through production networks, which can be dismantled only at considerable cost to economic welfare. Political leaders may resort to protectionist rhetoric but existing checks and balances, including pressure from firms involved in globalized production, will prevent outcomes that are inconsistent with stability of supply chain networks. Actual policies were less strident and more measured than is suggested by the anti-globalization rhetoric of President Trump. Moreover, protectionist measures against imports from China led less to US firms returning to manufacturing in the US, a reversal of globalized production, and more to a relocation of Chinese manufacturing to other countries in Asia, such as Cambodia, a reconfiguration of globalized production. His America First policy stance has encouraged more investment in US manufacturing but not, by extension, also to a winding back of the new form of manufacturing.

Finally, to return to the fundamental issue of income inequality as the source of much of today's political backlash against globalization, even if a reversal is improbable, income inequality and distributional issues cannot be ignored. In the short term, an incitement of fear and rage may help some governments hold their political support base intact, but this cannot be a long-term governance strategy. The root problem has to be tackled, and one solution, as it was in the period that Simon Kuznets (1955) studied in his analysis of income distribution, is political intervention. Capitalism as a system generates inequality, but the excesses of it can be managed, and in the contemporary period, fault lies not with globalization but with deregulation, a policy matrix that was adopted by most developed countries in the time that globalization was starting to take shape. We must remember that economics only provides us with prescriptions of how to increase and grow the economic pie, how that pie is then distributed is a political decision.

Bibliography

Alvaredo, F., Chancel, L., Piketty, T., Saez, E., and Zucaman, G. 2017. World Inequality Report 2018. *World Inequality Lab.* Paris.

Baldwin, R. and Evenett, S. 2009. *The Collapse of the Global Trade, Nurky Protectionism and the Crisis: Recommendations for the G20.* Geneva: The Graduate Institute.

Bergsten, F. and Noland, M. 1993. *Reconcilable Differences? United States-Japan Economic Conflict.* Washington, DC, Institute for International Economics.

Cattaneo, O., Gereffi, G. and Staritz, C. (eds). 2010. *Global Value Chains in a Postcrisis World: A Development Perspective.* The World Bank, Washington, DC.

Dore, R. 1997. The Distinctiveness of Japan. In: *Political Economy of Modern Capitalism: Mapping Convergence and Divergence.* Crouch, C. and Streeck, W. (ed.) London, Sage Publications.

Dyer, J. H. 2000. How Chrysler Created an American Keiretsu. *Harvard Business Review on Managing Value Chains.* Cambridge, Harvard Business School Press.

Economist, 2012. January 14.

Ferrarini, B. and Hummels, D. 2014. Asia and Global Production Networks: Implications for Trade, Incomes and Economic Vulnerability. In: *Asia and Global Production Networks.* Ferrarini, B. and Hummels, D, (eds.) Cheltenham, Edward Elgar.

Financial Times. 2018. Britain Faces a Simple Choice: Raise Taxes or Cut Services. Available at: www.ft.com/content/5495626e-94c1-11e8-b747-fb1e803ee64e.

Frankopan, P. 2017. *The Silk Roads: A New History of the World.* New York, Vintage Books.

Friedman, T. 2000. *The Lexus and the Olive Tree: Understanding Globalization.* New York, Anchor Books.

Gilpin, R. 2000. *The Challenge of Global Capitalism.* Princeton, Princeton University Press.

Hirst, P. and Thompson, G. 1996. *Globalization in Question: The International Economy and the Possibilities of Governance.* Cambridge, Polity Press.

JAMA. 2014. More American Than Ever. Tokyo, *Annual Contributions Report 2014–2015.*

Keohane, R. and Nye, J. 1989. *Power and Interdependence.* 2nd ed. New York, Harper Collins.

Keohane, R. and Nye, J. 2000. Introduction. In: *Governance in a Globalizing World.* Nye, J. and Donahue, J. (eds.) Washington, DC, Brookings Institution Press.

Koichi, S. 1992. The Internationalization of the Japanese Automobile Industry. In: *The Internationalization of Japan.* Hook, G. and Weiner, M. (eds.) London and New York Routledge.

Krugman, P. 2013. *End This Depression Now.* New York and London, W. Norton & Co.

Kuznets, S. 1955. Economic Growth and Income Inequality. *American Economic Review,* Vol. 45: 1–29.

Lubben, R. 1988. *Just-in-Time Manufacturing: An Aggressive Manufacturing Strategy.* New York, McGraw Hill Book Co.

Lund, S. and Tyson, L. 2018. Globalization Is Not in Retreat: Digital Technology and the Future of Trade. *Foreign Affairs:* 130–140.

Maswood, S. 1989. *Japan and Protection: The Growth of Protectionist Sentiment and the Japanese Response.* London and New York, Routledge and Nissan Institute of Japanese Studies, University of Oxford.

Monden, Y. 1993. *Toyota Production System: An Integrated Approach to Just-in-Time.* Norcross, G. (2nd ed.). Florida: Taylor & Francis.

Moore, K. and Lewis, D. 2009. *The Origins of Globalization.* New York, Routledge.

Moore, M. 2003. *A World Without Wall: Freedom, Development, Free Trade and Global Governance.* Cambridge and New York, Cambridge University Press.

Nelson, D. 1996. Making Sense of the 1981 Automobile VER: Economics, Politics and the Political Economy of Protectionism. In: *The Political Economy of Trade Protection.* Krueger, A. (ed.) Chicago and London, The University of Chicago Press.

Ohmae, K. 1999. *The Borderless World: Power and Strategy in the Interlinked Economy.* New York, Harper Business.

Pegels, C. 1984. *Japan vs the West: Implications for Management*. Boston, Kluwer Nijhoff Publishing.

Phillip, N. 2017. Power and Inequality in the Global Political Economy. *International Affairs*, Vol. 93, issue 2.

Posen, A. 2018. The Post-American World Economy: Globalization in the Trump Era. *Foreign Affairs*, Vol. 97, issue 2, 28–38.

Rodrik, D. 1997. *Has Globalization Gone Too Far?* Washington, DC, Institute for International Economics.

Sachs. J. 2005. *The End of Poverty: How We Can Make It Happen in Our Lifetime*. London, Penguin Books.

Sheard, P. 1994. Interlocking Shareholdings and Corporate Governance. In: *The Japanese Firm: Sources of Competitive Strength*. Aoki, M. and Dore, R. (ed.) New York, Oxford University Press.

Stangler, C. 2018. What's Really Behind France's Yellow Vest Protest? *The Nation*. Available at: www.thenation.com/article/france-yellow-vest-protest-macron.

The Striats Times. 2018. US Slaps Steep Tariffs on Imported Washing Machines and Solar Panels. Availabke at: www.straitstimes.com/world/united-states/trump-makes-first-big-trade-move-with-tariffs-aimed-at-asia.

Whittaker, D. H. 1997. *Small Firms in the Japanese Economy*. Cambridge: Cambridge University Press.

39

The IPE of global tax governance

Martin Hearson

Introduction

Though taxation has historically been less studied by scholars of international political economy than issues such as trade, investment or finance, recent years have seen a growing volume of scholarship addressing the causes and consequences of cooperation and discord between states over the taxation of cross-border economic activity. This growth in interest corresponds to a new popular politics of global tax governance following the global financial crisis. Since 2008, household-name multinational companies such as Apple, McDonalds and Starbucks have been the subject of front-page newspaper investigations and public protests. Leaked information from law firms in tax havens, such as the 'Panama' and 'Paradise' Papers, created political scandals across the globe, forcing out heads of state in countries as far apart as Pakistan and Iceland. Civil society campaigners in developed and developing countries alike have turned their attention to international taxation, exemplified by the creation in 2012 of the Global Alliance for Tax Justice, a coalition of civil society organisations on five continents.

This politicisation has raised the stakes for governments. In the Global North, civil society organisations ranging from the radical 'Uncut' and 'Occupy' movements to the more established development agencies and trade unions have seized on the issue of tax avoidance and evasion, at a time when large fiscal deficits, growing concerns about inequality and the politics of austerity have all contributed to the upsurge in popular concern about tax avoidance and evasion. In the Global South, the drivers have been different: doubts about the stability of aid flows, the lack of significantly increased government revenue following a boom in commodity prices in the 2000s, the controversial introduction of indirect taxes such as VAT, and a new discourse of 'domestic resource mobilisation' in development assistance.

The consequence of this politicisation has been a heightening of tensions between states. In 2015, for example, a United Nations summit in Addis Ababa on financing the new Sustainable Development Goals nearly ended in stalemate after developing countries dug their heels in over the UN's role in global tax governance. As early as 2009, a G-20 summit to discuss the response to the financial crisis also stumbled over a dispute between France and China over the publication of a list of 'tax havens'. One consequence of these changes has been a newfound willingness to revisit some of the foundations of the international tax regime, which date from the 1920s and 1930s. A regime previously premised on bilateralism and sovereignty-preservation increasingly now incorporates binding multilateral commitments and a credible enforcement threat against non-compliant jurisdictions.

The first part of this chapter gives a description of the institutions of global tax governance. The next section explains in more detail the three competing goals that have shaped states' actions in the creation of those institutions: eliminating double taxation, preserving tax sovereignty, and curbing tax competition. Next, two axes of conflict between different states that characterise negotiations over international tax institutions are introduced. The final section contrasts the state-centric ontology that has quite understandably dominated much IPE scholarship on the international tax regime with constructivist and critical perspectives. Taxation is by its nature a state-centric subject, since by many definitions there could be no tax without the state; yet, international tax policy is often guided by aim of reducing taxes on capital, rather than raising them.

Box 39.1 Definitions

Base erosion and profit shifting (BEPS). According to the OECD, this refers to 'tax planning strategies that exploit gaps and mismatches in tax rules to make profits "disappear" for tax purposes or to shift profits to locations where there is little or no real activity but the taxes are low resulting in little or no overall corporate tax being paid'. The BEPS project coordinated by the OECD, also involving G20 countries, seeks to reform international tax standards that have become open to exploitation by multinational firms.

Double taxation, single taxation and double non-taxation. Where a company or individual incurs a tax liability in more than one country, international tax instruments strive to ensure that any given transaction is taxed once and only once by the different countries with a claim on it (single taxation). If two countries' claims on the taxing rights overlap, this creates double taxation; if neither country claims the taxing rights, this creates double non-taxation.

Offshore financial centre. Any financial centre that mediates transactions between foreign residents is an offshore centre. The term is often used indistinguishably with 'tax haven', because tax havens, by providing a legal environment attractive to foreign residents, encourage funds to move from 'onshore' where they originated to 'offshore', where they are merely present on paper.

Tax avoidance. According to a common formal definition, tax avoidance practices are those designed to gain a tax advantage by contravening the intention of legislation, but not its letter. Such practices can be prevented through statutory anti-avoidance rules.

Tax haven. The classic definition comes from a 1998 OECD report, which named four criteria. A tax haven provides an environment in which foreign residents incur low or nominal tax rates, in combination with one or more of: no rules requiring a substantial economic presence to qualify for tax residence, a lack of transparency around the tax system, and an unwillingness to exchange information with other tax authorities.

Tax evasion. This refers to actions by a taxpayer to escape a tax liability that has arisen under the law of a country. Doing so generally involves concealing from the revenue authority the income on which the tax liability has arisen.

Tax planning. This refers to tax strategies designed to prevent a tax liability from arising. Unlike tax evasion and tax avoidance, tax planning does not contravene either the letter or the spirit of the law.

Tax treaty. Formally known as tax conventions on income and capital, bilateral tax treaties between countries were originally referred to as double taxation treaties. By concluding them, countries reach a negotiated settlement that restricts their ability to tax cross-border investment, to prevent double taxation.

Transfer pricing. This refers to the price of transactions occurring between related companies, in particular companies within the same multinational group. Because companies have an incentive to manipulate these prices to shift profits to places where they incur less tax, governments set rules to determine how transfer pricing should be undertaken.

The nuts and bolts of global tax governance

For IPE, the starting point in any analysis of the international tax regime is the taxes levied by governments on mobile factors of production: capital and labour. In practice, most of the attention in scholarship, and in this chapter, is on capital taxation, but it is true that taxation on highly paid labour, at least, is also subject to many of the same dynamics. States have recognised a need to coordinate their income tax systems since they first began to consolidate them in the interwar years.[1] These needs have been enhanced by the liberalisation of capital flows and the growth of multinational companies since the 1970s, which greatly increased the entanglement of countries' tax bases. Nonetheless, the institutions of global tax governance have until recently been premised on norms of sovereignty-preservation and decentralised bilateralism, with multilateral agreement limited to model bilateral agreements and non-binding guidance.[2]

The central institution of the international tax regime is the OECD's *Model Tax Convention on Income and Capital*, first agreed in 1963 and based on models developed by the League of Nations in the 1920s and 1930s. Most importantly, the OECD model treaty is the basis of over 3000 bilateral tax treaties negotiated between states. It carves up the tax base of cross-border economic activities between states, articulating an ideal-type negotiated outcome that can be modified in bilateral negotiations. The OECD model also incorporates various explicit and implicit principles of the international tax regime, alongside two sets of standards that have a life beyond the bilateral treaties: the OECD's Transfer Pricing Guidelines, which set out how the profits of multinational companies are attributed among the states in which they operate, and its standards for the exchange of tax information between countries. It is through the constant updating of the model and this associated guidance that the international tax system evolves. There are alternative models, especially that of the United Nations as well as several regional groupings such as the Common Market of Eastern and Southern Africa (COMESA) and Association of South-East Asian Nations (ASEAN). Each of these model conventions nonetheless takes the OECD model as its starting point, at least indirectly.

The OECD model and its associated standards do not have a 'hard law' status unless states commit to be bound by them through an actual treaty based on the OECD model. The number of such commitments is growing, but even beyond that, the reach of OECD soft law is becoming broader and deeper over time, and some have suggested that it has the status of customary international law.[3] Many countries, not only OECD members, use OECD model treaty provisions and transfer pricing standards as the basis of their domestic law. Texts such as the commentary to the OECD model treaty and the Transfer Pricing Guidelines have been referred to by courts as a source of authority, even where they do not form part of the law.

A shift towards more centralised, sovereignty-constraining economic governance began at the very end of the twenty-first century. The OECD is active across many areas of economic governance, and in most of these areas its approach combines two elements: first, member states and others involved on an ad hoc basis develop a set of standards through a consensus approach, then they conduct peer reviews of each other's compliance with those standards.[4] At the turn of the century, the OECD began to apply this peer review mechanism to taxation, increasing the pressure on countries (and offshore financial centres that are not strictly speaking countries in their own right) to comply with minimum standards for exchanging tax information with each other. This first attempt was generally regarded as a failure, due to the weaknesses of the standards and the absence of real ambition to enforce compliance with them.[5]

Following the global financial crisis, however, there has been a marked increase in the pace and ambition of change. The exchange of information standard has been progressively tightened, both in terms of content and through the creation of a body, the Global Forum on Transparency and Exchange of Information, for peer reviews. New rules dealing with aspects of countries' tax systems that allow multinational companies to avoid tax, developed through the OECD's Base Erosion and Profit Shifting (BEPS) project, are also now subject to peer review through the Inclusive Framework on BEPS. These bodies have expanded memberships, and in both areas, there are new binding multilateral agreements to quickly translate some of the new standards into hard law. Nonetheless, the effectiveness of these interventions is still debated, especially from the perspective of developing countries,[6] and global tax governance is still relatively decentralised and sovereignty-preserving in comparison to, say, the trade regime.

A trilemma of cooperation

What pressures explain this regime design and its recent changes? We can begin to explain it using three key observations about the conflict between multinational capital and governments seeking to tax it:

1   If a taxpayer has income in more than one state, it faces claims to taxation from more than one government. If the governments do not coordinate their actions, these may overlap, creating 'double taxation'. This is the primary stated aim of tax treaties and the model conventions on which they are based.
2   Governments want to retain their sovereignty, but cannot enforce taxes on mobile capital effectively without cooperation from other jurisdictions. Tax information exchange agreements are a key example of this. This tension is at the heart of regime design.
3   Governments' tax decisions will affect where mobile capital chooses to locate itself, leading to 'tax competition'. A distinction is often drawn between 'benign' or 'real' tax competition, in which lower effective tax rates are used to entice economic activity, and 'harmful' or 'virtual' tax competition, in which special tax rules entice money – but not substantial economic activity – for the sole purpose of avoiding and evading tax.

Philipp Genschel and Thomas Rixen suggest that these three elements of international conflict and cooperation lead to a trilemma: governments can reconcile two, but not three, of their key objectives of curbing tax competition, alleviating double taxation, and preserving tax sovereignty.[7] If they choose to build a regime that prevents double taxation while preserving tax sovereignty, some states will exploit the rules to enable harmful tax competition. To prevent the loss of revenue through tax competition while retaining sovereignty, states must adapt their own domestic tax systems to insulate themselves, but in doing so they will create double taxation. States can solve the problems of double taxation and tax competition simultaneously, but only by creating an enforceable global regime that limits tax sovereignty.

Double taxation

When a taxpayer has a potential tax liability in more than one state, what happens if all those states claim the right to tax it? The risk is that those claims will overlap, discouraging cross-border economic activity. Capital-exporting states have generally made the first move, introducing unilateral mechanisms into their tax systems that reduce the risk of 'double taxation' when their residents earn income abroad, for example by exempting the profits of multinational companies where they were earned abroad.[8] Nonetheless, multinational businesses and the governments of their home states have advocated since the 1920s for more comprehensive global cooperation among developed states,[9] as well as for the extension of that regime to all states through the conclusion of bilateral double taxation agreements with developing countries.[10] Double taxation was thus the problem that primarily animated the initial design of the international tax regime during the League of Nations era, a design that endures into the twenty-first century.

From the perspective of capital-exporting governments and multinational businesses, cooperation to relieve double taxation achieves several benefits over unilateral methods. It more comprehensively eliminates double taxation, because states can negotiate consistent rules and definitions, and put in place dispute settlement procedures where there are outstanding differences of interpretation. It also shares the cost of double taxation relief between states as a result of a negotiated outcome: if one country (most likely the net capital exporter) considers the revenue it has sacrificed through unilateral relief to be too great, it can negotiate with other countries to have them take on some of these costs, by accepting curbs on the extent to which they can tax investors.[11]

Between two developed countries where transactions are more complex and investment flows both ways, the cost of following inconsistent rules is greater, and the give-and-take of reaching an agreement is less likely to produce a lop-sided outcome. Between a developed and developing country, the picture is different. An agreement exports rules written among OECD states to the developing country,[12] and, where investment flows are largely one way, the treaty imposes many costs and fewer benefits on the developing country, and may be more akin to 'aid in reverse.'[13] Developing countries' enthusiastic participation in this regime is therefore a puzzle.

Sovereignty and administrative cooperation

A state may claim the right to tax a person in principle, either because they are one of its residents, or because they earn income within its borders. But there are practical constraints that may prevent it from exercising that right, and these constraints have shaped the development of international tax norms to date.[14] The two biggest are these: first, how can a state tax an entity with sources of income in multiple countries, if it cannot know whether or not the entity has given an honest account of its global financial position? Second, how can a state force a foreign resident to pay tax on income it has earned within the state's borders, if the foreign resident no longer has any income or assets in that state? In a condition of pure anarchy, states would be powerless to surmount these difficulties.

The solution has been to develop a set of international instruments through which states share information with each other and cooperate to collect revenue from cross-border taxpayers. This began with bilateral agreements for the exchange of taxpayer information on request, where the requesting authority had to demonstrate that the information was 'foreseeably relevant'. In recent years, however, states have moved towards a combination of bilateral and multilateral agreements, through which they can share bulk data on each other's taxpayers' affairs, make requests from each other for more detailed information as part of tax investigations, and even collect tax revenue on each other's behalf. Jurisdictions are now pressurised to enter into and comply with these agreements through the OECD Global Forum's peer review mechanism, which is backed by a threat of G20 sanctions, as well as the threat of unilateral sanctions from powerful states.[15] This system demonstrates that states recognise the need to give up some *de jure* sovereignty in order to enforce their sovereign taxing rights de facto. As Allison Christians puts it, it 'appears to shift the focus on tax sovereignty toward identifying affirmative duty in tax system design as a necessary element of respect for sovereignty itself'.[16] The speed and timing of this erosion of fiscal sovereignty, after decades in which the principle was defended, is in itself an interesting subject for further research.

These developments are surprising, because they contravene what scholars for many years considered to be a constant in the IPE of global tax governance: a norm of sovereignty-preservation.

Box 39.2 Taxation, the state and sovereignty

'Fiscal sociologists', among them Joseph Schumpeter and Charles Tilly, have recognised for a century that tax is an important part of any country's political and social characteristics, and hence that it has the power to help explain the development of those characteristics. A group of 'new fiscal sociologists' posit 'a new theory of taxation as a social contract that multiplies a society's infrastructural power'.[17] For the state to fulfil its side of the contract, and especially to safeguard the security of its citizens, it needs tax revenue. Because of this, sovereignty over taxation is a special priority for the state. Indeed, one of the foundational texts of realist international relations, Thomas Hobbes' Leviathan, ascribes to the sovereign not only 'the Right of making Warre, and Peace with other Nations' but also 'to levy mony upon the Subjects, to defray the expenses thereof'.[18] As Douglass North suggests, the state may even be defined as, 'an organization with a comparative advantage in violence, extending over a geographic area whose boundaries are determined by its power to tax constituents'.[19] This is the reason why states are thought to be especially concerned about their fiscal sovereignty: as Raymond Burke wrote, 'the revenue of the state *is* the state', which means that tax sovereignty *is* sovereignty.[20]

For many tax havens, the provision of secrecy, by deliberately withholding information from the tax authorities of other jurisdictions, has been part and parcel of their competitive strategy.[21] In recognition of this, the OECD originally used the term 'harmful tax competition' as an umbrella term for its work challenging tax havens. This proved to be a linguistic own-goal, since tax competition itself is widely endorsed by OECD members, and because it is not easy to define a boundary between harmful and legitimate tax competition without placing some OECD members themselves on the 'harmful' side.[22] Tax havens deployed the concept of fiscal sovereignty to fend off the OECD attack, an effective weapon because, as Palan argues, states could not intervene in each other's tax laws without contravening the norms of sovereignty on which the Westphalian state-system had been built.[23]

Tax competition

Governments have other priorities from tax policy than raising revenue, and perhaps the most important of these is the desire to stimulate investment and growth. Tax need not necessarily have a negative effect on either, but governments must take into account the behavioural effects resulting from the impact of taxation on taxpayers' economic incentives. They may reduce the incentive to work and invest, increase the incentive to avoid or evade taxes altogether, or encourage mobile economic actors to seek out less onerous tax regimes. While some of these incentive effects occur within each state regardless of the conditions outside, the effect of taxation on mobile taxpayers is to create strategic interactions between states, known as 'tax competition'. A large number of studies have attempted to model how corporate income taxation in the host state affects inflows of foreign direct investment (FDI). Meta-analyses of these studies find that a one-point increase in the corporate tax rate reduces FDI inflows by up to 3 per cent.[24] For developing countries, however, there is some evidence that long-term investment may not be as responsive to taxation, and especially to tax incentives.[25]

Despite these limitations, tax competition is not merely a descriptive theory: it is a powerful idea that influences policy. Some economists, originating with Charles Tiebout, regard tax competition as beneficial because it encourages states to consider the optimal balance between the provision of public services and levels of taxation.[26] Conversely, others argue that states should cooperate to limit a 'race to the bottom' from tax competition, which if unmitigated leads to inefficient outcomes.[27] Nonetheless, it is clear that governments believe there are gains from tax competition, and a broad consensus in the literature confirms that it takes place.[28] Corporation tax rates, for example, have fallen consistently since the 1960s, while burgeoning tax incentive regimes can be seen both in developing and developed countries, in spite of consistent advice from international organisations that such competition is unlikely to bring investment gains.[29] There are caveats to this account: tax rates are not the only elements of tax policy that determine how much companies pay, and evidence also suggests that political factors such as governing party ideology and prevailing societal norms can limit the potency of tax competition.[30]

Not all tax competition is equal. While the discussion above focuses on competition for real investment, which Peter Dietsch calls 'luring', governments may also use tax rules to attract paper profits and portfolio income, detached from any real activity, which can be described as virtual competition, or 'poaching'.[31] The two are connected, since a multinational company that can benefit by moving its paper profits may not be so sensitive to real tax competition, and hence tax avoidance may reduce the so-called real tax competition pressure on governments.[32] The OECD draws a similar distinction, discussing a range of outcomes from national tax rules in the global economy and reserving particular criticism for those where 'the effect is for one country to redirect capital and financial flows and the corresponding revenue from the other jurisdictions by bidding aggressively for the tax base of other countries' concluding that '[i]f the spillover effects of particular tax practices are so substantial that they are concluded to be poaching other countries' tax bases, such practices would be doubtlessly labelled "harmful tax competition"'.[33] Despite this, neither the OECD, nor other organisations such as the EU and the East African Community (EAC) that have tried, has succeeded in fully stamping out harmful tax competition among their members.

Two axes of conflict

Academic literature and policy debate on the international tax regime are animated by two main axes of conflict, which emerge from the abovementioned areas of cooperation and conflict. A first is between large states, which, because they have large tax bases, have the most to lose from tax competition, and small jurisdictions, which have more to gain. A second is between developed countries, which are predominantly exporters of capital, and developing countries, which import it; these two groups have different preferences in many areas of global tax governance. These two distinctions still apply today, a century after states began multilateral cooperation on tax matters, although the evolution of the global economy is beginning to create shifting alliances.

Small versus large states

Jurisdictions that don't have a large stock of capital or a large tax base from corporations have an incentive to engage in tax competition since in doing so they can attract significant amounts of foreign capital. Larger countries, in contrast, would struggle to attract enough capital from tax competition to make up for the lower tax revenue they would raise on their large existing tax base. Ronen Palan describes the consequent development of 'tax havens', often but not always small island states, as the 'commercialisation of state sovereignty', by which a jurisdiction offers residents of other countries the opportunity to adopt its nationality, attracting them with the benefits of an attractive tax regime, without actually moving physically to that state.[34] By becoming, on paper, a resident of this offshore jurisdiction, companies and wealthy individuals can exploit the self-imposed limits accepted by onshore countries in combination with the low tax rates of the offshore jurisdiction to lower their overall tax bills. Harmful tax competition thus exploits the existing structure of international tax institutions. In other instances, companies and individuals use the commercialised sovereignty of tax havens to conceal their wealth behind a veil of secrecy that cannot be penetrated by the onshore tax authorities of the countries where they are actually present. In these cases, large countries can only deal with this problem if they are willing and able to force smaller countries to comply.

When powerful states choose to challenge such behaviour, they use the rhetorical threat of brute force to pressure smaller jurisdictions to change their tax rules against their will, focused on reputational damage as well as the threat of retaliation.[35] For example, in 2009, G-20 members threatened countermeasures against states that did not comply with certain tax standards, linking an enforcement threat to the OECD's Global Forum. A number of individual states, including France and Brazil, and more recently the European Union, adopted blacklists of tax havens, users of which are penalised. In 2012, the United States went one step further through its Foreign Account Tax Compliance Act (FATCA), which unilaterally forced foreign banks to disclose information on any US citizens among their clients, with a much more tangible threat of sanctions against those banks.[36]

These developments notwithstanding, one of the great questions motivating the literature on global tax governance is why the world's most powerful states have been slow – and arguably have still failed – to tackle the tax haven problem, which has been visible since the 1960s.

As Box 39.3 outlines, international tax avoidance and evasion have significant fiscal costs, although the estimates are often disputed. Beyond the direct cost to the state, they also exacerbate inequality and damage confidence in the tax system. The OECD report on Harmful Tax Competition noted that large states can also engage in 'poaching' through harmful preferential tax regimes, and it is understandable that this should have been harder to stamp out. But large states surely have the motive and the capability to force smaller tax havens to comply with their wishes.

Box 39.3 The cost of tax avoidance and evasion

It is difficult to estimate the cost of tax avoidance and evasion, and many of the figures commonly used are disputed. There have, however, been three recent estimates by international organisations of the cost of multinational companies' base erosion and profit-shifting practices, which converge on an order of magnitude. An IMF working paper estimated the long-run costs to government revenues at equivalent to around one percent of GDP, around US$400 billion in OECD countries and US$200 billion elsewhere.[37] UNCTAD, looking specifically at developing countries, estimates a revenue loss 'in the order of' $100 billion from one particular type of tax avoidance, the use of interest payments to move taxable profits out of operating countries.[38] The OECD gives a global estimate for all countries of $100 to $240 billion, which is 4 to 10 per cent of corporate income tax revenues.[39] One more recent estimate suggests that 40 percent of corporate profits are shifted to tax havens, reducing corporate income tax revenue by as much as 18 percent in EU countries, and 7 per cent in developing countries.[40]

Estimates of the cost of tax evasion are more difficulty, because by definition it relies on secrecy. It is perhaps more reliable to estimate the amount of wealth held in tax havens. Such estimates range from that by Gabriel Zucman, who finds it to be eight percent of total household wealth ($7.6 trillion at the end of 2013) to James Henry of Tax Justice Network, who estimated the amount to be larger, at US$32 trillion.[41] To know how much of this offshore wealth is the proceeds of tax evasion, or generates income on which tax continues to be evaded, is harder. But we can say that, for example, the OECD estimates €93 billion has been reclaimed by governments through more effective exchange of information mechanisms put in place in 2008.[42] The International Consortium of Investigative Journalists, which published the leaked offshore documents known as the Panama Papers, claims that tax authorities used the information to recoup more than US$500 million in 2016 and 2017.[43] Thus, while the amounts involved are uncertain, they are certainly large.

Developed versus developing states

International tax cooperation has always been characterised by disagreements between developed countries on the one hand, which have broadly speaking preferred a regime that emphasises the right of a multinational's home state to tax its worldwide profits, and on the other hand developing countries, which prefer to divide those rights up between its host states. This disagreement was visible in the 1920s, when the first model treaties were developed under the auspices of the League of Nations, and again in the 1940s, when two model treaties emerged, the 'Mexico' Draft developed predominantly by Latin American countries, and the London Draft by Europeans. In the 1960s and 1970s, these models were updated by the Organisation for European Economic Cooperation (OEEC), which subsequently became the OECD, and by the Community of Andean Nations. The OECD model won out over the Andean model, which was never used outside of treaties signed within Latin America. The 1970s saw the emergence of a United Nations committee that eventually published its own model, closely based on the OECD model, but with some variations in the interests of developing countries (see the timeline in Box 39.4).

Given this global asymmetry between North and South, the dominant role played by the OECD in the design of international tax institutions is something of a puzzle. Developing and developed countries may have clashed over the status of the UN committee, but the momentum

---

Box 39.4 Timeline of key developments in international tax governance

1920s and 1930s: League of Nations agrees the underlying framework of international tax cooperation

1946: United Nations Fiscal Committee collapses

1960s and 1970s: problems created by capital mobility emerge: double taxation and double non-taxation

1963: OECD model tax treaty is created, eventually published in a revised format in 1977

1979: OECD transfer pricing guidelines are published

1980: United Nations model treaty is published

1997–2003: OECD harmful tax practices project largely fails to resolve the problems of tax havens

2009: Following the financial crisis, an era of intense cooperation begins with the G20 threatening sanctions on non-cooperative jurisdictions

2012: Base Erosion and Profit-Shifting project is launched

---

is clearly with the OECD. Most bilateral treaties use a combination of articles from the OECD and UN models, but the balance between the two is generally in favour of the OECD, even for treaties between countries that are not members of the OECD.[44] The OECD is far better resourced, its model is updated more frequently, its international meetings are better attended by developed and developing countries alike, and there is no UN equivalent to the proliferation of OECD soft law such as the transfer pricing guidelines and its peer-reviewed minimum standards. Indeed, the OECD's Committee on Fiscal Affairs has the weight of an intergovernmental body, while UN committee's members only participate as experts in a personal capacity. The creation of the Global Forum for exchange of information and the Inclusive Framework on BEPS may mark the end of the OECD's club model of making tax rules, at least in principle.

It is notable that proposals for a more 'ethical' international tax system generally focus on the issue of harmful tax competition, which affects both developed and developing countries, leaving the North–South tensions to one side. Peter Diestch's design for a more philosophically sound international tax institution, for example, leaves out this question on the grounds that it would make it too hard to reach consensus among states.[45] The popular proposal among critics to replace the existing system of transfer pricing with 'unitary taxation', where a globally agreed formula would allocate the tax base between states, leaves unanswered the distributional implications of such an agreed formula for developing countries.[46]

Turning to the tax haven problem, even here there are important differences between the interests of developed and developing states. First, the asymmetrical nature of economic flows and enforcement capacities means that developing countries need a different form of cooperation to developed countries. For example, complex corporate tax structuring is a problem for developed countries, while developing countries suffer from 'plain vanilla' structures that developed countries can often prevent quite easily.[47] In contrast, as capital importers, developing countries need access to information on multinational investors that may be more readily available to the developed countries in which they are headquartered.[48] The international tools of administrative cooperation formulated by developed countries may therefore not always meet the needs of developing countries. A second difference is that, while developed countries have the economic power to coerce tax havens into cooperating, developing countries who lack this coercive power must piggy-back on initiatives designed by others. To obtain information from less-cooperative tax havens, for example, they may need to participate in OECD exchange of information initiatives that are backed by the threat of G-20 countermeasures.

State-centric, constructivist and critical perspectives on global tax governance

The trilemma of cooperation, in combination with the two axes of conflict mentioned above, gives us a map of the key questions animating the IPE literature on global tax governance. These questions have been examined through three different lenses: a predominant approach that emphasises the interests and capabilities of states, a more recent constructivist strand that considers nation states to be less important and is more concerned with the sociological dynamics of the community of experts who make international tax standards, and critical scholarship, which is predominantly the preserve of activist scholars, rather than academic critical political economists.

State-centric perspectives

An 'open economy politics' lens is one way in which we could study the development of the international tax regime.[49] According to Thomas Rixen, one of the leading scholars working in this approach, governments aim to maximise national welfare while maintaining the support of three domestic interest groups: labour, individual capital and corporate capital.[50] In this view, business capital usually possesses the greatest instrumental power because it has a clear and shared preference, and it prefers the alleviation of double taxation.[51] Of course, governments need to raise revenue, and as Lukas Hakelberg demonstrates, they may also be influenced by the nature of their political constituencies, which shapes their incentives to reduce or increase the tax burden on labour, consumption and capital.[52]

The history of the international tax regime to date supports the idea that these interests at domestic level have combined through political institutions to create a strong first-order preference for cooperation between states to eliminate double taxation, by agreeing on a common set of rules for corporate taxation. As a second-order preference, each state also sought to organise cooperation in a manner that left it free to tax as much as possible, imposing greater restrictions on other states' taxing rights. As Rixen and Claudio Radaelli have argued, this created a coordination game in which institutions were needed to help states converge on one of multiple stable equilibria, without any need for a mechanism to enforce their prior commitments.[53] Powerful states could influence the content of cooperation rules to maximise their own gains, but it would still be in the interests of weaker states to participate despite rule content that imposed greater fiscal costs on them. This analysis explained the stability of multilateral rules for a century, as well as the proliferation of bilateral treaties based on the OECD model.[54]

The liberalisation of cross-border capital flows posed a challenge to this regime. On one hand, it exacerbated the problem of double taxation, increasing the need for cooperation, which led to an expansion in the amount of detail in the model treaties and the creation of the transfer pricing standards. On the other hand, it elevated the problem of harmful tax competition, which states found very difficult to resolve. Rixen, writing in the historical institutionalist tradition, argues that states sought to use existing international tax institutions, but were hamstrung by the institutions they had created, which lacked the mechanisms or the credibility to force compliance.[55] The tools of double taxation relief were also biased in favour of OECD members, which increased their incentives to defend them, in spite of their unsuitability.[56] Jason Sharman's explanation for the failure of an OECD initiative to counter harmful tax competition at the turn of the twenty-first century supports this emphasis on path dependence: he argues that the OECD lacked moral authority because of its partial membership, and had a way of working premised on soft power, which was inadequate to the task of forcing tax havens to comply.[57]

Authors in a more realist tradition question the premise that all powerful states have a preference for challenging tax havens.[58] Instead, they suggest that states focus on the impact of international cooperation on domestic industries' competitiveness. Where a country's multinational firms use tax havens to avoid or evade overseas tax, this gives them a competitive advantage that the government may seek to protect in international negotiations. Furthermore, large, developed countries also have finance sectors that themselves benefit from harmful tax competition: the City of London, for example, gains business through its connections with the United Kingdom's overseas territories and crown dependencies;[59] several states within the United States are themselves offshore financial centres. Research examining the use of financial centres by multinational companies suggests that those within or connected to powerful OECD member states are among the most important.[60]

Constructivist perspectives

While taxation is, unlike most areas that we might study in IPE, by definition a function of the state, it does not follow that it must be studied through a state-centric perspective. Tax law history literature on the development of the international tax regime commonly emphasises the expert-led quality of negotiations since their very origins at the League of Nations.[61] Indeed, the preface to one of the early reports from the League of Nations fiscal committee stresses that, 'although the members of the Committee are nominated by their respective Governments, they only speak in their capacity as experts, i.e., in their own name'.[62] One history of an early bilateral tax treaty notes that it was regarded as a 'personal project' of one of its negotiators.[63] Contemporary legal scholarship also emphasises the role of 'an intertwined epistemic community that holds an important and influential position in the law-making order' and which 'served as a driving force in the double taxation problem, both in terms of providing a forum for discussion and providing a base of expertise to structure the debate'.[64] Meanwhile, the offshore tax avoidance industry is built on the actions of a community of wealth managers, engaged in a 'cat and mouse' game with states.[65]

Some IPE scholars have taken this expert-led attribute as an explanation for many of the phenomena described earlier. States' negotiators may have been willing to sign up to tax instruments that exhibit a bias against them because of the difficulties of challenging the received wisdom within a community of experts, or indeed socialisation into that community.[66] The same dynamics may explain the failure of states to eliminate harmful tax competition, insofar as the social community developed in parallel with the double taxation institutions themselves, creating entrenched interests that defended existing institutions even though they were not suited to resolving the harmful tax competition problem.[67] The 'revolving doors' between senior tax roles in the public and private sector also give some support to a sociological corporate capture explanation, and date from the beginning of the international tax regime. The US was represented at the League of Nations by Thomas Adams, who was also an active participant in the work of the US and International Chambers of Commerce. His successor, Mitchell Carroll, also advised multinational firms on their tax affairs.[68]

Literature has also suggested that the designation of tax cooperation as a largely technical domain, combined with the elaboration of increasingly complex concepts and language, have insulated the policymaking process from intervention by political actors including civil society and even politicians. What has changed is that some of those actors have found ways to enter into the same expert discourse,[69] while political leaders have begun to exercise greater influence over previously autonomous technocrats.

Critical perspectives

There is surprisingly little scholarship in a Marxist tradition on global tax governance, perhaps because of Marx's own ambivalent position on the subject: the Communist Manifesto advocated 'very heavy and progressive' taxation, but as a means of destabilising the capitalist system rather than financing the state. Mainstream IPE scholarship, like that in development studies, is implicitly orientated towards the public policy challenge of raising more revenue in a progressive way. Critical IPE scholarship in a Marxist tradition is more sceptical of the state to begin with, so might be more wary of such a normative orientation.

Nonetheless, some of the theoretical lenses deployed by critical IPE scholars provide useful insights on the questions outlined earlier. For example, it is easy to analyse the expansion of the double taxation regime through the lens of imperialist powers seeking new markets for their monopolistic companies. In the early 1950s, Russia and other Communist countries objected to work on double taxation at the United Nations on the grounds that it 'was in reality intended to promote economic conditions favourable to the activities of British and American monopolies' and 'relieve investors from the highly-industrialised capitalist countries of the taxation which those less highly developed countries were entitled to enforce.'[70] Similarly, the strong influence exerted over the policymaking discourse by tax professionals from OECD states, including those explicitly working for multinational companies, seems easy to reconcile with a neogramscian approach to hegemony.

We certainly do find a thriving critical literature among activist scholars working on international tax. Most notably, the Tax Justice Network (TJN), founded by former tax professionals with decades' combined experience in law, economics and accounting in 2003. TJN was able to overcome the expertise gap that had acted as a barrier to civil society engagement, using the global tax community's technical language to enter the space previously dominated by tax professionals in businesses and government.[71] TJN developed alternative forms of knowledge that cast doubt on governments' motivations. Most notably, its Financial Secrecy Index acts as a counterweight to official lists of tax havens, supporting an argument that OECD member states support and enable, rather than oppose, tax avoidance and evasion.[72] Nick Shaxson's book *Treasure Islands* argues that the City of London and the British state played a large part in the emergence of offshore finance and that interdependencies between offshore territories and the UK today are too great for the UK to act as an effective opponent of harmful tax competition.[73]

Conclusion

As in many other areas of IPE scholarship, the global financial crisis has challenged previously uncontested assumptions about the international tax regime.[74] It appears to have created the political conditions – fiscal pressures and popular outrage – for large states to finally overpower small jurisdictions that acted as tax havens, although not to agree solutions that stamp out their own harmful tax practices. The North–South axis of conflict, previously more the preoccupation of legal scholars than IPE, is now becoming more important. While large states can all find a solution based on absolute gains to the problems of tax avoidance and evasion, which enlarge the tax pie, they are less able to deal with the distributional questions about how to divide up that pie, which were troublesome enough among a club of OECD members, before the arrival of the G20 and new institutions such as the Inclusive Framework.

From a constructivist perspective, the financial crisis also resulted in a politicisation of global tax governance. It should not be a great leap to move from literature that conceptualised the international tax regime as stable because it was relatively isolated from political pressures, to explanations of more recent change that depart from the disruption of this technocratic consensus by political actors. Again, it is tempting to focus here on the renewed vigour in the fight against tax havens, but equally interesting is the entry of new countries from outside the OECD into the heart of the policymaking process, which infuses the debate with new ideas and interests.

The process of academic knowledge formation itself has also been changed by these developments. Tax justice activists have, since the crisis (and earlier), shaped the incentives for governments and entered directly into debates in the transnational space. They have also contributed to the empirical research and theory of IPE scholars, developing a critical theory of global tax governance that challenges the motivations of powerful states and questions whether their actions serve the interests of their own citizens. This, in turn, challenges the assumptions embedded in academic scholarship, whether in law, economics or indeed IPE.

Notes

1 Jogarajan 2018.
2 Rixen 2008.
3 Avi-Yonah 2007.
4 Woodward 2009.
5 Sharman 2006.
6 Hearson 2018a.
7 Genschel and Rixen 2015.
8 Graetz and O'Hear 1997: 1025.
9 Picciotto 1992.
10 Hearson 2018b.
11 Dagan 2000.
12 Hearson 2018b.
13 Irish 1974.
14 Avi-Yonah 2007.
15 Hakelberg 2016.
16 Christians 2009: 13.
17 Martin, Mehrotra and Prasad 2009: 14.
18 Hobbes 1994: 184.
19 North 1981: 21.
20 Burke 1955: 105.
21 Palan, Murphy and Chavagneux 2010.
22 Sharman 2006.
23 Palan 2002.
24 Feld and Heckemeyer 2011; Mooij and Ederveen 2008.
25 Kinda 2014; Oman 2000.
26 Tiebout 1956.
27 Clausing 2016; Oates 1972.
28 Genschel and Schwarz 2011; Swank 2016.
29 Keen and Mansour 2009; Klemm and Abass 2012.
30 Basinger and Hallerberg 2004; Plümper, Troeger and Winner 2009.
31 Dietsch 2015.
32 Clausing 2016.
33 OECD 1998.

34 Palan 2002.
35 Sharman 2009.
36 Hakelberg 2016.
37 Crivelli, De Mooij and Keen 2015.
38 UNCTAD 2015
39 OECD 2015.
40 Tørsløv, Wier and Zucman 2018.
41 Henry 2012; Zucman 2015.
42 OECD 2018.
43 ICIJ 2017.
44 Hearson 2016; Wijnen and de Goede 2013.
45 Dietsch 2015.
46 Picciotto 2012.
47 OECD 2014.
48 High-Level Panel on Illicit Financial Flows from Africa 2015.
49 Lake 2009.
50 Rixen 2011.
51 Rixen 2010.
52 Hakelberg 2016.
53 'Game Theory and Institutional Entrepreneurship: Transfer Pricing and the Search for Coordination International Tax Policy'.
54 Chisik and Davies 2004; Hearson 2018c; Rixen 2010; Rixen and Schwarz 2009.
55 Rixen 2011.
56 Genschel and Rixen 2015.
57 Sharman 2006.
58 Hakelberg 2016; Hakelberg and Schaub 2018; Lips 2019.
59 Shaxson 2011.
60 Garcia et al. 2017.
61 Graetz and O'Hear 1997.
62 League of Nations 1927.
63 Evers 2013.
64 Christians 2010: 22; Ring 2006: 148.
65 Harrington 2016.
66 Hearson 2018b.
67 Buttner and Thiemann 2017; Wigan and Baden 2017.
68 Carroll 1978.
69 Picciotto 2015; Seabrooke and Wigan 2016.
70 United Nations 1951.
71 Seabrooke and Wigan 2016.
72 Cobham, Janský and Meinzer 2015.
73 Shaxson 2011.
74 Christensen and Hearson 2019.

Bibliography

Avi-Yonah, R. 2007. *International Tax as International Law*. New York: Cambridge University Press.

Basinger, S. and Hallerberg, M. 2004. Remodeling the Competition for Capital: How Domestic Politics Erases the Race to the Bottom. *American Political Science Review* 98, no. 2: 261–276.

Burke, E. 1955. *Reflections on the French Revolution*. London: Dent.

Buttner, T. and Thiemann, M. 2017. Breaking Regime Stability? The Politicization of Expertise in the OECD G20 Process on BEPS and the Potential Transformation of International Taxation. *Accounting, Economics, and Law: A Convivium* 7, no. 1: 1–16.

Carroll, M. 1978. *Global Perspectives of an International Tax Lawyer*. Hicksville: Exposition Press.

Chisik, R. and Davies, R. 2004. Asymmetric FDI and Tax-Treaty Bargaining: Theory and Evidence. *Journal of Public Economics* 88, no. 6: 1119–1148.

Christensen, R. C. and Hearson, M. 2019. The New Politics of Global Tax Governance: Taking Stock a Decade after the Financial Crisis. *Review of International Political Economy*, 26, no. 5: 1068–1088.

Christians, A. 2009. Sovereignty, Taxation and Social Contract. *Minnesota Journal of International Law* 18, no. 1: 99–153.

Christians, A. 2010. Networks, Norms and National Tax Policy. *Washington University Global Studies Law Review* 1: 0–38.

Clausing, K. 2016. The Nature and Practice of Tax Competition. In: *Global Tax Governance: What Is Wrong with It and How to Fix It*: 27–54. Colchester: ECPR Press.

Cobham, A., Janskỳ, P. and Meinzer, M. 2015. The Financial Secrecy Index: Shedding New Light on the Geography of Secrecy. *Economic Geography* 91, no. 3: 281–303.

Crivelli, E., De Mooij, R. and Keen, M. 2015. Base Erosion, Profit Shifting and Developing Countries. *IMF Working Papers*. Washington, DC: International Monetary Fund.

Dagan, T. 2000. The Tax Treaties Myth. *New York University Journal of International Law and Politics* 32: 939–939.

Dietsch, P. 2015. *Catching Capital: The Ethics of Tax Competition*. New York: Oxford University Press.

Evers, M. 2013. Tracing the Origins of the Netherlands Tax Treaty. *Intertax* 41, no. 6: 375–386.

Feld, L. and Heckemeyer, J. 2011. FDI and Taxation: A Meta-Study. *Journal of Economic Surveys* 25, no. 2: 233–72.

Garcia, J., Fichtner, J., Heemskerk, E. and Takes, F. 2017. Uncovering Offshore Financial Centers: Conduits and Sinks in the Global Corporate Ownership Network. *Scientific Reports* 7: 1–18.

Genschel, P. and Rixen, T. 2015. Settling and Unsettling the Transnational Legal Order of International Taxation. In: *Transnational Legal Orders*. Halliday, T. and Shaffer, G. (eds.). New York: Cambridge University Press.

Genschel, P. and Schwarz, P. 2011. Tax Competition: A Literature Review. *Socio-Economic Review* 9, no. 2: 339–370.

Graetz, M, and O'Hear, M. 1997. The 'Original Intent' of U.S. International Taxation. *Duke Law Journal* 46, no. 5: 1020–1109.

Hakelberg, L. 2016. Coercion in International Tax Cooperation: Identifying the Prerequisites for Sanction Threats by a Great Power. *Review of International Political Economy* 23, no. 3: 511–541.

Hakelberg, L. and Schaub, M. 2018. The Redistributive Impact of Hypocrisy in International Taxation: Hypocrisy and Redistribution. *Regulation & Governance* 12, no. 3: 353–370.

Harrington, B. 2016. *Capital without Borders: Wealth Managers and the One Percent*. Cambridge, MA: Harvard University Press.

Hearson, M. 2016. *Measuring Tax Treaty Negotiation Outcomes: The ActionAid Tax Treaties Dataset*. Brighton: Institute of Development Studies.

Hearson, M. 2018a. The Challenges for Developing Countries in International Tax Justice. *The Journal of Development Studies* 54, no. 10: 1932–1938.

Hearson, M. 2018b. Transnational Expertise and the Expansion of the International Tax Regime: Imposing 'Acceptable' Standards. *Review of International Political Economy* 25, no. 5: 647–671.

Hearson, M. 2018c. When Do Developing Countries Negotiate Away Their Corporate Tax Base? *Journal of International Development* 30, no. 2: 233–235.

Henry, J. 2012. *The Price of Offshore*. Available at: http://taxjustice.blogspot.ch/2012/07/the-price-of-offshore-revisited-and.html.

High-Level Panel on Illicit Financial Flows from Africa. 2015. *Illicit Financial Flows*. Addis Ababa: United Nations Economic Commission for Africa. Available at: www.uneca.org/sites/default/files/Publication Files/iff_main_report_26feb_en.pdf.

Hobbes, T. 1994. *Leviathan: With Selected Variants from the Latin Edition 1668*. Curley, E. (ed.). Indianapolis: Hackett Publishing.

ICIJ. 2017. More than $500 Million Recovered by Tax Authorities Worldwide Following the Panama Papers. *ICIJ*. Available at: www.icij.org/blog/2017/12/500-million-recovered-tax-authorities-worldwide-following-panama-papers/.

Irish, C. 1974. International Double Taxation Agreements and Income Taxation at Source. *International and Comparative Law Quarterly* 23, no. 2: 292–316.

Jogarajan, S. 2018. *Double Taxation and the League of Nations*. Cambridge: Cambridge University Press.

Keen, M. and Mansour, M. 2009. Revenue Mobilization in Sub-Saharan Africa: Challenges from Globalization. Vol. 9/157. *Working Paper*. Washington, DC: International Monetary Fund (IMF).

Kinda, T. 2014. The Quest for Non-Resource-Based FDI: Do Taxes Matter? *Working Paper 14/15*. Washington, DC: International Monetary Fund.

Klemm, A. and Abass, S. 2012. A Partial Race to the Bottom: Corporate Tax Developments in Emerging and Developing Economies. *Working Paper 12/28*. Washington, DC.

Lake, D. 2009. Open Economy Politics: A Critical Review. *The Review of International Organizations* 4, no. 3: 219–244.

League of Nations. 1927. *Report of the Committee of Technical Experts on Double Taxation and Tax Evasion.* Geneva: League of Nations.

Lips, W. 2019. Great Powers in Global Tax Governance: A Comparison of the US Role in the CRS and BEPS. *Globalizations* 16, no. 1: 104–19.

Martin, I., Mehrotra, A. and Prasad, M. 2009. The Thunder of History: The Origins and Development of the New Fiscal Sociology. In: *The New Fiscal Sociology.* Martin, I. W., Mehrotra, A. and Prasad, M. (eds.): 1–28. Cambridge: Cambridge University Press.

Mooij, R. and Ederveen, S. 2008. Corporate Tax Elasticities: A Reader's Guide to Empirical Findings. *Oxford Review of Economic Policy* 24, no. 4: 680–697.

North, D. 1981. *Structure and Change in Economic History.* New York: W. W. Norton.

Oates, W. 1972. *Fiscal Federalism.* New York: Harcourt Brace Jovanovich.

OECD. 1998. *Harmful Tax Competition: An Emerging Global Issue.* Paris: OECD. Available at: www.oecd.org/tax/transparency/44430243.pdf.

OECD. 2014. *Report to G20 Development Working Group on the Impact of BEPS in Low Income Countries (Parts 1 and 2).* Paris: OECD Publishing. Available at: www.g20.org/.

OECD. 2015. Measuring and Monitoring BEPS, Action 11–2015 Final Report. *OECD/G20 Base Erosion and Profit Shifting Project.* Paris: OECD Publishing. Available at: https://doi.org/10.1787/97892642 41343-en.

OECD. 2018. *OECD Secretary-General Report to G20 Finance Ministers and Central Bank Governors.* Paris: OECD Publishing.

Oman, C. 2000. *Policy Competition for Foreign Direct Investment: A Study of Competition among Governments to Attract FDI.* Paris: OECD Publishing.

Palan, R. 2002. Tax Havens and the Commercialization of State Sovereignty. *International Organization* 56, no. 1: 151–176.

Palan, R., Murphy, R. and Chavagneux, C. 2010. *Tax Havens: How Globalization Really Works.* Ithaca: Cornell University Press.

Picciotto, S. 1992. *International Business Taxation: A Study in the Internationalization of Business Regulation.* London: Weidenfeld & Nicolson.

Picciotto, S. 2012. *Towards Unitary Taxation of Transnational Corporations.* Available at: www.taxjustice.net/cms/upload/pdf/Towards_Unitary_Taxation_1-1.pdf.

Picciotto, S. 2015. Indeterminacy, Complexity, Technocracy and the Reform of International Corporate Taxation. *Social & Legal Studies* 24, no. 2: 165–84.

Plümper, T., Troeger, V. and Winner, H. 2009. Why Is There No Race to the Bottom in Capital Taxation? *International Studies Quarterly* 53, no. 3: 761–86.

Ring, D. 2006. International Tax Relations: Theory and Implications. *New York University Tax Law Review* 60: 83–154. NYU.

Rixen, T. 2008. *The Political Economy of International Tax Governance.* New York: Palgrave Macmillan.

Rixen, T. 2010. Bilateralism or Multilateralism? The Political Economy of Avoiding International Double Taxation. *European Journal of International Relations* 16, no. 4: 589–614.

Rixen, T. 2011. From Double Tax Avoidance to Tax Competition: Explaining the Institutional Trajectory of International Tax Governance. *Review of International Political Economy* 18, no. 2: 197–227.

Rixen, T. and Schwarz, P. 2009. Bargaining over the Avoidance of Double Taxation: Evidence from German Tax Treaties. *FinanzArchiv: Public Finance Analysis* 65, no. 4: 442–471.

Seabrooke, L. and Wigan, D. 2016. Powering Ideas through Expertise: Professionals in Global Tax Battles. *Journal of European Public Policy* 23, no. 3: 357–374.

Sharman, J. 2006. *Havens in a Storm: The Global Struggle for Tax Regulation.* Ithaca: Cornell University Press.

Sharman, J. 2009. The Bark is the Bite: International Organizations and Blacklisting. *Review of International Political Economy* 16, no. 4: 573.

Shaxson, N. 2011. *Treasure Islands: Uncovering the Damage of Offshore Banking and Tax Havens.* New York: St. Martin's Press.

Swank, D. 2016. The New Political Economy of Taxation in the Developing World. *Review of International Political Economy* 23, no. 2: 185–207.

Tiebout, C. 1956. A Pure Theory of Local Expenditures. *The Journal of Political Economy* 64, no. 5: 416–424.

Tørsløv, T., Wier, L. and Zucman, G. 2018. *The Missing Profits of Nations*. Cambridge, MA: National Bureau of Economic Research.

UNCTAD. 2015. International Tax and Investment Policy Coherence. In: *World Investment Report 2015*: 175–218. Geneva: United Nations Conference on Trade and Development.

United Nations. 1951. *Economic Committee: Summary Record of the One Hundred and Sixteenth Meeting*. IR40/9959. The National Archives, London. p7.

Wigan, D. and Baden, A. 2017. Professional Activists on Tax Transparency. In: *Professional Networks in Transnational Governance*. Seabrooke, L. and Folke, L. (eds.): 130–146. Cambridge: Cambridge University Press.

Wijnen, W. and De Goede, J. 2013. *The UN Model in Practice 1997–2013*. Amsterdam: International Bureau of Fiscal Documentation. Available at: www.un.org/esa/ffd/tax/ninthsession/CRP18_UN Model.pdf.

Woodward, R. 2009. *The Organisation for Economic Cooperation and Development*. London: Routledge.

Zucman, G. 2015. *The Hidden Wealth of Nations: The Scourge of Tax Havens*. Chicago: University Of Chicago Press.

40

The political economy of new technology – especially with an eye to the labour market

Bent Greve

Introduction

During the course of history, new technologies have always had an impact on people's life, and, also on, which is the central issue here: people's jobs. Jobs both in relation to the number and quality hereof. Technology is and has been an important driver for changes and development in societies, this also in such a way that there has been winners and losers of the changes, which can influence the social cohesion. The impact is not only on the labour market, but as this chapter will show might also have strong repercussions on the modern state form, the welfare states.

The chapter attempts to present an overview of the core theoretical arguments for change as a consequence of the development of new technologies such as artificial intelligence, robots and IT in a broader understanding. The chapter will proceed by looking into and presenting some of the existing studies pointing to changes in the number of jobs and job functions that might be done by use of new technology with a split between routine and non-routine jobs. This includes a short presentation of how these calculations has been done (such as Frey and Osborne 2013; Nedelkoska and Quintini 2018; PCW 2017; 2018a).

The presentation will be supplemented with some methodological considerations on how and if it is possible to estimate the possible change in the number of jobs, which jobs are most in danger and if it, at all, is possible to indicate something about the new types of jobs. Hereafter the focus will be on theoretical understanding of changes in the labour market including how to use classical theories of changes (dualization, insider/outsider) to understand what will happen and what division in societies this might lead to (Greve 2018; Rueda 2014; Yoon and Chung 2016).

The focus then moves to how welfare states differ, mainly in their approach to the labour market policy, including generosity of benefits, as the role of the welfare state might be even more important as a way of having economic stabilizers and ensuring at least some buying power for those at the margin of the labour market. The welfare state is thus expected to have a role, and, this might naturally be different in various types of welfare states.

Based on this, the next section will discuss choice and possible interventions if the aim is to ensure a set of options of choice for individuals and reducing the risk of strongly polarized societies. There will always be at least some delimitations in a chapter. Use of existing studies of expected changes will mainly focus on developed countries, even though new technology will also influence developing countries. Changes in, for example, size of outsourcing due to new technology is outside the scope of the chapter. The studies used will also mainly be those that have an international comparative approach and, thus, many national studies on the specific impact of changes on individual countries is not included. Quality of work is also only a more limited part of the chapter, this albeit despite the fact that new technology has been part of the ability to make working life more comfortable by reducing the most dangerous types of jobs with higher risks of accidents (see instead Bussemer, Krell and Meyer 2016; Gallie 2013; 2017). Given that there is no agreement on the speed of changes, the chapter cannot be precise in the timing of possible necessary changes, but the main part of the studies focus on the next 10–15 years, implying that the timeframe for the changes will be around 2025–2030.

Delete or expand news jobs?

This section will deal with what we know about the possible impact of new technology on the labour markets. Will it create or destroy jobs? Even if it both creates and destroys jobs what is then the overall outcome of the expected development? Are we at all able to make a solid forecast of the development in the number of jobs in the future? The section will first paint a short historical picture of the development, and then present some of the estimates of expected change in the number of jobs.

Gutenberg's printers, who could produce 180 Bibles in the time it took one person to produce 1 Bible, is probably the first historical example (MacGregor 2016). Historically, there has been major concern among employees about the consequences for the individual in terms of unemployment and the number of jobs when new technology were introduced (Mokyr and Vikers 2015). There are different names for the development, including The Second Machine Age (Brynjolfsson and McAfee 2014). This, or as labelled the Fourth Industrial Revolution (Schwab 2016), is in itself not a new phenomenon but a continuation of previous development. However, one argument is that this time the changes are more dramatic as artificial intelligence, robots and the use of algorisms to an even larger degree than earlier can replace workers. Fusion of technologies across physical, digital and biological domains are also new options. Part of the issue of how fast the development will be is that, even if technologies are available, then they shall first need to be implemented and, further, it is difficult to know which types of jobs and how many might be created.

Table 40.1 presents the possible changes of jobs in the digital economy.

Table 40.1 clearly indicates that manual jobs and jobs that have some kind of repetition will be those most in danger, whereas jobs with a human relationship as part of the job is less in danger. This follows the now historical interpretation of what types of jobs are at risk, by looking into routine and non-routine jobs. This split between routine and not-routine jobs, which is shown in Table 40.2, can then be linked to jobs that are analytical and interactive, or jobs involving manual tasks, thereby also indicating the possible risk of automization in the years to come.

The interesting issue is, what are routine jobs and/or jobs that can be split into routine elements? Splitting up jobs has increased the implication that more jobs are now at risk of being automated. It is this division between jobs that are affected as they can be automated and jobs not or only more limited, which in fact has been the central methodological approach influencing calculation of share of jobs in danger of being obsolete, for the now classical analysis (see Frey and Osborne 2013).

Studies are different, and the details used to calculate and analyse changes have varied. The assessment of how many jobs are at risk and which can be automated may depend on whether an

Table 40.1 Jobs in the digital economy

Jobs at greatest risk of automation/digitalization	Jobs at least risk of automation/digitalization	New jobs
Office work and clerical tasks	Education, arts and media	'Top of the scale'
• Sales and commerce • Transport, logistics • Manufacturing industry • Construction • Some aspects of financial services • Some types of services (translation, tax consultancy, etc.)	• Legal services • Management, human resources management • Business • Some aspects of financial services • Health service providers • Some types of services (social work, hairdressing, beauty care, etc.)	• Data analysts, data miners, data architects • Software and application developers • Specialists in networking, artificial intelligence, etc. • Designers and producers of new intelligent machines, robots and 3D printers • Digital marketing and e-commerce specialists • 'Bottom of the scale' • Digital 'galley slaves' (data entry or filter workers) and other 'mechanical Turks' working on the digital platforms (see below) • Uber drivers, casual odd-jobbing (repairs, home improvement, pet care, etc.) in the 'collaborative' industry

Source: Christophe Degryse (ETUI 2016) on the basis of data from Frey and Osborne, Ford, Valsamis, Irani, Head, Babinet (Available at: www.etui.org/Publications2/Working-Papers/Digitalisation-of-the-economy-and-its-impact-on-labour-markets).

Table 40.2 Risk of automization dependent on type of job

	Routine work	Non-routine work
Analytical and interactive task	Substantial substitution	Strong complementarities
Manual task	Substantial substitution	Limited opportunities for substitution or complementarity

Source: (Autor, Levy and Murnane 2003: 1286).

emphasis is placed on an approach based on tasks or on the types of jobs. If emphasis is placed on competences measured at the educational attainment level, this might give one result; however a different result may be gained from looking into details of different types of jobs. In addition, the uncertainty about the calculations is caused by whether companies actually incorporate new technology and at what speed they actually do, as this might be different from country to country depending on, among other things, the local wage level. It is uncertain how many new jobs, such as those depicted in Table 40.1, will be created and what types of jobs can and will be created in a world where the speed at which IT can take over job functions is growing. Measuring and defining skills might thus influence the result (Chlon-Dominczak and Zurawskik 2017).

Over time, many and varied studies have used different approaches. A recent study shows that 'one additional robot per thousand workers reduces the employment rate by 0.16–0.20

percentage points' (Chiacchio, Petropoulos and Pichler 2018: 1). The rise in the number of robots performing job tasks already and that, gradually, they will become better and able to do even more things than before, and things that are not expected, such as driving cars, is a strong indication that many jobs are at risk of being wiped away in the next 10–15 years.

In addition, the analyses focus on whether it is parts of different jobs or entire jobs that can and will be automated. Regardless of the choice of method, any projection will be at risk of under- or overestimating the consequences of new technology on the labour market. Methodological issues in measuring includes if and when implementation of technology takes place and, further, which new types of jobs will there be, as this will be difficult to predict. Therefore even those jobs presented in Table 40.1 might not actually be the types of roles that will exist 2030.

One of the first studies to examine changes in the labour market argued that 140 million full-time knowledge workers and half of the jobs in the US, and one-third in the UK, as we known in an earlys study are at risk (Frey and Osborne 2013). For Europe, a 2014 study concluded that 54 per cent of jobs at risk.[1]

Ongoing discussions are taking place regarding whether to look into jobs at risk of automation or tasks within a job role that could be automated (Pieterson 2018). Thus, it has been argued that, when looking at the varieties of task within a specific job, automation of jobs in the US will be reduced from 38 per cent to 9 per cent (Arntz, Gregory and Zierahn 2017). However, another study pointed out that 50 per cent of hours could be automated, with differences across countries (McKinsey & Company 2017). Therefore, even if only some tasks can be automated, this may have overall consequences for the number of jobs and, those where part of their task can be automated might do more of the types of jobs that cannot be, implying a reduction in the number of people needed to work in these specific areas.

Figure 40.1 shows the possible extent of automation on jobs, split into jobs at high risk of automation and those at risk of significant change.

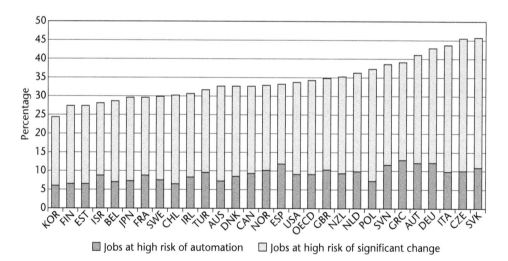

Figure 40.1   The risk of automation in OECD countries

Source: OECD 2017. Available at: www-oecd-ilibrary-org.ep.fjernadgang.kb.dk/docserver/empl_outlook-2017-en.pdf?expires=1528098709&id=id&accname=ocid195427&checksum=79E8A536A5871DF48CA5E79A45CADF3C, Figure 3.10.

Note
Reference: OECD 2017. *Employment Outlook.* Paris, OECD.

Figure 40.1 shows a variation from below 25 per cent (Korea) to more than 45 per cent in Slovakia. Part of the reason for the differences is how far the countries have already automated their production, but the difference can also be explained by changes towards service. The same kinds of results can be found in different estimates, albeit naturally with some variation in size. Another study confirms that, especially within Eastern Europe, in early 2030 the potential job loss is over 40 per cent compared to 20–25 per cent in East Asian and Nordic countries (PWC 2018). This is based upon knowledge of the use of qualification in different jobs today. Further-more, the study tries to estimate the impact based upon the expected implementation of algo-rithm, augmentation and autonomy waves. Overall, it is it especially manufacturing and trade that is at risk, whereas the pressure is lower in human health, social work and education. Different kinds of services might be at risk of being automated, including transport.

Studies sometimes differentiate between risk and high risk, and one study indicates that up to 30 per cent of jobs in the UK, 38 per cent in the US, 35 per cent in Germany and 21 per cent in Japan are at high risk of being wiped away (PWC 2017). Overall, there is knowledge that there will be a considerable loss of jobs. There will presumably also be new job opportun-ities in the coming years. Uncertainty relates, in particular, to the expectations for the creation of new types of jobs, as well as what time horizon there is for the change. However, there is no doubt that many jobs will change over the coming years, and with significant risk that people without education will have more difficulties in entering or staying in the labour market.

Theoretical understanding of changes in the labour market

Two theoretical concepts are central for an understanding of the consequence of changes in the labour market as a consequence of new technology: dualization (Greve 2016; Yoon and Chung 2016) and insider/outsider (Doeringer and Piore 1971). These concepts help in analysing and explaining the impact on developed societies. This includes risk of increase in inequality as, for example, increased dualization can have strong impact. This means that some individuals have stable jobs in high-income areas, whereas others work in low-income roles and are also often less secure in their job, if they have a job at all. These changes are also influenced by new types of work as the use of technology, such as working through platforms, implying that there also will be changes in employment structure (Valenduc and Vendramin 2016).

The insider/outsider issue is partly about whose interest is taken care of, on the under-standing that the position of outsiders is not represented in decision making and/or collective agreements on the labour market. This would, presumably, be a simplistic position to take, as it also includes a division between people included and excluded socially, especially given that for those of working age, having a job is important for social esteem. However, the point is that those who are outsiders will often have more precarious jobs and a lower income than insiders with stable and well-paid jobs.

Box 40.1 Insider/outsider and dualization

Insider/outsider theory refers to the fact that some workers have a high degree of security and often high-quality jobs with stable income, whereas outsiders have a high degree of insecurity, and are often in low-quality jobs with an unstable income.

Dualization refers to the fact that there are still low- and high-income jobs, whereas jobs with middle income are declining.

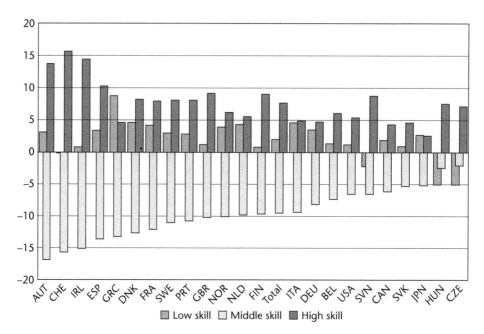

Figure 40.2 Polarization in OECD labour markets 1995–2015. Change in percentage point change in share of total employment, 1995 to 2015

Source: OECD 2017. Polarization in OECD labour markets 1995–2015: 121 Available at: www-oecd-ilibrary-org.ep.fjernadgang.kb.dk/docserver/empl_outlook-2017-en.pdf?expires=1528098709&id=id&accname=ocid195427&checksum=79E8A536A5871DF48CA5E79A45CADF3C DOI: http://dx.doi.org/10.1787/88893 3477957.

Note
OECD 2017. *Employment Outlook.* Paris, OECD.

These role may not the be the be same type of jobs that are always insider jobs. With the shift from classical production to more service-oriented production, for example, there has also been a move towards more non-standard employment, as this is more prevalent in the service sector; however, there might now also be an increase in those types of non-standard jobs in some high-skills services areas (Eichorst and Marx 2015). Thus, the risk of being an outsider increases in the years to come as a result of the fact that the number of stable jobs with high job-security will be reduced, and the level of skills is no longer necessarily the only factor related to type and security of jobs for those already in the labour market. However, there still seems to be a bias towards a higher risk for the unskilled, cf. also the already lower participation rate and continuous high unemployment rate of people with no or low educational qualifications in most countries. It can be argued that this can be a problem with non-standard work due to the fact that it already makes up one-third of all employment in the Organization for Economic Cooperation and Development (OECD) area and half the employment growth since 1990, and that the fact that it contributes to job-polarization and non-standard jobs is 'not always a stepping stone to stable employment' (OECD 2015: 37), and lastly, that there are lower wages, less training and, in general, less job quality.

In modern production, flexibility might even be more of a way of securing a limited number of people in stable jobs, where the flexibility to hire and fire will imply a growing number of outsiders. This could be achieved through the splitting of work into many and very small pieces, which can be performed by outsiders (Rueda 2014). The ability to split jobs into many small elements by the use of new technology is thus in itself a challenge for the labour markets, which one can expect to increase in the years to come.

Historically, dualization has revolved around the fact that there will be fewer jobs in the middle and more high-skilled and unskilled jobs (Goos, Manning and Salomons 2014; Rutledge and Guan 2015). It has also been seen as difficult to move from one kind of job to another, as historically depicted by Lindbeck and Snower (1988). This will presumably continue, although one of the issues is that more high-skilled jobs are under pressure, such as oncologists using IBM-s Watson, and law firms using computers to scan documents and computerized speech (Chelliah 2017). A possible exception for this trend might be personal care workers (Nedelkoska and Quintini 2018). That there has been polarization is shown in Figure 40.2.

There are also varieties between countries, but at the same time a strong tendency towards this partly reflects the downturn in manufacturing and agriculture alongside the rise in the service economy. In the US there has, at the same time, been a strong decline in employment in middle-skilled occupations (Cortes, Jaimovich and Siu 2017). That there has been dualization in the labour market seems obvious, but there also seems to be a trend, which has been labelled future insecure (Yoon and Chung 2016), that those who are not only insecure in the labour market also have a high risk of low income. This is partly due to involuntary part-time work and lack of benefits such as pension savings and social security in general.

A short note on welfare states, labour market policy and new technology

The core reason to have a section on welfare states is that, often, the main responsibility for supporting people who lose their job, both economically and in supporting them in getting back into the labour market, falls on the state. This means that, as pointed out in the debate on new social risk, lack of qualifications (low or obsolete) can be considered as one of the new social risks (Bonoli 2005). This type of intervention and size of risk, as discussed above, varies considerably across countries, as does the more specific emphasis on the type of active labour market policy to pursue (Bonoli 2010), which further can and presumably will change over time, and might even diffuse between countries. Welfare states are often clustered into a number of regimes following the path laid by Esping-Andersen (see Greve 2019).

Thus, at the outset, one could expect that the more generous welfare states, such as the Nordic ones, would, if the transition of the labour market becomes stronger and more persistent over a longer time spell, have more difficulties in coping with these transitions than liberal welfare states with less generous approaches, with the continental welfare states somewhere in between. There are naturally strong variations among countries and changes in the welfare systems are not the only consequence of decisions taken related to and given the pressure from changes in the labour market, even though this will have implications given that jobs seem to be high on the agenda in many countries. This is both due to the fact that people in jobs do not need, to the same degree as those who are the outsiders, support from the welfare state, but is also due to the fact that in most countries having a job is important for happiness (Council 2018; Ejrnaes and Greve 2017; Greve 2012). The consequence of changes in the labour market might thus not only influence the ability to finance the welfare states, but also the ability to get electoral support, as those losing their jobs (income and esteem as well) might prefer to vote for some who promise jobs and seem to have answers on how to create them (Diener et al. 2016).

A further problem for welfare states' development is that, not only will financing be difficult and that there will be jobs lost, but also the work in the platform economy, sometimes labelled the gig economy, will imply a more precarious work situation for many (see for example Hill 2015). A reason why this is a problem is that these roles have been on the rise (Evans and Gawer

2016), and this is expected to continue in the years to come. Those working in these environments will often have fewer rights, especially in countries where access to social security relies on having a job, and have less opportunity for a good family life (Böhnke and Cifuentes 2017). Böhnke and Cifuentes also point out that 'a high level of social security tends to weaken the influence of employment patterns on family satisfaction' (2017: 404). The platform economy raises issues on how industrial relations can function (Kilhoffer, Lenaerts and Beblavy 2017), and also, as a consequence of that, work is fragmented, provided by individual workers, facilitated by a platform and workers are seen as individual contractors (Minter 2017). In most welfare states the self-employed are not covered by welfare benefits. Those working on platforms further seem to be under-employed (Codagnone, Abadie and Biagi 2016). The volatility of income when trying to earn on the platform might also, in societies with less strong social security nets, imply fewer automatic stabilizers from the public-sector economy. Part of this also reflects that workers on the platforms can come from all around the world, using a global workforce (Pearson 2015).

The ability to finance welfare states also depends on the growth in the economies, so if new technology includes economic growth (McKinsey & Company 2017), then the issue is how the welfare states get their share of the economic development, as redistribution of the productivity gain might raise the well-being of all citizens (Sachs, Benzell and LaGarda 2015). Naturally, economic development does in itself not fully inform on the well-being of individuals (Greve 2017a).

Choice and options related to new technology

There are, as always, options available for societies, and and thus there is not only what has sometimes been labelled 'the necessary politics'. This section will briefly discuss two issues related to new technology. One being education, the other the issue of how to ensure financing of welfare states in the wake of new platforms and the use of new technology in the production of goods and services. The possible impact of changes in jobs do in many ways for developed countries resembles those in the wake of globalization, as this has implied they have had to adjust cost and have developed more split societies. This is because: 'Displacement destroys industry-specific human capital, leaving affected workers in positions for which they are poorly suited relative to nondisplaced workers' (Autor, Dorn and Hanson 2016: 232). This also implies the risk of regional divide in countries, depending on which regions are most affected by the changes.

A risk of automation is the reduction in the ability to get sufficient funds to pay for the welfare states, including income to those made redundant by new technology. There is also the risk of 'winner takes it all' by use of robots, and, therefore, it has been discussed whether one should tax robots (Guerreiro, Rebelo and Teles, n.d). The fact that, in order to continue with development with a high level of productivity, robots might be needed, needs to be balanced with how to ensure sufficient public-sector revenue. Even if robots in themselves are not taxed, it might be that companies need to be taxed in such a way that welfare states still have a reliable and stable income to finance their activities. This might be through tax on turnover, but also by international agreement on where the taxes will have to be paid, even by activities taking place on platforms.

Use of a variety of finance instruments might thus be important in order to be able to pay for welfare in the future. Moreover, for companies, even if they have to pay tax, if they are not able to get the qualified workforce this will reduce their options, and also, if those not in the labour market do not have any income to spend, then the companies will not, even at low prices, be able to sell their goods and services. Thus, a policy that helps to ensure at least a minimum living standard will also imply demand for goods and services. Given that there will always be economic up- and down-turns, then a welfare state with more can help reduce these changes in the overall economic activity with automatic stabilizers.

It could also be that there is a need for ensuring some social protection and health-safety measures, including a minimum wage, for those on the margin of the labour market as a consequence of new technology (Codagnone, Abadie and Biagi 2016). Additionally, a stronger focus has been placed on active labour market policy (ALMP), and especially up-skilling, which has not been historically strong in many countries, with the Nordic states being an exception (Bonoli 2010). Skill mismatch is further seen as lower in the Nordic welfare states, which among other things, has strong participation in lifelong learning (Chlon-Dominczak and Zurawskik 2017).

Concluding remarks

There is no doubt that technology will strongly influence labour markets around the globe. Jobs will be lost and many will have to find new types of jobs, if they can find one at all. There will be a possible dark side and a possible bright side (Greve 2017b). As it is, it is not possible to be very precise about the future development of the labour market (just look back at the last financial crisis) and this makes discussion on the future situation very difficult. However, whether it will be the dark side with the loss of many jobs without many new ones being created, or whether it will be the bright side, with as many new jobs created as destroyed, does not change the fact that many people will be affected. The implication here is that there will at least be a transition time where old qualifications will become redundant and some who have had their jobs, even for many years, will presumably not be employable. Therefore, dualization in the labour market has a high risk of increasing in the years to come, and there is also a possible stronger division between insiders and outsiders in the labour market.

It will be a global change as part of the new technology that will imply that humans need not apply, with the understanding that, even if they offer their work for very low wages, they will not get the job (Kaplan 2015). Thus, it is not only in the developed world that new technology will have a strong impact, but also, presumably, on a wider scale. Thus, there will be a need for welfare state intervention in order to help those people back into the labour market and/or provide them with an income so that they can have a reasonable living standard. If not, this will imply an increasing divide in societies with more people outside the core of society with a risk of stronger division, increasing the risk of more unstable societies.

Accordingly, welfare states will need to make decisions related to how and to what extent they will try to modify the play of market forces, as was also what one of the historical definitions of what welfare states are pointed to (Briggs 1961). Technology can imply better working conditions and economic development, but it can also create disturbances and changes that strongly influence our life. Still, there are options available related to using education (including lifelong learning), labour market and social security policy, that might help in reconciling change so that societies will not be even more unequal than they are today.

Notes

1 See http://bruegel.org/2014/07/chart-of-the-week-54-of-eu-jobs-at-risk-of-computerisation/, accessed 4 July 2018.

Bibliography

Arntz, M., Gregory, T. and Zierahn, U. 2017. Revisiting the Risk of Automation. *Economics Letters*, 159: 157–160.

Autor, D. Dorn, D. and Hanson, G. 2016. The China Shock: Learning from Labor-Market Adjustment to Large Changes in Trade. *Annual Review of Economics*, 8: 205–240.

Autor, D., Levy, F. and Murnane, R. 2003. The Skill Content of Recent Technological Change: An Empirical Exploration. *The Quarterly Journal of Economics*, 118(4): 1279–1333.

Böhnke, P. and Cifuentes, I. 2017. Employment Patterns and Family Satisfaction in Europe. Do Welfare and Labour Market Policies Intervene? *International Journal of Sociology and Social Policy*, 38(5/6): 394–410.

Bonoli, G. 2005. The Politics of New Social Policies: Providing Coverage against New Social Risks in Mature Welfare States. *Policy and Politics*, 33(3): 431–449.

Bonoli, G. 2010. The Political Economy of Active Labor-Market Policy. *Politics & Society*, 38(4): 435–457.

Briggs, A. 1961. The Welfare State in Historical Perspective. *Archives Européenes de Sociologie*, 2(2): 221–259.

Brynjolfsson, E. and McAfee, A. 2014. *The Second Machine Age. Work, Progress, and Prosperity in a Time of Brilliant Technologies*. London: W. W. Norton & Company.

Bussemer, T., Krell, C. and Meyer, H. 2016. *Social Democratic Values in the Digital Society. Challenges of the Fourth Industrial Revolution*. Available at: www.socialeurope.eu/book/op-10-social-democratic-values-in-the-digital-society.

Chelliah, J. 2017. Will Artificial Intelligence Usurp White Collar Jobs? *Human Resource Management International Digest*, 25(3): 1–3.

Chiacchio, F., Petropoulos, G. and Pichler, D. 2018. *The Impact of Industrial Robots on EU Employment and Wages: A Local Labour Market Approach*, (No. 2018/02). Bruegel working paper.

Chlon-Dominczak, A. and Zurawskik, A. 2017. *Measuring Skills Mismatches Revisited – Introducing Sectoral Approach*. IBS Working Paper 03/2017.

Codagnone, C., Abadie, F. and Biagi, F. 2016. *The Future of Work in the 'Sharing Economy. Market efficiency and Equitable Opportunities or Unfair Precarisation?* Brussels: Institute for Prospective Technological Studies, Science for Policy Report by the Joint Research Centre.

Cortes, G., Jaimovich, N. and Siu, H. 2017. Disappearing Routine Jobs: Who, How, and Why? *Journal of Monetary Economics*, 91: 69–87.

Council, T. 2018. *Global Happiness Policy Report 2018*. New York: Sustainable Development Solutions Network.

Diener, E. Heintzelman, S. J., Kushlev, K., Tay, L., Wirtz, D., Lutes, L. D. and Oishi, S. 2016. Findings All Psychologist Should Know From the New Science on Subjective Well-Being. *Canadian Psychology*, 58(2): 87–104.

Doeringer, P. and Piore, M. 1971. *Internal Labor Markets and Manpower Analysis*. Lexington: Health Lexington.

Eichorst, W. and Marx, P. (eds) 2015. *Non-standard Employment in Post-Industrial Labour Markets. An Occupational Perspective*. Cheltenham: Edward Elgar.

Ejrnaes, A. and Greve, B. 2017. Your Position in Society Matters For How Happy You Are. *International Journal of Social Welfare*, 26(3): 206–217.

Evans, P. and Gawer, A. 2016. The Rise of the Platform Enterprise. *The Emerging Platform Economy Series No. 1*. New York.

Frey, C. and Osborne, M. 2013. *The Future of Employment: How Susceptible are Jobs to Computerisation?* Oxford: Oxford University Press. Available at: http://enliza.es.

Gallie, D. 2013. *Economic Crisis, Quality of Work, and Social Integration: The European Experience. No Title*. Gallie, D. (ed.) Oxford: Oxford University Press.

Gallie, D. 2017. The Quality of Work in a Changing Labour Market. *Social Policy & Administration*, 51(2): 226–243.

Goos, M., Manning, A. and Salomons, A. 2014. Explaining Job Polarization: Routine-based Technological Change and Offshoring. *American Economic Review*, 104(8): 2509–2526.

Greve, B. 2012. The Impact of the Financial Crisis on Happiness in Affluent European Countries. *Journal of Comparative Social Welfare*, 28(3): 183–193.

Greve, B. 2016. *The Politics of Occupational Welfare, Labor Markets: Analysis, Regulations and Outcomes*. New York: Nova Science Publishers.

Greve, B. 2017a. How to Measure Social Progress? *Social Policy and Administration*, 51(7): 1002–1022.

Greve, B. 2017b. *Technology and the Future of Work. The Impact on Labour Markets and Welfare States*. Cheltenham: Edward Elgar.

Greve, B. 2018. At the Heart of the Nordic Occupational Welfare Model: Occupational Welfare Trajectories in Sweden and Denmark. *Social Policy and Administration*, 52(2): 508–518.

Greve, B. 2019. *The Routledge Handbook of the Welfare State*. 2nd edn. Greve, B. (ed.) Oxford: Routledge.

Guerreiro, J., Rebelo, S. and Teles, P. (n.d.) Should Robots be Taxed? *NBER Working Paper Series*.

Hill, S. 2015. *Raw Deal. How the 'Uber Economy' and Runaway Capitalism are Screwing American Workers*. New York: St. Martins Press.

Kaplan, J. 2015. *Humans Need Not Apply. A Guide to Wealth and Work in the Age of Artificial Intelligence*. London: Yale University Press.

Kilhoffer, Z., Lenaerts, K. and Beblavy, M. 2017. *The Platform Economy and Industrial Relations. Applying the Old Framework to the New Reality*. 2017/12. Brussels.

Lindbeck, A. and Snower, D. 1988. *The Insider-Outsider Theory of Employment and Unemployment*. Cambridge, MA: MIT Press.

MacGregor, N. 2016. *Germany. Memories of a Nation*. London: Penguin.

McKinsey & Company. 2017. *Shaping the Future of Work in Europe's Digital Front-runners*. Available at: www.mckinsey.com/~/media/McKinsey/Global.

Minter, K. 2017. Negotiating Labour Standards in the Gig Economy: Airtasker and Unions New South Wales. *The Economic and Labour Relations Review*, 28(3): 438–454.

Mokyr, J. and Vickers, C. 2015. The History of Technological Anxiety and the Future of Economic Growth: Is This Time Different? *Journal of Economic Perspectives*, 29(3): 31–50.

Nedelkoska, L. and Quintini, G. 2018. *Automation, Skills Use and Training*. OECD Social, Employment and Migration Working Papers, No. 202, OECD Publishing, Paris. Available at: http://dx.doi.org/10.1787/2e2f4eea-en.

OECD. 2015. *In it Together: Why Less Inequality Benefits All*. Paris: OECD Publishing.

OECD. 2017. *Employment Outlook*. OECD. Paris.

Pearson, T. 2015. *The End of Jobs. Money, Meaning and Freedom without the 9 to 5*. Austin, TX: Lioncrest Publishing.

Pieterson, W. 2018. *Digitization and Work: How Governments are Responding to Changing Labour Markets?* Brussels: DG Employment, Social Affairs and Inclusion. Available at: http://ec.europa.eu/social/mlp.

PWC. 2017. *Will Robots Steal Our Jobs? The Potential Impact of Automation*. Available at: www.pwc.co.uk/services/economics-policy/insights/uk-economic-outlook.html.

PWC. 2018. *Will Robots Really Steal Our Jobs? An International Analysis of the Potential Long-term Impact of Automation*. Available at: http://pwc.blogs.com/economics_in_business/2018/02/will-robots-really-steal-our-jobs.html.

Rueda, D. 2014. Dualization, Crisis and the Welfare State. *Socio-Economic Review*, 12(2): 381–407.

Rutledge, M. and Guan, Q. 2015. *Job Polarization and Labour Market Outcomes for Older, Middle-skilled Workers*. Center for Retirement Research at Boston College Working Paper, (2015-23).

Sachs, J., Benzell, Z. and LaGarda, G. 2015. *Robots: Curse or Blessing? A Basic Framework*. Cambridge, MA: Cambridge University Press.

Schwab, K. 2016. *The Fourth Industrial Revolution*. Davos: World Economic Forum.

Valenduc, G. and Vendramin, P. 2016. *Work in the Digital Economy: Sorting the Old from the New*. Brussels; European Union Institute.

Yoon, Y. and Chung, H. 2016. New Forms of Dualization? Labour Market Segmentation Patterns in the UK from the Late 90s Until the Post-crisis in the Late 2000s. *Social Indicator Research*, 128(2): 609–631.

41
Cyberpolitics and IPE
Towards a research agenda in the Global South

Maximiliano Vila Seoane and Marcelo Saguier

Introduction

Cyberpolitics is a field where the political, economic and ecological dynamics that shape contemporary international relations are being played out in relation to technological transformations. We are in a moment of transition towards data capitalism[1] that is characterized by the accumulation of capital by few large Internet companies and platforms (Srnicek 2016), based on the extraction, safeguarding, analysis and (ab)use of data for different purposes (Mayer-Schönberger and Cukier 2013). We call *digitalization* the ongoing process of turning every type of interaction into data. Digitalization is a fundamental vector of data capitalism insofar as the organization of production, decisions and identities are increasingly linked to the generation, availability and interaction with large volumes of data (popularly known as big data).

Digitalization has profound implications in terms of new forms of power and asymmetries among the many old and new actors of inter- and transnational politics. In effect, these new technological capabilities are concentrated in few leading Internet companies located in the US and China (McKinsey & Company 2017) and, to a lesser extent, in Canada, Israel, Russia and some European countries. This unequal distribution poses enormous challenges for the development prospects of countries and societies from the Global South, increasing the historical patterns of dependency between technologically advanced countries and the rest. Taking into account that China is one of the main leaders in digitalization, there are also new emerging center-periphery configurations in the Global South marked by striking technological asymmetries. Moreover, the accumulation of data by a few companies severely limits citizens' decisions over their data, facilitating new forms of surveillance and control for commercial and geopolitical purposes, as well as the violation of human rights such as the right to privacy.

Due to these and other problematic aspects of digitalization, it is essential to understand the relationship between politics and the changes produced by the new information and communication technologies. "Internet politics" (Chadwick and Howard 2009) and "cyberpolitics" are terms usually used in the social sciences to refer to the nexus between politics and technological changes. We adopt the prefix "cyber" in line with scholarly convention in the field of International Relations studies (IR). According to Choucri (2012: 4), cyberpolitics "refers to the conjunction of two processes or realities — those pertaining to human interactions (politics) surrounding the determination of who gets what, when, and how, and those enabled by the uses of a virtual space (cyber) as a new arena of contention with its own modalities and realities." Departing from this broad definition, we focus on the emerging dynamics of cooperation and competition between the key public and private actors that are currently shaping an emerging global political economy of data.

Cyberpolitics is becoming increasingly an area of interest in IR/International Political Economy (IPE) scholarship, mostly in research centers of technologically advanced countries of the Western Anglo-Saxon sphere. The mainstream research agenda on cyberpolitics is largely concerned with cyberwar issues and increasingly also with the study of the political and social significance of data (Madsen et al. 2016; Mahrenbach et al. 2018). To a lesser extent, the intersections between cyberpolitics and development studies is also becoming a site of research interest (Mahrenbach et al. 2018; Schia 2018; Taylor and Schroeder 2015).

In contrast, there is scarce research of cyberpolitics coming from technologically dependent countries and societies in the Global South. Some notable exceptions in Latin America examined novel initiatives that took place in the region, such as the Civil Rights Framework for the Internet in established in Brazil in 2014 and the cooperation agenda in cyberdefense and cybersecurity policies adopted by the Union of South American Nations (UNASUR) in 2012 (Abdenur and da Silva Gama 2015). These landmark initiatives captured the initial drive for research agenda on cyberpolitics for some time. Yet, this incipient literature tends to be largely descriptive, oriented to a policy informed readership, and lacking the conceptual and analytical depth that is needed to fully explore, understand and manage the complex political, economic and developmental implications of the digitalization processes worldwide and in the Global South particularly.

In this chapter we set out to interrogate *what role and implications have the digitalization process in the making of a new global political economy centered on data.*

To address this question in the first section we introduce a theoretical discussion to conceptualize digitalization as the political terrain of cyberpolitics. We draw from concepts of the neo-Gramscian perspectives of International Political Economy and of the field of Science and Technology Studies. In the second section we explore the implications of digitalization in four areas where cyberpolitics is being played out: cybersecurity; governance of digital trade and global finance; human rights and citizenship on the Internet; and the environment–sustainable development nexus. These areas are representative of the main arenas where dynamics of conflict and cooperation between key cyberpolitics actors are laying ground for the construction of digital world orders but are not the only ones. Finally, we conclude with a reflection about the importance of advancing research on cyberpolitics in countries and societies of the Global South.

The main claim of this chapter is that the digitalization process constitutes a set of practices in which relations of production and governance frameworks are being disputed as part of digital word (dis)orders historically specific to data capitalism in the making.

Box 41.1 Main concepts

Digitalization: The ongoing process of turning every type of interaction into data, a fundamental vector of data capitalism insofar as the organization of production, decisions and identities are increasingly linked to the generation, availability and interaction with large volumes of data (popularly known as big data).

Cyberpolitics: According to Choucri (2012: 4), cyberpolitics "refers to the conjunction of two processes or realities – those pertaining to human interactions (politics) surrounding the determination of who gets what, when, and how, and those enabled by the uses of a virtual space (cyber) as a new arena of contention with its own modalities and realities." For International Relations it is important to limit the analysis to actors and processes of cooperation and dispute at the inter- and transnational level.

Socio-technical relations of production: covers the totality of socio-technical relations that engender particular socio-technical forces.

Forms of governance: refers to historically contingent state/society/technology complexes.

Digital World (dis)order: the particular configurations of forces which successively define the problematic of how to organize cyberspace.

Hegemony: a form of dominance where elements of consensus prevail, but that does not exclude elements of coercion.

Socio-technical relations of production, forms of governance and digital world (dis)orders

In this section, we present a theoretical discussion to conceptualize the role of the digitalization; the terrain of cyberpolitics shaped by the dynamics of conflict and cooperation among actors structuring a new global political economy centered on data. To do so we revisit core concepts of the neo-Gramscian perspective of International Political Economy (IPE) in terms of their value and limitations for understanding the digitalization process. Furthermore, in the spirit of establishing bridges between both research traditions we bring in insights from the field of Science and Technology Studies (STS) in the effort to overcome shortcomings of such IPE concepts.

Since the seminal work of Robert W. Cox in the early 1980s the perspective of neo-Gramscian critique of IPE has contributed to understanding the unfolding configurations and forces of state–society relations as historically specific configurations associated with the transformations of global capitalism (Bieler and Morton 2004; Cox 1981, 1987; Cox and Sinclair 1996; Gill 2008). The concepts of *social relations of production, forms of state* and *world orders* are core categories of this perspective, which explain the structural relations that emerge as the outcome of dialectical relations between social forces at any given time in history.

For example, a possible relation is that antagonisms between different social forces, caused by changes of the social relations of production, can lead to the establishment of hegemony by one class over the rest. Thus, the hegemonic class becomes capable of modifying the forms of state, and if it reaches enough international projection, it can also alter the world order (Cox 1981: 138) which, in turn, conditions the actions of other states. Each conceptual category can be understood heuristically by analyzing the dialectical relationship between ideas, institutions and material capabilities (including technological ones).

The concept of hegemony is central to the definition of *world order* in this IPE perspective. Hegemony here differs from formulations of the Realists school in IR where it is associated with a quality of military supremacy of one state over others. Instead, a neo-Gramscian definition sees hegemony as a form of domination by a *social force* over others, exercised by the consent of sub-ordinate classes. Their acquiescence to a ruling elite takes place when ideas and values presented by a dominant ruling class are accepted as necessary and universal (when they are naturalized as "common sense"). Through consensus and coercion, dominant ideas, supported by material capabilities and by institutions, act as conditions of legitimacy on which social order is produced and reproduced (Cox 1981; Howson and Smith 2008; Robinson 2005).

Furthermore, as a relational concept, hegemony is always understood in contradiction with counter-hegemonic forces. These contest the legitimacy of a social order is maintained based on unequal relations of domination. Resistances can potentially modify the correlations of power between social forces, resulting in changes of the hegemonic order (Cox 1981: 144). IPE readings of global political economy processes apply the notions of hegemony and counter-hegemonic resistance beyond state-centered analyses. States, international organizations, transnational companies (TNCs) and global social movements are seen as forces that structure and shape the dynamics of neoliberal globalization as a historically specific configuration of world order (Gill 2008).

These IPE concepts provide a starting point to understanding the transformations that digitalization generates in the global political economy of data capitalism. Particularly, the kinds of shifting power relations associated with the prevalence that TNCs (particularly but not only in leading technology sectors) are gaining ideational, material and institutional capacities to appear as legitimate forms of private authority in global governance processes (Fuchs 2013; Hall and Biersteker 2002; Newell and Levy 2002). Nevertheless, these IPE concepts fall short to fully tackle the implications that technology is having in all spheres of human and non-human activity which has direct bearing on the dynamics of conflicts and cooperation that is the focus of cyberpolitics.

Concepts are always the product of a particular historical moment. The neo-Gramscian perspective has evolved in relation to analyses of changes in the world economy associated, first, with imperialism, the post-war international system and, later, with neoliberal globalization and its resistances. The extent to which data technology is imbricated in human and non-human processes at a global scale has no comparison with anything ever experienced, and thus requires new lenses to visualize its unfolding configurations and tensions. In other words, critical IPE concepts need to accommodate conceptually and analytically the mutations of global capitalism towards data-centered processes that are redefining socio-political, ecological and identity relations worldwide.

The understanding of "technology" is critical here. Neo-Gramscian IPE conceives technology as an objective factor influenced by and, at the same time, influencing social forces (Cox 1987: 21). Actors with the greatest "social power" determine the direction of technological change. To illustrate this point, let us think of nuclear technology in war, or the innovative technology applied in industrial processes as examples where the development, access and control of key technologies represent advantages vis a vis countries and economic sectors in terms of capacity to control the use and consequences of such technologies. This view of technology, as an instrument of power, is limited to understand some of the issues raised by digitalization. IPE considers technology as something external and separate from the social; a separation that is being challenged by the growing centrality that data processes have in all spheres of human activity, as much of the literature of Science and Technology Studies (STS) points out.

STS perspectives problematize a simplistic separation between the spheres of the "social" and the "technical." Moving away from instrumental understandings of technology, STS look instead at ontologies that better address the kinds of co-construction relations that take place between human actors and other non-human organisms with technological artifacts (Acuto and

Curtis 2014; McCarthy 2011). One implication of this view of technology is that the belief that the social group with more "power" always determines the direction of technological change is put under question (Bijker et al. 2012; Feenberg 1999; Latour 2005). This is because technology today allows types of agency which cannot be reduced to human decisions alone or else to linear processes; artificial intelligence being the extreme and paradigmatic example of this.

Based on these insights, in what follows we reformulate the IPE concepts that were presented earlier to accommodate a non-instrumental view of technology. We hope this effort enables us to grapple with the question of what role and implications the digitalization process has in the making of a new global political economy centered on data.

First, we refer to *socio-technical relations of production* to examine the networks between humans and other artifacts propitiated by digitalization in contemporary relations of production. Namely, we move beyond a focus on analyses of human actors as separate from technological process. This allows us to study the actions of various devices in our contemporary lives, which seem to act independently or locally, but which are really part of vast global networks of material and human elements. Such networks of human-artifacts are maintained by different practices, can act at a distance and transfer policy decisions through technological designs (Nahuis and van Lente 2008).

Cyberspace is an example of such networks (Deibert et al. 2013; Mueller et al. 2007). Cyberspace includes more than Internet. It also covers all the physical infrastructures of information and telecommunications, codes and protocols for "dialogue" between machines, regulations and norms. In this sense, cyberspace becomes a polycentric and transnational network structure. It raises various questions for the study of cyberpolitics in IR/IPE, such as what power actually means when states are being diminished in their capacities to implement unilateral decisions for the whole network (Choucri 2012) or when technology users can shape the functional boundaries of technology and its originally intended applications. It is also true that cyberspace is entirely built by humans (Betz and Stevens 2011), therefore, its structure is in continuous evolution, as well as the transnational threats it enables and the regulatory frameworks to govern it, which have a marked weakness to keep up to date.

Second, the concept of *forms of state* as originally formulated understands the state bureaucratic apparatus as occupied at a certain historical moment by particular social forces, which can establish multiple configurations of relationships with different social actors, such as companies, the church, media, etc. Besides, these social forces may extend their influence beyond the occupied state in question on a global scale (Bieler and Morton 2004: 87; Cox 1981: 141; Gill 2008). Although this conceptualization is superior to the idea of the state as a unitary structure, it is not enough to understand the growing influence in inter- and transnational politics of different types of actors and non-state networks that multiplied with globalization, such TNCs, networks of activists or terrorists, etc. The specificity of these networks is that they also build horizontal relationships, without necessarily having to control the state in order extend their influence on a global scale (Cox and Schechter 2002; Robinson 2005). This is evident on the Internet, where a wide range of "old" actors coexists with new ones, such as the creation of cyber armies by terrorist organizations or the emergence of transnational technology companies that in a short time accumulated an impressive power and influence worldwide.

Likewise, a standard definition of global governance focuses on the set of rules, norms and practices that include both the state as well as private and social actors as relevant stakeholders in global agenda issues. Such a mainstream view of global governance stresses the plurality of actors in processes of deliberation, decision-making and policy implementation and practices. Cox refers to "nebuleuse" to the constellation of actors in transnational networks that exercise governance functions and authority in an age of global capitalism (Cox and Schechter 2002).

However, global governance and nebuleuse both retain a vision of the "political" that has no technological dimension in its conception of agency-structure and power. Alternatively, we propose that governance is also carried out through technologies, such as algorithms (Ziewitz 2015). Therefore, we refer to *forms of governance* as historically contingent state/society/technology complexes which captures such diverse types of configurations.

Finally, taking into account that digitalization is the main driver of data capitalism, it is more precise to refer to *digital world orders* instead of world orders. We are interested in the dynamics of conflict and cooperation that take place in cyberspace. We question the idea of an order in cyberspace, suggesting that "disordered" conditions are likely without this meaning a situation of conflict ridden global processes. In this sense, we propose that the notion of "order" underpinning neo-Gramscian perspectives of IPE needs to be revisited, since it suggests stable and homogenous properties that are too rigid to make sense of more fluid, decentered, contested global processes of co-construction relations between human actors and other non-human organisms with technological artifacts.

In this discussion we have tried to show that the changes that digitalization produces in an emerging global political economy of data are not easily captured by instrumental views of technology and its correlates in other core concepts of critical IPE. What is needed is conceptual lenses that provide insights into the difficult issues and questions raised by data technologies. We are at a historical time when new forms of state-society-technology complexes are being established. Conceptualizing these transformations are inevitably a challenging task, particularly in the field of international relations studies where technology has received little attention (Mayer et al. 2014).

Cyberpolitics in the contours of digital world (dis)orders

Drawing on the theoretical discussion introduced in the previous section, here we explore the implications of digitalization in the global political economy of data in relation to cybersecurity; governance of digital trade and global finance; human rights and citizenship on the Internet; and the environment–sustainable development nexus. These areas are not comprehensive of all domains where data technologies are generating policy and research debates. Nor are the issues and debates presented in each case all that can be said about them. Nevertheless, these areas are strategic arenas where cyberpolitics is drawing new boundaries in defining agendas, actors' alliances and governance arrangements/practices. In these areas, the pathways for future digital world (dis)orders are being disputed.

Cybersecurity

Digitalization has changed significantly the agendas and practices of international security. This changes the global political economy as high-tech companies gain unprecedented weight in security and defense policies. Cybersecurity is the general term most used in relation to the defense against potential threats and/or attacks on the Internet and the protection of computer systems. However, its meaning has come to be associated with strategic military perspectives as was incorporated into a securitization discourse (Dunn Cavelty 2007), displacing the civilian interpretation of the term.

The US military was pioneer in the adaptation to the opportunities that digitalization opened for defense industry and military applications. This was determinant in the securitization of the cybersecurity agenda. In 2009 the US created its Cyber Command dependent on the National Security Agency (NSA) to carry out defensive and attack operations. Then, in 2011 the Pentagon classified cyberspace as a new field of war, along with traditional ones (air, space, sea and land).

The North Atlantic Treaty Organization (NATO) followed in 2016. Therefore, and referring to the theoretical discussion of the previous section, the focus of the mainstream literature on cybersecurity is on the analysis of military and intelligence state agencies, high-tech information companies and other related organizations. These are key actors, or socio-technical forces, driving of cybersecurity processes.

Furthermore, the debates in the cybersecurity literature reflect a "problem solving" approach (Cox 1981) to the potential risks posed by new technologies. The primary concern of scholarly production is to contribute to US capacities to maintain technological superiority and hence support its standing as a global power, which includes neutralizing risks and threats. Issues of great importance are the prospects of attack and deterrence techniques. The prospects of a cyberwar taking place is subject of intense debate (Junio 2013; Lynn III 2010; Rid 2012).

Those convinced of cyber-weapons risks often repeat well-known Realist perspective analyses, accusing countries such as China or Russia of being threats to the world order. Such is the case of Adam Segal (2013), who asserts that China, in order to reach the peak in technological development of its industries, supports systematic cyber-espionage campaigns against US companies and state agencies to steal their intellectual property and other valuable strategic data. In the same vein, Russia is credited with sophisticated "hybrid warfare" attack, which often involves a mixture of cyber-attacks, disinformation campaigns and the use of camouflaged soldiers, as in the cases of Estonia, Georgia, Ukraine and the United States in 2016.

From the perspective of international security, the malware known as StuxNet (Kello 2018) became a milestone in the study of cybersecurity, because it exemplifies the danger of cyber-weapons. It was allegedly created by the intelligence services of the US and Israel and was used in 2010 to sabotage the computer systems of the Natanz nuclear power plant in Iran. The original feature of StuxNet is that it was designed to attack the software that controls industrial processes, and specifically nuclear centrifuges, without resorting to a conventional military attack. In addition to the malware's source code causing considerable physical damage, it also infected other organizations using systems similar to those of the Iranian nuclear power plant. This generated consternation in the community dedicated to cybersecurity because of the risk of causing major damage beyond its initial military objectives.

The risks of cyber-attacks are particularly high in "critical infrastructures." This imprecise concept covers all types of industry or sectors that are critical for the normal functioning of societies, be it civil or military (e.g., banks, social security databases, electric power plants, transportation, etc.) (Deibert et al. 2013). These are no longer mere prospective scenarios. Several incidents demonstrated the damage that cyberattacks[2] can cause in contemporary societies in the process of digitalization. The recent global attack of WannaCry ransomware caused considerable physical damage by paralyzing the systems of companies, government departments, hospitals and individuals around the world. This malware was supposedly created by North Korean hackers based on leaks of cyber-weapons developed by the NSA.

Like all hegemony, order on the Internet is also based on a dimension of consensus-based cooperation. In effect, the US is the driver of the multistakeholder model for Internet governance,[3] which is believed to be a more democratic model than others. Decision processes includes states, firms, civil society organizations, international organizations and technical communities, among others. However, it is no secret that the main Internet governance companies and organizations are generally located in the USA. Therefore, the ideas and interests of these organizations have a superior influence to those of other countries in the development of the Internet and in the processes of digitalization. Hence, the promise of the multistakeholder model, despite its democratic intention, does not alter significantly the power dynamics that privileges the role of states and TNCs particularly those of the US (Carr 2014).

The most emblematic example of this trend is the Internet Corporation for Assigned Names and Numbers (ICANN), a non-profit organization based in Los Angeles, charged until 2016 with administering Internet domain names directly on behalf of the US Department of Commerce. For years, this was the cause of a dispute with initiatives from other countries that sought to transfer this responsibility to the United Nations Organization, in order to avoid the prevalence of US preferences over those of other countries, a tension that persists despite recent changes at ICANN (Jackson 2018).

Although the US and its coalition of socio-technical forces retain the leadership in the construction of a hegemony in data capitalism, it is not exempt from counter-hegemonic challenges (Ebert and Maurer 2013). One example of this is the criticisms about the abuse of the surveillance and control facilitated by data technologies following Edward Snowden's revelations. This former NSA agent exposed mass cyber-surveillance programs of the US and its allies in cooperation with transnational technology companies, revealing deep contradictions with the discourse of a free and democratic Internet that emanates from Western countries. The public outcry caused by these revelations did not produce changes in surveillance practices. Instead, the leaks paved the way for public policies that legalized such practices (Pohle and Van Audenhove 2017).

In this scenario, China indirectly accuses the US of having a "cyber hegemony" on the Internet, for not respecting the "cyber sovereignty" of other states. Based on this reading, it is not surprising that China uses its growing economic and technological capabilities to compete with the US on a par in terms of cybersecurity, electronic surveillance, and more recently, artificial intelligence and 5G technologies.

Another example of this counter-hegemonic competition is the establishment of rules to govern conflicts in cyberspace (Finnemore and Hollis 2016). The proposals of the Shanghai Cooperation Organization to limit the use of cybercrimes go in that direction. Yet, these proposals have not prospered due to US opposition on the grounds that such rules would limit freedom of expression and its ability to perform cyber-attacks (Maurer 2011). In response to these initiatives, NATO's Cooperative Cyber Defense Centre of Excellence developed two versions of the Tallinn Manual, written to adapt and internationalize its interpretation of international law for conflicts in cyberspace.

Governance of digital trade and global finance

Digitalization changes relations of production by modifying global trade and finance leading to a transition to digital economies. The governance of these key areas of the global political economy are critical arenas between competing actors.

Global data value chains have different types of actors, though the most influential ones are the companies based in the US (Amazon, Apple, Facebook, Gmail and Microsoft) and in China (Alibaba, Baidu and Tencent). These companies have a privileged position in the new configurations of a global political economy centered on data. They have structural power, which is derived from the increasing dependence that conventional international trade of goods and services has from "digital trade."

"Digital trade" refers to the set of transactions carried out through web portals and new forms of communication. Data transactions differ from the exchange of products or services, since there is no consent or payment for their cross-border flow, and yet they remain essential and of enormous value for data capitalism. The increase in cross-border data flows and automation (e.g., algorithms and robotics) accelerates international trade of goods and services (López-González and Jouanjean 2017).

Moreover, digitalization has enabled the expansion of global value chains that rest on deterritorialized forms of work that would be unthinkable without innovations in the data technology. New modalities of work are facilitated by the provision of services in the "cloud" that allows access to documents, emails and all types of data from various devices and in any moment that can be accessed via the Internet. These facilitate remote distance coordination between production units located in different parts of the world as well as the management to international trade logistics.

The pivotal role that TNCs in data technology sectors have in the global value chains has been characterized as the consolidation as the new monopolies of the twenty-first century. A form of transnational "privatized public infrastructure" (Plantin et al. 2016) is leading the development of new forms of production in the digital era and is partly responsible for their negative effects in terms of human rights and developmental. This has led to a debate about the need to have effective global regulatory instruments to avoid market concentration, tax evasion (Aaronson 2015) and complicity in human rights violations around the world.

Voices contrary to regulation claim that monopolistic concentration in digital sectors is necessary to offer global goods that would otherwise be difficult to produce. This position informs the lobbying practices of US companies in the US and in the European Union aimed at ensuring that the rules of the digital economy and digital trade are in tune with their interests. Likewise, the anti-regulation positions seek to prevent other states from implementing restrictions on the free flow of data across borders (e.g., data localization requirements in the countries where they operate), because they consider such policies as a restriction to freedom of access to the Internet.

In contrast, positions favorable to regulatory measures hold that they are essential state instruments to ensure that digitalization can be conducive to development-oriented policies, as well as consistent with national sovereignty rights. In short, what is at stake is the dispute over different forms of governance of digital trade, an area of the global economy that places additional strains on the state digital development strategies.

Equally, the actors and governance challenges of the global financial system are being changed by the emergence of FinTech. Cryptocurrencies, such as Bitcoin, are one of the most recent cases of new technological innovations in the sector, but not the only ones. These digital currencies are based on blockchain technology (De Filippi and Wright 2018), which allows to protect and exchange value in encrypted, decentralized and transnational networks.

Different actors are part of these new cryptocurrencies networks, such as technologists, investors, fans, citizens, but also money launderers and other criminals from around the world, promoting a new way of realizing and speculating with financial transactions. In its most radical expression, these new digital forms of exchanging value are inspiring the creation of "nations without borders", such as BitNation, as well as the implementation of smart contracts, which exemplifies the looming forms of algorithmic-decentralized governance.

According to Campbell-Verduyn and Goguen (2017) these processes of decentralization have a direct impact on the dominant intermediaries of global finance (e.g., companies such as JP Morgan, central and private banks). Their control capacities are being loosened by such new structures of money and value flows, causing new dilemmas for the stability of the global financial system and for efforts to curb money laundering. States and companies have responded by seeking to appropriate blockchain technology in an attempt to reverse their loss of control in global finances. In short, blockchain exemplifies the emergence of a new form of transnational governance, which has the potential to alter significantly the digital world order.

Human rights and citizenship on the Internet

The digitalization of contemporary societies is causing multiple impacts on preexisting ideas and practices on human rights and citizenship. Infringement to citizen's rights to privacy is one of the main problems associated with digitalization. Indeed, cybercrime (Holt and Bossler 2014) and the excessive use of devices capable of producing thorough electronic traces of our inter-actions with other humans and machines, allows companies to generate precise profiles on consumption, political preferences, spatial displacements, etc. (Ball et al. 2012) of its users, limiting citizens' online privacy. State security and intelligence agencies believe that the collec-tion of these large databases – in collaboration with the private sector – is essential to avoid contemporary threats, such as terrorism or organized crime. These practices are justified on the grounds that citizens need not fear from the analysis of data or metadata[4] if they have nothing to hide. However, following Snowden's revelations about the indiscriminate and disproportionate use of espionage capabilities by the US in collaboration with other states, the arguments used to justify massive electronic surveillance are seriously questionable (Bernal 2016).

This is not a new issue in international relations. Already in the 1990s Der Derian (1990) identified the strategic role of surveillance to discipline and normalize behaviors of others. Yet, in data capitalism the variety, speed and volume of data (big data) that states and companies can obtain from entire populations certainly constitutes a new phenomenon. That is to say, the current coercive practices of cyber-espionage and cyber-surveillance of major powers have con-firmed, and even exceeded, the wildest speculations and concerns of previous decades.

The regulation of increasingly powerful Internet TNCs in terms of their impacts on eco-nomic, political and social rights consists of a great challenge in an age of data capitalism. Com-panies have the ability to make decisions at a distance through algorithms that are often not transparent (DeNardis and Hackl 2015) generating impacts on the working conditions of their users. Many of these companies coordinate the offer of their digital products and services glo-bally, without necessarily operating physically in offshore jurisdictions, generating considerable disruptions in sectors that until recently were immune to digitalization.

The most striking example is Uber's incursion in the transport sector, whose rapid global expansion was accompanied by a disdain to comply with local regulations in the countries where it operates, causing conflicts with national labor regulations and trade unions that see workers' rights threatened and with states that have a limited capacity to regulate the company. Another recent landmark is that of the scandal of the firm Cambridge Analytica, which revealed how Facebook's lax data protection policies at the time paved the way for the collection and manipulation of its users' personal data to distribute political propaganda in different elections (such as in those in the USA, Argentina, Kenya and the United Kingdom).

The growing centrality of TNCs in offering all types of products and services is having signi-ficant impacts in terms of citizenship. Identities are increasingly mediated by algorithms and data that circulate in private and transnational Internet platforms with the effect of influencing the interactions that users may have (Jackson 2018). For instance, social media algorithms show their users content that corroborates their cultural, economic, political, etc. preferences, in order to retain them on the platform. This generates the so-called echo chambers effect, since users mostly access content that confirms their beliefs, limiting exposure to other positions, and pos-sibly impoverishing the necessary debate in democratic contexts (Helbing et al. 2017).

In turn, this phenomenon can facilitate the distribution of "fake news", which might shape the construction of political identities in ways in need of further research (Lazer et al. 2018). Likewise, another characteristic of these new mediations is that a large section of users are in jurisdictions different from those of origin of these companies, putting under pressure the traditional idea of citizenship based on our belonging to a nation-state in geographical terms. For these reasons, Isin and Ruppert (2015) invite us to think about the digital citizen as someone who claims rights, both of existing and new ones, and can be useful to investigate the novel and changing contours of digital and transnational citizenship in an era of data capitalism.

The impacts of digitalization on human rights and citizenship are changing relations of production and forms of governance. This has led to human rights organizations such as Amnesty International and Human Rights Watch to incorporate these issues into their agendas. Likewise, new transnational organizations specialized in digital rights were created, such as Privacy International, which contest what they consider to be unethical production practices of several Internet companies. It is also true that some of the Internet TNC are adopting—albeit slowly—cryptography in their services (e.g., WhatsApp), which make it difficult for third parties to access the content of messages, but which also limit state sovereignty in regulating the content through such channels (Buchanan 2016).

Finally, several states are legislating over the Internet and the use of data. On the one hand, initiatives to reform data protection laws stand out, such as the General Regulation of Data Protection of the European Union. These grant basic rights to users about their data and assigns responsibilities to organizations that collect and process data, although without reducing all the asymmetries between these two types of actors. On the other hand, other states are implementing policies of censorship, control and "nationalization" of the Internet, which challenge the multistakeholder model of governance (Deibert 2015).

Environment–sustainable development nexus

Big data techniques to collect real time information about the human–environment nexus are revolutionizing the science, politics and economics of adaptation and mitigation to climate change (Ford et al. 2016) and sustainable development. While digitalization presents opportunities it also poses risks for environmental and sustainable development policies related to the issue of ownership and potential uses of biological and environmental data.

The so-called "Fourth Industrial Revolution" is presented as an opportunity to tackle many of the world's current environmental problems (climate change, pollution, depletion of fishing stocks, toxins in rivers and soils, waste on land and oceans, loss of biodiversity and deforestation, etc.). New technologies are enabling societal shifts by having an effect on economics, values, identities and possibilities for future generations. This industrial revolution, unlike previous ones, is underpinned by the established digital economy and is based on rapid advances in artificial intelligence (AI), the Internet of Things, robots, autonomous vehicles, biotechnology, nanotechnology and quantum computing, among others. It is characterized by the combination of these technologies, which are increasing speed, intelligence and efficiency gains (World Economic Forum 2018).

The applications of big data technologies like AI and others enable new possibilities for monitoring environmental changes, such as changes in soil composition, water quality, patterns of species movements, to mention a few examples. Access to big data on the environment is critical for adequate policy and environmental governance responses. In particular, to devise informed mechanisms and processes of impact assessment on socio-ecological systems. This is relevant to understand the scale, intensity and direct/indirect impacts of climate change, resource-based industries (agriculture, mining, aquiculture, fishing, forestry, energy, etc.) and infrastructure projects (hydroelectrical, transport, irrigation infrastructures, etc.) (Gerlak et al. 2019).

Moreover, other technologies such as blockchain are also opening new possibilities for different approaches to environmental governance. Blockchain technology is being used in forest protection (Howson et al., 2019), and as a mechanism for smart contracts to register the ownership of environmental resources or the traceability of products, among others (Chapron 2017). This decentralized technology, where no single user can control the entire information structure, is proving a viable option to managing the problems associated with lack of trust between stakeholders connected to different aspects of environmental governance.

Digitalization of environmental data also presents some difficult issues such as the unequal conditions in terms of influence, advantages and power related to access to this information. Private ownership of environmental data favors economic concentration in leading actors in natural resource sectors. Likewise, in the internet platforms that provide the technologies to generate and manage environmental data by different users. Big data technologies make it possible to estimate more accurately the availability of biological and natural resources. It becomes a strategic commodity, as access to this technology translates into commercial advantages. It can also encourage illicit economic activities such as biopiracy, which consist in the commercial exploitation of animals, plants, microorganisms and other natural resources (Lucchi 2013).

The weight of environmental big data is not only related to the fact that only leading economic sectors can access and control information. It also depends on the generation of artificial barriers that limit the use of data by other states and actors who cannot pay for them (such as public policy decision makers in less resourceful states, researchers and the public in general). Restricted public ownership or access to environmental data undermines efforts to democratize the management, protection, and/or rational and sustainable use of natural and biological resources.

In fact, the booming market of companies providing big data services for the natural resource industries is in direct tension with states' goal of advancing opportunities for public access to information and participation in decisions concerning the environment (as contained in the Agenda 2030 of the Sustainable Development Goals, as the follow up of the 1992 UN Summit on Sustainable Development in Rio). Due to these criticisms, an open data movement has emerged as a counter-hegemonic socio-technical force advocating the notion of data as a public good (Leonelli 2013). Ensuring public access and control over environmental data is essential for the democratization of environmental governance.

Private ownership and control of environmental data contributes to creating conditions for the diffusion of a market-based approach to global environmental governance. Companies that have access to this technology are being presented as key stakeholders in bringing about effective responses to the environmental crisis and as means to realizing the aspirations of sustainable development. This is part of a narrative of eco-efficiency and environmental modernization that currently disputes the meanings and contents of an evolving discourse of "sustainable development." Companies that muster data technologies are seen to be best capable of responsibly managing resources with sustainability criteria. Let us think of the notion of "responsible mining" in relation to technology providing means of managing contamination risks and water usage in mining practices, or the evolving notion of an "intelligent agriculture" as the paradigm of efficient use of soil and water relying on big data and AI. In fact, this technological element can be seen as a more recent development of a longer process of building a narrative of "corporate responsibility" as a discursive strategy to offset regulatory demands stemming from mounting criticisms to business involvement in ecological destruction and human rights violations (Saguier 2012).

These ideas have a pretence to serve as part of a hegemonic consensus on which to structure global governance arrangement for the environment based on a market-based approach that has business actors as driving agents of change. Internet and high-tech companies have a pivotal role here since they command a neuralgic component of the value chains in resource-based sectors. Reflexions about alternative policy pathways to address the environmental crisis and the challenges of sustainable development challenges, which do not involve the determining role of business, are simply foreclosed or minimized from the global agenda (Saguier and Brent 2017).

The politics of environmental governance involve also state–company coalitions that dispute a share of the enormous market that the climate crisis opened for business investments. Germany and China are prime examples of states that have articulated solid alliances with private and public companies (Beveridge and Kern 2013; Wang et al. 2014) with great influence in shaping the politics of global environmental governance in terms of agenda setting, securing commercial contracts and investing in international legitimacy. Their global leadership in "green production" and renewable energy sectors are also explained by the disengagement of the US from the climate agenda under the Donald Trump government and of Brazil under Jair Bolsonaro.

Conclusions

In this chapter we set out to interrogate what role and implications the digitalization process has in the making of a new global political economy centered on data. To explore this theme, we reviewed the emerging issues, actors and processes in four strategic arenas of cyberpolitics. In these arenas we discussed ways in which digitalization is generating changes in the relations of production, governance and configurations of socio-technical forces that are currently disputing the direction of potentially different pathways towards world orders in cyberspace.

The challenges and dilemmas raised by digitalization are already a priority on the agenda of major powers and other transnational actors but remain marginal in the research communities of Global South countries and societies. In the effort to contribute to a research agenda on these issues we identify a few preliminary conclusions.

In terms of cybersecurity, we find that IR/IPE scholarship is mostly oriented to maintaining the hegemony of countries and Western social forces (led by US companies, security and defense agencies) on the Internet, both in terms of new forms to carry out cyberwar, as in elaborating norms and institutions that defend the neoliberal order of Internet Governance. The boundaries between public and private spheres in the security and defense sectors are increasingly blurred as the leading private high-tech companies have a leading role and influence in this industry and in public sector decisions and capabilities.

With respect to the governance of digital trade and global finance, we identify two opposite patterns. On the one hand, from the side of digital trade, there is a process of concentration in few TNCs from the US and China, which gives them excessive market power. This creates new ways of producing value, but also new governance challenges and questions about what type of data capitalism will prevail on the Internet. On the other hand, in terms of global finance, blockchain technology initiated an opposite process of decentralization, which threatens not only incumbent actors in charge of financial transactions, but also the global financial structure. That is, IPE perspectives on cyberpolitics can shed light on the new patterns of organization and regulation of trade, production and finance in the digital era.

Similarly, changes in the forms of production fostered by digitalization are generating new challenges in terms of human rights and citizenship practices and identities. These are being addressed by different states and civil society organizations in disparate ways. Nascent citizen movements have begun to contest and counteract the growing concentration of data that is (mis)used for security, commercial and political purposes. However, the extent to which such bottom-up forces can open up spaces of democratization and pluralization in the sphere of cyberpolitics is yet to be seen. Nonetheless, it is certain that citizen movements will tend to have growing influence as the awareness of the implications of new technologies gradually coalesce into new social demands and political agendas in different countries.

Finally, we highlight the challenges that emerge in relation to environmental data being considered a private versus a public good. Similarly, we mentioned the potential of new forms of decentralized environmental governance based on blockchain technology, but also a centralizing trend towards concentrated companies in the high tech and extractive sectors having growing authority and material leverage in environmental governance. This trend is inscribed in the efforts of countries like China and Germany to influence global environmental governance, based on innovations achieved at the national level through digitalization. What is crucial is to understand the shifting configurations of power involved in the construction of an environment–sustainable development nexus where technology places a pivotal role.

Notwithstanding the particular issues raised in these four arenas of cyberpolitics, we also argued that we face conceptual challenges in the effort to make sense of the implications of digitalization. In this respect, we proposed to go beyond instrumental understandings of technology as the only possible readings of the political and economic implications of the use of new data technologies. Although instrumental use will always be relevant to consider, our warning is to avoid assuming uncritically ideas of technological determinism; whereby actors' possession of technology translates necessarily into power.

Instead, we suggest to see social and technological spheres as co-produced. This means that what is relevant is to pay attention to technology designs as immanent of, and imbricated in, social contexts marked by dynamics of conflict and cooperation between socio-technical forces. Namely, seeing social contexts as constitutive of technology and not as mere backgrounds. That is to say, the particular designs of technology (its functional capability) are manifestations of specific relations between such forces and interests. This suggests that new data technologies are also being appropriated and adapted by different actors beyond the intent for which it was originally designed. This complicates power assumptions that rely on a conflated relation between actor's agency and technology control. In this chapter we cited some examples that illustrate trends of cyberpolitics as dimensions of decentered agency.

Notwithstanding the potential openings that cyberpolitics offers for exploring alternative uses of technology, for most other countries today it is not an exaggeration to say that they are under a kind of "digital imperialism." Although Snowden's revelations intensified tensions between the US and the European Union in terms of data protection, it has not led to significant changes. This is a hegemonic order in which that most data-dependent countries accept and rarely question. An order characterized by new forms of digital control, concentrated in a few transnational social actors that have increasing influence over data of varied kinds (personal, biological, environmental, military, etc.), is enabling the fine-grained surveillance of populations in ways that were impractical a few years ago.

Despite these trends, academic interest in cyberpolitics and digitalization is rather scarce in countries and regions that experience such new digital dependencies. We consider this problematic for two reasons. First, strategically, without some exceptions, researchers in the Global South are not thinking about how to deal with these new digital challenges, leaving such countries and societies even more vulnerable on initiatives of extra-regional actors. Second, by neglecting cyberpolitics and digitalization in the Global South, academics are missing the opportunity to expand our understanding of these processes by incorporating the national and/or regional specificities that that could extend IR/IPE research scholarship beyond the usual Western-centric paradigms.

The discussion we proposed in this chapter hopes to make a contribution in this direction. Although the issues and topics addressed are not the only ones where research is needed, we think that they are at least the indispensable ones to move forward in a collective and interdisciplinary way. At the same time, we must not lose sight of the importance of critical engagements with cyberpolitics research. The greatest challenge of all is to contribute to avoid, or at least manage, the worst elements of digitalization, as well as position alternatives to those preferred by the most powerful actors of data capitalism.

Notes

1 Researchers often use "digital capitalism" in the literature; however, we chose data capitalism, because it makes a clear reference to the central resource that this form of capitalism accumulates: data.
2 When speaking of "cyber-weapons", analysts refer to malware, which is a concept that includes software with malicious purpose that seeks to provoke some kind of damage in other systems or software. There are several types of malware, among them: worms, ransomware, rootkits, trojans and viruses.
3 It should be noted that in this section our observations are limited to the intersection between cybersecurity and Internet governance, and not to all the other connotations that tend to be discussed under the latter term, particularly in the context of the Internet Governance Forum.
4 Metadata refers to data about data, such as the telephone numbers that a specific line was contacted. Although such metadata does not expose the content of the communications, it reveals the network of contacts of the spied line, very valuable intelligence information.

Bibliography

Aaronson, S. 2015. Why trade agreements are not setting information free: the lost history and reinvigorated debate over cross-border data flows, human rights, and national security. *World Trade Review* 14(4): 671–700.
Abdenur, A. and Da Silva Gama, C. 2015 Triggering the norms cascade: Brazil's initiatives for curbing electronic espionage. *Global Governance* 21(3): 455–474.
Acuto, M. and Curtis, S. (eds.) 2014. *Reassembling International Theory: Assemblage Thinking and International Relations*. Basingstoke, UK: Palgrave Macmillan.
Ball, K., Haggerty, K. and Lyon, D. (eds.) 2012. *Routledge Handbook of Surveillance Studies*. Routledge International Handbooks. New York, USA: Routledge.
Bernal, P. 2016. Data gathering, surveillance and human rights: recasting the debate. *Journal of Cyber Policy* 1(2): 243–264.
Betz, D. and Stevens, T. 2011. *Cyberspace and the State. Toward a Strategy for Cyber-Power*. London, UK: Routledge.
Beveridge, R. and Kern, K. 2013. The Energiewende in Germany: Background, developments and future challenges. *Renewable Energy Law and Policy Review* 4(1): 3–12.
Bieler, A. and Morton, A. 2004. A critical theory route to hegemony, world order and historical change: neo-Gramscian perspectives in international relations. *Capital & Class* 28(1): 85–113.
Bijker, W., Hughes, T. and Pinch, T. (eds.) 2012. *The Social Construction of Technological Systems*. Anniversary edition. Cambridge, Massachusetts, USA: The MIT Press.
Buchanan, B. 2016. Cryptography and sovereignty. *Survival* 58(5): 95–122.
Campbell-Verduyn, M. and Goguen, M. 2017. The mutual constitution of technology and global governance: Bitcoin, blockchains, and the international anti-money-laundering regime. In: *Bitcoin and Beyond: Cryptocurrencies, Blockchains, and Global Governance*. London, UK: Routledge.
Carr, M. 2014. Power plays in global internet governance. *Millennium: Journal of International Studies* 43(2): 640–659.
Chadwick, A. and Howard, P. 2009. *Routledge Handbook of Internet Politics*. London, UK: Routledge.
Chapron, G. 2017. The environment needs cryptogovernance. *Nature* 545(7655): 403–405.
Choucri, N. 2012. *Cyberpolitics in International Relations*. Cambridge, Massachusetts, USA: The MIT Press.
Cox, R. 1981. Social forces, states and world orders: Beyond International Relations Theory. *Millennium. Journal of International Studies* 10(2): 126–155.
Cox, R. 1987. *Production, Power, and World Order: Social Forces in the Making of History*. New York, USA: Columbia University Press.

Cox, R. and Schechter, M. 2002. *The Political Economy of a Plural World: Critical Reflections on Power, Morals and Civilization*. RIPE series in: Global Political Economy. London, UK: Routledge.

Cox, R. and Sinclair, T. 1996. *Approaches to World Order*. Cambridge, UK: Cambridge University Press.

De Filippi, P. and Wright, A. 2018. *Blockchain and the Law: The Rule of Code*. Cambridge, Massachusetts, USA: Harvard University Press.

Deibert, R. 2015. The geopolitics of cyberspace after Snowden. *Current History* 114(768): 9–15.

Deibert, R., Rohozinski, R. and Crete-Nishihata, M. 2013. Cyclones in cyberspace: Information shaping and denial in the 2008 Russia-Georgia war. *Security Dialogue* 43(1): 3–24.

DeNardis, L. and Hackl, A. 2015. Internet governance by social media platforms. *Telecommunications Policy* 39(9): 761–770.

Der Derian, J. 1990. The (s)pace of international relations: Simulation, surveillance, and speed. *International Studies Quarterly* 34(3): 295–310.

Dunn Cavelty, M. 2007. Cyber-terror – looming threat or phantom menace? The framing of the US cyber-threat debate. *Journal of Information Technology & Politics* 4(1): 19–36.

Ebert, H. and Maurer, T. 2013. Contested cyberspace and rising powers. *Third World Quarterly* 34(6): 1054–1074.

Feenberg, A. 1999. *Questioning Technology*. Abingdon, Oxon, UK: Routledge.

Finnemore, M. and Hollis, D. 2016. Constructing norms for global cybersecurity. *The American Journal of International Law* 110(3): 425–479.

Ford, J., Tilleard, S., Berrand-Ford, L., Araos, M., Biesbroek, R., Lesnikowski, A., MacDonald, G., Hsu, A., Chen, C. and Bizikova, L. 2016. Big data has big potential for applications to climate change adaptation. *Proceedings of the National Academy of Sciences of the United States of America* 113(39): 10729–10732.

Fuchs, D. 2013. Theorizing the power of global companies. In: Mikler, John, ed. *Handbook of Global Companies*. Chichester: Wiley-Blackwell: 77–95.

Gerlak, A., Saguier, M., Mills-Novoa, M., Fearnside, P. and Albrecht, T. 2019. Dams, Chinese investments, and EIAs: A race to the bottom in South America? *Ambio* 49(1): 154–164.

Gill, S. 2008. *Power and Resistance in the New World Order*. 2nd ed. New York, USA: Palgrave Macmillan.

Hall, R. and Biersteker, T. 2002. *The Emergence of Private Authority in Global Governance*. Cambridge, UK: Cambridge University Press.

Helbing, D., Frey, B. and Gigerenzer, G., Hafen, E., Hagner, M., Hofstetter, Y., van den Hoven, J., Zicari, R.V. and Zwitter A. 2017. Will democracy survive big data and artificial intelligence? *Scientific American* 25, February.

Holt, T. and Bossler, A. 2014. An assessment of the current state of cybercrime scholarship. *Deviant Behavior* 35(1): 20–40.

Howson, P., Oakes, S., Baynham-Herd, Z. and Swords, J. 2019. Cryptocarbon: The promises and pitfalls of forest protection on a blockchain. *Geoforum* 100: 1–9.

Howson, R. and Smith, K. (eds.) 2008. *Hegemony: Studies in Consensus and Coercion*. Routledge Studies in Social and Political Thought. New York, USA: Routledge.

Isin, E. and Ruppert, E. 2015. *Being Digital Citizens*. London, UK: Rowman & Littlefield.

Jackson, S. 2018. A turning IR landscape in a shifting media ecology: The state of IR literature on New Media. *International Studies Review* 21(3): 518–534.

Junio, T. 2013. How probable is cyber war? Bringing IR theory back in to the cyber conflict debate. *The Journal of Strategic Studies* 36(1): 125–133.

Kello, L. 2018. *The Virtual Weapon and International Order*. New Haven, Connecticut, USA: Yale University Press.

Latour, B. 2005. *Reassembling the Social. An Introduction to Actor-Network Theory*. New York, USA: Oxford University Press.

Lazer, D., Baum, M., Benkler, Y., Berinsky,A. J., Greenhill, K. M., Menczer, F., Metzger, M. J., Nyhan, B., Pennycook, G., Rothschild, D., Schudson, M., Sloman, S. A., Sunstein, C. R., Thorson, E. A., Watts, D. J. and Zittrain J. L. 2018. The science of fake news. *Science* 359(6380): 1094–1096.

Leonelli, S. 2013. Why the current insistence on open access to scientific data? Big data, knowledge production, and the political economy of contemporary biology. *Bulletin of Science, Technology & Society* 33(1–2): 6–11.

López-González, J. and Jouanjean, M. 2017. *Digital Trade: Developing a Framework for Analysis. OECD Trade Policy Paper 205*: OECD.

Lucchi, N. 2013. Understanding genetic information as a commons: From bioprospecting to personalized medicine. *International Journal of the Commons* 7(2): 313–338.

Lynn III, W. 2010. Defending a new domain: The Pentagon's cyberstrategy. *Foreign Affairs* 89(5): 97–108.

Madsen, A., Flyverbom, M., Hilbert, M. and Rupert, E. 2016. Big Data: Issues for an international political sociology of data practices. *International Political Sociology* 10(3): 275–296.

Mahrenbach, L., Mayer, K. and Pfeffer, J. 2018. Policy visions of big data: Views from the Global South. *Third World Quarterly* 39(10): 1861–1882.

Maurer, T. 2011. *Cyber Norm Emergence at the United Nations: An Analysis of the Activities at the UN Regarding Cyber-security.* Cambridge, Massachusetts: Belfer Center for Science and International Affairs, Harvard Kennedy School.

Mayer, M., Carpes, M. and Knoblich, R. (eds.) 2014. The global politics of science and technology: an introduction. In: *The Global Politics of Science and Technology.* Berlin: Springer-Verlag: 1–35.

Mayer-Schönberger, V. and Cukier, K. 2013. *Big Data. A Revolution That Will Transform How We Live, Work and Think.* New York, USA: Houghton Mifflin Hartcourt Publishing Company.

McCarthy, D. 2011. The meaning of materiality: Reconsidering the materialism of Gramscian IR. *Review of International Studies* 37(3): 1215–1234.

McKinsey & Company 2017. *Artificial Intelligence: The Next Digital Frontier?* Discussion Paper. McKinsey Global Institute. Available at: www.mckinsey.com/~/media/McKinsey/Industries/Advanced%20 Electronics/Our%20Insights/How%20artificial%20intelligence%20can%20deliver%20real%20 value%20to%20companies/MGI-Artificial-Intelligence-Discussion-paper.ashx.

Mueller, M., Mathiason, J. and Klein, H. 2007. The Internet and global governance: Principles and norms for a new regime. *Global Governance* 13(2): 237–254.

Nahuis, R. and Van Lente, H. 2008. Where are the politics? Perspectives on democracy and technology. *Science, Technology & Human Values* 33(5): 559–581.

Newell, P. and Levy, D. 2002. Business strategy and international environmental governance: Towards a neo-Gramscian synthesis. *Global Environmental Politics* 2(4): 84–101.

Plantin, J., Lagoze, C., Edwards, P.and Sandvig. C. 2016. Infrastructure studies meet platform studies in the age of Google and Facebook. *New Media & Society* 20(1): 293–310.

Pohle, J. and Van Audenhove, L. 2017. Post-Snowden Internet policy: Between public outrage, resistance and policy change. *Media and Communication* 5(1):1–6.

Rid, T. 2012. Cyber war will not take place. *The Journal of Strategic Studies* 36(1): 5–32.

Robinson, W. 2005. Gramsci and globalisation: From nation-state to transnational hegemony. *Critical Review of International Social and Political Philosophy* 8(4): 559–574.

Saguier, M. 2012. Peoples' tribunals in Latin America. In: Reed, D., Utting, P. and Mukherjee-Reed, A. (eds) *Business Regulation and Non-State Actors: Whose Standards? Whose Development?* Abingdon, UK: Routledge: 250–265.

Saguier, M. and Brent, Z. 2017. Social and solidarity economy in South American regional governance. *Global Social Policy* 17(3): 259–278.

Schia, N. 2018. The cyber frontier and digital pitfalls in the Global South. *Third World Quarterly* 39(5): 821–837.

Segal, A. 2013. The code not taken: China, the United States, and the future of cyber espionage. *Bulletin of the Atomic Scientists* 69(5): 38–45.

Srnicek, N. 2016. *Platform Capitalism.* Cambridge: Polity Press.

Taylor, L. and Schroeder, R. 2015. Is bigger better? The emergence of big data as a tool for international development policy. *GeoJournal* 80(4): 503–518.

Wang, Z., He, H. and Fan, M. 2014. The ecological civilization debate in China. The role of ecological Marxism and constructive postmodernism—Beyond the predicament of legislation. *Monthly Review* 66(6): 37–59.

World Economic Forum. 2018. Harnessing Artificial Intelligence for the Earth. *Fourth Industrial Revolution for the Earth Series:* REF 030118. Available at: www3.weforum.org/docs/Harnessing_Artificial_ Intelligence_for_the_Earth_report_2018.pdf.

Ziewitz, M. 2015. Governing algorithms: Myth, mess, and methods. *Science, Technology & Human Values* 41(1): 1–14.

42
The IPE of regional energy integration in South America

Ignacio Sabbatella and Thauan Santos

Introduction

The current energy changes of global capitalism represent some challenges for the process of regional integration in South America. This chapter focuses on two changes. On the one hand, there is the transition to a low-carbon economy, especially after the Paris Agreement and the establishment of the Sustainable Development Goals (SDGs). In this sense, the promotion of renewable energies is an objective that countries are nationally assuming within the framework of the fight against climate change. On the other hand, the expansion of liquefied natural gas (LNG) international trade, driven by cost reduction and greater availability of resources. LNG trade is becoming more attractive than gas pipeline trade for importing countries in order to guarantee national energy security.

Thanks to its large endowment of energy resources, South America has a rich history of natural gas and electricity cross-border connections (initially through binational hydroelectric dams) dating back to the 1970s. However, the two global changes indicated seem to diminish the interest on the part of the countries to seek greater regional integration. Thus, the main purpose of this chapter is to analyze the impact of these changes in the global energy system, from a regional energy integration perspective.

To this end, we will start from the critical view of the International Political Economy (IPE), in its variant of the Latin American school, and the recent contributions of the IPE of energy to understand the nexus between global changes, regional integration and energy policies. Regional energy integration can be defined as a "process of strategic interconnection of energy networks in international corridors, which allows, under a common regulatory framework and adequate services, their agile and efficient circulation."[1] For that reason, we are going to focus on gas and electrical interconnection projects, although it is worth noting that there have also been many cooperation projects on oil exploitation between South American countries throughout history.

In order to address these issues, this chapter is divided into five sections. First, we will briefly examine the nexus between critical IPE, regionalism and energy from a Latin American perspective. Second, we will review the historical stages of energy integration in South America, taking into account both power and gas sectors. Third, we will describe the main current changes along the global energy system. Fourth, we will analyze the impacts of these changes over the energy integration process, questioning whether these challenges contribute to a greater or lesser propensity for regional energy integration. Finally, we will provide some final considerations.

Theoretical framework

We start from the critical view of the International Political Economy (IPE). From this perspective, it is possible to understand how capitalism leads to uneven development as some centers increase their wealth and growth at the expense of others.[2] Considering this inequality, the dependency theory was an approach unfolded in Latin America around the 1960s to explain the obstacles to development faced by poor countries, vulnerable as a result of economic exploitation from developed states.[3]

Besides dependency, after the World War II the Latin American critical tradition revolved around another axe: structuralism. Although they were considerably different, these intellectual traditions shared the consciousness of under-development. For *dependentists*, it was necessary a more radical political leadership for the left; while for structuralists, what was important was a renewed leading economic role for the state.[4]

Under the influence of Raúl Prebish, the Economic Commission for Latin America and the Caribbean (ECLAC) developed a structuralist analysis in the sense that it viewed the world economy as a system within which the center and the periphery are intrinsically related. Most of the economic problems of the periphery were associated with the specific economic structure that emerged from that interaction, because of the tendency to deterioration of the terms of trade.

While the structure of production in the center is homogeneous and diversified; the structure in the periphery, in contrast, is heterogeneous and specialized in primary products. To escape from these asymmetries, it was necessary to introduce a process of vigorous state-led industrialization.[5] In this context, regional integration was a key policy to create a broader market and sustain the process of industrialization. More generally, the initiatives and reflections on regional integration in Latin America have historically been oriented towards the search for autonomy, that is, greater freedom from extra-regional powers, and economic development, that is, the diversification of the regional productive structure.[6]

Regarding the link between critical IPE and regionalism, the World Order Approach (WOA) is skeptical about much of the really existing regionalism, but it points out that there is a potential for states-driven regional projects to mitigate the negative effects of globalization and contribute to a new era of social regulation and community.[7] In Latin America, several studies have combined a critical perspective of IPE with a positive evaluation of regional integration. The Latin American school of IPE has been considered a "hybrid model" that combines concepts of dependency, realism and interdependence. Therefore, its structuring axes are development, dependency and autonomy; its unit of analysis is the peripheral state in the world system; and its objectives are to maximize the power of negotiation and autonomy.[8] In this context, the role of some strategic sectors is highlighted, such as energy.

In general, Van de Graaf et al. synthesize the contributions of the main theories in IPE and their applications to energy: mercantilism/realism, liberalism, Marxism and constructivism.[9] They argue that, in the case of mercantilism/realism, energy is a strategic asset and can be a source of power; in liberalism, energy is treated as any other commodity and the role of liberalization and interdependence is observed due to international energy trade; in Marxism, a critical analysis is made of the beneficiaries of the exploitation of the resource, of the role of local elites, and of the country's risk of becoming resource-dependent; finally, constructivism reflects on the social construction of the concept of energy security and energy statistics. Throughout South American history, the tension between two models, with nuances, is remarkable: energy as a strategic resource, managed by state companies to promote industrial development, and energy as a commodity, exploited by private companies according to the maximization of their profits.

It is also worth mentioning that the classic IPE texts on the energy issue tend to focus almost exclusively on oil, given its relevance especially in the twentieth century, so there is little discussion about other sources and energy regimes.[10] Therefore, energy remains conceptually ill-defined and poorly understood in IPE terms, whether by the meager treatment of the concepts of the world of energy, or by the little existence of theoretical discussion about different sources and energy regimes. It was left as an essentially technical subject, relegated to the realm of policymakers and practitioners, to economists and to engineers.[11]

Besides, Van de Graaf and Colgan explain that states have traditionally regarded the energy sector as a crucial component of national sovereignty despite of the global benefits to be reaped from international cooperation.[12] Consequently, national energy governance still reigns above regional or global energy governance, thus becoming one of the main barriers to greater energy cooperation and integration. It is no wonder indeed that energy was a major driver in the beginning of European integration with the European Coal and Steel Community (ECSC) in 1951 and of European Atomic Energy Community (EURATOM) in 1957, but it took about 50 years before, finally, the European Union (EU) was able to agree in March 2007 on an "Energy policy for Europe."[13]

Often, energy integration is defended as an alternative policy in the (national) energy planning, corresponding to a policy of guaranteeing *energy security*. Although the concept of energy security arises in the twentieth century during the period of the oil shocks of the 1970s, there is no single and/or consensus definition about this concept "because it is polysemic, multi-dimensional and context-dependent on the nature of each country/region."[14]

A first definition of energy security is the uninterrupted availability of energy sources at an affordable price, as proposed by the International Energy Agency,[15] or "the efficient management of primary energy supply from domestic and external sources, reliability of the energy infrastructure and capacity of energy suppliers to meet current and future demand," according to the World Energy Council.[16] More broadly, Sovacool and Mukherjee claimed that energy security is a complex objective that includes questions on how to equitably provide available, affordable, reliable, efficient, environmentally benign, properly governed and socially acceptable energy services.[17] In the South American case, Palestini claims that regional energy integration is a winning strategy for all parties since it increases both the security and the energy efficiency of those countries with a low endowment of resources (such as Chile or Uruguay), as well as those with a less diversified energy matrix (such as Ecuador or Bolivia) and, also, it is an option for exporters that seek to diversify the final markets to insert their surplus production.[18] Ergo, and considering the diversity of resources that the different countries of the region have, it is possible to recognize (power and gas) energy integration as a strategic energy policy that guarantees regional energy security in a broad way, that is, considering the social (universal access) and environmental (mitigation of emissions and environmental impacts) dimensions to the concept of energy security when it comes to developing countries.[19]

Viewed as a whole, South America is a region that holds important and diversified renewable and non-renewable energy resources, that allow it to be characterized as a self-sufficient and even exporting region.[20]

South American energy integration

According to Latin American Energy Organization (OLADE), in 2015 primary energy supply in South America consisted of 34 percent oil; 28 percent natural gas; 10 percent hydro energy; 6 percent coal; 1 percent nuclear; and 21 percent others. Unlike the global energy matrix, natural gas occupies the second place and coal has a smaller share even than the hydro energy. Regarding electricity, the installed capacity accounted 57 percent hydro; 37 percent thermo; 1 percent nuclear; and 5 percent others (geothermal, solar and wind energy). Due to the existence of an electric mix strongly based on hydroelectricity, the emissions of Greenhouse Gases (GHG) are lower than the world average.[21] (We will return to this point in the next section.

The uneven distribution of energy resources in South America determines that some countries are exporters and others importers (see Table 42.1), which favors a gas and power integration development to optimize energy complementarity and supply security.[22]

However, due to the political and economic regional transformations, the integration process has not been linear. There are three stages or waves: autonomous regionalism, new or open regionalism, and post-liberal or post-hegemonic regionalism (see Table 42.2).

The autonomous regionalism was extended from the 1950s to the end of the 1980s and its objective was to increase the autonomy of the region against the centers of world power.[23] It was characterized by a state with an active role in regionalism, in which import-substitution industrialization (ISI) and the quest for a larger regional market to cultivate a demand for value-added products of the region were key components.[24]

The pursuit of complementarity in the field of energy has been present since the first initiatives focused on regional integration at a Latin American level.[25] At the beginning of the 1960s, the formation of the Latin American Free Trade Association (ALALC) in the intergovernmental sphere had as counterpart, in the field of companies (public and private), the emergence of the Regional Energy Integration Commission (CIER) in 1964, and the reciprocal Assistance of National Oil Companies of Latin America (ARPEL, now the Regional Association Of Oil, Gas And Biofuels Sector Companies In Latin America And The Caribbean) in 1965. In 1972 was created the Latin American Energy Organization (OLADE), with the purpose of conducting studies and promoting energy cooperation.

Table 42.1 Net exporters and net importers countries

Net exporters	Net importers	Main products
Venezuela	–	Oil
Colombia	–	Oil
Ecuador	–	Oil
Bolivia	–	Natural Gas
Paraguay	–	Hydro-electricity
Perú	–	Natural Gas
–	Uruguay	Oil
–	Argentina	Natural Gas
–	Chile	Natural Gas
–	Brazil	Natural Gas, Electricity
–	Surinam	Oil
–	Guyana	Oil

Source: Authors' own elaboration.

Table 42.2 Stages of South American energy integration

Stages	Main characteristics	Energy focus and results	Energy initiatives
1950s–1980s: Autonomous Regionalism	Active role of the state and ISI. Objective: autonomy. Geopolitics: competition between Ar–Br to expand their influence over the bordering countries.	Binational initiatives (state-led). High level of execution.	Yabog pipeline (Bo–Ar). Itaipu Dam (Bo–Br). Salto Grande Dam (Ur–Ar). Yacyretá Dam (Ar–Py).
1990s: New or Open Regionalism	Neoliberal hegemony. Trade liberalization. Reforms in the oil and gas and power sector: deregulation and privatization of state companies. Objective: maximize private profits. Low energy prices.	Binational initiatives (market-led). High level of execution but low sustainability. Multilateral initiatives: no impact.	Border pipelines: 7 between Ar–Ch; 2 Ar–Ur; 1 Ar–Br; 2 Bo–Br. Mercosur: MoU on Gas Exchange and Gas Integration; MoU concerning Electric Exchanges and Electrical Integration). Binational electrical interconnections.
2000s: Post-liberal or Post-hegemonic Regionalism	Neoliberal hegemony crisis. Factors: bilateral interconnection crisis; rising oil prices; Venezuelan energy diplomacy.	Multilateral (state-led). Low level of execution.	Southern Energy Ring; Great Southern Gas Pipeline; OPPEGASUR; South America Energy Council. Resume of gas exports Bo–Arg; Renegotiation of the gas contract Bo-Bra; gas pipeline Co–Ve. Binational electrical interconnections.

Source: Authors' own elaboration.

At the same time that the ISI model was prevailing as a predominant paradigm in the region, the electricity sectors have been shaped around the conception of the power industry as a natural monopoly based on the concept of sovereignty that privileges the use of national energy resources to the search for energy self-sufficiency. In that way, the interconnections[26] between countries were limited to very specific cases, usually with the purpose of enabling cross-border exchanges in very remote areas. In the meantime, studies were underway to explore the possibility of joint exploitation of the hydroelectric resources of bordering rivers.[27] Then, in this stage, binational hydro-electrical projects were conceived in strategic and geopolitical terms; either because the common efficient use of water resources arose as an innovative solution for the border disputes, such as the Itaipu case (Brazil–Paraguay), or to balance the neighbor countries relative forces in border areas, such as the Yacyreta case (Argentina–Paraguay).[28] Regarding the gas sector, the first gas interconnection project was materialized in 1972 with the startup of Yabog pipeline, which links Bolivia with Argentina. Its objective was less oriented to the Argentinian market supply than to the dictatorial governments' geopolitical relationship in the context of the competition between the main regional powers, Brazil and Argentina, to expand their influence over the bordering countries.[29]

During the 1990s, regional initiatives were framed in the neoliberal restructuring of South American economies in terms of unilateral and multilateral trade liberalization, unlike previous integration strategies characterized by protectionism and state intervention in pursuit of endogenous industrial development. In contrast with that "old regionalism" of postwar, the Inter-American Development Bank (IDB) called the initiatives of the last decade of the twentieth century "new regionalism,"[30] while ECLAC created the "open regionalism" concept.[31]

Under neoliberal hegemony, national reforms took place in the energy sector, with different levels of depth. The premise was the opening of private capital participation, the separation of the activities of the power chain (generation, transmission and distribution) and its independent regulation, open access to the transmission networks (including international connections) and distribution, opening to exchanges between companies of different countries (both in the market of contracts as in the opportunity), and creation of wholesale markets.[32] In this scenario, private companies promoted bilateral integration in order to maximize their profits and the states limited themselves to guaranteeing the general conditions for commercial exchange by signing protocols.

The most outstanding case was Argentina, whose reform enabled the overexploitation of existing natural gas reserves by private operators,[33] which turned over gas surpluses to neighboring markets through ten export gas pipelines (seven to Chile, two to Uruguay and one towards Brazil). In open regionalism terms, there was a predominance of "de facto" integration, driven by private interests, complemented by policy-driven integration in which the Argentinian government signed the necessary agreements with the neighboring countries to guarantee the commercial exchange of gas by gas pipelines. There were no agencies created to monitor the commitments assumed, nor mechanisms to anticipate situations of supply risk.[34] As Argentina abandoned the condition of importer to become an exporter, Bolivia strengthened its ties with Brazil in order to redirect the destination of its gas. For this purpose, two cross-border gas pipelines were built and launched between 1999 and 2002.

When it comes to power integration, due to the reforms of the decade, it was argued that while the countries were establishing policies aimed at creating efficient markets, the integration of their markets (developed in a competitive environment, transparency and clarity regarding the rules of the game) would be a natural consequence of these policies along the way to achieve the optimum of the whole. In this way, the existence of asymmetries and regulatory barriers became the main obstacles to be detected and removed. Hence the emphasis on the requirement that electricity sectors of the countries converge towards a similar model.[35]

Within Mercosur, the Memorandum of Understanding (MoU) on Electric Exchanges and Electrical Integration was signed in 1998 and the MoU on Gas Exchanges and Gas Integration in 1999, in which the States Parties undertook to develop individual markets' regional electricity and natural gas operated by both public and private companies under the rules of free trade and competition. Despite the fact that energy issues are dealt with in Sub-Working Group No. 9 (SGT 9), the legal regulations on energy integration have not made any progress in terms of incorporating mechanisms for the resolution of disputes or for regulating crisis situations, and there is evidence of the lack of a multilateral institutional framework to regulate and coordinate integration processes in the energy sector.

The integration processes forged in the 2000s have led to terms such as "post-liberal regionalism"[36] or "post-hegemonic regionalism"[37] since this regionalism emerges from the crisis of neoliberal hegemony, but it does not consolidate a new hegemony. From the victory of progressive parties in a large part of the region, the integration was relaunched with a primacy of the political agenda over the economy, the return of developmentalism and the active role of the state.

The post-liberal scenario was featured by multilateral energy initiatives and energy became a strategic axis of the regional integration agenda. Among the factors that gave impetus are: the increase in the international price of a barrel of oil; the questioning of privatization schemes through the extension of state control, nationalizations and/or mechanisms to capture oil revenues; the implementation of "energy diplomacy" from Venezuela by the government of Hugo Chávez; the diplomatic crisis between the governments of Argentina and Chile when Argentina was unable to comply simultaneously with domestic market supply and export commitments.

The main multilateral initiatives were the Southern Energy Ring;[38] the Great Gas Pipeline of the South;[39] OPPEGASUR,[40] but none was executed.[41] The creation of the Union of South American Nations (UNASUR) in 2008 consecrated energy as one of the central engines of integration. Under its orbit was the Energy Council of South America (CES), created by the Declaration of Margarita (2007) and composed of the Ministers of Energy of each country and set as its goal to draft the Energy Treaty of South America (TES). However, the existence of opposing energy models between the governments most focused on the state role and the governments pro-market, conspired against its operation. Due to the Argentinian supply crisis, in addition to the fall of multilateral projects, Chile had to install two LNG terminals to cover its internal demand. Likewise, Argentina has had to import Bolivian gas again to cover the growth of domestic demand encouraged by the economic reactivation. The Bolivian government imposed a condition to Argentina not to export its gas to Chile until the border demand that would allow Bolivia to enter the sea was met by Chile. However, the internal political problems that Bolivia went through in the following years and the slowdown in private investment after the nationalization of hydrocarbons prevented the Bolivian government from complying with the volumes committed. Bolivia had to prioritize the shipment of gas to Brazil, but even so was not enough to meet the volumes expected by the Brazilian market and, therefore, Brazil expanded its external supply of natural gas by contracting three Floating Storage and Regasification Units (FSRUs) between 2009 and 2014. Analogously, the Argentinian government resorted to the import of LNG through the installation of two FSRUs between 2008 and 2011.

Additionally, Colombia and Venezuela were interconnected through the Transcaribean gas pipeline in 2007. The duration of the contract was 20 years, Colombia expected to sell its gas to Venezuela during the first 4 years to cover its shortages in the western region and, at the end of that period, the supply from Venezuela to Colombia would be reversed. The delay in investments in Venezuelan territory did not allow the contract to be fulfilled, so supply from Colombia was extended until 2015.

In short, the multilateral initiatives in the post-neoliberal scenario, unlike the previous stage, had a strong state imprint and sought to transcend the commercial ties based on an economic and social development agenda. However, they were not executed due to historical, political, technical, economic, financial and regulatory obstacles.[42]

In addition to the rise in oil prices and the uncertainty in the availability of gas in the Southern Cone, there were important changes in the energy situation in the 2000s, generating a climate of distrust among countries regarding energy exchanges and in the investors in general. However, several interconnection projects were developed in LA, such as between Argentina–Brazil (2000–2001) and Ecuador–Colombia (2003–2006).

Created in 2000, the Initiative for the Integration of Regional Infrastructure in South America (IIRSA) was incorporated into the South American Council of Infrastructure and

Planning (COSIPLAN) in 2011, which is a forum for political and strategic discussion through consultation, evaluation, cooperation, planning and coordination of efforts and articulation of programs and projects in order to foster regional infrastructure integration among UNASUR member countries.[43] In the context of the Andean Community (CAN), the general framework for the subregional interconnection of electric systems and intracommunity exchange of electricity was established in 2002.[44] Recently, CAN is taking more accurate steps to integrate the electricity system of the member countries.

Figures 42.1 and 42.2 show the current status of energy interconnections and pipelines in South America. Figure 42.1 shows that cross-border interconnections are spatially concentrated in the Andes or Southern Cone, that justifies why different authors approach the South American energy integration as divided by two large blocs of countries.[45] Almost all countries have

Figure 42.1 Power plant and international interconnections in South America
Source: CIER (2017).

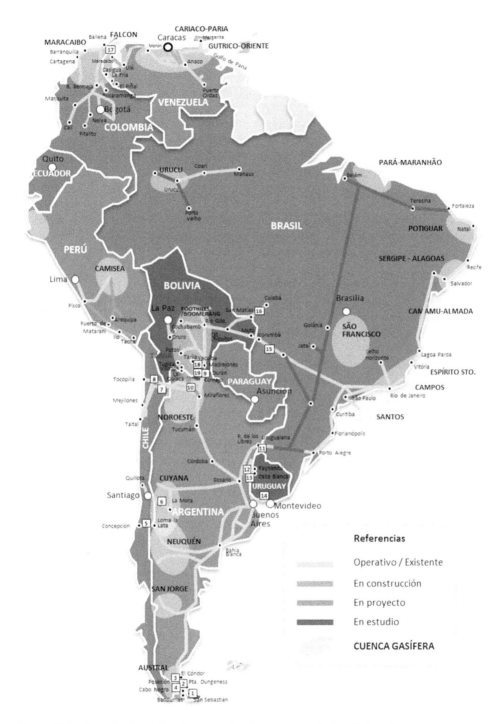

Figure 42.2 Gas pipeline networks and natural gas reserves in South America
Source: CIER (2017).

interconnections with a neighboring country. Figure 42.2 shows current gas pipeline networks and natural gas reserves in South America, as well as gas basins.

In addition to the three binational hydroelectric powers (HPs) already in operation – Itaipu (Br–Py, 14 GW), Salto Grande (Ar–Uy, 1.9 GW) and Yacyreta (Ar–Py, 3.2 GW) – Panambí (Ar–Br, 1.1 GW) and Corpus Christi (Ar–Py, 3.4 GW) dams are under study.[46] There are 22 international interconnections in South America,[47] some operating in 50 Hz and others in 60 Hz, with special participation of Argentina, Brazil, Colombia, Ecuador, Paraguay, Uruguay and Venezuela; in contrast, Bolivia, Chile and Peru are still relatively isolated from the electrical systems of neighboring countries.

Global energy changes

After a brief presentation of the stages of energy integration in South America, it is necessary to make an adequate analysis of the current global energy changes and their effects. There are at least three current changes underway in the global energy market:[48]

1   climate change and the need to decarbonize global economy;
2   geopolitical changes related to the rise of energy demand from developing countries such as China and India; and
3   increasing volatility in oil and gas (O&G) markets.

The first (and probably the most important) shift is related to the need to decarbonize global economy to face the impacts of climate change. The Paris Agreement was agreed by virtually every country in the world to reduce greenhouse gas emissions (GHG) in order to limit the average global temperature rise well below 2 degrees Celsius and as close as possible to 1.5 degrees Celsius, thus avoiding the most severe impacts of climate change such as increased droughts, floods and severe storms. Given the impossibility of reaching consensus on a single universal emission mitigation formula, it was agreed that each country decided its own goals for the period 2020–2030. From the point of view of equity, the per capita emissions of developing countries are generally much lower than those of developed countries. South American emissions as a whole represent only 3.2 percent of the total in 2017, according to BP data,[49] due to the strong preponderance of hydroelectric power as we have shown in the previous section. The historical responsibility not only of South America, but also of Latin America, in climate change is therefore very limited – especially if we consider the principle of "common but differentiated responsibility" (CBDR). However, the divergence of national interests of the countries of the region in relation to climate change has not allowed a common position in the international negotiations related to the climate regime. In this way, regional organizations such as Mercosur and UNASUR have not yet played a specific role in these negotiations.[50]

According to the International Energy Agency (IEA),[51] energy sector accounts for two-thirds of total GHG emissions and 80 percent of CO_2, so any effort to reduce emissions and mitigate climate change must include the energy sector. In this sense, the promotion of renewable energies is one of the main policies adopted at the national level. In some developed countries the transformation of their energy mixes with the aim of reducing CO_2 emissions began many years ago, while a few developing countries incorporated renewable energies in order to increase energy supply and improve access to energy electricity in isolated areas.[52] Since the Paris Agreement and the Sustainable Development Goals (SDGs),[53] the promotion of renewable energies has accelerated in both cases. Generally, the passage from the era of fossil fuels to the era of renewable energies is called energy transition (see Box 42.1). Although it is not the first energy

---

Box 42.1 What is energy transition?

Energy transition can be understood as a structural change in the system of energy supply and utilization. Sometimes it is the consequence of technological and economic transformations; sometimes, it is the product of political decisions.

Historically, transitions have taken several decades to consolidate. The 80 years that elapsed since 1830, when the contribution of coal to world energy exceeded 10 percent, until it reached its peak of about 45 percent by 1910 are proof of that. As a plus, in 55 years the share of oil in the energy matrix went from 10 percent (World War I) to just over 40 percent in the 1970s (Carrizo et al. 2016).

According to IRENA (2019), the ongoing concept of "energy transition" is used to mention the shift from fossil fuels to renewable energy sources. There are three main aspects that underpin the transition, all of them directly affected by technology development (Bueb et al. 2017):

1   *energy efficiency*, guaranteeing economic growth with lower energy inputs;
2   *renewables energies*, with solar and wind power standing out while other renewables have been growing more slowly – such as wave and tidal power, biofuels and waste (Kuzemko et al. 2018); and
3   *electrification*, since heat pumps and electric vehicles are pushing for the increase of renewable energies in transport, industry and construction.

Due to the very complex and dynamic nature of the energy transition, it is difficult to make precise predictions (IRENA 2019). What is known is that energy transition will require significant additional policy interventions (IEA–IRENA 2017) and the financial system will need to consider broader sustainability and energy transition requirements.

---

transition humanity has ever witnessed, the current energy transition from fossil fuels is already ongoing and should not be analyzed from a single lens – since it is not an exclusively technological or resource endowment issue.[54]

Even though renewables growing is unquestionable, oil and gas would still play a key role over the next two decades. In fact, there is a strong remnant embedded within what can be called "fossil fuel capitalism"[55] or "petro-market capitalism"[56] that underpin carbon intensity, what makes energy transitions to be path dependent (rather than revolutionary), cumulative (rather than fully substitutive) and carbon lock-in – limiting the agency of future generations.[57]

In this context, natural gas is seen as a cleaner option among fossil fuels. It produces around half the CO_2 emissions of coal when burned to generate power and it is the ideal complement to renewables as it can be a lower-carbon, cost-effective backup to the variability of wind, solar and hydropower generation. In this transition scenario, the global gas market is evolving rapidly due to two revolutions: the US shale revolution and the LNG revolution.[58]

The "shale revolution" evolving in the US since the late 2000s features the use of shale resources thereby increasing the country's production of oil and natural gas significantly and correspondingly reducing its imports and contributing to oversupply in global markets and decreasing prices.[59] The basis of the shale revolution was two significant technological innovations: horizontal drilling and hydraulic fracturing.

In 2017, the United States exported more natural gas than it imported, marking the first time since 1957 that the US has been a net natural gas exporter.[60] Exports have grown both by pipeline (to Canada and Mexico) and as LNG (to Mexico, South Korea, China, Japan).[61] With its greater flexibility, US LNG will increasingly challenge gas "superpowers" such as Russia and Qatar.[62] At the same time, the increasing global competition among gas exporters could affect the global competitiveness of the renewable sector.[63] Gas is becoming more accessible and affordable throughout the world due to the growth of the global gas market. This growth has been faster by ship than by pipelines. According to BP data, the global export of LNG grew 108 percent between 2005 and 2017, while the export via gas pipelines only increased by 39 percent. Thus, LNG went from representing 26.2 percent to 34.6 percent of total worldwide natural gas trade in that period. The data for 2017 indicates the existence of 19 exporting countries (led by Qatar, Australia, Malaysia, Nigeria and Indonesia) and 40 importing countries (led by Japan, China, South Korea, India and Taiwan), while 26.7 percent of the supply comes from Qatar, 72.9 percent of global demand comes from Asia. South America represents only 3 percent of the total demand.[64]

As part of the decarbonization transition, the role of LNG is forecast to grow not only for power supply, but also in new markets such as fuel for the haulage and maritime sectors.[65] The technology of LNG, in addition to new significant resources such as the US shale, is gradually turning natural gas into a global commodity (see Box 42.2). Also, flexible LNG solutions can be more viable than a gas pipeline scheme because it does not require political arrangements.[66]

For the reasons detailed in this section, regional integration faces two challenges. First, the incorporation of renewable energies is a goal that countries are nationally assuming within the framework of the fight against climate change. In that sense, Sung Kyu and Hye Yeong studied the case of Northeast Asian Energy Market and they arrived to the conclusion that a country will face great limitations in development potential and costs if it attempts to increase the share of renewable energy. Instead, they consider that building an energy grid between neighboring countries enables eco-friendly energy use. Joint, large-scale development and sharing of abundant renewable sources would allow a substantial increase of that share.[67] In the same line, Muñoz Maldonado et al. understand that regional integration in Latin America benefits renewable projects since large projects can be developed to meet high demands, take advantage of shared energy resources to interconnect the countries of the region and reduce costs.[68] In another order of ideas, Hurtado and Souza warn about the interest of core economies and global governance organizations to promote a massive transfer of green technology to non-central regions, especially after the 2008 financial crisis, with the objective of relaunching capitalist accumulation.[69] Actually, the development of renewable energy sources may be an opportunity for peripheral countries to develop endogenous technological capacities from the initial stage of a new leading sector. Undoubtedly, the technological aspect is key to the extension of margins of autonomy of a region such as South America.

Second, LNG appears as an attractive option to guarantee national energy security. However, LNG can also be used for a bilateral or multilateral integration strategy, especially when it is more efficient to share regasification infrastructure or when the physical connection between the exporter and the consumer within the same region faces geographical difficulties. In addition, natural gas is the backup source for more wind and solar energy, which are naturally intermittent and need peak gas plants. If an energy mix of renewable energies and natural gas (including LNG) is considered, it is possible to plan an integration policy that aims both to promote a cleaner energy matrix and to strengthen regional energy security.

Box 42.2 What is Liquefied Natural Gas (LNG)?

The waterway transport of Liquefied Natural Gas (LNG) represents an alternative to the transportation of natural gas by gas pipelines. LNG is a natural gas cooled to the point that condenses to liquid, by being exposed to a temperature of approximately 161°C and at atmospheric pressure. This process is carried out in liquefaction plants or Floating units of Production, Storage and Offloading (FPSO) in the exporting country and the volume is reduced by 600 times approximately, which makes it more economical to be transported between continents, in special vessels called methane tankers. The process of reconversion to a gaseous state is carried out at the port of destination through regasification plants or Floating Storage and Regasification Units (FSRU) in order to inject it into the gas pipeline network or for specific uses in the importing country.

As the distance in which the gas can be transported increases, the economic advantages of gas pipelines decrease compared to LNG. Indeed, though both transport networks are relatively fixed transport infrastructure, the capital and operational expenses for the pipeline systems grow exponentially with their length, while a LNG system has a single component which varies with distance: maritime transport, which was traditionally much more economic per each cubic meter transported (López 2012).

The first long-distance LNG transportation is considered to have been carried out in 1959, when the Methane Pioneer ship routed gas from Lake Charles in the US Gulf of Mexico to the Canvey Island regasification terminal in the United Kingdom. This way, the viability of this transportation system was demonstrated.

A few years later, both liquefaction and regasification projects began. The first commercial transactions were LNG sales from the Arzew terminal in Algeria (launched in 1964) to the United Kingdom. In the Pacific basin, the Kenai plant in Alaska began its activities in 1969, exporting LNG to Japan (Díaz Casado 2008). However, it was not until the twenty-first century that the costs of transporting LNG were brought down to levels that made it competitive with piped gas (Markus 2016).

Although the global LNG market does not stop expanding, it is still governed by different regional prices. In Europe, wholesale gas is sold mainly via long-term contracts. These contracts variously make use of gas hub-based or oil-linked pricing, and often both. In Asia and many emerging markets without established and liquid gas trading markets, the price of LNG is for the most part set via oil-linkages, supplemented by a smaller share of spot imports.

In contrast, gas prices in North America are largely set at liquid trading hubs, the largest and most important of which is Henry Hub in Louisiana. There the movements of gas prices are driven more by overall market fundamentals than by changes in the oil price (IGU 2018).

Impacts on regional energy integration

After analyzing the main global energy changes as well as its challenges, this section assesses its possible impacts on regional energy integration. As already highlighted, the energy transformation will dramatically reshape geopolitics in the twenty-first century, especially because countries that lack domestic fuel reserves may benefit from exploiting their renewable energy resources.[70] Thus, the much-sought transition to a low-carbon energy economy shall be a cornerstone of national (and regional) energy policies committed to the climate change.[71]

However, when discussing "regional integration" it is necessary to clarify a possible conceptual confusion that happens in the literature, since all of them deal with challenges to energy planning and involve technical, regulatory and economic factors.[72] The first one is "regional energy integration" (the focus of this chapter), which deals with the energy integration between different countries through investments in physical infrastructure and harmonization of regulatory frameworks. Given the fact that (energy) resources are unevenly distributed, regional (energy) integration can be understood as a feasible option for meeting concrete needs and a powerful way to promote regional energy security. The second possible meaning addresses the integration of different sources due to the complementarity of generation – often between hydro with wind and/or solar). The third idea copes with renewable energy integration into the power grids and electricity markets, that basically focuses on incorporating renewable energy, but also considers distributed generation, energy storage and thermally activated technologies. Among the main barriers to a wider integration of renewable energy systems, we can stress their (i) limited realizable potential; (ii) still limited competitiveness; and (iii) intermittence.[73]

Evaluating the world of energy from the regional (and not only national) perspective contributes to the perception that such interactions across political levels can rarely be understood by looking only at national or international processes on their own. Despite this, in some countries the abandonment of the search for regional energy self-sufficiency and the withdrawal towards energy security in national terms can be seen.

Therefore, analyzing the impacts of global transactions on regional energy integration requires understanding both their impact on investments in physical infrastructure as well as their impact on the institutional governance of energy markets. With particular regard to the infrastructure, Guler, Çelebi and Nathwani developed a conceptual framework of "Regional Energy Hubs" and propose a greater role for investing in transmission capacity for inter-regional trade. By doing so, the authors consider and integrate key geopolitical, economic, environmental and financial factors needed to foster investment for transmission, since it can help countries to face climate change policies, remove congestion bottlenecks in the systems, as well as reduce countries' emissions.[74]

With regard to institutional governance, it is critical to realize that the changes that are taking place will affect geopolitics and the interests of actors and elites at the subnational, national and regional levels. As a consequence, it will impact on the international economy, trade flows and commodity prices; however, unlike other traditional areas of IPE, energy is characterized by a remarkable weakness of global institutions.[75] In fact, there is no "governance gap", but a multitude of weak and fragmented institutional arrangements mainly due to the resource nationalism associated with state control over the energy sectors through property, trade, and subsidy policies.[76]

In the 1990s, the countries of the region were less involved in climate policies since GHGs were below the world average thanks to an electric mix strongly based on hydroelectricity. The main promotional policies implemented in Argentina and Brazil had as the main objective the diversification of electricity generation, attracting the private investments necessary to respond to the increase in demand. In the last decade, the incorporation of renewable energies was accelerated in order to attract foreign investments as well as to reduce GHG emissions in the energy sector. As for the instruments used, the auction system has been implemented by Argentina, Brazil, Uruguay and Peru. Chile has implemented the quota system with a market of negotiable green certificates since 2008. Bolivia and Ecuador have opted for a system of guaranteed premium rates (feed-in tariffs). In contrast, until 2014, Colombia, Venezuela and Paraguay had not implemented any incentive policy.[77]

Uruguay has been the most successful case, since in 2017 it produced 28 percent of its electricity from wind and solar energy, according to OLADE. Chile reached 10 percent that year,

Brazil more than 7 percent and Peru 2.5 percent. Argentina still has a little significant participation but it aim to reach 20 percent of renewable electricity generation by 2025. Although there are initiatives to stimulate the national production of renewable technologies, the main regional suppliers are multinational companies. It is worth noting that the economic and political problems associated with the dependence on technologies developed abroad. In this regard, Inchauspe and Barrera show that there is productive capacity at a regional scale that could potentially replace imports in the industrial chain of renewable technologies, mainly in wind energy.[78]

Considering natural gas, one asks if LNG is going to be an energy security option over integration by gas pipelines. Casas de las Peñas del Corral argues that "natural gas has the essential characteristics to be the catalyst of regional energy integration as well as being a fuel-bridge to a possible energy transition to renewable fuels" adding that "the potential synergies that can flow from natural gas developments have not been exploited by South American countries."[79]

The increase of LNG trade in South America in the last decade has been negatively evaluated in relation to the regional integration process. Kozulj points out that the LNG projects do not connect with an integration policy but with a strategy of security supply. The crisis of the bilateral integration model, as in the cases of Argentina–Chile and Bolivia with Brazil and Argentina, has driven the need to visualize LNG like a supply option to continue gas market development.[80] In the same line, Altomonte et al. asserts that traditional supply through gas pipelines was not enough to guarantee energy security and that was the reason for resorting to maritime transport, favoring "energy disintegration" in some cases.[81]

Gas-importing countries have opted to replace or complement their supply through LNG regasification terminals and thereby strengthen internal energy security strategies. Between 2008 and 2016, eight regasification terminals have been enabled in the main importing countries with a total capacity of 108.5 million m³/day (see Table 42.3). Chile had to turn to LNG due to the crisis of the exporting role of Argentina and the impossibility of having gas coming from Peru and Bolivia, given the historical boundary problems it maintains with both countries. In the cases of Brazil and Argentina, the supply of LNG was complementary to the supply of Bolivian gas. Colombia incorporated an FSRU in order to import LNG to feed three power generation plants and thus strengthen domestic supply when El Niño weather affects the operation of hydroelectric power plants. Despite this, the impact of the breach of the bilateral contract with Venezuela cannot be underestimated.

Simultaneously, Peru chose to install a liquefaction terminal in order to export its surpluses in the form of LNG to extra-regional countries instead of allocating them to the regional

Table 42.3 LNG terminals in South America

Country	Terminal	Location	Opening year	Capacity (MMm³/d)
Argentina	FSRU	Bahía Blanca (Bs. As.)	2008	17
Argentina	FSRU	Escobar (Bs. As.)	2011	17
Brazil	FSRU	Pecem (Ceara)	2009	7
Brazil	FSRU	Bahía Guanabara (Rio do Janeiro)	2009	14
Brazil	FSRU	Bahía	2014	22
Perú	Liquefaction Plant	Melchorita (Lima)	2010	17
Chile	Regasification Plant	Quintero (Valparaíso)	2009	17
Chile	Regasification Plan	Mejillones (Antofagasta)	2010	5.5
Colombia	FSRU	Cartagena	2016	11

Source: Authors' own elaboration based on data from GIIGNL (2017).

market. In addition, Venezuela canceled a liquefaction terminal project that was to have South America as its main destination. Therefore, importing countries were forced to source LNG from outside the South American region.

Overall, the volume of trade in pipelines continues to have a significant share on the total, close to half, despite the fact that in 2013 it was surpassed by the volume of LNG. In spite of the breach of the committed volumes by the Bolivian government, neither Brazil nor Argentina finished the bilateral tie. In contrast, the situation of bilateral integration between Colombia and Venezuela does seem to be stuck, since the problems of the Venezuelan gas sector were compounded by the deterioration of diplomatic relations between both governments.

The trend towards the commoditization of natural gas through LNG trade directly affects Venezuela and Bolivia as "regional powers" of trade by gas pipelines. At the same time, it is necessary to consider domestic and regional particularities for both cases. Venezuela faces political, economic and financial problems that prevent it from consolidating its gas production. Bolivia as a regional supplier faces two challenges: the development of the Pre-sal in Brazilian maritime territory and Vaca Muerta formation in Argentinian territory envisages a lower need for importing Bolivian gas for the main markets of the region. In turn, the ideological distancing of the new governments of Brazil and Argentina adds more pressure to the next renegotiations of purchase and sale contracts in 2019 and 2026, respectively.

In recent years, there has been a regional change of political orientation since the arrival of pro-market governments, especially in Brazil and Argentina, and the economic and political crisis that Venezuela is going through. In this context, there is a process of dismantling or disuse of the main integration organizations: UNASUR and Mercosur.

Conclusions

From the perspective of the Latin American school of IPE it has been possible to analyze how the energy changes of global capitalism are affecting the process of regional integration in South America. There is no causal determinism. Actually, the obstacles to South American integration are endogenous and historical. The existence of these obstacles, in addition to the global changes, seems to have diminished the interest in promoting regional integration policies. The incorporation of renewable energies and the increase in the flow of LNG have been adopted at the national level instead of being adopted as regional policies, suggesting uncertainty about the direction of regional energy integration.

The process of energy integration in South America has been strongly based on binational initiatives, especially hydroelectric power plants (HPP) and gas pipelines. At the different stages of regional energy integration presented, it was clear that few projects were bold enough to consider more than two states. It is therefore necessary to reflect on how far the promotion of renewable energy plants, including the impetus given by the Paris Agreement and the SDG Agenda, will be able to change this historical profile.

Still considering the relationship between renewable energies and HPPs, the dubious use of the concept of energy integration was discussed: sometimes it suggests a regional physical energy integration as well as harmonization of regulatory framework, sometimes it proposes an integration of different sources due to the complementarity of generation (often with wind and solar). It is also possible to glimpse a third meaning for energy integration, which specifically addresses the incorporation of intermittent renewable energies into distribution networks. One question that arises from the different interpretations of the concept is the following: can the exploitation of renewable energies on a national scale lead to the lesser need to seek integration with neighbors as a side effect?

Regarding natural gas, another question arises: if LNG is on the way to becoming a global commodity, will it be feasible to think of new gas pipeline projects that interconnect the countries of the region?

In order to answer these questions, it is necessary to rethink the regional integration project in light of the historical tensions: autonomy vs. dependency; state-lead vs. market-lead; regional self-sufficiency vs. national energy security; energy as strategic resource vs. commodity; own technology vs. foreign technology.

Despite the reduction in its priority, the energy integration projects in South America do not seem to be exhausted. The Arco Norte and the Andean Electrical Interconnection System (SINEA) projects are examples that countries in the region continue to think of regional alternatives to the national challenges that each one faces. Respectively involving four (Brazil, Guyana, Suriname and French Guiana) and five (Colombia, Ecuador, Peru, Bolivia and Chile) countries, both projects cover different areas (north and Pacific coast of the subcontinent) and add to national narrowing initiatives relations with neighboring countries.

Instead of proposing a strong role only for Brazil (which often occurs), we stressed that different countries have a central role in promoting regional energy integration, such as Argentina and Bolivia.

> The fact that they have borders with five countries each, water resources in abundance, and large-scale conventional and non-conventional reserves places them in a strategic position in promoting regional (physical) energy integration. Peru also plays a significant role, particularly due to its borders with four countries in the region and an enormous hydroelectric potential available.[82]

Besides, it is worth mentioning the particular situation of Argentina in relation to Chile. In 2016, the Argentinian government decided to import regasified LNG from the Chilean terminals through the pipelines that had been left in disuse in order to replace more expensive alternative fuels for the generation of electricity at the peak of winter demand. On the other hand, the impressive take-off of Vaca Muerta's unconventional gas production has reactivated private projects to export summer period surpluses to the Chilean, Brazilian and Uruguayan markets. That is to say, the process of regional gas integration may not be on the way to definitive exhaustion, but rather return to open regionalism under neoliberal principles.

It was shown that integrating is a political decision, not just a matter of technical and institutional/regulatory nature. Ergo, renewables and LNG can become an opportunity to create new pathways of regional energy integration. Thus, despite the side effects the expansion of renewables and LNG can cause in the process of energy integration in South America, they are expected to be able to promote the development of integration, ensuring sustainable regional energy security.

Notes

1 Ruiz–Caro 2010.
2 O'Brien and Williams 2016.
3 Dos Santos 2002.
4 Palma 2009.
5 Palma 2009.
6 Briceño Ruiz 2012.
7 Söderbaum 2005.
8 Tussie 2015.
9 Van de Graaf et al. 2016.
10 Santos 2018.
11 Kuzemko et al. 2018.

12 Van de Graaf and Colgan 2016.
13 Jong 2015.
14 Santos 2018.
15 See official website: www.iea.org/topics/energysecurity/.
16 World Energy Council 2017.
17 Sovacool and Mukherjee 2011: 5344.
18 Palestini 2016.
19 Santos et al. 2017.
20 UNASUR/OLADE 2012: 45.
21 Bersalli et al. 2018.
22 CAF 2013.
23 Briceño Ruiz 2012.
24 Quiliconi and Salgado 2017.
25 Fuser 2016.
26 Even if an interconnection usually promotes mutual benefits, its distribution can be very unequal and there may even be actors or countries that are adversely affected. Therefore, for electric integration projects to be sustainable over time, it is necessary to pay special attention to the mechanisms for sharing the benefits, otherwise these will become a permanent source of discord between the countries.
27 Ruchansky 2013.
28 Lambertini 2016.
29 Kozulj 2008.
30 IDB 2002.
31 ECLAC 1994.
32 Ruchansky 2013.
33 Barrera et al. 2012.
34 Sabbatella 2018.
35 Ruchansky 2013.
36 Sanahuja 2008.
37 Riggirozzi and Tussie 2012.
38 The Energy Ring project was promoted by Chile in order to face the fall of the Argentinian gas supply. The construction of a network of gas pipelines, interconnecting new and old pipelines, was envisaged with the gas coming from the Peruvian Camisea deposit – and possibly Bolivian gas – to supply the entire sub-region. Bolivia only participated as an observer, since it conditioned its full participation to the solution of its historical demand to go out to sea with Chile. Finally, Peru desisted to continue with the project for the reactivation of the border conflict with the same country and chose to prioritize the LNG export project through a liquefaction plant.
39 It was an initiative of the Chávez government to build an 8,000-kilometers pipeline that would unite Venezuela–Brazil–Argentina, interconnecting the rest of the countries in the region. The initiative was weak in terms of economic and environmental feasibility, and there was also some Brazilian reluctance to accept a project that would place Chavez Venezuela in a situation of regional leadership. The international economic crisis of 2008 also added financing problems. An additional factor was Venezuela's slow gas development.
40 In 2007, Argentina, Bolivia, and Venezuela – the first three producers in the region – agreed on the Energy Treaty for the Creation of an Organization of Gas Producing and Exporting Countries of South America (OPPEGASUR). The objective was to create a gas OPEC that would coordinate the investment, production, price and export policies of the countries in the region in terms of gas. The Brazilian government expressed its displeasure at being left out of the initiative. However, the initiative was truncated by the slow development of Venezuelan gas and the decline of production in Argentina.
41 Sabbatella 2015.
42 Sabbatella 2015; Santos 2018.
43 For example, in UNASUR–COSIPLAN 2016 Project Portfolio, there were 31 projects related to energy interconnection, totaling US$10,560.20 million – 18.4 percent of the energy investments and 5.5 percent of the total (Santos 2018).
44 Ruchansky 2013.
45 Santos 2018.
46 It seems that these projects are not going to be reactivated due to lack of financing but also because of the great social and environmental impacts that they can generate. Consequently, a reflection arises: the

promotion of alternative renewable energies (wind and solar, above all) can compete with large hydro-electric projects.

47 CIER 2017.
48 Van de Graaf and Colgan 2016.
49 Brazil leads the emissions with 1.4 percent of the total; then Argentina, 0.5 percent; Venezuela 0.4 percent; Chile and Colombia 0.3 percent; Peru 0.2 percent; Ecuador 0.1 percent; other countries 0.1 percent.
50 Tudela 2014.
51 See: www.iea.org/topics/climatechange/.
52 Bersalli et al. 2018.
53 The SDGs were adopted by world leaders at the United Nations in September 2015. They contain a specific goal on energy, which aims to provide universal access to modern energy services, double the rate of improvement in energy efficiency, and increase substantially the share of renewable energy in the global energy mix by 2030.
54 Grayson 2017.
55 Newell and Paterson 2010.
56 Di Muzio 2014.
57 Van de Graaf and Colgan 2016.
58 IEA 2017.
59 Aalto et al. 2017.
60 IEA 2018.
61 In 2016, as the Sabine Pass LNG terminal in Louisiana began to ramp up operations, US LNG exports increased. Sabine Pass now has four operating liquefaction units, with a fifth currently under construction. The Cove Point LNG facility in Maryland exported its first LNG cargo on March 1, 2018. Cove Point is the second currently operating LNG export facility in the United States, after Sabine Pass. Four other LNG projects are under construction and expected to increase.
62 Boersma and Losz 2018.
63 Aalto et al. 2017.
64 GIIGNL 2017.
65 IGU 2018.
66 Boersma and Losz 2018.
67 Kyu and Yeong 2016.
68 Muñoz Maldonado et al. 2017.
69 Hurtado and Souza 2018.
70 IRENA 2019.
71 Guler et al. 2018.
72 Santos 2018.
73 Codina-Gironès 2018.
74 Guler et al. 2018.
75 Van de Graaf et al. 2016.
76 Wilson 2018.
77 Bersalli et al. 2018.
78 Inchauspe and Barrera 2015.
79 Casas de las Peñas del Corral 2012.
80 Kozulj 2008.
81 Altomonte et al. 2013.
82 Santos 2018.

Bibliography

Aalto, P., Bilgin, M. and Talus, K. 2017. The political economy structures of energy transition: from shale gas to renewable energy. Paper presented at the *Internationale Energiewirtschaftstagung Klimaziele 2050: Chance für einen Paradigmenwechsel?* Vienna, Austria. Available at: www.eeg.tuwien.ac.at/conference/iaee2017/files/paper/639_Aalto_fullpaper_2017-06-17_08-57.pdf.

Altomonte, H., Acquatella, J., Arroyo, A., Jouravlev, A., Lardé, J. and Salgado, R. 2013. Recursos naturales en UNASUR: Situación y tendencias para una agenda de desarrollo regional. *ECLAC.* https://repositorio.cepal.org/bitstream/handle/11362/3116/1/S2013072_es.pdf.

Barrera, M., Sabbatella, I. and Serrani, E. 2012. *Historia de una privatización: cómo y por qué se perdió YPF.* Buenos Aires: Capital Intelectual.

Bersalli, G., Hallack, M., Guzowski, C., Losekann, L. and Zabaloy, M. 2018. La efectividad de las políticas de promoción de las fuentes renovables de energía: experiencias en América del Sud. *ENERLA II*, 2, no. 1: 158–174.

Boersma, T. and Losz, A. 2018. The new international political economy of natural gas. In: *The Handbook of the International Political Economy of Energy and Natural Resources.* Andreas, G., Keating, M. and Kuzemko, C. (eds.): 138–153. Northampton: Edward Elgar Publishing.

Briceño Ruiz, J. 2012. Autonomía y desarrollo en el pensamiento integracionista latinoamericano. In: *Integración Latinoamericana y Caribeña.* Briceño Ruiz, J., Rivarola, J. A. and Casas, A. (eds.): 27–78. Buenos Aires: Fondo de Cultura Económica, 2012.

Bueb, J., Richieri, L. and Le Clézio, A. 2017. Border adjustment mechanisms: Elements for economic, legal, and political analysis. In: *The Political Economy of Clean Energy Transitions.* Arent, D., Arndt, C., Miller, M., Tarp, F. and Zinaman, O. (eds.): 60–79. Oxford: Oxford University Press, UNU-Wider Studies in Development Economics.

CAF. 2013. Energía: una visión sobre los retos y oportunidades en América Latina y el Caribe. *CAF-ECLAC.* Available at: https://repositorio.cepal.org/bitstream/handle/11362/1505/1/Energia_CAF_CEPAL.pdf.

Carrizo, S., Núñez, M. and Gil, S. 2016. Transiciones energéticas en la Argentina. *Ciencia Hoy*, No. 147: 24–29. Available at: http://cienciahoy.org.ar/2016/01/transiciones-energeticas-en-la-argentina/.

Casas de las Peñas del Corral, A. 2012. Regional energy integration: A wide and worthy challenge for South America. *Journal of World Energy Law and Business*, no. 2: 166–173.

CIER. 2017. *Síntesis Informativa Energética de los Países de la CIER 2017. Información del sector energético en países de América del Sur, América Central y El Caribe.* Comisión de Integración Energética Regional. Available at: www.cier.org/es-uy/Lists/EstadisticasLD/S%C3%8DNTESIS%20INFORMATIVA_Datos2016_VF.pdf.

Codina-Gironès, V. 2018. *Scenario modelling and optimisation of renewable energy integration for the energy transition.* PhD thesis, Ecole Polytechniqué Federale de Lausanne. Available at: https://infoscience.epfl.ch/record/256112/files/EPFL_TH8780.pdf.

Díaz Casado, R. 2008. *GNL un mercado global.* Anales de Mecánica y Electricidad. Available at: www.icai.es/contenidos/publicaciones/anales_get.php?id=1551.

Di Muzio, T. 2014. Capitalizing a future unstable: Finance, energy and the fate of market civilization. *Review of International Political Economy* 19, no. 3: 363–88.

Dos Santos, T. 2002. *Teoría de la dependencia. Balance y perspectivas.* México: Plaza y Janés.

ECLAC. 1994. El regionalismo abierto en América Latina y el Caribe: La integración económica al servicio de la transformación productiva con equidad. *ECLAC.* Available at: https://repositorio.cepal.org/bitstream/handle/11362/2140/1/S9481108_es.pdf.

Fuser, I. 2016. A integração energética sul-americana e o impasse político regional: entre a "segurança jurídica" e o "uso soberano dos recursos naturais." *Observatorio da Energia.* Available at: https://observatorio daenergia.files.wordpress.com/2017/12/fuser-integrac3a7c3a3o-energc3a9tica_impasse-jurc3addico-ou-soberania.pdf.

GIIGNL. 2017. *The LNG industry Annual Report.* Paris: GIIGNL.

Grayson, M. 2017. Energy transitions. *Nature* 551, S133.

Guler, B., Çelebi, E. and Nathwani, J. 2018. A "Regional Energy Hub" for achieving a low-carbon energy transition. *Energy Policy* 113: 376–385. Available at: https://EconPapers.repec.org/RePEc:eee:enepol:v:113:y:2018:i:c:p:376-385.

Hurtado, D. and Souza, P. 2018. Geoeconomic uses of global warming: The "green" technological revolution and the role of the semi-periphery. *Journal of World-Systems Research*, 24, no. 1: 123–150.

IDB. 2002. Mas allá de las fronteras: el nuevo regionalismo en América latina. *IDB.* Available at: http://services.iadb.org/wmsfiles/products/Publications/1657428.pdf.

IEA. 2018. World Energy Investment 2018. *International Energy Agency.* Available at: https://webstore.iea.org/download/direct/1242?fileName=WEI2018.pdf.

IEA-IRENA. 2017. Perspectives for the energy transition: Investment needs for a low-carbon energy system. *OECD/IEA and IRENA.* Available at: www.irena.org/publications/2017/Mar/Perspectives-for-the-energy-transition-Investment-needs-for-a-low-carbon-energy-system.

IGU. 2018. World LNG *Report. IGU.* Available at: www.igu.org/sites/default/files/node-document-field_file/IGU_LNG_2018_0.pdf.

Inchauspe, M. and Barrera, M. 2015. Estudio sobre la cadena de bienes de capital para la energía eólica en el Mercosur: Un abordaje del desarrollo productivo y la asociatividad empresarial. In: *Socios en la integración productiva: la estrategia asociativa de las empresas en el Mercosur*. Trucco, P. (ed.): 109–146. Buenos Aires: Teseo.

IRENA. 2017. Rethinking energy 2017: Accelerating the global energy transformation. *International Renewable Energy Agency*. Available at: www.irena.org/documentdownloads/publications/irena_rethinking_energy_2017.pdf.

IRENA. 2018. Renewable energy statistics 2018. *International Renewable Energy Agency*. Available at: www.irena.org/-/media/Files/IRENA/Agency/Publication/2018/Jul/IRENA_Renewable_Energy_Statistics_2018.pdf.

IRENA. 2019. A new world: The geopolitics of the energy transformation. *International Renewable Energy Agency*. Available at: http://geopoliticsofrenewables.org/assets/geopolitics/Reports/wp-content/uploads/2019/01/Global_commission_renewable_energy_2019.pdf.

Jong de, J., Pellerin-Carlin, T. and Vinois, J. 2015. Governing the differences in the European Energy Union. *Jacques Delors Institute*. Available at: http://institutdelors.eu/wp-content/uploads/2018/01/pp.144governanceenergyunionjavinoisjdjongjdioct2015.pdf.

Kozulj, R. 2008. Situación y perspectivas del gas natural licuado en América del Sur. *ECLAC*. Santiago de Chile. Available at: https://repositorio.cepal.org/bitstream/handle/11362/6330/1/S0800091_es.pdf.

Kuzemko, C., Keating, M. and Goldthau, A. (eds.) 2018. Nexus-thinking in international political economy: What energy and natural resource scholarship can offer international political economy. In: *Handbook of the International Political Economy of Energy and Natural Resources*: 1–20. Northampton: Edward Elgar Publishing.

Kyu, L. and Yeong, J. 2016. The formation of the EU's Energy Union and its implications for the Northeast Asian Energy Market. *The Northeast Asian Economic Review* 4, no. 1: 11–22.

Lambertini, G. 2016. Estudio sobre convenios bilaterales que soportan las interconexiones energéticas en América del Sur. *OLADE*. Available at: http://biblioteca.olade.org/opac-tmpl/Documentos/old0371.pdf.

López, E. 2012. El gas natural licuado (GNL). *Revista Petrotecnia*, 53, no. 3: 84–88.

Markus, U. 2016. The international oil and gas price regimes. In: *The Palgrave Handbook of the International Political Economy of Energy*. Van de Graaf, T., Sovacool, B., Gosh, A., Kern, F. and Klare, M. (eds.): 225–246. Basingstoke: Palgrave.

Muñoz Maldonado, Y., Güiza, R. and Salazar, S. 2017. Análisis de integración regional con fuentes de energía renovable en América Latina y el Caribe. *ENERALC I*, 1, no. 1: 106–125.

Newell, P. and Paterson, M. 2010. *Climate Capitalism*. Cambridge: Cambridge University Press.

O'Brien, R. and Williams, M. 2016. *Global Political Economy: Evolution and Dynamics*. Basingstoke: Palgrave Macmillan.

Palestini, S. 2016. Energía de baja intensidad: gobiernos, mercados e instituciones en el regionalismo energético de América del Sur. *Caderno CRH*, 29, no. 3: 107–123.

Palma, J. 2009. Why did the Latin American critical tradition in the social sciences become practically extinct? In: *Routledge Handbook of International Political Economy (IPE): IPE as a Global Conversation*. Blyth, M. (ed.): 243–265. Abingdon and New York: Routledge.

Quiliconi, C. and Salgado, R. 2017. Latin American integration: Regionalism à la carte in a multipolar world? *Colombia Internacional* 92: 15–41.

Riggirozzi, P. and Tussie, D. (eds.) 2012. The rise of post-hegemonic regionalism in Latin America. *The Rise of Post-Hegemonic Regionalism:* 1–16. Dordrecht: Springer.

Ruchansky, B. 2013. Integración eléctrica en América Latina: antecedentes, realidades y caminos por recorrer. *CEPAL and GIZ*. Available at: https://repositorio.cepal.org/bitstream/handle/11362/4053/1/S2012999_es.pdf.

Ruiz-Caro, A. 2010. Puntos de conflicto de la cooperación e integración energética en América Latina y el Caribe. *CEPAL*. Available at: https://repositorio.cepal.org/bitstream/handle/11362/6349/1/S1000042_es.pdf.

Sabbatella, I. 2015. Integración petrolera y gasífera en Suramérica: buenas intenciones, pocos avances. In: *Del No al ALCA a UNASUR: Diez años después de Mar del Plata*. Karg, J. and Lewitt, A. (eds.): 165–177. Buenos Aires: Ediciones del CCC.

Sabbatella, I. 2018. Neoliberalismo e integración "de hecho" en el Cono Sur: Argentina como exportadora de hidrocarburos. *Revista Desafíos* 30, no. 1: 173–212.

Sanahuja, J. 2008. Del "regionalismo abierto" al "regionalismo post liberal." Crisis y cambio en la integración en América Latina y el Caribe. In: *Anuario de la integración regional de América Latina y el Gran Caribe 2008–2009*. Martínez, L., Peña, L., y Vazquez, M. (eds.): 11–54. Buenos Aires: CRIES.

Santos, T. 2018. *Regional Energy Security: Re-evaluating concepts and policies to promote energy integration in Mercosur*. PhD thesis, PPE/COPPE/UFRJ.

Santos, T., Pereira, A. and La Rovere., E. 2017. Evaluating energy policies through the use of a hybrid quantitative indicator-based approach: The case of Mercosur. *Energies* 10, no. 12: 2140–2115.

Söderbaum, F. 2005. The international political economy of regionalism. In: *Globalizing International Political Economy*. Philips, N. (ed.): 221–245. Basingstoke: Palgrave.

Sovacool, B. and Mukherjee, I. 2011. Conceptualizing and measuring energy security: A synthesized approach. *Energy* 36, no. 8: 5343–5355.

Tudela, F. 2014. Negociaciones internacionales sobre cambio climático: Estado actual e implicaciones para América Latina y el Caribe. *ECLAC*. Available at: https://repositorio.cepal.org/bitstream/handle/11362/37329/1/S1420809_es.pdf.

Tussie, D. 2015. Relaciones Internacionales y Economía Política Internacional: Notas para el debate. *Relaciones Internacionales*, no. 48: 155–175.

UNASUR/OLADE. 2012. UNASUR: un espacio que consolida la integración energética. *UNASUR/OLADE*. Available at: http://biblioteca.olade.org/opac-tmpl/Documentos/old0235.pdf.

Van de Graaf, T. and Colgan, J. 2016. Global energy governance: A review and research agenda. *Palgrave Communications* 2. https://doi.org/10.1057/palcomms.2015.47.

Van de Graaf, T., Sovacool, B., Gosh, A., Kern, F. and Klare, M. (eds.) 2016. States, markets, and institutions: Integrating international political economy and global energy politics. In: *The Palgrave Handbook of the International Political Economy of Energy*: 3–44. Basingstoke: Palgrave.

Wilson, J. 2018. The resource nationalist challenge to global energy governance. In: *Handbook of the International Political Economy of Energy and Natural Resources*. Goldthau, A., Keating, M., Kuzemko, C. (eds.): 50–61. Northampton: Edward Elgar Publishing.

World Energy Council. 2017. World Energy Trilemma Index 2017. *World Energy Council*. Available at: www.worldenergy.org/wp-content/uploads/2017/11/Energy-Trilemma-Index-2017-Report.pdf.

43

Industrial policy in Latin America

A theoretical discussion

Leticia Araya and Francisco Castañeda

Introduction

The discussion about how to achieve greater accelerated economic development within the countries of the Global South remains a major feature of debate within global academic and political forums. The concept of industrialization and how it might best be promoted is firmly back on the agenda of multilateral institutions and governments due to the fact that the previous policies promoted by the Washington Consensus (Williamson 2009: 1) do not appear to have worked properly.

Box 43.1 Measures promoted by the Washington Consensus for the Global South

Fiscal discipline, involving a drastic reduction in budget deficits, was implemented in a bid to tackle the large accumulated deficits that led to the crisis in the balance of payments and high inflation.

Reduced public spending, especially on social welfare. The Washington Consensus actually intended to redistribute spending to the promotion of economic growth and more targeted programmes for the poor, for example, from unjustified generalized subsidies to basic health care, education and infrastructure.

Improved tax collection based on the extension of indirect taxes, especially VAT. The aim was that the tax system should combine a broad tax base with moderate marginal rates.

Liberalization of the financial system and interest rates.

Maintenance of a competitive exchange rate.

External trade liberalization, by reducing tariffs and abolishing existing import barriers.

Provision of wide facilities/incentives to encourage foreign investment.

Privatization of public enterprises.

Strict enforcement of payment of the foreign debt.

Reinforced private property rights: protected by the legal system

(Source Williamson 2009)

After more than a decade of application of these policies, their results have been poor in terms of creating a more diversified productive structure and they have also tended to worsen the distribution of income. The neoliberal views promoted under the Washington Consensus did not mention the concept of industrial policy in their recommendations for promoting economic growth; policy was instead much more focused on deregulating markets, privatization, and reducing the size and influence of the state within Latin American economies. Certainly, experience would now suggest that the liberalization of productive sectors and deregulation is not enough to create a more sustainable form of economic growth (Stiglitz 2004: 2). These uneven results have created renewed interest in rethinking industrialization and its role in future economic development strategies. A new framework for industrial policy (as a new paradigm) is required to face the challenges that globalization poses for countries of the Global South.

The views on how the state can act to support the industrialization of an economy are many and are not necessarily exclusive. These views encompass such approaches as: nationalization (or creating a state-owned company); kick-starting a broader industrialization programme via selecting and supporting those private companies which appear to present the best possibilities for spreading the spillovers towards the rest of the economy's productive structures (generating a structural change); or, as has been pursued strongly in some recent public policy initiatives, states can act to support the participation of small to medium-sized enterprises (SMEs) along global value chains. However, the concept of industrialization is too complex to summarize briefly. Discussions about industrialization have to address the nature of the desired industrialization, which industries will be included within the industrialization process (i.e. which sectors will be targeted by the government) and the ways in which the pursuit of industrialization fits into the wider intentions of the state (this is related to whether the state has a developmental view of its role and whether it is prepared to allocate significant public resources to the industrialization objective).

The simplest neoliberal view is that a country should be able to make economic progress by exploiting its static comparative advantages (abundant land, cheap labour, etc.) and from there it can create industrial upgrading via limited public policies. The alternative structuralism view is that states should intervene to protect industrial markets ('infant industry') and achieve industrial upgrading (the developmental strategy). Both of these economic strategies have costs and benefits in the short and long term, and there exists a variety of evidence at both country and industry levels as to their impacts which are discussed in the ensuing sections of this chapter. Before this, however, it is perhaps useful to provide some basic definitions of industrial policy (Agosin 2008).

Accordingly, there are two main types of industrial policy. Horizontal Policy is applied across the industrial sector and is designed to correct market failures, for instance, the typical credit rationing that affects SMEs. This kind of policy (horizontal industrial policy) is the most common industrial policy ingredient within neoliberal economic strategies. Such policies are seen as neutral due to the fact that they do not favour any particular industrial sector, instead revolving around the identification of specific market failures which, according to the neoliberal perspective, must be corrected inside the system, without 'altering the allocation of resources' or the free operation of market forces.

Vertical Industrial Policy or Targeted Industrial Policy, on the other hand, is much broader in its scope and is applied under the assumption that the market, by itself, is slow and inefficient in developing new comparative advantages. The spillover effects from industrial activity are, in this view, not captured by market forces and government intervention is required to internalize the positive effects (spillovers) of this policy.

States and markets: the key contours of the debate over industrial policy

In the social sciences, the discussion about industrialization is an old one. In the early part of the twentieth century, the world economy collapsed (The Great Depression of 1929) to be followed by a surge of alternative new views on how to create economic growth. This intensified after the Second World War via a debate which can be divided in terms of economic policy between those countries that wanted to intervene directly to promote industrialization and those that believed that the establishment of a mainly free market would in itself act to improve the standard of their economies.

According to Wade (1990: 8) the problems facing many developing countries in the 1950s were those of: low private savings, dependence on primary product exports, declining prices of exports in relation to imports, small internal markets, limited skills, few entrepreneurs adept at large scale organization, and pervasive underemployment. Within this context, the state was seen as not only responsible for maintaining the macroeconomic balance and the supply of public goods, but also for augmenting resources and transferring them to capital formation. During this period, therefore, for most countries the state was seen as the engine of economic development. The view was that when the market is left to operate alone, it generates less investment than is socially optimal, and in this context the state becomes an activist in the economic agenda.

Drawing upon these kinds of arguments, Latin America, from the 1930s until the 1970s, applied a strategy called import substitution industrialization (ISI). It was a trade and economic policy that advocated replacing imports with domestic production. It was based on the premise that a country should attempt to reduce its foreign dependency through the local production of industrialized products. ISI was applied in many countries in Latin America (and elsewhere), where it was implemented with the intention of helping countries to become more self-sufficient and less vulnerable by creating jobs and relying less on other nations. ISI was based primarily on the domestic market and worked by having the state lead economic development through nationalization, the subsidization of vital industries (including agriculture, power generation, etc.), increased taxation to fund these activities, and a highly protectionist trade policy which implied high tariffs. Thorp (1998: 150) points out that ISI promoted the development of a great number of functions and instruments in the public sector. There emerged a new class of technocrat, with knowledge in economics, planning, management and engineering. They were relevant in the creation of new development and financial institutions (such as the development banks). Also, there emerged with it a new industrial bourgeoisie.

But ISI was gradually abandoned by developing countries in the 1980s and 1990s due to disappointment with the results and its ability to respond to changing global circumstances (Palma 2009). Palma argues further that the industrialization process benefitted only a small segment of the population (during and after ISI), creating social segregation.

ISI drew theoretically upon the works of Raúl Prebisch (1973) and was a major part of the economic strategies developed and promoted across the region by the Commission Economica para Latinoamerica y el Caribe (CEPAL), known as the Economic Commission for Latin America and the Caribbean (ECLAC) in English. CEPAL's recommendation of state-induced industrialization through governmental spending was influenced by Keynesian models as well as the infant industry arguments adopted by some highly industrialized countries, such as the United States, until the 1940s. ISI is also often associated with dependency theory, although the latter adopts a much broader sociological outlook which also addresses cultural elements thought to be linked with underdevelopment (Larrain 2014: 26).

ECLAC supported this process of industrialization and recommended several tools and means, such as easy credit, infrastructural support and favourable foreign exchange measures, but

Table 43.1 Indicators of growth and trade balance performance for three different periods

Country	Period	Years	Growth rate (%)	Import elasticity (%)	Export elasticity (%)	Change in productivity gap (%)
Argentina	IS golden Age	1950–1973	3.49	0.42	0.71	–
	Pre-Reform	1974–1990	0.34	-3.1	14.29	0.84
	Post-Reform	1991–2003	1.81	2.66	3.81	0.91
Brazil	IS golden Age	1950–1973	7.2	0.8	0.78	–
	Pre-Reform	1974–1990	4.07	-0.27	1.98	0.55
	Post-Reform	1991–2003	1.83	3.74	3.64	0.76
Chile	IS golden Age	1950–1973	3.64	1.45	0.6	–
	Pre-Reform	1974–1990	1.63	-0.38	3.81	1.6
	Post-Reform	1991–2003	5.34	2.07	1.7	0.65
Colombia	IS golden Age	1950–1973	5.2	0.57	0.88	–
	Pre-Reform	1974–1990	4.12	0.82	1.28	0.58
	Post-Reform	1991–2003	2.71	2.35	1.64	1.03
Mexico	IS golden Age	1950–1973	6.56	0.66	0.69	–
	Pre-Reform	1974–1990	4.58	0.58	2.37	0.67
	Post-Reform	1991–2003	2.88	4.42	3.23	0.68
Peru	IS golden Age	1950–1973	5.12	1.19	0.99	–
	Pre-Reform	1974–1990	0.75	-5.46	2.85	-0.92
	Post-Reform	1991–2003	3.74	1.87	2.19	0.78
Uruguay	IS golden Age	1950–1973	1.55	-0.12	-0.25	–
	Pre-Reform	1974–1990	3.67	-0.14	4.23	1.33
	Post-Reform	1991–2003	1.03	3.44	3.02	0.77
Latin America	IS golden Age	1950–1973	3.04	0.58	0.74	–
Weighted Average	Pre-Reform	1974–1990	3.12	0.58	2.42	0.43
	Post-Reform	1991–2003	2.45	3.64	3.31	0.74

Source: Palma 2003.

Note
The table reports average growth rates of income, elasticities of imports and exports. The change in productivity gap is the percentage change in productivity for the country relative to the same change in the international technological frontier.

mainly through protectionism. Tariff barriers were imposed or increased on all those industrial imports whose production was to be substituted. According to (Kay 1989: 38): 'ECLAC hoped that ISI strategy would transform industry into the most dynamic sector and lead to a higher rate of economic growth than that achieved by the export sector'. It was hoped that the manufacturing sector was a relevant part of national income.

But from the 1960s, ISI began to be subjected to a growing critique from the political right and left. Critics pointed to the inability of the ISI strategy to either generate sufficient internal resources or foreign currency to carry out the industrialization process effectively. It was also argued that ISI required too much subsidization and ended up protecting inefficient industries which did not achieve international competitiveness. All of this meant that there were frequent foreign currency shortages and later, excessive foreign borrowing. The final straw for the model came during the 1980s debt crisis when the growing current account deficit reached a peak in 1981 which put excessive pressure on the policy of maintaining currencies which could stimulate the acquisition of capital goods, a major feature of ISI policy (Lustig 1988: 55). Other authors (Franko 1999) have also pointed out the role of clientelism and the reliance on low levels of technological upgrading in limiting the development of economies of scale in the case of Latin American industrialization.

Here we begin to see the influence of neoliberal critiques of industrialization policy which argue that extensive government intervention within ISI strategies tended to create rent-seeking or political clientelism (Todaro 1997: 86–87). This reflects the influence of 'public-choice theory', also known as the new political economy approach, which argues that government intervention is inherently problematic. In this view, politicians, bureaucrats, citizens and states act solely from a self-interested perspective. This means citizens (and institutions and businesses) use political influence to obtain special benefits called 'rents' from government policies (e.g. import licences or rationing foreign exchange). Bureaucrats, in this theory, use their positions to extract bribes from rent-seeking citizens and to operate protected businesses on the side. This perspective therefore implies that the best government is a minimal government. Interestingly, in the Asian context (Khan and Jomo 2000: 121) the idea of rent-seeking has been seen in a different way. In this approach, the rent-seeking mechanism operates because of the logic of free market forces. In this context, the government is seen as acting as an allocator of rents among different industries and sectors wanting industrialization and the possibility to absorb unemployment. The state protects sectors through high tariffs (infant industry), delivering licenses, promoting subsidies in credit and technological transference, etc. However, in turn, the state controls the results of these industries in terms of industrial value added and keeping 'tension' in this scheme.

The World Bank has been one of the chief architects of the evolving neoliberal perspective on industrialization. Its code of good governance, for example, points out what it sees as the determinants for sustainable economic growth which strongly reinforce the case for non-intervention in the economy. The application of the Washington Consensus since the onset of the debt crisis basically reduced the influence of industrial policies, establishing, at least in its own mind, neutrality in the allocation of resources. Also, at a financial level, neoliberal policies reduced the independence of monetary and exchange policies that might have been used to boost aggregate demand or induce a different pattern of productive structure. The World Bank's code of good governance is open to critical analysis due to the fact that it assumes a homogenous world in which poor countries have the same characteristics as rich countries but are affected by factors that prevent them from catching up (corruption, lack of democracy, state failures, market failures, etc.). Moreover, developing countries are structurally different in how their social regulation systems operate.

Neostructuralism emerged post-ISI as an answer to these capitalist forces (Sunkel 1993: 2) and as an attempt at formulating an alternative to neoliberalism. Sunkel claims that that neostructuralism shares the basic structuralism tenet that the sources of underdevelopment in Latin America do not originate in policy-induced distortions (determined economic policies). Sunkel points out that underdevelopment in Latin America is rooted in history and is structural and endogenous.

Accordingly, a new approach towards the industrial policy is required. It should be based on the analysis of disaggregated outcomes (not solely on growth), and also on the generation of employment and changes in the pattern of distribution of income (Stallings and Peres 2000: 7). The income would depend on level of skill, and that different jobs within firms would attract levels of pay that reflected the level of skill required objectively.

Links between the lost decade in Latin America and de-industrialization policies

The Washington Consensus was a phrase coined by John Williamson to describe the recipe established in the 1980s by the International Monetary Fund (IMF) and the World Bank to develop a series of policies derived from the neoliberal perspective, as described above, to stimulate economic recovery and reconstruction following the onset of the debt crisis (chiefly in Latin America and Africa). The 1980s therefore saw a major change in the orientation of economic development strategies and hence attitudes towards industrial policy and it is often referred to as the lost development decade in Latin America (Ffrench-Davis 2007). This lost decade began with the Mexican default in 1982, when Mexico declared that it could no longer meet its external debt payments with international agencies and other entities. Other countries threatened to follow. This was a result, among other factors, of the industrialized countries deciding, due to a range of economic problems, to increase interest rates which raised the cost of national borrowing in Latin America at a time of enhanced need and also caused capital flight. It led to the inevitable devaluation of Latin America's domestic currencies, together with significant increases in inflation rates.

The economic crisis that this generated (not just in Latin America) allowed the international financial institutions to significantly enhance their influence over the governments of the region that led to the emergence of a different approach towards economic development and industrialization which, as suggested above, was heavily influenced by the neoliberal ideas of the Washington Consensus). This created the basis of structural adjustment policies and reduced the ability of the state to generate an autonomous and national industrial policy to diversify their economies away from their dependence upon commodities and raw materials (Lustig 1988: 50). The need for foreign trade (in order to generate the resources to pay their external debt) increasingly led the Latin American economies towards specialization within economic activities determined by the comparative advantages promoted by the mainstream proponents of international trade (i.e. the commodities and raw materials referred to above). It created a growth without social counterbalances which was very dependent on international cycles. Devés (2004: 116) reinforces the previous setting. He claims that in the modernization proposal of neoliberalism, the recurrent topics were to reduce the size of state, decrease the public expenditure and mainly to exclude the state of the production of goods and services; the need of macroeconomic equilibriums, the insistence in comparative advantages, reduce tariffs and give security to the international capital. It reduces finally the capacity of the state to guide the economic process.

Certainly, the term 'industrial policy' is missing in the recommendations of the Washington Consensus. There was such a level of distrust in the role of the state in the economies that any type of state intervention was considered out of place. With these policies, Latin American countries in the 1980s did not alter their productive patterns in a structurally significant way. Besides, the Washington Consensus did not take into account ethnic factors, distribution of income, infrastructure and inadequate networks (Moncayo 2003: 80). In other words, the Washington Consensus recommended a move towards a freer market economy without considering the historical and socioeconomic–political context.

Why industrial policy?

Chang (2003: 61) acknowledges three important justifications for industrial policy in Southeast Asian countries:

1 The need to coordinate complementary investments in the presence of significant economies of scale and capital market imperfections.
2 The role that the state is able to play as the organizer of domestic firms into implicit cartels in their negotiations with foreign firms or governments.
3 Policies to deal with learning externalities (e.g. subsidies for industrial training).

The most important goal of industrial policies is achieving sustained economic growth through industrialization. Therefore, there is an old belief based on past industrializations that heavy industries (manufacturing) are the leader industries which will boost growth. This process would cause an increase in labour demand by firms. So full employment is an objective of industrial policy which must be embedded into a macro-framework which encompasses numerous things from taxation and research and development (R&D) expenditure to fiscal and monetary policy.

For the last couple of decades, the idea of the developmental state, which could contribute directly to economic growth, has been laid to one side. There is, however, no acknowledgement that the path that was taken by Northern industrial economies to their current economic status originated precisely in the kind of policies they currently criticize. Finally, however, particularly after the subprime crisis, there has begun to be a breakdown within the Washington Consensus and the emergence of a vague post-Washington Consensus which addresses the problems of the old consensus mainly via theories of market imperfections (Fine 2001: 13).

In contrast to import substitution, however, this approach still tends to evolve towards an open economy industrial policy where the objective is to increase economic openness by enhancing flows of knowledge, foster productive innovation and promoting non-traditional exports. It does, nonetheless, seem to represent a reasonable solution to the old schemes of industrialization in Latin America in the 1960s, and of those freer market economy schemes. According to the definitions of industrial policy and its variants outlined above, post-Washington Consensus-influenced perspectives would probably be defined as horizontal industrial policy, designed to correct market failures (particularly asymmetries of information). It will depend greatly on the political will of policy makers in individual countries whether such approaches become more ambitious (perhaps, for example, selecting and protecting those sectors with the highest economic potential).

What is clear is that productivity growth is the key to enhancing the quality of life of a nation's citizens, as well as determining its ability to compete in global markets. Economic development implies structural transformation, moving from low productivity activities towards high productivity activities, from simple agriculture and simple manufacturing to more modern manufacturing and agricultural processes. Industrialization, broadly speaking, has as its goal the increase of both labour productivity and economic activity as a whole. The types of policy can include measures (e.g. taxation incentives) designed to attract foreign investment, which can be relevant for specific sectors, as well as more general interventions oriented towards the promotion of exports. Both of these should be considered as part of industrial policy. A typical problem on the political agenda is how to protect certain industries, which are considered dynamic, with positive externalities (spillover effects).

Fajnzylber (1992) contributes to this debate claiming that for overcoming of syndrome of 'empty box' (dichotomy between growth and equity), a productive transformation was required in order to significantly boost labour productivity, support international competitiveness based on technical progress, strengthen and widen the Latin American entrepreneurial base, and develop relations of cooperation in the long term (with a strategic view) among government, entrepreneurs and workers.

Ul Haque (2007: 3), supporting the use of industrial policy, points out that government intervention becomes necessary when competition alone does not force firms to innovate and undertake productivity enhancing investments. The argument is that market forces alone do not provide enough information about the profitability of resources that do not exist (e.g. new skills or new technology). So, the comparative advantage doctrine is of limited value in designing policy if the intention is to increase investment and human capital as well as knowledge. Rodrik (1998) notes: 'whatever it is that serves as the driving force of economic development, it cannot be the forces of comparative advantage as conventionally understood'. The main criticism of the policy to limit state intervention to the correction of market failures is that it is a weak industrial policy. The emphasis upon correcting market failures leads to emphases upon the provision of education, infrastructure and risk capital as well as R&D funding. In this type of industrial policy there are not any direct market interventions by the state in terms, for example, of creating a state enterprise to develop and strengthen new niche markets or the selection of strategic sectors with high economic potential. Also, the World Bank's code of good governance, explored earlier, emphasizes the importance of contracts and fulfilment of property rights. While these elements are obviously important within any industrial strategy, the approach to policy making within the successful economies of East Asia was clearly much broader in its orientation. Overall, it would appear that the correction of market failures as an orientation for a 'sound industrial policy' is too limited and too optimistic.

However, elsewhere in the literature, Felipe (2010: 69), for example, the term industrial policy is reserved for any type of selective intervention or government policy that attempts to alter the structure of production towards sectors that are expected to offer better prospects for economic growth. The term is used somewhat pejoratively by neoliberal commentators who view this type of intervention as degenerating into 'picking winners' (Khan and Jomo 2000: 95) where government officials decide what activities and sectors to promote with frequently spurious and politically motivated rationality.

Rodrik (1998), nevertheless, points out that even this type of more profound industrial policy is justified by the existence of market failures although these are not the typical market failures addressed by the traditional interventions of public policy. These market failures are highly uncertain due to their location and magnitude. One example comes from considering measures designed to address those coordination externalities that weaken the entrepreneurial drive to restructure and diversify low-income economies. Coordination efforts between the public and private sectors can bring positive effects to society in terms of investments which can be complementary and so obtain the minimum scales of production necessary to develop new businesses and new ventures. In other words, the state can be a strategic partner to the private sector reducing the risks faced by the private sector (technology transference, subsidies for location outside the big cities, state agencies promoting credit, etc.).

Clearly then successful industrial policy requires collaboration between the state and private sectors in order to identify and act upon areas where the country has comparative advantage. Nevertheless, the state also has to take into account broader issues such as the need to pursue full employment and balanced development together with the balance of activity between the regions and provinces, otherwise development can become concentrated, monopolistic and monopsonist.

The proposals of Rodrik are appropriate in general terms. However, he does not mention explicitly the need for an effective SMEs policy. How do SMEs fit into value chains and clusters? How do they get the upgrading to enhance processes and products? It is perhaps logical to assume that in the first stage, countries require large companies (as in the South Korean chaebols) operating in the chosen value chains and clusters in order to take advantage of faster economies of scale, better channels of distribution, better logistics, etc. Nevertheless, in order not to commit past mistakes, industrial policy principles should contain and add explicit exploration of the participation of SMEs across value chains and explicitly include sectoral interlinkages within them. In this way, the public funds allocated to promote industrial policies would not only be captured by large companies inside the chosen value chains and clusters. Further, SMEs are intensive in labour in comparison to large companies, which permit them to meet the objectives of full employment (or at least to reduce the gaps in relation to full employment).

One way of exploring this issue comes through the framework of 'rent-seeking management'. This framework presents industrial policy as providing a way of dealing with rent-seeking that is different to that promoted by competitive markets. Within this perspective there is an assumption that all economic agents and enterprises will seek an undue economic profit (monopolies, special protection, capture of the authority, etc.). In other words, rents are distributed on a non-competitive basis. This theory promotes the idea that the state can put rules and pressure on firms (professional bureaucratic rules, medium and long term targets of production, value

Table 43.2 Financing products used by SMEs

	Percentage of SMEs					
	Argentina	*Colombia*	*Chile*	*Mexico*	*Peru*	*Venezuela*
Financing products	–	40.5	–	–	–	–
Term loans	–	–	38.7	–	–	2.8
Short-terms loans	–	–	–	–	40.0	–
Working capital loans	–	–	23.4	–	6.5	7.5
Medium-long term loans	–	–	–	–	–	–
Investment loans	–	–	–	–	–	–
Term loans with fixed asset guarantee	4.4	–	18.8	2.7	–	0.3
Loans supported by public programmes	2.7	–	8.1	–	–	0.3
Lines of credit	25.7	29.4	75.1	29.8	18.0	–
Overdrafts	28.8	–	–	4.3	20.6	0.7
Check/document discounting	35.4	2.7	5.1	1.4	10.1	3.4
Leasing	4.3	8.9	12.6	1.2	5.9	0.3
Factoring	1.9	1.8	7.5	1.1	1.7	0.3
Foreign trade financing	2.9	5.6	13.2	2.0	5.2	3.0
Credit card	–	13.9	–	–	11.2	–
Letter of credit	2.1	1.0	14.6	1.5	7.8	0.3
None	30.8	29.8	13.2	64.9	29.1	51.3

Source: De la Torre, S., Martinez, P. and Schmukler 2008: 2289.

added, employment creation etc.) so that the rent-seeking of firms is managed by the state through a professional bureaucracy. This form of managing rent-seeking is developed through contracts between the state and large firms in order that the latter meet their own growth objectives while also simultaneously fulfilling the requirements of public policy (high quality employment, determined ratio of exports, etc.). In this way, the state acts as a power balance protecting firms in chosen sectors (via special tariffs, credit, subsides, allocation of tenders, etc.) but simultaneously, these companies (by a 'special contract' with the state) must upgrade processes, products, and develop the ability to export and exploit new market niches, etc. (Khan and Jomo 2000: 74). In other words, the state grants some benefits (mostly temporary) but it demands results (fulfilment of the targets) in terms of its national public policy.

Khan (2003) explains that countries that follow the recommendations of good governance promoted by the World Bank and the Washington Consensus have low economic growth in comparison with those countries that challenge the productive status quo (especially those countries that have an active industrial policy as a targeted – picking the winners). Therefore, there are negative consequences of a lack of political leadership and its effects on economic stagnation. Stagnation occurs, according to Khan, where the state creates rents through unstable property rights, market distortions, etc., without having a clear process of development in the long term. In Khan's theory, it should be possible to manage these rents so that pressure is put on the productive sectors to unleash gains in productivity.

Industrial policy: specific issues

In the previous subsections, the main theories of industrial policy in regard to their conceptual perspectives and institutional dynamics were analysed. However, in order to be successful, industrial policy requires determined institutional arrangements that encompass numerous things from institutions that promote industrial activities (credit, technology, foreign direct investment(FDI)) to sound practices that encourage productive diversification. In this section, the major elements of an industrial policy will be mentioned and explained (based on a review of the literature).

FDI policy

Industrial Policy is also not isolated from policies concerning FDI. If laissez-faire policies are applied to investment in terms of not directing the flows of investment, only a weak industrial policy can be developed. Furthermore, within industrial policy there has frequently been a strong interest in setting subsidies and reducing tariffs in order to attract foreign investments in areas, which present a high potential for economic growth.

One of the key discussions concerning the relationship between industrial policy and FDI relates to the relationship between levels of FDI and trade openness. The neoclassical view suggests that only openness provides a guarantee of higher FDI, but this view does not deal with the quality of investments and in which sectors they are invested (the neutrality principle). Also, contrary to conventional neoclassical wisdom, many East and South East Asian countries have had restrictive policies towards FDI. Only Malaysia and Hong Kong have had liberal attitudes towards the involvement of transnational corporations (TNCs). Singapore also sought to attract TNCs, but the government deliberately directed investment towards its priority areas, such as infrastructure, education, training and investment incentives. There is a big debate in the literature about the role of TNCs and FDI within industrialization in the Global South. However, it appears that the most successful cases of economic development in the twentieth century occurred in countries where FDI was strategically restricted and heavily controlled in terms of entry, ownership, technology transfer and local content requirements (Japan, South Korea, Taiwan and Finland) (Akkemik 2009: 22). In the case of South Korea, as discussed above, rapid industrialization began from a very low base. It meant that the South Korean government was not willing to accept the investment of foreign companies without receiving benefits for its economy (joint ventures, training, endogenous growth).

Generally, during the infant industry protection stage, most South East Asian economies (except Japan) started with the assembly of simple consumer products (low level of knowledge). This simple economic structure is what the neoliberal strategy would have recommended, and current policy would certainly not have sought to challenge this current productive structure. Later, during the transition to a knowledge economy, technology creation became more important. During the 1980s, there was rapid growth in the production and export of technology-intensive manufactures in South Korea, Singapore and Taiwan. In the 1990s, these countries shifted a part of their productive resources to new products in information technologies (complex software, semiconductors, telecommunications, etc.). This was facilitated by state incentives that encouraged productive diversification and the development of new niche markets (Chang 2006: 29).

Industrial upgrading and international trade

In the 1950s, developing countries participated in international trade largely through the exchange of exported primary products for the importation of manufactured goods. This pattern of specialization expanded national exports, but it can be seen as 'immiserizing growth' due to the worsening of the terms of trade of these primary products vis-à-vis manufactured goods, and the impact of this on national income levels over time as the prices of processed products rise while primary products decline. This phenomenon is due to oversupply combined with low elasticity of international demand for primary products (Franko 1999: 51). For decades, therefore, those devising and implementing economic development strategies have sought to find the most appropriate ways of switching production towards products with greater value added (processed or manufacturing). Success in this endeavour will, it is argued, allow enhancement of the living standards of the population over the medium term. Globally, there is a great fragmentation of production across countries and regions. A growing number of countries are specializing in manufacturing at different levels of industrial processing. This pattern of specialization poses many of the same problems as those facing primary producers. The manufacturing sector is being affected by low entry barriers, oversupply and decreasing terms of trade, leading to some of the segments of these markets being 'commodified'. This means that the products are not different enough and have the same characteristics. The levels of competition therefore are high (Franko 1999: 55). Within this context, there are several agents (firms and countries) suffering from the same immiserizing growth due to this pattern of specialization. The search for industrial upgrading is, therefore, the search for mechanisms and strategies for transiting from dependence upon the commodity segments of the market (primary and manufacturing goods) in order to escape the problems of declining terms of trade (Amighini 2006).

According to Amighini (2006: 221), industrial upgrading can be attained by:

a   Shifting production to other non-commodified segments within the same market (this shift is called vertical process integration).
b   De-commodifying the products in which a country is specialized. That is, countries and firms should be able to create entry barriers to the markets they specialize in and so increase product differentiation.

This would suggest (Amighini 2006: 223) that a country upgrades in a sector when two conditions are fulfilled:

a   it produces a higher-value product than its competitors; and
b   it competes in international markets, without losing market share.

Any increase in export earnings that results solely from a rise in market share without an increase in unit value should not be considered product upgrading. It is not upgrading because it is not related to any innovation and improvement in a market segment and because it could lead to an immiserating type of growth if increasing exports create downward pressures on prices.

Localizing industrial policy

Most economists research into industrial policy at a national level, although they consider regions and economic sectors as units of analysis. Economic geographers, however, have a much more direct interest in the local and regional dimensions of economies and have, for example, focused their analyses upon the inter-relationships between regional and local factors (territories), global commodity chains (and global production networks) and the territorial dimensions regarding how the surplus is distributed along these chains (Bellandi and Di Tommaso 2006: 342).

According to this view, the processes of industrial development in a territorial context relate to the interplay between two different units of analysis: the industry, with its organization and territorial characteristics, and the locality, with its socioeconomic characteristics and evolutionary processes.

The locality includes:

a   the territory under a specific form of local government;
b   a locality with a socioeconomic identity, corresponding to a set of towns, villages, rural areas near to one another;
c   a locality of industry: a locality characterized in social and economic terms.

The previous sections have demonstrated the many facets of industrial policy and illustrated many of the arguments used by those supporting their application. What is clear, however, is that it is necessary to take into account the socio-economic characteristics of regions and localities before embarking upon any strategy for industrial upgrade. This sensitivity to territory is crucial in the design of industrial policy regardless of whether the industry is natural resource-based or knowledge-intensive. In the case of South Korea and Taiwan, for example, there were stringent local content rules creating support industries, protection of local suppliers and subcontracting promotion within the territories experiencing rapid industrial growth (Lall 2006: 86). This was meant to promote local capabilities in the territory and it was consistent with the concept of endogenous development. The implications for Latin America are clear. An industrial policy that does not take into account the specifics of regions and territories will not deliver balanced and sustainable economic development that can help correct the regional imbalances in opportunities for labour as well as the economic space for SMEs.

Different perspectives on the role of the state in industrialization

Drawing upon the preceding discussions, we can identify some basic divisions in the literature over the fundamental intentions of industrial policy and industrial upgrading. In the discussions explored in the previous sections, upgrading is typically limited to upgrading production. According to Puppim de Oliveira (2008: 3), one way to upgrade firms and clusters in developing countries is linking them with global chains and markets, especially in developed markets. Nevertheless, the traditional view of upgrading (a narrowly economistic view) poses some problems. Certainly, upgrading means improvements in the production or economic sphere and upgrading in SME clusters would allow these firms to have better processes or products. Nevertheless, upgrading as currently articulated pays little attention to labour, social and environmental conditions. As well as bringing economic benefits, upgrading can also cause pollution, lay off workers and squeeze salaries. Therefore, one of the main criticisms of this traditional view of upgrading is that it does not take into account these negative dimensions. To contribute towards sustainable development, social upgrading that embodies all these dimensions is required. However, to date, even the developmental dynamic has largely not been able to deliver an answer to this challenge in most Latin American economies. Therefore, any new industrial policy (that can take us beyond the limitations of the post-Washington Consensus) will need to, through state institutions, reflect these weaknesses and explicitly include the conditions of workers (salaries, social rights and training) as well as respect for the environment in its objectives. It should also include affirmative action to strengthen the SME sector in terms of the allocation of state resources (credit, technology transfer, etc.).

Traditionally, industrial upgrading can be understood as those processes which add industrial value to the supply of existing resources. Basically, in this view, the current comparative advantages of any economy are the baseline from which to enhance economic growth. In other words, it is necessary to use existing resources to generate industrialization. In the modern version of this perspective, neoliberal commentators promote the role of a facilitating state which creates the conditions for the private sector to exploit these comparative advantages. Such perspectives do not think of big leaps forward: in this neoliberal logic, a rapid and accelerated transformation and industrial upgrading is unthinkable. On the other hand, the developmental view argues that the state can help the private sector to exploit the current comparative advantages in a more active way, for example by selecting sectors and industries with a higher presence of positive externalities (employment, technology, economies of scale, etc.).

As discussed above, in Latin America the ISI strategy was adopted in the 1950s to seek an industrial development that would reduce dependency on the more advanced countries. The ISI strategy tried to attain a form of development that was autonomous from the centre core (that is, the industrialized countries). It also had deep roots in structuralism theories which held that the disequilibrium experienced in Latin American economies originated from the unequal distribution of land within most countries. As it was argued, the ISI strategy had led to higher agriculture prices (raising the domestic inflation rate across the region) due to the inability of the farms to achieve higher productivity (recognition of this led to the initiation of agrarian reform processes across Latin America in the 1960s). However, Kay (2002: 1087) remarks on a missing thread; it is the relation between agrarian reform and industrialization. He claims that East Asia overtook Latin America, in spite of the fact that Latin America started its process of industrialization several decades earlier. In his analysis, the agrarian reform in South Korea and Taiwan were carried out before that any significant industrialization (while agrarian reforms in Latin America happened after that industrialization had been established, with the exception of Mexico). Also, the landlord class in South Korea and Taiwan was swept from power, while in Latin America, the landlords retained power and influence during the first stage of the industrialization process, and so were able to block or delay any reform of the land tenure system. In order to explain the superior performance of these Asian countries, Kay adds to this set of factors the ability of the state in South Korea and Taiwan, to design and implement strategies and policies conducive to development (transforming the land tenure system and agrarian social relations, while Latin America was immersed in a polarized and entrenched class structure).

Under ISI, Latin American countries increased tariffs to avoid external competition in order to protect national industry and the internal market. However, this led to constraints in the availability of capital for intermediate goods imports, which were necessary in this first stage of industrialization. The Latin American economies did not have enough technological experience to initiate this ISI process without foreign technological experience. The scarcity of capital, as well as the traditional problems in the balance of payments (insufficient currencies) led to what has been interpreted as the poor performance of these policies (Lustig 1988). Nevertheless, when the results of economic growth in Latin America are analysed, what is clear is that ISI-focused industrialization created more accelerated economic growth in the ISI golden age (1950–1973) than was achieved in the 1980s. Although most Latin American countries returned to more sustained economic growth during the 1990s with far more externally oriented approaches, it appears to have been the incorporation of China and India into the global economy (which boosted commodity prices) which underlies this success rather than any successful Latin American industrialization strategy (Ffrench-Davis 2009). Basically, the point is that in the period during which the state played a far stronger role in planning and directing the economy in Latin America, economic growth levels were relatively high, although it must be recognized that specific elements of the strategy also brought other disequilibrium such as high inflation rates, and it focused too much on the small internal markets.

Returning to our earlier discussion about the role of specific tools of industrial policy, the ISI strategy involved the use of multiple tools – tariffs, state support to industrial processes, control of exchange rates, interest rates and others – which were not always compatible and not necessarily aligned. For example, while high tariffs protected the domestic economy (local producers and entrepreneurs) to stimulate local employment, simultaneously this same high tariff created problems of foreign exchange scarcity and affected the balance of payments. Also, the high tariffs made the importation of capital goods, which were crucial for a sustained industrial process, far too expensive.

Many Latin American countries also tried to initiate accelerated processes of industrialization through the development of State-Owned Enterprises (SOEs). These initiatives tended to emerge when the protection of domestic industry (through trade policy, the implicit subsidy of a low exchange rate and the availability of cheap credit) had not been sufficient to create the sort of new industries in which governments were interested (Reyes and Sawyer 2011: 154). Brazil in the 1970s, for example, attempted to develop computer and aerospace industries using SOEs without the participation of the private sector. The development of SOEs also reflected the view in some cases that natural resources are the patrimony of the local population which raises complex political questions about the exploitation of these resources even by domestic firms (Castañeda, Barría and Astorga 2015: 19). Many countries in Latin America chose to develop their natural resources using SOEs. In some cases, such as the copper industry in Chile and the oil industry in Brazil, SOEs have been extremely successful.

Across all of these examples, it is clear to see the central importance of the state. In the ISI national strategy, the role of the state is much more interventionist than in the export-oriented industrialization (EOI) strategy. In the ISI strategy, the state is involved in production and actively uses an industrial policy (export-promotion schemes, joint ventures with domestic partners as a requirement for accessing the internal market, etc.). Also, as part of this industrial policy, tariffs were used to avoid external competition and discretionally to favour certain industrial sectors. In turn, in the EOI strategy, governments are mainly facilitators creating the conditions for sustained economic growth and they are not directly involved in production. In this strategy, the role of the state has been important in terms of shaping the relationships between the local firms (typically SMEs) and the large buyers overseas. There will be more gains for society (higher levels of employment, long term relationships in contracts between SMEs and the big buyers, technological learning and appropriation of rents across the chain remaining mostly in the domestic economy) if the state can assist firms in moving from simple assembly towards a more complex industrial organization. In both cases, governments create the broader conditions through which industrialization strategies can prosper through investment in the physical infrastructure required for an intensive export path (communication networks and transportation), subsidies for raw materials, lower customs duties for imported inputs that are used in export production (equivalent to a tax reduction), special and devoted financial institutions to satisfy the niche of SMEs through state guarantees, etc.

It is important to note that industrial upgrading (moving to the next stage) must not be seen from a static point of view. The role of the state is fundamental in industrial upgrading. For instance, East Asian countries (Hong Kong, South Korea, Taiwan and Singapore) moved rapidly from the assembly phase of export (utilizing export processing zones located near major ports) to a more generalized system of incentives that applied to all export-oriented factories in their economies. Another example is China which in the last 20 years has seen a radical change in its productive structures. Market openness has transformed production patterns, but openness is not enough. Within its productive structure, there is a clear trend in exports towards products with higher value added. Resource-based manufacturing has fallen sharply, decreasing its share in total exports by 30 per cent between 1985 and 2000. This industrial upgrading has been achieved via the state-sanctioned introduction and learning of specific new technologies, the creation of defined economic zones free of taxes and duties, the establishment of a local environment willing to accept higher entrepreneurship and a real opportunity for local communities to be able to absorb new technologies and new forms of learning.

The rediscovery of industrial policy and the current contours of industrial policy

After the 'lost decade' in Latin America in the 1990s, the Washington Consensus emerged as a perfect recipe for Latin American countries due to debt crisis. The almost unique application of private property rights, private initiative, devaluing the role of the state in society, the reduction of public expenditure as well as inflation control were the characteristic elements of this new consensus. But the so-called Total Productivity Factors (TPF) were only growing in most Asian countries, while in Latin America, renewed economic growth was basically influenced by the high price of commodities. This created a discussion about which type of industrial policy it was necessary to apply. According to Stiglitz (2004: 2), there was a failure in understanding economic structures within developing countries focusing on too narrow a set of objectives and on too limited a set of instruments.

Most recommendations of the Washington Consensus were limited, narrow and, despite their claims, contrary to the measures that had been taken by East Asian countries, which were broader and more interventionist. The Washington Consensus was too concerned with the efficiency of exchanges, and let the political system moderate the distributional effects of these exchanges. In the light of the failures of the Washington Consensus, a new post-Washington Consensus has emerged that seeks to find a role for both the market and the state. Stiglitz (2004: 3) points out that there is no theoretical underpinning to the belief that in the early stages of development, markets by themselves will lead to efficient outcomes. Central to the new post-Washington Consensus are the importance of national systems of innovation, limiting the freedom of capital flows and the idea that these need to be governed when necessary, local and territorial development, the development of SMEs, improving the contexts of credit and technological transference and, hence, launching a new industrial policy.

In contrast to traditional import substitution, a modern industrial policy is an open industrial economic policy with the objective of increasing economic openness by enhancing flows of knowledge and fostering productive innovation and promoting non-traditional exports. However, the role of the state is important for the coordination of investment efforts and for avoiding coordination failures to ensure long term stability and to incorporate all the relevant actors (trade unions, entrepreneurs, local politicians). Also, there are contradictory views with regard to the state of development in the previous century. This developmental concept was applied in the twentieth century and was more related to large entrepreneurial conglomerates (state-owned and private companies). After serious and large financial crises in the last few years, there is an apparent reawakening of the Western nations (Kyung-Sup, Weiss and Fine 2012: 3) for developmental measures although quite what the concept means today is certainly open to debate (in fact, the same authors point out that the World Bank itself is positing 'a need to rethink development'. The excessive financialization of economies is creating the conditions for posing a new debate over national development policy within which the discussion of industrial policy takes a central role.

One general theme that has emerged is that generally the literature has neglected analysis of the participation of SMEs in industrial policies. Another missing element has been a focus on the working conditions of labour, particularly if the industrial strategy is based on natural resources (natural endowment) or in the creation of new niche markets (picking new industrial sectors). Certainly, any attempt to accelerate industrial upgrading in the region must tackle these problems.

Bibliography

Agosin, M. 2008. *Políticas de Innovación y Competitividad En Chile*. Departamento de Economía Universidad de Chile.

Akkemik, K. 2009. *Industrial Development in East Asia: A Comparative Look at Japan, Korea, Taiwan, and Singapore*. Singapore, Hackensack, NJ: World Scientific.

Amighini, A. 2006. Upgrading in International Trade: Methods and Evidence from Selected Sectors in Latin America. In *Upgrading to Compete: Global Value Chains, Clusters, and SMEs in Latin America, Upgrading to Compete*: 221–250. Washington, DC: IDB.

Bellandi, M. and Di Tommaso, M. 2006. The Local Dimensions of Industrial Policy. In *International Handbook on Industrial Policy*: 342–362. Cheltenham: Edward Elgar. Available at: https://ideas.repec.org/h/elg/eechap/3451_17.html.

Castañeda, F., Barría, D. and Astorga, G. 2015. *Is the OECD Model Suitable for Strategic Public Enterprises in Terms of National Development? Reflections from CODELCO Case, Chile*. Available at: https://ideas.repec.org/p/crc/wpaper/1518.html.

Chang, H. 2003. The Market, the State and Institutions in Economic Development. *Rethinking Development Economics* 1: 41–60.

Chang, H. 2006. *The East Asian Development Experience: The Miracle, the Crisis and the Future*. London: Zed Books.

de la Torre, A., Soledad Martinez Peria, M. and Schmukler, S. L. 2008. Bank Involvement with SMEs: Beyond Relationship Lending. Policy Research Working Paper Series 4649, The World Bank.

Devés, E. 2004. *El Pensamiento Latinoamericano Em El Siglo XX: Las Discusiones y Las Figuras Del Fin de Siglo. Los Años 90*. Buenos Aires: Biblos.

Fajnzylber, F. 1992. Industrialización En América Latina: De La Caja Negra Al casillero Vacío. *Nueva Sociedad* 118: 21–28.

Felipe, J. 2010. *Inclusive Growth, Full Employment, and Structural Change: Implications and Policies for Developing Asia*. 2nd ed. London: Anthem Press. Available at: https://doi.org/10.7135/UPO9781843313557.

Ffrench-Davis, R. 2007. América Latina después del Consenso de Washington. *Quórum: Revista de pensamiento iberoamericano*, (18): 141–51. Available at: www.redalyc.org/articulo.oa?id=52001813.

Ffrench-Davis, R. 2009. Crisis Global, Flujos Especulativos y Financiación Innovadora Para El Desarrollo. *CEPAL* No. 97. Available at: www.cepal.org/es/publicaciones/11271-crisis-global-flujos-especulativos-financiacion-innovadora-desarrollo.

Fine, B. (ed.). 2001. Neither the Washington Nor the Post-Washington Consensus: An Introduction. In Lapavistas, C. and Pincus, J. (eds) *Development Policy in the Twenty-First Century: Beyond the Post-Washington Consensus*. London: Routledge.

Franko, P. 1999. *The Puzzle of Latin American Economic Development*. Lanham, MD: Rowman & Littlefield.

Kay, C. 1989. *Latin American Theories of Development and Underdevelopment*. London: Routledge. Available at: www.tandfonline.com/toc/rwhi20/.

Kay, C. 2002. Why East Asia Overtook Latin America: Agrarian Reform, Industrialisation and Development. *Third World Quarterly* 23 (6): 1073–1102. Available at: www.jstor.org/stable/3993564.

Khan, M. 2003. State Failure in Developing Countries and Strategies of Institutional Reform. *Revue d'Economie Du Developpement* 17 (2–3): 5–48.

Khan, M. and Jomo, K. 2000. *Rents, Rent-Seeking and Economic Development: Theory and Evidence in Asia*. Cambridge: Cambridge University Press.

Kyung-Sup, C., Weiss, L. and Fine., B. (eds) 2012. Introduction: Neoliberalism and Developmental Politics in Perspective. In *Developmental Politics in Transition: The Neoliberal Era and Beyond*: 1–23. International Political Economy Series. London: Palgrave Macmillan.

Lall, S. 2006. *Industrial Policy in Developing Countries: What Can We Learn from East Asia?* Cheltenham: Edward Elgar. Available at: www.elgaronline.com/view/9781843768364.00011.xml.

Larrain, J. 2014. Modernity and Identity: Cultural Change in Latin America. In *Latin America Transformed*: 42–58. London: Routledge.

Lustig, N. 1988. Del Estructuralismo Al Neoestructuralismo: La Búsqueda de Un Paradigma Heterodoxo. *Cadernos Colección Estudios CIEPLAN* (25): 35–50.

Moncayo, E. 2003. Resultados de Las Reformas Del Consenso de Washington En Los Países Andinos: Estabilización Incompleta, Profundización de Los Desequilibrios Sociales y Crecimiento Precario. *Economía y Desarrollo* 2 (1): 73–95.

Palma, G. 2003. The Latin American Economies during the Second Half of the Twentieth Century – from the Age of ISI to the age of The End of History. In *Rethinking Development Economics*. Chang, H.-J. (ed.): 107–125. London: Anthem Press.

Palma, J. 2009. Flying Geese and Waddling Ducks: The Different Capabilities of East Asia and Latin America to 'Demand-Adapt' and 'Supply-Upgrade' their Export Productive Capacity. In *Industrial Policy and Development: The Political Economy of Capabilities Accumulation*. Cimoli, M., Dosi, G. and Stiglitz, J. (eds). Oxford: Oxford University Press.

Prebisch, R. 1973. Problemas Teóricos y Prácticos Del Crecimiento Económico. *CEPAL*. Available at: https://repositorio.cepal.org//handle/11362/2958.

Puppim de Oliveira, J. 2008. *Implementation of Environmental Policies in Developing Countries: A Case of Protected Areas and Tourism in Brazil*. Albany, NY: State University of New York Press.

Reyes, J. and Sawyer, C. 2011. *Latin American Economic Development. Routledge Textbooks in Development Economics*. Abingdon: Routledge.

Rodrik, D. 1998. The New Global Economy and Developing Countries: Making Openness Work. *The New Global Economy and Developing Countries: Making Openness Work*. Overseas Development Council, Washington, DC, distributed by John Hopkins University Press; Policy Essay: 24.

Stallings, B, and Peres, W. 2000. *Growth, Employment, and Equity: The Impact of the Economic Reforms in Latin America and the Caribbean*. Washington, DC: Brookings Institution Press.

Stiglitz, J. 2004. The Post Washington Consensus. *The Initiative for Policy Dialogue*, 1–15.

Sunkel, O. ed. 1993. *Development from Within: Toward a Neostructuralist Approach for Latin America*. Boulder, CO: Lynne Rienner.

Thorp, R. 1998. *Progress, Poverty and Exclusion: An Economic History of Latin America in the 20th Century.* Washington, DC; Baltimore: Inter-American Development Bank; Johns Hopkins University Press.

Todaro, M. 1997. *Economic Development.* New York; London: Longman.

Ul Haque, I. 2007. *Rethinking Industrial Policy: United Nations Conference on Trade and Development.* Geneva: Unctad.

Wade, R. 1990. *Governing the Market: Economic Theory and the Role of Government in East Asian Industrialization.* Princeton, NJ: Princeton University Press.

Williamson, J. 2009. A Short History of the Washington Consensus. *Law & Business Review America.* 15 (1): 7. Available at: https://scholar.smu.edu/lbra/vol. 15/iss1/3.

44

The IPE of global corporations

John Mikler

Introduction

In 1970 there were around 7,000 global corporations (Clapp 2005). According to United Nations Conference on Trade and Development (UNCTAD) (2011) there are now over 100,000 with nearly 900,000 foreign affiliates. A global dimension to almost all major corporations is now taken for granted. What are global corporations though? The term is perhaps a little too obtuse, and there are other more precise ones that might be worth considering instead. These include multinational corporations (MNCs), transnational corporations (TNCs) and multinational enterprises (MNEs). MNCs are defined as such because they invest, produce and sell their products and services in more than one national jurisdiction. Labelling corporations as TNCs stresses their transnationality, which goes beyond conceiving them as operating in several jurisdictions to seeing them as passing through/across borders as if these were irrelevant. The MNE term, most often used in the international business literature, encompasses aspects of both in the sense that modern business involves the management of supply chains and operations across multiple national territories. The label of 'global corporation' encompasses aspects of all three terms, while not being clearly defined by any of them (see Box 44.1). Yet whatever the definitional fuzziness, in all cases there is the sense that while the governments of states are bound by their territorial jurisdictions, the world's major corporations are not, and that this is increasingly the norm as they potentially operate 'as if the entire world (or major regions of it) were a single entity' (Levitt 1983, p. 92).

Politically, it is easy to form the view that global corporations rival states, as they therefore also potentially undermine the scope and policy efficacy of states' sovereignty. Some commentators, notably Korten (2015), have suggested that they do so to such an extent that they potentially 'rule' instead of states. Whether or not they do, or the extent to which they do, is surely a topic worth pursuing for any student or scholar of international political economy (IPE). It is rather surprising then, that instead of explicitly focusing on global corporations, much of the debate about their political power in IPE is far more obtuse. Much of the time it revolves instead around the extent and desirability of markets, and the market forces that are said to underpin neoliberal globalisation. This is certainly true of the early globalisation literature which laid the foundations for such debates. For example, the redoubtable Susan Strange looked at the

---

Box 44.1 Defining global corporations

MNC: A corporation that invests, produces and sells its products and services in more than one national jurisdiction.

TNC: A corporation that operates and has interests in several national jurisdictions, and which does so as if the borders between them were irrelevant. It passes through/across borders essentially as if they were not there.

MNE: A corporation that embodies aspects of both MNCs and TNCs, but emphasising its networked attributes in the sense that modern business involves the management of supply chains and coordinating networks of operations across multiple national territories. This is important to recognise because global corporations like Walmart, Apple, Gap and Nike actually produce no goods themselves. Instead, their core function in the production process is contracting and logistical management of their global supply chains.

Global corporation: A corporation that exhibits attributes of MNCs, TNCs and MNEs to the extent that it may be said to operate on a global scale. This is a somewhat tautological definition, yet it is the one used by the *Financial Times* (n.d.) which defines such a corporation as one with at least 20 per cent of its sales in each of at least three continental markets.

---

world order that emerged with the end of the Cold War and declared that 'where states were once the masters of markets, now it is markets which, on many crucial issues, are the masters over the governments of states' (Strange 1996, p. 4). She stressed the political impact not of global corporations, but of the marketisation of global economic *relations*. From this perspective, disembodied market forces and market imperatives do not produce governance in the sense of purposive control over national destinies. They undermine it, to instead produce a 'diffusion of authority away from national governments (that) has left a hole of non-authority, ungovernance it might be called (Strange 1996, p. 14).

Pitched ideological battles have been fought on the basis of this view. The demise of states' power has been celebrated by those who see the economic, social and political benefits produced by free markets (e.g. Fukuyama 1992; Bhagwati 2004; Wolf 2004), while critical voices have demanded a global alternative to the structural basis for the class relations producing the marketisation of political processes and relations at all levels (e.g. Kitching 2001; Coburn 2011). It is surely not unimportant to consider whether states in charge versus markets that are free are desirable, how a more economically interconnected world drives the embrace or rejection of this viewpoint, and whether or not this state of affairs has come to pass. However, the result is often an analysis that focuses on the power of globally mobile *capital* over labour and democratically elected state representatives, and the way corporate economic *interests* are served that clash with citizens' aspirations. These interests are then primarily seen in economic terms, so that in addition to global corporations being given less prominence than they should be afforded in these debates, they are often cast as market rather than political actors (e.g. see Broome 2014).

The purpose of this chapter is to make a contribution to re-animating debates about the political power of global corporations in IPE. In the first section, they are located in the main IPE theoretical traditions *vis a vis* conceptualising globalisation. A transformationalist perspective of them as relationally 'entangled' with states is suggested as the most useful starting point for critically unpacking the power relations between them. Drawing on a three faces of power approach for understanding global corporate power, in the second section it is demonstrated that global corporations wield their power instrumentally, structurally and discursively. Their political power is not just a function of the material wealth they possess and the economic processes they control, but of them constructing themselves as legitimate self-governors. The case is made for why their discursive power reinforces their instrumental and structural power by increasing perceptions of their legitimacy. Therefore, the degree to which one particular IPE tradition or another is ideationally accepted as self-evident frames not just the manner in which globalisation is conceptualised, but also the political power global corporations are seen as being entitled to wield.

IPE theories and globalisation

The main IPE traditions exist in a trichotomy of nationalist, liberal and Marxist approaches. Or at least, as Watson (2008) suggests, these approaches are often the starting point for teaching and an initial understanding of IPE. For nationalism, this includes neo-mercantilism, economic nationalism, the developmental state literature and state capitalism as said to be embodied by the rise of China and the 'Beijing Consensus'. For liberalism, this includes embedded liberalism (in the national and international organisations that establish global regulatory regimes), and neo-liberalism as a new form of liberal ideology, or a radical extension of it, as embodied in the 'Washington Consensus'. For Marxism, this includes neo-Marxist traditions such as World Systems theory, Gramscianism and critical theory. This of course is not an exhaustive list, and the contributions in Parts I and II of this Handbook explain them and other more critical approaches in greater detail. The aim here is simply to more explicitly locate global corporations in the IPE theoretical traditions and the lenses they provide for conceptualising globalisation.

Nationalist accounts see the state as the key unit of analysis, focusing on its interest in economic wealth due to the mutually supportive relationship it has with power and sovereignty (e.g. see Viner 1948). Wealth produces power, and power is employed in pursuit of greater wealth, and therefore it is natural that the state should be interested in the relationship between these two sides of the same sovereignty 'coin'. For example, it is seen as necessary and natural that a state should take charge to strategically promote development, as exemplified by the Northeast Asian developmental states of Japan and South Korea that experienced rapid industrialisation post-World War Two (e.g. Evans 1995; Johnson 1995; Weiss and Hobson 1995; Woo-Cummings 1999). Once industrialised, many industrialised states are seen as continuing to perform a guiding hand in coordinating economic activity, rather than leaving this to the invisible hand of competition in markets, with this exemplified by continental European and East Asian varieties of capitalism (e.g. see authors such as Streeck and Yamamura 2001, 2003; Schmidt 2002; Walter and Zhang 2012). The role of the state, complex and variegated as it may be, is therefore seen as central. And it may well be so with respect to the rise of global corporations too. While it could be contended that global corporations are market actors responding to global market forces and acting globally in their economic interests, it may also be observed that just ten states are the headquarters for 84 per cent of those listed on the FT Global 500. These are the world's largest corporations on the basis of stock market capitalisation, and those based in the US alone account for 42 per cent of them (*Financial Times* 2016). With the emergence of Brazil, Russia, India, and China (collectively known as the BRICs) as economic powers it may no longer be as true as it once was that 'a statistical profile for the current corporation indicates that it is predominantly Anglo-American' (Harrod 2006, pp. 27–28), but it remains the case that the home bases of the world's largest corporations are like a map of global economic power. Therefore, it seems reasonable to think that economically powerful states are cognisant of the fact that they are the headquarters of these corporations, and that wherever possible they need to be controlled and directed to ensure they serve the national interest, including as they operate beyond and across national boundaries.

Of course, if this is not possible it logically follows that global corporations potentially undermine even these powerful states' ability to act. This is seen as desirable in liberal accounts which stress the benefits of economic development and opportunity for all individuals produced by free markets. The result is an attack on the state in order to relocate power in market actors' hands, with neoliberal accounts seeing this as inevitable in addition to desirable given undeniable global market forces. The political zeal of the attack was especially evident as the Cold War drew to an end, as neoliberal globalisation came to be seen as the inevitable result of a less divided and more homogeneously free market capitalist world. As Harvey (2005, p. 11) explains, where liberalism was once 'embedded' in the sense that 'entrepreneurial and corporate activities were surrounded by a web of social and political constraints ... the neoliberal project is to dis-embed capital from these constraints'. But whether the state creates a liberal order or removes itself to ensure a neoliberal one, an obsession with competitive markets in which firms complete for profits has come to predominate in debates. This is increasingly at odds with the reality of a world in which most markets appear to be oligopolistic. The point about most major corporations having a global dimension to their operations as noted in the introduction notwithstanding, it is also the case that according to Nolan et al. (2002; see also Tepper and Hearn 2019) already by the turn of the twentieth century no more than five global corporations controlled each of the world's major industries. Around a third of these had one corporation which accounted for over 40 per cent of global sales. The competitiveness which may have once characterised markets, and of which liberals stress the desirability, is now challenged by oligopolistic structures produced be concentrated market power in global corporations' hands.

On the other hand, it could be contended that although the markets in which global corporations operate are highly concentrated, they are not oligopolistic in nature because a small number of huge global corporations are engaged in fierce competition with one another. Liberals might then claim that efficiently maximised profits and economic opportunities are still being produced by free markets, despite their concentration. Even if they are though, Marxists would see maximised exploitation and alienation. This is because their focus on class relations defined by the capitalist mode of production leads them to see those who control the means of production (i.e. the boards and shareholders of corporations – increasingly one and the same according to authors such as Lazonick and O'Sullivan 2000; and Lazonick 2014) subordinating those who do not in the search for greater profits. Neo-Marxists like Sklair (2001) have declared the emergence of a 'transnational capitalist class' that accompanies the territorial and market concentration referred to above. This class constitutes a ruling elite that controls the global economy, with global corporations as the key organisational basis for doing so. This ruling elite then co-opts or strategically incorporates states in pursuit corporate interests, resulting in the institutionalisation of regulations and policies that serve these interests at the expense of labour, the public good and democratic processes. The result is a world in which inequality inevitably results from the global expansion of capitalism, underpinned by governments that are either powerless or serve the interests of capital. As such, while a nationalist account is supported by evidence for the geopolitical patterns suggested by the major global corporations' headquarters, Marxists would expect that the governments of these states are not actually in charge. Trade statistics lend support to such claims, because it is global corporations, not states, that are responsible for the data reported on international trade. In fact, they are estimated to be responsible for as much as 80 per cent of global trade because the vast majority of trade today is intra-firm rather than inter-state (Dobbs et al. 2015; see also Bonturi and Fukasaku 1993; see also Karliner 1997). Trade occurs on the basis of the control of global supply chains, rather than on the basis of Ricardian comparative advantage between states. This produces the global class relations neo-Marxists identify: one of core and periphery states and regions, increasingly prone to crisis and ultimately doomed to collapse (Wallerstein 1984, 2004).

So, there are implications flowing from each of the major IPE traditions for theorising global corporate power. Corporations are framed as serving/undermining the national interest (nationalism), replacing the state (liberalism, but more especially neoliberalism), or serving the capitalist class (Marxism, and contemporarily neo-Marxism). There are also normative implications – i.e. whether or not these outcomes are desirable. Taken in turn, these traditions suggest that global corporations must be either controlled and guided to serve the state, freed from the heavy hand of states' control to promote global growth and opportunity for the world's peoples, or curtailed and where possible eliminated to deliver the emancipation of the oppressed majority.

The different frames are also related to how globalisation is conceptualised, which Martell (2007) identifies as having occurred in three sequential waves: globalists, sceptics and transformationalists. The globalists predicted the decline of the nation state in the wake of the end of the Cold War, with all states losing sovereignty albeit to differing degrees. Therefore, if global governance is not possible, neoliberalism is inevitable, and this will produce a world in which global markets are in charge. However, it could equally be contended that it means global corporations are in charge, not free markets, with states acceding to their demands. The sceptics responded that not as much had changed as the globalists asserted, so that states remain central as do regional blocs in international relations. International (i.e. relations between states), as opposed to global power relations remain important. Therefore, political agency on the part of states remains possible. If this is the case, while global corporations attempt to influence states, the latter remain able to choose to act, and how to act, in order to ensure that the national interest is served (e.g. to control or free markets, and to embrace, modify or reject capitalism). The transformationalists occupy a middle ground, not just rejecting but also modifying the earlier pronouncements of the globalists. In seeing politics as globally transformed, they accept that nation states remain important, but also reconstructed in how they can act in a more economically interconnected world. A key aspect of this reconstruction is the need to share sovereignty with each other, as well as non-state actors like global corporations, in order to retain political agency. Given that the waves of theorising globalisation are sequential, the transformationalist wave may be thought of as the current mainstream perspective. As the term implies, globalisation is a set of processes not an outcome. It is not an 'ism' but a process of 'isation', and therefore while the globalist and sceptical accounts are possible outcomes, they are not inevitable. This is the central point of authors such as Held et al. (1999), Dicken (2015), and contributions to be found in collections such as Hay and Marsh (2000) and Held and McGrew (2003), whose works are emblematic of the literature rejecting the inevitable epochal change prophesised by the globalists, as well as sceptical claims that little had changed.

These three waves can be viewed through the 'lenses' of the IPE traditions. For example, from a nationalist–transformationalist perspective the role of a state is to share sovereignty with its global corporations in the national interest, given that a conception of what this entails is no longer as confined by national geographical borders as was once the case. It is not so much that disembodied market 'forces' have taken over, but that in a more interdependent world there are more actors involved, and global corporations are central among these. Rather than the inevitability of the neoliberal state, with this involving a ceding of state sovereignty to market actors through processes of deregulation and privatisation, it could also be contended that this

763

potentially produces a *publicisation* of corporations that assume responsibility for performing state functions rather than competing in markets to primarily serve economic functions. As argued in Mikler (2011, 2012), the result is the increasing mutual *entanglement* of corporate–state interests. This somewhat abstruse term is useful from a transformationalist perspective, as it does not assume that one or the other is in charge, although depending on the issue this may be the case. However, the starting point for understanding power relations needs to be an analysis of shared sovereignty (on the part of states) and authority (on the part of corporations), in the dominant national, regional and global contexts in which this occurs (see Box 44.2).

Box 44.2 Corporate–state 'entanglement'

The mutual entanglement of states and global corporations draws on Mann's conception of infrastructural power: 'the institutional capacity of a central state … to penetrate its territories and logistically implement decisions' (Mann 1993, p. 59). A state's territories could be narrowly conceived as those defined by its borders, but with globalisation he finds that 'the transnational and the national have surged together' (Mann 2000, p. 41). In other words, the conception of the national interest must now encompass global spaces. This leads Weiss (2006, p. 173) to make the point that, rather than questions of which actors are in control, as is stressed by liberals and Marxists and animates much of the debate between globalists and sceptics, in reality 'global and national networks of interaction are not competing for space, but are intertwined'. Putting it more simply, in a more economically interdependent world there are more actors involved, and there is the need for an actor-centred analysis in understanding the intertwining of national and global networks. This includes analysing the power dynamics inherent in the mutual entanglement of global corporations with states.

For example, Weiss (2006, 2010) says states must have the capacity to engage in 'governed interdependence' via state–business alliances operating on the basis of 'reciprocal consent'. This involves states and corporations mutually serving each other's interests, but with the state strategically in the governing lead. One does not necessarily have to accept that this must be the case though. It could be contended that corporations, rather than states, must strategically be in the lead, or that the class relations underpinning capitalist relations of production make this inevitable. As such, a more liberal or Marxist, rather than a nationalist, rendering of the relationship is equally possible.

Before moving on to the next section it is important to acknowledge, as Gilpin (1987, p. 25) does, that the main IPE theoretical traditions are also essentially 'three ideologies' to be embraced or rejected not just on the basis of interests, but also beliefs. This means that the power of ideas should be considered. There are a range of more ideational approaches in IPE, some of which are quite radical as they focus on ideas to such an extent that political actors – whether these be states, corporations or other non-state actors – do not actually exist so much as ideas about them do. But in general, the point of more ideational approaches is that ideas, as well as structures of power that inform and underpin material interests, have explanatory power. For example, as Finnemore and Sikkink (2001, p. 393) note, constructivists 'focus on the role of ideas, norms, knowledge, culture and argument in politics, stressing in particular the role of collectively held or "intersubjective" ideas and understandings of social life'. As such, '(a) human interaction is shaped primarily by ideational factors, not simply material ones; (b) the most important ideational factors are widely shared or "intersubjective" beliefs, which are not reducible to individuals; and (c) these shared beliefs construct the interests and identities of purposive actors' (see also Adler 1997; Price and Reus-Smit 1998; Ruggie 1998; Wendt 1999; Amin and Palan 2001; Hay 2006; Widmaier 2016). Therefore, to the extent that either a nationalist, liberal or Marxist perspective may be seen as self-evident, and determining which wave for conceptualising globalisation holds most weight, depends on the dominant ideas about the interests and standpoints of the actors involved. This is not to say that empirically observable evidence in support of each of the perspectives is lacking. However, widely held intersubjective beliefs are the 'filters' through which this evidence is explained and assessed.

The result is that whether or not globalisation exists, the form it takes, and whether or not this form is desirable, are all also matters of the accepted wisdom produced by an 'ideas game'. As Bell (2013, p. 115) puts it:

> Ideas can have real effects and the impacts of globalization become almost a self-fulfilling reflex. If policy-makers believe a (neoliberal) 'golden straightjacket' exists, then, in effect, it exists.

Relatedly, if global corporations are believed to possess not just the ability but right to exercise their power, given the environment that is produced in which they operate, then we may as well say they do indeed have the right to do so. They can also lose that right. Whether global corporations become more politically powerful than states and the societies they represent is therefore not just a matter of material capabilities. Ideas about them, which they purposively construct and attempt to influence, shape and potentially enhance the power they possess.

Three faces of power

A 'three faces of power' framework for understanding global corporate power, as suggested by Fuchs (2007), is useful for unpacking the complexity of this. She explains how, for analytical purposes, global corporations' political power may be seen as instrumental, structural, and discursive (see Box 44.3). Of course, in reality political power is not so easily divided up. However, her framework draws on a rich tradition in political analysis that is mostly applied to states and their polities, but which she demonstrates may also be usefully employed to understand corporate political power. It also further helps in drawing and understanding the links between the main IPE traditions and waves of conceptualising globalisation.

Box 44.3 Three faces of power

Fuchs' (2007) three faces of power framework is useful for understanding the complexity of the political power global corporations possess, and how they exercise it. It also stresses their relational entanglement with states and other non-state actors, in the sense that they wield their power with and over others in their exercise of it.

Instrumental power: As per Dahl's (1957, p. 201) definition, this means that 'A has power over B to the extent that he can get B to do something that B would not otherwise do'. Therefore, it is about leverage exercised to achieve a desired end (i.e. it is instrumentally motivated) between purposive actors (i.e. it is exercised relationally). For global corporations, it is evident in their

---

lobbying expenditure and efforts, as well as relations with influential policy-makers. If such lobbying and connections are successful, they may produce corporate–state relations that are said to be akin to a 'revolving door'.

Structural power: As Bachrach and Baratz (1962) put it, this means 'A devotes his energies to creating or reinforcing social and political values and institutional practices that limit the scope of the political process to public consideration of only those issues which are comparatively innocuous to A'. Structural power emphasises the manner in which issues are organised 'in' and 'out' of politics via actors' capacity for agenda-setting. To be able to do this, a political actor must possess underlying control of processes and resources. In the case of global corporations this is evident through their dominance of the markets for their goods and services, their size relative to states and their resulting ability to threaten to withhold investment, or to disinvest, in particular states if policy-makers do not take account of their interests. This puts them in a 'privileged position' by comparison to other non-state actors.

Discursive power: As Lukes (1974, p. 23) explains, 'A may exercise power over B by getting him to do what he does not want to do, but he also exercises power over him by influencing, shaping or determining his very wants'. Discursive power focuses on the power of ideas, and is therefore the hardest to observe. It is also potentially the most important because it relates to the creation of one actor's interests in another's. This goes beyond having access and being influential with the right contacts, or being in a structurally powerful position to determine outcomes, to the *right* to get them. Global corporations engage in an 'ideas game' to establish their discursive legitimacy not just to influence policy agendas, but to set them. One of the clearest examples of this in practice is their declared embrace of corporate social responsibility to enhance acceptance of their claims that they are legitimate global self-governors.

Instrumental power

Instrumental power focuses on the direct influence of one actor on another in order to achieve a desired outcome. As per Dahl's (1957, p. 201) definition, this means that 'A has power over B to the extent that he can get B to do something that B would not otherwise do'. Instrumental power is therefore about leverage exercised to achieve a desired end (i.e. it is instrumentally motivated) between purposive actors (i.e. it is exercised relationally). In international relations it can be seen in realist conceptions of an anarchical world where coercion and conflict between states to achieve desired ends is endemic, and results in a power balance or imbalance that produces stability or conflict. Likewise in nationalist IPE accounts. But in terms of the political power of global corporations, it is most clearly seen in efforts to directly lobby and influence policy-makers to produce desired outcomes.

For example, the UK's Chartered Institute of Public Relations estimates the public relations industry is worth around £6.5 billion, of which approximately 30 per cent is focused on private sector lobbying to influence 'public affairs'. The motivations for this are described by Parvin (2007, p. 10) as follows:

> If lobbying, in its widest sense, did not produce commercial results and consequently improve profits, then it is reasonable to assume that it would not be carried out at all. Businesses make their investment in the expectation that they will see a worthwhile return and it is this interaction between the political process and profit that fuels scepticism about the role and influence of lobbying.

In other words, the expenditure is instrumentally motivated by the achievement of enhanced material outcomes. But it is the relational aspect rather than the resources deployed which are most salient to understanding instrumental power. Access to policy-makers may be bought, and indeed it may buy the policy-makers themselves if it involves a corruption of the policy-making process. However, corporations with senior office holders who have the right connections may not need to buy access at all. If this is the case, then their lobbying activities are not as transparently evident. For example, it may be that corporate board members and government officials have gone to the same schools or universities, or belong to the same clubs, or belong to the 'transnational capitalist class' of elites referred to above. There is evidence that they may do so, because Wilks-Heeg et al. (2012) find that 46 of the top 50 publicly listed corporations in the UK have a member of parliament as either a director of shareholder. The result is that 'British business and political elites are not distinct entities: they are deeply intertwined' (Jones 2014, p. 71). The extent of their entanglement leads Moran (2008, p. 74) to conclude that they are 'incorporated into the policy-making elite'.

Such corporate–state connections exist in all states to one degree or another. They produce government–business relations that have been referred to as akin to a 'revolving door' (Levy and Egan 1998, p. 342; see also Newell 2000; Newell and Levy 2006; Falkner 2008; Sell 2009; Tienhaara 2014). The lobbying efforts and connections established mean that corporations are in a position to 'capture' the regulatory agencies of states on behalf of corporate interests (e.g. Weidenbaum 2004; Carpenter and Moss 2014). There is also growing acceptance that because of the global nature of their operations, global corporations are well-suited to lobbying for their interests across and between, as well as within, states. For example, Mattli and Woods (2009, p. 9) suggest that

> the view that most regulatory issues start out as domestic problems before globalisation makes them international issues underplays the fact that a good deal of transnational regulation is motivated by uniquely transnational problems; and that transnational institutional structures may offer privileged access to some actors, biasing global regulatory outcomes in ways difficult to comprehend from a purely domestic perspective.

This is particularly evident in the case of the European Union (EU). Characterised as a 'microcosm of globalisation' (Weber 2001, p. 4) for the supranational governance and the interconnection of its member states that characterise its operations, Fuchs (2007, p. 85) also dubs it 'the world's largest playground for interest groups' representing corporations. In fact, Ronit and Schneider (1997; see also Coen 2009) find that the overwhelming majority of EU lobbying is corporate, by comparison to interest groups focused on social, labour and environmental issues.

There are many examples of the extensive lobbying efforts of corporations, and of corporate influence exercised over and with governments nationally and internationally. And it should be noted that this suggests that there is a fundamentally territorial aspect to this face of power. This is because although corporate interests and operations may be increasingly global, the relational aspect of instrumental power means that it must be exercised *somewhere*. This is obviously the case at the national level, but it is also the case for international organisations and intergovernmental groups that remain comprised of states, and which operate on the basis of negotiations and agreements between them. Such territoriality is potentially less the case for the second structural face of power.

Structural power

Structural power emphasises the manner in which issues are organised 'in' and 'out' of politics due to political actors' capacity for agenda-setting. As Bachrach and Baratz (1962; see also Strange 1988) put it, it means 'A devotes his energies to creating or reinforcing social and political values and institutional practices that limit the scope of the political process to public consideration of only those issues which are comparatively innocuous to A'. To be able to do this suggests the possession of underlying control of processes and resources. Global corporations' size and economic dominance suggest they certainly do, and therefore that they are in a position to punish or reward states for the provision of favourable conditions both within and between their territories. They are effectively in what has been termed a 'privileged position' by comparison to other non-state actors (e.g. environmental non-government organisations) because of their indispensability to the economic bases of states and the global economy (Tienhaara 2014, p. 166; see also Lindblom 1977; Frank 1978; Cox 1987).

Market concentration, and the oligopolistic nature of the world's major industries it suggests, means that the visible hand of the state and the Smithian invisible hand of the market have both been replaced by a visible handful of huge corporations. As Crouch (2011, p. 49) puts it, there has been a 'corporate takeover of the market' (see also the earlier work of Chandler 1977 in respect of the US specifically). The world's 500 largest corporations on the basis of their annual revenues together accounted for US$31.2 trillion in sales in 2015 (Fortune 2015). By comparison the size of the global economy in the same year was estimated to be US$73.5 trillion (World Bank 2016). This means that 40 per cent of the global economy was accounted for by these 500 non-state entities. UNCTAD and International Monetary Fund (IMF) data further indicate that the top 20 most global non-financial corporations' sales were greater than the combined gross domestic product (GDP) of the bottom 138 states, and the combined expenditure of the bottom 166 states. On the basis of GDP, many of the top 20 corporations are as large as middle income or emerging states such as Algeria and Portugal. A comparison with national expenditure may be more accurate because a state's budget is analogous to a corporation's sales, these being an indicator of how much it has spent on purchasing inputs (labour, resources, investments, goods, advertising, corporate image-making, lobbying, consultants etc.) to produce its surpluses. On the basis of national expenditure, these top 20 global corporations are as large as many of the top 30 high income states. Only the major industrialised countries like the US, Germany, Japan and (relatively recently) China may be said to rival them in terms of economic size (UNCTAD 2014; IMF 2015).

As noted above, the same dominance is evident in trade relations because the vast majority of trade data reported is intra-firm rather than inter-state in nature. That trade occurs on the basis of internal corporate global supply chain management strategies, rather than national comparative advantage, means global corporations can impose economic costs or confer benefits for certain policy choices by moving their operations to wherever conditions are most favourable. It should be noted that this is relatively easy because their operations do not necessarily require a physical presence. Global corporations like Walmart, Apple, Gap and Nike actually produce no goods themselves, but instead their core function in the production process is the logistical management of contractors and subcontractors in a range of states. For example, Nike employs 800,000 workers in a global network of 600 factories, none of which it owns but which it controls from its headquarters in the US (Dicken 2015, p. 160). Likewise, Walmart does not own any manufacturing operations but contracts over 100,000 suppliers to produce its products (LeBaron 2014; Walmart 2017). The result is that just the *possibility* of such corporations shifting the operations within their global supply chains may be sufficient for them to shape public policy. They effectively play states off against one another not on the basis of natural endowments, but on the basis of favourable treatment. As states compete with each other for the economic benefits global corporations may confer or withhold, over time Wilks (2013, p. 166) suggests this has the potential to produce global corporations that are 'no longer dependent clients of their home states and the new global partnerships between states and corporations are more likely to be manifest in collaborations in transnational networks and sharing in regulation and economic governance'.

Clearly, their size and economic dominance mean that the economic fortunes of even the most powerful states are dependent on the decisions made by global corporations. As a result, they are in a strong position even before they instrumentally lobby or bargain for their interests. They may not even need to do so, as instead they may count on their indispensability to national economies, as well as the global economy. But when they do need to do so, their structural power enhances their instrumental power by enhancing their policy leverage. Because they may credibly threaten states' economic fortunes by deciding to invest or disinvest in their territories, the representatives of global corporations need to rely less on arguing, representation, cajoling, threatening and influencing policy-makers. Such 'displays' attract more critical attention and tend to suggest that an argument needs to be made, and that it may be lost. In addition, both these first two faces of power are enhanced when they possess discursive power.

Discursive power

Discursive power focuses on the role played by ideas. It is therefore the hardest to observe, while also potentially the most important, because it relates to the creation of one political actor's interests in another. As Lukes (1974, p. 23) explains, 'A may exercise power over B by getting him to do what he does not want to do, but he also exercises power over him by influencing, shaping or determining his very wants'. This goes beyond paying for access through lobbying or being influential with useful contacts. It also goes beyond being in a structurally powerful position to influence, and maybe determine, policy outcomes. It is about to the *right* to get them. If power is 'the production, in and through social relations, of effects that shape the capacities of actors to determine their own circumstances and fate' (Barnett and Duvall 2005, p. 3), then this is surely the most powerful face of it. As Elbra (2014) puts it, 'interests do not need to be pursued if they can be created', and essentially through creating 'truths' about policy that are widely accepted, global corporations can promote the 'projection of a particular set of interests as the general interest' (Levy and Newell 2002 p. 87).

Discursive power underpins perceptions of legitimacy. It creates 'a generalised perception or assumption that the actions of an entity are desirable, proper, or appropriate within some socially constructed system' (Suchman 1995, p. 574). The rise of the phenomenon of corporate social responsibility (CSR) is one of the clearest examples of this in practice. Through their declared embrace of it, global corporations signal that they are not just motivated by economic interests, but by being servants of the public good. Their aim is to be perceived as acting virtuously as an end in itself, and maybe even to claim that they may be globally self-governing. Whether this is actually true or not in reality is a matter of ongoing debate. It may seem naive to easily accept it is, yet from a more pragmatically materialistic perspective corporate reputation can be seen as an intangible asset (Gotsi and Wilson 2001; see also O'Callaghan 2007). In fact, international business scholars have claimed a 'business integrity thesis' has emerged which accepts firms now 'proactively build reputational capital for strategic advantage' (Jackson 2004, p. 3). According to this thesis, shareholders are interested in profitable businesses that return rewards in the form of high dividends, but they also wish to see corporations in which they invest mitigate financial risks by adhering to socially accepted norms. It may also be the case that corporations seen to be acting in the public good are able to charge higher prices for their products and services, and to build brand loyalty.

Acting through CSR initiatives to create the sense that what is in their private interest is also in the public interest may also allow global corporations to claim a reduced need for government regulation. The 'iron law of responsibility' says that whomever does not use power in ways that society considers responsible will tend to lose it (Lawrence et al. 2005, p. 47; originally Davis and Blomstrom 1966). Corporations perceived to be 'doing the right thing', or to be 'trustworthy', may be capable of claiming the legitimate right to self-regulation. They may also be in an enhanced position to receive the regulatory and financial support they desire on the basis that they deserve it. They do not have to fall back on structural and instrumental forms of power, but rather may claim their *right* to not just influence but set the policy agenda, and to be entitled to get what they want. If global corporations must rely more on threats and rewards, or making demands based on their economic dominance, then the continuity of, and commitment to, their agendas and interests is always threatened. If support for them is given grudgingly, then this suggests potential for their agendas and interests to be controlled by others who will have the upper hand in setting the agenda.

Putting it simply, power that is believed to be exercised responsibly comes to be institutionalised as 'normal', or at the very least 'tolerable' (Wilks 2013, p. 177), because it is perceived to be legitimate. It does not need to be continually asserted and imposed. As Kolleck (2013, p. 147) notes, 'the discursive power of global companies is … based on legitimacy and acceptance of business-friendly norms and ideas,' and therefore discursive power that leads to legitimacy reinforces instrumental and structural power by institutionalising widely accepted norms of behaviour on the basis of it. As noted above, it may even shape widely accepted beliefs as self-evident about the nature of globalisation and the operation of the global economy, such as the desirability of free and deregulated markets, to the benefit of global corporations which can increase their economic, political and social control not just in the states where they are headquartered, but wherever they operate and have interests.

Conclusion

Global corporations control their markets, which tend to be highly concentrated. It seems easier to believe that these operate oligopolistically rather than competitively. They also control trade flows, because they control their global supply chains, and therefore are in a position to make the rules for how the global economy operates. They are huge. In terms of their size they rival even the most economically powerful states. For reasons such as these, it is more useful to locate them as political rather than (or at least in addition to) market actors in IPE, and to theorise them as such. The point made in this chapter is that global corporations' power is a function of them exercising leverage given their material wealth, whether instrumentally or structurally, with this enhanced by discursively constructing themselves as legitimately entitled to wield it. For global corporations, the third face of discursive power is the political 'prize' that facilitates the creation of a world in the image of their interests – i.e. to make it appear that, as global political actors, their interests are synonymous with those of all states and a global society.

This means that any of the waves of conceptualising globalisation and the major IPE traditions are potentially be applicable, but that the role played by global corporations must be central to understanding the power dynamics. The role states play is traditionally seen as governing on behalf of their citizens, but depending on the nature of the normative basis of the power corporations wield relationally with states, they may instead give preference to the interests of global corporations. Whether or not this is desirable depends on support for such a situation (i.e. a liberal versus Marxist perspective) or the extent to which it serves the national interest (i.e. a nationalist perspective). Therefore, an ideational approach such as constructivism is also useful to understand the basis and support for one perspective versus another, and how this becomes institutionalised over time as self-evident.

What has also been suggested is that relational 'entanglement' between states and global corporations always applies. As such, a transformationalist conception of globalisation is the most tractable starting point for analysis, given that politically the focus is on the way in which states which are territorially constrained share sovereignty with global corporations that are not. There has not been the room to explore the implications of this here, but it suffices to say that it raises questions such as whether global corporations act on behalf of 'their' states on the international stage, or *vice versa*. Likewise, whether the power global corporations wield is a function of the power of their home states, or *vice versa*. States remain *loci* of political power in a more globalised world, and the role played by their governments versus global markets is important. But any serious student or scholar of IPE needs to also consider the role played by global corporations.

Bibliography

Adler, E. 'Seizing the Middle Ground: Constructivism in World Politics.' *European Journal of International Relations* 3, no. 3 (1997): 319–363.

Amin, A. and R. Palan. 'Towards a Non-Rationalist International Political Economy.' *Review of International Political Economy* 8, no. 4 (2001): 559–577.

Bachrach, P. and M. Baratz. 'Two Faces of Power.' *American Political Science Review* 56 (1962): 947–952.

Barnett. M. and R. Duvall. 'Power in Global Governance.' In *Power in Global Governance*, edited by M. Barnett and R. Duvall, Cambridge: Cambridge University Press, 2005.

Bell. S. 'How Governments Mediate the Structural Power of International Business.' In *The Handbook of Global Companies*, edited by J. Mikler, Oxford: Wiley Blackwell, 2013.

Bhagwati, J. *In Defense of Globalisation*. Oxford: Oxford University Press, 2004.

Bonturi, M. and K. Fukasaku. 'Globalisaton and Intra-firm Trade: An Empirical Note.' *OECD Economic Studies* 20, Spring (1993): 145–159.

Broome, A. *Issues and Actors in the Global Political Economy*. Basingstoke: Palgrave Macmillan, 2014.

Carpenter, D. and D. A. Moss, eds. *Preventing Regulatory Capture: Special Interest Influence and How to Limit It*. Cambridge: Cambridge University Press, 2014.

Chandler, A. D. Jr. *The Visible Hand: The Managerial Revolution in American Business*. Cambridge: Harvard University Press, 1977.

Clapp, J. 'Transnational Corporations and Global Environmental Governance.' In *Handbook of Global Environmental Politics*, edited by P. Dauvergne. Cheltenham: Edward Elgar, 2005.

Coburn, E. 'Resisting Neoliberal Capitalism: Insights from Marxist Political Economy.' In *Relations of Global Power: Neoliberal Order and Disorder*, edited by G. Teeple and S. McBride. Toronto: University of Toronto Press, 2011.

Coen, D. 'Business Lobbying in the European Union.' In *Lobbying the European Union: Institutions, Actors and Issues*, edited by D. Coen and J. Richardson. Oxford: Oxford University Press, 2009.

Cox, R. W. *Production, Power and World Order: Social Forces in the Making of History*. New York: Columbia University Press, 1987.

Crouch, C. *The Strange Non-Death of Neoliberalism*. Cambridge: Polity Press, 2011.

Dahl, R. 'The Concept of Power.' *Behavioral Science* 2 (1957): 201–215.

Davis, K. and R. Blomstrom. *Business and its Environment*. New York: McGraw Hill, 1966.

Dicken, P. *Global Shift: Mapping the Changing Contours of the World Economy*. 7th ed. New York: The Guilford Press, 2015.

Dobbs, R., T. Koller, S. Ramaswamy, J. Woetzel, J. Manyika, R. Krishnan, and N. Andreula. *Playing to Win: The New Global Competition for Corporate Profits*. McKinsey Global Institute, 2015. Accessed 8 September 2016. www.mckinsey.com/business-functions/strategy-and-corporate-finance/our-insights/thenew-global-competition-for-corporate-profits.

Elbra, A. 'Interests Need Not be Pursued if They Can be Created: Private Governance in African Gold Mining.' *Business and Politics* 16, no. 2 (2014): 247–266.

Evans, P. *Embedded Autonomy: States and Industrial Transformation.* Princeton: Princeton University Press, 1995.

Falkner, J. *Business Power and Conflict in International Environmental Politics.* Basingstoke: Palgrave Macmillan, 2008.

Financial Times. Definition of Global Multinational Enterprises, no date. Accessed 28 October 2016. http://lexicon.ft.com/Term?term=global-multinational-enterprises.

Financial Times. FT Global 500 2015, 2016. Accessed 5 June 2015. www.ft.com/ft500.

Finnemore, M. and K. Sikkink. 'Taking Stock: The Constructivist Research Program in International Relations and Comparative Politics.' *Annual Review of Political Science 2001* 4 (2001): pp. 391–416.

Fortune. *Fortune Global 500*, 2015. Accessed 11 November 2015. http://fortune.com/global500/.

Frank, A. G. *Dependent Accumulation and Underdevelopment.* London: Macmillan, 1978.

Fuchs, D. *Business Power in Global Governance.* Boulder: Lynne Rienner Publishers, 2007.

Fukuyama, F. *The End of History and the Last Man.* New York: Avon Books, 1992.

Gilpin, R. *The Political Economy of International Relations.* Princeton: Princeton University Press, 1987.

Gotsi, M. and A. M. Wilson. 'Corporate Reputation: Seeking a Definition.' *Corporate Communications: An International Journal* 6, no. 1 (2001): 24–30.

Harrod, J. 'The Century of the Corporation.' In *Global Corporate Power*, edited by C. May. Boulder: Lynne Rienner Publishers, 2006.

Harvey, D. *A Brief History of Neoliberalism*, Oxford: Oxford University Press. 2005.

Hay, C. 'Constructivist Institutionalism.' In *The Oxford Handbook of Political Institutions*, edited by M. Moran, M. Rein and R. E. Goodin. Oxford: University of Oxford Press, 2006.

Hay, C. and D. Marsh eds. *Demystifying Globalisation.* Basingstoke: Palgrave Macmillan, 2000.

Held, D. and A. McGrew eds. *The Global Transformations Reader.* Cambridge: Polity Press, 2003.

Held, D., A. McGrew, D. Goldblatt and J. Perraton. *Global Transformations.* Cambridge: Polity Press, 1999.

IMF. *World Economic Outlook Database: April 2015 Edition*, 2015. Accessed 12 January 2016. www.imf.org/external/pubs/ft/weo/2015/01/weodata/index.aspx.

Jackson, K. T. *Building Reputational Capital: Strategies for Integrity and Fair Play that Improve the Bottom Line.* Oxford: Oxford University Press, 2004.

Johnson, C. *Japan: Who Governs? The Rise of the Developmental State.* New York: Norton, 1995.

Jones, O. *The Establishment and How They Get Away With It.* London: Allen Lane, 2014.

Karliner, J. *The Corporate Planet: Ecology and Politics in the Age of Globalization.* San Francisco: Sierra Club, 1997.

Kitching, G. *Seeking Social Justice through Globalization: Escaping a Nationalist Perspective.* Pennsylvania: Pennsylvania State University Press, 2001.

Kolleck, N. 'How Global Companies Wield Their Power: The Discursive Shaping of Sustainable Development.' In *The Handbook of Global Companies*, edited by J. Mikler. Oxford: Wiley Blackwell, 2013.

Korten, D. *When Corporations Rule the World.* 2nd ed. Oakland: Berrett-Koehler Publishers, 2015.

Lawrence, A., J. Weber and J. Post. *Business and Society: Stakeholders, Ethics, Public Policy.* 11th ed. New York: McGraw Hill, 2005.

Lazonick, W. 'The Big Idea: Profits Without Prosperity.' *Harvard Business Review* September (2014): 46–55.

Lazonick, W. and M. O'Sullivan. 'Maximizing Shareholder Value: A New Ideology for Corporate Governance.' *Economy and Society* 29, no. 1 (2000): 13–35.

LeBaron, G. 'Subcontracting Is Not Illegal, but Is It Unethical? Business Ethics, Forced Labour, and Economic Success.' *Brown Journal of World Affairs* 20, no. 2 (2014): 237–249.

Levitt, T. 'The Globalization of Markets.' *Harvard Business Review* 61, no. 3 (1983): 92–102.

Levy, D. L. and D. Egan. 'Capital Contests: National and Transnational Channels of Corporate Influence on the Climate Change Negotiations.' *Politics and Society* 26, no. 3, (1998): 337–362.

Levy, D. L. and P. J. Newell. 'Business Strategy and International Environmental Governance: Towards a Neo-Gramscian Synthesis.' *Global Environmental Politics* 2, no. 4, (2002): 84–101.

Lindblom, C. *Politics and Markets.* New York: Basic, 1977.

Lukes, S. *Power: A Radical View.* London: Palgrave Macmillan, 1974.

Mann, M. *The Sources of Social Power. Volume II: The Rise of Classes and Nation-States.* Cambridge: Cambridge University Press, 1993.

Mann, M. *Globalisation and Modernity*. Unpublished manuscript, Department of Sociology, UCLA, 2000.

Martell, L. 'The Third Wave in Globalization Theory.' *International Studies Review* 9, no. 2 (2007): 173–196.

Mattli, W. and N. Woods. 'In Whose Benefit? Explaining Regulatory Change in Global Politics.' In *The Politics of Global Regulation*, edited by W. Mattli and N. Woods. Princeton: Princeton University Press, 2009.

Mikler, J. 'Sharing Sovereignty for Policy Outcomes.' *Policy and Society* 30, no. 3 (2011): 151–160.

Mikler, J. 'Still Stalled on the Road to Neoliberal Globalisation? The Endurance of National Varieties of Capitalism.' In *Neoliberalism: Beyond the Free Market*, edited by D. Cahill, L. Edwards, and F. Stilwell. Cheltenham: Edward Elgar Publishing, 2012.

Moran, M. 'Representing the Corporate Elite in Britain: Capitalist Solidarity and Capitalist Legacy.' In *Remembering Elites*, edited by M. Savage and K. Williams. Oxford: Blackwell, 2008.

Newell, P. *Climate for Change: Non-state Actors and the Global Politics of the Greenhouse*. Cambridge: Cambridge University Press, 2000.

Newell, P. and D. L. Levy. 'The Political Economy of the Firm in Global Environmental Governance.' In *Global Corporate Power*, edited by C. May. London: Lynne Rienner Publishers, 2006.

Nolan, P., D. Sutherland, and J. Zhang. 'The Challenge of the Global Business Revolution.' *Contributions to Political Economy* 21, no. 1 (2002): 91–110.

O'Callaghan, T. 'Disciplining Multinational Enterprises: The Regulatory Power of Reputation Risk.' *Global Society* 21, no. 1 (2007): 95–117.

Parvin, P. *Friend or Foe? Lobbying in British Democracy*, London: Hansard Society, 2007. Accessed 11 August 2015. www.hansardsociety.org.uk/wp-content/uploads/2012/10/Friend-or-Foe-Lobbying-in-British-Democracy-2007.pdf.

Price, R. and C. Reus-Smit, 'Dangerous Liaisons? Critical International Relations Theory and Constructivism.' *European Journal of International Relations* 4, no. 3 (1998): 259–294.

Ronit, K. and V. Schneider. 'Organisierte Interessen in Nationalen und Supranationalen Politokologien: Ein Vegleich der G7 Lander mit der Europaischen Union.' In *Verbande in Vergleihender Perpektiv*, edited by U. von Alemann and B. Wessels. Berlin: Edition Sigma, 1997.

Ruggie, J. 'What Makes the World Hang Together? Neo-utilitarianism and the Social Constructivist Challenge.' *International Organization* 52, no. 4, (1998): 855–887.

Schmidt, V. *The Futures of European Capitalism*. Oxford: Oxford University Press, 2002.

Sell, S. 'Corporations, Seeds, and Intellectual Property Rights Governance.' In *Corporate Power in Global Agrifood Governance*, edited by J. Clapp and D. Fuchs. Cambridge: MIT Press, 2009.

Sklair, L. *The Transnational Capitalist Class*. Oxford: Blackwell, 2001.

Strange, S. *The Retreat of the State: The Diffusion of Power in the World Economy*. Cambridge: Cambridge University Press, 1996.

Strange, S. *States and Markets: An Introduction to International Political Economy*. London: Pinter Publishers, 1988.

Streeck, W. and K. Yamamura, eds. *The Origins of Nonliberal Capitalism: Germany and Japan in Comparison*. Ithaca: Cornell University Press, 2001.

Streeck, W. and K. Yamamura, eds. *The End of Diversity? Prospects for German and Japanese Capitalism*. Ithaca: Cornell University Press, 2003.

Suchman, M. C. 'Managing Legitimacy: Strategic and Institutional Approaches.' *Academy of Management Review* 20, no. 3 (1995): 571–610.

Tepper, J. and D. Hearn. *The Myth of Capitalism: Monopolies and the Death of Competition*. Hoboken: John Wiley and Sons, 2019.

Tienhaara, K. 'Corporations: Business and Industrial Influence.' In *Routledge Handbook of Global Environmental Politics*, edited by P. G. Harris. Abingdon: Routledge, 2014.

UNCTAD. *World Investment Report 2011*. Web Table 34: Number of Parent Corporations and Foreign Affiliates, by Region and Economy 2010, 2010. Accessed 20 July 2015. http://unctad.org/Sections/dite_dir/docs/WIR11_web%20tab%2034.pdf.

UNCTAD. *World Investment Report 2014*. Web Table 28: The World's Top 100 Non-Financial TNCs, Ranked by Foreign Assets 2013, 2014. Accessed 20 October 2015. http://unctad.org/Sections/dite_dir/docs/WIR2014/WIR14_tab28.xls.

Viner, J. 'Power Versus Plenty as Objectives of Foreign Policy in the Seventeenth and Eighteenth Centuries.' *World Politics* 1, no. 1 (1948): 1–29.

Wallerstein, I. *The Politics of the World Economy: The States, the Movements and the Civilizations*. Cambridge: Cambridge University Press, 1984.

Wallerstein, I. *World Systems Analysis: Am Introduction*. New York: Basil Blackwell, 2004.

Walmart. *Apply to Be a Supplier*, 2017. Accessed 18 December 2018. http://corporate.walmart.com/suppliers/apply-to-be-a-supplier.

Walter, A. and X. Zhang, eds. *East Asian Capitalism: Diversity, Continuity and Change*. Oxford: Oxford University Press, 2012.

Watson, M. 'Theoretical Traditions in Global Political Economy.' In *Global Political Economy*, edited by J. Ravenhill. 2nd ed. Oxford: Oxford University Press, 2008.

Weber, S. 'Introduction.' In *Globalization and the European Political Economy*, edited by S. Weber. New York: Columbia University Press, 2001.

Weidenbaum, M. *Business and Government in the Global Marketplace*. 7th ed. Upper Saddle River: Prentice Hall, 2004.

Weiss, L. 'Infrastructural Power, Economic Transformation, and Globalization.' In *An Anatomy of Power: The Social Theory of Michael Mann*, edited by J. A. Hall and R. Schroeder. Cambridge: Cambridge University Press, 2006.

Weiss, L. 'The State in the Economy: Neoliberal or Neoactivist?' In *The Oxford Handbook of Comparative Institutional Analysis*, edited by G. Morgan, J. L. Campbell, C. Crouch, O. K. Pedersen and R. Whitley. Oxford: Oxford University Press, 2010.

Weiss, L. and L. Hobson. *States and Economic Development: A Comparative Historical Analysis*. Cambridge: Polity Press, 1995.

Wendt, A. *Social Theory of International Politics*. Cambridge: Cambridge University Press, 1999.

Widmaier, W. *Economic Ideas in Political Time: The Rise and Fall of Economic Orders from the Progressive Era to the Global Financial Crisis*. Cambridge: Cambridge University Press, 2016.

Wilks, S. *The Political Power of the Business Corporation*. Cheltenham: Edward Elgar, 2013.

Wilks-Heeg, S., A. Blick, and S. Crone. *How Democratic is the UK? The 2012 Audit*. Liverpool: Democratic Audit, 2012. Accessed 20 July 2015. http://democracyuk-2012.democraticaudit.com/.

Wolf, M. *Why Globalisation Works*. New Haven and London: Yale University Press, 2004.

Woo-Cumings, M. ed. *The Developmental State*. Ithaca and London: Cornell University Press, 1999.

World Bank. *Gross Domestic Product 2015*. World Development Indicator Database, 11 October, 2016. Accessed 1 November 2016. http://databank.worldbank.org/data/download/GDP.pdf.

45

The International Political Economy of cities and urbanization

Insights from Latin America

Michael Lukas and Gustavo Durán[F1]

Introduction

Entering the third decade of the twenty-first century, it has been widely accepted that Henri Lefebvre was right when in 1968 he proclaimed a coming urban revolution. Indeed, today humanity is a majority urban species and by 2050 even more than three-quarters of the world's population is predicted to be living in urban areas (United Nations, Department of Economic and Social Affairs, Population Division 2019). However, far more important than this quantitative aspect of global urbanization is the qualitative shift whereby, following Lefebvre, urbanization rather than industrialization has become the major driving force of capitalist development. Today, from Berlin to Santiago, from Lagos to Manaus and from Shenzen to Dubai, the world is seeing a planetary construction boom, hyper-densification in global city-centers and the rapid sprawling of urban peripheries, facilitated through the increasing integration and globalization of real estate and finance capital. However, it is not only in and around cities where urbanization unfolds. Through the construction of transnational infrastructural networks the urban fabric extends into the most remote areas of planetary space. The Initiative for the Integration of Regional Infrastructure in South America (IIRSA), for instance, is by far the most ambitious project of infrastructure roll-out South America has seen since colonization. The construction of roads, waterways, ports, energy and communications networks seeks to increase and accelerate commodity exports (soybeans, timber and minerals, for instance) especially to the rapidly growing Asian and Chinese markets. In all, 335 projects have been identified as part of IIRSA, with an overall budget of US$37.4 billion.[1] Of course, this already gigantic and for South America unprecedented project looks tiny compared to Chinas "project of the century," the "New Silk road" where intercontinental infrastructure projects are planned to be built for up to US$1.3 trillion by 2027.[2]

The issue of urbanization thus today is of ever increasing economic, political and environmental relevance and it does not surprise that there is a renewed interest to make sense of urbanization from an International Political Economy (IPE) perspective, that means to analyze the dialectical relationship of planetary urbanization and global capitalist development. In this chapter we focus on Latin America. Latin America is of particular interest because it has been the forerunner of massive urbanization in the developing world. The region hosts some of the largest mega-cities in the world and today 80 percent of its population are living in urban areas. Since the times of colonial domination Latin America has been integrated into the world economy as a provider of natural resources with in most countries only incipient processes of industrialization throughout the twentieth century. This form of dependent development in the urban realm led to what Caldeira (2017) has called peripheral urbanization, a mode of space production whereby cities have been largely constructed by their residents, giving way to widespread informal settlements characterizing the region's urban condition in important ways until today. With globalization and the neoliberal turn in the 1980s and 1990s, Latin American cities, citizens and territories became ever deeper integrated into global capitalism and its new financialized regime of accumulation. Through structural adjustment and neoliberal reforms pushing free trade, liberalization, flexibilization and privatization, national and transnational corporate capital not only got access to the abundant national resources in the region's hinterlands, extending the extractive frontiers, but also began to invest heavily in the modernization of all types of urban infrastructure, from super-modern highway systems, high-rise condos, office parks and shopping malls, to huge gated communities on the urban outskirts. With Swyngedouw (2018), what we see here is the Latin American expression a new "financialized capitalist urbanity."

In this chapter we provide an overview of recent research into this new financialized capitalist urbanity from an IPE perspective at the intersection of Marxist human geography, urban studies, economic geography and planning theory. First, we construct a theoretical framework based on the most influential theoretical approaches on capitalist urbanization: geo-historical materialism, world-systems analysis and global city theory, planetary urbanization and global urbanism. In the next section, we revise the recent literature on cities and urbanization in Latin America based on the outlined theoretical framework. We present evidence of global city formation in Latina America, the role of different types of megaprojects in urban restructuring and coupling urban space to financialized capital circuits, discuss the fast growing literature on urban financialization, especially housing, and new forms and conceptualizations of extended urbanization, that is, the operationalization of hinterlands. In the last section we conclude that there is a need to strengthen IPE research on Latin America in general and particularly the integration of different theoretical perspectives to overcome a certain fragmentation. We also state that what is missing in the literature is to take into account more strongly the specificity of Latin American political economies.

Conceptualizing the IPE of cities and urbanization: a theoretical framework

In this section we present what we consider to be the most important theoretical approaches on the IPE of cities and urbanization and that taken together provide a framework for the analysis of the entanglements of urbanization and global capitalism in Latin America. We start with David Harvey's formulations on the urban process under capitalism since his work on capital switching and the spatial fix has become a sort of common sense for the studying of the IPE of cities and urbanization in the international research community. Thereafter, we present work that approaches urbanization from a world-systems perspective, especially world and global city theory, particularly influential in Latin America in the 1990s and 2000s. Finally, we present the more recently emerging work on planetary urbanization and global urbanism which seeks to overcome the city-centered earlier approaches and makes urban research more relational and much broader in scope, bringing together cities and hinterlands on a planetary scale.

The urban process under capitalism

In the 1970s David Harvey (1973) and Manuel Castells (1977) revolutionized the study of urbanization: ever since "the city was no longer to be interpreted as a social ecology, subject to natural forces inherent in the dynamics of population and space," rather "it came to be viewed instead as a product of specifically social forces set in motion by capitalist relations of production" (Friedmann 1986: 69). Especially Harvey (1973; 1978; 1982/2006) with his theoretical work on the urbanization of capital created a whole new field from where until today some of the most intriguing insights into capitalist urbanization can be drawn. In his geo-historical materialism, Harvey (1978) analyzes "the urban process under capitalism" based on Marx' theory of capitalist accumulation and class struggle and develops three major concepts of interest here: the three circuits of capital, capital switching and the spatial fix.

In his dialectical analysis of "the structure of flows within a system of production and realization of value" (ibid.: 103), Harvey identifies three closely interwoven but distinct circuits of capital. The primary circuit is that of commodity production where capitalists create surplus value through the exploitation of labor power and the organization of the work process. Due to inner contradictions of the capitalist mode of production there is a tendency towards overaccumulation at the level of the primary circuit, that means, that "too much capital is produced in aggregate relative to the opportunities to employ that capital" (ibid.: 106). Particularly in times of overaccumulation, capital is being switched from the primary to the secondary (or tertiary[3]) circuit, which is made up of urban infrastructure and what he calls the built environment:

> a vast, humanly created resource system, comprising use values embedded in the physical landscape, which can be utilized for production, exchange and consumption ... [and] comprises a whole host of diverse elements: factories, dams, offices, shops, warehouses, roads, railways, docks, power stations, water supply and sewage disposal systems, schools, hospitals, parks, cinemas, restaurants – the list is endless.
>
> *(Harvey 1982/2000: 233)*

An important aspect of the built environment is that it is "essential to both creating and storing surplus value" (Aalbers 2019: 15). It is essential to the *creation* of surplus value in the sense that industrial commodity production needs a particular physical infrastructure of fixed assets within and through that the production, exchange and consumption processes take place. When the factory system appeared in the nineteenth century, cities such as Manchester and London were the first to be adjusted to make space for the physical infrastructure of a new mode of production (and reproduction). Today, in the time of late capitalism and postmodern consumer culture, the ruins of industrial capitalism (warehouses, ports, railway stations) are transformed into lofts, cultural centers and new consumption spaces. Similarly, as global capitalism in the 1970s turned towards a new international division of labor and complex global production networks, in cities around the world new physical infrastructure had to be installed to host and spatially organize this new round of capitalist modernization in global city-centers. Second, the built environment is essential for *storing and investing* surplus value, both in times of "regular" capitalist accumulation and when capital seeks an (ultimately impossible) solution to the problem of overaccumulation. Surplus capital is flowing into real estate production and the construction industry, that means into fixed assets and the creation of new spatial configurations. Because for individual capitalists it is very difficult to organize this kind of "spatial fix" to capital's crisis tendency, what is needed is a functioning capital market for the expansion of credit and fictitious capital and state institutions that together work, in the words of Harvey, as "a kind of collective nerve center governing and mediating the relations between the primary and secondary circuits of capital" (Harvey 1978: 107). As Harvey (1978; 1982; 2011) and many other authors following in his line (Wu 1997; Christophers 2011; Shin and Kim 2015) have shown, these spatial fixes take place at different moments and at different spatial scales, from city-regions, to national urban systems, to the planetary scale.

To explain the principles of capital switching and the spatial fix, Harvey (1978; 2011) himself has given various historical–empirical examples, from the large-scale transformation of Second Empire Paris under Baron Haussmann in the nineteenth century, over Robert Moses "meat axe-urbanism" in New York and the subsequent generalization of suburbanization in the United States. It was through credit-financed construction of highways and other large-scale infrastructure projects that Moses ushered in "the total re-engineering (using new construction technologies pioneered during the war) not just the city but the whole metropolitan region" and "defined a way to absorb the capital and labor surpluses profitably … where would the capital sur-plus have gone had it not been for the making of the New York metropolitan region, Chicago, Los Angeles and other places of their ilk after 1945?" (Harvey 2011: 169). Thus, in the United States an overaccumulation crisis (the Great Depression) necessitated a new spatial fix initiated by government infrastructure and housing programs, and then developed a life of its own as a "suburban way of life" which provided for many years of economic prosperity and political stability. Neither Paris nor New York nor suburbanization generalized were all about new infrastructure and buildings for surplus absorption, but the new spatial structures established new lifestyles that in turn made new products necessary: houses, refrigerators, automobiles, air conditioning and much more (Harvey 2008).

With the crisis of the Fordist-regime of accumulation in the 1970s, "urbanization underwent yet another transformation of scale. It went global. […] This transformation in scale makes it hard to grasp that what may be going on globally is in principle similar to the processes that Haussmann managed so expertly for a while in Second Empire Paris" (Harvey 2011: 172, 174). It is this global process of the generalization of credit-financed intensification of urbanization that Lefebvre (1968/2011) called an urban revolution and Merrifield (2013) the principle of "Neo-Haussmanization." The new planetary scale and scope of urbanization implies that, unlike in previous rounds of capitalist modernization, cities in Asia, Latin America and parts of Africa now play a central role in the absorption of capital: "These metropolitan economies are becoming the production hearths of a new globalism" (Smith 2002: 89). Following the principle of Haussmann (or Moses), credit-financed urbanization processes are now on the rise worldwide, be it in Dubai, Sao Paulo, Santiago, Madrid, Mumbai, Hong Kong or London. And while Chinese banks have been investing in the subprime market in the US, Goldman Sachs is active in Mumbai, capital from Hong Kong in Baltimore and German real estate funds in Santiago de Chile. There is a real estate boom today that spans the globe:

> Building booms have been evident in Mexico City, Santiago de Chile, in Mumbai, Johannesburg, Seoul, Taipei, Moscow, and all over Europe (Spain and Ireland being the most dramatic), as well as in the cities of core capitalist countries such as London, Los Angeles, San Diego and New York.
>
> *(Harvey 2011: 173)*

As in previous rounds of urbanization-centered crisis strategies, the massive investments currently being made in the built environment are credit-financed and closely linked to financial–market innovations and global neoliberalization. Only through these innovations and deregulation policies in relation to capital movements, investment opportunities are comparable and available worldwide today, and (excess) capital can globally search for viable investment opportunities. It is in that context that financialization has become one of the major research arenas in urban studies and that for Soederberg and Walks (2018: 109)[4] "finance is a key *reason* for increasing inequalities" and "the key *way* that urbanization is supplanting industrialization as the key driver of capitalist development."

World-systems analysis and global city networks

A different entry point into the study of cities and urbanization processes in global capitalism has been inspired by world-systems research.[5] Distinctive of world-systems approaches is that at its core lies the analysis of the integrated world economy in which the international spatial division of labor is structured by core-periphery relations, that means, economic and political relations that are marked by power asymmetries and unequal exchange between core and peripheral economies, between developed and underdeveloped societies. In the 1960s and 1970s in dependency theory this general framework has been applied to conceptualize urbanization processes and patterns in Latin America. From that perspective, the explosive growth of the metropolitan cities through rural-to-urban migration was interpreted as "dependent urbanization" (Castells 1977: 40). The structure of Latin American economies characterized by a high-productivity export sector, subsistence agriculture and the lack of endogenous industrialization here lead to dependent urbanization in the form of overurbanization, new urban population that could not be absorbed by the formal labor nor housing markets. As Maricato (2017) states for the Brazilian context, the dependent form of Latin America's integration to the world economy meant that "industrialization and low wages resulted in urbanization and low wages," the auto-construction of housing and entire parts of the city being an important contribution to the accumulation of capital throughout the period of industrialization in Latin America and until today. While influential in urban studies throughout the region in the 1960s and 1970s, the theories of dependent urbanization were criticized already at the time from a theoretical point of view, mainly because of its extreme structuralism (Pradilla 1982) and ever since have lost ground.

Inspired by dependency theory and Wallerstein's world-systems analysis, urban planner John Friedmann (1986) in a highly influential article pioneered the conceptualization of the role of cities in the changing international division of labor that set in with the crisis of Fordist capitalism in the 1970s. In the late 1980s it had become clear that capitalist restructuring led to the relocation of production processes from core western countries to peripheral economies in the Global South and East, leading to production processes that were organized on a truly global scale, but with a distinct geography. Friedmann (1986: 70) stated that within that new

> single (spatial) division of labour different localities – national, regional, and urban subsystems – perform specialized roles. Focusing only on metropolitan economies, some carry out headquarter functions, others serve primarily as a financial centre, and still others have as their main function the articulation of regional and/or national economies with the global system.

Importantly, Friedmann claimed that most of "contemporary urban change" in terms of metropolitan functions, labor relations and the physical form of cities are *externally induced* adaptations to worldwide processes such as the direction and volume of "transnational capital flows," "the spatial division of the functions of finance, management and production" and "the employment structure of economic base activities" (ibid.).

It was Saskia Sassen (1991) who took the world–city hypothesis a step further by relating it more directly to the emerging discourse on economic globalization. She analyzed how far "globalization has reasserted the centrality of cities" in global capitalism (Rossi 2017: 52) and showed that logistical functions and decision making power increasingly became concentrated in leading global cities as New York, London, Tokyo and Paris, relying however on a hierarchically structured inter-urban network that also integrates second and third-tier global cities in the Global South. A defining feature of global city theory is the centrality it gives to the transnational flows of information, money and capital. The fact that these flows transcend national boundaries of control and regulation and are managed through a cross-border network of global cities profoundly affects economic, political and spatial aspects of urban development in many cities around the world (Parnreiter 2015a: 21).

The restructuring of global capitalism and the heightened role for cities has had its correlate in the emergence of new city functions and new city forms. For instance, with the rise of the significance of advanced producer services there is a new demand for premium-networked office space and on the supply side a massive influx of transnational capital into the real estate and construction sector is taking place. As can be observed in cities around the world, global city functions are clustering in expanding Central Business Districts (CBDs) in inner-city locations and new industrial and technological districts are emerging on the outskirts of cities. In that sense, new city functions, in political and economic terms, and new city forms, are only two sides of the same coin of urban rescaling under globalization (Lukas 2018). In sum, global city theory and global city formation works on two scales: that of the networked-hierarchy of functional linkages between cities on the global inter-urban scale and that of socio-spatial transformation on the intra-urban scale. On the global scale of analysis, it is analyzed in how far some cities operate as the command and control centers of economic globalization, as headquarters for transnational corporations and clusters of advanced producer and financial service firms. On the intra-urban scale, it is analyzed how the socio-spatial configuration of cities changes with its integration into the globalizing world economy.[6]

Planetary urbanization and global urbanism

A recent body of work of high influence in Latin America is that on planetary urbanization, principally put forward by Neil Brenner (2014) and colleagues and which draws on Lefebvre's hypothesis of the generalization of capitalist urbanization and the "implosion–explosion" of spaces. With this metaphor derived from nuclear physics, Lefebvre described the simultaneous and dialectically related processes of agglomeration and territorial concentration of capital, people and infrastructure in urban centers and metropolitan regions on the one hand (understood as the moment of concentrated urbanization), and the dispersion of disjunct urban fragments, infrastructures and practices throughout a previously non-urban realm, that means, metropolitan hinterlands, the countryside and remote peripheral locations of planetary space (understood as the moment of extended urbanization). As Brenner (2014: 17) states,

> the notion of implosion-explosion thus comes to describe the production and continual transformation of an industrialized urban fabric in which centers of agglomeration and their operational landscapes are woven together in mutually transformative ways while being co-articulated into a worldwide capitalist system.

This agenda has many implications for urban research and also IPE, the most important being on the one hand, to overcome "methodological cityism," that means to put cities as bounded entities as main research interests. As Harvey (1996; cited in Brenner 2014) said, "the 'thing' we call a city is the outcome of a process we call urbanization." On the other hand, planetary urbanization addresses the need to overcome the urban–rural dualism, where the urban and the rural as societal and territorial realms historically have been understood as separate entities and not part of the same process of capitalist territorial development.

Rooted in the same epistemological turn towards processual and relational thinking which informs the concept of planetary urbanization (and other theoretical developments as global production networks), in the last decade there has been a huge output on the transnational dynamics of urban policy making (McCann and Ward 2011; Baker and McGuirk 2016). The focus in that literature is on the globally interconnected processes of assembling policies, plans and programs and the actor networks and epistemic communities that sustain it. In empirical terms, this research has shown that a tightly networked global informational infrastructure exists today, through which ideas, policy fragments and best practice models are produced and diffused. A crucial role in this circulatory process is exercised by the "global intelligence corps" (Rapoport 2015: 111) of urban development expertise, consisting of a loose and expanding network of politicians, planners, consultants and activists who not only mobilize ideas, practices and models, but are themselves globally mobile. These "traveling technocrats" (Larner and Laurie 2010), "international masterplanners" (Rapoport 2015) and "persuasive practitioners" (Montero 2017) specialize in diagnosing urban problems and providing solutions to urban decision makers in cities that increasingly try to enhance their cities' competitiveness and global visibility. A characteristic of this emerging field of global urbanism is a strong simplification in the rhetorical packaging of the problems to be addressed, the solutions recommended and the policy processes that are mobilized as best practices. The network re-produces itself and its knowledge at the international meetings and conferences – together with the resulting documents and policy recommendations – of international organizations such as OECD, World Bank or UN-Habitat (Kaika 2017). The fact that UN-Habitat's World Urban Forum in 2014 was held in Medellín, the Habitat III-conference 2016 in Quito and that Chilean architect Alejandro Aravena in the same year received the Pritzker Prize indicates that Latin American cities and their planners are an integral part of the global circuits of urban knowledge production and policy diffusion. As Justin McGuirk (2015: 25) shows, Latin American cities and its persuasive practitioners have been particularly successful in positioning themselves as oriented towards issues of socio-spatial inclusion, social urbanism and participatory planning, offering a whole new "urban repertoire." From another perspective, however, they are part of the "global urban intellectual and professional technocracy (that) has spurred a frantic search for a 'smart' socio-ecological urbanity ... under the banner of radical techno-managerial restructuring, the focus is squarely on how to sustain capitalist urbanity so that nothing really has to change!" (Swyngedouw and Kaika 2014).

Research arenas on the IPE of cities and urbanization in Latin America

In this section we present some of the major lines of research into contemporary urbanization processes in Latin America. While not being exhaustive, taken together these lines might give a good picture of the IPE of urbanization in Latin America. First, we present work on globalization and global city formation that has been particularly influential throughout the 1990s and 2000s, but continues to be important today. Second, we focus on the related topic of urban megaprojects. We identify four types of urban megaprojects of particular importance in Latin America and that provide clues of how urban space in Latin America is plugged in to global capitalism. Third, we present research on urban financialization that has burgeoned in the last ten years or so. Both the demand and supply sides of housing provision in Latin America have changed dramatically in the last 30 years through the expansion of (mortgage) credits to ever wider segments of society on the one hand and the integration of the real estate and finance industries on the other. Fourth, we revise what is maybe the most stimulating field of IPE work on urbanization in Latin America, that of planetary and extended urbanization and global urbanism. Here links are made between the specifically Latin American development model of neo-extractivism, territorial transformations at different scales, and the political and planning dynamics emerging around the extension of extractive frontiers in a world economy organized through global production networks.

Globalization and global city formation

Especially throughout the 1990s and 2000s, the study of urban development in Latin America was highly influenced by the international debate on economic globalization in general and global city theory in particular. Latin American authors as De Mattos (1999) and Ciccollela (1999), among many others, observed the emergence of new city functions and the transformation of the economic base of cities leading to new urban forms and projects. In general terms, from the 1990s onwards, urban transformation in Latin America has been understood as "intimately related to the flows of foreign capital and the production of new urban objects, materially and symbolically related to the process of economic globalization and the socio-cultural paradigm of postmodernism" (Ciccolella 1999: 24). For cities like Mexico City, Santiago and Buenos Aires the appearance of "artefacts of globalization and transformations in metropolitan landscapes" (Ciccolella 1999: 13) have been described, being the major features shifting centralities in the form of new urban downtowns, business parks, luxury hotels and the upsurge of gated communities on the urban outskirts.

In a highly influential study with impact in Latin America, Beaverstock, Smith and Taylor (1999) grounded world and global city theory in empirical terms. Studying the world–city network based on the capacity of cities to provide advanced producer services (accounting, advertising, banking and law), they identified 55 world cities – which they classified hierarchically into alpha, beta and gamma in terms of their degree of world–city-ness – and 67 further cities that showed some evidence of world–city formation. While all the alpha world cities at that time were found to be located in the developed and rapidly industrializing world (New York, Chicago, Los Angeles, London, Paris, Frankfurt, Milán, Tokyo, Hong Kong and Singapore), five Latin American cities were considered to be beta and gamma world cities (Mexico City and Sao Paulo in the beta and Caracas, Santiago and Buenos Aires in the gamma category), and the other six cities as being in a state of world–city formation (Rio de Janeiro, Bogotá, Lima, Montevideo, Brasilia and Tijuana). While Latin American cities at the end of the 1990s were actually in a process of articulation to the dynamic of globalization, this was taking place in a secondary role, thus "in its fundamental aspects not representing big changes with respect to the international division of labor that existed at the end of the Keynesian–Fordist phase" (De Mattos 2010).

In a more recent study Parnreiter (2015a) updated the analysis of the role of Latin American cities in the global economy, combining conceptual insights of global city theory, world-systems analysis and the work on global production chains, also extending the indicators being considered in the analysis of economic centrality.[7] In general terms, the study confirms the ongoing exceptional importance of New York, London, Tokyo and Paris as the urban powerhouses of global capitalism. Unsurprisingly, Asian and especially Chinese cities do show ever higher levels of economic centrality, the most important cities in that context being Peking, Hong Kong,

Singapore and Shanghai. With a view to Latin America, the most important cities in the region were found to be Sao Paulo, Rio de Janeiro, Mexico City, Santiago de Chile and Bogotá, analyzed in terms of the location of headquarters of transnational companies (TNCs). While being marginal in terms of sales and profits of TNCs (2.5 percent of worldwide sales), it is interesting that some Latin American cities show very high growth rates of sales between 2006 and 2014, above all Bogotá and Medellín, with 6162 percent and 907 percent, respectively. In terms of aggregated value in producer services, the second indicator analyzed, Latin American cities generate 5.6 percent of all aggregated value. Here São Paulo, Mexico City, Santiago de Chile and Buenos Aires lead the regional ranking. However, again cities considered as peripheral to the world economy show the highest growth rates, such as San José, Santa Cruz, Montevideo, Bogotá, Lima, Santo Domingo and Caracas (Parnreiter 2015a: 15). With a view to global connectivity, the third indicator, Sao Paulo and Mexico City show very high numbers, as do, on a minor scale, Buenos Aires and Santiago de Chile. As alpha World Cities these urban centers link major economic regions and states into the world economy. Lima, Bogotá, Caracas, Montevideo, Rio de Janeiro, Guatemala, Panamá, San José and Quito are considered to be "beta World Cities," that means as "important world cities that are instrumental in linking their region or state into the world economy." Again, the highest growth rates are shown in smaller and less central cities, such as Querétaro y Puebla, Cali, San Salvador, Cordoba, Guatemala and Lima.

In general terms then, what has been confirmed is that Latin American cities still play a secondary role in the world economy, especially with a view to formal economic power (sales and headquarters),[8] but are important in terms of what Parnreiter (2015a) calls organizing and globalizing power. Especially Sao Paulo and Mexico are heavily integrated into the global city network through their strong producer service sectors, but many other cities are showing strong growth rates with a view to producer services and global inter-urban connectivity. However, while the work on global cities highlights very important aspects of the integration of Latin American cities into the world economy, it has a bias. In the words of Coe et al. (2010: 143)

> an excessive concentration on APS or, for that matter, any other sector produces a caricatured view of complex organizational ecologies and sector dynamics that not only produce the underlying dynamics of contemporary cities, but also enable these cities to be interconnected and thus constitute global networks.

Especially, the crucial role of many Latin American cities for resource extraction cannot be addressed, neither can the links between capital cities and their hinterlands (Scholvin, Breul and Revilla Diez 2019). Here, establishing links with the emerging field of planetary urbanization might be helpful, as will be developed below.

Urban megaprojects

A central insight of global city theory – and research inspired by it on Latin America – is that economic globalization leads to "a [new] geography of centralities and marginalities at different geographical scales" (Rossi 2017: 58). While at the global inter-urban scale some cities are much more central than others to the organization of economic globalization, at the intra-urban scale the dialectic of centrality and marginality – or integration and exclusion – can be seen between globally integrated parts of cities, and parts of the same city that are excluded from globalizing dynamics, or almost any dynamism of formal economic activity at all. As particularly important vehicles for the integration of Latin American cities into the world economy, different types of urban megaprojects have been identified (Lungo 2005). While there is not one definition of what is a megaproject, based on the existing empirical research for Latin America four types of megaprojects can be identified (see Table 45.1): new urban downtowns, urban regeneration projects, transportation and logistics projects and integrated peri-urban projects. While all four types of projects are highly complex and serve multiple functions and rationales, it can be stated that new urban downtowns and transportation and logistics projects are more closely related to the location of new global city functions and global production networks, while urban regeneration and integrated peri-urban projects have their basic purpose in capital switching and the appropriation of ground rents. From a different angle, new urban downtowns and urban regeneration projects are tendentially located in city-centers, while transportation and logistics and peri-urban projects are part of the drivers of urban outward growth. The former two, thus, being an expression and vehicle of implosion and the latter two being vehicles of the explosion of urban space. What most of these projects have in common is that they invoke global imaginaries and are part and parcel of the transnational circulation of policy and planning ideas. More often than not, they are based on exceptional planning measures and some sort of formal or informal partnership between public and private sector. Sometimes megaprojects are related to megaevents, as in the case of the soccer world cup and Olympic Games in Brazil (see Box 45.1).

With view to new urban downtowns, Parnreiter (2015b: 22) states that

> because all the financial institutions, legal and accountancy firms and business consultancies that have followed their clients to Latin American, African or Asian cities require high quality office spaces, and because existing inventory in the cities could neither quantitatively nor qualitatively accommodate this demand, the need to literally house the global city led to the production of new downtowns.

In Mexico City for instance, one of the best documented cases of new downtown formation, a new corporate geography has emerged since the 1980s when Mexico embarked on the strategy

Table 45.1 Different types of urban megaprojects in Latin America

Type	Primary function	Geographical location	Examples
New urban downtowns	Host corporate headquarters, advanced producer services and other globalization related functions	City centre	Santa Fe, Mexico City; Avenida Paulista, Sao Paulo; Nuevas Las Condes, Santiago de Chile
Urban regeneration projects	Appropriation of land rents, new consumption practices	City centre and peri-central areas	Puerto Madero, Buenos Aires; el Malecón, Guayaquil; Costanera Center, Santiago de Chile
Transportation and logistics projects	Organization of flows, transnational connectivity and the circulation of information, goods and people	Peri-central areas and peri-urban spaces	Airports, Container ports; highway systems, logistic parks, retail; Iranduba University City, Manaus
Integrated peri-urban projects	Appropriation of land rents, new consumption practices	Peri-urban spaces	Nordelta, Buenos Aires; Piedra Roja, Santiago de Chile

Source: own elaboration.

Box 45.1 Porto Maravilha (Rio de Janeiro – Brazil)

Despite being the main gateway to the city for customs and the tourism industry (arrival of cruise ships), the port area of Rio de Janeiro has been in constant decline for most of the twentieth century. Faced with this situation, the Porto Maravilha project, a private–public operation led by the Federal Government of Rio de Janeiro based on the Barcelona model of urban regeneration through international megaevents, seeks to induce urban revitalization and the empowerment of public space. The project covers an area of five million square meters of mostly public assets under the Federal Government's concession to the port administration Companhia DOCAS. It seeks to materialize through a public–private investment alliance through the re-functionalization of the territory in question, generating self-financing potential mechanisms from the private sector, with state support, in this case the city of Rio de Janeiro. The overall stated objective in terms of financial managements has been to promote economic viability in the management of urban land through private investment. Contreras (2014: 11) explains that the Porto Maravilha megaproject

> is carried out through of the Operação Urbana Consorciada da Região do Porto do Rio de Janeiro 2009 (OUCPRJ), financed through the issuance of Certificates of Additional Potential of Construção (CEPACS) – necessary titles for anyone wishing to build in the port and who are negotiated in the market-, issued by a fund created especially for this transaction, the Imobiliário Porto Maravilha investment fund (FII PM).

To date, more than US$3,000 million have been invested by public and private actors, in addition to the overall more than 13,000 million invested for the Olympic Games of 2016 (Sarue 2018).

The revitalization of the port area, one of the main legacies of the 2016 Olympic Games, has since its inception been marked by various controversies, and public opinion has been highly critical about the operation. The permanent use value of many of the sites constructed for the sports event has been questioned since the beginning and during the process corruption cases appeared. For example, the former managers of la Caixa involved in the Porto Maravilha project were summoned in corruption cases in Operation Lava Jato, as the construction companies Odebrecht, OAS and Carioca Christiani-Nielsen are shareholders of the Porto Novo Concessionaire in charge of the project. The consortium (Porto Novo among others) instrumentalized land and public resources of the workers' fund (FGTS) to take advantage of real estate bonds with a minimum margin of value capture by the public sector (Contreras 2014: 12). After the Olympic Games of 2016 much of the sports equipment and infrastructure in fact has been abandoned and the local administration is not capable of taking charge of it (as an example the sports facilities of Barra de Tijuca are now abandoned). On the other hand, the public–private agreement established for the realization of the project has suffered severe problems due to the inability of the private sector to realize the committed investment committed. In reaction, the Prefecture of Rio de Janeiro has transferred public resources to the Porto Novo Concessionaire (in charge of the execution) so that works could be continued. This situation has alarmed public opinion, thus the Porto Maravilha project highlights a general feature of urban megaprojects throughout the region and beyond, that private investors seek to capture ground rents while the public sector takes the financial risk and the citizens' new public spaces do not meet real popular demand.

of liberalization and globalization culminating in the NAFTA-agreement in 1994. Parnreiter (2015b) in that context describes the enormous growth of downtown office space from 3.7 million square meters in 1997 to 7.1 million square meters in 2011, concentrated in several business districts as Santa Fe, Paseo de la Reforma and Polanco, all located in the center of the vast metropolitan region which is Mexico City. Especially the development of Santa Fe has been spectacular; the area transformed from a garbage dump in the 1950s to a new globally connected Central Business District (Jones and Moreno-Carranco 2007). The decisive factor explaining that growth according to Parnreiter is global city formation and thus particularly a strong growth and geographical concentration of the producer service sector:

> In the last decade, financial and real estate services together increased their participation in the product of the Federal District by 65.9% (from 21.4 to 35.5%) and in urban employment by 47.7% (from 7.7 to 11.5%) (INEGI 1999; 2009). This growth has been pushed by the massive influx of global firms. In 2010, of the 175 global producer firms analyzed by GaWC (Globalization and World Cities Research Network), 89 had offices in Mexico City (Taylor et al. 2013).
>
> *(Parnreiter 2015b: 24)*

While thus there is a highly increased demand of global firms for premium-networked spaces in the secondary global city Mexico City, requiring an "externally induced adaptation" to worldwide processes in Friedmann's (1986) terms, this adaptation is organized locally through modifications of the planning system. In Mexico the exceptional measures for site-specific planning have been, first, the Specific Zones for Controlled Development (ZEDEC), and later the Corridors of Integration and Development (CIDs). What Parnreiter (2015b: 26) describes for Mexico, that "the geographical orientation of planning shifted scales, from 'planning for all' (the whole city) to 'planning for the exceptions', the so-called strategic projects" which relied furthermore on concerted public–private partnership backed up by authoritarian top-down planning, is a very common trait of the planning for competitiveness and transnational capital in globalizing cities in Latin America.

Probably the best-known case of urban regeneration megaprojects in Latin America is Puerto Madero, the redevelopment of a 170-hectare de-industrialized waterfront located right in the administrative and financial city center of Buenos Aires. In the early 1990s the site sparked the interest of real estate developers and in 1992 one of its 16 old docks was used for the Exhibition of the Americas and a public–private development corporation was set up. As Guano (2002: 188) described,

> the success of the exhibition struck the imagination of investors. In no time the old warehouses were transformed into offices and lofts, which were sold in even less time for astronomic figures. An irresistible Puerto Madero fever spread to the city's wealthiest companies and businesses and property prices escalated rapidly.

By 2009, in Puerto Madero 2.3 million square meters had been constructed and total public and private investment totaled US$1.7 million. For Guano (2002) and Cuenya and Corral (2011), Puerto Madero is a paradigmatic case of how urban megaprojects become symbols for the world–cityness and modernity of Latin American metropolises and also the entrepreneurial governance and planning logic of the neoliberal state that foments land speculation through the flexibilization of planning and urban marketing, as mentioned above. Through these pro-growth urban politics, over 20 years the defunct Puerto Madero site was transformed into one of the most expensive real estate locations in Latin America and allowed the appropriation of monopoly-land rents by private developers, that is, the extraction of rents without redistribution (Guano 2002). Furthermore, "the Manhattan on the Río de la Plata" serves as one of the most important areas for the new consumer culture of local middle classes and elites, that at Puerto Madero "admire the spectacle of transnational modernity surrounding them" (Guano 2002: 190).

An example for the combination of transportation and integrated peri-urban megaprojects is the northern periphery of Santiago de Chile (Lukas 2014). Especially in the Chicureo sector an unprecedented modernization process of urban–regional infrastructure took place, based on large private investments enacted through new planning and financing schemes. The most striking features have been, on the one hand, the layout of a hypermodern grid of intra- and inter-urban toll roads through a system of franchising highway concessions and, on the other, huge master-planned, new urbanist-style communities grouping residential, retail, recreational and educational functions in a single land plot (Lukas and López-Morales 2018). It is important to note that the urbanization of the former rural zone was strategically conceived and actively produced by a coalition of large economic groups with access to financial capital, traditional large-scale land holders and the state. While the economic groups-cum-developers since the 1980s bought up cheap agricultural and by-then non-urbanizable land, developing master plans for their integrated peri-urban megaprojects, in 1997 the state provided a new zoning orientation named "conditional planning" (planificación por condiciones). This major institutional and political adjustment and the production of urbanizable land for the financialized development industry implied a whole new way of organizing peri-urban growth and particularly a new way of linking land use and transportation planning and its financing. In fact, a toll-road was designed by the land developers, subsidized by transnational infrastructure contractors and heavily subsidized by public coffers, in essence the state enabling monopoly rents for the economic-groups-cum-developers. By now, the Chicureo area has turned not only into the new upper-class district of Santiago where land prices exploded, as had been conceived by the developers, it is also a highly fragmented and financialized landscape that is expanding according to the rhythms of financial investors as pension funds and investment trusts.

To sum up, the study of urban megaprojects in Latin America serves "to understand global processes from a localized and spatialized perspective," one that is largely lacking in the global inter-urban accounts of the global cities literature (Moreno-Carranco 2013: 188). What has been shown in urban megaproject research is that they are key instruments for the creative destruction of city space, and are necessary for the spatial location of new logistical functions of cities and the global organization of transnational flows of money, information and goods. Megaprojects also work as sinks for excess capital, as sites for the appropriation of ground rents and the location of new consumption spaces. Furthermore, megaprojects respond to specific modernizing imaginaries of political elites and the state.

Urban financialization

The described urban megaprojects are only the most iconic expressions of a massive building and speculation boom in Latin America which is linked to the privatization and financialization of many crucial aspects of urbanization such as (social) housing provision, highway systems and natural resources such as land and water.

One of the major fields of financialization in Latin America is that of housing provision, whereby "a shift from an incremental development process towards a large-scale speculative homebuilding system" (Monkkonen 2011: 2) has taken place, very much in line with what

Rolnik (2013) describes as "a glob al U-turn" in housing and urban policy agendas. Under the driving forces of globalization and neoliberalism and highlighting the strategic role of the real estate industry for economic growth, states have withdrawn from the direct provision of social housing and instead installed market-based housing finance models. This, "together with the increased use of housing as an investment asset within a globalized financial market, has profoundly affected the enjoyment of the right to adequate housing" (Rolnik 2013). For Latin America, the best documented cases of housing financialization through new housing policies are those of Brazil and Mexico. In Brazil, the Minha Casa Minha Vida (My House My Life) housing program launched in 2009 is regarded a major subsidy for construction firms with view to the impacts of economic crisis. It resulted "in 3.9 million units by 2014 with the goal of building 27 million units by the end of 2018" and as such is considered to be "the largest home-ownership and construction/mortgage subsidy scheme ever launched in the world" (Aalbers 2019: 4). While it has created ownership rights for households that lacked those rights beforehand, thus addressing a pressing social problem similar in many other Latin American societies, it also pushed low-income households into mortgage debts that in future economic crisis might become an economic burden too heavy to handle. Also in Mexico the scale of subsidized housing production is impressive (see Box 45.2). In the Metropolitan Area of Mexico City "between 2000 and 2015, an overall number of 686.926 housing units were authorized in 409 different residential developments," targeting low-income population in low-quality projects in peripheral locations that often lack basic urban infrastructure (Soederberg 2015; Janoschka and Salinas 2017).

Box 45.2 Infonavit (Mexico)

The Institute of the National Housing Fund for Workers (Infonavit) is a decentralized agency founded in 1972 with the enactment of the Infonavit Law. Its goal is to guarantee the constitutional right to the access to housing by Mexican workers. The backbone of the Infonavit system is a national fund where employers contribute with 5 percent of the salary of each worker in order to obtain a housing loan or the right to have their savings returned to them. To make the access of housing effective, the government partnered with private developers to develop affordable housing on a large scale. From 2001 to 2012, an estimated 20 million people – one-sixth of the population of Mexico – took refuge in this housing policy led by the Mexican state, especially in poorly equipped large-scale housing colonies on the outskirts of large Mexican cities. In a study of 2010, Infonavit determined that only in the period between 2006 and 2009 26 percent of the homes delivered have been abandoned. Despite this situation of abandonment and non-payment of credits, the institution delivered further loans for 1.8 million homes in the following years. In an investigative article the *Los Angeles Times* highlighted that in the period from 2001 to 2012 about 14.8 million housing solutions have been delivered, reaching its peak in the year 2008 (moment of the financial crisis of the United States). The Mexico housing policy with Infonavit as its back bone is thus an example of how the financialization of housing leads to the massive relocation of the popular sectors to the urban peripheries, and is not meeting needs in terms of access to urban infrastructure or the financial realities of workers.

But financialization does not only affect the demand-side of housing production through new subsidy- and mortgage schemes, it also affects the development industry and its business and location strategies. At least for Mexico, Brazil and Chile it has been described how the neoliberal policies of flexibilization and liberalization of capital flows have facilitated the emergence of a powerful real estate and development industry (Lukas 2014; Sanfelici and Halbert 2015; Janoschka and Salinas 2017). As Sanfelici and Halbert (2015: 3) state,

> in so-called 'emerging' countries that adopted neoliberal reforms, the role of financial markets in the financing of firms increased, while, at the same time, global capital availability has escalated, especially in the 2000s. The development industry is no exception: cash-consuming developers are eager to resort to private equity funds and stock markets to boost their growth.
>
> *(Rouanet and Halbert 2015)*

Where previously small and medium-sized real estate and construction firms operated in local markets, today there is a tendency towards market concentration and vertical integration of the different moments in the development process, leading to ever larger corporations and further triggering the integration of real estate and finance capital. There are different ways that concentration and integration proceeds: through mergers, acquisitions, joint ventures and partnerships between developers; developers partnering with international private equity firms at the corporate level; developers attracting financial investors by issuing stocks and bonds; and finance capital entering the direct ownership of properties or financing of specific development operations (Sanfelici and Halbert 2015).

These processes of concentration and integration with finance capital in the development industry lead to "spatial oligopolies," whereby "the real estate market has become dominated by a reduced number of companies that cluster in specific cities and regions," as Janoschka and Salinas (2017: 45) describe for Mexico City.

> In the Metropolitan Area of Mexico City, concentration is alarming: For instance, the company Desarrollos Inmobiliarios Sadasi was granted permission for building 62,700 housing units in the municipality of Tecámac, equivalent to more than two-thirds of the aggregate. On the other hand, in the neighboring Zumpango municipality, another big player in the housing market, GEO Hogares Ideales (Casas GEO), dominates the local market with 71,780 housing units approved by local authorities – nearly 80 percent of the total sum. Similar concentrations exist in other municipalities, thus indicating the existence of market agreements.
>
> *(Ibid.)*

Also Sanfelici and Halbert (2015: 3) mention that "four developers were responsible for one-quarter of all new housing launchings in the metropolitan area of Sao Paulo" and López-Morales (2016: 91) identifies in Santiago de Chile "a semi-monopoly of property-firms that control land supply" in the market of urban regeneration. Another effect of horizontal and vertical integration is a push towards economies of scale and ever bigger development projects, the new urban periphery of Santiago described above being only one of many examples, similar projects can be found in the major urban centers of Brazil, Mexico and Buenos Aires. As Gasic (2018) describes for Santiago de Chile, especially on the urban peripheries we see a special sort of peri-urban land grabbing, whereby institutional investors buy up large-scale land banks. Here, with Harvey, "the land becomes a form of fictitious capital, and the land market functions simply as a particular branch— albeit with some special characteristics—of the circulation of interest-bearing capital. Under such conditions the land is treated as a pure financial asset which is bought and sold according to the rent it yields" (1982/2006: 347).

Extended urbanization and transnational planning

In a certain way, research on planetary urbanization and the entanglements of concentrated and extended forms of urbanization has the potential to bring several of the aforementioned research fields together and, at the same time, broaden and deepen the analysis of the IPE of urbanization in Latin America. First of all, expanding the notion of the urban and urbanization beyond what previously was the central focus of urban research, the bounded entity called city and what happens within and between cities, allows for an understanding of the multi-scalar and multi-dimensional aspects of uneven territorial development that is characterizing the region. With the expansion of the extractive frontiers in the agro-industry, mining, fishing and forestry sectors, it becomes clear that urbanization processes are reaching far beyond the confines of the mega-cities and their peripheries. In a quite similar way to what has been argued in the phase of the debate on dependent urbanization, Brazil Monte-Mór and Castriota (2018: 341) see a "double process of industrialization and urbanization of the agrarian world," whereby "the contemporary rural submerges either in industrial processes (like agribusinesses) and their productive logic, or else in urban extensive processes focused on everyday life and the quality of collective reproduction" (Monte-Mór and Castriota 2018: 342). Other authors stretch "the notion of extended urbanization to the mines and fields in all corners of the earth from where concentrated forms of urbanization (i.e. cities and suburbs) are being provisioned" (Keil 2017: 176). Arboleda (2016) for instance, working on the small Chilean mining town Huasco, sheds light on the operational landscapes that function as "metabolic vehicles of planetary urbanization" and thus deepens the understanding of "the combined process of metropolization and extended urbanization" (Monte-Mór 2014: 112). Related to this kind of reasoning and the analysis of the entanglements of expanding extractive frontiers and urbanization processes are studies that focus on the extension of infrastructural networks and logistic chains – as the Initiative for the Integration of the Regional Infrastructure of South America (IIRSA in Spanish, see Box 45.3) – into regions that where previously not part of urban studies, such as the rainforests in Mexico, Ecuador, Brazil and Venezuela (Kanai 2014; 2016; Wilson 2014; Wilson and Bayón 2017).

Thus, if one looks at extended urbanization as the current form of explosion of capitalist investments inexorably related to the location of infrastructures in previously remote spaces, a new way of understanding the urban peripheries of Latin America is opened. The enclaves based on the extraction of land rent through agroindustrial, mining, oil, fishing or forestry complexes are connected by increasingly ambitious plans for new roads, ports, waterways or airports throughout the region. In the case of Ecuador, two emerging axes of urbanization show the configuration of new nodes linked to resource extraction. In the coastal region, a new inner-coastal urban axis has emerged from the existence of service cities and the commercialization of agrarian goods such as bananas, rice and palm, with high rates of migration from the countryside to new cities in rhythms consistent with the expansion of agribusiness that have led to extensive urban peripheries. In the Amazon region, multimodal infrastructure plans are combined with the expansion of capital flows in the opening of the oil, mining and agroindustrial frontiers, so that small service towns have become new cities, as well as new enclave ports are boosting new urbanization areas (Bayón 2019). In both cases, the new production and connectivity nodes generate new forms of urbanization in the peripheries, new spaces of capital, that have as their counterpart new forms of precarious living conditions for new urban dwellers.

An example of how to bring together different IPE approaches through the combined consideration of concentrated and extended forms of urbanization and its relation to global urbanism can be derived from recent research on the territorial organization and spatial division of

---

Box 45.3 IIRSA

The IIRSA South American Regional Integration Initiative project was formed in 2000 as an agreement of the 12 countries of the region (Colombia, Venezuela, Ecuador, Peru, Guyana, Chile, Paraguay, Uruguay, Bolivia, Surinam, Argentina and Brazil, member countries of the Union of South American Nations (UNASUR)). With the support of the Inter-American Development Bank (IDB), the Andean Development Corporation (CAF) and the Financial Fund for the Development of the Plata Basin, IIRSA includes 335 infrastructure projects worth US$37.5 billion. It seeks to enhance the continents' integration into the world economy by breaking up the geographical isolation of its peripheries. As its backbone, major development corridors are projected, such as the Montero Bulo Buloque Railway Bioceanic Corridor that links Brazil, Peru, Bolivia and Chile, or the Campo Grande highway corridor that seeks to link Sao Paulo in Brazil with Argentina, Paraguay and Chile. Also a range of hydroelectric plants are projected in or close to environmentally fragile places such as national parks and indigenous territories, areas protected by the laws of the countries themselves. No wonder that many of IIRSA's projects have espoused social and environmental conflicts. At the citizen level, indigenous communities close to these projects have been identified as those most affected, such as the cases of hydroelectric plants and road development in the Amazon basin, who have also established resistance to deforestation, state corruption and bad practices of the private sector that executes these projects. In the southern part of South America, criticisms also emerge regarding the development of monocultures that desertify and exacerbate the drought of extensive territories, such as soy in Argentina. The development of hydroelectric projects on the other hand generates large human displacements due to the flooding of valleys and streams for the generation of energy, in addition to the environmental effects of the energy interconnection processes (high voltage cables). However, the main threat of IIRSA might be the accumulated effect of all associated activities, a definite change of the region's integration into the world economy and the subsumption of until now remote places and indigenous communities to resource extraction and capital accumulation. Unsurprisingly, the IIRSA projects are highly prone to corruption so pervasive in the construction sector and, in fact, several projects have been linked to the continent-wide Odebrecht corruption scandal.

---

labor of the transnational mining industry in Chile (Phelps, Atienza and Arias 2015; Lukas and Brueck 2018; Vergara-Perucich 2018). There national and transnational corporations of the extractive industries (such as the Chilean state enterprise CODELCO, the Chilean Luksic group and the BHP Billiton, the world's largest private mining company) operate complex logistic chains that entail copper mines high in the Andean mountains in the region of Antofagasta, different transport infrastructures (railway systems, road networks, pipelines) that connect the mines in the hinterlands to port facilities in the coastal city of Antofagasta and shipping companies that transport the mineral from Antofagasta to the mostly Asian markets. While the region of Antofagasta thus is operationalized by the transnational extractive industries, local economic development and agglomeration dynamics in the city of Antofagasta is very poor. Rather, it is in Santiago where there "are signs of something of an agglomeration of mining services suppliers in Santiago" (Phelps, Atienza and Arias 2015). It is a "spatially delimited quarter in the capital city" that plays "the main intermediary role in the global supply chain of mining production and firms can benefit from the existence of urbanization economies" (Phelps, Atienza and

Arias 2015). Here the mining companies have their headquarters and mining suppliers and producer services are concentrated. The extractive regions and their gateway cities such as Antofagasta serve mere logistical functions for global production networks and their lead firms, while command and control functions and wealth derived from research extraction are concentrated in Santiago (Vergara-Perucich 2018). However, in order to make Antofagasta more competitive in the attraction of advanced human capital and to pacify social protest against mining-related urban precariousness and mineral pollution, in 2013 BHP Billiton set up one of the most ambitious initiatives of strategic urban planning in Latin America (CREO Antofagasta), showing emerging links between the transnational circuits of resource extraction and global urbanism.

Conclusion

In this chapter we have provided a brief overview of recent lines of research of the IPE of cities and planetary urbanization, with special regard to contributions from and on urbanization in Latin America. What has been addressed are the multiple ways in which Latin American cities and regions are integrated into the global economy and are shaped by the latest rounds of capitalist modernization. The large metropolises that saw massive urbanization in the period of import substitution industrialization (ISI in the twentieth century are still the dominating urban centers, today providing global city functions for the integration of national extractive economies to the world economy. Beyond these global logistical and operational functions, which lead to the creation of specific sites and zones for their realization as in the form of new urban downtowns, it has also been shown how the deep neoliberalization since the 1970s and 1980s led to the financialization of housing supply and demand, this in turn leading to socio-spatial transformation processes as the installation of megaprojects of urban regeneration, large-scale low-quality housing projects and new financialized peri-urban landscapes for the appropriation of ground rents on the urban peripheries. What is only recently beginning to be addressed is how concentrated and extended forms of financialized urbanization are dialectically intertwined and together facilitate the extraction of value and the increasing and combined assumption of urban and rural space under the rule of financialized capital accumulation.

What, from our point of view, could significantly strengthen IPE research on cities and urbanization in Latin America is its integration with theories that help to address the regional specificity of its integration into the world economy. Global city formation, urban megaprojects, urban financialization and extended urbanization in Latin America take place in a post-colonial context of very high concentration of economic and political power and in weak democracies that are characterized by the capture of the state through transnational-oriented local elites.

Footnote

1 **Acknowledgements:** Felipe Hernández, Manuel Bayón, Daniel Zárate, Caridad Santelices, Isaac Araujo.

Notes

1 See: www.internationalrivers.org/campaigns/initiative-for-the-integration-of-regional-infrastructure-in-south-america.
2 See: www.bloomberg.com/quicktake/china-s-silk-road.
3 The tertiary capital cycle at Harvey includes social spending in relation to the reproduction of labor power (education, health and ideological cooptation and overt repression, among others), development and research. Again, the potential for productive investment is exhausted after some time, and neither in this area the fundamental crisis of capitalism can be overcome (Harvey 1978: 108).

4 Broadly understood, financialization is "the increasing predominance of financial instruments, practices and mechanisms over the actual production of goods or services in order to yield profits" (Arboleda 2016:4).

5 There are different variants of the world system discussion, with maybe Braudel, Cardoso and Faletto, Wallerstein and Arrighi representing the major foundational works more urbanization-centered accounts were based on.

6 Global city theory has been criticized from various angles: the lack of real relational thinking, understanding the city as bounded entity. Another critique to global city research is that its vocabulary was taken over by city boosters around the world. City leaders look at and cite the international rankings, since to be of global relevance gives prestige to political leaders and attracts more investment. However, global city theory in itself can hardly be blamed for that partial and abusive appropriation of its arguments.

7 Parnreiter (2015b) considers three indicators in order to address the centrality of Latin American economies and its major cities: first, the location of headquarters of lead firms in global production networks (GPN) (that informs about the geography of "formal corporate power" in the global economy); second, the added value in advanced producer services (that informs about the geography of "organizational power"); and, third, the geography of global network connectivity as calculated by the Globalization and World Cities (GaWC) research group which analyzes inter-urban connectivity in terms of the flows of information, capital, professionals, among other aspects (and that informs over the geography of "globalizing power").

8 The most important sectors are banking and finance (with the Brazilian Banco Bradesco, Banco do Brasil and Itau Unibanco Holding leading), mining and petroleum (Petrobas y Ecopetrol) and telecommunications (América Móvil, former Telmex, in Mexico).

Bibliography

Aalbers, M. 2019. Financial Geographies of Real Estate and the City: A Literature Review. *Financial Geography Working Papers Series* No. 21. KU Leuven/University of Leuven.

Arboleda, M. 2016. Spaces of Extraction, Metropolitan Explosions: Planetary Urbanization and the Commodity Boom in Latin America. *International Journal of Urban and Regional Research* 40(1): 96–112.

Baker, T. and McGuirk, P. 2016. Assemblage Thinking as Methodology: Commitments and Practices for Critical Policy Research. *Territory, Politics, Governance* 5(4): 425–442.

Bayón, M. 2019. *Una mirada de la Amazonía a través de su urbanización en Geografía Crítica para detener el despojo de los territorios: teorías, experiencias y casos de trabajo en Ecuador*. Bayón and Torres [Coord]. Quito: Abya Yala.

Beaverstock, J., Smith, R. and Taylor, P. 1999. A Roster of World Cities. *Cities* 16(6): 445–58.

Brenner, N. 2014. *Implosions – Explosions: Towards a Study of Planetary Urbanization*. Berlin: Jovis Verlag Gmb.

Caldeira, T. 2017. Peripheral Urbanization: Autoconstruction, Transversal Logics, and Politics in Cities of the Global South. *Environment and Planning D: Society and Space* 35(1): 3–20.

Castells, M. 1977. *The Urban Question: A Marxist Approach*. Cambridge, MA: MIT Press.

Christophers, B. 2011. Revisiting the Urbanization of Capital. *Annals of the Association of American Geographers* 101(6): 1347–1364.

Ciccolella, P. 1999. Globalización Y Dualización En La Región Metropolitana De Buenos Aires: Grandes Inversiones Y Reestructuración Socioterritorial En Los Años Noventa. *EURE* 25(76): 5–27.

Coe, N., Dicken, P., Hess, M. and Wai-Cheung, H. 2010. Making Connections: Global Production Networks and World City Networks. *Global Networks* 10(1): 138–149.

Contreras, E. 2014. Las alianzas público privadas y la gentrificación del Puerto Histórico de Río de Janeiro. Caso: Porto Maravilha. *Working Paper Series Contested Cities*: 1–16. DOI: 2341–2755.

Cuenya, B. and Corral, M. 2011. Empresarialismo, Economía Del Suelo Y Grandes Proyectos Urbanos: El Modelo De Puerto Madero En Buenos Aires. *EURE (Santiago)* 37(111): 25–45.

De Mattos, C. 1999. Globalización Y Expansión Metropolitana: Lo Que Existía Sigue Existiendo. *EURE (Santiago)* 25(76): 29–56.

De Mattos, C. 2010. Globalización Y Metamorfosis Metropolitana En América Latina: De La Ciudad a Lo Urbano Generalizado. *Revista De Geografía Norte Grande* 47: 81–104.

Friedmann, J. 1986. The World City Hypothesis: Development and Change. *Urban Studies*, 23(2): 59–137.

Gasic, I. 2018. Inversiones E Intermediaciones Financieras En El Mercado Del Suelo Urbano. Principales Hallazgos a Partir Del Estudio De Transacciones De Terrenos En Santiago De Chile, 2010–2015. *EURE (Santiago)* 44(133): 29–50.

Guano, E. 2002. Spectacles of Modernity: Transnational Imagination and Local Hegemonies in Neoliberal Buenos Aires. *Cultural Anthropology* 17(2): 181–209.

Harvey, D. 1973. *Social Justice and the City*. Athens: University of Georgia Press.

Harvey, D. 1978. The Urban Process under Capitalism: A Framework for Analysis. *International Journal of Urban and Regional Research* 2(1–3): 101–131.

Harvey, D. 1982/2006. *The Limits to Capital*. London: Verso.

Harvey, D. 2011. *The Enigma of Capital and the Crises of Capitalism*. London: Profile Books.

Janoschka, M. and Salinas, L. 2017. Peripheral Urbanisation in Mexico City. A Comparative Analysis of Uneven Social and Material Geographies in Low-income Housing Estates. *Habitat International* 70: 43–49.

Jones, G. and Moreno-Carranco, M. 2007. Megaprojects: Beneath the Pavement, Excess. *City: Analysis of Urban Trends, Culture, Theory, Policy, Action* 11(2): 144–164.

Kaika, M. 2017. Don't Call Me Resilient Again!: The New Urban Agenda as Immunology … or … What Happens When Communities Refuse to be Vaccinated with "Smart Cities" and Indicators. *Environment and Urbanization* 29(1): 89–102.

Kanai, J. 2014. On the Peripheries of Planetary Urbanization: Globalizing Manaus and Its Expanding Impact. *Environment and Planning: Society and Space* 32(6): 1071–1087.

Kanai, J. 2016. The Pervasiveness of Neoliberal Territorial Design: Cross-border Infrastructure Planning in South America since the Introduction of IIRSA. *Geoforum* 69: 160–70.

Keil, R. 2017. Extended Urbanization, "Disjunct Fragments" and Global Suburbanisms. *Environment and Planning D* 36(3): 494–511.

Larner, W. and Laurie, N. 2010. Travelling Technocrats, Embodied Knowledges: Globalising Privatisation in Telecoms and Water. *Geoforum* 41(2): 218–226.

Lefebvre, H. 1968/2011. *The Urban Revolution*. Minneapolis, MN: University of Minnesota Press.

López-Morales, E. 2016. A Multidimensional Approach to Urban Entrepreneurialism, Financialization, and Gentrification in the High-Rise Residential Market of Inner Santiago, Chile. *Research in Political Economy Risking Capitalism* 31: 79–105.

Lukas, M. 2014. Neoliberale Stadtentwicklung in Santiago de Chile. *Akteurskonstellationen und Machtverhaeltnisse in der Planung staedtebaulicher Megaprojekte*. Kiel: Geographisches Institut der Universität.

Lukas, M. 2018. Urban Rescaling. In: Orum, A. (ed.) *The Wiley-Blackwell Encyclopedia of Urban and Regional Studies*. Hoboken, NJ: Wiley-Blackwell.

Lukas, M. and Brueck, A. (2018). Urban Policy Mobilities und globale Produktionsnetzwerke: Städtische Planung in Chile als Legitimationsinstanz extraktiver Industrien. *Suburban – Zeitschrift fuer kritische Stadtforschung* 6(2/3): 69–90.

Lukas, M. and López-Morales, E. 2018. Real Estate Production, Geographies of Mobility and Spatial Contestation: A Two-case Study in Santiago De Chile. *Journal of Transport Geography* 67: 92–101.

Lungo, M. 2005. Globalización, grandes proyectos y privatización de la gestión urbana. *Urbano* 8(11): 49–58.

Maricato, E. 2017. The Future of Global Peripheral Cities. *Latin American Perspectives* 44(2): 18–37.

Merrifield, A. 2013. The Urban Question under Planetary Urbanization. *International Journal of Urban and Regional Research* 37(3): 909–922.

McCann, E. and Ward, K. 2011. *Mobile Urbanism: Cities and Policymaking in the Global Age*. Minneapolis, MN: University of Minnesota Press.

McGuirk, J. 2015. *Radical Cities: Across Latin America in Search of a New Architecture*. London: Verso.

Monkkonen, P. 2011. Housing Finance Reform and Increasing Socioeconomic Segregation in Mexico. *International Journal of Urban and Regional Research* (4): 757–772.

Monte-Mór, R. 2014. Extended Urbanization and Settlement Patterns: An Environmental Approach. In Brenner, N. (ed.) *Implosions/Explosions*. Berlin: Jovis, 260–267.

Monte-Mór, R. and Castriota, R. 2018. Extended Urbanization: Implications for Urban and Regional Theory. *Handbook on the Geographies of Regions and Territories*. Berlin: Jovis: 332–345.

Montero, S. 2017. Persuasive Practitioners and the Art of Simplification: Mobilizing the "Bogotá Model" through Storytelling. *Novos Estudos CEBRAP* 36(1): 59–76.

Moreno-Carranco, M. 2013. Global Mexico under Construction. The Santa Fe Megaproject in Mexico City. In: Irazábal, C. (ed.) *Transbordering Latin Americanisms: Liminal Places, Cultures, and Powers (T) Here*. New York: Taylor and Francis: 187–214.

Parnreiter, C. 2015a. Strategic Planning, the Real Estate Economy, and the Production of New Spaces of Centrality. The Case of Mexico City. *Erdkunde* 69(1): 21–31.

Parnreiter, C. 2015b. Las Ciudades Latinoamericanas En La Economía Mundial: La Geografía De Centralidad Económica Y Sus Transformaciones Recientes. *Economía UNAM* 12(35): 3–22.

Phelps, N., Atienza, M. and Arias, M. 2015. Encore for the Enclave: The Changing Nature of the Industry Enclave with Illustrations from the Mining Industry in Chile. *Economic Geography* 91(2): 119–146.

Pradilla, E. 1982. Autoconstrucción, explotación de la fuerza de trabajo y políticas del Estado en América Latina. In Pradilla, E. (ed.) *Ensayos sobre el problema de la vivienda en América Latina*. México DF: UAM-Xochimilco.

Rapoport, E. 2015. Globalizing Sustainable Urbanism: The Role of International Masterplanners. *Area* 47(2): 110–115.

Rolnik, R. 2013. Late Neoliberalism: The Financialization of Homeownership and Housing Rights. *International Journal of Urban and Regional Research* (3): 1058–1066.

Rossi, U. 2017. *Cities in Global Capitalism*. Cambridge: Polity Press.

Sanfelici, D. and Halbert, L. 2015. Financial Markets, Developers and the Geographies of Housing in Brazil: A Supply-side Account. *Urban Studies* 53(7): 1465–1485.

Sarue, B. 2018. Quando grandes projetos urbanos acontecem? Uma análise a partir do Porto Maravilha no Rio de Janeiro. *Scielo* 61(3): 581–616.

Sassen, S. 1991. *The Global City. New York, London, Tokyo*. Princeton, NJ: Princeton University Press.

Scholvin, S., Breul, M. and Revilla Diez, J. 2019. Revisiting Gateway Cities: Connecting Hubs in Global Networks to Their Hinterlands. *Urban Geography* 40(9): 1291–1309.

Shin, H. and Kim, S. H. 2015. The Developmental State, Speculative Urbanisation and the Politics of Displacement in Gentrifying Seoul. *Urban Studies* 53(3): 540–559.

Smith, N. 2002. New Globalism, New Urbanism: Gentrification as Global Urban Strategy. *Antipode* 34(3): 427–450.

Soederberg, S. 2015. Subprime Housing Goes South: Constructing Securitized Mortgages for the Poor in Mexico. *Antipode* 47(2): 481–499.

Soederberg, S. and Walks, A. 2018. Producing and Governing Inequalities under Planetary Urbanization: From Urban Age to Urban Revolution? *Geoforum* (89): 107–113.

Swyngedouw, E. and Kaika, M. 2014. Urban Political Ecology. Great Promises, Deadlock … and New Beginnings? *Documents d'Anàlisi Geogràfica* 60(3): 459–481.

Swyngedouw, E. 2018. The Urbanization of Capital and the Production of Capitalist Natures. *The Oxford Handbook of Karl Marx*. Oxford: Oxford University Press: 538–56.

United Nations, Department of Economic and Social Affairs, Population Division. 2019. *World Urbanization Prospects: The 2018 Revision (ST/ESA/SER.A/420)*. New York: United Nations.

Vergara-Perucich, J. 2018. Aplicaciones De La Teoría Implosión/explosión: Relación Entre La Región Metropolitana De Santiago De Chile Y Los Territorios Productivos Regionales. *EURE (Santiago)* 133(44): 71–90.

Wilson, J. 2014. The Violence of Abstract Space: Contested Regional Developments in Southern Mexico. *International Journal of Urban and Regional Research* 38(2): 516–538.

Wilson, J. and Bayón, M. 2017. Fantastical Materializations: Interoceanic Infrastructures in the Ecuadorian Amazon. *Environment and Planning: Society and Space* 35(5): 836–854.

Wu, F. 1997. Urban Restructuring in China's Emerging Market Economy: Towards a Framework for Analysis. *International Journal of Urban and Regional Research* 21(4): 640–663.

46
Migration and international political economy

Fabiola Mieres[1]

Introduction

At the turn of the twenty-first century, migration has emerged as a critical political and policy challenge in matters such as integration, displacement, safe migration and border management (IOM 2018: 13). Perceptions that migration is one of the key 'problems' in developed countries remain high (Castles 2012). Challenges abound not only in terms of the number of migrants that a country should accept, but also around governance mechanisms put in place for a government to become more effective in 'managing' flows. Competing governance mechanisms for migration question the nature of the 'global governance' of migration, if we accept that any form of global governance exists. According to the United Nations, the estimated number of international migrants worldwide increased over 17 years between 2000 and 2017, reaching 258 million in 2017 (UNDESA 2017). During the same period, the stock of international migrants grew by an average of 2.3 per cent. Despite the increase in absolute numbers, the share of international migrants in proportion to the population of the world has remained relatively stable, between 1970 and 2017 at around 2.2 to 3.5 per cent (UNDESA 2017). If international migrants are only 3.5 per cent of the global population, what is all the fuss?

The answer is not straightforward and would require a deep multidisciplinary historiography on migration that exceeds the scope of this chapter. Migration is generally a highly sensitive topic where the debate tends to be dominated by opinion rather than evidence (Skeldon 2012: 229). However, reflecting on migration from an 'IPE standpoint' can provide initial insights to unpack the complexities around migration in the global political economy. Many advances have been made in the discipline of IPE since O'Brien's (2000: 89) denounce of workers being largely invisible in the study of International Political Economy (IPE). Almost 20 years of scholarship in IPE (and its Global Political Economy (GPE) variant) has cast a light on many aspects of workers, including migrant workers, and production in the global economy as it pertains to labour movements across borders (Pellerin 2015; Phillips 2011; Talani 2015; Taylor 2008). Notwithstanding, the study of migration has too infrequently been approached through the lenses of the theoretical constructs and core debates of IPE (Phillips 2011: 2). This chapter takes stock of labour migration within IPE and offer pathways to rethink IPE through a migration lens. Theorising and understandings of migration within IPE entail overcoming polarising debates, both within perspectives of what constitutes IPE, and within the migration literature eclipsed in 'migration studies'. Implications of this exercise are theoretical and carry methodological consequences and allow important aspects such as gender, social reproduction, skill, segmentation and developmental impacts of migration to be addressed more systematically and critically.

This chapter reflects on labour migration within core IPE perspectives rather than addressing the 'IPE of labour migration' at length. This latter exercise is a much more ambitious task which involves analysing at more depth different regions, migration corridors, integration to the global economy through trade, investment, (global) production, industrialisation and the institutional framework (domestic and international) in understanding the socio-economic factors at the global level that drive particular forms of labour migration, either permanent, circular, temporary, seasonal, forced displacement, refugees, and so forth. This chapter has opted to provide an initial overview of some elements of IPE and GPE theorising that reflect (or lack of) engagement with migration and some key concepts in migration studies that allow G(I)PE to enrich its analysis on the role of migrant workers in the global economy.

Let us begin with the simplest distinction that renders 'migration' a reality and that refers to 'internal' vs. 'international'. Internal migration involves people who move within the borders of their own countries, for example from rural to urban areas, and vice-versa. The focus of this chapter is on 'international migration' which is the act of moving across international borders from a country of origin (also called country of emigration) to a country of destination (also called immigration), and in particular, it will focus on 'international labour migrants', people who cross borders for the purpose of work (see Box 46.1).

Box 46.1 Who is a migrant?

The most commonly used definition of a migrant worker lies within the International Convention on the Protection of the Rights of All Migrant Workers and Members of Their Families (CMW), 1990, by which a migrant worker is a 'person who is to be engaged, is engaged, or has been engaged in a remunerated activity in a state of which he or she is not a national'. While there is no universally agreed definition of migration or migrant, several definitions are widely accepted and have been developed in different settings, such as those set out in the United Nations Department of Economic and Social Affairs' (UNDESA) 1998 Recommendations on Statistics of International Migration (IOM 2018: 14). Definitions and categories of migrants are shaped by geographical, legal, political, temporal and methodological factors: length of stay, citizenship, place of residence, etc. Countries opt for different responses, which also brings problems of homogenisation of migration statistics. In capturing 'international labour migration' for instance, the International Labour Organization (ILO) developed guidelines to advise countries in that exercise. In that light, the term international labour migration refers to the process and outcome of international labour migration including i) international migrant workers, that is, workers who cross borders; ii) for-work international migrants, i.e. international migrants who are looking to work; and iii) return international migrant worker (ILO 2018). In turn, a refugee is someone who has been forced to flee his or her country because of persecution, war or violence. A refugee has a well-founded fear of persecution for reasons of race, religion, nationality, political opinion or membership in a particular social group. Most likely, they cannot return home or are afraid to do so. War and ethnic, tribal and religious violence are leading causes of refugees fleeing their countries (UNHCR n/d). In recent years, large-scale movements and refugee situations around the world have been recognised to have labour market implications. However, migrants and refugees have different needs and a different set of protections by international law, what traditionally distinguishes them is the 'voluntary' nature of migration versus that of 'forced' for refugees. However, in reality, the distinction is not always obvious and the term 'mixed migration' is some-times used to capture the complexity of the flows (Van Hear et al. 2009).

Source: ILO 2018; IOM 2018; UNHCR (n/d); Van Hear et al. 2009

Any traditional view on International Relations (IR) and its associated subfield of IPE as it has been called in the 'American School' (Cohen 2008; Maliniak and Tierney 2011) has been blind to the issue of migration. This will become clearer in the following section but suffice it to high-light here that this view depends highly on what we understand 'IPE' to constitute. As IPE began to broaden and incorporate other paradigms, schools of thought and *problématiques* (Phillips 2011), the view that migration has been close to absent is not accurate. This is no surprise given the openness of more critical approaches within IPE and GPE to inter- and cross-disciplinarity, which lies at the heart of migration studies as well.

To address migration within IPE, the chapter is structured as follows: First, dynamics on migration are presented; second, preoccupations with security and sovereignty reflect approaches in 'mainstream IPE' that explain why the issue has been caught up so slowly; third, so-called 'critical approaches' are analysed to understand globalisation and the roots of inequality that explain labour migration. Fourth, we reflect on some key aspects of migration research and IPE such as gender, social reproduction, skill, segmentation, development and global production that are crucial towards unpacking the 'global political economy of migration'. Finally, conclusions are drawn suggesting ways of carrying the 'migration and/within IPE' research agenda forward.

Migration dynamics in the global economy

The number of international migrants in the world has continued to rise reaching 258 million in 2017 (UNDESA 2017: 1). In terms of where these migrants are located by levels of income, high-income countries host almost two-thirds of all international migrants representing 64 per cent of all migrants worldwide, equal to 165 million. Middle or low-income countries host 36 per cent (92 million) of the world's migrants. Compared to 2000, the share of international migrants living in high-income countries increased slightly while the share of middle and low-income countries fell (UNDESA 2017). By geographic regions, more than 60 per cent of all international migrants live in Asia or Europe: 80 million in Asia and 78 million in Europe. North America hosted the third largest number of migrants (58 million), followed by Africa (25 million), Latin America and the Caribbean (10 million) and Oceania (8 million).

Despite this growth in numbers, international migrants accounted for 2 per cent or less of the total population of Africa, Asia and Latin America and the Caribbean. In contrast, in Europe, North America and Oceania, they comprised at least 10 per cent of the total population. Moreover, the number of international migrants worldwide has grown faster than the world's population, and that is why the share went up from 2.8 in 2000 to 3.4 per cent in 2017. This pace varies across regions: Oceania recorded the fastest growth at 2.7 per cent, Latin America and the Caribbean at 2.2 per cent, while Europe and North America, where the number of migrants has already been high, showed a slower pace of change at 1.9 and 2.1 per cent respectively (UNDESA 2017: 6).

A relatively small number of countries hosts more than 50 per cent of all international migrants. Table 46.1 shows that the largest number of migrants live in the United States of America, around 50 million (19 per cent of the world's total).

Table 46.1 Twenty countries or areas hosting the largest number of international migrants, 2000 and 2017 (millions)

Country	2000	Country	2017
USA	34.8	USA	49.8
Russian Federation	11.9	Germany	12.2
Germany	9	Saudi Arabia	12.2
India	6.4	Russian Federation	11.7
France	6.3	UK	8.8
Ukraine	5.5	United Arab Emirates	8.3
Canada	5.5	Canada	7.9
Saudi Arabia	5.3	France	7.9
UK	4.7	Australia	7
Australia	4.4	Italy	5.9
Pakistan	4.2	Spain	5.9
Kazakhstan	2.9	India	5.2
Iran	2.8	Ukraine	5
China, Hong Kong, SAR	2.7	Turkey	4.9
United Arab Emirates	2.4	South Africa	4
Italy	2.1	Kazakhstan	3.6
Cote d'Ivoire	2	Thailand	3.6
Jordan	1.9	Pakistan	3.4
Israel	1.9	Jordan	3.2
Japan	1.7	Kuwait	3.1

Source: UNDESA (2017: 6).

Another important dimension includes regions of origin. The number of international migrants originating from Asia showed the largest increase between 2000 and 2017, at 40.7 million, followed by the migrant population born in Africa (14.7 million), in Latina America and the Caribbean (12.9 million), in Europe (11.6 million), in Northern America (1.2 million) and in Oceania (700,000). In relative terms, however, the number of international migrants originating in Africa experienced the largest increase since 2000 (68 per cent), followed by the population of migrants born in Asia (62 per cent), in Latin America and the Caribbean (52 per cent) and in Oceania (51 per cent).

It is worth noting that migration is still a 'regional phenomenon' as it takes place primarily between countries that are located within the same world region. In 2017, this is the case of Europe, where 67 per cent of the international migrants originate from that block, while in Asia, 60 per cent reside in a country located in their region of birth. The same is evidenced for Oceania (60 per cent) and Africa (53 per cent). In contrast, international migrants from Latin America and the Caribbean (84 per cent) and Northern America (72 per cent) reside primarily outside their region of birth (UNDESA 2017: 12).

These regional dynamics are also contrasted by the fact that Asia represents the origin of the majority of persons who are living outside their region. Most of the Asian international migrants were living in Europe (20 million), North America (17 million) and Oceania (3 million). In North America, 26 million migrants are from Latin America and the Caribbean and five million Latin Americans live in Europe (UNDESA 2017: 13). At the global level, one-third of all international migrants come from only ten countries with India, Mexico, the Russian Federation and China topping the list (see Table 46.2).

Table 46.2 Twenty largest countries or areas of origin of international migrants, 2000 and 2017 (millions)

Country of origin	2000	Country of origin	2007
Russian Federation	10.7	India	16.6
Mexico	9.6	Mexico	13.0
India	8.0	Russian Federation	10.6
China	5.8	China	10.0
Ukraine	5.6	Bangladesh	7.5
Bangladesh	5.4	Syrian Arab Republic	6.9
Afghanistan	4.5	Pakistan	6.0
UK	3.9	Ukraine	5.9
Kazakhstan	3.6	Philippines	5.7
Pakistan	3.4	UK	4.9
Germany	3.4	Afghanistan	4.8
Italy	3.1	Poland	4.7
Philippines	3.1	Indonesia	4.2
Turkey	2.8	Germany	4.2
State of Palestine	2.8	Kazakhstan	4.1
Indonesia	2.3	State of Palestine	3.8
Poland	2.1	Romania	3.6
Portugal	2.0	Turkey	3.4
USA	2.0	Egypt	3.4
Republic of Korea	2.0	Italy	3.0

Source: UNDESA (2017: 13).

Contemporary migration is complex and the above figures reflect trends in 'stocks'. Nevertheless, migration 'flows' (i.e. movements) are harder to estimate and UNDESA's database of migration flows only encompasses 45 countries (IOM 2018: 21). In addition, the presence of undocumented (irregular) migration presents difficulties for gaining statistics, while varying lengths of stay of migrants that are not always reported complicate data collection, and the lack of accurate reporting remains a difficulty as well. Capturing data on migration flows persists a challenge as countries mostly record inflows (and not always outflows).

Box 46.2 Migration and its measurement

Migration constitutes the 'third' demographic variable, but unlike 'births' and 'deaths', it is not a unique event but a continuous process across time and space (Skeldon 2012: 230). This complicates technical definitions and together with political and legal factors, there is no universally agreed definition. UNDESA produces estimates of the number of international migrations globally based on data provided by nation-states (UNDESA 2017). The UN Recommendations on Statistics of International Migration defines an international migrant as any person who has changed his or her country of usual residence, distinguishing between 'short-term migrants' (those who have changed their country of usual residence for at least three months, but less than one year) and 'long-term migrants' (those who have done so for at least one year) (IOM 2018: 15). Not all countries use this definition, therefore, differences in concepts as well as data collection methodologies hinder full comparability of these statistics. In turn, the ILO estimates the

> number of migrant workers based on UNDESA, the Organisation for Economic Co-operation and Development (OECD) and Statistical Office for the European Union (EUROSTAT). In 2017, it was estimated that 164 million people are migrant workers worldwide who constitute 4.2 per cent of all workers. From the previous estimate in the year 2013, there was an 11 per cent increase (ILO 2018: ix).

International migration matters for IPE not only because the movement of people have characterised humans for millennia, and migration per se is attached to 'nation-states' as a person to be considered a 'migrant' needs to move from one independent state or territory to another, and the question of length of residence matters for definitional purposes. It also matters for transformations in the global economy such as the globalisation of trade, services, the fragmentation of production in geographically dispersed and distributed (global) supply chains, progress in digital technologies, and the outsourcing of production among other factors are key preoccupations of scholars of IPE which have implications for the movement of people and workers. In this vein, migration (and international migration mostly) entails distilling the analytical categories that have been subject to the study of IPE in traditional approaches (also called 'mainstream'), namely the 'nation-state' and its role vis-à-vis migration. The analytical categories used to address migration are related to the circumstances (structures) and motivations (agency) for moving. The issue of migration raises important and challenging questions about the legitimacy and authority of 'state power' and therefore, the boundaries of political membership.[2]

In this light, IPE as a discipline[3] in its more critical variants, allows for integration of structure and agency and it facilitates an approach to understanding the social foundations of the global political economy (Phillips 2011; Taylor 2008) as related to the role of labour migrants in the global economy. By analysing and unpacking the 'social foundations' of the global economy, we can shed light on the everyday power relationships that underpin the global economy through the forms of power, politics and contestation of the agents that carry out migration (migrant themselves), who are inseparable from the 'everyday material life' which is traditionally analysed in political economy through the role of markets, wealth generation, distribution and welfare under strict assumptions of rationality, complete information, rational expectations and other key tenets of neoclassical paradigms (see Taylor 2008) which also permeate more 'mainstream' approaches' in IPE associated with the American School.[4] In the next section, we move on to analysing how 'mainstream IPE' has conceptualised migration.

Sovereignty and security: migration in mainstream IPE

If IPE is understood as 'subfield' of the broader discipline of IR, then the political science literature on migration and international relations has rendered exceptionally thin, even though a number of scholars have begun to turn their attention to the inquiry of the role of migration in the international system (Hollifield 2012: 5–6).

Classical IR theory has been historically preoccupied with the role of 'nation-states' in an anarchic world, and from 1945 to 1990, inquiries and theoretical developments were dominated by the Cold War, and international relations theorists tended to divide politics into two categories: high and low. Theories were also binary in the sense that worldviews were either 'realist' or 'idealist'. The realist version of IR is concerned with 'high politics' which includes national security, foreign policy, issues around war and peace, and the balance of power among other topics. In turn, 'low politics' is related to all other aspects that pertain to economics and the social dimension. In this vein, migration (and labour migration most specifically) would fit 'low politics' and therefore, should not be a focus of scholars of IR who are concerned with high politics, and thus as Hollifield (2012: 6) points out:

> Unless it can be demonstrated that a social or economic phenomenon like migration clearly affects relations among states to the point of upsetting the balance of power, the study of migration should be left to economists, sociologists, anthropologists, and other scholars of low politics, especially those with a more transnational or idealistic view of international relations, driven by agency and devoid of power considerations.

As the world moved into further economic liberalisation in the 1970s, and there was an increase in international trade and foreign direct investment, the rise of multinational corporations began to pose questions about conflict and cooperation, not only in international security, but in the economic realm. Scholars such as Joseph Nye, Robert Gilpin, Robert Keohane and Stephen Krasner began to theorise economic interdependence with its different facets, and from a classical IR standpoint, the 'subfield of IPE' was born. Therefore, as of mid and late 1990s, the discipline of IR and IPE began to recognise that large population movements across borders can have an effect in security and sovereignty of nation-states (Weiner and Russell 2001).

'Mainstream IPE' theories place their unit of analysis in the nation-state defined in terms of 'interests'. Thus, everything that pertains to international migration is analysed from the standpoint of the role of nation-states in allowing (or not) migration with an exclusive focus on power, interest and structure.[5]

From a realist or neorealist perspective, in debates about the role of migration, economic–nationalist perspectives would place themselves to the side of restrictive immigration positions, arguing that the nation-state is a self-contained category with shared values and would therefore support restrictions that protect domestic workers from the (assumed) competitive pressures argued to be caused by migrants. For these approaches, nation-states do exercise power over their borders without having to provide a justification for it – the necessary conditions for migration to occur may be social and economic, but the sufficient conditions are political and legal (Hollifield 2012: 4).

In contrast, liberal IPE approaches focus on understanding the 'national interest' from the point of view of the different actors (social and economic) that compete to influence the nation-state. For liberal theorists, international politics can be reduced to an economic game in which a problem of collective action needs to be resolved by understanding the preferences that make up those competing interests (Milner 1997). Therefore, institutions play a key role in unpacking the politics and policies of liberal states where the possibilities of cooperation expand the understanding of the international system as 'anarchic'. The system is still anarchic but it can be tamed by the presence of international institutions whose presence make actors' expectations converge (Keohane 1984; Krasner 1982).

Under this liberal paradigm, there is a demand for international cooperation in the area of migration with the view of managing the flows (this could potentially explain the adoption of two Global Compacts on Migration and Refugees in December 2018, see Box 46.3).

Nation-states would have incentives to cooperate in managing migration to contain the flows, even though in the past, these incentives at the global level were almost non-existent, and some nations recruited workers through bilateral agreements such as the Bracero Program in the United States during the 1940s and 1960s, and the German Gastarbeiter (Guest worker) Program in the 1960s (Calavita 2010, Castles and Miller 2009).

If we assume that there is an agreement on the number of migrants that are allowed in a particular nation-state, the debate then turns to issues around rights, citizenship, national identity

---

Box 46.3 Global compacts for migration and refugees

Within the 2030 Agenda for Sustainable Development, migration is recognised in the UN Sustainable Development Goals (SDGs) as one of the means to reduce inequality within and among countries and as a call on countries to adopt well-managed migration policies (Target 10.7), protect the rights of migrant workers, especially women (Target 8.8), and reduce remittance transfer costs (Target 10.c). In December 2018, the Global Compact for Refugees (GCR) and the Global Compact for Safe, Orderly and Regular Migration (GCM) were adopted. These non-binding agreements lay out a set of principles, objectives and partnerships for the governance of refugees and migration. They both recognise that refugees and migrants are entitled to the same universal human rights and fundamental freedoms, however, these are distinct groups governed by separate legal frameworks. The GCM lays out a number of 23 objectives for 'safe, orderly and regular migration' which include issues from data collection on migration for evidence-based policies, enhance availability and flexibility of pathways for regular migration, facilitate fair and ethical recruitment and prevent, combat and eradicate trafficking in persons in the context of international migration, strengthen international cooperation and global partnerships among others. The GCM is an exercise in coordination and cooperation in the 'global governance of migration', however, many governments have expressed their non-adherence to these set of guidelines as they contradict their 'national interests'. As of early 2019, examples of some of these governments include the United States, Austria, Hungary, Chile, Brazil and Poland.

Source: Intergovernmental Conference to Adopt the Global Compact for Safe, Orderly and
Regular Migration, A/CONF.231/3, Available at: https://undocs.org/en/A/CONF.231/3

---

and the role of migrants in labour markets (Cornelius et al. 2004). This is the case in liberal–democratic states of the OECD for instance. Ruhs (2013) extends the analysis beyond OECD countries to show that 'bringing the state back in' in migration debates means dealing with the trade-off between 'numbers vs. rights' when it comes to the protection of migrant rights and the regulation of labour migration. In a nutshell, Ruhs' argument posits that in deciding and defining an immigration policy, nation-states operate within the trade-off of determining how many migrants to allow, and with which rights – the corollary being that some countries might decide to allow higher number of migrants at the expense of rights.

One of the key problems with both approaches from the mainstream tradition in IPE lies not only in the rationality attributed to the nation-state per se, but the fact that the nation-state is the life and soul as unit of analysis. This obscures the multifaceted nature of international migration as well as the variegated cultural, economic and social processes that types of migration entail. This trend followed what Wimmer and Glick Schiller call the 'second variant of methodological nationalism: naturalisation' by which empirical-oriented social sciences have systematically taken for granted nationally bounded societies as the natural unit of analysis (Wimmer and Glick Schiller 2002: 579). The following section looks into approaches that try to overcome 'methodological nationalism' in different ways.

Globalisation and the roots of inequality: critical approaches in IPE

No one has taken a purely realist approach to the study of international migration that would require us to infer the behaviour of nation-states as reflected in their policy choices from the structure of the international system (Hollifield 2012: 8). However, territoriality is an important dimension of nation-states as they exercise control over its boundaries through notions of migration and immigration. The problematisation of territoriality has been a key endeavour of human geographers (Collyer and King 2015, Delaney 2005). Much of the focus of migration research within this paradigm suits strands of IPE associated with a critical tradition as it also allows to explore the intertwined and co-constitutive relationship between structure and agency (Elias 2010; Kofman 2015; Pellerin 2015; Phillips 2011).

Another example of questioning territoriality in migration studies comes from the 'transnational turn' which posits that 'transmigrants' or 'transnational migrants' are immigrants whose daily lives depend on multiple and constant interconnections across international borders and whose public identities are configured in relationship to more than one nation-state (Glick Schiller et al. 1995: 48). The term has been developed to challenge assertions that treat migrants as 'uprooted', as if migrants had no linkages with their home communities (Basch et al. 1994; Glick Schiller et al. 1992).[6]

A critical IPE[7] standpoint looks at migration dynamics from a political economy perspective that analyses the supply and demand of migrant labour as well its articulation with transnational migrant networks, production structures and nation-state policies that give migration and labour migrants' experiences variegated outcomes. In this way, global labour migrations are framed as a result of changes in the configuration of *power* in global capitalism which produce certain dislocations by transnational capital and particular demands of certain types of labour are created (Bauder 2011; Cohen 1987). As a result of complex transformation in global production and the mobility of capital, migrant workers become – according to some scholars – a structural necessity (Basok 2002; Preibisch 2010). To fill 'labour shortages', migrants become the option by some nation-states which put in place different schemes to attract this labour to particular sectors, such as agriculture, construction, fishing and the service economy. Much has been written about the vulnerabilities experienced by migrant workers in these sectors and the challenges of legal protection (Vosko 2018).

Governments have put in place different temporary migration schemes to attract a specific pool of workers for a short period of time under strict contractual relationships. These temporary migration schemes take different forms, and range from *kafala* systems in the Gulf (Jureidini 2014) to different seasonal agriculture programs in agriculture (Chattier 2019) or by signing bilateral labour agreements (see Wickramasekara 2011).

In some variants of critical IPE scholarship, the fact that labour markets are socially constructed is not a novelty (Bauder 2011; Pellerin 2015), and therefore, approaches that study labour migration take into account the different and conflicting roles of actors involved in the movement of people: from government regulations, to the role of corporations and diverse actors involved in the business of migration which have also been termed the 'migration industry' (Gammeltoft-Hansen and Sørensen 2013; Hernández-León 2005).

An important contribution from critical IPE scholarship lies in the engagement with processes termed 'globalisation' from a truly critical position. This involves an analysis of the winners and losers from the transformations in the economy and the social relations within and across nation-states that render the process unequal and with different consequences for all the actors involved. In this vein, the view that contemporary globalisation is an expanding force connecting markets, nation-states and people in a 'current age of migration' (Castles and Miller 2009) also shows that labour migration has been asymmetrical and uneven. Migration from the South to the North has received vast academic and policy attention (Kofman 2015) while South–South migration has been underestimated, even though this trend has begun to change, as the body of literature expands to address concerns in the Global South. For example, the recently labelled 'migration crisis from Venezuela' calls for further understanding of these South–South flows (see Box 46.4).

A critical engagement with globalisation naturally allows a better understanding of inequality. Many approaches in migration research have seen the causes of migration at the heart of inequality, either in wages (neoclassical economics), labour market opportunities which are differentiated by skill levels, lifestyles of migrants and access to information and social networks among many other factors. Income and wealth inequalities between origin and destination countries exacerbate flows. Traditions within neoclassical economics have influenced this way of thinking for many years, in which wage differentials continued to be the main variable for explanation of movement. Inspired by initial studies on internal migration from rural to urban areas, the argument was that urban labour markets would absorb supplies of labour in rural areas, thus raising wages. As the labour supply in urban areas would increase, then wages would fall again giving place to the equalisation of wages between rural and urban areas, and therefore, internal migration would stop (Lewis 1954). This simple 'model' was expanded to explain international migration between countries at the 'macro level', that is, without taking into account the individual considerations as to why some people would decide to migrate. Critical scholars have engaged with other factors that explain the whole set of complexities around labour movement which include not only wage differentials, but also different motivations of migrants and their families as well as the institutional mechanisms at the global, regional and national levels that restrict labour migration for some groups, and allows others (such as highly skilled workers who are not traditionally called 'migrants').

In sum, critical scholars of IPE have contributed to broadening the unit of analysis by their plural engagement with other disciplines, therefore nation-states, migrants, multinationals

---

Box 46.4 What constitutes a 'migration crisis'?

In the last years, the scale and rate of international migration and refugee movements have attracted vast attention in the media and policy circles. However, the wide-ranging and unimaginable responses to these 'crises' also attract attention. It is important to take a historical view in assessing the concept of 'crisis' to shed light on the nature of power dynamics in the world economy that make us pose the question in light of 'crisis for whom?'. Between the end of the eighteenth and nineteenth centuries, the process of creating newly independent nation-states became relevant, with examples such as the US (1776), Haiti (1804), Mexico (1810), Honduras (1821) and Belgium (1830). The process of replacing empires with nation-states took also the form of forced population transfers, attempts to create homogenous national spaces with populations mapped onto territory (Bhabha 2018: 17). The proper idea of 'international' migration became more apparent.

Taking a long-view of history as suggested by Bhabha (2018) allows us to think critically of the ethical dimensions and implications of trying to 'fix' these 'migration crises'. Without critical historical thinking, measures to reduce 'distress migration' will fail in the medium and long term, without attention to legitimate quests for greater social, political, and economic equality (Bhabha 2018: xiv). The language of 'crisis' obscures the complexity of these movements by imposing a fixed and dominant framework – the perceived threat to the already present community – over the other critical and relevant variables which include the possibility of social enrichment, of local and geopolitical enhancement, of interconnectivity and technological gain (Bhabha 2018: 30).

(the role of capital), international organisations and many actors have been included in the analysis also across spatial lines (problematising regions, cities and localities).

Key migration issues within IPE

This section aims to shed light on important aspects of migration that have been approached from a 'migration studies' as well as some strands of 'critical IPE' which advocate for a deep study of the social foundations that underpin the global economy. These issues entail a whole set of intertwined complexities in migration processes. They cover gender and social reproduction, debates around skills, segmentation in labour markets, the migration and development nexus and global supply chains and labour chains.[8]

There is also the need to adopt the framing of 'migrants' and not 'migration' to emphasise the place of human beings front and centre in contemporary debates (Pearson and Sweetman 2019: 1). Amid so-called 'migration crises' (see Box 46.4), many scholars believe it imperative to 'humanise' debates around migration. An important contribution comes from feminist theory in migration studies and IPE that shift our attention to the *gendered* norms and patterns of labour migration as well as dismantling misconceptions and myths about women migrant workers and their work. Feminist approaches have been key in highlighting the role of 'global care chains' (Hochschild 2000) to describe women's care for children transnationally. Hochschild (2000) studied the case of Filipino women migrant workers in the United States who provided childcare to families while other women in the Philippines were taking care of their children. In this way, a 'chain' of care work across borders depicts how domestic workers depend on other women care-givers to provide care for the families that stay in the origin country.

The topic of care leads to rethinking production beyond the productive capacities of migrants, but also to highlight the nature of the social relations that underpin capitalist economies. Therefore, if we understand socio-economic inequalities to be embedded in the functioning of the global capitalist economy, then gender inequalities are fed within them too. The connections between production and *social reproduction* – that is, the way people care for each other in families, communities, and nations (Bastia and Piper 2019: 16) needs to come to light and critical feminist scholarship has been key in giving visibility to social reproduction in the global economy (e.g. Elias 2010 among others).

A focus on the gendered dynamics of migration also allows to unpack the *segmentation* that takes place in labour markets. Within the body of literature on labour market segmentation, the constitution and formation of segments continues to be much debated (Cain 1976; Fine 1998; Osterman 1975). The concept of segments evolved to illustrate the variability and unpredictability of outcomes within labour markets that obey to complex regulatory mechanisms. One of the important implications of this approach is that the evolving traditions of theorists of segmentation posit that when addressing labour market issues, the idea of causality differs substantially from neoclassical economics, since the emphasis on socially constructed segments leads to multi-causal explanations.

When it comes to migration, migrants have been found to be segmented according to different categories – race, citizenship, gender, ethnicity, etc. – Bauder (2006) demonstrated the social, cultural and institutional natures of the link between international migration and the regulation of labour markets by showing how migrants and immigrants perform distinct roles in society and in the labour market. Inspired in the work of Peck (1996) and Bourdieu (1984), Bauder brings back the notion of labour markets being socially constructed and shows how income and wages are not the only variables explaining migrant labour integration in Berlin and Vancouver.

Labour market segmentation approaches applied to the study of migration focus on the labour market demand in richer countries for migrant workers based on employers' demands while governments facilitate these demands by putting in place specific visa systems of different temporary nature (and in specific sectors, for example in agriculture). Scholars who have been involved in using these approaches range mainly from anthropology, sociology and economic geography (Samers and Collyer 2017).

Another important element in driving forms of segmentation in labour markets lies in 'skills'. A country that emphasises skills as the primary criterion upon which to issue visas will experience a different pattern in the growth and composition of its immigrant population from that of a country that constructs a policy-mix based on family reunification and refugee status (Bettel and Hollifield 2010: 6).

In the empirical literature on migration that looks at skills from a human capital perspective, scholars have historically relied on measurable proxies of 'skills' such as years of education, professional training and host country language skills (Stark and Bloom 1985). These data constraints have encouraged a 'dichotomy' between the 'skilled and highly skilled' and 'low-skilled' or sometimes even labelled 'unskilled'. As Hagan et al. (2015:11) pointed out: 'categories such as unskilled and even low skilled function as a black box: obscuring, instead of revealing, the social processes by which certain workers perform distinct jobs that also require knowledge, competences and tacit skills'. By studying Mexican migrants in the US over a five-year study, Hagan et al. (2015) show how social skills can sometimes translate into entrepreneurial activities of return migrants in Mexico from the United States, and they conceptualise the learning of skills as a lifelong and gendered process that is not restricted to an individual's time in school or in the workforce, it also shaped by the migratory cycle, experience and context.

Another manifestation of the dichotomy vis-à-vis skills is highlighted by Faist (2018: 289):

> with respect to the highly skilled mobiles, spatial movement is often considered economically efficient and thus desirable by policy-makers and even researchers. Apparently, no social integration is involved with respect to this categorization. Allegedly, a win–win situation applies: countries of origin, countries of destination, and the highly skilled themselves all benefit from cross-border ties. In this perspective, national economic competitiveness in global markets leads to higher productivity.

And furthermore,

> the discursive juxtaposition of category 'labour migrants' vs. category 'highly-skilled in itself is an outcome of upholding and reproducing social inequalities on a national and global scale, in this case the social mechanism of hierarchization of migrants and highly skilled mobiles.
>
> *(Faist 2018: 289)*

Skills' debates lead also to notions of development. The relationship between international migration and development is complex. People are motivated to migrate internationally because of poverty and lack of opportunities at home, and then migration can potentially enable not only their personal improvement but also lead to development at home – by sending remittances. These connections are referred to as the 'migration–development nexus' (Van Hear and Sørensen 2003). One of the fundamental questions here lies in understanding the relationship between economic development and migration, and vice versa. An argument that has been put forward by Martin and Taylor (1996) states that for the very poor, financial resources are a constraint to migration, therefore, when economic development provides access to more financial capital it encourages more people to seek opportunities abroad up until a point of development in which financial capital is no longer a constraint and people (in theory) fulfil their aspirations in the home country, and thus, international migration declines (the 'migration hump'). This is a generalisation that has been further researched and questioned giving place to mixed views on the migration–development nexus. Another important aspect within this debate relates to the role of remittances in development (Özden and Schiff 2007). Pessimists argue that remittances do not spur development because households spend the extra money on conspicuous consumption (rather than investment), they also drive inequalities between communities that receive remittances and those that do not, and may create dependency on a remittance economy (for examples of these arguments see Castles and Miller 2009, and Faist 2008). On the other hand, optimists argue that remittances can foster investment, contribute to poverty alleviation in developing countries and are a source of income for countries (Adams and Page 2005).

Another aspect of the migration–development nexus refers to 'brain drain', the loss of skilled labour in developing countries due to international migration. In recent years, the negative aspect of 'brain drain' has been articulated through a 'brain gain' as debates turned to 'circular migration' referring to the movement back and forth of skilled migrants between countries of origin and destination, bringing in 'social remittances' (Levitt 1998) which include ideas, and social practices which contribute to the construction of schools, social organisations and other institutions (on top of financial remittances previously discussed).

The final aspect to cover in this section refers to global production and its organisation through vast networks of (global) supply chains which expand across geographies fragmenting the labour process (Cattaneo et al. 2010; Gereffi et al. 2005). Barrientos (2013) showed how contracting practices within these global supply chains (or global production networks) may lead to instances of unfree labour and how the presence of 'labour chains' should be analysed in the context of the commercial dynamics that drive global production in different sectors, which demand particular forms of migrant labour. In this way, production structures intersect with migration regimes rendering different outcomes in recruitment forms with different provisions on protection and outcomes on rights (Andrees et al. 2015; Mieres 2018). The issue of labour chains and the ways in which migrant workers are incorporated in vast networks of production has brought to light the exploitation of migrant workers and it has also encouraged a new area of 'recruitment regulation' to include not only nation-states but other actors such as multinationals at the top of the supply chains which should embrace 'ethical' or 'fair' recruitment practices (Gordon 2015).

The way forward: how migration reshapes the discipline of IPE

This chapter reviewed 'migration' from an I(G)PE standpoint with a special focus on labour migrants. It provided a roadmap to understand how classical conceptualisations of IPE rooted in IR have been blind to the issue of migration, and how this omission is corrected by more critical strands of I(G)PE.

Perspectives rooted in 'critical' I(G) PE have been dealing with many of the issues addressed by migration scholars but without necessarily talking to each other. Critical IPE has been thorough in its theorisation of globalisation and unequal power structures, and labour movement across borders also lie at the heart of these. We are seeing advances in the field and cross-fertilisation in the conversations. IPE would greatly enrich from a more mature engagement on issues around scale and space with a specific 'migration lens'. This is needed to enrich traditions of IPE that are already dealing with the functioning of labour markets, either domestically and across borders, and taking migration policies both as 'dependent' and 'independent' variables to unpack its complexities.

The rich tradition of inter and cross-disciplinary engagement both of migration studies and critical IPE is key to advance on theorisations around the 'global political economy of migration'. In determining the research questions, the complex interactions and linkages between macrostructures and agency need to be determined, and how these change over time, so that a lens on 'temporality' can be added to migration within IPE. This would allow to further explore why people cross borders, what types of migration are being driven, how migrants (through the different visas and statuses) are incorporated into receiving societies, either in labour markets but also beyond. In this way, the everyday power relationships that critical IPE scholars seek to analyse will become more apparent, with its contradictions, complexities and changes.

It is not enough for IPE scholars to analyse the social foundations of the global economy, to truly unpack power imbalances a much more robust and substantive engagement in normative debates around 'open' vs. 'closed borders' in migration is needed. Empirical studies of migration can also engage with normative work on migration as it can inform debates around justice which are pretty much centred on a few countries from the 'Global North' as Song notices that political theorists have tended to focus on issues of migration in North America, Europe and Oceania because these are the places where many of them live (2018: 399). The rich empirical work on migration from the Global South can inform these debates from an 'IPE standpoint' by questioning the nature of the 'brain drain', the impacts of migrant relatives on those who stay and the role of remittances from a global distributive justice perspective that takes inequality seriously. Also, in contemporary issues, the formation and development of the 'migration crisis' in the Global South – of different nature and generating mixed flows – challenges assumptions on what constitutes a 'crisis', 'crisis for whom' and with what power consequences. These are new issues that I(G)PE scholars can begin to engage with in order to advance an integrative agenda on migration within IPE while fully recognising the gendered nature of the processes that underpin these evolving circumstances.

Notes

1 This chapter expresses the views of the author and it does not reflect the official views of the ILO.
2 Important normative issues around justice also arise, and a wide literature in philosophy and political theory addresses these. Limitations of space do not allow an exploration here but interested readers should consult Ruhs and Chang (2004), Carens (2013) and Song (2018).
3 The author subscribes to the notion that IPE has matured as a discipline in itself.
4 See Cohen (2008) and Phillips and Weaver (2011).
5 Structure understood as the anarchical system, and the position of nation-states within this structure, which constitute the level of analysis à la Waltz (see Waltz 1979).
6 However, not all migrants are transnational; this is an aspect that varies according to case studies and conceptualisations of migrants as units of analysis.
7 There are many strands of 'critical IPE', see Shields et al. (2011).
8 Due to space constraints, the selected issues reflect core areas for IPE thinking.

Bibliography

Adams, R. H. and Page, J. 2005. Do International Migration and Remittances Reduce Poverty in Developing Countries? *World Development*, 33(10): 1645–1669.
Andrees, B., Nasri, A. and Swiniarski, P. 2015. *Regulating Labour Recruitment to Prevent Human Trafficking and to Foster Fair Migration: Models, Challenges and Opportunities*. Geneva: ILO.
Barrientos, S. 2013. Labour Chains': Analysing the Role of Labour Contractors in Global Production Networks. *Journal of Development Studies*, 49(8): 1058–71.

Basch, L., Glick, N. and Szanton-Blanc, C. 1994. *Nations Unbound: Transnational Projects and the Deterritorialized Nation-State.* New York: Gordon and Breach.

Basok, T. 2002. *Tortillas and Tomatoes: Transmigrant Mexican Harvesters in Canada.* Montreal: McGill-Queen's University Press.

Bastia, T. and Piper, N. 2019. Women Migrants in the Global Economy: A Global Overview (and Regional Perspectives). *Gender & Development,* 27(1): 15–30.

Bauder, H. 2006. *Labor Movement: How Migration Regulates Labor Markets,* Oxford: Oxford University Press.

Bauder, H. 2011. The Regulation of Labor Markets through Migration. In Phillips, N. (ed.) *Migration in the Global Political Economy.* London: Lynne Rienner Publishers: 41–60.

Bhabha, J. 2018. *Can We Solve the Migration Crisis?* Cambridge: Polity Press.

Bourdieu, P. 1984. *Distinction: A Social Critique of the Judgement of Taste.* Cambridge: Harvard University Press.

Brettel C. B. and Hollifield, J. F. 2015. *Migration Theory. Talking across Disciplines.* London: Routledge.

Cain, G. 1976. The Challenge of Segmented Labor Market Theories to Orthodox Theory: A Survey. *Journal of Economic Literature,* 14(4), 1215–1257.

Calavita, K. 2010. *Inside the State: The Bracero Program, Immigration, and the I.N.S.* New Orleans: Quid Pro Books.

Carens, J. 2013. *The Ethics of Immigration.* Oxford: Oxford University Press.

Castles, S. 2012. Understanding the Relationship between Methodology and Methods. In Vargas-Silva, C. (ed.) *Handbook of Research Methods in Migration.* Cheltenham: Edward Elgar: 7–25.

Castles, S. and Miller, M. J. 2009. *The Age of Migration: International Population Movements in the Modern World,* 4th Ed. Basingstoke: Palgrave.

Cattaneo, O., Gereffi, G. and Staritz, C. (eds) 2010. *Global Value Chains in a Postcrisis World: A Development Perspective.* Washington, DC: World Bank.

Chattier, P. 2019. Beyond Development Impact: Gender and Care in the Pacific Seasonal Worker Programme. *Gender & Development,* 27(1): 49–65.

Cohen, B. 2008. *International Political Economy: An Intellectual History.* Princeton: Princeton University Press.

Cohen, R. 1987. *The New Helots: Migrants in the International Division of Labour.* Aldershot: Avebury.

Collyer, M. and King, R. 2015. Producing Transnational Space: International Migration and the Extra-Territorial Reach of State Power. *Progress in Human Geography,* 39(2):1 85–204.

Cornelius, W., Tsuda, T., Martin, P. and Hollifield, J. (eds) 2004. *Controlling Immigration: A Global Perspective.* Palo Alto: Stanford University Press.

Delaney, D. 2005. *Territory: A Short Introduction.* Oxford: Blackwell.

Elias, J. 2010. Making Migrant Domestic Work Visible: The Rights-based Approach to Migration and the Challenges of Social Reproduction. *Review of International Political Economy,* 17(5): 840–859.

Faist, T. 2008. Migrants as Transnational Development Agents: An Inquiry into the Newest round of the Migration-Development nexus. *Population, Space and Place,* 14(1): 21–42.

Faist, T. 2018. *The Transnationalized Social Question: Migration and Politics of Social Inequalities in the Twenty-First Century.* Oxford: Oxford University Press.

Fine, B. 1998. *Labour Market Theory: A Constructive Reassessment.* London and New York: Routledge.

Gammeltoft-Hansen, T. and Sorensen, N. (eds) 2013. *The Migration Industry and the Commercialization of International Migration.* London: Routledge.

Gereffi, G., Humphrey, J. and Sturgeon, T. 2005. The Governance of Global Value Chains. *Review of International Political Economy,* 12(1): 78–104.

Glick-Schiller, N., Basch, L. and Szanton-Blanc, C. 1992. *Towards a Transnational Perspective on Migration: Race, Class, Ethnicity and Nationalism Reconsidered.* New York: New York Academy of Sciences.

Glick-Schiller, N., Basch, L. and Szanton-Blanc, C. 1995. From Immigrant to Transmigrant: Theorizing Transnational Migration. *Anthropological Quarterly,* 68(1): 48–63.

Gordon, J. 2015. *Global Labour Recruitment in a Supply Chain Context.* Geneva: ILO.

Hagan, J., Hernandez-Leon, R. and Demonsant, J. 2015. *Skills of the 'Unskilled': Work and Mobility among Mexican Migrants.* Oakland: University of California Press.

Hernández-León, R. 2005. *The Migration Industry in the Mexico-US Migratory System.* California Center for Population Research: *Working Paper Series.* Available at http://escholarship.org/uc/item/3hg44 330#page-1.

Hochschild, A. 2000. Global Care Chains and Emotional Surplus Value. In Hutton, W. and Giddens, A. (eds) *On the Edge: Living with Global Capitalism.* London: Jonathan Cape: 130–146.

Hollifield, J. 2012. Migration and International Relations. In Rosenblum, M. and Tichenor, D. (eds) *Oxford Handbook of the Politics of International Migration*. Oxford: Oxford University Press.

International Labour Organization. (ILO). 2018. *Guidelines: Concerning Statistics of International Labour Migration* (Geneva). Available at: www.ilo.org/wcmsp5/groups/public/-dgreports/-stat/documents/meetingdocument/wcms_648922.pdf.

International Organization for Migration (IOM). 2018. *World Migration Report 2018*. Geneva: IOM.

Jureidini, R. 2014. *Migrant Labour Recruitment to Qatar: Report for Qatar Foundation Migrant Worker Welfare Initiative*. Doha: Bloomsbury Qatar Foundation.

Keohane, R. 1984. *After Hegemony: Cooperation and Discord in the World Political Economy*. Princeton: Princeton University Press.

Kofman, E. 2015. Globalization and Labour Migrations. In Edgell, S., Gottfried, H. and Granter, E. (eds) *The SAGE Handbook of the Sociology of Work and Employment*. London: Sage Publications.

Krasner, S. 1982. Structural Causes and Regime Consequences: Regimes as Intervening Variables. *International Organization*, 36(2): 185–205.

Levitt, P. 1998. Social Remittances: Migration Driven Local-level Forms of Cultural Diffusion. *International Migration Review*, 32(4): 926–948.

Lewis, A. 1954. Development with Unlimited Supplies of Labour. *The Manchester School*, 22: 139–192.

Maliniak, D. and Tierney, M. 2011. The American School of IPE. In Phillips, N. and Weaver, C. (eds) *International Political Economy: Debating the Past, Present and Future*. London: Routledge.

Martin, P. and Taylor, J. 1996. The Anatomy of the Migration Hump. In Taylor, J. (ed.) *Development Strategy, Employment and Migration: Insights from Models*. Paris: OECD.

Mieres, F. 2018. Migration, Recruitment and Forced Labour in a Globalising World. In: Triandafyllidou, A. (ed.) *Handbook of Migration and Globalisation*. Cheltenham and Northampton: Edward Elgar Publishing: 155–169.

Milner, H. 1997. *Interests, Institutions, and Information: Domestic Politics and International Relations*. Princeton: Princeton University Press.

O'Brien, R. 2000. Labour and IPE: Rediscovering Human Agency. In Palan, R. (ed.) *Global Political Economy: Contemporary Theories*. London: Routledge.

Osterman, P. 1975. An Empirical Study of Labor Market Segmentation. *Industrial and Labor Relations Review*, 28(4): 508–521.

Özden, Ç. and Schiff, M. (eds) 2007. *International Migration and Economic Development and Policy*. Washington, DC: The World Bank and Palgrave MacMillan.

Pearson, R. and Sweetman, C. 2019. Introduction: Gender, Development, and Migrants in a Global Economy. *Gender & Development*, 27(1): 1–13.

Peck, J. 1996. *Workplace: The Social Regulation of Labor Markets*. New York: Guilford.

Pellerin, H. 2015. Global Foreign Workers. Supply and Demand and the Political Economy of International Labour Migration. In Talani, L. and McMahon, S. (eds) *The International Political Economy of Migration*. London: Edward Edgar Publishing: 145–166.

Phillips, N. (ed.) 2011. *Migration in the Global Political Economy*. London: Lynne Rienner Publishers.

Phillips, N. and Weaver, C. (eds) 2011. *International Political Economy: Debating the Past, Present and Future*. London: Routledge.

Preibisch, K. 2010. Pick-your-own Labor: Migrant Workers and Flexibility in Canadian Agriculture. *International Migration Review*, 44(2): 404–441.

Ruhs, M. 2013. *The Price of Rights: Regulating International Labor Migration*. Princeton: Princeton University Press.

Ruhs, M. and Chang, H. 2004. The Ethics of Labor Immigration Policy. *International Organization*, 58(1): 69–102.

Samers, M. and Collyer, M. (eds) 2017. *Migration*. 2nd Ed. London: Routledge.

Shields, S., Bruff, I. and Macartney, H. (eds) 2011. *Critical International Political Economy*. London: Palgrave Macmillan.

Skeldon, R. 2012. Migration and its Measurement: Towards a More Robust Map of Bilateral Flows. In Vargas-Silva, C. (ed.) *Handbook of Research Methods in Migration*. Cheltenham: Edward Elgar: 229–248.

Song, S. 2018. Political Theories of Migration. *Annual Review of Political Science*, 21: 385–402.

Stark, O. and Bloom, D. 1985. The New Economics of Labor Migration. *American Economic Review*, 75(2): 173–178.

Talani, L. 2015. International Migration: IPE Perspectives and Impact of Globalization. In Talani, L. and McMahon, S. (eds) *The International Political Economy of Migration*. London: Edward Edgar Publishing: 17–36.

Taylor, M. 2008. (ed.) *Global Economy Contested: Power and Conflict Across the International Division of Labour*. London: Routledge.

UNHCR. n/d. *Who is a Refugee?* Available at: www.unrefugees.org/refugee-facts/what-is-a-refugee/.

United Nations, Department of Economic and Social Affairs, Population Division (UNDESA). 2017. *Trends in International Migrant Stock: The 2017 Revision*. United Nations database, POP/DB/MIG/Stock/Rev.2017.

Van Hear, N., Brubaker, R. and Bessa, T. 2009. *Managing Mobility for Human Development: The Growing Salience of Mixed Migration, Human Development Research Paper* 2009/20. UNDP.

Van Hear, N. and Sørensen, N. (eds) 2003. *The Migration-Development Nexus*. Geneva: IOM.

Vosko, L. 2018. Legal but Deportable: Institutionalized Deportability and the Limits of Collective Bargaining among Participants in Canada's Seasonal Agricultural Workers Program. *Industrial Labor Relations Review*, 71(4): 882–907.

Waltz, K. 1979. *Theory of International Politics*. Reading, MA: Addison-Wesley Publishing Company.

Weiner, M. and Russell, S. (eds) 2001. *Demography and National Security*. New York: Berghahn Books.

Wickramasekara, P. 2011. *Circular Migration: A Triple Win or a Dead End? Global Union Research Network Discussion Paper No. 15*. Geneva: International Labour Organization.

Wimmer, A. and Glick Schiller, G. 2002. Methodological Nationalism and Beyond: Nation-State Building, Migration. *Global Networks*, 2(4): 301–334.

47

International political economy and the environment

Gian Delgado Ramos

Introduction

The current global ecological crisis is so profound that it has been suggested that an epoch-scale boundary has been crossed, from the Holocene to the so-called Anthropocene (Crutzen 2002). Such a new geological epoch, a statement still in debate (Lewis and Maslin 2015), postulates that anthropogenic changes are of such a scale that they might be observable in future geological stratigraphic records. There is, however, no general agreement on when such epoch apparently began. Some date it when fossil fuels became the main energy source of capitalism, as early as the end of the eighteenth century with the use of coal. Others, at some point around halfway through the twentieth century, when a "Great Acceleration" started, noticed "a remarkable discontinuity in the human enterprise" that speed up most of economic, social and environmental indicators (Steffen et al. 2011).

The globalization of the economy, only possible by an accelerated development of the means of production and circulation of goods and services, has progressively coupled economic growth with energy and material consumption and environmental degradation. Material and energy consumption have increased, for the case of some materials – like cement – at higher rates than economic growth and certainly above population growth rates (Steinberger, Krausmann, and Eisenmenger 2010). This intense transformation of nature has caused a persistent transgression of the planetary boundaries, meaning the environmental limits within which humanity can safely operate (Steffen et al. 2015).

Biophysical impacts include the rise in global temperature and sea levels, ocean acidification and coral bleaching, biodiversity loss, deforestation, water, soil and air pollution, among others that take place at the global level, but also at the local and regional levels, which in turn can create synergies and feedbacks at all time and spatial scales.

Anthropogenic climate change has been unequivocally recognized in the Fifth Assessment Report of the Intergovernmental Panel on Climate Change – IPCC (IPCC 2014a) as well as in the *Global Warming of 1.5 Report*, which estimates that global warming is likely to reach 1.5°C between 2030 and 2052 if it continues to increase at the current rate (IPCC 2018). Land degradation, understood as the many processes that drive the decline of biodiversity, ecosystem functions or ecosystem services has been assessed by the (IPBES 2018), while the depletion or degradation of several key resources by the *GEO 5 and GEO 6 Report*, which warn, among other issues, that the current state of the environment is already constraining conventional development in some parts of the world (UNEP 2012; 2019).

The evolution of such global environmental conditions has certainly shaped the international environmental politics approaches, evolving from one centered on the availability/scarcity of natural resources (e.g., timber, fossil fuels, minerals or water), to others focused on the impacts of industrial practices, the concerns regarding population growth and, more recently, global environmental problems and the interplay of economic globalization and environmental regulation (Stevis and Assetto 2001).

In the following section some theoretical, as well as other aspects of International Political Economy and the Environment (IPE&E) are analyzed.

Mainstream theoretical perspectives on sustainability and their influence on IPE&E

The importance of environmental issues to international political economy (IPE) is definitely without discussion. How those issues are understood and in what way their priority is defined within the IPE body of knowledge is, nevertheless, far from being sufficient or consistent. International relations and the international political economy and environment (IPE&E) perspectives that emanate from the first one, tend to limit their analysis on how environmental problems and solutions arise and are framed, with the exception of intergovernmental negotiations (Stevis and Assetto 2001). This means that viewpoints, languages and tools of valuation, preferences and priorities in play are usually neglected. How IPE&E is framed, defines the degree of understanding on the social forces involved and their unequal capabilities and incidence over decision-making process, but moreover, reveals who is served and who is excluded under a given political imagination framework (Stevis and Assetto 2001).

Tracking IPE&E framing from a historical viewpoint offers more clarity for understanding how it has evolved and varied in specific sociopolitical and economic contexts. The modern idea of sustainability in which IPE&E is rooted actually is not new and has been extensively documented (Caradonna 2014). The first indications are identified around the concern on decline of resources, mainly due to the overexploitation of forests which supplied biomass, and other resources, to the local and incipient regional economies. It was a context in which population growth began to be seen as a problem for food supply (Malthus 1826). With the arrival of the second industrial revolution, which actually established regional economies and promoted a growing use of coal, concerns regarding the eventual exhaustion of local, regional and even national reserves of coal emerged in England (Jevons 1866), which was at that time the epicenter of capitalist relations of production. In such a context, and due to the intensification of socio-ecological impacts, mainly but not only in industrial cities, the desirability of a "steady state" of the economy was proposed, an alternative that, as visualized, wouldn't have to imply a setback of the human condition (Mill 1848); this proposal would later be recovered by H. Daly (1974).

By the end of the nineteenth century, in a context in which the third industrial revolution created the basic conditions for an internationalized economy, a clear rupture was set between conservationists and preservationists; among their main representatives in USA was, on one hand Gifford Pinchot, from the US Forest Service who was a conservationist, and on the other, the Club Sierra which had a preservationist viewpoint. While the former vision implied a reasonable use of natural resources, the latter considered that nature, mainly certain hotspots, should not be altered. It was not until the economy and its implications began to become globalized that the first signs for an IPE and later-on for an IPE&E began to be manifested. Accordingly, after two world wars that enabled a recovery of the international economy that suffered from a crisis of accumulation (Panitch and Gindin 2013), a rising consumption dynamic of energy and materials took off, producing in turn the germinal conditions for a global environmental consciousness.

The notion of sustainability as a social, environmental and economic ideal is thus a recent phenomenon that emerged from such postwar developmentalism that was highly criticized due to its environmental impacts (Carson 1962; Hardin 1968), but mostly because it implied the eventual exhaustion of key natural resources, mainly the conventional oil reserves (NRC Council 1962). The latter actually happened a few years after the meeting of Club of Rome (1968) when, in addition to the global oil shock of 1973, a peak oil in USA was experienced and was later apparently outstripped by the exploitation of unconventional reserves (i.e., shale oil and shale gas) (EIA 2015). As subscribed by Clapp and Helleiner (2012), "IPE was born in the 1970s, largely in response to changes in the 'real world'," with the breakdown of the Bretton Woods Monetary System, the oil shock, accumulated trade conflicts, the continuity of the so-called cold war and the growing demands of the Global South for a new political and economic order (e.g., the non-aligned movement of 1976).

As early as 1984, environmental implications of international trade, industrial activities and extractive activities by multinational corporations began to be considered within IPE, including issues of pollution havens (Lofdahl 1998; Pazienza 2014). Following the publication of the Brundtland Report in 1987 and the 1992 Rio Earth Summit, the notion of "sustainable development" arose, becoming increasingly present in political, social and academic narratives, including those of IPE&E (Clapp and Helleiner 2012). Since then, its mainstream perspective assumes that economic growth is not only compatible with sustainability, but necessary to attain it. Within such understanding, a *weak sustainability* approach has been embraced (UNEP 2011; WCED 1987).

More critical voices also emerged from the scientific world that was worried about the undesirable implications of certain technologies such as agrochemicals (Carson 1962) or nuclear energy (Caldicott 1978). As a result, some argued for a transformation of the relationship between human beings and nature, suggesting a reformulation of the economy and its ends. Consequently, different viewpoints emerged, from those like bio-economy (Georgescu-Roegen 1971), eco-development (Mellos 1988), deep ecology (Naess 1989), post-development (Escobar 1995) or eco-Marxism (Bellamy 2000; Gorz 2013), to proposals seeking conviviality (Illich 1973), the expansion of human capabilities (Sen 1999), de-growth pathways (D'Alisa et al. 2015), a prosperity without growth (Jackson 2017), or the "common good of humanity" (Delgado 2014). Of all that diversity, what it is evident is that the notion of sustainability is clearly a philosophical and political matter because it involves a reflexive exercise on how good life, the meaning of life, and the future of humanity are pictured (Delgado 2019a; O'Neill et al. 2018).

In any case, and considering the above, it can be argued that two general approaches dominate IPE&E perspectives nowadays, which in turn embrace distinctive postures on politics and sustainability, from reformist to anti-capitalist, and from those strong technocentric, to those strong ecocentric:

1   A sort of *conventional or mainstream approach* based on the dominant understanding of sustainable development that perceives environmental problems from a point of view that usually lacks critical sociopolitical analysis. In this approach, problems are seen in a generalist or aggregated way, while solutions are perceived as "recipes" that can be transplanted from

place to place (a sort of globalization of "best practices" or of greener technology transfer, typically executed in a top-down manner).

2   More *critical approaches* in which environmental problems are analyzed by taking into consideration the behavior and power structures in play, and thus, by acknowledging specific viewpoints, values, preferences and interests (Stevis and Assetto 2001). Normatively speaking, a critical approach expands IPE&E accountability on environmental politics, including building processes and capabilities for social and environmental just policies at different scales, an issue that is neither self-evident nor unproblematic as it constitutes what has been described as a "wicked problem" (Rittel 1973). Such critical approaches pay attention to alternative imaginaries of sustainability, its complexity and diversity at different spatial and temporal scales, as it seeks to transcend any arrangement in which environmental problems may become "the new opium for the masses", as provocatively expressed by Zizek (2008).

The affinity of IPE scientific literature with environmental issues tends to focus on the relationship of the environment, sustainable development and policy in a context of a globalized economy; climate change and its relationship with sustainable development, (neoliberal-) development and governance; as well as on the political ecology surrounding development, particularly within a neoliberal economic context.

Specifically, IPE&E scholarship focuses on global economic structures and processes, and to a certain degree, on the power relationships within them, therefore exploring:

a   How international economic regimes and institutions have addressed environmental issues, including environmental protectionism (Bechtel et al. 2012) or, more recently, the environmental footprint of military institutions, such as the Pentagon. This type of approach is vast. It embraces initiatives from the World Bank, the World Trade Organization or the International Monetary Fund and other regional developing banks (e.g., the Asian Development Bank or the Inter-American Development Bank); measures considered within foreign direct investment (FDI) schemes and trade agreements or treaties (e.g., North America Free Trade Agreement); arrangements taken within international cooperation or aid schemes either North–South or South–South; as well as other concerted plans of action for coping with climate change (UN Framework Convention on Climate Change and its Kyoto Protocol and its subsequent Paris Agreement), reverse land degradation (UN Convention to Combat Desertification and its Global Mechanism to assist countries in the mobilization of financial resources) or ending the ozone-layer depletion (Montreal Protocol on Substances that Deplete the Ozone Layer). It also includes the evaluation of international agendas such as Agenda 21 (1992–2000), the Millennium Development Goals (2000–2015) and, more recently, the adoption 2030 Agenda for Sustainable Development (2015–2030).

b   The economic provisions of international environmental initiatives as, for example, those arranged in trade provisions, financing arrangements (such as the Climate Fund) or carbon markets (see Layfield 2013; Newell 2014), among other actions within the context of international commerce (e.g., World Trade Organization rules and environmental policies or the investment-policy environment of the OECD Multilateral Agreement on Investment), cooperation, and finance (e.g., the environmental and social standards of the World Bank).

c   The nature of private governance regimes addressing the economy–environment interface (Christmann and Taylor 2012), due to four key issues: public concern, growth of green consumerism (mainly in the Global North), the diffusion of ecological knowledge and values, and the strengthening of the environmental regulatory framework (Williams 2001). It includes the literature on private environmental governance as a mechanism that helps to steer and coordinate corporate behavior, for example by improving the financial disclosure of climate risks within financial markets (by participating, for example, in projects such as the UNFCCC Non-state-Actor Zone for Climate Action – NAZCA, the Investor Network on Climate Risk – INCR, or the Climate Disclosure Standard Board – CDSB) (Zadek 2013). It also includes the actions taken by multinational corporations, either individually or through alliances, towards auto-regulatory schemes (i.e., corporate environmental and social responsibility measures) such as corporate certification mechanisms or eco-labeling (a voluntary certification that identifies products or services proven environmentally preferable overall), and voluntary standards for improving corporate environmental performance (e.g., ISO14000 and ISO14001; the International Air Transport Association's measures for coping climate change; the Round Table on Responsible Soy; or the Extractive Industries Transparency Initiative; among other private governance regimes related to soft-regulatory measures for cosmetics, novel technologies and other products and services).

d   The impacts of transnational environmental crime, which involves trading or smuggling across borders species, resources and pollutants in violation of prohibition or regulation established by multilateral environmental agreements (Elliott 2014).

IPE&E scholarship has a diversity of interpretations of the processes, incentives and actions mentioned above. Hence the findings will depend on the analytical lenses used.

A conventional or *mainstream approach* will recognize the value of market-oriented and policy centered measures, which are seen as key mechanisms for moving forward a "transformative agenda" that can embrace both economic development and sustainability, as stated by the 2030 Agenda for Sustainable Development. At the bottom of such understanding there is a belief, on one hand, that there is no inherent conflict between a capitalist economy and the environment, and on the other, that innovation and greener technology can improve both the economy and the environment. In fact, from a neoclassical economic point of view, environmental quality may be correlated to income as the *Environmental Kuznets Curve* – EKC sustains; a reading that has been amply criticized, even to the point of questioning its existence, at least when looking at environmental problems on a planetary scale (Dasgupta et al. 2002; Perman and Stern 2003).

As stated by the International Chamber of Commerce (ICC), "the ICC firmly believes that economic growth and open trade provide the best conditions in which to address key environmental challenges" (ICC 2009). Therefore, and from what can be perceived as a Global North perspective, "trade openness may engender an international ratcheting up of environmental standards as higher regulatory environmental standards of richer and greener countries spread to countries stating out with lower environmental standards" (Spilker et al. 2017). Limitations may come from a lack of information, technologies or existing capacities, but not from a contradictory nature of current relations of production; the weight that government delegations, certain industry groups and international institutions have in setting the agenda; or the approach used in itself. Decoupling economic growth from energy and material consumption is therefore seen as a solution, a vision that ensures that the existing economic and political structures can be preserved with certain modifications (Williams 2001).

A *critical approach* will seek to reveal instead, the existing contradictions between developmentalism and sustainability and, consequently, of the decoupling myth (Polimeni et al. 2015). It will also expose the asymmetrical power relationships in play and question the effectiveness of the proposed measures in the face of the dimension of environmental challenges and their impacts, such as climate change or biodiversity loss. Accordingly, free trade may induce overexploitation of labor and the environment, even more when national policies seek to profit from specialization (the idea of profiting from existing comparative advantages). The uneven international division of labor that supports the specialization of the Global North in manufactured goods and developing means of production while the Global South, at least most of it, continues to overexploit labor and the environment, but also reinforces its dependency through the importation of goods, technologies and capital from the Global North, has been extensively criticized since the 1950s, mostly by the dependency theory (Cardoso and Faletto 1979; Prebish 1950) and most recent by others, including the literature dealing with the so-called neoextractivism (Brand et al. 2016; Gudynas 2010). Such uneven international division of labor from a critical IPE&E viewpoint may be seen as the basis for the Global North to transfer most of the environmental costs of production and consumption to the Global South. For example, while the socioecological impacts of oil palm production are mostly experienced in the Global South, in countries like Indonesia, Malaysia or Thailand its transformation to biodiesel and its consumption tends to be seized by several countries of the Global North pursuing to be green, at least within their frontiers (in fact, this situation led to the approval of the Procedure 2016/2222(INI) on palm oil and deforestation of rainforests by the European Parliament).

An IPE&E critical approach also analyzes how problem framing and conflict management, as implemented in most international institutions, usually leads to a narrow or politically aseptic understanding of environmental issues (Irwin 2001), but also to a displacement of decision-making process from the national and local realms, where grassroot movements may exercise some influence, to the international arena (Williams 2001). Accordingly, it can also allow the recognition of how the clash of weak and strong sustainability viewpoints actually, "facilitates the formation of alliances around the principles of environmental economics and environmental management" (Williams 2001), because the institutions and actors with decision-making power, usually identified themselves with a weak sustainability position.

Besides the discrepancies and tensions between different IPE&E approaches, it has to be pointed out that relevant issues are still missing or have not been sufficiently studied by IPE&E scholars such as the spread and intensification of consumer culture and the consequent need for reducing consumption patterns (mostly in the Global North) and promoting a circular economy (Cohen 2010; Dauvergne 2008); the globalization of risk and the scalation of technological unwanted implications (Beck 1992; EEA 2001; 2013); the emergence, distribution and articulation of environmental justice organizations (see: EJOLT (www.ejolt.org); Byrne et al. 2017; Sandler and Pezzullo 2007); the even more profound global inequality and its drivers (Alvaredo et al. 2018); gender and global politics (Shepherd 2010); the environmental implications of global financial speculation, including urban and land speculation (Cotula 2012; Delgado 2019b); the role of international cooperation, private foundations and alike in framing the global environmental agenda and structuring networks of key actors and alliances; or furthermore, a comprehensive understanding of the existing synergies, cobenefits and trade-offs among the diversity of action agendas currently underway at the international level (which, for example, is indeed a challenge for a fruitful implementation of Sustainable Development Goals (SDGs) (ISC 2017)).

Building a common action agenda for coping with climate change and biodiversity and ecosystem services degradation

Established in 1988 by the UN General Assembly, the Intergovernmental Panel on Climate Change seeks to provide with regular meta-analysis on the current state of scientific knowledge on climate change to the 195 signing members of the United Nations Framework Convention on Climate Change (UNFCCC). Since then and until 2019, the IPCC has published five Assessment Reports. The first Assessment Report was issued in 1990, followed by others in 1995, 2 years before the adoption of the Kyoto Protocol; in 2001 which focused on adaptation; in 2007 when the IPCC received the Nobel Prize; and in 2014 before the negotiations that led to the Paris Agreement. Currently the IPCC is under its Sixth Assessment Report cycle. The expected report will be published in 2021–2022. Besides the Methodology Reports that provide practical guidelines for the preparation of GHG inventories under the UNFCCC, the IPCC has also published 14 Special Reports on key issues such as the "Global Warming of 1.5°C" (IPCC 2018). It has also sponsored a group of experts for delineating a "Research and Action Agenda on Cities and Climate Change Science" (Prieur-Richard et al. 2018).

For all such reports, thousands of scientists around the globe volunteered within a process that has pushed forward the co-generation of information for policymaking. The IPCC does not conduct research in its own, it evaluates the existing scientific literature and certain gray literature in order to identify the strength of scientific agreement and where further research is needed. The co-generation of meta-analysis is supported on the articulation of scientists at a global scale for working in a multidisciplinary manner, even sometimes reaching interdisciplinarity, which in turn has enabled a positive environment for promoting other inter- and transdisciplinary efforts beyond the IPCC structure and its assessing outcomes. This is a major step that has changed science–policy interface at the international level, while impacting scientific practices at different scales. IPCC impact on scientific publications and science has undoubtedly increased with each Assessment and Special Report, as scientometric analyses show (Vasileiadou et al. 2011).

In general, it is assumed that there is a high rigor in the IPCC review process, despite the fact that there is indeed room for improvement, for example in what respects to a better coordination among working groups (Schiermeier 2010), and a desirable reduction of both physical and economic bias and of scientific fields separation which is a part and consequence of the division of the IPCC assessing work in three working groups (scientific basis of climate system and climate change; vulnerability of socioeconomic and natural systems; and mitigation of climate change) (Bjurström and Polk 2011).

The IPCC has received critiques and additional recommendations. From errors in the 5th Assessment Report (Schiermeier 2010); the lack of Global North and Global South balanced participation (Delgado 2018; Vasileiadou et al. 2011)); the limited expertise on indigenous knowledge, understanding and experience (Ford et al. 2016); and gender-related issues within the IPCC (Gay-Antaki and Liverman 2018); to a diversity of aspects on procedures, governance and management, conflict of interest policy and communications strategies (InterAcademy Council 2010).

It has also confronted a diversity of pressures from both governments delegations and the private sector. On one hand, the first ones demand relevant, complete, accurate but non-prescriptive assessments due to the interest of some signatories of the UNFCCC for keeping non-binding targets, indeed a reason to point out that the apparent "policy-neutrality" may be extremely misleading (Havstad and Brown 2017b). Furthermore, such neutrality, based on a questionable assumption of a model science that accepts that scientific practice does not requires epistemic value-laden judgments, implies that decisions on standards of evidence can be deferred "by simply communicating the evidence plus its attendant probabilities and leaving it for others to choose the 'correct' evidential standards" (Havstad and Brown 2017a).

On the other hand, the private sector either seeks to undermine the credibility and legitimacy of the IPCC (like the Global Climate Coalition or the Information Council for Environment have intended), or insists on keeping regulations at the national level while playing an important role during the final stage of their preparation through the conventional process of commenting, but also by the means of a direct dialogue in order to ensure that the private sector viewpoints and, in some cases, proactive actions, are somehow incorporated (this do not refers to any alleged conflict of interests due to business-related associations of the IPCC (*The Economist* 2010)). In fact, the 5th Assessment Report positively subscribes that the private sector has an indispensable role to play in addressing climate change, and therefore foresees it necessary to enable appropriate environments for business action (IPCC 2014b). Organized civil society also participates in such a process, but it is usually limited to certain international non-governmental organizations (NGOs) that are usually linked to international institutions, mainly the United Nations (UN) and the World Bank. Grass root movements are thus excluded, constraining their action to the national and local contexts, which, as said, can be seen as a way to reduce their eventual impact in international politics (Newell 2012; Williams 2001).

With a similar goal as the IPCC, the Intergovernmental Science-Policy Platform on Biodiversity and Ecosystem Services (IPBES) was established in 2012 for strengthening science–policy interface for biodiversity and ecosystem services for the conservation and sustainable use of biodiversity, long-term well-being and sustainable development. With over 130 member states, the IPBES works in four areas: assessments, policy support, building capacity and knowledge, and communications and outreach. It publishes global, regional or sub-regional assessments on biodiversity and ecosystem services, in addition to thematic reports. The IPBES Global Assessment, published in May 2019, follows almost a decade and a half after the only global report on the issue, the *Millennium Ecosystem Assessment*, published in 2005.

IPBES's four regional reports were published in 2018 for Africa, America, Asia Pacific, Europe and Central Asia, along with the *Land Degradation and Restoration* report. Such reports came after the publication of the first thematic assessment on *Pollination and Food Production* (2016) and the methodological assessment report on *Scenarios and Models of Biodiversity and Ecosystem Services* (2016).

Based on the work of volunteer scientists, IPBES assesses current scientific knowledge useful for decision-making, as the IPCC does, but it also reviews information about practices based on indigenous and local knowledge through a technical support unit on the issue, hosted by UNESCO; the latter, along with capacity building and policy support, are indeed major differences with the IPCC (Brooks et al. 2014). IPBES's work involves – as observers – NGOs organizations, conventions and civil society groups. Several memorandums of cooperation have been signed as well with key partners such as the Convention on Biological Diversity, the Convention on International Trade in Endangered Species of Wild Fauna and Flora, the Convention to Combat Desertification, Future Earth and the International Union for Conservation of Nature.

The IPCC and IPBES's experiences are without doubt valuable experiences for enhancing science–policy interface while moving forward a more robust scientific multidisciplinary knowledge at an international scale. However, certain key aspects have to be considered, such as how scientific networks not communities, are themselves engaged in policy, but mostly, into politics; how such networks are conformed unevenly; and how the powerful groups within it dominate certain agendas and the way they are framed, including the proposed solutions or actions. It is in that sense that transparency and openness play a determining and increasing role in the success of experiences similar to IPCC and IPBES, but moreover, on the degree to which the main findings actually influence policy and decision making (Vasileiadou et al. 2011; Vohland et al. 2011). In that sense, the 2030 Agenda for Sustainable Development still has work to do (Coopman et al. 2016; ISC 2017). See Box 47.1.

Box 47.1 Transformational pathways, SDGs and the production of knowledge

The 2030 Agenda for Sustainable Development is assumed as an integrated effort composed of 17 goals or SDGs. Each SDG has set a variety of targets related to one or more dimensions of the mainstream understanding of sustainable development. As such targets can generate positive, competing or clear-cut negative interactions with each other. A better understanding on how those interactions may impact the concrete advancement of the 2030 Agenda is indubitably desired. Multidisciplinary approaches are thus being used to identify the elements that mutually support each other, but also those that generate trade-offs (Coopman et al. 2016; Kanie 2017; ISC 2017). Ideally, inter- and transdisciplinary approaches would push further the implementation and the outcomes of SDGs as they may allow to question the very foundations from which the Agenda departs, particularly in relation to sustainability framing. Since the 2030 Agenda, as said, is based on a mainstream understanding of sustainability (i.e., sustainable development), tensions between different SDG targets are thus to be expected, particularly among those intended to promote economic growth, sustainability and social justice. Considering the above, the 2030 Agenda therefore confronts two challenges. On one hand, enhancing SDG's interactions on the basis of a more robust understanding on how nexuses, cobenefits and trade-offs may variate depending on the scales and the political, socioeconomic and cultural contexts. On the other, reframing the Agenda itself on the basis of a more critical approach, a broader social participation and even by embracing co-production processes of knowledge for decision-making in which the figure of the expert is still relevant but certainly not enough due to the reflexive and context-dependent nature of sustainability and the meaning of "good life." In this context it is to be noticed that the Global South faces particular challenges, not just because most of the expected population and the expansion of the built environment may be experienced there, but also due to the correlation and persistence of diverse issues such as of poverty, inequality, lack of public services, low levels of education, economic and technological dependencies, limited funding and credit, constrained capacity building, poor accountability and corruption. Actions to be taken can thus not be transplanted from place to place, a fact that demands a reconsideration of how governance is understood and implemented. In order for the Agenda to be meaningful for both the North and the Global South, and for it to have a real transformational power, a "transformational way of thinking" is required to enable a "coproduced transformative governance", namely, innovative top-down and bottom-up modes of participation and decision making. The identification of main gaps or misalignments at the local level and across spatial scales, as well as the search for potential conduits for resolution within a reasonable timeframe of action, will be a first relevant step towards a transformative governance and transformative actions that involve governments (at all levels), economic units, different types of institutions (including universities) and lay people, or all inhabitants that may be either affected in a business as usual scenario or benefit from a tangible and profound transformation of the relationship between human beings and nature.

IPE&E has followed but also adopted dissimilar positions in relation to the above, moving from a conventional reading to a more critical one. Yet, even when IPE&E scholarship has contributed to such a debate, it is for the most part still trapped in disciplinary and multidisciplinary practices that constrains its full potential. If interdisciplinarity is understood as a way of producing novel, comprehensive and complex knowledge on the basis of reframing the mainstream research questions and narratives, and if transdisciplinarity means introducing as well different kinds of knowledge and practices, including the co-production of knowledge, critical IPE&E approaches may particularly benefit as succinctly explored in the following section.

Towards inter- and transdisciplinary IPE&E knowledge

Reducing IPE&E gaps or weaknesses by approaching hybrid disciplines and fields of knowledge and promoting more collaborative research and co-production schemes of knowledge could enable a more comprehensive approach to global environmental change and its implications, which take place in specific socio-cultural, historical and political contexts. It may also enhance a more fluid and productive dialogue between the diversity of IPE&E perspectives that could enable a deeper reflection, not only about IPE&E evolution, but of the very nature of knowledge production and the objectives it pursues.

IPE&E scholarship can broaden its horizons by transcending linear, simplified and fragmented approximations that tend to characterize mainstream IPE&E approaches.

Moving towards inter- and transdisciplinary approaches may help to consolidate a critical science with socioecological awareness, which in itself implies a holistic, multidimensional and multicriterial vision. The resulting interaction and articulation of epistemologies, theories and methodologies may actually translate into the renovation or reformulation of the narratives regarding nature, society, politics and culture; a defiance that would compel a vision able to address the prevailing reality and the possible futures that can be derived from it. The latter is usually an objective of contemporary hybridized disciplines such as ecological economics, political ecology, environmental anthropology, environmental history, social ecology, among others, which to some degree have already enriched IPE&E literature.

To the extent that such hybridized disciplines interact with each other, but moreover, with other types of knowledges and practices besides the scientific ones, new "fields of knowledge" could emerge and evolve, enabling a more vigorous advancement of informed and successful transformational pathways (for a further description of such process see Delgado 2015).

Knowledge co-production is useful for policy and decision making as it is a localized process, but also because it is carried out with and ideally for the people. The co-production of knowledge for policy cannot be a neutral exercise. It demands elucidating at least the following issues: (1) how the co-production itself is defined, framed and put into practice; (2) which languages and communication tools are more constructive and useful; (3) who are the actors involved or that should be involved; (4) how concepts are constructed; (5) which are the assumptions behind definitions, assessments, measurements and valuations; and (6) which are the expected outcomes from one or another analytical perspective. Since this has vast implications for problem framing (according to who and for whom there is a problem or challenge to be confronted; in what sense, scale of value and vision of desirable or undesirable future), novel IPE&E perspectives may need to answer a key question within environmental politics: how to frame environmental issues for both people and nature, all in a context of inclusion, equality, justice and compliance with planetary boundaries (Delgado 2015; O'Neill et al. 2018).

Recognizing that all methodology involves a particular worldview from which a set of objectives emanate that may well influence and even limit or disrupt the existing epistemological and ontological positions, a novel IPE&E scholarship should ideally maintain principles of openness and transparency, beginning by making explicit its objectives, components, values and given weights. It may also benefit from fostering a constructive dialogue and spaces of trust among actors, not only scientific ones, but others, including the civil society, which is particularly important as their members can supervise, question and even reformulate the work of scientists and their interaction with policy-makers (Ungar and Strand 2005).

Conclusion: transformations towards sustainability?

Developing transformational pathways towards sustainability implies more than transitional efforts and certainly even more than incremental changes as both are based on a reformist approach to sustainability in which there are no fundamental changes of the system. In the best case, an improved version of the existing system might be pursued.

Transformations towards sustainability therefore,

> refer to fundamental changes in structural, functional, and cognitive socio-technical-ecological systems that lead to new patterns of interactions and outcomes [...] transformations towards sustainability however, are likely to be deeply political and contested because different actors will be affected in different ways, and may stand to gain or lose as a result of change.
>
> *(Patterson et al. 2017)*

Because transitional and transformational pathways are not necessarily mutually exclusive, the latter demands, normatively speaking, recognizing the contradictory nature of capitalism in order to transcend it. As is well known, capitalism has produced staggering wealth while degrading the natural basis that supports both capitalism and life itself (Foster 2002; O'Connor 1991). Such contradictory nature, not necessarily constrained to capitalist relations of production, also encompasses the vast capability to produce poverty, informality and inequalities of all types, including racial and gender ones (IPSP 2018). Social inequalities are consequently relevant for a comprehensive understanding of the above-mentioned discontinuity and its implications because the transgression of ecosystems has not been equally produced, but also because the capabilities of human beings to tackle undesirable impacts and to eventually promote a change are without doubt uneven (Biermann et al. 2016). In other words, the so-called Anthropocene is not a consequence of an ascending species, on the contrary, "intra-species inequalities are part and parcel of current ecological crisis" (Malm and Hornborg 2014).

Yet, and as already said, while some back reformist-action pathways or even transformational ones (Hopwood et al. 2005), others still believe that green liberalism still is the answer (Steinberg 2010). In any case, as Newell puts it, a globalizing capitalist political economy, "provides the context in which the challenges of sustainability have to be met given the imperative of near-term action" (Newell 2012). It is a complex and multifaceted challenge as the main drivers of environmental systems' destabilization tend to have high inertia and path-dependencies and, thus, may potentially act as barriers to successful and timely action (UNEP 2012); a context that indeed places the *politics of policy* in a permanent contested position, as prominently explained in Ferguson's *anti-politics machine* (Ferguson 1994).

In this context, and in order to continue to be relevant, IPE&E will need to evolve, ideally coproducing new knowledge capable of offering comprehensive answers to the changing socio-ecological crisis that humanity faces. Accordingly, IPE&E may actively play a significant role in the construction of a new political era for sustainability, one based on a radical transformative thinking and frank transformative actions that take into account local–regional features, capacities, constraints and potentialities, as well as global dynamics, including North–South and South–South interactions.

Bibliography

Alvaredo, D., Chancel, L., Piketty, T., Saez, E. and Zucman, G. 2018. *World Inequality Report 2018*. World Inequality Lab. On-line: https://wir2018.wid.world/files/download/wir2018-full-report-english.pdf.

Bechtel, M., Bernauer, T. and Meyer, R. 2012. The green side of protectionism. *Review of International Political Economy* 19(5): 837–866.

Beck, U. 1992. *Risk Society: Towards a New Modernity*. London: Sage.

Bellamy, F. 2000. *Marx's Ecology: Materialism and Nature*. New York: Monthly Review Press. USA.

Biermann, F., Bai, X., Bondre, N., Broadgate, W., Chen, C., Dube, O., Erisman, J., Glaser, M., Van der Hel, S., Lemos, M., Seitzinger, S. and Seto, K. 2016. Down to earth: Contextualizing the Anthropocene. *Global Environmental Change* 39: 341–350.

Bjurström, A. and Polk, M. 2011. Physical and economic bias in climate change research. *Climatic Change* 108 (1–2): 1–22.

Brand, U., Dietz, K. and Lang, M. 2016. Neo-Extractivism in Latin America – one side of a new phase of global capitalist dynamics. *Ciencia Política* 11 (21): 125–129.

Brooks, T., Lamoreux, J. and Soberón, J. 2014. IPBES ≠ IPCC. *Trends in Ecology & Evolution* 29 (10): 543–545.

Byrne, J., Glover, L. and Martínez, C. 2017. *Environmental Justice. Discourses in International Political Economy*. Vol. 8. New York: Routledge.

Caldicott, H. 1978. *Nuclear Madness*. New York and London: Norton.

Caradonna, J. 2014. *Sustainability. A History*. Oxford: Oxford University Press.

Cardoso, F. and Faletto, E. 1979. *Dependency and Development in Latin America*. Berkeley: University of California Press.

Carson, R. 1962. *Silent Spring*. Boston, MA: Houghton Mifflin.

Christmann, P. and Taylor, G. 2012. International Business and the Environment. In: *The Oxford Handbook of Business and the Natural Environment*. Oxford: Oxford University Press.

Clapp, J. and Helleiner, E. 2012. International political economy and the environment: Back to the basics? *International Affairs* 88 (3): 485–501.

Cohen, M. 2010. The international political economy of (un)sustainable consumption and the global financial collapse. *Environmental Politics* 19 (1): 107–126.

Coopman, A., Osborn, D. and Ullah, F. 2016. *Seeing the Whole. Implementing the SDGs in an Integrated and Coherent Way*. Stakeholder Forum; Newcastle University. On-line: https://sf.stakeholderforum.org/fileadmin/files/SeeingTheWhole.ResearchPilotReportOnSDGsImplementation.pdf.

Cotula, L. 2012. The international political economy of the global land rush. *Journal of Peasant Studies* 39 (3–4): 649–680.

Crutzen, P. J. 2002. Geology of mankind. *Nature* 415: 23.

D'Alisa, G., Demaria, F. and Kallis, G. 2015. *Decrecimiento. Vocabulario para una nueva era*. Barcelona: Icaria.

Daly, H. 1974. The economics of the steady state. *The American Economic Review* 64 (2): 15–21.

Dasgupta, S., Laplante, B., Wang, H. and Wheeler, D. 2002. Confronting the Environmental Kuznets Curve. *Journal of Economic Perspectives* 16 (1): 147–168.

Dauvergne, P. 2008. *The Shadows of Consumption*. Massachusetts: MIT Press.

Delgado, G. (coord). 2014. *Buena Vida, Buen Vivir*. Mexico City: CEIICH, UNAM.

Delgado, G. 2015. Complejidad e interdisciplina en las nuevas perspectivas socioecológicas. *Letras Verdes* 17: 108–130.

Delgado, G. 2018. ¿Hacia una transición urbana sustentable en América Latina? *Observatorio del Desarrollo* 7 (20): 7–24.

Delgado, G. 2019a. *Asentamientos urbanos sustentables y resilientes*. Mexico City: CEIICH, UNAM.

Delgado, G. 2019b. Real estate industry as an urban machine. *Sustainability* 11 (7): 1980.

Economist. 2010. A time for introspection. *The Economist*. On-line: www.economist.com/science-and-technology/2010/02/04/a-time-for-introspection.

EEA. 2001. *Late Lessons from Early Warnings: The Precautionary Principle 1896–2000*. Copenhagen: European Environment Agency.

EEA. 2013. *Late Lessons from Early Warnings: Science, Precaution, Innovation*. Luxembourg: European Environment Agency.

EIA – Energy International Agency. 2015. *World Shale Resource Assessments*. On-line: www.eia.gov/analysis/studies/worldshalegas/.

Elliott, L. 2014. Governing the International Political Economy of Transnational Environmental Crime. In: *Handbook of the International Political Economy of Governance*: 450–468. Cheltenham: Edward Elgar.

Escobar, A. 1995. *Encountering Development: The Making and Unmaking of the Third World*. Princeton: Princeton University Press.

Ferguson, J. 1994. *The Anti-Politics Machine. Development, Depoliticization and Bureaucratic Power in Lesotho*. Minnesota: Minnesota Press.

Ford, J., Cameron, L., Rubis, J., Maillet, M., Nakashima, D., Cunsolo, A. and Pearce, T. 2016. Including indigenous knowledge and experience in IPCC assessment reports. *Nature Climate Change* 6(4): 349.

Foster, J. 2002. Capitalism and Ecology. The Nature of the Contradiction. *Monthly Review* 54 (4): 6–16.

Gay-Antaki, M. and Liverman, D. 2018. Climate for women in climate science. *Proceedings of the National Academy of Sciences* 115 (9): 2060–2065.

Georgescu-Roegen, N. 1971. *The Entropy Law and the Economic Process*. Harvard: Harvard University Press.

Gorz, A. 2013. *Capitalism, Socialism, Ecology*. London: Verso.

Gudynas, E. 2010. *The New Extractivism of the 21st Century*. Washington DC: Center for International Policy.

Hardin, G. 1968. The tragedy of the commons. *Science* 162 (3859): 1243–1248.

Havstad, J. and Brown, M. 2017a. Inductive risk, deferred decisions, and climate science advising. In: *Exploring Inductive Risk*. Richards, K. and Elliott, T. (eds.): 101–126. New York: Oxford University Press.

Havstad, J. and Brown, M. 2017b. Neutrality, relevance, prescription and the IPCC. *Public Affairs Quarterly* 31 (4): 303–324.

Hopwood, B., Mellor, M. and O'Brien, G. 2005. Sustainable development: Mapping different approaches. *Sustainable Development* 13 (1): 38–52.

ICC. 2009. *ICC Recommendations on Trade and Climate Change*. Paris: International Chamber of Commerce. On-line: https://cdn.iccwbo.org/content/uploads/sites/3/2009/02/ICC-recommendations-on-trade-and-climate-change.pdf.

Illich, I. 1973. *Tools for Conviviality*. New York: Harper & Row.

InterAcademy Council. 2010. *Climate Change Assessments. Review of the Processes and Procedures of the IPCC*. On-line: https://archive.ipcc.ch/pdf/IAC_report/IAC%20Report.pdf.

IPBES. 2018. The IPBES Assessment Report on Land Degradation and Restoration. *Intergovernmental Science-Policy Platform on Biodiversity and Ecosystem Services*. Bonn.

IPCC. 2014a. *Climate Change 2014*. IPCC. Cambridge: Cambridge University Press.

IPCC. 2014b. *Fifth Assessment Report. Climate Change 2014: Mitigation of Climate Change. Summary for Policy Makers*. IPCC. Cambridge: Cambridge University Press.

IPCC. 2018. *Global Warming of 1.5 °C*. IPCC (IPCC). On-line: www.ipcc.ch/sr15/.

IPSP. 2018. *Rethinking Society for the 21st Century. Vol. 1: Socio-economic transformations. International Panel on Social Progress*. Cambridge: Cambridge University Press.

Irwin, Rosalind. 2001. Posing Global Environmental Problems from Conservation to Sustainable Development. In: *The International Political Economy of the Environment*. Dimitris, A. and Stevis, V. (eds.): 15–38. London: Lynne Rienner.

ISC. 2017. *A Guide to SDG Interactions: From Science to Implementation*. International Science Council. On-line: https://council.science/cms/2017/05/SDGs-Guide-to-Interactions.pdf.

Jackson, T. 2017. *Prosperity without Growth. Foundations for the Economy of Tomorrow*. New York: Routledge.

Jevons, W. 1866. *The Coal Question*. London: Macmillan.

Kanie, N. and Biermann, F. 2017. *Governing through Goals. Sustainable Development Goals as Governance Innovation*. London: MIT Press.

Layfield, D. 2013. Turning carbon into gold: The financialisation of international climate policy. *Environmental Politics* 22 (6): 901–917.

Lewis, S. and Maslin, M. 2015. Defining the Anthropocene. *Nature* 519: 171–180.

Lofdahl, C. 1998. On the environmental externalities of global trade. *International Political Science Review* 19 (4): 339–355.

Malm, A. and Hornborg, A. 2014. The geology of mankind? A critique of the Anthropocene narrative. *The Anthropocene Review* 1 (1): 62–69.

Malthus, T. 1826. *An Essay on the Principle of Population*. London: Macmillan.

Mellos, K. 1988. Theory of Eco-development. In: *Perspectives on Ecology*: 59–74. London: Palgrave Macmillan.

Mill, J. S. 1848. *Principles of Political Economy, with Some of Their Applications to Social Philosophy*. London: Longmans.

Naess, A. 1989. *Ecology Community and Lifestyle*. Cambridge: Cambridge University Press.

Newell, P. 2012. *Globalization and the Environment*. Cambridge; Massachusetts: Polity Press.

Newell, P. 2014. The international political economy of governing carbon. In: *Handbook of International Political Economy of Governance*. Phillips, A. and Payne, N. (eds.): 414–432. Cheltenham: Edward Elgar.

NRC – National Research Council. 1962. *Energy Resources*. Washington: The National Academies Press.

O'Connor, J. 1991. On the two contradictions of capitalism. *Capitalism, Nature, Socialism* 2 (3): 107–109.

O'Neill, D., Fanning, A., Lamb, W. and Steinberger. J. 2018. A good life for all within planetary boundaries. *Nature Sustainability* 1 (2): 88–95.

Panitch, L. and Gindin, S. 2013. *The Making of Global Capitalism*. London: Verso.

Patterson, J., Schulz, K., Vervoort, J., Van der Hel, S., Widerberg, O., Adler, C., Hurlbert, M., Anderton, K., Sethi, M. and Barau, A. 2017. Exploring the governance and politics of transformations towards sustainability. *Environmental Innovation and Societal Transitions* 24: 1–16.

Pazienza, P. 2014. *The Relationship between DFI and the Natural Environment*. New York; London: Springer.

Perman, R, and Stern, D. 2003. Evidence from panel unit root and cointegration tests that the Environmental Kuznets Curve does not exist. *Australian Journal of Agricultural and Resource Economics* 47 (3): 325–347.

Polimeni, J., Mayumi, K., Giampietro, M. and Alcott, B. 2015. *The Jevons Paradox and the Myth of Resource Efficiency Improvements*. London: Routledge.

Prebish, R. 1950. *The Economic Development of Latin America and its Principal Problems*. Economic Commission for Latin America. New York: CEPAL.

Prieur-Richard, A., et al. 2018. *Global Research and Action Agenda on Cities and Climate Change Science*. IPCC Cities. On-line: www.wcrp-climate.org/WCRP-publications/2019/GRAA-Cities-and-Climate-Change-Science-Full.pdf.

Rittel, H. 1973. Dilemmas in a general theory of planning. *Policy Sciences* 4 (2): 155–159.

Sandler, R. and Pezzullo, P. 2007. *Environmental Justice and Environmentalism*. Massachusetts: MIT Press.

Schiermeier, Q. 2010. IPCC flooded by criticism. *Nature* 463: 596–597.

Sen, A. 1999. *Development as Freedom*. Oxford: Oxford University Press.

Shepherd, L. 2010. *Gender Matters in Global Politics*. New York: Routledge.

Spilker, G., Koubi, V. and Bernauer, T. 2017. International political economy and the environment. In: *Oxford Research Encyclopedia of Politics*. Thompson, W. (ed.) Oxford: Oxford University Press.

Steffen, W., Persson, Å., Deutsch, L. Zalasiewicz, J., Williams, M., Richardson, K., Crumley, C., Crutzen, P., Folke, C., Gordon, L., Molina, M., Ramanathan, V., Rockström, J., Scheffer, M., Schellnhuber, H. J. and Svedin, U. 2011. The Anthropocene: From global change to planetary stewardship. *AMBIO* 40 (7): 739.

Steffen, W., Richardson, K., Rockström, J., Cornell, S., Fetzer, I., Bennett, E., Biggs, R., Carpenter, S., de Vries, W., de Wit, C., Folke, C., Gerten, D., Heinke, J., Mace, G., Persson, L.,Ramanathan, V., Reyers, B. and Sörlin, S. 2015. *Planetary Boundaries: Guiding Human Development on a Changing Planet* 347 (6223): 1259855.

Steinberg, T. 2010. Can Capitalism Save the Planet? *Radical History Review* (107): 7–24.

Steinberger, J., Krausmann, F. and Eisenmenger, N. 2010. Global patterns of materials use. *Ecological Economics*. 69 (5): 1148–1158.

Stevis, D. and Assetto, V. (eds.). 2001. *The International Political Economy of the Environment*. London: Rienner Publishers.

UNEP 2011. *Green Economy. Pathways to Sustainable Development and Poverty Eradication*. Nairobi: UNEP.

UNEP. 2019. *Global Environmental Outlook – GEO 6*. Cambridge: Cambridge University Press.

UNEP. 2012. *Global Environmental Outlook – GEO 5*. Nairobi: UNEP.

Ungar, P. and Strand, R. 2005. Complejidad: Una reflexión desde la ciencia de la conservación. *Nómadas* 22: 36–46.

Vasileiadou, E., Heimeriks, G. and Petersen, A. 2011. Exploring the impact of the IPCC Assessment Reports on science. *Environmental Science & Policy* 14 (8): 1052–1061.

Vohland, K., Mlambo, M., Domeignoz, L., Jonsson, B., Paulsch, A. and Martinez, S. 2011. How to ensure a credible and efficient IPBES? *Environmental Science & Policy* 14 (8): 1188–1194.

WCED. 1987. *Our Common Future*. World Commission on Environment and Development. https://sswm.info/sites/default/files/reference_attachments/UN%20WCED%201987%20Brundtland%20Report.pdf.

Williams, M. 2001. In search of global standards: The political economy of trade and the environment. In: *The International Political Economy of the Environment*. Dimitris, A. and Stevis, V (eds.): 39–61. London: Lynne Rienner.

Zizek, S. 2008. *Censorship Today: Violence, or Ecology as a New Opium for the Masses*.

Zadek, S. 2013. Will business save the world? In: *The Handbook of Global Companies*: Wiley Online Library. Chapter 28: 474–491. https://onlinelibrary.wiley.com/doi/10.1002/9781118326152.ch28.

48

Conceptual hinges between international political economy and Economic Intelligence

Some disciplinary challenges

Fredy Rivera and Lester Cabrera

Introduction

Realist theoretical tradition and positivist approaches of international relations erroneously positioned intelligence as a process that is exclusive to national security and defense organizations that also involve politics outside of the state. However, under an international system that prioritizes economic and commercial factors in addition to the strategic goals of the different actors that form a part of that system, states face the necessity of determining the characteristics, evolution, and deployment of economic rationalities to make better decisions and with this improve or maintain the levels of development that the societies they represent intend to reach. Under that premise, Economic Intelligence emerges as a part of the effort by state decision-makers to achieve better positioning within the world economic and commercial architecture. However, trying to understand this international system from a purely commercial perspective or through positions that prioritize the role of interests and the greatest possible maximization of profits ostensibly limits the capacity for understanding and analyzing the political and strategic factors that affect the complex realities under which nations operate and make decisions.

Keeping in mind the existence of the political element linked to decisions regarding regional and international markets necessarily implies that other analytical perspectives and ideas emerging from International Political Economy (IPE) should be implemented to harmonize the intersection between politics and economics in international contexts. This disciplinary exercise, without holistic implications, opens the door to the integration of new categories stemming from Economic Intelligence and brings about greater results for the strategic application of state and corporate decisions. In this sense, the combination of intelligence factors and IPE goes beyond the results that could be obtained through a foreign policy that operates with conservative and traditional approaches.

Thus, the relationship between IPE and Economic Intelligence is carried out and visualized not only within the field of decisions made by states but it also substantially modifies a number of concepts and processes that are evident in both disciplines. In particular, it introduces the geoeconomic analytical basis, the level and complexity of the processes of interdependence, and the notion of security in broader terms than those exposed by realists or liberals to enhance the complexity in the diagnosis of the international system, and the possible decisions made by nations in this context. As this dynamic is achieved, merging additional theoretical and disciplinary spheres, the "hinge" function emerges based on the mentioned concepts and the disciplinary perspectives of IPE and intelligence. Therefore, this chapter investigates those "conceptual hinges," incorporating the relevant areas of Economic Intelligence that serve to reduce the level of uncertainty within the decision-making process at the highest levels of state.

To achieve this objective, an analysis is carried out on the implications and difficulties represented by the separate disciplines as well as the issues that emerge from establishing links between them. Thus, in broadening the conceptual field, the "hinges" cannot be considered as exclusive segments. Instead, they acquire relevance through the interrelationships with other concepts upon broadening each of the disciplinary perspectives that they represent. IPE and Economic Intelligence, in addition to being linked through the mentioned concepts, also reflect areas of attention that modify the traditional analytical perspectives that stem from international relations, foreign policy, and national security.

It concludes that the crossing, exchange, and interpretation of the "conceptual hinges" between IPE and Economic Intelligence can demystify the sheltered nature of intelligence that states deploy in their interdependent actions. In addition, the chapter suggests theoretical and analytical tools that can be used in the debate surrounding development in nations and states in contexts of complexity and globalization.

The necessity of a discussion about Economic Intelligence

The efforts to imbue intelligence with a scientific and transdisciplinary quality have been valid for at least three decades. The exchange of knowledge and academic recognitions have moved along a difficult institutional path full of misunderstandings and political ignorance on the part of the establishment in many countries. While the initial debates were channeled through the particular interests of the Anglo-Saxon community, concerned with historical analysis or with the organizational structure of intelligence services with an emphasis on the U.S. context, the growing academic production from diverse regions remains significant for the social sciences, generating concerns and conceptual advances, as well as epistemic and methodological exchanges with economics, political science, geopolitics, and other theoretical fields that include communication, anthropology, and sociology, to name some areas of interdisciplinary research.

Intelligence – assumed as a space of knowledge that condenses various methods, subject matters, and projections in internal and foreign policy – has also been researched in terms of the analysis of neo-institutionalism and international law. It would be inaccurate to highlight the historical, economic, and sociopolitical studies related to national security without mentioning the role played by military and police intelligence services during political periods driven by military dictatorships.

In general terms, many analytical and operational fields from distinct disciplines converge in the field of Intelligence but from the strategic point of view. This is seen as the highest level of intelligence based on its inclusive capacity to define national interests and objectives, as well as to plan in function of these goals and to protect them (McDowell 2009). The classic concept of Strategic Intelligence formulated by Sherman Kent in the middle of the twentieth century, has not been subject to substantial changes but has incorporated diverse methodological, theoretical, and technologies aspects to comprehend the current reality and use it as a significant element for future planning (Berkowitz and Goodman 1989: 3–4).

Intelligence in general, and Economic Intelligence in particular, encompass a series of elements tied to appreciation and comprehension, especially within the prevailing context of globalization. Beyond the general perceptions that equate it to a secret activity that includes dark segments in its implementation, intelligence constitutes a key function for the performance of any contemporary state because the distinct internal and external actors that intervene in political and economic situations require accurate, objectively analyzed, and verified information to make better decisions. Those decisions are understood not only from the perspective of security or national interests that must be protected, but they also involve other aspects of daily life within the society in which the state must make decisions that allow it to improve its development (Hildebrand and Hughes 2017). However, the classic conception of intelligence includes intrinsic elements that complicate its treatment, systemization, and comprehension. Within these elements, it is possible to point to the epistemic root, an object of study, and a methodological approach.

Box 48.1 Intelligence: a definition

In this work, we use the framework used by Julian Richards (2001), to explain that it is difficult to provide a unique definition of Intelligence. From his point of view, Intelligence is not the same for the entire world. We need to know how different cultures analyze information, for what purpose, and if that multiple orientations share some point in the analysis process. But at the same time, Richards provides that Intelligence cannot be fully understood, if we don't consider some levels of execution (strategic, operational, and tactical level). And if we add that Intelligence could be seen as a bad or blurrier activity in the eyes of society, the complexity of the context is high to create or assume a categorical position about a concept of Intelligence.

Nevertheless, we consider Intelligence not only as a concept, but also as a category of study. In that sense, Intelligence is the activity created by a requirement, from the public or private sector, considering information recollected and processed under a scientific method, to achieve objectives in order to take better decisions, and thus, reduce uncertainty. But also, we need to consider that one of the most important things in Intelligence is the necessity of constant feedback, especially when we consider some different analysis methods because, only through that, should it be possible to understand if the current method is the most accurate option to make a better diagnosis of demanded process.

In the proposal definition, the main elements to build Intelligence are, from one perspective, the analysis, and the relation between decision-making and the reduction of uncertainty, for another. Those aspects are the base of any definition of Intelligence, no matter what sphere of work this definition is applied to (public or private sector).

Considering the epistemological base or origin, the discussion is centered on whether intelligence constitutes its own field of study or discipline. And despite that this approach is not new, the perspective of its evolution, the context in which it applies, and the regional and cultural differences of each particular country mean that the epistemic uncertainties related to intelligence remain valid (Rogg 2018).

Although there is no singular conceptualization about the epistemological nature of intelligence, it is possible to visualize a link between positivist currents and the form in which intelligence has been studied. The works that have been made about the subject, particularly those derived from Anglo-Saxon traditions and reasoning, conceive intelligence as a description of events, related to experiences linked to situations of conflict or, alternatively, as a way of constructing and planning for vital decisions where intelligence plays a role (Richards 2010). However, in the twenty-first century, a significant portion of the studies about intelligence began to include a different epistemic root, criticizing the extreme positivism and generating approaches that look to interpret events beyond what is evident. An example of that is the incorporation of the cultural variable in different analyses and perspectives of intelligence, especially applied to interpretations regarding terrorism and other conflicts (Somiedo 2012).

Intelligence also possesses a complexity in explanations and implications when it comes to classifying this field of study. According to Julian Richards, intelligence has been approached from two main perspectives throughout history. First, there is a notion related to the comparison of intelligence systems, on an internal state level and in international scope as well. That point of view emphasizes organizational and bureaucratic criteria, leaving aside the processes revolving around the analysis and production of intelligence. This perspective is explained by the strong influence of US political science on the understanding of intelligence systems, taking as a base the configurations within the state and specifically the controls and counterbalances that an intelligence system must take into consideration (Richards 2010).

The second point of view observes that intelligence systems are also considered as part of the object of investigation, especially in the area of strategic studies. However, the focus of comparison derives from the failures in intelligence services and more concretely in the consequences that those errors have provoked when intelligence services have been unable to warn about violent actions with a regional and worldwide impact (Buckley 2017; Jackson 2008).

Beyond the existing problems revolving around the theoretical and disciplinary classification of intelligence, it is necessary to remark that there are common issues related to the erroneous identification made between intelligence and the distinct areas of national security, incorrectly understanding intelligence exclusively as part of security (Bulger 2016). When we speak of traditions and structure of thought, we refer precisely to those that have for decades related intelligence with realism and positivism in the field of international relations. In effect, the states that have opted to use security-related intelligence preferentially as a functional tool for inclusion in regional and global spaces have not managed to achieve their objectives in an integral manner, considering this perspective an area of Strategic Intelligence thought (Hastedt 1998).

Box 48.2 Dimensions of intelligence

There are different dimensions of Intelligence. But despite the many perspectives made by academics, the general dimensions of Intelligence are:

- As a product. Intelligence is worthless if cannot produce some consequence in the decision-making process, either to reinforce a decision or change some part of it. But to do that, Intelligence should be applied in a document, in order to assure that the analysis has been made.
- As a process. This perspective of Intelligence is related to the Intelligence Cycle. To create Intelligence, we need to pass some areas inside that cycle, often starting with the political or technical requirement; then comes the gathering of information and data, and next, the stage of analysis as a unique part. Then, the next step in this cycle is the dissemination to the key actors, to create a policy or take action, as a final part of the cycle.

- As an institution. Often, Political Science observes Intelligence as an institution. That means that Intelligence can be located as a part of the public apparatus or bureaucracy of the state. Therefore, it is possible to find some organization, with its own name, dedicated to producing Intelligence inside the government. From this perspective, Intelligence has fluctuations inside the check and balance dichotomy, and also people with political responsibility in charge of these institutions.
- As a function. This dimension is similar in comparison to the last one. When we define Intelligence as a function, we look at Intelligence as a part of the state organization. In this sense, Intelligence can be considered as another branch of the multiple functions of the government, but without an "intelligence" name. In other words, Intelligence should be seen as a normal governmental activity, even if this activity doesn't have the level of institutionalization that requires and locates the actors or departments that carry out that function.
- As a field of study. Intelligence has transited a long road to be part of the Strategic Studies beyond the contributions of disciplines as Political Science or even the military area. This is because Intelligence has been located as a part of Political Science from the institutional point of view, and with the military sphere through the application. But now, Intelligence has been trespassing national borders and is positioned as a unique field of study, with its own concepts and theoretical approaches.

Thus, there are different fields and dimensions of intelligence that are applied to diverse areas in the public sector as well as the private sector and have as a primordial element obtaining high-quality processed information. This is a sort of hermeneutic resource that is employed to make better decisions and reduce the level of uncertainty in obtaining results. One of the dimensions of intelligence that seeks to protect the security of a country – understood as the relational set of state and private institutions along with the population as a whole – is Economic Intelligence. One of the principal goals of this form of intelligence is safeguarding the economic, financial, and business interests of a particular country through the structuring and systemization of state information on an internal and external level (Gonzáles and Larriba 2011).

Another definition is offered by Jeffrey Herzog, who mentions that "Economic Intelligence is information about how those outside the collecting organization's country develop material goods that are interpreted and presented to inform policymakers" (Herzog 2008: 302). Finally, the other interpretation of Economic Intelligence comes from Gustavo Díaz, who indicates, "Economic Intelligence definitely has a clear state component since it helps states achieve regional gains by gathering information – that is interpreted and spread in time – to reduce the uncertainty of those in charge of the decision-making process" (Díaz 2016: 157).

Based on the definitions mentioned, it is possible to find some points and criteria to establish a better understanding of the concept. First, Economic Intelligence is a perspective of analysis and a set of actions that are associated with the protection and defense of the interests of the state. In other words, Economic Intelligence looks at the position of a particular country to achieve national and international goals. The political and strategic interpretation carried out by the state regarding "its interests" is linked with the economic, financial, and commercial positioning that a specific nation requires. In this sense, Economic Intelligence is configured as a tool of the state and for the state, reinforcing its actions, monitoring the contingencies of markets and corporations, and controlling possible threats that could emerge in regional and global spaces.

This last factor can be observed by keeping in mind that the security of a state is no longer limited exclusively to the protection of material elements or related to the classic institutions of security and defense. Economy and its evolution, especially in a negative sense, are considered among the non-conventional threats that can strongly affect states and their societies (Chandra and Bhonsle 2015). In present times, it would be unthinkable to consider national security not linked to Economic Intelligence when it comes to analyzing, for instance, the negative consequences that a nation would suffer from being infiltrated by international organized crime groups. These kinds of links, arising from the international economy, have not received sufficient attention from the academic sectors that work on issues related to international relations and political economics.

Economic Intelligence is related to the protection and safeguarding of a nation's objectives and interests because it adds certainty to the performance of the state actors and businesses through the analysis and assessment of correct decisions. It reduces levels of uncertainty and contingencies in confronting volatile economic scenarios by general models that can explain the success or failure of political intervention or strategy. In addition, similar to all intelligence cycles, Economic Intelligence obtains, provides, and distributes sensitive and sophisticated information between the politicians responsible for making transcendental decisions. This data and knowledge are acquired through distinct mechanisms or operations – some of which are open and others are reserved and secret – that will serve to achieve the planned objectives.

The application and analysis of Economic Intelligence have a double dimension. On one side is the internal facet of the nations, and on the other is the external scope related to regional and international settings that form the basis of observation and intervention, constituting the foundation to establish guidelines for increasing or decreasing levels of development. But although all the definitions signal the relevance of the international aspect, they also mention the diagnostics that are elaborated to improve the decision-making process, are from inside the state apparatus. (Olier 2016).

It is important to mention that Economic Intelligence positioning cannot be considered as homogeneous or free of complexities. One example of this is the confusion that exists, in conceptual terms, among interpretations related to Economic Intelligence, and those that are referred to Competitive Intelligence. According to Eric Nenzhelele, this last concept is a form that businesses possess to enhance their competitive structure in relation to other actors in similar areas or goals. Competitive Intelligence is also directly associated with the manner in which businesses establish a diagnostic process with respect to the international environment that surrounds them to take better decisions (CITEX 2011; Nenzhelele 2015).

The tendency to link Economic Intelligence with Competitive Intelligence reflects not only in the conceptual environment but also in practice. This happens because the same actors intervene in similar fields but not the same. In effect, while the state can be a participant in the execution of a better Competitive Intelligence process, it is also true that the final result of such intervention is not seen in the state structure but on private business. Competitive Intelligence has a range of action that crosses internal and external spaces, and in turn, it depends on the objectives, interests, and even the actual nature of the business, which may have a national or transnational focus. On the other hand, Economic Intelligence preferentially focuses its analysis specifically on the international system, in pursuit of achieving a better positioning for the state.

In the current international context, a state that does not possess a structure to alert about the importance of the use of Economic Intelligence not only establishes an incomplete parameter regarding the processes that affect it or could affect it; it also works against the achievement of development objectives proposed. Therefore, the relevancy of Economic Intelligence is focused not only in the fact that it is a tool to help the state on an internal level, but it also allows states to position themselves in a more effective manner within an international context dominated by the process of globalization (Cohen 2008). In this sense, IPE appears to be a discipline that attracts, articulates, and condenses distinct aspects related to the process of globalization, the contingencies of the political dynamics of state and corporate actors, and the threats, challenges, and complexities related to security that imply for the countries the need to intervene in regional or global economic affairs involving large amounts of volatility and uncertainty. And at the same time, IPE offers a theoretical and conceptual architecture while permitting the development of interdisciplinary bridges and links with intelligence, especially in areas that are relevant to its comprehension from an economic perspective, broadening the range of activities related to the previous field of study.

International political economy as a disciplinary spectrum

At the moment when we consider the factors that influence economic and strategic decision making by states, the process of globalization represents a panorama filled with uncertainties and insecurities that affect distinct social and political actors. Globalization itself may not be understood exclusively by considering the intervention of commercial logic and interests; it also needs to be conceivable as a dynamic that unites technological, cultural, and geopolitical dimensions (Mahrenbach and Shaw 2019). Under this perspective, it is necessary to incorporate a point of view that helps achieve an understanding of this variety of factors. Thus, articulating the relationships generated between the state and the market, IPE serving as an optimal and broad disciplinary framework to analyzing different phenomena (Tussie 2015).

IPE has a series of analytical currents ranging from classical conceptions that view the state as an actor subject to market logic, to critical perspectives that question capitalist models in different levels of analysis (Gill 2016). In this sense, it is evident that all countries, independent of their ideological formats, needs consider Economic Intelligence as a necessary resource to achieve better positioning in international markets as well as to achieve other goals and promote their national development. The intelligence analysis and recommendations that result from the process of incorporating IPE categories will not be interpreted by states as isolated units, nor will they prioritize the market as an abstract and omnipresent notion in the economic and commercial sphere. The IPE analytical categories minimize the realist and positivist focus coming from international relations, as well as the currents anchored in national security doctrines. IPE permits a differentiation and visualization of other national and regional actors, locating and analyzing sociopolitical processes arising from the complex relationships within globalization (Rosamond 2003).

One of the categories employed in IPE and international relations to better understand the contexts for the state's application of Economic Intelligence, is the level of autonomy at the moment to make decisions. While it is true that the decisions made by a state will be executed in relation to its interests as well as the potential effects on the society it represents, it is also true that this premise can be ambiguous and inexact due the nature of the actual international environment. Generally, the state is considered as a rational actor, and its decisions are independent of what may be decided by any other actor; but that perspective becomes ambiguous according to the level of autonomy that the state has to reach a specific decision that does not depend entirely on the country itself. In this perspective, states objectives and interests are mixed with other actors, resulting in the necessity to evaluate decisions in a different way (Abdelal 2009).

Therefore, as a result of commercial exchange and the multitude of actors that are part of the international economic system, countries cannot make decisions in a totally independent manner, as the consequences of these decisions have an impact that extends beyond their borders

(Kirshner 2009). Thus, it is possible to make a relationship between Economic Intelligence and IPE, as the decision-making process entailed in reasoning from the perspective of Economic Intelligence cannot be separated from the criteria that are considered in other spheres, especially the private sector. Accordingly, decisions of a country find themselves subordinated to the reactions of other international actors, minimizing the role of the state. This may cause a certain level of confusion with respect to the use of Competitive Intelligence, but it is evident that the influence of IPE within the field of Economic Intelligence reinforces the role of the state regarding the comprehension of international political phenomena. But in this matter, it is necessary to incorporate other analytical tools that are ascribed to private business but without giving them a primary role in the process (Díaz 2016).

Economic Intelligence observes and analyzes the positioning that states may have within regional and global markets. Considering that countries are located and operate inside the international global system, Economic Intelligence could allow them to strengthen their performance or to maintain the necessary safeguards against eventual critical situations or threats. However, the fact of making decisions, or even not making them, would imply a change of perception regarding the state. Therefore, if a country seeks to project an international image that helps it gain a better position with respect to different markets, the information and data that it compiles could amount to be a before and after, in terms of the projection and materialization of its national objectives and interests (Olier 2013).

Having accurate knowledge of previous conditions, along with the necessity of being able to interpret updates and transformations to regional and international scenarios, constitutes one of the substantial factors of Economic Intelligence and its relationship with IPE. An adequate process for diagnosing international context, always from the economic–commercial point of view, implies a political strategy, but the process of collecting information from different sources does not necessarily mean that a decision is made in the short term because actors or countries often act in a shifting manner within the international economic system, when they directly or indirectly signal their interests and objectives. In these situations, Economic Intelligence becomes a great resource for monitoring and take early alerts, in order to states have available to increase the certainty of their decisions and fulfill their goals (Olier 2016).

As has been mentioned, Economic Intelligence is a tool that is functional to the institutions of a country immersed in a complex international context. Thus, Economic Intelligence tries to be an assistant or a guide to reduce the uncertainty of strategic political decisions, but it also offers a structure of analysis that can warn about the potential relationships between entering certain international contexts and the consequences of these decisions on national politics. That warning capacity places the theoretical and methodological discussion of IPE in a key position because of the role of political culture in the composition and understanding that or gives form to the Economic Intelligence process and its relationship to national development (Gonzáles and Larriba 2011).

Box 48.3 The use of Economic Intelligence: Spain as a case study

Spain's case is a very interesting model of example because that country saw the necessity to expand their "country brand" beyond European surface. But at the same time, the different governments, since 2011, understood that the past model of security to the country should not be able to confront threats in the new international and regional context. So, in order to connect both perspectives, the Spanish government created a Strategy of National Security, including the concept of Economic Intelligence. In this case, despite the protagonist of the armed forces or national police in the maintenance of internal and external security, private actors also have a role to play in Spain's security. This perspective considers Spain's economic environment as an opportunity, but also as a considerable threat, if the government does not take actions to promote their national interest in different levels. Nevertheless, to do that, Spain's decision-makers had to think differently, from a security–military paradigm to a broader perspective, where economics is one of the main elements to achieve security and, most important, a better level of national development. In a country historically beaten by terrorism as a Spain, with groups like ETA, this change of thinking was a huge movement, not only in terms of institutions but also in expressions of international positioning. In context, Spain's Strategy of National Security includes Economic Intelligence, as a tool to achieve international objectives, and in that way, increase their perception of security to maintain levels of development according to the needs of their society.

Considering this perspective that links development with the process of Economic Intelligence is where it's possible to find a bridge between these two notions. That interaction offers some analytical surprises. For instance, a country that achieves moderate economic growth or an eventual better positioning within the international markets does not necessarily bring about a positive evolution in its levels of development (Blyth 2003).

Economic Intelligence, used in conjunction with an explanatory framework coming from IPE looking to safeguard the interests and objectives of a country, also maintains a strong political and social component. With it, the development notion becomes a part of an evaluation of the objectives and interests of the state as well as the process that should be carried out to achieve these goals. Economic Intelligence substantially affects economic security and sustainability of a country and, in turn, plays a role in the state's perspectives on developing itself and protects its population (Díaz 2016; Olier 2016).

These conceptions about the autonomy that may exist in making a decision within the international economic environment, the level of impact that a decision has within the Economic Intelligence process, and the incorporation of non–economic elements but it has a significant influence on a nation's economy, such as development, are keys to explain Economic Intelligence. In this sense, it is necessary to obtain explanatory and analytical categories to enlarge the discussion between disciplines. In that perspective, IPE provides a theoretical context to understand the mentioned categories. The impact of this reasoning can be seen in Table 48.1.

Table 48.1 Impact of IPE in economic intelligence

	Decision-making process	Positioning and international projection	Elements and analytical process
Economic Intelligence	Relatively autonomous	The process implies an improvement to the state	Economic, with a link to security aspects
Economic Intelligence and IPE	Subordinated to the behavior and decisions of other actors, including those within the state	Recognized as a process that can generate negative effects	Economic, political, and social, among the most relevant

Source: Authors' own elaboration.

The previous classification is not absolute or definitive because the diverse interpretive perspectives of IPE can generate constant changes in the notion of Economic Intelligence, specifically when this last concept is considered as a field of study itself (Balaam 2013). Through the precepts of Economic Intelligence and the postulates derived from IPE, it is possible to observe different concepts that serve as axes or bridges between both disciplines. That is one of the main challenges that the link between Economic Intelligence and IPE generates, to achieve a better theoretical comprehension of the international context and also the actions and decisions of the states.

Conceptual hinges: geoeconomy, interdependence, and security

Given that IPE establishes new categories and contributions for a better understanding of Economic Intelligence, it becomes necessary to specify the links and areas between both disciplines. The first area is related to centering the discussion on those aspects in which IPE directly influences the interpretation of Economic Intelligence. On this level, the "conceptual hinges" permit a better understanding of the implications of both Economic Intelligence and IPE on the analysis and decision-making process that accompany the execution of intelligence in any country or even in a corporate environment (Rivera 2012). But also the implications of the "conceptual hinges" are translated through the meaning of positioning on both a territorial and spatial level that a state has with respect to the international economy (geoeconomy), the grade and nature of the dependence it has on other international actors (interdependence), and finally, the protection that could be provided to society through the utilization of Economic Intelligence (security).

The second area is related to the use and meaning of the concept "hinge," considering two elements. First, that concept could serve as a joining axis, with the capacity to be deployed in two or even more fields of knowledge, addressing shared objects of study and multidisciplinary commonalities. In this sense, IPE and Economic Intelligence present the challenge of theorizing and analyzing specific fields of study on a macro, middle, and micro level. And in the second place, the concept "hinges" also recognize the interrelationship between IPE and Economic Intelligence, permitting the modification and broadening of traditional conceptualizations with enhancements such as studies related to globalization, the state, transnational organized crime, international relations, security, and politics. Thus, the schallenge grows because new perspectives of thought for each of the mentioned disciplines generate greater levels of complexity in the fields of study themselves, as is reflected in Figure 48.1.

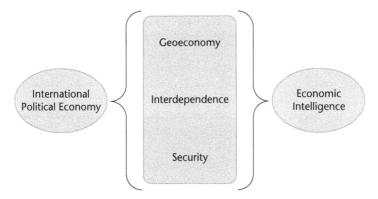

Figure 48.1   "Conceptual hinges" between IPE and economic intelligence
Source: Authors' own elaboration.

Another relevant point related to Economic Intelligence is that the concept of the hinge cannot be understood without the presence of distinct disciplinary components. According to that premise, it is necessary for a better understanding of the of the field to take into account the multiple bridges inside each group; but at the same time, each group cannot be observed as an independent element because, in its complexity, it needs to have a relation with the other discipline. In other words, IPE and Economic Intelligence cannot be conceived as a singular and unique perspective of thought. Thus, for instance, elements and processes that share a basis of geoeconomic analysis can be applied to understand aspects related to a country's level of interdependence with others, or even if the entrance of certain international commercial and economic actors into a territorial space could signify a threat from a state point of view. A similar situation happens with the perspectives of interdependence and security, which acquire a multifaceted perspective within the contexts of IPE and Economic Intelligence, at the moment to know their scopes in the decision-making process.

Geoeconomics is the first term related to the "conceptual hinges," which can be defined as a field of study that takes as its main research object the influence that economics instruments have within the understanding of territorial spaces (Olier 2012). In this sense, geoeconomics' perspective of a particular country will have the international system as a principal context to apply its decisions, derived from the international market logic and from different actors that intervene on it. However, the main element derived from geoeconomic positioning is the use of territorial dimension to achieve a better place within the global economy (Blackwill and Harris 2016).

Upon establishing a link between IPE and Economic Intelligence regarding the concept of geoeconomics, it is possible to establish some union points. First, an adequate diagnosis derived from the Economic Intelligence process can help countries decide how to invest or promote their interests, reducing or increasing interdependence, taking into consideration the economic and commercial environment. Geographical location of countries and their involvement within the global economic system should not be ignored, not only for the distances and time required to transfer goods but also principally for the creation of strategies that facilitate access to the exact sites that offer relevant economic value. One of the main examples in this part is the eventual decision to improve port and airport infrastructure, taking into account the capacity of the economy to increase its importation and exportation levels. In the same line, the projection of a territorial space can offer some value for a particular economic activity, such as islands, straits, or even determined regions with strategic benefits (Baracuhy 2019).

Another point related to geoeconomics that establishes a hinge between IPE and Economic Intelligence involves the establishment, amplification, or cancelation of regional integration agreements in the commercial sphere. When considering an international negotiation related to a regional project, the geoeconomic implications for any country are modified as a consequence of that international agreement because the territorial perspective is extended from a local/national market to one with regional qualities. Nevertheless, even under that point of view, the geoeconomic perspective of a country change in terms of territorial projection, considering that although a state may have a perspective toward a regional space in particular, when it takes the decision to jointly to a specific integration project, that vision can change due to the interests of the regional bloc (Vivares 2018).

The geoeconomic perspectives of any country are tied to the notion of interdependence. In general terms, interdependence can be described as a process that has a somewhat paradoxical double vision. On one hand, it is understood that mutual dependence and collaboration helps to prevent conflicts between countries. But on the other hand, interdependence incentivizes the conflict points between actors involved in the process, as a result of exposing some vulnerabilities of the state, increasing the perception of insecurity. In other words, there is a consequence of transparency in a relation among states and the possibility of a threat when that mutual trust is betrayed (Mastanduno 2012: 220).

Without judging the different theoretical and analytical considerations with respect to interdependence, the direct relationship that concept has with IPE and Economic Intelligence stems from the state's necessity of knowledge in order to increase or decrease the levels of commercial and political relationships with a country, or even with a specific regional area. Determining the capacity of a state to reduce its levels of dependence toward a group of countries requires passing through an initial detailed study from the Economic Intelligence perspective because the consequences of a bad decision in that area can negatively affect national development. Therefore, Economic Intelligence becomes a tool that can establish parameters in the decision-making process, considering that may result in an increase or decrease in mutual dependence.

Nevertheless, the consideration of interdependence goes much further than increasing or decreasing the process of interchange of goods and services in the commercial sphere. The concept implications also have repercussions in the complexity that can be seen in the relationships between countries, or even in specific areas such as economic and commercial segments, where it is possible to see outcomes on a political, cultural or social level. Under this logic of thought, although the perspective of interdependence can affect different areas of a society, in general terms, the state is the institution charged with observing the evolution of consequences, both negative and positive, of interdependence process. In this sense, the state can be interpreted as an institution to tries to resolve conflicts and, at the same time, finds a way to improve levels of social development (O'Brien and Williams 2007). Besides, although there can be multiple observable consequences of interdependence on distinct societal areas, there is a tendency to link interdependence with a commercial architecture in which the principal effects of the process express themselves. Thus, the state, by means of its institutional capacity, can help to establish permanent parameters that evaluate the level of interdependence and autonomy in its decisions.

The relationship between IPE and Economic Intelligence, through interdependence, for more complete comprehension, it is possible to present under a double perspective. The first perspective is related to IPE and the parameters around the composition of the international system, especially in commercial and economic aspects. In that way, interdependence becomes an area in which Economic Intelligence can be deployed to evaluate eventual consequences of the link with a determined number of actors, always considering the positioning of the state in a commercial context. In second place, Economic Intelligence can help to make decisions about the need to increase links with one or many countries, for which it becomes necessary to establish clear and pertinent objectives about the role of a country or corporation in the international economic and commercial system. But also, Economic Intelligence allows the deciphering of a better diagnostic, considering current and future needs of the state, without forgetting that the principal objective of that discipline is to increase the perception of security to obtain a better development.

Finally, the last hinge between IPE and Economic Intelligence is related to security. But in this sense, security is understood from the perspective of the necessity to safeguard the objectives and interests of the state, despite the complexity and amplitude that the concept mentioned implies. Thus, the notion of security does not have a traditional meaning when it comes to establishing a link between Economic Intelligence and IPE given that these disciplines offer a wider view of the phenomena and processes that affect the security of societies. Accordingly, this broadening not only carries with it an understanding of the behavior of security actors, as the role of armed forces or national police, but it also incorporates other actors that, although they may not be security oriented, participate in the process of security as a part of the state (Dent 2009).

It has also been observed that, when incorporating notions of IPE and Economic Intelligence within the composition of security institutions, the broadening also involves new parameters to analyze the contexts in which a country is involved, principally from an economic and commercial perspective. This can be explained because institutions and their actors require technical and scientific specialization beyond the classical security understanding. But at the same time, that specialization helps to articulate a better security system in all institutional capacity of the state, despite the monopoly of the legitimate force used by traditional security actors (Morgan 2007). Thus, it becomes necessary in this hinge to incorporate new actors within the logic of the state for the adequate management and implementation of a diagnosis, which incorporates economic and commercial processes, and a multidimensional sense to the traditional concept of national security.

New outlines, parameters, and theoretical concepts of IPE should be evaluated with the tools provided by Economic Intelligence. In this way, the hinges create links between themselves, in addition to establishing scenarios and guidelines that in turn generate a need to connect the aspects of the interaction between these two disciplines.

Conclusions

Talk of "conceptual hinges" is not only confined to covering vocabulary and terminological precision; it also generates an approximation to the different processes that emerge from a conceptual discussion between IPE and Economic Intelligence. On this point, although some specific linking elements are established, that cannot be considered as an inclusive exercise; the disciplinary relationships between IPE and Economic Intelligence can even be understood through processes such as the declining relevance of the traditional concept of national sovereignty and the intervention of non-state international actors beyond traditional westphalian-state borders.

It is important to mention that the "conceptual hinges" give the green light to understand that a state, beyond its intended model of development and its ideology, must consider the action and consequences of Economic Intelligence in its regional and international projection. This can be understood under the prism of the different guidelines that the state plans and considers, to takes strategic decisions in order to reduce the risk factors and vulnerability. And in this sense, the intelligence and security apparatus should be prepared to warn about any threat to the state plans.

Thus, states and also corporations cannot avoid the use and interpretation of both disciplines in two relevant aspects. First, given that IPE is a discipline capable of analyzing and theorizing about implications of development for society and the state, it opens up points of intervention for the categories coming from Economic Intelligence that incorporate the study of the motivations around decisions made at the highest level of the state. Second, the incorporation of IPE to the matrix of analysis of intelligence through the "conceptual hinges," opens the door to a cultural process related to the "demystification" of the intelligence functions associated with spying, secretive, infiltration, and conspiracy. From this point of view, Economic Intelligence, while it looks to provide a perception of greater certainty, security, and autonomy within the decision-making process, does not have a direct relationship with the traditional conception of national security.

Recognizing this situation, especially in countries that have a conflicted past when it comes to the function of intelligence, opens up possibilities of creation and the legitimacy of new analysis to understand development under the complex, shifting, and asymmetrical contexts related to globalization. The "conceptual hinges" also help the construction of a direct bridge between academic discussion and putting into practice these reflections in internal and foreign policy.

Bibliography

Abdelal, R. 2009. Constructivism as an approach to international political economy. In *Routledge Handbook of International Political Economy (IPE)*. Blyth, M. (ed.): 62–76. New York: Routledge.

Balaam, D. 2013. *Introduction to International Political Economy*. New York: Routledge.

Baracuhy, B. 2019. Geo-economics as a dimension of grand strategy: notes on the concept and its evolution. In *Geo-Economics and Power Politics in the 21st century: The Revival of the Economic Statecraft*. Wigell, M. Scholvin, S. and Mika, A. (eds.): 14–27. London: Routledge.

Berkowitz, B. and Goodman, A. 1989. *Strategic Intelligence for American Security*. Princeton: Princeton University Press.

Blackwill, R. and Harris, J. 2016. *War by other means: Geoeconomics and Statecraft*. Cambridge: Harvard University Press.

Blyth, M. 2003. IPE as a global conversation. In *Routledge Handbook of International Political Economy (IPE)*. Blyth, M (ed.): 1–20. New York: Routledge.

Buckley, J. 2017. Intelligence and Organized Crime – Paradigms and Paradoxes. In *The Palgrave Handbook of Security, Risk and Intelligence*. Dover, R., Huw D. and Goodman, M. (eds.): 137–156. London: Palgrave Macmillan.

Bulger, N. 2016. The Evolving Role of Intelligence: Migrating from Traditional Competitive Intelligence to Integrated Intelligence. *The International Journal of Intelligence, Security, and Public Affairs* 18 (1): 57–84.

Chandra, S. and Bhonsle, R. 2015. National Security: Concept, Measurement and Management. *Strategic Analysis* 39 (4): 337–359.

CITEX. 2011. *Methods and Practices in Competitive Intelligence: A Handbook for Small and Medium-sized Enterprises*. Madrid: Instituto de Comercio Exterior.

Cohen, B. 2008. *International Political Economy. An Intellectual History*. Princeton: Princeton University Press.

Dent, C. 2009. Economic Security. In: *Contemporary Security Studies*. Collins, A. (ed.): 239–255. New York: Oxford University Press.

Díaz, G. 2016. From Cooperation to Competition: Economic Intelligence as Part of Spain's National Security Strategy. *International Journal of Intelligence and CounterIntelligence* 29 (1): 151–164.

Gill, S. 2016. Critical Global Political Economy and the Global Organic Crisis. In *The Palgrave Handbook of Critical International Political Economy*. Cafruny, A., Talani, L. and Pozo, G. (eds.): 29–48. London: Palgrave.

Gonzáles, J. and Larriba, B. 2011. *Inteligencia Económica y Competitiva: estrategias legales en las nuevas agendas de Seguridad Nacional*. Valencia: Tirant lo Blanch.

Hastedt, G. 1998. Seeking Economic Security through Intelligence. *International Journal of Intelligence and Counter Intelligence* 11 (4): 385–401.

Herzog, J. A. 2008. Using Economic Intelligence to Achieve Regional Security Objectives. *International Journal of Intelligence and CounterIntelligence* 21 (2): 302–313.

Hillebrand, C. and Hughes, G. 2017. The Quest for a Theory of Intelligence. In: *The Palgrave Handbook of Security, Risk and Intelligence*. Dover, R. Huw D. and Goodman, M. (eds.): 1–25. London: Palgrave Macmillan.

Jackson, P. 2008. Introduction: Enquiries into the "Secret State". In *Exploring Intelligence Archives*. Hughes, G., Jackson, P. and Scott, L. (eds.): 1–12. New York: Routledge.

Kirshner, J. 2009. Realist Political Economy: Traditional Themes and Contemporary Challenges. In: *Routledge Handbook of International Political Economy (IPE)*. Blyth, M. (ed.): 36–47. New York: Routledge.

Mahrenbach, L. and Shaw, T. 2019. Continuities and Change in IPE at the Start of the Twenty first Century. In: *The Palgrave Handbook of Contemporary International Political Economy*. Shaw, T., Mahrenbach, L. C., Modi, R. and Yi-chong, X. (eds.): 1–24. London: Palgrave.

Mastanduno, M. 2012. Economic Statecraft. In *Foreign Policy: Theories, Actors, Cases*, Smith, S., Hadfield, A. and Dunne, T. (eds.): 204–221. New York: Oxford University Press.

McDowell, D. 2009. *Strategic Intelligence. A Handbook for Practitioners, Managers, and Users*. Toronto: The Scarecrow Press.

Morgan, P. 2007. Security in International Politics: Traditional Approaches. In *Contemporary Security Studies*. Collins, A. (ed.): 13–34. New York: Oxford University Press.

Nenzhelele, E. 2015. Competitive Intelligence Tools Used by Small and Medium-sized Enterprises. *Journal of Governance and Regulation* 4 (3): 191–200.

O'Brien, R. and Williams, M. 2007. *Global Political Economy: Evolution and Dynamics*. New York: Palgrave.

Olier, E. 2012. *Geoeconomía: Las claves de la economía global*. Madrid: Pearson Educación.

Olier, E. 2013. Inteligencia Estratégica y seguridad económica. *Cuadernos de Estrategia* 162: 9–34.

Olier, E. 2016. Inteligencia económica. In *Conceptos Fundamentales de Inteligencia*, Díaz, A. (ed.): 233–240. Madrid: Tirant lo Blanch.

Richards, J. 2010. *The Art and Science of Intelligence Analysis*. New York: Oxford University Press.

Rivera, F. 2012. *La seguridad perversa: Política, democracia y derechos humanos en Ecuador 1998–2006*. Quito: FLACSO Ecuador.

Rogg, J. 2018. 'Quo Vadis?' A Comparatist Meets a Theorist Searching for a Grand Theory of Intelligence. *Intelligence and National Security* 33 (4): 541–552.

Rosamond, B. 2003. Babylon and On? Globalization and International Political Economy. *Review of International Political Economy* 10 (4): 661–671.

Somiedo, J. 2012. El papel de la epistemología en el análisis de inteligencia. *Inteligencia y seguridad: Revista de Análisis y Prospectiva* 12: 241–272.

Tussie, D. 2015. Relaciones Internacionales y Economía Política Internacional: notas para el debate. *Relaciones Internacionales* 48 (24): 155–175.

Vivares, E. 2018. The IPE Puzzle of Regional Inequality, Instability, and the Global Insertion of South America. In *Regionalism, Development and the Post-Commodities Boom in South America*. Ernesto Vivares (ed.): 1–24. London: Palgrave Macmillan.

49

The IPE of money laundering and terrorist finance

William Vlcek

Introduction

The political economy of money laundering and terrorist finance operates at an intersection of finance and security. As clear from the terms used, money and the financial system are the objects of concern for government agencies responsible for protecting society from criminals and terrorists. The concern dates from the late 1970s and, in the beginning, it involved illegal drugs trafficking where one approach for interdicting the activity was to deprive the criminals of their ill-gotten gains. Action to address this issue at an international level was orchestrated by the G7 club of wealthy developed economies. The scope of concern spread from laundering the proceeds of the illegal drugs trade to include terrorist financing in 2001, and further mission creep over the subsequent decade brought in concerns over financing the proliferation of weapons of mass destruction and tax evasion. The essential point is that money with an illegal or criminal origin has been deemed a threat to the economy and society at large.

The measures implemented to deal with illegal money are present throughout the financial system and beyond, to include what the Financial Action Task Force (FATF) identified as 'designated non-financial businesses and professions' (DNFBPs). The latter firms include casinos, dealers in precious metals and stones, lawyers and real estate agents (Financial Action Task Force 2012: 19–20). In essence, any economic transaction has the potential for serving to launder the proceeds of crime. It is for this reason, dear Reader, that you are asked to provide proof of identity and proof of address when you open an account at a bank, at any other financial institution or with a DNFBP. And this is why you may be asked to explain the source of your money, because the firm needs to be able to demonstrate that it has not knowingly accepted illegal money and become part of the money laundering process. The chapter explores the nature of the political economy of money laundering and terrorist finance in the following three sections, beginning with an explanation of the evolution of this global financial governance regime. The second section explores the operation of these measures to combat money laundering and terrorist finance in practice while the third section considers the enforcement mechanisms used by this global financial regime and the unintended consequences they produced.

Box 49.1 Acronyms and terms

- AML/CFT – Anti-Money Laundering/Combating the Financing of Terrorism
- BMPE – Black Market Peso Exchange
- CDD – Customer Due Diligence
- CoE – Council of Europe
- DNFBPs – Designated Non-Financial Businesses and Professions
- FATF – Financial Action Task Force
- FSRB – FATF-Style Regional Body
- IVTS – Informal Value Transfer Service
- KYC – Know Your Customer
- NCCT – Non-Cooperative Countries and Territories
- PEP – Politically Exposed Person
- Predicate crime – this is the illegal activity which produced the money which needs to be laundered
- STR – Suspicious Transaction Report

Evolution of a global financial regime

The origin of the term 'money laundering' is often attributed to the use of a laundromat for moving illicit money into the legal economy (see Box 49.2). For some authors, it may be explained with a longer history, perhaps by reference to the informal value transfer methods that have been used for thousands of years and predating the modern banking system (see Box 49.4). Whatever the origin for the term, these attributions are vacant of any recognition for the socially constructed nature of the law, and therefore of the determination made by society for what is considered legal/illegal in the domestic political economy. Thus, for an economic transaction to represent money laundering the underlying money must be the product of a prior, or *predicate*, criminal activity. The socially constructed origins for money laundering in conjunction with the effort to impose the AML legal structure in other socio-legal contexts (such as a domestic political economy outside of Europe and North America) produces the tensions, resistance and unintended consequences touched on in the following sections. Terrorist finance and the efforts to combat it are similar, because with reference to that old saw, 'one man's terrorist is another man's freedom fighter', the designation of terrorist finance exposes the constructed nature behind the naming of one group as 'terrorists' and yet another group as 'resistance fighters', 'freedom fighters' or 'rebels'. Without entering into the debate over the definition of terrorism as a form of political violence, it is a definition which should emphasise methods rather than political objectives, but this chapter is an exploration of *political* economy and thus politics are an essential element. The political dimension of naming an individual or group as 'terrorist' has implications for the implementation and enforcement of international guidance to combat terrorist financing at the national level, as will be explained further below.

Another political economic point to recognise in any discussion of money laundering is the unscientific origin for the commonly repeated assertion that it represents '2–5 per cent of global gross domestic product (GDP)'. This claim originated with a speech in 1998 by Michel Camdessus, when he was the Managing Director of the International Monetary Fund (IMF). A number of scholars subsequently endeavoured to put empirical facts behind the claim, or to offer their figure for the amount of global capital consisting of laundered money (Levi 2002; Sharman 2011: 18–20; Walker 1999). An earlier study by the US Congress Office of Technology Assessment included the more precise estimate of US$300 billion, citing a State Department factsheet from 1992 on money laundering that in turn was referencing the FATF. This study went on to explain in this footnote, 'it appears that this estimate was first generated by one U.S. government analyst as "mostly a guess"', which over time became a fact-by-repetition (Eckert and Biersteker 2010: 261; US Congress Office of Technology Assessment 1995: 2). The desire for a headline figure to represent the scale of money laundering in the world economy is laudable, but it involves an effort to measure the immeasurable, the undeclared capital of an unknown number of people engaged in a variety of illegal or illicit practices producing income that must somehow be made to appear 'legal' or 'clean'. Efforts to understand and measure the scale of terrorist finance are also confronted by determining the unknowable in its entirety. After the terrorist act, estimates are derived from the evidence left behind by the terrorist group, but the estimate is relevant for that singular event and extrapolating from the one to the many is problematic (Eckert and Biersteker 2010; Levi 2010).

Anti-money laundering

As already indicated, the concern over money laundering arose in the 1970s alongside the growth in illegal drugs trafficking. The first point to understand is that the process of 'money laundering' serves to make money from an illegal source appear as if it is money originating from a legal source of income. The possession of illegal money as the proceeds of crime became one way for pursuing the suspected criminal in the absence of any other evidence for illegal conduct. Thus the oft-repeated story of the American gangster Al Capone, who was convicted of tax evasion (for failing to declare his illegal income and paying the income tax due on it) and not for any of the other crimes he is suspected to have committed (Naylor 1994: 21). Money laundering was formally criminalised in the United States in 1986, however, the US government recognised that criminals would simply move their criminal proceeds outside the country and send it back to their US bank account. From the bank's perspective it would be a legitimate wire transfer from the foreign bank, and thus it would circumvent the intentions of the Money Laundering Control Act of 1986. International cooperation was necessary, leading to the establishment of the Financial Action Task Force in 1989 (see Box 49.3). With any initial membership comprised of the leading developed economies, international cooperation against money laundering seemed to be achieved.

Box 49.2 The money laundering process

The origin that is frequently offered for the term 'money laundering' (and is perhaps apocryphal) involves a gangster who owned several laundromats. Because a laundromat is a cash-intensive business it is relatively straightforward to introduce cash from other, criminal, sources to be deposited and declared as income from the laundromat business. Clearly this technique would also work with any other cash-intensive business, such as a car wash, fast food outlet or a corner shop. Captured by this practice is the money laundering process itself, the action or series of actions taken to disguise the origins or ownership of money, when that money came from some criminal activity. The objective is to present the appearance, to banks, government officials and neighbours that all of one's income is from legal legitimate sources.

The process of money laundering is widely explained as consisting of three steps – placement, layering and integration. The placement step involves getting the criminal money into the financial system in the first place, which is the function performed by the laundromat. But this initial step may not be enough to avoid questions, requiring the second step of layering. The layering step consists of a series of transactions intended to disguise the origins of the money and to make it difficult, if not impossible, to trace the money back to its original, criminal source. It may require transferring the money between several bank accounts, using it to purchase goods that are then sold to someone else, or it may include co-opting the services of a lawyer or accountant as a further move to conceal the origin of the money behind non-disclosure and privacy obligations. Successful layering leads to the third step, integration, which is simply the point at which the money is available for use and to all appearances came from a legitimate source.

The critical feature with money laundering beyond the process is the determination that the money in question had a criminal origin and is therefore illegal money. This determination is made through the existence of a *predicate* crime, the criminal act or activity that generated the money. It is this criminal act that makes the money illegal and creates the desire to launder the money before being able to use it as legitimate money. The list of predicate crimes is long and the indicative guidance is provided at pages 112–113 of the FATF's *International Standards on Combating Money Laundering and the Financing of Terrorism & Proliferation: The FATF Recommendations* (2012). The list of 'designated categories of offences' for predicate crimes includes: robbery, kidnapping, trafficking/smuggling, corruption/bribery, piracy, terrorism and tax crimes. The practices used to conduct money laundering have evolved in reaction to AML enforcement. The FATF members study and share the 'methods and trends' of these evolving money laundering practices and release public reports on them and how they may be countered (see www.fatf-gafi. org/publications/methodsandtrends/).

The action taken against money laundering in the sixteen original FATF member states, however, led to the use of banks in other states and territories without similar AML laws, a situation that would be prominently revealed a decade later. In 1999 the US government found that billions of dollars of suspicious money from Russia had passed through banks in New York City and were transferred to offshore banks in the Pacific (General Accounting Office 2000; Minority Staff of the Permanent Subcommittee on Investigations 2001). The New York City financial community sought to deflect blame for contributing to this capital flight and probable money laundering by imposing private sanctions on their correspondent banking relationships with the offshore banks resident in the small island destinations for the Russian money. The FATF formalised these private sanctions as international sanctions when it produced a blacklist of 'non-cooperative countries and territories' (NCCT). This NCCT list was comprised of states and territories that were not members of the FATF, and had not implemented the Forty Recommendations against money laundering created for the FATF member states (Financial Action Task Force 2000a; 2000b). The NCCT blacklist approach ended in 2006 when the last listed country was determined to be compliant with the FATF's demands. The NCCT approach was very contentious because it served to impose the obligations of membership on states and territories that were not members of the club. The FATF continues to be concerned for insufficient AML enforcement in some areas of the world economy, consequently it has continued to identify states of high-risk for money laundering along with its guidance for guarding against it (Vlcek 2018b: 108). In 2001, attention shifted to combating the financing of terrorism (CFT), following a logic that stopping the financing of terrorism was a crucial tactic for preventing terrorism.

Box 49.3 The Financial Action Task Force

The Financial Action Task Force (FATF) is presently composed of thirty-six state/territory members and two multinational organisation members (see www.fatf-gafi.org/about/membersandobservers/). There are also two observer states, which provides a preliminary status to full membership, along with a further group of observer multinational organisations including United Nations (UN) agencies, the IMF and World Bank. In addition to the global membership and focus of the FATF, it also has regionally focused associate members. These FATF-style regional bodies (FSRBs) provide a regional peer network of member states to share knowledge and expertise as well as identify trends and region-specific money laundering activities. The FSRB may have one or more members that also are a member of the FATF and this overlapping membership facilitates knowledge transfer and continuity among the organisations.

The FATF was established in 1989 with the initial directive to study the methods employed to launder criminal money with the goal of designing procedures to identify, prevent and convict those involved in money laundering (Financial Action Task Force 1990a). The crime of money laundering was established as a mechanism for combating illegal drugs trafficking into the US in the 1980s. Clearly, US domestic law would be easily circumvented by moving the money to a foreign bank and then transferring it back to the US, requiring an international solution in order to advance the US domestic 'war on drugs'. Working with the other members of the G7, the FATF was established to design and implement an international solution (Sharman 2011: 20–26). The first edition of the FATF Forty Recommendations was released in 1990, with subsequent revisions to clarify and adjust the scope of the Recommendations to incorporate additional responsibilities (Financial Action Task Force 1990b; 2001b; 2003; 2012). Central to the work of the FATF was not only the identification of the methods and trends used for money laundering by its members, but also the predicate crimes producing the illegal money to be laundered (e.g. Financial Action Task Force 2013b).

Combating the financing of terrorism

At the beginning of the twentieth century, the problem of political violence was recognised under the name of 'anarchism', and international cooperation was coordinated by the 1902 'Treaty for the Extradition of Criminals and for Protection Against Anarchism' (Alexander, Browne and Nanes 1979). The concern over anarchism faded but political violence re-emerged in the 1960s with the hijacking of airliners to bring attention to the hijackers' political demands and for hostages to exchange for political prisoners. A series of international conventions covering terrorist threats to civil aviation, hostages, internationally protected persons, maritime navigation and nuclear material were ratified between 1963 and 1990 (see: www.un.org/en/counterterrorism/legal-instruments.shtml). During this period of time, however, these acts of political violence were generally framed as state-sponsored terrorism and the financial support for them was attributed to a state sponsor (often Libya during the 1970s and 1980s). In many cases this understanding was accurate, but it did not cover all terrorist groups and their violent acts. In Europe during the 1970s, groups such as the Red Army Faction (aka, Baader-Meinhof Gang), the Red Brigades and the Irish Republican Army financed themselves through extortion, kidnapping and robbery. Recognising this fact, the Council of Europe (CoE) proposed in 1980 a Recommendation on 'Measures Against the Transfer and Safekeeping of Funds of

Criminal Origin' (Rec(80)10E). The CoE is a multinational organisation promoting human rights, democracy and the rule of law across the region broadly seen as forming Europe, and it views organised crime and terrorism as a threat to rule of law. The measures outlined by the Recommendation were to identify and confiscate the profits from crimes committed by a terrorist group as one measure to interdict their terrorist activity (Council of Europe 1980).

The CoE initiative was a bit ahead of its time, it was not ratified and the efforts to combat these European terrorist groups remained substantially an individual national problem. The United Kingdom, for example, enacted the Prevention of Terrorism (Temporary Provisions) Act 1989. The Act included provisions to tackle the 'Financial Assistance for Terrorism', but was concerned solely with the Troubles in Northern Ireland and financial support to 'acts of terrorism connected with the affairs of Northern Ireland' and not terrorism more generally. The paramilitaries in Northern Ireland were financed by a mixture of contributions and criminal conduct, with some of the proceeds of crime invested in legitimate businesses which generated profits as well as providing a method for laundering money. At the same time, financial support for the IRA was a persistent point of criticism made by the UK government against the US government. There was a perception in the UK that US federal, state and local law enforcement did very little to prevent IRA fundraising by Irish–Americans. In particular there was NORAID, the Irish Northern Aid Committee, which ostensibly raised money for humanitarian purposes with collection cups found at shops and pubs throughout the greater Boston, Massachusetts area (Horgan and Taylor 1999).

While the CoE effort to address the issue of terrorist financing was unsuccessful, in 1999 the US raised the topic of terrorist financing at a meeting of the FATF (Financial Action Task Force 2001a). The issue gained importance for the US government following al Qaida's 1993 bombing attack on the World Trade Center and the 1998 bombings of the US embassies in Kenya and Tanzania. The proposal was to apply AML methods against terrorist finance, but it met with resistance from other FATF members. The FATF's annual Report on Money Laundering Typologies for 2000–2001 discussed the results of its experts' examination of terrorist finance's similarities to money laundering. The conclusions highlighted the differences and the group's failure to overcome those differences and achieve consensus. The problem was that while the practices of concealment used by money launders and terrorist financiers may be similar, not all sources of money for terrorist finance were illegal (e.g. donations or charitable contributions). Absent a predicate crime, the money used to finance terrorism could not therefore be countered with AML legislation (Financial Action Task Force 2001a).

The perspective on using AML laws to pursue terrorist finance changed in 2001. Following the terrorist attacks in the US in September, the FATF held an extraordinary plenary meeting in Washington, DC in October 2001. The meeting produced eight Special Recommendations on Terrorist Financing and the first Recommendation was ratification of the 1999 International Convention for the Suppression of the Financing of Terrorism (Financial Action Task Force 2001b). This initial Recommendation was necessary because in September 2001 only four states had ratified the UN treaty (Botswana, Sri Lanka, United Kingdom and Uzbekistan) and a year later that figure had increased to fifty states. With the implementation of the Special Recommendations (and ratification of the Convention) a state would have criminalised the financing of a terrorist act or group, and established the predicate crime necessary to incorporate terrorist finance into the structures created for AML enforcement. While these Special Recommendations of the FATF were applicable only to its members, the UN Security Council adopted Resolution 1373 at its meeting on 28 September 2001. This Resolution directed substantially the same actions for the members of the UN, the criminalisation of terrorist finance and action to suppress terrorist groups (United Nations Security Council 2001). Four years later, the UN

Security Council went further, when it 'strongly urged' states to fully implement the FATF's Forty Recommendations (United Nations Security Council 2005).

The scope of responsibility for the FATF expanded to include measures to counter the financing behind the proliferation of weapons of mass destruction, along with explicitly identifying corruption and tax crimes as predicate offences for money laundering. This expansion led to increased coordination between the FATF and other international organisations by framing the concealment of bribes and untaxed income as money laundering. All of these changes were consolidated in the 2012 revision of the Forty Recommendations, 'International Standards on Combating Money Laundering and the Financing of Terrorism & Proliferation' (Financial Action Task Force 2012). The FATF maintains and reinforces the need for continual scrutiny against locations of potential weakness in the global regime against money laundering and terrorist finance with its semi-annual pronouncement identifying states which require additional 'due diligence measures' because of a heightened risk for potential money laundering and terrorist finance. The public statements updating the current watch list of 'high-risk and other monitored jurisdictions' are available at the FATF website.

AML/CFT in practice

The FATF crafted the Forty Recommendations to serve as guidance for national legislation and action against money laundering, and subsequently also against terrorist finance and the financing of the proliferation of weapons of mass destruction. Once the relevant legislation has been ratified the task of implementing the processes and procedures of AML/CFT falls primarily on the private sector – banks, other financial service firms, and the identified non-financial firms and professions – involved in the everyday economy. In the 1990s, AML practices were relatively basic, with law enforcement officials investigating the finances of suspected criminals with particular attention paid to those believed to be involved in the illegal drugs trade. Financial institutions, predominantly retail banks, filed suspicious transaction reports (STRs) when a bank transaction exceeded the 10,000 threshold (a magic number applied whether the transaction was denominated in US dollars, Canadian dollars, Deutsche marks, French francs, etc.) The figure of 10,000 had been identified as high enough to minimise disruption for most ordinary financial transactions while also low enough to identify the suspicious transaction that may be money laundering. The AML activity at this time mainly considered the first step in the money laundering process, the placement of the illegal money into the financial system (see box, The money laundering process). Alongside these STRs banks implemented a 'Know Your Customer' (KYC) procedure, which involves confirming and recording the customer's identity, address and in many instances source of income. The procedure requires the presentation of recognised documents demonstrating legal identity and residence, such as passports, driver's licenses, household bills, company invoices, and pay statements. In 1996 KYC was required under the implementation of an EU Directive for EU Member States while in the US banks conducted KYC checks on a voluntary basis pending new federal regulations (*Money Laundering: FinCEN's Law Enforcement Support, Regulatory, and International Roles* 1996).

In the US it became increasingly common to add a money laundering charge alongside any other criminal charge producing illegal income (Adams 2000). If convicted of a money laundering charge any assets that may have been acquired using the illegal income were forfeited and seized by law enforcement agencies. Asset forfeiture served to punish the convicted and offered a warning to other people considering crime as a source of income. Simultaneously, asset forfeiture carries a moral weight, that 'crime does not pay', and therefore it was the responsibility of the state to ensure that convicted criminals should not benefit from their criminal conduct

(Alldridge 2003). In the case of the US, the forfeited assets did not become part of the general revenue fund for the local or national government. Rather, forfeited assets are shared among the law enforcement agencies involved in the arrest of the convicted person. This situation leads some observers to suggest that asset forfeiture incentivises the law enforcement agency to pursue suspects with assets to be seized, in order to supplement their budget (Holcomb, Kovandzic and Williams 2011). In other jurisdictions the forfeited assets are transferred to the government and proceeds accounted as government revenue, but local judicial processes and the domestic political economy can challenge efficient application of this form of AML punishment (Thoumi and Anzola 2010).

The experience with the initial version of the FATF's Forty Recommendations revealed gaps and deficiencies in the legislation produced to follow its guidance. Moreover, criminals are rational actors and they responded to the implementation of AML laws by shifting money laundering activities to businesses and locations not covered by the law. A revised set of the Forty Recommendations was published in 1996, but legislation in the US and EU to implement the expanded scope to address additional forms of money laundering was resisted by businesses and politicians. The legislation remained in draft until circumstances changed and agreement for expanding the scope of AML laws was readily available. Events in September 2001 changed perspectives on AML policy and enforcement, and on 26 October 2001 President George W. Bush signed into law the USA PATRIOT Act, full name – Uniting and Strengthening America by Providing Appropriate Tools Required to Intercept and Obstruct Terrorism Act of 2001 (USA PATRIOT Act 2001). This new law incorporated much of the previous draft legislation which had been criticised for increasing the scope of government surveillance with an accompanying decline in personal privacy. Confronted by the threat of terrorism, the balance between liberty and security shifted to comply with citizen demands for security (Vlcek 2008).

In the EU, the proposal to amend the money laundering Directive and incorporate the revised Forty Recommendations was released in 1999 and it encountered similar resistance in the European Parliament. One concern was the expansion of the scope of predicate crimes beyond illegal drugs trafficking to include any 'serious crime' and a second concern was the inclusion of additional business activities responsible for reporting potential money laundering activity. The latter aspect was challenged by the legal profession whose members now would be obligated to report suspected money laundering and felt it represented a step too far in expanding the scope of AML. The argument made was that it represented a human rights violation, because an obligation to report potential money laundering based on information provided by a client impinged on client-attorney privilege (Mitsilegas 2003: 95–102). As was the case in the US, the 2001 terrorist attacks provided the political will to overcome resistance in the European Parliament to the expanded scope of AML legislation.

Even though many of the same measures were applied the attention given to combating terrorist finance since 2001 overshadowed on-going AML activity. Media reports highlighted the additional challenges faced by people with providing KYC information in order to keep an existing account open, much less opening a new account. Awareness for the $10,000 threshold for a STR seeped through society, with references made in US crime dramas when a character's $9,000 bank transfer was judged an effort to 'keep it under the $10,000 reporting limit'. In turn, widespread knowledge of the reporting threshold motivated the rational criminal to avoid it, but limiting transactions to $9,000 would not be sufficient. Regulatory officials in the US had directed banks to report any suspicious transactions over $5,000 in 1996 (Hecker 1996: 4, footnote 3). The solution to avoid the reporting requirement is to structure multiple transactions below the threshold, a technique known as 'smurfing', by way of reference to the children's animated show, 'The Smurfs', which is inhabited by a large number of small, blue characters.

Smurfing involves the use of multiple, small transactions to avoid the reporting threshold that will in sufficient quantity achieve the transfer of substantial amounts of money (Reuter and Truman 2004: 30).

But none of the AML measures enforced with such diligence after September 2001 would have successfully identified the hijackers involved in the terrorist attacks. Investigations found that the hijackers had funded themselves using bank transfers, credit cards, traveller's cheques and cash, and never in an amount large enough to have triggered a STR. In fact, 'Even in hindsight, there is nothing … to indicate that any [STR] should have been filed or the hijackers otherwise reported to law enforcement.' (Roth, Greenburg and Wille 2004: 141). This quotation comes from the 'Monograph on Terrorist Financing' appended to the report of the National Commission on Terrorist Attacks on the United States. It investigated the nature and methods of financing behind al Qaida and the large coordinated attack in the US. In addition to the scale of money behind the events of 11 September 2001, the monograph highlighted the role of charities to collect and disguise al Qaida's financing and it discussed the use of informal value transfer systems (IVTS) to move economic value around the world outside of the formal financial system (see Box 49.4). The latter revelation exposed Western elites to the continued operation of informal methods of transferring money not only in the Global South, but simultaneously throughout the Global North. Initial efforts to understand the modalities of IVTS and prevent their use by terrorist financiers outside the scope of financial system surveillance further revealed the significant sums of money involved, substantially consisting of the aggregated small sums of remittances sent home by migrant workers. Data collection on migrant remittances became part of the World Bank agenda, leading to the recognition that migrant remittances exceeded official development aid flowing to many of these developing economies (World Bank 2011: 17). (See Chapter 46, this volume.)

Box 49.4 The informal value transfer system

The informal value transfer system (IVTS) operates as an alternative to retail banks and predates the origins of modern banking. The IVTS provided a form of long distance transfer and financial intermediation long before the creation of the banking system that we know today. A brief example from China will illustrate the process, when an alternative financial intermediation practice developed during the T'ang dynasty. This value transfer mechanism was named fei-ch'ien (flying money) and facilitated the trade between the Southern provinces and the Imperial capital. A Southern merchant sold their goods in the capital, and then exchanged the money received for a certificate from the Imperial court. The merchant exchanged the certificate for money with the local government on their return home. The money provided to the Imperial court served to offset taxes owed by the Southern provincial government and that government used its locally collected taxes when redeeming the Imperial court certificate (Cassidy 1994). The operational aspects from this illustration are the fact that an easily portable form of wealth is not involved, no coins, gold, other precious metals or gems. Rather the certificate represented a claim on value (money) that could be exchanged for the currency used in the Southern provinces. And it could be safely carried past bandits and highway robbers because they would not be able to exchange it. Networks of informal value transfer operated along the trade routes of the Indo-Pacific region, facilitating trade along the Silk Road and from the coast of China, across the coasts and islands of Southeast Asia to the coast of East Africa (El Qorchi, Maimbo and Wilson 2003: 16–18).

There are a number of culturally specific names for an IVTS, but it was 'hawala' which gained widespread attention and recognition following the 2001 terrorist attacks. Hawala re-emerged in the global political economy for use by South Asian migrants living and working in the Middle East and the United Kingdom in the 1960s and 1970s to send money home. A similar IVTS developed between Latin America and the United States, the Black Market Peso Exchange (BMPE). The BMPE originally was used to circumvent currency restrictions by Columbian importers for settling their overseas accounts, and came to be used by Colombian migrants in the US to send money home. It became a leading tool of the Columbian drug cartels in the 1980s to evade AML action in the US and transfer the proceeds of the cocaine trade in the US back to Columbia (Cassara 2015: 33–48). The association with money laundering and terrorist finance of BMPE and hawala served to demonise the IVTS as a whole among the media in Europe and North America. But it was the operation of the IVTS supporting migrant remittances that highlighted its function in the contemporary global financial system. These 'informal' methods offered more cost-effective and efficient means for moving money from a developed economy to a developing economy. Moreover, the IVTS provided money transfer services to locations without easy access to retail banking or other money transfer businesses (Lindley 2009).

The increased attention placed on the mis-use of charities and IVTS, along with smurfing to avoid suspicious transaction reporting, underscores the point that essentially any economic transaction may serve to facilitate money laundering or terrorist finance (see Box 49.5). The recognition of this fact led the FATF to expand the scope of businesses and professions with a reporting obligation beyond just banks, and the range of predicate crimes producing illegal money for laundering beyond illegal drug trafficking. They are listed in the latest edition of the Forty Recommendations, while Recommendation 15 covers 'New Technologies' and therefore any method currently not on the list. This Recommendation specifies that countries need to be aware of new innovations in finance and their potential to perform money laundering and terrorist finance (Financial Action Task Force 2012: 17). Recent new payment technologies of concern include prepaid debit/credit cards, virtual currencies like Bitcoin and internet-based payment systems such as PayPal. While the full extent of actual use of these payment methods is not known, the FATF offers several case studies to demonstrate that already they have been used for money laundering and/or terrorist finance (Financial Action Task Force 2015a: 35–39). The potential for anonymity provided by a new payment technology is the source for concern and it motivates the desire to ensure the inclusion of AML/CFT surveillance into any new technology (Financial Action Task Force 2010).

Beyond the concern with new payment methods because they may offer anonymity, there are other ways a person with money to launder may conceal their identity and the FATF seeks to prevent these methods as well. A simple one is just to have someone or something else instead be identified as the 'owner' of the income. This method gained extensive public exposure through the Panama Papers revelation of people concealed behind a company, trust or foundation which 'owned' the assets or were part of the layering step in the money laundering process (see: www.icij.org/investigations/panama-papers/). Among the people revealed were a number of politicians using an offshore company to conceal their assets. The term used by the FATF for this area of concern is the 'politically exposed person' (PEP), someone that is or has occupied a prominent position in government (elected, civil service, military or state-owned enterprise). As suggested by those individuals revealed in the Panama Papers, the PEP is a risk for money laundering because they may possess income that exceeds their official salary. The term is also applied to the families and close associates of the person in government, because they may be acting on their behalf or they may have illicit income due to the relationship (Financial Action Task Force 2013a). The Panama Papers story highlights two further aspects confronting the effective implementation of AML/CFT. First is the role of intermediaries and facilitators (e.g. lawyers and accountants) in the money laundering process, by setting up the companies used or in other instances by using their firm's bank account to pass client money through to perform a step in the layering process (Sharman 2017: 47–48). And the second aspect of concern is the identification of beneficial ownership of the asset, whether company, real estate or yacht, when it may be publicly listed as someone else (a nominee) or it could be another company (Financial Action Task Force 2018). The latter aspects are the subject of increased enforcement attention, at the national level as well as by international organisations such as the FATF.

Enforcement mechanisms and consequences

The FATF assures compliance with the Forty Recommendations through a process of peer-review assessment that produces a Mutual Evaluation Report on the jurisdiction reviewed. The mutual evaluation process begins with the completion of a detailed questionnaire on the country's implementation of AML/CFT standards by the relevant local staff. The questionnaire report is provided to a team of experts drawn from other members of the FATF or FSRB and this team then visits the jurisdiction to gather additional data themselves. Any issues raised from their review of the questionnaire report will be included in their inquiries, and during the visit a preliminary mutual evaluation report is prepared. This initial version is discussed with government officials and evaluation scores may be adjusted as a result. The mutual evaluation report is reviewed at the next plenary meeting of the FATF/FSRB, where there may be further discussion and possible revisions of the text and scores assigned. The agreed final version will be approved by the members at the plenary meeting and made publicly available on the FATF/FSRB website (Sharman 2011: 138–146). Sharman describes this process as a form of socialisation where the members and their representatives are inculcated into the processes and practices of this community for the global implementation of AML/CFT. In addition to the collegiality of this socialisation process, there is to a certain extent a measure of peer pressure present. A jurisdiction does not want to be viewed as less rigorous than it neighbours are with enforcing AML/CFT measures, or to end up on the FATF's list of high-risk countries. Should either situation occur, then economic relations with its neighbours and other countries could be hampered by increased due diligence on financial transactions. In turn, increased due diligence would introduce friction in finance and trade flows with consequences for the domestic economy (Vlcek 2012: 647–649).

The expansion of the scope of the Forty Recommendations has revealed problems with imposing financial surveillance structures designed for a developed economy and using them to identify money laundering in a developing economy financial system which is far less reliant on retail banking. For example, it is difficult to operate a 'know your customer' system when a large segment of the population lacks the necessary official identity documents. Consequently, countries with low formal financial system participation and a significant part of the population without official identity documents may be less rigorous with enforcement of KYC requirements, in the view of the team of outside experts conducting the evaluation (e.g. Financial Action Task Force & Eastern and Southern Africa Anti-Money Laundering Group 2009: 108). The FATF responded to this challenge by producing a 'risk-based' approach for implementing and enforcing AML/CFT in 2007 (Financial Action Task Force 2007). This approach was considered in the mutual evaluation of South Africa because the government had approved special 'low-risk' bank accounts to encourage financial inclusion (De Koker 2009). Unsurprisingly, the implementation of measures against terrorist financing can be as problematic as with money laundering. There may be a perception that terrorist financing is a problem in other countries, 'that it does not happen here', which delays legislation. Another barrier is the determination or definition of the 'terrorist', which has delayed the introduction of CFT in Brazil for many years. Senior members of the Brazilian governments from 2003 to 2016, including the President, were members of the Workers Party (Partido dos Trabalhadores, PT). During the period of the military dictatorship (1964–1989) the PT was identified as 'terrorists' and in government was suspicious of any counter terrorism legislation (Lasmar 2019). Brazil's historical experience hampers the introduction of CFT legislation and the FATF has highlighted this 'deficiency' in statements following the plenary meetings since the publication of Brazil's Mutual Evaluation report in 2010 (e.g. Financial Action Task Force 2016).

Box 49.5 A different case? The financing of ISIS[1]

The Islamic State in Iraq and Syria (also known as, Islamic State in Iraq and the Levant, ISIL, and Daesh) transitioned from an insurgent group in a conflict region into controlling a large piece of territory because it possessed a monopoly of the use of force (as a substitute for the local state). In achieving this status, the methods for financing the organisation expanded as well as requiring the group to operate and simulate the functions of a government for the territory it controlled. The situation was similar to that of other insurgent groups categorised as a terrorist organisation that also controlled territory, including the Liberation Tigers of Tamil Eelam (LTTE) in Sri Lanka and Revolutionary Armed Forces of Colombia (FARC) . Controlling territory includes the capacity to operate similar to a state, by collecting taxes and tolls, charging for different forms of fees and extracting revenue from the resources found within the territory under control. For ISIS in Syria it meant controlling much of the territory with crude oil production and providing substantial revenue at the time global crude oil prices were at a peak in 2014 (Lister 2014).

Nonetheless, ISIS was treated as a different case of terrorist financing, demonstrated by the publication of an FATF report specifically addressing the 'Financing of the Terrorist Organisation Islamic State in Iraq and the Levant (ISIL)' (Financial Action Task Force 2015b). This report highlighted not only the use of natural resources to finance the group, but also its use of extortion (taxation), kidnapping for ransom, private donations and the sale of cultural artefacts. With the exception of the latter, these sources of income replicate the activities of other terrorist organisations, like the LTTE and al Qaida. The smuggling and sale of ancient cultural artefacts was different, and supplanted pre-existing criminal activity in the region. At the same time, it attracted media attention because profiting from the sale of cultural artefacts was in stark contrast to the widely publicised destruction of pre-Islamic archaeological sites and artefacts by ISIS (Pringle 2014; Shabi 2015).

Note

1 This discussion is based on my contribution to Rashmi Singh, Jorge Lasmar and William Vlcek 'Cultural Genocide and Terrorism Financing: ISIS and the Erasure of History', presented at the 59th ISA Annual Convention, 4–7 April 2018, San Francisco, USA with research assistance provided by Colleen A. M. Gargiulo.

The FATF is currently in its fourth round of mutual evaluations, indicating that the member states will have been evaluated as many as three times previously (depending on length of membership in the FATF or FSRB). Each round of evaluations is conducted with regard to the current version of the Forty Recommendations when the round began, and the present round is assessing countries using the procedures developed for conducting a mutual evaluation following the guidance of the 2012 edition. New to this latest round of evaluations will be those features introduced to the Forty Recommendations in 2012, including the new measures for countering the proliferation of weapons of mass destruction and the refinements made to explicitly target the money laundering connected to bribery, corruption and tax crimes. This is not to suggest that the value and efficacy of the mutual evaluation process has been unchallenged. Jackie Johnson, for example, considered a set of sixteen third round reports, which were the first to include the Special Recommendations on Terrorist Financing (Financial Action Task Force 2001b). The methodology applied in her analysis found a decline in the level of compliance measured by the third round reports when compared to earlier evaluations (Johnson 2008). In addition, the IMF commissioned a report to assess the AML/CFT component of its Reports on the Observance of Standards and Codes (ROSCs). One objective for this assessment was to analyse third round reports and the evaluation methodology in order to develop recommendations for the fourth round. Part of the goal is to improve the quality of the evaluations while also recognising the variety of economic circumstances among evaluated countries. The report offers a critical assessment of the AML/CFT regime, over and above the methodology employed by the FATF and IMF for measuring its success. And it contains extensive recommendations for improving AML/CFT practices in order to produce improved methods for evaluating AML/CFT implementation leading to a more effective international regime (Halliday, Levi and Reuter 2014).

The mutual evaluation process managed by the FATF with assistance from the FSRBs is the enforcement mechanism over the states and territories obligated to implement the Forty Recommendations. It evaluates the success of states and territories to enforce their AML/CFT legislation not only on the money launders and terrorist financiers resident in their jurisdiction, but also their enforcement over the multitude of private actors on the front line – financial firms, DNFBPs, lawyers, accountants, etc. An entire industry has grown to provide services to these private actors, training their compliance staff and maintaining databases of named individuals and firms under sanctions or accused of money laundering and terrorist finance (Liss and Sharman 2015). The cost of compliance has been estimated at nearly 10 per cent of a financial firm's annual operating costs, and that figure does not include any fines and penalties if the firm is found to have failed to satisfy the expectations of AML/CFT legislation. The US governments (federal, state and local, specifically New York City law enforcement agencies) have been particularly diligent at imposing their compliance expectations on any firm doing business in the New York City financial centre, or simply conducting business denominated in US dollars. Prominent examples include BNP Paribas ($8.9 billion), HSBC ($1.9 billion), and Standard Chartered ($667 million) (Barrett, Matthews and Johnson, 2014; Ensign 2015; Too big to jail: HSBC and Standard Chartered 2012). Clearly, the dominant position of the US dollar in the world economy gives the US government the leverage to enforce its view of AML/CFT compliance (Zarate 2013).

Just as criminals have responded to increased AML/CFT enforcement by moving to other forms of economic activity to launder money, financial firms also have responded to the increased attention given to AML/CFT enforcement. In part, their response has been to increase their compliance activity, while at the same time acting to reduce their exposure to potentially risky business transactions. The issue is that a business activity may be acceptable and legitimate today, but become categorised as illegitimate in the future. This risk reduction activity is known as 'derisking' and involves closing the accounts of individuals and businesses that may be risky, such as money transfer companies, which echoes the private sanctions imposed by New York City banks in 1999 on their Pacific Island counterparts. Derisking on a larger scale involves closing the correspondent banking accounts of financial firms located in jurisdictions perceived as high risk as well as closing the firm's branches and subsidiaries in these same jurisdictions (Wright 2016). The FATF was forced to issue a public statement after its October 2014 plenary meeting declaring that derisking was not solely due to heightened AML/CFT enforcement, but may be due to 'concerns about profitability, prudential requirements, anxiety after the global financial crisis, and reputational risk.' (Financial Action Task Force 2014) There remains a perception, however, that AML/CFT enforcement risks motivates a large part of the derisking activity, in order to avoid US enforcement action, penalties and fines.

Conclusions

The full variety and complexity of IPE issues with money laundering and the financing of terrorism could not be covered in the space of this one chapter. A number of other areas which the reader may wish to explore further include the AML/CFT regime as a form of global governance and the debates seeking to explain the widespread implementation of the Forty Recommendations (Hameiri and Jones 2016; Hülsse 2007; Nance 2015). One feature of the AML/CFT regime receiving particular attention for its potential applicability in other global governance initiatives is the FATF's use of 'blacklisting' as a mechanism to achieve compliance (Eggenberger 2018; Sharman 2009). Yet notwithstanding its wide implementation, some industries have been slow to incorporate AML/CFT practices, such as real estate agents, and they are receiving increased attention (Financial Crimes Enforcement Network 2017; Transparency International 2017). Finally, the scope of impact in developing economies extends beyond derisking and the issues with identity documents for KYC. Continued economic development and the problem with financial inclusion may also be hampered by the requirements imposed with AML/CFT implementation (Vlcek 2018a).

The international regime created to address money laundering and extended to include terrorist finance and other multinational concerns has become an integral part of global trade and finance. It affects the everyday life of individuals and companies, and the international enforcement structure has produced unintended consequences for individuals, companies and entire countries through the practices of derisking. Yet the implementation and enforcement of AML/CFT laws and regulation has not achieved its ultimate goal of stopping illegal drugs trafficking or international terrorism. It has, however, succeeded in making them much more difficult and expanding the scope of predicate crimes for money laundering to include all forms of illegal money provides governments and prosecutors with a tool against corruption and bribery. A prominent example for the utility of this tool is the Operation Car Wash ('Operação Lava Jato') corruption investigation in Brazil of the multinational construction company Odebrecht, which spread to involve a number of other countries where the Brazilian firm operated (Kassab and Rosen, 2019). The AML/CFT global governance regime will continue to evolve, to include additional new payment methods and to assure that new financial technologies are designed to prevent their use as a vehicle for money laundering and terrorist finance.

Bibliography

Adams, T. 2000. Tacking on money laundering charges to white crimes: What did Congress intend, and what are the courts doing? *Georgia State University Law Review* 17, no. 2: 531–573.

Alexander, Y., Browne, M. and Nanes, A. 1979. eds. *Control of Terrorism: International Documents*. New York: Crane, Russack and Company.

Alldridge, P. 2003. *Money Laundering Law: Forfeiture, Confiscation, Civil Recovery, Criminal Laundering and Taxation of the Proceeds of Crime*. Oxford: Hart Publishing.

Barrett, D., Matthews, C. and Johnson, A. 2014. BNP Paribas Draws Record Fine for 'Tour de Fraud'. *Wall Street Journal*. Available at: http://online.wsj.com/articles/bnp-agrees-to-pay-over-8-8-billion-to-settle-sanctions-probe-1404160117.

Cassara, J. 2015. *Trade-Based Money Laundering: The Next Frontier in International Money Laundering Enforcement*. Hoboken, NJ: John Wiley & Sons, Inc.

Cassidy, W. 1994. *Fei-Chien, or Flying Money: A Study of Chinese Underground Banking*. W.L.R. Cassidy & Associates. Available at: www.alternatives.com/crime/flyingmo.html.

Council of Europe. 1980. Measures Against the Transfer and Safekeeping of Funds of Criminal Origin: Recommendation and Explanatory Memorandum. In *Rec(80)10E*.

De Koker, L. 2009. The money laundering risk posed by low-risk financial products in South Africa. *Journal of Money Laundering Control* 12, no. 4: 323–339.

Eckert, S. and Biersteker, T. 2010. (Mis)Measuring Success in Countering the Financing of Terrorism. In *Sex, Drugs, and Body Counts: The Politics of Numbers in Global Crime and Conflict*. Andreas, P. and Greenhill, K. (eds): 247–263. Ithaca, NY: Cornell University Press.

Eggenberger, K. 2018. When is blacklisting effective? Stigma, sanctions and legitimacy: the reputational and financial costs of being blacklisted. *Review of International Political Economy* 25, no. 4: 483–504.

El Qorchi, M., Maimbo, S. and Wilson, J. 2003. *Informal Funds Transfer Systems: An Analysis of the Informal Hawala System*. Washington, DC: International Monetary Fund.

Ensign, R. 2015. HSBC Money-Laundering Case Yields $116 Million Bounty for Queens D.A. *Wall Street Journal*. Available at: www.wsj.com/articles/hsbc-money-laundering-case-yields-116-million-bounty-for-queens-d-a-1436891783.

Financial Action Task Force. 1990a. *Financial Action Task Force on Money Laundering Report*. Available at: www.fatf-gafi.org/.

Financial Action Task Force. 1990b. *The Forty Recommendations of the Financial Action Task Force on Money Laundering*. Available at: wwwfatf-gafi.org.

Financial Action Task Force. 2000a. *Report on Non-Cooperative Countries or Territories*. Available at: www.fatf-gafi.org/.

Financial Action Task Force. 2000b. *Review to Identify Non-Cooperative Countries or Territories: Increasing the World-Wide Effectiveness of Anti-Money Laundering Measures*. Available at: www.fatf-gafi.org/.

Financial Action Task Force. 2001a. *Report on Money Laundering Typologies, 2000–2001*. Available at: www.fatf-gafi.org/.

Financial Action Task Force. 2001b. *Special Recommendations on Terrorist Financing*. Available at: www.fatf-gafi.org/.

Financial Action Task Force. 2003. *The Forty Recommendations*. Available at: www.fatf-gafi.org/.

Financial Action Task Force. 2007. *Guidance on the Risk-Based Approach to Combating Money Laundering and Terrorist Finance: High Level Principles and Procedures*. Available at: www.fatf-gafi.org/.

Financial Action Task Force. 2010. *Money Laundering Using New Payment Methods*. Available at: www.fatf-gafi.org/.

Financial Action Task Force. 2012. *International Standards on Combating Money Laundering and the Financing of Terrorism & Proliferation: The FATF Recommendations*. OECD/FATF, 2012. www.fatf-gafi.org/.

Financial Action Task Force. 2013a. *Best Practices Paper – The use of the FATF Recommendations to combat corruption*. Available at: www.fatf-gafi.org/.

Financial Action Task Force. 2013b. *The Role of Hawala and Other Similar Service Providers in Money Laundering and Terrorist Financing*. FATF/OECD. Available at: www.fatf-gafi.org/.

Financial Action Task Force. 2014. *FATF Clarifies Risk-based Approach: Case-by-case, Not Wholesale De-risking*. Available at: www.fatf-gafi.org/.

Financial Action Task Force. 2015a. *Emerging Terrorist Financing Risks*. Available at: www.fatf-gafi.org/.

Financial Action Task Force. 2015b. *Financing of the Terrorist Organisation Islamic State in Iraq and the Levant (ISIL)*. Financial Action Task Force. Available at: www.fatf-gafi.org/.

Financial Action Task Force. 2016. *Outcomes of the Plenary Meeting of the FATF, Paris, 19–21 October 2016*. Available at: www.fatf-gafi.org/.

Financial Action Task Force. 2018. *Concealment of Beneficial Ownership*. FATF/OECD. Available at: www. fatf-gafi.org/.

Financial Action Task Force, and Eastern and Southern Africa Anti-Money Laundering Group. 2009. *Mutual Evaluation Report – Anti-Money Laundering and Combating the Financing of Terrorism: South Africa*. Paris.

Financial Crimes Enforcement Network. 2017. *Advisory to Financial Institutions and Real Estate Firms and Professionals*. Washington, DC: U.S. Department of the Treasury.

General Accounting Office. 2000. Suspicious Banking Activities: Possible Money Laundering by U.S. Corporations Formed for Russian Entities. In *Report to the Ranking Minority Member*. Permanent Subcommittee on Investigations, Committee on Governmental Affairs, United States Senate. Washington, DC: General Accounting Office.

Halliday, T., Levi, M. and Reuter, P. 2014. *Global Surveillance of Dirty Money: Assessing Assessments of Regimes to Control Money-Laundering and Combat the Financing of Terrorism*. Champaign, IL: Center on Law and Globalization.

Hameiri, S. and Jones, L. 2016. Global Governance as State Transformation. *Political Studies* 64, no. 4: 793–810.

Hecker, J. 1996. Money Laundering: U.S. Efforts to Combat Money Laundering Overseas. Statement of JayEtta Z. Hecker, Associate Director, International Relations and Trade Issues. In *Committee on Banking and Financial Services, House of Representatives*. Washington, DC: General Accounting Office.

Holcomb, J., Kovandzic, T. and Williams, M. 2011. Civil asset forfeiture, equitable sharing, and policing for profit in the United States. *Journal of Criminal Justice*, 39, no. 3: 273–285.

Horgan, J. and Taylor, M. 1999. Playing the 'green card' – financing the provisional IRA: Part 1. *Terrorism and Political Violence*, 11, no. 2: 1–38.

Hülsse, R. 2007. Creating demand for global governance: The making of a global money-laundering problem. *Global Society*, 21, no. 2: 155–178.

Johnson, J. 2008. Third round FATF mutual evaluations indicate declining compliance. *Journal of Money Laundering Control*, 11, no. 1: 47–66.

Kassab, H. and Rosen, J. 2019. South America. In *Corruption, Institutions, and Fragile States*: 135–159. Cham: Palgrave Macmillan.

Lasmar, J. 2019. When the shoe doesn't fit: Brazilian approaches to terrorism and counterterrorism in the post-9/11 era. In *Non-Western Responses to Terrorism*. Boyle, M. (ed.): 221–245. Manchester: Manchester University Press.

Levi, M. 2002. Money laundering and its regulation. *Annals of the American Academy of Political and Social Science*, 582, no. 1: 181–194.

Levi, M. 2010. Combating the financing of terrorism: A history and assessment of the control of 'threat finance'. *British Journal of Criminology*, 50, no. 4: 650–669.

Lindley, A. 2009. Between 'dirty money' and 'development capital': Somali money transfer infrastructure under global scrutiny. *African Affairs*, 108, no. 433: 519–539.

Liss, C. and Sharman, J. 2015. Global corporate crime-fighters: Private transnational responses to piracy and money laundering. *Review of International Political Economy*, 22, no. 4: 693–718.

Lister, C. 2014. *Cutting off ISIS' Cash Flow*. *Markaz*. Available at: www.brookings.edu/blog/markaz/2014/10/24/cutting-off-isis-cash-flow/.

Minority Staff of the Permanent Subcommittee on Investigations. 2001. *Report on Correspondent Banking: A Gateway for Money Laundering*. Washington, DC: U.S. Senate Committee on Government Affairs.

Mitsilegas, V. 2003. *Money Laundering Counter-Measures in the European Union: A New Paradigm of Security Governance Versus Fundamental Legal Principles*. The Hague, London, New York: Kluwer Law International.

Nance, M. 2015. Naming and Shaming in Financial Regulation: Explaining Variation in the Financial Action Task Force on Money Laundering. In *The Politics of Leverage in International Relations: Name, Shame, and Sanction*. Friman, R. (ed.): 123–142. London: Palgrave Macmillan UK.

Naylor, R. 1994. *Hot Money and the Politics of Debt*. 2nd ed. Montreal: Black Rose Books.

Pringle, H. 2014. ISIS cashing in on looted antiquities to fuel Iraq insurgency. *National Geographic*.

Reuter, P. and Truman, E. 2004. *Chasing Dirty Money: The Fight Against Money Laundering*. Washington, DC: Institute for International Economics.

Roth, J., Greenburg, D. and Wille, S. 2004. *Monograph on Terrorist Financing*. Washington, DC: National Commission on Terrorist Attacks on the United States.

Shabi, R. 2015. Looted in Syria – and sold in London: The British antiques shops dealing in artefacts smuggled by Isis. *The Guardian*. Available at: www.theguardian.com/world/2015/jul/03/antiquities-looted-by-isis-end-up-in-london-shops.

Sharman, J. 2009. The bark is the bite: International organisations and blacklisting. *Review of International Political Economy*, 16, no. 4: 573–596.

Sharman, J. 2011. *The Money Laundry: Regulating Criminal Finance in the Global Economy*. Ithaca, NY; London: Cornell University Press.

Sharman, J. 2017. Illicit global wealth chains after the financial crisis: Micro-states and an unusual suspect. *Review of International Political Economy*, 24, no. 1: 30–55.

Thoumi, F. and Anzola, M. 2010. Asset and money laundering in Bolivia, Columbia and Peru: A legal transplant in vulnerable environments? *Crime, Law and Social Change*, 53, no. 5: 437–455.

Too big to jail: HSBC and Standard Chartered. 2012. *The Economist*.

Transparency International. 2017. *Doors Wide Open: Corruption and Real Estate in Four Key Markets*. Berlin.

US Congress Office of Technology Assessment. 1995. *Information Technologies for Control of Money Laundering*. Washington, DC: US Government Printing Office.

United Nations Security Council. 2001. Resolution 1373 (2001). In *S/RES/1373 (2001)*.

United Nations Security Council. 2005. Resolution 1617 (2005). In *S/RES/1617 (2005)*.

USA PATRIOT Act. 2001. Uniting and Strengthening America by Providing Appropriate Tools Required to Intercept and Obstruct Terrorism: 107–56.

Vlcek, W. 2008. A Leviathan rejuvenated: Surveillance, money laundering, and the war on terror. *International Journal of Politics, Culture and Society*, 20, no. 1–4: 21–40.

Vlcek, W. 2012. Power and the practice of security to govern global finance. *Review of International Political Economy*, 19, no. 4: 639–662.

Vlcek, W. 2018a. Global financial governance and the informal: Limits to the regulation of money. *Crime, Law and Social Change*, 69, no. 2: 249–264.

Vlcek, W. 2018b. Privatising Security in Finance: Measures Against the Money Threatening Society. In *Security Privatization: How Non-security-related Private Businesses Shape Security Governance*. Bures, O. and Carrapico, H. (eds): 101–122. Cham, Switzerland: Springer International Publishing.

Walker, J. 1999. How big is global money laundering? *Journal of Money Laundering Control*, 3, no. 1: 25–37.

World Bank. 2011. *Migration and Remittances Factbook 2011*. 2nd ed. Washington, DC: IBRD/World Bank.

Wright, A. 2016. *De-Risking and its Impact: The Caribbean Perspective*. St Augustine, Trinidad and Tobago: Caribbean Centre for Money and Finance.

Zarate, J. 2013. *Treasury's War: The Unleashing of a New Era of Financial Warfare*. New York: Public Affairs.

Index

For Product Safety Concerns and Information please contact our EU
representative GPSR@taylorandfrancis.com
Taylor & Francis Verlag GmbH, Kaufingerstraße 24, 80331 München, Germany

www.ingramcontent.com/pod-product-compliance
Ingram Content Group UK Ltd.
Pitfield, Milton Keynes, MK11 3LW, UK
UKHW011455240425
457818UK00021B/845